INTERNATIONAL ENCYCLOPEDIA OF

DANCE

A project of Dance Perspectives Foundation, Inc.

FOUNDING EDITOR

Selma Jeanne Cohen

AREA EDITORS

George Dorris   Nancy Goldner   Beate Gordon
Nancy Reynolds   David Vaughan
Suzanne Youngerman

CONSULTANTS

Thomas F. Kelly   Horst Koegler   Richard Ralph
Elizabeth Souritz

VOLUME 3

OXFORD UNIVERSITY PRESS

New York   1998   Oxford

OXFORD UNIVERSITY PRESS

Oxford   New York
Athens   Auckland   Bangkok   Bogotá   Bombay
Buenos Aires   Calcutta   Cape Town   Dar es Salaam
Delhi   Florence   Hong Kong   Istanbul   Karachi
Kuala Lumpur   Madras   Madrid   Melbourne
Mexico City   Nairobi   Paris   Singapore
Taipei   Tokyo   Toronto   Warsaw
and associated companies in
Berlin   Ibadan

Copyright © 1998 by Oxford University Press, Inc.

Published by Oxford University Press, Inc.,
198 Madison Avenue, New York, New York 10016

Oxford is a registered trademark of Oxford University Press

This work was initiated with funds granted by the
National Endowment for the Humanities,
a federal agency

Library of Congress Cataloging-in-Publication Data
International encyclopedia of dance : a project of Dance
Perspectives Foundation, Inc. / founding editor, Selma Jeanne Cohen;
area editors, George Dorris et al.; consultants, Thomas F. Kelly et al.
p.   cm.
Includes bibliographical references and index.
1. Dance—Encyclopedias.   2. Ballet—Encyclopedias.   I. Cohen,
Selma Jeanne, 1920-.   II. Dance Perspectives Foundation.
GV1585.I586   1998   97-36562   792.6′2′03—dc21   CIP
ISBN 0-19-509462-X (set)
ISBN 0-19-512307-7 (vol. 3)

Printing (last digit): 9 8 7 6 5 4 3 2

Printed in the United States of America
on acid-free paper

FIREBIRD, THE. [*This entry comprises two articles on ballets choreographed to Igor Stravinsky's score: the first is a brief description of Michel Fokine's original production; the second is a survey of later productions.*]

Fokine Production

French title: *L'Oiseau de Feu.* Ballet in one act and two scenes. Choreography: Michel Fokine. Music: Igor Stravinsky. Libretto: Michel Fokine. Scenery: Aleksandr Golovin. Costumes: Aleksandr Golovin and Léon Bakst. First performance: 26 June 1910, Théâtre National de l'Opéra, Paris, Ballets Russes de Serge Diaghilev. Principals: Tamara Karsavina (The Firebird), Michel Fokine (Ivan Tsarevich), Vera Fokina (Tsarevna), Aleksei Bulgakov (Kastchei).

Produced during the second season of Diaghilev's Ballets Russes in Paris, *L'Oiseau de Feu* was an immediate success. The result of a close collaboration of choreographer, composer, and designers, it had all the elements of exoticism so characteristic of Diaghilev's early Saisons Russes: a fantastic libretto based on Russian folklore, elaborately beautiful sets and costumes, dramatic dancing, and the strange and ravishingly beautiful idiom of the musical score. Parisian audiences were delighted with the ballet, and critics claimed that it heralded a new direction for the art of dance.

Fokine's libretto draws heavily from Russian fairy tales, blending the stories of Ivan Tsarevich (Prince Ivan), a magical "bird of light," and Kastchei the Immortal, a wicked magician who rules a world of monsters. While hunting in the forest, Prince Ivan strays into the enchanted realm of Kastchei. There he encounters and captures the mysterious Firebird, who, in exchange for her freedom, gives him a magic feather by which he may summon her if he is ever in danger. Ivan then comes across twelve tsarevnas (princesses) who live in captivity under Kastchei. Enticed to join them in a round dance, he falls in love with the most beautiful of them and persuades her to try to escape. Before they can do so, they are discovered by Kastchei and his retinue of monstrous creatures. In the ensuing "Dance of the Impure Kingdom," staged in the form of a dance symphony, one of the monsters advances upon Ivan, threatening to inflict the curse of Kastchei

upon him. But Ivan waves the magic feather, calling forth the Firebird, who flies in and casts a spell, causing the monsters to dance to exhaustion and allowing Ivan to smash the egg that contains Kastchei's soul—thus breaking his dominion, destroying the Kingdom of Evil, and freeing the princesses and their suitors, knights who had been turned to stone while attempting to overcome Kastchei. In the end, in a scene of great pomp and majesty, Prince Ivan and the lovely Tsarevna are wed and crowned to rule over the entire kingdom.

THE FIREBIRD: Fokine Production. Michel Fokine as Ivan Tsarevich and Tamara Karsavina as the Firebird in the original production of Fokine's 1910 ballet. (Photograph from the Dance Collection, New York Public Library for the Performing Arts.)

In devising this libretto, Fokine not only created opportunities for beautiful and dramatic dancing but also skillfully and clearly set up the opposition of good and evil on which so many fairy tales are based. Kastchei the Immortal and his Impure Kingdom are the embodiment of evil and ugliness, while the Firebird is a wonderful creature of light and beauty, which have power to elevate and transform the world. Prince Ivan and the princesses represent the social structure of human beings, those for whom the fantastic forces of good and evil do battle. Ivan Tsarevich is the traditional fairy-tale hero possessed of a magical object, a feather from the Firebird, that makes him invincible.

In his choreography for the various characters in the ballet, Fokine employed a variety of expressive forms of dance, using the idiom of classical ballet for the dazzling Firebird, violent and grotesque movements for Kastchei and his retinue, and a free form of plastique for the gentle princesses. Such variety, however, in no way created a sense of stylistic disharmony; on the contrary, *L'Oiseau de Feu* was later recognized as being, in a stylistic sense, one of the most completely integrated of all Fokine's choreographic efforts, a perfect match for the marvelous musical program in Stravinsky's innovative score, his first commission for a ballet. It brought both Fokine and Stravinsky great acclaim, and it made Tamara Karsavina, who created the role of the Firebird, the darling of critics and other balletomanes all over Europe.

BIBLIOGRAPHY

Beaumont, Cyril W. *Complete Book of Ballets*. Rev. ed. London, 1951.

Garafola, Lynn. *Diaghilev's Ballets Russes*. New York, 1989.

Horwitz, Dawn Lille. *Michel Fokine*. Boston, 1985.

Lester, Keith. "Fokine's *Firebird*." *The Dancing Times* (April 1968):354–356.

Reynolds, Nancy, and Susan Reimer-Torn. *Dance Classics*. Pennington, N.J., 1991.

Schouvaloff, Alexander, and Victor Borovsky. *Stravinsky on Stage*. London, 1982.

Taruskin, Richard. "From *Firebird* to *The Rite*: Folk Elements in Stravinsky's Score." *Ballet Review* 10 (Summer 1982):72–87.

Vaughan, David. "Fokine in the Contemporary Repertory." *Ballet Review* 7.2–3 (1978–1979):19–27.

Vershinina, I. I. *Rannie balety Stravinskogo*. Moscow, 1967.

GALINA N. DOBROVOLSKAYA
Translated from Russian

Later Productions

Igor Stravinsky's colorful and evocative score (original 1910) has inspired many choreographers to create new versions of *The Firebird*. Some are danced to the suite that Stravinsky made in 1945, which he himself preferred to the complete score; a few use the 1919 suite, which is shorter still. As the following sampling suggests, the ballets fall into three general categories: (1) those that follow Michel Fokine's scenario, albeit with minor variations in detail; (2) those that discard the Russian folkloristic elements but preserve the fairy-tale plot; and (3) those that

introduce an entirely new plot and setting. Common to all is a theme that can be summarized as the struggle and ultimate triumph of good over evil.

Fokine's ballet served as the model for revivals by Adolph Bolm (Ballet Theatre, 1945), Serge Lifar (Paris Opera Ballet, 1954), and Serge Grigoriev and Lubov Tchernicheva (Sadler's Wells Ballet, 1954)—this last considered by some observers as closest in spirit to the original. Grigoriev, the *régisseur* of the Ballets Russes de Serge Diaghilev, undoubtedly knew Fokine's choreography well; in addition, Margot Fonteyn was coached in the title role by Tamara Karsavina, the original Firebird. The Sadler's Wells production also utilized the designs that Natalia Goncharova had made for Diaghilev in 1926.

George Balanchine's version, first mounted by New York City Ballet in 1949, is arguably the best-known and longest-lived revival of *The Firebird* in the United States. Balanchine wished to emphasize the dancing, and a strong point of this production was the choreography for

THE FIREBIRD: Later Productions. In George Balanchine's *Firebird*, mounted in 1949 for the New York City Ballet, Francisco Moncion and Maria Tallchief created the leading roles. Scenery and costumes were designed by Marc Chagall. Balanchine made major revisions in his choreography in 1970, 1972, and 1980. (Photograph from the Dance Collection, New York Public Library for the Performing Arts. Choreography by George Balanchine © The George Balanchine Trust.)

the Firebird role, as powerfully danced by Maria Tallchief. Marc Chagall's jewel-toned sets and costumes, originally created for Ballet Theatre's 1945 production, were purchased by New York City Ballet. In 1970, Balanchine revised *The Firebird* in collaboration with Jerome Robbins, who choreographed the monsters' *danse infernale.* The extreme youth of Gelsey Kirkland, who danced the Firebird in that production, heightened the asexual, nonhuman quality of the role. In an effort to bring the ballet closer to realizing Chagall's fantasies, Balanchine introduced a new costume for the Firebird in 1972, reproducing the bird-headed female figure on Chagall's drop curtain. However, the ballerina's movements were so severely limited by the wings, long train, and bird headdress of this costume that, in 1985, New York City Ballet reinstated Tallchief's red tutu, along with the choreography she had danced. Brian Macdonald's version for the Royal Swedish Ballet in 1966 and the Harkness Ballet in 1967 also followed Fokine's scenario, but his otherwise conventional Firebird was accompanied by two identically costumed Reflections.

John Neumeier choreographed two versions of *The Firebird* that retained the fairy-tale plot while transposing the action to a futuristic world. In the Frankfurt Opera Ballet's production of 1970, the hero was literally swallowed by Kastchei, a glass-walled robot with a closed-circuit television for an eye. By destroying the correct valve, the hero saves himself and restores human shape to Kastchei's monsters. When Neumeier staged the ballet for the Vienna State Opera Ballet in 1983, he again conceived

Kastchei as a malevolent robot, this time armed with a death-dealing wand. Upon his defeat by a soldier and a young girl, the dying sun revives and floods the blighted land with light, and the girl's carefully guarded flower blooms into an enormous tree.

THE FIREBIRD: Later Productions. Heinz Spoerli first staged *Der Feuervogel* for the Basel Ballet in 1973. Twenty years later, in 1993, he made a new version for the Ballett der Deutschen Oper am Rhein, Düsseldorf-Duisberg. Simona Noja and Juan Boix danced the leading roles. (Photograph by Gundel Kilian; used by permission.)

ure. She emerges triumphant at last, dressed in bridal white and ready for a new life of love and fulfillment.

In Ferenc Barbay's reductionist version of *The Firebird*, performed at the Munich Ballet Festival in 1981 to Isao Tomita's synthesizer adaptation of Stravinsky's music, the ballet is recast as a pas de deux for two men—identified as the Firebird and the Sorcerer—who square off for their dance duel on a bare stage. As in other versions, the Firebird is the victor here.

In both its Russian and non-Russian incarnations, *The Firebird* continues to challenge choreographers of imagination. The many different successful realizations of the ageless theme of good versus evil embodied in Stravinsky's score are proof of *The Firebird*'s ability to speak in a multitude of voices that appeal to diverse tastes and times.

BIBLIOGRAPHY

Balanchine, George, with Francis Mason. *Balanchine's Complete Stories of the Great Ballets.* Rev. and enl. ed. Garden City, N.Y., 1977.

Barnes, Clive. "The Firebird" (parts 1–2). *Dance and Dancers* (April–May 1963).

Garafola, Lynn. *Diaghilev's Ballets Russes.* New York, 1989.

Karsavina, Tamara. "Firebird." *The Dancing Times* (May 1954): 483.

Maynard, Olga. "The Firebird." *Dance Magazine* (August 1970): 43–57.

Reynolds, Nancy. *Repertory in Review: Forty Years of the New York City Ballet.* New York, 1977.

SUSAN AU

Theatrical spectacle set the tone of Vicente Nebrada's staging for the Royal Winnipeg Ballet in 1982, which included a light show. His streamlined Firebird, dressed in a red unitard, confronts a turbaned music-hall Magician with a wife and a retinue of triple-bodied reptiles. Three of the leading characters in John Taras's version for the Dance Theatre of Harlem in 1982 were presented in terms of universal symbols: the Young Man, the Princess of Unreal Beauty, and the Prince of Evil. The story, similar to Fokine's, unfolded in a tropical rain forest.

Maurice Béjart departed from both Russian local color and fairy tale in his 1970 staging of *The Firebird*, first produced by the Paris Opera Ballet and later by Béjart's own Ballet du XXᵉ Siècle. His male Firebird, dressed in red tights, emerges from a group of drably costumed revolutionaries, whom he leads to victory against an unseen foe. Although he dies in the struggle, a second Firebird rises phoenixlike in his place, and the whole group is ultimately transformed into red-clad Firebirds.

The protagonist of Glen Tetley's 1981 production of *The Firebird* for the Royal Danish Ballet is a young woman oppressed by shadowy figures—a man who may be her father or guardian and a group of governesslike women. In a garden filled with leaping gray creatures, she meets a young man who fights on her behalf against the father fig-

FITZJAMES SISTERS. Louise and Nathalie Fitzjames, originally surnamed Fijan, were French dancers who performed at the Paris Opera during the 1830s and 1840s.

Louise Fitzjames (born 10 December 1809 in Paris, date and place of death unknown) began to study dance with Auguste Romieu at the age of ten and later became the last pupil of Auguste Vestris, who had reigned as the leading male dancer of the late eighteenth century. She also studied with Filippo Taglioni, the father of the celebrated Marie, who allowed Louise "the unprecedented privilege of sharing his private class with his daughter" (Guest, 1982).

She made her debut at the Paris Opera on 1 October 1832 in *Les Pages du Duc de Vendôme* and was immediately engaged by the director, Louis Véron, who also gave her the role of the Abbess, which was originally created by Marie Taglioni, in the opera *Robert le Diable*. This role became her own; she first assumed it on 31 December 1832 and subsequently danced it more than 230 times. Giacomo Meyerbeer, the composer of the opera, commemorated her two-hundredth performance by sending her a bronze bust of himself.

She created the role of the *prima ballerina* of La Fenice in *La Jolie Fille de Gand*, choreographed by Monsieur Albert and first performed on 22 June 1842. The cast included Carlotta Grisi, Lucien Petipa, Monsieur Albert, and Joseph Mazilier. She also created roles in the ballet *divertissements* of the operas *Stradella* (1837), choreographed by Jean Coralli, with music by Louis-Abraham Niedermeyer; *Le Drapier* (1840), choreographer unknown, with music by Fromental Halévy; and *Les Martyrs* (1840), choreographed by Jean Coralli, with music by Gaetano Donizetti. In addition, she danced Taglioni's roles of Zulma in *La Révolte au Sérail* and Zoloë in *Le Dieu et la Bayadère.*

Although she enjoyed the status of a principal dancer and was praised for the correctness of her technique, her tall, thin figure was not admired by audiences of the time (she was, in fact, caricatured as an asparagus in an imaginary ballet of vegetables), and she never achieved the stature of a major ballerina.

Nathalie Fitzjames (born 1819 in Paris, date and place of death unknown) was destined for greater things. As a child she was so precocious that Jean-Louis Aumer chose her to create the role of Cupid in his ballet *La Belle au Bois Dormant,* first presented at the Paris Opera on 27 April 1829. She further benefited from the interest of Alexandre Aguado, marquis de Las Marismas del Guadalquivir, who was the lover of her elder sister Alexandrine and an associate of Henri Duponchel, the new director of the Paris Opera. At Aguado's behest the management began to groom Nathalie as a replacement for Taglioni and Fanny Elssler, and in the spring of 1837 the Italian choreographer Antonio Guerra was commissioned to create a ballet for her. The scenario of this ballet, *Les Mohicans,* was loosely adapted by Léon Halévy from James Fenimore Cooper's novel *The Last of the Mohicans* (1826). The ballet, which premiered on 5 July 1837, was not a success and received only two performances, but Nathalie formally became a member of the Paris Opera on 1 October 1837.

Although she never attained the heights projected for her, she was a competent dancer with particular strength in character dances such as "La Tyrolienne" in the opera *Guillaume Tell* and "La Mauresca" in the opera *La Vendetta.* She created the role of the peasant girl Lilia in Joseph Mazilier's ballet *Le Diable Amoureux,* first presented on 23 September 1840. Nathalie was also associated with the ballet that became the epitome of the Romantic era, *Giselle,* choreographed by Jean Coralli and Jules Perrot, with music by Adolphe Adam. At its first performance on 28 June 1841 she was partnered by Auguste Mabille. She danced the Peasant pas de deux in the first act of the ballet to interpolated music by Friedrich Burgmüller.

Nathalie danced Taglioni's role of Zoloë in *Le Dieu et la Bayadère* and the role of Thérèse in *La Somnambule,* thereby revealing a flair for drama. She was a talented singer as well, and on a single evening in 1842, before the court at Versailles, she sang two acts of *Lucia di Lammer-*

FITZJAMES SISTERS. Nathalie Fitzjames and Auguste Mabille in the Peasant pas de deux, danced to music by Friedrich Burgmüller, in *Giselle* (1841). Lithographed music cover by Guillet, Paris, c.1842. (Courtesy of Madison U. Sowell and Debra H. Sowell, Brigham Young University, Provo, Utah.)

moor, mimed two acts of *La Muette de Portici,* and danced the Peasant pas de deux from *Giselle.* During her residency at the Paris Opera she also found time, in 1838, to appear as a principal dancer at Her Majesty's Theatre in London.

At the end of September 1842 Nathalie left the Paris Opera to tour Italy, where she became the first ballerina to dance *Giselle* in Florence and Genoa. In the autumn of 1850 she traveled to the United States as the ballerina of an opera company directed by the impresario Max Maretzek. She made her American debut on 27 November 1850 at the Astor Place Opera House in New York City, dancing in Lucien Petipa's staging of *Paquita.* During the spring of 1851 she appeared in Brooklyn, New York, dancing with a "bloomer troupe." Toward the end of her career she returned to Paris, where she created a principal role in Arthur Saint-Léon's *opéra-ballet Le Danseur du Roi,* first performed on 22 October 1853 at the Théâtre Lyrique.

BIBLIOGRAPHY
Guest, Ivor. *The Romantic Ballet in Paris.* 2d rev. ed. London, 1980.
Martel. "Some Lesser Stars of the Victorian Era" (parts 1–4). *The Dancing Times* (July 1917–October 1917).
Moore, Lillian. "Forgotten Dancers of the Nineteenth Century." *Dance Magazine* (December 1953): 25–30.
Moore, Lillian. *Images of the Dance: Historical Treasures of the Dance Collection, 1581–1861.* New York, 1965.

SUSAN AU

FLAMENCO DANCE. A Gypsy, or *calo*, ritual form of song and dance performed in the southern, coastal regions of Spain, flamenco dance allows its performers a sensuous display of the upper torso through arm work or *(braceo)* and articulate hand gestures *(florea)*. The legs and feet attack the floor in a stacatto, percussive pounding of machine-gun rapidity of footwork *(zapateado)*.

Flamenco dance is to be distinguished from the Spanish classical style of dancing (called *escuela bolera*) as well as regional folk dances, such as the jota of Aragon and the Andalusian sevillanas. Stylistic similarities between eighteenth-century *contradanzas*, such as the *sarabande*, the *pavane*, and the *chaconne* can be seen in the relationship between head, arms, and feet in the fourth position *desplante* that ends most flamenco dances. The spatial relationship between arms extended outward to a demi-second position and upward to a high fifth position and the crossed *(croisé)* placement of the legs and feet in direct alignment with the upper body suggest the historical interchange between Spanish classical dance and flamenco technique.

Flamenco is danced by the body, sung by the voice, and played on guitars by Gypsies at their weddings, baptisms, festivals, and fiestas. It is danced both out of happiness and as an expression of grief. It is the oral history medium through which Gypsies communicate to one another their lives, thoughts, feelings, and performance ability. Perhaps the most powerful element of flamenco dance is the moment of *duende* ("trance"). This is an epiphenomenal moment. Although performers do not fall to the floor, they are thought to fall, mentally, into a liminal state of consciousness after fifteen minutes of repetitive footwork sequences: their attention becomes inwardly focused; their lips vibrate, as if resonating the pulse of the beat or a heartbeat; sweat begins to trickle down the cheeks and neck, and performers continue to dance, unaware of fatigue and physical stress on the feet, legs, and body.

Some Gypsies believe that a spiritual presence inhabits their dancing and that, at the moment, they are "in the flamenco." In his lecture in Cuba, Spanish poet Federico García Lorca called this moment the time when *los sonidos negros* ("the dark sounds") visit the performer's body. The distinction between this world and the next, between mortality and death, join in the body of the performer as he or she becomes totally absorbed by the rhythm *(compás)*. As a poet and a voice for the Gypsy people, García Lorca wrote numerous poems (*The Gypsy Ballads*, 1924–1927) in an attempt to describe the amorphous and fleeting nature of trance-induced blackness.

History. The origins of flamenco dance remain much disputed. Historians Ricardo Molina (1967) and Mañuel García Matos (1971, 1987) trace flamenco's origins to the ninth century, with the first mass migrations of the people now called Gypsies from the Punjab region of India, through Persia (Iran) to Egypt and North Africa, and then, into Spain. Molina argues that flamenco music had its genesis during the enlightened reign in the Iberian Peninsula of the Moorish king ʿAbd al-Raḥmān II, the Umayyad emir of Córdoba from 822 to 852, under whose patronage the poet and court musician Zyriab composed ten thousand songs. "The Black Nightingale," as Zyriab was known, invented a five-string lute that was ancestral to the modern guitar. The Moors (North African Muslims) had conquered the Iberian Peninsula in 711 and had ruled in grandiose courts until the final battles of Granada in 1492, which allowed the Catholic monarchs Ferdinand V of Aragon and Isabella of Castile to complete the *reconquista* ("reconquest") and to unite Spain as a Catholic country, expelling non-Christians.

Molina further argues that the integration of Moorish court music with Gypsy *cante* ("songs") laid the groundwork for flamenco as a Mozarabic creation. Connections between Indian *kathak* dance and North African *danse du ventre* can be seen in the interchange among guitarist, dancer, and singer, in the curvilinear motions of torso and arms, and in the articulation of the fingers (the *mudrás*). The *cantaor*'s ("singer's") wailing *(afílla)* is reminiscent of the call to prayer of Islam's muezzin. A Jewish influence may also exist in the emphasis on *duende* (spiritual trance). In 1469, at the royal wedding of Ferdinand to Isabella, Jews had performed the ecstatic dance of Palermo.

Some historians have argued that flamenco emerged only after the reunification of Spain, with the loss of Mozarabic cultural cohesion. The resulting severity of Spain's *reconquista* and the installation of the Spanish Inquisition provoked an artistic reaction expressed through flamenco. In 1480 Ferdinand and Isabella in their reuniting of northern and southern Spain forced all Gypsies into *gitanerías* (Gypsy enclaves), where they remained until the seventeenth century, when the crown allowed them to settle in villages and work as field laborers. Because many Gypsies remained attached to a nomadic form of life, others argue that the creation of flamenco as a Gypsy music and dance form did not begin until the latter part of the eighteenth century, when Charles III decreed that Gypsies were allowed to work in other occupations, some connected with the bullring. Most of the early iconography of flamenco dance dates only to the eighteenth century, in the form of engravings, etchings, and a few paintings, the most famous of which were executed by Francisco Goya.

The Edad del Oro, the golden age of flamenco, is generally considered to have begun in the 1780s. Two forms of flamenco song and dance emerged: *cantes jondos* and *cantes chicos*. The *cantes chicos* (*rumbas flamencas, tan-*

guillos, bulerías, alegrías, farrucas, zambras moras, and *fandangos*) grew out of the *cantes jondos*. The *cantes chicos* require technical proficiency but not the emotional commitment involved in the *cantes jondos'* individualistic interpretations.

The *cantes jondos (soleares, tientos, tangos,* and *seguiriyas)* are performed in a twelve-count phrase, with cut time and ¾ meter, to remain a test for a performer's creativity. The bases of *cantes grandes* expression are *caña, carcelera, tonas—martinete, debla—carrios, playeras, siguiríyas, polos,* and *soleares*. Out of these songs grew the flamenco dances we see performed today as well as the exchange of stylistic and rhythmic formulations between the Andalusian folk dances and the *flamenco andaluz.*

Among the great flamenco *cantaors* from the eighteenth to the mid-twentieth century were Tío Luis el de la Juliana (1750–1830); El Planeta (1785–1860); Diego el Fillo (1800–1878); Silverio Franconetti (1831–1893); Tomás el Nitri (1830–1890); María Borrico (1810–1880); La Adonda (1830–1890); Juan Pelao (1845–1910); La Sarneta (1837–1910); Manuel Torre (1878–1933); Pepe Nuñez de la Matrona (1887–1980); and probably, the most famous woman *cantaor,* "La Niña de Los Peines," Pastora Pavon (1890–1969).

The singers of flamenco's golden age were accompanied by dancers who adapted their rhythmic and choreographic styles to the *cante* while retaining a continually evolving formulation of the *flamenco baile* ("flamenco dance"). Among the first *bailaoras* ("dancers") to create the flamenco we know today were Juana Vargas, called La Macarrona (1860–1947), and Magdalena Seda, called La Malena (1870–1953). Both created completely individualistic, novel interpretations of *cantes jondo* and *cantes chico* songs; when they danced, fellow Gypsies knew in advance what to expect from them.

Most Gypsy performances of the late eighteenth and early nineteenth centuries took place around the camp fire, in the hills of Granada, in the Sacromonte, and in the *barrio* Santa Cruz in Seville. With no "proper" theater for flamenco performance as we know it today, flamenco remained, until the middle of the nineteenth century, a ritualistic experience for the great Gypsy clans—the Amayas, Ortegas, and Vargases, whose dynasties retained their influence in the twentieth century. In addition, Gypsies occasionally performed for "outsiders," both members of the land-owning aristocracy and travelers, such as John Singer Sargent, Prosper Merimée, Chauteaubriand, and Théophile Gautier—all of whom wrote and painted, portraying their Western vision of Andalusian life.

The golden age of "pure" flamenco was succeeded by a period of commercial performance in Europe's bars, music halls, and the first *café cantante,* founded by Silverio

FLAMENCO DANCE. Eighteenth- and nineteenth-century Gypsy dancers usually performed for members of their own family but occasionally danced for travelers. This engraving was made by C. Laplante after an original by Gustave Doré. (Reprinted from Lilly Grove, *Dancing,* London, 1895, p. 216.)

Franconetti in Seville in 1842, called the Café sin Nombre (the No-Name Café). By the end of the nineteenth century, dozens of such cafés flourished in Madrid, Barcelona, and Seville, and they profoundly influenced the development of flamenco. The changes in performance atmosphere, from outdoor patio to indoor stage and from a family setting to a small *tablao* ("platform") located in the back of a bar, emphasized the physical beauty of the female figure and the relationship between the male musician and the female dancer—thus divorcing flamenco from its original venues to create the sensuous, seductive, and mythic image we have of flamenco dancing today.

The *café cantante* enabled both musicians and dancers to earn a living as *gitanas flamencas*. Most important for the dance itself, the musicians were placed upstage, while the women danced to their accompaniment within the *cuadro,* or corps de ballet. The prettiest and youngest women, wearing long flounced dresses *(batas de colas),* performed at the front of the tiny stage. Men sitting nearby asked for specific women to dance and then paid them, occasionally arranging a "private" concert in another room. The dancers and musicians earned just enough to live on. The display of the dancer's body, her cascading ruffled dress, dangling earrings, hair combs, and *mantilla* made her the object of attention for the entire audience. The singer, once the most important performer in executing the traditional flamenco rhythms, now became her rhythmic accompaniment, ready to shift the *compás* in order to accompany her. With pamphlets and posters, advertising specific performers on specific nights, the *café cantante* became a commercial enterprise that formed the model for today's *tablados*, existing in major cities worldwide.

By the early twentieth century, the *cafés cantantes* were replaced by the music-hall stages of Madrid, Barcelona, Paris, London, and in the big cities of South America. Flamenco became a necessary staple of the music-hall era, but it also became an "act" wedged between other "acts." The women beautified the stage with their movement and costumes, and their male accompanists were pushed even farther upstage (*atrás*), their talents relegated to the guitar. The *cante* also began to change, becoming a melody that enhanced the guitar's arpeggios. As a storytelling

medium, as a Gypsy form of communication, *cante* had no place on the music-hall stage. Instead, the voice took on an operatic quality, perhaps the result of Italian-influenced *afílla* singing or because of the increasingly popular appeal of the male singers *en travesti* (in female dress) who appeared before or after a *bailaora*. With the softer, lighter tonality of traditional flamenco songs, the period known as *operisma* emerged.

Some stages were so small that dancers had to learn to dance around themselves. A typical male-female duet, the *martinete*, for example, could be danced in a space as wide as a large dinner table. Entire *cuadros* of ten female dancers, one dancing after another, would either take to the stage one-by-one or crowd it, allowing just enough space for the soloist to execute a shortened *soleá por bulerías* or a group *alegrías*, the typical finale. Often, each number contained the germ of a narrative situation. Men dressed as women singing shrill, comedic, operatic songs would often perform between flamenco solos, to diversify an entire performance. There could be as many as twenty separate dances within a single flamenco act. Sometimes a film would be shown in the middle: a Charlie Chaplin comedy, for example. Three shows could be performed per night. Some Gypsies continued to perform as well as they could. Others just performed, viewing a non-Gypsy audience as unknowledgeable, therefore unworthy of true

FLAMENCO DANCE. The cascading ruffled dress (*batas de colas*) complements the dancer's sensual display of the upper torso. *(left)* María Dolores, onstage with the Ximénez-Vargas Ballet Español, c.1964. *(right)* Sara De Louis, in a courtyard in Spain. (Photographs from the archives at Jacob's Pillow, Becket, Massachusetts.)

flamenco performance, and such performances continue to dominate nightclubs in Madrid.

Spanish artists and intellectuals of the early twentieth century criticized the corruption of a native art form; Federico García Lorca and composer Manuel de Falla viewed the growth of commercial flamenco as the bastardization of a utopian ethic that had lost its authenticity. With commercial venues, intellectuals influenced twentieth-century flamenco performance in several ways. The first important step toward a reconstruction of Gypsy flamenco began with Falla's *El Amor Brujo* in 1915 and his collaboration with librettists María Sierra and Gregorio Martínez Sierra for a pantomime version of *El Sombrero de Tres Picos* (1917–1919), which was danced by Gypsies in Madrid. A more elaborate ballet version, *Le Tricorne* (1919), was presented by Serge Diaghilev's Ballets Russes at London's Alhambra Theatre on 22 July 1919, choreographed by Léonide Massine, with flamenco coaching by Felix García and set designs by Pablo Picasso.

In 1922, in Granada, García Lorca and Falla organized the first flamenco Concurso de Cante Jondo, a competition of *"cante primitivo andaluz."* Gypsy flamenco performers came from pueblos around Andalusia to compete. The title's emphasis on "primitive, Andalusian *cante*" made socioeconomic, anthropological, and aesthetic statements, conflating the purity of Andalusian *cante* with its primitive nature—here was a folk form that had to be saved. The competition and other theatrical events were attempts to reposition flamenco as high art. They were statements of how folk forms might be adapted to modernist purposes and disseminated among a sophisticated cosmopolitan public appreciative of its authenticity and its newness. By 1936, when García Lorca was executed by Franco's forces, Gypsy flamenco performers had begun to recapture the authenticity of their art within a modernist context, touring their own shows.

The rebirth of flamenco in the 1910s and 1920s marked the beginning of its neoclassical period. Internationally renowned performers such as La Argentina (Antonia Mercé; 1888–1936), Vicente Escudero (1892–1980), Carmen Amaya (1913–1963), La Argentinita (Encarnación López; 1895–1945), and José Greco (born 1919) as well as the large traveling companies of Antonio and Rosario (Antonio Ruiz Soler and Rosario Florencia Pérez Podilla) and Ximénez-Vargas (Roberto Ximénez and Manolo Vargas) reenvisioned flamenco as a twentieth-century art form. Flamenco's movement vocabulary had been enlarged; gestures were bigger and footwork traveled across the entire stage, not just executed around the body of the performer. The spatial dimensions were altered to fit extensive scenery and lighting designs for audiences altogether unfamiliar with the flamenco genre. Most important to these performers' individual and collective successes was the way in which each fused the style and format of the traditional flamenco dances with Spanish classical dance and folk dances from various regions of Spain. These dancers paved the way for the radical departures from traditional songs to a more total theater that today calls for a complete fusion of music, dance, and *mise-en-scène:* the rhythms of the dancer and the guitarist are becoming one.

Argentina, Argentinita, Vicente Escudero, Antonio Rosario, and the Italian-American José Greco represent some of the best-known artists to have emerged from the music-hall era and onto concert stages in Spain, western Europe, and South and North America. Argentinita's sister, Pilar López, continued the traditions of both Argentina and Argentinita after their premature deaths. As neoclassical performers, soloists, and directors of major touring companies, these two performers brought fame and fortune to many flamenco Gypsy and non-Gypsy artists.

These dancers were traditional flamenco performers who widened the possibilities for flamenco through their incorporation of the *escuela bolera* into a *soleá por bulerías*, using castanets to accompany rapid footwork sequences instead of only the guitar or voice. The rhythms and the accents remained the same, but the elements—bodily, scenic, vocal—were manipulated to create a vision of flamenco heretofore unseen.

Although most early twentieth-century performers adapted text, costumes, lighting, and music to play to houses of greater than four thousand people, Carmen Amaya, perhaps the greatest interpreter of the flamenco rhythms, retained the traditional Gypsy setting for her performances whether they took place at New York's Town Hall or Buenos Aires's Teatro Colón. Amaya won international renown for the daring solos she executed dressed in a *bailaor*'s white suit, allowing her hair to come unraveled toward the end of the intense footwork sequences for which she earned her fame. Like Antonio, Amaya appeared in a number of Hollywood films, but she did not adapt stories and scene designs or use Spanish classical dances in her choreography. Amaya entertained audiences around the world, making no attempt to envision the stage space as a painting or a sculpture, as did Argentina, or anything but a floor on which to dance.

The virtuosic, prolific, and international fame gained by these artists paved the way for the post–Spanish Civil War artists of the 1950s, 1960s, and 1970s who performed during and after the death in 1975 of Spain's dictator Generalisimo Francisco Franco (ruled 1939–1975). Like Argentina and Argentinita, José Greco, Antonio and Rosario, Ximénez-Vargas, María Rosa, and Mario Maya populated their stages with as many as forty dancers in a single piece. Antonio, in particular, drew on classical ballet jumps and leaps to create an acrobatic performance space, in which he extended the possibilities of the male-female partnership in flamenco, using the entire stage to fall in love while executing his fancy footwork *(zapateado)*.

Flamenco performance in the post-Franco era has been prolific, rich with the jazz fusion and musical innovations of Paco de Lucia, the singing of Camaron de la Isla, and the films of Carlos Saura and Antonio Gades. Perhaps coinciding with the death of Franco, this 1970s and 1980s richness in the evolution of the formal elements of flamenco music as it relates to flamenco choreography has forever changed the face of flamenco performance. While retaining a Gypsy aura, the works of Antonio Gades, Mario Maya, Manolete Manolo Marín, Christina Hoyos, Concha Vargas, Rafael de Córdoba, Mathilde Choral, Blanca del Rey, Mariemma, La Tati, Carmen Cortés, Fernanda Romero, José Antonio (a director of the Ballet Nacional de España), El Guito, El Farruco, Merché Esmeralda, Nacho Duato, Manuela Vargas, Manuela Carrasco, the Grecos, Belén Maya, María Rosa, La Tona, Juana Amaya, and Antonio Canales, have all asserted choreographic and musical influences on the form. Antonio Canales's work with guitarist José Jiménez is very interesting in that, like the work of Mario Maya in the 1960s and 1970s, Canales attempts to create a stage space in which dance becomes rhythm, and guitar and song become the dance, so that the narrative becomes one of total rhythm in the service of total theater.

These innovations must be seen in the context of a chiefly neo-Gypsy interest that clearly rejects the neoclassical foundation. In Spain, this syncretic revolution, led

FLAMENCO DANCE. The rhythms of percussive footwork *(zapateado)* are often augmented by handclapping or castanets. *(above)* Flamenco dancer Inesita, c.1954. *(left)* Roberto Ximénez (kneeling) and Manolo Vargas (standing) with members of their company, c.1958. (Photographs from the archives at Jacob's Pillow, Becket, Massachusetts.)

by Canales, Maya, Marín, and the Grecos, opens up traditional flamenco by placing emphasis on the physical parameters of the body as it stands and rotates in high-heeled boots and shoes. The new flamenco body is thinner, longer, slick, and faster. It can turn like Vicente Escudero, the greatest male *bailaor* in history; jump like Antonio Ruiz Soler, the eccentric flamenco dancer of the late 1950s; and also stand on pointe, play castanets, and act, following the modernist approach to flamenco first imported to New York in 1916 by La Argentina. No one has yet to top the footwork of Carmen Amaya, the 1940s flamenco diva.

Antonio Canales may be said to lead the new flamencos. Half-Spaniard, half-Gypsy, the inventor of flamenco's most complex footwork sequences, he exists both inside and outside Gypsy culture. In a stunning display of male virtuosity, his *farruca* becomes the metaphysical embodiment of flamenco's future. In choreography, stature, and theatrical emphasis, Canales merges the technical, acrobatic style of the 1990s with the dance-theater world of the 1920s, fragmenting the traditional *baile flamenco* and reintroducing elements of a *soleá por bulerías* as the stuff of musical theater, adding a sculpted *escuela bolera* arm to the Art Deco line he demonstrates with his lower torso.

The seemingly prescient philosophy common to many flamenco performers in both Spain and the Americas is reminiscent of García Lorca and Falla's search for an authentic return to *flamenco puro* as it was performed in the Sacromonte. Yet it begs an awareness of the discoveries of both the boundaries and possibilities of a multicultured art form—one deep, rich, and ready for serendipitous exploration in the service of art and the preservation of Spanish and Gypsy performance history.

Although a majority of flamenco-identified dancers are Spanish, an important group of non-Spanish dancers includes Carola Goya, Matteo Marcellus Vittuci (scholar and dancer, known as Matteo), Teo Morca, Marianno Parra, Pilar Rioja, María Benítez, Carlota Santana, La Conja y Pedro Cortés, Susanna di Palma, and Pablo Rodarte.

Carola Goya, Matteo, Teo Morca, and María Benítez, in particular, as performers, company directors, and teachers, kept flamenco alive in the United States during the 1950s to 1970s' American boycott of fascist Spain, by touring small towns between New York and California. These performers, along with José Greco, whose work in Spain and the United States linked Spain to America through performance. With an increasingly large Hispanic population in North America, the rise of flamenco companies and studios has been timely, accepted, and acknowledged by both dance scholars and artists as an important phenomenon in a creolized American culture. At the end of the twentieth century, flamenco has become a global phenomenon, with performers in Spain, the Americas, Japan, Sweden, France, Israel, England, and Australia keeping it alive.

[*See also* Castanets; Escuela Bolera; Ximénez-Vargas Ballet Español; *and the entries on Amaya, Antonio and Rosario, La Argentina, La Argentinita, Escudero, Gades, Greco, López, and Rioja.*]

BIBLIOGRAPHY

Acton, Thomas. *Gitanos.* Madrid, 1983.

Balouch, Aziz. *Spanish Cante Jondo and Its Origin in Sindhi Music* (1955). Hyderabad, 1968.

Baroja, Pío. *Obras completas.* 8 vols. Madrid, 1946–1951.

Bennahum, Ninotchka. "A Most Civil War." *Village Voice* (17 December 1996).

Bennahum, Ninotchka. "Seduction in Andalusian Flamenco." In *Dancing Female Lives and Issues of Women in Contemporary Dance*, edited by Sharon Friedler and Susan Glazer. London, 1997.

Bennahum, Ninotchka. "La Argentina." Ph.D. diss., New York University, 1997.

Blas Vega, José. *Diccionario enciclopédico ilustrado del flamenco.* 2d ed. Madrid, 1990.

Brihuega, Jaime. *Los vanguardias artísticas en España, 1909–1936.* Madrid, 1981.

Castro, Américo. *The Structure of Spanish History.* Translated by Edmund L. King. Princeton, 1954.

Escudero, Vicente. *Mi baile.* Barcelona, 1947.

France, Anatole. "Antonio Argentina." *L'Illustration* (1928).

García Lorca, Federico. *Collected Poems.* New York, 1991.

García Matos, Manuel. *Danzas populares de España: Andalucía.* Madrid, 1971.

García Matos, Manuel. *Sobre el flamenco: Estudios y notas.* Madrid, 1987.

Grande, Félix. *Memoria del flamenco* (1929). 2 vols. 2d ed. Madrid, 1987.

Levinson, André. "Argentina" and "The Spirit of the Spanish Dance." In *André Levinson on Dance: Writings from Paris in the Twenties*, edited by Joan Acocella and Lynn Garafola. Middletown, Conn., 1991.

Manuel, Peter. "Andalusian Gypsy and Class Identity in the Contemporary Flamenco Complex." *Ethnomusicology* 33 (1989).

Martin, John. "The Dance: La Argentina." *New York Times* (1928).

Matteo [Matteo Marcellus Vittucci]. *The Language of Spanish Dance.* Norman, Okla., 1990.

Mitchell, Timothy. *Flamenco Deep Song.* New Haven, 1994.

Molina, Ricardo. *Misterios del arte flamenco.* Seville, 1967, 1986.

Pahlen, Victor. "Flamenco Art Linked to Spain's Proud Past." *New York Times* (April 1941).

Persia, Jorge de. *I concurso de cante jundo, 1922–1992.* Granada, 1992.

Pohren, D. E. *Lives and Legends of Flamenco.* Madrid, 1964.

Pohren, D. E. *The Art of Flamenco.* Seville, 1972.

Pohren, D. E. *A Way of Life.* Madrid, 1980.

Serrano, Juan, and Jose Elgorriaga. *Flamenco, Body and Soul.* Fresno, Calif., 1990.

Schreiner, Claus, ed. *Flamenco.* Translated by Mollie C. Peters. Portland, Ore., 1990.

Thiel-Cramer, Barbara. *Flamenco: The Art of Flamenco, Its History, and Development until Our Days.* Translated by Sheila Smith. Lidingo, Sweden, 1991.

Triana, Fernando el de la. *Arte y artista flamencas.* Madrid, 1957.

NINOTCHKA BENNAHUM

FLAMES OF PARIS, THE. Russian title: *Plamya Parizha*. Ballet in three acts and seven scenes. Choreography: Vasily Vainonen. Music: Boris Asafiev, based on music of the French Revolutionary era. Libretto: Vladimir Dmitriev and Nikolai Volkov. Art direction: Sergei Radlov. Scenery and costumes: Vladimir Dmitriev. First performance: 7 November 1932, State Academic Theater for Opera and Ballet, Leningrad. Principals: Olga Jordan (Jeanne), Natalia Dudinskaya (Mireille de Poitiers), Nina Anisimova (Thérèse), Vakhtang Chabukiani (Jérome), Konstantin Sergeyev (Antoine Mistral).

The action takes place in the third year of the French Revolution. The destiny of the main character, Jeanne—daughter of the peasant Gaspar of Marseille—is closely linked to events of insurgent Paris. The unjust and decadent court of King Louis XVI is opposed by the noble spirit of the common people, Jérome of Marseille, the Basque Thérèse, and the actors Antoine Mistral and Mireille de Poitiers, who help the insurgents to expose the conspiracy between army officers and aristocrats. To the music of revolutionary songs, the people storm the Tuileries Palace and wipe out the defenders of the monarchy. The people dance in Paris squares celebrating victory.

The production was twice revived on the Kirov stage: in 1936 in the original three-act, seven-scene version, and in 1950 in a new version of four acts and five scenes. In 1933 the ballet was staged in Moscow by the Bolshoi Ballet, with Anastasia Abramova as Jeanne; Marina Semenova as Mireille de Poitiers; Nadezhda Kapustina and Valentina Galetskaya alternating as Thérèse; Vakhtang Chabukiani and Aleksei Yermolayev as Philippe (the renamed role of Jérome). At the Bolshoi the ballet was revived twice: in 1947 with Olga Lepeshinskaya as Jeanne, Sofia Golovkina as Mireille de Poitiers, and Yermolayev as Philippe, and in 1960 with Raisa Struchkova as Mireille de Poitiers, Susanna Zvyagina as Thérèse, and Georgi Farmaniants as Philippe. Various choreographers in many Soviet cities (Sverdlovsk, Kharkov, Perm, Novosibirsk) as well as in eastern European cities (Budapest, Bratislava, Kosice, Leipzig, Prague, Brno) restaged the ballet.

The Flames of Paris is a pioneering Soviet ballet classic: it culminates in the taking of the royal palace, and it shows the people's revolutionary ardor and quest for freedom. The dance language of the folk scenes ranges from the unhurried "speech" of the Provençal natives to the excited "exclamations" of Jérome's variation and Thérèse's fiery dance.

BIBLIOGRAPHY

Asafiev, Boris, et al. *Plamya Parizha*. Leningrad, 1934.
Beaumont, Cyril W. *Complete Book of Ballets*. Rev. ed. London, 1951.
"The 'Danse des Citoyens.'" *The Dancing Times* (January 1936): 507–508.
Dorris, George. "Music for Spectacle." *Ballet Review* 6.1 (1977): 45–55.
Raffé, W. G. "Ballet in the U.S.S.R." *The Dancing Times* (January 1936): 505–509.
Roslavleva, Natalia. *Era of the Russian Ballet* (1966). New York, 1979.
Sollertinskii, Ivan. *Stati o balete*. Leningrad, 1973.
Swift, Mary Grace. *The Art of the Dance in the U.S.S.R.* Notre Dame, 1968.

IGOR V. STUPNIKOV
Translated from Russian

FLINDT, FLEMMING (born 30 September 1936 in Copenhagen), Danish dancer, choreographer, and director. In 1946 Flindt entered the ballet school of the Royal Theater in Copenhagen, where his most important teachers were Harald Lander and Vera Volkova. He became a member of the Royal Danish Ballet in 1955 but left Denmark that same year to join London's Festival Ballet as a principal dancer. In 1957 he was back in Copenhagen for a brief interval as a principal but soon left to join the Paris Opera Ballet, where he was *danseur étoile* from 1960 to 1966. During the twelve years that Flindt directed the Royal Danish Ballet, from 1966 to 1978, modern dance found its way to Copenhagen.

Flindt began his career as a classic *danseur noble*. He danced all the princes in the international repertory as well as all the male heroes in the August Bournonville ballets, Gennaro in *Napoli* and James in *La Sylphide* being the most important of these. His technique was competent and controlled, but he was most impressive when he combined steps with character, especially when the latter had a touch of the bizarre, as with such characters in his own ballets as the Dancing Master in *The Lesson* (1963) and the title role in his choreographic masterpiece, his version of *The Miraculous Mandarin*, produced in 1967, as well as the title role in Roland Petit's *Le Loup*. It was Petit who gave Flindt his first chance to show his true strength as a character dancer by giving him the role of Don José in *Carmen* in 1960.

Flindt was the foremost Danish choreographer after Harald Lander. His first ballet, *The Lesson*, was made for Danish television in 1963. Based on Eugène Ionesco's play of the same title, *The Lesson* magnificently conveyed the play's atmosphere of terror, fear, and death. Flindt worked with Ionesco again on *The Young Man Must Marry* (1965), a parody of bourgeois life and an erotic nightmare; with music by Per Nørgård, it was a highly original work. Another Ionesco play, *Jeux de Massacre*, was the basis for the 1971 Flindt ballet *The Triumph of Death*, which was hughly successful in Denmark. A strong, intense portrayal of the fall of Western civilization, the ballet received extra publicity because some of its scenes were danced in the nude—something that had never been done before by the Royal Danish Ballet. In addition, the production attracted a new, young audience because of the swinging beat of

Thomas Koppel's music, which was played by the Danish group Savage Rose. Flindt called it a dance drama rather than a ballet, and indeed Flindt's talent for dramatic effect may well have been his greatest strength as a choreographer.

Flindt is a man of the theater and a showman more than an original choreographer. His showmanship became evident in *The Three Musketeers*, first performed in 1966, as well as in the third act of his version of *Swan Lake*, produced in 1969. Flindt staged a rather cold but impressive *Sacre du Printemps* on television in 1968, and in 1978 he produced another dance drama, *Salomé*, with music by Peter Maxwell Davies and with his wife, Vivi Flindt, dancing the title role. Staged in the circus building in Copenhagen, *Salomé* showed Flindt's ability to exploit the unusual setting of the circus arena as well as the highly erotic element of Salomé dancing in the nude. *Salomé* was an exploration of the dark side of life, which always seemed to inspire Flindt most, often with impressive results. Drawn to the dark

FLINDT. One of the controversial scenes from Flindt's *Triumph of Death* (1971), in which some dancers appeared nude. This photograph was taken during a 1976 performance at the Metropolitan Opera House, New York. (Photograph © 1984 by Johan Elbers; used by permission.)

but nonetheless always aiming for the light, Flindt stood midway between a Jean Genet and an August Bournonville.

Flindt did choreograph some ballets more in the classical tradition, including *The Four Seasons*, to the concertos by Antonio Vivaldi, and *The Nutcracker*. Flindt's version of *The Nutcracker*, with sets and costumes by Bjørn Wiinblad, had a Biedermeier, or harmonic, quality, very much in the tradition of the Royal Danish Ballet.

Flindt left his mark on ballet in Copenhagen. He performed the classical repertory on which the Danish ballet tradition was founded. His *The Toreador* in 1978, based on an 1840 Bournonville ballet, represented an intelligent approach to that tradition—something to be respected but also to be played with. In the same vein he staged Bournonville's *Wedding Festival at Hardanger* with the Norwegian National Ballet in Oslo in 1982. The story was Bournonville's, and Flindt's choreography was in the style of Bournonville. Nevertheless, Flindt's true interests were the modern trends in dance. He gave new types of dancers, such as Vivi Flindt and Johnny Eliasen, new possibilities in the repertory, and he brought numerous modern choreographers to Copenhagen, especially from the United States, among them Paul Taylor, Glen Tetley, José Limón, Murray Louis, Eliot Feld, and John Neumeier. In 1981 Flindt became director of the Dallas Ballet; he left in 1989.

After his years in Dallas, Flindt went on working as a freelance choreographer. For Rudolf Nureyev he created *The Overcoat* (1989), after the short story by Russian writer Nikolay Gogol, and *Death in Venice* (1991), after the novel by Thomas Mann. For the Royal Danish Ballet he created the full-length ballet *Caroline Mathilde*, also in 1991, about the tragic fate of a young English princess who came to Denmark in the 1760s to marry the mad king Christian VII. The dance, with a new score by Peter Maxwell Davies, once again showed Flindt's talent for the psychological and erotic dance drama.

[*See also* Royal Danish Ballet.]

BIBLIOGRAPHY

Anderson, Jack, and George Dorris. "A Conversation with Svend Kragh-Jacobsen." *Ballet Review* 5.4 (1975–1976): 1–20.

Aschengreen, Erik. "Flindt, Flemming." In *Dansk biografisk leksikon.* 3d ed. Copenhagen, 1979–.

Aschengreen, Erik. *Balletbogen.* Copenhagen, 1982.

Duff, Helen. "Dancing in Copenhagen." *The Dancing Times* (December 1978):156–157.

Jackson, George. "Falling in Love Again." *Dance View* 9 (June (1992):31–37.

Lundgren, Henrik. "50 år Flemming Flindt." *Politiken* (29 September 1986).

Nugent, Ann. "Altered States." *Dance Theatre Journal* 12 (Autumn 1995):16–20.

Tomalonis, Alexandra. "Bournonville's Gifts." *Dance View* 9 (June 1992):42–54.

ERIK ASCHENGREEN

FOKINE, MICHEL (Mikhail Mikhailovich Fokin; born 23 April [5 May] 1880 in Saint Petersburg, died 22 August 1942 in New York), Russian choreographer. The ballets of Michel Fokine were the basis of the repertory for all the Ballets Russes companies. He created seventeen works for Serge Diaghilev between 1909 and 1914, and contributed substantially to the companies headed by René Blum, Colonel Wassily de Basil, and Sergei Denham. Fokine's works include some of the most famous ballets in history, and certainly some of the most significant of the early twentieth century, among them *Les Sylphides, Le Carnaval, Schéhérazade, The Firebird, Le Spectre de la Rose,* and *Petrouchka.* Only *Les Sylphides (Chopiniana),* however, has survived in repertory as an undisputed masterpiece and a hallmark of twentieth-century plastique. If Fokine had choreographed no other ballet, his stature in dance history would still have been assured.

Fokine was noted as a "reformer" of ballet—a champion of expressivity over pure dance in the tradition of Franz Hilverding, Gaspero Angiolini, John Weaver, and Jean-Georges Noverre. His choreography in the Diaghilev era revitalized ballet, creating new forms and expanding the ballet vocabulary, and his one-act ballets compressed dancing and pantomime into a unified expression. Fokine rebelled against the display of technique for its own sake rather than for the portrayal of emotion. He also railed against a set choreographic form, advocating instead the creation of a framework according to dramatic requirements.

Training and Early Career. Fokine entered Saint Petersburg's Imperial Theater School in 1889 and studied with Platon Karsavin, Nikolai Volkov, Aleksandr Shiriaev, Pavel Gerdt, and Nikolai Legat. His first performance was in Marius Petipa's *The Talisman;* while still a student he performed leading roles in other Petipa ballets, such as *The Magic Flute* and *La Fille Mal Gardée.* Upon graduation with first prize in his class of 1898, Fokine immediately entered the Maryinsky company as a soloist, making a successful debut on 26 April in the pas de quatre from *Paquita.* He performed both character and classical roles in the Maryinsky repertory, including Bernard de Ventadur and Jean de Brienne in *Raymonda,* the pas de trois and Siegfried in *Swan Lake,* Pierre in *La Halte de Cavalerie,* Bluebird and Prince Désiré in *The Sleeping Beauty,* Harlequin in *Harlequinade,* Lucien in *Paquita,* Solor in *La Bayadère,* and the pas de trois in *The Fairy Doll.* He was promoted to *premier danseur* in 1904. He was Anna Pavlova's regular partner; they created leading roles in the Petipa-Ivanov ballet *The Awakening of Flora.* In 1901 he appeared outside Russia for the first time, in Budapest and Vienna, with a small troupe organized by Marie Petipa.

Fokine was accepted in the postgraduate "class of perfection" taught by Christian Johansson, whom he revered as "a living museum of choreographic art," and he thus became interested in ballet pedagogy. He began teaching at the Imperial Theater School in 1902 in the girls' department, and in 1908 also began teaching boys. Among his pupils were Bronislava Nijinska, Lydia Lopokova, Olga Spessivtseva, Elena Smirnova, Elena Lukom, Elisaveta Gerdt, Lubov Tchernicheva, Marie Piltz, Pierre Vladimiroff, Aleksandr Gavrilov, Andrei Lopukhov, and Nikolai Ivanovsky. Fokine deviated from the standard school syllabus by emphasizing musicality, developing *épaulement* and expressive use of the head, and giving his pupils problems in dance composition and lectures on beauty and aesthetics. He was promoted to *professeur de danse* in 1904.

In 1905 Fokine married his former student Vera Antonova. She was his constant companion until his death, serving as an interpreter of his ballets and becoming perhaps his most influential artistic adviser. She also shared teaching duties with him in their New York studio in the 1920s.

From the beginning of his career with the Maryinsky company, Fokine was unhappy with what he perceived to be its stagnant ballet traditions. He scorned the apparent lack of seriousness, citing the inappropriate costumes of the ballerinas, the direct appeals to the audience by dancers stepping out of character, and the interruption of the ballets by outbursts from the audience. In Fokine's notion of art, dance had to aim for dramatic cohesion, preserving the unities and aiming for a strict consistency of illusion. He felt that ballet could not be serious unless it expressed drama or emotion.

Fokine's first formal realization of these precepts was an introduction outlining his proposed reforms in a 1904 libretto for *Daphnis et Chloë,* which he submitted to Vladimir Teliakovsky, director of the Imperial Theaters. Although the ballet was not produced at that time, these notes formed the basis of Fokine's famous letter to the *Times* of London, 6 July 1914, in which he decreed his Five Principles of ballet reform: (1) movement must be appropriate to locale and period; (2) dramatic action should be advanced through movement; (3) the total body should be expressive, eliminating set mime and hand gestures; (4) the entire corps de ballet should express the theme; and (5) music should unify the theme, and the sets and costumes should be appropriate to the era of the ballet. These principles were also given formal expression in "The New Ballet," published in the Russian journal *Argus* on 1 November 1916. These reforms clearly harken back in spirit to those set down by Jean-Georges Noverre in his *Lettres sur la danse* (1760), a work with which Fokine was familiar.

In 1900 Fokine had seen touring Siamese court dancers, and their influence can be found in the exoticism of his early ballets. But even more important for him was the arrival of Isadora Duncan in Saint Petersburg in December 1904. There is little doubt that Duncan had a profound influence on Fokine, particularly in her use of music by great composers (rather than pieces commissioned from hacks) and in her use of the entire body in a natural manner for emotional and pictorial expression; the actual extent of her influence, however, has been the subject of much debate. Diaghilev cited Duncan as the root of Fokine's ballet and thus of the Ballets Russes enterprise, but Fokine himself was angered by this assertion; he admired Duncan but also admitted a profound uneasiness about her. Fokine said that he did not find new ideas in her, but rather a kindred spirit who was developing her art along lines parallel to his own. Fokine asserted that he had already studied the art of ancient Greece before he saw Duncan, and there are in fact profound differences between their approaches.

While Duncan opted for abstraction in her "natural" approach to Greek art, attempting to distill its essence, Fokine took a literal, curatorial approach in his borrowing of Greek themes and poses (as he would do later in his oriental and Slavic pieces). Fokine did not reject the idea of drama and storytelling in ballet; he simply wanted more verisimilitude, while Duncan aimed for the abstract. While Duncan was rejecting the artificiality of ballet technique, Fokine was insisting that his dancers have a technical basis; he was quarreling with the misuse of technique, not with its existence.

Shortly after Duncan's visit Fokine choreographed his first ballet, *Acis and Galatea,* to music by Andrei Kadlets and based on a theme from Ovid's *Metamorphoses,* for the annual student performance of 1905, using some ideas from his unproduced *Daphnis* libretto. The school's management did not allow him freedom to stage the ballet according to his own notion of Greek style; he had to provide choreography that employed turnout, pointe work, and virtuosic technique. However, there were compromises: the costumes were a hybrid, with Grecian tunics and pointe shoes, and there was a nonballetic plastique using variation of levels, relaxed poses, and asymmetrical groupings inspired by the frescoes of Pompeii. For the same program Fokine also choreographed *Polka with a Little Ball* and what would become Pavlova's signature piece, *The Dying Swan.* Fokine annually mounted productions for the school performances during his tenure on the faculty.

In 1906 Fokine began regularly choreographing for benefits, a practice he continued until he left Russia. His first work for professionals was Anton Rubinstein's *La Vigne* in April 1906, in which dancers—including Lydia Kyasht, Marie Petipa, Tamara Karsavina, Pavlova, and Fokine himself—portrayed qualities of wine. Marius Petipa sent Fokine a note congratulating him on this ballet and predicted a great career, a compliment that Fokine treasured as the greatest of his life. On 23 February 1907

Fokine created an entire charity evening at the Maryinsky, for which he choreographed the two-act *Eunice* to music by Konstantin Shcherbachev, and the first version of *Chopiniana.* In *Eunice,* with a libretto by Count Stenbok-Fermor taken from Henryk Sienkiewicz's novel *Quo Vadis?,* Fokine was able to apply his reforms relatively unhampered. He used no turnout, pointe work, or other pyrotechnics, opting instead for a plastique approach in the Duncan Grecian style, emphasizing the ensemble. The dancers were dressed in draperies rather than tutus, but the management forced the use of tights, on which Fokine ordered toes painted to simulate bare feet. In the cast were Matilda Kshessinska as the slave Eunice, who performed a sword dance; Pavel Gerdt as Petronius; and Pavlova as Actea.

On 27 March 1906 students and junior company members danced Fokine's revision of Petipa's *A Midsummer Night's Dream,* with some new dances that included "Vol de Papillons," a pas de deux for Elena Smirnova and Vaslav Nijinsky; "The Valse Fantasia" (to inserted music by Mikhail Glinka); and "The Battle of the Elves and Bats." For the school performance of 15 April 1907 Fokine choreographed *The Animated Gobelin,* which he was invited to set on the Maryinsky company in an expanded version called *Le Pavillon d'Armide,* with libretto and designs by Alexandre Benois; it debuted on 25 November 1907. The Saison Russe enterprise in dance began with Diaghilev's desire to present *Pavillon* in Paris, where it was the opening ballet of his first season in 1909. [*See* Pavillon d'Armide, Le.]

In his choreography for charity performances Fokine was able to bypass the administration and strictures of the Imperial Theaters. He staged *Bal Poudré,* to music by Muzio Clementi, at the Pavlov Hall in Saint Petersburg—a work he considered too risqué for repetition. At another charity performance on 8 March 1908 *Une Nuit d'Égypte* (also called *Egyptian Nights*), to music by Anton Arensky, premiered, with a libretto that had been written by Petipa and choreographed by Lev Ivanov in 1900 but never performed. It was staged in a mock Egyptian style of flat profile and angular lines, with the dancers in dark body makeup and appropriate costumes from the Maryinsky wardrobe, supplemented by a few new ones by Léon Bakst. It entered the regular Maryinsky repertory on 19 February 1909, with Pavel Gerdt as Mark Antony, Olga Preobrajenska and Nijinsky as Favored Slaves, Pavlova as Veronica, Fokine as Amoun, Aleksei Bulgakov as the High Priest, and drama student Elisaveta Timme in the nondancing role of Cleopatra. Although Fokine was aiming for an authentic Egyptian look, the dance of the slaves with silk scarves was, according to Nijinsky, "à la Duncan." The ballet was known as *Cléopâtre* after it entered the Diaghilev repertory in 1909.

One of the most famous dances in the twentieth-century repertory, *The Dying Swan*, to music by Camille Saint-Saëns, was presented at a charity performance on 22 December 1907. Fokine had initially worked out the choreography on Pavlova in less than half an hour for the student performance of 1905, and it was specifically designed for her gifts. It became indelibly associated with her image as she performed it throughout her career. [*See* Dying Swan, The.] For the same performance Fokine choreographed *Dance with a Torch (Danse Assyrienne)* for Karsavina. In February 1908, for a charity performance at the Maryinsky, Fokine choreographed *Nocturne* for Kshessinska and Nijinsky. For another charity ball on 20 February 1910 he created *Le Carnaval,* whose *commedia dell'arte* characters were based on Robert Schumann's notes to his score. This ballet also entered the Diaghilev and Maryinsky repertories. [*See* Carnaval, Le.]

In 1907 Fokine began choreographing a series of dances to the music of Chopin, which evolved into his acknowledged masterpiece, *Les Sylphides* (still known as *Chopiniana* in Russia). Ironically, it is this abstract ballet—far removed from the type of dramatic ballet he made his life's mission—that carries Fokine's name to succeeding generations. The first version consisted of five short independent scenes—four character dances and a classical pas de deux for Pavlova and Anatole Obukhoff—presented as a *divertissement* for a charity performance on 10 February 1907. The following year Fokine staged *Danses sur la Musique de Chopin*, which with new orchestration by Maurice Keller was presented in its entirety at another charity performance on 8 March 1908. A ballet in the Romantic style, the second *Chopiniana* had twenty ballerinas in white costumes, with Nijinsky in the only male role. The character work from the first *Chopiniana* had been eliminated; the Waltz in C-sharp Minor had been retained and used as the basis for the entire ballet. On 19 February 1909 *Chopiniana* finally entered the Maryinsky repertory. On the second 1909 Ballets Russes program in Paris, *Les Sylphides*, renamed by Diaghilev in homage to Parisian Romantic ballet, premiered, with the Prelude in A Major replacing the Polonaise in A Major as an overture and new orchestrations arranged by several noted composers. For this ballet Nijinsky created a new image for the male dancer as an equal to the ballerina. [*See* Sylphides, Les.]

By 1908 Fokine was emerging as a rival and open competitor to Nikolai Legat, the Maryinsky's official ballet master and choreographer. Fokine's demands, bluntness, irritability, and intolerance for tradition created a rift in the company and made the older dancers especially antagonistic toward him. However, there was a small group at the Imperial School and Theater who were devoted to Fokine and his ideas (these "Fokintsy" had dubbed themselves "the innovators"), among whom were Nijinsky and Nijinska. The other Maryinsky camp, the "Imperialitsy"

led by Legat and Kshessinska, considered Fokine their principal enemy.

Diaghilev's Ballets Russes. In 1908 Benois, a friend of Fokine's and the first of the *Mir isskustva* group to recognize Fokine's abilities, advanced Fokine's views to Diaghilev, whom the choreographer had known only slightly as a theater official years before. Diaghilev asked Fokine to prepare an entire repertory, which he would present in Paris in 1909, engaging Fokine as premier danseur as well as ballet master. The first performance of Diaghilev's Ballets Russes at the Théâtre du Châtelet on 19 May 1909 consisted of *Le Pavillon d'Armide* and the newly commissioned *Polovtsian Dances* from the second act of Aleksandr Borodin's opera *Prince Igor*. During this season only, the work was performed as part of the entire act of the opera, with the accompaniment of a complete chorus. The Slavic barbarity of Nikolai Roerich's decor and the seething masses whirling and jumping in rhythmic frenzy—particularly in the ending, in which the men repeatedly hurled themselves into the air and crashed onto the floor—created a sensation and made Adolph Bolm as the Polovtsian Chief an immediate star. This dance and others by Fokine that followed in the next three seasons helped to form the mystique of the Russian dancer as wild, natural, semibarbaric, emotional, and theatrical; however, as Nijinska pointed out, even the "wild hordes" danced in a perfect circle and crossed the stage in an even pattern, not unlike the symmetry of Petipa.

The second program on 2 June 1909 consisted of *Cléopâtre, Le Festin,* and *Les Sylphides*. For *Cléopâtre,* to Arensky's original score Diaghilev added new music, a pastiche of pieces by Nikolai Rimsky-Korsakov, Mikhail Glinka, Modest Mussorgsky, Aleksandr Glazunov, Nikolai Tcherepnin, and Sergei Taneyev. The spectacular Bakst decor was a turning point in theatrical decoration. A private student of Fokine, Ida Rubinstein, mimed Cleopatra, making her entrance as a mummy who is slowly unwrapped from her veils. Fokine danced Amoun to Pavlova's Ta-Hor (as the character Veronica was renamed), and Nijinsky was the Favorite Slave. For this version Fokine created "Bacchanale" to Glazunov's Autumn movement of *The Seasons*, in which women were pursued by a satyr; this dance thrilled Paris and became the prototype for the erotic melodramas of the early Ballets Russes repertory. Fokine reworked the "Bacchanale" as a pas de deux, which after much protest was finally presented in Saint Petersburg in 1910 by Pavlova and Laurent Novikoff. (Newly arranged by Mikhail Mordkin, it later became a signature work in Pavlova's repertory.) Fokine created the "Hopak," "Trepak," and "Finale" for the suite of character dances called *Le Festin*. After the sensational 1909 season Fokine received the Palme Académique from the French government.

For the 1910 season, Fokine created *Schéhérazade, The*

Firebird (under the title *L'Oiseau de Feu*), and *Les Orientales*, and he revived *Le Carnaval*. *Schéhérazade* was the first true creation of the Diaghilev collaborators designed specifically for the Saison Russe. Its orgy scene and the vibrant colors of Bakst's decor profoundly influenced both ballet and fashion. [*See* Schéhérazade.] *The Firebird* had been announced but was not ready for the 1909 season; it received its premiere on 24 June 1910. The first Diaghilev ballet with commissioned music, it launched the career of composer Igor Stravinsky, who found himself famous overnight. *The Firebird* was based on a mélange of the folktales of Aleksandr Afanasiev; Fokine was credited as librettist, although it seems clear that many others contributed. Stravinsky and Fokine worked closely in developing the choreography and the score. With Karsavina as the Firebird, Fokine as Ivan Tsarevich, Fokina as the

Tsarevna, and Bulgakov miming Kastchei, Fokine created a realistic interpretation of the fairy tale. [*See* Firebird, The, *article on* Fokine Production.] Fokine saw the importance of this ballet in its containing no "conversations" and in its establishment of a truly collaborative working process with the composer. *Les Orientales*, to music by Glazunov, Christian Sinding, Arensky, and Grieg, orchestrated by Stravinsky, a suite of dances featuring Nijinsky, was certainly influenced by the Siamese dancers Fokine had seen in Saint Petersburg.

During the creation of *Firebird*, Diaghilev and Fokine had begun to quarrel, and Diaghilev complained to Karsavina that Fokine's work was old-fashioned. Diaghilev resented Fokine's independence and threatened to sell all the Fokine ballets and to work instead with Aleksandr Gorsky or Nijinsky. By 1911 Diaghilev wanted to get rid of Fokine, considering him stubborn, conceited, and narrow. There is no doubt that Diaghilev also wanted to create his own choreographer. He felt that Fokine's ballets were limited because they evoked the past, concentrating

FOKINE. *Le Pavillon d'Armide*, with designs by Alexandre Benois, was presented during Diaghilev's first Saison Russe in Paris. This photograph was taken at the open dress rehearsal on 18 May 1909 at the Théâtre du Châtelet. (Photograph from the Dance Collection, New York Public Library for the Performing Arts.)

FOKINE. Aleksei Bulgakov as Kastchei and Michel Fokine as Ivan Tsarevich in *The Firebird* (1910). Kastchei, master of monsters, embodiment of evil, and ruler of the Impure Kingdom in Fokine's ballet, is also the subject of an opera by Nikolai Rimsky-Korsakov, *Kashchei the Immortal*. (Photograph from the Dance Collection, New York Public Library for the Performing Arts.)

on distant lands and local color rather than speaking to the modern world. Nijinsky, too, was unhappy with Fokine's sacrifice of structure to his notion of realism.

In 1911, however, Fokine was still the sole choreographer for the Ballets Russes and obtained prolonged leave from the Maryinsky to choreograph new ballets: *Petrouchka* to music by Stravinsky, *Le Spectre de la Rose* to Carl Maria von Weber, *Narcisse* to Tcherepnin, and *Sadko—Au Royaume Sousmarin* to Rimsky-Korsakov. He also supplied additional choreography for a truncated *Swan Lake*. Receiving its premiere 13 June 1911, *Petrouchka* arguably has the most famous ballet score ever written, with which Fokine was said to have had great difficulty. Nijinsky created the role of Petrouchka, Karsavina was the Ballerina, and Alexandre Orloff the Moor, and there was an ensemble of more than one hundred. It was one of the great successes of the Ballets Russes repertory. [*See* Petrouchka.]

Based on a poem by Théophile Gautier and set to Carl Maria von Weber's "Invitation to the Dance," *Le Spectre de la Rose* was first performed on 6 June 1911. The ballet became indelibly associated with its dancers, Karsavina as the Young Girl and Nijinsky an astonishment as the Spirit of the Rose. Based on Nijinsky's incomparable elevation, this was the most difficult and longest male variation in the ballet repertory, culminating in a huge leap out of the window. Nijinsky's performance in this role became part of ballet legend. His strange androgyny and distortion of the classical *port de bras* as the incarnation of a rose, along with the sleepwalking of Karsavina as the young girl, created a dreamlike atmosphere within Bakst's Biedermeier decor. The ballet became the most popular work in the Ballets Russes repertory.

Sadko—Au Royaume Sousmarin, taken from Rimsky-Korsakov's eponymous opera, was a one-act ballet sung by a chorus and danced entirely by the ensemble, with decor by Boris Anisfeld. With a commissioned score by Tcherepnin and a libretto by Bakst, *Narcisse* was another "Greek" ballet; Fokine choreographed it only reluctantly because his heart was set on the postponed *Daphnis et Chloë*. The cast included Nijinsky as Narcisse, Karsavina as Echo, Fokina as the Boetian Girl, and Nijinska as a Bacchante. The static libretto worked against the ballet, and even with Karsavina and Nijinsky it was not a success. Bakst and Fokine incorporated many of their ideas for *Daphnis,* and the ensemble movements were clearly in the Duncan style; however, Nijinska claimed that the choreographic style of *L'Après-midi d'un Faune* was carried over by Nijinsky and herself into their interpretations in this ballet.

Despite the conflict between the two men, Diaghilev persuaded Fokine to leave the Maryinsky permanently and named him choreographic director for the 1911 season, at a large salary. Fokine worked quickly, and Diaghilev's demands on him—nothing less than the creation of an entire repertory each season—were prodigious. The 1912 season was filled with tension as Fokine created three ballets for the company. On 13 May 1912 Diaghilev presented *Le Dieu Bleu* to a score by Reynaldo Hahn, based on Hindu legends adapted by Jean Cocteau. It was notable chiefly for the extravagance of Bakst's costumes and decor; less successful was the choreography in pseudo–Hindu-Siamese style. *Thamar,* premiering on 20 May 1912, was another pseudo-Oriental ballet, basically a variation on *Cléopâtre* and *Schéhérazade,* with extraordinary Bakst decor and some pointe work for the men. Fokine faithfully reproduced authentic Caucasian Georgian dances to the superb Mily Balakirev score. Karsavina and Bolm were highly praised, and the ballet was warmly received in London. The evil Georgian queen was one of

Karsavina's best-known roles, and the ballet lasted well into the 1930s.

Fokine's final work for Diaghilev in 1912 was *Daphnis et Chloë,* with a masterful score by Maurice Ravel, the project on which Fokine had worked from the outset of his choreographic career. Fokine's libretto concerning Pan and his two worshippers had first been submitted in 1904 to the Maryinsky directorate and then shown to Diaghilev in 1910. However, Ravel's score was not ready until 1912, by which time Diaghilev was no longer interested in Fokine. *Daphnis* was staged as an eighteenth-century pastoral, with Nijinsky as Daphnis, Karsavina as Chloé, and Bolm as Darkon. Diaghilev was concentrating at the time on Nijinsky's *L'Après-midi d'un Faune* and paid little attention to Fokine's pet ballet. Bakst's original decor had already been used for *Narcisse,* and the new one he provided was unsuitable; Diaghilev also gave Fokine recycled costumes. This inattention and an unwieldy libretto gave the ballet, which premiered on 5 June 1912, little chance for success. Fokine was furious with Nijinsky and accused him of copying the style of *Daphnis* in his *Faune;* however, Nijinska claimed that Fokine appropriated the style of *Faune* in his dance for the three nymphs, and that Bolm's "Dance of Darkon" in *Daphnis* was a travesty of *Faune.*

Break with Diaghilev. Fokine resented Nijinsky's new role as choreographer and acrimoniously left the company following the Paris season of 1912. However, public perception still assumed Fokine to be the choreographer of Nijinsky's *Le Sacre du Printemps,* much to the dismay of its composer, Stravinsky, who saw in Fokine an "exhausted artist," clever but not a genius and incapable of imagining appropriately modern choreographic forms.

While working for Diaghilev, Fokine had continued to choreograph and perform in Russia. In April 1910 he staged the Venusberg scene from Richard Wagner's opera *Tannhäuser* for a charity benefit. Other ballets (*Chopiniana, Une Nuit d'Égypte, Le Carnaval, Polovtsian Dances*) were being taken into the Maryinsky repertory by

FOKINE. Scene from the original Diaghilev production of *Petrouchka* (1911), with Alexandre Orloff as the Moor (center), wielding a sickle, Vaslav Nijinsky as Petrouchka, cowering on the floor, and Tamara Karsavina as the Ballerina, covering her ears. (Photograph from the Dance Collection, New York Public Library for the Performing Arts.)

Teliakovsky, who was disappointed in the ballets of Legat. In 1911 Fokine staged dances for Gluck's opera *Orfeo ed Euridice*. On 10 March 1912 staged two new works at the Maryinsky with dancers from Diaghilev's company: Balakirev's *Islamey* was another Oriental fantasy based on *The Arabian Nights*; Robert Schumann's *Papillons* was a sequel to *Le Carnaval*. Both ballets entered the Maryinsky repertory. Fokine also performed at the Maryinsky during his Diaghilev years.

After leaving Diaghilev in 1912 Fokine returned to the Maryinsky to stage the operas *Judith*, by Aleksandr Serov, and *The Pearl Fishers*, by Georges Bizet. In 1913 he contributed two ballets to Pavlova's repertory. *Les Préludes* to Franz Liszt, a choreographic essay on Lamartine's *Poetic Meditations*, was in the manner and spirit of Isadora Duncan; it was later transferred to the Maryinsky. *The Seven Daughters of the Mountain King* (also known as *The Three Palms*), to music by Aleksandr Spendiarov, was an ambitious Oriental ballet with modernist decor by Anisfeld. Fokine then staged the dances for Ida Rubinstein in Gabriele D'Annunzio's play *La Pisanella*, produced in Paris. Fokine had taught Rubinstein privately in Saint Petersburg and had choreographed the "Dance of the Seven Veils" for her in Oscar Wilde's *Salomé*, presented at the Mikhailovsky Theater in 1908 in a production designed by Bakst and directed by Meyerhold. He had also choreographed D'Annunzio's *Le Martyre de Saint-Sébastien* for her in 1911. That year Fokine had also begun an association with the Royal Swedish Ballet, returning regularly through 1914 to restage his works.

Return to the company.   After Diaghilev's dismissal of Nijinsky, Fokine was reengaged in 1914 as *premier danseur* and choreographic director to reset old ballets and create new ones. His contract specified that Nijinsky's works were to be dropped from the repertory and that Fokine was to dance Nijinsky's roles. Fokine brought *Papillons*, exactly as it had been staged in Saint Petersburg. *Die Josephslegende*, with an undanceable Richard Strauss score and a libretto by Hugo von Hofmannsthal and Count Harry Kessler, introduced nineteen-year-old Léonide Massine in the role of Joseph. The action of the biblical tale was transferred to Renaissance Venice in the sets of José Maria Sert; Bakst's costumes were in the style of Veronese. *Josephslegende* was criticized for its reliance on mime, but Massine was not yet fully trained as a dancer and Maria Kuznetsova as Potiphar's Wife was a better singer than dancer. With music by Maximilian Steinberg, *Midas* was another Greek ballet, this one concerning a contest between Pan and Apollo, that featured Karsavina and Bolm. *Midas* is generally dismissed as inconsequential, although Benois has championed it.

Rimsky-Korsakov's *Le Coq d'Or* was Fokine's last ballet for Diaghilev and one of his greatest. The libretto by Vladimir Belsky was based on a poem by Aleksandr

FOKINE. After his break with Diaghilev in 1912, Fokine returned to Saint Petersburg and resumed work at the Maryinsky Theater. He is seen here, c.1914, with his wife Vera Fokina in his *Chopiniana*. (Photograph from the Dance Collection, New York Public Library for the Performing Arts.)

Pushkin. Karsavina danced the Queen of Shemakhan, which became her favorite role. The decor and costumes by Natalia Goncharova and the staging of the opera with the dancers portraying the sung roles (the singers were relegated to tiered stands on the sides of the stage) aroused great attention, but the composer's widow disliked the staging and forced Diaghilev to withdraw it from the repertory. However, Fokine restaged the ballet, his favorite, in 1937 in an all-dance version for Colonel W. de Basil's Ballets Russes.

Fokine rehearsed the 1915 repertory but left the Ballets Russes before the United States tour. According to Fokine's memoirs, Diaghilev sailed to the United States without settling his debts, and Fokine refused to work for him again. Nonetheless, Fokine's works were given by Diaghilev through his last season.

To Russia.   Following his final break with Diaghilev, Fokine returned to Russia, remaining in Petrograd throughout World War I. During this period he choreographed only seven short ballets, some opera dances, and a few concert numbers. In December 1915 two ballets, *Eros* and *Francesca da Rimini*, which had been choreographed for charity performances, entered the Maryinsky repertory. Set to Tchaikovsky's "Serenade for Strings," *Eros* was based on Valerian Svetlov's tale "The Angel of Fiesole." It bore some resemblance to *Les Sylphides* and *Le Spectre de la Rose*, as Fokine attempted to reconcile his quest for a natural plastique with classical technique. *Francesca da Rimini*, set to Tchaikovsky's symphonic poem concerning an episode from Dante's *Divine Comedy*, was choreographed as a series of tableaux. Fokine also choreographed in 1915 Glazunov's *Stenka Razin*, a ballet on Russian national themes with pantomime scenes, folk dances, and Oriental dances. In 1916 he choreographed Paul Dukas's *The Sorcerer's Apprentice*, which he later reproduced at New York's Lewisohn Stadium and in Buenos Aires.

Only one work of this period, *Jota Aragonesa* (1916), is recognized as among Fokine's greatest. Set to the famous Spanish overture by Glinka, this was a suite of brilliant character dances in which soloists moved naturally in and out of the ensemble dances. The choreography employed those elements of Spanish dance closest to classical ballet; *battements*, *glissades*, and small, skidding jumps were arranged with classical harmony, symmetry, and order. It was revived by the Ballet Russe de Monte Carlo. Apart from this ballet, however, critical reaction in Russia was unfavorable. Fokine's last association with the Maryinsky came in November 1917 when he staged Glinka's opera *Ruslan and Ludmila*. In 1918 Fokine left for a Scandinavian tour, never to return.

Fokine desperately wished to resume a loose association with the Maryinsky, but the Soviet government would not guarantee his freedom to travel to the West. He was forced to choose between total commitment to the Soviet Union or an uncertain artistic life in the United States and Europe. The last twenty years of his life were spent in constant travel in order to dance, choreograph, and reset his works. Fokine hated the commercialism of the American theater, where he worked for the next decade. During the last years of his life he longed for traditions, and he wanted to establish an institution in the United States comparable to the Maryinsky.

In 1923, negotiations were set in motion for Fokine, his reputation now officially reinstated, to return to the Maryinsky for a two-day jubilee to celebrate his quarter-century there with the ballet (even though he had not been present for the final five years). The jubilee was held and a monograph was issued, but Fokine stayed away rather than risk denial of an exit visa. Like Diaghilev, Fokine was severely disappointed by his inability to repeat his Western success within Russia. But this success, founded on exoticism, lost its appeal at its source, where interest centered in the formal. The publication of the Russian edition of his autobiography was important for Soviet dance history, as was Yuri Slonimsky's introduction, "Fokine and His Time," which placed Fokine within the Soviet aesthetic.

To Sweden and the United States. Fokine and his family left Russia in March 1918, crossing the Baltic on sleds packed with their belongings. They went to Stockholm, where Fokine staged *Petrouchka* at the Royal Theater. He also choreographed large outdoor spectacles in Stockholm in September 1918—Beethoven's

Moonlight Sonata and *The Four Seasons* to music by Grieg, Schubert, and Tchaikovsky, with a cast of eight hundred. He then settled in Denmark, where he taught and staged performances. The Fokines took part with Rolf de Maré in planning Les Ballets Suédois, which was to be directed by Jean Börlin, a Swedish dancer who studied with Fokine in Copenhagen. During that company's first season in Paris in 1920, Börlin staged dances from *Chopiniana*.

Musicals, concerts, and charities. America had first seen Fokine ballets in unauthorized versions staged by Theodore Koslov for Gertrude Hoffman's Saison Russe in 1911. Eleven Fokine ballets had also been included in the repertory of the 1916 and 1917 Ballets Russes American tours. In 1919 the producer Morris Gest brought Fokine to New York to stage the dances for act 2 of the Broadway musical *Aphrodite*, which opened at the Century Theatre on 1 December 1919. He staged a similar production for Gest the following year called *Mecca*, yet another pageant of the Orient for which Fokine choreographed a processional and a ballet, "Memories of the Past," followed by a bacchanale led by Martha Lorber and Serge Pernikoff.

Sponsored by Morris Gest, Sol Hurok, Richard G. Herndon, and others, Fokine and his wife gave concerts, recitals and lecture-demonstrations in the United States in the 1920s. Their first concert in New York, on 30 December 1919 at the Metropolitan Opera House, included *Salomé*, *Chant d'Automne*, *Gypsy Dance*, *Bacchus*, *Panaderos*, and a suite of eight Russian dances, all but *Gypsy Dance* using music by Russian composers. Fokine turned to Mozart for his one-act *Le Rêve de la Marquise*, first presented at the Metropolitan Opera House on 1 March 1921. Set in the eighteenth century, it tells of a Marquise (Fokina) who dreams that the statue of a Faun (Fokine, who also danced the Marquis) comes alive and pursues her into a park pool. Other concert repertory included *Poland—Three Moods: Happiness, Revolt, Sadness*, to music by Chopin, *Moonlight Sonata*, *Amoun and Berenice* to Arensky, *Passepied* to Delius, *Mazurka* to Delibes, *Humoresque* to Dvořák, and *Etude Symphonique* to Schumann. On 23 January 1933 the Fokines gave their last public performances in Toronto.

The Fokines had hoped to have a concert career in the United States, but they were forced to adapt to American tastes for revue and spectacle. Fokine's work in the American theater included "The Ballet of Perfumes," to Brahms, for Lydia Lopokova in *The Rose Girl*, a 1921 Shubert-produced musical. On 3 September 1921 Fokine's ballet *Thunderbird* opened as part of the Dillingham revue *Get Together* at the New York Hippodrome. The libretto, attributed to Vera Fokina, was based on an Aztec legend, and the ballet had choreographic and thematic links to *The Firebird*, *Swan Lake*, and *The Dying Swan*. With decor by Willy Pogany and music by Balakirev, Borodin,

Rimsky-Korsakov, and Tchaikovsky, the ballet featured Fokina as Nahua and the Thunder-bird and Fokine as Aztlan. Fokine also contributed two ballets—*Frolicking Gods*, to Tchaikovsky's "Nutcracker Suite," and *Farljandio* to music by Victor Herbert, both led by Martha Lorber and Serge Pernikoff—to the sixteenth *Ziegfeld Follies*. His "Ballet of the Flowers" was led by Marilyn Miller in *Rosalie*, a 1928 musical.

In the 1920s Fokine also choreographed incidental dances for plays such as *Johannes Kreisler* (1922), *Casanova* (1923), Max Reinhardt's *The Miracle* (1924), the Oriental spectacle *Hassan* (1923–1924), and *The Tenth Commandment* (1926). Work in other New York productions included ballet numbers in *Sweet Little Devil* (1924), *Skygirl* (1923), *Grand Street Follies* (1928), and the 1936 revivals of *Floradora* and *Blossom Time* by the San Carlo Opera Company.

Fokine also staged dances for the revues, vaudeville

FOKINE. During the 1920s, Fokine worked mainly in the United States, as a freelance choreographer and performer. This studio portrait shows him in costume for his *Cléopâtre*, originally presented in 1909 in Paris. The curly wig seen here is typical of the sort worn by ballet dancers in the early 1900s. (Photograph by Mishkin; from the Dance Collection, New York Public Library for the Performing Arts.)

acts, and concerts of established stars. For Gertrude Hoffman and her American Ballet he choreographed *Mazurka*, *Pas Espagnol*, and the Oriental ballet *Shaytan's Captive* to music from *Raymonda*. He also contributed Hoffman's ballets for the musical revue *Hello, Everybody* (1923). Gilda Gray, "the Shimmy Girl," studied with Fokine; he choreographed *Russian Toys* to music by Rimsky-Korsakov for her 1922 nightclub act. This ballet was also included on programs by Fokine and his students and was later revived under the name *Igrouchki* for the Ballet Russe de Monte Carlo, with Alexandra Danilova as the Goose Girl. As he had in Russia, Fokine contributed ballets to American charity functions. These included *La Fontaine Animée, Caucasian Sketches, Ballet Espagnol, The Mountain Queen*, and *Danse Grecque*.

From 1922 through 1927, Fokine choreographed prologues for movie palaces; each week he was required to stage new shows that ran three or four times a day. The 1922 prologue repertory included *Les Sylphides, Polka, Waltz*, and *The Adventures of Harlequin*, a *commedia dell'arte* ballet, and in 1927 *Faust*. The Fokines appeared in a nightclub engagement in 1926, and in 1924–1925 the Fokine Dancers toured on the Keith-Albee vaudeville circuit with a new ballet, *The Immortal Pierrot*, to music by Beethoven, revived in 1926 and 1934.

Fokine appeared at the Hollywood Bowl in August 1929, having rechoreographed his 1910 Venusberg scene from *Tannhäuser* as *Bacchanale*. In 1929 he gave up his New York home and studio to move to Hollywood and choreograph for films, but no offers materialized and the Fokines retreated to New York in early 1931.

Teaching and the American Ballet Company. Fokine had opened his first studio in the United States in 1921, sharing teaching duties with Fokina and their son, Vitale. Fokine taught Italian technique as he had learned it in Russia, adding a third dimension to the "flat" exercises. The classes emphasized style over technique, aiming for fluidity, natural progression, and orchestration of the entire body in a movement. Fokine taught that the torso and head were involved in every movement, and he favored an asymmetrical twist. His American pupils included Patricia Bowman, Paul Haakon, Betty Bruce, Harold Haskin, Eugene Loring, Nora Kaye, Helen Tamiris, John Taras, Annabelle Lyon, Lincoln Kirstein, and Ruth Page. He also taught summer teachers' courses and, in 1925–1926, classes in "Plastique and Dance" at Artef.

The Fokine American Ballet Company made its debut on 26 February 1924 at the Metropolitan Opera House in New York. The company of sixty dancers, all students of Fokine, included his son. In the repertory were *The Dying Swan, Le Rêve de la Marquise, Antique Frieze* (probably a version of *Danse Grecque*), and *Olé Toro*, a comic work previously performed as *Capriccio Espagnol*. There were also two premieres. *Les Elfes*, a plotless work similar to

FOKINE. With his own company, billed as the American Ballet Company, Fokine appeared as Perseus in his *Medusa* (1924), at the Metropolitan Opera House, New York. (Photograph by Goodwin; from the Dance Collection, New York Public Library for the Performing Arts.)

Les Sylphides with the dancers clad as wood sprites, was choreographed to the same music Fokine had used for *A Midsummer Night's Dream;* it was later restaged for the Ballet Russe de Monte Carlo. *Medusa,* to Tchaikovsky's Sixth Symphony ("Pathétique"), was a staging of the Greek myth, with Fokina as Medusa, Fokine as Perseus, Nelly Savage as Pallas, and Jack Scott as Poseidon.

Fokine never had the permanent American company he had envisioned, owing to lack of financial backing, and his group assembled only for individual engagements. After its debut the company did not reappear in major engagements until August 1927, when Sol Hurok presented them at Lewisohn Stadium. They reappeared there in 1934, performing to an audience of seventeen thousand with an additional ten thousand turned away. Over the years the company's repertory included *Oriental Dances, Voices of Spring, The Adventures of Harlequin,* and *The Sorcerer's Apprentice,* in addition to Fokine standards. At various times the company included Bowman, Haakon, Lyon, Kaye, Loring, Vitale Fokine, Albertina Vitak, Pauline Koner, Thalia Mara, George Chaffee, and George Church. When Fokine returned to Europe, Vitale took

over the direction of the group, which continued to give sporadic performances through 1940. At Jones Beach in July 1936 two solos Fokine had choreographed for Bowman premiered—*Persian Angel* told of an angel who becomes human and dances herself to death; in *Tennis* (for which Fokine used music from *Coppélia*) Bowman played four sets of tennis in four minutes—and in summer 1937 *None But the Lonely Heart.*

Globetrotting. Although Fokine used the United States as his base in the 1920s and became an American citizen in 1932, he occasionally traveled to Europe to perform in concert tours and stage revivals. In 1925 the Fokines returned to Stockholm to rehearse his ballets, and he toured with Fokina in Scandinavia, the Baltic countries, and Germany. In Berlin in 1925 he staged *Fra Mina* to Schumann, an unsuccessful work based on Anatole France's "The Saintly Satyr." He also choreographed the dances for *A Midsummer Night's Dream* at London's Drury Lane in 1925. The Fokines returned to Europe for a brief tour in 1929.

FOKINE. A studio portrait from the 1920s of Fokine as Harlequin in *Le Carnaval* (1910), his ballet based on *commedia dell'arte* characters. (Photograph from the Dance Collection, New York Public Library for the Performing Arts.)

FOKINE. Vera Fokina and Michel Fokine in *Le Spectre de la Rose* (1911), performed by Fokine's company on a tour of Germany in 1925. (Photograph from the Dance Collection, New York Public Library for the Performing Arts.)

By the 1930s, Fokine was disheartened by the conditions of American show business and he spent most of the decade abroad. In 1931 he spent five months at the Teatro Colón in Buenos Aires, restaging the *Polovtsian Dances*, *Le Carnaval*, a new version of *The Sorcerer's Apprentice*, *Le Spectre de la Rose*, *Les Sylphides*, *Schéhérazade*, and a new version of *The Adventures of Harlequin*. In Paris in 1935 he staged *Psyché* to music by César Franck and *Mephisto Valse* to Liszt for Olga Spessivtseva's Concert de Danse. That year he also created four ballets for Ida Rubinstein: *Sémiramis* to music by Arthur Honegger, *Diane de Poitiers* to Jacques Ibert, and Ravel's *La Valse* and *Boléro*. In residence at the Teatro alla Scala in Milan in 1936 he choreographed dances for Saint-Saëns's opera *Samson et Dalila* and the ballet *The Love for Three Oranges* to music by Simoni and Giulio Sonzogno.

The Ballet Russe companies. It was not until 1936, with his engagement as choreographer-in-chief for René Blum's Ballets de Monte-Carlo, that Fokine reentered the mainstream of European ballet. From their beginnings, both Blum's and de Basil's Ballet Russe companies had been based on the Fokine repertory. With the Blum engagement Fokine entered a new period of creativity. He restaged most of his Diaghilev ballets and some later works, including *Les Elfes*, *Igrouchki*, and *Jota Aragonesa*. He also choreographed three new ballets—*L'Épreuve d'Amour*, *Don Juan*, and *Les Éléments*—which were critical successes but have not survived in repertory.

Reported to be one of Fokine's finest works, *L'Épreuve d'Amour* premiered in Monte Carlo on 4 April 1936 with a score that was formerly attributed to Mozart but is now thought to be *Der Rekrut*, divertissements by various Viennese composers. The ballet was a *chinoiserie*, with libretto by Fokine and André Derain, and a masterful Derain decor. It contained elements of both farce and fantasy, and both classical and character dancing. The cast included Vera Nemchinova as the Chinese Maiden, André Eglevsky as her lover, and Hélène Kirsova as the Butterfly.

With a libretto by Fokine based on Molière's play, the mimetic "choreodrama" *Don Juan* was Fokine's version of the eighteenth-century *ballet d'action*. In the 25 June 1936 London premiere Anatole Vilzak appeared as Don Juan, Jeannette Lauret as Donna Elvira, Jan Yazvinsky as the Commander, Louis Lebercher as Sganarelle, and Eglevsky as the Jester. Particularly noted was the virtuosic "Dance of the Jesters," and the "Dance of the Furies" accelerated to a fever pitch of speed and intensity. As a whole, however, it was regarded as visually lavish but generally uninteresting.

Les Éléments, to music by Bach, premiered at the London Coliseum on 26 June 1937. It was choreographed in the eighteenth-century heroic style and featured the dancers as Flora and Zephyr, with other gods, sprites, and natural elements of vapor, rain, flowers, a volcano, and ocean waves. Created for Fokine's own American company in 1924, *Les Elfes* was revived by both Blum's and Denham's Ballet Russe companies. *Igrouchki* was also revived in 1939 by Blum.

When Blum's company disbanded in 1937, Fokine replaced Massine as ballet master for the Ballet Russe of Colonel de Basil, which had performed *Les Sylphides* as the opening of its first London program on 5 July 1933. It already possessed a large repertory of Fokine works, staged by Serge Grigoriev. Fokine revised his older ballets to great critical praise and created three new ones.

A new *Le Coq d'Or* in a straight ballet version, with a score edited by Tcherepnin, was staged in 1937. A mixture of pageantry and comedy, it featured marvelous sets and costumes by Goncharova. The dramatic ballet was largely mime, characterization, and decor, but there were fine roles, particularly the Queen of Shemakhan for Irina Baronova, the Golden Cockerel for Tatiana Riabouchinska, King Dodon for Marc Platt (then called Platov), and the Astrologer for Harcourt Algeranoff. The ballet was noted for its wit, satirical viewpoint, and detailed characterizations as well as for the unified designs of mass movement for the corps.

When the de Basil company became known as Educational Ballets (under the titular leadership of German Sevastianov), Fokine choreographed two more ballets. *Cendrillon,* to a score by Frédéric d'Erlanger, premiered in London on 19 July 1938, with Riabouchinska as Cinderella, David Lichine as the Prince, Tamara Grigorieva as the Good Fairy, and Raissa Kuznetsova as the Cat. It featured pre-Renaissance decor by Natalia Goncharova but was hampered by its unsuccessful score; still, the pageant interlaced with comedy and broad farce for the Stepsisters was thought to have naiveté and charm.

FOKINE. The ensemble of the Ballets Russes de Monte Carlo in Serge Grigoriev's 1935 staging of *Schéhérezade,* originally choreographed by Fokine in 1910. (Photograph by Raoul Barbà; from the Dance Collection, New York Public Library for the Performing Arts.)

In 1937 Fokine had begun to work with Sergei Rachmaninov on *Paganini,* a theme suggested by the composer. This psychological ballet, which also dealt with philosophical ideas, was based on the legend of the violin virtuoso selling his soul to the devil in return for perfection in his art—drawing parallels between the life of Paganini and Fokine's own. The complicated production in three scenes, designed by Serge Soudeikine, premiered on 30 June 1939. The title role, performed by Dmitri Rostov, was mainly mime, but there was highly virtuosic dance for the rest of the cast, which included Riabouchinska as the Florentine Beauty, Baronova as Divine Genius, Yurek Lazowski as Scandal, Alberto Alonso as Gossip, and Grigorieva as Guile. The ballet was hailed as a great work, but it began to lose its appeal in the late 1940s. Fokine toured to Australia with de Basil (then called the Covent Garden Russian Ballet) in 1938–1939.

Sergei Denham's Ballet Russe de Monte Carlo had a large repertory of Fokine ballets acquired from Blum. Most programs that this "American" Ballet Russe brought to audiences across the United States from 1938 to 1963 contained at least one Fokine ballet.

Ballet Theatre.   In 1939 Fokine joined the newly formed Ballet Theatre as its first choreographer and head of his own "Fokine wing." Its first program in January 1940 opened with *Les Sylphides*, newly staged for the company, as did all opening seasons for the next fifteen years, and the work became a signature piece for Ballet Theatre; when Mikhail Baryshnikov took over American Ballet Theatre, he restaged it in the Kirov Ballet tradition. Fokine's careful restaging of *Le Carnaval*, also on the opening program, brought it new life, with Bolm as Pierrot and Bowman as Columbine. *Le Spectre de la Rose* was restaged in 1941 and *Petrouchka* in 1942. The Fokine image dominated Ballet Theatre in its first years, and the company in effect became the American home of which Fokine had dreamed. It was filled with former Fokine students and dancers.

FOKINE. The *Polovtsian Dances* from *Prince Igor*. The highlight of act 2 of Aleksandr Borodin's opera, Fokine's ballet was originally presented in May 1909 during the opening season of Diaghilev's Ballets Russes. This scene is from his 1936 restaging for René Blum's Ballets de Monte Carlo. (Photograph by Raoul Barbà; from the Dance Collection, New York Public Library for the Performing Arts.)

For Ballet Theatre, Fokine choreographed *Bluebeard*, to music by Jacques Offenbach, arranged by Antal Dorati, which premiered at the Palacio de Bellas Artes in Mexico City on 27 October 1941. The four-act ballet had a libretto by Fokine after the comic opera by Ludovic Halévy and Henry Meilhac, and decor by Marcel Vertès. It starred Antony Tudor as King Bobiche, Anton Dolin as Bluebeard, Lucia Chase as Queen Clementine, Alicia Markova as Floretta, George Skibine as Prince Sapphire, Irina Baronova as Boulotte, and Nora Kaye, Maria Karnilova, Rosella Hightower, Miriam Golden, and Jeannette Lauret as Bluebeard's wives. A parodic farce with love scenes, duels, masques, and slapstick, *Bluebeard* was set in a mythical sixteenth-century kingdom and told of the sad old age of King Bobiche, plagued by his wife's infidelity and the philanderings of Baron Bluebeard. It became a staple of the Ballet Theatre repertory on its Hurok tours and was still in the repertory in 1960, when it was taken to the Soviet Union.

The Russian Soldier premiered at the Boston Opera House on 23 January 1942, with decor by Mstislav Dobujinsky. The work featured Yurek Lazowski as a young

FOKINE. Alexandra Danilova (center) as the Goose Girl in Fokine's 1938 revival of his *Igrouchki*, for the Ballet Russe de Monte Carlo. Also known as *Russian Toys*, this peasant comedy, set to music by Rimsky-Korsakov, was originally created in 1922 as a nightclub act for Gilda Gray, the inventor of the Shimmy. (Photograph from the Dance Collection, New York Public Library for the Performing Arts.)

Russian soldier who envisioned his life as he lay on a battlefield waiting for Death (Donald Saddler). The work was filled with pageantry and *trepak*-style dances. Its main appeal was its timely appearance during World War II, but it was criticized as running contrary in theme to its programmatic score, Sergei Prokofiev's *Lieutenant Kijé Suite*.

Fokine's last work for Ballet Theatre was *Helen of Troy*, to Offenbach's *La Belle Hélène*. It was meant to be a companion piece to *Bluebeard* and used the same collaborators. Fokine fell ill during rehearsals and was unable to polish the production, but it was premiered at the Palacio de Bellas Artes in Mexico City on 8 September 1942, with Donald Saddler as Menelaus, Baronova as Helen, Dolin as Paris, and Ian Gibson as Hermes. After Fokine's death from pneumonia, the ballet was rechoreographed by David Lichine and George Balanchine.

The "Fokine problem" has been one of the great debates in dance criticism at the end of the twentieth century. Although his preeminence was accepted in the West throughout the first half of the century, the extent of his importance is a matter of debate in the second. Fokine's reputation has suffered with a change in taste, which has come to accept the Maryinsky dance-centered standards and its neoclassical offspring rather than Fokine's dramatic style. As David Vaughan (1978–1979) pointed out, of the approximately eighty ballets Fokine choreographed, only eight remain in the current repertory, and all except *Le Coq d'Or* (second version) are from the Diaghilev era. Even these ballets are regarded in the main as historical curiosities. Dale Harris (1980) asserted that much of the feeling for these works is nostalgic, looking back to this last flowering of pre–World War I European culture.

Most of the ballets are in the curious position of being venerated by historians while remaining essentially unrevivable. The very fact that they centered on the evocation of character and place rather than on pure movement elements makes them especially difficult to revive. They featured dramatic-mimetic roles to be filled by specific interpreters. The original performances, particularly those of Nijinsky, were an inherent part of the choreography, and it is this legend rather than reproducible formal movements that have survived.

Fokine himself eschewed the modernist aesthetic. He usually chose to work with traditional nineteenth-century and early twentieth-century music, particularly by Russian composers. After *Petrouchka*, he avoided the use of Stravinsky's music. Fokine also ended his career as a guardian of his own tradition and a champion of classical technique. A famous confrontation with Martha Graham in 1931 prompted his article "A Sad Art," first printed in *Novoe russkoe slovo*, which described their disagreement regarding the "basis" of natural movement.

There is no question that Fokine changed the course of ballet. He was a pathbreaker in dispensing with classical technique and structure, according to the needs of style and internal logic. Favored with the extraordinary interpreter and technician Nijinsky, Fokine also took part in a revitalization of male dancing, creating for the *danseur* expressive roles that would stand equal to those created for the ballerina.

[*See also* Ballets Russes de Monte Carlo; Ballets Russes de Serge Diaghilev; *and the entries on the principal figures mentioned herein.*]

BIBLIOGRAPHY

Anderson, Jack. *The One and Only: The Ballet Russe de Monte Carlo.* New York, 1981.
Beaumont, Cyril W. *Michel Fokine and His Ballets.* London, 1935. See Appendix C for a complete list of choreographed works.
Borisoglebskii, Mikhail. *Proshloe baletnogo otdeleniia Peterburgskogo teatral'nogo uchilishcha, nyne Leningradskogo gosudarstvennogo khoreograficheskogo uchilishcha: Materialy po istorii russkogo baleta.* Vol. 2. Leningrad, 1939.
Buckle, Richard. *Diaghilev.* New York, 1979.
Fokine, Michel. "The Principles of Ballet" (1916). *The Dancing Times* (June 1932): 223–225.
Fokine, Michel. *Memoirs of a Ballet Master.* Translated by Vitale Fokine. Edited by Anatole Chujoy. London, 1961. Includes a complete list of choreographed works.
Fokine, Michel. *Protiv techeniia: Vospominaniia baletmeistera.* Edited by Yuri Slonimsky. Leningrad, 1962.
Garafola, Lynn. *Diaghilev's Ballets Russes.* New York, 1989.
García-Márquez, Vicente. *The Ballets Russes: Colonel de Basil's Ballets Russes de Monte Carlo, 1932–1952.* New York, 1990.
Goldman, Debra. "Mothers and Fathers: A View of Isadora and Fokine." *Ballet Review* 6.4 (1977–1978): 33–43.
Harris, Dale, and David Vaughan. "A Conversation with P. W. Manchester." *Ballet Review* 6.3–4 (1978–1979): 57–90, 108–125.
Harris, Dale. "The Fokine Legacy." *Ballet News* 2 (September 1980): 28–31.
Horwitz, Dawn Lille. *Michel Fokine.* Boston, 1985.
Horwitz, Dawn Lille. "Michel Fokine: Choreography of the Thirties." In *Proceedings of the Eleventh Annual Conference, Society of Dance History Scholars, North Carolina School of the Arts, 12–14 February 1988,* compiled by Christena L. Schlundt. Riverside, Calif., 1988.
Kirstein, Lincoln. *Fokine.* London, 1934.
Kirstein, Lincoln. "Homage to Michel Fokine." In Kirstein's *Ballet: Bias, and Belief.* New York, 1983.
Koner, Pauline. "With Fokine." *Ballet Review* 17 (Spring 1989): 16–26.
Krasovskaya, Vera. *Russkii baletnyi teatr nachala dvadtsatogo veka,* vol. 1, *Khoreografy.* Leningrad, 1971.
Macdonald, Nesta. "Mikhail Fokine and 'Modern Dance.'" *Dance and Dancers* (August 1992): 17–21.
Money, Keith. *Pavlova: Her Art and Life.* New York, 1982.
Nijinska, Bronislava. *Early Memoirs.* Translated and edited by Irina Nijinska and Jean Rawlinson. New York, 1981.
Payne, Charles, et al. *American Ballet Theatre.* New York, 1977.
Perron, Wendy. "The Far-Flung Fokine Family." *Ballet Review* 18 (Summer 1990): 48–58.
Poesio, Giannandrea. "Balletic Mime." *The Dancing Times* (June 1990): 895–899.
Pudełek, Janina. "Fokine in Warsaw, 1908–1914." *Dance Chronicle* 15.1 (1992): 59–71.
Sokolov-Kaminsky, Arkady. "Mikhail Fokin in St. Petersburg, 1912–1918." *Dance Research* 10 (Spring 1992): 53–58.
Sorley Walker, Kathrine. *De Basil's Ballets Russes.* New York, 1983.
Teliakovsky, Vladimir. "Memoirs: St. Petersburg Ballet." Translated by Nina Dimitrievich. *Dance Research* 9 (Spring 1991): 26–39.
Vaughan, David. "Fokine in the Contemporary Repertory." *Ballet Review* 7.2–3 (1978–1979): 19–27.

ARCHIVE.   Michel Fokine Archives, Phyllis Fokine, Jackson Heights, New York.

SUZANNE CARBONNEAU

FOLIA. Known in Spanish as *la folia* and in French as *les folies d'Espagne,* the *folia* was a boisterous, noisy type of dance accompanied by singing and instruments (guitar, castanets, and flute), attested from Renaissance times in Portugal and Spain. In the early seventeenth century it spread to Italy and later came to the court of Louis XIV in France. The term *folia* also refers to the music—the bass line and chords of the accompaniment, several versions of which exist—that has served as a point of departure for numerous compositions from the seventeenth century to the present day.

Aside from literary references, little is known of the *folia* before the seventeenth century. It was associated with the theater of Spain's Golden Age (c.1550–1650), as a component of the unrelated interludes and ballets that were inserted at pauses in the main dramatic work. A vivid description is given by Sebastian de Covarrubias in *Tesoro de la lengua castellana o española:*

> The folia is a very noisy dance of Portugese origin. Many dance figures come from it, accompanied by the noisy *sonajas* [a wooden ring holding metal disks] all of which make a loud noise and other instruments. Some dancers carry others on their shoulders, and some young men dress themselves as young maids, who, with pointed sleeves, go making turns and sometimes dancing. And the *sonajas* play with such great noise

FOLIA. Example 1. Violin part for the dance "Folie d'Espagne" as found in Feuillet's *Recüeil de dances*, published in 1700.

and so rapidly that everyone seems to be out of their minds; thus the dance is called folia, from the Tuscan word *folle*, meaning emptiness, madness, without brains.

(Covarrubias, 1611)

Other writers associated the *folia* with occasions such as fertility rites or Carnival festivities; it was also said to be connected with the Renaissance *moresca*, or Morris dance. The earliest preserved music is in the *Musica libri septem* of Francisco de Salinas (1577).

The *folia* changed when it went to other parts of Europe, and at the French court of Louis XIV it was refined to conform to French taste. Four theatrical pieces from about 1700, entitled "Folie d'Espagne," survive in choreographic notation, two by Louis Pecour and two by Raoul-Auger Feuillet. The music, which is sixteen measures long and in a moderate triple meter, keeps repeating continuously, usually from four to six times. Variations were undoubtedly improvised, though only a single unadorned violin part appears with the dance notation (see example 1). Castanets and a special use of the arms were apparently characteristic, since Feuillet's *Chorégraphie* (1700) provides one couplet of a *folie d'Espagne* showing exactly when to sound the castanets and move the arms in conjunction with the steps and music. The steps are those common to French court dancing of the time (for example, *pas de bourrée*, *coupé*, and *temps de courante*), but with special use of virtuosic movements, such as elegant leg gestures, pirouettes, and *battements*. The choreographies accumulate energy gradually, with a high point approximately in the middle of the piece, and return to quietness at the end.

The *folia* music has been investigated by musicologists, notably Richard Hudson (1971), who brilliantly delineated the structures on which improvisation was based. However, the dance itself, despite an immense popularity in Europe over several centuries and despite the availability of sources, still awaits attention by scholars and performers of Baroque dances. Among composers who wrote *folia* variations are Girolamo Frescobaldi, Arcangelo Corelli, Marin Marais, Jean-Henri D'Anglebert, Domenico Scarlatti, Franz Liszt, and Sergei Rachmaninov.

[*For related discussion, see* Ballet Technique, History of, *article on* French Court Dance.]

BIBLIOGRAPHY

Cotarelo y Mori, Emilio. *Colección de entremeses, loas, bailes, jácaras, y mojigangas.* Madrid, 1911.

Covarrubias, Sebastian de. *Tesoro de la lengua castellana o española.* Madrid, 1611.

Hudson, Richard. "The *Folia* Dance and the *Folia* Formula in Seventeenth-Century Guitar Music." *Musica Disciplina* 25 (1971): 199–221.

MEREDITH ELLIS LITTLE

FOLK DANCE HISTORY. The concept of folk dance has its origin in the identity of "the folk." Though dancing has been an integral part of community festivities throughout history, it was not until the late eighteenth and early nineteenth centuries that a certain strata of European society acquired the label "the folk" and folk culture became an object of scholarly inquiry. Folk dance did not sustain any scholarly interest until the 1890s—more than one hundred years after the first studies of other folk cultural forms. The definition of folk dance is inextricably tied to this history of folk cultural studies.

In the second half of the eighteenth century a cultural revitalization movement took root in Germany that, as it grew, led to intellectual developments throughout Europe. German philosopher Johann Gottfried von Herder advocated embracing native German language and culture, which had been disparaged by the upper classes for centuries in favor of more fashionable foreign elements. Among Herder's many influential ideas was the concept of *das Volk* ("the folk"): the embodiment of pure national culture in the common man who had, through the centuries, remained close to the national spirit and uncorrupted by artificial fads. Through the revelation of folk customs and traditions, Herder believed, Germans would rediscover their national soul.

From those seeds sprouted a general philosophy of nationalism that spread throughout Europe and became increasingly romanticized through the nineteenth century. In the wake of the French Revolution, the European upper classes grappled with the implications of changing social tenets further intensified by the throes of industrialization. This was especially acute in England where intellectuals seized the concept of nationalism in an effort to inform their view of those unprecedented transformations. In the face of social trauma and change, nineteenth-century scholars idealized the folk and looked to their seemingly pure national culture as some antidote to the uncertainties of the present. However, unlike Herder, who viewed folk culture as a rich resource for the future, these later scholars saw in folk culture only the vestiges of a grander past.

The growth of Romantic nationalism prompted a flurry of collecting and scholarly studies focused on folk cultural forms and performance genres such as folk song, folk poetry, and traditional crafts. Dance garnered little attention, however, and was generally mentioned only in passing, occasionally in reference to the performance of ballads but mostly as part of an account of some seasonal festival. Nineteenth-century intellectual categories did not classify dance as an artistic genre along with folk music and folk drama; instead, dance was considered one of the many elements of folk custom, usually losing precedence to ceremonial display, costume, agricultural practices, and games. The development of another intellectual trend, evolutionism, offers some clues to the reasons behind the neglect of folk dance.

Cultural Evolution. The theory of cultural evolution was based on Darwin's biological theory. It proposed that all human cultures evolved through the same unilineal stages, from primitive savagery to civilization. The writings of two English theorists, Herbert Spencer and Edward Burnett Tylor, were particularly influential in the second half of the nineteenth century, and the evolutionary theme they espoused permeated contemporary intellectual thought. European scholars believed that Africans and Australian Aborigines, for example, illustrated the primitive end of the spectrum, whereas educated European society illustrated civilization. European folk culture fell somewhere in between, for several reasons. First, the folk were considered to be rural peasants who lived a simple existence in relatively homogeneous, agricultural communities. Second, the folk, or rural peasants, were generally illiterate and therefore not privy to the "higher" knowledge and expression found through reading and writing. Third, many aspects of folklife were considered survivals of primitive customs or beliefs because they appeared irrational to scholars. It was thought that many of those seemingly primitive survivals in folklore were symbolic vestiges of pagan religion because, scholars believed, religion was of overarching importance in all primitive societies.

This spirit of evolutionism (social Darwinism), which assumed the necessary progression from the primitive to the civilized, was also applied to individual forms of cultural expression. Both Spencer and Tylor commented specifically on dance. In his book *Anthropology* (1881), Tylor wrote, "Such an example shows how, in the lower levels of culture, men dance to express their feelings and wishes. All this explains how in ancient religion dancing came to be one of the chief acts of worship." Spencer devoted an essay, entitled "Dancer and Musician," to the evolution of the two genres and professional performers. He stated,

Why dancing ceased to be a part of religious worship [in civilized societies], while music did not, we may readily see. In the first place dancing, being inarticulate, is not capable of expressing those various ideas and feelings which music, joining with words, is able to do. (Spencer, 1885)

These comments illustrate two important beliefs: that dancing is an elemental and emotional expression, not capable of transmitting intellectual messages, and that dancing is central to primitive religious worship. Though nineteenth-century scholars did not comment on why they avoided studying dance, these beliefs were undoubtedly influential. Dancing was ascribed low status in the hierarchy of human expressive forms, and its study might have been seen as a trivial pursuit. Additionally, if dancing was indeed a passionate force in pagan religious ritual, upstanding Christian intellectuals may have found it somewhat threatening—ardent proof that their own primitive roots lay close under the surface of good breeding (Friedland, 1987).

Scholarly Attention. Though dance did not receive much scholarly attention, no energy was spared in the investigation of other folk cultural forms, especially literary genres. In the last quarter of the nineteenth century, the evolution-tinged view of dance as a primitive, and therefore ancient, activity was incorporated into a theory propounding the origin of the ballad. Intriguing accounts of ballads being sung and improvised as accompaniment to a simple line or chain dance inspired this view.

Perhaps the most profound evidence in support of this theory was found in the Faeroe Islands, where such singing and dancing would continue for hours as the assembled company progressed through ballads having as many as 165 verses. The literary structure of the Faeroese ballads was also an old form that had all but vanished from the contemporary ballad repertories found on the European continent. Faeroese ballads were first compiled in 1781 and 1782, and the first collection was published in 1822; a new edition followed in 1851. Awareness of the Faeroese dance-ballad tradition appears to have played a pivotal role in historical thinking on ballad origins and development.

Folklorist Andrew Lang discussed this dance connection in some detail in his entry on the ballad in the *Encyclopaedia Britannica* (9th ed., 1879). Lang wrote that "features in European ballad poetry . . . all sprang from the same primitive custom of dance, accompanied by improvised song." Lang cited evidence of ongoing dance-ballad traditions in France, Italy, Greece, and Russia and noted that

in those lands where a blithe peasant life still exists with its dances, . . . we find ballads identicle [*sic*] in many respects with those which have died out of oral tradition in these [British] islands. (Lang, 1879)

Lang's comments set the stage for a full-scale scholarly war, that would erupt in the early 1890s, over the origin of the ballad. Perhaps more important, through these comments and ensuing discussions, dance finally gained some currency in scholarly circles. Whether the association with a revered literary form such as the ballad lent dance some credibility or whether the time was ripe for other reasons is unclear. It is clear, however, that by the 1890s the dance forms and customs found in European folk communities were being allotted more space in essays on local festivities. Lilly Grove's book *Dancing* (1895) included whole chapters on national dances, though distinctions between folk and nonfolk materials were somewhat blurred. Sir James G. Frazer's mammoth work *The Golden Bough* (1890) presented comparative examples of magic and religious materials from all over the world and included a generous sampling of dance customs. Though Frazer's examples are problematic because he made no distinction between firsthand observation and armchair speculation, it is significant that he included many European folk dance customs.

Even as dance began to garner more attention in the 1890s, a peculiarity persisted. Through more than a century of interest in the folk and their culture, many new compound terms came into use, such as folk song, folklore, folk culture, folk art, and folklife. All these terms clearly indicated that the subject at hand was of the folk, thrived in folk communities, and was cultivated through folk tradition. Throughout that century, the term *folk dance* was not used, even in passing references. Virtually every possible synonym was used: national dance, peasant dance, rustic dance, village dance, regional dance, country dance, ritual dance. Sometimes the names of individual dance types were used, such as Sword Dance or maypole dance, but generally the most common term was simply "dance." The inconsistency of applying the folk prefix remains a puzzling issue. Recent research suggests that the first use of the term *folk dance* in different European languages (or the consistent use of a single synonym) signals the beginning of concerted interest in that region's traditional dance.

Folk Pedigree. The time lag between the early development of folk cultural studies and the initial, focused interest in folk dance is important. From the first efforts to collect and document folk dance traditions, which burgeoned in the 1890s through the first two decades of the twentieth century, the term *folk dance* was used in a retrospective sense. That is, it incorporated the model of the folk and folk culture promulgated through nineteenth-century scholarship, inspired by Romantic nationalism and evolutionism. Thus, *folk dance* encompassed those dances found in folk communities. In general, communities deemed folk communities were those that resembled nineteenth-century peasant villages, since there was lim-

ited written documentation of earlier peasant dance activity. Therefore, as the study of folk dance developed, the authenticity of dance materials was judged according to a kind of folk pedigree that was based on certain key factors extracted from nineteenth-century models.

This folk pedigree emphasized the origins and transmission of dances, and to a lesser extent dance forms and styles and the function of dance in specific performance contexts. Origins were particularly important because Romantic, evolutionary philosophy suggested that folk dance, like all aspects of folk culture, was an expression of pure national culture. Many scholars believed that folk dances were survivals from ritual and ceremonial customs derived from ancient, primitive religious practice (Friedland, 1987). It was also commonly held that authentic folk dances were composed communally and subject to standards of form and aesthetics mediated by the folk community at large. In this way folk dances, like ballads, were thought to be quintessential creations of the common people. How folk dances were transmitted was another important consideration for early dance scholars. They believed that the process of passing on knowledge from one generation of community members to the next preserved authenticity. Therefore, dances transmitted and learned within this traditional system were considered unadulterated folk forms because they would, at all times, be prone to communal judgments.

The function of folk dances in different social and celebratory events was also a factor in assessing folk pedigree. The belief that folk dances were survivals of more primitive rituals suggested that the dances originally had some primitive symbolic or ceremonial functions, such as to show devotion to a deity or to petition spirits for good luck. Scholars believed that primitive societies did not appreciate art for art's sake. Some folk dances appeared to retain ceremonial functions. So, for example, as part of festivities celebrating the return of spring, peasants danced while simultaneously plaiting ribbons around a tall pole in the center of a dance circle. This was the Maypole dance, performed in many parts of Europe. Members of many folk communities imputed nothing more to the dance than a gesture to ensure good luck. In the evolutionary view of nineteenth-century scholars, however, the pole represented the ancient fertility symbol of a sacred tree and the dance's original function was to supplicate pagan gods and spirits to oversee successful crops. Many folk dances, however, seemed to have no apparent ceremonial elements. Scholars believed that group social dances functioned as a vehicle of communal expression. Similarly, couple dances were thought to function primarily as a means of courtship.

Finally, dance form and style also played an important role in scholars' adjudication of folk dance authenticity. As dances were documented, collectors sought to establish the oldest and purest form: that which had been known longest in the community and had not been corrupted by outside influences. Collectors also valued the performance style of natural or indigenous dance that seemed untutored when compared to sophisticated fashions of the time. The early documentation of dance forms and styles led to the codification of folk dances. As dances were observed and recorded, and then judged authentic according to origins, transmission, function, form, and style, they were used to set standards of legitimacy against which new versions and regional variants might be compared. The folk pedigree of dances was, therefore, retrospectively tied to nineteenth-century models of folk culture—both real and imagined.

Popular Dance. At the same time this retrospective philosophy yielded an idealized notion of folk dance, a contrasting category developed: popular dance. Popular dance differed from folk dance in origins, function, form, and style. Unlike folk dance, which originated as the primeval, communal expression of the folk, popular dance was thought to be a recent innovation, promoted by known individuals such as dancing masters, or a new hybrid form consisting of borrowed and adapted foreign elements. The origins of popular dance could not be traced to antiquity, and popular dance forms and styles were a fashionable pastiche of patterns not native to a folk community. Also contrary to folk dance, popular dance functioned merely as social diversion and carried no vestige of ceremonial meaning (Friedland, 1987).

By the early twentieth century, when folk dance research began in earnest, most community performance repertoires consisted of a mixture of folk and popular dances. Scholars distinguished the two categories by tracing the folk pedigree of dances and creating authoritative texts of what they believed were the most authentic folk dance forms and customs. Popular dances were dismissed as impure, bourgeois products that offered little insight into national heritage and aesthetics.

This distinction between folk and popular dance was predicated on the idealized notion of the folk as vessels of a pristine past. This ideal, however, did not reflect the varied and complex everyday life of European peasants (Burke, 1978). Contrary to that ideal of unself-conscious homogeneity, peasant culture was intensely stratified according to occupation, wealth, and status. Some were rich while others were poor. There were freemen and serfs, and some peasants could read and write (Burke, 1978).

Community dance traditions have always been responsive to the beliefs and values that pervade everyday life and have always adopted elements of vernacular culture that proved the most effective and satisfying vehicles for expression. Communities have always had vernacular dance traditions in the sense that the dances and customs were "integral to the everyday life and beliefs of a given group of people, irrespective of whether that dancing might also be classified as folk or popular" (Friedland, 1987). Vernacular dance subsumes the motley conglomeration of real-life performance repertories that might include dance forms with impeccable folk pedigrees, "imported" couple dances such as the waltz or fox trot, the "Virginia Reel" learned in elementary school gym class, and contemporary rock-and-roll or disco improvisation. Vernacular dance becomes common parlance to a given group of people who, through shared experience, become a dance community.

Vernacular dance can potentially include anything, as long as its meaning is consonant with community beliefs and expression. Folk and popular dance are subsets of vernacular dance, each delimited by selected criteria established according to different analytical perspectives. The term *folk dance*, on the other hand, is inextricably tied to the nineteenth-century view of the folk as guardians of the pure national soul and folk culture as the repository of customs descended from ancient religious ritual. The term *folk dance* is valuable only when this historical connection is maintained. Folk dance is that subset of dance forms and customs that can be traced to folk communities and repertories so defined by nineteenth-century concepts; it is a historical term that refers to a particular interpretation of the history of human culture and expression.

The Study of Folk Dance. Because the concept of folk dance developed out of the study of European peasant culture, the term has been applied most often to European and European-derived dance traditions and traditions found in analogous non-European peasant societies. Even though nineteenth-century scholars were interested in the dance customs of Native Americans in the United States, these were considered primitive, not folk, societies, and their dances were therefore considered primitive, not folk, dances. This nineteenth-century conceptual boundary between primitive and folk dance persisted through much of the twentieth century (Sachs, 1933; Kurath, 1949). Its prevalence has decreased significantly since the 1960s.

Before the advent of modern audiovisual technology, the history of dancing in any culture was documented through oral history of bygone eras, written accounts, and pictorial representations. There are written and pictorial references to dancing and dance-related customs in Western civilization dating to the early Greeks. (Lawler, 1964). Chronicles of dancing cover much of pre-Christian Europe (Backman, 1952) and extend through the Middle Ages and the Renaissance (Sutton et al., 1980) to the late eighteenth century, when many commentators became more conscious of burgeoning nationalism and the romanticization of the common people.

Social and ceremonial dancing in Wales, for example, is recounted by several travelers who toured the region during the last quarter of the eighteenth century (Williams, 1933). Informal gatherings in farmhouse kitchens were scenes of harp and flute playing, singing, and clog dancing. In 1798, an Englishman observed a dance event in a South Wales public house and noted the unfamiliar and complicated figures of the Welsh dances performed to the music of a harp and the competitive clog dancing that concluded the festivities. He bemoaned the disappearance of such spirit in his hometown dances and was "astonished at the agility and skill which these rustics displayed" (Williams, 1933).

A collection of dances performed in the Basque province of Guipúzcoa, compiled by Juan Ignacio Iztueta, appeared in 1826 (De Barandiaran, 1980). Iztueta not only documented thirty-six regional dances and two types of dance melodies but also analyzed a repertory of fifteen dance steps used to improvise different combinations specifically wedded to the characteristics of individual tunes. The Guipúzcoan dances included a broad range of secular and ceremonial forms including circle dances, stick and sword dances, and religious processionals.

As scholars began to study folk songs and ballads in greater detail, discussions of dancing increased. In his 1833 study of Christmas carols, William Sandys speculated the song was originally "intermingled with dancing, or a sort of divertisement [sic]." Several French scholars of the mid–nineteenth-century studied the contemporary performance of ballads in different French provinces and observed how they were sung to accompany group dancing. Théodore Hersart La Villemarqué noted how, in Brittany, verses were improvised while dancing. Jérôme Bujeaud and Théodore de Puymaigre wrote about the close relationship between the dancing and ballad texts. These accounts, and similar ones offered by scholars in many parts of Europe, were tremendously influential and fueled the debates over ballad origins that helped bring dance closer to the scholarly spotlight toward the end of the nineteenth century.

In the 1890s, a flurry of articles published by English folklore collectors discussed the ceremonial dances performed during seasonal festivals. May Day was celebrated with different types of garland dances and processions. In the Oxfordshire village of Bampton, Whitsuntide was marked by the performance of Morris dancers costumed in white and festooned with bells and ribbons (Manning 1897). In Ireland, wedding celebrations included social dancing, and one account from county Mayo, in 1892, noted how a gang of "straw-boys," or male mummers, disguised in women's clothes and conical masks arrived to dance with the bride and contribute to the revelry (Haddon, 1893). Lilly Grove's history of dancing reflected a heightened awareness of national dance and discussed it in greater depth than previous studies, though Franz Böhme's 1886 regional survey of German folk dances is a notable exception (1886; see Lange, 1980). Grove espoused an integrative view: "The dances of a country are not something extraneous to it; they have grown up with the people, and possess their peculiarities, as a garment fits itself to the shape of the wearer" (1895).

In Sweden the study of folk culture was approached in a holistic way, focusing not only on individual traditions such as ballad singing but also on the interrelated complex of traditional elements that shaped rural, preindustrial peasant communities. The first open-air folklife museum, Skansen, was developed in 1891 by Artur Hazelius to display regional building types and everyday customs and technology in a naturalistic setting. The enthusiasm for this collecting and documenting of folk culture extended to dance customs, and in 1893 Hazelius helped found the Svenska Folkdansens Vänner, or Friends of Swedish Folk Dance (Rehnberg, 1939). This organization sought to preserve folk dances from different regions of Sweden by documenting them, and encouraging their performance and revival. These efforts set the stage for major folk dance study and revival movements in the twentieth century.

Increasing Interest in Folk Dance. During the years 1900 to 1920, there was an upsurge of interest in folk dance throughout most of Europe and North America. Many national folk dance organizations were founded during this period and most of them not only promoted the revival of folk dance performance but also established archives. In 1899, a Swedish demonstration troupe performed a program of regional folk dances in Copenhagen and inspired their Danish audience to adopt Swedish folk dancing as a recreational activity. By 1901, the Foreningen til Folkedansens Fremme (Danish Association for the Promotion of Folk-Dancing) was founded. With some support from the Danish government, along with the help of many dedicated collectors, the society helped coordinate the documentation of folk dances, folk music, and traditional regional costumes. This collecting effort spanned the first three decades of the twentieth century and resulted in the publication of a series of booklets beginning in 1904. Each booklet contained dance descriptions linked to tunes issued in corresponding music booklets; the first volume also included illustrations of different styles of buttons, clasps, and belt buckles for folk dance costumes. These booklets were widely used in the teaching and revival of folk dances. The Danish folk dance revival was also aided by far-reaching educational programs that, along with the society's collecting and documenting activities, served as a model for similar organizations in other countries.

A major folk dance revival movement also developed in England, largely because of the work of Cecil Sharp. Beginning in 1907, Sharp published a series of books recording Morris, sword, and country dances found in different regions of England and some adapted from the seventeenth-century country dance manuals of John Playford. Many dance traditions were dwindling by the time Sharp sought to notate individual dance forms. He reconstructed some dances based on incomplete accounts and, in other cases, chose what he deemed the most representative version of a dance to publish in his dance manuals (Sharp and MacIlwaine, 1912; Forrest, 1985). In 1909 educators officially incorporated English folk dance in the physical education curriculum of elementary and secondary schools. Consequently, Sharp's published materials, workshops, and lectures became indispensable for training a new army of folk dance instructors. In 1911 the English Folk Dance Society was established, an organization that soon provided for the educational and performance activities that helped to cultivate a new national awareness of English folk dance. Sharp also instigated the teaching of English folk dance in a few locations in the United States, where he traveled and lectured repeatedly between 1914 and 1918 (Karpeles, 1967). [*See the entry on Sharp.*]

A folk dance movement of a different nature began in the United States in the first few years of the twentieth century. In most European countries, folk dance revivals first grew out of a nationalistic impulse to preserve folk culture and then infiltrated different types of child and adult education as healthful, expressive, and patriotic recreation. In the United States, however, interest in folk dance sprang first from physical education and the organized-play movement, which was striving to entice immigrants out of the streets and into public playgrounds and recreation centers where they might engage in "cooperative" team games and pastimes (Goodman, 1979). Educators compiled instructional books of folk dances and singing games, using as models European manuals such as those issued by Scandinavian folk dance societies. Initially there was little effort to include any dances that might be considered American; the overwhelming presence of newly arrived European immigrant children in many American urban centers confronted educators with a multicultural reality. Luther H. Gulick, an influential figure in the organized-play movement, believed that these sentiments lay at the heart of the folk dance movement:

> We in America have recognized the value of the labor which the immigrants have brought to us, but we have not appreciated the wealth of tradition and experience which is embodied in the race-history of our immigrants; yet the great social com-

posite that is developing in America not only is an embodiment of the physical abilities of the old countries, but also includes strands of their rich aesthetic life.   (Burchenal, 1909)

In 1905, Elizabeth Burchenal established the folk dance movement within the Playground Association of America in New York City. Her work through the ensuing thirty years helped set standards for folk dance educators throughout the United States. Beginning in 1909, she published an influential and widely used series of books devoted to folk dances from many countries, based largely on her firsthand observations. During her travels in Europe she visited the various national folk dance societies and revival groups and shared with them a mutual belief in the rich aesthetic expression of folk dance. Burchenal believed that folk dances were more than a novel form of physical exercise; their essence was a spirit that could be understood if dancers "laugh from sheer pleasure in the dance itself." Another essential ingredient was an accompanying musician who could not only feel the music's "folk quality" but also impart to it "charm and irresistible rhythm" (Burchenal, 1909).

Burchenal did not distinguish between dances she found in written sources, dances reconstructed by national folk dance societies, dances learned from immigrants living in the United States, and dances performed in an unbroken century of tradition in rural New England communities. Because she was an educator used to teaching large numbers of school children, however, she did classify dances according to whether they were best suited for grass playgrounds, dirt surfaces, or indoor playgrounds. Despite her lack of attention to the provenance of specific dances, Burchenal laid the foundation upon which generations of American recreation specialists would build. She was also one of the earliest collectors of American folk dances and concentrated her efforts in New England, especially in Maine. In 1916 she helped found the American Folk-Dance Society and served as its president. The society was suspended during World War I and was later reconstituted at the League of Nations as the United States Section of the International Commission on Folk-Arts.

The widespread collecting, revival, and educational activities that developed during the first two decades of the twentieth century helped to sharpen the focus of the growing number of scholars interested in folk dance materials. Even before World War I they discussed the need for more rigorous research methods that would yield a fuller understanding of cultural context and performance process. One early plea for more scientific description urged that careful attention be paid to dance names and related technical terms and their explanation; social contexts for dancing and the structure of the performance repertory; information about the musical instruments and instrumentation; historical characteristics of the dances and dance performance; the nature of the dance performance space, the position of dancers within it, and the direction in which dances progress; information about accompanying music, verbal texts, and dance performance including notated transcriptions with tempo markings; and data regarding location, informants, date, and fieldworker (Zoder, 1911). Discussions such as this encouraged new directions in folk dance research, which blossomed into more sophisticated structural and cultural analyses in the following decades.

New Breed of Studies. Though the revival fervor and efforts to compile folk dance instruction manuals continued unabated, by the late 1920s and early 1930s a new breed of scholarly studies began to explore the cultural and historical contexts of folk dance traditions, as well as individual dance forms. Such historical and contextual issues were especially compelling in Latin America, where rich and varied regional dance traditions exhibited a heritage of dance forms brought from Europe, new creations combining diverse elements into localized tradition, and the influence of indigenous form, style, and custom. In 1927, Jorge Furt traced the origins and development of *gaucho,* or cowboy, dances found primarily in Argentina, Chile, and Peru. He combed through old written materials, including personal letters and travelers' diaries, and attempted to chart how dance forms and variants evolved, when they moved to different geographical regions, and how they were adapted to new environments and local beliefs.

Similar historical studies using a wide range of written and archival resources examined the evolution of folk dance forms throughout Scandinavia (Nielsen, 1933; Heikel, 1938) as well as many parts of Europe (for example, Williams, 1932). The rich dance tradition of the Auvergne region of France was subject to both historical analysis and contemporary observations (Delzangles, 1930). The variety of dance forms integral to celebrating rites of passage, religious and civic festivities, and simple social gatherings and reunions were recorded along with the music and songs that accompanied the dances.

An ethnographic approach pervaded studies in Hungary where, in the 1930s, concerted efforts were made to document folk dance and dance music with written accounts, still photography, and motion pictures (Martin, 1982). The first volume of Ljubica and Danica Janković's pioneering structural analysis and notation of dance forms, along with the recording of music, song texts, and contextual data, formed the foundation of their copious and influential studies published throughout the following four decades.

While the development of historical and ethnographic approaches to folk dance traditions were strengthened by the inclusion of primary data from firsthand, contemporary observation, German musicologist Curt Sachs relied on inconsistent second- and third-hand written accounts to construct a history of dance (Sachs, 1933; Youngerman, 1974). Though he included examples of folk dances from many parts of the world, Sachs held an evolutionary perspective that harkened back to outdated nineteenth-century notions and consequently did not assist the development of more modern theoretical studies.

In the United States, the educational folk dance movement and various offshoot revival activities continued, including campaign instigated by automobile magnate Henry Ford to revive American square dancing. Ford's actions received nationwide publicity and helped to promote renewed popular interest in regional American dance traditions. Around the same time, the distinctive New England tradition of longways contra dances and four-couple quadrilles was described by Tolman and Page in a unique, native account of the ongoing dances in a small New Hampshire town (1937). Through the late 1930s, information about traditional dancing was collected, along with many other aspects of regional culture, under the auspices of the Federal Writers' Project. The depth and scope of these collecting efforts varied from one state to the next, and the materials remain largely unpublished. Some collectors recorded beliefs, regional expressions, and personal experience narratives regarding dancing, as well as the verbal texts of square dance calls and figures (for example, see Welsch, 1966).

In 1935 English author Violet Alford published her first popular travelogue of European folk dances and customs, (Alford and Gallop, 1935; cf. Opera Nazionale Dopolavoro, 1935), which was soon followed by her account of Pyrenean calendar customs (Alford, 1937). Alford's books presented the subject of folk dance to a popular audience through the next three decades, combining a novelistic writing style with descriptions and photographs of folk dance customs and performance.

World War II and Beyond. Though World War II disrupted millions of lives across the globe, the intense interest in folk dance as a symbol of national identity seemed undeterred. The revival of folk songs and dances in Switzerland grew out of an earlier revival of traditional regional costume (Witzig, 1941). Commentators recounted the history of dancing in traditional Dutch festivals along with many folk dance forms, their accompanying music and songs, and popular folk dance revival activities (Van der Ven-Ten Bensel and Van der Ven, 1942). Many new collections of regional French folk dances appeared (for example, Blanchard, 1943; Guilcher, 1947). The history and symbolism of the Catalonian dance the *sardana* was explored in detail (Capmany, 1948; Pépratx-Saisset, 1946). The indigenous festivals of the Andes, featuring syncretic dance forms and customs, were documented in a spectacular photo essay by Pierre Verger

(1945). New collections of Latin American folk dances appeared, especially in Argentina (Flury, 1947; Vega, 1952).

During the following decades, the historical study and documentation of folk dance proliferated and became more focused on specific geographic regions, such as the Westphalia and Saar districts of Germany (Salmen, 1954; Von der Au, 1954), and on specific subcultures, such as the Canadian descendants of French settlers in Quebec (Doyon, 1950; Barbeau, 1956 and 1963) and of Scottish settlers in Nova Scotia (Thurston, 1954; Flett and Flett, 1964). There was also increasing discussion of the interrelationship of folk dance forms and customs in neighboring geographic regions and the transmission of traditional culture (for example, Wolfram, 1951; Kurath, 1949 and 1956; Sanders, 1951). Growing self-awareness and interaction within the scholarly community broadened perspectives and encouraged overviews of the field (Kurath, 1960). One such survey, by Lekis in 1958, reviewed folk dance forms and customs, their geographical distribution, and related research from virtually all of Latin America. The refinement of the unique Latin American perspective on traditional culture, subject to both syncretic and Creole cultural phenomena that challenged the historical model of "pure" folk dance, also inspired one of the earliest uses of the term *bailes vernáculos* ("vernacular dance") (Larralde, 1952).

In general, through the 1950s and 1960s, closer networks of communication developed between folk dance researchers, educators, and revivalists, many of whom participated in all phases of folk dance activism. Organizations such as the International Folk Music Council (now the International Council for Traditional Music) brought scholars together, both in person and in print. In addition to articles discussing nearly every European nation and many countries in the New World and Africa, the society's journal provided other important resources. Book reviews and notices of publications constituted a valuable chronicle of current scholarship.

Since the 1960s new avenues of research have been explored that have reached beyond the foundation of repertory and contextual studies. Analyses of rhythmic formulas (Proca Ciortea, 1969) and motive types (Martin and Pesovár, 1961) have yielded insight into the structure of dance variants and the process of performance. The interrelationship of rural and urban dance traditions in a given geographic region (Ilijin, 1965; Lange, 1974), and the differences in the performance style and expression of closely related dance traditions (Gellerman, 1978) have also been investigated. The use of movement notation systems has continued to expand (see Kurath, 1960; Lange, 1980), especially as a tool in the structural analysis pursued by many eastern European scholars. There has also been increased discussion of definitions of folk dance and methods of inquiry (Hoerburger, 1965, 1968; Kealiino-

homoku, 1972; Lange, 1984) such as comparative choreography (Forrest, 1984) and the reconstruction of dance forms (Rodriguez de Ayestarán, 1984).

Historical studies of dance forms and performance contexts have furthered the understanding of dance traditions in many parts of Europe (Louis, 1963; Sarmela, 1969; Breathnách, 1977). Fieldwork data and firsthand observations have been incorporated into discussions of regional traditions and specific dance forms (Guilcher, 1963; Kligman, 1981; Beal, 1984). Yet others have examined the nature of change in a dance tradition (Proca Ciortea, 1978–1979) and the place of dancing in a complex of traditional community performance genres (Falassi, 1980). Growing interest in North America has prompted recent studies of Canadian traditions and pictorial representations of dancing (Quigley, 1985; Voyer, 1986; Sarrasin, 1984; Shifrin, 1984). Widely different regional traditions centering on a variant of the American square dance have also received attention (Kimball, 1988; Tyler, 1992; Winslow, 1972; Bethke, 1974; Feintuch, 1981; Lavita, 1983; Burns and Mack, 1978). In the United States, where scholarship did not develop alongside fervent folk dance education and revival movements, a new generation of researchers is exploring the diversity of dance traditions found in contemporary, multicultural American society.

[*For related discussion, see* European Traditional Dance *and* Methodologies in the Study of Dance, *article on* Ethnology.]

BIBLIOGRAPHY

Alford, Violet, and Rodney Gallop. *The Traditional Dance.* London, 1935.

Alford, Violet. *Pyrenean Festivals, Calendar Customs, Music and Magic, Drama and Dance.* London, 1937.

Au, Hans von der. *Heit is Kerb in unserm Dorf: Tänze rechts und links der Saar.* Kassel, 1954.

Backman, Eugène Louis. *Religious Dances in the Christian Church and in Popular Medicine.* Translated by E. Classen. London, 1952.

Barbeau, Marius. "'Rondes' from French Canada." *Journal of the International Folk Music Council* 8 (1956).

Barbeau, Marius, ed. *Dansons à la ronde/Rondelays.* Ottawa, 1963.

Beal, Daniel Sundstedt. "Two Springar Dance Traditions from Western Norway." *Ethnomusicology* 28 (1984).

Bethke, Robert D. "Old-Time Fiddling and Social Dance in Central St. Lawrence County." *New York Folklore Quarterly* 30 (1974).

Blanchard, Roger. *Les danses du Limousin.* Paris, 1943.

Böhme, Franz M. *Geschichte des Tanzes in Deutschland.* 2 vols. Leipzig, 1886.

Breathnach, Breandán. *Folk Music and Dances of Ireland.* Rev. ed. Dublin, 1977.

Burchenal, Elizabeth. *Folk-Dances and Singing Games.* 3 vols. New York, 1909–1922.

Burchenal, Elizabeth. *Folk-Dances of Denmark.* New York, 1915.

Burke, Peter. *Popular Culture in Early Modern Europe.* New York, 1978.

Burns, Thomas A., with Doris Mack. "Social Symbolism in a Rural Square Dance Event." *Southern Folklore Quarterly* 42 (1978): 295–327.

Capmany, Aurelio. *La sardana a Catalunya*. Barcelona, 1948.

Cawte, E. C., et al. "A Geographical Index of the Ceremonial Dance in Great Britain." *Journal of the English Folk Dance and Song Society* 9.1 (1960): 1–41.

De Barandiarán, Gaizka. "Basque Music." In *The New Grove Dictionary of Music and Musicians*. London, 1980.

Doyon, Madeleine. "Folk Dances in Beauce County." *Journal of American Folklore* 63 (1950).

Falassi, Alessandro. *Folklore by the Fireside: Text and Context of the Tuscan Veglia*. Austin, 1980.

Feintuch, Burt. "Dancing to the Music: Domestic Square Dances and Community in Southcentral Kentucky, 1880–1940." *Journal of the Folklore Institute* 18 (1981): 49–68.

Flett, J. F., and T. M. Flett. *Traditional Dancing in Scotland*. London, 1964.

Flury, Lázaro. *Danzas folklóricas Argentinas*. Buenos Aires, 1947.

Forrest, John. *"Morris and Matachin": A Study in Comparative Choreography*. London, 1984.

Forrest, John. "Here We Come a-Fossiling." *Dance Research Journal* 17 (Spring-Summer 1985): 27–42.

Friedland, LeeEllen. "Dance: Popular and Folk Dance." In *Encyclopedia of Religion*. New York, 1987.

Furt, Jorge M. *Coreografía gauchesca*. Buenos Aires, 1927.

Gellerman, Jill. "The Mayim Pattern as an Indicator of Cultural Attitudes in Three American Hasidic Communities." *CORD Dance Research Annual* 9 (1978): 111–144.

Goodman, Cary. *Choosing Sides: Playground and Street Life on the Lower East Side*. New York, 1979.

Grove, Lilly M. *Dancing*. London, 1895.

Guilcher, Jean-Michel. *Dix danses simples des pays de France*. Paris, 1947.

Guilcher, Jean-Michel. *La tradition populaire de danse en Basse-Bretagne*. Paris, 1963.

Haddon, Alfred C. "A Wedding Dance-Mask from Co. Mayo." *Folk-Lore* 4 (1893).

Heikel, Yngvar. *Dansbeskrivningar*. Finlands Svenska Folkdiktning, 6. Helsinki, 1938.

Hoerburger, Felix. "Folk Dance Survey." *Journal of the International Folk Music Council* 17 (1965).

Hoerburger, Felix. "Once Again: On the Concept of 'Folk Dance.'" *Journal of the International Folk Music Council* 20 (1968): 30–32.

Hofer, Mari Ruef. *Popular Folk Games and Dances*. Chicago, 1907.

Ilijin, Milica. "Influences réciproques des danses urbaines et traditionnelles en Yougoslavie." *Studia musicologica* 7 (1965).

Janković, Ljubica S., and Danica S. Janković. *Narodne igre*. 8 vols. Belgrade, 1934–1964.

Karpeles, Maud. *Cecil Sharp: His Life and Work*. Chicago, 1967.

Kealiinohomoku, Joann W. "Folk Dance." In *Folklore and Folklife: An Introduction*, edited by Richard M. Dorson. Chicago, 1972.

Kimball, James. "Country Dancing in Central and Western New York State." *New York Folklore* 14 (1988).

Kligman, Gail. *Calus: Symbolic Transformation in Romanian Ritual*. Chicago, 1981.

Kurath, Gertrude Prokosch. "Dance: Folk and Primitive." In *Dictionary of Folklore, Mythology, and Legend*. New York, 1949–.

Kurath, Gertrude Prokosch. "Dance Relatives of Mid-Europe and Middle America: A Venture in Comparative Choreology." *Journal of American Folklore* 69 (1956).

Kurath, Gertrude Prokosch. "Panorama of Dance Ethnology." *Current Anthropology* 1 (1960): 233–254.

Lange, Roderyk. "On Differences between the Rural and the Urban: Traditional Polish Peasant Dancing." *Yearbook of the International Folk Music Council* 6 (1974).

Lange, Roderyk. "The Development of Anthropological Dance Research." *Dance Studies* 4 (1980): 1–36.

Lange, Roderyk. "Guidelines for Field Work on Traditional Dance: Methods and Checklist." *Dance Studies* 8 (1984): 7–47.

Larralde, Jorge Andrés. *Coreografías de danzas folklóricas*. Buenos Aires, 1952.

LaVita, James A. "Allemande Left with Your Left Hand: Structure in Modern Western Square Dancing." *International Folklore Review* 3 (1983).

Lawler, Lillian B. *The Dance in Ancient Greece*. Middletown, Conn., 1964.

Lekis, Lisa. *Folk Dances of Latin America*. New York, 1958.

Louis, Maurice L.–A. *Le folklore et la danse*. Paris, 1963.

Manning, Percy. "Some Oxfordshire Seasonal Festivals: With Notes on Morris-Dancing in Oxfordshire." *Folk-Lore* 8 (1897).

Martin, György, and Ernő Pesovár. "Determination of the Motif Types in Dance Folklore." *Acta Ethnographica Academiae Scientiarum Hungaricae* 12 (1963): 162–210.

Martin, György. "A Survey of the Hungarian Folk Dance Research." *Dance Studies* 6 (1982): 9–45.

Matthews, Gail V. S. "Cutting a Dido: A Dancer's Eye View of Mountain Dance in Haywood County, N. C." Master's thesis, Indiana University, 1983.

Nielsen, H. Grüner. *Vore aldste folkedanse, langdans og polskdans*. Copenhagen, 1917.

Nielsen, H. Grüner. "Dans i Norge." In *Idrott och lek, utgiven av Johan Götlind*, edited by H. Grüner Nielsen. Nordisk Kultur, vol. 24. Oslo, 1933.

Opera Nazionale Dopolavoro. *Costumi, musica, danze e feste popolari italiane*. Rome, 1935.

Pépratx-Saisset, Henry, ed. *La Sardane: La danse des Catalans, son symbole, sa magie, ses énigmes*. Perpignan, 1955.

Porter, James, and A. L. Lloyd. "Europe." In *The New Grove Dictionary of Music and Musicians*. London, 1980.

Proca Ciortea, Vera. "On Rhythm in Rumanian Folk Dance." *Yearbook of the International Folk Music Council* 1 (1969).

Proca Ciortea, Vera. "The 'Calus Custom' in Rumania: Tradition, Change, Creativity." *Dance Studies* 3 (1978–1979): 1–43.

Quigley, Colin. *Close to the Floor: Folk Dance in Newfoundland*. St. John's, Newfoundland, 1985.

Rehnberg, Mats. *Swedish Folk Dances*. Stockholm, 1939.

Rodríguez de Ayestarán, Flor de María. "Methodology in the Reconstruction of Extinct Folk Dances." *Dance Studies* 8 (1984): 67–74.

Sachs, Curt. *World History of the Dance*. Translated by Bessie Schönberg. New York, 1937.

Salmen, Walter. "Grundriss einer Geschichte des Tanzes in Westfalen." *Westfälische Forschungen* 7 (1953–1954): 129–136.

Sanders, Olcott. "The Texas Cattle Country and Cowboy Square Dance." *Journal of the International Folk Music Council* 3 (1951).

Sardys, William. *Christmas Carols, Ancient and Modern*. London, 1833.

Sarmela, Matti. *Reciprocity Systems of the Rural Society in the Finnish-Karelian Culture Area*. Translated by Matt T. Salo. Helsinki, 1969.

Sarrasin, Francine. "L'iconographie de la danse dans les gravures et les dessins canadiens." *Canadian Folklore Canadien* 6 (1984).

Sharp, Cecil, and Herbert C. Macilwaine. *The Morris Book*. 5 vols. London, 1909–1913. 2d ed. London, 1912–1924.

Shifrin, Ellen. "Traditional French-Canadian Dance Iconography: A Methodology for Analysis." *Canadian Folklore Canadien* 6 (1984).

Sutton, Julia, et al. "Dance." In *The New Grove Dictionary of Music and Musicians*. London, 1980.

Thurston, Hugh A. *Scotland's Dances*. London, 1954.

Tolman, Beth, and Ralph Page. *The Country Dance Book.* New York, 1937.

Tyler, Paul Leslie. "'Sets on the Floor': Social Dance as an Emblem of Community in Rural Indiana." Ph.D. diss., Indiana University, 1992.

Vega, Carlos. *Las danzas populares Argentinas.* Buenos Aires, 1952.

Ven-ten Bensel, Elise van der, and D. J. van der Ven. *De volksdans in Nederland.* Naarden, 1942.

Verger, Pierre. *Fiestas y danzas en el Cuzco y en los Andes.* Buenos Aires, 1945.

Voyer, Simonne. *La danse traditionnelle dans l'est du Canada: Quadrilles et cotillons.* Quebec, 1986.

Welsch, Roger L., comp. *A Treasury of Nebraska Pioneer Folklore.* Lincoln, Neb., 1966.

Williams, W. S. Gwynn. *Welsh National Music and Dance.* London, 1933.

Winslow, David John. "The Rural Square Dance in the Northeastern United States: A Continuity of Tradition." Ph.D. diss., University of Pennsylvania, 1972.

Witzig, Louise. *Volkstänze der Schweiz.* Zurich, 1941.

Wolfram, Richard. *Die Volkstänze in Österreich und verwandte Tänze in Europa.* Salzburg, 1951.

Youngerman, Suzanne. "Curt Sachs and His Heritage: A Critical Review of *World History of the Dance* with a Survey of Recent Studies that Perpetuate His Ideas." *CORD News* 6 (July 1974): 6–19.

Zoder, Raimund. "Wie zeichnet man Volkstänze auf?" *Zeitschrift des Vereins für Volkskunde* 21 (1911).

LeeEllen Friedland

FOLK DANCE SOUNDS. Many forms of dance are performed silently or with instrumental musical accompaniment, but folk and traditional dances are often accompanied by vocal sounds such as chants, howls, screams, squeals, and ululations. These are distinct from "calls," which direct dancers to do certain steps or figures. Calls are used mainly in European quadrilles and the Lancers (a nineteenth-century set of quadrilles) and in American square dancing.

Vocal sounds express a dancer's emotions, whether using pure sound, nonsense words, or words with meaning. Often spectators join in. The most commonly used and most familiar sounds are "hey," "hup," and "hi." In Greece, "hup" is expanded to "opa"; in Serbia, to "hupat-soop." In Japan, dancers softly sing out a gentle "a-yoi-yoi," whereas in Scotland, male Highland dancers break forth into loud shouts of "hooch"—pronounced with a deep, guttural initial /h/ sound. The audience often responds with the same "hooch" at a well-executed *pas de basque* or an exciting reel. In Cape Breton, Canada, dancers, musicians, and audience members often let out a rising, high-pitched "yow" sound (which is shared with Irish set and *ceilidh* dancers on both sides of the Atlantic); also common are cries of *suas e* or *suas i* (literally, "up with it" in Gaelic) or its idiomatic English equivalent, "drive it," and the more elaborate *suas a bhodaich* ("drive it, old man"). Another common sound is the sibilant /s/ or "tss, tss" used in the Balkans and in the Middle East. In Germany, Austria, and Switzerland, dancers may shout "ya-hooey" or "ya-ha-ha-hooey." In the Appenzell section of Switzerland, this changes slightly to mimic the sound of dogs howling at the moon, and the musicians join in the howls. In Slovakia, a high-pitched "ooo-eee-ooo-eee" is used, and in the former Yugoslavia it is sounded as "eee-ya-eee-ya-eee-ya-ya."

Ululation, a wailing lament, is important in Middle Eastern dancing, especially in Turkey. In the Arab world, the favorite dance words are "yach teh," "yabooey," "ya-habibi," and "hizzy, hizzy." This last is similar in meaning to the 1940s American "hubba, hubba"—meaning "what a pretty girl."

In the Balkans, folk dances are replete with a great many shouts, such as *adje* ("let's go"), *igra kolo* ("let's dance the kolo"), and *veselo* ("happily dance"). In Spain and Mexico, *olé* ("bravo"; "well done") is ubiquitously used, and there are many nuances to its pronunciation. The /o/ sound can be quite long, with a short inflection on the last syllable, but inflections vary with the manner and movement of each dancer. In Mexico, dance sounds include shouts of *arriba* ("on your feet"; "up you go"), *andale* ("get it going"), *echale* ("throw it"; "fling it"), and encouraging trills of rolling /r/ sounds. In Spain, shouts may include *así se baila* ("dance like that"), *bien lo hecho* ("do it good"), *eso es* ("that's it"), *viva yo* ("hurrah for me"), and even a purely nondance word, *alcachofas* ("artichoke"). Most of these shouts are used in flamenco dancing.

Many dances are accompanied by the singing or chanting of verse couplets improvised on the spot—usually some gossip about the dancers. In the Ukrainian *hutzul* dance, *kolomeyka*, for example, this verbal skill is as important as the dancing. Thousands of such ditties have been collected and published by the Ethnographic Institute of the Taras Shevchenko Society in Lviv, Ukraine. At Ukrainian weddings, the verses for the dance are earthy, aimed at arousing the bridal couple into a nuptial mood. Scottish Gaelic culture boasts a special genre of unaccompanied song for dancing called *puirt-a-beul* ("mouth music"), whose verses were in times past similarly extemporized. Mouth music makes extensive and virtuosic use in its tongue-twisting choruses of the so-called Gaelic vocables, nonsense syllables with deep roots in the language that some scholars believe represent remnants of ancient Gaelic words (vocables also occur in other highly rhythmic songs, especially work songs). The hundreds of different vocables may be combined in infinite ways; typical examples are "Hó hi ri ri ri ri ù," "I bhì a dà, u à idil à," or "Air fail a lail ó, horó; air fail a lail é." *Puirt-a-beul* are preserved in the Gaelic-speaking areas of Scotland and Cape Breton, but are today seldom used for dancing.

Since shouts and sounds are an integral part of folk dance, many societies have special terms for them. In Romania, they are called *strigature;* in the former Yugoslavia, *poskocice;* in the Appenzell region of Switzerland, *sauerle;* in Spain, *gritos;* and in Russia, *chastushki.* Many folk dance recordings provide a good source for hearing these sounds in context.

MARY ANN HERMAN

FOLK TALE, A. Danish title: *Et Folkesagn.* Ballet in three acts. Choreography and libretto: August Bournonville. Music: Niels William Gade, Johan Peter Emilius Hartmann. Scenery: Christian Ferdinand Christensen, Troels Lund. Costumes: Edvard Lehmann. First performance: 20 March 1854, Royal Theater, Copenhagen. Principals: Juliette Price (Hilda), Wilhelm Erik Funck (Junker Ove), Froken Birthe (Petrine Fredstrup), Ferdinand Hoppensach (Diderik), Edvard Stramboe (Viderik).

In his own opinion his "most perfect and finest choreographic work," Bournonville's *A Folk Tale* weaves comedy, pathos, dancing, mime, and elements of several Danish legends into a Danish fairy tale. The ballet is set in sixteenth-century Jutland on Midsummer's Eve. Hilda, a human girl, lives inside a hill with the sorceress Muri and her troll sons, who vie for Hilda's affections. As a baby, Hilda was kidnapped from her father's manor house in exchange for the troll child Birthe. Capricious Birthe (who has been raised as heiress to the manor) and her guests frolic at a woodland picnic. When night falls, her distracted, melancholy fiancé, Junker Ove, remains behind in the forest; here he encounters Hilda, is caught up in the frenzied dance of the elf maidens, and loses his senses. In a dream, Hilda envisions her childhood nursery and a cross, symbolic of her Christian origins. At the height of a drunken troll celebration, she and the kindly troll Viderik flee from the hill. Once above ground, Hilda restores Ove's sanity with water from a sacred well, thereby overcoming the power of the hidden forces of nature. Birthe is recognized as a troll and must accept her true nature, and Hilda is restored to her rightful estate. The ballet ends idyllically with the happy wedding of Hilda and Ove, celebrated to the lilting strains of the "Bridal Waltz," and with a group of seven Gypsies performing a bravura pas de sept.

With its rich symbolism, *A Folk Tale* remains one of Bournonville's clearest and most finely delineated expressions of optimism and the triumph of faith and love. Its music is considered the finest score written for ballet in Denmark. Major productions include those of Harald Lander and Valborg Borchsenius (1940/41), Hans Brenaa (1969), and Kirsten Ralov (1979).

[*See also* Royal Danish Ballet *and the entry on* Bournonville.]

A FOLK TALE. Silja Schandorff as Hilda (second from left), flanked by Michael Bastian as Diderik and Sorella Englund as Viderik, with Jette Buchwald as Muri. Based on Danish fairy tales, the story is set in sixteenth-century Jutland. The scenery for this 1991 Royal Danish Ballet production was designed by Queen Margrete II of Denmark. (Photograph © 1991 by Rigmor Mydtskov; from the Archives and Library of the Royal Theater, Copenhagen.)

BIBLIOGRAPHY

Aschengreen, Erik, et al., eds. *Perspektiv på Bournonville.* Copenhagen, 1980.

Bournonville, August. "The Ballet Poems of August Bournonville: The Complete Scenarios." Translated by Patricia McAndrew. *Dance Chronicle* 3.2 (1979)–6.1 (1983).

Bournonville, August. *My Theatre Life* (1848–1878). Translated by Patricia McAndrew (Middletown, Conn., 1979).

Clarke, Mary. "A Real Royal Ballet: *A Folk Tale* in Copenhagen." *The Dancing Times* (November 1991):144–147.

PATRICIA MCANDREW

FOLKWANG TANZSTUDIO. A training center in Essen, Germany, the Folkwang Tanzstudio became one of the prime movers of the new German dance theater in the late 1960s . It remains important both as a school and as a venue for performances of works by advanced students, alumni, and teachers.

In 1927, the city of Essen, located in the industrial region of the Ruhr Valley, founded a school of the applied arts, the Folkwang Schule. The following year, 1928, a dance department was created, the Folkwang-Tanstheater-Studio, headed by Kurt Jooss, Sigurd Leeder, Aino Siimola, Frederick (Fritz) Cohen, and Elsa Kahl. When the department was closed in 1929, the faculty and students joined the dancers of the Essen Opera House, and a company known as the Folkwang Tanzbühne soon emerged. From 1929 untill Jooss immigrated in 1933 to Paris with the renamed Folkwang Ballett Essen, the company frequently performed ballets by Jooss, who had based his new dance aesthetic on his association with Rudolf Laban. In Paris in 1932, Jooss had won first prize for his work *The Green Table*, set to music by Fritz Cohen, in the choreographic competition organized by the Archives Internationales de la Danse. In 1933 he relocated the company to Paris and named it Les Ballets Jooss.

After his return to Essen in 1949, Jooss once more directed the ensemble, now known as the Folkwang Tanztheater, until its dissolution in 1953. During the 1963/64 season, the group was revived as the Folkwang Tanzstudio, the school's master class. After Jooss's retirement in 1968, the company's former solo dancer Hans Züllig became its director. In that year Pina Bausch, one of the most important representatives of the new dance theater, introduced her choreography into the Folkwang repertory. She was the company's leading choreographer until her move to the Wuppertal Tanztheater in 1973. Bausch was succeeded by Reinhild Hoffmann and Susanne Linke, who created their own choreography with the ensemble. After Hoffmann took over the Bremer Tanztheater in 1978, Linke, as artistic director, made the Folkwang Tanzstudio into an increasingly independent, internationally successful group. More than any other educational institution, the Folkwang Schule and its affiliated Folkwang Ballett have influenced the course of German dance—before World War II as an important center for the teaching and practice of interpretive dance, and since the war as fertile ground for the new German dance theater. In addition to being an excellent steppingstone for young choreographers, the Folkwang has continued to play an important role in the evolution of aesthetic style in dance.

[*See also the entries on the principal figures mentioned herein.*]

BIBLIOGRAPHY

Choreography and Dance 3.2 (1993). Special issue on Kurt Jooss.

Coton, A. V. *The New Ballet: Kurt Jooss and His Ork.* London, 1946.

NORBERT SERVOS
Translated from German

FONTEYN, MARGOT (Margaret Hookham; born 18 May 1919 in Reigate, England, died 21 February 1991 in Panama City), *prima ballerina assoluta* of the Royal Ballet. Margot Fonteyn started taking ballet lessons in Ealing, England, at the age of four. In 1928, her family moved to China, where in Shanghai she studied with George Goncharov, a former member of the Bolshoi Ballet. Back in

FONTEYN. In 1936, Fonteyn created the role of the Woman in the Ball Dress in Frederick Ashton's romantic ballet *Apparitions*, mounted for the Vic-Wells Ballet. Her beautiful ball dress was designed by Cecil Beaton. (Photograph from the Dance Collection, New York Public Library for the Performing Arts.)

FONTEYN. In *The Sleeping Beauty*, Fonteyn established herself as the quintessential interpreter of the title role, the Princess Aurora. Here she is seen, center stage, with Michael Somes as Prince Florestan and other members of the Sadler's Wells Ballet in the new production that was presented at the Royal Opera House, Covent Garden, in January 1946. (Photograph from the Dance Collection, New York Public Library for the Performing Arts.)

England in 1933, she attended the academy run by Serafina Astafieva, a former Maryinsky dancer, and in 1934 joined the Sadler's Wells School in London. While still a student she made her debut with the Vic-Wells Ballet (it became Sadler's Wells and eventually the Royal Ballet) as a Snowflake in *The Nutcracker;* she also appeared in several opera ballets when the company took part in the summer opera season at Covent Garden.

In the fall of 1934, while still a student-member of the corps de ballet, she danced her first solo role: Young Tregennis in *The Haunted Ballroom* by Ninette de Valois, the company's founder and director. De Valois quickly saw her potential and cast her in a succession of small featured parts—Lilian in Frederick Ashton's *Lord of Burleigh,* the Mazurka in *Les Sylphides,* and the Creole Girl in Ashton's *Rio Grande,* originally created by the Vic-Wells's ballerina Alicia Markova for the Camargo Society.

In 1935, Fonteyn became a regular member of the Vic-Wells and took over some of the roles relinquished by Markova, who had left the company. In November, at the age of sixteen, she created the part of the Bride in Ashton's *Le Baiser de la Fée.* In December, she danced Odette in the full-length *Swan Lake* (Ruth French was the Odile), a debut that affirmed her status as the first potential *prima ballerina* to emerge from within the company's ranks.

The facts of Fonteyn's early career are unremarkable. What happened subsequently is the stuff of theatrical legend. Although Fonteyn confirmed her ascendancy in 1946 as Aurora in the new production of *The Sleeping Beauty,* with which Sadler's Wells Ballet opened its first season at Covent Garden, London, she was hardly a household name. Apart from Paris, where in 1948 she enjoyed a great success with Roland Petit's Ballets de Paris, she was scarcely known beyond the confines of Great Britain until 9 October 1949, when she made her New York debut in *The Sleeping Beauty.*

Nevertheless, Fonteyn played a crucial role in the ultimate success of British ballet, for which reason she has a permanent place on the Royal Ballet's roster as its sole *prima ballerina assoluta.* Without Fonteyn to take on classics, the Vic-Wells Ballet might not have weathered the loss of Markova in 1935. Further, from 1935 with *Le Baiser de la Fée* to 1958 with *Ondine,* she was the chosen

FONTEYN. In 1949, the Sadler's Wells Ballet made a triumphant tour of the United States. Besides *The Sleeping Beauty*, which became the company's signature work, Fonteyn appeared in *Swan Lake*, partnered by Robert Helpmann as Prince Siegfried. Here they are seen in act 3, at a critical moment in the Black Swan pas de deux. (Photograph from the Dance Collection, New York Public Library for the Performing Arts.)

instrument of Frederick Ashton's creative will, helping to determine the bent of his imagination.

Over the years, Fonteyn's roles in works such as *Symphonic Variations, Scènes de Ballet,* and *Daphnis and Chloe* have been taken over by other dancers with great success. Yet each of these ballets owes an enormous amount to Fonteyn's individual qualities: her faultless line, her lyricism, her musicality, the radiance that suffused her simplest movements. The climax of an Ashton ballet made for her was likely to be a moment of quiet ecstasy, of inward fulfillment—Chloe restored to Daphnis and carried aloft in tranquil joy; the gentle, subsiding close of the ballroom pas de deux in *Cinderella;* the final tableau of *Symphonic Variations.* These reflect qualities that once seemed purely local in interest.

Fonteyn herself spoke of her fears that her essentially lyrical style would have no appeal for American audiences. Yet it was her triumph as Aurora that ensured the acceptance of British ballet in the United States. Fonteyn's American career began when she was at the peak of her powers. The dancer who ran onto the stage of New York's Metropolitan Opera House as Princess Aurora in 1949 was fully formed. *Daphnis and Chloe, The Firebird, Ondine,* and *Marguerite and Armand* were still ahead, but in these works her qualities were only deepened and refined (though it must be emphasized that she never ceased to distill her art until the end of her career).

From the start, she was without peculiarities. Edwin Denby once said that he had never seen such good manners on stage. Although in her autobiography she speaks about her chronic lack of confidence, she rarely communi-

cated anything but the serenity that comes from deep-seated self-assurance. Occasionally, she appeared remote, abstracted. In certain comic roles, for which she clearly had no temperamental affinity (above all, Swanilda and Mam'zelle Angot), her dancing revealed more willpower than spontaneity, and her smile became unnervingly fixed. For the most part, however, she communicated a firmly held belief that she could hold the audience's attention without a display of assertiveness. Her appeal was based on an irresistible modesty of demeanor that sprang from the purity of her style, as formed by Ashton from the heritage of nineteenth-century Russian ballet.

Fonteyn grew up in an artistic environment that differed from those dominating ballet in Europe and the United States before World War II. Tamara Toumanova and Irina Baronova, her exact contemporaries, were famous when Fonteyn was still a beginner. By comparison, Fonteyn was nurtured gently and obscurely, developing slowly in an atmosphere remote from box-office demands and public adulation. She belonged to a company with its own school, a permanent home, and the obligation to perform only once a week. She took on act 2 of *Swan Lake* at sixteen: Odette at sixteen, Giselle at seventeen, Odette-Odile at nineteen, Aurora two-and-a-half months later. She never had to force, either technically or interpretively. Even in her callowest days she seems to have projected a sense of poise. Part of an established hierarchy, she never had to make her way. She inherited the position of ballerina from Markova by the command of Ninette de Valois. Her rank in the company was ordained through the recognition of her merit and promise, not through the struggle to outdo others. The only kind of success she had to consider was artistic.

The wartime closing of Sadler's Wells Theatre quickened the rate of Fonteyn's development and brought her and the company face-to-face with the conditions of the commercial theater: nine shows a week before enormous, often undiscriminating audiences; poor rehearsal conditions; cross-country touring. By the mid-1940s, Fonteyn was giving more performances in a month than she had given in an entire year before 1939. She learned how to make her quiet lyricism more theatrical and was transformed from a romantic to a classical ballerina. The emphasis of her Odette shifted from pathos to nobility and took on a note of genuine tragedy. At the same time she remained highly effective in a wide range of *demi-caractère* roles.

Fonteyn in those years was not physically strong, but few roles took her beyond her capabilities. Only the thirty-two *fouettés* in *Swan Lake's* act 3 defeated her; she got through them, but they were loose-jointed and unstable. Whereas a Markova would substitute a brilliant sequence of *échappés*, Fonteyn did not funk the *fouettés;* they were part of the role and therefore an obligation that she fulfilled by dancing them as well as she could.

Fonteyn owed a lot to Robert Helpmann—a strong stage personality, he brought out her womanliness and was a faultless partner. With Helpmann, Fonteyn developed a rapport she found with no one else. Neither Michael Somes nor Rudolf Nureyev ever gave her the same security; Somes lacked confidence in himself, whereas Nureyev offered her incentives to excel herself, to take risks. By 1949 the Fonteyn-Helpmann partnership was a miracle of coordination. From the first bemused pas de deux in the Vision Scene of *The Sleeping Beauty* until the exultant wedding celebration, there was a progression toward fulfillment that Fonteyn never subsequently equaled. At the climax of the last-act pas de deux, her turns behind the Prince's outstretched arm before the fish dive were so secure and swift that one never saw her take up the supporting foot.

The ultimate proof of Fonteyn's brilliance was her ability to make her last-act variation into the climax of the entire evening—to transform into the apex of Aurora's good fortune a simple dance designed to supply a lyrical contrast for the grand adagio that precedes it and the strong male solo and boisterous coda that follow. (In 1949, there was no male solo, and the coda was used for the Three Ivans.) Fonteyn's triumph was compounded of all her virtues: the slow opening section showed off her noble proportions, her perfect placement, the clarity and continuity of her line from fingertips to feet, and the ballerina head and face that gave focus to the body's expressiveness by directing the audience's attention where she willed it to be. In the sequence to the perky violin solo, as she flicked her wrists while raising her arms, she would draw the rhythm taut by raising her eyes a fraction later than her arms.

The same kind of *rubato* informed her phrasing of the *petits battements frappés* to the *pizzicati*, so that she seemed to be flirting with the music. Yet in the final section her fast, sure *piqué* turns were thrilling precisely because they accorded so exactly with the music's strong, driving rhythm. The dance exemplified Fonteyn's musicality; her gift was not simply to dance as if the music originated in her body but also to ride the music like a surfer, impelled by and partaking of its primal energy.

The combination of Tchaikovsky scores and Petipa choreography was ideally suited to Fonteyn's gifts; that of Tchaikovsky and George Balanchine was not. The distillation of nineteenth-century grandeur in Balanchine's *Ballet Imperial,* presented by Sadler's Wells Ballet the year after its American debut, suited her not at all, being too concentrated for her essentially lyrical style. By 1950, Fonteyn was not lacking in strength or technique, but she could never master the dynamics of *Ballet Imperial.* Bal-

FONTEYN. Of the many ballets Frederick Ashton made for Fonteyn, perhaps none suited her so well as *Ondine* (1958). As the water spirit who falls in love with a mortal, Palemon, portrayed by Michael Somes, she was the epitome of sparkling fluidity. (Photograph © 1958 by Zoe Dominic; used by permission.)

anchine's visit to London made it clear that Fonteyn was not going to be able to widen her range in any significant way. Before this, she had made little effect in Léonide Massine's *Le Tricorne* and *Mam'zelle Angot* and never worked with him again.

The problem was not one of national temperament, because de Valois, usually thought of as the most English of choreographers, had been unable to provide her with one single memorable role. Fonteyn's range, it became apparent, did not extend much beyond the classics and Frederick Ashton—though later on, she did make a superb, impersonal Firebird. What she did best was probe and intensify.

In the late-1950s, Fonteyn's *Swan Lake* achieved a new tragic grandeur. From the Soviet Russians, finally performing in the West, Fonteyn learned greater freedom of movement, fuller use of the arms, and more impetuous phrasing. In act 3, her back and shoulders were particularly seductive. She used her head and her glittering smile to attract and rebuff Siegfried. Her eyes were wanton. Her *arabesque penchée* at the end of the adagio was like an arrow flying to its mark. *Fouettés* notwithstanding, she brought the excitement to an extraordinary pitch.

These were years of steadily increasing popularity. In Britain, she was made Dame in 1956—the first dancer to be so honored in mid-career. Her accolade was followed by the granting of a Royal Charter to Sadler's Wells Ballet, henceforth known as the Royal Ballet. It is doubtful that this would have happened without Fonteyn, though the reverse is just as true. She gave the company glamor, and it gave her the opportunity to achieve it. Above all, it gave her Ashton, who from 1946 on provided her with a series of consummate roles: *Symphonic Variations*; the Spirits of the Air pas de deux from *The Fairy Queen*; *Scènes de Ballet*; Death in *Don Juan*; Cinderella; Chloe; the long pas de deux of *Tiresias*, act 2; Sylvia; The Queen of the Air in *Homage to the Queen*; La Péri; *Birthday Offering*; and Ondine. By the time she came to the last, she was dancing with extraordinary lambency. Her great set pieces summed up her allure and, especially in the climactic pas de deux, during which Palemon kisses her and dies, added to it an overwhelming sense of romantic passion. In this period Chloe remains her greatest creation. The dance she performed as a captive of the pirates was singularly eloquent: the fear in her eyes; the manner in which her shoulders pushed forward while her arms were held rigid before her as she struggled to free her bound hands; her stabbing *piqués* as she begged for pity.

The change in Fonteyn's status in 1959, from a member of the Royal Ballet to guest artist—which was effected, it seems, without her prior knowledge—simply acknowledged what had been true for some time. Fonteyn's career was no longer automatically identifiable with the company and, except in the United States, where her box office appeal was a necessary adjunct to the Royal Ballet's success, the company no longer depended utterly on her.

FONTEYN. In 1963, Ashton created *Marguerite and Armand* for Fonteyn and Rudolf Nureyev, a young Russian dancer who had recently defected from the Soviet Union. Based on *La dame aux camélias*, the famous novel by Alexandre Dumas *fils*, it depicts the passionate romance of Marguerite Gautier, a courtesan, and Armand Duval. As Marguerite, Fonteyn is seen here amid a group of admirers. Uniquely her own, the role was never danced by anyone else. (Photograph from the Dance Collection, New York Public Library for the Performing Arts.)

FONTEYN. The partnership of Fonteyn and Nureyev quickly became legendary, as each seemed perfectly attuned to the other. In 1965, they performed the pas de deux from *Le Corsaire* in the film *An Evening with the Royal Ballet.* (Photograph from the Dance Collection, New York Public Library for the Performing Arts.)

More and more did Fonteyn seem like a link with the past. The present was in other, younger hands. There was a sense of consummation about her career: in 1954, she succeeded Dame Adeline Genée as president of the Royal Academy of Dancing; in 1959, she was awarded an honorary degree by Oxford; in 1961, she was highly praised in the Soviet Union during the Royal Ballet's visit to Moscow and Leningrad. Each season looked as if it would be her last.

Rudolf Nureyev changed all that. Through him, she discovered fresh sources of energy. At the culmination of her career, she was suddenly made aware of capabilities in herself as yet unrealized. She has spoken about the partnership as a challenge she accepted in full awareness of its dangers. In it she competed not with Nureyev, but with herself, with what she had been until then. From February 1962, when they first appeared together (at Covent Garden, in *Giselle*), Fonteyn danced with a new largeness of utterance, a weightier lyricism than she had ever before understood was possible for her to achieve.

Nureyev aroused the audience with his strength, his passion, his prowess; Fonteyn with her assurance and the sense of exultance that emerged from it. Without ever de-

veloping a virtuoso technique, she became, in effect, a virtuoso. In *Le Corsaire*, she made so kinetically vivacious a response to the music and phrased it with so keen a sense of climax that she seemed to have performed prodigious technical feats. Yet in those first three or four years with Nureyev—in taking on a more generous, ample, and annunciative style—she never lost the qualities that had made her a great ballerina. For all the excitement she produced in *Le Corsaire*, she exemplified all the virtues of her classical heritage: grace, order, modesty, proportion, a sense of her own limitations, inner strength, and the unerring instinct for beauty of movement.

The partnership became one of the indispensable sights of the 1960s. Oddly enough, when Ashton devised a work for them, he gave Fonteyn the opportunity to be uniquely herself, but gave Nureyev something far less personal. *Marguerite and Armand*, created in 1963, when Fonteyn was nearly forty-four, was a tribute to everything she had achieved, a fable of her popular triumphs, her artistic attainments, and her inevitable decline. Whereas Armand was a generalized portrait of the young, handsome lover, Marguerite was the summation of Fonteyn's career—a role that seized with infinite tact upon her gift for simultaneously moving and exciting the audience. Unlike many of the ballets in which she appeared during this period (among them, Roland Petit's *Paradise Lost* and *Pelléas and Mélisande;* John Cranko's *Poème de l'Exstase;* and Martha Graham's *Lucifer*), *Marguerite and Armand* was artistically seemly. Like *The Dying Swan* for Pavlova, it projected an ultimate truth in metaphorical form about Fonteyn as both a dancer and a human being. Luckily, it survives on film.

Fonteyn never retired formally. In 1981, she played Lady Capulet, a nondancing role, in Nureyev's *Romeo and Juliet*. In 1984, she took part in a gala at New York City's Metropolitan Opera, for which Ashton, who also appeared, arranged a little mime scene to music from *The Sleeping Beauty*, as an act of homage to her in the city that had played a decisive part in her career.

The real end of Fonteyn's career had already been acknowledged at Covent Garden in May 1979, shortly after her sixtieth birthday. There, the curtain rose on Ashton's *Salut d'Amour à Margot Fonteyn* to find the ballerina sitting in a chair. With the aid of gestures and movements of the head she began silently to retrace her career as an Ashton dancer, referring briefly to all the great roles he had created for her, first at Sadler's Wells, then at Covent Garden. At the end of the evening she danced her old role of the Debutante in Ashton's *Façade* with Sir Robert Helpmann, who was then seventy years old.

Now that Fonteyn's performances are part of dance history, it is pointless to dwell on the decline in evidence during her final seasons as a ballerina. But for those who saw her only on those nights when she was all legend and no substance, the greatness she achieved and maintained for more than two decades—say, from 1948 to 1970—must be affirmed.

BIBLIOGRAPHY
Ballet Review 21 (Summer 1993): 21–43. Symposium entitled "Remembering Margot Fonteyn."
Bland, Alexander. *Fonteyn and Nureyev: The Story of a Partnership.* London and New York, 1979.
Fonteyn, Margot. *Margot Fonteyn: Autobiography.* London, 1975.
Fonteyn, Margot. *Pavlova Impressions.* London, 1984.
Harris, Dale. "Snowflake to Superstar." *Ballet Review* 4.6 (1974): 67–79.
Hastings, Baird. "Margot Fonteyn, 1919–1991." *Ballet Review* 19 (Spring 1991): 20–35.
Manchester, P. W. *Vic-Wells: A Ballet Progress.* London, 1942.
Money, Keith. *The Art of Margot Fonteyn.* London, 1965.
Money, Keith. *Fonteyn: The Making of a Legend.* London, 1973.
Money, Keith. *Fonteyn and Nureyev: The Great Years.* London, 1994.
Vernon, Gilbert. "Margot Fonteyn: A Personal Tribute." *Dance Chronicle* 14.2–3 (1991): 221–233.

DALE HARRIS

FOOTWEAR is not essential to dance. The dances of many countries and periods have been performed without shoes. In the early twentieth century, the absence of shoes became a distinguishing characteristic when Isadora Duncan, her followers, and her imitators danced in their bare feet.

Protection is not the only reason for dancers to wear foot coverings. Some types of footwear, such as the pointe shoe worn by ballet dancers, extend the dancer's range of movement. Shoes with hard soles or heels, sometimes augmented by metal plates as on tap-dancing shoes, allow the dancer to enrich the acoustic qualities of the dance. Specific types of footwear may add to the authentic appearance of a national costume, for example, the use of boots in the character dances of many classical ballets. High-heeled shoes are worn to lend an air of fashion and glamour, while soft-soled oxford-style jazz shoes give a more casual appearance. Athletic shoes, such as sneakers, have also found their way to the dance stage.

Dance shoes may be made of a number of materials, among them leather, satin, canvas, velvet, and wood. They may be cut in many different styles. Some differ little in appearance from ordinary shoes, although they may be made of lightweight, pliable materials. Others, such as pointe shoes and tap-dancing shoes, are highly specialized forms developed for dancing. The modern dance sandal was also designed especially for dancing; it protects the ball of the foot while leaving the toes and heel free. Most modern dancers, however, prefer bare feet, jazz shoes, or sneakers.

In the Western world, shoes have had a significant influence on the development of dance technique. Ingrid Brainard, a noted scholar of fifteenth-century dance, has pointed out that long-toed shoes such as the *poulaine*, popular in Europe between the eleventh and thirteenth centuries, had the negative effect of inhibiting the wearer's range of movement; yet heeled shoes, introduced in the seventeenth century, enhanced the stamping steps of contemporary dances.

Pointe shoes (also called toe shoes), a unique type of female footwear, evolved in response to the development of academic ballet technique. Although toe-dancing is synonymous with ballet in the public mind, it was incorporated in ballet technique only in the nineteenth century. Ballerinas of the seventeenth and eighteenth centuries wore high-heeled shoes. In the eighteenth century, Marie Camargo is said to have removed the high heels from her dancing shoes to achieve greater technical facility; however, Lillian Moore suggests that she did so toward the end of her career, since portraits of her in action depict her in conventional high-heeled shoes.

By the beginning of the nineteenth century, professional ballet dancers wore light, flexible satin slippers tied with ribbons around the ankles, much like the shoes worn at that time in the ballroom. The pliability of these slippers allowed the dancer to rise onto the tips of her toes, although in those days she remained there only for a few seconds. No one knows exactly when pointe work was introduced, but verbal and pictorial evidence points to a date between 1810 and 1820. It won full acceptance as a part of ballet technique in 1832, after Marie Taglioni's triumph as the airy heroine of *La Sylphide*.

Early pointe shoes were strengthened by darning; cotton wadding was inserted into them to protect the dancer's toes. Later the shoes were further stiffened with glue, starch, or sewn-on ribbons or tapes. In a description of pointe shoes published in 1866, Théophile Gautier notes that the sole of the shoe "does not reach the top of the foot, but ends squarely, leaving about two finger-breadths of material projecting" and that "the inside of the shoe is lined with strong canvas and, at the very end, a strip of leather and cardboard, the thickness of which depends on the lightness of the wearer" (Guest, 1981). These shoes were still relatively light and flimsy compared to the blocked or boxed pointe shoe that came into use near the end of the nineteenth century.

Even today, the box of the pointe shoe is made not of wood, as is often believed, but of many layers of cloth (linen, felt, canvas, and others) held together by a special glue whose formula is jealously guarded by the manufacturer. The box supports the sides of the foot and forms a flat base upon which the toes stand. The dancer's arch is supported by a strong, springy inner shank and a short leather sole that, as in the shoes of Gautier's day, does not extend to the toes. The fabric under the toes is pleated to allow the dancer to spread her toes and grip the floor. The sides and top of the shoe are made of satin-covered cloth, with a drawstring around the top to ensure the close fit of the shoe. Pointe shoes are generally worn in a size two to three times smaller than the dancer's street shoes; they must fit well enough to feel like part of the foot. Many dancers say they like to "feel the floor" through their shoes.

Pointe shoes are assembled almost entirely by hand although machines are used for a few steps, such as cutting out material for the box and sewing on the drawstring. The dancer sews on the ribbons that are tied around the ankle. Professional dancers usually have their shoes custom-made to detailed specifications. Professional ballet companies supply the shoes used by their dancers in rehearsals and performances.

Each dancer has her own favorite rituals for breaking in the shoes, which are too stiff to dance in when they come from the manufacturer. Favorite methods include slamming a door on them or striking them against a wall. Individual dancers have different preferences as to the softness of their shoes; these preferences may also vary depending on the technical requirements of the role to be danced.

In preparing for a performance, the dancer must ensure that her shoes will not slip or come off. She may glue or sew the shoes to her tights, spit on or sew the knot of the ribbons, or dip her feet in water so the wet shoes will dry tightly around her feet. To avoid slipping on the stage dancers rub the soles of their shoes in rosin or sprinkle water, a gritty household cleanser, or even a soft drink on the stage.

The soft ballet shoes worn by men and beginning ballet students are similar to pointe shoes in appearance, but they lack the box and are usually covered with leather or canvas instead of satin. The male dancers of the Royal Danish Ballet still preserve a fashion dating back to the 1820s; their black shoes with a triangle of white leather set into the vamp are worn in the ballets of August Bournonville. Men's shoes are not tied with ribbons; one or two strips of elastic may be sewn on at the instep, although some dancers dispense with this entirely. Like women's shoes, men's shoes are fitted closely to the foot and require breaking in before they are used.

The making of ballet shoes had become a specialized industry by the middle of the nineteenth century. Janssen, Crait, Ebermann, and Niccolini were among the leading manufacturers. The firm of Crait still survives today as the official supplier of shoes to the Paris Opera, a position it has held since 1879. Other manufacturers of note are (in alphabetical order) Anello and David, Capezio, Freed, Gamba, Porselli, Repetto, Schachtners, and Selva. Most dancers have a preferred manufacturer and, perhaps, even a preferred craftsman within the firm.

Tap-dancing shoes, another specialized type of footwear, are made with leather uppers and wooden heels. The taps, thin metal plates usually made of aluminum alloy, are fixed to the front and heel of the shoe with nails, screws, or rivets. Taps may be selected in a variety of shapes or sizes that depend on the type of sound the dancer wishes to produce.

Today it is not unusual to see dancers in a ballet company performing in high heels or jazz shoes. Modern dancers, no longer identified by their bare feet, may don jazz shoes, sneakers, or even soft ballet shoes. Although a certain amount of training is required to use some types of shoes correctly, such as pointe shoes and tap-dancing shoes, choreographers today generally have their dancers wear the type of shoes that best suits the movement style of a specific work.

[*See also* Designing for Dance.]

BIBLIOGRAPHY

Barringer, Janice, and Sarah Schlesinger. *The Pointe Book: Shoes, Training, and Technique*. Princeton, 1991.

Draper, Paul. "Shoes and Taps." *Dance Magazine* 33 (March 1958): 60–61.

Gale, Joseph. "The Taming of the Toe Shoes." *Newsday* (24 August 1975).

Guest, Ivor. "Costume and the Nineteenth Century Dancer." In *Designing for the Dancer*, by Roy Strong et al. London, 1981.

Horosko, Marian. "If the Shoe Fits. . . ." *Dance Magazine* 60 (April 1986): 80–81; 60 (May 1986): 98–99.

Sorine, Daniel S., and Stephanie Riva Sorine. *Dancershoes*. New York, 1979.

Terry, Walter. *On Pointe!* New York, 1962.

Tobias, Tobi. "Toe Shoes: The Satin Thorns under Every Ballerina's Feet." *New York Times* (21 September 1975).

Tools of the Trade. Capezio brochure, c.1965.

SUSAN AU

FOREGGER, NIKOLAI (Nikolai Mikhailovich Greifenturn [Foregger]; born 6 [18] April 1892 in Moscow, died 8 June 1939 in Kuibyshev, Russia), director and choreographer. The sole descendant of an aristocratic Russo-German family, Nikolai Foregger was considered one of the most innovative and controversial of all the Soviet directors and choreographers of the early 1920s. Largely forgotten after 1930, Foregger pioneered the use of movement grids for actors (which he called *tafiatrenazh*), mechanical dances, eccentric dance parodies of Western popular dances, and short, colorful propaganda displays that featured a wide variety of grotesque and acrobatic activity. Under his tutelage many future Soviet filmmakers and choreographers—experimental artists such as Sergei Eisenstein, Boris Barnet, Sergei Yutkevich, Vladimir Fogel, and Luda Semenova—received their earliest schooling.

A graduate of Kiev University's Department of Philology in 1915, Foregger developed an overriding interest in recreating seventeenth- and eighteenth-century French farces and pantomimes. After serving a brief apprenticeship at Aleksandr Tairov's Kamerny Theater in Moscow in 1916 and 1917, Foregger choreographed several pieces to the music of Maurice Ravel and Claude Debussy in Petrograd. It was at this time that Foregger began to blend the stylized gestures of the Renaissance French theater and the *commedia dell'arte* with those of the modern circus and puppet show.

During the Revolution, Foregger spent a year with a Red Army agit-prop train in Ukraine. In 1920 he returned to Moscow and inaugurated his Theater of the Four Masks, a contemporary Soviet *commedia dell'arte*. Operating out of his own apartment, Foregger presented comic propaganda performances that began to attract the attention of arts luminaries such as Vladimir Mayakovsky, Osip Brik, and Aleksandr Rodchenko. In December 1921 Foregger's bitingly satirical burlesque, *The Parody Show,* designed by Yutkevich and Eisenstein, demonstrated how perfectly executed grotesque and stylized acting could find a new niche between theater and dance. Attacking the theatrical pretentions of the Moscow Art Theater and Tairov as well as the naiveté of the current agit-prop, Foregger quickly became the focal point of a theater-mad Moscow.

On 5 January 1922, Foregger presented his best-known production, *Good Treatment for Horses.* Written by Vladimir Mass, *Good Treatment* revealed the vulgar bourgeois temperament as a rich capitalist couple tour a new constructivist Moscow. In the third act, the local capitalists enter a slightly decadent Moscow cabaret, where they are amazed and awed at the new Western dances and jazz. Combining *tafiatrenazh* with illustrations from a Berlin manual on American jazz, Foregger created an entirely new kind of eccentric dance. The real audience was so captivated by "Mucky from Kentucky," the "Dance of the Ku Klux Klan," and the fictitious couple that this third act reappeared in *Better Treatment for Horses* and *Improved Treatment for Horses.*

Now called MASTFOR (a Russian acronym for Foregger's workshop, Mast[erskaya] For[eggera]), Foregger's troupe acquired a permanent theater space in October 1922 and offered more than thirty different programs of sketches and dances in eccentric and constructivist costuming. As his popularity grew, so did his inventiveness: fox trots, tangos, apache dances, and shimmies merged with aerial somersaults, pyramid building, folkloric leaps, and mechanical bows and swings. Although his theater and the adjacent Praga Restaurant were long rumored to be centers of large-scale black-marketing, gambling, and prostitution, tickets to the MASTFOR became the most difficult items to find in Moscow.

Formally presented on 13 February 1923, MASTFOR's *Dance of Machines* created a sensation throughout the Soviet avant-garde. Precise human enactments of linchpin rotations on locomotive wheels, pistons within expanding cylinders, and turning flywheels, handpumps, and lathes impressed even Foregger's bitterest enemies. Celebrating the new "god of the machine," the MASTFOR dancers found a novel use for their old comical, mechanical gestures.

At the height of its fame in January 1924 the MASTFOR cabaret was destroyed by fire. Foregger and some of his leading performers worked in other theaters, but with much less success because their original work was already widely imitated. By 1927 Foregger had failed in attempts to rebuild the MASTFOR in Leningrad and once again in Moscow. Choreographing for the amateur Blue Blouse movement and other leftist theaters of satire, Foregger temporarily kept his name and movement innovations alive. In 1929 he returned, probably in "voluntary exile," to Ukraine, where he worked in semiobscurity as a ballet master and an opera director in Kharkov—creating there the frequently performed ballet *Ferendzhi* (1930)—and then in Kiev. In 1938 he became ballet master in Kuibyshev, Russia, where he died.

BIBLIOGRAPHY

Foregger, Nikolai. "Experiments in the Art of the Dance." Translated by David Miller. *Drama Review* 19 (March 1975): 74–77.

Gordon, Mel. "Foregger and the Dance of the Machines." *Drama Review* 19 (March 1975): 68–73.

Ritm i kultura tantsa. Leningrad, 1926.

Sheremetyevskaya, Natalia. "Nikolai Foregger: Postanovshchik tant-sev." *Teatr* (May 1972).

Souritz, Elizabeth. "Soviet Ballet of the 1920s and the Influence of Constructivism." *Soviet Union/Union Soviétique* 7.1–2 (1980): 112–137.

Swift, Mary Grace. *The Art of the Dance in the U.S.S.R.* Notre Dame, 1968.

ARCHIVES.   The Kitchen, New York, which holds programs for a series of performances (1983) from the theater of Foregger and Meyerhold and films of the Soviet theater, 1924–1935.

MEL GORDON

FORLANA (It., *furlana;* Fr., *forlane, fourlane*). A lively couple dance in compound duple meter, the forlana derives its name from Friuli, the region of its origin, which lies to the northeast of Venice. A courtship dance in which the man and woman repeatedly approach and flee each other, the forlana has existed as a folk dance, in the ballroom, and on the stage. Its strong associations with Venice have led to its use in theatrical evocations of that city and its famous masquerades during Carnival season. The most concrete choreographic descriptions of the forlana come from early eighteenth-century France, where the forlana flourished as both a theatrical and a ballroom dance for a number of years.

Italy. The early history of the forlana is obscure. It may have derived from Slavic dances, as Friuli was subject to a substantial amount of immigration from the Slavic parts of Europe. The dance was already in existence in the late sixteenth century, for there are two duple-meter dances called *ballo furlano* in Pierre Phalèse's collection of dances *Chorearum molliorum collectanea* of 1583. In 1609, Jean-Baptiste Duval, secretary of the French ambassador to Venice, reports watching an evening of galliards, passamezzos, and dances *"à la fourlane"* (Écorcheville, 1914). Duval did not specify what characterized the Friulian style of dancing, but in 1683 a French visitor to Venice described the Carnival festivities there for *Le Mercure galant*, saying, "The prettiest of [the Venetians'] dances is the *fourlane*. It is done by two or four people, with an equal number of men and women, who turn in a circle while jumping and agitating their feet with marvelous speed and lightness. They then approach each other, still turning in the same way, and sometimes take each others' arms which they interlace and pass above their heads." To

James, Earl of Perth, who visited Venice in 1695, the forlana seemed "somewhat like the way our Highlanders dance, but the women do it much more prettily than the men." These and others accounts by visitors reveal that the forlana was done both as part of street festivals and in ballrooms, sometimes by aristocrats dressed as "country people."

Both the circling figure and the vigor of the dance are attested to by Casanova, who described in his memoirs a forlana that he and a partner performed in Constantinople in 1744. After dancing six forlanas in a row, "I was burning hot and out of breath, for there is no national dance more violent." His partner, however, was unruffled, and "during the turning part of the dance, which is the most difficult part, she seemed to float." In 1762 Giovanni Gallini remarked that

> the favorite dance of the Venetians, is what they call the Furlana, which is performed by two persons dancing a-round with the greatest rapidity. Those who have a good ear, keep time with the crossing their feet behind; and some add a motion of their hands, as if they were rowing or tugging at an oar.

In the nineteenth century, the forlana appears to have been danced very little, although in 1894 Gaspare Ungarelli classified it as among those dances still in use. It was danced occasionally on the operatic stage, however, when a bit of Venetian local color was desired, as, for example, the forlana danced by masqueraders at the end of act 1 of Amilcare Ponchielli's *La Gioconda* (1876). In 1914 a ballroom version of the forlana bearing little resemblance to the traditional dance was created by Enrico Pichetti in response to the concern of Pope Pius X over the increasing popularity of the tango. The sudden thrust of the forlana into the spotlight sparked a renewed interest in the dance. Despite the support of the pope, the success of the ballroom forlana was short-lived. The forlana has, however, enjoyed a modest revival as a folk dance in twentieth-century Italy.

France. At the dawn of the eighteenth century, the French fascination with the lavish Venetian Carnival season found expression in a series of ballets and *opéra-ballets* with Venetian themes performed at the Paris Opera, among them André Campra's *Carnaval de Venise* (1699), Michel de La Barre's *La Vénitienne* (1705), and Campra's *Les Fêtes Vénitiennes* (1710). The forlana, along with its close relatives the *vénitienne* and the *saltarello*, fig-

FORLANA. Example 1. André Campra's *Ballet des Fragments de M. de Lully* (1702).

...

ured prominently among the dances used to evoke the ambience of Venice, particularly the masked balls. Of these three dance types, fourteen French choreographies survive in Feuillet notation, all but one of them dances for a single couple. Although drawing their inspiration from Venice, these dances are clearly French in technique, step vocabulary, and layout of the figures. Some of the choreographies are transcriptions of the forlanas as they were danced by the professional dancers of the Opera; others made use of the tunes of the well-known stage forlanas but were choreographed for inclusion in the various collections of ballroom dances that appeared starting in 1700. All the choreographed forlanas are in 6/4 time and have one step-unit per bar. Most of the tunes are built on repeated two-bar phrases, often with dotted figures in the first measure of the pair and a ♩♪♪ rhythm in the second. (See Example 1.)

The structure of the music is not binary, as in most French dance music of the period, but a rounded form in which the eight measures of the first section are repeated at the end of the dance following a middle section or sections. By making use of such devices as step repetitions, pairing of steps, and changes in direction, the choreographies generally adhere to the phrase structure of the music without slavishly imitating every musical repeat.

The forlana reached the height of its popularity in France during the first quarter of the eighteenth century. Along with many other French dances, it was also in use on the other side of the channel, as the three English forlana choreographies show. That the forlana also reached the German-speaking countries can be seen in various musical forlana settings, including one by Johann Sebastian Bach, and by the inclusion of a forlana for a gondolier in Gregorio Lambranzi's series of theatrical dance pictures. A similar nautical character is ascribed to a forlana from Jean-Philippe Rameau's ballet *Les Indes Galantes* (dance added after 1743), which is subtitled "Sailors' Dance." When Jean Jacques Rousseau stated in his *Dictionnaire de musique* in 1768 that the forlana was a dance popular in Venice particularly among the gondoliers (a remark since repeated by numerous lexicographers), he was perhaps reporting on practices more in use among the gondoliers on the stages of Europe than on the canals of Venice.

Although the forlana declined in popularity as a dance after 1725 (Rameau wrote only two in all of his stage works), some of the forlana tunes were reused as the melodies for *contredanses*.

[*See also* Ballet Technique, History of, *article on* French Court Dance.]

BIBLIOGRAPHY

Alm, Irene. *Theatrical Dance in Seventeenth-Century Venetian Opera.* Chicago, 1997.
Casanova, Giacomo. *Mémoires.* Vol. 1. Paris, 1880. See page 420.
Cofini, Marcello. "Furlana." In *Die Musik in Geschichte und Gegenwart.* 2d ed. Vol 3 (1995). Kassel, 1949–.
Échorcheville, Jules. "La forlane." *La revue musicale* 10 (1 April 1914): 11–28.
Galanti, Bianca Maria. "Furlana." In *Enciclopedia dello spettacolo.* Rome, 1954–.
Gallini, Giovanni. *A Treatise on the Art of Dancing.* London, 1762.
Lambranzi, Gregorio. *Neue und curieuse theatralische Tantz-Schul. Deliciae theatrales.* Nuremburg, 1716. Translated by Friderica Derra de Moroda as *New and Curious School of Theatrical Dancing* (London, 1928).
Little, Meredith Ellis, and Carol G. Marsh. *La Danse Noble: An Inventory of Dances and Sources.* Williamstown, Mass., 1992.
Mercure galant (April 1683): 52–58.
Nettl, Paul. *The Story of Dance Music.* New York, 1947.
Seefrid, Gisela. *Die Airs de danse in den Bühnenwerken von Jean-Philippe Rameau.* Wiesbaden, 1969.
Terry, Carole Ruth. "La saltarelle nouvelle: From the *XXe et VIe Recueil de dance pour l'année 1722* by Mr Pécour." D.M.A. Project, Stanford University, 1977.
Ungarelli, Gaspare. *Le vecchie danze italiane ancore in uso nella provincia bolognese.* Rome, 1894.

REBECCA HARRIS-WARRICK

FORNAROLI, CIA (Lucia Fornaroli; born 16 October 1888 in Milan, died 16 August 1954 in Riverdale, New York), Italian ballet dancer, choreographer, and teacher. Fornaroli studied at the ballet school of the Teatro alla Scala in Milan with Adelaide Viganò, Achille Coppini, Caterina Beretta, and Raffaele Grassi. Enrico Cecchetti, with whom she perfected her art, esteemed her so highly that he considered her the most suitable to transmit his own teaching method. Fornaroli, after performing some minor roles at La Scala, made her debut as *prima ballerina* during the 1910/11 season at the Metropolitan Opera in New York City, where she remained until the end of the 1913/14 season. During 1914 and 1915, she appeared at the Teatro Principal in Barcelona, the Teatro Real in Madrid, and the Teatro Colón in Buenos Aires.

Returning to Italy, Fornaroli began a period of intense activity, during which she danced at the Teatro Costanzi in Rome (1916–1920) and at La Scala (1918) and also acted in a number of silent films. As an actress, Fornaroli worked for the Caesar and the Cines companies, performing in the films *L'Annelo di Perrot* (1917), *Cuorie e Tuffi* (1917), *Frou-Frou* (1918), and other productions until 1920.

Between 1922 and 1929, Fornaroli was *prima ballerina* at La Scala. In 1923 she collaborated with Angelina Gini in choreographing *Mahit*, a ballet-fable with singing, composed by Riccardo Pick-Mangiagalli, in which she also danced the principal role. That same year she choreographed the dances for a production of Gustave Charpentier's opera *Louise*, conducted by Arturo Toscanini, and participated in exhibitions by the Italian-Viennese Ballet (Irene Sironi Ballet) with Bianca Gallizia and Vincenzo

Celli at the Vienna Volksoper. In 1924 she danced in Franco Alfano's opera *La Leggenda di Sakuntala* at La Scala and appeared in the Italian opera seasons in Berlin and in Vienna.

During the late 1920s, Fornaroli participated in a number of historic productions at La Scala. On 7 February 1925, she danced in the premiere of Giovanni Pratesi's *Il Convento Veneziano*, set to the score by Alfredo Casella, and on 9 May 1926 she performed the role of the Ballerina in *Petrouchka*, choreographed by Boris Romanov and conducted by Igor Stravinsky, with Vincenzo Celli as the Moor and Anatole Oboukhoff in the title role. The next year she danced the same role with Enrico Cecchetti as the Old Showman and Celli as Petrouchka, in the version by Pratesi. In 1928 she appeared in two new works by Pratesi: *Vecchia Milano*, set to a libretto by Giuseppe Adami and music by Franco Vittadini, and *La Leggenda di Giuseppe (Die Josephslegende)*, set to the score by Richard Strauss, who also conducted at the premiere performance. In 1929, after the death of Cecchetti and following his wishes, Fornaroli became director and teacher at the ballet school of La Scala.

Upon leaving La Scala in 1932, Fornaroli became the choreographer for the International Music Festival in Venice, and in 1933 she formed her own company, the Compagnia del Balletto Italiano da Camera, at the Teatro del Casinò Municipale in San Remo. For this company she composed, among other works, *La Berceuse*, with music by Pick-Mangiagalli; *Gli Uccelli* (The Birds), with music by Ottorino Respighi; and her own version of *L'Histoire d'un Pierrot*, to music by Mario Pasquale Costa. In the choreographic productions for her company, Fornaroli's attention to contemporary research in music was evident, especially in her choice of Italian composers who were revitalizing musical theater, such as Gian Francesco Malipiero (*Pantea*; Venice, 1932) and Ildebrando Pizzetti (*Concerto dell'Estate*, 1933), as well as in the revival of music by such early masters as Claudio Monteverdi (*Il Combattimento di Tancredi e Clorinda*; Venice, 1932) and Antonio Vivaldi (*La Primavera*, 1933).

In 1938, Fornaroli's husband Walter Toscanini, the son of the eminent conductor, immigrated to the United States under pressure of the fascist regime in Italy, and Fornaroli followed him. They spent the last years of their lives in and near New York City, where Fornaroli established herself as a popular teacher. In 1940 she held master classes for Ballet Theatre, and in 1944 she founded the Cecchetti Method School of Classical Dancing, which she directed for a number of years.

Fornaroli was a dancer of great charm and musicality, a versatile, cultivated artist, conscious of the value of dance as an art. She shared with her husband the love for books; their rich collection of documents on dance is today preserved in the Dance Collection of the New York Public Library for the Performing Arts. Among her pupils were ballerinas such as Bice del Frate, Ria Teresa Legnani, Maria Melò, Wanda Nardi, Eugenia Sala, Attilia Radice, Regina Colombo, and Nives Poli.

BIBLIOGRAPHY
L'arte della danza e dell'arte di Cia Fornaroli. Milan, 1923.
Celli, Vincenzo. "Serata d'onore: A Tribute to the Lovely Italian Ballerina, Cia Fornaroli." *Dance Magazine* (January 1955): 23–25, 71–73.
May, Helen. "With Cecchetti at La Scala." *The Dancing Times* (July 1928): 401–403.
Moore, Lillian. "The Metropolitan Opera Ballet Story." *Dance Magazine* (January 1951): 20–48.
Moore, Lillian. "The Romance of a Dance Collection." *Dance Magazine* (December 1955): 32–35.
Page, Ruth. "Classwork: Cia Fornaroli Toscanini." In Page's *Class: Notes on Dance Classes around the World, 1915–1980.* Princeton, N.J., 1984.
Rossi, Luigi. *Il ballo alla Scala, 1778–1970.* Milan, 1972.
Veroli, Patrizia. "Un grande maestro ritorna alla Scala: Lettere inedite di Enrico Cecchetti a Cia Fornaroli (1925–1928)." *La danza italiana* n.s. 1 (1996).
Veroli, Patrizia. "Una rivolta antimanzottiana: I Balletti da Camera di Walter Toscanini e Cia Fornaroli (San Remo, 1933)." *Chorégraphie* 9 (1997).
Veroli, Patrizia. "The Toscaninis' Wide-Ranging Impulse for a Ballet Renaissance (Milan, La Scala, 1921–1932)." *Dance Chronicle* (1997).

ARCHIVE. Walter Toscanini Collection of Research Materials in Dance, New York Public Library for the Performing Arts.

CLAUDIA CELI
Translated from Italian

FORSYTHE, WILLIAM (born 30 December 1949 in New York), American dancer, choreographer, and company director, active in Germany. Having begun his dance training with Jonathan Watts at the Joffrey Ballet School, William Forsythe continued his studies in the classes of Maggie Black and Finis Jhung. He began his professional career in 1971 as a dancer with the Joffrey Ballet (then called the City Center Joffrey Ballet), leaving that company in 1973, with his wife, dancer Eileen Brady, to join the Stuttgart Ballet. As an expatriate, he would make his home in Germany for more than twenty years.

In Stuttgart, Forsythe began to choreograph in 1976 with *Urlicht*, a pas de deux for himself and his wife, to music by Gustav Mahler. As a resident choreographer of the Stuttgart Ballet from 1977 to 1981, he contributed *Daphne* (1977, to music by Antonin Dvořak), *Flore Subsimplici* (1977, to music by Georg Friedrich Handel), *From the Most Distant Time* (1978, to music by György Ligeti), and *Dream of Galilei* (1978, to Krzysztof Penderecki's First Symphony). He also worked for other companies, including the Basel Ballet (*Bach Violin Concerto in A Minor*, 1977) and the Montepulciano Festival (*Folia*, 1978, to music by Hans Werner Henze).

Forsythe came into his own with the 1979 Stuttgart premiere of *Orpheus*, a full-length ballet with music by Henze and libretto by Edward Bond; it was a contemporary reinterpretation of the myth, full of expressionist fervor and social criticism. He followed this with *Time Cycle* (1979, to music by Lukas Foss), *'Tis Pity She's a Whore* (1980, to music by Thomas Jahn), *Tancred and Clorinda* (1981, to music by Claudio Monteverdi), and *Whisper Moon* (1981, to music by William Bolcolm).

Beyond Stuttgart, Forsythe also choreographed *Page 1 —Love Songe—Old Records* (1979, to the songs of Dionne Warwick and Aretha Franklin) for the Munich State Opera Ballet; *Say Bye-Bye* (1980, to music by Jürgen Vater) for the Netherlands Dance Theater; and *Nacht aus Blei* (Night of Lead; 1981, to music by Hans-Jürgen von Bose) for the German Opera Ballet in Berlin. His freelance choreography continued with the one-act *Gänge I* (1982) and *Mental Mode* (1983, to music by Igor Stravinsky) for the Netherlands Dance Theater; the full-length *Gänge* (1983, to music by Jahn) for the Frankfurt Ballet;

Square Deal (1983), a "ballet without dance" for the Joffrey Ballet; *France/Dance* (1983) for the Paris Opera Ballet; and *Berg AB* (1983), a filmed work to Alban Berg's three pieces for orchestra, for the Vienna State Opera Ballet.

Forsythe was appointed artistic director of the Frankfurt Ballet in 1984. He also continued to choreograph for other companies. His creations for Frankfurt included *Artifact* (1984), to music by Bach and others; *LDC* (1985), to music by Tom Willems; *Isabelle's Dance* (1986), a musical with a score by Eva Crossmann-Hecht; *Skinny* (1985), choreographed with Amanda Miller, to Forsythe's own score; *Die Befragung des Robert Scott* (1986, to music by Willems; *Same Old Story* (1986), to music by Willems; *Big White Baby Dog* (1986), to a text from *Empty Speech* by Anne Waldman; *The Loss of Small Detail* (1987), to music by Willems; *Impressing the Czar* (1988), with music by Beethoven, Crossmann-Hecht, Stuck, and Willems; and *The Vile Parody of Address* (1988), with music by Crossmann-Hecht for a first version and music by Bach in a later version. Outside work included *Steptext* (1985), to music by Bach, for Aterballetto; *New Sleep* (1987), to music by Willems, for the San Francisco Ballet; *Same Old*

FORSYTHE. Members of the Frankfurt Ballet in a 1988 performance of Forsythe's *Skinny* (1986). (Photograph © 1988 by Linda Vartoogian; used by permission)

Story (1987), presented by the Frankfurt Ballet in Hamburg and at a dance festival in New York); *In the Middle, Somewhat Elevated* (1988), to music by Willems, for the Paris Opera Ballet; and *Behind the China Dogs* (1988), to music by Leslie Stuck, for the New York City Ballet.

At the end of 1988 Forsythe was appointed director of the ballet section of the state theaters of Frankfurt am Main, with a five-year contract beginning with the 1990/91 season. By this time Forsythe had developed the formula for his conceptual ballets, which do not adhere to a fixed style but incorporate elements from many trends in contemporary arts and thought. His productions have used language, song, film, video, sculpture, and electronic sounds, as well as amplified noises produced by the dancers. His themes draw from the lives of the dancers as well as the history of dance, including the academic vocabulary; the latter often lends a classical sheen even to his most experimental works. Forsythe often designs costumes and moving sculptural objects for the stage, as well as composing electronic music.

Forsythe has occasionally referred to Rudolf Laban and his Space Harmony movement as his artistic ancestor, but his ballet craft owes a great deal to George Balanchine. He also admires the American architect Daniel Libeskind. He combines these elements in an enigmatic, movement-propelled style of dance; its fragmentary nature both baffles and fascinates audiences.

The attraction of Forsythe's work has contributed to bringing capacity audiences to performances in Frankfurt, as well as in Paris, where since 1990 he has conducted an annual residency at the Théâtre Musical du Châtelet. The Frankfurt Ballet, which makes frequent international tours, in 1996 employed eighteen female and twenty-one male dancers; their highly individual physiques and talents contribute creatively in the development of new choreography.

Forsythe continues to create occasionally for other companies and to oversee revivals of his works by, for example, the New York City Ballet, the Paris Opera Ballet, the Royal Ballet (London), and the National Ballet of Canada. Since being appointed director at Frankfurt, he has added many new works to the repertory, all to music by Willems unless otherwise noted: *Enemy in the Figure* (1989); *Slingerland* (1989), to music by Gavin Bryars; *Limb's Theorem* (1991); *Snap, Woven Effort* (1991); *Herman Schmerman* (1992), for New York City Ballet; *Alie/na(c)tion* (1992); *As a Garden in This Setting* (1993); *Quintett* (1993), to music by Bryars; *Self Meant to Govern* (1994); *Firstext* (1995), choreographed with Dana Caspersen and Antony Rizzi for the Royal Ballet; *Eidos/Telos* (1995); *Invisible Film* (1995), to music of Bach, Handel, and Henry Purcell; *Of Any If And* (1995); and *Six Counter Points* (1996), choreographed with Caspersen, to music by Beethoven, Willems, and Franz Schubert.

FORSYTHE. Simona Noja and Jukka Aromaa in a production of Forsythe's *In the Middle, Somewhat Elevated* (1988) by the Ballett der Deutschen Oper am Rhein, Düsseldorf-Duisberg. (Photograph © 1993 by Gundel Kilian; used by permission.)

In 1996 Forsythe's contract with Frankfurt was extended through 1999. By that time he had come to be considered perhaps the most creative ballet director in Europe. In 1988 he received the German Critics' Prize, and in 1996 the Denis de Rougemont Prize.

BIBLIOGRAPHY

Boxberger, Edith. "A Change of Paradigms in Dance." *Ballett International / Tanz Aktuell* 2 (February 1994): 28–32.

Driver, Senta. "A Conversation with William Forsythe." *Ballet Review* 18 (Spring 1990): 86–97.

Driver, Senta. "Two or Three Things That Might Be Considered Primary." *Ballet Review* 18 (Spring 1990): 81–85.

Jeschke, Claudia. "American Theatricality in Contemporary German Dancing: John Neumeier and William Forsythe." In *Proceedings of the Fifteenth Annual Conference, Society of Dance History Scholars, University of California, Riverside, 14–15 February 1992,* compiled by Christena L. Schlundt. Riverside, Calif., 1992.

Langer, Roland, and Richard Sikes. "New Directors, Part II: William Forsythe." *Dance Magazine* (January 1986): 49–51.

Meisner, Nadine. "Dangerous Dancing." *Dance and Dancers* (January–February 1992): 12–13.

Rauner, Gaby von, ed. *William Forsythe, Tanz und Sprache.* Frankfurt am Main, 1993.

Regitz, Hartmut. "Ballett mit anderen Augen sehen: Uraufführung in Frankfurt, 'Gänge' von William Forsythe." *Ballett-Journal / Das Tanzarchiv* 31 (March 1983): 27–28.

Servos, Norbert. "The Dancer and His Double: Gänge by Forsythe/Simon/Jahn in Frankfurt." *Ballet International* 6 (May 1983): 28–30.

Stuart, Otis. "Forsythe's Follies." *Ballet Review* 15 (Fall 1987): 41–44.

HORST KOEGLER

FORTI, SIMONE (also known as Simone Morris and Simone Whitman; born 25 March 1935 in Florence, Italy), dancer and choreographer. Forti grew up in Los Angeles, attended Reed College, San Francisco State College, and has degrees from Hunter and Bank Street Colleges. Her teachers have included Anna Halprin, Robert Dunn, Marshall Ho, and Bonnie Bainbridge Cohen.

After performing with Halprin from 1955 to 1959, Forti moved with her then husband, the sculptor Robert Morris, to New York, where she was influenced by happenings, the work of the composer La Monte Young, and observations of children's play. Her early works, including *See-Saw* and *Rollers* (both 1960) and the evening *5 dance constructions + some other things* (1961), which included *Slant Board* and *Huddle*, were based on game and play structures and the compositional strategy of allowing "one thing" to happen for a duration. Although never a member of Judson Dance Theater, Forti influenced many choreographers who were. From 1962 to 1966, she worked with her then husband Robert Whitman on his happenings. Her *Huddle* was performed for Fluxus programs in the early 1960s.

Forti proposes a theory of dance art that accepts and values both the real and the commonplace. In her dances, everyday movements and objects that we rarely notice in daily life are transformed into defamiliarized occasions for contemplation. Several of Forti's works in the late 1960s focused on the sound rather than the movement qualities of dancers' actions. For instance, in *Face Tunes* (1967), Forti invented a simple machine that allowed her to draw the profiles of faces while she played their shapes on a slide whistle. In the 1970s she collaborated with musicians Charlemagne Palestine and Peter Van Riper, and her dance-theater pieces of the 1980s again emphasized the vocal activities of the performers.

Much of Forti's work in the 1970s and 1980s was based on observations of plant and animal movements and of the kinesthetic perceptions of such basic human movements as crawling, circling, and balancing. These include *Planet* (1976), a large group piece that speaks of evolution, and *Jackdaw Songs* (1982), a solo in which the choreographer observes bird movements.

From 1986 to 1991 she performed with a small group of dancers as Simone Forti and Troupe, a company devoted to developing "natural/geologic/historic portraits" of specific locations (structured group improvisations with talking and movement). In her solos of the 1980s and 1990s, which she calls "animations," Forti creates improvised narratives in which movement and text evolve from a common source, ranging from world events (*News Animations*, 1987) to the structure of cabbage plant roots.

Forti has taught prodigiously, throughout the United States, Canada, and Europe, and in Japan, Australia, and Venezuela. From 1991 to 1997 she appeared frequently in Nam June Paik's Video Opera performances in the United States, Europe, and Japan. Forti has published extensively in *Contact Quarterly* and the *Movement Research Performance Journal*. She has received many grants, fellowships, and awards, including a New York Dance and Performance award (Bessie) for sustained achievement in 1995.

BIBLIOGRAPHY

Banes, Sally. *Terpsichore in Sneakers: Post-Modern Dance.* 2d ed. Middletown, Ct., 1987. Includes a bibliography.

Forti, Simone. *Handbook in Motion.* Halifax, N.S., 1974.

Forti, Simone. "Home Base." *Contact Quarterly* (Summer 1980).

Forti, Simone. "Thoughts on *To Be Continued.*" *Contact Quarterly* 19 (Winter/Spring 1994): 13–21.

Forti, Simone, and Yvonne Rainer. "Tea for Two." *Contact Quarterly* 15 (Spring/Summer 1990): 27–31.

SALLY BANES

FOSSANO, IL. *See* Rinaldi, Antonio.

FOSSE, BOB (Robert Louis Fosse; born 23 June 1927 in Chicago, died 23 September 1987 in Washington, D.C.), American actor, dancer, choreographer, and film director. Fosse began his career as a performer in nightclubs when he was only thirteen. A professional entertainer during his teens, he did his first choreography, a club routine to "That Old Black Magic," in 1942. After serving in naval entertainment units in the Pacific, he studied at the American Theatre Wing and appeared on stage and television during the late 1940s and early 1950s. He acted and danced in three films for Metro-Goldwyn-Mayer (MGM) in 1953, *The Affairs of Dobie Gillis*, *Give a Girl a Break*, and *Kiss Me, Kate*; in *Kiss Me, Kate* he also prepared a short dance for Carol Haney and himself that later led to *The Pajama Game*, his first choreographic assignment on Broadway. Subsequently he choreographed *Damn Yankees* (1955), *New Girl in Town* (1957), and *Redhead* (1959), which he also directed. Meanwhile, he choreographed the films *My Sister Eileen* (1955), *The Pajama Game* (1957), and *Damn Yankees* (1958).

Although Fosse continued to perform occasionally (the title role in a 1961 revival of *Pal Joey*, the Snake in the 1974 film *The Little Prince*), he became principally a stage and screen choreographer and director. On Broadway he did *How to Succeed in Business without Really Trying* (1961), *Little Me* (1962), *Sweet Charity* (1966), *Pippin* (1972), *Chicago* (1975), and *Dancin'* (1978), and he directed and choreographed the films *Sweet Charity* (1969),

FOSSE. In the Hollywood film *Kiss Me, Kate* (MGM, 1953), Fosse, Tommy Rall, and Bobby Van danced to "Tom, Dick, and Harry" as they wooed the glamorous Ann Miller. Each male dancer performed in his own distinctive style of movement. Fosse's characteristic turned-in legs and pelvic thrust are evident here. (Photograph from the Film Stills Library, Museum of Modern Art, New York; used by permission.)

Cabaret (1972), and *All That Jazz* (1979) as well as the award-winning television special *Liza with a Z* (1972). Demonstrating his increased interest in other kinds of projects, Fosse directed the nonmusical films *Lenny* (1974) and *Star 80* (1983). In 1986 he returned to Broadway where he wrote, choreographed, and directed *Big Deal*, a musical with a predominantly black cast. The show was a failure, however, and was overshadowed by a revival that same year of *Sweet Charity*, which Fosse had also supervised.

Fosse's choreographic style emphasized eccentricity, isolation, and fragmentation. He repeatedly stressed that the unique aspects of his dancing resulted from his own physical limitations, relating him to the eccentric dancers of the 1930s and 1940s. The isolation technique of jazz dance contributed an off-center body, turned-in legs, and unique arm movements. Hat routines, high-stepping walks, and upper arms hugging the body were recurrent images in Fosse's work as well. In film he emphasized the isolation and fragmentation of his dances by a heightened use of close-ups and jump cuts. Fosse's interest in dance influenced all his work, and he used that interest to become involved in every aspect of stage and film production.

[*See* Film Musicals, *article on* Hollywood Film Musicals; *and* United States of America, *article on* Musical Theater.]

BIBLIOGRAPHY

Beddow, Margery. *Bob Fosse's Broadway.* Portsmouth, N.H., 1996.

Challender, James W. "The Function of the Choreographer in the Development of the Conceptual Musical: An Examination of the Work of Jerome Robbins, Bob Fosse, and Michael Bennett on Broadway between 1944 and 1981." Ph.D. diss., Florida State University, 1986.

Gardner, Paul. "Bob Fosse Off His Toes." *New York* (16 December 1974).

Grubb, Kevin Boyd. *Razzle Dazzle: The Life and Work of Bob Fosse.* New York, 1989.

Hodgson, Moira. "Film: When Bob Fosse's Art Imitates Life, It's Just 'All That Jazz.'" *New York Times* (30 December 1979).

Wood, Robert E. "Cloven Hoofer: Choreography as Autobiography in *All That Jazz.*" *Post Script* 6.2 (1987).

JEROME DELAMATER

FOUETTÉS. *See* Ballet Technique, *article on* Turning Movements.

FOUNTAIN OF BAKHCHISARAI, THE. Choreographed poem (after Aleksandr Pushkin's poem of the same name). Choreography: Rostislav Zakharov. Music: Boris Asafiev. Libretto: Nikolai Volkov. Scenery: Valentina Khodasevich. Production supervision: Sergei Radlov. First performance: 28 September 1934, State Academic Theater for Opera and Ballet, Leningrad. Principals: Galina Ulanova (Maria), Olga Jordan (Zarema), Konstantin Sergeyev (Vatslav), Mikhail Dudko (Girei).

In 1838 the newspaper *Severnaia Pchela* informed its Saint Petersburg reading public of Filippo Taglioni's intention to stage the ballet *The Fountain of Bakhchisarai* for his daughter Marie. His plan was never realized. However, in 1854 the famous Russian ballerina Elena Andreyanova performed her own version of *The Fountain of Bakhchisarai*, to a selection of pieces by several composers, while on tour in Voronezh; her performance was a success with the public. In 1890 A. Y. Alekseev staged the work as a pantomime with dance on the outdoor stage at the Krestovskii Theater in Saint Petersburg. In the final scene the action was transferred into the otherworld, and the climax was filled with extravagant special effects. Foma Nijinsky, the father of the famous dancer Vaslav Nijinsky, turned his attention to the theme of the poem and produced a ballet he called *The Victim of Jealousy* in 1892. He lent a religious-mystical quality to the work, and in the finale celestial bodies burned brightly as the spirit of the heroine Maria soared above them.

The Fountain of Bakhchisarai inaugurated the era of Pushkin-based Soviet ballets. The ballet's creators aspired to capture as far as possible the spirit of Pushkin's poem, which easily translated into the language of the stage. The action is laid in the castle of a Polish prince during a fête. At the height of the festivities a group of Tatar warriors, led by the khan Kerim-Girei, bursts into the castle. The castle burns during the ensuing battle. The prince himself perishes, as does his daughter's fiancé, Vatslav, having heroically battled the Tatars. Girei is captivated by the beauty of the young princess Maria. But she rejects his love and lives in solitude in a remote room in the khan's palace. Tormented by jealousy, Zarema, the previous favorite wife of the khan, kills Maria. In honor of the murdered Maria, the khan orders that a fountain be erected, called the Fountain of Tears. The ballet begins and ends with the mournfully prostrate figure of the khan near the fountain.

The creators of the ballet were concerned not only with the plot but also with the message of Pushkin's poem. As

THE FOUNTAIN OF BAKHCHISARAI. Galina Ulanova as Maria, Tatiana Vecheslova as Zarema, and Mikhail Dudko as Girei in Rostislav Zakharov's original production, Leningrad, 1934. (Photograph from the Dance Collection, New York Public Library for the Performing Arts.)

the basic principle for the ballet Rostislav Zakharov took the writer Vissarion Belinsky's words about the rebirth and enlightenment of a savage soul under the influence of love. The compositional structure of the ballet was innovative. Determined not to limit himself to any canons, the choreographer created the ballet by proceeding solely from the intrinsic meaning of Pushkin's poem. There was no stylistic divergence between classical and character dance; *polonez, mazur,* and *krakowiak* were danced in a Romantic style.

The ballet resolved many of the pressing problems that were facing Soviet ballet at the time. In the performance classical dance merged with Polish folklore motifs, crowd scenes were vibrant with energy, the pas de deux became intrinsically more significant, and during the course of the action there were no dances intended simply as diversions from the main action. In this work the choreographer implemented the creative principles of Konstantin Stanislavsky and Vladimir Nemirovich-Danchenko as applied to the art of ballet. He strove to permeate the performance with action, to make everything in it logical, well founded, and psychologically motivated. The poetically inspired dancing of Galina Ulanova as Maria, the fiery ardor of Olga Jordan as Zarema, the romantic fluidity of Konstantin Sergeyev as Vatslav, and the spare pantomime of Mikhail Dudko's Girei all served to convey the work's main idea.

Several generations of dancers achieved fame in *The Fountain of Bakhchisarai*—Tatiana Vecheslova, Alla Shelest, Raisa Struchkova, Maya Plisetskaya, Petr Gusev, Aleksandr Lapauri—all of whom retained the work in their repertory for many years. The ballet has been in the repertory of the Maryinsky Ballet since its premiere, and until the 1960s it was danced by Moscow's Bolshoi Ballet after Zakharov staged it for the company in 1936. It was also staged by all of the regional and national theaters of the USSR as well as those in eastern Europe.

BIBLIOGRAPHY

Asafiev, Boris. *Bakhchisaraiskii fontan.* Moscow, 1955.

Barnes, Clive. "Bolshoi Ballets: *The Fountain of Bakhchisaray.*" *Dance and Dancers* (December 1956): 15–18.

Beaumont, Cyril W. *Supplement to Complete Book of Ballets.* London, 1942.

Bogdanov-Berezovskii, V. M., N. D. Volkov, and V. A. Manuilov. *Bakhchisaraiskii fontan.* Leningrad, 1934.

Dorris, George. "Music for Spectacle." *Ballet Review* 6.1 (1977): 45–55.

MacMahon, Deirdre. "'Corridor to the Muses.'" *Ballet Review* 12 (Spring 1984): 57–65.

Raffé, W. G. "The Newer Soviet Ballet: *The Fountain of Bakhchisarai.*" *Dancing Times* (August 1935): 471–474.

Roslavleva, Natalia. "Stanislavski and the Ballet." *Dance Perspectives,* no. 23 (1965).

Sulcas, Roslyn. "The Fountain of Bakhchisaray." *Dance Magazine* (March 1995): 98–99.

Zakharov, Rostislav. *Iskusstvo baletmeistera.* Moscow, 1954.

NIKOLAI I. ELYASH
Translated from Russian

FOUR STEP BROTHERS, a group of tap dancers whose formula of fast rhythm, acrobatic leaps, and boogie-woogie jitterbug-style tap dancing made them a popular tap act. The Four Step Brothers were not actually brothers. Maceo Anderson (born 3 September 1910 in Charleston, South Carolina) founded the group in 1927. William ("Red") Walker (born in Virginia, died c.1932 in New York City); Al Williams (born c.1915 in Waycross, Georgia, died 3 May 1985 in Sherman Oaks, California); and Sylvester ("Happy") Johnson (born in Washington, D.C., died in the 1940s) were the other members. Over the years, the Four Step Brothers included Freddy James; Sunshine Sammy, who appeared in the act for six months in 1944 for the motion pictures *Greenwich Village* and *Shine On, Harvest Moon;* Prince Spencer (born 3 October 1917 in Jenkinsville, South Carolina), who joined the act in 1941; and Rufus Lee ("Flash") McDonald (born 16 March 1919 in Saint Louis, Missouri, died 20 March 1991 in Saint Louis), who joined in 1942. The "brothers" adopted their style directly from the streets—with handclapping, encouraging yelps, fast tempos, and the ceaseless topping of one another's tap steps. While the names and faces of the Four Step Brothers changed, the formula, the "challenge," remained the same: each dancer strove to top the others by heightening the complexity and speed of his steps.

Hiding behind a costume rack at Harlem's famous Cotton Club in the mid-1920s, four eager adolescent boys waited for Duke Ellington to pass. Recalled Maceo Anderson:

Finally Duke Ellington came out to get some water at the fountain . . . We run out and said, "Mr. Ellington! Mr. Ellington! We want to get on and we want to dance—see, see this?" And we fell on our knees and jumped all around.   (Frank, 1994)

The boys were promptly booted out of the club. After accosting Ellington several more times, they finally were given their chance and stayed at the Cotton Club for four years.

The Four Step Brothers toured abroad extensively, dancing for kings and queens, and played every important nightclub and theater in the United States, including Radio City Music Hall, the Roxy, and the Paramount Theater in New York City. From the 1930s onward, they appeared in twenty-eight motion pictures, including *It Ain't Hay* (1943), *Rhythm of the Islands* (1943), *Greenwich Village* (1944), *That's My Gal* (1947), and *Here Come the Girls* (1953). They were guests on television variety shows hosted by Bob Hope, Milton Berle, and Dean Martin and Jerry Lewis.

[*See also* Tap Dance.]

BIBLIOGRAPHY

Frank, Rusty E. *Tap! The Greatest Tap Dance Stars and Their Stories, 1900–1955.* Rev. ed. New York, 1994.

Stearns, Marshall, and Jean Stearns. *Jazz Dance: The Story of American Vernacular Dance.* Rev. ed. New York, 1994.

RUSTY E. FRANK

FOUR TEMPERAMENTS, THE. Ballet in five parts. Choreography: George Balanchine. Music: Paul Hindemith; *Theme with Four Variations (According to the Four Temperaments).* Scenery and costumes: Kurt Seligmann. Lighting: Jean Rosenthal. First performance: 20 November 1946, Central High School of Needle Trades, New York, Ballet Society. Principals: Beatrice Tompkins, José Martinez, Elise Reiman, Lew Christensen, Gisella Caccialanza, Francisco Moncion; William Dollar (Melancholic); Mary Ellen Moylan and Fred Danieli (Sanguinic); Todd Bolender (Phlegmatic); Tanaquil Le Clercq (Choleric).

Through a concentrated examination and transformation of ballet vocabulary, George Balanchine augmented the language's expressive potential in *The Four Temperaments,* mounted on a commissioned score by Paul Hindemith. The look of the work was totally new, for Balanchine subjected individual components of a dance phrase to distortion, inversion, and unconventional juxtaposition. Other dance and nondance movements were also ab-

THE FOUR TEMPERAMENTS. (*left*) A studio portrait of Todd Bolender in costume for the third variation, Phlegmatic, from the original production. (*right*) The Dutch National Ballet in the finale of a 1960 performance. Since 1951 *The Four Temperaments* has been danced in practice clothes and without scenery. (Left photograph by Carl Van Vechten; used by permission of the Estate of Carl Van Vechten. Right photograph by Siegfried Regeling; from the Dance Collection, New York Public Library for the Performing Arts. Choreography by George Balanchine © by Edward Bigelow.)

sorbed into the technique. Yet the ballet is firmly rooted in the *danse d'école*.

Although distantly related to Balanchine's ballet *Apollo* (1928), *The Four Temperaments* demonstrates a more versatile and assured use of the classical language. In the earlier work, Balanchine began to perceive the laws governing groups of movements akin to classical music harmony; he more fully explored these relationships in the later ballet. The three main themes are stated in the opening part, danced by three successive couples. Motifs stated in the first theme (flexed feet, *arabesque penchée* between the partner's legs, *attitude* wrapped around the partner's torso) are developed and transfigured in the subsequent two themes and four variations, so that the composition becomes more cohesive, expansive, and probing than a straightforward theme-and-variations form.

The score, for string orchestra and piano, was commissioned by Balanchine for *The Cave of Sleep*, to be produced with Pavel Tchelichev's costumes and decor, for the American Ballet Caravan's South American tour in 1941. It was never presented. Instead, Balanchine choreographed a ballet to the score for the opening program of Ballet Society in 1946.

Each variation was named after one of the four humors of medieval cosmology—Melancholic, Sanguinic, Phleg-

matic, and Choleric—to indicate musical mood rather than literal stage direction. Unfortunately, Kurt Seligmann, a visual artist interested in alchemy and black magic, created intrusively literal decor and costumes that obscured the movement and wreaked havoc with the dancers. Nonetheless, the cast carried on bravely. The cumbersome apparel was simplified to practice clothes when the work was mounted for the New York City Ballet in 1951, a revision that was favorably received.

Balanchine defined his spatial territory and motive statements in the first three themes. Side-to-side turns in the first section become complete revolutions in the second; rhythms become increasingly complex.

The ballet contains two extraordinary roles for men, the Melancholic and Phlegmatic variations. In the former, the dancer attempts to penetrate space with wide leaps and yearning backbends, only to collapse inward. A menacing corps of women further constricts his freedom. Unlike Melancholic, the indolent Phlegmatic does not try to break free from the supported arabesques of his sexy, jazzy corps. He relishes languor and delights in his rhythmically complex tap dance.

The allegro Sanguinic variation, which precedes Phlegmatic, is also full of sexy side poses and syncopated rhythms for its extroverted ballerina and her partner. The ballet's denouement (often reworked by Balanchine) is led by the amazonian Choleric, who crashes through space. She is the center of the ballet's "universe" as the ensemble revolves around her, recapitulating thematic material to a soaring, C-major apotheosis in the score.

The Four Temperaments has remained in the repertory of the New York City Ballet almost without interruption for more than four decades. Balanchine modified certain acrobatic elements in the Melancholic variation, originally danced by William Dollar, to suit the talents of later performers, and over the years he made numerous choreographic changes in the finale. Since 1960, the work has been mounted for many companies around the world, including the Royal Swedish Ballet, La Scala Ballet, the Paris Opera Ballet, the Royal Danish Ballet, the Vienna State Opera Ballet, the National Ballet of Canada, the Düsseldorf-Duisberg Ballet, the Ballet du Grand Théâtre de Genève, the Royal Ballet (London), Les Grands Ballets Canadiens, Ballet-Théâtre Contemporain (Amiens), the Göteberg Ballet, and the Zurich Ballet. In the United States it has been danced by the Boston Ballet, the Pennsylvania Ballet, the San Francisco Ballet, Ballet West, the Chicago Lyric Opera Ballet, Pacific Northwest Ballet, and Dance Theatre of Harlem.

BIBLIOGRAPHY

Acocella, Joan. "The Four Humors." *Ballet Review* 14 (Winter 1987): 16–19.

Ashley, Merrill, et al. "Celebrating *The Four Temperaments*." *Ballet Review* 14 (Winter 1987): 16–35; 15 (Spring 1988): 38–59.

Balanchine, George, with Francis Mason. *Balanchine's Complete Stories of the Great Ballets*. Rev. and enl. ed. Garden City, N.Y., 1977.

Choreography by George Balanchine: A Catalogue of Works. New York, 1984.

Croce, Arlene. Review. *The New Yorker* (8 December 1975). Reprinted as "Momentous" in Croce's *Afterimages* (New York, 1977).

Denby, Edwin. Review (December 1946). Reprinted as "Extraordinary Fascination" in Denby's *Looking at the Dance* (New York, 1949).

Graff, Ellen. "*The Four Temperaments* and *Orpheus:* Models of a Modern Classical Tradition." *Ballet Review* 13 (Fall 1985): 54–59.

Kirstein, Lincoln. *Thirty Years: The New York City Ballet*. New York, 1978.

Reynolds, Nancy. *Repertory in Review: Forty Years of the New York City Ballet*. New York, 1977.

Reynolds, Nancy. "Balanchine: An Introduction to the Ballets." *Dance Notation Journal* 6 (Winter–Spring 1988–1989): 15–74.

Scholl, Tim. *From Petipa to Balanchine: Classical Revival and the Modernization of Ballet*. New York, 1994.

Terry, Walter. Reviews. *New York Herald Tribune* (23 November 1951, 25 February 1953, 7 May 1953).

Wilkins, Darrell. "*The Four Temperaments:* An Interpretation." *Ballet Review* 21 (Summer 1993): 81–87.

NOTATED SCORE. *The Four Temperaments*, Benesh notation (1973).

VIDEOTAPE. *The Four Temperaments*, performed by New York City Ballet, "Choreography by Balanchine" (part 1), *Dance in America* (WNET-TV, New York, 1977).

REBA ANN ADLER

FOX TROT. See Social Dance, *article on* Twentieth-Century Social Dance to 1960. *See also* Ballroom Dance Competition.

FRACCI, CARLA (born 20 August 1936 in Milan), Italian ballet dancer. In 1946, when she was ten years old, Carla Fracci reluctantly accompanied her father, a street-car conductor, to be enrolled in the ballet school of the Teatro alla Scala in Milan. For her first five years there she studied, with no great conviction, in the classes of Paolina Giussani, Edda Marginoni, Esmée Bulnes, and Vera Volkova. In 1950, however, the appearance of Margot Fonteyn at La Scala in *The Sleeping Beauty* profoundly changed Fracci's attitude toward dance and made her want to continue her studies. She, along with other students of the ballet school, was onstage, dressed as a page and holding a mandolin, when Fonteyn made her entrance from the top of an immense staircase. She descended, as Fracci has often said, straight into the young girl's heart, where she remained as a paradigm of elegance and perfection. After this experience, Fracci resumed her studies with authentic passion and great determination.

Having been graduated from La Scala Ballet School in 1954, Fracci made her *passo d'addio* ("farewell step"), the final, public examination of students of a ballet school attached to an opera house, in 1955. During her performance, the staff and administration of La Scala became aware that a bright new star had risen, a young woman with a symmetrical face, a slim body, and a sweet, communicative smile. By coincidence, Fracci's examination was held on the same date as the premiere of a new production of the opera *La Sonnambula*, starring Maria Callas and directed by Luchino Visconti. That same evening she met Visconti's assistant, Beppe Menegatti, whom she married nine years later and who contributed much to her development as an artist and to the success of her career.

Fracci was immediately accepted into La Scala's corps de ballet, and before very long her great moment arrived. In 1956, substituting for the French ballerina Violette Verdy, Fracci danced the title role in Alfred Rodrigues's production of *Cinderella* and, a little like the heroine, ultimately emerged triumphant. In her first starring role in a full-length ballet, she gave a touching performance of great tenderness and beauty. Soon thereafter she was promoted to solo dancer and was named *prima ballerina* two years later, in 1958.

The early years of Fracci's career were marked by a series of successes in most of the great roles of the classical and neoclassical repertories. On the international level, her chief promoter was Anton Dolin, who, at the Nervi Festival in 1957, decided to give her the role of Fanny Cerrito in his *Pas de Quatre*, in which she danced with three ballerinas of formidable reputations: Yvette Chauviré, Alicia Markova, and Margrethe Schanne. In 1959 Dolin also invited her to appear as a guest with London Festival Ballet in the title role of *Giselle*, under his direction, with John Gilpin as Albrecht. Without doubt, it was this title role, and then that of August Bournonville's *La Sylphide*, that established Fracci's image as a Romantic ballerina and that dominated her career for the next ten or fifteen

FRACCI. Carla Fracci poses during filming of a television version of *Giselle*, act 2. As Italy's *prima ballerina*, Fracci was most admired for her performances in the nineteenth-century Romantic ballets. (Photograph © 1968 by Judy Cameron; from the Dance Collection, New York Public Library for the Performing Arts.)

years. Wearing a long white tutu, a crown of flowers on her head, and little gossamer wings on her shoulders, Fracci gradually became for the Italian public a modern incarnation of Marie Taglioni, a sort of Italian madonna and the first diva of ballet to become as popular as a movie star.

In Fracci's campaign to reinvent the image of the ballerina and to promote the art of dance in Italy, she was greatly assisted by Beppe Menegatti, who encouraged and aided her in forming her own company for performances away from La Scala. Although La Scala provided Fracci with great prestige, it was the performances with her own company that won her the affection and acclaim of the public and that made her a nationally recognized figure.

In 1971, Fracci made a decisive break with La Scala Ballet, blaming the company for not using her enough and for failing to mount new productions for her. Her departure was not entirely unexpected by La Scala's management, for Fracci had earlier expressed dissatisfaction and had sought more interesting work outside Italy. In

1967 she had, in fact, found a home away from home in American Ballet Theatre, which offered a rich and varied repertory and frequent performances in New York and other cities of the United States. In this company she met Erik Bruhn, the great Danish *danseur noble*, who became her favorite partner and teacher. Fortunately, the television version of their *Giselle* (1970) survives, although no trace remains of *La Sylphide*, another high point of their artistic collaboration. Fracci often returned to La Scala as a guest ballerina, usually dancing with Paolo Bortoluzzi and then, in the early 1980s, even more often with Rudolf Nureyev in his productions of such classic ballets as *Don Quixote* and *Romeo and Juliet*.

Besides the heroines of the classical ballet repertory and leading parts in many contemporary works, Fracci had opportunities to perform a variety of unusual roles. At La Scala in 1966 she appeared as Gelsomina, the brutalized but indomitably cheerful waif in Mario Pistoni's *La Strada*, a ballet based on the film by Federico Fellini. The following year, at the Maggio Musicale Fiorentino (May Music Festival in Florence), and then again at La Scala in 1974, she danced the role of Civilization in Ugo dell'Ara's reconstruction of Luigi Manzotti's spectacular ballet *Excelsior*, originally mounted in 1881. Her performance was a prime example of careful, clever re-creation of the technique and style of a certain type of Italian ballerina of the later nineteenth century—brilliant, nimble, and stimulating, with roguish eyes and a bewitching smile.

In her performances with her own company and as a guest in the ballet companies of various Italian theaters, Fracci set about expanding her range as a dancer-actress, always under the guidance of her husband. She enriched her persona as a *femme fatale* in such roles as the Lady of the Mountain in Loris Gai's *The Stone Flower* (1973) and as the Fairy in his production of *Le Baiser de la Fée* (1975). In creating the title role of John Butler's *Medea*, mounted for the 1975 Spoleto Festival, she danced opposite Mikhail Baryshnikov as Jason and began to show herself as mistress of an entirely new kind of role: in place of the ethereal, disembodied spirit there appeared a visceral, terrestrial image, no longer a ghostly wili or sprightly sylphide, but a vengeful, passionate fury. In stark contrast, in Alfred Rodrigues's *Mirandolina* (1981), based on a comedy by Carlo Goldoni, she was a piquant and sexy soubrette.

As a dramatic actress, Fracci interpreted with great success the role of Giuseppina Strepponi in a serialized biography of Giuseppe Verdi televised in Italy in 1982 and later, in an English-language version, in Great Britain, the United States, and other Anglophone countries. She also portrayed Tamara Karsavina in the 1980 film about Nijinsky directed by Herbert Ross, as well as heroines in many television specials in Italy and abroad. A documentary film, *An Hour with Carla Fracci,* was broadcast on Italian television in 1973.

Fracci's later successes, besides an ongoing series of guest appearances with American Ballet Theatre—where she danced the Accused (Lizzie Borden) in Agnes de Mille's *Fall River Legend* in 1991—are linked to her husband's special brand of dance theater at the Teatro San Carlo and the Teatro Mercandante in Naples. Their productions have included *Nijinsky Memorie di Giovinezza* (April 1989), *Cocteau–Opium* (November 1989), and *Eleonora Duse–Isadora Duncan: Adieu et au Revoir* (February 1990). The Nijinsky program, enhanced by the presence of Vladimir Vasiliev and Eric Vu-An, was a notable success.

In the later years of Fracci's dancing career, particularly in her partnership with the young Romanian Gheorghe Iancu, it became apparent that her true strength was not so much her technical command or her Romantic aura of impalpable femininity, but rather her versatility as an actress. At the height of her powers, her ability to interpret new and different characters, based on a thoughtful analysis of psychological motivations, led the critic Clive Barnes to nickname her "the Duse of the Dance." As her physical powers as a dancer waned, her abilities as a dramatic actress extended her career in new and interesting directions.

BIBLIOGRAPHY

Agostini, Alfio. "Lettera aperta a Carla Fracci." *Balletto* (April–May 1982).

Agostini, Alfio. "Carla Fracci, La stellissime." *Danser* (April 1986).

Arruga, Lorenzo. *Perchè Carla Fracci.* Venice, 1974.

Arruga, Lorenzo. "Carla Fracci." *Musica Viva* (November 1982).

Costume (April–September 1974). Issue dedicated to Fracci.

Doglio, Vittoria, and Elisa Vaccarino. *L'Italia in ballo.* Rome, 1993.

Fracci, Carla. *La mia vita sulle punte.* Milan, 1978.

Gruen, John. *The Private World of Ballet.* New York, 1975.

Lewis, Jean Battey. "Talking to Carla Fracci." *Dance View* 10 (Summer 1993): 2–4.

Migel, Parmenia. "A Romantic Ballerina in Our Times: Carla Fracci." *Dance Magazine* (December 1984): 42–47.

Ottolenghi, Vittoria. *I casi della danza.* Rome, 1981.

Testa, Alberto. "Carla Fracci passo per passo." *Balletto* (April–May 1982).

Testa, Alberto, et al. *Il balletto nel novecento.* Turin, 1983.

Tobias, Tobi. "Visiting Fracci." *Dance Magazine* (January 1974): 51–66.

VITTORIA OTTOLENGHI
Translated from Italian

FRANCA, CELIA (Celia Franks; born 25 June 1921 in London), British Canadian dancer, choreographer, teacher, and company director. Franca began her ballet training at London's Guildhall School of Music and at the Royal Academy of Dancing. Among her teachers were Stanislas Idzikowski, Judith Espinosa, Antony Tudor, and Marie Rambert. In 1936, at age fifteen, she appeared in the West End revue *Spread It Abroad,* choreographed by Walter Gore, before joining Ballet Rambert as a member of the corps de ballet. In the corps or as a soloist, she appeared in most of the works in the company repertory and was especially pleased to be cast in works by Antony Tudor. In 1937, she appeared in the ensemble of the original production of his *Dark Elegies* and danced a featured role in his *Jardin aux Lilas* as well as taking on leading dramatic roles in works by other choreographers. In 1938 she choreographed her first ballet for Ballet Rambert, *Constanza's Lament,* set to music by Beethoven, and in 1939

FRANCA. During the early years of the National Ballet of Canada, Franca danced principal roles in most of the company's productions. In 1953, she appeared as Giselle, here seen making her first entrance in act 1. (Photograph by Ken Bell; used by permission of the National Ballet of Canada.)

she created her first major character role, that of the Dope Fiend in Walter Gore's production of *Paris Soir.*

Soon thereafter Franca left Ballet Rambert to dance with the short-lived Three Arts Ballet (Ballet des Trois Arts), for which she made her second work, *Midas* (1939). In 1940 she appeared with the Arts Theatre Ballet, with the International Ballet, and once again with Ballet Rambert, where she created the role of the Bird in Frank Staff's production of *Peter and the Wolf.* After joining the Sadler's Wells Ballet in 1941 she became known as one of the company's most distinguished young *demi-caractère* dancers, creating roles in Robert Helpmann's *Hamlet* (1942) and *Miracle in the Gorbals* (1944) and in Andrée Howard's *Le Festin d'Araignée* (1944).

Launching a free-lance career in 1946, Franca created *Khadra* (1946), set to music by Sibelius, and *Bailemos* (1947), to music by Massenet, for the Sadler's Wells Theatre Ballet and, for BBC television, *Dance of Salome* (1949), and *The Eve of Saint Agnes* (1950). Meanwhile, she studied and performed with Ballets Jooss, and in 1948 she joined the newly formed Metropolitan Ballet as soloist and ballet mistress. With this company she created leading roles in ballets by Frank Staff and Rosella Hightower and danced, for the first time, the role of Swanilda in *Coppélia.* In 1950, she returned once more to appear as guest artist with Ballet Rambert, dancing in repertory favorites by Antony Tudor, Frederick Ashton, and others.

The year 1950 was to prove of special significance in Franca's career, for it was then that she was approached by a group of Canadian ballet lovers with an invitation to imigrate to Canada and help found a new company, modeled on the Sadler's Wells Ballet. Unable to resist the opportunity, Franca moved to Toronto in 1951 and became founding artistic director of the National Ballet of Canada. Her unflagging energy and determination helped the company to survive its problematic early years. Despite criticism in some quarters for what was seen as an excessively conservative artistic policy, Franca remained as artistic director for more than two decades, until 1974. By then the National Ballet had achieved internatioanl recognition as a classical company of well-schooled dancers.

Although Franca staged some of her own ballets for the company, she was determined to build a solid classical repertory. She thus concentrated on mounting full-scale productions of the nineteenth-century classics: *Giselle, Coppélia, Swan Lake,* and *The Nutcracker.* By the time she resigned her post, she had given the National Ballet a handsome repertory of full-length works. Moreover, she had introduced ballets by a wide range of internationally recognized choreographers—Frederick Ashton, George Balanchine, Antony Tudor, Roland Petit, Eliot Feld, John Cranko, and many others—while also fostering the works of the company's first resident choreographer, Grant Strate.

Franca danced with her company until 1959, appearing, notably, in the title roles of *Giselle* and *Lady from the Sea,* by the Canadian choreographer Elizabeth Leese. She returned to the stage in the mid-1960s in a series of memorable character roles: Carabosse in Rudolf Nureyev's production of *The Sleeping Beauty;* Madge, the witch, in Erick Bruhn's production of *La Sylphide;* Lady Capulet in John Cranko's *Romeo and Juliet;* and the Pianist in Flemming Flindt's *The Lesson.* She also choreographed major new productions of *The Nutcracker* (1964) and *Cinderella* (1968). In 1975, she restaged one of the perennial favorites in the company repertory, Antony Tudor's *Offenbach in the Underworld,* first mounted in its definitive version for the National Ballet in 1955.

Retaining the honorific title of founder, Franca continued to work periodically with the National Ballet of Canada after she gave up the post of artistic director in 1974, coaching, restaging productions, and making occasional guest appearances until 1983. From her home in Ottawa, she remains active as a teacher, lecturer, and artistic consultant. Awarded many honors, she was made an officer of the Order of Canada in 1967 and a companion of the Order in 1985; she received the Canada Dance Award in 1984, was named to the Order of Ontario in 1987, and was given the Governor General's Performing Arts Award in 1994.

[*See also* National Ballet of Canada.]

BIBLIOGRAPHY

Bell, Ken, and Celia Franca. *The National Ballet of Canada: A Celebration.* Toronto, 1978.

Davidson, Gladys. "Celia Franca." In Davidson's *Ballet Biographies.* London, 1974.

Maynard, Olga. "Celia Franca and the National Ballet of Canada." *Dance Magazine* (May 1974): 83.

Neufeld, James. *Power to Rise: The Story of the National Ballet of Canada.* Toronto, 1996.

Whittaker, Herbert. *Canada's National Ballet.* Toronto, 1967.

Wyman, Max. *Dance Canada: An Illustrated History.* Vancouver, 1989.

MICHAEL CRABB

FRANCE. [*To survey the dance traditions of France, this entry comprises ten articles:*

The first article explores popular and traditional dance; the following five articles focus on the history of theatrical dance; the seventh and eighth discuss dance education; the concluding articles provide a brief history of scholarship and writing. For further discussion of theatrical dance, see entries on individual companies, choreographers, and dancers.]

Recreational Dance

To the French of today the word *recréatif* ("recreational") suggests an amusement of secondary importance, but recreational dancing held an important place in the social life of their ancestors. It features in medieval illustrations and literature. Dance in the sixteenth century was associated both with military display and with social success. Seventeenth-century humanists assigned dance an educational value; like horseback riding and skill with weapons, it was one of a gentleman's expected accomplishments. King Louis XIV worked several hours a day under the direction of his dancing master. Eighteenth-century French society was devoted to the *contredanse* and the *menuet*. Even in the nineteenth century, the military had compulsory courses for officers and *assauts de danse* (dance examinations in classical ballet) taught by a ballet master. Rural people too regarded dancing as an indispensable social activity for their communities.

The history of recreational dance in France to some extent reflects changes in socioeconomic structure. As a middle class rose in the eighteenth century, its members increasingly assumed the social graces formerly limited to the aristocracy, including court dances. This democratization progressed through the nineteenth century, when rural and working-class people slowly absorbed and adapted the dances of the urban elites.

Diffusion, however, does not entirely explain the diversity of recreational dances through history. It is possible to categorize popular dances according to their source as traditional—transmitted from generation to generation more or less unchanged—or as folkloric, which denotes a dance that spread from an elite milieu and was transformed over the years into another legitimate expression, perhaps incorporating traditional regional elements. For example, the *bourrées* of rural central France had less complex figures than did the *contredanses* of the aristocracy, but they also added original steps and stylistic features.

At the beginning of the twentieth century, traditional dances still existed in great diversity in France's provinces, particularly in the form of chain dances—especially prevalent in Brittany and Gascony—and circle dances. There were also step, figure, and couple dances. In the circle dances, the dancers often sing to accompany their performance. Especially prevalent in western France, this genre is exemplified by the three-step circle dance of Normandy, the *dans-tro* and *dans vanch* of Brittany, and the *hanter-dro* and *laridés* of Morbihan.

Opening the circle into a chain emphasized the role of the leader. Examples of the chain dance are the *rondeau* of the Grande Lande, the Breton *gavottes* of Léon and the

FRANCE: Recreational Dance. Early nineteenth-century social dancers perform La Poule, the third figure of the *quadrille français*. The quadrille, a group dance for four couples facing in a square formation, was popular throughout nineteenth-century French ballrooms. This caricature, from *Observations sur les modes et les usages de Paris*, shows a gentleman kissing the hand of his partner. (Metropolitan Museum of Art, New York; Harris Brisbane Dick Fund, 1938 [38.38.5]; photograph used by permission.)

Quimper region, and the *branle* of Ecueillé in Berry. More recently the chain has been shortened into a quartet, with two women placed between two men, as in the *gavotte* of Aven in Haute Cornouaille. The chain sometimes preserves its pattern while loosing its steps, as in the popular Provençal *farandole*. The couple dance, in some cases as the last stage in the evolution of the chain dance, appears in the *gavotte* of Pont-l'Abbé in Brittany, the *kas-abah* of Vannes, and the *branle* of Ossau.

With the transition from circle to chain and couple dances, singing was replaced by instrumental accompaniment: flute, drum, and oboe in Occitania; bagpipes and *vielle* in Gascony and the Vendée; or Breton pipes and *bombardon* in Brittany. Sometimes a clarinet was used, and the violin appeared almost everywhere; the accordion was introduced around the beginning of the twentieth century. The new musical repertory and arrangement of

FRANCE: Recreational Dance. An early nineteenth-century caricature entitled *La Sauteuse* shows the abandon of the early waltz but also the era's more refined ballet technique required for the era's social dances, here demonstrated in the use of turnout. (Metropolitan Museum of Art, New York; Harris Brisbane Dick Fund, 1938 [38.38.5]; photograph used by permission.)

dancers allowed displays of virtuosity—especially by the leader of a chain—not possible in the older circle dances.

This musical innovation was not universal, however. Interior parts of Brittany, for example, retained the circle dance with sung accompaniment until the twentieth century. Brittany had no instrumental tradition, and the circle most appropriately expressed the region's social relations.

Figure dances were not readily accepted in their original urban form and generally were performed only in simple form in regions where the chain dance was dominant. Rural figure dances such as the Breton *jabadaos* or Landes *congos* are very limited in comparison with urban figure dances, consisting of little more than advancing and withdrawing, crossing, Dos-à-Dos, Moulinets, Rights and Lefts, and Ladies' Chain.

Where tradition offered no obstacle to the adoption of figure dances, they were usually remodeled. In central France the *bourrée* was blended with existing dances to produce *bourrées* in duple time (in Berry, Bourbonnais, and Basse-Auvergne) and in triple time (the *montagnardes* of Haute-Auvergne). To the south, the *rigaudon* became naturalized in Provence, Languedoc, the Vivarais, the Dauphiné, Bresse, and part of Nivernais.

Some modifications of older dances were a deliberate rather than a folk process. Thus the Catalan *sardana*, a circle dance that alternates long and short steps, was codified by Pep Ventura in the late nineteenth century into a form that today is its only manifestation. The *sardana* reached Catalan France early in the twentieth century and replaced the local *contrepas* and *ball*.

In addition to chain and circle dances, the Basque region, Béarn, and Bigorre, particularly in the Soule Valley, cultivated dance ceremonies and spectacles. The technique, derived from eighteenth-century ballet, was taught in rural areas by dancing masters trained with the military. Similar dances flourished in Provence and Languedoc. The *bacchuber*, a sword dance performed by young men of the village of Pont-de-Cervières in the Briançonnais, was another dance spectacle, accompanied by onomatopoetic sounds chanted by a female chorus. Another example was the *danse du Baiar* of Esquieze in Lavedan.

Dance historians and ethnographers became interested in traditional dances too late to obtain a clear picture of the *branles* of Savoy and the Franche-Comté, or of the repertories of such regions as Alsace, Lorraine, northern France, and the Île de France, where urban dances became predominant at an early date. Once the figure dance had been adopted, the path was clear for such new couple dances as the waltzes, polkas, and schottisches that inundated France after 1850.

The traditional and folk dance repertory has inspired diverse attempts at reconstruction and revival. Some of these involved choreographers and classically trained dancers; an example is the national dance ensemble of Jacques Douai and Thérèse Palau. More often, however, the tradition was degraded and infantilized by teaching in schools, summer camps, and youth groups, despite the attempts of such organizations as the Centre d'Entraînement aux Méthodes d'Éducation Active to improve folk dance education. Folk dance experienced revivals in the international youth hostel movement, during the 1930s, then again in the 1950s and 1960s. In the late 1960s, folk dancers tried to establish it as a leisure activity for adults; they organized "folk balls," which still enjoy some popularity.

One approach to the study of folk dance in France holds that patterns of dance have resulted from historical factors, including those of regional and local social organization. Isolated communities with a collective, interdependent lifestyle are said to favor circle dances. The breakdown of the circle into a chain and later into couples expresses a reorganization from the collective life to the modern system in which the autonomous couple is considered an adequate social unit. The spread of figure dances in the eighteenth century is regarded as part of a general trend toward cultural exchange, liberation from traditional mores, and the rise of the middle class.

This approach is extended into the psychosocial realm by the view that the content of certain forms, particularly the couple dance, changed over the years. Processional couple dances such as the *bassedanse* and the *pavane* assume the presence of an appreciative audience as well as the two partners. The *contredanse* emphasized the relationship of the dancers more but remained without intimacy, subject to the approval of society. Not until the end of the nineteenth century did the couple come to perform solely as an isolated, sexually defined unit, and outside viewers become intrusive.

Although recreational dance styles developed at varying times and places in different ways, they continued to evolve. They have been shaped by the historically possible relationships of their society in their own time.

[*See also* Chain and Round Dances. *For related discussion, see* European Traditional Dance.]

BIBLIOGRAPHY

Albert, Monsieur [François Decombe]. *L'art de danser à la ville et à la cour.* Paris, 1834.

Arbeau, Thoinot. *Orchesography* (1589). Translated by Mary Stewart Evans. New York, 1948.

Arena, Antonius de. *Ad suos compagnones studiantes.* Lyon, 1528. (Edition A.D.P. of 1520, Créteil, 1990.)

Blanchard, Raphaël. *Le Bac'ubert.* Paris, 1914.

Bonnet, Jacques. *Histoire générale de la danse, sacrée et profane.* Paris, 1723.

Bouillet, J.-B. *L'album auvergnat.* Moulin, 1848.

Cahusac, Louis de. *La danse ancienne et moderne, ou, Traité historique de la danse.* 3 vols. The Hague, 1754.

Cellarius, Henri. *The Drawing-Room Dances.* London, 1847.

Dassance, L. "Les Sauts Basques et les vieilles danses labourdines." *Bulletin du Musée Basque* 3 (1926): 21–30.

Feuillet, Raoul-Auger. *Chorégraphie, ou L'art de décrire la dance, par caractères, figures et signes démonstratifs, avec lesquels on apprend facilement de soy-même toutes sortes de dances.* Paris, 1700. Translated by John Weaver as *Orchesography, or, The Art of Dancing* (London, 1706).

Gasnault, François. *Le bal populaire a Paris au XIX's.* Paris, 1990.

Gougaud, Louis. "La danse dans les églises." *Revue d'histoire ecclésiastique* 15 (1914): 5–22.

Guilcher, Jean-Michel. *La tradition populaire de danse en Basse-Bretagne.* Paris, 1963.

Guilcher, Jean-Michel. *La tradition de danse en Bearn et Pays Basque Français.* Paris, 1984.

Guilcher, Jean-Michel. *La contredanse et les renouvellements de la danse française.* Paris, 1969.

Guilcher, Jean-Michel. "L'enseignement militaire de la danse et les traditions populaires." *Arts et traditions populaires* 18 (1970).

Guilcher, Jean-Michel. "Aspects et problèmes de la danse populaire traditionnelle." *Ethnologie* 1 (1971).

Guilcher, Yves. "Dance as a Reflection of Society." *Choreography and Dance* 2.1 (1992): 77–107.

Harruguet, S. "La danse en Basse Navarre." *Bulletin du Musée Basque* 4 (1927).

Ponsich, Pierre. "Contrepas et Sardane en Catalogne et Roussillon." In *La sardane,* edited by Henry Pépratx-Saisset. Perpignan, 1955.

Rameau, Pierre. *Le maître à danser.* Paris, 1725. Translated by Cyril W. Beaumont as *The Dancing Master* (London, 1931).

Rokseth, Yvonne. "Danses cléricales du XIIIe siècle." In *Mélanges 1945,* vol. 3, *Études historiques.* Paris, 1947.

Sachs, Curt. *World History of the Dance.* Translated by Bessie Schönberg. New York, 1937.

Toulouze, Michel. *L'art et instruction de bien dancer.* Paris, 1488.

YVES GUILCHER
Translated from French

Theatrical Dance, 1581–1789

Between 1581, when the famous *Balet Comique de la Royne* was presented, and 1669, when Louis XIV danced for the last time in public, the *ballet de cour* enjoyed its golden age. The French taste for dancing developed under its influence. [*See* Ballet de Cour.]

Wealthy private patrons in Paris and in the provinces vied in presenting dance performances in their homes. They were encouraged in this during the seventeenth and eighteenth centuries by the flourishing of the *ballets de collège* and the teaching of classical dance, a fundamental part of education at that time. [*See* Ballet de Collège.]

In addition, there were troupes of traveling actors, initially Italians such as the celebrated Gelosi of Venice, who came to France in 1577. Later, French groups arose, heirs of the Confrères de la Passion, which had held a monopoly on religious plays during the sixteenth century. At the demand of their noble or plebeian audiences, these groups interpolated dances into their performances, which otherwise consisted of burlesque pantomimes de-

FRANCE: Theatrical Dance, 1581–1789. Jacques Patin's illustration of satyrs for the 1581 production of *Le Balet Comique de la Royne*, commissioned by Catherine de Médicis. The ballet, performed in the Salle de Bourbon of the Louvre, was part of the festivities in honor of the wedding of the duc de Joyeuse to Mademoiselle de Vaudemont. (Private collection.)

rived from the *commedia dell'arte* or from the French comedians of the Pont-Neuf.

Some actors and actresses were also dancers. Moreover, dancing often served as a kind of apprenticeship for new actors, some of whom—for example, Jean Dauberval—abandoned acting for ballet. In the seventeenth century, the directors of companies such as those of the Hôtel de Bourgogne, the Théâtre du Marais, and the Illustre Théâtre de Molière commonly engaged professional dancers for their *intermèdes* (danced interludes).

Héroard mentions in his *Journal* of 1622 a "grand ballet" from the city, in the style of the Italian comedy. Was this already a professional troupe? The first such troupe whose existence is officially documented was that of Horace Morel, who obtained a royal patent. In 1632, at the Jeu de Paume du Marais du Temple, he presented *Le Ballet de l'Harmonie Universelle* and *Le Ballet des Effets de la Nature*, followed in 1633 by *Le Ballet des Cinq Sens*, all with librettos by Guillaume Colletet. Though highly praised, these efforts had no successors, probably for financial reasons.

The *pièces à machines* (special-effects spectacles), such as *La Toison d'Or* (1661), upon which the troupe of the Marais based its success, featured much dance, which attracted the court. This trend was reinforced by the influence of Molière's comic ballets. Actors vigorously contested the patent obtained by Jean-Baptiste Lully in 1672 for the Académie Royale de Musique, since it stripped them of the right to engage musicians and dancers. However, the Comédie Française, founded in Paris in 1680,

stubbornly succeeded in retaining until the end of the eighteenth century a variable number of dancers, among whom were Marie Allard, Marie-Madeleine Guimard, Mesdemoiselles Dangeville, Rey, and Camasse, and Angiolo Vestris and Jean Dauberval.

The Comédie Française joined with the Paris Opera in attacking the Italian actors and the small popular theaters of the Foires Saint-Germain, Saint-Laurent, and Saint-Ovid. These companies, temporarily deprived of the right to use speech, substituted expressive gestures, pantomime, and dance. Many celebrated dancers, among them Marie Sallé, made their debuts here before going on to the Opera. At the Opéra-Comique, founded in 1724, Noverre mounted in 1754 *Les Fêtes Chinoises* and *La Fontaine de Jouvence*, among other successes.

Expelled by Louis XIV in 1697, the Comédie Italienne was recalled by the Regent in 1716, and in 1762 it was combined with the Opéra-Comique. It continued to attract excellent choreographers, the most renowned being Jean-Baptiste de Hesse. The small-scale but picturesque ballets it presented enjoyed great favor, leading to the development, during the reign of Louis XVI, of the theaters of the Boulevard du Temple and the rise of new troupes, among them, Nicholas Audinot and his Théâtre de l'Ambigu-Comique and Nicolet's theater. These companies displayed a freedom of invention, satirical verve, and a search for originality that contrasted with the tradition-bound pomp of the Opera. Yet, though the Opera was often irritated by the freewheeling ways of the boulevard theaters, it was more and more influenced by them toward the end of the eighteenth century.

During this period dancers were also employed by many traveling troupes working in the provinces. Important opera houses were founded in Rouen, Lyon, Marseille, Bordeaux, and Dijon. They vied in attracting both new and established artists such as Marie Camargo, Louis

Dupré, Jean-Georges Noverre, Maximilien Gardel, Jean Dauberval, Antoine-Bonaventure Pitrot, the Malter brothers, and the Viganò family. Ballet life in France was thus characterized by great mobility, and performers moved about frequently, attesting to the general success of choreographic spectacles.

[*For further discussion, see* Balet Comique de la Royne, Le; Ballet Technique, History of, *article on* French Court Dance; and Paris Opera Ballet. *See also the entries on the principal figures mentioned herein.*]

BIBLIOGRAPHY

Beauchamps, Pierre. *Recherches sur les théâtres de France.* 3 vols. Paris, 1735.

Campardon, Émile. *Les spectacles de la foire, 1595–1791.* Paris, 1877.

Campardon, Émile. *La troupe italienne.* Paris, 1877.

Chazin-Bennahum, Judith. "The Contribution of Jean-Jacques Rousseau to Ballet." In *Proceedings of the Ninth Annual Conference, Society of Dance History Scholars, City College, City University of New York, 14–17 February 1986,* compiled by Christena L. Schlundt. Riverside, Calif., 1986.

Chazin-Bennahum, Judith. "Wine, Women, and Song: Anacreon's Triple Threat to French Eighteenth-Century Ballet." *Dance Research* 5 (Spring 1987): 55–64.

Christout, Marie-Françoise. *Le ballet de cour de Louis XIV, 1643–1672.* Paris, 1967.

Christout, Marie-Françoise. *Le ballet occidental, XVIe–XXe siècle.* Paris, 1995.

Coeyman, Barbara. "Theatres for Opera and Ballet during the Reigns of Louis XIV and Louis XV." *Early Music* 18 (February 1990): 22–37.

Dictionnaire de la musique du France. Paris, 1992.

Foster, Susan Leigh. *Choreography and Narrative.* Bloomington, 1996.

Franko, Mark. *Dance as Text: Ideologies of the Baroque Body.* New York, 1993.

Fuchs, Max. *La vie théâtrale en province au XVIIIe siècle.* Paris, 1933.

Fuchs, Max. *Lexique des troupe de comédiens au XVIIIe siècle.* Paris, 1944.

Guest, Ivor. *The Ballet of the Englightenment: The Establishment of the Ballet d'Action in France, 1770–1793.* London, 1996.

Harris-Warrick, Rebecca. "La Mariée: The History of a French Court Dance." In *Jean-Baptiste Lully and the Music of the French Baroque,* edited by John Heyer. New York, 1989.

Harris-Warrick, Rebecca. "Interpreting Pendulum Markings for French Baroque Dances." *Historical Performance* 6 (Spring 1993): 9–22.

Hilton, Wendy. *Dance of Court and Theatre: The French Noble Style, 1690–1725.* Princeton, 1981.

Kougioumtzoglou-Roucher, Eugénia. "Aux origines de la danse classique: Le vocabulaire de la belle danse, 1661–1701." 2 vols. Ph.D. diss., Université de Paris XIII, 1991.

LaGorce, Jérome de. *Opéra à Paris au temps de Louis XIV.* Paris, 1993.

Lancelot, Francine. "Les ornements dans la danse baroque." *Les goûts réunis,* no. 2 (1982): 72–78.

Pitou, Spire. *The Paris Opéra: An Encyclopedia of Operas, Ballets, Composers, and Performers.* Westport, Conn., 1983–.

Rice, Paul F. *The Performing Arts at Fontainebleau from Louis XIV to Louis XVI.* Ann Arbor, 1989.

Samard, Evelyne. "Les danses guerrières dans le ballet de cour en Savoie au XVIIe siècle." In *Le ballet aux XVIe et XVIIe siècles en France et à la Cour de Savoie,* edited by Marie-Thérèse Bouquet. Geneva, 1992.

Schwartz, Judith L., and Christena L. Schlundt. *French Court Dance and Dance Music: A Guide to Primary Source Writings, 1643–1789.* Stuyvesant, N.Y., 1987.

Swift, Mary Grace. "The Three Ballets of the Young Sun." *Dance Chronicle* 3.4 (1979–1980): 361–372.

Vaccarino, Elisa. "Il balletto alla corte di Torino, ovvero la diligenza per Lione." *La danza italiana* 4 (Spring 1986): 49–57.

MARIE-FRANÇOISE CHRISTOUT
Translated from French

Theatrical Dance, 1789–1914

In France, the year 1789 marked the beginning of a prolonged political and social struggle that surrounded the overthrow of the monarchy and the establishment of the First Republic. Although the French Revolution (1789–1799) caused a major social upheaval, neither theatrical dance nor social dance was diminished in any appreciable way. The activities of dancing teachers to the ladies of the court were, of course, curtailed, but all well-bred people already knew how to dance the popular social dances of the salons: the *menuet,* the *pavane,* and the *courante.* At the height of the Revolution, during the most troubled times, people sang and danced with a recklessness fueled by their insecurity about the future: no one could predict whom the guillotine would next claim. After the storming of the Bastille in 1792, the song and dance called "La Carmagnole" came into vogue as an expression of the fears, hopes, and joys inspired by this event. The dancers formed a huge circle while singing, turning slowly, and striking the ground during the verse, then speeding up for the refrain.

Theaters appear to have continued functioning with relatively little disruption, and public balls were numerous. According to the historian Gaston Vuillier (1898), on the day after the Reign of Terror began, on 5 September 1793, twenty-three theaters and eighteen hundred balls were open in Paris. The public balls, which charged admission, had begun nearly a century earlier as a family-oriented activity but had become more commercial over time. Only briefly interrupted by the excesses of the Revolution, they were resumed in 1794 and 1795 in even greater splendor.

The Revolution did frighten some dancers of the Paris Opera into dispersing to the provinces, where they frequently resettled in Bordeaux, Lyon, or Marseille. The quality of performances in Paris was thus temporarily affected, but the political and social changes that occurred during the Revolution ultimately contributed to the growth of theatrical dance. The monopoly on dance that the Opera had shared with the Comédie Italienne in Paris was broken by an edict of 1791, which permitted lesser theaters to stage ballets. Just as important was the emergence of a rising middle class, whose members filled the cheapest seats in the theaters. This audience had little interest in intellectual matters or in the formal conventions of the old order. It wanted simply to be entertained. One of the most popular new theatrical forms, melodrama, blended the formerly clear-cut genres of tragedy and comedy, combining the sublime with the grotesque. The rising Romantic movement would also exert an influence on the popular theater, which imitated the Romantics' interest in history, local color, and the supernatural.

The Romanticism of the supernatural world had not yet reached the ballet stages of France, however. Stories based on history or local color were still the order of the day. Jean Dauberval's *La Fille Mal Gardée*, first presented in Bordeaux in 1789, was based on a simple libretto that responded to the tastes of the time: a mother wants to marry her daughter to a rich simpleton, but the girl contrives to get the poor, but more presentable, young man she prefers. The pantomime and country dances, one of which was a ribbon dance in the Montpelleran style, were warmly received by the public. [*See* Fille Mal Gardée, La.] Bordeaux was the scene of a great deal of choreographic activity in the last decade of the eighteenth century and the first half of the nineteenth. Not only Dauberval but Jean-Baptiste Blache, Charles-Louis Didelot, and Jean-Louis Aumer spent much time there, as did Carlo Blasis and the Petipa family.

In Paris, ballet performances could be found at many secondary theaters in addition to the Opera. In 1797 the Théâtre de la Gaîté hired Eugène Hus as ballet master; this post was later filled by Jean-Baptiste Hullin, whose ballet *Amélie* made a sensational hit with its "Negroes' Dance." Jules Perrot, destined to become one of France's great choreographers, made his Parisian debut at the Théâtre de la Gaîté in 1823, in roles emulating those of the well-known comic dancer Charles-François Mazurier.

The Théâtre de l'Ambigu-Comique, which had been dormant during the Revolution began to present melodramas interspersed with ballets in 1798. Among its dancers were Charles-Louis Didelot and Louis Duport, both of whom would make great names for themselves. In 1799, the Théâtre de l'Ambigu-Comique produced one of Louis Milon's earliest ballets, *Pygmalion*, which recalled the paintings of Jean-Honoré Fragonard. The groupings of the chorus were particularly admired for their resemblance to those seen in Greek bas-reliefs. During this time the waltz reigned supreme in the salons of Paris. This dance had been presented on stage as early as 1787 in Vincenzo Martini's opera *Una Cosa Rara*; it reappeared in 1800 at the Paris Opera in Pierre Gardel's ballet *La Dansomanie*.

Fashionable life returned with the reign of Napoleon I, who had established the government of the Consulate at the end of 1799 and brought the French Revolutionary Wars to an end in 1802. Lavish celebrations marked the New Year in 1803, Napoleon's coronation in 1804, and the Carnival season in 1805. The first great ball of the Empire period (1804–1814) took place in 1806. At the Paris Opera, the cunning Gardel, who had adroitly masterminded the festivals of the Revolution, now mounted extravagant spectacles, often with a mythological motif, designed to flatter the emperor. Gardel shared his despotic sway over the Opera only with Milon; other choreographers were forced to seek positions in lesser theaters in Paris or in the provinces.

After Napoleon's rise to power, the directors of the Opera endeavored to restore its prerevolutionary tradition of elegance and refinement, but its high ticket prices and its frigid artistic atmosphere kept many people away. The general public now preferred to patronize the more informal secondary theaters, where they nonetheless demanded the ballets, beautiful decors, and elaborate stage effects they had been in the habit of applauding at the Opera. These demands provoked fresh activity in the boulevard theaters.

The leader of these theaters was the Théâtre de la Porte-Saint-Martin, nicknamed the "Opera of the Boulevard." Its building had in fact been occupied by the Paris Opera until 1794. Open to all the new ideas and trends that foreshadowed Romanticism, the Porte-Saint-Martin was a source of talent where many male dancers and choreographers worked before being engaged by the Opera. In 1802, Jean-Louis Aumer arranged *divertissements*, including a brilliant sun festival, in Guilbert de Pixérécourt's play *Pizarro* in this theater, and in 1806 he staged *Jenny, ou Le Mariage Secret*, which treated a popular Romantic theme, madness. His ballet *Les Deux Créoles*, also created in 1806, coincided with Gardel's ballet based on the same story, *Paul et Virginie*, produced at the Opera. Some viewers preferred Aumer's version because it seemed less refined and more dynamic.

Louis Henry, who had been trained at the Opera, worked briefly at the Porte-Saint-Martin. His ballet *Les Sauvages de Floride* (1807) was praised by Julien-Louis Geoffroy in the *Journal des débats* for its "joyous dances, pathetic situations, and voluptuous movements." At Gardel's insistence, however, Napoleon ordered the Porte-Saint-Martin to close in 1807. It subsequently reopened to present historical plays, gymnastic demonstrations, and melodramas, but each time a production achieved success, the theater was once again ordered to close. This cycle continued until the abdication of Napoleon in 1814.

Gardel and Milon, the despots of the Paris Opera, opposed all innovation, causing many of their compatriots to seek work in other European countries, especially Germany and Italy. When they returned, they brought new styles and ideas with them. Louis Henry, for example, returned to the Porte-Saint-Martin in 1814, following a sojourn in Italy, and introduced in his ballets a greater emphasis on drama, influenced by the works of Salvatore Viganò and Gaetano Gioja. Jean Coralli worked at the same theater between 1825 and 1829, staging, in a melodramatic version of *Faust*, a *pas de sylphides* that foreshadowed all the "white ballets" of the Romantic era. The comic dancer Charles-François Mazurier continued to be a leading attraction during these years. He combined acrobatics and miming so successfully in his impersonation of the monkey hero of *Jocko, ou Le Singe du Brésil* that he often drew tears from his audience.

The ostentatious social life of the Empire period revived the demand for private dance instruction. Vying for wealthy pupils, the dancing masters sought to enhance their reputations by introducing some of the conventions of theatrical dancing into social dances. Quadrilles of the time often included steps such as *entrechats* and *jetés battus,* and some social dances resembled little ballets.

By the 1830s, classical conventions were beginning to lose their hold on the Opera as well as at the boulevard theaters. Victor Hugo's drama *Hernani,* Hector Berlioz's *Symphonie Fantastique,* and Giacomo Meyerbeer's opera *Robert le Diable* shared the contemporary goal of activating the senses as well as the intellect of the spectator. The boulevard theaters' innovations in stage effects and lighting (creating wind, storms, fires, and flying dancers) also began to pervade the Opera, which had introduced gas lighting on stage in 1821. Scenery acquired such importance that the director of the Opera, Henri Duponchel, sent the designer Pierre Ciceri to Italy to study scenographic techniques. Intermissions were introduced to facilitate changes of scenery, which had formerly been accomplished in full view of the audience.

Ballets of this time tended to focus on three characters: a heroine, a hero, and a villain. Previously, the choreographer had written his own libretto as well as assembled various pieces of music into a score, but during this period men of letters began to create ballet scenarios. The playwright Eugène Scribe wrote the libretto for *La Somnambule* in 1827; Théophile Gautier and Jules-Henri Vernoy, marquis de Saint-Georges, would collaborate on the story for *Giselle* in 1841. Novels, plays, and operas supplied the plot lines of such ballets as *Le Diable Boiteux* (1836) and *La Jolie Fille de Gand* (1842).

The rise of full-blown Romanticism on the ballet stage is generally dated from the premiere of Filippo Taglioni's *La Sylphide* at the Paris Opera on 12 March 1832. [*See* Sylphide, La.] Thereafter, the Paris Opera made major contributions to the Romantic movement, including its original production on 28 June 1841 of *Giselle,* which has been called the quintessential Romantic ballet. [*See* Giselle.] However, most of the leading ballerinas of the period, the supreme interpreters of Romantic ballet, were not French; they were foreign-born. Marie Taglioni, who popularized use of the pointes with her ethereal dancing in *La Sylphide,* was Swedish-Italian. Carlotta Grisi, the first

Giselle, was Italian, as was Fanny Cerrito. Lucile Grahn was Danish, and Fanny Elssler was Austrian.

Elssler, who became Taglioni's greatest rival, introduced the fashion for balleticized national dances with her performance of the Spanish-flavored *cachuca* in Coralli's *Le Diable Boiteux* (1836). Dancers from Spain had appeared in Paris in 1833 after the theaters of Madrid had been closed following the death of King Ferdinand VII. Balleticized versions of Spanish dances have remained perennially popular on the stages of France down to the present day.

During the reign of Louis Phillippe (1830–1848), the can-can, a popular derivation of the quadrille, became the rage at public balls. Carnival balls, like the Bal Mabille, were held practically everywhere in France. In the 1840s the building of railroads allowed the spread of new dances throughout the country. The polka, the waltz, and the quadrille replaced older dances such as the *branle,* the *rigaudon,* and the *gavotte.* A few dances survived: the *bourrée,* principally in Auvergne; the *sardane,* in the Basque country; and the *farandole,* in Provence. The Poles

FRANCE: Theatrical Dance, 1789–1914. A lithograph showing the dancer-acrobat Charles Mazurier in his most famous role, the title character in Frédéric Blache's *Jocko, ou Le Singe du Brésil* (1825). Widely copied and plagiarized, this work was produced in Stuttgart by Filippo Taglioni as *Danina, oder Jocko der Brazilianische Affe* (1826). Based on a French melodrama, the ballet tells the tale of Danina, a beautiful Brazilian, who saves an ape from being bitten by a snake; the ape later returns her kindness by preventing her son from being kidnapped. (Photograph from the Dance Collection, New York Public Library for the Performing Arts.)

introduced the mazurka, and the English the schottische. After Louis Phillippe relinquished his throne, public balls lost favor. During the unsettled years of the Second Republic (1848–1852), many Hungarians and Italians came to Paris in hope of influencing the political situation, and their national dances, too, soon began to be seen on Parisian stages.

As the impact of the Romantic ballet dwindled in the 1850s, opera began to take its place in the affections of the public, although ballet *divertissements* were still incorporated into many operas. Beginning in 1852, a new middle class composed of bankers and industrialists rose to power along with Napoleon III. During his reign (1852–1870), called the Second Empire period, this group of theatergoers preferred operettas to ballet. Jacques Offenbach was in his heyday; he opened his own theater, Bouffes-Parisien, in 1855 and produced one hit operetta

FRANCE: Theatrical Dance, 1789–1914. Carlotta Grisi and Lucien Petipa in the "Valse Favorite" from act 1 of *Giselle, ou les Wilis*, which premiered at the Académie Royale de Musique in 1841. This lithograph, by Formentin & Cie., was printed on a music cover in Paris, c.1842. (Courtesy of Madison U. Sowell and Debra H. Sowell, Brigham Young University, Provo, Utah.)

FRANCE: Theatrical Dance, 1789–1914. Costume design for an Andalusian dancer in Jean Coralli's *Le Diable Boiteux*, which premiered at the Académie Royale de Musique in 1836. This contemporary engraving is by Maleuvre, from the *Petit galerie dramatique*, Paris. (Courtesy of Madison U. Sowell and Debra H. Sowell, Brigham Young University, Provo, Utah.)

after another, including *Orphée aux Enfers* (1859), *La Belle Hélène* (1864), and *La Vie Parisienne* (1866).

Italian ballerinas continued to dominate the Parisian stage. Carolina Rosati, who had made her debut at the Théâtre Italien in 1851, was followed shortly afterward by Amalia Ferraris. Both ballerinas appeared in Joseph Mazilier's *Marco Spada* (1856) at the Opera. One French ballerina of the time, Emma Livry, did win widespread public and critical acclaim, in performances of *La Sylphide* and subsequently in *Le Papillon* (1860), choreographed especially for her by Marie Taglioni to music by Offenbach. She held every promise of being a worthy successor to the great Taglioni, but her career and life were tragically cut short in 1862 when her tutu caught fire from a gas jet during a rehearsal on the Opera stage.

The Second Empire period produced few ballets of any distinction. One exception, Arthur Saint-Léon's *La Source* (1866), was notable mainly for the portions of its score composed by Léo Delibes. After this, nothing noteworthy was produced at the Opera until Saint-Léon choreo-

FRANCE: Theatrical Dance, 1789–1914. A portrait of Giuseppina Bozzacchi, who created the role of Swanilda in Saint-Léon's *Coppélia* (1870). Six months after her spectacular success at the Paris Opera, she died of smallpox on her seventeenth birthday. (Photograph from the Dance Collection, New York Public Library for the Performing Arts.)

performers. Luigi Manzotti's spectacles, produced at the Théâtre Eden in the 1880s, were particularly successful. Virginia Zucchi was the star of *Excelsior* (1883), a paean to modern technology that reflected contemporary faith in industry as the cure-all for past ills.

In 1892, the American dancer Loie Fuller, who had been turned down by the Opera, made her debut at the Folies-Bergère. She was the first performer in France to exploit the possibilities for exotic theatrical effects of electric lighting, which had been introduced to the Parisian stage years before, in the 1840s. One critic described her *Serpentine Dance* as "undulating, luminous, filled with a strange grace that was a true revelation to the Parisians" (Vuillier, 1898). Fuller became the darling of her era. Henri de Toulouse-Lautrec designed posters for her; the glassmaker Émile Gallé was inspired by her innovative lighting effects.

The early years of the twentieth century were dominated by the ballerina Carlotta Zambelli at the Paris Opera and the Spanish dancer Carolina Otéro in the music halls. Isadora Duncan made her first appearances in Paris, inspiring painters and sculptors such as Auguste Rodin, Émile-Antoine Bourdelle, and José Clara. The musician Gustave Charpentier wrote, "She has created a new vocabulary." Her first successful season in Paris coincided with that of the Ballets Russes. [*See* Ballets Russes de Serge Diaghilev.]

The advent of the Ballets Russes in Paris in 1909 is a recognized turning point in the art of ballet. But it had little immediate effect on ballet productions at the Opera and other theaters. The Opera's major ballet production of 1909 was *Javotte*, a work created by Léo Staats as a starring vehicle for Zambelli and himself. The Opera main-

graphed *Coppélia*, to Delibes's masterful score, a few years later. It was finally presented in May 1870, on the eve of the Franco-Prussian War. [*See* Coppélia.]

Although the defeat of France in the war, the rise of the Commune in 1871, and the burning of the Opera in 1873 were all hindrances to artistic creation, they did not stifle it altogether, and the Opera continued to produce new works during the early years of the Third Republic. Louis Mérante's ballet *Yedda* (1879), with Rita Sangalli in the leading role, exploited the Japanese style of decoration that had come into vogue during the reign of Napoleon III. In the following year, he created *La Korrigane*, based on a Breton folk tale adapted by the poet François Coppée.

Music halls became more and more popular toward the close of the century. [*See* Music Hall, *article on* French Traditions.] They presented not ballets but extravagant revues that sometimes featured as many as five hundred

FRANCE: Theatrical Dance, 1789–1914. A postcard showing four female dancers in the corps of the Paris Opera Ballet, including Carlotta Zambelli (right), who later became a *prima ballerina* of the company, and three others identified only by their last names as Boos, Piodi, and Vangoethen. (Photograph from the Dance Collection, New York Public Library for the Performing Arts.)

tained its conservatism until Jacques Rouché, former head of the Théâtre des Arts, became its director in 1914. Rouché had earlier organized several concert programs at the Théâtre du Châtelet for the dancer Natalia Trouhanova, who often used music by contemporary French composers. *La Péri*, to music by Paul Dukas; *Istar*, to music by Vincent d'Indy; and *Adélaïde*, to Maurice Ravel's *Valses Nobles et Sentimentales* were works featured in her repertory. Rouché followed her example when he arrived at the Opera, introducing the music of Ravel and Albert Roussel. Nevertheless, on the eve of World War I, choreography on the Opera's stage continued to be entirely academic. It would remain so until the coming of Serge Lifar in 1929.

[*See also* Paris Opera Ballet *and the entries on major figures and dance types mentioned herein.*]

BIBLIOGRAPHY

Boulenger, Jacques. *De la walse au tango.* Paris, 1920.
Chapman, John V. "Silent Drama to Silent Dream: Parisian Ballet Criticism, 1800–1850." *Dance Chronicle* 11.3 (1988): 365–380.
Chapman, John V. "Jules Janin and the Ballet." *Dance Research* 7 (Spring 1989): 65–77.
Chapman, John V. "The Paris Opéra Ballet School, 1798–1827." *Dance Chronicle* 12.2 (1989): 196–220.
Chazin-Bennahum, Judith. *Dance in the Shadow of the Guillotine.* Carbondale, Ill., 1988.
Guest, Ivor. *The Ballet of the Second Empire.* London, 1974.
Guest, Ivor. *The Romantic Ballet in Paris.* 2d rev. ed. London, 1980.
Lawson, Joan. "Masters of the Ballet of the Nineteenth Century" (parts 1–6). *The Dancing Times* (November 1939–April 1940).
Louis, Maurice L.-A. *Le folklore et la danse.* Paris, 1963.
Louis, Maurice L.-A. *Danses populaires et ballets d'Opéra.* Paris, 1965.
Meglin, Joellen A. "Representations and Realities: Analyzing Gender Symbols in the Romantic Ballet." Ph.D. diss., Temple University, 1995.
Michel, Marcelle. "Apothéose et décadence de la danse classique sous la Révolution et l'Empire." Ph.D. diss., Sorbonne, 1955.
Pitou, Spire. *The Paris Opéra: An Encyclopedia of Operas, Ballets, Composers, and Performers*, vol 2, *Rococo and Romantic, 1715–1815*; vol. 3, *Growth and Grandeur, 1815–1914.* Westport, Conn., 1983–.
Schwartz, Jane D. "The Role of the Male Dancer in the Era of the Romantic Ballet, 1824–1864." Ph.D. diss., University of California, Los Angeles, 1972.
Soria, Henri de. *Histoire pittoresque de la danse.* Paris, 1897.
Vuillier, Gaston. *La danse.* Paris, 1898.

MONIQUE BABSKY
Translated from French

Ballet since 1914

Theatrical dance in France after 1914, outside the Paris Opera Ballet, was dominated by foreign soloists and companies. The annual seasons of Serge Diaghilev's Ballets Russes, extending from 1909 to 1929, had restored Paris to its former position as the focal point of the dance world. The appearances of Isadora Duncan, Anna Pavlova, and La Argentina added luster to the French dance scene. Most of these artists, however, looked upon French audiences as highly discerning arbiters of taste and both respected and feared their judgments.

In addition, a number of foreign dancers and companies made Paris their base of operations and employed French writers, artists, and musicians as collaborators. Les Ballets Suédois, a company organized by the Swedish patron of the arts Rolf de Maré in 1920, numbered Jean Cocteau, Blaise Cendrars, and Paul Claudel among its librettists, Georges Auric, Darius Milhaud, and Francis Poulenc among its composers, and Fernand Léger and Francis Picabia among its designers. Its modernist experiments—such as *Relâche* (1924), for which Picabia designed a backdrop of automobile headlamps and René Clair made a film—drew the attention of the artistic world. [*See* Ballets Suédois.]

That same year, a French patron, Comte Étienne de Beaumont, organized a ballet season called Les Soirées de Paris, for which he enlisted the talents of Cocteau, Léonide Massine, Pablo Picasso, and Georges Braque. The first performances of Massine's popular ballets *Le Beau Danube* and *Gaîté Parisienne* were given under these auspices. The next year, 1925, Bronislava Nijinska formed a chamber ballet group based in Paris. She was invited in 1928 to become the chief choreographer of Ida Rubinstein's company, for which she created the ballets *Le Baiser de la Fée*, *La Valse*, and *Boléro*, the last to a score that Rubinstein had commissioned from the French composer Maurice Ravel.

In 1931, Rolf de Maré founded the Archives Internationales de la Danse (AID) in Paris under the curatorship of Pierre Tugal. This organization also sponsored exhibitions and lecture demonstrations, published a magazine, and ran a studio for experimental works. It held its first choreographic competition in Paris in 1932, awarding the first prize to Kurt Jooss for *The Green Table*.

The year 1932 is also notable in the history of ballet in France for the first appearance in Paris of the Ballets Russes de Monte Carlo, newly founded by Colonel Wassily de Basil and René Blum around a nucleus of former members of Diaghilev's Ballets Russes. During a two-week season in June at the Théâtre des Champs-Élysées, the company scored a triumph with George Balanchine's *Cotillon*, *La Concurrence*, and *Le Bourgeois Gentilhomme*. The company's only other Parisian appearance before World War II was in 1934, when it presented Massine's *Choreartium* and David Lichine's *Les Imaginaires*. [*See* Ballets Russes de Monte Carlo.]

The single season of Les Ballets 1933, sponsored by the English art patron Edward James, was also presented at the Théâtre des Champs-Élysées. This company, directed by Balanchine, Boris Kochno, and Vladimir Dimitriev, featured Tilly Losch, Tamara Toumanova, and Roman Jasinski in a repertory of six works by Balanchine that included *Mozartiana* and *Les Sept Péchés Capitaux*. The French artists André Derain and Christian Bérard and the composers Darius Milhaud and Henri Sauguet also contributed to this season. [*See* Ballets 1933.]

Another short-lived company, Les Ballets de la Jeunesse, was founded in Paris in 1937 by the Russian ballerina Lubov Egorova, the French poet Jean-Louis Vaudoyer (who had suggested the libretto for Michel Fokine's *Le Spectre de la Rose* in 1911), and F. Barrette. Although this company lasted only a year, it introduced such dancers, as George Skibine, Geneviève Moulin, Tatiana Leskova, Edmond Audran, and Youly Algaroff.

The Paris Opera Ballet began to reclaim its former glory during the 1930s under the leadership of Serge Lifar. Its progress was disrupted, however, by the outbreak of World War II. Some of the dancers who fled Paris found a haven in the Nouveaux Ballets de Monte Carlo, organized in 1942, which performed *Les Sylphides*, *Petrouchka*, and other works from the Diaghilev repertory. The company was reorganized in 1945 as the Nouveau Ballet de Monte Carlo, with Lifar as its artistic director and a roster of dancers that included Yvette Chauviré, Janine Charrat, Renée ("Zizi") Jeanmaire, Alexandre Kalioujny, and Vladimir Skouratoff. Lifar choreographed *Dramma per Musica*, *Chota Roustaveli*, and *Nautéos* for this company prior to his return to the Opera in 1947. In that year the company was purchased by the Marquis de Cuevas, who rechristened it the Grand Ballet du Marquis de Cuevas and gave it a new repertory and new personnel led by the American dancers Rosella Hightower, Marjorie Tallchief, and William Dollar.

The Opéra-Comique in Paris, which had been amalgamated with the Paris Opera in 1939, regained independent status in 1946 when Jean-Jacques Etchévery was appointed its ballet master. Charrat and Massine also choreographed for this company, which included dancers such as Solange Schwarz, Christiane Vaussard, and Paul Goubé. After a hiatus in the 1950s, the company resumed activity in 1957 under the direction of Gérard Mulys.

In the mid-1940s a new generation of French dancers and choreographers began to strike out on their own. The leaders were Roland Petit, Jean Babilée, and Janine Charrat, who, unlike the other two, was not a product of the Paris Opera. They were aided by the dance critic Irène Lidova, who helped them organize the independent dance concerts called Soirées de la Danse at the Théâtre Sarah-Bernhardt in 1944. In the following year Petit founded the Ballets des Champs-Élysées, with Boris Kochno, Diaghilev's former secretary, as artistic director. Jean Cocteau and Christian Bérard also lent their support. [*See* Ballets des Champs-Élysées.]

This company provided an important outlet for experimental work that could not be mounted at the more conservative Opera and eventually shaped a style of choreog-

FRANCE: Ballet since 1914. Serge Lifar choreographed his neo-Romantic ballet *Les Mirages* for the Paris Opera Ballet in the spring of 1944. Shortly after its premiere, the Allies landed on the beaches of Normandy, and the doors of the Opera were shut. After the liberation of Paris, Lifar, under suspicion of collaboration with the Nazis, was banned from the Opera. When he returned in 1947, *Les Mirages* was mounted once again and proved a great success. In this scene, the Young Man (Michel Renault, right) and his Shadow (Yvette Chauviré, center) arrive at the kingdom of the Moon (Denise Bourgeois, left). The Shadow was one of the greatest roles of the beloved ballerina known as "La Chauviré Nationale." (Photograph from the Dance Collection, New York Public Library for the Performing Arts.)

raphy that came to be regarded as distinctively French: theatrical, daring, chic, and sexy. Charrat created a version of Igor Stravinsky's *Jeu de Cartes* (1945), with the dazzling Babilée as the virtuosic Joker. Petit's *Le Jeune Homme et al Mort* (1946), upon which he collaborated with Cocteau, shocked audiences with its juxtaposition of a tale of sexual cruelty and the noble strains of Bach's *Passacaglia*. *L'Amour et Son Amour* (1948), a modern retelling of an ancient Greek myth, was choreographed by Babilée with himself in the role of Eros and his wife Nathalie Philippart as Psyche. In contrast to these new works was Victor Gsovsky's revival of Filippo Taglioni's *La Sylphide*, with Nina Vyroubova in the title role and Petit as her hapless lover. In addition to Charrat, Petit, and Babilée, who were all exceptional dancers as well as choreographers, the company's roster included Jeanmaire, Ethéry Pagava, Irène Skorik, Algaroff, and Skouratoff. Leslie Caron, who later gained fame as a film actress, first attracted the public's notice as the enigmatic Sphinx in David Lichine's *La Recontre*, created for the company in 1948.

In 1948 Petit founded a new company, Les Ballets de Paris. His first creation for this company was *Les Demoiselles de la Nuit*, in which Margot Fonteyn, appearing as a guest artist, played a cat who turns into a woman for the sake of her human lover. The company's greatest success, however, was *Carmen* (1949), which elevated Jeanmaire to stardom in the role of the tempestuous gypsy. *Le Loup* (1953) introduced the young ballerina Violette Verdy as a bride who falls in love with the wolf she has been tricked into marrying. The visual impact of these works was enhanced by Petit's use of outstanding designers: Léonor Fini, Antoni Clavé, and Carzou.

Charrat also formed her own company, which was initially given her name in 1951; it was later called Ballets de France. One of her most lauded works was *Les Algues* (1953), a disturbing ballet danced to a *musique concrète* score. As though to comment ironically on the ballet *Giselle*, it depicted a young man who pretends to be mad in order to join his beloved in a lunatic asylum.

Babilée, Pierre Lacotte, and Maurice Béjart also founded companies in the 1950s as showcases for their choreography. Béjart's Ballets de l'Étoile, founded with Jean Laurent in 1953, presented his first important work, *Symphonie pour un Homme Seul* (1955). Its theme of the

FRANCE: Ballet since 1914. Roland Petit's *Le Loup* (1953), a production of Les Ballets de Paris de Roland Petit, with Violette Verdy as the Fiancée and the choreographer himself as the Wolf. (Photograph from the Dance Collection, New York Public Library for the Performing Arts.)

vicissitudes of modern man pointed the way for many of his future works. In 1957 the company was renamed Ballet-Théâtre de Paris. It was later absorbed by the Ballet du XXᵉ Siècle, the Brussels-based company that Béjart headed from 1960 to 1987. Lacotte directed the Ballet de la Tour Eiffel and, in the 1960s, the Ballet National Jeunesses Musicales de France. Although both of these companies toured widely, Lacotte gained his greatest fame only in the 1970s, when he began to reconstruct historical ballets such as *La Sylphide* for the Paris Opera Ballet and other companies. Babilée's company, which bore his name, was established in 1956 and made several foreign tours, displaying his gifts both as a choreographer and a dancer.

Milorad Miskovitch and Irène Lidova were the artistic directors of the Ballet des Étoiles de Paris, which originated as Les Ballets 1956 and changed its name yearly until 1961. Oriented toward soloists, it presented Veronika Mlakar, Ethery Pagava, Irène Skorik, Milko Sparemblek, Miskovitch, and others in a repertory of works by Charrat, Béjart, Lifar, Skibine, and John Taras.

Beginning in the 1960s, an increasing number of ballet companies were founded outside Paris. The choreographer Joseph Lazzini was responsible for fostering much dance activity in Marseille. He also contributed to the repertory of Ballet-Théâtre Contemporain, which was formed in 1968 in Amiens and moved to Angers in 1972. Under the direction of Françoise Adret and Jean-Albert Cartier, it was responsible for the creation of a remarkable repertory of contemporary works before it was disbanded in 1978. [*See* Ballet-Théâtre Contemporain.]

Other notable companies established outside Paris include the Ballet du Nord, the Ballet du Rhin, and Ballet-Théâtre de Nancy. The Ballet du Nord, established in Lille but now based in nearby Roubaix, is directed by Jean-Paul Comelin, a former dancer with the Paris Opera Ballet, London Festival Ballet, and several companies in the United States. Jean Babilée was the first director of the Ballet du Rhin, founded in 1972 in Strasbourg. Now directed by Jean-Paul Gravier, this company of forty dancers performs regularly in Strasbourg and in the neighboring towns of Mulhouse and Colmar.

The Ballet-Théâtre Français de Nancy was formed in 1978 with Jean-Albert Cartier as artistic adviser and Hélène Trailine as ballet mistress. It stated as its goal the performance of all the major twentieth-century dance works, from Serge Diaghilev's era to the present. It embarked on this project in January 1979 with the performance of John Taras's *Designs with Strings*, George Balanchine's *La Sonnambula*, and Janine Charrat's *Concerto de Grieg* and *Jeu de Cartes*. Later revivals included John Cranko's *L'Estro Armonico;* Léonide Massine's *La Boutique Fantasque*, with Lorca Massine dancing the role created by his father; Serge Lifar's *Aubade;* and Bronislava

Nijinska's *Les Biches*. In 1982, the company staged an Homage to Diaghilev with guest artists Dominique Khalfouni, Eva Evdokimova, and Rudolf Nureyev appearing in Vaslav Nijinsky's *L'Après-midi d'un Faune* and Michel Fokine's *Petrouchka* and *Le Spectre de la Rose*. The 1983 season at the Théâtre du Châtelet in Paris included Birgit Cullberg's *Miss Julie*, with Nureyev and Evdokimova. In 1988, Patrick Dupond, a *danseur étoile* at the Paris Opera, was named to replace Cartier and Trailine. He stayed until December 1990, when he became Nureyev's successor as director of the Paris Opera Ballet. The current artistic adviser of the company, now called the Ballet National de Nancy et de Lorraine, is Pierre Lacotte, who has begun to diversify the company's repertory.

Cartier and Trailine are now, respectively, general director and artistic director of the Ballet de Nice, a company of thirty dancers. The Ballet National de Marseille, the largest company in the south of France, has been directed since 1972 by Roland Petit, who has created more than forty new works for it. A prolific choreographer, Petit's creations in Marseille range from *Pink Floyd Ballet* (1972) to original versions of classics such as *Coppélia* (1975) and *The Nutcracker* (1976) to *Tout Satie* (1988) and *Les Valses de Ravel* (1989). Interesting work is now also being done by Ballet-Théâtre de Bordeaux, a company of thirty-six dancers under the direction of Eric Vu-An.

In addition to the activities of established companies, ballet is also encouraged in France by the numerous dance festivals held there, which play host to both French and foreign companies. The Festival International de Danse, for instance, has been held annually in Paris since 1963. Aspiring choreographers may find a stage at the choreographic competitions called Ballet pour Demain, which has been held yearly since 1969 in Bagnolet. France also has its own version of the popular ballet competition, the first of which took place in Paris in 1984.

[*See also* Paris Opera Ballet *and the entries on the principal figures mentioned herein.*]

BIBLIOGRAPHY

Biennale internationale de la danse. Lyon, 1984.
Bourcier, Paul. *Histoire de la danse en Occident.* Paris, 1978.
Brunel, Lise. *Nouvelle danse française.* Paris, 1980.
Cirillo, Silvana, ed. *Corpo, teatro, danza: Béjart, Blaska, Petit.* Brescia, 1981.
Divoire, Fernand. *Découvertes sur la danse.* Paris, 1924.
Divoire, Fernand. *Pour la danse.* Paris, 1935.
Dorris, George. "Diaghilev and de Maré in Paris." *Dance Chronicle* 15.1 (1992): 106–113.
"Dossier spécial Marseilles." *Pour la danse* (April 1979): 16–32.
Encyclopédie du théâtre contemporain, 1917–1950. Paris, 1959.
Exposition du cinquantenaire du Théâtre des Champs-Elysées au théâtre et au Musée Bourdelle, Paris: 1er avril et 29 mars 1913–1963. Paris, 1963.
Foster, Susan Leigh. *Choreography and Narrative.* Bloomington, 1996.
Garafola, Lynn. *Diaghilev's Ballets Russes.* New York and Oxford, 1989.
García-Márquez, Vicente. *The Ballets Russes: Colonel de Basil's Ballets Russes de Monte Carlo, 1932–1952.* New York, 1990.
Koenig, John Franklin. *La danse contemporaine.* Paris, 1980.
Levinson, André. *La danse d'aujourd'hui.* Paris, 1929.
Lidova, Irène. *Ma vie avec la danse.* Paris, 1992.
Lobet, Marcel. *Le ballet français d'aujourd'hui de Lifar à Béjart.* Brussels, 1958.
Michaut, Pierre. *Le ballet contemporain, 1929–1950.* Paris, 1950.
Michaut, Pierre. "Ballet in France in 1951–1952." *Dance News Annual* (1953): 188–200.
Reyna, Ferdinando. *Histoire de la danse.* 2d ed. Paris, 1984.
Pritchard, Jane. "André Derain in Paris." *The Dancing Times* (February 1995): 479–487.
Scheuer, L. Franc. "Les Ballets de la Jeunesse." *The Dancing Times* (February 1938): 160–162.
Shaïkevitch, André. *Serge Lifar et le destin de ballet de l'Opéra.* Paris, 1971.
Thuilleux, Jacqueline. *Les années Dupond du Ballet français de Nancy.* Nancy, 1990.
Tugal, Pierre. "Ballet in Paris, 1946–1947." *Ballet Annual* 2 (1948): 80–89.

MONIQUE BABSKY
Translated from French

Modern Dance before 1970

Since the turn of the twentieth century, when modern dance began to emerge in other countries, France lagged behind, perhaps a penalty for being the birthplace of classical ballet. The pioneers of modern dance had to fight harder and for a longer period in France than elsewhere against the prevailing belief that dance could only be a pretty, harmonious, innocuous entertainment for the upper classes.

The first stirrings of the new dance were much the same as in other European countries and subject to the same influences—Loie Fuller, Isadora Duncan, Michel Fokine, and other pioneers. Since the early nineteenth century, however, France has had a truly indigenous art form, the traditional mime theater. From Gaspard Debureau, the creator of Pierrot, to the great teacher Étienne Decroux and Marcel Marceau, this genre shared with the new dance a concern for expressing the condition of humanity through movement.

Between the two world wars the strongest influences were Rudolf Laban, Mary Wigman, Duncan, Émile Jaques-Dalcroze, and Orientalist dance. Modern dance provoked the interest of poets and writers rather than that of musicians and painters, who were more involved with ballet. A few farsighted men of the theater—such as Jacques Copeau, who produced experimental work at the Vieux-Colombier—played a considerable part in fostering free or expressive dance. It could be said that in the 1920s and 1930s there was an École de Paris of dance similar to that of painting, including immigrant artists, and little known except to an elite. Among these artists were Lisa Duncan, one of Isadora's adopted daughters; George

Pomiès, the first French male dancer to express contemporary themes; and Renée Odic Kintzel, also a musician and writer, who advocated the classical Greek concept of physical and spiritual harmony. There were also political exiles who sought shelter in France in the 1930s, who had major influence on the subsequent development of French modern dance; they included Dussia Bereska (Laban's former assistant), Jean Weidt, Heinz Finkel, Ludolf Schild, Doryta Brown, Julia Marcus, and Mila Cirul, a former member of Wigman's company and a romantic, flamboyant dancer who taught until a great age.

In 1931, the Archives Internationales de la Danse, recently founded by Rolf de Maré, became a home and showcase for modern dance. Over the years it sponsored international activities that promoted new dance and recognized outstanding achievements; at its initial competition in Paris in 1932, Kurt Jooss won the first prize for *The Green Table*. Internationalism long characterized French modern dance: at the Archives Internationales de la Danse competition in Copenhagen in 1947, the first prize went to Ballet des Arts, a French company directed by the German dancer Jean Weidt, who created *La Cellule*, with Françoise Dupuy in the leading role. In 1958, at the first festival and competition for modern dance in France, Les Ballets Modernes de Paris of Dominique and Françoise Dupuy won the first prize for *Épithalame*, a rapturous work danced in silence, which was created by Englishman Deryk Mendel.

From the 1920s there existed a typically French dance genre that the general public considered synonymous with modern dance—the *danse rythmique*, of the "health-and-beauty" school of thought, promulgated especially by Irène Popard. Today jazz dance perhaps fulfills this niche. In most cases this was an offshoot of gymnastics, with a whiff of Duncan and a dash of Dalcroze; it was somewhat stilted and affected. It became very popular as a form of movement training for children and nonprofessionals and as an alternative to ballet.

Dancers whose influence brought a fresh image of dance to a wide public were Marguerite Bougai, Jean Serry, and Janine Solane. They all had an orthodox classical background and worked out individual aesthetic codes and teaching methods which, though rooted in ballet technique, put the accent on personal expression.

This was the era of the solo recital. There were practically no professional modern dance companies. Other factors beyond the obvious economic ones may explain this lack. Perhaps no individual was powerful enough to gather others about him or her, or possibly the dancers were hampered by a fierce sense of individualism and a native difficulty in achieving team spirit. It is true that at this time in France there seems to have been no innovator of international stature.

By 1946 a new generation of French dancers were rising who shared much the same background as those already in the field. During this postwar period there was an understandably widespread move to promote national identity and art for the people. Groups such as Travail et Culture undertook to bring theater to an untapped public, incidentally rehabilitating folk music and dance. But there were still difficult years for modern dance, which was considered wildly avant-garde and suffered damning reviews from the critics. Fruitful work was done by Jean Dorcy's Danse et Culture group, which presented young dancers and choreographers in lecture-demonstrations and performances all around the country. A few years later a similar project, the Théâtre d'Essai de la Danse, was introduced under the aegis of the discerning dance critic Dinah Maggie.

By the 1950s splendid pioneering work had been done by Françoise and Dominique Dupuy, who with their company, Les Ballets Modernes de Paris, had won the first prize for their *Epithalame* at the first festival and competition for modern dance in France in 1958.

Three foreign-born dancers with Wigman backgrounds settled in Paris in the 1950s and made their marks as teachers as well: Jerome Andrews from the United States, Jacqueline Robinson from England, and Karin Waehner from Germany. They co-founded one of the first professional modern dance companies in France, Les Compagnons de la Danse. Later, Jerome Andrews founded his own company, La Compagnie Jerome Andrews and rapidly became a leading figure in the French modern dance world, a compelling, passionate dancer and choreographer. In 1958 Waehner formed her own group, les Ballets Contemporains, which performed until 1986. A performer of tremendous vitality, as a choreographer she had explored many avenues (having studied with Louis Horst, Martha Graham, José Limón, and Merce Cunningham), but in the early 1980s, she returned to the profound humanity of the Wigman heritage.

Robinson, even more faithful to the Wigman heritage, and whose choreography is remarkable for its expressive directness, musical purity and clarity of style, founded in 1955, long before modern dance became appreciated in France, L'Atelier de la Danse, a performing space and meeting ground for modern dancers.

Other noteworthy dancers of the time include the Russian-born Olga Stens, whose elegant style combined a classical and Wigman background and whose specialty was character dancing; and independent, Swiss-born Anne Gardon, also with a Wigman background, a remarkable dancer with a lyrical, dramatic highly personal style. Raymonde Lombardin, who also had an eclectic background, worked for the theater and danced with Paul d'Arnot, a Uruguayan dancer trained by Clotilde and Alexandre

Sakharoff in a repertory that ranged from folk to expressionist dances. Madeleine Lytton, a pupil of Lisa Duncan and guardian of that heritage, also worked for the theater and for the cinema, and did research on early dance genres.

The 1960s witnessed the growth of public interest as the number of dancers and companies rose, along with artistic standards. A definite influence was that of Maurice Béjart, whose spectacular neoclassical works awakened in France a vast public that had hitherto been unaware of the power of dance. A mutual exchange began around 1970, when many French dancers went to study in the United States and American dancers came to perform and teach in France at international festivals, cultural centers, and numerous theaters. Martha Graham initially exerted the strongest influence, although the Humphrey-Limón technique was also imported. Later Alwin Nikolais's influence could be traced, first through Susan Buirge and then through Carolyn Carlson, who both settled in France; and then, very definitely, that of Merce Cunningham.

BIBLIOGRAPHY

Baril, Jacques. *La danse moderne (d'Isadora Duncan à Twyla Tharp)*. Paris, 1977.

Bereska, Dussia. "Méthode Rudolf von Laban." *Archives internationales de la danse* 3 (November 1935): 18–19.

Brunel, Lise. *Nouvelle danse française*. Paris, 1980.

Caen, Édouard, et al. *Danser c'est vivre: Georges Pomiès*. Paris, 1939.

Cirul, Mila. "La formation de la personnalité." *Archives internationales de la danse* 3 (November 1935): 20–21.

Copeau, Jacques, et al. *Les registres du Vieux Columbier*. 2 vols. Edited by Marie-Hélène Dasté and Suzanne Maistre Saint-Denis. Paris, 1979–1984.

Divoire, Fernand. *Découvertes sur la danse*. Paris, 1924.

Divoire, Fernand. *Pour la danse*. Paris, 1935.

Empreintes: Écrits sur la danse. Paris, 1977–.

Frank, Waldo. *The Art of the Vieux Colombier*. New York, 1918.

Gradinger, Malve. "'You Are Your Own Sculptor': Interview with Karin Wähner." *Ballett International* 9 (April 1986): 31–35.

Hommage à Olga Stens. Paris, 1980.

Imbert, Charles. "Soirées de Paris (Lombardin et Béjart)." *La danse* (March 1956): 8–10.

Mila Cirul/Hedy Pfundmayr. Vienna, 1922.

Robinson, Jacqueline. *L'aventure de la danse moderne en France, 1920–1970*. Paris, 1990.

Robinson, Jacqueline. "Hommage à Marguerite Bougai." *Saisons de la danse*, no. 260 (September 1994): 38.

Tugal, Pierre. "Ballet in Paris, 1946–1947." *Ballet Annual* 2 (1948): 80–89.

JACQUELINE ROBINSON

Modern Dance since 1970

Modern dance in France, which had previously been influenced by expressionism in modern dance in Germany, changed its focus in the 1970s with the implantation of a modern-dance company, the Groupe de Recherches Théâtrales de l'Opéra de Paris (GRTOP), at the heart of the

FRANCE: Modern Dance since 1970. Michèle Prélonge in Régine Chopinot's *Délices*, at the Festival de Châteauvallon in 1983. Based on love stories by Hervé Guaville, and a film by Picq and Palacio, Chopinot's choreography depicts a group of tense, solitary women searching for love. (Photograph by Jean-Luc Dugied; used by permission.)

Paris Opera. The appointment of Carolyn Carlson as the group's *étoile chorégraphe* turned the attention of the French to the United States and to progressive trends in modern dance choreography. In addition, a number of American modern dance troupes were invited to perform at the Festival International de Danse in Paris, the Autumn and Summer Festivals, the Maisons de la Culture (cultural centers), and the Théâtre de la Ville (Paris). French companies such as Ballet-Théâtre Contemporain and the Théâtre du Silence included works by American choreographers in their repertories. A few American dancers, such as Susan Buirge, settled in Paris and started their own schools.

Influenced by Alwin Nikolais, Merce Cunningham, and postmodern dance, abstraction took a leap forward. The summer workshops at Villeneuve-lès-Avignon and the

FRANCE: Modern Dance since 1970. One of Maguy Marin's most notable works, *May B* depicts characters from the plays of Samuel Beckett in a grotesque and absurd world. *May B* is here performed by dancers of the Ballet-Théâtre de l'Arche, at the Théâtre de la Ville, Tours, in 1984. (Photograph by Jean-Luc Dugied; used by permission.)

Centre National de Danse Contemporaine (CNDC) in Angers (directed by Nikolais from 1978 to 1981 and by Viola Farber from 1981 to 1983) were put in the hands of American choreographers. They trained an entire generation of dancers who were encouraged to choreograph by Ballet pour Demain, a competition held in Bagnolet. The government also set up a system of subsidies to promote the opening of a Maison de la Danse.

A new type of French dance was born that gradually detached itself from its American models. By 1984 more than one hundred new groups had sprung up, many of which discovered their own styles in a subtle web of cultural and sociological influences. These groups can be characterized by their diversity and their return to the notion of spectacle, a more rigorous approach to technique, and an increasing concern with professionalism. Marked by the violence and lack of meaning in the contemporary world, dance themes varied from one choreographer to another, and sometimes from one work to another, depending upon the work's motivations. Major influences include the theatricality of Pina Bausch, the cinema of Wim Wenders, the music of Nina Hagen or the Talking Heads, literature ranging from Marguerite Duras to cartoons, and contemporary painting.

Extremely mobile, French dance in the 1980s expanded in every direction. The choreographers mentioned below are among the most representative examples of the decade. Many produced their works in the United States.

After training at the Beaux-Arts school in Grenoble and the Cunningham studio in New York, Jean-Claude Gallotta, winner of the Ballet pour Demain award in 1980, established the Groupe Émile Dubois in Grenoble with the help of the city and national governments. In his early works *(Pas de Quatre, Waslav Désirs,* and *Ulysse 1),* the abstract quality of the movement revealed the influence of American choreographers such as Cunningham, Lucinda Childs, and Yvonne Rainer. Gradually, however, Gallotta's work began to demonstrate greater sensitivity to human qualities. Beginning with *Yves P.,* his choreography grew richer in connotations that intertwined literature and cinema. *Ulysse 84,* which was presented in the United States, seductively embellished a postmodern structure with theatrical human motifs that bordered on the comic. *Les Aventures d'Ivan Vaffan,* a grand epic fresco, turned

FRANCE: Modern Dance since 1970. Jean-Claude Gallotta's *Les Aventures d'Ivan Vaffan,* performed at the Lyon Biennale in 1984. An imaginary character created by Gallotta, Ivan Vaffan lives in a tribe whose movement combines ancestral gestures and contemporary speed. The dancers are Deborah Salmirs, Eric Alfieri, Pascal Gravat, Robert Seyfried, Lucie Moormann, and Corine Métral. (Photograph by Jean-Luc Dugied; used by permission.)

straightforwardly to farce, with sexual images charged with eroticism.

Other choreographers, such as Cremona and Michel Hallet-Eghayan in Lyon and Jean Pomarès in Paris, worked in an abstract style based on pure movement. In the work of Dominique Bagouet of Montpellier and Quentin Rouillier of Caen, formal values and a sense of theater seemed to be balanced. However, while Bagouet, who was largely inspired by music, underlined the personalities of his characters *(F. et Stein, Insaisies)*, Rouillier engaged in an alchemy of the universal *(Saisons)*.

French dance soon returned, if not to storytelling, at least to theatricality. Caroline Marcade found her place somewhere between the search for identity *(Pierre Robert)* and the naive tale. In *Deuxième Légende* (1984), which marked her arrival in Le Havre, she worked in close collaboration with the scenery and music, emphasizing the visual and dreamlike aspect of the dance.

Maguy Marín has been absorbed by the social nature of human beings. Fascinated by crowds and the average individual, she captures them in their environment, carrying her portraits to the point of caricature. She uses her dancers' own personalities as a starting point, drawing from their characters the visceral images that appear in her works. The exiles of *Babel-Babel* parade in darkness; Samuel Beckett's common people move through *May B* with rhythmical small steps; dead chickens are thrown on the ground in *La Jeune Fille et la Mort* before a mute and stupid family lined up on chairs. Marín received her first choreographic award for *Nieblas de Niño* in 1978 in Bagnolet. For Marín, the shock of the image and the rhythm of the movements count more than the movements themselves or their technique. Her work displayed a new realism in the French style, which no longer had anything in common with either ballet or modern dance.

Régine Chopinot's themes synthesized contemporary energy and lunacy with violent, fragmented movement that emphasizes the individuality of the interpreters. Each work has its own identity, created by the specific artistic team assembled as collaborators: dancers, actors, musicians, costume designers, photographers or video artists, and writers. *Via* (1984) centers on pure dance, and the extravagant costumes of J. P. Gaultier's *Délices* (1983) brings together a cinematic and photographic decor, a literary theme with mythical references to the couple, and the superimposition of many levels of meaning. Between the absurd, the erotic, the decadent, and the intellectual, Chopinot affirmed a torn and ironic personality that carries movement to a high technical level, even while she created relaxation and breathing spaces.

In 1972 Hideyuki Yano brought from his native Japan new relationships between dance and the body. The work of François Verret and the Compagnie de l'Ésquisse (led by Regis Obadia and Joëlle Bouvier) comes in part from

FRANCE: Modern Dance since 1970. The choreography of Fred Bendongué integrates elements of *capoeira*, traditional African music and dance, with modern and ballet idioms. He is seen here (left) with members of his Compagnie Azanie, Myrian Wandji and Harry Albert, in his work *À la Vue d'un Seul Oeil* (Seen with One Eye), at the Majestic Theater, Brooklyn Academy of Music, New York, 1996. (Photograph © 1996 by Jack Vartoogian; used by permission.)

Yano, although these choreographers moved toward a new type of expression deriving from contact improvisation. While Verret emphasized theatricality through the interplay of decor, actors, and music (Tazartès), Obadia and Bouvier concentrated on movement. Approaching Buto in their exploration of the dark regions of the human soul, their choreography addresses the physical expression of emotions. Works such as *Terre Battue, Noces d'Argile* (1981), and *Vertée* (1984) utilized primitive gestures, violent collisions between dancers, and brutal falls to the floor.

Marie-Christine Gheorghiu, a rock-music fan (*Pôle à Pôle*, 1983), and Karine Saporta also displayed affinities with this current of violence. The acrobatic virtuosity of Saporta's *Hypnotic Circus*, a piece for three dancers bouncing on a mattress, was remarked on at the American Dance Festival in Durham, North Carolina, in 1983. Daniel Larrieu intelligently combined everyday movements with absurd situations. Resembling the postmoderns in their choreographic process, his *Un Sucre ou Deux?* (1983) and *La Peau et les Os* (1984) worked on the details of movement with finesse. Josette Baiz treated children like responsible adults and turned them into authentic performers capable of dancing with adults. More successful than *Cheval d'Argile*, which was based on the German dramatist Heinrich von Kleist, her *Barbe-Bleue*, in punk style, displayed the children's astonishing possibilities. In *Prudence* (1984) she plunged into an erotic and ambiguous world borrowed from the Marquis de Sade.

While older companies such as Rivoire, Gerard, Wood, Witzman, Ramseyer, Four Solaire, Martinez, Atlani, Buirge, Wäehner, Dupuy, and others should not be forgotten, many new companies are worthy of notice: Patarozzi, Ecchymose, Lolita, Diasnas, Beau Geste (an offshoot of the CNDC), and Matos, who works with computers and video. In the 1990s, a new generation of choreographers is bringing something new and more elaborate to French dance audiences. Some of them are in residence with the help of government, as are Preljocaj in Aix-en-Provence, Duboc in Belfort, Monnier in Montpellier (after the death of Bagouet), Diverres in Rennes, Robbe in Brest, and Raffinot in Le Hâvre. More independent, the younger choreographers try to create a new language, to express with dance the absurdity or the violence of society.

BIBLIOGRAPHY

Adolphe, Jean-Marc. "New Dance in France." *Ballett International* 11 (August–September 1988): 22–28.

Adolphe, Jean-Marc. "The Source and the Destiny." *Tanz International* 2 (January 1991): 22–29.

Adolphe, Jean-Marc. "La nouvelle danse française" (in English). In *The Dance Has Many Faces*, edited by Walter Sorell. 3d ed. Pennington, N.J., 1992.

Adolphe, Jean-Marc. "A Dance of Disaster." *Ballett International/Tanz Aktuell* (January 1994): 10–13.

Baillon, Jacques, et al. *Régine Chopinot/Rosella Hightower.* Paris, 1990.

Béchaz, André. "Les trois coups de l'ennui." *Saisons de la danse*, no. 241 (December 1992): 22–23.

Biennale internationale de la danse. Lyon, 1986.

Bonis, Bernadette. "French Choreographers Creating New Worlds." *Ballett International* 12 (November 1989): 28–31.

Bourcier, Paul. "L'école germanique et sa lignée américaine." In Bourcier's *Histoire de la danse en Occident.* Paris, 1978.

Bourgade, Yves. "Fifty Years of Opera Ballet and Its Audiences." *Choreography and Dance* 2.1 (1992): 29–34.

Bozzini, Annie. "They Film as They Dance." *Tanz International* 2 (January 1991): 36–41.

Brunel, Lise. *Nouvelle danse française: Dix ans de chorégraphie, 1970–1980.* Paris, 1980.

Brunel, Lise. "Les entre-deux de Susan." *Saisons de la danse*, no. 261 (October 1994): 15–16.

Christout, Marie-Françoise. "Americans in Paris." *Dance and Dancers* (January 1978): 34–35.

Choplin, Antoine, and Patricia Kuypers. *Ellipses: Regards sur 10 chorégraphes contemporains.* Lille, 1993.

Cixous, Hélène, et al. *Karine Saporta, Peter Greenaway.* Paris, 1990.

Compagnie L'Ésquisse: Joëlle Bouvier, Régis Obadia. Paris, 1986.

Dance in France: Choreographers and Companies. Paris, 1988.

Diénis, Jean-Claude. "Pleins-feux: Invitations à la danse." *Danser* (October 1993): 34–41.

L'Ésquisse: Joëlle Bouvier, Régis Obadia. Paris, 1991.

France '85 dans/theater. Brussels, 1985.

Gallotta, Jean-Claude. "Introducing Gallotta." *Dance and Dancers* (September 1989): 14–15.

Goater, Delphine. "Régine Chopinot: Au loin, l'Atlantique." *Saisons de la danse*, no. 243 (February 1993): 39–40.

Gradinger, Malve. "Surface Values." *Ballett International* 9 (February 1986): 20–25.

Hardy, Camille. "Compagnie Maguy Marín." *Dance Magazine* (December 1995): 119–121.

Hersin, André-Philippe. "Maguy Marín." *Saisons de la danse*, no. 254 (February 1994): 8–10.

Izrine, Agnes. "Régine Chopinot: À 33 ans elle découvrait la mer." *Danser* (April 1986): 34–37.

Jordan, Stephanie. "A Taste of Paris." *Dance and Dancers* (July 1989): 21–24.

Kaplan, Peggy Jarrell. *Portraits of Choreographers.* New York, 1988.

Koenig, John Franklin. *La danse contemporaine.* Paris, 1980.

Lescault, Gilbert. *Daniel Larrieu.* Paris, 1989.

Louppe, Laurence, et al. *Jean-Claude Gallotta: Groupe Émile Dubois.* Paris, 1988.

Louppe, Laurence. "The Origins and Development of Contemporary Dance in France." *Dance Theatre Journal* 7 (Summer 1989): 2–9.

Manning, Emma. "The French New Wave." *Dance Australia* (October–November 1995): 44–48.

Michel, Marcelle. "Carolyn Carlson, ou l'espace-rêve." *Danser* (July–September 1983): 16–19.

Michel, Marcelle. *La danse au XXeme siècle.* Paris, 1995.

Passet, Dominique. "Karine Saporta." *Danser* (June 1986): 38–41.

Robertson, Allen. "Danse Nouvelle: The New Wave of French Modern Dance." *Ballet News* 5 (July 1983): 14–17.

Thirion, Jean-François. "Structure-conjoncture: Le danse contemporaine française interpellée." In *La danse: Art du XXe siècle.* Lausanne, 1990.

Vaccarino, Elisa. *Altre scene, altre danze: Vent'anni di balletto contemporaneo.* Turin, 1991.

Verrièle, Philippe. "Karine Saporta." *Saisons de la danse*, no. 257 (June 1994): 43–45.

LISE BRUNEL
Translated from French

Classical Dance Education

Since the sixteenth century in France, the teaching of theatrical dance has taken many forms. Initially linked with the development of the court ballet, the discipline became academic in the seventeenth century. After the golden age of classical dance in the eighteenth century, it passed through vicissitudes in the late nineteenth to renewal in the twentieth. Dance instruction contributed to the development of a recognizable French style, which though affected by various foreign influences during its evolution, continued to respect the basic principles originally defined by its dance teachers.

Italian dancing masters appear to have played an important role in the Valois court of the sixteenth century. Henri II and Catherine de Médicis hired Pompeo Diobono and Virgilio Bracesco to teach their children, and their daughter Marguerite de Valois was the pupil of Paul de Rège, a Frenchman. Traditionally dancing was taught by members of the minstrels' guilds, who were also violinists. The custom of playing the violin to accompany lessons continued for three centuries; by the seventeenth century the instrument had become the *pochette*, a pocket-sized fiddle, long and slender enough to be slipped into a deep pocket. Aspiring teachers had to study for six years and then pay a licensing fee to the guild. With the development of classical technique at the end of the seventeenth century, the most famous masters sought—not without difficulty—to abolish this outdated guardianship, which was stubbornly defended by Guillaume Dumanoir, the head of the guild.

The sovereigns of France set an example by engaging renowned dancing masters such as Bocan (Jacques Cordier), who taught Louis XIII and five queens (Anne of Austria, the queen of Sweden, Henrietta and Elisabeth of France, and Catherine of Brandenburg). Denys Cordier was dancing master to the king and queen in 1643, but the young Louis XIV began his studies with Françoise Prévost. There were many dancing masters in Paris and other cities during the seventeenth century; Orléans was particularly famous in this regard. Foreigners came to France for additional training, and French dancing masters were invited all over Europe, particularly in the eighteenth century. They disseminated the technique developed at the instigation of Louis XIV, who protected the purity of the French school by founding the Académie Royale de Danse in 1661. The academy's thirteen members were chosen from among the most renowned dancing masters of the time. It existed until the French Revolution in 1789, numbering among its members such illustrious artists as the Dumoulin brothers, Louis Dupré, François Marcel, Jean-Barthélemy Lany, Gaëtan Vestris, Pierre Gardel, Jean Dauberval, and Jean-Georges Noverre. In the twentieth century it was resurrected in name by Serge Lifar.

Dance technique as codified by Pierre Beauchamps was widely taught in the *collèges* (secondary schools) and in high society by dancers from the Paris Opera, such as Louis Pecour, Claude Ballon, Françoise Prévost, Michel Blondy, and especially François Marcel. Dancing was a part of any good education. Raoul-Auger Feuillet's publication of *Chorégraphie* (1700), followed by Pierre Rameau's *Le maître à danser* (1725), served to spread the French school outside Paris.

When Jean-Baptiste Lully took over the Paris Opera in 1672, Anne-Louis Lestang taught its dancers under the supervision of Beauchamps and later of Pecour. However, the shortcomings of subsequent teachers made reforms necessary. In 1713 Louis XIV decreed a new Réglement de l'Opéra, which founded the Conservatoire de Danse. Every Tuesday, Thursday, and Saturday, dancers and even singers were required to attend free lessons given by a *maître de salle*, frequently supervised by the ballet master, in an annex to the theater on the rue Saint-Nicaise. The Conservatoire's regulations gradually became stricter, and soon a preliminary physical examination was required. A new set of regulations in 1776 reinforced discipline.

When Jacques-François Deshayes died in 1797, Noverre applied for the vacant post of director. Pierre Gardel, who ultimately won the appointment, imposed rigid disci-

pline. The school admitted sixty selected pupils between the ages of six and ten, who remained there until the age of eighteen. In 1821 their teachers were Georges Maze, Romain, and Louis Milon (for mime). Beginning in 1819 Jean-François Coulon and Auguste Vestris taught a *classe de perfectionnement* for the dancers in the company. The school was successively directed by Jean-Baptiste Barrez, Maze, and Charles Petit.

Paradoxically, conditions at the school deteriorated during the triumph of the Romantic ballet in Paris. The students had to pay their teachers, who were so poorly compensated by the administration that they lost interest in teaching. Installed in quarters in the rue Richer, the Conservatoire de Danse de l'Opéra was reorganized in 1860 under the supervision of Marie Taglioni, who succeeded Louis-François Gosselin as the teacher of the *classe de perfectionnement*. Twenty-three or more students were divided among six classes: elementary, girls, boys, pantomime, *exercice de ballet*, and the *classe de perfectionnement*. By a kind of apprenticeship contract the pupil was linked exclusively with the Paris Opera for five years; the course of study lasted until the age of twelve (thirteen, starting in 1915). Only in 1919, at the instigation of Jacques Rouché, were pupils required to work for certificates of primary education at a school reserved for them.

Madame Dominique, who had taught the elementary class since 1860, succeeded Taglioni as the teacher of the *classe de perfectionnement* in 1872, and was followed in turn by Zina Mérante (*née* Richard), Madame Théodore, and Rosita Mauri. Carlotta Zambelli then reigned over the *classe de perfectionnement* until her retirement. Albert

FRANCE: Classical Dance Education. Matilda Kshessinska, one of Russia's great ballerinas, opened a studio in Paris in 1929. Here she instructs Tatiana Riabouchinska, c.1935. (Photograph from the Dance Collection, New York Public Library for the Performing Arts.)

FRANCE: Classical Dance Education. Young boys in class at the Paris Opera Ballet School, c.1971. Patrick Dupond is in the front row, at center. (Photograph by Colette Masson; used by permission of Agence Enguerand/Iliade, Paris.)

Aveline directed the school until 1950. Among his successors were Harald Lander and Geneviève Guillot.

In 1960 the school was reorganized to add further academic studies to dance instruction, permitting students to pursue their *baccalauréat* (equivalent to a U.S. high school diploma). After her appointment as director in 1972, Claude Bessy infused the school with new life. She reorganized its structure in 1976, enriching the classical course of instruction with classes in historical dance, folk dance, character dancing, jazz, mime, adagio, variations, and repertory. Teachers since 1983 have included Gilbert Mayer, Daniel Franck, Serge Golovine, Cyril Atanassoff, Liliane Garry, and Christiane Vaussard.

Separated into five divisions, thirty-six boys and forty-eight girls (95 percent are of French origin, while the remainder must have resided in France for more than five years) are rigorously selected and trained for six years. Public classes and performances provide a means of testing the students and giving them stage experience. The current high level of instruction prepares the students to become members of the Paris Opera Ballet, where company classes are often taught by the same teachers or by guest instructors such as Violette Verdy, Jean-Pierre Bonnefous, Toni Lander, and Peter Martins.

In the twentieth century, a parallel course of official dance instruction has been offered by the Conservatoire National de Musique in Paris, which has around seventy-five students. Among their teachers have been Solange Schwarz, Yves Brieux, and Christiane Vlassi. First-prize winners are engaged either by the school or by the Paris Opera company. Actually directed by Quentin Rouillier, the Conservatoire de Danse de Paris offers a course of modern and classical dance (three to five years) to thirty-six students. Martine Clarey is maître de ballet, and the senior class gives performances and tours as the Junior Ballet.

In 1980 another national conservatory was established in Lyon. There are also thirty state-supported regional conservatories in the provinces, supervised by the Dance Department of the Ministry of Culture, which hires the teachers and ensures the quality of instruction, which is free of charge. National music schools, which are administered in the same way, are also supervised by the mayoral governments, which oversee the management of the many municipal conservatories intended for nonprofessionals. These schools have shorter hours but are also subject to official control. The courses, qualifications of the teachers, and technical standards are defined by the Ministry of Culture.

The Dance Department of the City of Paris, headed in the 1980s by Claire Sombert, instituted classes in twenty *arrondissements* (sectors of Paris). The advanced classes are intended to prepare professional-level students who may then enter the new Conservatoire de Danse Marius Petipa. About two thousand students follow this course in Paris, participating in examinations and performances for which prizes are offered. Their technical instruction is generally supplemented by theoretical courses in dance history, solfeggio, theater, and musical expression.

Private instruction, almost the only manner of teaching dance in earlier centuries, has not ceased to play an important role in France. During the nineteenth century, teachers such as Auguste Vestris and Madame Dominique enjoyed an international reputation. In the twentieth century, teachers of the caliber of Léo Staats, Brieux, and Zambelli established themselves in Paris. A number of studios were also opened by Russian emigrés, among them Lubov Egorova, Olga Preobrajenska, Matilda Kshessinska, Vera Trefilova, Alexandre Volinine, Tatjana Gsovsky, Nicholas Zvereff, Boris Kniasseff, and Madame Roussane. They attracted prestigious students from all over the world, who came to absorb tradition in the decrepit but illustrious setting of the Studio Wacker (later transformed into the conservatory of dance of Paris's Ninth Arrondissement). The renewal of French dance owes a great deal to their contributions.

These teachers have been succeeded by Paul Goubé, Raymond Franchetti, Nora Kiss, Nina Tikanova, Juan Giuliano, and others who teach on a private basis. The Ministry of Culture's Directoir de la Danse established a national diploma that is now required of all future teachers. Such a requirement facilitates stricter control of the teacher's competence and insures closer attention to the laws of physiology by standardizing classes for amateurs, many of whom are adults.

BIBLIOGRAPHY

Chapman, John V. "The Paris Opéra Ballet School, 1798–1827." *Dance Chronicle* 12.2 (1989): 196–220.

Christout, Marie-Françoise. "La danse au Conservatoire de Paris." In *Le Conservatoire de Paris, 1795–1995*. Paris, 1995.

Feuillet, Raoul-Auger. *Chorégraphie, ou L'art de décrire la dance, par caractères, figures et signes démonstratifs, avec lesquels on apprend facilement de soy-même toutes sortes de dances*. Paris, 1700. Translated by John Weaver as *Orchesography, or, The Art of Dancing* (London, 1706).

Guest, Ivor. *The Ballet of the Second Empire*. London, 1974.

Rameau, Pierre. *Le maître à danser*. Paris, 1725. Translated by Cyril W. Beamont as *The Dancing Master* (London, 1931).

ARCHIVES. Direction de la Danse, Direction des Affaires Culturelles de la Ville de Paris. Ministry of Culture, Paris.

MARIE-FRANÇOISE CHRISTOUT
Translated from French

Modern Dance Education

Modern dance is taught today in France at many official or state-controlled schools, but its primary nurturing ground has always been private studios. Since 1993, however, a state diploma has been compulsory for classical, contemporary, and jazz dance teachers, and to offer the required professional training, private schools must be approved by the Ministry of Culture and must follow strict regulations and curricula. Among the state-run schools are the national and local conservatories of music and dance, which only recently have included modern dance classes.

After some attempts in the 1950s by such pioneers as Mireille Arguel to include dance in university curricula, the first university dance department in France was founded at the Sorbonne in Paris in 1981. It offered a course of specialized studies, including modern dance, and led to the equivalent of a master of fine arts degree. It ceased, however, in 1990. Most of the national physical education colleges, or Centres Régionals d'Éducation Physique et Sportive, include modern dance training as an optional subject.

The Centre National de Danse Contemporaine, the first state-subsidized modern dance school, was founded in Angers in 1978. Its first director was the American choreographer Alwin Nikolais, who was followed in 1981 by another American, Viola Farber. Today the CNDC is directed by the fine dancers and choreographers Joëlle Bouvier and Regis Obadia. The school accepts a limited number of young dancers with previous training and gives them the opportunity to work with various choreographers and perform in diverse venues.

In the early days, several individuals played an important role as teachers, whether through personal charisma or through a particular methodological approach. During the 1930s François Malkowski, a Duncan-inspired dancer, based his work on the study of natural rhythms and functional gesture, gearing his teaching more toward the layman than the professional dancer. Yvonne Berge, who had studied in Salzburg with Isadora Duncan's sister Elizabeth, founded a school that still remains a home of the Duncan spirit. Jean Serry, who left the Paris Opera where he trained, sought to breathe life into the classical vocabulary. After the war he was connected with Travail et Culture and staged pageants and choric works. Till his death in 1987 he taught his technique, *danse vivante*, a synthesis of classical and modern dance that was particularly aimed toward children.

After early training in classical ballet, Janine Solane studied with Ellen Tels, a pupil of Irma Duncan. She evolved a method called *danse classique naturelle*, which retained much of the ballet vocabulary but softened its characteristic vertical stance by introducing asymmetrical and sinuous lines. Her work reveals expressiveness and musicality, and she has trained many dancers who became innovators in their own right.

By 1946 three German dancers had brought to France a new seriousness of approach inherited from Laban, combining technical and pedagogical soundness with creative audacity. They were the choreographer Jean Weidt, founder of Ballets 38 and later Ballets des Arts; Heinz Finkel, who was also a musician; and Ludolf Schild, Weidt's student, whose studio, Salle Pleyel, was a nursery for the new generation.

In the 1950s three other dancers from abroad opened studios in Paris and became influential in modern dance teaching. Jerome Andrews, an American, brought to his teaching a wide range of experience with most of the major figures in American modern dance (Ruth St. Denis, Ted Shawn, Martha Graham, Doris Humphrey, and Hanya Holm), but he had studied most intensively with Mary Wigman. He gave his students an integrated technical training refreshingly free of aesthetic dogma and called on the deep individuality of each student—hence his own name for his work, "deep dance." German-born Karin Waehner also studied with Wigman. For the Ministry of Youth and Sport, she pioneered teaching modern dance in state colleges for physical education; She also served as a professor of dance at the renowned music academy Schola Cantorum and at the Conservatoire de la Rochelle. Jacqueline Robinson, who came from England and was also a student of Mary Wigman, founded L'Atelier de la Danse in Paris in 1955. This center not only was the first school to offer professional training in modern dance but also provided a venue for modern dance classes, performances, and seminars at a time when modern dance was little known and had few performing spaces. Robinson has also made a major contribution to teaching modern and creative dance for children. Today she specializes in teaching dance composition and the relationship of dance with music; she has also written several books on dance.

Laura Sheleen of the United States, who later specialized in dance therapy, was among the first to introduce

Graham technique, providing rigorous training. In the north of France, remarkable work was done for more than thirty years by Anne Marie Debatte, who taught a luminous style of creative dance, mostly to nonprofessionals, and her school—Danse Creation—now directed by Andrée Lamotte, is of a very high standard.

Among the more influential teachers of recent years are Françoise and Dominique Dupuy, who founded one of the most comprehensive dance schools in France, Rencontres Internationales de Danse Contemporaine. Other important private schools that offered professional training were the Centre International de la Danse in Paris, with a faculty composed mostly of guest teachers from the United States, and the École Supérieure d'Études Chorégraphiques, which included modern dance in its wide curriculum.

The younger generation includes many dancers who have established themselves as teachers as well as performers, choreographers, and company directors. Among them are Arlet Bon, Susan Buirge, Maïté Fossen, Christine Gérard, Elsa Wooliaston, and the late Hideyuki Yano. Today studios, summer schools, and short courses all over the country offer training in modern dance technique. A private organization, the Fédération Française de Danse, links schools and companies and promotes the activities in the nonprofessional area.

BIBLIOGRAPHY

Arguel, Mireille. *Danse et enseignement, quel corps?* Paris, 1980.
Arguel, Mireille. *Danse, le corps enjeu.* Paris, 1992.
Bernard, Michel. *L'expressivité du corps.* Paris, 1976.
Berge, Yvonne. *Vivre son corps.* Paris, 1975.
Brunel, Lise. *Nouvelle danse française.* Paris, 1980.
Divoire, Fernand. *Découvertes sur la danse.* Paris, 1924.
Divoire, Fernand. *Pour la danse.* Paris, 1935.
Empreintes: Écrits sur la danse. Paris, 1977–.
Hersin, André-Philippe. "L'animation chorégraphique en milieu scolaire." *Saisons de la danse,* no. 210 (February 1990): 9–12.
Pinok & Matho. *Expression corporelle-mouvement et pensée.* Paris, 1976.
Robinson, Jacqueline. *Éléments du langage chorégraphique.* Paris, 1981.
Robinson, Jacqueline. *Danse chemin d'éducation.* Paris, 1993.
Robinson, Jacqueline. *L'enfant et la danse.* 2d ed. Arques, 1993.
Romanelli, Ermanno. "Alwin Nikolais e Dominique Dupuy." *Danza & danza,* no. 38 (November 1989): 4.
Solane, Janine. *Pour une danse plus humaine.* Paris, 1950.
Serry, Jean. *Par le mouvement.* Friburg, 1970.
Waehner, Karin. *Outillage chorégraphique.* Paris, 1993.

JACQUELINE ROBINSON

Dance Research and Publication

The first French works of dance scholarship date back to the sixteenth century; a notable early work is Thoinot Arbeau's *Orchésographie* (1588). The seventeenth century brought studies of greater depth, such as François de Lauze's *Apologie de la danse* (1623), based on the treatises of classical antiquity. In 1641 Monsieur de Saint-Hubert published a brief treatise on how to compose successful ballets, *La manière de composer et faire réussir les ballets.* Père Marin Mersenne devoted several chapters of his *Harmonie universelle* (1636) to dance theory. The Abbé d'Aubignac wrote *La pratique du théâtre* (1647), which dealt with another aspect of dance; his thoughts were useful to many organizers of ballets and *comédie-ballets.* The Abbé Michel de Pure devoted one-third of his *Idées des spectacles anciens et nouveaux* (1668) to ballet. Later, Père Claude-François Ménéstrier, himself a composer of ballets, wrote two seminal works: *Des représentations en musique anciennes et modernes* (1681) and *Des ballets anciens et modernes* (1682).

A number of eighteenth-century works on aesthetics contained extensive discussions of ballet; among them were the Abbé Jean-Baptiste Du Bos's *Réflexions critiques* (1719) and Charles Batteux's *Les beaux-arts* (1746). Michel de Marolles dedicated a chapter of his 1755 *Mémoires* to the principal ballets of the reign of Louis XIII. Substantial works on dance history were also written during the eighteenth century, such as Louis de Cahusac's *La danse ancienne et moderne* (1754), which promoted dramatic dance well before Jean-Georges Noverre's more famous *Lettres sur la danse et les ballets* (1760). Later, the theme was extended in François l'Aulmaye's *De la saltation théâtrale* (1790), which dealt with the pantomimes of ancient Rome.

More popular works appeared in the nineteenth than in the eighteenth century. *La danse et les ballets* (1832) by Castil-Blaze described leading performers of the time, and Auguste Baron's *Lettres à Sophie* (1825) recounted imaginary conversations between a dancer and her fans. The brilliantly perceptive reviews of Théophile Gautier were written between 1836 and 1870.

The twentieth century brought important publications in both history and aesthetics. Henry Prunières stressed the role of music in dance in his *Le ballet de cour en France* (1914); Marie-Françoise Christout's *Le ballet de cour de Louis XIV* (1967) dealt chiefly with *mise-en-scène.* The reviews of André Levinson in the 1920s and 1930s praised the beauty and precision of classical ballet. Important contributions to dance aesthetics were made by Paul Valéry, especially in "L'âme et la danse" (1925), and by Raymond Bayer in *L'esthétique de la grâce* (1933).

Few French publishers have taken a special interest in dance. Although a few autobiographies have appeared, dance books have consisted largely of photographic collections with a preface or commentary, or reprints of rare early works. Dance writing has appeared mostly in musicological or theatrical contexts. For example, the firm of Albin-Michel published a number of issues of *Ballet/Danse,* dealing with contemporary artists and ballets, as part of the Avant Scène series.

The scholarly journal *La recherche en danse* began publication in 1982 with Jean-Claude Serre as editor. Contributions have ranged from discussions of ballet technique to analysis of folk dance genres and perspectives on contemporary performance styles. Many of the articles have originated in papers delivered at colloquia organized by Serre at the Sorbonne.

Long the province of a few specialists, dance scholarship presently interests an increasing number of students and researchers. However, because the methods are so diverse and the results so disparate, it is difficult to tell precisely how many of these efforts will prove to be significant.

The creation of a *baccalauréat* degree (secondary school diploma) with a dance option has contributed to directing more students toward the study of dance as a whole. The new degree requires more extensive and more precise knowledge of theory and history than was demanded previously. After receiving this degree, young dancers can pursue research at a university while practicing their art and developing their creative skills in choreography. At the Sorbonne in Paris, students can obtain a university diploma of the first degree (equivalent to a U.S. bachelor's degree) after passing an examination in a major subject area. The university diploma of the second degree (similar to a master's degree) is awarded to those who have completed a dissertation. For example, Carole Trévoux, a dancer with the Ballet du XXᵉ Siècle, studied the creative process in Maurice Béjart's work *Dionysios*, in which she also performed.

Dance researchers, often coming from diverse disciplines—history, aesthetics, musicology, sociology—devote their doctoral theses (for the diploma of the third degree) to dance. Thesis work may be as highly developed as Françoise Reiss's work on Nijinsky or Nathalie Lecomte's on orientalism in the ballet of the seventeenth and eighteenth centuries. A work submitted as a doctoral thesis must be previously unpublished and prepared under the guidance of a professor who holds a doctorate.

MARIE-FRANÇOISE CHRISTOUT
Translated from French

Contemporary Criticism

The appearance of a regular, independent chronicle of dance events in the daily or weekly French press was a phenomenon of the 1970s. Previously it was strictly linked to the music section. The dance critic does not yet occupy as important a place in France as in America, and a single dance critic is the rule for a daily, weekly, or monthly publication. Only the two specialized reviews, *Les saisons de la danse* and *Danser*, have several critics.

As temporary collaborators for most journals, dance critics for the daily press in France find themselves practically limited to two or three articles per week. This always tacit, informal agreement limits the impact that dance could have on the public at large. It is clear that the press has a role to play in the development of theatrical dance, a role it cannot, under these conditions, completely fulfill. Thus, not all events are covered and small companies are often abandoned in favor of large ones, the avant-garde in favor of the institution. The Parisian premiere of Maurice Béjart or of the Opera or of a new work at the Théâtre de la Ville is not discussed. A festival of contemporary dance in Toulouse, Lille, or Rennes, or in Paris in a little theater or in the suburbs may pass in silence. It is here of course that the personality of the critic and his relationship with the publication's editor-in-chief becomes a factor. The quantity of choice is often set by what is expedient at the time and depends on the space left free by film or literary events on the cultural pages, which are themselves dependent on the pages devoted to politics and society.

Le monde, Le Figaro, and *Le parisien* guarantee regular reports in the form of rather brief critical reviews, concerned with contemporary creations as well as with the ballet. *L'express* or *Le quotidien* favor the prestigious companies above all and the ballets of the highest quality. *Le nouvel observateur* and *L'evènement du jeudi* treat essentially contemporary work and savor the occasion to support contemporary dance, though it has to meet quite a high standard. *Libération* publishes the longest articles and chooses its subjects from among contemporary works. Often they prefer to support young dance companies rather than flatter the fashionable choreographers. Stopped in 1988, *Le matin de Paris* attended closely to present interests, with a preference for contemporary work, new dance, and the avant-garde.

Les saisons de la danse observes ballet with as much interest as modern dance and keeps an open mind in investigating the avant-garde. *Danser* offers general articles, notes, reports, and interviews, generally on quite eclectic subjects, rather than critical reviews.

Attacking or defending the productions that he or she sees, the French critic gives proof of his solicitude, preferring value judgments to analysis of content or to the process of the work's construction. Technical perfection, as well as aesthetic emotion, is much prized in France: theatricality outweighs abstraction, and the familiar has limited success.

Although it would not be correct to speak of different "schools" of criticism, it seems nevertheless that the unconditional supporters of ballet do not accept modernism as an equally high level of spectacle, and the defenders of modern dance are not inevitably inclined to the avant-garde. It is necessary then to point out that with the new generations, rather literary critics, for whom writing is, above all, an exercise in style, appear to write merely to enhance their self-importance. There are, however, some exceptions who consider the artistic course of a creator and the evolution of the choreographic art both in general and in the context of other arts and of society.

Lise Brunel
Translated from French

FRANCISQUI, JEAN-BAPTISTE (*fl.* 1793–1808), French-born dancer, choreographer, and producer. One of the most talented and prolific of the dancer-choreographers to bring ballet to the United States, Francisqui produced more than one hundred and twenty-five ballets and pantomimes during his American career, from 1793 to 1808. No other ballet master in the country approached his choreographic output in terms of sheer bulk or prodigious variety. His name, a venerable one in French theatrical annals, was also spelled *Francisguy, Francisquy,* or *Francisque;* however, he used *Francisqui* most often. The name dated back to 1715, when a family of dancers with that name was active at Bordeaux, where he was said to have been born.

Francisqui volunteered little information concerning his European career other than, according to theatrical advertisements of the time, that he danced at "The Opera House, Paris." A "M. Francisque" was listed as a student at the Académie Royale de Musique in 1777 and 1778. According to the *Almanach des spectacles,* he was promoted to an *"élève"* who danced daily at the Paris Opera by 1783 and, by the next year, was ranked at the head of his class. He joined the corps de ballet in 1785 and continued to dance at the Opera for one more year.

The young Francisqui was engaged as *première danseur* at the Martinique Théâtre in July 1788; he remained on Martinique through April 1788. He then traveled to Saint Domingue (Haiti) but fled in 1791 during the slave uprising. As soon as he had scrambled safely aboard ship, he and his little troupe, as he put it, were "plundered by Privateers, and conducted to Providence, where they experienced a number of misfortunes" (Charleston *City Gazette and Daily Advertiser,* 8 February 1794). Thus his American career began (and apparently ended) in misfortune.

Francisqui hastily announced an "exhibition" in Savannah, on 28 November 1793 and followed with a repeat performance in Charleston. He performed in Jean-Jacques Rousseau's *Pygmalion;* a pastorale ballet; a comedy; and a Comédie Italienne ballet, *The Two Hunters and the Milkmaid.* On 26 March 1794 he and his three friends joined a rival group of refugees to form the Charleston French Theatre. Their repertory included "dancing, pantomime, ballets or dances, harlequin pantomimes, rope dancing with many feats and little amusing French pieces; and to satisfy many who wish it, the grand pieces of the French theatre" (Charleston *City Gazette and Daily Advertiser,* 26 March 1794).

Francisqui's partner in the theater was Alexandre Placide, a celebrated French pantomimist and acrobat who also directed harlequinades and comical ballets. [*See the entry on Placide.*] Francisqui complimented Placide's acrobatic skills by drawing on his experience at the Paris Opera to produce the sophisticated *ballets d'action* of Maximilien Gardel, Jean Dauberval, and Jean-Georges Noverre. The leading dancers, besides Francisqui, were Placide, Suzanne Douvillier, Laurent Spinacuta, Louis-Antoine Duport, Peter Fayolle, little Miss Duthe, and the Vals.

Francisqui toured with Placide to Richmond and other small southern cities until 1796, when the troupe split up. In March he made his New York debut with his small company and immediately was asked to join the Old American Company for the rest of the season. Madame Val and Anna Gardie were the leading *danseuses.* He traveled to Newport, Rhode Island, in company with actors from Harper's troupe. In Boston, Francisqui was appointed ballet master for the new Haymarket Theatre during the winter of 1796 and spring of 1797. The *Columbian Centinel* critic confessed that he had "never witnessed more taste, elegance and ease" in any dancer and praised the Frenchman's dancing style as "the most elegant ever seen by an American audience."

Francisqui shared the position of ballet master with Jean-Marie Lege, who had once danced with the Placides at Jean-Baptiste Nicolet's theater in Paris. Lege later charged that Francisqui jealously prevented him from demonstrating his true talents. A choreographer's war erupted after Lege signed a new contract with a rival theater. The critic in the *Massachusetts Mercury* adjudged Lege the winner in the *paysannerie* (country village comedies), whereas Francisqui evidently was more impressive in the *danseur noble* and *demi-caractère* roles.

In Boston Francisqui later became attached to Philippe Lailson's circus, an elaborate spectacle that combined equestrian performances with ballet and opera. Francisqui rode the circuit from Boston to New York and Philadelphia from 1797 to 1798 until Lialson declared bankruptcy.

Francisqui dropped out of sight on the East Coast and resurfaced in the Spanish colony of Louisiana in September 1799. He spent the next nine years in New Orleans, where he resided in a large double house with his wife, three children, and four servants. The main source of his prosperity was his dancing school with its attendant subscription balls. His children's balls were so popular that uninvited adults would crowd the young scholars off the ballroom floor. Patrons delighted in his innovative use of a brass dance band for the waltzes but preferred that it alternate with a traditional string orchestra for the *contredanses.*

Francisqui did not totally abandon his stage career for a dancing master's life. On the contrary, he was instrumental in establishing the ballet troupe of the New Orleans Opera, an illustrious company that performed from 1792 to 1919. As ballet master, he trained soloists as well as his corps de ballet drawn from students at his school. Suzanne Douvillier, his partner, had previously danced with him in Charleston, Philadelphia, and New York; both had studied at the Paris Opera. [*See the entry on Douvillier.*]

Francisqui even directed the opera company on a series of international appearances at a time when U.S. theatrical companies recruited English actors to staff their stages. From 1800 to 1803, at the close of each theatrical season, he led the company on annual tours to Havana, Cuba, where they presented French opera and ballets. The Havana critics extolled Francisqui's "agility and poise in treading the boards" (Tolon and Gonzalez, 1961) and noted that his excellent training and long professional experience were readily apparent.

Francisqui's last recorded appearance in New Orleans occurred on 19 May 1808 at his newly organized theater on Saint Philippe Street shortly before it folded. Louis Douvillier, who probably was his partner in the enterprise, was taken to court for bankruptcy proceedings. Well before that, however, Francisqui and his family had mysteriously disappeared, never again to be seen on American territory as far as can be ascertained. It would not be surprising, however, ultimately to discover that this adventuresome entrepreneur continued to dance and teach elsewhere continents away.

FRANKLIN. Known for his energy and clean-cut good looks, Franklin was ideally cast as the Hussar in Léonide Massine's *Le Beau Danube.* (Photograph by Maurice Seymour; used by permission.

BIBLIOGRAPHY

Almanach des spectacles de Paris, ou Calendrier historique et chronologique des théâtres. Paris, 1778–1786.

Columbian Centinel (Boston) (28 and 31 December 1786).

Costonis, Maureen Needham. "The American Career of Jean-Baptiste Francisqui, 1793–1808." *Bulletin of Research in the Humanities* 85 (Winter 1982): 430–442.

Costonis, Maureen Needham. "The French Connection: Ballet Comes to America." In *Musical Theatre in America,* edited by Glenn Loney. Westport Conn., 1984.

Massachusetts Mercury (10 February 1797).

Moore, Lillian. "When Ballet Came to Charleston." *The Dancing Times* (December 1956): 122–124.

Seilhamer, George O. *History of the American Theatre.* Vol. 2. Philadelphia, 1889.

Tolón, Edwin Teurbe, and Jorge António González. *Historio del teatro en la Habana.* Havana, 1961.

Waldo, Lewis P. *The French Drama in America.* Baltimore, 1942.

MAUREEN NEEDHAM

FRANKLIN, FREDERIC (born 13 June 1914 in Liverpool), British-American dancer, choreographer, teacher, and ballet director. Frederic Franklin studied dance with Mrs. E. M. Kelly, Marjorie Kelly, and Shelagh Elliott-Clarke in his hometown of Liverpool, continuing his training in London with Nicholas Legat, Lydia Kyasht, Lydia Sokolova, and Anton Dolin and in Paris with Lubov Egorova. He made his debut in 1931 at the Casino de Paris with the legendary music-hall star Mistinguett. He danced in vaudeville (tap dancing as a member of The Lancashire Lads), in West End musicals, and in supper clubs with Wendy Toye before joining the Markova-Dolin Ballet as a soloist from 1935 until 1937.

In 1938 Franklin joined the Ballet Russe de Monte Carlo as *premier danseur* and remained a dominant artistic force in that company into the 1950s. This is the company that spent World War II in the United States; it was disbanded in the early 1950s, refounded by Franklin and Maria Tallchief in 1954, but finally vanished in the 1960s. While with the company, Franklin created a lasting impression in an enormous repertory of roles as a member of the original casts in Léonide Massine's *Gaîté Parisienne, Seventh Symphony, Rouge et Noir, The New Yorker, Labyrinth,* and *Saratoga;* in Frederick Ashton's *Devil's Holiday;* in Agnes de Mille's *Rodeo;* and in Ruth Page's *Billy Sunday* and *The Bells.* He also danced in George Balanchine's *Serenade, Night Shadow, Mozartiana, Poker Game,*

Le Baiser de la Fée, Danses Concertantes, and *Raymonda,* and in Page's *Frankie and Johnny.* Franklin could dance classical roles as well; he danced the roles of Albrecht in *Giselle,* Siegfried in *Swan Lake,* Franz in *Coppélia,* the Prince in *The Nutcracker,* and the Favorite Slave in Michel Fokine's *Schéhérazade.*

Walter Terry described Franklin's attraction as follows: "Loaded with energy and blessed with the most engaging grin in ballet, he exuded virility, zest and a clean-cut boyishness that endeared him to women of all ages and earned him the respect of those legions of American men who thought ballet was 'sissy stuff.'"

In the summer of 1944, Franklin danced with the Ballet Russe de Monte Carlo on Broadway in *Song of Norway.* At Balanchine's urging, Franklin was named ballet master in the fall of 1944. This appointment, along with Franklin's legendary partnership with Alexandra Danilova, brought about an artistic renaissance in the company. Ironically, however, the universal demand for appearances by Franklin and Danilova precluded the advancement of younger dancers and may have contributed to the company's ultimate demise.

In 1949 Franklin and Danilova appeared as guest artists with the Sadler's Wells (now Royal) Ballet at the Royal Opera House, Covent Garden, London. In 1951 Franklin formed the Slavenska-Franklin Ballet with another Ballet Russe partner, Mia Slavenska. They created the leading roles of Stanley and Blanche in Valerie Bettis's *A Streetcar Named Desire.* The company toured the United States, Canada, and Japan. Following a brief return to the Ballet Russe, Franklin toured South America with Danilova.

In 1959 Franklin became co-director of the Washington Ballet. His affability, professionalism, and experience as ballet master—de Mille called him the "inner motor" of the Ballet Russe—made him eminently qualified for this appointment. Franklin went on to found the National Ballet in 1962, holding the post of director from 1962 to 1974; he also became artistic adviser at American Ballet Theatre and the Chicago Ballet (1973–1974). From 1975 to 1977 he was co-artistic director of the Pittsburgh Ballet. He joined the Cincinnati Ballet as resident choreographer in 1977 and served as artistic director from 1984 to 1986. He also took on many assignments with ballet companies throughout the United States and Europe, staging the ballets of Fokine, Massine, Balanchine, and Page as well as several nineteenth-century classics.

Franklin also staged his own original compositions, such as *Tribute* (music by César Franck; Ballet Russe, Boston, 1961) and *Poème Lyrique* (music by Maurice Ravel; choreography by Claudia Lynch; Cincinnati Ballet, 1983). For his original staging of *Giselle* in a Louisiana bayou setting, performed by Dance Theatre of Harlem, he received the Society of West End Theatres' 1984 Laurence Olivier Award for Best Choreographer of the Year.

Although from the 1960s on Franklin focused on staging and coaching, his stage career also continued, with outstanding performances of character roles, including Drosselmeyer in *The Nutcracker,* Doctor Coppélius in *Coppélia,* Friar Laurence in *Romeo and Juliet,* the Eunuch in *Schéhérazade,* and Madge the Witch in *La Sylphide.* In recognition of his contributions "to the vitality and popularity of dance in America, through his dynamic performances and inspired teaching," Franklin received the 1985 *Dance Magazine* Award; he also received the Capezio Award in 1992.

BIBLIOGRAPHY
Anderson, Jack. *The One and Only: The Ballet Russe de Monte Carlo.* New York, 1981.
Anderson, Jack. "Danilova and Franklin." *Ballet Review* 9 (Winter 1982): 75–81.
Denby, Edwin. *Dance Writings.* Edited by Robert Cornfield and William MacKay. New York, 1986.
Franklin, Frederic, et al. "NYCB and DTH: Anniversary Reflections." *Ballet Review* 22 (Fall 1994): 14–28.
Kerensky, Oleg, and Charles Witherspoon. "Curtain Up." *Dance and Dancers* (October 1989).
Maynard, Olga. "Frederic Franklin: A Life in the Theater." *Dance Magazine* (June 1974): 44–58.
Terry, Walter. "Franklin's Fifty Years on Stage." *Dance Magazine* (April 1982): 112–113.

VIDEOTAPE. "Billy Sunday: Baseball, Bible, and Ballet" (WCET-TV, Cincinnati, 1984).

ANDREW MARK WENTINK

FRÄNZL FAMILY, Austrian family of dancers who made a major contribution to ballet in Vienna. Notable members were the brothers Fritz and Philipp Fränzl and four of Fritz's six children: Fritzi, Hedy, Rudi, and Willy.

Fritz Fränzl (Friedrich Josef Fränzl; born 13 July 1863 in Vienna, died 24 February 1938), dancer and teacher. Fritz Fränzl was in the corps de ballet of the Vienna Court Opera from 1881 and was a mime from 1904 to 1915. He taught dance and was president of the Austrian association of dancing teachers.

Philipp Fränzl (born 1865 in Vienna, died 1917), dancer. Phillip Fränzl joined the corps of the Vienna Court Opera in 1881 and was a mime from 1915 to 1931.

Fritzi Fränzl (Friederike Fränzl; born 21 October 1896 in Vienna, died 24 April 1958), dancer. Joining the corps de ballet of the Vienna Court Opera in 1912, Fritzi Fränzl became its leader in 1918, and soloist from 1920 to 1932.

Hedy Fränzl (Hedwig Fränzl; born 21 May 1901 in Vienna) joined the corps de ballet of the Vienna Court Opera in 1917 and, following her sister Fritzi, became corps leader in 1920. From 1927 to 1931 she was a soloist.

Rudi Fränzl (Rudolf Fränzl; born 23 October 1894, died 26 January 1974), dancer and choreographer. Rudi Fränzl joined the corps de ballet of the Vienna Court Opera in

1911 and was a soloist from 1921 to 1945. He also choreographed interludes for operas and revues and ran a school.

Willy Fränzl (Wilhelm Fränzl; born 5 June 1898 in Vienna, died 24 June 1982), dancer and teacher. Willy Fränzl joined the corps of the Vienna Court Opera in 1914, became a soloist in 1921, and was first soloist from 1938 to 1962. He served as assistant ballet master from 1935 to 1962, as a teacher from 1938 to 1962, and as head of the ballet school from 1937 to 1945. He danced principal roles in *Die Prinzessin von Tragant, Die Josephslegende, Klein Idas Blumen* (Little Ida's Flowers), *Schlagobers* (Whipped Cream), and *Der Taugenichts in Wien* (Ne'er-do-wells in Vienna). Willy organized many dance evenings, both in Austria and abroad, and he choreographed interludes for operas and *divertissements* for the Salzburg and Bregenz festivals. At the Vienna Opera he supervised new stagings of ballets by Josef Hassreiter, Heinrich Kröller, and Margarete Wallmann, and made sure that *Die Puppenfee* was retained. He is known first and foremost for his interpretations of the Viennese waltz for the opening of the Vienna Opera Ball. With his wife Lucia Bräuer (born 23 June 1923), a soloist from 1946 to 1967, he ran one of the most prominent ballet and ballroom dancing schools in Vienna.

BIBLIOGRAPHY

Amort, Andrea. "Die Geschichte des Balletts der Wiener Staatsoper, 1918–1942." Ph.D. diss., University of Vienna, 1981.
Matzinger, Ruth. "Die Geschichte des Balletts der Wiener Hofoper, 1869–1918." Ph.D. diss., University of Vienna, 1982.
Raab, Riki. "Grabstätten von Ballettmitgliedern des Kärntnertortheaters, der k. k. Hofoper und Staatsoper, Wien." *Jahrbuch des Vereins für Geschichte der Stadt Wien* 28 (1972).

RUTH SANDER
Translated from German

FROMAN, MARGARITA

FROMAN, MARGARITA (Margarita Petrovna Froman; born 27 October 1890 in Moscow, died 24 March 1970 in Boston), dancer, choreographer, teacher, and director. Froman came from a family of dancers. She graduated from the Moscow Ballet School in the class of Vasily Tikhomirov and joined the Bolshoi Theater Ballet in 1909. For the following three seasons (1910–1912) she appeared with the Ballets Russes de Serge Diaghilev and in 1916 accompanied the group on its American tour. In 1921 she settled in Zagreb, in the former Yugoslavia, along with her three brothers, Maksimilijan, Pavel, and Valentin. Working as a *prima ballerina*, choreographer, teacher, and director during the next three and a half decades, Froman emerged as the most important female ballerina-choreographer active in Yugoslavia in the first half of the twentieth century. Alone and in collaboration with her brothers, she provided the impetus for the revival of ballet in her adopted country.

Froman introduced Yugoslav audiences to works choreographed by Arthur Saint-Léon, Marius Petipa, and Michel Fokine. Among these were *Swan Lake* and *Coppélia* (1921); *Schéhérazade, Le Papillon,* and the *Polovtsian Dances* from *Prince Igor* (1922); *Petrouchka* and *Thamar* (1923); *Le Carnaval* (1924); *Raymonda, Firebird,* and *Don Juan* (1928); *The Little Humpbacked Horse* (1929); and *The Nutcracker* (1931). In addition, Froman choreographed what are considered masterpieces of the Yugoslav repertory, notably *The Gingerbread Heart* (1924) and *Imbrek with the Nose* (1935) to music by Krešimir Baranović and *The Legend of Ochrid* (1949), to music by Stevan Hristić. In 1956 Froman immigrated to the United States, where she settled in Boston and taught at a ballet studio run by her brother Maksimilijan.

BIBLIOGRAPHY

Maynard, Olga. "The Dance in Yugoslavia." *Dance Magazine* (May 1977): 67–82.
Obituary. *Dance News* (May 1970): 11.

MILICA JOVANOVIĆ

FUCHS, AUGUSTA

FUCHS, AUGUSTA. *See* Augusta, Madame.

FUJIMA FUJIKO

FUJIMA FUJIKO (Tanaka Kimiko; born 31 October 1907 in Tokyo), dancer and choreographer. Fujima Fujiko became the student of Fujima Kan'emon II, the head *(iemoto)* of the Iemoto branch of the Fujima school of Japanese traditional dance *(nihon buyō)*, at the age of eight and has remained at the center of the school ever since. Her skill and years of experience have raised her to a position second only to the *iemoto,* and her importance to the branch can be seen in the fact that the past two *iemoto* have been taught by her strict hand. Her position has been made even more important since the current *iemoto,* Fujima Kan'emon VI *(kabuki* actor Onoe Tatsunosuke III), took the title at the age of sixteen. Fujiko's own prestige has helped maintain the reputation of the Iemoto branch of the Fujima school as one of the finest in Japanese dance despite the inexperience of its leader.

Fujiko's style has been described as "lustrous touches within solid movement"—a style that is suitable for *tachiyaku* (male character) dances; indeed, it is at these types of dances that she has excelled. Among her most famous dances are *Kikujido,* based on a Chinese legend in which the title character learns that the fountain of youth lies in the dew of chrysanthemums, and *Kagekiyo,* in which a famous warrior visits his lover in the pleasure quarters of Kyoto. Fujiko herself has described how the dancer portraying Kagekiyo must show the sensuality of a romantic lead without losing the fact that Kagekiyo is a strong samurai general. *Kagekiyo* became one of Fujiko's trademark dances, and for it she received the 1955 Education Minister's Theater Festival Prize.

Both of the dances mentioned are accompanied by the *tokiwazu* style of music, a somewhat lofty and rigid style often used for dances with strong male roles. Fujiko often choreographs *tokiwazu* dances for the *kabuki* theater; examples include *Masakado* and *Seki no To* (The Snow-Covered Barrier).

Fujiko has committed her life to maintaining the quality of dance within the Iemoto branch of the Fujima school and throughout the classical Japanese dance world. If her image is somewhat subdued compared to that of many of her peers, her skill and position as the leading transmitter of classical dance are well known and have won her numerous awards and honors, including being designated a National Living Treasure by the Japanese government in 1985.

[*See also* Japanese Traditional Schools; Kabuki Theater; *and the entry on* Azuma Tokuho.]

BIBLIOGRAPHY
Eguchi Hiroshi, ed. *Nihon buyo zenshu.* Vol. 2. Tokyo, 1981.
Onaka Hiroshi. *Gendai no shozo: Hyakunin no buyo-ka.* Edited by Gunji Masakatsu. Tokyo, 1985.
Sato Kikuo, ed. *Ningen kokuho.* Tokyo, 1991.
Toin Masuno. "Ningen kokuho, Fujima Fujiko-sensei." *Hogaku to Buyo* 36 (July 1985):28–29.

VIDEOTAPES. National Theater Library, Tokyo.
MATTHEW JOHNSON

FUJIMA KANJŪRŌ, hereditary stage-name of Sōke Fujima Ryū, the head family of the Fujima school (founded in 1781) of *nihon buyō,* the Japanese traditional dance genre associated with *kabuki.* The stage-name was first used by Fujima Kanbei (d. 1769). Fujima Kanjūrō IV choreographed *Fujimusume* (Wisteria Maiden) and *Sanja Matsuri,* important works in the repertory of the Fujima school.

Fujima Kanjūrō VI (1900–1990), who was given the name by the acclaimed *kabuki* actor Kikugoro VI, choreographed a number of masterpieces of *nihon buyō* for *kabuki.* His choreographic work, which he pursued with vigor through the Taisho and Shōwa eras, includes *Yamauba* and *Oimatsu.* He was designated an Important Intangible Cultural Property in 1960 and was honored by the Japan Arts Academy in 1962.

He was succeeded by his daughter Fujima Koko (b. 1945), who became Fujima Kanjūrō VII. She studied with her father and made her debut in *Kamuro* at the Kabukiza at age six. Her works include *Tsunemasa* and *Kanemaki Dōjōji.*

[*For further general discussion, see* Japanese Traditional Schools.]

BIBLIOGRAPHY
Makoto Sugiyama and Fujima Kanjuro. *An Outline History of the Japanese Dance.* Translated by Shigeyoshi Sakabe. Tokyo, 1937.
HASEGAWA ROKU
Translated from Japanese

FULLER, LOIE (Mary Louise Fuller; born 22 January 1862 in Fullersburg [now Hinsdale], Illinois, died 2 January 1928 in Paris), American-born actress, dancer, and choreographer. Fuller was born in a tavern during an especially cold northern Illinois winter. Her father, Ruben, was a skilled fiddler and dance caller, and her mother, Delilah, had wanted to be an opera singer before her marriage. Thus Fuller grew up surrounded by country dancing and music and, encouraged in her youthful ambitions by her parents, picked up a keen sense of phrasing and rhythm at an early age.

When Fuller was twelve years old she acted in nearby Chicago; during the next two years she gave temperance lectures and Shakespearean and poetry recitations. From 1878 to 1879 she toured with the Felix A. Vincent Company, which performed *Aladdin,* a pantomime spectacle filled with magical scene transformations. In ill-equipped theaters, smooth transformations were achieved by artful arrangements of gauze curtains and the calcium lights that illuminated them, as well as by shifting and modulating multiple slide projections thrown onto the fabric by magic lanterns (precursors of the modern slide projector). These important principles of stagecraft, absorbed by the adolescent Fuller, would be essential to her aesthetic development.

From 1881 to 1889 the hard-driving young actress (billed as "Mary Louise," "Louise," and finally "Loie") performed in western melodramas and musical burlettas in New York City and the Midwest. Some highlights of this period were *Davy Crockett* (1882) and *Twenty Days, or Buffalo Bill's Pledge* (1883). In 1886 she became a full-time contract actress with the Bijou Opera House Theater Company in New York City, which specialized in lightweight musical parodies and farces. Her most successful Bijou role was the lead in *Little Jack Shepherd,* in which she played the boy's role of Jack, dressed in tights or the somewhat risqué outfit of boy's knee-length knickers; during the play's run, in the spring of 1887, she caught the eye of Colonel William B. Hayes, a man-about-town and nephew of former president Rutherford B. Hayes. In October 1887 Fuller played the lead in *The Arabian Nights* at the Standard Theatre; the production featured a "steam curtain" whose vapors were illuminated by multicolored lights. Such exuberant stagecraft was typical of American popular entertainments of the era, when unrestrained experimentation resulted in the spectacular stage effects beloved by the audiences of the rising middle classes. It was the perfect school for Fuller.

In 1889 Colonel Hayes, who had financed some of Fuller's theatrical ventures, proposed marriage. In May 1889 they contracted a secret common-law marriage; in August Fuller left for London, where she produced *Caprice*. The play quickly folded, and she briefly visited the Paris Exposition Universelle, where she was particularly impressed by the Palais d'Électricité and the illuminated fountains of the Champs de Mars, where thirty-foot (nine-meter) sprays of water were lit by multicolored electric lights beaming up through a glass-bottomed pool. Back in London in 1890, she was hired as a second-

company member of the Gaiety Theatre, home of the Gaiety Girl and the skirt dance, which would be seminal in the evolution of Fuller's own early solo choreography.

Returning to the United States in 1891, Fuller performed her version of the skirt dance while touring with *Quack, MD* (a comedy that dealt with the subject of hypnotism). Wearing a long skirt pinned up beneath her breasts in Empire style, she pretended to be hypnotized as she danced; holding up the sides of the long skirt and letting it stream behind her, she ran about the stage, turning, alighting in poses, and swirling the soft fabric about her, enchanting the audience with her ethereal and lyrical dance. Immediately setting to work to choreograph her dance carefully, she discovered, by experimenting with a large piece of fine ivory silk in front of a full-length mirror, that each movement of her body caused predictable ripples and shimmerings in the silk and that by controlling her body's actions she could sculpt the iridescent fabric into abstract configurations that billowed about her. In teaching herself how to choreograph for body and silk, Fuller unlocked one of her most important choreographic concepts. From the beginning she was intrigued by images that began with the human body and radiated outward as costume extended the range of motion and took on shapes and a life of its own.

In November 1891 Fuller was hired to perform her *Serpentine Dance* between the acts of a comedy, *Uncle Celestine*. While on out-of-town tryouts with *Celestine* she had William B. Hayes arrested on charges of bigamy (in fact, the colonel was betraying three wives simultaneously). The situation was resolved when Hayes made a $10,000 out-of-court settlement with Fuller.

FULLER. Manipulating winglike projections of silk in a costume made for her *Danse Blanche*, which she wore in several other dances, Fuller created images of insects, the elements, and flowers. Here, she dances a whirlwind *(above)* and a butterfly *(right)* during an outdoor photography session c.1898. (Photographs probably by Samuel Joshua Beckett; from the Dance Collection, New York Public Library for the Performing Arts.)

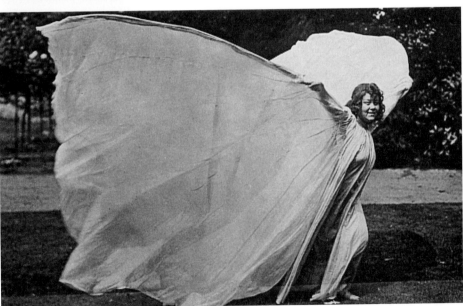

When *Uncle Celestine* opened in New York on 16 January 1892, only Fuller and the *Serpentine Dance* received rave reviews. Even so, when Fuller asked for a raise she was fired and replaced with an imitator, Minne (Renwood) Bemis. Angered, she moved to the Madison Square Theatre as an entr'acte specialty dancer in Hoyt and Thomas's *A Trip to Chinatown*. Yet personal and professional problems continued to plague her. In March she tried unsuccessfully to stop Bemis's imitation of her dance. The judgment went against her and became a landmark case in copyright law affecting dance choreography. *Fuller v. Bemis* (*Federal Reporter*, 50 (1892), S. 929) stated that copyright protection could not be applied to the "devising of a series of graceful movements" because it in no way comprised a dramatic composition. In June she broke her contract with Hoyt and Thomas. In July, accompanied by her mother, she left for Europe, where she hoped to receive the serious artistic recognition she had been denied at home.

In October, after a short, disastrous German tour, Fuller arrived in Paris, which she later described as a port after the storm. She was hired by the Folies-Bergère, Paris's largest music hall, as a headliner dancer, replacing another New York serpentine dancer and imitator, Maybelle Stewart. On 5 November 1892 she presented *Serpentine, Papillon, Violet*, and *XXXX* (later named *La Danse Blanche*). In 1892 the Folies-Bergère had switched from gaslight to electric light only for stage illumination. In order to darken the house in preparation for Fuller's performance—still a radical theatrical practice in 1892—the gas lights in the auditorium had to be extinguished by the ushers. The excitement and tension of waiting for the house to be darkened added to the suspense and anticipation. The stage, stripped of decor, was lined with black chenille curtains, and the floor was covered with black velvet. A blaze of light kindled the inky blackness of the stage. Illuminated in a bath of iridescent color, the figure of the dancer appeared, now revealed, now concealed in the silken clouds of her costume. As she turned and danced, she tossed the gossamer material high in the air. It wafted about her in the shapes of enormous butterflies and flowers that unfurled and curled in on themselves, twined upward, then floated in the air like outspread wings painted in pastel hues. The dancer then drew the silks about her, disappearing once more in the fabric, which closed around her like petals of a lily bud.

An immediate sensation, Fuller was called the creator of a new dance art and thus received the eloquent critical and popular acclaim she had so ardently desired. Fuller's timing had been perfect; it was as if Paris had specially prepared itself to receive her luminous dance. Fuller's arrival coincided with the blooming of Art Nouveau, the development of symbolist performance theories, and the conversion of theaters from gas to electric illumination.

With the first fluctuations of her silks, Fuller took Art Nouveau on stage, where the symbolist found in her dreamlike images a perfect reciprocity between idea and symbol. Fuller's enigmatic and entranced presence (just as in *Quack, MD*) allowed for the supremacy of image, which freed dance from the restrictions of character and narrative and forged the path toward modern abstraction.

Hailed as *la fée lumineuse* ("the luminous fairy"), Fuller was written about by poets and critics, among whom were Georges Rodenbach, Rastignac, Jean Lorrain, and Roger Marx. In 1893 France's most prestigious literary figure, Stéphane Mallarmé, praised her dance in his essay "Considerations sur l'art de Loïe Fuller."

By 1893 artists were depicting Fuller's image, and her figure swathed in swirling silks became one of the most visible icons of the era. Henri de Toulouse-Lautrec, Fernand Sigismond Bach, Jean de Paléologue, Jules Chéret, George de Feur, and numerous others created lithograph posters of Fuller, and she was sculpted by such artists as Pierre Roche, François-Raoul Larche, François Rupert Carabin, Eugène Carrière, Théodore Rivière, and Henri Levasseur. Popular images of Fuller abounded: there were dresses, perfumes, scarves, bonnets, vases, lamps, toys, and stoves à la Loïe. Parisian stages blossomed with flotillas of imitators and parodies, including a performing circus dog and a lion-tamer act.

Fuller's use of the diacritic in her name also dates from this period. The dieresis was originally added by the French press to aid French speakers in the correct pronunciation of her name; without the diacritic, *Loie* in French would appear to be a homonym for *loi* (meaning "law," pronounced /lwah/). Though plain and simple Loie (a common Midwestern American nickname for Louise) had been Fuller's professional stage name for many years, appearing *sans accent* in all her early American playbills, Fuller came to love the European aura the diacritic lent her name, especially when written in script, and often, though inconsistently, added it to her signature.

For protection, Fuller patented her costume designs and lighting devices. The most famous and popular of her solos, *La Danse du Feu* (Fire Dance), first performed in 1895 as one dance in her full-length *Salomé*, used underlighting. She danced on a thick glass plate that had been set into one of the traps in the stage floor; the beam of a powerful light that shone up from beneath the stage illuminated the hem of her costume, giving the impression that it had caught fire. To the rushing music of Wagner's *Ride of the Walkyries*, the flames rose, seeming to engulf her until she appeared to become the heated center of volcanic eruptions; the flames then began to diminish, until nothing could be seen but flecks of burning embers, a tiny beam of light catching the edges of the silk as it floated high above the stage. Fuller's first lighting design for *Fire Dance* called for complicated, multifocused cross beams, but she quickly simplified this to underlighting alone.

This evolution toward simple abstraction characterized the progression of Fuller's solo choreography between 1892 and 1900. Beginning with serpentine and flower shapes, she later began to create dances that suggested waves, mists, fire, and great winged creatures. By enlarging her costume and holding long, curved bamboo canes in her hands, she extended the radius of her costume ten feet to either side. She attempted to replicate firmament by projecting slides of the stars and the moon onto silks that lazily circled her in the shape of a helix.

From 1893 on Fuller toured Europe and the United States, performing in prestigious variety houses on mixed bills as the featured performer. She spent her life trying to place dance in respected theaters where it would stand on its own merits. As a highly respected artist she had surprising but intermittent success. This situation did not change until after 1910, when other dance pioneers joined the modern dance revolution.

Fuller was an odd figure within the avant-garde. Although she had many acquaintances within elite artistic groups and attended various elegant salons, she was never interested in becoming a member of one of those inner circles. She liked to picture herself as an intuitive genius who stumbled into art as if by happy accident. Nonanalytical and nonintellectual, she was not interested in theories nor in salon performances. Gifted with formidable energy and curiosity, she continually worked out her ideas in practice. She designed all her costumes and scenic settings and made all of the glass color filters for her lights. In fact, Fuller's scenic innovations of 1892 precluded many of the theories of Adolphe-François Appia and Gordon Craig, yet she is rarely credited for her contributions. Until the early 1900s Fuller was the strikingly singular pioneer of modern dance. It was her work that paved the way for the acceptance of later dancers who rather than she are considered the founders of the modern dance movement.

For the 1900 Paris Exposition Universelle, Art Nouveau architect Marcel Sauvage designed Le Théâtre de Loïe-Fuller, where Fuller presented the Japanese dancer and actress, Kawakami Sadayakko, known as Sada Yakko, to an enthralled public. Both Ruth St. Denis and Isadora Duncan were impressed by Fuller and Yakko's performance at the exposition.

In 1901 Fuller met Isadora Duncan. She immediately recognized Duncan's astonishing talents and was interested in managing the young dancer. Duncan needed help to establish her career, and the two women agreed that she would join Fuller's troupe for her 1901–1902 European tour. Fuller often carried a pick-up troupe with her on tour to perform her group work, *Ballet de Lumière*, the choreography for which was refined and reshaped

FULLER. *Fire Dance*, photographed in 1896. The light shining up through a glass plate at Fuller's feet created the illusion that she was ringed by flames. (Photograph from the Dance Collection, New York Public Library for the Performing Arts.)

throughout her career. Duncan joined Fuller in Berlin and then traveled with the group to Vienna and Budapest, where Fuller introduced her to the influential critics and patrons in specially arranged performances.

It quickly became apparent that although the two women respected each other artistically they hated each other personally. After only a few months, in early 1902, Duncan left Fuller's company and struck out on her own. Fuller was angry, sure that Duncan had exploited her for her connections and had left when she was no longer of use. Her anger may have been justified, but it is also true that Fuller had tried to control Duncan's career, which the younger innovator could not abide.

In 1902 Fuller met Crown Princess Marie of Romania, and after this friendship was renewed in 1913, it became one of the most important of her life. Another important friend of Fuller's was Auguste Rodin, whom she first met in the mid-1890s. She considered Rodin the greatest of all artists, and she continually championed him and his art throughout her life, sometimes acting as a kind of informal agent in selling his work. When she toured the United States in 1903, she brought with her a collection of Rodins. Unfortunately, the United States was not yet ready for his art, and she returned to Paris without having sold anything.

Fuller was an impassioned amateur scientist, and when Marie and Pierre Curie, two of her most treasured friends, politely refused in the early 1890s to give her the radium she requested, Fuller determined to develop her own source of "cool" light to use on her costumes. Through the years she worked at extracting phosphorescence from strontium salts and pitchblendes. In 1904 she premiered a series of *Radium Dances* in which luminous phosphorescent paint decorated all her costumes. Their radiant glow (achieved by exposing the paint to light, causing it to shine in the dark) was described by critic André Bidou as the free-form play of floating abstract designs and linear streaks tinted in brilliant hues against a blue background. Fuller was paralleling, in performance, experiments of line, shape, and color that were being made in art.

In 1907 Fuller began writing her autobiography, *Fifteen Years of a Dancer's Life* and produced her second full-length *Tragédie de Salomé* to music by Florent Schmitt. The production was not the unqualified success she had hoped for, and during its run her mother came down with severe pneumonia; she died soon thereafter. It may have been in response to this loss that Fuller decided to form a school and a company in 1908. She was forty-six, myopic, and no longer possessed a body that could be pleasing on stage. More importantly, she was eager to expand her group compositions, which at this point in her choreographic evolution interested her more than performing.

Fuller now called herself "the mother of natural dancing." By "natural" she meant that the dancers would not be taught a restricting technique. They wore short, sleeve-

FULLER. *A Midsummer Night's Dream,* performed c.1916, with Fuller (center) and her "muses." Fuller's production for her company of young dancers created a fantastic landscape of light, fabric, scenery, and choreography. (Photograph from the Dance Collection, New York Public Library for the Performing Arts.)

less tunics and danced in bare feet. Their movements were unaffected and natural to the body. Because no two people do the same thing at the same time in real life, Fuller saw no reason why they should do so in dancing, so she had her dancers use gestures that were unique to them as individuals. For example, one girl was pigeon-toed, so Fuller choreographed movement for her that capitalized on this. Ranging in age from three to eighteen years, her dancers were chosen for their native grace and expressiveness. Fuller called them the "muses." She said, "They were not learning, but attaining. . . . The so-called 'faults,' when understood, are frequently just the things most worthy of development." According to three of her former dancers, Fuller never criticized; she simply suggested different ways of moving.

Before beginning to choreograph, Fuller would gather the girls together in the studio and have them listen to the music played repeatedly by her pianist until they absorbed the flow and phrasing of the musical rhythms. She then asked each one to improvise, eventually incorporating some of their material into her finished dance. The final sequencing of the dance phrases piece was always set precisely with elaborate orchestrations of lights and the play of silks. But within their phrases, the girls apparently were always permitted their own individual interpretations in performing the movement. Fuller held exhaustive rehearsals until the piece was exactly as she wanted it.

In March 1909 the company's first public performance at the Théâtre Mariguy was well received and the company was immediately contracted for another appearance. In addition to stage productions, l'École de Loie Fuller began giving outside performances in which sunlight, moonbeams, and breezes illuminated and wafted the great silken scarves. From September 1909 to March 1910 the company performed in the United States, appearing in New York, Boston, Philadelphia, and Washington, and then returned to Paris and the Riviera for the spring season. During the next years the school settled down to what would become its usual schedule: fall and early winter performances in Paris and London, late winter tours, often to the Riviera, a spring season in Paris, and intermittent performances in the summer months.

In 1911 Fuller choreographed the first of a series of seminal shadow dances. Refined and reshaped throughout the rest of her career, these choreographic investigations into shadows and movement in two dimensions reverberated with contemporary artistic investigations in cubism.

Although Fuller had accompanied her dances with serious music since 1894 (compositions by Felix Mendelssohn, Hector Berlioz, Edvard Grieg, Henry Purcell, Richard Wagner, and Ludwig van Beethoven were some of those she used), after 1909 she increasingly turned to modern composers. Between 1911 and 1914 she choreographed dances to Claude Debussy, Aleksandr Scriabin, Igor Stravinsky, Armande de Polignac, Nikolai Rimsky-Korsakov, Darius Milhaud, and other members the group of modern French composers known as *les six*. She was stretching her images to the outermost edges of modernism: the silks had grown in size, covering the entire stage, and the dancers moved through a plastic, mobile, and radiant environment. Sometimes they were invisible, setting the silks in billowing motion; when they emerged, they were caught in fantastic landscapes in which the essential metaphor was the fusion of art and technology.

World War I brought a temporary halt to Fuller's choreographic experiments. Although the company appeared in California in 1915 and in London in 1915 and 1916, it performed old repertory pieces and then disbanded for the duration of the war. Fuller became a tireless relief worker, raising hundreds of thousands of dollars for Belgium and Romania. In the United States, with Alma Spreckles, wife of California sugar king Adolph Spreckles, Fuller established a relief organization and funds and began developing plans to establish a fine arts museum in California that would house a large collection of Rodin's works. (This project was realized in 1924 with the opening of the Palace of the Legion of Honor museum in San Francisco.)

Between 1918 and 1921 Fuller's creative interests turned to directing and producing a full-length dance-drama film. Fuller had re-assembled her troupe after the war, and they danced in the film, called *La Lys de la Vie*, a surreal fantasy based on a fairy story written by Queen Marie of Romania. No prints of *La Lys de la Vie* have survived, but film fragments and photographic stills taken from the film footage as well as reviews of the 1921 premiere described unusual slow-motion effects, reversed negative–positive images, disembodied hands and heads flying through the air, and the incorporation of outdoor settings along the Riviera coast, where the natural effects of rolling fog and cloudy mists were beautifully employed. During this time the company (now completely turned over to the competent management of Gabrielle Bloch, Fuller's longtime lover, secretary, and occasional financial supporter) still performed and toured, but on a greatly reduced schedule.

From 1922 to 1923 Fuller's interest turned once more to choreography, and she revived and reworked her shadow dances in flaming colors. In 1924 and 1925 *L'Homme au Sable, L'Ombres Gigantesques (La Danse de la Sorcière),* and *La Grande Voile (La Mer)* received rave reviews, and another generation of critics was calling the sixty-three-year-old Fuller a brilliant revolutionary in dance. Since 1892 she had choreographed approximately 128 dances. Although many of the dances appear to have been reworkings of earlier pieces, it remains a prodigious output.

Loie Fuller's contributions are impressive. The first American dancer to be acclaimed the creator of a new, modern dance form, Fuller paved the way for the acceptance of modern dance and dancers in the twentieth century. She was prized and praised by the Symbolists of the 1890s; ironically, it was this American dancer from the theater of popular entertainments who was able to realize their most elusive theories on stage. Fuller predicted the stagecraft of the 1900s when she stripped the stage of scenery and used light and fabric as scenic decor, sculpting abstract shapes with the ineffable materials of light, color, silk, and the motion of the human body. She invoked the admiration of the Futurists because she tamed the "terrible" power of electricity by fusing art and technology. Fuller had an appreciative eye for talent, and managed Sada Yakko, Maud Allen, and Isadora Duncan. In producing her film, *La Lys de la Vie,* Fuller ingeniously exploited natural, exterior settings and achieved startling effects with negative–positive image reversal in her final print. And, with her brilliantly colored shadow-dance images she was, in fact, envisioning a design potential that would be realized with technicolor film.

In January 1926 Fuller had an operation to remove a large cyst from her breast; it was the first indication of the carcinogenic contamination she had been exposed to over the years. She dyed all her costumes herself, working over great vats of analine dyes with highly carcinogenic fumes; when she painted her costumes with phosphorescent paint, often she would moisten the brush with her saliva before dipping it into the paint, thus repeatedly dosing herself with minute quantities of deadly substances. She recovered from the operation but never regained her former strength.

Fuller joined Queen Marie on her tour of the United States in the fall of 1926. This trip was intended as a pleasant goodwill visit, but it turned instead into an exhausting and grandiose affair of state—and a personal nightmare for Fuller. The stage performance of *La Lys de la Vie* at the Metropolitan Opera was an underrehearsed failure, the house partly empty. Fuller, now very ill, was maligned as an opportunist who was financially exploiting her highness's trip, and it was repeatedly suggested that a dancer was not fit company for a queen. Petty jealousies prevailed onboard the queen's royal train, and although Fuller kept to her bed and rarely appeared in public, she could not escape being humiliated by the rumors and innuendoes. She cut her trip short and left the royal train in November, and one week later the queen was abruptly called to the bedside of her sick husband. The two women exchanged many letters but never met again.

Fuller's once-formidable energies continued to wane during 1927. In the summer, however, she enjoyed one last burst of creative power and began work on a film based on the E. T. A. Hoffmann story "Der Sandmann." Suffering from various ailments, she was forced to her bed on 27 December and died six days later of pneumo-

nia. Fuller had asked to be cremated, and in the many eulogies published after her death, it was often noted how fitting it was that the woman who had lived in flames should be finally consumed by them.

[*See also* Artists and Dance, 1760–1929.]

BIBLIOGRAPHY

Doughty, Heather. "The Choreographer in the Courtroom: Loie Fuller and Léonide Massine." In *Proceedings of the Fifth Annual Conference, Society of Dance History Scholars, Harvard University, 13–15 February 1982,* compiled by Christena L. Schlundt. Riverside, Calif., 1982.

Fuller, Loie. *Fifteen Years of a Dancer's Life.* Boston, 1913.

Harris, Margaret Haile, and Sally R. Sommer. "Choreochronology of Loie Fuller." In *The Complete Guide to Modern Dance,* edited by Don McDonagh. New York, 1976.

Harris, Margaret Haile. *Loie Fuller: Magician of Light.* Richmond, Va., 1979.

Harris, Margaret Haile. "Loie Fuller: The Myth, the Woman, and the Artist." *Arts in Virginia* 20 (Fall 1979).

Kermode, Frank. "Poet and Dancer before Diaghilev." In Kermode's *Puzzles and Epiphanies.* New York, 1962.

Loie Fuller: Getanzter Jugendstil, edited by Jo-Anne Birnie Danzker. Museum Villa Stuck, München, 1995.

Sommer, Sally R. "Loie Fuller." *Drama Review* 19 (March 1975): 53–67.

Sommer, Sally R. "The Stage Apprenticeship of Loie Fuller." *Dance Scope* 12 (Fall-Winter 1977–1978): 23–34.

Sommer, Sally R. "Loie Fuller's Art of Music and Light." *Dance Chronicle* 4.4 (1982): 389–401.

SALLY R. SOMMER

FUOCO, SOFIA (Maria Brambilla; born 16 January 1830 in Milan, died 3 June 1916 in Carate Lario, Como), Italian ballet dancer. The daughter of a well-known painter, Maria Brambilla was enrolled at the age of seven in the ballet school of the Teatro alla Scala, where she was trained by Carlo Blasis. She soon became one of the group of his favored pupils known as Les Pleiades. Her first appearances at La Scala were in 1839, when she was only nine years old. In 1843, when she was thirteen, she replaced an indisposed ballerina, scored a success, and was subsequently appointed *prima ballerina assoluta* at La Scala. On the occasion of this appearance she took the stage name of Sofia Fuoco, a name underlining the liveliness of her temperament. (*Fuoco* signifies "fire," "flaming," "ardor," or "passion" in Italian.) In 1846 she danced in a revival by Filippo Taglioni of Jules Perrot's *Pas de Quatre,* sharing the stage with such well-known ballerinas as Marie Taglioni, Carolina Rosati, and Carolina Vente.

Widely hailed in Italy, Fuoco excited a similar enthusiasm among the French public when she appeared at the Paris Opera on 10 July 1846 in *Betty, ou La Jeunesse de Henri V* by Joseph Mazilier. "La Fuoco" conquered all the French critics, earning acclaim even from the exacting Théophile Gautier. Writing about her debut in *La presse*

(20 July 1846), he spoke of her dancing in very favorable terms, having been impressed by the precision and vivacity of her technique. He saw her as a skilled dancer, endowed with a style all her own characterized by an amazing rapidity in the execution of steps. Fuoco continued to make appearances at the Paris Opera until 1850. In 1847 she danced in London, at Drury Lane and Covent Garden, and in 1848 she appeared at the Teatro Real in Madrid and at the Liceo in Barcelona. From that time onward, Fuoco divided her time between giving performances in Italy and making appearances abroad, in France and Spain. She appeared in numerous ballets created for her by Italian choreographers, including *Il Prestigiatore* (1852) by Blasis, *Zuleika* (1852) by Antonio Coppini, *Armilla, ossia La Cetra Incantata* (1854) by Antonio Monticini, *Kabdelaj, o La Figlia del Profeta* (1854) by Emanuele Viotti, and *Le Nozze di Ninetta e Nane* (1854) by Dario Fissi.

As fascinating and impetuous on stage as she was reserved in her private life, La Fuoco was the focus of an authentic cult, formed by fans who were dazzled by her acrobatic vituosity. Each of her appearances at La Scala, usually accompanied by her favorite partner, Dario Fissi, was greeted with great enthusiasm. When she appeared in the title role of Jules Perrot's *Catarina, ou La Fille du Bandit* at La Scala in 1853, a critic reported the event as follows:

> It would take too long to describe what La Fuoco and her feet do in the five acts of *La Figlia del Bandito*, one of her favorite dances. It would take too long to repeat what the audience does with its voice, its hands, and even with its feet to acclaim La Fuoco. . . . Above all rhymed and unrhymed poetry, one prefers that unsurpassable poetry La Fuoco achieves on the stage.   (Monaldi, 1910)

Despite such references to poetry, Fuoco was essentially a virtuoso dancer, a technician immensely skilled in pointework, rather than an interpretive artist. As such, she enjoyed enormous popularity throughout her career, which lasted until the late 1850s. After that time, little is known of her life; she apparently enjoyed a comfortable retirement in her home near Lake Como. Upon her death in 1916, she gave her villa in Carate Lario to the Como Hospital and left a generous bequest to the charitable fund administered by La Scala.

BIBLIOGRAPHY

Gabanizza, Clara. "Brambilla, Maria." In *Dizionario biografico degli Italiani.* Rome, 1960–.

Girardi, Michele, and Franco Rossi. *Il Teatro La Fenice: Cronologia degli spettacoli, 1792–1936.* Venice, 1989.

Gautier, Théophile. *Gautier on Dance.* Translated and edited by Ivor Guest. London, 1986.

Guest, Ivor. *The Romantic Ballet in England.* London, 1972.

Guest, Ivor. *The Romantic Ballet in Paris.* 2d rev. ed. London, 1980.

Jürgensen, Knud Arne. *The Verdi Ballets.* Parma, 1995.

Kuzmick Hansell, Kathleen. "Il ballo teatrale e l'opera italiana." In *Storia dell'opera italiana,* vol. 5, pp. 175–306. Turin, 1987.

Monaldi, Gino. *Le regine della danza nel secolo XIX.* Turin, 1910.

Rossi, Luigi. *Il Ballo alla Scala, 1778–1970.* Milan, 1972.

Ruffin, Elena, and Giovanna Trentin. "Catalogo generale cronologico dei balli teatrali a Venezia dal 1746 al 1859." In *Balli teatrali a Venezia (1746–1859).* Milan, 1994.

Tintori, Giampiero. *Duecento anni di Teatro alla Scala: Cronologia opere-balletti-concerti, 1778–1977.* Gorle, Bergamo, 1979.

ARCHIVE.   Walter Toscanini Collection of Research Materials in Dance, New York Public Library for the Performing Arts.

CLAUDIA CELI
Translated from Italian

G

GABOVICH, MIKHAIL (Mikhail Markovich Gabovich; born 24 November [7 December] 1905 in Velikiye Gulyaki, Russia, died 12 July 1965 in Moscow), dancer, teacher, and ballet critic. Gabovich received his primary training in ballet at a private studio run by Maria Gorshenkova, a former soloist at the Maryinsky Theater. He later studied at the Moscow Ballet School under Aleksandr Gorsky and Vasily Tikhomirov. Upon graduation in 1924 he was accepted into the Bolshoi Ballet, where he quickly gained prominence. With a commanding stage presence, he made his mark as a classical dancer in the lyrical-romantic mold. Having begun with minor solo roles of the classical repertory, he moved into the forefront of the Bolshoi's soloists. Between 1930 and 1936 he took the leading male roles in classical ballets such as *La Bayadère, The Sleeping Beauty, Don Quixote, Swan Lake, Chopiniana, Giselle,* and *Raymonda.* In these roles, which were the high points of his career, he displayed the relaxed freedom and naturalness of an actor's interpretation and treatment. He took a creative approach to his roles, and having absorbed the best of what his teachers had to offer, he worked hard to expand his range.

Gabovich cooperated closely with leading Soviet choreographers such as Kasyan Goleizovsky, Vasily Tikhomirov, Lev Lashchilin, Vasily Vainonen, Rostislav Zakharov, and Leonid Lavrovsky in working on new productions. In 1927 Gabovich contributed to the creation of Lashchilin and Tikhomirov's *The Red Poppy,* the first Soviet ballet, in which he danced the role of the Phoenix. In a series of Bolshoi first performances he appeared as the actor Antoine Mistral in Vainonen's *The Flames of Paris* (1933); as Vatslav in *The Fountain of Bakhchisarai* (1936), Vladimir in *The Prisoner of the Caucasus* (1938), Andrei in *Taras Bulba* (1941), Prince Charming in *Cinderella* (1945), and Evgeny in *The Bronze Horseman* (1949), all by Zakharov; and Romeo in *Romeo and Juliet* (1946) and Ma Li-Chen in *The Red Poppy* (1949), both by Lavrovsky. In 1946 Gabovich became Galina Ulanova's permanent partner. It was in close collaboration with her that he created his best roles—Romeo, Albrecht in *Giselle,* and Vatslav.

Gabovich had a high standard of execution, clean line, and strict classical form. He was able to imbue each character with human qualities, but always couched in terms of poetic imagery. Unfortunately, his career was short-lived; an injury sustained in an accident forced him into early retirement at the height of his powers. In 1951 he started teaching at the Moscow Ballet School. Among his first students was Vladimir Vasiliev, who would subsequently become the principal male dancer of the Bolshoi. He also trained Evgeny Valupin, who later became a well-known dance teacher, and Yuri Papko, a leading dancer and ballet master. Gabovich also worked long and fruitfully as a scholar and critic. He published a series of works on ballet theory, including a book and a collection of articles, reviews, and essays. He received the title People's Artist of the Russian Federation in 1951.

BIBLIOGRAPHY

Gabovich, A. M., ed. *Mikhail Gabovich.* Moscow, 1977.
Gabovich, Mikhail. "Moscow Critic Analyses New York City Ballet Work." *Dance Magazine* (December 1962): 4.
Gabovich, Mikhail. *Dushoi ispolnennyi polet.* Moscow, 1966.
Greskovic, Robert. "The Grigorovich Factor and the Bolshoi." *Ballet Review* 5.2 (1975–1976): 1–10.
Razumnii, Vladimir. "Dramatism schastlivoy sudby." *Sovetskii balet,* no. 2 (1987).
Volkov, Nikolai D. "Distinguished Artists of the Moscow Ballet." *The Dancing Times* (October 1944): 13–14.

GALINA V. INOZEMTSEVA
Translated from Russian

GABZDYL, EMERICH (born 20 July 1908 in Ostrava-Vítkovice, Moravia, died 12 September 1993 in Ostrava), Czech dancer, choreographer, and teacher. At age fourteen Gabzdyl joined the Ostrava ballet, where his teacher and director was the Italian Achille Viscusi. Under his firm and fastidious tutelage, the young Gabzdyl quickly developed. At age eighteen he signed a soloist contract and began to choreograph operas and operettas. When, in 1927, Professor Max Semmler guest-produced, in Ostrava, *Die Josephslegende,* he chose Gabzdyl for the title role. This role produced new opportunities for Gabzdyl: first an engagement in Bratislava (1928–1929) Followed by, in the same role, guest performances in Semmler productions in Austria, Switzerland, and Germany. Gabzdyl even taught in Semmler's Berlin school (1930–1932).

A new world of dance opened up for Gabzdyl in Berlin. Having been trained in old Italian classical dance, he now discovered German dance, with its singular emphasis on expression. Germany's rapidly deteriorating political situation, however, forced Gabzdyl to return to the Czechoslavak Socialist Republic and accept the post of first soloist in Brno (1932–1938). During this time he created many stage characters, including Abderakhman in *Raymonda*, Apollo in *Apollon Musagète*, and the Prodigal Son. His debut as a choreographer was in a production of Prokofiev's *Chout* in 1935; Gabzdyl also performed as a tenor in operettas. In 1938 he accepted an offer to become a director in his native Ostrava, where, over the next thirty-two years, he danced and sang, choreographed, and directed a company. Gabzdyl created a true era in the Ostrava ballet. He gradually built a large (fifty-member), hard-working, and ambitious company; he himself danced in many roles (Romeo, Rothbart in *Swan Lake*, Khan, Girei in *The Fountain of Bakhchisarai*, and Don Juan). In 1968, at age sixty, he portrayed the character of Old Magdón in *Maryčka Magdónova* (music by Jiří Bažant).

During his career Gabzdyl produced seventy-five ballets and choreographed one hundred and twenty operas and one hundred and thirty operettas; his performances numbered in the thousands. His repertory did not have a distinct personal style; the time, place, and public did not allow for that. In spite of this, however, he was responsible for the staging of several new works, including *Ondráš* (1951), *Jack and the Devil* (1954), *Florella* (1960), and *Well of Love* (1967). Gabzdyl also trained a long line of dancers, among them, Marta Drottnerová, Vlasta Pavelcová, and Albert Janíček; in 1953–1954 Gabzdyl was professor of choreography at the Prague Academy of Musical Arts. The culmination of his theatrical career came in 1970, when he was offered the post of ballet director of the Prague National Theater, from which he retired in 1974.

BIBLIOGRAPHY

Dance View (Spring 1993).
Gabzdyl, Emerich, and Vladimír Vašut. *V hlavní roli Emerich Gabzdyl*. Ostrava, 1988.
Rey, Jan. "Change and Growth in Czechoslovakia." *Dance and Dancers* (October 1960): 14–17.
25 let divadelní činnosti. Ostrava, n.d.
Státní divadlo v Ostravě, 1919–1979. Ostrava, 1979.
Schmidová, Lidka. *Československý balet*. Prague, 1962.
Vašut, Vladimír, and Emerich Gabzdyl. *V hlavní roli Emerich Gabzdyl*. Ostrava, 1988.

VLADIMÍR VAŠUT
Translated from Czech

GADD, ULF (born 8 March 1943 in Göteborg), Swedish dancer, choreographer, and ballet director. After studies from 1950 to 1960 with Mila Gardemeister in Göteborg, Gadd was engaged at the Royal Swedish Ballet in Stockholm, where he soon won public and critical acclaim for his technical brilliance and characterization as the Bluebird in *The Sleeping Beauty* and in the title role in Ivo Cramér's *The Prodigal Son*. He was awarded the Prix Nijinsky in 1967 for his pure classical dancing. After a season with the Harkness Ballet in the United States, he returned in 1968 to his hometown and its opera house, the Stora Teatern (Great Theater), where he danced roles including solo parts in Harald Lander's *Études* and Roland Petit's version of *Carmen*.

In 1969, Gadd made his choreographic debut with *Ebb och Flod* (Ebb and Flood), set to Georg Philipp Telemann's *Wassermusik*, which he also staged for London Festival Ballet in 1972. In 1970, he made a breakthrough with a powerful version of *The Miraculous Mandarin*, which he also staged for both the Royal Swedish Ballet and American Ballet Theatre in 1971 and for the Berlin Opera Ballet in 1972.

In 1970 Gadd toured London, Paris, and Stockholm with a short-lived company called Les Nouveaux Ballets Suédois. In 1972 he returned to Göteborg as dancer and choreographer; from 1976 through 1988 he held the post of ballet director at the Stora Teatern, which he turned into one of Scandinavia's most creative dance companies. He has been a guest choreographer at the Cullberg Ballet and at the Royal Swedish Ballet, where in 1974 he staged a controversial version of *The Sleeping Beauty*.

Following *The Miraculous Mandarin*, Gadd focused on dramatic ballets, often with dark and violent undercurrents. In 1973 he created a new version of one of the best-known ballets from the 1920s repertory of Les Ballets Suédois in Paris, *Maison de Fous* (The Madhouse), with music by Viking Dahl. His first full-length work was *Kalevala* (1975), based on the Finnish national epic and set to music by Jean Sibelius. He further developed the full-length ballet in dance-theater pieces created in collaboration with the designer Svenerik Goude: *Drottning Kristina* (Queen Christina) in 1978; *Coppélia* in 1979, to music by Léo Délibes; *Diaghilews Ryska Balett* (Diaghilev's Russian Ballet) in 1980; *Gösta Berlings Saga* (The Tale of Gösta Berling) in 1981, based on Selma Lagerlöf's famous novel, to music by Franz Berwald; *Ringen* (The Ring) in 1983, to music by Richard Wagner; *Den Dunkles Danser* (The Darkling Dances) in 1984, to the ballet music for *Kratt* by Eduard Tubin; and in 1985 *Tango Buenos Aires 1907*, based on a medley of Argentine tango music.

In these full-length works by Gadd and Goude, dance and theater are equally important. They work together as a unit, always very ambitious, creating a large format, often spectacular design, with exciting visual flow. In contrast to this grand-scale theatrical dance, Gadd successfully created an intense chamber version of *Le Sacre du Printemps* in 1982.

Gadd left Göteborg after the 1987/88 season to settle in Bali and study Balinese dance and music. He returned in the autumn of 1996, as ballet director at the Göteborg Opera (formerly called the Stora Teatern).

BIBLIOGRAPHY

Gadd, Ulf. "Om Göteborgsbaletten och Orfeus i synnerhet." *Dans* (November 1974): 49–53.

Garske, Rolf. "We Cannot Go Back: Interview with Ulf Gadd." *Ballett International* 12 (January 1989): 20–25.

Näslund, Erik. "Widerstand ja! Gegnerschaft nein! Ulf Gadd, Ballettdirektor und Chefchoreograph in schwedischen Göteborg." In *Ballet 1984: Chronik und Bilanz des Ballettjahres,* edited by Horst Koegler et al. Velber bei Hannover, 1984.

Percival, John. "Old, New, Borrowed, and Blue in Gothenburg." *Dance and Dancers* (December 1974): 24–26.

Percival, John. "The Gifted Goths." *Dance and Dancers* (May 1975): 16–18.

Williams, Peter, and John Percival. "Regional Ballet Comes to London." *Dance and Dancers* (July 1975): 27–31.

ERIK NÄSLUND

GADES, ANTONIO (born 1936 in Elba), Spanish flamenco dancer. The great Spanish flamenco dancer Antonio Gades is neither a Gypsy nor an Andalusian; he was born in the province of Alicante. His father, a worker and a supporter of the Republican government, was seriously wounded at the close of the Spanish Civil War (1936–1939). Antonio Gades went to live in Madrid, where he was put to work at an early age.

Having fortuitously found a school of dance, Gades was in the early 1950s hired to dance in a cabaret in Santander. Here he was discovered by Pilar López, in whose company he danced from 1952 to 1961. López had followed in the footsteps of La Argentinita, who raised elements of Spanish folk dance to the technical and theatrical level of ballet. Another of his teachers was Vicente Escudero, whom he met in 1955.

In 1961 Gades studied academic technique in Rome and became Anton Dolin's assistant in *Boléro.* He was invited by Gian-Carlo Menotti to participate in the Spoleto Festival and in the Ballet des Deux Mondes, where he staged dances for a production of Bizet's opera *Carmen* conducted by Thomas Schippers, with Carla Fracci and Milorad Miskovich. In 1962 he staged *Pavane pour une Infante Défunte* and *Le Rétable de Don Cristobal,* followed by *El Amor Brujo* at the Teatro alla Scala, Milan. These successes in Italy did not lead him to turn his back on Spain. In 1963 he returned to his native country and founded his first small company.

Staged in a Barcelona *tablao* (nightclub), *Los Tarantos* brought Gades a brilliant success, and he was engaged for the 1963/64 New York World's Fair. In 1964 Fraga Iribarne, a minister in Spain's government, then led by the dictator Francisco Franco, mobilized the press against Gades's tragicomedic version of *Don Juan.* His choreography for *El Sombrero de Tres Picos,* in which he danced the

GADES. During the late 1960s and the 1970s, the Antonio Gades Spanish Dance Company toured widely and enjoyed great success. Gades is pictured here with musicians of his company in a 1972 performance. (Photograph from the Dance Collection, New York Public Library for the Performing Arts.)

role of the Old Faruca, also made a political statement against the Spanish regime.

In 1978 Gades was asked to establish the National Ballet of Spain. He lasted barely two years as its director; his fondness for the regional dances of Galicia and the Basque country clashed with the nationalist view. Nevertheless, he succeeded in staging *Bodas de Sangre* (Blood Wedding), inspired by Federico García Lorca's play, and *El Rango* (Rank), using a mixture of Gregorian chant and flamenco guitar music. In 1980 he founded his own troupe, with Cristina Hoyos, Juan Antonio, and Enrique Esteve. He restaged the same two works in the rigorous and spectacular form of a flamenco suite.

In 1981 Carlos Saura made a motion picture based on *Bodas de Sangre,* filming the ballet without sets or costumes, in the company's rehearsal hall; the result was a ballet that seemed still sparer and purer. After this success Saura and Gades prepared a *Carmen* for both cinema and stage; in the film a dramatic intrigue develops between the dancers, which is superimposed on the story line inspired by Prosper Mérimée's novel. The ballet version is a spare montage of flamenco song and dances for which Bizet's music occasionally serves as a counterpoint. Cristina Hoyos played the role of Carmen on the stage, and Laura del Sol in the film. Gades and Saura subsequently collaborated on *El Amor Brujo* to music by Manuel de Falla. Completed in 1986, the film became the basis of a staged version that has toured extensively.

Gades's work is a logical step in the evolution of Spanish dance. Noting that flamenco dancers based their dancing on a limited number of steps when they improvised,

Gades gave up the romantic conception that flamenco's beauty depends on mysterious inspiration or *duende*. Pilar López, the heir of La Argentinita, initiated Gades into the art of the theater. It was not enough to stage solos and pas de deux: it was necessary to design movements for groups and to pay great attention to lighting. In terms of style, Gades's master was Vicente Escudero, who was taught to dance by the Spanish Gypsies of Valladolid; he had succeeded in eliminating every trace of mannerism and vulgarity from flamenco. Traditionally, the flamenco dancer concentrated his attention on the movements of the legs and the tapping of the heels, but Escudero developed the arms, positioning his hands like flames above his head. Gades inherited Escudero's demanding nature and his sense of modernity. He designs with the rigor of a geometer or painter, but he is careful not to dampen the spontaneity or weaken the brilliance of his dances.

BIBLIOGRAPHY

Carmen: Ballet Antonio Gades con Cristina Hoyos. Barcelona, 1985.
Lartigue, Pierre. *Antonio Gades: Le flamenco.* L'Avant-Scène/Ballet-Danse, no. 14. Paris, 1984.
Lartigue, Pierre. *L'Art de la pointe.* Paris, 1992.
Schmidt, Jochen. "Ballet Espagnol Antonio Gades." *Das Tanzarchiv* 21 (August 1973): 91–92.

PIERRE LARTIGUE
Translated from French

GAGAKU is a general term for all the music and dance of the Japanese Imperial Household Agency. Although it is not uncommon to find the term for court dance, *bugaku*, used in contradistinction to *gagaku*, *bugaku* is, in fact, the dance form of two strands of the *gagaku* tradition (*togaku* and *komagaku*, discussed below).

In origin, the term *gagaku* was synonymous with the Chinese *yayue*, the ancient tradition of music and dance of the so-called Confucian ritual. The Japanese tradition, in fact, owes it origin to the court banquet and entertainment tradition of Tang-dynasty China (618–906 CE) and to the many forms of music and dance popular at the Tang court. In Japan, *gagaku* also came to include music that had earlier been introduced from the Three Kingdoms of what is present-day Korea. In addition, *gagaku* now includes the various forms of traditional Shintō ritual music and dance, which were developed in Japan before the introduction of any music and dance from mainland Asia.

Japanese *gagaku* was well established by the late eighth century CE and has survived in a continuous, unbroken teacher-to-pupil and father-to-son tradition since that time. Even so, *gagaku* has undergone numerous gradual changes over the years, and certain elements of the tradition have been lost. From its beginnings till today, *gagaku* has been the almost exclusive prerogative and responsibility of a single group of professional musicians' guilds. These families presently constitute Japan's Music Department of the Imperial Household Agency. Today, the tradition consists of three large repertories, each with its own dances, music, and special instrumentation: the largest repertory is *togaku*, or "Tang music"; *komagaku* is the repertory of music from Korea; the Shintō ritual group consists of a number of separate musical pieces and dances. Although *togaku* and *komagaku* trace their names and forms back to traditions of mainland Asia, most compositions in each repertory were probably composed by Japanese courtiers.

The dance forms of *togaku* and *komagaku* are referred to collectively as *bugaku*. *Togaku* actually has two forms of performance—*bugaku*, or dance performances, and *kangen*, instrumental recitals. The difference is not merely that *bugaku* is danced whereas *kangen* is limited to instrumental performance; rather, the same musical composition is given different phrasing, tempo, and instrumentation, depending on whether it is a *bugaku* or *kangen* performance. Of all *gagaku* forms, *togaku* requires the most complex instrumentation; its *kangen* form uses three kinds of wind instruments, two kinds of stringed instruments, and three kinds of percussion instruments, including a gong and drums. In *bugaku* (danced) performances of *togaku*, the stringed instruments are omitted and larger versions of the percussion instruments are usually employed, lending the performance a greater rhythmic stability.

Komagaku is traditionally performed in only its *bugaku*, or danced, form, and there is no special name for instrumental performance of *komagaku*. Here, the accompanying ensemble consists of two different kinds of wind instruments and three kinds of percussion instruments. The ritual Shintō music and dances are not traditionally performed outside the context of Shintō shrine ceremonies. Again, no separate instrumental form of the music exists. Song is an important part of the Shintō ritual repertories; instrumentation is limited to two wind instruments, a single stringed instrument, and two pairs of clappers, each played by one of the leading singers. Of the Shintō song-and-dance cycles, the *mikagura* is the most ancient and sacred. The others, *Kume mai*, *Yamato mai*, and *Azuma asobi* (named for locales), while still vital parts of the court Shintō ritual repertory, are in their present form thought to have been modeled on the form and style of the *mikagura*.

Whereas individual pieces of the Shintō ritual repertories are grouped together in the large song-and-dance cycles to which they belong and therefore have a fixed sequence of performance, *togaku* and *komagaku* are rather freely combined and mixed in performance. Thus, in a

GAGAKU. A ceremonial genre of music and dance from the Japanese imperial court, *gagaku* has had a continuous performance tradition since the eighth century. Here, an instrumental ensemble plays while four dancers manipulate spears. (Photograph from the archives of The Asia Society, New York.)

typical *bugaku* performance, dances using *togaku* music are contrasted with those using *komagaku* music. Within the *togaku* and *komagaku* subdivisions of the *gagaku* tradition are various categories of rhythmic type and compositional form that add to the richness and complexity of a performance program.

Besides the *gagaku* performances that they give in the Imperial Palace in Tokyo, the imperial court musicians also perform periodic services at many of the major Shintō shrines throughout the country—in particular at the Meiji Shrine in Tokyo—as well as frequent public concerts outside the palace. In addition to the musicians of the Imperial Household, several more recently established *gagaku* groups perform in Tokyo; there are also a few groups in Kyoto, and groups of *gagaku* musicians are attached to the Tenno temple in Osaka, the Kasuga Shrine in Nara, and the Ise Shrine. In each case, the tradition of

dance and musical performance is essentially the same as that of the musicians of the Imperial Palace.

[*For related discussion, see* Japan, *overview article. For more general discussion, see* Bugaku *and* Music for Dance, *article on* Asian Music.]

BIBLIOGRAPHY

Garfias, Robert. *Music of a Thousand Autumns: The Togagku Style of Japanese Court Music.* Los Angeles, 1975.

Harich-Schneider, Eta. *A History of Japanese Music.* London, 1973.

Malm, William P. *Japanese Music and Musical Instruments.* Tokyo, 1959.

Togi, Masataro. *Gagaku: Court Music and Dance.* Translated by Don Kenny. New York, 1971.

Wolz, Carl. *Bugaku: Japanese Court Dance.* Providence, R.I., 1971.

ROBERT GARFIAS

GAÎTÉ PARISIENNE. Ballet in one act. Choreography: Léonide Massine. Music: Jacques Offenbach. Scenery and costumes: Comte Étienne de Beaumont. First performance: 5 April 1938, Monte Carlo, Ballet Russe de Monte Carlo. Principals: Nina Tarakanova (The

Glove Seller), Eugénie Delarova (The Flower Girl), Jeannette Lauret (La Lionne), Léonide Massine (The Peruvian), Frederic Franklin (The Baron), Igor Youskevitch (The Military Officer), Casimir Kokitch (The Duke), Irène Fabergé (La Cantinière), Robert T. Irwin (Tortoni).

Gaîté Parisienne was the second of Léonide Massine's fanciful comic ballets and is one of the most popular and enduring of all his works. It was the first ballet created for the new Ballet Russe de Monte Carlo company established in 1938 with Massine as artistic director. The timelessness of the work depends not on its choreographic invention nor on the scantily woven plot, but on the ingenuity of its creator in presenting a lively and colorful entertainment.

The story line centers on the adventures of a rich Peruvian who arrives in a fashionable Paris restaurant looking for a good time. The waiters and maids are preparing the main room for the evening. Various flirtations transpire between the Peruvian, the Flower Girl, and the Glove Seller. The Baron enters and diverts the attention of the girls. His entrance is followed by more customers, including the Duke, the elegant beauty La Lionne, and the Military Officer. With the humor of a slapstick comedy, a fight breaks out over petty jealousies. Finally, the restaurant is cleared before the guests reenter to watch the can-can girls perform. When it is time to leave, the leading characters have paired off and depart, leaving the Peruvian trembling in utter despair.

Most critics agree that the choreography of *Gaîté Parisienne* is not of the same quality as in some of Massine's other ballets, but most also acknowledge that it has real audience appeal. Massine, in fact, was very clever in his construction of the ballet. The action is constant, the energy of his characters was high, and the colors of the costumes and decor were vibrant. In his movement characterization, Massine exaggerated the comical traits of the personalities. The Peruvian, for example, was constantly moving in excited anticipation, using his Latin good looks to woo the women while spinning and fluttering all over the room.

In 1941, Warner Brothers Studios made a short film of the ballet, titling it *The Gay Parisian*. Many revivals of the ballet have been presented all over the world; Massine himself staged it for Ballet Theatre in New York (1942), at the Teatro alla Scala in Milan (1948), at the Teatro Municipal in Rio de Janeiro (1955), for the Marquis de Cuevas Company in Brussels (1958), and for London Festival Ballet (1973).

GAÎTÉ PARISIENNE. Alexandra Danilova as the Glove Seller and Frederic Franklin as the Baron in a moment of romantic abandon in their pas de deux. Although Danilova did not create the Glove Seller, she made the role her own and became famous for it. On opening night of the Ballet Russe de Monte Carlo's 1941 New York season, the audience greeted Danilova's entrance with an ovation, which thereafter became a tradition. (Photograph by Dwight Godwin; from the Dance Collection, New York Public Library for the Performing Arts.)

BIBLIOGRAPHY
Beaumont, Cyril W. *Complete Book of Ballets*. London, 1937.
Fusillo, Lisa A. "Léonide Massine: Choreographic Genius with a Collaborative Spirit." Ph.D. diss., Texas Woman's University, 1982.
Krokover, Rosalyn. *The New Borzoi Book of Ballets*. New York, 1956.

LISA A. FUSILLO

GALEOTTI, VINCENZO (Vincenzo Tomasselli; born 5 March 1733, possibly in Florence, died 16 December 1816 in Copenhagen), dancer and ballet master. Galeotti held the post of Royal Danish ballet master from 1781 until his death. He became a Danish citizen in 1812 and in 1814 was named a Knight of the Order of Dannebrog, as the first artist at the Royal Theater.

Galeotti was a pupil of Gaspero Angiolini, and probably also of Jean-Georges Noverre in Stuttgart. Galeotti's wife, Antonia Guidi, was an Italian ballerina who worked under Noverre. Galeotti performed as solo dancer in the Venetian theaters of San Moisè in 1759 and San Benedetto in 1761. He spent the next fifteen years as ballet master and solo dancer in Venice and briefly (1767) in Turin. In 1769 Galeotti came as solo dancer with the Italian opera to the

King's Theatre, London, where the following year he was appointed ballet master. After returning to Venice, in March 1775 Galeotti was engaged by the Royal Theater in Copenhagen as ballet master and solo dancer. His wife was also engaged; she died in 1780.

In October 1775, twenty days after his arrival in Copenhagen, Galeotti presented his first major ballet, *Kongen paa Jagt* (The King at the Hunt), probably a version of Gaspero Angiolini's *Il Re alla Caccia*, which he had staged in Genoa in 1774 under the title *La Caccia d'Enrico Quarto*. Further inspired by Angiolini, Galeotti presented *Bønderne og Herrerne på Lystgaarden* (Peasants and Masters at the Villa) in December 1775 and *Zigeunernes Leir* (The Gypsy Camp) in January 1776.

During his first decade in Copenhagen, Galeotti staged his own versions of famous ballets by Angiolini and Noverre. At first he used Italian violin scores orchestrated by the Danish musician Johannes Darbes. Later Claus Schall, a former ballet pupil, took over the work of orchestration. In November 1780 Schall composed his first original ballet music for Galeotti's *Kjaerligheds og Mistankens Magt* (The Power of Love and Suspicion). They collaborated on dozens of ballets and *divertissements*.

The ballets from Galeotti's first period stayed in the repertory for decades. Among his greatest successes were *Den Forladte Dido* (Dido Abandoned) in October 1777 and *L'Orphelin de la Chine* in January 1780. Even though dancers and critics knew that these works were derivative, all were deeply impressed and enthusiastic in their descriptions of Galeotti's genius. Two important contemporary sources are the first Danish theatrical periodical, *Den dramatiske journal*, written by Rosenstand-Goiske, and the observations in Antoine Bournonville's diary.

When the Royal Theater was founded in 1748, the art of professional ballet in Denmark was born as well. Galeotti did not try, as did ballet masters in the company's first twenty-five years, to adapt ballet to the art the court preferred—comic or serious opera. Instead, he used the ideals of *ballet d'action* and underlined the theatrical, dramatic side of the art of dance, establishing an attitude toward ballet in Denmark that to some extent prevails even today. Galeotti also pioneered by supporting the education of Danish children as artists, to make the Royal Ballet the first purely national company in Europe (outside Italy and France). The only non-Danish dancer of importance whom Galeotti engaged was Antoine Bournonville, the father of August Bournonville.

Galeotti's ballet *Amors og Balletmesterens Luner* (The Whims of Cupid and the Ballet Master) premiered on 31 October 1786 and is still performed. The music was composed by Jens Lolle, a violinist from the Royal Orchestra. Members of the company preserved the choreography during the long Bournonville period (1792–1823); nearly every time Bournonville left for engagements abroad,

Amors returned to the repertory. Ballet master Emil Hansen made the first notation of its choreography for its centennial performance. Comparison with the original score shows that the current version has lost only sixteen beats (a solo by Cupid) and that all tempi have survived.

Amors shows that Galeotti was an inventive choreographer. Its story is simple: couples come to the temple of Cupid asking to be united and blessed. In the printed program Galeotti says that he created the ballet to prove that he could interest the audience through a series of independent pas de deux, but he does not describe the witty inner structure. *Amors* is built like a miniature court ballet: it repeats the conventional sequence of *danse sérieuse*, *demi-classique*, and *grotesque*, and then ends in a grand ballet in which the wicked Cupid/Ballet Master mixes the couples in an extraordinary way. This subtlety of Galeotti's was later forgotten, so that the character of the two pas de deux changed, but not the choreography. The most important difference is that the "Negro Dance" was originally not a grotesque but a serious dance, reflecting the eighteenth-century idea of the Noble Savage. The Royal Ballet has performed *Amors* more than five hundred times. Harald Lander staged it for the Paris Opera in 1952, and Elsa-Marianne von Rosen staged it for the eighteenth-century Drottningholm Court Theater in 1969.

A new direction in Galeotti's career came on 30 January 1801, when the sixty-seven-year-old ballet master presented *Lagertha*, with music by Claus Schall. The story was written by Christen Pram, who used the medieval Danish historian Saxo's description of a Viking heroine, Lagertha, and her unfaithful husband. *Lagertha* was a turning point not only in its use of a Nordic theme for a big heroic ballet, but also in its music. It introduced the Nordic features that characterized all Scandinavian Romantic music for nearly a century to follow. *Lagertha's* costuming, designed by Danish artist Nicolai Abildgård, was the first attempt to dress ancient Scandinavian theatrical heroes in authentic historical costume instead of Greco-Roman styles.

Galeotti is also known for two other ballets, early attempts to adapt Shakespearean plays. He created *Romeo og Giulietta* in 1811 and *Macbeth* in 1816, only a few months before his death. Into old age Galeotti continued to present his versions of international successes, including *Nina, ou La Folle par Amour* (1802), *Inez de Castro* (1804), *Bluebeard* (1808), and *Choromania* (1811).

Apart from almost sixty ballets, Galeotti helped to develop standards of dance and mimed scenes in drama, comedy, musical comedy, and opera at the Royal Theater. He gave the Royal Danish Ballet its identity and national character. He did not share the obsession of August Bournonville with creating ballets of the highest dramatic standard. Galeotti's choreography, especially for the leading characters in his tragic ballets, was more easygoing and probably more lyrical than that created by his famous successor.

[*See also* Royal Danish Ballet.]

BIBLIOGRAPHY

Beaumont, Cyril W. *Ballets Past and Present: Being a Third Supplement to the Complete Book of Ballets*. London, 1955.

Fog, Dan. *The Royal Danish Ballet, 1760–1958, and August Bournonville: A Chronological Catalogue*. Copenhagen, 1961.

Fridericia, Allan. "Amor og Balettmästarens nycker." In *Drottningholm teaterns suvenirprogram*. Copenhagen, 1969.

Kragh-Jacobsen, Svend. *The Royal Danish Ballet*. Copenhagen and London, 1955.

Winter, Marian Hannah. *The Pre-Romantic Ballet*. London, 1974.

ALLAN FRIDERICIA

GALLET, SÉBASTIEN

GALLET, SÉBASTIEN (born 1750, died 10 June 1807 in Vienna), French dancer and ballet master. Gallet was a student of Jean-George Noverre, for whom he danced in court ballets. In 1770 he appeared at Versailles in *Castor et Pollux*, with music by Jean-Philippe Rameau, and, at the marriage of the Dauphin and Marie-Antoinette on 17 May, in *Persée*, set to music by Jean-Baptiste Lully. Both were choreographed by Michel-Jean Bandieri de Laval. At Fontainebleau he danced in *Le Devin du Village*, with music by Jean-Jacques Rousseau, and *La Fête de Flore*, choreographed by Laval. Gallet then left France but returned to make his debut at the Paris Opera on 6 August 1782 in *Roland* (scored by Niccolò Piccinni), with his mistress Eléonore Dupré. Dismissed in 1783 for unknown reasons, he once again went abroad.

Having abandoned his career as a dancer, in 1791 Gallet returned to the Paris Opera as a choreographer. His *Bacchus et Ariane*, with music by Rochefort, premiered on 11 December, with Auguste Vestris, Mesdemoiselles Millière and Coulon, and Marie-Adrienne Chameroy, was highly successful. Noverre described it: "The arrival of Bacchus, followed by the bacchantes, the fauns, the spirits of the woods, and the elderly Silenus, offered to an enchanted audience the *tableau vivant* of the bacchanales of antiquity." Gallet was named assistant ballet master to Pierre Gardel, but, disheartened by the difficulties he encountered, he again left the Opera. He was welcomed in Vienna, Milan, Naples, and London. In Bordeaux, between 1796 and 1800, he presented *Les Circonstances Embarrassantes*, *Acis et Galathée*, and *L'Offrande à Terpsichore*.

As a dancer and ballet master at the King's Theatre in London, after *Apollon Berger* on 27 December, 1796, Gallet directed numerous ballets in 1797, 1798, and 1803, including *Les Délassements Militaires* (1797), *Les Rivaux Généreux* (1798), *La Fête de Vénus* and *La Fôret Enchantée*, presented on 4 December 1802, and *Laurette* (1803). He applied the principles of Noverre, an ardent defender of the *ballet d'action*, who in turn regarded his former pupil as one of the most ingenious choreographers.

BIBLIOGRAPHY

Baron, Auguste A. F. *Lettres à Sophie sur la danse*. Paris, 1825.

Chazin-Bennahum, Judith. *Dance in the Shadow of the Guillotine*. Carbondale, Ill., 1988.

Massaro, Maria Nevilla. "Balli e ballerini fra Padova e Venezia." *La danza italiana* 5–6 (Autumn 1987): 77–88.

Noverre, Jean-Georges. *Lettres sur les arts imitateurs en général et sur la danse en particulier*. 2 vols. Paris, 1807. Edited by Fernand Divoire as *Lettres sur la danse et les arts imitateurs* (Paris, 1952).

Swift, Mary Grace. *A Loftier Flight: The Life and Accomplishments of Charles Louis Didelot*. Middletown, Conn., 1974.

JEANNINE DORVANE
Translated from French

GALLIARD

GALLIARD (It., *gagliarda*; Fr., *gaillarde*; Sp., *gallarda*). The galliard was the most vigorous, virtuosic, and joyous dance type of the sixteenth and early seventeenth centuries. In addition to its various manifestations as a social dance, it was a virtuoso showpiece for male dancers in theatrical presentations.

The galliard was usually performed in moderate triple or compound duple meter (3/2 or 6/2). The term *galliard* means "spirited and virile"; the names of the galliard's fundamental step pattern of five leapt changes of weight with kicks in six beats (It., *cinquepassi*; Fr., *cinque pas*; Eng., sinkapace) were often used synonymously for the dance itself. By the late seventeenth and early eighteenth centuries, both step and dance type were in a slow to moderate simple duple meter as shown in five extant eighteenth-century choreographies. The galliard is still a traditional folk dance in parts of Italy, and aspects of its style are evident in other traditional dances (e.g. the tarantella).

As with most sixteenth-century dances, the galliard's origins are unknown; some argue for Lombardy, others Rome. The earliest extant reference seems to be in a late fifteenth-century epic poem by Matteo Boiardo, *Orlando Innamorato*, but the poem was completed by Francesco Berni in 1531 and the galliard reference is in one of Berni's stanzas. It is known with certainty that the galliard's earliest documented musical appearance is in Pierre Attaingnant's *Dix-huit basses dances* and *Six gaillards et six pavanes* (both Paris [?], 1529, 1530), and its earliest choreographic reference is by Antonius Arena, in about 1528, in a text in comical macaronic verse that, in this case, emphasizes the galliard's leaping vigor: "It is a bold dance which makes us gasp for breath" (Arena, 1528). It is known that later comments continue to underscore its athleticism (e.g., Bishop Lanfranco says, "As for the Pavana and Gagliarda, let them be as vivacious as they can so that even the very benches, chairs, and vases start to dance" (1549). English literary references abound, as in this excerpt from a scene in William Shakespeare's *Twelfth Night*:

SIR TOBY: What is thy excellence in a galliard, knight?

SIR ANDREW: Faith, I can cut a caper.

SIR TOBY: And I can cut the mutton to't.

SIR ANDREW: And I think I have the back-trick simply as strong as any man in Illyria.

SIR TOBY: Wherefore are these things hid? wherefore have these gifts a curtain before 'em? are they like to take dust, like Mistress Mall's picture? why dost thou not go to church in a galliard and come home in a coranto? My very walk should be a jig; I would not so much as make water but in a sink-a-pace. What dost thou mean? Is it a world to hide virtues in? I did think, by the excellent consitution of thy leg, it was formed under the star of a galliard.   (*Twelfth Night,* act 1, scene 3)

The popularity of the dance in Italy and France is well documented in instruction material from the second half of the sixteenth century. The earliest known major source is Lutio Compasso's *Ballo della gagliarda* (1560), with descriptions of 165 variations; the sheer number speaks for the dance's popularity and suggests at the very least a twenty-five-year history. Fabritio Caroso's *Il ballarino* (1581) begins a virtual explosion of published instructions for basic step patterns and galliard variations, lasting at least until 1620, including those of (Ludovico Jacobilli) (1615). Caroso's instructions are predominantly for entire galliard movements of *balletto* suites; they are the first with music and clear time values for some steps. Caroso's second manual, *Nobiltà di dame* (1600), gives "corrections" of much of his earlier material, as well as new steps and dances.

Cesare Negri's manual *Le gratie d'amore* (1602), reissued as *Nuove inventioni di balli* (1604), is the most comprehensive of all in treating the galliard (see below). Thoinot Arbeau (1588) gives almost twenty variations with music and precise rhythmic values, but no complete dance. Prospero Lutii of Sulmona (1589) has thirty-two *partite, et passeggi* (variations and passages traversing the floor), and Livio Lupi (1600, 1607) provides an astounding two hundred variations. Neither Lutii nor Lupi, however, gives adequate rhythmic instructions, music, or complete dances. Clearly, the lists of galliard variations were designed to assist those who felt unable to improvise their own; however, they also reinforce the view that an extremely important aspect of the dance was improvisation.

In England only an Inns of Court manuscript by John Ramsey (Bodleian Library, Douce 280) from about 1600 gives directions, cryptically citing the basic galliard's pattern of weight changes. Ramsey merely mentions that there are more elaborate steps, "learned only by practise." Appropriately, complex galliard variations of several bars' length were termed *tricks* in English; a "galliard trick of twenty," for example, probably refers to the number of leg gestures in a particular variation.

Of all the sources, Negri (1602, 1604) provides the most complete picture of the dance. The first section of *Le gratie d'amore* lists dancing masters of the time, specifying their expertise—among which dancing the galliard brilliantly and making up new tricks clearly signifies much: "Stefano, son of Manzino of Bologna, in vaulting to horse, somersaulting . . . and in dancing the galliard is marvelous" (Negri, 1602, 1604, p. 3, my translation). Negri's second section incorporates a detailed and lengthy portion of seventy pages of galliard steps and variations, including many carefully detailed descriptions of individual step variants, with hints as to time values, and many complex step combinations of up to six bars (thirty-six beats). Although without music, there are precise instructions on the duration and number of leg gestures *(botte)* of each variation (e.g., "*29 botte & sei tempi di suono*"—that is, twenty-nine gestures in six bars of music). Negri even includes occasional comments on the comparative difficulty of one or another variation. He also specifies and illustrates (uniquely) performance details such as bodily gesture (quiet, erect torso; relaxed arms; direct gaze) as well as aspects of costume (e.g., in the more strenuous variations, the gentleman may remove his cape and sword but not his hat). Negri's many variations have lengths that are regular (four bars and multiples) or irregular (three-, five-, or six-bar *tempi di gagliarda*). Here too are male feats that have been associated with Western dance for centuries: for example, *intrecciate* (or capers) of various types, multiple turns on the ground *(girate)*, or the same in the air *(salti tondi)*. Negri is the first ever to depict a *barre*—a chair and table—for use when practicing. The technical demands here, and in Lutii and Lupi, go far beyond Arbeau's (Caroso occupies a middle ground), revealing both virtuosity and improvisatory techniques that even today's professionals may find challenging (e.g., three successive turns in the air in six minim beats). In his third section, Negri and Caroso, give precise choreographies of full galliard movements in *balletto* suites, with music.

Unquestionably, ladies also danced galliards vigorously, but without the full male pyrotechnics. Caroso and Negri give some special women's variations that are less strenuous than the men's. Although in the galliard choreographies of the multimovement *balletti*, the ladies are usually told to duplicate or slightly simplify their partners' steps, they receive scant attention in the separate listings of galliard variations. (Negri describes four lady's variations requiring quick footwork.) Some sources state that ladies dance lower than gentlemen (Arbeau and Caroso). Never, however, do their variations include the male feats mentioned above—not even a single *girate* (pirouette). This omission suggests strongly that such techniques were truly reserved for males.

Determining exactly the original step pattern of the galliard when it was first mentioned in 1528 is impossible for lack of information. Even after 1560 it is complicated by the rapid appearance of hundreds of complex galliard steps, variations, and passages. Nevertheless, many of the simpler variations in all sources share traits, confirm the term *sinkapace* (or *cinq pas*): five changes of weight in one galliard pattern *(tempo di gagliarda)* of six minim beats, with vigorous kicks and a leap ending with a *cadenza* (Fr., *saut majeur* and *posture*)—a high caper that could be ornamented (note the parallel usage to the musical term *cadenza* to signify a showy ending). It may thus be surmised that this pattern was basic, at least after about 1550 (e.g., Arbeau's and Negri's basic patterns seem to be virtually identical; Caroso's is the same as one variation of Arbeau's). Separate rules for the individual components of the step pattern (e.g., It., *zoppetto, passo in aria, ricacciata, cadenza, sottopiede;* Fr., *petit saut, grève, saut majeur, posture, entretaille*) allowed their use outside the galliard as well. In fact, it is not known whether steps or pattern came first chronologically. Nevertheless, when in the sources the terms *tempo di gagliarda, cinque passi in gagliarda, cinq pas,* or *sinkapace* appear, they imply the six-minim pattern as a whole, however simple or complex its footwork, and they demonstrate that the writer was thinking of the galliard.

As a social dance, the galliard in its typical choreographic paths was a wooing dance for one couple. Normally it included simultaneous passages that introduced and interspersed variations performed alternately, The active partner showed off while the "inactive" partner often danced a simple walking passage *(passegio)*. The whole was essentially a "solo-with-accompaniment" form, with refrains of simultaneous dancing in which the passing and repassing of partners was also customary. Other showy dance types, such as the *tordiglione,* canary, and *passo e mezzo,* also used this alternating pattern. In Negri especially, one common galliard path involved the linking of arms, with full turn and return to place, or a half turn (or one and a half turns) to change places on a reverse **S** path (e.g., Negri's "Torneo Amoroso"). Ample evidence shows that the galliard could be part of group dances, mixers, or two-couple dances following still other paths; it was, besides, ideal for showy male theatrical dance (as in Emilio de'Cavalieri's *ballo,* to his own music, "The Descent of Rhythm and Harmony," in the final Medici *intermedio* to "La Pellegrina" of 1589).

Only Caroso and Negri give completely independent galliard choreographies: Caroso's "Gagliarda di Spagna," in both his books, is atypically barred in duple, but with three-bar groupings. Both Caroso and Negri have a few *balletto* suites that are predominantly galliards (Negri's "Alta Mendozza" and Caroso's "Bellezza d'Olimpia"); they

Ruade droicte.

GALLIARD. Many hundreds of galliard steps and variations are documented after 1560. With the right gesture leg bent behind in this illustration, Thoinot Arbeau described a movement he called "Ru de vache" used in a galliard variation. The movement of the gesture leg from back to front was described as similar to that of a cow. (Reprinted from Arbeau, 1588, p. 46.)

are intertwined at the beginning and end with steps associated with the pavan. In most cases, however, the galliard is a single movement of a *balletto* suite (usually one of the triple after-dances to an unnamed first movement, and thus related to the pavan-galliard combinations in many musical collections). The sources that simply give instructions for variations, however, place the responsibility on the dancers for improvising a complete dance (such extemporizing was a typical aspect of all the performing arts of the period). By about 1580, then, the social galliard could be either a section of a solo couple or group dance, a mixer (Caroso's "Il Piantone"), or an entirely discrete dance (Negri's "Bianco Fiore"). Such freedom of usage attests to the galliard's importance between 1525 and 1625, one hundred years that may truly be called the Age of the Galliard.

Of the three salient characteristics by which a dance type is recognized—step patterns, paths, and music—the music of a typical galliard is perhaps the most easily recognizable. Its rhythmic pattern is basic and characteristic: six strong beats of a triple or compound duple meter with a characteristic dotted rhythm marking the *cadenza:*

Hemiola in music and dance also occurs frequently, but not necessarily simultaneously. Furthermore, the existence of duple galliards (see, as cited, Caroso's "Gagliarda di Spagna") is an indication that meter alone does not always define a galliard.

Galliard tempo was obviously subject to the relative simplicity or complexity of the steps, as well as to the strength and height of the dancer (see Arbeau). If it is allowed that as it aged the dance grew more complex, then it is also possible that it grew slower to accommodate the increasing number of divisions of the beat; this assumption seems borne out by various sources (e.g., Arbeau, Esquivel Navarro). It was never a rapid dance in musical terms, however, because of the time required even in simple galliard patterns for the leaping changes of weight. Certainly in solo male or solo couple dances the musicians adjusted their tempo so that the male dancer could comfortably demonstrate his high elevation; in group dances, undoubtedly, a generally acceptable tempo was adopted.

As in *balletto* suites, galliard sections were included in much of the extant theatrical dance music of the time, such as Claudio Monteverdi's *balli* or the figured dances for many that were centerpieces of the Italian *intermedio*, the French *balet*, and the English masque. From the tiny handful of extant theatrical choreographies (only by Negri and Cavalieri), it is known that the techniques of the ballroom galliard were adapted for use on the stage.

A number of dance types of the period are closely related to the galliard, such as the tordion/*tordiglione, passo e mezzo, pavaniglia, volta, piantone,* and *zoppa.* (The *saltarello,* however, despite many modern allegations, and despite its compound duple meter, is not related to the galliard in the manuals.) Also, many musically recognizable galliards appear in instrumental or vocal collections, such as Giovanni Gastoldi's *Balletti,* and Monteverdi's *Scherzi musicali,* whose use for dancing is uncertain, and in individual songs such as John Dowland's "Can She Excuse My Wrongs." Their telltale galliard rhythm nevertheless reflects its popularity.

References to the galliard continued to appear in dance and music manuals through the first half of the seventeenth century. All three major new choreographic sources of the time—F[rançois] de Lauze in England in 1623, Marin Mersenne in France in 1636, and Juan de Esquivel Navarro in Spain in 1642—agree on the galliard's brilliant virtuosity. In de Lauze, however, the dominance of the dance has given way to the courante, and some disparaging remarks of his, likening high "tricks" to those of a *baladin* (professional entertainer), hint at a change in the style of social dance in northern Europe. In southern Europe, although Esquivel Navarro refers to the galliard's moderate tempo, he applies most of its flashy foot and air work (which he only partially describes) to many dance types. That he admires such technical virtuosity and that in 1630 Caroso's *Nobiltà di dame* was reissued and Negri's

Le gratie d'amore translated into Spanish (in manuscript and without music) suggest a continuation of the virtuoso tradition in southern Europe. A growing separation between northern and southern styles of social dance may have occurred, but the sixty-year gap in dance manuals (1640–1700) remains to be filled before such a separation can be known for certain.

In 1700 Raoul-Auger Feuillet described a *pas de gaillarde,* which seems unrelated to the *cinq pas* or its components of the sixteenth and seventeenth centuries. Pierre Rameau (1725) and Kellom Tomlinson (1735) explained the new version as a step in duple time. The five extant *gaillard* choreographies in Feuillet notation are from the late seventeenth and early eighteenth centuries. The step vocabulary of these dances is so unlike those of the sixteenth-century galliard as to represent either a new dance type with the same name, or one whose developmental history from the sixteenth-century dance has yet to be uncovered. There is an impressive concurrent (1660–1736) musical repertory labeled galliard that shares the same distinctive musical characteristics as the tunes for the five choreographies. This reality further supports a theory that the eighteenth-century galliard was an independent and well-defined, though comparatively minor, dance step and type (see, e.g., Tomlinson, 1735, pl. VII). There is no evidence of the dance at any European court after the 1730s.

Today the galliard continues as a folk dance in parts of Italy. It includes leaping turns in an embrace position reminiscent of the *volta* or *nizzarda;* also, the leaping kicks of some modern *saltarelli* and tarantellas resemble those in the sixteenth-century galliard. Manifestations of aspects of the galliard can be seen in a number of other European folk dance traditions, as in the footwork in traditional Morris dance (the caper, foot-up, and "galley" or "gallery" step). In many Balkan dances much of the tricky footwork can be named according to step types associated with the galliard in sixteenth-century sources. Much of the complex air work once associated primarily with the galliard may now be seen in Basque dance and classical ballet. In many folk dances of Europe the crossing paths and arm or elbow turns are there, too. The likenesses are suggestive, but the history remains murky. Whether the dance drew on traditional footwork and figures or vice versa is unknown. The galliard is a dance whose complete history is as yet untold, but whose historical vigor is indubitable.

The similarity of steps and style of the sixteenth-century galliard to some current European folk dance traditions, as well as to aspects of ballet, supports a theory of a centuries-long history of step vocabulary and daring male feats in Western dance, of which the galliard was the chief late Renaissance representative. Earlier fifteenth-century references to jumps, full turns, and flourishes by Guglielmo Ebreo da Pesaro when he became Giovanni Ambrosio seem to support this theory. Thus, though unknown chronological links prohibit a continuous narrative, the lusty style and showy air work (with an erect torso) associated with the galliard may simply represent the sixteenth-century phase of a long tradition in Western dance.

[*See also the entries on Arbeau, Caroso, and Negri. In addition, many of the dance types mentioned herein are the subjects of independent entries.*]

BIBLIOGRAPHY: SOURCES

Alessandri, Filippo degli. *Discorso sopra il ballo.* Terni, 1620.

Arbeau, Thoinot. *Orchésographie et traicte en forme de dialogve, par leqvel tovtes personnes pevvent facilement apprendre & practiquer l'honneste exercice des dances.* Langres, 1588, 1589. Facsimile reprint, Langres, 1988. Reprinted with expanded title as *Orchesographie, metode, et teorie en forme de discovrs et tablatvre povr apprendre a dancer, battre le Tambour en toute sorte & diuersité de batteries, Iouët du fifre & arigot, tirer dis armes & escrimer, auec autres honnestes exercices fort conuenables à la Ieunesse.* Langres, 1596. Facsimile reprint, Geneva, 1972.

Arbeau, Thoinot. *Orchesography.* 1589. Translated into English by Mary Stewart Evans. New York, 1948. Reprint with corrections, a new introduction, and notes by Julia Sutton, and representative steps and dances in Labanotation by Mireille Backer. New York, 1967.

Arena, Antonius. *Ad suos compagnones studiantes.* Lyon, 1528. Translated by John Guthrie and Marino Zorzi in "Rules of Dancing by Antonius Arena." *Dance Research* 4 (Autumn 1986): 3–53.

Attaignant, Pierre. *18 basses dances.* Paris, 1529–1530.

Attaignant, Pierre. *Six galliardes et six pavanes.* Paris, 1529–1530.

Caroso, Fabritio. *Il ballarino* (1581). Facsimile reprint, New York, 1967.

Caroso, Fabritio. *Nobiltà di dame.* Venice, 1600, 1605. Facsimile reprint, Bologna, 1970. Reissued with order of illustrations changed as *Raccolta di varij balli.* Rome, 1630. Translated into English with eight introductory chapters by Julia Sutton, the music transcribed by F. Marian Walker. Oxford, 1986. Reprint with a step manual in Labanotation by Rachelle Palnick Tsachor and Julia Sutton, New York, 1995.

Cavalieri, Emilio de'. "Intermedio VI." In Cristofano Malvezzi's *Intermedii et concerti, fatti per la Commedia rappresentata in Firenze nelle Nozze del Serenissimo Don Ferdinando Medici et Madama Christiana di Loreno, Granduchi di Toscana.* Venice, 1591. Translated and edited by D.P. Walker as *Les Fêtes de Florence: Musique des intermèdes de "La Pellegrina."* Paris, 1963.

Cavalieri, Emilio de'. *La rappresentazione di anima e di corpo* (1600). Facsimile reprint, Bologna, 1967.

Compasso, Lutio. *Ballo della gagliarda.* Florence, 1560. Facsimile reprint with introduction by Barbara Sparti, Freiburg, 1995.

Davies, John. *Orchestra, or A Poem of Dancing.* London, 1596.

Esquivel Navarro, Juan de. *Discursos sobre el arte del dancado* (1642). Facsimile reprint, Madrid, 1947.

Feuillet, Raoul-Auger. *Choreographie, ou L'art de décrire la dance, par caractères, figures et signes démonstratifs, avec lesquels on apprend facilement de soy-même toutes sortes de dances.* Paris, 1700. 2d. ed., 1709, 1713. Facsimile reprint, New York, 1968; also Hildesheim and New York, 1979.

Guglielmo Ebreo da Pesaro (also known as Giovanni Ambrosio). *De pratica seu arte tripudii.* Milan and Naples (?), 1463, 1471–1474. In Paris, Bibliothèque Nationale, f.ital.973 and f.ital.476. Transcribed and translated by Barbara Sparti as *On the Practice or Art of Dancing.* Oxford, 1993. Other MS copies or versions under the same title c.1461–1510.

Jacobilli, Ludovico. *Modo di ballare.* Circa 1615. Manuscript located in Foligno, Biblioteca Jacobilli, AIII.19, ff.102–104.

Lauze, F[rançois] de. *Apologie de la danse, 1623.* Translated by Joan Wildeblood, and with original text, as *A Treatise of Instruction in Dancing and Deportment.* London, 1952.

Lupi, Livio. *Libro di gagliarde, tordiglione, passo e mezzo, canari e passeggi.* Palermo, 1600. Rev. ed., Palermo, 1607.

Lutii, Prospero. *Opera bellissima nella quale si contengono molte partite, et passeggi di gagliarda.* Perugia, 1589.

Maisse, André Hurault de. *A Journal of All That Was Accomplished by Monsieur de Maisse, Ambassador in England from King Henry IV to Queen Elizabeth* (1597). Translated by G.B. Harrison and P.A. Jones. London, 1931.

Mancini, Giulio. *Del origine et nobiltà del ballo* (c.1623–1630). Facsimile reprint with introduction by Barbara Sparti, Freiburg, 1996.

Manuscripts of the Inns of Court. Located in Bodleian Library, Rawl.Poet.108,ff.10v–11r;British Library, Harley 367, pp. 178–179; Bodleian, Douce 280, ff.66av–66bv (202v–203v); Bodleian, Rawl.D.864, f.199v, ff.203r–204; Royal College of Music, MS 1119, title page and ff.1–2, 23v–24r; Inner Temple, Miscellanea vol. 27.

Mersenne, Marin. *Harmonie universelle* (1636–1637). Facsimile reprint, Paris, 1963. English translation of Book 2 by J.B. Egan. Ph.D. diss., Indiana University, 1962.

Negri, Cesare. *Le gratie d'amore.* Milan, 1602. Reissued as *Nuove invenzione di balli.* Milan, 1604. Translated into Spanish by Don Balthasar Carlos for Señor Condé, Duke of Sanlucar, 1630. Manuscript located in Madrid, Biblioteca Nacional, MS 14085. Facsimile reprint of 1602, New York and Bologna, 1969. Literal translation into English and musical transcription by Yvonne Kendall. D.M.A. diss., Stanford University, 1985.

Tomlinson, Kellom. *The Art of Dancing Explained by Reading and Figures.* 2 vols. London, 1735. Facsimile reprint, London and New York, 1970.

Zuccolo da Cologna, Simeon. *La pazzia del ballo* (1549). Facsimile reprint, Bologna, 1969.

BIBLIOGRAPHY: OTHER STUDIES

Aldrich, Putnam. *Rhythm in Seventeenth-Century Italian Monody.* New York, 1966.

Brooks, Lynn Matluck. *The Dances of the Processions of Seville in Spain's Golden Age.* Kassell, 1988.

Brown, Alan. "Galliard." In *The New Grove Dictionary of Music and Musicians.* London, 1980.

Commune di Roma Assessorato all Cultura. *La danza tradizionale in Italia, mostra documentaria.* Rome, 1981.

Donington Robert. "Volta." In *The New Grove Dictionary of Music and Musicians.* London, 1980.

Esses, Maurice. *Dance and Instrumental Diferencias in Spain during the Seventeenth and Early Eighteenth Centuries.* Stuyvesant, N.Y., 1992.

Feldmann, Fritz. "Historische Tänze der musikalischen und choreographischen Weltliteratur" (parts 1–2). *Volkstanz in Tanzarchiv* 4–5 (1960–1961).

Heartz, Daniel. "Sources and Forms of the French Instrumental Dance in the Sixteenth Century." Ph.D. diss., Harvard University, 1957.

Heartz, Daniel. *Preludes, Chansons, and Dances for Lute Published by Pierre Attaingnant, Paris, 1529–1530.* Neuilly-sur-Seine, 1964.

Jones, Pamela. "The Relation between Music and Dance in Cesare Negri's 'Le gratie d'amore' (1602)." 2 vols. Ph.D. diss., University of London, 1988.

Jones, Pamela. "The Editions of Cesare Negri's *Le Gratie d'Amore:* Choreographic Revisions in Printed Copies." *Studi Musicali* 21 (1991): 21–33.

Little, Meredith Ellis, and Carol G. Marsh. *La Danse Noble: An Inventory of Dances and Sources.* Williamstown, Mass., 1992.

Matteo [Vittucci, Matteo Marcellus] with Carola Goya. *The Language of Spanish Dance.* Norman, Okla., 1990.

Meyer, Ernst Hermann. "Allemande." In *Die Musik in Geschichte und Gegenwart.* 1st ed., vol. 1, 1949–1951. Kassel, 1949–1979.

Moe, Lawrence H. "Dance Music in Printed Italian Lute Tablatures from 1507 to 1611." Ph.D. diss., Harvard University, 1956.

Mönkemeyer, Helmut, ed. *Cesare Negri: "Nuove inventioni di balli."* 2 vols. Rodenkirchen, 1970. Music only, transcribed for guitar.

Mönkemeyer, Helmut, ed. *Fabritio Caroso: "Il ballarino."* 2 vols. Rodenkirchen, 1971. Music.

Pirrotta, Nino, and Elena Povoledo. *Music and Theatre from Poliziano to Monteverdi.* Translated by Karen Eales, Cambridge, 1982.

Sonner, Rudolf. "Arbeau, Thoinot." In *Die Musik in Geschichte und Gegenwart.* Vol. 1, 1949–1952. Kassel, 1949–1979.

Steele, Mary Susan. *Plays and Masques at Court during the Reigns of Elizabeth, James I, and Charles I, 1558–1642.* London, 1926.

Sutton, Julia. "Reconstruction of Sixteenth-Century Dance." In *Dance History Research: Perspectives from Related Arts and Disciplines,* edited by Joann W. Kealiinohomoku. New York, 1970.

Sutton, Julia. *Renaissance Revisited: Twelve Dances Reconstructed [in Labanotation] from the Originals of Thoinot Arbeau, Fabritio Caroso, and Cesare Negri.* New York, 1972.

Sutton, Julia, and Charles P. Coldwell. Review of Helmut Mönkemeyer's *Fabritio Caroso: "Il ballarino."* Notes 30 (1973): 357–359.

Sutton, Julia. "Arbeau, Thoinot"; "Caroso, Fabritio"; and "Negri, Cesare." In *The New Grove Dictionary of Music and Musicians.* London, 1980.

Sutton, Julia. "Triple Pavans: Clues to Some Mysteries in Sixteenth-Century Dance." *Early Music* 14.2 (1986): 174–181.

Sutton, Julia. "Musical Forms and Dance Forms in the Dance Manuals of Sixteenth-Century Italy: Plato and the Varieties of Variation." In *The Marriage of Music and Dance: Papers from a Conference Held at the Guildhall School of Music and Drama, London, 9th–11th August 1991.* Cambridge, 1992.

Sutton, Julia, and Sibylle Dahms. "Ballo, Balletto." In *Die Musik in Geschichte und Gegenwart.* 2d ed., vol. 1, 1994. Kassel 1994–.

VIDEOTAPE. Julia Sutton. *"Il Ballarino (The Dancing Master),"* a teaching videotape featuring a glossary of steps and three sixteenth-century Italian dances by Caroso and Negri (Pennington, N.J., 1991).

JULIA SUTTON
with Elizabeth Kurtz and Carol G. Marsh

GALLINI, GIOVANNI (Giovanni-Andrea Gallini, also known as Sir John Gallini; born 7 January 1728 in Florence, died 5 July 1805 in London), dancer, choreographer, impresario, and writer. Gallini studied dancing in Paris under François Marcel and danced at the Académie Royale de Musique until at least 1754. He went to London shortly afterward, appearing at Covent Garden on 17 December 1757 in the pantomime-ballet *The Judgement of Paris* and in a comic dance *The Sicilian Peasants.* In the 1758/59 season at the King's Theatre, he directed dances for an opera by Gioacchino Cocchi and began to gain fame as a dancer. By 1759/60 Gallini was principal dancer at the King's Theatre and director of all the opera dances there. In the 1761/62 season, he began his profitable association with Johann Christian Bach, providing ballets for his first London opera, *Orione,* and for his *Zanaida.* Gallini was at Covent Garden again in 1763/64 as director of dances and at the King's again the following season.

At about that time, Gallini's career was given a boost by his marriage to Lady Elizabeth Bertie, sister of the fourth earl of Abingdon. Although the marriage was not acceptable to society, it brought Gallini renown and position.

Soon after his arrival in England, Gallini began taking private pupils in genteel dancing; he became one of the most fashionable and gifted teachers and committed his methods and philosophy to record. His two elegant theoretical publications are historical and social apologies for his art. *A Treatise on the Art of Dancing* (1762) and the undated *Critical Observations on the Art of Dancing* borrow silently and liberally from John Weaver's *An Essay towards a History of Dancing* (1712), but Gallini's style and procedure are free of the tangled allusions of Weaver's pioneering study. Gallini adds something of his own, while refining and practically applying his arguments for social dance. He displays shrewd judgment in calculating what is acceptable to English society—it clearly helped him to number earls, prime ministers, leaders of society, and courtiers among his pupils.

Gallini's works also reveal an interest in non-European dance, unusual at that time, and present radically dissenting views on the usefulness of notation. His written works are important as the testimony of an outstanding teacher and as a reflection of the style of dancing practiced at court and in society in the late middle years of the eighteenth century.

In 1775 Gallini opened a magnificent concert hall, the Hanover Square Rooms, for musical events and balls. The Great Hall provided a home for the subscription concerts of Johann Christian Bach and Karl Friedrich Abel. It remained one of the leading concert halls in London for many years, at which George III was a regular patron.

By diversifying and multiplying his business activities, Gallini became very wealthy. In 1778 he purchased the mortgage on the King's Theatre in the Haymarket and became its proprietor in 1783 and again from 1785 to 1789. As a theater proprietor, Gallini traveled in Europe to engage singers and dancers. Many of the finest dancers and dancing masters came to London at his invitation: Jean Dauberval, Charles Le Picq, James Harvey D'Egville, Jean-Baptiste Hus, Antoine-Bonaventure Pitrot, Louis Nivelon, Simon Slingsby, and Auguste Vestris. During one European visit Gallini received the Knighthood of the Golden Spur from the pope and henceforth styled himself Sir John Gallini. His transformation into an English gentleman was completed in 1784, when he purchased the manor of Yattendon in Berkshire and became lord of the manor.

At the King's Theatre in the late 1780s, Gallini provided dancing of the highest standard available. Along with Charles-Louis Didelot, Pierre Gardel, and Marie-Madeleine Guimard, he brought Jean-Georges Noverre, who led a large troupe of French dancers and produced his important ballet *L'Amour et Psyché* at the theater on 29 January 1788.

The King's Theatre burned down on 17 June 1789; after a brief interlude spent providing opera and dance at Covent Garden, Gallini's managerial association with the theater came to an end. In 1791 he may have led the orchestra at the King's Theatre, Dublin. He remained interested in the theater to the end of his life and continued to teach dancing. On the day before he died, Gallini taught in the afternoon and attended Covent Garden in the evening.

BIBLIOGRAPHY

Gallini, Giovanni. *Critical Observations on the Art of Dancing, to Which Is Added a Collection of Cotillons or French Dances.* London, c.1770.

Guest, Ivor. "Letters from London: Guimard's Farewell to the Stage." *Dance Chronicle* 18.2 (1995): 207–215.

Price, Curtis A., et al. *Italian Opera in Late Eighteenth-Century London,* vol. 1, *The King's Theatre, Haymarket, 1778–1791.* London, 1995.

Ralph, Richard. "Sir John Gallini." *About the House* (Summer 1979).

RICHARD RALPH

GAMELAN. [*To discuss gamelan and its relationship to Indonesian dance, this entry comprises two articles. The first presents Balinese traditions and the second focuses on Javanese traditions. For related discussion, see* Indonesia.]

Balinese Traditions

The general term for Bali's dozen or so types of instrumental music ensembles, the word *gamelan* is derived from *gamel*, "to handle." The Balinese make a clear distinction between *gamelan krawang*, or bronze instruments, and other kinds of ensembles, such as the bamboo *gambang, jogéd bumbung,* or the *gaguntangan* ensemble of *arja* dance drama. The distinctive features of Bali's major gamelan styles highlight shimmering resonances of gongs, gong-chimes, and metallophones, ranging five octaves and differing from those of neighboring Java in their explosive sonorities and phrasings. Although Balinese gamelan is chiefly an ensemble of percussion, the bamboo flute *(suling)* is an important component of many genres, and a two-stringed bowed lute *(rebab)* is essential to at least one extant genre.

Gamelan styles are associated with specific contexts of ceremony, entertainment, or recreation. *Gamelan bebonangan* or *balaganjur,* is generally used for ceremonial processions from one temple or shrine to another, or from a shrine to a ritual bathing place such as a spring, river, or seacoast. A number of *bonang,* or gong-chimes, provide an interlocking melodic figure along with large cymbals, gongs, and drums.

The four-tone *gamelan angklung* is most often associated with cremations and related ceremonies for the dead, although it may be included in other ceremonies, or even (if a more appropriate gamelan is unavailable) in dance and dramatic performances.

The stately, traditional *gamelan gong* accompanies ritual dances within a temple, *topéng* plays, and ceremonial *baris* drill dances. It also possesses a repertory of music, *gending gong,* which is performed at specific times during large temple ceremonies.

The twentieth-century *gamelan gong kebiar* often draws from this traditional repertory, but its livelier, streamlined sound is at its best in performance with *kebiar*-style dances. *Gong kebiar* is presently considered appropriate for almost any dance and theater form.

Nonetheless, although *gong kebiar* has all but replaced the traditional *arja* ensemble, most performers still prefer the old *geguntangan* instrumentation, which highlights the dancers' singing and the subtle interplay of music and dance. The bamboo *suling* flute, small *kendang* drums, small *rincik* cymbals, and *guntang,* the bamboo-tube zither which substitutes for the gong, are featured in this ensemble.

The free-flowing modal qualities of *arja* are derived from the more formalized and larger *gamelan gambuh,* which may utilize four distinct modes in a performance. Here four large *suling,* each 35 inches long, and a *rebab* are the only melodic instruments, joined by two small *kendang* and an assortment of unusual percussion. *Gambuh* compositions are a resource for the *semar pegulingan* ensemble, and also for any other gamelan requiring accompaniment for specific dramatic characters derived from the *gambuh* theater. The lyrical melodic style and modal shadings reveal a strong connection with the theater, expressing dramatic moods and varieties of characterization.

Instrumental music in Bali generally utilizes a four-tone or five-tone octave, whether in the *sléndro* tuning of *gendér wayang* or the *pélog* tuning of most other genres. The bamboo flute produces additional pitches and tonal shadings, as do singers joining with a gamelan. The five-tone *pélog* tuning is actually derived from an older seven-tone *saih pitu* system that is still used by such ensembles as *gamelan gembuh, semar pegulingan,* and *gamelan gambang.*

Traditionally instrumental music is not notated, and musicians learn their parts by rote. The music is highly structured, however, and the only room for improvisation is in the leading drum part or that of the flute, both of which are still tightly bound by rhythmic or melodic form. In contemporary schools, music is taught using a system of cipher (Kepatihan) notation.

In addition to the unusual visual impact of finely crafted bronze instruments, Balinese gamelan is distinctive in its styles of melodic and rhythmic interlocking and in its precise system of tuning based on acoustical beats. The precision with which a gamelan is tuned to slightly varying cycles per second, or *ombak*, creates the steady "waves" of resounding, pulsing bronze. This is also accomplished by stretching or compressing successive octaves.

The process of Balinese gamelan manufacture includes three main stages: casting the molten metal into a workable shape; shaping the metal into its ultimate form by hammering and stretching in the manner of blacksmithing; and finally, fine-tuning each instrument by scraping and filing. The earliest stage of the gamelan-making process, mixing the ingredients of the bronze alloy *krawang*, has not been in general practice in Bali. Instead, old Javanese or Balinese instruments were melted down to forge new ones. The gamelan-smiths, called *pandé gong* or *pandé krawang*, are highly respected and regarded with awe, an attitude toward metallurgical craftsmen found in many cultures. The unique collection of tuned gongs, chimes, and flat metallophones associated with the gamelan styles of Bali and Java appears to have developed sometime between the construction of the ninth-century temple at Borobudur and the arrival of the first Dutch expedition in 1595.

Balinese gamelan, in its most expanded form, is organized into seven areas of instrumental stratification ranging over five octaves:

1. Basic statement of the melody within a one-octave range.
2. Articulation at regular time intervals of the basic melody, generally every four tones.

GAMELAN: Balinese Traditions. Dancers move to the distinctive interlocking rhythms of a Balinese gamelan, an instrumental ensemble composed chiefly of bronze percussion instruments, including gongs, cymbals, and metallophones. (Photograph from the Dance Collection, New York Public Library for the Performing Arts.)

3. Full melodic expression, ranging from two to three octaves.

4. Doubling and paraphrasing in the octave above.

5. Ornamental figuration of the melody.

6. Punctuation of larger time intervals—the general function of the various gongs and gong-chimes.

7. Drumming, which conducts the group as well as providing a rhythmic undercurrent; one or two musicians will each play a two-headed drum (kendang) with their hands or a single mallet.

The instruments fall into several broad categories. Idiophones, primarily self-sounding and percussive, include a great range of gongs, varying in size and tone. Besides the large gong itself, there are the *kempur, bendé, kajar, kelenang, kempli, kemong kentong*, cymbals (*céngcéng* and *rincik*), bells (*gentorak*), xylophones (*gambang, caruk, and jogéd bumbung*), and metallophones such as *saron* and the iron-keyed *salundéng*. Melodic gong-chimes, such as *reong, trompong*, and *bonang*, are also in this group. Idio-aerophones comprise various metallophones with bamboo resonators (*bumbung*), each of which is tuned to a specific pitch. The vibrating tube contributes much of the acoustic effect. Included here are *gendér* (of ten, thirteen, or fifteen keys), *gangsa, jublag* or *calung, jegogan, kantilan*, and *saron*. Membranophones are wooden drums (*kendang*) with a membrane of skin stretched over openings at both ends. The *rebana* is a rare, one-headed drum used for *janggér* performances. Aerophones consist of end-blown bamboo flutes. Finally, these are chordophones—the two-stringed bowed lute (*rebab*) and the bamboo-tube zither (*guntang*).

[*See also* Baris; *and* Kebiar. *For information on* arja, gambuh, *and* topéng, *see* Indonesia, *article on* Balinese Dance Theater.]

BIBLIOGRAPHY

Bandem, I Madé. *Prakempa: Sebuah Lontar Gambelan Bali*. Denpasar, 1986.

Dibia, I Wayan. "Arja: A Sung Dance-Drama of Bali." Ph.D. diss., University of California, Los Angeles, 1992.

Herbst, Edward. *Voices in Bali: Energies and Perceptions in Vocal Music and Dance Theater*. Hanover and London, 1997.

Hitchcock, Michael, and Lucy Norris. *Bali, the Imaginary Museum: The Photographs of Walter Spies and Beryl de Zoete*. New York, 1995.

Hood, Mantle. "Sléndro and Pélog Redefined." *Selected Reports in Ethnomusicology* 1 (1966): 28–48.

Hood, Mantle, et al. "Indonesia." In *New Grove Dictionary of Music and Musicians*, London, 1980.

Hood, Mantle. *The Evolution of Javanese Gamelan*. 3 vols. New York, 1980.

Hood, Mantle. "The Enduring Tradition: Music and Theater in Java and Bali." In *Indonesia*, edited by Ruth McVey, pp. 438–560. New Haven, 1983.

Kunst, Jaap. *Hindu-Javanese Musical Instruments*. 2d ed., rev. and enl. The Hague, 1968.

Kunst, Jaap. *Music in Java*. 2 vols. Translated by Emile van Loo. 3d ed. The Hague, 1973.

Kusumo, Sardono W. "Studi Lingkungan." In *Sewindu LPKJ*, edited by Edi Sedyawati and Wiyoso Yudoseputro. Jakarta, 1978.

Lindsay, Jennifer. *Javanese Gamelan*. Kuala Lumpur, 1979.

McPhee, Colin. "The 'Absolute' Music of Bali." *Modern Music* 12 (1936): 163–169.

McPhee, Colin. *A House in Bali*. New York, 1946.

McPhee, Colin. *A Club of Small Men*. New York, 1948.

McPhee, Colin. "Children and Music in Bali." In *Childhood in Contemporary Cultures*, edited by Margaret Mead and Martha Wolfenstein. Chicago, 1955.

McPhee, Colin. *Music in Bali*. New Haven, 1966.

McPhee, Colin. "The Balinese Wayang Kulit and Its Music." In *Traditional Balinese Culture*, edited by Jane Belo. New York, 1970.

Mead, Margaret. "The Arts in Bali." In *Traditional Balinese Culture*, edited by Jane Belo. New York, 1970.

Ornstein, Ruby. *Gamelan Gong Kebjar: The Development of a Balinese Musical Tradition*. Ph.D. diss., University of California, Los Angeles.

Rembang, I Nyoman. "Gamelan Gambuh dan Gamelan Lainya di Bali." In *Panitithalaning Pagambuhan*, edited by I Madé Bandem. Denpasar, 1975.

Seebass, Tilman. "A note on Kebyar in Modern Bali." *Orbis Musicae* 9 (1985): 103–21.

Sumandhi, I Nyoman. "Gending Iringan Wayang Kulit Bali." In *Pakem wayang parwa Bali*. Denpasar, 1978.

Sumarsam. "Inner Melody in Javanese Gamelan Music." *Asian Music* 7.1 (1976).

Sumarsam. *Gamelan: Cultural Interaction and Musical Development in Central Java*. Chicago, 1995.

Tenzer, Michael. *Balinese Music*. Singapore, 1992.

Wallis, Richard. "The Voice as a Mode of Cultural Expression in Bali." Ph.D. diss., University of Michigan, 1980.

EDWARD HERBST

Javanese Traditions

The generic term *gamelan* refers to an ensemble composed primarily of metallophones and gong-type instruments that produce tones when struck with mallets. The other instruments of a complete gamelan include a wooden xylophone (*gambang*), a set of two-headed drums (*kendhang*), a two-stringed fiddle (the *rebab*), a plucked zither-type instrument (*celempung* or *siter*), a bamboo flute (*suling*), and male and female singers. Most gamelan instruments have fixed pitches and employ two tuning systems (*laras*): the five-toned *sléndro* and the seven-toned *pélog*. A complete gamelan is therefore a double set—*sléndro* and *pélog* gamelan—although they never play simultaneously.

The development of today's gamelan music can be traced to the late 1500s, and its precursor can be traced to the tenth century. Throughout its development, one finds the interaction of three musical components: the loud ensemble, the soft ensemble, and the singing of various poetic forms. The loud ensemble consists of various combinations of drums, gong-type instruments, and me-

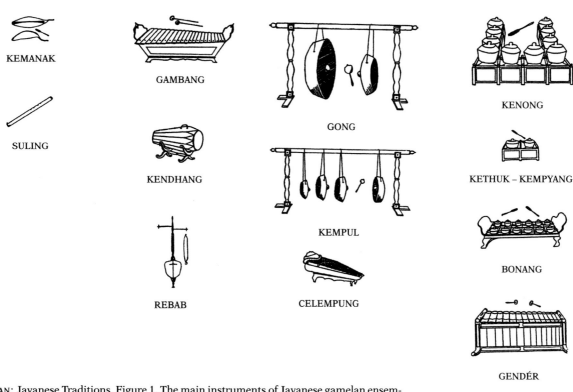

GAMELAN: Javanese Traditions. Figure 1. The main instruments of Javanese gamelan ensembles (not drawn to scale). Most of the percussion instruments vary in size, depending on their register. All are played in a sitting or kneeling position. The *rebab* (two-stringed spike fiddle) is shown from the front, with the bow alongside; its long slender tuning pegs protrude on either side at the top. The *kemanak* are elongated stick-beaten handbells used only in the accompaniment of certain ritual court dances. The predominant central Javanese gamelan, including the instruments in both pentatonic *sléndro* and heptatonic *pélog* tunings, comprises one set of *kenong* (for one player), a *kethuk* and two *kempyang* (all three for one player), four *bonang* (for two players), six *gendér* (for two players), sixteen *saron* (for eight players), two *slenthem* (for one player), three *gambang* (for one player), three *kendhang* (played by one drummer, the ensemble's leading musician), an array of *gong* and *kempul* (divided among three players), a *rebab*, a *suling*, a *celempung*, a female solo singer, and a small choir of about five male singers. (Drawings by Sumarsam © The University of Chicago; used by permission.)

tallophones—all played with unpadded mallets. The soft ensemble consists of various combinations of metallophones—played with padded mallets—as well as the flute and stringed instruments.

Loud and soft presentation is still a stylistic feature of today's gamelan practice. In the soft style, the loud-sounding instruments are played softly. In the loud style, the soft-sounding instruments may be played, or they may not be included. In most cases, the singing blends with the soft style. In some gamelan compositional genres, the singing is a melodic feature, as in the *palaran* genre used to accompany the *langendriyan* dance opera. The shift from the soft to the loud style (or the reverse) is a characteristic feature in gamelan accompaniment

to dance or to dance drama, since it creates dynamic tension.

Stratified Melodic Layers. In gamelan, melodic structures are based on the stratification of pulsing. Some instruments play pulsing melodic patterns in a high level of density; another group plays in a medium density; yet another plays in a low density. Stratification also applies to the melodic ranges of gamelan instruments, since some instruments have a wide melodic range, some a medium range, and others a narrow range. The instruments function in the ensemble based on both their melodic range and their density stratum. The one-octave metallophone instruments of the *saron* family play within a relatively low density level and bear the melodic skeleton of a com-

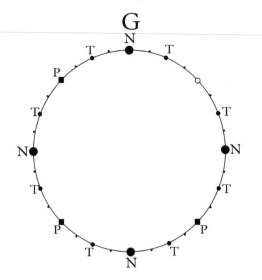

GAMELAN: Javanese Traditions. Figure 2. This circle shows the *ladrang gongan* at thirty-two beats per cycle. The letters denote the strokes of various gamelan instruments. G stands for *gong ageng,* N for *kenong,* K for *kempul,* and T for *tethuk.* (Drawings by Sumarsam © The University of Chicago; used by permission.)

position. The wider-range instruments play elaborate melodies in a medium density and perform leading melodies (they are the rebab, the long metallophone *gendér barung,* and the two-row set of gongs *bonang barung.*) Other wide-range instruments play at a high density level and carry supporting melodies (they are the *gambang,* the *celempung,* and the high-pitched set of *gendér* and *bonang*). The intermittently played *suling,* a male chorus *(gérong)* and female solo singing *(sindhèn),* also perform supporting melodic roles.

Formal Structure: Gongan Cycle. A gamelan composition is composed in one of several fundamental structural units, the length of which is determined by the number of pulses it contains (16, 32, 64, 128, or 256). The stroke of a large gong *(gong ageng)* is very important in marking the end of the main unit, giving a feeling of balance and closure. Repeating or moving cyclically, the structural unit is called *gongan.*

There are several formal structures, each delineated by the length of the *gongan* and by the way other gong-type instruments mark important accents in that *gongan.* The *kenong* (a set of large kettle gongs) divides the *gongan* into two or four equal phrases. The *kempul* (a set of hanging gongs) subdivides the *kenong* phrases and is further subdivided by the *kethuk* (a small kettle gong). In a few formal structures, such as *srepegan,* the *kenong* and *kempul* play in rapid succession (every beat or every other beat). Compositions in these structures usually accompany the exits and entrances of dancers and fight scenes. Javanese dancers are keenly aware of the formal structure of a composition. They execute transitional movement

(singgetan) toward the stroke of *kenong* or gong, at which point a new movement begins.

Irama. The tempo and meter of gamelan are encompassed by the concept called *irama,* which involves both the rhythm (fast, medium, or slow) and the expanding and contracting tempo of the *gongan* cycle. *Irama* also comprises the slowing down or speeding up of the basic beats played by the *saron* metallophones, accompanied by the rise and fall of the density level for some instruments in relation to the basic beats. The drummer, through a number of musical signals woven into the drumming of rhythmic patterns, sets the *irama* and keeps a steady tempo. The drummer also controls transitions to slower or faster meter and signals the end of the piece.

There are four drumming styles, which consist of both simple and elaborate rhythmic patterns. The patterns of the most elaborate *kendhang ciblon* style are directly related to the rhythmic movements of some dances, such as *gambyong* and *golèk.* The patterns of *kendhang ciblon* also accompany fight scenes in dance or in dance drama; freely improvised, the drum accentuates the sound effects of the fight.

[*See also* Indonesia, *article on* Javanese Dance Traditions. *For related discussion, see* Music for Dance, *article on* Asian Traditions.]

BIBLIOGRAPHY
Becker, Judith O. *Traditional Music in Modern Java: Gamelan in a Changing Society.* Honolulu, 1980.
Hood, Mantle. *Javanese Gamelan in the World of Music.* Yogyakarta, 1958.
Kunst, Jaap. *Hindu-Javanese Musical Instruments.* The Hague, 1968.
Lindsay, Jennifer. *Javanese Gamelan: Traditional Orchestra of Indonesia.* Singapore, 1992.
Sumarsam. *Gamelan: Cultural Interaction and Musical Development in Central Java.* Chicago, 1995.

SUMARSAM

GARDEL FAMILY, German-French family of musicians, dancers, and choreographers. Most notable were the brothers Maximilien and Pierre, and Pierre's wife Marie Gardel.

Maximilien Gardel (Maximilien-Léopold-Philippe-Joseph Gardel, also known as Gardel the elder; born 18 December 1741 in Mannheim, died 11 March 1787 in Paris), dancer, ballet master, and choreographer. Son of Claude Gardel, ballet master at the court of King Stanislas I of Poland, Maximilien became a student at the Paris Opera in 1755. In 1760 the journal *Le Mercure* noted his successes in the *chaconne* in *Dardanus* (music by Jean-Philippe Rameau), in which he danced a role created by Gaëtan Vestris, and in *Ismène* (music by Jean-Féry Rebel and François Francoeur), in which he performed with Mademoiselle Carville, Gaëtan Vestris, and Thérèse Vestris. After his brilliant performance in *Zaïs* (music by

Rameau), critics compared him to Gaëtan Vestris, the pre-eminent male dancer of the era.

In 1767 a sister, Agathe Gardel, whose *danse noble* was admired, appeared in *Hippolyte et Aricie* (music by Rameau), but despite her talent she soon left the Opera. In 1768 Maximilien Gardel, together with Marie-Madeleine Guimard and Jean Dauberval, was applauded in a pastorale by Jean-Joseph Mondonville entitled *Daphnis et Alcimadure*. On 21 January 1772, he replaced Vestris in *Castor et Pollux* (music by Rameau), defying tradition by dancing the role of Apollo without a mask and wig—an innovation recommended by dance authority Jean-Georges Noverre. On 7 September 1773, after a performance of *L'Union de l'Amour et des Arts* (music by Étienne-Joseph Floquet), the German critic Friedrich Melchior von Grimm wrote, "The god Vestris dances an *entrée* (in this case a chaconne) with the demigod Gardel, a phenomenon hitherto believed to be impossible."

Although Gardel was not the equal of his illustrious father, he had brilliant technical qualities—strength, balance, elegance, and precision; an alleged lack of expression, however, diminished his art. He interpreted such works of Noverre as *Iphigénie en Aulide, Orphée et Euridice, Alceste,* as well as Christoph Willibald Gluck's *Armide* and *Les Horaces,* but he apparently did not apply to his own ballets Noverre's basic principles, nor did the master treat him with much kindness.

In 1773 Maximilien was named deputy ballet master with Dauberval. When Noverre departed in 1681 he became official ballet master, a post he held until his death. He retired from dancing to devote himself to choreography. His works were inspired particularly by popular comic opera and vaudeville, genres in which dance and song were combined. They included *La Chercheuse d'Esprit,* based on a work by Charles-Simon Favart (presented at Fontainebleau, 1777); *Ninette à la Cour,* a ballet pantomime (1778); *Mirza et Lindor* (music by François-Joseph Gossec, 1779); *La Rosière,* a *ballet d'action* (1783); *L'Oracle* (1784); *Le Premier Navigateur, ou Le Pouvoir de l'Amour* (music by André-Modeste Grétry, 1785); *Le Coq au village,* inspired by a comic opera by Favart (1787); and *Le Déserteur,* (music by Ernest Müller). The last work, a pantomime-ballet based on Michel-Jean Sedaine's comic opera, was performed before the court at Fontainebleau in 1786 and at the Paris Opera on 16 January 1788. Maximilien also mounted numerous *divertissements* for operas by Niccoló Piccinni (*Diane et Endymion,* 1784), Grétry (*La Caravane du Caire,* 1784; *Panurge dans l'Île des Lanternes,* 1785), and Antonio Sacchini (*Oedipe à Colone,* 1786).

Noverre dealt harshly with Maximilien's work, perhaps because he was bitter over the intrigues of Gardel and Dauberval, who wanted his post as ballet master. In 1779 he wrote, "Since Mr. Gardel took possession of Terpsi-chore's scepter, the entertainments and ballets connected with poems are being mercilessly sacrificed to pantomimes in which brilliant execution, gracefulness, and harmony of movements are replaced by vague meanderings, meaningless gestures, and an expression so weak and so monotonous that one needs the help of vaudeville to give them meaning." Grimm was equally severe, crediting Gardel with "little inventiveness, little wit, and little interest." Nonetheless, his profound knowledge of his art, his conscientious work, his search for balance in groupings, and his careful execution of steps made him a respected choreographer, and his ballets, performed by such prestigious artists as Marie-Madeleine Guimard and Auguste Vestris, enjoyed much success.

Pierre Gardel (Pierre-Gabriel Gardel; born 4 February 1758 in Nancy, died 18 October 1840 in Paris), dancer and choreographer. The younger son of Claude Gardel, Pierre ("Gardel the younger") learned violin and dance at a very early age. He joined the Paris Opera in 1771 and made his debut in 1772 in Jean-Benjamin Laborde's *La Cinquantaine* and Rameau's *Castor et Pollux.* In 1773 he danced a pas de deux with the charming Mademoiselle Dorival in Floquet's *L'Union de l'Amour et des Arts,* earning notice for his skill and gracefulness. He appeared in Gluck's *Iphigénie en Aulide* in 1774, and in 1775 he danced in Grétry's *Céphale et Procris* and Gossec's *Philémon et Baucis.* He appeared in *La Chercheuse d'Esprit* (choreographed by his brother Maximilien) on 1 March 1778.

Pierre was named *premier danseur noble* in 1780. In 1781 and 1782 he danced at the King's Theatre in London, with August Bournonville, Louis Nivelon, and Mesdemoiselles Théodore and Simonet, under Noverre's direction, achieving success in Noverre's *Renaud et Armide, Médée et Jason,* and *Adèle de Ponthieu.* An accomplished artist, he shone at the Paris Opera and the court.

Pierre, following his brother's example, began his career as a choreographer with a *divertissement* for *Dardanus* (music by Sacchini) in 1784. In 1786 he and Maximilien composed and choreographed *Les Sauvages, ou Le Pouvoir de la Danse.* The following year, upon the death of Maximilien, Pierre was named ballet master.

His best works enjoyed exceptional success. *Télémaque dans l'Île de Calypso* (music by Müller), created in 1790, was performed 416 times over thirty-six years. His most famous ballet, *Psyché,* also with music by Müller, was performed 1,160 times in thirty-nine years. *Le courrier des spectacles* called it "possibly the most imposing ballet and most magical spectacle the theater can offer." Inspired by mythology, it offered inventive, contrasting scenes, including a charming vignette of Terpsichore giving Psyche (Marie Miller, Pierre's future wife) a lesson in dancing, and a tableau of the Furies dragging the heroine into their infernal dances. In the same vein, *Le Jugement de Pâris* (music by Franz Joseph Haydn, Ignaz Pleyel, Étienne-

Nicolas Méhul) combined a fantastic setting with expressive pantomime. In 1793 an enthusiastic welcome greeted his spectacle of the gods transported in magnificent chariots or descending from heaven on a cloud, with the young Paris (Auguste Vestris) "depicting his character through the gaiety, grace, and sensuality of his dance." In 1792 Gardel composed an interlude based on Rouget de Lisle's "Marseillaise." Entitled *L'Offrande à la Liberté*, it was performed 130 times between 1792 and 1797, familiarizing all of Europe with the republican anthem.

After 1795 Pierre largely ceased dancing and devoted himself to choreography. *La Dansomanie* (music by Méhul), a pantomime folly first performed on 14 June, 1800, is a cheerful, tender, mocking work in which every action is a pretext for dancing; characters with evocative names reveal their personalities through their variations. Mr. Duléger, the Dansomaniac, tries to perform "two *jetés battus* and one *entrechat*." His valet, Pasmoucheté, falls

GARDEL FAMILY. Pierre Gardel, as the title character in his *Télémaque dans l'Île de Calypso*, writes the name of his beloved, Eucharis, in the sand. Premiered on 23 February 1790 at the Académie Royale de Musique, Gardel's popular ballet was performed frequently during the next four decades. This engraving by Jean Prud'hon, after Sébastien Coeuré, is from *Galerie théâtrale* (Paris, 1812–1834). (Courtesy of Madison U. Sowell and Debra H. Sowell, Brigham Young University, Provo, Utah.)

while imitating him. Mr. Flic-Flac, a dance master, initiates the Dansomaniac into the most sophisticated techniques, listed in the libretto as "double, triple, and quadruple *temps de cuisse*, *pas* in which the legs are thrown forward one after the other, pirouettes on the instep, *valses*, and arabesques, all those steps that ridicule our city dances and only too often spoil those of our theaters." The suitors of the young Phrosine (Marie Gardel) compete for her hand; Dumarsept (Auguste Vestris), disguised as a Basque, wins her because "happiness leads him, lightness sustains him, the graces surround him." This folly ends in a general gaiety, with the lovers being united "provided they'll go on dancing." Noverre noted that this ballet "offers every type of dance, and is full of gaiety and charming steps." In it the waltz made its first appearance at the Opera.

Pierre Gardel created new works prolifically. They included *Achille à Scyros* (music by Luigi Cherubini, 1804) and *Paul et Virginie* (music by Rodolphe Kreutzer), performed before the court at Saint-Cloud on 12 June 1806, and at the Opera on 24 June. The latter was a drama set on a distant island, inspired by the novel by Bernardin de Saint-Pierre, and interpreted by Louis-Joseph Saint-Amans as Paul, Marie Gardel as Virginie, and Auguste Vestris as Domingo, an African servant; it is a precursor of Romantic ballet. So is *L'Enfant Prodigue* (music by Henri-Montan Berton), featuring subjects beloved of nineteenth-century authors: the exotic, emotions pushed to hysteria, and the intervention of the supernatural. The libretto describes "the dazzling costumes of the Egyptians and the tumultuous dances of peoples in ecstasy," followed by the rags and tragic pantomime of the unfortunate hero Azaël (Auguste Vestris), "devoured by remorse, in despair at his continued survival to his shame, death in his face, torment in his heart." Only inspiration from an angel makes his touching recovery possible.

With his assistant Louis-Jacques Milon, Gardel created numerous *divertissements* for operas, including Antonio Salieri's *Tarare*, Grétry's *Amphitryon* and *Aspasie*, Cherubini's *Démophon*, *Anacréon, ou L'Amour Fugitif*, and *Les Abencérages*, and Gaspare Spontini's *Vestale* and *Fernando Cortez*. Gardel composed the dances for Mozart's *Don Giovanni* when it was performed for the first time at the Paris Opera on 17 September 1805. He also composed the dances for *The Sleeping Beauty*, a fairy-tale opera by Michele Carafa.

According to a Monsieur Papillon, an administrator at the Opera, "Gardel owes to nature the most perfect physique she can create. It can also be said that he has done everything to take best advantage of this gift so generously given." He combined with his natural elegance a remarkable nobility and an expressive physiognomy perfect for tragic pantomime. As a performer he excelled both in his brother's ballets and in his own works, particularly *Télémaque dans l'Île de Calypso* and *Psyché,* in which he was admired in the role of Apollo.

As a choreographer, Pierre Gardel demonstrated "as much imagination as taste," according to Noverre, who added, "His compositions were brilliantly successful, and (something quite rare) they have retained the charms and freshness of their first youth." Gardel strove to put dance at the service of action without neglecting musicality. His musical knowledge complemented his mastery of the steps and determined their harmony. The choreographer, he said, "must be a consummate musician, or nature must have endowed him with perfect measure and a perfect ear." He imparted to ensembles a lively sense of theater and transmitted to his performers, wrote Noverre, a fondness for "an execution as difficult as it was perfect." As director of the Opera's School of Dance after 1802, he inculcated in his students, through rigorous precision of gesture, the style essential to dance. One of his students, Carlo Blasis, based his famous Code on the teachings of Pierre Gardel, to whom he dedicated it. Shrewd and even opportunistic, Gardel managed to hold onto his position despite the political upheavals of the French Revolution. Above all, he was able to maintain the quality of dance and to ensure an unbroken transition from a tradition inherited from the *ancien régime* to the flowering of the Romantic age.

Marie Gardel (Marie-Elisabeth-Anne-Boubert, also known as Marie Miller; born 8 April 1770 in Auxonne, died 18 April 1833 in Paris), dancer and teacher. Pierre's wife Marie Gardel was a stepdaughter of the composer Ernest Müller (Miller), whose name she used until her marriage. She entered the dance school of the Opera, where she studied with the Poco brothers. She made her debut in 1783 or 1784 at the Théâtre du Nicolet and about two years later danced before the court at Fontainebleau in Rameau's *Dardanus;* the queen was moved by her grace. She was warmly welcomed when she made her debut at the Opera on 13 January 1786, in the same work. On 14 December 1790, she appeared in Pierre Gardel's *Psyché.* In 1794 she married Pierre Gardel. A *demi-caractère* dancer after 1792, she performed in *Psyché* and in other ballets by her husband. *Le courrier des spectacles* noted that she danced Psyche "with much intelligence and grace." On 23 October 1806, she won great applause in a pas de trois with the beautiful Clotilde Malfleuroy and Auguste Vestris in the last act of the opera *Le Triomphe de Trajan* by Louis-Luc de Persuis and Jean-François Lesueur. She also created a leading role in *Lucas et Laurette* (music by François-Charlemagne Lefèvre, choreography by Louis-Jacques Milon). She left the stage in 1816, reappearing in 1819 in *La Dansomanie,* after which she devoted herself chiefly to teaching with her husband.

Noverre praised Marie Gardel's gifts lavishly:

I should need new words and new sentences in order faithfully to depict for you her rare talents. Her dancing is dazzling; diamonds burst from her feet, as it were; the polish of her execution is delicate; the most difficult phrasings and the most complicated series of steps are executed by this rival of Terpsichore with as much ease as perfection; she has a fine sense of measure and an impeccable ear, which impart to her dancing great precision and a novel charm. When I admire her, she reconciles me with the pirouette, because she does it so smoothly, she ends it with a lovely pause, and no unpleasant stress on her part forewarns the public that she is about to do it. . . . She is to dance what the Venus de Medici is to sculpture.

BIBLIOGRAPHY

Chapman, John V. "Forgotten Giant: Pierre Gardel." *Dance Research* 5 (Spring 1987): 3–20.

Chapman, John V. "The Paris Opéra Ballet School, 1798–1827." *Dance Chronicle* 12.2 (1989): 196–220.

Chazin-Bennahum, Judith. *Dance in the Shadow of the Guillotine.* Carbondale, Ill., 1988.

Grimm, Friedrich Melchior von. *Correspondance littéraire, philosophique et critique.* 17 vols. Paris, 1812–1814.

Guest, Ivor. *The Romantic Ballet in Paris.* 2d rev. ed. London, 1980.

Guest, Ivor. "La dansomanie." *The Dancing Times* (November 1985): 127–129.

Noverre, Jean-Georges. *Lettres sur les arts imitateurs en général et sur la danse en particulier.* 2 vols. Paris, 1807. Edited by Fernand Divoire as *Lettres sur la danse et les arts imitateurs* (Paris, 1952).

Price, Curtis A., et al. *Italian Opera in Late Eighteenth-Century London,* vol. 1, *The King's Theatre, Haymarket, 1778–1791.* London, 1995.

Swift, Mary Grace. *A Loftier Flight: The Life and Accomplishments of Charles Louis Didelot.* Middletown, Conn., 1974.

Winter, Marian Hannah. *The Pre-Romantic Ballet.* London, 1974.

JEANNINE DORVANE
Translated from French

GARDIE, ANNA (died 20 July 1798 in New York City), French dancer. Four years after Madame Gardie made her Philadelphia debut on 26 April 1794 in Jean-François Arnould-Mussot's pantomime-ballet *La Fôret Noire,* her career ended in tragedy. Gardie's pathetic story has long mesmerized historians, who have credited her, incorrectly, with being America's first ballet star and the first to present "serious" ballet in the United States.

Anna Gardie trained and danced at Cap-François, Haiti, and continued her career as an actress at one of the little theaters of Paris. She danced in Philadelphia from April through December 1794. When her contract was not renewed, she transferred to New York City and danced with Jean-Baptiste Francisqui; later she traveled to Hartford, Connecticut; Boston; New York again; and Newport, Rhode Island. In early October 1796 she returned to Boston, where she danced, on and off, until December 1797. Her American repertory included more than fifty roles, half in pantomime-ballets and the rest in harlequinades or character dances performed during the entr'actes.

Several journalists remarked on her "ravishing" beauty and dramatic talents. Representative is the *Massachusetts Mercury* critic who praised the accuracy with which she adapted "her every attitude, gesture, and expression to the various traits, and arduous transitions" in her role as an Indian princess.

Gardie never remained long employed at any theater, no matter how much she was admired by the critics or her fellow actors. On 31 January 1798 the impoverished dancer advertised her benefit performance, "in distress," in Boston, and she later offered free services to the New York theater in exchange for a benefit performance. The remedy brought no relief. She resolved to separate from Louis Stephen Gardie, her aristocratic lover—he to return home to France, she to Haiti. Distraught at their impending separation, he slew her, then killed himself. The tragedy took place at New York's Fraunces Tavern on the night of 20 July 1798. She was buried in Saint Mary's churchyard; he, in Potter's Field, now Washington Square.

BIBLIOGRAPHY
Columbian Centinel (Boston) (7 November 1795, 28 July 1798).
Costonis, Maureen Needham. "The French Connection: Ballet Comes to America." In *Musical Theatre in America*, edited by Glenn Loney. Westport, Conn., 1984.
Costonis, Maureen Needham. "French Ballet in Eighteenth-Century Saint Dominique." In *Proceedings of the Sixth Annual Conference, Society of Dance History Scholars, the Ohio State University, 11–13 February 1983*, compiled by Christena L. Schlundt. Milwaukee, 1983.
Dunlap, William. *History of the American Theatre.* 2 vols. London, 1833.
Dunlap, William. *Diary of William Dunlap.* 3 vols. Edited by Dorothy C. Barck. New York, 1930.
Durang, Charles. *History of the Philadelphia Stage between the Years 1749 and 1855.* 7 vols. Philadelphia, 1868.
Massachusetts Mercury (Boston) (17 February 1795).
Moore, Lillian. "The Dance: The Slain Ballerina, a Bit of Americana." *New York Herald Tribune* (16 June 1963).
Odell, George C. D. *Annals of the New York Stage.* Vol. 1. New York, 1927.

MAUREEN NEEDHAM

GARIFUNA DANCE. The Garifuna people of Belize and Honduras, also known as black Caribs, are descendents of a unique Maroon (escaped slave) society that formed on the island of Saint Vincent in the Lesser Antilles during the seventeenth and eighteenth centuries. Their ethnohistory reaches back to Amazonia in the heart of South America through the Carib and Arawak cultures of the Caribbean; it was altered since the late 1600s by a strong infusion of African culture. Garifuna music and dance retain both African and Native American stylistic features, as well as those of more recent European and Central American influences.

The Garifuna culture developed when shipwrecked and runaway slaves from West Africa settled among the Island Carib people who were themselves a mixed people, descended from the Arawakan Iñeri and Carib conquerors from what is now Venezuela. By 1700, Africans greatly outnumbered Island Caribs. The Africans took Carib women as wives and adopted Carib language, body decoration, manioc (cassava, an edible starchy root) technology, shamanism, and other cultural elements. After losing Saint Vincent to the British in 1797, the Garifuna were exiled to Honduras, and from there they spread along the Caribbean coast from Nicaragua to Belize. Many thousands have now emigrated to the United States, where they maintain their identity largely through the performance of traditional music and dance.

Garifuna musical influences include exposure to French Jesuit (Roman Catholic) missionaries, Spanish music both sacred and secular, the music of other Afro-Caribbean peoples such as Haitians, Jamaicans, and Cayman Islanders, and British and French performing traditions such as quadrilles and marching bands. From the Spanish the Garifuna adopted the guitar, violin, and flute, the *Juego de Tiras* (Dance of the Moors), and song genres such as the *bolero*, *paranda*, *serenada*, and *berusu*.

Above all, Garifuna music today retains a strong African element, expressed in drumming, drum lore, several dances, and the relationship among drummers, dancers, and audience. Native American roots, however, have not been lost; specific song styles related to manioc technology, healing, and ancestor worship have been retained.

Song types and dance beats are generally synonymous. There are more than a dozen different types of songs (*oremu*). Handmade log drums fitted with a single-skin head and with strings or wire stretched across as a snare are played without sticks. These accompany both sacred and secular music. A few song forms are sung to guitar accompaniment alone. One type, the *uyanu*, is sung a capella (with no music) in irregular meter by a line of performers linked by their little fingers, who make stylized gestures without crossing the feet.

Punta is the first rhythmic pattern children learn and the most popular social dance, included at all parties and required at Garifuna *beluria*, the Nine-Nights Ceremonies, which are held after a death. The *punta* expresses the politics of Garifuna sexuality. The dance, performed by two people (usually a man and a woman, occasionally two women), is a competitive display of skill, sometimes bordering on mock combat. The humor in both the dance and the song is ribald and often scandalous. *Punta* songs are composed, often by women, to expose a rival or comment on unacceptable behavior. Similar dances are found in African-American communities throughout Latin America and the Caribbean.

The most spectacular Garifuna dance is the *wanaragua*, a street masquerade similar to the Jamaican Jonkonnu.

Performed at Christmas by troupes of men dressed as either men or women, this dance was once widespread throughout West Indian slave communities. At one time it celebrated a saturnalian reversal of roles, during which the plantation masters opened their homes to slaves and feasted them on Christmas Day. The dancers, dressed as white men, perform in a menacing manner to scare the onlookers. The Garifuna costume consists of crowns made of macaw feathers and crepe paper, cowrie-shell kneebands, and whiteface masks of molded and painted metal screen. Dancers, drummers, and accompanying female singers form troupes and visit houses at Christmas, receiving delicacies, coins, or rum. The Garifuna version traditionally opened with the arrival of the *warrine*, a Carib figure dressed in plantain leaves. The music is very fast and polyrhythmic. [*See* Jonkonnu Festival.]

The *chumba* is one of the oldest Garifuna dance forms known today. Solo dancers come before the drums, saluting them with staccato movements that often descend in stages to a level where the dancers' backs are on the floor. The *chumba* requires subtle communication between drummers and dancers.

The *sambai* is not commonly performed today. Its beat seems related to *wanaragua*, but it is danced with a stomping step by both men and women. The *gunjai* is a circle dance in which partners exchange at the call "Sarse." It is clearly European in origin but shows Latin stylistic influences. The *hunguhungu* is a processional in triple meter, a secularized version of the sacred *hugulendu* dancing.

One of the reasons that the Garifuna have retained the integrity of their traditional dance is that their religious rituals require dance. These rituals continue to be practiced despite an official Roman Catholicism. The roots are found in both African and Carib beliefs about the power of ancestral spirits and the need to placate them. A series of post-mortem rituals incorporate trances of possession by ancestor spirits, shamanism, herbalism, and an extensive corpus of sacred music. By these means angry spirits are honored and their destructive power redirected toward healing.

At the *dugu*, the most elaborate Garifuna ritual, the sacred drums play only one beat, a unison triple meter unlike the polyrhythms of African and Garifuna secular music. The participants are required to sing and dance nearly constantly for three to four days and nights, performing a sacred dance step called the *hugulendu*. This somber, tightly bound shuffle, sometimes staged in a circle, was, in 1665, reported to be danced by the Island Carib. The symbolic action of the ceremony (the name of which literally means "treading down") is the suppression of the troublesome ancestral spirits' power. This reflects the Island Carib custom of treading down the grave with the feet, demonstrated today by the sacred shuffle step. When pos-

sessed, however, Garifuna dancers' movements change dramatically, becoming far less repetitive or bound and using more space, assuming African-style body movements. Drummers maintain the same beat but shift the accents, which shifts the stress of the dancers' steps.

The *mali*, the most sacred dance, is performed many times in the course of a *dugu* ceremony. It is led by the chief healer (*buyei*) who shakes gourd rattles and leads the congregation around the temple in a long series of movements with a complex floor plan.

Among Belizeans, the remarkable strength and longevity of Garifuna dance styles has been based on maintaining the traditional religion as well as incorporating the celebration of secular holidays—including Garifuna Settlement Day, 29 September.

[*See also* Belize *and* Caribbean Region.]

BIBLIOGRAPHY

Cayetano, Sebastian. *Garifuna History, Language, and Culture of Belize, Central America, and the Caribbean.* Belize City, 1993.

Crawford, Michael, ed. *Black Caribs: A Case Study in Biocultural Adaptation.* New York, 1984.

Foley, Kenan. "Garifuna Music Culture." Master's thesis, State University of New York, Binghamton, 1994.

González, Nancie L. Solien. *Sojourners of the Caribbean: Ethnogenesis and Ethnohistory of the Garifuna.* Urbana, Ill., 1988.

Palacio, Myrtle. *The First Primer on the People Called Garifuna.* Belize City, 1993.

Porter, Robert W. "History and Social Life of the Garifuna in the Lesser Antilles and Central America." Ph.D. diss., Princeton University, 1984.

Whitehead, Neil L., ed. *Wolves from the Sea: Readings in the Anthropology of the Native Caribbean.* Leiden, 1995.

RECORDINGS.   Carol Jenkins and Travis Jenkins, *Traditional Music of the Garifuna of Belize* (New York: Ethnic Folkways Records, 1982), and *Dabuyabarugu, Inside the Temple: Sacred Music of the Garifuna of Belize* (New York: Ethnic Folkways Records, 1982).

CAROL JENKINS

GASKELL, SONIA (born 14 April 1904 in Vilkaviskis, Lithuania, died 9 July 1974 in Paris), Dutch dancer, choreographer, and ballet director. Gaskell studied with Lubov Egorova in Paris and danced there in Serge Diaghilev's Ballets Russes as well as in several small companies and cabarets. In 1939 she followed her Dutch husband Philip Bauchhenss to Amsterdam, where she schooled generations of Dutch ballet dancers in the Russian technique. She was also one of the most influential postwar pioneers and laid the foundation for a Dutch ballet tradition with her consecutive companies, Ballet Studio '45 (1945), Ballet Recital (1949–1951, 1952–1954), the Netherlands Ballet (1954–1961), and the Dutch National Ballet (from 1961). As a choreographer she created more than twenty ballets, but none remained long in the repertory.

Gaskell's insistence on technical perfection, her love of dance history, and her interest in new developments made her one of the dominant figures of ballet in the Netherlands. For example, in the 1950s she advocated the abstract ballets of George Balanchine, which were then not well known in Europe; furthermore, in 1959 she commissioned Paul Taylor to create a modern dance piece, and from 1961 she had her dancers taught Graham technique, first by Pearl Lang, who also made dance pieces for her company. However, Gaskell's intellectual and demanding approach to dance, coupled with her strong, authoritarian personality, also made her one of the most controversial figures in the Dutch dance world. Conflicts abounded, with two dramatic climaxes: the loss of many of her dancers in 1959, who went on to found the Netherlands Dance Theater; and her own departure from the Dutch National Ballet in 1968. Thereafter, she mainly worked as a member of the board of the dance department of the United Nations Educational, Scientific, and Cultural Organization. Gaskell was named a Knight of the Orde van Oranje-Nassau and was promoted in 1966 to Officer.

[*See also* Netherlands, *article on* Theatrical Dance since 1945.]

BIBLIOGRAPHY

Loney, Glenn. "Evolution of an Ensemble." *Dance Magazine* (March 1974): 34–39.

Utrecht, Luuk. *Het Nationale Ballet 25 jaar: De Geschiedenis van Het Nationale Ballet van 1961 tot 1986.* Amsterdam, 1987.

Weetering, Conrad van de, and Luuk Utrecht. *Sonia Gaskell.* Zutphen, 1976.

LUUK UTRECHT

GAUDRAU, MICHEL (born 1692 in Paris, died 14 February 1751 in Bayonne, France), dancer, teacher, and author. Born to Jeanne Rolland and Charles Gaudrau, a maker and merchant of silk cloth in Paris, the young Michel was probably apprenticed to Raoul-Auger Feuillet, from whom he learned the now-famous but at the time new system of dance notation. In October 1708, at the age of sixteen, Michel Gaudrau made his professional debut at the Académie Royale de Musique in the role of a Chinaman in act 5 of the *Pastorale Héroïque: Issé.* As a member of the ballet corps, he continued to appear in all the Paris Opera productions until 1715, when he left France altogether to become the dancing master to the royal family of Spain. This elevated position followed the publication of his book—a collection of Guillaume-Louis Pecour's latest dances for the ballroom and stage—which he had recorded in the Feuillet notation. Published around 1713, this splendid work is one of the major sources of information for the study of eighteenth-century theatrical dancing.

Once settled in Spain, Gaudrau changed his name to Don Miguel Godro and married a compatriot, Marie Madeleine Carlier, daughter of René Carlier, the French architect who designed the Retiro Gardens in Madrid. Several children were born of the union, and three sons survived him—Ricardo, Miguel-Angel, and Luis Godro—but none became a dancer.

When Michel Gaudrau died in Bayonne on 14 February 1751, he was buried in the cloister of the ancient cathedral.

BIBLIOGRAPHY

Astier, Régine. "Michel Gaudrau, un danseur presqu'ordinaire." *Les goûts réunis,* no. 3 (January 1983).

Astier, Régine. "La vie quotidienne des danseurs sous l'ancien régime." *Les goûts réunis,* no. 3 (January 1983).

Gaudrau, Michel. *Nouveau recueil de dance de bal et celle de ballet, contenant un très grand nombres des meillieures entrées de ballet de la composition de Mr. Pécour.* Paris, 1713.

Whitley-Bauguess, Paige. "An Eighteenth-Century Dance Reconstruction." *Dance Notation Journal* 5.1 (Spring 1987): 11–24.

RÉGINE ASTIER

GAUTIER, THÉOPHILE (Pierre-Jules-Théophile Gautier; born 31 August 1811 in Tarbes, France, died 23 October 1872 in Paris), French critic and man of letters. As the youngest of the masters of French romanticism, Gautier deserves better than his present neglect as a critic and man of letters. Often, he is remembered solely for having worn a flamboyant red vest to the premiere of Victor Hugo's drama *Hernani* (1830); his true worth, however, was recognized by poet Charles Baudelaire, whose dedication in *Les fleurs du mal* (1857) called Gautier "the impeccable poet" and "the perfect magician of French letters." Gautier's poems in *Emaux et camées* (1852) typify the art-for-art's sake movement, a view he held as early as 1835 and presented in the preface to his novel *Mademoiselle de Maupin.*

As a critic, Gautier wrote for two major Parisian dailies, *La presse* (1836–1855) and *Le moniteur universel* (1855–1868); they contain the bulk of his artistic and theatrical criticism. His dramatic criticism, another series of weekly articles, includes more than two hundred separate mentions of dance and dancers. Reviews of ballet premieres at the Paris Opera are the most important. He also discusses revivals of earlier works and ballets at other theaters as well as debuts by both French and foreign dancers and by national dance troupes. Gautier had a gift for recounting plots and describing the persons of the female dancers in highly detailed, colorful images. In his famous description of Fanny Elssler dancing the *cachucha*, for example, he noted how "her swooning arms flutter about her drooping head, her body curves back, her white shoulders almost brush the floor."

Further articles by Gautier include the five essays in *Les beautés de l'Opéra* (1845), among them the studies of *Le Diable Boiteux* and *Giselle.* He was one of the few who tried to prove Elssler's superiority over Marie Taglioni when Elssler assumed her roles in *La Sylphide* and *La Fille du Danube*. For Carlotta Grisi he campaigned even more avidly, providing at least part of the libretto for a production of *Giselle* in 1841. His love for Grisi was never-ending; her name, the last word he spoke on his deathbed. Grisi's disinclination to return his love resulted in his twenty-five-year liaison with her sister Ernesta, by whom he fathered two daughters.

The first volume of reprints from Gautier's dramatic criticism, *L'histoire de l'art dramatique en France*, appeared in 1858. With the completion of the sixth volume the following year, a large selection of his reviews from 1837 to 1852 became readily accessible. Criticisms of many ballets are included, but there are numerous misdatings and omissions. The totality of his dance writings can be studied properly only by reviewing the original newspapers. Serge Lifar, in his biography *Carlotta Grisi* (1941), supposed a lessening of Gautier's interest in her solely because his reviews of her later ballets and many mentions of her career are not included in *L'histoire*.

Gautier wrote ballet libretti—the only man of letters to recognize the potential of ballet as a medium of poetic expression. Six of his libretti were performed: five at the Paris Opera and one at the Théâtre de la Porte-Saint-Martin. For Grisi, he contributed one for *Giselle* in 1841 and one for *La Péri* in 1843; they were two of her greatest successes. About "Achmet and *La Péri*," he wrote, "matter and spirit, desire and love, meet in the ecstasy of a dream." For Fanny Cerrito, he provided two other libretti: in 1851, *Pâquerette*, an overlong work choreographed by Arthur Saint-Léon, and, in 1854, *Gemma*, a melodrama about mesmerism in seventeenth-century Naples, with choreography by Cerrito; both were failures, though Saint-Léon did tour with *Pâquerette*, and in the late 1860s there was even talk of a Paris revival. In 1858, the year Gautier's *Yanko le Bandit* was mounted at the Porte-Saint-Martin, he adapted a Hindu epic for Amalia Ferraris at the Opera: as *Sacountala*, choreographed by Lucien Petipa, it was performed twenty-four times and was an artistic success.

Gautier also wrote six ballet libretti that never were realized. His first would have presented Elssler as Cleopatra. Another was commissioned by composer and would-be London impresario Louis Antoine Jullien; letters by Hector Berlioz, its intended composer, have revealed that its subject was Goethe's *Wilhelm Meister*. Gautier's *La Statue Amoureuse* dates from about 1853, whereas his final three ballets all belong to the last years of his life. Mariano Fortuny's painting *Le Mariage dans la Vicaria de Madrid* (1870) was the creative spark for a one-act work featuring Gautier's beloved Spanish dances. He also proposed both *The Pied Piper of Hamelin* and Goethe's *Erlkönig* as possible subjects of a ballet to the young composer Jules Massenet, who chose the former. The finished libretto was the last work Gautier wrote before his death.

[*See also the entries on the principal figures mentioned herein.*]

BIBLIOGRAPHY

Baudelaire, Charles. *Les fleurs du mal*. Paris, 1857.

Binney, Edwin, 3rd. *Les ballets de Théophile Gautier*. Paris, 1965.

Chapman, John V. "Silent Drama to Silent Dream: Parisian Ballet Criticism." *Dance Chronicle* 11.3 (1988):365–380.

Gautier, Théophile. *Histoire de l'art dramatique en France depuis vingt-cinq ans*. 6 vols. Leipzig, 1858–1859. Reprint, Geneva, 1968.

Gautier, Théophile. *Théâtre: Mystère, comédies et ballets*. New ed. Paris, 1882.

Gautier, Théophile. *Gautier on Dance*. Translated and edited by Ivor Guest. London, 1986.

Guest, Ivor. *The Ballet of the Second Empire*. London, 1974.

Guest, Ivor. *The Romantic Ballet in Paris*. 2d rev. ed. London, 1980.

Guest, Ivor. *Jules Perrot: Master of the Romantic Ballet*. London, 1984.

Levinson, André. *Meister des balletts*. Potsdam, 1923.

Lifar, Serge. *Giselle: Apothéose du ballet romantique*. Paris, 1942.

Lifar, Serge. *Carlotta Grisi*. Translated by Doris Langley Moore. London, 1947.

Priddin, Deirde. *The Art of the Dance in French Literature from Théophile Gautier to Paul Valéry*. London, 1952.

Richardson, Joanna. *Théophile Gautier: His Life and Times*. London, 1958.

Senninger, Claude-Marie. *Théophile Gautier: Une vie, une oeuvre*. Paris, 1994.

Taplin, Diana Theodores. "On Critics and Criticism of Dance." In *New Directions in Dance*, edited by Diana Theodores Taplin. Toronto, 1979.

Ubersfeld, Anne. *Théophile Gautier*. Paris, 1992.

EDWIN BINNEY, 3RD

GAVOTTE. A French dance, probably of folk origin, dating from the sixteenth century or earlier, the *gavotte* is still performed in folk versions in several areas of France today. The *gavotte* developed in the sixteenth century into a popular court dance and continued to be performed as both a social and a theatrical dance through the nineteenth century.

Michael Praetorius states in *Terpsichore* (1612) that the dance originated with the peasants of Gavotte, in the Alpine region near Gap in southeastern France. An alternate derivation of the term is from the central French-dialect word *gavaud*, meaning "bent leg," a feature of one of the *gavotte* steps included in Thoinot Arbeau's description of the dance. According to Arbeau's *Orchésographie* (1588), the *gavotte* was similar to the double *branle*, a social dance performed by a number of couples in a circle. Like the double *branle* it was in duple meter with four- and eight-bar phrases, but the addition of hops to the double steps gave it a lively character. The *gavotte branles* differed from the ordinary *branles* in at least two other ways: steps from the *galliarde* were interspersed into the doubles sequences, and each couple in turn danced alone in the

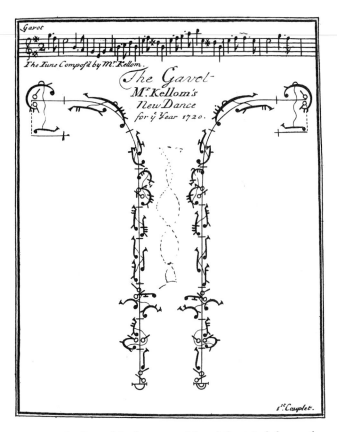

GAVOTTE. Performed both as a social and theatrical dance, the *gavotte*'s characteristic step pattern included the frequent use of an *assemblé* preceded by a step called *contretemps de gavotte*. In this example of a ballroom *gavotte*, recorded in Feuillet notation, the eight measures of music correspond to the eight measures of steps. (Reprinted from Kellom Tomlinson, *Six Dances Composed by Mr. Kellom Tomlinson*, London, 1721.)

middle of the circle, after which they kissed all the other dancers.

During the first third of the seventeenth century the *branle* suite became standardized, normally consisting of five different *branles* followed by a single *gavotte*. Numerous collections of dance music confirm that the *gavotte*, as part of the *branle* suite, was danced at most of the important courts of northern Europe throughout the century. In Pierre Rameau's *Le maître à danser* (1725) the *branle* suite was said to have been danced at the opening of formal court balls during the reign of Louis XIV (at least until the 1680s—it is clear that Rameau is not describing contemporary practice). Unfortunately, few choreographic descriptions of the seventeenth-century *branle/gavotte* survive. According to De Lauze in *Apologie de la danse* (1623), the dance was so well known that a description of the steps and actions was unnecessary. (He does mention that at least three different *gavottes* were still being danced, and that significant regional variants existed.) Marin

Mersenne's description in *Harmonie universelle* (1636) is quite similar to Arbeau's, adding some further details about the "solo" section of the dance.

Toward the end of the seventeenth century a new type of *gavotte*, not connected to the *branle* suite, coexisted with the older *branle/gavotte*. These individual *gavottes* first appeared in the ballets and operas of Jean-Baptiste Lully; at least thirty-seven are found in his theatrical works between the years 1653 and 1687. The pieces, usually in binary form (two repeated strains of music), retain the duple meter and four-bar phrases of the earlier *gavotte*. In addition, they are characterized by a distinctive rhythmic structure in which the melody begins halfway through the bar, usually with two upbeats: ♩♩|♩. We do not know what dances were originally performed to Lully's *gavotte* music, as only two notated choreographies survive. Both were published more than thirty years after the music was composed and were probably choreographed for revivals of his works. An additional ten *gavotte* choreographies are preserved in Feuillet notation, eight of them published between 1714 and 1722. Seventeen other notated choreographies, set to *gavotte* music but not called *gavottes*, also survive in manuscripts and prints dating from around 1700 to 1756.

These twenty-nine surviving *gavottes* and *gavotte*-type dances can be divided into three categories based on step vocabulary and number of dancers. (Like all "French" dances of this period, each *gavotte* has a unique floor pattern and step sequence and was intended to be danced to specific music.) The theatrical dance, usually for one or two men or women, included difficult steps and was sometimes in a much slower tempo. The social dance (*danse à deux*) was performed at court or at other formal balls. Although these dances use a large step vocabulary, they can usually be distinguished from other Baroque dance types by their frequent use of the *assemblé* to create short, well-defined dance phrases. The *assemblé* is often preceded by a *contretemps de gavotte*, a step combination that functions as a choreographic cadential pattern. The third type of *gavotte* choreography is a much simpler dance for two or more couples, in which only a few step-units, other than the cadential pattern referred to above, are used. Examples of this type, "Le Cotillon" (1705) and "Le Gavotte du Roi" (1716), may be remnants of the *branle/gavotte* tradition. Although Raoul-Auger Feuillet refers to a *"pas de gavotte"* in his 1706 *contredanse* treatise, neither he nor other contemporary writers define this step. A description does appear in Josson's *Traité* (1763) that is similar to the cadential pattern mentioned earlier.

The *gavotte* continued to be danced in the theater even after it was no longer popular as a social dance. The composer Jean-Philippe Rameau used it more than any other dance type in his stage works (1733–1764), and danced *gavottes* were also included in works by Gluck and Wolfgang Amadeus Mozart. In late eighteenth-century England, a *menuet* and *gavotte* were often danced as entr'acte entertainment, and both dance types were still being performed at the Paris Opera as late as 1817.

Through much of the nineteenth century the term *gavotte* seems to have been synonymous with the "Gavotte de Vestris," a theatrical duet by the famed dancer Gaetano Vestris first performed in the 1760s or 1770s. Although no notation or description of the original dance survives, several nineteenth-century versions do exist in verbal descriptions, dance notations, or both. The music is still in duple meter with four- and eight-bar phrases; however, the characteristic rhythmic pattern beginning in the middle of the bar is no longer present. Although similarities of steps and spatial patterns exist among these versions the differences between them are great enough, particularly in the level of difficulty, that it might be more accurate to speak of "Gavotte de Vestris" interpretations rather than a single dance. A late-nineteenth-century version of the "Gavotte de Vestris" by Giraudet is for two couples, with considerable simplification of the steps and an alteration of the dance/music relationships.

A number of different folk dances called *gavottes* are still performed today in France, particularly in Basse-Bretagne. Examples include the Gavotte de Pont-Aven, the Gavotte de Quimper, and the Gavotte des Montagnes. These dances encompass a great variety of steps, floor patterns, and other performance traditions.

[*See also* Ballet Technique, History of, *article on* French Court Dance; *and* Social Dance, *article on* Court and Social Dance before 1800.]

BIBLIOGRAPHY

Hammond, Sandra Noll. "The 'Gavotte de Vestris': A Dance of Three Centuries." In *Proceedings of the Seventh Annual Conference, Society of Dance History Scholars, Goucher College, Towson, Maryland, 17–19 February 1984*, compiled by Christena L. Schlundt. Riverside, Calif., 1984.

Little, Meredith Ellis. "Gavotte." In *The New Grove Dictionary of Music and Musicians*. London, 1980.

Warner, Mary Jane. "Gavottes and Bouquets: A Comparative Study of Changes in Dance Style between 1700 and 1850." Ph.D. diss., Ohio State University, 1974.

CAROL G. MARSH

GAYANÉ. Originally performed under the title *Happiness* in 1939, this ballet in four acts was first staged in Armenia. Aram Khachaturian, the composer, took into account the limited possibilities of a ballet company that had not yet reached maturity. Hence, the ballet contained a large number of pantomime and play scenes, and many ethnic dances, which lent it the character of a musical-choreographic rhapsody on folk themes, rather than an integrated musical drama. Despite the indisputable mer-

its of the music, the libretto was soon radically revised by the author. Seeking to enrich and develop the ballet, Khachaturian revised the score and created large passages of new music—a series of dramatized dance episodes based on symphonically developed themes. This became the new score, *Gayané*.

The first professional production of the ballet, choreographed by Nina Anisimova to a libretto by Konstantin Derzhavin, was presented by the Kirov Ballet on 9 December 1942 in Perm, where the company resided during World War II. "The birth of *Gayané*, a beautiful flower in the middle of a raging war, assumed great political significance by awakening a heart-rending nostalgia for peaceful life, constructive work, and love, the spiritual values that were being defended in the great battle against the Nazis" (Katonova, 1980). The ballet takes place on a collective farm in Armenia. Gayané, the daughter of the collective chairman, is in love with Armen, whose rival for her affections is Giko. Aided by Giko, a spy has infiltrated the territory and when he is captured with Gayané's imperiled assistance, Giko is imprisoned. With danger averted and Gayané now able to marry Armen, a grand celebratory finale takes place, which includes the well-known "Saber Dance." In this production Gayané was danced by Natalia Dudinskaya, Armen by Konstantin Sergeyev, and Giko by Boris Shavrov, with Anisimova in an archetypal portrayal of socialist labor and freedom.

The stage life of the ballet largely determined the history of Armenian ballet. After the production of *Happiness* by Ilya Arbatov in 1939 and *Gayané* by Anisimova in 1942, Maxim Martirosian revived it in 1971. In each new production the ballet seemed to be nearing its perfect embodiment. In 1974 another premiere, by the choreographer Vilen Galstian, was staged. For it Khachaturian made a special music edition that contributed to the ballet's vividness and originality. The mutual understanding among the composer, choreographer, and designer (Minas Avetisian), their knowledge of the national temperament, and the modern spirit of the production brought the music, choreography, and decor into complete harmony. The ballet in this version was added to the company repertories in Novosibirsk, Cairo, and Gdansk, and the ballet company of the Ruse Theater in Bulgaria staged it in 1983. Armenian dancers presented it in Moscow, Leningrad, Kiev, Tbilisi, Buenos Aires, Mexico City, Damascus, Tunis, Paris, and Marseille. Other significant productions were done by Sergei Sergeyev in Kiev in 1974, Natalia Danilova in Kuibyshev (now Samara) in 1952, Vasily Vainonen for the Bolshoi Ballet in Moscow in 1957, Boris Eifman for the Maly Opera and Ballet Theater in Leningrad in 1972, and Imre Keres in Wiesbaden in 1972. The ballet has also been seen in Berlin, Leipzig, Bratislava, and Kosice.

BIBLIOGRAPHY

Danilov, Sergei. "Leningrad." *Dance Magazine* (April 1946): 43–44.

Katonova, Svetlana. *Muzyka sovetskogo baleta.* 2d ed. Leningrad, 1990.

MacMahon, Deirdre. "'Corridor to the Muses.'" *Ballet Review* 12 (Spring 1984): 57–65.

Shneerson, Grigorii M. *Aram Khachaturian* (in English). Moscow, 1959.

Tigranov, Georgii. *Balety A. Khachaturiana.* 2d ed. Moscow, 1974.

KATARINEH SARYAN
Translated from Russian

GEISHA DANCE. The term *geisha* is a common word in Japanese for a *geigi* (or *geiko* in the Kamigata region), literally, a person skilled in the performing arts. Geisha dance is not an established form like *kabuki* dance; the Japanese themselves would say "dances by geisha" rather than "geisha dance."

The geisha tradition developed gradually in the pleasure districts of Japanese cities beginning in the late seventeenth century. The tradition represents a synthesis of the arts and skills of two groups, one primarily entertainers, the other primarily prostitutes. Originally some geisha were men proficient in martial arts, but by the late eighteenth century, women geisha had established themselves as entertainers, dancers, and performers on a stringed instrument, the *shamisen*. By the late nineteenth century, the term *geisha* had come to mean a skilled hostess serving businessmen and politicians.

The influence of the geisha tradition on dance and music cannot be overlooked. In present-day Japan, however, the number of trained geisha is decreasing drastically as entertainment forms change with modernization. Today, geisha dance is performed in two different settings. The first, and more common, of these is the less theatrical, being an entertainment performed for men in the small *tatami* room of a restaurant. It is characterized by movements adapted to a limited space: the use of the limbs is restricted, and gestures are used to illustrate songs in a more literal fashion than in *kabuki* dance. Geisha dance is more subtle and quiet than *kabuki* dance, and many accompanying songs are short and center on themes of love.

In a second form, geisha dance is given as a public performance in the manner of a revue on a proscenium stage, usually once a year. Three well-known concerts are Miyako Odori and Kamogawa Odori, in Kyoto, and Azuma Odori, in Tokyo. (Besides these, geisha-dance concerts are given by other groups in Tokyo, Kyoto, Osaka, Nagoya, and other cities.)

Miyako Odori is a popular Kyoto tourist attraction performed by geisha of the Gion district. Started in 1872 by Yachyo Inoue III of the Inoue school, the prominent traditional dance school of Kyoto, it is now performed every spring.

Kamogawa Odori is a dance revue started in 1872 by geisha of the Ponto-chō district along the Kamo River in Kyoto. The choreography has varied through the years and tends to be more modern than that of Miyako Odori.

Azuma Odori, started in 1925, is performed every spring and fall by geisha of the Shimbashi district in Tokyo. Although stopped during World War II, it was revived in 1948. Because the choreography for Azuma Odori has often been done by headmasters of Japanese classical-dance schools, this concert is much more akin to full-scale dance drama than are the others. Azuma Odori has fostered the meteoric rise of geisha stars such as Marichiyo.

BIBLIOGRAPHY

Dalby, Liza C. *Geisha.* Berkley, Calif., 1983.

Geino-shi Kenkyu-kai (Association for the History of Performing Arts Studies, Hayashi, Tasusaburo, Editor). *Nihon no Koten Geino* (The Classic Arts of Japan). Tokyo, 1970.

Gunji, Masakatsu. *Buyo* (Dance). Tokyo, 1970.

Katayama, Keijiro. *Inoue Yachiyo Geiwa* (Monologues of Inoue Yachiyo on Her Art). Tokyo, 1967.

SACHIYO ITO

GELABERT, CESC (born 9 February 1953 in Barcelona), Spanish dancer and choreographer. Gelabert started studying dance in 1969 at the Anna Maleras Studio in Barcelona and became a member of her company, the first modern-jazz dance group in Spain. In 1972 he presented his first work, and in 1973 he choreographed a solo, *Acció O.* Solos are a constant feature of his career, reflecting his individuality. At the beginning, he was more self-taught than trained by others, but he studied various modern dance styles and alternative techniques. He also studied architecture at the University of Barcelona from 1971 to 1976.

In 1978, Gelabert applied for a scholarship from the March Foundation but was turned down because his work was considered unclassifiable. Nonetheless, he went to New York, where he studied for two years, performing his solos at the Cunningham Studio, The Kitchen, La Mama E.T.C., and Danspace, and collaborating with other artists. In 1980 he returned to Barcelona and met Lydia Azzopardi, a British dancer trained at the London Contemporary Dance School, with whom he started a long collaboration. She was crucial in his career, improving his technique and bringing maturity to his work. His style is now intimate and eclectic, with a personal movement that flows from within.

From 1980 to 1985, Gelabert and Azzopardi presented their work in Spain, France, Germany, England, Mexico, Italy, and New York. In 1986 they formed the Gelabert-Azzopardi Company. Their productions fall into three categories: solos such as *Bujaraloz* (1982), *Suspiros de*

España (1984), *Vaslav* (1989), and *Variació de Muriel* (1994); company productions such as *Desfigurat* (1986), *Requiem* (1987), *Belmonte* (1988), *El Sueño de Artemis* (1991), *Kaalon Kaakon* (1992), *Augenlid* (1993), and *El Jardiner* (1993); and collaborations in theater and opera, of which the most important are *La Vera Storia, Mephistofeles, Cristobal Colon, Le Rossignol,* and *El Público*. Gelabert's collaborations with well-known musicians such as Carlos Santos and plastic artists such as Frederic Amat, along with his sense of contemporaneity, have made him popular with the general public.

Apart from dancing and choreographing, Gelabert has taught extensively in La Fàbrica (Barcelona), elsewhere in Spain, and abroad. He is considered the pioneer of a new generation of young dancers and choreographers in Spain, and throughout his career he has been involved in researching and experimenting with choreographic issues.

Gelabert did the choreography for the arrival of the torch in Empuries, Catalonia, for the 1992 Olympic Games in Barcelona. He received the Premio Nacional de Dansa in 1983, the Ciutat de Barcelona award in 1987, and the Gold Medal of Merit for the Arts in 1994.

BIBLIOGRAPHY
"Cesc Gelabert and Lydia Azzopardi." *Dance and Dancers* (November 1984): 28–30.
García, J. M., and Ferrer Martí Rom. *Cesc Gelabert.* Barcelona, 1990.
García Otzet, Montse, et al. *Dansa: Noves tendencías de la coreografía catalana.* Barcelona, 1994.
Goodwin, Noël. "Gelabert/Santos." *Dance and Dancers* (January 1986): 19–20.
Kumin, Laura. "A Look at Contemporary Dance in Spain." *Dance Magazine* (August 1993): 38–41.
Llorens, Pilar, et al. *História de la danza en Cataluña.* Barcelona, 1987.
Rodrigo, Eulália. "Els solos del pioner." *Escena* (March 1995).

NÈLIDA MONÉS I MESTRE

GELTSER. Known for her formidable classical technique and acclaimed for her interpretations of *demi-caractère* roles, Geltser also excelled in national dances. Here she is seen in costume for a Russian dance, c.1910. (Photograph from the Dance Collection, New York Public Library for the Performing Arts.)

GELTSER, EKATERINA (Ekaterina Vasil'evna Geltser; born 2 [14] November 1876, died 12 December 1962 in Moscow), Russian dancer. The daughter of the Bolshoi Theater male dancer and ballet teacher Vasily Geltser, Ekaterina graduated from the Moscow ballet school, where she studied under I. D. Nikitin and José Mendes. From 1894 to 1896 she danced at the Bolshoi Theater in Moscow, then went to Saint Petersburg where she appeared at the Maryinsky Theater as a member of the corps de ballet and in classical and character ensembles in Marius Petipa's ballets. She also continued her education there with Christian Johansson. In 1898 she returned to the Bolshoi to take leading roles in the restagings of Petipa ballets, such as Thérèse in *La Halte de Cavalerie* and Princess Aurora in *The Sleeping Beauty*.

Geltser's creative originality and talent flowered fully after she began working under the choreographer Aleksandr Gorsky, who produced his first ballet at the Bolshoi Theater in 1899 and assumed leadership of its ballet troupe in 1902. Influenced by the successful productions of the Moscow Art Theater and Savva Mamontov's Private Opera, Gorsky sought to achieve the utmost artistic integrity of his ballet productions on the basis of full-blooded story lines, graphic scenic effects, colorful stage designs, and complete naturalness and authenticity of dramatic action. A successful and convincing solution of this task called for enhancing the acting of dance roles and for a serious, meaningful message to convey. Geltser shared Gorsky's philosophy and took the title roles in many of his productions.

A ballerina with virtuosic technique, Geltser combined her technical brilliance with fluid movements and a soft line. At the same time she was an excellent mime and was capable of conveying genuine human emotions and sentiments. In different periods Geltser danced in Gorsky's best ballets, his versions of classics as well as originals, appearing as Odette-Odile in *Swan Lake*, Medora in *Le Corsaire*, Lise in *La Fille Mal Gardée*, Kitri in *Don Quixote*, the Tsar-Maiden in *The Little Humpbacked Horse*, the Shepherdess in *Love Is Quick!*, Eunice in *Eunice and Petronius*, and the title role in *Raymonda*. Her talents unfolded to the full when she created the powerful and memorable title role in *Salammbô* (1910), which embodied Gorsky's philosophy and artistic principles. Geltser's permanent partner was Vasily Tikhomirov, who also conducted the class in which she polished her technique.

In 1910 Geltser traveled to Berlin, then to Brussels for a series of guest performances, and also danced in Paris as a part of Diaghilev's Ballets Russes Saisons Russes. The following year she danced in London together with Tikhomirov and a group of Bolshoi Theater dancers, traveling to the United States with Mikhail Mordkin later in the year. Geltser also appeared on tour in every major city in Russia to consolidate her reputation as one of the country's best ballerinas.

After the Revolution of 1917 Geltser, Tikhomirov, and Gorsky were among the first prominent personalities of the Russian ballet who were active in building the edifice of a new Soviet culture and in promoting new trends born of the revolution, withal they continued to advocate the classical heritage and offered spirited resistance to its would-be destroyers. Geltser created new roles more in tune with the spirit of the times. One example was her profoundly human portrayal of Esmeralda in Tikhomirov's version of the eponymous ballet in 1926. In 1927 Geltser created a moving and heroic image of the Chinese dancer Tao-Hoa in one of the first Soviet ballets on a contemporary subject, *The Red Poppy*, choreographed by Lev Lashchilin and Tikhomirov.

In 1935 Geltser left the Bolshoi Ballet and until 1941 toured throughout the Soviet Union, appearing both in major cities and in the remotest corners of the country. She was one of the first ballerinas in the Soviet Union to win the prestigious title People's Artist of the Russian Federation, which was conferred on her in 1925. In 1943 she was awarded a national prize in recognition of her services to the country.

BIBLIOGRAPHY

Guest, Ivor. *Ballet in Leicester Square*. London, 1992.
Iving, Victor. "Catherine Geltser." In *The Soviet Ballet*, by Yuri Slonimsky et al. New York, 1947.
Krasovskaya, Vera. *Russkii baletnyi teatr nachala dvadtsatogo veka*, vol. 2, *Tantsovshchiki*. Leningrad, 1972.
Martynova, Olga M. *Ekaterina Geltser* (in Russian). Moscow, 1965.
Roslavleva, Natalia. "Moscow Assoluta." *Dance and Dancers* (April 1963): 23–25.
Smakov, Gennady. *The Great Russian Dancers*. New York, 1984.
Souritz, Elizabeth. *Soviet Choreographers in the 1920s*. Translated by Lynn Visson. Durham, N.C., 1990.
Swift, Mary Grace. *The Art of the Dance in the U.S.S.R.* Notre Dame, 1968.

ARCHIVE.   Leningrad State Theatre Library, Lunacharsky.

NATALIA Y. CHERNOVA
Translated from Russian

GENDER STUDIES. *See* Methodologies in the Study of Dance, *article on* New Areas of Inquiry.

GENÉE, ADELINE (Anina Margarete Kirstina Petra Jensen; born 6 January 1878 in Hinnerup, Denmark, died 23 April 1970 in Esher, England), Danish-born British ballet dancer, choreographer, and teacher. The daughter of a farming family, Nina Jensen was at an early age placed in the charge of her uncle, Alexander Genée, and his wife, Antonia Zimmermann, who directed a small touring ballet company. As Adeline Genée (so called in honor of the great opera singer Adelina Patti), she made her stage debut with this company at the age of ten and was soon playing major roles. In 1896, the company was engaged at the Berlin Opera and that same year appeared at the Munich Opera, where Adeline danced Swanilda in *Coppélia* for the first time.

These early performances led to a six-week engagement at the Empire Theatre in London, where she made her debut on 22 November 1897 in Katti Lanner's *Monte Cristo*. Genée's success was such that her engagement was extended, and in time she became the regular star ballerina of the Empire. She was featured there in a succession of ballets, mostly choreographed by Lanner and produced under the supervision of the designer C. Wilhelm. Among the most celebrated of these were *The Press* (1898), *Old China* (1901), *The Milliner Duchess* (1903), *High Jinks* (1904), *The Dancing Doll* (1905), *Cinderella* (1906), and *The Débutante* (1906), all by Lanner, and *The Belle of the Ball* (1907), choreographed jointly by Fred Farren and Alexander Genée.

The Empire was a music hall, and the ballets there—although presented by a large, permanent company and with considerable magnificence—were conceived to appeal to a wide and largely unsophisticated public. For a long time the management fought shy of presenting the type of works that were the normal fare in the opera houses on the Continent. It was not until 1906, when Genée found herself in a position to insist, as a condition of accepting reengagement, that *Coppélia* should be produced there by her uncle. She was confident that it would be well received, for she had successfully danced in it, first in Munich and later, in 1902, during a short guest season at the Royal Theater in Copenhagen, where she had been partnered by Hans Beck. In fact, *Coppélia* gave Genée the greatest success of her career and drew from Max Beerbohm the tribute that "she was born a comedian, and a comedian she remains, light and liberal as foam" (Beerbohm, 1906).

In 1908, Genée decided to conquer new fields and embarked on her first visit to the United States. She appeared in an extravagant production entitled *The Soul Kiss*, which opened in Philadelphia on 18 January and enjoyed a long run of sixteen weeks at the New York Theater. She returned briefly to the Empire on her return to London, but her dancing career was subsequently restricted to foreign tours and occasional London seasons that she herself presented with Wilhelm's artistic collaboration. She returned to the United States for the 1908/09 season (appearing in a new version of *The Soul Kiss*), in 1909/10 *(The Silver Star)*, and in 1910/11 *(The Bachelor Belles)*. All these productions were spectacular musical shows with a strong dance element, featuring Genée in some of the most effective numbers from her repertory, such as her famous "Hunting Dance." The last production was unsuccessful, and shortly after it closed she announced her impending retirement.

Nonetheless, Genée continued her dancing career intermittently and appeared in a number of short seasons under her own direction. The standard of the new ballets that she presented reflected her own taste, which was largely influenced by the fastidious Wilhelm. *A Dream of Roses and Butterflies* (Coliseum, London, 1911) was a charming but slight *divertissement*. *La Camargo* (Coliseum, London, 1912) was a more substantial work in which Genée, who had become interested in the history of ballet, appeared as the celebrated eighteenth-century ballerina Marie Camargo.

Genée's interest in history later inspired *La Danse*, a survey of ballet history from 1710 to 1845. In it she appeared successively as Françoise Prévost, Camargo, Marie Sallé, Marie-Madelaine Guimard, and Marie Taglioni. *La Danse* was first given at the Metropolitan Opera House, New York, in 1912, at the beginning of Genée's last overseas tour as a ballerina, in which she crossed the United States from coast to coast and moved on to Australia and New Zealand. She gave a farewell season in London in 1914, partnered by Alexandre Volinine, but this was not to be her last stage appearance. During World War I she participated in several more seasons and choreographed two other ballets for the Coliseum in London, *The Dancer's Adventure* (1915) and *The Pretty Prentice* (1916). Her last season was in 1917, although she continued to appear occasionally in charity performances.

In 1920, Genée was one of the five founding members of the organization of teachers of ballet that later became the Royal Academy of Dancing. She was elected its presi-

GENÉE. The lives and careers of her predecessors held special interest for Genée. In *La Camargo*, premiered at London's Coliseum on 20 May 1912, she appeared as Marie Camargo, famed French dancer of the early eighteenth century. Genée devised the choreography herself, to music arranged by Dora Bright; the elaborate scenery and costumes were designed by C. Wilhelm. (Photograph by Elliott & Fry, London.)

dent, a post she held until 1953; throughout that time she played the predominant role in its development. In 1932 Genée led a group of English dancers on a visit to Copenhagen, dancing with Anton Dolin in a charming eighteenth-century evocation, *The Love Song*, which they performed shortly afterward on television.

Genée's name is perpetuated in the annual awards offered by the Royal Academy of Dancing and in the Adeline Genée Theatre in East Grinstead, Surrey. Queen Elizabeth II of England made her a Dame Commander of the British Empire in 1950, and King Frederick IX of Denmark honored her with an Ingenio et Arti Award and invested her in the Order of Danneborg in 1953.

BIBLIOGRAPHY
Flitch, J. E. Crawford. *Modern Dancing and Dancers.* London, 1912.
Guest, Ivor. *Adeline Genée: A Lifetime of Ballet under Six Reigns.* London, 1958.

Guest, Ivor. *Adeline Genée: A Pictorial Record.* London, 1978.

Guest, Ivor. *Ballet in Leicester Square.* London, 1992.

Hardy, Camille. "The American Debut of Adeline Genée." In *New Directions in Dance*, edited by Diana Theodores Taplin. Toronto, 1979.

Parker, Henry Taylor. "Two Ballerinas: Adeline Genée and Anna Pavlova." In Parker's *Motion Arrested: Dance Reviews of H. T. Parker.* Edited by Olive Holmes. Middletown, Conn., 1982.

Perugini, Mark E. *The Art of Ballet.* London, 1915.

IVOR GUEST

GENNARO, PETER. *See* Jazz Dance.

GENRES OF WESTERN THEATRICAL DANCE.

A genre has been defined as the sum of the qualities and structures common to the art works of a period or group. As times and cultures change, so do some of the qualities and structures of the works. Since we tend to retain certain names to identity types of art works, we may look to see which qualities and structures may continue to identify the type.

The origins of the genre we know as ballet can be traced to the *balletti*, of early sixteenth-century Europe, which were semistaged versions of the social dances of the day. By 1581 Balthasar de Beaujoyeulx called his *Le Balet Comique de la Royne* "geometrical groupings of people dancing together," adding that there would also be music and a story. Together, these would satisfy "the eye, the ear, and the intellect." The basic elements of a "ballet" were established.

Since the first ballet dancers were not professionals, but rather members of a monarch's court, they were expected to move with erect nobility of carriage as well as with precision. Soon, their technical dexterity, especially when it appeared effortless, was found attractive to audiences, so dancers were eager to develop it. They learned that rotating the legs outward from the hip gave them greater freedom of movement, and the *en dehors* position became a hallmark of ballet. As technical dexterity became increasingly important, the verticality of the body had to be controlled, so that the movement would appear effortless. A basic vocabulary of movements—steps, jumps, and turns—was established.

With the advent of nineteenth-century romanticism, the sylph became an important heroine, and—to portray her ethereal character—ballerinas learned to dance on their toes; thus lightness *sur les pointes* became another emblem of ballet. The male performer, though not so concerned with lightness, still had to meet increasing technical demands. The strict verticality of the body enabled both dancers to accomplish movements that appeared to flow effortlessly. They moved with grace.

Even in the eighteenth century, complaints were made about concentrating on technical dexterity rather than on dramatic expression. Jean-Georges Noverre urged then that choreographers give more attention to movements that designated emotions than to those that demonstrated the physical accomplishments of the performer. Nevertheless, some dramatic situations demanded movements that contradicted the generic qualities of ballet—its confident verticality, its elegant grace, and its lightness. There were evil villains; there were scenes of tragedy. In the late nineteenth century, a solution was found: dramatic episodes were conveyed by means of pantomime; the dancing was interspersed with scenes telling the story by means of gestures.

Then Michel Fokine appeared and demanded that every movement in a ballet be made to express dramatic character and situation. Pantomime, he urged, should be replaced with movements that were "the development and ideal of the sign." Eliminating mere gestures, meant devising new dance movements that would tell the story. In the twentieth century, a diversity of styles was developed within the genre of ballet. Dancers adept in the basic technique—with legs turned out, body erect—had the skill to perform classical movements in neoclassical ways. There were choreographers, including George Balanchine, who occasionally asked them to move in sharply angular paths rather than in flowing lines, with percussive thrusts into the floor rather than lyrical soaring into the air. But *en dehors* and verticality continued to hold sway over the scene.

Meanwhile, however, some choreographers had found the ballet vocabulary and its inherent qualities completely inadequate to serve their needs. In the early twentieth century, Isadora Duncan had looked to nature, Ruth St. Denis to the Orient. For those who felt strongly that dance should deal with contemporary issues, renunciation of the balletic genre became a necessity. The new generation rejected pictures of simple beauty and harmony in order to deal with the struggles and emotional turmoil of their own world. Freeing themselves from generally accepted codes of behavior, they claimed the right to make personal statements. In each case, an individual statement required the invention of an individual vocabulary. The classical vocabulary had to be abandoned.

A wide range of styles was about to develop. In general, the *en dehors* position was rejected, while the emphasis on verticality gave way to a vigorous torso. Apparent ease was abandoned as illusion yielded to the acknowledgment of weight and the humanity of effort. Mary Wigman saw World War I as ending the rule of ballet. Then the audience wanted dance that honestly reflected its own emotional experiences. Martha Graham rejected the upright body for a torso that contracted with passion and released as its tension was resolved. Where Graham stressed internal conflict, Doris Humphrey saw the person fighting the tug of gravity, a symbol of all the forces that threaten security, so her movements were based on the threat of the fall, the triumph of the recovery. These two choreographers started with the feeling or idea that needed to be expressed; then came the movement, not chosen from a preestablished set of possibilities, but organically engendered by the feeling.

Others were stimulated by such ideas to devise their own movements—those that would say what they wanted to say. Expression, rather than an established vocabulary, was the key to the identity of this genre.

These choreographers, starting in the 1920s and 1930s, founded what became known as modern dance. John Martin, then dance critic of the *New York Times*, later objected, urging that it should never have been called "modern dance"; a more appropriate title would have been "expressive dance." He was right. In the 1960s, what came to be called postmodern dance began, with choreographers who chose to eliminate expression and the individual techniques designed to serve it. The decades that followed displayed a number of approaches to this developing genre.

Actually, as early as the 1950s Merce Cunningham had begun to construct dances that were not expressive. Asked how he went about composing a dance, he tended to say that he started with a step—not with a character or a story. He started with a movement and added other movements, often by chance procedures. Though he did not call attention to their skills, his dancers needed considerable ability to perform his work.

In the 1960s, however, the emergence of a new group of choreographers agreed to Cunningham's abstraction but rejected his use of accomplished movement. These became known as the founders of postmodern dance. They preferred natural actions, without particular grace or skill. They agreed, however, with Cunningham's use of occasionally less rigid structures, which they designed by arbitrary accumulation or improvisation. In time, however, other approaches were adopted, among them the use of multimedia, theatricality, and even narrative. Sally Banes solved the problem of identity by suggesting a period of analytic postmodern followed by one of metaphoric postmodern. What next?

Still to be considered are the genres of jazz dance and tap dance, forms that share a number of qualities. Both have developed largely through the work of individual performers, with improvisation playing an important role in each. Jazz stems from dance movements that were brought from Africa to the West Indies and then to the southern United States, where they were featured in nineteenth-century minstrel shows and carnivals. Typical are isolated movements of various parts of the body, which are usually extemporaneous. The rhythms, which are syncopated and contrapuntal, are much more typical than are any particular movements.

Tap dance, performed to similar rhythms, stems in part from the African origins of jazz but also from the Irish jig, a peasant festival dance performed by couples in rapid 6/8 time, and to clog dance, an old English form in which male dancers moved in a circle, beating the ground with their feet in heavy wooden shoes. What counts in tap dance are movements of the legs and feet. Emphasis is on the exacting, percussive sounds of the feet, while the upper body usually remains flexible and relaxed. Precision is essential, but so is the illusion of facility, qualities that tap shares with classical ballet.

As the twentieth century draws to a close, attention is being paid to ways of preserving traditional genres, not only for the sake of retaining important repertory but also for use by dancers and choreographers of the future. At the same time, there have been increasing instances of the merging of genres. Tap dance invaded ballet in 1944 with Jerome Robbins's *Fancy Free*. Numbers of modern dancers have been attracted to the disciplined training of classical ballet, and modern dance choreographers have been tempted to utilize their skills of lightness, flow, and grace. Meanwhile, some ballet companies have turned to modern dance choreographers for new repertory, acquiring works that demand weight and sharpness of execution.

Some choreographers have drawn on their own varied backgrounds, as has Jiří Kylián, who has composed works blending his knowledge of classical ballet, Graham technique, and Slavonic folk dance. Janaki Patrik's Kathak Ensemble has presented "Ka-Tap," combining Eastern and Western dances that share elements of improvisation and rhythmic footwork. It seems most likely that both preservation and experimentation will continue.

[*For related discussion, see* Avant-garde Dance; Ballet Technique, History of; Jazz Dance; Modern Dance Technique; *and* Tap Dance. *See also the entries on the principal figures mentioned herein.*]

BIBLIOGRAPHY

Cohen, Selma Jeanne, and Katy Matheson, eds. *Dance as a Theatre Art: Source Readings in Dance History from 1581 to the Present.* 2d ed. Princeton, 1992. Contains extensive bibliographies for ballet, modern, and postmodern dance.

Daly, Ann, ed. "What Has Become of Postmodern Dance?" *Drama Review* 36 (Spring 1992).

SELMA JEANNE COHEN

GEORGI, YVONNE (born 29 October 1903 in Leipzig, died 25 January 1975 in Hanover), German dancer, choreographer, and teacher. Like many leading figures of German interpretive (or expressionist) dance, Georgi began her training in 1920 at Émile Jaques-Dalcroze's school in

Hellerau, then switched to Mary Wigman's school in Dresden. In 1923 she gave her first dance evening in Leipzig, followed by numerous guest appearances, some of them jointly with Gret Palucca. A contemporary critic, Rudolf Lämmel, summarized her style:

> Like her personality, her dancing is characterized by unusually effective inspiration. Her art never becomes acrobatic; rather, it is often reminiscent of Wigman's art. Hers is an artistically distinguished, likable personality whose influence on the viewer results from its rare harmony.   (Lämmel, 1928)

In 1924 Georgi danced as a soloist for Kurt Jooss in Münster. In 1925 she accepted her first engagement as ballet mistress in Gera, where the first ballets she choreographed, including *Saudades do Brazil* to music by Darius Milhaud, brought her immediate attention, leading to her engagement as ballet director in Hanover from 1926 to 1931. With a strong gift for theatricality, she aimed to build a solid repertory, seeking to combine preservation of

GEORGI. A leading figure of German interpretive dancing (*Ausdruckstanz*), Georgi was admired for her evocative, yet enigmatic dances. She is seen here in *Waltz*, set to music by Frederick Wilckens. (Photograph by A. Binder; from the Dance Collection, New York Public Library for the Performing Arts.)

the classical heritage with the encouragement of experimentation. This synthesis of tradition and innovation remained the determining factor in all her choreographic work; it accompanied a strong interest in pedagogy.

Shortly after her arrival in Hanover in 1926, Georgi founded a school in which she trained the next generation of dancers. Her first major ballet evening, with *Petrouchka* and *Pulcinella* (1926)—in which the Wigman student Harald Kreutzberg was a guest performer—won over the audience. Major premieres followed: *Das Seltsame Haus* (music by Paul Hindemith), *Baby in der Bar* (music by Wilhelm Grosz), and *Tanzsuite* (music by Egon Wellesz). These productions brought renown to the Hanover Theater. Her collaboration with Kreutzberg produced a series of duo evenings in which they appeared very successfully in concerts in Germany and other countries. In 1928 they appeared for the first time in New York. Their collaboration ended with the choreography of *Le Train Bleu*, with music by Milhaud, in 1931 for the Berlin State Opera. After this Georgi moved to Amsterdam, where she organized her own ballet evenings, established a school, and founded a ballet company that later became the Ballets Yvonne Georgi.

Between 1933 and 1935 Georgi was ballet director in Hanover and made extensive tours. During this period she turned increasingly to classical dance, with such important presentations as *Deutsche Tänze*, to music by Franz Schubert in 1933, *Coppélia*, to music by Léo Delibes in 1934, and *Die Geschöpfe des Prometheus*, to music by Ludwig van Beethoven in 1935. During World War II she worked in the Netherlands, where she produced regular seasons with her resident company in Scheveningen and collaborated as choreographer in theater and opera productions. In 1950 she filmed *Ballerina* with Ludwig Berger in Paris. In 1951 she returned to Germany, and until 1954 she was the director of the Düsseldorf Ballet, producing *Les Animaux Modèles*, to music by Francis Poulenc; *Das Goldfischglas*, to music by Juriaan Andriessen; and *The Rite of Spring*, set to music by Igor Stravinsky.

In the summer of 1954 Georgi choreographed the first performance, at Alpbach in the Tyrol, of Gottfried von Einem's *Glück, Tod und Traum*. In fall of the same year she returned to Hanover for good. Under her motto "Diversity of dance cultivation," she began once again to build up a repertory that corresponded to her concept of a synthesis of classical and modern dance. She believed that these two modes of dance expression should coexist equally, not as mutually exclusive opposites. Classical productions of Tchaikovsky's *The Nutcracker* (1955) and *Swan Lake* (1965) and Prokofiev's *Cinderella* (1968) and *Romeo and Juliet* (1969), seen for the first time in Hanover, were joined by modern ballets such as *Ruth*, to music by Heimo Erbse in 1959, and three *Electronic Ballets*, to music by Henk Badings in 1957, 1958, and 1960. Georgi considered these modern pieces her most interesting and best works.

During her residence in the Netherlands, Georgi had become acquainted with the Dutch composer Henk Badings, who wrote the music for her 1942 version of *Orpheus and Eurydice,* and with whom she would continue her fruitful collaboration in Hanover. A number of regional premieres established the outstanding position of the Hanover Ballet during the postwar period. Georgi's most important works of the period included, in addition to the *Electronic Ballets, Der Mohr von Venedig* (1956, to music by Boris Blacher); *Le Loup* (1957, to music by Henri Dutilleux); *Agon* (1958, to music by Stravinsky); *Das Einhorn, der Drache und der Tigermann* (1959, to music by Gian-Carlo Menotti); *Hamlet* (1962, to music by Blacher); *Metamorphoses* (1962, to music by Richard Strauss); *Demeter* (1964, to music by Blacher); *The Golem* (1965, to music by Francis Burt); *Paradis Perdu* (1969; to music by Marius Constant); *Jeux Venetiens* (1969, to music by Witold Lutosławski); and *Klein Zack* (1970, to music by Nikolai Karetnikov).

Georgi fulfilled her pedagogical goals as director of the Dance Department of the Institute for Music and Theater in Hanover, where she continued as ballet director until 1973. Yvonne Georgi was undoubtedly one of the most creative dance personalities to come out of Germany; she succeeded in combining the discoveries of modern dance with the traditions of classical ballet.

[*See also* Germany, *article on* Theatrical Dance, 1600–1945; *and* Netherlands, *article on* Theatrical Dance, 1900–1945.]

BIBLIOGRAPHY

Georgi, Yvonne. *Anmerkungen zum Theatertanz.* Dresden, 1934.
Koegler, Horst. *Yvonne Georgi* (in German). Velber bei Hannover, 1963.
Lämmel, Rudolf. *Der moderne Tanz.* Berlin, c.1928.
Schäfer, Rolf Helmut. *Yvonne Georgi* (in German). Brunswick, 1974.
Wille, Hansjürgen. *Harald Kreutzberg—Yvonne Georgi* (in German). Leipzig, 1930.

HEDWIG MÜLLER
Translated from German

GEORGIA. Situated in the southern portion of the Caucasus Mountains and bordering the eastern shore of the Black Sea, the Republic of Georgia is known to natives as Sakartvelo. In ancient times, the western region was known as Colchis, land of the Amazons and the fabled Golden Fleece; the eastern part was called Iberia. There is archeological evidence of ancient dance here: a scene on a silver bowl found on the eastern tip of the Black Sea and dating back to the second millenium BCE shows the rite of *perkhuli* performed by masked hunters to worship the Svanetian goddess of hunting, Dali. In time this dance incorporated acrobatic movements *(fundruki)* and warlike intonations, evolving into the pantomimic war dance *kho-*

GEORGIA. Wearing flexible leather boots, two men of the Georgian State Dance Company perform a characteristic bent-toe dance. (Photograph © 1988 by Jack Vartoogian; used by permission.)

rumi, which depicts the search for the battleground, the sighting of the enemy, the battle itself, and the victory celebration. The Greek historian Xenophon, writing in the fourth century BCE, noted that Georgian tribes performed military songs and dances as a prelude to battle.

Many of the earliest dances were apparently of ritual origin. A bone plate from the second millenium BCE, depicting a dancing woman, may represent a female ritual usually performed during the harvest season before statues of the goddess of fertility. The *partsa* was performed in honor of Dali, a peace-loving goddess who dwelt in the forest. Hunters were especially favored by Dali after one saved her infant child from a wolf. In these early dances, men formed a circle and placed a woman at each of the four cardinal points. According to Georgian dance scholar, Avtandil Tataradze, these dances and the songs that accompanied them were dedicated to Amirani, Dali's son, suggesting a shift from a matriarchial society to a patriarchial one.

A dance from the Kartuli-Kakhetian region was dedicated to the sun goddess Nana. After the introduction of Christianity in 337 CE, the song that accompanied the dance to Nana gradually lost its original purpose and came to serve as a lullaby. The dance *samaya* derives its name from the Georgian word for three, *sami,* since it was traditionally performed by women in groups of three. It was dedicated to the goddess of fertility, the moon, and was performed to celebrate the birth of a family's first female child. In spite of its pre-Christian associations, the dance is depicted in a fresco in the cathedral of Mtskheta, the former capital of Georgia. The transition to farming and cattle-breeding gave rise to new rites with magic ritual dances, notably the two-tiered and three-tiered *perkhuli,* in

GEORGIA. Members of the Georgian State Dance Company perform a women's line dance from Abkhazia, on the Black Sea coast at the western end of the Caucasus Mountains. (Photograph from the Dance Collection, New York Public Library for the Performing Arts.)

which one circle of men stands on the shoulders of another group standing on the ground (reflecting the harvest of orchard fruits), the masked agricultural ceremony *berikaoba*, and other rites praising the generosity of nature or depicting work on the land. Ancient couple dances were linked to fertility cults. Romantic couple dances were also known; the most ancient to survive is the *kartuli*.

In addition to these ancient ritual and ceremonial dances, there are work, game, courtship, and comic dances. They comprise solo, pair, and group dances, and dances performed by men, women, and mixed groups. Differences in the regional and social origin of these dances have resulted in a rich variety of styles ranging from the *parikaoba*, a men's combat dance from the highlands, to the *kintauri*, a mischievous nineteenth-century dance of Tbilisi's merchants.

The most common dance rhythms are 2/4, 4/4, and 6/8; only the *khorumi* uses the irregular 5/4 rhythm. Dance tunes were traditionally played on stringed and woodwind instruments. More recently the accordion has been used to accompany dance. Some dances are done to choral singing. The two-headed drum used in Georgian dance music is called a *dole*.

Unending conflicts with foreign invaders—Persians, Arabs, Mongols, and Turks—nurtured a warlike spirit in the Georgians. This warrior tradition is apparent in the men's dances, the most distinctive element of which is toe dancing, done only by males. Unlike the pointe shoe used in classical ballet, the supple leather boots worn by Georgian dancers have no reinforcement or special supports. Ten or more different types of movements are executed on the bent toes, including standing, spinning, and jumping on the toes of one or both feet. In many of the dances,

such as the *kartuli*, the upper body must remain immobile while the feet execute quick, precise movements. While the origin of Georgian toe-dancing is unknown, it is thought by some to be an imitation of birds, such as the eagle and falcon, which were sacred to ancient Georgians. The bent toe position resembles talons, and the outstretched arms mimic wings. Another theory suggests that the step developed from traversing narrow mountain paths while clinging to the sheer cliff face. Men's dances also include competitions featuring acrobatic leaps and jumps, and rapid turns that include knee spins. Some dances are performed with sword and shield; other dances involve flinging daggers into the floor.

Women's dances require an aloof, regal demeanor. In couple dances, the woman never openly tries to attract her partner and barely deigns to notice his presence. Arm movements are soft and flowing, with graceful wrist circles. While the torso is held erect and still, the feet move with fast, light steps that require great agility and strength. Because these movements are hidden by long skirts, women's dances such as the *narnari* create an illusion of effortless gliding across the stage. Mountain dances are an exception; there, calf-length dresses show off lively footwork, performed with a bold and playful attitude.

Georgian court dances such as the *davluri* (sometimes called "Georgian minuet") and the *simd* have a distinctively medieval look, reflecting the golden age under the rule of Queen Thamar (1184–1213) when the kingdom became one of the strongest in the Near East. During Thamar's reign Shota Rustaveli created the literary masterpiece *The Knight in Panther Skin*, dedicating it to his sovereign. The epic poem's themes of chivalry and heroism, and the idealized lovers Tinatin and Avtandil, are depicted in a celebrated couple dance, the *kartuli*. The conduct of the male toward his partner is strictly governed by a set of rules, among which is that he must never touch the woman, not even with the fabric of his coat, for to do so shows a lack of respect and could be interpreted as an insult by her family. At the Georgian court there were groups of professional dancers. In addition to performing national dances, the women of the companies also mastered and performed the dances of neighbors such as the Persians and Turks.

The chivalry of the Middle Ages can also be seen in the dances of the Khevsurs, who live in the Georgian highlands and trace their ancestry to the Crusaders. Their traditional costumes have elaborate embroidery featuring a cross motif, and the men sometimes wear chain mail. One contemporary Khevsur dance depicts the ancient Georgian tradition of forcing an end to a bitter duel: so great was the respect for women that if one were to remove her headdress and throw it between two combatants, they would end their fight immediately.

Georgia was annexed by Russia in 1801. Writers such as Leo Tolstoy and Mikhail Lermontov, and composers such as Mily Balakirev, Aleksandr Borodin, and Petr Tchaikovsky found inspiration in Georgian culture, music, and dance. (The "Arabian Dance" in Tchaikovsky's *The Nutcracker* is based on a Georgian lullaby.) Later, in the early twentieth century, Georgian dance would be depicted in Serge Diaghilev's Ballets Russes production *Thamar*, based on Lermontov's eponymous poem.

Russia also influenced the development of Georgian dance. In 1851 Russian and foreign classical ballets were staged at the newly opened opera house in the capital, Tbilisi. The small ballet company there was directed by Fedor Manokhin from Moscow. In the 1880s and 1890s, ballet companies from the Imperial Theaters performed there. Isadora Duncan appeared at Tbilisi's opera house, and various classical works were staged for the resident company during the first quarter of the twentieth century. The first studio for the classical training of local dancers was established in Tbilisi by a former soloist, Mana I. Perini. The first professional Georgian ballet dancer, Aleksidze Songulashvili, was trained in this studio and later opened the first school for Georgian dance. After 1921, when the Soviet government was established in Georgia, many classical ballets were produced in Tbilisi.

In the early twentieth century expeditions to distant areas of the republic and early festivals of amateur art stimulated revivals of nearly forgotten dances. Nina Ramishvili, cofounder of the Georgian State Dance Ensemble, joined the Tbilisi Theater of Opera and Ballet in 1927, performing as a soloist for twelve years. Her husband, Iliko Sukhishvili, a classically trained dancer and leading soloist and choreographer with the company, decided to create a Georgian dance company. He and his wife traveled throughout Georgia collecting folk dances and interpreting them for the concert stage. The Turkish-influenced dances of Adzharia, which required that men and women dance separately, were adapted for mixed performances. In 1935 Sukhishvili won first place at the World Folk Dance Festival. The Georgian State Dance Company has since traveled and performed for audiences all over the world. Another ensemble, Rustavi, under the direction of Anzor Erkomaishvili and Fridon Sulaberidze, also specializes in traditional Georgian dance and has toured extensively.

In June 1938 a Georgian ballet, *The Heart of the Hills*, premiered at Leningrad's Kirov Theater, with choreography by Vakhtang Chabukiani and music by Andrei Balanchivadze. Using classical structure and vocabulary, the ballet adapted traditional Georgian dances. Young girls in traditional costume glided across the stage on pointe in the *lekouri*. Next came the competition dance the *lezghinka*, during which the ballet's proletarian hero Georgi clashed with Prince Zaal. Central to the action is the Adzhar dance *khorumi*, which was accompanied by percussion instruments. By blending elements from traditional Georgian dance and classical ballet, Chabukiani developed a dynamic narrative of class conflict. The ballet received numerous subsequent productions. [*See the entry on Chabukiani.*]

Many works from the classical repertory were staged in Georgia during the 1930s. In 1935 Vasily Litvenko was named chief choreographer at the Tbilisi Theater of Opera and Ballet. Among his important productions was *Ferendzhi* (1932), in which he applied cinematic techniques of fragmentation and interlocking material to develop the plot. He was also the creator, with David Dzharishvili, of the first Georgian ballet on a modern theme, *Maltakva* (1938). Dzharishvili played an important role in the theatrical staging of Georgian folk dances. From 1934 to 1951 he was the director of the school founded by Perini, which is today the ballet school for the Tbilisi Theater of Opera and Ballet. He also wrote books on Georgian folk dance and devised a system for its recording, *Symbols for the Notation of Georgian Choreography* (1961).

In 1941 Tbilisi's ballet company was led by Chabukiani; ten years later he also became director of the new ballet school. He staged a number of new ballets in Tbilisi as well as new productions of his *Heart of the Hills* and *Laurencia*. In 1972 Georgi Aleksidze was appointed chief choreographer of the Tbilisi ballet company; he staged classical works and also created new ones based on national legends. Mikhail Lavrovsky, who came from Moscow's Bolshoi Theater, was named company director in 1982. He attracted attention with his production of George Gershwin's *Porgy and Bess* as well as his reconstruction of *Serenade* by the most famous of all Georgian choreographers, the expatriate George Balanchine. Aleksidze returned as chief choreographer in 1984, at which time a small, experimental group became attached to the theater and frequently traveled abroad.

BIBLIOGRAPHY

Allen, W. E. D. *A History of the Georgian People.* London, 1971.

Asitiani, Zaur V. *Tri siuzhetnykh tantsa.* Tbilisi, 1979.

Essad-Bey. *Twelve Secrets of the Caucasus.* Translated by G. Chychele Waterston. New York, 1931.

Gray, Laurel Victoria. "'Thamar': A Study in Russian Orientalism." *Arabesque* (July–August 1983): 14–15.

Gray, Laurel Victoria. "In Search of Ethnic Dance in the USSR." *Viltis* 43 (June–August 1984): 12–44; 44 (May 1985): 10–11.

Gray, Laurel Victoria. "Georgians Conquer Seattle." *Jareeda* (July 1990): 12–14.

Gray, Laurel Victoria. "Georgians Invade New York." *Chashma* (Autumn 1990): 4–14.

Gray, Laurel Victoria. "The Goddess Dances: Women's Dance of Georgia." *Habibi* (Fall 1995): 17, 39.

Gvaramadze, Lili. *Gruzinskii tantseval'nyi fol'klor.* Tbilisi, 1987.

Lakov, Nikolai A., and Vera P. Sokolovskaia. *Kostiumy k tantsam narodov SSSR.* Moscow, 1964.

Lang, David Marshall. *The Georgians.* New York, 1966.

Mepisashvili, Rusudan, and Vakhtang Tsintsadze. *The Arts of Ancient Georgia*. Translated by Alisa Jaffa. New York, 1979.

Suny, Ronald G. *The Making of the Georgian Nation*. Stanford, Calif., 1988.

Tkachenko, Tamara. *Narodnyi tanets*. 2d ed. Moscow, 1967.

LAUREL VICTORIA GRAY
Based on materials submitted by Elena Gvaramadze

GEORGIADIS, NICHOLAS (born 14 September 1923 in Athens), costume and stage designer. Nicholas Georgiadis studied architecture in his native Athens and at Columbia University before winning a scholarship in theater design to London's Slade School of Art in 1954. There he was promptly selected by Kenneth MacMillan to design *Danses Concertantes*, the first professional ballet venture for both men and the beginning of a long collaboration. Georgiadis's emphasis in this early period was on strong color contrasts; in MacMillan's *House of Birds* (1955) and *Noctambules* (1956), he reacted to edgy modern scores and surreal scenarios with designs of angular outline colored with stinging intensity.

A new realism in Georgiadis's work in the late 1950s was consistent with MacMillan's changing themes, exemplified by the confined gray and brown space of the Kafkaesque *The Burrow* (1958) or the suggestive Edwardian detail of *The Invitation* (1960). His collaboration with Rudolf Nureyev on the 1964 Vienna Opera production of *Swan Lake* was Georgiadis's first design for a nineteenth-century classic; a year later, the architectural grandeur and textured richness of his sets and costumes for MacMillan's *Romeo and Juliet* almost made it seem a classic itself. Challenged by the pomp and scale of the Bolshoi's production, the Royal Ballet's *Romeo* returned opulence and splendor to the ballet stage in Britain. For the market scenes, Georgiadis created a staircase of burnished gold and luminous pink marble, filling the stage and carrying the action onto several levels while allowing the dancing full sweep. His chapel for Friar Laurence glowed with the darkly brilliant colors of Byzantine icons, binding Renaissance Verona to Prokofiev's Eastern harmonics. The designs, traditional but never derivative, became essential elements of the drama and the ballet's success.

The heavy sumptuousness that marked Georgiadis's continuing work on the classics could be overwhelming, as in Nureyev's versions of *The Sleeping Beauty* (1970) and *Raymonda* (1972) for the Zurich Ballet. Working again with MacMillan at the Royal Ballet, Georgiadis moved toward dramatic allusiveness in *Manon* (1974), in which menacing poverty was manifest in a backdrop of rags lurking behind the surface elegance of Rococo Paris. The imperial Vienna of MacMillan's *Mayerling* (1978) required sets simplified for rapid scene changes and relied on iso- lated images rather than broad stage pictures; mannequins lining the royal apartments and guarding the ballroom conveyed the sinister atmosphere of court surveillance. For MacMillan's *Prince of the Pagodas* (1989), Georgiadis again departed from his characteristically sumptuous effects with castles that were moved around like chess pieces and a walled city with translucent pagodas.

Both in his theatrical work and as codirector of the theater design department at Slade, Georgiadis has influenced a generation of younger British designers.

[*See also* Scenic Design.]

BIBLIOGRAPHY
Crichton, Ronald. "*Romeo's* Designer: Nicholas Georgiadis." *The Dancing Times* (April 1965).

Georgiadis, Nicholas. Interview. *Dance and Dancers* (June 1966): 32–34.

Reuling, Karl F. "Gifts of a Greek." *Opera News* (May 1973).

Thorpe, Edward. "Georgiadis." *Dance Gazette* (October 1982): 21–25.

Williams, Peter. "Nureyev's Beauty." *Dance and Dancers* (June 1975): 36–38.

CLAUDIA ROTH PIERPONT

GERDT FAMILY, Russian ballet dancers. The father, Pavel, noted dancer and teacher, became a model for subsequent generations of Russian ballet dancers. His daughter Elisaveta also distinguished herself as a dancer, teacher, and coach.

Pavel Gerdt (Ger., Paul Friedrich Gerdt; Rus., Pavel Andreevich Gerdt; born 22 November [4 December] 1844 in Volynkino, Russia, died 30 July [12 August] 1917 in Vamaljoki, Finland). Gerdt graduated from the Saint Petersburg Theater School, where he studied under Aleksandr Pimenov and Jean Petipa, and in his final years under Marius Petipa and Christian Johansson. These teachers passed on to the aspiring artist the technique perfected by western Europe's foremost dancers: Pimenov had studied under Charles Didelot; Marius Petipa, Auguste Vestris; and Johansson, August Bournonville. In his art Gerdt blended the best of each school of ballet represented by his teachers. Drawing on this wealth of experience, refracted through the prism of Russian choreographic traditions, and on his own creative vision, he evolved a singular style that was destined to become a model for subsequent generations of Russian ballet dancers.

Gerdt's first major artistic challenge came in 1867 with the role of the fisherman Matteo in *Ondine, ou La Naïade*, a ballet first staged in 1851 by Jules Perrot to the music of Cesare Pugni. A year before his death Gerdt made his last stage appearance in the role of Gamache in *Don Quixote*, a version created by Aleksandr Gorsky in 1902 to the music of Ludwig Minkus. Gerdt's eventful artistic career spanned nearly fifty years. He appeared in title roles in all of the productions staged in Saint Petersburg by Jules

Perrot, Arthur Saint-Léon, Marius Petipa, Lev Ivanov, and Michel Fokine. His finest creations were the products of collaborations with Petipa and Ivanov: it was Gerdt who first danced the roles of Prince Désiré in *The Sleeping Beauty* (1890), Prince Whooping Cough in *The Nutcracker* (1892), Prince Siegfried in *Swan Lake* (1895), and Abderakhman in *Raymonda* (1898), breaking new ground in each of them. Male dancers of that period were somewhat limited in their choice of technique. To produce a greater dramatic effect Gerdt relied heavily on his mime skills, which, coupled with meticulously polished body positions and movements, helped him to convey characters with greater meaning.

In 1880 Gerdt began teaching at the Saint Petersburg Theater School. As an enthusiastic devotee of classical ballet, Gerdt set his students off on an artistic adventure by stirring their intelligence and imagination. Among his pupils were Anna Pavlova, Tamara Karsavina, Agrippina Vaganova, and Michel Fokine. Late in his career Gerdt began to choreograph: in 1901 he collaborated with Ivanov, and on Ivanov's death completed, the ballet *Sylvia* with music by Léo Delibes, and in 1902 he staged *Javotte* to the music of Camille Saint-Saëns.

Elisaveta Gerdt (Elisaveta Pavlovna Gerdt; born 17 [29] April 1891 in Saint Petersburg, died 5 November 1975 in Moscow). Elisaveta was Pavel Gerdt's daughter; her mother, Aleksandra Shaposhnikova, was a ballerina with the Maryinsky Theater company. Elisaveta Gerdt studied at the Saint Petersburg Theater School under Michel Fokine, graduating in 1908. While still a student she appeared as Armide in Fokine's experimental production *The Animated Gobelin* (the first Russian version of his well-known ballet *Le Pavillon d'Armide*). Later, as a soloist with the Maryinsky company, she was involved in productions of Fokine's *Chopiniana* and *Le Carnaval*. Other celebrated dancers also had a strong influence on Gerdt. She was quoted in *Sovietskii Balet* (Struchkova, 1982) as saying, "If asked to divulge the source of my strength and technique and who served as a model for my dancing style, I would name Ekaterina Vazem and Enrico Cecchetti. And who was it that cultivated my taste, excellent form, dignity, elegance, charm, and style—Pavel Gerdt, Christian Johansson, and Olga Preobrajenska."

In 1910 Gerdt danced the role of Theresa in *Halte de Cavalerie* and in 1911 she recreated the roles of the Lilac Fairy in *The Sleeping Beauty* and Dawn in *Coppélia*. She danced numerous leading roles, including Princess Aurora in *The Sleeping Beauty*, Odette-Odile in *Swan Lake*, the Sugarplum Fairy in *The Nutcracker*, the Tsar-Maiden in *The Little Humpbacked Horse*, Aspicia in *La Fille du Pharaon*, the title role in *Raymonda*, Nikia in *La Bayadère*, and Myrtha in *Giselle*. By 1924 Gerdt had danced forty-two different roles. Her dancing radiated harmony and precision and her interpretations were marked by sophistication and academic virtuosity, qualities pivotal to Gerdt's artistic integrity. A contemporary referred to her as a "highly cultured actress, a custodian of old traditions who looked regal in all her roles" (Mikhailov, 1978). A classical ballerina by temperament and training, Gerdt nonetheless danced in two experimental productions of the Soviet choreographer Fedor Lopukhov, *The Red Whirlwind* (1924) and *Pulcinella* (1926).

Elisaveta Gerdt retired from the stage in 1928 and devoted herself to teaching the ballerinas' class at the State Academic Theater of Opera and Ballet and the Class of Perfection at the Leningrad Choreographic Institute; she was an artistic director there between 1930 and 1932. In 1934 she moved to Moscow, where she taught at the Moscow Ballet School and also coached Bolshoi soloists until 1960; from 1936 to 1937 she directed the school. As

GERDT FAMILY. Pavel Gerdt's flair for mime created dramatic effects in many ballets. It also helped him prolong his career past his physical prime. He is seen here, c.1880, gesturing as Solor in Marius Petipa's *La Bayadère*. (Photograph from the Dance Collection, New York Public Library for the Performing Arts.)

GERDT FAMILY. Elisaveta Gerdt danced the role of the Lilac Fairy in the 1911 revival of Petipa's *The Sleeping Beauty* for the Imperial Ballet of the Maryinsky Theater, Saint Petersburg. (Photograph from the Dance Collection, New York Public Library for the Performing Arts.)

a teacher Gerdt not only instilled in her pupils a sense of independence in mastering the basics and laws of classical dance, but also sought to stimulate their creativity by getting them to spell out thoughts and emotions through poses and gestures. She gave priority to dance exercises that reinforced a correct stance and drills that emphasized the ability of the arms to flow and bend. Among the beneficiaries of her teaching methods were many prominent ballerinas, including Alla Shelest, Maya Plisetskaya, Violetta Bovt, Raisa Struchkova, and Ekaterina Maximova.

BIBLIOGRAPHY

Gerdt, Elisaveta. "Zhizn v balete i vo imia baleta: K 100-letiiu so dnia rozhdeniia E. P. Gerdt." *Sovetskii balet*, no. 2 (1991).
Goldstein, Michael. "Paul Gerdt." *Das Tanzarchiv* 21 (August 1973): 70–74.
Gregory, John. "Legendary Dancers: Pavel Gerdt." *The Dancing Times* (November 1987): 129.
Gregory, John. *The Legat Saga*. 2d ed. London, 1993.
Guest, Ivor. *The Divine Virginia: A Biography of Virginia Zucchi*. New York, 1977.
Karsavina, Tamara. "Family Album: Pavel Andreevitch Gerdt." *The Dancing Times* (June 1964): 462.

Kholfina, Serafima. *Vospominania masterov moskovskogo baleta.* Moscow, 1990.
Krasovskaya, Vera. *Russkii baletnyi teatr vtoroi poloviny deviatnadtsatogo veka.* Leningrad, 1963.
Krasovskaya, Vera. *Russkii baletnyi teatr nachala dvadtsatogo veka,* vol. 2, *Tantsovshchiki.* Leningrad, 1972.
Mikhailov, Mikhail M. *Molodye gody leningradskogo baleta.* Leningrad, 1978.
Pleshcheyev, Aleksandr. *Nash balet.* 2d ed. St. Petersburg, 1899.
Relkin, Abbie. "In Pavlova's Shadow." *Ballet News* 2 (January 1981): 26–29.
Roslavleva, Natalia, and Joan Lawson. "Yelizaveta Gerdt." *The Dancing Times* (May 1964): 414.
Smakov, Gennady. *The Great Russian Dancers.* New York, 1984.
Struchkova, Raisa. "Kakaia blagorodnaia i polnaia zhizn." *Sovetskii balet*, no. 1 (1982).
Wiley, Roland John, trans. and ed. *A Century of Russian Ballet: Documents and Accounts, 1810–1910.* Oxford, 1990.

RAISA S. STRUCHKOVA
Translated from Russian

GERMAN OPERA BALLET. *See* Berlin Opera Ballet.

GERMANY. [*To survey the dance traditions of Germany, this entry comprises five articles:*
>Traditional and Social Dance
>Theatrical Dance, 1600–1945
>Theatrical Dance since 1945
>Dance Education
>Dance Research and Publication

For further discussion of theatrical dance, see entries on individual companies, choreographers, and dancers.]

Traditional and Social Dance

Located in central Europe, the unified German state was formed first in the mid-nineteenth century from the petty German states, duchies, and principalities that had been part of the Holy Roman Empire—a political entity from the tenth century that gave rise to both Austria and Germany. Its complex history begins with the Carolingian Empire of Charlemagne, whose empire from 800 CE was considered the successor state to the Western Roman Empire (defunct since 476), though it soon divided into east (German) and west (French) realms. When Otto I restored control in the east, he was crowned emperor of the new Holy Roman Empire in 962 by the Roman Catholic pope. The empire was soon in conflict with the various popes and against the rising power of local princes: in the thirteenth century its claims to Italy were given up; in the fourteenth century its control over the princely states was lost. Direct rule remained only in personal domains—

considerable territory in the case of the Habsburgs, who ruled from the fifteenth century onward. The Protestant Reformation (beginning in 1517), ongoing wars with the invading Ottoman armies (in the territory between the Balkans and Vienna), and battles with France further weakened what remained of the empire until its final collapse in 1806 during the Napoleonic Wars.

From 1840 to 1861, Frederick William IV reigned in Prussia and increased Prussia's role as leader of the German Confederation. The Revolutions of 1848, however, led to Frederick's appeasing the rebels by embracing German nationalism and granting a liberal constitution; other German states did the same. Internecine German politics and wars, the 1870–1871 Franco-Prussian War, and the threat of socialism brought Germany into the twentieth century—with World War I (1914–1918) ending the reign of Kaiser Wilhelm and setting the stage for the interwar governments (including that of the National Socialists, the Nazi party), World War II (1939–1945), and the partition of Germany between West and East from 1945 to 1991.

Folk dance in Germany is documented in reports and artworks from as early as the first century CE, but the origins of the diverse folk dances known today are sometimes obscure. When folk dances were first classified early in the nineteenth century, individual dances were known by descriptive names (sword dance, circle dance, jumping dance, seven-leap, spinner, and so on), by their performers (farmers, apprentices, butchers, and others), or by the names of the events at which they were performed, such as fairs, weddings, or religious festivals. Some regional dances were named for their localities.

The study of folk dance is a relatively young discipline in Germany. The term *Volkstanz* is restricted to traditionally transmitted dances and dance games that have fixed functions and practice among rural and working people. A specific folk dance was usually performed only by specific social and occupational groups, not throughout the society. Dances are usually associated with specific regions, and regional variants of general dance types are recognized. Under this definition, for example, the dances of southern German herdspeople, living far from the cities, are folk dances, even though the same dances may be known among other social and regional populations.

Throughout history, innumerable new dances arose in what is now Germany through exchange and borrowing—for example, between urban and court social dancing and the traditional dances of neighboring ethnic groups. The borrowed dances were adapted to their new social contexts, assimilated, modified, and merged with the existing tradition. Thus folk dances have provided the basis for stylized and standardized social dances such as the allemande, *Strassburger*, German galop, *Styrienne*, *Tyrolienne*, *Rheinländer*, and waltz. Conversely, middle-class and court social dances were often remodeled into folk dances, as occurred with the *Tampet*, the *Kegel*, and many of the quadrilles.

Early Folk Dance. Only a few illustrations of pre-medieval German dances and dancers have survived as decorations on objects excavated from graves by archaeologists. Most of these depictions are of weapons dances, done with swords and shields, or dances done either to celebrate religious festivals, such as Midsummer, or to exorcise demons. The Roman historian Tacitus (55–120 CE) provided a detailed description of the weapons dances of young German men, which were performed at sacrifices, as memorials, and for entertainment. Based on sources from the fringes of the Germanic world, such as the Faeroe Islands, and from medieval accounts, we can be certain that this dancing was accompanied by the singing of traditional epics and that the dances were done in a circle formation, with simple combinations of steps. These "ballad dances" might also be used to reproach and mock members of a clan whose behavior had violated group norms.

When the Frankish, Saxon, and Thuringian tribes of Germany converted to Christianity in the eighth century, dance remained an important part of their observance, as it had been in their pre-Christian religions. Not until the late Middle Ages (twelfth to fifteenth centuries) did class distinctions become reflected in the dance repertory, with the content, symbolism, and style of performance developing differently in different social contexts. By the twelfth century, traditional dance among the nobility was restricted by numerous prohibitions issued by church authorities against dances believed to have pagan associations. New dances therefore came into being chiefly through wandering minnesingers and troubadours. New couple dances, mostly processional, served exclusively to entertain the elite. Nobles led the dances, dressed in costly garments and wearing precious jewels. Instrumental music provided accompaniment, played on newly invented or introduced instruments, which differentiated court music from the dance music of peasants. In this period, German folk dance became truly distinct from elite social dance, although the two genres continued to influence each other.

Rural Folk Dances. The traditional dances of German countryfolk were characterized by vital, spirited hopping and jumping, which contrasted with the dignified, measured steps of court dances. In rural areas, the occasions for dancing and entertainment included Carnival, Easter, ember days, sowing, the driving out of the cattle, May Day, the feasts of Saint John the Baptist and Saint Martin, the anniversary of the local church's dedication, and the winter solstice.

Although many dance festivals were linked with Christian holidays, their roots were in pre-Christian times; this is especially true of the festivals for the pressing of new wine, Carnival, the bell dances, and the dances performed by masked young men between Christmas and Epiphany. The dancers were often equipped with noisemakers, such as bells, clappers, or rattles, and were sometimes disguised with masks. Their purpose was to protect humans, animals, and the fields from evil spirits and to safeguard the site of the dance from sickness, bad weather, and fire. In southern Germany such processions existed, in greatly modified form, until the twentieth century; they were often performed with religious trappings (particularly during the Counter-Reformation of the sixteenth century) to veil their pagan origins, which the church had attacked intermittently since the eighth century.

In contrast to such ritual dances, social folk dancing gradually became more widespread and important after medieval times. It occurred as part of the celebrations of major life events, such as baptisms and weddings, at seasonal festivals such as harvest, and at church dedication anniversaries. The works of such artists as Dürer, Geham, and Aldegrever depict various kinds of group dances, including circle, round, and couple dances; they suggest various styles but do not reveal much about specific movements. Some of the old dance names reflect their lively, cheerful nature. Old documents and popular songs and musical scores report titles indicating jumping, calling, dancing in a line, spinning, or circling. Also popular among villagers were social dance games, such as the nose and spoon dances, and dances involving athletic skill, such as egg or rooster dances.

The musical accompaniment for peasant dances before the seventeenth century was generally provided by the bagpipe and treble shawm, sometimes with the addition of a bowed instrument and/or a hurdy-gurdy—all depicted in old illustrations. Other instruments were seldom seen in rural areas. According to the pictorial evidence, the musicians were not separated from the dancers on a podium or gallery, as they were for court and urban occasions; rural musicians and dancers belonged to the same class and sat at the same table.

In the mid-seventeenth century, village dances began to include the music of stringed instruments, oboes, horns, dulcimers, and trumpets, played by amateur local performers. This innovation was accelerated in Saxony, Thuringia, and Franconia by the formation of rural adjuvant groups—local associations of enthusiasts formed to sing and play instruments at evangelical religious services under the direction of the choirmaster or minister, with the church supplying the instruments.

Rural dances in summer were held in the open under the trees and winter dances indoors on the threshing floor, with food and drink always abundant. No detailed choreographic descriptions of these dances survive.

Early Urban Dance. The development of dance in the towns followed a different pattern. As early as the twelfth century, urban artisans formed guilds to protect their trades against exploitation by the feudal aristocracy and to maintain monopolies. The guilds organized public dances, obtaining permits from the city council or from the owners of large estates. The cost of these permits was high, whether in money or in other pledges of loyalty. The guild pageants usually consisted of chain dances in which the dancers were linked by holding swords, circlets, kerchiefs, pretzels, sausages, or other objects. They moved through such choreographic figures as the snake, chain, and passage, usually finishing with the woven rose or circle. Individual guilds dressed their selected dancers, numbering between twenty and sixty, in distinctive and magnificent costumes that were owned by the guild; they carried symbols of their occupations and guilds. Only one guild could hold a dance on a given day.

Like the rural celebrations, these pageants had roots in pre-Christian practices; however, they soon lost any religious significance for both performers and spectators and took on other meanings, such as thanksgiving or wishes for success. The most famous guild dances were the circle dances of the coopers (barrelmakers), which survived into modern times in southern Germany, and the sword dances of the butchers, cutlers, shoemakers, and bakers. The guilds also organized many masked dances for Carnival, such as bearded-mask dances and Moorish dances.

The guild dancers were accompanied by music played on reed pipes and military drums; cornets and flutes are rarely seen in illustrations. The use of the trumpet was restricted to the aristocracy, but a few imperial cities purchased the right to have trumpets blown by appointed functionaries on special occasions.

The social dances organized by urban artisans were held either in the guild's premises—a workshop or barn—or in a hall rented from a city, guild, or inn. Festivals in-

GERMANY: Traditional and Social Dance. In contrast to more dignified court forms, traditional dances were often characterized by spirited hopping and jumping. This sixteenth-century engraving shows two peasant couples dancing outdoors. (Reprinted from Lilly Grove, *Dancing*, London, 1895, p. 294.)

volving the entire population, such as the feast of Saint John, were held in the marketplace. Festive torch and lantern dances were organized for family social events. Certain group dances were especially popular with young people: the *Caprioletanz* was a wild, leaping dance, often attacked and forbidden by church and civil authorities; in the *Schmoller*, couples danced around and kissed, the name being based on gestures and actions suggesting malice and sulking (from *schmollen*, "to sulk"). The pigeon dance, in which each couple had to imitate figures performed by the lead dancer, was the occasion for great merriment.

The first borrowings of dances from neighboring peoples to the west and east undoubtedly developed in this urban milieu. Every master craftsman had to spend several years as a journeyman, and apprentices traveled widely, adopting new dances and bringing them home. To these introduced dances people added elements of their native tradition, thus creating new folk dances. Many of these remodeled folk dances eventually reached court society, where they might become fashionable for a time before filtering back to their original source, often with new modifications. Most printed collections of court music from the sixteenth and seventeenth centuries contain a few examples of dances that must have been close to urban folk dances; and the professional musicians who used these scores probably had a more varied collection of instruments than peasant and artisan bands did, since flutes, wooden cornets, and a wide variety of stringed and plucked instruments appear in illustrations.

German courts did not develop the spectacular dance pageants or masques that were a feature of the Italian, French, and English courts of this period. Dance as entertainment for spectators figured in urban school dramas (*Gymnasium* performances), which reflected the tastes of the middle class. There were grotesque dances in the style of *commedia dell'arte*, dances with movements modeled on the gestures of artisans, and lively pantomimes that often mocked the nearby peasantry.

Contredanse and Quadrille. Toward the end of the seventeenth century *contredanses* spread through both rural and urban Germany. These dances originated in northern Europe and particularly in England, where they were known as "country dances." English musicians had performed in Germany as early as the mid-sixteenth century, playing at dances and popular entertainments at the royal courts of Dresden and Dessau and at the great annual markets and trade fairs in Leipzig and Frankfurt-am-Main. During the same period, troupes of English actors and puppeteers toured the German countryside.

The *contredanses* were enthusiastically adopted, particularly in northern and central Germany. Obviously related to known peasant dances, they were soon reinterpreted and expanded to create specifically German dances. These usually involved four couples facing one another in a column, square, or circle. The square dances were generally called quadrilles.

The *contredanses* often included symbolic representations of work or tools (the mill wheel, the mill, or weaving, for example); these movements were artistically incorporated with other combinations of steps and figures. Special figures such as the star, rose, wheel, mill, carousel, chain, and cross-ring occur repeatedly in the various dances.

Descriptions of many quadrilles have survived. Identified dance types include the pin, hand, smile, ballet, kiss, and hunter, named after characteristic movements or contexts. Dances called the *Fingerschottisch*, *Föhringer Kontra*, *Achterrüm*, *Hopskontra*, and *Tampet* are found throughout northern Germany. In rural areas and in isolated parts of northern Germany these *grossen bunten Tänze* ("big variety dances"), as they were collectively known, were performed until the early twentieth century, especially by older people at weddings and church dedication anniversaries.

Recent Regional Dances. Regional dances of southern Germany in the seventeenth century included the *Dreher* ("spinning top"), *Schleifer* ("slide," also known as the *Deutsche*, or "German dance"), and many forms of the *Ländler* (or *Laendler*), a slow dance in 3/4 time. These dances included precursors and early versions of the Viennese waltz, and in rural areas, they coexisted with it into modern times.

The *Schuhplattler* is a vigorous courtship dance with many complex movements, difficult to perform and to depict. They include such figures as The Small Window, The Large Window, and The Bridge as well as the lifting of the female partner and kissing. The sequence of the figures and the brilliance of the footwork depend on the inspiration and skill of individual dancers or couples. In another type of courtship dance, the *Dreisteirer*, two women compete for the attention of one man. Courtship dances, which included many mime sequences, were performed until recently throughout southern Germany and Austria.

The *Zwiefachen* are rhythmic couple dances in which the meter varies continually among 2/4, 3/4, and 4/4. The *Bandl* ("ribbon" dance), performed at spring and harvest festivals, is a circle dance done around a maypole or harvest crown; by the end of the dance the ribbons held by the dancers are wrapped in geometric patterns around the pole.

Popular Social Dance. The quick, or Vienna, waltz became popular in the early to mid-nineteenth century. As is evident from the *Fichtelbücher* (manuscript melodic notebooks), it spread quickly throughout Germany, and by 1850 it was the most popular dance among rural Germans.

At the beginning of the nineteenth century the schottische, a circle dance in a moderately quick 2/4 tempo,

GERMANY: Traditional and Social Dance. By the mid-nineteenth century, the popularity of couple dances, including the quick waltz, the Bavarian polka, and the galop, was widespread. This 1890s couple is seen in a waltz position. (Reprinted from Lilly Grove, *Dancing,* London, 1895, p. 298[a].)

was particularly widespread. The Bavarian polka and the *Rheinländer*—and their many variants—developed somewhat later. In the mid-nineteenth century the mazurka (or *Warschauer*) arrived from Poland and spread throughout Germany, where it was varied according to regional preference. The mazurka merged with other dances and entered the folk tradition under such names as *Berliner Stillstand, Geus up de Deel, Rück en Bittken, Krauttreter, Massianer,* and *Dreh dich mal um.* It was soon followed by the *Schnellpolka* ("quick polka") and *Galopp* ("galop"). In addition, social dance games—such as the Basket Waltz, Cube Waltz, Broom Dance, Apron Dance, and March Waltz—were popular at private parties and village assemblies.

Modern Folk Dance Movements. Around the beginning of the twentieth century, enthusiastic teachers involved with the youth movement began to notice the dances of the rural population, which differed markedly from the fashionable social dances of the time in their grace, naturalness, and multiplicity of forms, movements,

and musical accompaniment. They believed that the discipline and sensitivity required for the performance of pattern dances, together with the healthfulness and pleasure of folk dancing, would help in the spiritual reform that was the goal of the German youth movement. Berlin and Hamburg became centers of the dance preservation movement and the sites of folk dance conferences and teaching.

In the 1920s, collectors and dance teachers began to create new folk-style community dances based on traditional forms, which they called new folk dances, youth dances, or social dances. These scholar-choreographers included Julius Blasche, Anna Helms-Blasche, Ilse Berthold-Baczynski, Ludwig Burkhardt, Heinrich Dieckelmann, Dolf Giebel, Erich Janietz, Gernot Nietzsche, and Arthur Nowy. The folk dance preservation section of the youth movement combined the performance of the dances with a social regimen that forbade the use of alcohol and tobacco and encouraged dancing in the open air. These efforts at spiritual reform came to an abrupt end in 1933, when the youth groups were either banned or co-opted into Nazi organizations.

After World War II, many organizations in northern Europe became concerned with preserving folk dance. They joined in national and regional associations, organized conferences and courses, and published informational materials, such as the magazines *Der Volkstanz, Fröhlicher Kreis,* and *Information über Tanz.* Their sphere of interest extended to English and American country and square dances.

After the mid-1950s, the folk dances of the European communist countries were incorporated into the programs of East German youth and performing groups. Since the 1960s, other German dance groups have been formed to reconstruct and perform historical dances; much of this was sponsored by the East German government, which also organized festivals featuring folk dance, such as the Rudolstadt Festival, inaugurated in 1955.

Traditional German folk dances are today used in movement training in the elementary schools and are performed in many regions in folk costume, both socially and for audiences. Senior citizens' groups and social dancers continue to perform dances that have been handed down in their local region. Folk dance is also used as part of dance and movement therapy, adapted as needed for special groups. The magazine *Der Tanz,* founded in 1956, is a principal source of information.

BIBLIOGRAPHY

Angerstein, Wilhelm. *Volkstänze im deutschen Mittelalter.* Berlin, 1868.
Au, Hans von der. "Das Volkstanzgut im Rheinfränkischen." Ph.D. diss., University of Giessen, 1939.

Au, Hans von der. *Heit is Kerb in unserm Dorf: Tänze rechts und links der Saar.* Kassel, 1954.

Bauer, Anton. *30 altbayrische Tänze.* Leipzig, 1928.

Bauer, Anton. *Wir tanzen Zwiefache.* Berlin, 1935.

Bloch, Paul Jacques. "Der deutsche Volkstanz der Gegenwart." Ph.D. diss., University of Giessen, 1927.

Böhme, Franz M. *Geschichte des Tanzes in Deutschland.* 2 vols. Leipzig, 1886.

Bröcker, Marianne, ed. *Tanz und Tanzmusik in Überlieferung und Gegenwart.* Bamberg, 1992.

Burgauner, Christoph. *Tanzen in Deutschland.* Munich, 1986.

Burkhardt, Ludwig. *Mädel wasch dich.* Kassel, 1954.

Dieckelmann, Heinrich. *Kleines Volkstanzlexikon.* Hamburg, 1958.

Fladerer, O., et al., eds. *Deutsche Volkstänze.* Kassel, 1928–. By 1968, fifty-seven volumes on folk dance had been published, representing every German region.

Goldschmidt, Aenne. *Handbuch des deutschen Volkstanzes.* Berlin, 1967.

Helms-Blasche, Anna, and Julius Blasche. *Bunte Tänze.* 12 vols. Frankfurt-am-Main, 1953–.

Helms-Blasche, Anna. *Bunte Tänze, wie wir sie suchten und fanden.* Leipzig, 1957.

Hoerburger, Felix. *Die Zwiefachen.* Berlin, 1956.

Hoerburger, Felix. *Volkstanzkunde.* 2 vols. Kassel, 1961.

Horak, Karl. *Volkstänze der Deutschen in Mittelpolen.* 4 vols. Plauen, 1936–1937.

Horak, Karl. *Donauschwäbische Volkstänze.* Munich, 1954.

Horak, Karl. *Tiroler Volkstänze.* 4 vols. Schwaz, 1954–1960.

Ilmbrecht, Otto. *Westfälische Heimattänze.* Hamburg, 1931.

Ilmbrecht, Otto. *Bückeburger Heimattänze.* Hamburg, 1937.

Janietz, Erich, ed. *Volkstänze für Volkstanzgruppen.* 6 vols. Leipzig, 1955–1960.

Klotzsche, Volker. *Tanzen seit 1945: Personen, die den Laientanz massgeblich beeinflusst haben.* Remscheid, 1988.

Koschier, Franz. *Kärntner Volkstänze.* 2 vols. Klagenfurt, 1963.

Kück, Eduard, and Elfriede Rotermund-Schönhagen. *Heidjers Tanzmusik.* 3d ed. Berlin, 1929.

Lager, Herbert, and Ilka Peter. *Perchtentanz in Pinzgau.* Vienna, 1940.

Lose Blätter für Laientanzgruppen. Leipzig, 1953–. Journal edited by Erich Janietz.

Meyer, Gertrud. *Volkstänze.* 5th ed. Leipzig, 1921.

Oetke, Herbert. *Aus der Entwicklung des deutschen Volkstanzes.* Berlin, 1954.

Oetke, Herbert. *Der Deutsche Volkstanz.* 2 vols. Berlin, 1982.

Petermann, Kurt. *Tanzbibliographie.* Vol. 1. Leipzig, 1966. See chapter 6 for a complete bibliography of German folk dance.

Petermann, Kurt. *Wechselbeziehungen zwischen Volks- und Gesellschaftstanz.* Berlin, 1983.

Peters, Marie. *Mecklenburgische Bauerntänze.* Schwerin, 1911.

Peters, Marie, and Otto Ilmbrecht. *Alte Tänze aus Mecklenburg.* Schwerin, 1927.

Salmen, Walter. *Der fahrende Musiker im europäischen Mittelalter.* Kassel, 1960.

Schützenberger, Erna, and Hermann Derschmidt. *Spinnradl.* Landsberg, 1959.

Schultz, Willi. *Deutsche Paartänze.* Leipzig, 1927.

Schultz, Willi. *Schüddel de Büx.* Leipzig, 1928.

Witzmann, Reingard. *Der Ländler in Wien.* Vienna, 1976.

Wolfram, Richard. *Deutsche Volkstänze.* Leipzig, 1937.

Wolfram, Richard. *Die Volkstänze in Österreich und verwandte Tänze in Europa.* Salzburg, 1951.

Zoder, Raimund. *Altösterreichische Volkstänze.* 4 vols. Vienna, 1922–1937.

Zoder, Raimund, and Hans Joachim Moser. *Deutsches Volkstum in Volksschauspiel und Volkstanz.* Berlin, 1938.

Zoder, Raimund. *Österreichische Volkstänze.* 3 vols. Vienna, 1948–1958.

Zoder, Raimund. *Volkslied, Volkstanz und Volksbrauch in Österreich.* Vienna, 1950.

KURT PETERMANN

Theatrical Dance, 1600–1945

Theatrical dance first appeared in Germany in the princely courts of Berlin, Brunswick, Darmstadt, Dresden, Düsseldorf, Hanover, and Stuttgart. Among early documented performances were Darmstadt's *Die Befreiung des Friedens* (The Liberation of Peace) in 1600 and Dresden's *Ballett von dem Orpheo und der Euridice* in 1638. Like other court ballets of the time, these works were sung as well as danced. Some of the ballet masters came from France and Italy, but German names also appear in the records.

With Jean-Georges Noverre's appointment as ballet master to the court of Württemberg by Duke Carl Eugen in March 1760, dance developments centered on Stuttgart, which is listed together with Lyon as the place of publication for Noverre's famous *Lettres sur la danse et sur*

GERMANY: Theatrical Dance, 1600-1945. This copper engraving by Christoph Weigel depicts a seventeenth-century dancing master. It was printed in Abraham a Santa Clara's *Etwas für Alle* (Nuremberg, 1699). (Courtesy of Madison U. Sowell and Debra H. Sowell, Brigham Young University, Provo, Utah.)

le ballet (1760). For the first time in Germany, ballet was considered equal to opera as an instrument of status and power, even though it continued to be performed mostly with opera. Thus the social status of the ballet was considerably raised, although its artists continued to be treated as dependents of the duke.

Ballet performances at Stuttgart and the nearby Ludwigsburg castle rose to unprecedented splendor and topped even those in Paris. With an enlarged corps de ballet of some fifty dancers, supplemented by such famous guests as Gaëtan Vestris, Maximilien Gardel, Jean Dauberval, and Anna-Friederike Heinel, Noverre realized his "reform ballets," for which he enlisted the help of composers such as Niccolò Jommelli, Florian Deller, and Johann Joseph Rudolph, with Louis Boquet and Giovanni Servandoni as designers. Thus Stuttgart and Ludwigsburg witnessed the creation of *Admète et Alceste* (1761), *La Mort d'Hercule* (1762), *Psyché et l'Amour* (1762), *Médée et Jason* (1763), *Orpheus und Eurydike* (1763), *Hypermnestra*

GERMANY: Theatrical Dance, 1600–1945. Minna Kitzinc and Anna Sellinc as English sailors in Paul Taglioni's *Flick und Flocks Abenteuer* (1858). This lithograph is by Louis Veit, after a photograph by L. Haase, and was printed in Eduard Bloch's *Album der Bühnen-Costüme* (Berlin, 1859). (Courtesy of Madison U. Sowell and Debra H. Sowell, Brigham Young University, Provo, Utah.)

(1764), *Alexandre* (1765), *Antoine et Cléopâtre* (1765), *Das Fest des Hymenäos* (1766), and *Der Raub der Proserpina* (1766). These works were prototypes of the gradually emerging *ballet d'action* and were analogous to the rationalist reforms introduced by Gluck in opera.

Although the Age of Enlightenment thus gradually influenced the ballet stage, its artists were still subject to the ruler's despotism. Thus when the duke's boundless extravagance left him low on funds, he cut down on his theater expenditures, with the result that the ballet company was considerably reduced and Noverre left for Vienna. By 1767 Stuttgart's first ballet miracle had come to an end.

During the six years of Noverre's direction, however, Stuttgart had presented a widely observed example of what German ballet might achieve. Small wonder, then, that other German rulers tried to emulate the Stuttgart model. Ballet became a plaything of the powerful, dependent on the whims and tempers of monarchs, today pampered, tomorrow dropped. Most German ballet enterprises were therefore short-lived, shifting from one court to another, sometimes turning up even at small residences such as Darmstadt or Kassel. In Munich, the ballet master Peter Legrand enjoyed moderate success and collaborated with Mozart on his opera *Idomeneo, Rè di Creta* (1781). The most successful ballet master in Germany after Noverre left was Étienne Lauchery, who had started his career in Mannheim and continued in Kassel (1764–1772, returning 1780–1786), Mannheim again (1772–1778), Munich (1778–1780), and Berlin (1788–1813).

Although ballet remained a feature of court opera houses in Berlin and Munich and perhaps also in Dresden (where most theatrical records were destroyed during World War II), it was not really comparable to the developments in Paris, London, Vienna, Milan, or Saint Petersburg, where ballet masters and dancers considered Germany provincial. The free cities of Hamburg, Frankfurt, and Leipzig had their own municipal theaters, maintaining their own ballet companies if enough money was available and otherwise relying on traveling troupes that offered mixed bills of plays, operas, and musical theater.

Not until 1826 did Germany witness a premiere of a ballet that entered the international repertory. It was Filippo Taglioni's *Jocko der Brasilianische Affe* (Jocko the Brazilian Ape), the fruit of his 1824–1828 stay in Stuttgart, with his daughter Marie in one of the leading roles. Its heavily sentimental, exotic subject (a Brazilian beauty saves an ape from being bitten by a snake, a favor reciprocated when Jocko, the ape, saves her child from being kidnapped) is typical of the petit-bourgeois, idyllic ballets that dominated the repertory during the Restoration period in Germany. Pre-Romantic ideas, subjects, and forms began to trickle in from Friedrich Horschelt in Munich and from Constantin Michel Telle and Antoine Titus in

Berlin. The Romantic ballet movement gained ground through imports from Paris and Vienna, with ballets such as *La Sylphide* (Berlin, 1832), *Giselle* (Berlin, 1843), and *La Péri* (Berlin, 1848) quickly making the rounds of German stages. There were, however, few genuine Romantic ballets from German sources apart from *Giselle;* Paul Taglioni's *Undine* (Berlin, 1836) was a rare example. It is characteristic that none of the great German composers of this era—not Schumann, Mendelssohn, or Brahms, let alone Wagner—ever thought of composing a ballet.

The age of industrialization that followed the revolution of 1849 favored the flight of ballet into the world of dreams on the one hand and the promotion of the middle-class idyll on the other. Representative ballets include Paul Taglioni's *Satanella, oder Metamorphosen* (Berlin, 1852) and *Flick und Flocks Abenteuer* (Berlin, 1858). Only the revised version of *La Fille Mal Gardée*, with new music commissioned by Paul Taglioni from Peter Ludwig Hertel for its Berlin premiere in 1864, succeeded in moving from the world of German-language theater into international circles.

While Wagner was creating music dramas that revolutionized the foundations of opera, and was building the ideal theater for the embodiment of his ideas in Bayreuth, ballet in the German theaters remained an auxiliary to the opera and an entertainment for a populace eager for distraction. The fact that Adèle Grantzow, born in Brunswick, preferred to make her dance career in Paris and Saint Petersburg is indicative of the lack of prospects on the German ballet stage at that time. The activity of Lucille Grahn in Leipzig (1858–1861) and Munich (1869–1875) as ballet mistress had as few artistic consequences as that of Katti Lanner in Hamburg (1857–1866). In 1861 Paul Taglioni in Berlin produced the German premiere of *Coppélia*, and in 1884 Charles Guillemin produced *Sylvia* there. Both ballets quickly made the rounds of German stages, in each case with new staging by the local ballet master. Around the end of the nineteenth century the ballet most frequently performed in the German theaters was undoubtedly *Die Puppenfee* (The Fairy Doll), an import from Vienna and the embodiment of an art whose products offered as much artistic sustenance as the creations of the royal court bakeries.

What Germany saw of genuinely significant ballet before 1914 it owed to the guest performances of foreign companies. In 1908 Anna Pavlova made the first of her many visits to Germany. In 1909 the ballet of the Maryinsky Theater in Saint Petersburg gave a few performances in Berlin, and in 1910 Serge Diaghilev's troupe gave what amounted to a general rehearsal for the forthcoming season in Paris.

The fact that these companies did not have any long-term influence in Germany is explained chiefly by the enthusiasm at the time for all types of artistic or expressive

GERMANY: Theatrical Dance, 1600-1945. In Paul Taglioni's *Satanella, oder Metamorphosen* (1852), Charles Müller, depicted here, appeared as Carlo, a Heidelberg student who is seduced by the she-devil Satanella and betrays his betrothed. This lithograph, after a photograph by Marowsky, was printed in Eduard Bloch's *Album der Bühnen-Costüme* (Berlin, 1859). (Courtesy of Madison U. Sowell and Debra H. Sowell, Brigham Young University, Provo, Utah.)

dance, seen as an alternative to classical, academic dance, which was attracting increasing attention under the names *Neuer Tanz* ("new dance"), *Ausdruckstanz* ("expressive dance"), and *Freier Tanz* ("free dance"). In 1902 Isadora Duncan made her debut in Munich; in 1904 she appeared as the Principal Grace in the bacchanae in the Bayreuth staging of *Tannhäuser* and founded her school in Berlin-Grunewald. In 1906 Ruth St. Denis began a series of triumphant guest performances in Germany. The two Americans became cult figures for many young German women who saw in dance a new means of finding their identity.

Interest in this other, freer, and more individual type of dance went hand in hand with the awareness of the body manifested in the gymnastics schools of various systems (such as those of Bess Mensendieck and the Émile Jaques-Dalcroze Institute in Dresden-Hellerau) that opened up

GERMANY: Theatrical Dance, 1600-1945. A school dedicated to unifying the arts, crafts, science, and technology, the Bauhaus encouraged artists to experiment in many media. Trained as a painter and sculptor, Oskar Schlemmer became director of the Bauhaus stage in 1922. In this improvisation, entitled *Meta, or The Pantomime of Places* (1924), placards boasting commands such as "enter," "suspense," "passion," and "conflict," determined the performers' actions. This and other Bauhaus stage works revealed the characteristic sense of play often accompanying radical innovation. (Photograph reprinted from Walter Gropius, *The Theater of the Bauhaus,* Middletown, Conn., 1991, p. 44.)

everywhere. In 1910 Rudolf Laban also founded a school in Munich; it became a gathering point for people for whom a renewal of the art of dance was important. They included Mary Wigman, who had come to see the Dalcroze system of rhythmic gymnastics as too restrictive. She became Laban's assistant and also worked with him in his schools in Ascona (Monte Verità) and Zurich. It is thus possible to speak of a new departure in German dance even before 1914, when the creative dance energies flowered that had been lying fallow during the centuries of dominance of classical, academic ballet in the theaters.

The great age of *Ausdruckstanz* was the period of the Weimar Republic. The political collapse of 1918, the reexamination of the values and notions of order that had governed bourgeois society until then, and the questioning of all artistic standards induced remarkable creativity, and dance benefited. The new dance sought to emancipate dance from literary and musical influences and to concentrate on pure movement as a medium in its own right. A wide variety of dance personalities performed in dance evenings before audiences, usually outside the established theaters; hence this new form was sometimes called "podium dance" or "concert dance," in contrast to theater dance.

Only a few of the prominent representatives of *Ausdruckstanz* obtained long-term appointments in municipal or state theaters. One was Yvonne Georgi in Hanover; Kurt Jooss was engaged first in Münster and then in Essen; and Laban worked between 1930 and 1934 at the Berlin State Opera. Most of them used their schools as a base, working with groups selected from among their students. Wigman and Gret Palucca worked in Dresden; Berthe Trümpy worked with Vera Skoronel in Berlin, where Margarete Wallmann was also active; and Jean Weidt appeared with the Red Dancers at workers' meeting and Communist Party functions. Prominent solo dancers of this time were Clotilde von Derp, Niddy Impekoven, Valeska Gert, Lotte Goslar, Lisa Czobel, Alexander Sakharoff, Harald Kreutzberg, and Alexander von Swaine.

In addition to the schools maintained by Laban in various locations (Mannheim, Hamburg, Würzburg, and Berlin), Wigman and Palucca had studios in Dresden, Wallmann and Trümpy in Berlin, and Jooss in Essen (the dance division of the Folkwang Schule). These studios produced most of the dancers who presented dance evenings all over Germany during the 1920s and the early 1930s. The first conventions of dancers were held in Magdeburg in 1927, in Essen in 1928, and in Munich in 1930; the delegates discussed the social as well as the artistic problems of their profession. These conventions also served as a platform for the appearances of well-known individual dancers and groups (particularly Jooss and Weidt) whose work reflected the contradictions and the versatility of the age, but without any deliberate reflection on performers' social and political roles.

Compared with this enormous creativity and vitality, ballet at the opera houses remained rather insignificant, although new ballets to music of such composers as Stravinsky, Prokofiev, Ravel, and de Falla appeared on German stages, choreographed by local ballet directors. One innovation of the 1920s was the "movement choir" (*Bewegunschöre),* based on Laban's cosmic dance philosophy, which sometimes consisted of hundreds of performers in mass choreographies forming a portion of the "dancing cosmos." Laban's influence as the inventor and developer of his system of movement notation was meritorious, but the cosmic mysticism he preached made it easier for the Nazis to appropriate the *Ausdruckstanz* movement when they came to power in 1933. Six months earlier, Jooss had produced *The Green Table,* which remains the culmination of this dance genre. Jooss's pacifist beliefs and activities were an annoyance to the Nazis, who were probably relieved when Jooss and his dancers failed to return to Germany after a foreign tour in 1933.

The conformism of the German dance scene after 1933 encountered little resistance from the artists. Laban soon followed Jooss into exile, Georgi went to the Netherlands, and Hanya Holm had already been sent by Wigman to found a New York branch of her Dresden institute. Wigman and Palucca withdrew into their schools. Those who remained behind and wanted to continue performing in public were forced to adapt to the National Socialist (i.e., Nazi) principles of physical development formulated by Rudolf Bode and others. The most striking expressions of these principles occurred in the rhythmic mass spectacles at the Olympic Games in Berlin in 1936 and at the National Socialist Party celebrations in Nuremburg, where choreography was turned into a drill book for mass formations. The German Master Workshops for Dance, founded in 1936 in Berlin, was an umbrella organization and central pedagogical institution for German dance. It was unable to sustain the once-powerful *Ausdruckstanz* movement against gradual decline and disappearance.

Ballet productions at the opera houses became rare. Classical ballet eked out a hand-to-mouth existence at the Berlin Variété with Tatjana Gsovsky, Evgenia Eduardova, and their students. (Ultimately Eduardova was obliged to emigrate because her husband, the dance writer Joseph Lewitan, was Jewish.) Guest appearances by in-

GERMANY: Theatrical Dance, 1600-1945. (*top*) Mary Wigman and her dancers in *Totenklage* (Lament for the Dead) from *Women's Dances* (1934). Her motif of women mourning harks back to her earlier *Totenmal* (1930). (*middle*) The Fächerdamen (The Fan Women) from scene 2 of Yvonne Georgi's *Don Morte,* Hanover, 1928. The dancers are probably Grete Beckmann, Alice Hammerich, Ilke Schellenberg, and Edith Taegener. (*bottom*) Yvonne Georgi and Harald Kreutzberg in *Pavane,* one of a series of collaborative duets the two made from the late 1920s through 1931. This photograph is by Maurice Goldberg. (Photographs from the Dance Collection, New York Public Library for the Performing Arts.)

ternationally famous companies became very rare. The Original Ballet Russe of Colonel de Basil and Les Ballets de Léon Woizikovski were among the few companies that still came to Germany. Among the few young German dance figures who survived the Nazi era with their integrity intact was Dore Hoyer, who had danced with Wigman.

[*See also* Ausdruckstanz *and the entries on major figures mentioned herein.*]

BIBLIOGRAPHY

Behr, Samuel Rudolph. *L'art de bien danser, oder Die Kunst wohl zu Tantzen* (1713). Leipzig, 1977.

Bie, Oskar. *Das Ballett.* Berlin, 1905.

Bittrich, Gerhard. *Ein deutsches Opernballett des siebzehnten Jahrhunderts.* Leipzig, 1931.

Böhme, Fritz. *Der Tanz der Zukunft.* Munich, 1926.

Böhme, Fritz. *Tanzkunst.* Dessau, 1926.

Brandenburg, Hans. *Der moderne Tanz.* 3d ed. Munich, 1921.

Forster, Marianne. "Reconstructing European Modern Dance: Bodenwieser, Chladek, Leeder, Kreutzberg, Hoyer." In *Dance Reconstructed*, edited by Barbara Palfy. New Brunswick, N.J., 1993.

Hammond, Sandra Noll. "A Nineteenth-Century Dancing Master at the Court of Württemberg: The Dance Notebooks of Michel St. Léon." *Dance Chronicle* 15.3 (1992): 291–315.

Howe, Dianne S. *Individuality and Expression: The Aesthetics of the New German Dance, 1908–1936.* New York, 1995.

Karina, Lilian, and Marion Kant. *Tanz unterm Hakenkreuz: Eine Dokumentation.* Berlin, 1996.

Koegler, Horst. "In the Shadow of the Swastika: Dance in Germany, 1929–1936." *Dance Perspectives*, no. 57 (Spring 1974).

Laban, Rudolf von. *Die Welt des Tänzers.* Stuttgart, 1920.

Laban, Rudolf von. *Choreographie.* Jena, 1926.

Laban, Rudolf von, and Mary Wigman, eds. *Die tänzerische Situation unserer Zeit: Ein Querschnitt.* Dresden, 1936.

Lambranzi, Gregorio. *Neue und curieuse theatralische Tantz-Schul: Deliciae theatrales.* Nuremberg, 1716.

Little, Meredith Ellis. "French Court Dance in Germany at the Time of Johann Sebastian Bach: *La Bourgogne* in Paris and Leipzig." In *Report of the Twelfth Congress, International Musicological Society [Berkeley 1977]*, edited by Daniel Heartz and Bonnie C. Wade. Kassel, 1981.

Little, Meredith Ellis. *Dance and the Music of J. S. Bach.* Bloomington, 1991.

Maack, Rudolf. *Tanz in Hamburg: Von Mary Wigman bis John Neumeier.* Hamburg, 1975.

Manning, Susan A. *Ecstasy and the Demon: Feminism and Nationalism in the Dances of Mary Wigman.* Berkeley, 1993.

Müller, Hedwig. *Mary Wigman: Leben und Werk der grossen Tänzerin.* Weinheim, 1986.

Müller, Hedwig, and Patricia Stöckemann, eds. *Jeder Mensch ist ein Tänzer: Ausdruckstanz in Deutschland zwischen 1900 und 1945.* Giessen, 1993.

Oberst, Günther. *Englische Orchestersuiten um 1600: Ein Beitrag zur deutschen Instrumentalmusik nebst einer Bibliographie der Tanzliteratur bis 1600.* Wolfenbüttel, 1929.

Oberzaucher-Schüller, G., ed. *Ausdruckstanz: Ein mitteleuropäische Bewegung der ersten Hälfte des 20. Jahrhunderts.* Wilhelmshaven, 1992.

Partsch-Bergsohn, Isa. *Modern Dance in Germany and the United States: Crosscurrents and Influences.* Chur, Switzerland, 1994.

Petermann, Kurt. *Tanzbibliographie: Verzeichnis der in deutscher Sprache veröffentlichten Schriften und Aufsätze zum Bühnen-, Gesellschafts-, Kinder-, Volks- und Turniertanz sowie zur Tanzwissenschaft, Tanzmusik und zum Jazz.* 4 vols. Leipzig, 1966–1982.

Preston-Dunlop, Valerie, and Susanne Lahusen, eds. *Schrifttanz: A View of German Dance in the Weimar Republic.* London, 1990.

Rannow, Angela, and Ralf Stabel, eds. *Mary Wigman in Leipzig.* Leipzig, 1994.

Rydberg, Olaf. *Die Tänzerin Palucca.* Dresden, 1935.

Schär, Christian. *Der Schlager und seine Tänze im Deutschland der 20er Jahre.* Zurich, 1991.

Schlicher, Susanne. "The West German Dance Theatre: Paths from the Twenties to the Present." *Choreography and Dance* 3.2 (1993): 25–43.

Servos, Norbert. "Pathos and Propaganda? On the Mass Choreography of Fascism." *Ballett International* 13 (January 1990): 63–67.

Taubert, Gottfried. *Rechtschaffener Tantzmeister, oder Gründliche Erklärung der frantzösischen Tantz-Kunst* (1717). Leipzig, 1976.

Walther, Suzanne K. *The Dance of Death: Kurt Jooss and the Weimar Years.* Chur, Switzerland, 1994.

Wigman, Mary. *The Language of Dance.* Translated by Walter Sorell. Middletown, Conn., 1966.

Wilkins, Darrell. "Aesthetics and Cultural Criticism in William Forsythe's *Impressing the Czar*." *Ballet Review* 22 (Spring 1994): 61–66.

HORST KOEGLER

Theatrical Dance since 1945

The political division of Germany after World War II into four occupation zones administered by the victorious powers led to divergent developments in East and West Germany and in the divided former capital of Berlin. The representatives of *Ausdruckstanz* who had stayed in Germany or had returned from exile soon recognized that it was impossible to return to the conditions of 1933. Under the influence of companies from Russia, France, England, and the United States, an interest in and commitment to classical, academic ballet gradually crystalized, while foreign modern dance troupes, most of them from the United States, encountered undisguised rejection.

Theatrical Dance in West Germany, 1945–1989. The reconstruction of the country, its society, and its economy in the Federal Republic of Germany (FRG) and West Berlin included a ballet boom unparalleled in German history. A return to *Ausdruckstanz* and an appropriation of the forms and materials of American modern dance occurred only during the period of intensified political activism around the end of the 1960s. By then, most of the pioneers of *Ausdruckstanz* had died after harrowing years of decline.

For simplicity, we can divide the West German postwar dance scene into a reconstructive phase, which lasted until 1968 and was preoccupied with classical, academic dance, and a subsequent phase characterized by inclusion of forms of expression that were neither classical nor academic. The center of development shifted from city to city—from Munich to West Berlin to Hanover, and even to smaller cities such as Wiesbaden and Wuppertal, which

GERMANY: Theatrical Dance since 1945. The Bavarian State Ballet, Munich, in Rudolf Kölling's production of *Le Sacre du Printemps* (1949), with Irina Cladiwowa (center) as the Chosen Virgin. Costumes and scenery were designed by Wily Hempel. (Photograph from the Dance Collection, New York Public Library for the Performing Arts.)

hosted notable dance companies from time to time but were unable to develop a critical mass of dance support. Even before Tatjana Gsovsky took up residence at the West Berlin City Opera in the mid-1950s, the Munich State Opera under Marcel Luipart had already attracted attention with the scandal-ridden premiere of Werner Egk's *Abraxas*. [See Abraxas.] In Düsseldorf and then for many years in Hanover, Yvonne Georgi worked to achieve a Franco-German *entente cordiale* in ballet. In Wuppertal, Erich Walter created a model company that attracted wide attention as it sought to create a German variant of George Balanchine's neoclassicism.

The number of ballet performances at opera houses increased slowly and steadily, but frequent changes of ballet directors at these houses contributed to unstable organizations. Companies existing independently of the theaters included the *Abraxas* touring company, which had settled in northern Germany, Gsovsky's Berlin Ballet, and the Folkwang Ballet, which had been revived by Kurt Jooss after his return to Essen.

These companies, however, were short-lived. The West German postwar ballet renaissance took place in the opera houses, and it was shaped by foreign ballet directors and choreographers, most of whom remained for only a few seasons. Still more alarming was the increasing importation of foreign dancers because of the lack of German talent. Victor Gsovsky came from France to the Munich State Opera, and Aurelio Milloss came to Cologne from Italy; both men had worked in Germany before. Other immigrants included Alan Carter, who came to Munich from England; Walter Gore, to Frankfurt from England; and Todd Bolender, to Cologne from the United States.

Stuttgart engaged Nicholas Beriozoff, who established the basis on which John Cranko created his Stuttgart "ballet miracle" in the 1960s—the purposeful organization of a company, a repertory, and a school that became a model for many endeavors elsewhere and gave Germany its first internationally famous ballet company. Cranko attracted other talents from England, including Peter Wright, Anne Woolliams, and particularly Kenneth MacMillan, who after his Stuttgart successes as a guest choreographer served from 1966 to 1969 as ballet director at the Deutsche Oper in Berlin.

During the short time in which it was directed by Dore Hoyer, the Hamburg State Opera Ballet never rose above

GERMANY: Theatrical Dance since 1945. The Capulet Ball scene from John Cranko's famous production of *Romeo and Juliet*, staged for the Stuttgart Ballet in 1962. Marcia Haydée as Juliet (right) kneels before Alan Beale and Ruth Papendick as Lord and Lady Capulet. (Photograph from the Dance Collection, New York Public Library for the Performing Arts.)

mediocrity. During the 1960s, however, under the direction of Peter van Dyk, it became the German port of entry for the choreographies of Balanchine, who made personal appearances and who in 1962 organized the festivities for Igor Stravinsky's eightieth birthday. This celebration was the occasion for the first performance of Balanchine's *Agon* in Europe, to an audience already familiar with his *Apollo* and *Orpheus*.

The enthusiasm of the 1950s and 1960s for ballet made the Federal Republic the preferred destination of major companies from both East and West. They in turn accelerated the boom in classical ballet. *Giselle, Swan Lake,* and *The Sleeping Beauty* were performed continually, not only in Berlin, Stuttgart, and Munich but also in Düsseldorf, Wuppertal, Bonn, and Mannheim. There was a concomitant surge in the introduction of ballets from the international modern repertory, by such choreographers as Balanchine, Frederick Ashton, Antony Tudor, Jerome Robbins, Birgit Cullberg, Glen Tetley, Roland Petit, Janine Charrat, Maurice Béjart, Hans van Manen, and Rudi van Dantzig. John Cranko's full-length Stuttgart ballet productions, such as *Onegin* and *The Taming of the Shrew,* created a school and awakened the desire for major story ballets.

Even before Cranko's death in 1973 at the age of forty-five, some of the junior choreographers he had encouraged became independent. Ashley Killar went to England and then to South Africa, Gray Veredon to Cologne, John Neumeier to Frankfurt and then to Hamburg, and Jiří Kylián to the Netherlands Dance Theater. The American Neumeier, in particular, quickly won international fame with his novel dramaturgic concepts and his revisions of the classics. Under his energetic and purposeful direction, the Hamburg Ballet became a serious competitor to Stuttgart, especially because, after Cranko's death, the Stuttgart company had trouble retaining first-rate choreographers. Marcia Haydée, Cranko's successor, endeavored to remedy the problem by encouraging the development of such choreographers as William Forsythe and Uwe Scholz. Beginning in the early 1960s there was a proliferation of efforts, through "ballet days" and "ballet weeks," to give local audiences and interested outside observers the opportunity once a season to see a concentrated survey of the work being done.

Among the companies that intensively promoted the classics was the German Opera Ballet in Berlin, directed since 1972 by Gert Reinholm, previously acting director, as the successor to Tatjana Gsovsky. Another was the Munich State Opera Ballet, under the direction of Ronald Hynd for the 1984/85 season. (Since Heinz Rosen's departure in 1969 there has been a new ballet director practically every two years, the last ones being Lynn Seymour, Edmund Gleede, and Ronald Hynd, and, since 1989, Konstanze Vernon.) Stuttgart, Hamburg, and Düsseldorf must also be mentioned.

The change in the political climate of the Federal Republic toward the end of the 1960s, the formation of a nonparliamentary opposition, the demand for greater employee participation in management, and the increasing awareness of the political and social relevance of work all affected the dance scene. In Berlin a movement formed around Gerhard Bohner and Frank Frey to protest the rigid structures of the Deutsche Oper. They found a forum for their activities in the Academy of the Arts, which opened its doors to the diverse currents of modern and postmodern dance flooding in from the United States. In Cologne, Johann Kresnik, along with a series of choreographers such as Jochen Ulrich, Helmut Baumann, Gray Veredon, and Jürg Burth (all formerly in opera ballet) were at the center of the new movement. Modern dance strongly influenced all these people, and all of them assumed that theater has a social function. This is also true of Pina Bausch and Reinhild Hoffman, both of whom came from the Folkwang Schule in Essen. For them, engagement with the means and techniques of theater are more interesting than the heritage of classical ballet.

Using as its models the Netherlands Dance Theater and the remodeled Ballet Rambert of England, the Cologne Opera Ballet reorganized itself as the Cologne Dance Forum, directed by Ulrich since 1978. Here the primary training is in Graham technique. Kresnik also shocked the German ballet establishment in Bremen with his *Politrevue*. He has worked in Heidelberg (1979–1989) and Bremen (1989–1994) and now is at the Berlin Volksbühne.

Pina Bausch, who began working in Wuppertal in 1973, became perhaps the strongest and most individualistic personality on the dance theater scene. Her Wuppertal productions have attracted international attention. Ger-

hard Bohner's effort to embody his ideas of dance theater within the framework of the Darmstadt State Theater were short-lived. After a brief interval in Bremen, Bohner caused a sensation, both at home and abroad, with his staging of *Triadic Ballet* and *Bauhaus Dances*. In Bremen, Hoffman became co-director with Bohner, then sole director, before moving to Bochum in 1987.

Women now clearly dominate the dance scene. The Bremen theater, directed by the choreographer Heidrun Vielhauer and the actress Rotraut de Neve from 1986 to 1989, is now run by Susanne Linke and Urs Dietrich. The Frankfurt Theater am Turm temporarily housed the troupes of Vivienne Newport and Amanda Miller. Birgitta Trommler has her own company in Münster; Rosamund Gilmore leads the Laokoon Dance Group; and in Berlin one of the leading free groups is headed by Sasha Waltz.

Somewhere between ballet and dance theater stands William Forsythe in Frankfurt. His classical base is considerable, but he has reconsidered and inverted the fundamentals of the syntax of the *danse d'école*.

Early in the 1980s a number of companies were established, some in small cities and towns, operating without any connection to a theater and performing in halls, vacant factories, sheds, and barns, with no guarantee of continuation. They consist of dancers to whom artistic self-realization is more important than material gain.

In the mid-1980s the West German dance scene offered an extremely complex and contradictory picture that

GERMANY: Theatrical Dance since 1945. Members of the Pina Bausch Wuppertal Tanztheater in a 1980s revival of *The Seven Deadly Sins* (1976). In the creation of this landmark work, Bausch developed her method of forming movement and spoken text generated by the dancers into a new-style *Tanztheater*. (Photograph © 1987 by Ulli Weiss; used by permission.)

extended from the Stuttgart Ballet to the Berlin Dance Factory. Even the small municipal theaters maintained permanent ballet ensembles year-round in order to perform opera and operetta. As the 1980s drew to a close, artistic dance in West Germany had come to enjoy a vitality and a creativity that did not need to hide behind the legendary 1920s. Theatrical dance enjoyed steadily growing audiences and an increasing number of performances.

Theatrical Dance in East Germany, 1945–1989. The history of dance in East Germany was intimately connected with the social development of the German Democratic Republic (GDR). The establishment of socialism and the continually increasing aesthetic demands of the society were the driving forces behind this development, which was not always linear but rather characterized by contradictions and oppositions.

Immediately after the end of World War II, when the day-to-day material needs of the population posed insu-

GERMANY: Theatrical Dance since 1945. William Forsythe's *Orpheus*, with Reid Anderson as Apollo (center) and Richard Cragun as the title character, staged for the Stuttgart Ballet in 1979. This full-length ballet was set to music by Hans Werner Henze and a libretto by Edward Bond. (Photograph © by Madeline Winkler-Betzendahl; used by permission.)

perable problems, progressive representatives of modern dance who had suffered persecution under the Nazis began with remarkable strength and optimism to shape a new dance culture. Using the art of dance as their medium, they helped rebuild the cultural ruins left by twelve years of fascism.

On 1 July 1945 Gret Palucca reopened her school in Dresden, which had been closed by the Nazis in 1939; in the same month she gave a public solo performance. On 15 June 1945 Henn Haas founded the Weimar Theater of Dance, which also had its own training workshop. After several weeks of intensive rehearsals, on 21 August this ensemble staged the premiere of the ballet *Princess Turandot* (music by Gottfried von Einem), a humanistic work of opposition to tyranny and cruelty. Around the same time Mary Wigman founded her dance studio in Leipzig, and in the fall Dore Hoyer took over the leadership of the former Wigman school in Dresden. In 1946 Marianne Vogelsang established a department of dance at the *Musikhochschule* (music academy) in Rostock, and Grita Krätke opened a dance studio in the theater in Schwerin.

Palucca gave preference to the works of composers who had been persecuted for racial reasons and banned during the Nazi era. Progressive themes, such as Wigman's three choric studies entitled *Aus der Note der Zeit* (Out of the Need of the Age), were an indictment of war. Hoyer created for her students a dance cycle based on pictures by Käthe Kollwitz, and Vogelsang based *Die Sieben Todsünden* (The Seven Deadly Sins) on studies by Ernst Barlach.

After his return from exile, Jean Weidt founded his own school in Berlin in 1948. In 1951 his dance group became the nucleus for the National Folk Art Ensemble of the GDR. He staged a number of ballets on contemporary themes for this group, including *Gesang für Helden* (Song for Heroes) and *Der stählerne Schritt* (The Steel Step).

In contrast to the modern dance groups, which were often able to convey artistic experiences with very modest material means, the theater ballet groups had great difficulty in resuming their work. Henn Haas with his Dance Theater was an exception. For his touring group, which had no obligations to opera or operetta, he endeavored to build a contemporary repertory that included themes of social criticism. Works such as *Das Abenteuerliche Herz* (The Adventurous Heart) and *Das Zauberfell* (The Magic Skin), both created in 1945, *Eine Vision des Irdischen Glücks* (A Vision of Earthly Happiness) of 1948, and *Apokalyptische Reiter* (Apocalyptic Rider) of 1949 were revolutionary creations on the ballet stage. This ensemble also performed traditional ballets.

Under the direction of Tatjana Gsovsky from 1945 to 1952, the Deutsche Staatsoper in East Berlin and its repertory became models for the many ensembles that were established in every theater in the GDR. Almost all the major theaters had training schools (known as ballet or dance studios) to prepare the next generation of dancers. After the establishment of state training schools subsequent to the founding of the German Democratic Republic in 1949, these schools were phased out.

The period between 1949 and 1961 was characterized by numerous disputes over linking contemporary dance to social realism. With Martin Spork's discussion of realism and formalism in dance in 1952, in an article in the magazine *Weltbühne* (World Stage), the field of modern dance was opened to the view of the critics. The new postulates of cultural policy were the full-length story ballet, based on literary works but with a contemporary and progressive or historical and revolutionary content.

Soviet ballet and its repertory provided models. Great attention was paid to the training provided at the three state ballet schools, in Dresden (the Palucca school), in East Berlin (the State Ballet School, founded in 1951), and in Leipzig (the School for Dance, founded in 1952). New knowledge, training methods, and experience related to this highly stylized language of movement were provided by Soviet specialists working as teachers and coaches and by students trained in the Soviet Union. At the same time these experts transmitted Soviet contemporary ballet, which was shaped by resources of classical, academic dance and folklore and which was based on literary sources.

A dance conference held in March 1953 declared that "the classical and national heritage in the field of dance consists of classical ballet and German folk dance." Unfortunately, the representatives of modern dance did not counter this lopsided perception with the necessary decisiveness, because they lacked artistic consensus. Modern dance thus retreated to the training workshops, but instruction continued. Marianne Vogelsang was active in Berlin from 1951 to 1957; thereafter, instruction in this branch of dance ceased there. In Leipzig the basics of *Ausdruckstanz* continued to be taught as a supplementary technique. Not until the 1970s did ballet choreographers rediscover the possibilities of modern dance and adapt it to their own work.

In subsequent years numerous new ballet works resulted from collaborations between composers and choreographers. The composers Karl-Rudi Griesbach, Wolfgang Hohensee, Victor Bruns, Fritz Geissler, Kurt Forest, and Wolfgang Hudy all contributed to this growth. New works came into being both through commissions from the state and through the personal initiative of musicians and choreographers.

Daisy Spies directed the ballet of the German State Opera from 1952 to 1955. In 1952 she staged *Cinderella*, followed by *Das Recht des Herrn* (The Lord's Law), with music by Bruns, and *Der Bekehrte Spiesser* (The Converted Philistine), two contemporary works that met the ideological requirements of the dance conference and that were

GERMANY: Theatrical Dance since 1945. John Neumeier, longtime director of the Hamburg Ballet, appears here (front), with Ivan Liška and Jean-Jacques Defago, in his four-hour *Saint Matthew Passion* (1981), set to the music of J. S. Bach. (Photograph © by Holger Badekow; used by permission.)

performed in a number of theaters in the GDR in various choreographic versions.

Lilo Gruber succeeded Spies and directed the company until 1970. Through her work, the German State Opera Ballet in Berlin became a center for the Soviet style of dance. Her staging of Aram Khachaturian's *Gayané* (1955) set new standards for relevant dramatic choreography. The ballet *Neue Odysee* (1957), set to music by Bruns, depicted the wandering of a man returning home after World War II. Gruber also staged classical works. The contemporary ballet *Ballade vom Glück* (Ballad of Happiness; 1967, music by Kurt Schwaen) was not very successful, but it too was characteristic of Gruber's commitment to explosive contemporary subjects.

Grita Krätke served as ballet mistress and choreographer of the German State Opera from 1963 to 1971. From 1951 to 1962 she was a teacher at the State Ballet School in Berlin. She created several highly regarded works for the company repertory, including *Die Sieben Todsünden der Kleinbürger* (The Seven Deadly Sins of the Petit Bourgeois; 1963, music by Kurt Weill), *Der Verlorene Sohn* (The Prodigal Son; 1964, music by Sergei Prokofiev), *Die Erschaffung der Welt* (The Creation of the World; 1965, music by Darius Milhaud), *Petrouchka* (1965, music by Igor Stravinsky), *Serenade für Streicher* (Serenade for Strings; 1965, music by Tchaikovsky), and *Don Quixote* (1969, mu-

GERMANY: Theatrical Dance since 1945. Wolfgang Stollwitzer and Sonia Santiago in the Stuttgart Ballet's production of *Cobra*, choreographed by Roberto de Oliveira to music by John Zorn. (Photograph © by Felipe Alcoceba; used by permission.)

sic by Leo Spies). Particular interest was aroused by a contemporary transposition of the Romeo and Juliet story entitled *Romeo und Julia und die Finsternis* (Romeo and Juliet and the Darkness; 1962, music by Forest). A television version was produced in 1964.

The ballet of the Metropol Theater, an operetta house in East Berlin, under the direction of Anni Peterka, participated intensively and successfully in the reconstruction of dance in the GDR. Between 1951 and 1961 eight premieres were staged, with music by young composers. One program included the first "murder mystery" ballet, *Grand Hotel* (music by Hans-Klaus Langer), together with the thought-provoking *Legende von der Wegwarte* (Legend of the Chicory; music by Gerhard Keil), a ballet opposing war and militarism. Unfortunately, this tradition was lost after Peterka's departure.

During the 1950s the ballet of the Comic Opera (Komische Oper) was unable to devote much attention to ballet, although ballet evenings organized by Sabine Ress, Ilse Meudtner, and Gertrud Steinweg drew upon quite demanding music. The choreographic and interpretive standards did not approach the level of the two other Berlin ballet ensembles until 1965, when Tom Schilling took over the direction.

The National Folk Art Ensemble (Staatliche Volkskunstensemble) of the GDR took up residence in Berlin in 1951, followed by the Erich Weinert Ensemble in 1956. The dance groups of both ensembles promoted folk dance in stage versions and used it in an effort to embody contemporary subjects and to use dance as a propaganda medium. Problems of the reform of agriculture (collectivization), the struggle against atomic weapons and militarism, and the development of socialist consciousness were subjects for their dance performances.

Ballet groups were also created in the many GDR theaters outside Berlin. In Dresden from 1956 to 1964, Tom Schilling directed the ballet ensemble of the State Opera, where his predecessors (Bernhard Wosien, 1948–1949; W. Kreideweis, 1949–1951; and Erwin Hansen) had created an efficient company. Schilling began his career in Weimar in 1953 as the youngest choreographer in the GDR. His early work included highly successful stagings of contemporary Soviet compositions. He formed a stylistically homogeneous ensemble for which he set high artistic standards.

Emmy Köhler-Richter directed the ballet in Weimar from 1956 to 1958 and then served until 1978 as ballet director of the Municipal Theater in Leipzig. In addition to the customary repertory, she organized the premieres of *Fanal*, a *Spartacus*-style ballet set to music by W. Hohensee (1961), *Till Eulenspiegel* (1965, music by Uwe Ködderitzsch), and *Die Idee* (The Idea; 1976, music by Peter Herrmann). Her individualistic interpretations of classical ballets *(The Sleeping Beauty, Swan Lake,* and *Romeo and Juliet)* were criticized, but under her direction the ballet of the Leipzig Theater developed into a leading ensemble in the GDR.

Vera Bräuer was the leader of the ballet company in Rostock from 1954 to 1976. In addition to the standard repertory, she staged one world premiere and ten GDR premieres of contemporary Soviet and Czech ballet works. Her choreographies introduced important works from the repertory of the socialist countries to inhabitants of the Baltic area. Many of these works were subsequently performed in other theaters, including *Das Fest von Coqueville* (The Festival of Coqueville; 1956, music by Julius Kalas), *Mario und der Zauberer* (Mario and the Magician; 1958, music by Franco Mannino), *Der Gefangene im Kaukasus* (The Prisoner of the Caucasus; 1958, music by Boris Asafiev), *Esmeralda* (1959, music by Reinhold Glière et al.), *Der Eherne Reiter* (The Brass Rider; 1960, music by Glière), and *Don Quixote* (1961, music by Jaroslav Doubrava).

Henn Hass, ballet master in Halle from 1957 to 1970, premiered a new work almost every year. One of the most inventive choreographers of this period, he collaborated with many composers not only as a choreographer but also as a librettist. His numerous choreographic works include *Kreuz-Bauer Ulrike* (1958, music by Carl-Heinz Dickmann), *Froschzarin* (Frog Tsarina; 1959, music by Waldemar Findeisen), *Annos* (1962, music by Wolfgang Hudy), *Eckensteher* (Loafer; 1965, music by Ralph Rank), *Fridolin* (1967, music by Hans J. Wenzel) and *Flucht vor Göttern* (Flight before the Gods; 1969, music by Hohensee). Much interest in ballet was also evident at theaters in Karl-Marx-Stadt (now called Chemnitz), Cottbus, Gera, Erfurt, Dessau, Magdeburg, Schwerin, and Zwickau.

In 1965 Tom Schilling founded the dance theater of the Comic Opera, transposing the principles of Walter Felsenstein's realistic musical theater to the dance. His scenic productions were distinguished by his great fantasy of movement, his sensitive response to music, and his continuous search for innovation. His artistic creations ranged from small satirical movement scenes to full-length works of social criticism. He formed an ensemble with a style and capability indelibly stamped by his personality. The milestones of his career include Berlioz's *Fantastic Symphony* and Uwe Ködderitzsch's *Impulse* (both 1967); Debussy's *La Mer* and Fritz Geissler's *Der Doppelgänger* (both 1969); Hans Werner Henze's *Undine* (1970); George Katzer's *Schwarze Vögel* (Blackbird; 1975); Siegfried Matthus's *Revue* (1977); *Swan Lake* (1978); Katzer's *Neuer Sommernachtstraum* (New Summer Night's Dream; 1981); Schubert's *Abendliche Tänze* (Evening Dances; 1979) and *Wahlverwandtschaften* (Kindred by Choice; 1983); and *Romeo and Juliet* (third version, 1984).

Among other successful ensembles, Hermann Rudolph built a ballet ensemble in Karl-Marx-Stadt that rivaled the leading troupes of Berlin, Dresden, and Leipzig in its appeal to audiences. Rudolph's stagings were characterized by a highly musical style of movement. His *Drei Schwangeren* (Three Pregnant Women), set to music by Gioacchino Rossini, was taken over by the German State Opera Ballet in Berlin. Rudolph's mastery of chamber dance is evident in his choreographies, which include *Psychogramme* (1977, music by Alexander Schurbin), *Eins plus Eins* (One plus One; 1979, music by Friedrich Goldmann), *Das Duell* (The Duel; 1980, music by Stravinsky), and *Dunkle Serenade* (Dark Serenade; 1980, music by Alban Berg).

During the 1970s a new generation of choreographers began to emerge, including Dietmar Seyffert, Harald Wandtke, Emöke Pösztenyi, Joachim Ahne, Arila Siegert, Volker Tietböhl, Stephan Lux, Veit-Ulrich Müller, and Brigitte Preuss. Particularly successful choreographies created by Seyffert include *Die Seele des Komödianten* (The Soul of the Actor; music by Ruggiero Leoncavallo), *Die Infantin und ihr Narr* (The Infanta and Her Fool; music by Heitor Villa-Lobos), *David und Goliath* (music by Tilo Medek), and a ballet for an audience of children, *Geschichte vom Häschen* (Story of the Rabbit; music by Erhard Ragwitz).

Harald Wantke deliberately linked with the movement

vocabulary of *Ausdruckstanz* and organized public improvisational evenings with his dancers in Dresden. His choreographies include *Triptychon* (music by Jean Françaix), *Rattenfänger* (The Pied Piper; music by Vaclav Kucera), *Die Gefesselte Hexe* (The Captured Witch; music by Udo Zimmermann), and *Apocalyptica* (music by Milko Keleman).

Pösztenyi, for many years a solo dancer with the GDR television ballet, received awards for some of his choreographies presented at GDR ballet competitions. They include *Der Dompteur* (The Tamer), *Alltag der Venus* (The Daily Life of Venus), and *H2O*, all set to music by Günter Fischer; *Katzenspiele* (Cats' Play; music by Rudolf Maros); and *Erwartung* (Anticipation; music by Istvan Miloslav).

A "dance time" program held regularly in Berlin beginning in 1978, under the artistic direction of Weidt, provided choreographers with a stage on which to present new works. Stefan Lux, a teacher at the ballet school in Berlin, became known for works with progressive subjects, including *Kinderkreuzzug* (Children's Crusade; music by Benjamin Britten), *Gavroche* (music by Tchaikovsky), and *Was Haben Sie mit dem Regen Gemacht?* (What Have They Done with the Rain?; music by Dmitri Shostakovich). Inge Berg-Peters, known for excellent work in Gera since 1975, created a noteworthy ensemble at a district theater, staging one ballet premiere a year.

During the 1980s, audiences at dance performances in East Germany grew steadily, reflecting the expanding artistic abilities of choreographers and performers. Dance in the GDR achieved the social recognition it merits among the arts and enjoyed widespread popularity.

Theatrical Dance since 1989. The reunification of Germany in 1989 meant little change in the West German dance scene, which continued very much as before, but the situation of theatrical dance in East Germany underwent drastic alterations. In the former German Democratic Republic, now generally referred to as the New Federal States (as opposed to the Old Federal States of the former West Germany), all pretenses of "socialist realism" in theatrical performances were dropped, almost overnight, as people tried to adjust to Western standards. There were, however, no immediate personal consequences of the changed political climate. No artistic directors, choreographers, dancers, teachers, or journalists were fired because they had been supporters of communism and the socialist system, although later a few people were asked to resign their positions when it became known that they had been regular members or informants of the State Security Services.

In West Berlin, the German Opera Ballet (Ballett der Deutschen Oper Berlin), also known as the Berlin Opera Ballet, continued on the course set by Gert Reinholm during his many years as artistic director, basing its repertory on the works of guest choreographers from all over the world. When Reinholm retired in 1990, he was succeeded by Peter Schaufuss, who stayed for five seasons. Under his directorship a certain rejuvenation among the dancers took place, but the repertory was not enriched. To mark the centennial of Tchaikovsky's death in 1993, Schaufuss mounted new productions of *Swan Lake, The Sleeping Beauty,* and *The Nutcracker* in which he tried, unsuccessfully, to identify Tchaikovsky with the male protagonist in each ballet. When Schaufuss became aware that his ambitions were not appreciated, he asked to be released from his contract at the end of the 1994/95 season. Despite a widespread search for a suitable successor, none could be immediately found. Ray Barra was lured from his semiretirement and installed as acting director for two seasons, with few discernible artistic results. Richard Cragun, formerly a principal dancer with the Stuttgart Ballet, assumed the post of artistic director in the autumn of 1996.

At the Staatsoper Unter den Linden, Berlin's historic opera house, Egon Bischoff continued in the role of artistic director of the ballet company, with a repertory now extended to include ballets by Balanchine, Nureyev, and Cranko. He was succeeded by Michaël Denard, formerly a star of the Paris Opera Ballet, in 1992. After Maurice Béjart had staged Bartók's *Miraculous Mandarin* and Schoenberg's *Transfigured Night* in 1993, he was appointed chief guest choreographer, and he thereafter revived a number of his ballets for the company. Patrice Bart from the Paris Opera Ballet staged *Don Quixote;* Roland Petit created *Dix, or Eros and Death;* and Pierre Lacotte attempted to reconstruct Jean Coralli's dances for Auber's opera *Le Lac des Fées,* which proved to be a major flop. Then, rather suddenly, the management became displeased with Béjart, and Denard resigned at the end of the 1995/96 season, leaving the company, which is considered Berlin's premier classical ballet troupe, adrift.

At the Komische Oper (Comic Opera) in Berlin, Tom Schilling was for many years the highly popular chief choreographer of what at this house was called *Tanztheater,* by which was meant not the Pina Bausch type of *Tanztheater* but rather ballet that emphasized dramatic content. After Schilling's resignation as artistic director in 1993, Doris Laine from Helsinki acted as a sort of deputy artistic director for two seasons, and in 1994 Mark Jonkers from Holland was installed as artistic director, with his compatriot Jan Linkens as chief choreographer. They aimed to build a contemporary repertory, inviting occasional guest choreographers such as Birgit Scherzer, Cesc Gelabert, François Raffinot, and Vicente Saez, but no clear programmatic contours emerged, and more and more of Schilling's ballets were brought back to rekindle the waning audience interest.

Each of Berlin's three opera houses—the Deutsche Oper, the Staatsoper Unter den Linden, and the Komische Oper—has a ballet company of its own, and each has a substantial history of performance. However, because artistic results have been so meager in recent years and because each house is facing heavy budget cuts, there have been serious discussions about the future of ballet in Berlin and about the possibilities of merging the companies into more economical units. As Berlin's fourth company, Johann Kresnik's Choreographic Theater, established in 1994 as part of the Volksbühne (Folk Theater), pursues its highly individual course of agit-prop and social-critical productions, attracting vast crowds of primarily young people.

Berlin also has a very lively "free dance" scene, consisting of smaller, modern-oriented, independent groups. Some of the *Freier Tanz* groups are connected to a school—such as the Tanzfabrik Berlin (Berlin Dance Factory), run by Claudia Feest and Dieter Heitkamp—while others try to survive by giving performances and touring—such as Jutta Hell and Dieter Baumenn's Rubato, Sasha Waltz & Guests, Joseph Tmim's Toladá Dance Company, and a group formed around choreographer Jo Fabian. As program director of the Hebbel Theater, Nele Hertling has successfully turned her house into a showcase for experimental local choreography and contemporary companies from all over the world.

Outside Berlin, one of the most interesting ballet companies of the New Federal States is connected to the Dresden State Opera. Under the artistic directorship of Vladimir Derevianko since 1944, this company concentrates on a repertory designed to showcase its director as a star dancer. Most new works are mounted by guest choreographers, and a strong tie exists with Hamburg's John Neumeier. The house choreographer is the still youthful Stephan Thoss, who comes from the Palucca school and who tries to synthesize the *danse d'école* with elements of Palucca's *Neuer künstlerischer Tanz* ("new artistic dance").

The once flourishing modern dance scene in Dresden, at its peak when Wigman and Palucca were working there during the 1920s, has shrunk to insubstantiality. The Palucca school is still functioning, but it has failed to generate genuine creativity. Arila Siegert tries to uphold the modern dance tradition as a solo performer and in her occasional guest choreographies for companies in Berlin, Leipzig, and Dessau. There is hope, however, that modern dance will be revitalized. The Hellerau buildings of the former Jaques-Dalcroze Institute, which during Russian occupation had been used as barracks for Soviet soldiers, are now being renovated and could provide an ideal home for a new center of contemporary dance.

Leipzig is another center of current dance activity. The Leipzig Ballet has enjoyed a remarkable rise since Uwe Scholz was appointed artistic director and chief choreographer in 1991. His own works dominate the repertory of

GERMANY: Theatrical Dance since 1945. Members of the Deutsche Oper am Rhein, Düsseldorf, in Heinz Spoerli's third version (1994) of *A Midsummer Night's Dream*. (Photograph © by Felipe Alcoceba; used by permission.)

the company, to the exclusion of all others. The city also boasts the Tanztheater Schauspielhaus Leipzig, a small group of modern-oriented dancers attached to the playhouse. Under the energetic choreographic leadership of Irina Pauels, this troupe specializes in works of social criticism with strong dramatic content.

There are opera houses and municipal theaters in many other cities of the New Federal States that have ballet companies or dance theater companies attached to them. Theatrical dance is regularly presented in Schwerin, Rostock, Magdeburg, Cottbus, Gera, Weimar, Erfurt, Görlitz, Chemnitz, and elsewhere. Although an interesting program or some specially talented dancer may occasionally be discovered in these cities, little of their dance activities attracts, or merits, national attention.

In the Old Federal States, the former West Germany, the main ballet companies are attached to opera houses in major cities. They include the Hamburg Ballet (Ballett der Hamburgischen Staatsoper), directed by John Neumeier; the Düsseldorf-Duisburg Ballet (Ballett der Deutschen Oper am Rhein Düsseldorf-Duisburg), directed by Heinz Spoerli from 1990 to 1996 and now by Youri Vámos; the Frankfurt Ballet (Ballett der Städtischen Bühnen Frankfurt am Main), directed by William Forsythe; the Stuttgart Ballet (Ballett der Württembergischen Staatstheater Stuttgart), directed by Marcia Haydée from 1987 to 1996 and now by Reid Anderson; and the Munich State Opera Ballet, now called the Bavarian State Ballet (Bayerisches Staatsballett), directed by Konstanze Vernon, to be succeeded in 1998 by Ivan Liška. Munich has

another significant ballet company, the Ballett des Staatstheaters am Gärtnerplatz, attached to the city's second opera house, which specializes in *opéra comique*. Directed by Philip Taylor, this company also gives regular ballet performances.

Leading the *Tanztheater* companies are those at Wuppertal, directed by Pina Bausch, and Bremen, directed by Susanne Linke and Urs Dietrich. The dance theater at Bochum, where Reinhild Hoffmann worked for several seasons, was disbanded because of economic pressures. This threat has also affected several smaller companies, compelling them to reduce the number of dancers employed. The Cologne Dance Forum, for example, was formerly a constituent company of the state opera house, but since 1995 it has functioned as an independent troupe; it continues under the direction of Jochen Ulrich.

Other independent dance companies featuring repertories of contemporary works include the S.O.A.P. Dance Theater (Rui Horta) and the Pretty Ugly Dancecompany (Amanda Miller), both in Frankfurt; the Düsseldorf Neuer Tanz (Wanda Golonka and V. A. Woelfl); the Iwanson Dance Company of Munich (Jessica Iwanson); the Ismael Ivo Company of Stuttgart-Weimar; the Stuttgart ensemble TrANZFORM (Daniela Kurz); and the Folkwang Studio Essen (Lutz Förster). Companies with repertories falling somewhere between ballet and dance theater are attached to most municipal theaters in Germany. Among those attracting occasionally wider attention are in Brunswick (Pierre Wyss), Gelsenkirchen (Bernd Schindowski), Essen

(Martin Puttke), Bonn (Pavel Mikulastik), Saarbrücken (Birgit Scherzer), and Mannheim (Philippe Talard).

Although it must yield pride of place to music, theatrical dance is a highly valued performing art in Germany. Each year the German Association of Dance Pedagogues awards the German Dance Prize at a gala performance in Essen, honoring outstanding achievement in the field. Recent recipients have included Hans van Manen (1993), Maurice Béjart (1994), Pina Bausch (1995), Tom Schilling (1996), and Philipp Braunschweig (1997).

[*See also* Ausdruckstanz; Bavarian State Ballet; Berlin Opera Ballet; Hamburg Ballet; Stuttgart Ballet; *and the entries on major figures mentioned herein.*]

BIBLIOGRAPHY
Ballet in Berlin, 1945–1978. Berlin, 1978.
Becker, Ute. *Die Oper in Stuttgart: 75 Jahre Littmann-Bau.* Stuttgart, 1987.
Cranko, John. *Über den Tanz: Gespräche mit Erich Schäfer.* Frankfurt, 1974.
Cuson, Tom. "Finding Forms That Fit New Contents." *Tanz Aktuell* 5 (July–August 1990): 6–11.
Dauber, Angela, ed. *Marianne Kruuse.* Hamburg, 1986.
Derra de Moroda, Friderica, ed. *The Dance Library.* Munich, 1982.
Ehrlenbruch, Gerda. *Die freien Gruppen in der Tanzszene der Bundesrepublik.* Frankfurt am Main, 1991.
Enkelmann, Siegfried, et al. *Ballett in Deutschland.* 2 vols. Berlin, 1954, 1957.
Grund, Dominique. "Ballett: Klassischer Tanz und kulturelle Entwicklung in Deutschland." *Tanz Aktuell* 6 (May–June 1991): 6–13.
Jeschke, Claudia. "American Theatricality in Contemporary German Dancing." In *Proceedings of the Fifteenth Annual Conference, Society of Dance History Scholars, University of California, Riverside, 14–16 February 1992,* compiled by Christena L. Schlundt. Riverside, Calif., 1992.
Karina, Lillian, and Marion Kant. *Tanz unterm Hakenkreuz.* Berlin, 1996.
Kilian, Hannes, and Klaus Geitel. *John Cranko: Ballett für die Welt.* Sigmaringen, 1977.
Koegler, Horst. *Yvonne Georgi.* Velber bei Hannover, 1963.
Koegler, Horst. *Stuttgart Ballet.* London, 1978.
Koegler, Horst. "Three Hundred Legs and No Head." *Ballett International / Tanz Aktuell* (January 1994): 28–33.
Köllinger, Bernd. *Tanztheater: Tom Schilling und die zeitgenössische Choreographie.* Berlin, 1983.
Maack, Rudolf. *Tanz in Hamburg: Von Mary Wigman bis John Neumeier.* Hamburg, 1975.
Neumeier, John. *John Neumeier und das Hamburger Ballett.* Hamburg, 1977.
Neumeier, John. *Traumwege.* Hamburg, 1980.
Nevill, Timothy, trans. *Ballet and Dance in the Federal Republic of Germany.* Bonn, 1988.
Nietzschmann, Jürgen. "Ballet Island GDR: Dance Development and Its Characteristics in the Socialist System." *Ballett International* 13 (September 1990): 19–23.
Partsch-Bergsohn, Isa. *Modern Dance in Germany and the United States: Crosscurrents and Influences.* Chur, Switzerland, 1994.
Petermann, Kurt. *Tanzbibliographie: Verzeichnis der in deutscher Sprache veröffentlichten Schriften und Aufsätze zum Bühnen-, Gesellschafts-, Kinder-, Volks- und Turniertanz sowie zur Tanzwissenschaft, Tanzmusik und zum Jazz.* 4 vols. Leipzig, 1966–1982.
Regitz, Hartmut, ed. *Tanz in Deutschland: Ballett seit 1945.* Berlin, 1984.
Regitz, Hartmut. "Will Dance Become a Contemporary Art?" *Tanz Aktuell* 5 (July–August 1990): 12–17.
Scheper, Dirk, ed. *Gerhard Bohner: Tänzer und Choreograph.* Berlin, 1991.
Schmidt, Jochen, and Hans-Dieter Dyroff, eds. *Tanzkultur in der Bundesrepublik Deutschland.* Bonn, 1990.
Schmidt, Jochen. *Tanztheater in Deutschland.* Berlin, 1992.
Schumann, Gerhard. *Palucca: Porträt einer Künstlerin.* Berlin, 1972.
Stöckemann, Patricia, and Hedwig Müller. "Berlin, 1945–1949." *Tanzdrama Magazin* (June 1995): 9–23.
Tanzarchiv International 1 (February 1990): 16–26; 1 (March 1990): 22–30; 1 (June 1990): 24–25; 1 (October 1990): 20–27. Surveys of the dance scene in Cologne, Hamburg, Munich, and Aachen.
Vollmer, Horst. "Racist Murders and Artistic Normalcy." *Ballett International* 16 (February 1993): 26–27.
Vollmer, Horst. "New Beginning in the Midst of Change." *Ballett International / Tanz Aktuell* 12 (December 1994): 34–39.
Winkler-Betzendahl, Madeline, and Horst Koegler. *Ballett in Stuttgart: Werkstattgespräch mit John Cranko.* Stuttgart, 1964.

ARCHIVES. The Deutsches Tanzarchiv in Cologne is Germany's biggest collection of materials relating to dance. It includes books, magazines, photographs, programs, posters, newspaper cuttings, films, and videotapes as well as memorabilia from the estates of many people from the dance world.

HORST KOEGLER

Dance Education

Until the eighteenth century, court dance was taught to German nobility at the courts and schools, chiefly by French dance teachers, while guild members taught German traditional dances to their peers. With the rise of the middle class in the cities, the dance culture of the nobility spread there, propagated by German dance teachers trained in Paris. A German dance literature based on the Paris Académie also developed, beginning with a French court dance teacher in Eisenach, Louis Bonin, who later taught dance at the university in Jena; he was the author of *Der Neueste Art der galanten und theateralischen Tanzkunst* (1711–1712). Teachers at other universities followed, such as Gottfried Taubert, whose *Rechtschaffener Tantzmeister* (Leipzig, 1717) was the starting point for the further development of schools and dance literature.

Court dance teachers, university dance teachers, and court opera ballet masters (positions often held by the same person) taught the nobility, students, the middle class, and the court opera's corps de ballet; this last consisted of pupils, actors, and soloists, many of whom were trained outside Germany. Their successors were recruited from the court opera schools but seldom rose above the status of actors, occupying the lowest social and artistic position in the theater. Dancers retained this inferior status in Germany until as late as the 1940s. No famous dancing master had emerged in the German states to create a permanent ballet school or ballet tradition or to raise the general status of dance. The various German courts sponsored operas that rarely toured and depended on a generosity often diminished by expensive wars.

Training in "high dance," was a social requirement for the nobility, along with riding and fencing. Until World War II, every serious ballet school taught this style, along with etiquette. Licensed social dance teachers had a more thorough knowledge of theory and practice than any ballet school graduate. High dance was part of a system of German liberal education advocated by Wilhelm von Humboldt, the early nineteenth-century scholar and statesman. In schools, the influence of the reforms instituted by the educator and social reformer Johann Heinrich Pestalozzi (1746–1827) survived until recently. Pestalozzi was the originator of the teacher training schools, which sought to harmonize the powers of the intellect, the emotions, and the body. Along with Pestalozzi, the popular educator Friedrich Fröbel, who studied early childhood education, founded kindergartens that also combined social training with dance. The general population of the late eighteenth and early nineteenth centuries was still taught dancing by obscure traveling teachers, while craftsmen, farmers, and musicians preserved the traditions of folk dances and festivals.

The status of high dance and ballet is best described in an 1843 survey by Franz Anton Roller, bearing the impressive title (in translation) of "Systematic manual for the educational art of dance and physical training from birth to full growth of the human being—prepared for the educated public, for instruction in physical education, and as instruction for those who wish to become practicing artists and effective teachers in this art." It was published in Weimar, in connection with the tricentennial of the Royal Prussian State School in Pforta. Roller was a theatrical dancer and, after 1805, a teacher of educational dance and gymnastics. The twenty-eight chapters of Roller's manual describe human development from early childhood to the polished young dancer, interspersed with observations on dance education from its basic stages to advanced French dance techniques. Roller's efforts "to support Nature in her work intelligently and as well as possible" are reminiscent of Jean-Jacques Rousseau's theories. After he left the stage, Roller learned dance theory and found fault with the exclusively practical instruction given to ballet students. "Artists and teachers are two different kinds of persons," who must be united, he protested. He also complained of the ignorance of traveling dance masters.

Friedrich Albert Zorn's profound work *Grammatik der Tanzkunst* was published in Leipzig in 1887. Zorn had been a dance teacher at the Imperial Russian Richelieu Gymnasium in Odessa since 1846, and his book, a thorough study of all dance genres of the day, was approved and accepted by the Academy of Dance Teaching, the association of dance teachers. The product of extensive travel and studies of European dance literature, as well as correspondence with choreographers Paul Taglioni and Arthur Saint-Léon, this book was for several decades the basis of dance teaching in Germany. Zorn recognized the need for dance notation and, following Saint-Léon, he de-

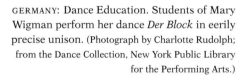

GERMANY: Dance Education. Students of Mary Wigman perform her dance *Der Block* in eerily precise unison. (Photograph by Charlotte Rudolph; from the Dance Collection, New York Public Library for the Performing Arts.)

veloped the *Strichmänchen* ("stick figure") system and added it to his work. His call for a large association of "solid" dance teachers was aimed at forming additional cultural institutions and against mercenary instructors who could impart neither artistry nor physical skill.

During the period between the two world wars, the theaters once patronized by the nobility were transformed into state and municipal theaters. Ballet was only slightly affected by the development of *Ausdruckstanz* (expressive dance) in the 1920s and 1930s. Under Adolf Hitler (1933–1945), the dance publicist and critic Fritz Böhme was given a free hand to establish the German Master Workshops for Dance in Berlin, but the Nazi regime undermined the creative development of this school, partly by the removal of people legislated as "undesirable elements." The school and the dance library created by Böhme were destroyed during the war, although the library was reestablished in 1950. The resulting vacuum, and certain divisions between ballet and modern dance, dance and training, and dance and the state, as well as a postwar era of Cold War conflict, hindered the creation of a national ballet school and a national ballet.

The concept of a comprehensive dance education changed dramatically at four junctures: (1) in the mid-nineteenth century, when François Delsarte presented a new analysis of the body gestures and language of actors; (2) about 1900, when Isadora Duncan's Berlin School (directed chiefly by Elizabeth Duncan) was established; (3) in 1911 when Émile Jaques-Dalcroze established a sanctuary for his rhythmic gymnastics; and (4) when Rudolf Laban gathered a creative community around him at Monte Verità. These were all starting points for central European dance movements that gave rise to countless new movements and an explosion of schools in Germany. In all the major cities there were Wigman, Palucca, Laban, and other schools representing the rhythmic, gymnastic, and improvisational methods in many variations. This development was reflected in sports institutes, public schools, and ballet schools, and also in some opera ballet ensembles that tended toward modernism.

Professional instruction is now divided more or less evenly between classical dance on one hand and folklore and modern dance on the other with theoretical subjects such as music and dance history. General dance education ends at the age of fifteen or sixteen; after that, training becomes more specialized. Commonly taught are Russian, English, American, and French techniques, and methods drawn from Vaganova in varying degrees. *Ausdruckstanz*, which has been influenced by American modern dance, particularly the Martha Graham technique, has been supplemented by jazz dance.

The physical education institutes teach the basics of modern dance, creative expression and international folklore. Before unification, in East Germany, the People's Theater organizations had their folklore groups, and regional labor associations trained social workers, public school teachers, and freelance group directors in every kind of dance felt to be of educational value—even meditation and dance therapy. Classical dance, however, remained the province of ballet schools.

Despite this abundance of dance techniques and an astonishing increase in the number of schools and students, there is still ample room for growth in dance education. Students have limited choices, teacher training is minimal, and artistic and intellectual subjects are neglected in favor of technical mastery. The qualifications of teachers and choreographers are hard to ascertain as schools multiply, and competent instruction is not easily available to the general public. The isolation of students in professional dance training from social and political life can result in frustration as they try to make the transition to professional careers. Essentially, the problems of the dance school have changed little since 1800. Since demand for the literature is rare, dance notation is an individual hobby.

A decline of dance has been bemoaned in every age, but individual teachers always succeed in creating excitement and in disseminating knowledge. Despite its limitations, the work of the German ballet school is beginning to hold its own against the traditional schools of other countries. Practical training is on its way to becoming universal; consistency in training should follow.

BIBLIOGRAPHY. There is no comprehensive history of dance education in Germany in the sense of a history of pedagogy. The entire German-speaking world, including Switzerland and Austria, and its sphere of influence (i.e., Poland, Czechoslovakia, Hungary, Holland, and Belgium) would have to be included in such a history.

Internationally known German histories include Albert Czerwinski, *Geschichte der Tanzkunst* (Leipzig, 1862); Rudolph Voss, *Der Tanz und seine Geschichte* (Berlin, 1869); Franz M. Böhme, *Geschichte des Tanzes in Deutschland*, 2 vols. (Leipzig, 1886); Karl Storck, *Der Tanz* (Bielefeld, 1903); Oskar Bie, *Der Tanz* (Berlin, 1905); Max von Boehn, *Der Tanz* (Berlin, 1925); John Schikowski, *Geschichte des Tanzes* (Berlin, 1926); Helmut Günther and Helmut Schäfer, *Vom Schamanentanz zur Rumba* (Stuttgart, 1959); and Joseph Gregor, *Kulturgeschichte des Balletts* (Vienna, 1944). These volumes provide historical information, dances, and steps, but not pedagogical evaluations; this is also true of most teaching manuals. A number of monographs and biographies would have to be assembled before a complete picture of pedagogy in dance could be drawn.

KURT PETERS

Dance Research and Publication

The history of dance writing and publication in Germany is the history of individual approaches to special subjects and the methods used therein. Until the turn of the twentieth century, dance was studied only in conjunction with art history, philosophy, education, drama, and musicology. During the course of the twentieth century, however, various developments led dance research out of its traditional obscurity toward its acceptance as a scholarly and academic discipline. This emancipatory process unfolded in several phases: the years before World War I, the period between the two world wars, in postwar Germany, and since reunification.

Before World War I. At the turn of the twentieth century, writers still thought of dance—that is, ballet—as an integral part of fine arts and/or education, but the first performances of Isadora Duncan and, later, of Diaghilev's Ballets Russes broadened their view. Discussing the validity of old and new dance forms, these writers focused for the first time on dance *per se,* for example, the aesthetics of dance style. This approach stimulated the production of a number of dance histories, among them works by cultural historian Max von Böhn and art historian Oscar Bie.

The 1920s and 1930s. The writers of German dance literature changed with the introduction of early expressive dance, called *Ausdruckstanz;* here, the dancer *(not the observer)* spoke and wrote. The personality, thoughts, and feelings of the individual dancer, that is, the dancer's particular nature, became the starting point for dance creation as well as for writing about it. Rudolf Laban and Mary Wigman, however, went a conceptual step further, transforming their individual views into universal dance philosophies and founding schools.

Laban's *Die Welt des Tänzers* (The World of the Dancer, 1920) elaborates on the metaphysics of modern dance; his *Choreographie* (1926) is not only the first educational manual of so-called natural dancing, it is also the first documentation of the author's innovative method of dance notation. Whereas Laban's writings combined the practical side of movement and its theoretical and historical foundations, Wigman's many articles concentrated on her cosmological philosophy of dance. A collection of her early writings, *Die Sprache des Tanzes* (The Language of Dance), was published in 1963.

In addition to the wide range of publications written by dancers, writers from various related disciplines, such as art, theater, and education, supported and broadened the theory of *Ausdruckstanz* and thereby established a critical dialogue between themselves, the theorists, and the practitioners. For example, dramatist and critic Hans Brandenburg published *Der moderne Tanz* (The Modern Dance) in 1912. Dance and music critic Fritz Böhme not only authored several books, among them *Der Tanz der Zukunft* (The Dance of the Future, 1926), he also edited, between 1927 and 1933, with Joseph Lewitan, the most important German dance periodical of the interwar period, *Der Tanz* (The Dance). Musician and music critic Alfred Schlee was instrumental in the publication of *Schrifttanz,* Laban's dance newsletter, which appeared between 1928 and 1931. Curt Sachs's *Eine Weltgeschichte des Tanzes* was published in Berlin in 1933 and soon was translated into several other languages; the English version, *World History of the Dance,* was published in 1937 and the work is still considered the standard of its kind. Three dance conferences held between 1927 and 1930 were devoted to theoretical discussions of the social and aesthetic issues facing contemporary dance in Germany. As subsequently documented in books and articles, the discussion of these issues shows the insidious political affiliation of German dancers with the national-socialist (Nazi) ideology as well as its influence on dance.

After World War II. Intended or not, the embarrassing connection between *Ausdruckstanz* and the Nazis led, after World War II, to a renaissance of the ballet and a concomitant suppression of the innovative trends of the prewar period; the formal classical style again dominated the dance scene as well as the field of dance writing and publication in what had become a divided Germany.

A few books on ballet were published in West Germany; among them were Max Niehaus's semiacademic *Ballett* in 1954 and, in 1962, *Ballett-Gestalt und Wesen* (Ballet-Gestalt and Essence), a scholarly interpretation of ballet aesthetics by Gerhard Zacharias, following Carl Jung's psychoanalytical approach. In the area of period dance reconstruction, Karl Heinz Taubert worked on both the theory and practice of social and court dances. He also taught these subjects and in 1968 published *Höfische Tänze: Ihre Geschichte und Choreographie* (Court Dances: Their History and Choreography). East German publications, meanwhile, tried to rewrite the history and appearance of the "capitalist" art form of dance, in conformity with the premises of socialist ideology.

Dance writing and publication in both Germanys in the 1950s and 1960s was a conservative endeavor, reflecting what were considered to be the cultural values of the past, excluding the Third Reich. Archives were founded in the West and the East, by critic and former dancer Kurt Peters in Cologne (West) in 1948 and by musicologist Kurt Petermann in Leipzig (East) in 1957. Both institutes are still active. In 1985 the Cologne archive was sold to the city and Frank-Manuel Peter became its curator. After Petermann's death in 1984 the Leipzig archive operated in various organizational states; since 1993 it has become an independent institution, collaborating with Leipzig University as well as with the Academy of Music and Theater. Petermann's chief interest had been the collection of folk dances; in addition he compiled a comprehensive bibliography of all facets of dance, published as *Tanzbibliographie* (Bibliography of Dance; 1966–1987). Petermann also initiated the publication of *Documenta Choreologica,* a series of annotated reprints of dance theory and educational German texts. Peters's orientation was theatrical dance. He collected prewar and contemporary dance material and, in 1953, founded the first German postwar dance periodical, *Das Tanzarchiv.* Peters also established the documentary approach to dance criticism, which was typical for the post–World War II period.

From 1980 on *Das Tanzarchiv* collaborated with *Ballett Journal,* edited by Eberhard Gockel and Ulrich Steiner, to feature articles on dance history and dance education. Another significant periodical in West Germany was *Ballett;* published between 1965 and 1987, this yearbook, edited first by the influental dance critic Horst Koegler and later by Hartmut Regitz, included articles on special subjects, reviews, and a chronology of dance performances in subsidized state theaters. From 1958 until reunification *Der Tanz* was the only periodical published in East Germany that focused on amateur dance.

A major sociocultural change took place in West Germany in the 1970s, while the political situation in East Germany kept it culturally immobile. Along with the social reforms instituted in response to the student revolts of 1968, the body itself came to be viewed as a major political entity, and this resulted in structural changes in the world of dance. Free dance groups were established alongside the permanent companies working at the theaters, and a new dance genre, the Tanztheater, emerged. The new emphasis on the body also stirred and broadened interest in dance, and in the course of dance becoming accepted and—finally—popular, more periodicals were founded in West Germany. Their critical approach attempted to locate German dance events in international as well as interdisciplinary contexts.

The bilingual *Ballett International,* which integrated *Ballett Info* (1978–1981) and was edited by Rolf Garske between 1982 and 1993, included actual reviews as well as historical and cultural surveys. *Tanz Aktuell,* founded by Johannes Odenthal in 1986, explored dance primarily in the context of body experience and art; in 1994 it merged with *Ballett International* with Odenthal as editor in chief. *Tanzdrama,* in contrast, searches for the roots of national dance. Published by the Mary Wigman Society and edited by Hedwig Müller, the periodical was started in 1987–1988 and features historical articles that deal primarily with expressive, modern dance forms.

As mentioned earlier, the expanding range of periodicals and their particular emphases produced a new, broader understanding of dance. In the field of academic writing and publication, however, dance scholars needed time to study the structural changes taking place in dance as well as the development of Tanztheater and its possible influence on new dance forms (and vice versa); thus Tanztheater became the topic of interest during the 1980s in both Germanys, whereas new dance forms became the focal point in the 1990s.

West German dance authors concentrated on Tanztheater's search for the individual expression of personal experience. In so doing they discovered the genre's relationship to *Ausdruckstanz,* which they came to see as the lost history of their parents' generation of dance, and their writings on Tanztheater therefore assumed a strong interest in dance history. A number of biographies of the protagonists of *Ausdruckstanz* and Tanztheater—Pina Bausch, Anita Berber, Gerhard Bohner, Valeska Gert, Dore Hoyer, Kurt Jooss, Mary Wigman—reflected this emphasis, as did publications charting the development and characteristics of Tanztheater, among them *TanzTheater* (1987) by theater and dance historian Susanne Schlicher and *Tanztheater in Deutschland* (1992) by critic Jochen Schmidt.

The theoretical treatment of Tanztheater was a major concern of East German authors as well, though they interpreted the term in an exclusively dramaturgical, narrative sense, according to their continuing political situation, namely, as a highly complex interplay between sociopsychologically based realistic theater theory and its effect on dance. (See, for example, Bernd Köllinger's *Tanztheater* [1983].) Other East German publications were oriented to education and compared issues related to what was called modern dance with those associated with traditional dance, that is, ballet. Discourse on modern dance dealt mainly with the pre–World War II creative development of dancer-theorists now seen as politically acceptable representatives of German dance. The achievements of Rudolf Laban and Mary Wigman, for example, became the subject of various conferences held in the East—and, interestingly enough, in the West. The complexity of the *Ausdruckstanz* movement was rediscovered in 1986, during the first scholarly dance symposium held in Bayreuth, West Germany, and this discovery resulted in a series of conferences organized by the then emerging societies concerned with dance, such as the Mary Wigman Society, founded in 1986, and the German Society for Dance Research, founded in 1987.

Since Reunification. The 1990s were characterized by two trends. The search for roots continued (see *Mary Wigman in Leipzig,* edited by Angela Rannow and Ralf Stabel, 1994), but in addition, new interdisciplinary approaches unbounded by the subjective limitations of the periodicals began to extend the borders of dance beyond those that had confined it to the fine arts. Other scholarly disciplines, such as history and sociology, and new critical methods, such as structuralism, started to interpret dance as cultural practice or as an independently structured work of its own; see, for example, Rudolf Braun and David Guggerli's *Macht des Tanzes—Tanz der Mächtigen* (The Power of Dance—Dance of the Powerful; 1993), Gabriele Klein's *FrauenKörperTanz* (Women Body Dance; 1992), and Gaby von Rauner's *William Forsythe—Tanz und Sprache* (—Dance and Language; 1993).

As physical and psychological therapy and sports increasingly used the dance experience as a tool of expression as well as a medium for nonverbal communication, the number of publications in this field grew. Examples of this trend include *Tanztherapie: Theorie und Praxis* (Dance Therapy: Theory and Practice), edited by Elke Willke (1991), and the annual *Tanzforschung* (Dance Research), edited since 1990 by Michael Klein. This multidisciplinary research documents the extent to which the subject of dance has developed from an aspect or ingredient of other disciplines into a self-contained discipline able to contribute independently to scholarly discussion.

BIBLIOGRAPHY

Bie, Oskar. *Der Tanz.* Berlin, 1900.

Bohner, Gerhard. *Tänzer und Choreograph.* Berlin, 1991.

Bremer Tanztheater Reinhild Hoffmann, 1978–1986. Bremen, 1986.

Feister, Karen. "Beitrag zur Grundlegung einer Berlinischen Dramaturgie des Tanztheaters auf der Basis der Tanztheater-Arbeit an der Komischen Oper Berlin im Zeitraum 1975–82." Ph.D. diss., Universität Berlin, 1983.

Fischer, Lothar. *Anita Berber: Tanz zwischen Rausch und Tod, 1918–1928 in Berlin.* Berlin, 1984.

Kant, Marion. "Romantisches Ballett: Eine Auskunft zur Frauenfrage." Ph.D. diss., Universität Berlin, 1983.

Markard, Anna, and Hermann Markard. *Jooss.* Cologne, 1985.

Müller, Hedwig. *Mary Wigman.* Berlin, 1986.

Müller, Hedwig, et al. *Dore Hoyer: Tänzerin.* Cologne, 1992.

Müller, Hedwig, and Patricia Stöckemann. ". . . jeder Mensch ist ein Tänzer": Ausdruckstanz in Deutschland zwischen 1900 und 1945. Giessen, 1993.

Oberzaucher-Schüller, Gunhild. *Ausdruckstanz: Eine mitteleuropäische Bewegung in der ersten Hälfte des 20. Jahrhunderts.* Wilhelmshaven, 1992.

Peter, Frank-Manuel. *Valeska Gert: Tänzerin, Schauspielerin, Kabarettistin.* Berlin, 1985.

Regitz, Hartmut, ed. *Tanz in Deutschland: Ballett seit 1945.* Berlin, 1984.

Servos, Norbert, and Gert Weigelt. *Pina Bausch Wuppertal Dance Theater, or, The Art of Training a Goldfish: Excursions into Dance.* Cologne, 1984.

Tanztheater International: Akademie-Gespräche 1987 mit Antonio Gades, Maurice Bejart, Pina Bausch, John Neumeier und Patricio Bunster. Berlin, 1988.

CLAUDIA JESCHKE

GERT, VALESKA (born 11 January 1892 in Berlin, died March 1978 in Kampen, Sylt, Germany), German dancer. As a solo dancer, Gert was the embodiment of the Roaring Twenties and the most famous and most impassioned opponent of the German interpretive or expressionist school and its introspective style. A member of no particular school and with no formal dance training, Gert developed a unique style of pantomime grotesque dance. Artistically and personally she was the diametric opposite and antagonist of Mary Wigman, but she was no less prominent.

Prior to World War I Gert worked as an actress with Max Reinhardt, and subsequently with expressionist artists as well as with Bertolt Brecht and Fritz Kortner. In 1918 she began appearing in solo dance evenings. Her costumes were colorful and flashy and her pantomimes as graphically striking as expressionist paintings; her movements had undertones of aggression, wildness, and shamelessness. On stage, she became ecstatic when the audience screamed and howled at her dancing. Her art was one of merciless attack; it had nothing of the softness and meditative approach of interpretive dance.

Gert's life, like her dancing, was frenetic, fueled by the joy of life, noise, and feeling. She was allied with the artistic movements of expressionism and Dadaism, and the middle class was her favorite target. With vicious sarcasm she satirized the moral ideas and behavior of the supposedly decent citizenry, portraying figures from the underside of bourgeois life—prostitutes, pimps, and gamblers. Her sketches were mostly scenes from daily life. In such studies as *Die Canaille*, one of her most famous dances, she uncompromisingly depicted the joys and sorrows of a prostitute. Her dances bore such titles as *Der Tod, Circus, Kinowochenschau, Pferderennen,* and *Laster.*

Gert toured other countries and was particularly successful in the Soviet Union. In Berlin she appeared in revues and at her own cabaret, the Kohlkopp. Her productions included Oscar Wilde's *Salomé,* which she produced as a grotesque movement piece. She also worked as a movie actress, appearing in *Die freudlose Gasse* with Greta Garbo (1925), Jean Renoir's *Nana* (1926), *Tagebuch einer Verlorenen* with Louise Brooks (1929), and G. W. Pabst's *Die Dreigroschenoper* (1931). During the 1920s her dance evenings were a meetingplace for the intellectual avant-garde of Berlin.

After the Nazi ascendance in 1933, however, Gert could appear safely only outside Germany. She became a British subject and lived temporarily in London, but she was drawn back to Berlin until the growing antisemitism made life there impossible for her. In 1938 she immigrated to the United States. She worked in New York and Provincetown, Massachusetts, and eventually opened a New York nightclub-cabaret called the Beggar's Bar, which became a famous artists' hangout. Tennessee Williams was her protégé.

In 1949 Gert returned to Germany via Switzerland. In Berlin she founded the Hexenküche Cabaret and resumed her pantomimes and cabaret sketches of social criticism, but she was unable to pick up the thread of her earlier fame: German audiences had forgotten her. In 1950 she moved to Kampen, a town on the island of Sylt, off the western coast of Schleswig-Holstein, and opened the Ziegenstall. She appeared there in her pantomimes and occasionally did film work, appearing in Federico Fellini's *Juliet of the Spirits* (1965). She spent the rest of her life in Kampen, where she was an eccentric cult figure in a small intellectual and artistic circle.

BIBLIOGRAPHY

Gert, Valeska. *Mein Weg.* Leipzig, 1931.

Gert, Valeska. *Die Bettlerbar von New York.* Berlin, 1950.

Gert, Valeska. *Ich bin eine Hexe.* Munich, 1968.

Gert, Valeska. *Katze von Kampen.* Percha, 1973.

Gert, Valeska. "Mary Wigman and Valeska Gert" (1926). *Tanzdrama* 19 (1992): 20–23.

Hoffmann, Christine. "Deutschsprachige Ausdruckstänzerinnen und ihre Emigration." *Tanzforschung Jahrbuch* 4 (1993): 43–59.

Keersmaeker, Anne Teresa de. "Valeska Gert." *Drama Review* 25 (Fall 1981): 55–66.

Peter, Frank-Manuel. *Valeska Gert: Tänzerin, Schauspielerin, Kabarettistin.* Berlin, 1987.

HEDWIG MÜLLER
Translated from German

GHANA. [*To survey dance traditions in Ghana, this entry comprises two articles. The first article provides an overview of ceremonial and recreational dance; the second is a brief history of scholarship and writing.*]

An Overview

Ghana is a small country on West Africa's coast whose several ethnic groups live both within and beyond its borders to the north, east, and west. The country, which is divided into ten regions, consequently has historical, linguistic, religious, and cultural ties to societies beyond its national frontiers. About three million of Ghana's people live in the Northern and Upper Regions (part of the West African savanna belt), sharing cultural affinities with the Sudanese cultural sphere; while Ghana's rain-forest belt and the coastal plain together have a population of approximately ten million. Arab Muslim cultural influences are apparent in the Northern Region in the drums and other musical instruments, praise chanting style, and religious celebrations, which syncretize traditional indigenous practices with those of Islam. One example is the Damba Festival in the northern regions, in which the chief receives pledges of loyalty and adulation from his subjects and, after leaping over a live cow, performs the stately *damba* dance of twirls and calculated half turns in his richly decorated regal tunic, which flares out in a radiance of whirling colors. Christian influences, dating from the colonial era, are evident in the Central Region, coastal areas, and in the Asante (Ashanti) Region.

There are many occasions within the life cycle of Ghana's traditional societies in which dance serves as an art form; it is also used as a language to express thoughts, emotions, spirit-quality and aspirations as significant milestones in the course of the cycle. There are dances for the installation of chiefs and priests. Ghanaians dance to express their joy and grief, love and hatred; they dance to bring prosperity and to shun calamity or tragedy; they dance their religion; they dance to pass the time. These dances can be classified into two main categories, ceremonial and recreational. Social needs and interrelated functions, however, tend to produce some degree of overlap in the use of particular dances.

Ceremonial Dances. Ghanaian ceremonial dances occur as part of the rites of passage that mark important milestones within the life span of each individual and ethnic community, such as births, initiation or puberty rites, hunting, fishing, sowing and harvesting, thanksgiving, funerals for human beings and dangerous wild beasts, and the accidental killing of a totemic animal related to a clan.

Ghana's court dances serve several functions within each ethnic community. Many of these dances have developed because each local traditional dignitary is recognized as the patron of a given ethnic group and the titular custodian of their music and dance heritage. Rulers maintain official drum and dance ensembles, which are diligently rehearsed to meet the heavy requirements of the court. Ordinary citizens may dance to the court drums if they comply with the traditional courtesies that must be shown to the drums, the drummers, the royal persons present, the rite, and the occasion. In Akan society, this involves baring the shoulders, bowing, and dancing barefooted as a sign of respect, and using only those gestures that are appropriate to one's station and office. In Akan cultural areas, some of the dances deal with the chief not only as a political and military leader, but also as a high priest and spiritual link with ancestors through whom prayers are directed to God. However, Akan people insist that this is not "ancestor worship." Praise singing with *dondo* (hourglass drum) accompaniment recounts the achievements and valor of the chief's predecessors, which he is assumed to have inherited. The *kete* court dance uses gestures to symbolize and enhance the dignity and achievements of the king's office and to inspire the loyalty of the courtiers. The Asantehene's *kete* is special; the accompanying music of flute and voice recounts the tragedies and triumphs of the king and his people and their will to succeed. The ceremony is a regal masque, a historical pageant that dramatizes the king's leadership role.

Before the chief of Sandema (Sandemanaaba) his marksmen and bodyguards don their ceremonial warriors' costumes, which are camouflaged to merge with the savanna environment. Their vests are encrusted with talismans on the chest and back, and they are armed with bows, arrows, and light wooden hoe (adze) handles with stepped harpoon tips. They perform the *lelik* warrior dances for the chief to assure him of their readiness to follow him into battle to terrify and destroy his foes and win victory.

In contrast, the Akan warrior dances solo to the *fontomfrom* drums to offer the same message. Another example exists in the Ashanti Region, where a special group has its own saber-rattling dance, which it performs with the Asantehene to remind citizens that its members are the *abrafɔɔ*, law-enforcement officers and executioners. The variegated and broken stacatto rhythms and the chattering dialogue of the *aperede* drum ensemble, the booming sound of the main drum, and changes of tempo facilitate captivating dance movements.

On some occasions, the chief sends his drummers and musicians on royal missions to perform at funerals. Royal ambassadors are dispatched with appropriate drummers and dancers to indicate the king's intentions should his demands not be met; for such a mission, he sends *fontom-from* performers to scare his hosts with the menacing, challenging sounds and matching vigorous and aggressive movements and gestures of this drum-and-dance ensemble. The chief can also select a particular drum ensemble for team or open massed dancing during a festive or formal occasion. In addition, youths often entertain the chief as an indication of their loyalty. Although the chief dances with them, he has to be supported, because of the heavy burden of gold jewelry and talismans he wears. He is guided by his courtiers to make his movements appear majestic.

Festivals in Ghana serve many social needs. Each commemorates the past and serves as a strong bond between the living and the dead; it creates an atmosphere of spiritual communication through a chief, priest, or the head of a clan or family. This spiritual channel leads to the source of life, the creator, who is also the giver of the good things of life.

A festival, like the Adɛɛ festival of the Asante, may last a day, or even longer for a Grand Adɛɛ (Adɛɛ Kɛseɛ). The Golgo festival, for example, lasts ten days, with specific dramatic dance activities for each day. At midnight, on day one, the eerie and moanful sounds of distant flute music can be heard, and the paths to the scattered villages are closed. The Tendama (priest-chiefs) perform a circular ritual dance on a distant flat hilltop in the moonlight, moving counterclockwise; periodically, they halt and take hoeing postures to mime harvesting, weeding, and replanting. This is followed by a quick step backward and a sudden leap upward, with arms stretched taut toward the heavens; the previous movements are then repeated. Meanwhile, a male chorus alternately performs heavy rhythmic progressive jingling stamps with lusty chanting. The members wear costumes of a bygone age, a loincloth and a large high domed turban. Each warrior carries quiver of arrows on his back, along with a deerskin; the left hand holds a shield and the right a long sword. A soloist chants a taunting and provocative song, and the others respond with a deep grunt, followed by a choral refrain made effective by the sound of the boat-shaped jingles tied to their right legs. The dancers manipulate their swords in coordination with different steps and body positions. The stamping develops into syncopated gesture steps that vary the jingling sounds and the heavy stamps

in counter-rhythmic patterns. While the men dance in serpentine formation (because the dance arena is strewn with great boulders and huts), the Tendama march, twist, and wave their staffs of office from side to side to ward off evil spirits.

Far to the south, a similar festival, a harvest thanksgiving of the Ga-Labadi people, is performed with similar provocative songs, taunts, and foot-stamping; here, however, the dancers' fists are thrust upward. Invariably, communal dancing highlights the end of festivals in atoll regions. Similarities exist among the various cultural groups in their acts of worship, although Christian missionaries until recently banned converts from all activities connected with dancing.

The traditional priest or priestess does not choose to be one but is driven by a spiritual agent that cannot be resisted. On the prescribed day of worship, attendants summon the spirits of the shrine to come and enter the body of the priest, who then falls into a trance. The priest performs as a physical and spiritual healer in a room with a shrine. Outside, a female chorus informs the spirit that they are assembled to honor it and invites the priest to come forth, which he or she does after the healing

GHANA. A dancer from the University of Ghana ensemble in the early 1960s, performing an action designed to make his costume flare in *damba* or *takai*. (Photograph by Willis E. Bell; reprinted from Opoku, 1965.)

GHANA. Men and women from the University of Ghana ensemble perform a *yeve* dance. The *yeve* is a secret society, which has a private, ceremonial language understood only by members. *Yeve* dances typically follow initiation rites. (Photograph by Willis E. Bell; reprinted from Opoku, 1965.)

process. The arena is first cleared of evil spirits by sprinkling white powder. The first spinning dance—the whirlwind of power—is followed by *adaban,* which establishes an impenetrable enclosure for a series of character dances that portray the attributes of the particular spirit possessing the priest. Through intensive training and practice, the priests are able to project appropriate visual characterizations of the supernatural beings. The priest or priestess is the medium who communicates with the spirit world on behalf of the living. The dance of the priests is one of triumph over evil and the joy of knowing that people are not alone in life on earth.

Among the Akan and the Adangbe, similar celebrations end the puberty rites of instruction. As J. H. Kwabena Nketia has written,

> Musical processions to ritual places, feasts in the home, singing and dancing parties . . . mark the end of the training, at which time each girl is richly adorned with precious beads, gold ornaments and ankle buzzers for display and dancing in the market place. For several days the girls go round the town performing the *dipo* dances, and collecting money from those who watch them. (Nketia, 1963)

In all of Ghana's regions, some of the most expressive dances are connected with dramatic and emotional funerals for ordinary citizens, members of guilds or social groups, or chiefs. The Akan *abofoo* (hunter's dance) may be performed in honor of a great hunter at his funeral; his sons may reenact in dramatic dance-mime the most notable hunting adventure of the deceased. Similarly, after killing a *sasaboa* (a beast embodying a demonic spirit) a hunter leaves it in the forest and rushes to his village, wailing and singing dirges for the dead beast. Fellow hunters accompany him to the site to cut up the animal and carry the meat to the village. A grand funeral is subsequently performed to appease the beast's spirit as the hunter re-creates the events leading to the kill. Funerals of occupational or paramilitary groups or associations may lack the pomp and majesty of royal funerals but are rich in dramatic and emotional dance expression. The dances of hunters' guilds, which are performed both at funerals and to honor living master hunters, are mimed stories performed to special drum music; they use weapons, animal skins, skulls, and horns as props, and other hunters dance to represent prey.

Recreational Dances. As in other African countries, recreational dancing in Ghana includes community storytelling, which combines imaginative narration with singing, clapping, drumming, and a highly developed style of miming and dancing. A distinctive characteristic of this form of storytelling is the interruption of the narrative by conventional formulas; a scene from a completely different story may also be acted out with interaction between the actor-dancers and the singing and dancing chorus. Numerous organizations vie with one another to create new forms of drum music with related melodies, texts, and complementary dances to satisfy the social demand for entertainment and interaction between old and young, male and female.

Dance clubs are generally patterned after ethnic sociopolitical organizations, with offices and responsibilities comparable to those of the chief or queen mother. Each club has the head of the community as its chief patron and performs at the palace on ceremonial occasions. A club may entertain publicly or be available for hire. The dancers use the movement forms and dynamic preferences of their representative traditional groups, which allows members of the same ethnic group to participate readily in the creation of new dances. Existing dance formations or combinations of one or two given social units may be used in a new dance, which can induce other youths to adopt it and add their own variations. Public competitions are held. Sometimes a new dance takes hold among several ethnic groups to link whole communities together. One such dance is the *konkoma,* a recreational youth dance which grew from a simple crossing sidestep with a dramatic dead stop into a suite of related slow fast steps, body swings, and pelvic rotations with various rhythms and tempos.

Characteristically, Ewe ethnic groups form dance clubs when they move away from their homelands; thus migrants from Ghana's northern upland regions congregate in villages and towns at the Zongo enclaves far from home to maintain ethnic solidarity. In contrast, the Akan rarely practice their dances beyond their traditional boundaries. Christians were for a long time forbidden to dance upon threat of expulsion from their church. Today, however, with better understanding of the purpose of dance, drumming and dancing have become part of the Christian service. Whole Masses are said with drumming and dancing by Bishop Sarpong at the Kumase Catholic Church.

At the Kumasi Cultural Centre, a unique dance club known as Agoromma was formed with the aim of having traditional dancers share their knowledge of festival and funeral dances with Western-educated Africans, lecturers, and others who have no traditional dance training. Agoromma's inclusion and performance of dances from other ethnic groups has become a model for district, regional, and national clubs.

Kwame Nkrumah, Ghana's first president (1960–1966), discovered the appeal of drumming and dancing to Ghana's multicultural population. He saw in the dance, not only a general communicative device but also a means of creating mutual understanding among Ghana's various ethnic groups as well as creating a path toward one distinctive national identity. The opening of Ghana's parliament includes a traditional ceremony comparable to those used on the most important regal occasions.

The task of implementing Nkrumah's idea was entrusted to Albert Opoku. It was decided to base the National Dance Company in an institution of higher learning. This was because a sound knowledge of traditional music and dance is traditionally expected from educated persons, and is a required qualification for chieftaincy. Aided by the experience and scholarship of such people as Philip Gheho (musician, drummer, and dancer, and the first executive chairman of the Arts Council of Ghana), ethnomuciocologist J. H. Nketia (the first African director of the Institute of African Studies), and chief Nana Kobina Nketsia (cultural adviser to the president), Opoku recruited master drummers to form a multicultural and multi-ethnic drum ensemble, the nucleus of what would become the Ghana Dance Ensemble. Its members first alternated as supporting drummers for each other; they then learned to play the unfamiliar master-drum forms of various ethnic groups for the group's twelve young dancers (six of each sex).

The full ensemble was trained to perform a variety of ethnic dances, returning to the various regions to refine their performances and to collect fresh dance material. The ensemble was renamed the National Dance Company of Ghana after its highly successful performances at the Mexico City Olympic Games. The company's performances on a subsequent tour of universities in California and New York were well received by the American press, and culminated in a highly successful season at Madison Square Garden. Previous performances had been staged as part of cultural exchange programs at diplomatic missions. The purpose of the American tour was to discover the company's world rating as professionals. The ensemble has continued to tour internationally. The school of dance, a companion establishment to the ensemble, has attracted students and researchers from Europe, Asia, the United States, and other African countries.

As Nketia noted at the inauguration of the dance company, "In our training, we have insisted not only on correctness of movement but also on the quality of move-

ment required by experts in our society. We have followed the warning that a dance form which does not re-create or revitalize itself stagnates and dies!" The company and the University of Ghana have enabled Ghana to supply teachers of drumming and dancing to institutions worldwide in addition to the programs available within the country at the School of Performing Arts, the Institute of African Studies, and the International Center for African Music and Dance at the university. One time members of the company, who have established drum and dance schools abroad, visit Ghana often to give their students a chance to observe social and ritual occasions and the dances that suit them. The units within the university stand for excellence, authenticity, and the best in Ghana's rich dance heritage.

Recent exhibition dances by Burma Camp school chil-

GHANA. Dancers and musicians from the University of Ghana ensemble in the early 1960s. This company, later called the National Dance Ensemble of Ghana, performed a variety of dances representing several ethnic groups. (Photograph by Willis E. Bell; reprinted from Opoku, 1965.)

dren, by dancers from the Volta Region, and by the Hewale Dance Club at the symposium and workshop at the International Center for African Music and Dance, promise both continuity and change in accordance with time-tested traditional practice.

[*See also* Costume in African Traditions; Mask and Makeup, *article on* African Traditions; *and* West Africa.]

BIBLIOGRAPHY

Blum, Odette. "Dance in Ghana." *Dance Perspectives*, no. 56 (Winter 1973).

Blum, Odette. "An Initial Investigation into Ghanaian Dance." In *A Spectrum of World Dance*, edited by Lynn Ager Wallen and Joan Acocella. New York, 1987.

Frosch-Schröder, Joan. "Things of Significance Do Not Vanish." *UCLA Journal of Dance Ethnology* 15 (1991): 54–67.

Frosch-Schröder, Joan. "Recreating Cultural Memory." *UCLA Journal of Dance Ethnology* 18 (1994): 17–23.

Jonas, Gerald. *Dancing: The Pleasure, Power, and Art of Movement.* New York, 1992.

Jones, A. M. *Studies in African Music.* 2 vols. London, 1959.

Locke, David. *Kpegisu: A War Drum of the Ewe.* Tempe, Ariz., 1992.

Nketia, J. H. Kwabena. *Drumming in Akan Communities of Ghana.* Edinburgh, 1963.

Nketia, J. H. Kwabena. "Golden Stool: Asante Center and Periphery; Asante Court Music." *American Museum of Natural History: Anthropological Papers.* Vol. 65. New York, 1987.

Nketia, J. H. Kwabena. "Proposal for the Establishment of an International Center for African Music and Dance at the University of Ghana, Legon." *World of Music* 34.1 (1992): 139–143.

Opoku, Albert Mawere, and Willis Bell. *African Dances: A Ghanaian Profile.* Legon, 1965.

Opoku, Albert Mawere. "Golden Stool: Asante Center and Periphery; Asante Court Dances." *American Museum of Natural History: Anthropological Papers.* Vol. 65. New York, 1987.

Opoku, Albert Mawere. "The Presentation of Traditional Music and Dance in the Theatre." *World of Music* 18.4 (1976): 58–67.

ALBERT MAWERE OPOKU

Dance Research and Publication

Because dance is an avenue of expression, in Ghana it has generally been closely related to the themes and purposes of social occasions as well as to the interests, attitudes, and beliefs of Ghanaian culture. Dance in Africa usually proceeds from deep emotion and motivation. As the renowned choreographer and dance teacher Albert Mawere Opoku has written:

> [The dances] speak to the mind through the heart. In the European sense, drama is a fact of life on which a spotlight is thrown to remind society of inner conflicts, strengths and weaknesses, failures and successes, hopes and fears as instruments which make us what we are. . . . The dance serves a similar purpose in our society and is to us what the conventional theatre is to other racial groups.

Dance in all its forms in Ghana is therefore seen as embracing all facets of life—physical, spiritual, mundane, and sacred.

Ghana's dance can be categorized as either indigenous—traditional—or modern. These categories sometimes overlap, complement, and supplement each other. The evolution of the modern dance form was made possible by research, borrowing, adaptation, and the reorganization of the basic indigenous dances.

Traditional Ghanaian Dance. Foreign colonialists condemned African culture as "heathen" or un-Christian and almost crippled indigenous performing arts; dance perhaps suffered most. Modern research has been hampered in efforts to document and catalog traditional dance by mutual distrust between foreign recorders and traditionalist performers.

The earliest resources for research in traditional dance were the performers of cult and vocational dances, who comprised the potential initiates and persons of royal lineage. New initiates into the *akom* or *yeve* cults were introduced to the cults' dance movements and symbolic values at only certain prescribed times. Researchers thus had limited access to the intricacies of these dances and limited insight into their spiritual, sacred, and secular characteristics and influences. The lack of modern recording devices also made full description difficult. Fortunately, the dances' historical consistency ensured that sacred lyrics, drum languages, and text formulas would survive to be recorded later. Instruction in court dances was likewise limited to royal heirs and other royal persons.

During such celebration festivals as the Kundum, Aboakyir, and Daniba, opposing dance groups in Ghana present performances in which they ridicule and castigate one another. In fact, during festivals a chief and his supporters have specific license to ridicule and insult opponents and rival factions. Usually the dancers investigate their opponents' recent scandals and interweave such histories with their culture's social and spiritual values and symbols. Many of the symbolic movements, lyrics, and drum patterns seen in today's dances originated from this ancient and refined method of research.

Contemporary Ghanaian Dance. Dating from the country's independence from Great Britain in 1957, "contemporary" or "modern" in this sense means ancient, traditional dance that has been uncovered by historical research and reconstructed for theatrical presentation. The colonial period saw the abandonment of many indigenous dances and ceremonies because they were considered by Christian missionaries as incompatible with the aims of conversion.

The early independence era of President Kwame Nkrumah (1960–1966) emphasized the African personality; with it came recognition by Ghana's dance scholars that if the nation's dances were to be preserved as part of a national cultural treasure, they had to be researched, reorganized, and taught to dancers. Cadres of Nkrumah supporters soon traveled throughout the country to organize interschool, interdistrict, and interregional dance competitions (other arts competitions also were established). By tradition, some parents had already taught dance gestures and their meanings to their children, but the movement accelerated as school teachers themselves became educated in dance traditions.

The vocational, the social, and the festival dances were the first and most easily transmitted; these were followed by the specialized royal and court dances. Practitioners of the most exclusive form, the cult dances, remain the most secretive and least open to revealing their art; researchers have found that uncovering and documenting them takes much patience, money, and tact.

Research has also proceeded along academic lines, especially with the establishment of the Institute of African Studies at the University of Ghana. Schools of music and performing arts (formerly dance and drama) were also established at the university, where the National Ghana Dance Ensemble was initiated by Nkrumah in 1962. Research has also been conducted along similar lines by the Arts Council of Ghana, the Cultural Centre, and Ghana Television Services.

Academic scholars and artists still must go to rural communities with open intentions and goodwill gifts to gain the cooperation of the indigenous dances' custodians and masters. In such ways have basic movements, drum patterns, and lyrics been taught to researchers, who have recorded them on audiotape, videotape, and film—although the absence of mutual trust has sometimes led to distortions in the collected information. The Cultural Centre in Kumasi has been generally successful, because of its central location—it is the capital of the Ashanti (Asante) Region, one of ten Ghanaian regions—and the relative homogeneity of Asante culture. There, local masters and custodians of indigenous Asante dances have been forthcoming, and their influence has been a constant in the Cultural Centre's theatrical productions. Unaffiliated individuals and groups also have done research into various dances with remarkable results.

The entire repertory of dances adapted and learned by the Ghana Dance Ensemble, now the National Dance Company of Ghana, based at the National Theater, are enhanced on occasion by visiting indigenous performers, who pass on their knowledge to students. Other practitioners—especially those of cult, court, and vocational dances—have refused to reveal their secrets, despite the dances' aesthetic appeal. For example, a *yeve* cult group was invited to perform by the Ghana Dance Ensemble in 1986; however, the custodians declined to perform certain sequences, fearing that their gods would be displeased if these were performed outside the cult's shrine.

The lack of modern recording equipment, especially video cameras, has presented another significant problem in modern dance research. Still photographs have been the most used method of capturing dances, but they fail to record the subtle movements that make the dances flow naturally. Most researchers have not been familiar with Labanotation or other movement notation systems, and so have recorded dances by memory, which limits detail and leads to misinterpretations. For example, as Albert Mawere Opoku has noted, researchers long thought that the northern Ghanaian *lobi* was a "trembling" dance; analysis has shown it to be akin to *agbadza* dance of Ghana's Volta Region.

Indigenous Ghanaian dance movements and gestures have been borrowed for use in Western dance forms such as ballet and jazz. Such adaptation is largely unmindful of the traditional context and symbolism of the movements and gestures and is thus superficial. Nonetheless, some enterprising artists have successfully used borrowed materials, such as Adjetey Cowak, who won the 1987 World Dancing Competition in London. Similar borrowings of indigenous dance elements can also be seen in cabarets, in hotels, and nightclubs by performers onstage and by patrons on the dance floor.

BIBLIOGRAPHY

Blum, Odette. "Dance in Ghana." *Dance Perspectives*, no. 56 (Winter 1973).
Jones, A. M. *Studies in African Music.* 2 vols. London, 1959.
Mawere-Opoku, Albert. "Thoughts from the School of Music and Drama." *Okyeame* 2.1 (1964): 51–65.
Nketia, J. H. Kwabena. *Drumming in Akan Communities of Ghana.* Edinburgh, 1963.

SOPHIA D. LOKKO

GHOST DANCE. The Ghost Dance of 1870 and 1890 was a Native American world-renewal religion. The religion took many forms, but its principal ideas were that the spirits of the dead would be raised, the buffalo would return, and European settlers would be driven away. A dance was the central focus of the ritual.

Precursors of the Ghost Dance may date back to Aztec religion. The languages of the Aztec and Northern Paiute are related and the latter are the originators of the Ghost Dance. Preceding the Ghost Dance, however, and coming from Nevada to the Plains, was the widespread Sun Dance—a painful, trance-inducing ordeal, with dancing under the hot sun from dawn to dusk. The Cheyenne emphasized that the ritual performance of the Sun Dance would reanimate the earth and its life—that is, renew the world.

The tribes of the northwestern plateau between the Rocky and Cascade ranges believed in the impending destruction and renewal of the world, when the dead were to return. Dance ceremonies would hasten the advent of that day. Leslie Spier, who in the 1930s designated such a ceremony the Prophet Dance, believed that it was this dance that gave rise to both the 1870 and the 1890 Ghost Dance of the Northern Paiute.

The Ghost Dance of 1870 was developed by a Northern Paiute medicine man, usually referred to as Wodsiwob, of Walker Lake Reservation, Nevada. The dance spread east to the Ute of Utah and the Shoshone of Idaho but was more important in Oregon and northern California. The 1870 Ghost Dance persisted through one generation to contribute to the rise of the 1890 Ghost Dance. The form of the dance—men and women holding hands and circling by stepping sideways—is both the ancient and the modern form of Northern Paiute social dancing.

Various factors contributed to the development of the Ghost Dance. One was based on ancient Northern Paiute (or Paviotso) shamanism, in which an individual gained power and knowledge through personal visions. [See Shamanism.] The Paiute were acquainted with the messianic hope and resurrection of the dead taught by Christianity; the consecrated undergarments worn by Mormons in the area to ward off harm may have inspired Ghost Dance shirts, to which similar power was attributed. Transportation by horse and then railroad, and communication by the U.S. postal service, facilitated the spread of ideas. The increasing domination of Native Americans by European settlers, with the accompanying destruction of the aboriginal ways of life, was the context in which the Ghost Dance developed.

The Ghost Dance of 1890 became more renowned than that of 1870 because it spread to the Great Plains and the warrior tribes of the Sioux, Cheyenne, Comanche, Kiowa, and others. The ritual comprised two types of dances. In the general dance, all participants held hands and moved in a circle by means of simple sidesteps. The stately steps were performed in unison, fairly slowly. Wovoka or John Wilson, the teacher of the Ghost Dance of 1890, announced that the God of the Christian Bible had instructed him, during a trance, to use the Paiute Round Dance as part of the sacred ceremony to help Him renew the world. In the second dance type, a frenzied twisting, turning, and gazing at the sun ended with the participant falling into a trance. Such individuals were seeking special communication with God, in imitation of the original vision reported by Wovoka after his trances in 1889.

The two types of dancing represent variations in leadership and in membership. The priest who had learned the proper rules and procedures directed sedate and orderly worship. The converts who were seeking to have personal encounters with supernatural powers tried to enlarge and broaden their religious teachings by receiving direct supernatural instruction under the new revelation. Most devotees failed in their attempts to modify the original instructions of the prophet Wovoka, so for the most part the Ghost Dance remained an orderly, slow circle dance accompanied by group singing and praying.

The U.S. government tried to ban the Ghost Dance, believing that it would lead to an uprising. Sioux Ghost Dancers, trusting that their Ghost Dance shirts would protect them from enemy bullets, were massacred by the army at Wounded Knee Creek, in South Dakota, on 29 December 1890. Although it is commonly believed that the movement ended at that time, large crowds continued to dance the Ghost Dance in Oklahoma after 1908, and small groups of believers persisted in South Dakota for decades.

[*See also* Native American Dance.]

BIBLIOGRAPHY

Barney, Garold D. *Mormons, Indians, and the Ghost Dance Religion of 1890.* Lanham, Md., 1986.

Du Bois, Cora Alice. *The 1870 Ghost Dance.* Berkeley, 1939.

Kroeber, A. L., and E. W. Gifford. *World Renewal: A Cult System of Native Northwestern California.* Berkeley, 1949.

Mooney, James. *The Ghost-Dance Religion and the Sioux Outbreak of 1890.* Washington, D.C., 1896.

Osterreich, Shelley Anne. *The American Indian Ghost Dance, 1870 and 1890: An Annotated Bibliography.* New York, 1991.

Spier, Leslie. *The Prophet Dance of the Northwest and Its Derivatives.* Menasha, Wis., 1935.

Stewart, Omer C. "The Ghost Dance." In *Anthropology on the Great Plains,* edited by W. Raymond Wood and Margot Liberty. Lincoln, Neb., 1980.

Vaillant, George C. *The Aztecs of Mexico.* New York, 1956.

OMER C. STEWART

GIGAKU. A Japanese performing art, *gigaku* is no longer extant, although traces of it remain in dances that were assimilated into *bugaku,* the official dance genre of the Japanese imperial court, and in the *gyōdō,* the still-performed, popular Buddhist processions. The precise origins of *gigaku* (lit., "skilled musical entertainment") are uncertain, but the form was introduced into the Japanese islands along with Buddhism from southern China via Korea. Mimashi, a dancer from Paekche, Korea, is credited with bringing *gigaku* to Japan in 612 CE.

Under the patronage of the imperial court, *gigaku* became the ceremonial entertainment during religious festivals at Buddhist temples. It reached a peak of great popularity during the eighth and ninth centuries, until *bugaku* supplanted it as the official entertainment both at court and in the major centers of worship.

After a period of decline (tenth through twelfth centuries), during which performances continued in Buddhist temples far from Edo, the capital, *gigaku* slowly disappeared between the thirteenth and sixteenth centuries. Our knowledge about the content and style of a *gigaku* performance is based on a late but reliable source: a description in the *Kyōkunshō* (1233), a compendium of *gagaku* sources by Chikazane Koma. Moreover, about 250 original *gigaku* headmasks, many of which date from the seventh and eighth centuries, are still preserved in the Shōsōin in Nara, the National Museum in Tokyo, and elsewhere. Similarities between some *gigaku* masks and late Roman comedy masks seem to support the suggestion of a link between Japan and the Mediterranean world.

A *gigaku* performance opened with a colorful procession of numerous dancers and musicians (playing flutes, drums, and cymbals), during which ritual masked dances were performed. One of these was *Gohō-jishi* (Lions in Five Directions); two men played the lion, accompanied by two others, who played lion cubs. The main dramatic feature of the *gigaku* performance was the mimed dance play *Konron* (or *Kuron*), whose plot centered on the villain Konron's sexual attack on two maidens. The maidens are eventually rescued by the hero, the Buddhist guardian-god Rikishi. Konron's phallus symbol, tied to a rope, is swung by Rikishi during his quick final dance celebrating the victory of virtue over lust—or of Buddhism over non-Buddhist magic. Three playlets—mimed parodies of didactic nature—followed, including one recounting the humiliation of a monk who has fathered a child and must wash swaddling clothes and another humorously mimicking a drunken king. An orchestral performance and a final majestic procession concluded the pageantry.

[*See also* Bugaku.]

BIBLIOGRAPHY

Araki, James T. *The Ballad-Drama of Medieval Japan.* Berkeley, 1964.
Kleinschmidt, Peter. *Die Masken der Gigaku, der ältesten Theaterform Japans.* Wiesbaden, 1966.
Lucas, Heinz. *Japanische Kultmasken.* Kassel, 1965.
Ortolani, Benito. *The Japanese Theatre: From Shamanistic Ritual to Contemporary Pluralism.* Rev. ed. Princeton, 1995.
Yoshinobu Inoura. *A History of Japanese Theater,* vol. 1, *Noh and Kyogen.* Yokohama, 1971.

BENITO ORTOLANI

GIGUE. The origins of the term *gigue* and the Baroque court and theater dance genre of that name are uncertain. Most likely, *gigue* derived from the Old French verb *giguer,* "to leap, gambol, or frolic." This derivation is also cited for the English term *jig:* "Used variously for types of music and dance it contains the idea of vigorous up and down movement, of which the dance is expressive" (Dean-Smith, 1980, p. 648). This term seems to encompass many different kinds of dances, all called jig but not necessarily related specifically in content or form, such as the English sixteenth-century bawdy song and dance genre and country dances. All, however, do have a vigorous and frolicsome spirit, the essential quality of movement that seems to link these dances to one another. The spirit suggested by the term is certainly reflected in the French court dance form that has been described as "gay and skipping" (Brossard, 1703), "airy and light" (Tomlinson, 1735), and "lively" (Rousseau, 1768). The steps and technique of the French *gigue* as it was practiced at the European courts of the late seventeenth and early eighteenth centuries are, however, unique to a style of dancing sometimes simply referred to as French dancing. It was described by Pierre Rameau in his *Le maître à danser* (1725) and by other dancing masters of the time.

Raoul-Auger Feuillet published the first known, notated *gigue* choreography in 1700. However, the growing popularity of the dance form during the second half of the seventeenth century is evidenced by the increasingly frequent inclusion of *gigues* in the works of Jean-Baptiste Lully (1632–1687). The first dance called a *gigue* in Lully's *ballets de cour* appears in 1660, and sixteen more appear in his works through 1687.

Approximately a dozen *gigues* from the ballroom and theater dance repertory of the early eighteenth century are available in *chorégraphie* (eighteenth-century dance notation). These notations provide examples of *gigues* performed by one couple (ballroom and theater) and as solos (theater). Two publications of dances by Raoul-Auger Feuillet and Guillaume-Louis Pecour contain the earliest known examples of *gigue* choreographies. The "Gigue pour Homme," a theatrical *gigue,* and the "Gigue à Deux," a dance for which no clear indication is given for its intended performance in either the ballroom or theater, can be found in Feuillet's *Recüeil de dances,* published in 1700. Pecour's "La Contredance," a *danse à deux* for the ballroom, can be found in another *Recüeil de dances* published by Feuillet in that same year.

The liveliness and gaiety of the *gigue* were expressed in springing steps, such as *contretemps* and *jetés.* The theatrical *gigue* was a virtuoso dance composed of *pas battus,* multiple pirouettes, and other nameless, intricate *pas composés* that demonstrate the technical prowess of the professional dancer. The ballroom *gigue,* although simpler in its step vocabulary than that for the theater, certainly did not lack in vivacity. It demanded stamina, agility, and a sure technique. The *gigue* served to demonstrate skill and lightness of step; however, as in all Baroque court dances, the required agility had to be accompanied by a calm and elegant deportment.

In the music of this period two distinct styles of the *gigue* emerged: French and Italian. The meter of the French *gigue* was 3/8, 6/8, or 6/4, while the Italian *giga* was usually written in 12/8. All surviving choreographies are in the French style, with one *pas composé* equaling one measure of compound double time; with few exceptions, they are written in 6/4 meter. To date, no choreographic examples of the *giga* have been found.

Characteristic of the French *gigue* is the dotted rhythm, ♩. ♪ ♩ ♩. ♪ ♩, which may be reflected in the performance of the *pas composés.* Neither the dance manuals of the time nor the notation indicates this rhythm for performing step because dancing masters did not differentiate between double and compound double time (Hilton, 1981).

However, the dotted rhythm clearly complements the music to which the dance is performed and emphasizes its characteristic skipping quality. *Pas composés* that contain more than two single steps, such as the *pas de bourrée*, are generally performed in this dotted rhythm. Basic *pas composés* commonly found in the *gigue* and their corresponding rhythms in 6/4 meter include *pas de bourrée*, ♩♩♩.; *contretemps de gavotte*, ♩♩♩.; two *demi-contretemps*, ♩♩♩♩; and *pas de sissonne*, ♩. ♩..

Dance phrases in *gigues* can be quite long and irregular—that is, nine or fifteen measures. The "Gigue pour une Femme Seul Dancée par Mlle. Guiot à Opéra de Tandrede" (Pecour, 1712) is composed of two lengthy phrases of twenty-two and thirty measures with no repetitions of particular movement sequences or patterns. This dance phrasing does not mirror the phrase structure of the accompanying music, which is composed of two strains of eleven and fifteen measures, both repeated, with the resulting musical pattern A-A-B-B.

The "Gigue à Deux" (Feuillet, 1700) is one of the few examples of a dance in the Baroque style in which the dance patterns and steps as well as the musical strains are repeated (Hilton, 1981). The musical pattern consists of two strains (A and B) structured as follows: A, nine measures, repeated; a linking passage of four measures; B, eight measures, repeated; the last four measures of B. The dance is composed of two figures, each repeated. The steps in the figures are repeated as well, with different steps occurring only in the linking passage and in the last four measures of the dance.

Today, reconstructions of the French *gigue* are danced at a moderate to quick tempo. The complexity of a choreography and, to a lesser degree, the technical skill or preference of the dancer determine the tempo of a particular *gigue* within this range. A *gigue* for the theater, such as the "Gigue pour une Femme" in Pecour (see above), containing more brilliant and complex footwork than that of a *gigue* for the ballroom, can be danced at a slightly slower tempo to accommodate the demands of the choreography. However, the buoyant quality of movement may be lost if the tempo is too slow. On the other hand, an excessively fast tempo may also rob the *gigue* of this springing quality, leading to unclear execution of the steps.

Extant *gigue* choreographies, particularly those for the theater, provide some of the most lively technical and stylistic challenges of the Baroque dance repertory. With their brisk, complex footwork, they illustrate the refined dance technique of both the courtiers and professional dancers of the period.

[*See also* Ballet Technique, History of, *article on* French Court Dance.]

BIBLIOGRAPHY

Brossard, Sébastien de. *Dictionary of Music* (1703). Translated and edited by Albion Gruber. Henryville, Pa., 1982.

Dean-Smith, Margaret. "Jig." In *The New Grove Dictionary of Music and Musicians*. London, 1980.

Hilton, Wendy. *Dance of Court and Theatre: The French Noble Style, 1690–1725*. Princeton, 1981.

Little, Meredith Ellen. "The Dances of J. B. Lully." Ph.D. diss., Stanford University, 1967.

Little, Meredith Ellis. "Gigue." In *The New Grove Dictionary of Music and Musicians*. London, 1980.

Rousseau, Jean-Jacques. *A Dictionary of Music* (1768). Translated by William Waring. 2d ed. London, 1779.

Tomlinson, Kellom. *The Art of Dancing Explained by Reading and Figures*. 2 vols. London, 1735.

Witherell, Anne L. *Louis Pécour's 1700 Recueil des danses*. Ann Arbor, Mich., 1983.

SUSAN F. BINDIG

GILMOUR, SALLY (born 2 November 1921 in Malaya), British ballet dancer. At the age of five, Sally Gilmour saw Anna Pavlova dance in Singapore, where her parents had moved in 1922, and decided she wanted to be a dancer. When the family moved to London in 1930, she studied first with Tamara Karsavina and, after the great ballerina gave up her studio in 1933, with Antony Tudor and Marie Rambert at Rambert's school in Notting Hill Gate. In 1936 Gilmour made her first appearances in Sun-

GILMOUR. This classic image, often reproduced, shows Charles Boyd and Sally Gilmour in the principal roles of Andrée Howard's *Lady into Fox*, made for Ballet Rambert in 1939. Gilmour portrayed Silvia, the lady of the title, and Boyd was Her Husband, from whom she was driven to escape by her vulpine nature. (Photograph by Gilbert Adams.)

day night performances of the Ballet Club, dancing in the pas de trois and in the pas de quatre of cygnets (the "Four Little Swans") from *Swan Lake* and as a Nymph in Frederick Ashton's *Mars and Venus*. Her first created role was Maria in Wendy Toye's version of *Cross-Garter'd* (1937), based on Shakespeare's play *Twelfth Night*. In the following season she created roles in Andrée Howard's *Croquis de Mercure* (1938) and in Walter Gore's *Valse Finale* (1938) and *Paris-Soir* (1939).

Gilmour achieved instant recognition as one of the great dramatic dancers of her generation when she created the title role of Silvia in Howard's *Lady into Fox* (1939), based on David Garnett's novel. The same year she revealed a delightful sense of comedy in Frank Staff's *Czernyana*, seen again in her charming portrayal of the doomed Duck in his *Peter and the Wolf* (1940). She danced many roles in the Rambert repertory, such as Caroline in Tudor's *Jardin aux Lilas* and the Lady Friend in Ashton's *Les Masques*. She was deeply moving in *Confessional*, based on Robert Browning's poem, created for her by Walter Gore and first performed at the Oxford University Ballet Club in 1941.

From 1943 onward, Gilmour was principal dancer of Ballet Rambert, creating roles in other ballets by Gore, including *Simple Symphony* (1944), *Mr. Punch* (1946), *Concerto Burlesco* (1947), and *Winter Night* (1948). She reached the peak of her powers with her performance of *Giselle* in Rambert's memorable production in 1946 and as Tulip, the sailor's African bride, in Howard's *The Sailor's Return* (1947), also based on a novel by David Garnett.

After Ballet Rambert's Australian tour, 1947–1949, during which she was married, Gilmour left the company and, following a brief freelance career, settled in 1953 in Australia, where she worked for the Royal Academy of Dancing until she returned to London in 1972. After resettling in London, Gilmour assisted in the revival of works by Ashton, Gore, and Staff, as well as the original version of Tudor's *Dark Elegies* for Ballet Rambert.

BIBLIOGRAPHY

Beaumont, Cyril W. "Sally Gilmour." *Ballet* 3 (June 1947): 20–36.
Clarke, Mary. *Dancers of Mercury: The Story of Ballet Rambert*. London, 1961.
Crisp, Clement, et al., eds. *Ballet Rambert: Fifty Years and On*. Rev. and enl. ed. [Ilkley, England], 1981.
Rambert, Marie. *Quicksilver: The Autobiography of Marie Rambert*. London, 1972.

PETER WILLIAMS

GILPIN, JOHN (born 10 February 1930 in Southsea, Hampshire, died 5 September 1983 in London), British ballet dancer, teacher, actor, and company director. After early training, from the age of seven, with Tina Pierce and Barbara Spencer-Edwards, John Gilpin won a scholarship to the Cone-Ripman School in 1939. At the age of thirteen, he became the youngest dancer ever to win the highest award at the Royal Academy of Dancing, the Adeline Genée gold medal. Gilpin's first professional stage appearances were as a child actor in J. M. Barrie's *Peter Pan* (1942–1943) and Daphne du Maurier's *Years Between* (1944; also in the film version). He also acted in radio plays and in films.

Gilpin joined Ballet Rambert as a soloist in 1945 and danced many roles in the company's repertory. Among them were Jack Ketch in Walter Gore's *Mr. Punch* (1946), the Rabbit Catcher in Andrée Howard's *The Sailor's Return* (1947), and leading roles in Gore's *Plaisance* (1947) and *Winter Night* (1948). During his five years with the company, he established himself as an outstanding artist.

When Ballet Rambert temporarily disbanded after its 1947–1949 Australian tour, Gilpin went to France and

GILPIN. Harald Lander's *Études* provided just the sort of role that suited Gilpin's classical virtuosity. Pictured here in a performance with London Festival Ballet, he seems to soar above the heads of the female ensemble in a momentary display of exceptional *ballon* and elegant line. (Photograph by Hannes Kilian; used by permission.)

joined Roland Petit's Ballets de Paris, creating the roles of Le Roi de Nougat in Frederick Ashton's *Le Rêve de Léonor* and a Bandit in Petit's *Carmen* (both 1949). In 1950 he moved to Le Grand Ballet du Marquis de Cuevas, where he danced many principal roles.

Returning to England in the autumn of 1950, Gilpin became one of the first male stars of the newly formed London's Festival Ballet. By this time his virtuosity, brilliant technique, and noble style had established him as one of Britain's foremost classical dancers. His association with the company lasted for twenty years, apart from a period in 1961–1962 when he appeared as a guest artist with the Royal Ballet.

Gilpin danced principal roles in the classics—*The Nutcracker, Giselle, The Sleeping Beauty, Swan Lake*—as well as in revivals from Serge Diaghilev's repertory, such as Michel Fokine's *Les Sylphides* and *Le Spectre de la Rose*. He also created many roles in contemporary ballets, including Ashton's *Vision of Marguerite* (Faust; 1952), Michael Charnley's *Symphony for Fun* (1952) and *Alice in Wonderland* (The White Rabbit; 1953), Ruth Page's *Vilia* (Danilo; 1953), Nicholas Beriozoff's *Esmeralda* (Pierre Gringoire; 1952), Anton Dolin's *Variations for Four* (1957), and Jack Carter's *London Morning* (The Sailor; 1959) and *Beatrix* (The Marquis; 1966). His most famous roles were in works recreated for London's Festival Ballet, such as Léonide Massine's *Beau Danube* (The Hussar), Harald Lander's *Études* (1955), and Carter's *Witch Boy* (1957). He was artistic director of the company from 1965 to 1967.

Over three decades, Gilpin partnered many of the greatest ballerinas of the time and appeared as guest artist with many of the world's leading companies. His active dancing career was cut short by illness and injury in the 1970s (his last performance was in *Carmina Burana* with Ballet Clasico de Madrid in 1978), but Gilpin continued to mount ballets, teach, and coach. In 1980 he appeared in a play based on his life, *Invitation to the Dance*, written for him by Maxim Mazumdar, in Canada and America. He died of a heart attack in 1983.

BIBLIOGRAPHY
Gilpin, John. *A Dance with Life*. London, 1982.
Gruen, John. *The Private World of Ballet*. New York, 1975.
Lidova, Irène. "John Gilpin." *Saisons de la danse* (December 1972).
Swinson, Cyril. *John Gilpin*. London, 1957.

PETER WILLIAMS

GIOJA, GAETANO (born c.1760 in Naples, died 30 March 1826 in Naples), Italian ballet dancer, choreographer, and teacher. Gioja's father, the choreographer Antonio Gioja, entrusted the young Gaetano's dance training to Giuseppe Traffieri, a prominent dancer and choreographer in Naples. Gaetano Gioja (spelled *Gioia* in modern

Italian) made his first recorded appearance on stage in the 1775/76 season at the Teatro Regio in Turin, where he danced a *quartetto grottesco* in Giuseppe Canziani's *L'Amante Travestita*. In subsequent years, he danced in Turin, Florence, Naples, Rome, and other Italian cities. In 1789 he started his career as a choreographer, presenting his ballets in Vicenza and Turin, and in the 1789/90 season he staged *Antigone* at the Teatro San Benedetto in Venice.

In 1791 Gioja was named *primo ballerino serio assoluto* at the Teatro alla Scala in Milan, and in the same year in Madrid he danced at the Teatro de los Caños del Peral with the company directed by Domenico Rossi. In 1793 Gioja's name as a choreographer was already so well established that he was engaged for the inauguration of the Teatro São Carlos in Lisbon, where he presented *A Bailerina Amante, A Felicidade Lusitana*, and *I Dispetti Amorosi*, to music by himself, Antonio Leal-Moreira, and Domenico Cimarosa, respectively. Throughout his career, Gioja often composed the music for his ballets or adapted it from works of famous contemporary composers, occasionally using musical reminiscences in order to depict the psychology of characters.

In December 1793, Gioja returned to La Scala as choreographer and principal dancer, and during the last years of the century he consolidated his fame with productions of his ballets in several Italian theaters. In 1800 and 1801 he was in Vienna to stage some of his ballets, among them *Alceste* (1800), *Zulima und Azem* (1800), and *Das Urtheil des Paris* (The Judgment of Paris; 1801). At this same time, Salvatore Viganò was also in the Austrian capital, creating *Die Geshöpfe des Prometheus* (The Creatures of Prometheus; 1801). It has been often alleged that Gioja's exposure to Viganò's *Creatures* in Vienna marks a watershed between his early creations and his mature style.

Kathleen Hansell (1987, 1992, 1996) casts some doubts on this claim, on the basis of an analysis of Gioja's conspicuous ballet production up to this date and of the earlier reviews that praise his fertile imagination and his ability to find new expressive means. She says that the influence of the Viennese years on Gioja is more apparent in his subsequent choices of instrumental music for his ballets and in the exploiting of the new lighting techniques developed by the *Zauberoper*. Because of the wide diffusion of his productions, Hansell claims that Gioja's influence on Italian dance theater, and even more on opera, may have been greater than Viganò's, as is shown for example by the fact that Gaetano Donizetti chose for three of his operas subjects previously staged with success by Gioja, like *Gabriella di Vergy* and *Kenilworth*. Further proof of the mutual exchanges between Gioja's ballets and opera comes from *Nina* (1794) and *Gli Orazi e Curiazi* (1798), with music adapted, respectively, from operas by Nicolas Dalayrac and Domenico Cimarosa with identical titles; these are two of the few documented examples in this period of ballets that use a single opera as a source for their music.

Having left Vienna in 1802, Gioja went to Naples where he created within six years a score of ballets for the Teatro San Carlo. *Andromeda e Perseo* (1803) caused the admiring astonishment of a public "that was not accustomed to seeing the artifices of painting shown live and true by choreodrama" (Ritoni, 1838). *Il Ritorno di Ulisse in Itaca* (1805), although overloaded with episodes, was also lauded because of the moving scene of recognition between Ulysses, Penelope, and Telemachus, surrounded in a choral embrace by the people of Ithaca. In 1806 Gioja presented *I Minatori Valacchi*, a tragic ballet, and *Saffo, o sia Il Salto di Leucade*, in which he set the protagonist the difficult task of expressing, through the mute language of gesture, the melody played by the orchestra. (A celebrated interpretation of this role was given by Marietta Conti at La Scala in 1819.)

In 1807, Gioja created the work acknowledged to be his masterpiece: *Cesare in Egitto*, with music by Wenzel Robert Gallenberg, a heroic, tragic pantomime in four acts and five scenes defined by Viganò as "the prince of heroic ballets." The subject of this ballet reflected the ideals of the Napoleonic Empire in its full splendor. Bonaparte himself, fascinated by the staging of the exploits of the great Roman general, personally congratulated Gioja after attending a performance of the ballet in 1809 at La Scala. Among Gioja's inventions for *Cesare in Egitto* was the scene of Cleopatra's apotheosis, in which she appeared as Venus, surrounded by zephyrs, the three Graces, nymphs, bacchantes, and genies. When the work was revived in 1815 at La Scala, Jean and Teresa Coralli appeared as Caesar and Cleopatra and Gaetana Abrami took the part of Ptolemy. The music for this production, by several composers, was arranged by Gioja.

Gioja also worked in many other Italian cities, including Turin, Venice, Florence, and Rome. For the Teatro Argentina in Rome, he revived *Gli Orazi e Curiazi* in 1812. At the Teatro La Pergola in Florence, he mounted *Orfeo ed Euridice* (1811) and *Niobe* (1814), among others. Of all his works presented at La Pergola between 1811 and 1820, the most famous was *Gabriella di Vergy* (1819). Set to music by Paolo Brumbilla and Petro Romani and excerpts from the operas of Gioacchino Rossini and Giacomo Meyerbeer, *Gabriella* was called by Giulio Ferrario a work of "the highest beauty" and judged to be a "fairly dangerous undertaking" because of its savage subject (Ferrario, 1836).

Gabriella di Vergy, which takes place in the Middle Ages, brought together some romantic elements—particularly the tragic destiny of the protagonist, who, only through death, frees herself from the conflict between her conjugal duties and her internal passion. When the ballet was performed at La Scala in 1822, the vast range of Gabriella's intense states of mind were portrayed by Antonia Pal-

lerini, Viganò's favorite dancer. Gioja's *Gabriella* was similar to Viganò's *Mirra* (1817): the heroine of each ballet struggled with a secret passion and was destined to find release from her torment only in death. *Gabriella di Vergy* was produced in many theaters in Italy and abroad, and it was still in the repertory of La Scala in 1842. Other widely produced ballets by Gioja were *Gundeberga* (1814) and *L'Ingegno supera l'Età* (1818).

Gioja worked at La Scala for several seasons between 1809 and 1824. From 1821 to his death he was regularly engaged by the Teatro San Carlo in Naples and was appointed, by royal decree, director of the Scuola di Pantomima (School of Pantomime). At the time of his death in 1826, Gioja had composed more than ninety-five ballets in many genres, covering the most diverse subjects. The work of this prolific artist, already celebrated during his lifetime, was characterized by the exclusion of virtuosity as an end in itself, by balance between solo and choral parts, by clear and dramatic plots, and by true expression of feelings, in the achieved synthesis between dance and pantomime. The comparison between Gioja and Viganò, both considered by their contemporaries as unsurpassed in their art, was recurrent in the evaluation of Gioja's oeuvre. His most successful ballets, some of which continued to be produced after his death, were considered masterpieces even by the critics who preferred the works of Viganò.

[*See also the entry on Viganò.*]

BIBLIOGRAPHY

Celi, Claudia. "Il balletto in Italia: Il Ottocento." In *Musica in scena: Storia dello spettacolo musicale*, edited by Alberto Basso, vol. 5, pp. 89–138. Turin, 1995.

Cohen, Selma Jeanne. "Freme di Gelosia! Italian Ballet Librettos, 1766–1865." *Bulletin of the New York Public Library* 67.9 (November 1963): 555–564.

Cohen, Selma Jeanne. "Virtue (Almost) Triumphant." *The Dancing Times* (March 1964): 297–301.

Ferrario, Giulio. *Il costume antico e moderno*. Livorno, 1836.

Guest, Ivor. "L'Italia e il balletto romantico" *La danza italiana* 8–9 (Winter 1990): 7–25.

Hadamowsky, Franz. *Die Wiener Hoftheater (Staatstheater)*, vol. 1, *1776–1810*. Vienna, 1966.

Hansell, Kathleen Kuzmick. "Il ballo teatrale e l'opera italiana." In *Storia dell'opera italiana*, vol. 5, pp. 175–306. Turin, 1987.

Hansell, Kathleen Kuzmick. "Gioia, Gaetano." In *The New Grove Dictionary of Opera*. London, 1992.

Hansell, Kathleen Kuzmick. "Gaetano Gioia, il ballo teatrale e l'opera del primo Ottocento." In *Creature di Prometio: Il ballo teatrale dal divertimento al dramma*, Studi di Musica Veneta no. 23, pp. 191–237. Venice, 1996.

Monaldi, Gino. *Le regine della danza nel secolo XIX*. Turin, 1910.

Raimondi, Ezio, ed. *Il sogno del coreodramma: Salvatore Viganò, poeta muto*. Bologna, 1984.

Regli, Francesco. *Dizionario biografico dei più celebri poeti ed artisti melodrammatici, tragici e comici, maestri, concertisti, coreografi, mimi, ballerini, scenografi, giornalisti, impresarii, ecc. ecc. che fiorirono in Italia dal 1800 al 1860*. Turin, 1860. Facsimile reprint, Bologna, 1990.

Ritorni, Carlo. *Commentarii della vita e delle opere coreodrammatiche di Salvatore Viganò e della coreografia e de' corepei.* Milan, 1838.

Rossi, Luigi. *Il ballo alla Scala, 1778–1970.* Milan, 1972.

Ruffin, Elena. "Il ballo teatrale a Venezia nel secolo XIX." *La danza italiana* 5–6 (Autumn 1987): 151–179.

Winter, Marian Hannah. *The Pre-Romantic Ballet.* London, 1974.

Zambon, Rita. "Sulle traccie dell'immortale Astigiano." *Chorégraphie* 1/2 (Autumn 1993): 73–84.

CLAUDIA CELI
Translated from Italian

GIRIAMA DANCE. A small Bantu-speaking group of agriculturalists, the Giriama inhabit the coast of Kenya between Malindi and Mombasa. They originated from the Nyika or Mijikenda group of nine tribes, probably migrating around 1600 from Shungwaya in southern Somalia.

Giriama dances are well known for their energy, virtuosity, and accessibility to the rapidly expanding coastal tourist trade in East Africa. The original functions of the dances were celebratory or ritualistic. Dances were performed at special occasions such as weddings and, until the end of the nineteenth century, at initiation ceremonies of the Kambi (the ruling *rika* or age set). They were also closely associated with secret societies and the exorcism of evil spirits.

Arthur M. Champion, a member of the Administrative Service in Kenya from 1909 until 1935, described the *uganja, chengi chengi, kijimbi,* and *kifudu* funerary dances.

Nowadays the most commonly performed dances are the *gonda* and the *mabumbumbu,* which are performed by groups of six to twelve dancers, with a core of adolescent girls and two or three older men. These dances are in the form of call and response, with the structure dictated by an accompanying song. A verse sung by a lead singer, who is often also the lead dancer, accompanies a relaxed step in which the dancers bend their knees and swing their hips to an underlying drum rhythm. This alternates with a succession of fast, vigorous steps characterized by the girls' hip-shaking gestures, which are performed either in a crouched position, standing, or while they are moving forward diagonally. During this movement phase, *gonda* and *mabumbumbu* dancers also undulate the pelvis back and forth and perform vertical jumps, spinning turns, and combinations of running, kicking, marching, and stamping steps interspersed with shoulder shaking. In the *mabumbumbu,* the girls sometimes go down on their knees and shake their shoulders parallel to the ground. All steps are performed in unison, with the men leaping around the girls or standing behind them, vigorously shaking their own elbows and forearms. When the girls revert to the relaxed step, the men perform acrobatic solos featuring gymnastic stunts.

The dancers stand either in two lines or in a compact set of couples—girls in front and men behind—all facing the same direction. The dancers are accompanied by three to six drummers playing single-membrane, wooden-stool drums called *bumbumbu* (hence *mabumbumbu* dance).

The girls, traditionally bare-breasted, wear *marindas* (sisal or grass skirts), which accentuate their hip-shaking; feathers attached to their backs to enhance their shoulder-shaking; and bells or rattles at their knees or ankles. The men wear long wrappers and have feathers attached to their elbows and forearms.

The *gonda* and *mabumbumbu* are considered traditional Giriama dances, but how old they are or in what ways they have developed is not clear. They exist as part of a living tradition rather than as preserved relics of a past culture, and new dance steps derived from the latest Western dance trends, imported to Mombasa nightclubs, are constantly being incorporated.

[*For related discussion, see* Digo Dance. *See also* Central and East Africa *and* Sub-Saharan Africa.]

BIBLIOGRAPHY

Brantley, Cynthia. *The Giriama and Colonial Resistance in Kenya, 1800–1920.* Berkeley, 1981.

Champion, Arthur M. *The Agiryama of Kenya* (1914). Royal Anthropological Institute of Great Britain and Ireland, Occasional Paper, no. 25. London, 1967.

VALERIE A. BRIGINSHAW

GISELLE. Full title: *Giselle, ou Les Wilis.* Ballet in two acts. Choreography: Jean Coralli and Jules Perrot. Music: Adolphe Adam and Friedrich Burgmüller. Libretto: Théophile Gautier and Jules-Henri Vernoy de Saint-Georges. Scenery: Pierre Ciceri. Costumes: Paul Lormier. First performance: 28 June 1841, Théâtre de l'Académie Royale de Musique, Paris. Principals: Carlotta Grisi (Giselle), Lucien Petipa (Loys/Albrecht), Adèle Dumilâtre (Myrtha, Queen of the Wilis).

Giselle has earned its place among the staples of the ballet repertory. It has provided innumerable ballerinas with a proving ground for their dancing and dramatic skills, so much so that Cyril Beaumont's equating the ballerina's role of Giselle with the actor's role of Hamlet has become an aphorism. The *premier danseur,* too, can find considerable challenge in the role of Albrecht. Yet the ballet is more than a vehicle for two principal dancers. It has been called "the quintessence of the Romantic ballet" (Guest, 1980), and a great deal of its appeal stems from our perception of it as perfectly representative of its time.

Through its long history the ballet has undergone many changes in its choreography, music, scenario, sets, and costumes. Elements have been cut, then reinstated. Yet it has always retained a recognizable basic plot, which may be summarized as follows.

GISELLE. With Ballet Theatre during the late 1940s and the 1950s, Alicia Alonso and Igor Youskevitch frequently appeared as Giselle and Albrecht. Here they are seen in act 1, enacting the mime scene as she plucks petals from a daisy to discover if "he loves me" or "he loves me not." Many would contend that the partnership of Alonso and Youskevitch in *Giselle* has been unrivaled, at least in the United States, in this century. Worldwide, their fame is matched only by Alicia Markova and Anton Dolin in Great Britain, Yvette Chauviré and Serge Lifar in France, Natalia Makarova and Mikhail Baryshnikov in the United States, and Carla Fracci and Erik Bruhn on the stages of several nations. (Photograph from the Dance Collection, New York Public Library for the Performing Arts.)

Synopsis.   Giselle is a peasant girl whose two greatest loves are dancing and Loys, a peasant who is actually Albrecht, a nobleman in disguise. The huntsman Hilarion, who loves Giselle and is jealous of Loys, finds evidence of Loys's true rank in his knightly sword. When the Duke of Courland, his daughter Bathilde, and their retinue visit Giselle's village during the course of a hunt, Hilarion brings forth this evidence and unmasks Albrecht. Bathilde recognizes him as her fiancé, and Giselle, heartbroken at this revelation, goes mad and dies.

In act 2 of the ballet, Giselle is inducted into the band of wilis, female spirits who emerge from their graves at midnight to dance and to force any man they meet to dance

with them until he dies. Hilarion enters their forest domain and falls prey to them. When Albrecht arrives to mourn at Giselle's grave, Giselle seeks to protect him, but the queen of the wilis demands his death. The lovers dance together, and just as Albrecht is about to succumb to exhaustion, dawn breaks and the wilis lose their power over him. Giselle, whose love for him has endured beyond death, bids him a final farewell.

History.   The ballet was the brainchild of the French poet and critic Théophile Gautier, who found the germ of his idea in Heinrich Heine's *De l'Allemagne* (1835). Gautier was much taken by Heine's account of Slavic legends of *vilas*, spirits of maidens who died before their wedding day. Despite their attractive appearance, they were vampires who took revenge on the male sex by dancing men to death.

Gautier initially planned to base the ballet's first act on Victor Hugo's poem "Les Fantômes"; Giselle was to be a guest at a ball who is enchanted by the queen of the wilis. This idea was altered when he began to work with the professional scenarist Jules-Henri Vernoy, marquis de Saint-Georges, who changed the setting of the first act to a rustic village on the Rhine, sometime during the medieval period. Gautier credited him with devising the action that led to the "pretty death" that ended the first act. Act 2 remained closer to Gautier's original conception of the nocturnal dances of the wilis, who were characterized as girls who died from dancing rather than as frustrated brides.

The title role of the ballet was intended for Carlotta Grisi, who had just made her debut at the Paris Opera in February 1841. The scenario was first shown to Jules Perrot, her mentor and lover, who took it to the composer Adolphe Adam. A prominent feature of Adam's score was the use of five major musical leitmotifs, which serve to underscore dramatic developments and link act 1 to act 2.

Jean Coralli, the chief ballet master at the Paris Opera, was named as choreographer. He was responsible for the ensemble dances, including the highly praised dances of the wilis in act 2. He also choreographed the peasant pas de deux in act 1, danced to interpolated music by Frédéric Burgmüller.

The role of Giselle, however, was choreographed by Perrot. This was no secret, although for financial reasons he was not credited in the scenario or playbills; had he been listed as a collaborator, he would have been entitled to a share of the royalties. In a period when much of the dramatic content of a ballet was conveyed through mime, Perrot tried as much as possible to use dance to express the action. He was undoubtedly helped in this by the scenario, since dancing is Giselle's passion and the wilis' form of revenge. The role of Giselle impressed J. Chaudes-Aigues, the reviewer of *Le moniteur des théâtres*, with its seemingly inordinate amount of dancing:

From one end of *Giselle* to the other the poor child is perpetually in the air or on her pointes. In the first act she runs, flies and bounds across the stage like a gazelle in love. . . . And yet this is nothing compared to what is in store for her in the second act. Here . . . she must be a thousand times lighter and intangible, since she is a shade. . . . Giselle is a Sylphide with not a moment's rest.
(Guest, 1980)

At the first performance of *Giselle* on 28 June 1841, Grisi was supported by Lucien Petipa as Loys/Albrecht (or Albert, as he is still called in Paris Opera productions; Gautier introduced the name Albrecht in his essay on the ballet in *Les beautés de l'Opéra*, 1845). That first cast also included François Simon as Hilarion, Elina Roland as Giselle's mother Berthe, Caroline Forster as Bathilde, and Adèle Dumilâtre as Myrtha, the Queen of the Wilis. The peasant pas de deux was danced by Nathalie Fitzjames and Auguste Mabille.

The first production included some elements that are rarely seen today. In act 1, Giselle told Loys in mime that she had dreamed that he loved a beautiful noblewoman. The Duke of Courland, Bathilde, and several other members of the hunting party made their entrance on horseback. At the end of the ballet, Bathilde arrived to reclaim Albrecht. The choreography has also changed since the first production; for example, Giselle's solo in act 1 has long given way to a dance with hops on pointe that require blocked shoes and a strong pointe technique, neither of which had yet been developed in the Romantic era.

Some features of the first production that were cut have been restored with the renewal of interest in historical authenticity. Among these is a mime scene in which Berthe recounts the legend of the wilis to Giselle and the villagers and cautions her daughter against her excessive love of dancing. The peasant pas de deux may be cut because it is felt to delay the action—or retained because the peasant couple's happiness illustrates the tragedy of Giselle's love for Albrecht. It may also be danced by more than one couple (e.g., as a pas de quatre or pas de six).

Several writers have explored the links between *Giselle* and the Romantic movement in art, literature, drama, music, and ballet. These links can be found both in details and in the ideas underlying the ballet. The name Albert was previously used by Gautier in his poem "Albertus" (1832) and in his novel *Mademoiselle de Maupin* (1835).

GISELLE. Galina Ulanova, *prima ballerina* of Moscow's Bolshoi Ballet, and members of the female ensemble in the joyful dance of Giselle and her girlfriends, c.1955. (Photograph from the Dance Collection, New York Public Library for the Performing Arts.)

Peasants had loved noblemen in the ballets *Clari* (1820) and *Nathalie* (1821; revived, 1832). Several of Coralli's earlier ballets had treated the theme of a girl seduced and abandoned by a nobleman; among these was *L'Orgie* (1831), his first ballet for the Paris Opera.

There was something of an epidemic of mad scenes on stage in the early nineteenth century; they occurred in plays, operas (notably *Lucia di Lammermoor* and *I Puritani*, both in 1835), and in the ballets *Nina, ou La Folle par Amour* (1813), *La Fille du Danube* (1836), and *L'Ecumeur de Mer* (1840), the last composed by Adam. The equation of beauty, youth, and madness also owed something to the revival of interest in Shakespeare's plays, particularly *Hamlet;* Eugène Delacroix and other artists painted scenes of Ophelia's madness and death. In 1840 Fanny Elssler revived *Nina* at the Paris Opera, earning Gautier's praise as "a worthy sister to Ophelia, a white and slender vision" (Guest, 1980).

The choreography of the ballet also reflects contemporary interests. Edwin Binney (1965) points to Heine's many references to nocturnal dances and the idea of dancing to death; he also cites the reawakening interest among antiquarians in the medieval "Dance of Death" in art and literature. Although act 2 of *La Sylphide* (1832) is often cited as the direct inspiration for the wilis' dances, Coralli had created a prototypical "white ballet" as early as 1828 in a melodrama based on Goethe's *Faust*.

The idea of art for art's sake, attributed to Gautier and espoused by many artists and critics after 1830, is paralleled by the conception of *Giselle* as a ballet about dancing. The Romantic cult of the artist had resulted in the separation of art and life; to many artists, art was primarily the pursuit of the beautiful rather than an agent of social and political change. *Giselle* was not intended as a manifesto against class distinctions; Albrecht's rank serves as a plot device rather than a real cause for grievance. As Gautier's original concept attests, the real interest of *Giselle* was dancing. The importance of dancing in the role of Giselle foreshadowed the increasing dominance of dancing in Perrot's ballets, particularly those of the late 1840s (e.g., *Les Éléments, Les Quatre Saisons*), which are basically suites of dances linked by the merest thread of story.

The medieval setting of *Giselle* stemmed largely from a revival of interest in the Middle Ages that began in the mid-eighteenth century and was shared by many literary and artistic groups besides the Romantics. Although medieval themes and styles could be used to illustrate a moral (e.g., to contrast the religious faith of the Middle Ages with contemporary godlessness), the medievalism in *Giselle* is somewhat superficial, a form of fancy dress. It has much in common with the troubadour style in art and literature, which tended to sentimentalize and trivialize the medieval, and with the "Intimate Romantic" type of painting identified by Roy Strong as "familial or amorous drama" combined with "personal, domestic glimpses of earlier ages."

Although Albrecht is nominally a duke, count, or prince, the ballet virtually ignores his function as a ruler of other men; it is entirely focused on his personal life. This concern with the individual and his inner being, rather than with the social group and its interactions, was one of the distinguishing marks of the Romantic movement both in art and in life. In her analysis of the Romantic hero, Lilian R. Furst describes a type of man who could well be Albrecht: "a sort of *homme fatal*," a member of the leisured class, self-absorbed, self-centered, cherishing illusions that can be crushed by a single experience. He "all too frequently exerts a disruptive, indeed destructive force."

Erik Aschengreen sees Albrecht as a man motivated by "a feeling of an incomplete existence . . . [that] causes him to seek something, though he hardly knows what." *Giselle* thus combines two Romantic preoccupations: disillusionment with this world and a quest for something beyond. Aschengreen summarizes *Giselle* as "a drama of the Romantic who seeks the unity of existence, but this time, disillusioned, must resign himself to the fact that there is an unbridgeable gulf between ideals and reality."

This search or quest, which is also central to *La Sylphide*, can also degenerate into escapism and thrill-seeking. John Chapman sees *Giselle* as an example of *juste–milieu*, or middle-of-the-road art, "an illusive, otherworldly vision in a classical language with erotic undertones." It did not intend to break new ground, either stylistic or thematic; rather, it was designed as middle-class entertainment, appealing to the audience's taste for the sensuous and exotic. This argument is convincing in the light of the original ending of the ballet, in which Bathilde returned to reclaim Albrecht. Here the more dangerous aspects of Romanticism are kept firmly in check: the mad girl dies, midnight terrors are dispelled by daylight, and the everyday world exerts its benevolent control. When this ending was changed, a darker meaning could be read into the ballet, as a Moscow critic did in 1850: "The bewitched Albrecht would return to the glade the following night in the hope of finding the spirit of Giselle again. He is not afraid of the evil of the wilis, nor of their fatal dances, nor of death itself" (Guest, 1970).

Giselle was restaged in London at Her Majesty's Theatre in March 1842, with choreography credited to André Deshayes and Perrot, who danced Albrecht to Grisi's Giselle. The ballet revealed its full dramatic stature in 1843, when Fanny Elssler assumed the title role at Her Majesty's. The intensity and conviction of her acting elevated act 1 into a scene of true pathos.

The French choreographer Antoine Titus was responsible for the first Russian staging, presented in Saint Petersburg in December 1842 with Elena Andreyanova in the title role. In Milan, Antonio Cortesi choreographed his version as a four-act *Giselle* to music by Giovanni Bajetti; it was first danced by Fanny Cerrito at La Scala in 1843. An American choreographer and dancer, Henry Wells, presented his own version of *Giselle* in New York in November 1841. The first American staging of the Coralli-Perrot version was presented in Boston in 1846 by Mary Ann Lee, who also danced the title role.

Despite its success, *Giselle* did not become a permanent

fixture at the Paris Opera, although it was given a new and more elaborate production in 1863 to mark the Paris Opera debut of Marfa Muravieva. It was dropped from the repertory in 1868 and was not revived until 1924.

Giselle, however, continued to be performed in Russia. Lucile Grahn danced it there in 1843, Elssler in 1848. In 1850, Perrot restaged it in Saint Petersburg for Grisi, revising much of it and strengthening its dramatic scenes.

Marius Petipa, who assisted Perrot with this restaging, continued to rework the ballet's choreography, scenario, and music until as late as 1889, although his 1884 revision is usually cited as the most influential. One of his major changes was the expansion of the wilis' dances into a *grand pas de wilis*. His choreography, recorded in Stepanov notation, was brought to the West by Nikolai Sergeyev, who revived the ballet for several companies, first for the Paris Opera Ballet in 1924. He also worked with

GISELLE. Carla Fracci (on floor) as Giselle and Erik Bruhn (kneeling) as Albrecht, with members of the ensemble of American Ballet Theatre, in a 1967 performance of the Mad Scene at the end of act 1. (Photograph from the Dance Collection, New York Public Library for the Performing Arts.)

GISELLE. (*above, left*) Yvette Chauviré, *premiere danseuse étoile* of the Paris Opera Ballet, in act 2, c.1950. (*above, right*) Alicia Markova and Anton Dolin danced with Ballet Theatre and with their own company in the late 1940s. (*below, left*) Natalia Makarova and Mikhail Baryshnikov, stars of American Ballet Theatre, in act 2, 1974. (Photograph above, left, from the Dance Collection, New York Public Library for the Performing Arts. Photograph above, right, by Fred Fehl; used by permission. Photograph below, left, © 1974 by Max Waldman; used by permission.)

Alicia Markova and Anton Dolin, who danced the principal roles with the Vic-Wells Ballet and toured extensively with their own company with *Giselle*. The Petipa version was also the basis of the *Giselle* reintroduced to the West by Diaghilev's Ballets Russes in 1910, with Tamara Karsavina and Vaslav Nijinsky in the leading roles. This became the basis of most twentieth-century productions.

Giselle allows considerable latitude in the interpretation of dramatic details and individual characterizations. Soviet productions, for example, often portrayed Hilarion as a sympathetic character, thus affirming his inherent virtue as a man of the people. Some Western productions also present him as an appealing young man who leaves gifts of flowers or game at Giselle's door. Gautier (1845) described him, however, as an unattractive, farouche man, whose love for Giselle is "un de ces amours qui ressemblent fort à de la haine" (one of those loves that strongly resembles hate).

Albrecht is also played with varying degrees of sympathy. Gautier (1845) intended him to be likable despite his faults: "Albrecht n'a trompé Giselle qu'à demi, et seulement sur sa qualité. En lui disant qu'il aimait, il était complètement sincère" (Albrecht only deceived Giselle partially, and only in his social rank. In telling how he loved her, he was completely sincere). A somewhat harsher interpretation is sometimes given: the premier danseur Erik Bruhn saw him as a playboy who "does not dream that Giselle will take his attentions so seriously."

Giselle's death may be caused by an actual wound from Albrecht's sword, inflicted upon herself in her madness (an interpretation that Gautier seems to support), or by the effects of shock and sorrow on a weak heart. According to Frank Ries, Petipa used the latter version because suicide was not acceptable on the nineteenth-century Russian stage. In recalling a hand-wiping gesture that Giselle makes, as though to get rid of blood, the English ballerina Moira Shearer states that Karsavina confirmed, "Oh yes, she stabs herself. It's the sword that kills her" (Newman, 1982). In 1945, Edwin Denby described Alicia Alonso's Giselle as "no tubercular ballerina-peasant but a spirited girl who stabs herself."

The characterization of Giselle as physically frail is, however, corroborated by the 1841 scenario, in which Berthe confides to Loys that Giselle is delicate and the

doctor has warned her against overexerting herself. Some ballerinas show this debility by making Giselle grow breathless and exhausted after her first dance with Albrecht and the villagers.

Surprisingly few attempts have been made to transpose the ballet's setting from medieval Germany or to reinterpret its action in terms of modern psychological theories. An exception is Mats Ek's *Giselle* (1982), which presents a fey, almost grotesque heroine in a stylized landscape replete with fertility symbols. Act 2 of Ek's ballet takes place in an insane asylum, where the white-gowned patients enact the part of the wilis. In 1984, the Dance Theatre of Harlem introduced a Creole *Giselle* set in the bayou region of Louisiana.

Giselle has inspired many adaptations and parodies, among them William Moncrieff's melodrama *Giselle, or The Phantom Night Dancers* (1841), the opera *The Night Dancers* (1846) by George Soane and Edward James Loder, and Myra Kinch's satirical ballet *Giselle's Revenge* (1953). *Grise-aile*, a series of caricatures, was published by Alcide Joseph Lorentz in *La Revue Philipon* (1842).

An enumeration of the famous Giselles of the past and present would occupy many pages; only a few can be mentioned here. Anna Pavlova, for example, famed as a dancer-actress, invested her mad scene with a feeling of terror that communicated itself to the spectator. Olga Spessivtseva's Giselle was compounded of dramatic fire, a lyrical dancing style, and an appearance of deceptive fragility. Galina Ulanova depicted a carefree girl who is transformed by tragedy into a being capable of transcendental love. Alicia Markova, a mistress of period style, was often compared to a Romantic lithograph come to life; her acting gave subtle emotional color to her weightless, precise dancing. Natalia Makarova's approach stressed

GISELLE. Laurent Hilaire (kneeling, at left) as Albrecht, Isabelle Guérin (bowing, at center) as Giselle, and Karin Averty (standing, at right) as Myrtha, Queen of the Wilis, with members of the female ensemble, in act 2, at the Paris Opera, 1995. (Photograph by Colette Masson; used by permission of Agence Enguerand, Paris.)

Giselle's spirituality in both the first and second acts; her death merely freed her from earthly concerns without altering her essential nature.

Giselle has repeatedly attracted dancers, choreographers, audiences, and scholars. Its capacity to absorb changes without losing its character has allowed many different *Giselles* to coexist, each valid in its own way. This capacity for change, perhaps, has given the ballet its vitality and longevity. Like all great works of art, it is both timeless and a product of its time.

[*Many of the figures mentioned herein are the subjects of independent entries.*]

BIBLIOGRAPHY.   Théophile Gautier's writings about *Giselle* can be found in *Les beautés de l'Opéra*, written in collaboration with Jules Janin and Philarète Chasles (Paris, 1845); *Théâtre: Mystère, comédies et ballets*, new ed. (Paris, 1882); and *The Romantic Ballet*, edited and translated by Cyril W. Beaumont, rev. ed. (London, 1947). Edwin Binney 3d, in *Les ballets de Théophile Gautier* (Paris, 1965), gives much information about the sources and genesis of the ballet.

Specialized studies of *Giselle* include Cyril W. Beaumont's *The Ballet Called Giselle*, 2d rev. ed. (London, 1945); Doris Hering's *Giselle and Albrecht* (New York, 1981); Serge Lifar's *Giselle: Apothéose du ballet romantique* (Paris, 1942); Evan Alderson's "Ballet as Ideology: *Giselle* Act II," *Dance Chronicle* 10.3 (1987): 290–304; Marian E. Smith's "What Killed Giselle?," *Dance Chronicle* 13.1 (1990): 68–81; and Frank W. D. Ries's "In Search of Giselle," *Dance Magazine* 53 (August 1979): 59–74.

Synopses and useful commentaries can also be found in George Balanchine and Francis Mason, *Balanchine's Complete Stories of the Great Ballets*, rev. and enl. ed. (Garden City, N.Y., 1977), and in Cyril W. Beaumont's *Complete Book of Ballets* (London, 1937). Joan Lawson's *A History of Ballet and Its Makers* (New York, 1964) contains a detailed analysis of the ballet's musical and choreographic leitmotives. John Mueller's "Is Giselle a Virgin?" in *Dance Chronicle* 4.2 (1981): 151–154, is a study of dramatic motivations. Giannandrea Poesio's "Giselle," *The Dancing Times* (March 1994): 563–573, provides an analysis of the scenario and choreography. Various dancers recall their first performance in the ballet in Germaine Prudhommeau, "Giselle première," *Danser* (October 1991): 35–40.

Ivor Guest's many books on nineteenth-century ballet describe various productions of *Giselle* in their historical context; these include *The Romantic Ballet in Paris*, 2d rev. ed. (London, 1980); *Jules Perrot* (London, 1984); *The Romantic Ballet in England* (London, 1972); *Fanny Elssler* (London, 1970); *Fanny Cerrito*, 2d rev. ed. (London, 1974); and *The Ballet of the Second Empire* (London, 1974). A wider scope is covered in his *Le ballet de l'Opéra de Paris* (Paris, 1976), while an unusual topic is treated in his "Parodies of *Giselle* on the English Stage, 1841–1871," *Theatre Notebook* 9.2 (1955): 38–46.

Russian and American productions are respectively described in Natalia Roslavleva's *Era of the Russian Ballet* (1966; reprint, New York, 1979) and Mary Grace Swift's *Belles and Beaux on Their Toes: Dancing Stars in Young America* (Washington, D.C., 1980). Gorsky's production is discussed in Elizabeth Souritz, *Soviet Choreographers in the 1920s*, translated by Lynn Visson (Durham, N.C., 1990). Barbara Newman's *Striking a Balance: Dancers Talk about Dancing*, rev. ed. (New York, 1992), includes commentaries on the ballet by Alicia Alonso, Moira Shearer, and Igor Youskevitch. Erik Bruhn's "Beyond Technique," *Dance Perspectives*, no. 36 (1968), contains his reflections on the ballet.

Analyses of *Giselle* as a Romantic work of art can be found in Erik Aschengreen's "The Beautiful Danger: Aspects of the Romantic Ballet," *Dance Perspectives*, no. 58 (Summer 1974); Richard Buckle's "Monsters at Midnight, Part 3," *Dance and Dancers* 17 (June 1966): 22–27; and John V. Chapman's "An Unromantic View of Nineteenth-Century Romanticism," *York Dance Review*, no. 7 (Spring 1978): 28–40. Useful insights into *Giselle's* Romantic background are also provided by Lilian R. Furst's "The Romantic Hero, or Is He an Anti-Hero?" in her *Contours of European Romanticism* (Lincoln, Neb., 1979); Arnold Hauser's *The Social History of Art*, vol. 3, *Rococo Classicism, and Romanticism*, translated by Stanley Godman (1951; reprint, New York, 1985); Hugh Honour's *Romanticism* (New York, 1979); Roy Strong's *Recreating the Past: British History and the Victorian Painter* (London, 1978); and William Vaughan's *German Romantic Painting* (New Haven, 1980).

SUSAN AU

GISSEY, HENRY (born 19 January 1621 in Paris, died 4 February 1673 in Paris), French sculptor and costume designer. The son of Germain Gissey, *sculpteur ordinaire de la chambre du roi* ("sculptor in ordinary of the king's chamber"), Henry Gissey had a brilliant career as a designer at the court of Louis XIV after he designed the costumes for the choreographic sections of *Le Ballet des Noces de Pélée et Thétis* in 1654. His models must have been highly esteemed, because in 1660 he was named *dessinateur du Cabinet du roi* ("designer of the king's cabinet"). However, he became famous particularly for his costumes for the *carroûsel* (horse ballet) held in front of the Louvre and the Tuileries in 1662. This gained Gissey admission, in 1663, to the Academy of Painting, an honor enjoyed by very few designers of revels. He also had the honor of submitting projects for fireworks and funerals, as well as of collaborating on performances of the *comédie-ballets* by the two "great Baptists," Molière (Jean-Baptiste Poquelin) and Jean-Baptiste Lully. His name remains linked with the creation of *George Dandin* (1668), *Le Bourgeois Gentilhomme* (1670), and the tragicomedy *Psyché* (1671). For this last work he created no fewer than thirty-six designs, which reveal the variety of his inspiration and the qualities of his style.

From his predecessors, particularly from Rabel and Stefano della Bella, Gissey inherited a complete descriptive vocabulary capable of evoking a character. He developed these expressive possibilities to assist the spectator to follow the plot more easily. Here, with a deliberate choice of balance and elegance, he followed the rule known as "appropriateness of costumes," which for more than a century was to be followed with particular devotion by his successors Jean Berain, Claude Gillot, Jean-Baptiste Martin, and Louis Boquet.

BIBLIOGRAPHY
Beaumont, Cyril W. *Five Centuries of Ballet Design*. London, 1939.
Christout, Marie-Françoise. *The Ballet de Cour in the Seventeenth Century* (in French and English). Geneva, 1987.
La Gorce, Jérôme de. "Les costumes d'Henry Gissey pour les représentations de *Psyché*." *Revue de l'art*, no. 66 (1984): 39–52.
Montaiglon, Anatole de. *Henri de Gissey de Paris: Dessinateur ordinaire des plaisirs et des ballets du roi*. Paris, 1854.

JÉRÔME DE LA GORCE
Translated from French

GITANA, LA. Russian title: *Gitana, ispanska Pia tsy-ganka*. Ballet in a prologue and three scenes. Choreography: Filippo Taglioni. Music: Hermann Schmidt and Daniel Auber. Libretto: Filippo Taglioni. First performance: 5 [17] December 1838, Bolshoi Theater, Saint Petersburg. Principals: Marie Taglioni (Lauretta), Nikolai Osipovich Golts (Ivan).

This ballet was Marie Taglioni's answer to Fanny Elssler—living proof that she, too, could succeed in the type of national dances in which her rival Elssler excelled. Choreographed for her by her father, Filippo, during their first trip to Russia, the work contained not only a mazurka but also a Spanish dance similar to Elssler's famous *cachucha* in *Le Diable Boiteux* (1836). *La Gitana* was very popular both in Russia and in London, where Antonio Guerra restaged Taglioni's choreography at Her Majesty's Theatre in June 1839, with Marie Taglioni in the title role.

The ballet depicted a young aristocratic girl, Lauretta, who is kidnapped by Gypsies as a seven-year-old child. Ten years later she is seen dancing at a fair by Ivan, the son of the governor of Nijni Novgorod, and the two fall in love. He pursues the Gypsies and restores Lauretta to her home, where the sight of her childhood surroundings brings back memories of her earlier life.

By coincidence, *La Gitana* was similar in title to Joseph Mazilier's *La Gipsy*, choreographed at the Paris Opera in January 1839 as a vehicle for Elssler. The settings and plots of the two ballets were actually very different, although both concerned aristocratic girls kidnapped by Gypsies. The role of Sarah in *La Gipsy* appears to have been much more full-blooded than Marie Taglioni's Lauretta, exploiting Elssler's dramatic gifts as well as her genius for character dancing. In contrast to *La Gitana*, the ending of *La Gipsy* is starkly tragic: Sarah stabs to death her rival, who has caused the death of her lover. Lauretta is more passive and peaceable. The ethereality of Marie Taglioni's Sylphide evidently crept even into her interpretation of *La Gitana*'s Spanish dance: an English reviewer likened her to "a deer standing with expanded nostril and neck uplifted to its loftiest height, at the first scent of his pursuers in the breeze. It was the very soul of swiftness embodied in a look!" (Guest, 1972).

The dual nature of both Sarah and Lauretta, who are at once aristocrats and Gypsies, evinces the Romantic era's ambivalence about the figure of the outsider, the man or woman who lives beyond the bounds of conventional society. Gypsies, with their roving lifestyle and aura of enticement and danger, were perfect representatives of the breed. Esmeralda of Victor Hugo's novel *Notre-Dame de Paris* (1831) lent her name to Jules Perrot's ballet of 1844, which gave her not only the heroine's place but a happy ending, unlike that of Hugo's novel. The firebrand Carmen of Prosper Mérimée's eponymous novel (1845) has also

been enacted in balletic as well as operatic and cinematic forms. Unlike these two authentic Gypsies, however, Sarah and Lauretta are really high-ranking women who are eventually restored to their true stations, and even their Gypsy lovers are revealed to be nobly born. They enjoy the best of two worlds: the alluring freedom from constraint of Gypsy life and the more solid and enduring, if less interesting, benefits of upper-class wealth and privilege. August Bournonville's *A Folk Tale* (1854) would similarly bring its changeling heroine from the fascinatingly fey yet unruly world of the trolls to the orderly comforts of a Christian home.

BIBLIOGRAPHY

Beaumont, Cyril W. *Complete Book of Ballets*. London, 1937.
Guest, Ivor. *The Romantic Ballet in England*. London, 1972.
Levinson, André. *Marie Taglioni* (1929). Translated by Cyril W. Beaumont. London, 1977.

SUSAN AU

GLAZUNOV, ALEKSANDR (Aleksandr Konstantinovich Glazunov; born 10 August 1865 in Saint Petersburg, died 21 March 1936 in Paris), Russian composer and pedagogue. Glazunov was born into a cultured, affluent family. His father was a good amateur violinist and his mother an excellent pianist. During his childhood, Glazunov voluntarily attended lectures at the University of Saint Petersburg and at the age of nine began taking lessons in piano and elementary music theory from Elenovsky, a well-known pianist. Also at this time Glazunov began to compose. In 1878, his mother asked Mily Balakirev, with whom she was acquainted, to continue her son's musical education.

Glazunov absorbed elementary principles with astonishing speed and retention. In 1879, Balakirev showed Nikolai Rimsky-Korsakov an orchestral score written by the fourteen-year-old Glazunov. He was so impressed that he accepted Glazunov as a student at once, later writing that Glazunov's musical development "progressed not by the day, but literally by the hour." During his study with Rimsky-Korsakov, Glazunov learned to play nearly every instrument in the orchestra, which served as preparation for his brilliant handling of the orchestra, as reflected in his ballets. Glazunov became known outside Russia through the interest of Franz Liszt, who sponsored his earliest concerts and conducted the first one in Weimar in 1884.

Glazunov composed three major commissioned ballets and, throughout his career, wrote music of such melody, sweep, texture, and sensuous appeal that choreographers have dipped into his oeuvre for at least thirty other ballets. In his ballet music, and in nearly all his program music for the stage, Glazunov extended principles developed by Petr Ilich Tchaikovsky, with all of the older composer's grace and melody yet without his symphonic underpinning. Nevertheless, Glazunov's gift of melody, elegance of form, and special scoring, especially for viola and cello, provided a sensibility that honored the choreography.

As a composer, Glazunov existed only to make music for music's sake. Although the former Soviet Union designated him People's Artist of the Republic, Glazunov was just as apolitical as he was traditional. His three ballets, all commissioned for Marius Petipa to choreograph, were composed from 1896 to 1899, during the composer's prime: the three-act *Raymonda* premiered in January of 1898, the one-act works, *Les Ruses d'Amour* and *The Seasons*, in January and February of 1900.

In *Raymonda* the vigorous Hungarian folk elements, suitably balletized, provide a striking contrast to the classical variations with their skillfully characterized melodies and rhythms. Glazunov's skill in providing rhythmic variety is especially apparent in the wedding *divertissement* that makes up the last act, supported by typically brilliant orchestration. [*See* Raymonda.] The use of strongly differentiated moods is also seen in *The Seasons;* the chill of winter, the delight of spring, the languor of summer, and the bacchanal of autumn, shift each mood by imaginative changes of rhythm and orchestral color. The gentler *Les Ruses d'Amour,* which has been neglected in the West, reflects its eighteenth-century setting in both orchestration and rhythms but also shows Glazunov's gift for sweeping Romantic melodies.

Glazunov was appointed a professor at the Saint Petersburg Conservatory in 1899 and its director in 1905. Soon after, it became clear that his finest composing days were behind him as he retreated into the academicism that was by then the signature of his generation; he was no longer the standard against which Russia's musical youth measured itself. He was a highly regarded teacher, however, and among his students was the young Dimitri Shostakovich. Glazunov left Russia in 1928 and settled in France, where he died in 1936.

BIBLIOGRAPHY

Abraham, Gerald. "Glazunov: The End of an Episode." In Abraham's *On Russian Music.* London, 1939.

Bakst, James. *A History of Russian-Soviet Music.* New York, 1966.

Calvocoressi, M. D., and Gerald Abraham. *Masters of Russian Music.* London, 1936.

Cohen-Stratyner, Barbara Naomi. "Glazunov." In *Biographical Dictionary of Dance.* New York, 1982.

Evans, Edwin. "Bacchanale." *The Dancing Times* (February 1940: 277–278.

Fedorova, Galina. *A. K. Glazunov* (in Russian). Moscow, 1947.

Günther-Glazunov, Elena. "Auf der Suche nach einem verlorenen Schatz." *Ballet-Journal/Das Tanzarchiv* 38 (June 1990): 46–49. Letters from Fokine to Glazunov.

Harris, Dale. "Glazunov." In *The Encyclopedia of Dance and Ballet.* New York, 1977.

Kriukov, Andrei. *Alexander Konstantinowitsch Glasunow.* Berlin, 1988.

Kunitsyn, Oleg. *Balety A. K. Glazunova.* Moscow, 1989.

Leonard, Richard Anthony. "The Second Generation." In Leonard's *A History of Russian Music.* New York, 1957.

Molden, Peter L. "Glazounov and the Ballet" (parts 1–2). *The Dancing Times* (July–August 1987).

Montagu-Nathan, Montagu. "Alexander Konstantinovich Glazounov." In *The Music Masters,* vol. 4, *The Twentieth Century,* by W. R. Anderson et al. Harmondsworth, 1957.

Mundy, Simon. *Alexander Glazunov.* London, 1987.

Schwarz, Boris. *Music and Musical Life in Soviet Russia, 1917–1970.* London, 1972.

Schwarz, Boris. "Glazunov, Alexander." In *The New Grove Dictionary of Music and Musicians.* London, 1980.

Souritz, Elizabeth. *Soviet Choreographers in the 1920s.* Translated by Lynn Visson. Durham, N.C., 1990.

Venturini, Donald J. *Alexander Glazounov: His Life and Works.* Delphos, Ohio, 1992.

JOSEPH GALE

GLIÈRE, REINHOLD (Reinhold Moritsovich Glier; born 30 December 1874 [11 January 1875] in Kiev, Ukraine, died 23 June 1975 in Moscow), composer. Glière's great interest in folklore as a source of musical language comprehensible to the listener with a broad taste in music, and his studies with famous classical composers, led to the leading position he occupied in the cultural development of the newly formed Soviet Union. Glière graduated from the Moscow Conservatory in 1900, having studied polyphony and form with Sergei Taneyev, composition with Mikhail Ippolitov-Ivanov, and harmony with Anton Arensky. He was acquainted with luminaries of Russian music such as Nikolai Rimsky-Korsakov, Vladimir Stasov, and Aleksandr Glazunov.

Glière left an enormous body of compositions, including six operas and three symphonies, but his major works were his ballets. The most important of these was *The Red Poppy* (1927). Its score reveals a mature composer who knew the specific character of the genre well. Glière had previously composed for dance. The Ellen Rabenek Studio presented his ballet-pantomime *Chrysis* (1912) in choreography by Tatiana Savinskaya and Vera Voskresenskaya to a libretto by Natalia Mill after Pierre Louÿs's *Les Chansons de Bilitis* and *Aphrodite;* Aleksandr Gorsky's rechoreographed version of 1921 was never staged. *Cleopatra* (1925), based on Aleksandr Pushkin's "Egyptian Nights," was staged as a ballet-melodrama by Leonid Baratov for the music studio of the Moscow Art Theater as part of a Pushkin Evening on 11 January 1926. It incorporated exotic dances, an element that was to recur in Soviet ballet. That year Glière revised and expanded Cesare Pugni's score for the ballet *La Esmeralda,* newly choreographed for the Bolshoi Ballet by Vasily Tikhomirov; these revisions formed part of the score used by Agrippina Vaganova for her staging of the ballet at the Kirov Theater in 1935 and by Vladimir Burmeister for his in 1950 at the Stanislavsky and Nemirovich-Danchenko Musical Theater. After *The Red Poppy* (1926), Glière's ballet *The Comedians* (1930), based on Lope de Vega's *Fuente Ovejuna*, was choreographed by Aleksandr Chekrygin for the Bolshoi Ballet in 1931 (a new version, retitled *A Daughter of Castile*, was choreographed by Aleksei Chichinadze for the Stanislavsky and Nemirovich-Danchenko Musical Theater in 1955).

The Red Poppy, choreographed by Lev Lashchilin and Tikhomirov, was a milestone in the annals of Soviet ballet because, for the first time in any state-run theater's repertory, the contemporary struggle for liberation was treated in a full-length work with artistic persuasiveness and with "the people" as the collective hero. Glière achieved an organic blend of classical traditions and new material to create a new idiom. He wove into the fabric of the composition elements of Soviet and Chinese folklore, drawing on the full range of classical choreography—adagio, variations, scenes, character and folk dances, mass or ensemble dances, and large pantomimic formations. The music of the ballet was characterized by striking melodic and harmonic language and rich orchestration built on vivid dramatic contrasts. [*See* Red Poppy, The.]

These features of the composer's style were developed further in the ballet *The Bronze Horseman*. Based on the eponymous poem by Pushkin, the ballet premiered at the Kirov Theater in 1948, with choreography by Konstantin Sergeyev (it was staged at the Bolshoi Theater in 1949, choreographed by Rostislav Zakharov). The psychological presentation of the lyrical characters Parasha and Evgeny contrasts with the epic majesty of Peter the Great and Saint Petersburg, which represent the power of the Russian state. The ballet is distinguished by its wholeness of form, a carefully worked-out dramatic design, and its system of dominant themes.

Glière's last ballet, *Taras Bulba* (1952), based on Gogol's story, also celebrated the heroic past. It was never staged.

In recognition of his work for the development of Soviet art, Glière was awarded the title of People's Artist of the USSR (1938) and the State Prize of the USSR (1946, 1948, and 1950).

BIBLIOGRAPHY

Belza, Igor F. *R. M. Glier* (in Russian). 2d ed. Moscow, 1962.
Glière, Reinhold. *Stat'i i vospominaniia.* Edited by V. A. Kiseleva. Moscow, 1975.
Katonova, S. V. *Baleti R. M. Gliera.* Moscow, 1960.
Krebs, Stanley Dale. *Soviet Composers and the Development of Soviet Music.* New York, 1970.
Lewin, S. I. "Dva baleta R. M. Gliera 'Krasnii tsvetok,' 'Mednii vsadnik.'" In *Muzyka sovetskovo baleta,* edited by L. N. Raaben, pp. 126–162. Moscow, 1962.
Yagolim, B. S. *R. M. Glier: Notograficheskii spavochnik.* Moscow, 1964.

GALINA A. GULYAEVA
Translated from Russian

GLUCK, CHRISTOPH WILLIBALD

GLUCK, CHRISTOPH WILLIBALD (Christoph Willibald Ritter von Gluck; born 2 July 1744 in Erasbach, Upper Palatinate, died 15 November 1787 in Vienna), German composer. Two categories of dance and ballet appear in Gluck's work: (1) dance as independent ballet and ballet pantomime; (2) dance in the context of his operas, such as *ballo* and *ballet-aria*, or *balli pantomimi* and *balli ballati* (Gluck's terminology).

Independent Ballets. In contemporary sources, the independent ballets were mainly called *ballo* or *ballet*, but those called *ballet pantomime* by Gaspero Angiolini particularly occupied Gluck in Vienna from 1759 to 1765. His most important partner, as choreographer and solo dancer, was Angiolini. After the rejection and failure of the ballet pantomimes *Sémiramis* and *Iphigénie*, produced jointly with Angiolini in January and May of 1765, Gluck withdrew from pure dance theater while Angiolini continued. The integration of the dance—as ballet and pantomime—into opera continued to occupy Gluck's creative thinking till the end of his life.

Gluck confronted the task of composing ballet music professionally for the first time when Joseph Starzer, whose responsibility this had been since 1752, followed Franz Hilverding to Saint Petersburg in the winter of 1758/59. In the salary accounts of the Viennese court (*État des personnes engagées*) for 1759, Gluck is mentioned as a *compositeur des airs* (composer of ballet music) with an annual salary of Fl 500. Angiolini, Hilverding's successor as choreographer at the Burgtheater, received a salary of Fl 840 for choreographing the ballets. In the same position and again with a salary of Fl 500, Gluck appeared in 1759 and 1760 also at the Kärntnertor Theater where Karl Bernardi was choreographer. In the 1761/62 season Franz Asplmayr replaced Gluck at the Kärntnertor Theater while Giuseppe Scarlatti took over from Gluck at the Burgtheater (1762/63). In 1763/64, Gluck, with Florian Gassmann, was responsible for the ballet music at both Viennese theaters. During these years Gluck is referred to as *direttore generale della musica* ("director general of music") "including the ballet music to be composed." His salary was 1650 florins.

During the years 1759 to 1765, Gluck's composition of ballet music in the broadest sense included independent "big" and "small" ballets, dances in Italian operas, such as *Orfeo ed Euridice*, and dances in *opéras comiques* such as *La Rencontre Imprévue* (The Unforeseen Encounter). The music that Gluck composed for independent ballets from the middle of April 1759 to the first one that is actually connected with his name, *Don Juan, ou Le Festin de Pierre* (1761), a ballet pantomime, appears to be lost. It seems likely, however, that identifications will occur once the many substantial anonymous collections and library holdings with attributions to Gluck have been investigated.

The same is true of the ballets composed by Gluck for *opéras comiques* during this period. The ballet music for Gluck's *Le Diable à Quatre*, preserved in manuscript score in Dresden, is probably not identical with the "new ballet of domestic servants" that concluded the premiere performance at the court theater in Laxenburg, near Vienna, on 28 May 1759 (Khevenhüller-Metsch, 1907–). Chloé's aria "Avec Quelle Ardeur" in *La Cythère Assiégée* (1759), designated as a *menuet avec danse* (the trio is played by the orchestra only) according to Bruce Brown (1991), may "be the earliest example of music meant specifically for dancing that we have from his pen." The amalgamation of sung airs and dance became possible through the talents of singer-dancers or dancer-singers, such as Louise Bodin, *prima ballerina* of the Burgtheater, who is also said to have sung leading roles in *opéra comique*. Gluck used instruments—for example, tambours, castanets, and tambourines—to correspond with the exotic themes of some of his ballets, including *Les Turcs*, *Le Port de Marseille*, and *Le Prix de la Danse*.

The announcement of and reactions to the first performance of the ballet pantomime *Don Juan, ou Le Festin de Pierre* at the Burgtheater on 17 October 1761 bear witness to the importance of the event. The outstanding impression achieved by Gluck and Angiolini is also reflected in more contemporary judgments. The expressive possibilities and the synthesis of music, pantomime, and dance astonished and greatly interested the eyewitnesses, responses that have remained constant from Franz Liszt in 1854 to more recent reformers and innovators such as Isadora Duncan, Rudolf Laban, Michel Fokine, Heinrich Kröller, and Aurelio Milloss. The division of the "grand" ballet pantomime into three acts or *parties* corresponds to the stage settings: street, banqueting hall, and cemetery. It also takes into account that both Don Juan and the Komthur appear at the end as ghosts. Gluck's music, which combines dance and pantomime for the representation of a full drama, was created through the close collaboration of the composer with the choreographer Angiolini, who himself danced the role of Don Juan. Still under discussion is the existence of two authentic versions of the score. The hypothesis that version A, the "long" version consisting of a sinfonia and thirty-one numbers, belongs to the 1770s must now be revised. It is fairly clear that the long version had already been performed by Angiolini and Gluck in Vienna in the early 1760s, as can be inferred from the extraordinarily large number of personnel and props, and even more so from the existence of the role of the servant in the third solo part in the revival on 5 April 1763.

The Transition to Ballet in Opera. As a counterpart to the tragic dance drama *Don Juan*, Angiolini produced, again in close contact with Gluck, *La Cythère Assiégée* (1759), an *opéra comique*, at the Burgtheater on 15 Sep-

tember 1762. Angiolini's second *Dissertation* (1765) indicates that the work was "reduced to a Ballo Pantomimo," and his *Lettere* (1773) notes that this was accomplished "without even introducing a sylvan note, the new texture notwithstanding." The success of this experiment, a danced comedy to the music of a comic opera, was overshadowed by Gluck's first Italian reform opera, *Orfeo ed Euridice*, which was performed three weeks later.

It was not until 4 October 1764, the name day of Emperor Franz Stefan, that Gluck again presented a ballet of his own at the Burgtheater: *Alessandro*. The scenario of this ballet is lost. The music consists of an introduction and seven numbers, beginning with a march and concluding with a *grande chaconne* that Gluck used again in the *divertissement* of his 1776 Paris version of his 1767 opera *Alceste*, after having used other parts of the ballet in his operas *Iphigénie en Aulide* and *Orphée*, both performed in Paris in 1774. Angiolini's name is neither mentioned in conjunction with Gluck's *Alessandro*-ballet nor a revival in Laxenburg on 21 May 1765.

The year 1765 brought to a poignant conclusion Gluck's composition of his ballet-pantomimes. His *Sémiramis*, a "tragédie en ballet," was first performed at the Burgtheater on 31 January 1765, on the occasion of the remarriage of Emperor Joseph II. The work found "absolutely no approval," says Khevenhüller-Metsch, probably not just because it was "far too pompous and sad for a wedding celebration." The action, in three acts after the model of Voltaire's tragedy, unfolds as an *action complète* in only twenty minutes. The horrible events are almost a reversal of the Oedipus drama: Queen Semiramis has removed her husband Ninus so that she may marry her own son, Ninias, who is unaware of the blood relationship. In compliance with the punishment decreed by the gods for murder and incest, Ninias kills his wife and mother Semiramis. When Ninias is about to kill himself, his suicide is prevented. Only three personages take active part in the representation: Semiramis, Ninias, and the Ghost of Ninus, who plays a major role in the ballet. Gluck fulfilled to the letter Angiolini's requirement that everything speak in the music and wrote what was probably his most modern score: a sinfonia and fifteen numbers, divided among the three acts. Frequently the individual numbers merge seamlessly, one with the next; the convention of separate dance pieces in the traditional manner was abandoned. Each *reigen*, or round dance (nos. 9a and 9b), is treated as a solemnly stepped hymn. Further light is thrown on the connection between Gluck's music and Angiolini's scenario by the reintroduction of much of the *Sémiramis* music in Gluck's *Iphigénie en Tauride* (1778).

Iphigénie, another Gluck-Angiolini ballet collaboration, had been performed on 19 May 1765 in Laxenburg. Both the scenario, based on a tragedy by Jean Racine, and the music are lost. As a gesture of respect and to assuage the court audience, shocked by *Sémiramis*, a happy ending was introduced. According to Gluck's admirer Archduke Leopold, the music pleased everyone greatly. The revival of the long, sad ballet of *Iphigenia* on 18 August 1765, the occasion of the archduke's wedding celebrations, was the last theater event witnessed by the balletomane Emperor Franz Stefan. Because of the death of the emperor, the performance of Angiolini's *Ballo d'Achille* did not take place. The story for the (now lost) scenario probably came from Pietro Metastasio's poem of the same name; Metastasio himself had considered the subject particularly suited for choreographic representation. Because Metastasio's *Achille in Sciro* shows connections to Racine's and also to Angiolini and Gluck's *Iphigénie*, one is tempted to think of Gluck as the composer of the music to Angiolini's *Ballo d'Achille* as well. It is also conceivable, partly because Gluck was overburdened with commitments in 1765, that Angiolini himself wrote the music as he had done in 1764 for *Le Muse Protette dal Genio d'Austria.* The musical authorship, however, has to be reevaluated in view of a *Ballo d'Achille* attributed to Gluck and designated as authentic by Rudolf Gerber, but considered more than doubtful by Klaus Hortschansky. Until this controversy is settled, one has to consider Gluck the composer of the *Ballo d'Achille* choreographed by Angiolini in 1765.

Dance in Opera. In Gluck's great Italian operas of the 1760s in Vienna, the traditional division of tasks in the composition of the music becomes evident: music for the opera proper was separate from music for the dances and ballets connected with it, including the final ballet, or a ballet performed after the opera, or both. As composer for both opera and ballet, Gluck was probably responsible for the *pasticcio* ("patchwork") *Arianna,* first performed on 27 May 1762 at Laxenburg, *Orfeo ed Euridice,* which premiered on 5 October 1762, and *Paride ed Elena,* which premiered on 3 November 1770, the latter two operas first performed at the Burgtheater. On the other hand, the ballet music for the second version of Gluck's *Ezio,* first performed on 26 December 1763 at the Burgtheater, is by Gassmann. Franz Asplmayr composed the music for the "grotesque" Noverre ballet, *Les (Petits) Riens,* that was appended to the Italian *Alceste,* which premiered on 26 December 1767 at the Burgtheater. For later Viennese performances of *Alceste,* probably Starzer's ballet *La Festa d'Alceste* was used. Unclear is the situation surrounding *Telemaco,* first performed on 31 January 1765 at the Burgtheater. All extant scores end with Circe's orchestral recitative (curse and destruction of the world); the subsequent reconciliatory ballet mentioned in the libretto is missing. Angiolini was choreographer and solo dancer until 1765, including *Telemaco;* Noverre was responsible for *Alceste* and *Paride ed Elena.*

The dimensions and functions of the ballets in the above works differ greatly. *Arianna,* for which the music is lost, contained two pas de deux, as well as one or more ballets with a total of fourteen dancers; for revivals in Schönbrunn and at the Burgtheater with its large ballet, it was newly composed with a new solo for Madame Campioni. The four *balli* in *Orfeo ed Euridice* are integrated into the action. The first *ballo* consists of shepherds and nymphs, followers of Orpheus, in act 1, scene 1; the second *ballo,* of hellish spectres who attempt to terrify Orpheus in act 2, scene 1; the third *ballo,* of the happy shadows in the Elysian Fields in act 2, scene 2; the fourth *ballo,* of heroes and heroines, with Amor, Orpheus, and Eurydice in act 3, scene 3. Lively discussions surrounded especially the third *ballo,* whose subject was taken from the fourth book of Virgil's *Aeneid.* In the final ballet, the return of Eurydice was feasted and the triumph of Amor was celebrated; the twenty-six dancers included three solo singers; two gentlemen and two ladies in a pas de quatre; and, in "the Concerts" of soloists and corps de ballet, fourteen female and male dancers as well as five children (as *amorini*).

Unlike the dances in the reform opera *Orfeo ed Euridice,* the two *balli* composed by Gassmann for Gluck's *Ezio* stand outside of the action of the opera. The theme of the first *ballo* was "the love of Teti and Peleo" (Louise Bodin and Angiolini), characters disturbed by the jealousy of Neptune (Turchi the younger). The harbor of Algiers provided the background for a confrontation between Spaniards and Moors in the second *ballo.*

Telemaco was praised in the *Gazette de Vienne,* particularly the adaptation of the "ballets connected with the piece" to the "different situations." This was apparently said in reference not only to the festive dance in act 1, scene 1, the only scene in Gluck's score containing ballet music, but also to other scenes and to the act finales, the second of which is a subject of controversy even today. Karl Geiringer (in Gluck, 1962) conjectures that "an older dance scene" was used for the concluding ballet of the opera and suggests the fourth *ballo* from *Orfeo ed Euridice.*

Alceste, premiered on 26 December 1767 at the Burgtheater, was the first work resulting from Gluck's collaboration with Noverre, who, according to Khevenhüller-Metsch, had just been "greatly applauded" for his "ballet pantomime with machines" in *L'Apothéose d'Hercule* with Gaëtan Vestris. J. V. Sonnenfels notes that *Alceste* was received enthusiastically, but also critically. After the "pompous" and "sinister" opera, the applause for *Les (Petits) Riens,* the ballet "in the grotesque taste" that Noverre had added, was all the more lively. In his *Lettres* (1803), Noverre paints a vivid picture of his collaboration with Gluck, who, in despair over the wooden immobility of the singers in the chorus, joyfully accepted the choreographer's brilliant suggestion to position the singers in the wings, while the best dancers acted on stage. The total integration of dance and pantomime, of the *balli ballati* and the *balli pantomimi*, corresponded exactly with Gluck's ideas. The problem of the ending, which had not been satisfactorily resolved in Vienna, resisted a solution in Paris as well. Although a *chaconne* was supposed to have followed the great chorus, public taste demanded an extensive final ballet. François-Joseph Gossec eventually was permitted to expand Gluck's six-section *divertissement* with the *grande chaconne* from *Alessandro* as its finale.

Paride ed Elena, premiered on 3 November 1770 at the Burgtheater, likewise found a mixed reception. Although the public, according to Khevenhüller-Metsch, was generally critical of the "uneven and somewhat peculiar taste" of Gluck and Calzabigi's opera, Noverre's ballets, according to Zinzendorf, were found to be "enchanting," presumably because in these Gluck's intention to contrast the national characters of the Phrygians and Trojans had been perfectly realized. There were two dance scenes each in acts 1 and 2, and one in act 4.

In Paris, Gluck came face to face with the French tradition and its love for *divertissements*, which forced him once again to confront the problem of the opera finale. A turning point came with the second version of *La Cythère Assiégée* in 1775, when Gluck insisted on retaining the final chorus and rejected the addition of a ballet by Pierre-Montan Berton. It was his intention then and for his future operas that a chorus or a vocal ensemble be the final piece, not a dance or ballet, whether composed himself or by someone else. The impulse for this rigorous, aesthetically highly significant decision derived from the criticism that had been leveled at Gluck's ballet-arias: "Then," Gluck wrote, "I will not be reproached in all the journals that my ballets are weak, mediocre, etc.: and so on; the filthy dogs shall not hear any by me anymore" (Gluck, 1962). In the summer of 1776 Gluck considered composing new dances for a revival of *La Cythère Assiégée* with Noverre in Paris in 1777. This, however, did not happen.

Historical Perspective. The term *reform* can be applied to Gluck; his theater dance was a logical continuation of the reform and renewal of the *danza seria* that Hilverding had begun and whose ultimate goal it was to create a complete story as dance drama, a total ballet, rather than a multitude of small, incidental details. Gluck's most important partner after Hilverding, next to Calzabigi, was Angiolini. Count Giacomo Durazzo deserves the credit for having brought Gluck, Angiolini, and Calzabigi together. The unwavering sense of purpose with which they worked during the time span of a mere four years, from 1761 to 1765, is comparable to Gluck's carefully planned activities during the years of the Paris reform of the 1770s: In both instances the envisaged goal was achieved; both times there was initial success, notorious and inflammatory, of *Don Juan* and *Iphigénie en*

Aulide respectively; both times Gluck experienced failures toward the end, in *Sémiramis* and *Echo et Narcisse* respectively.

In Noverre, Gluck had found, since *Alceste* in 1767, a second congenial partner who, unlike Angiolini, pursued his own goals and interests; even so, Noverre and Angiolini had very similar ideals concerning the *danza parlante* and the *danse en action*. While Angiolini emphasized the prime importance of music in the creative process and thus paid the ultimate compliment to the highly respected composer Gluck, for Noverre everything began with the imagination of the choreographer and with the expression to be conveyed by the movements of the dance. Eventually, Gluck appears to be a mere musical executor of the "steps, gestures, attitudes, expressions of the different personalities" dictated by Noverre. However, Noverre's description of the creation of the dances of the Scythes for *Iphigénie en Tauride* leaves unmentioned the fact that Gluck had already accomplished the characterization of the Scythes as "savages" in their choruses in which singing and dancing are combined. Wolfgang Amadeus Mozart was profoundly impressed by this scene, particularly by Gluck's music, and became the star witness for Gluck's genius as a composer of powerfully expressive stage dances. Any Gluck performance should keep this endorsement firmly in mind.

[*For related discussion, see* Austria, *article on* Theatrical Dance. *See also the entries on* Angiolini, Hilverding, *and* Noverre.]

BIBLIOGRAPHY

Abert, Anna Amalie. *Christoph Willibald Gluck.* Munich, 1959.

Arend, Max. *Zur Kunst Glucks: Gesammelte Aufsätze.* Regensburg, 1914.

Bacher, Otto. "Ein Frankfurter Szenar zu Glucks Don Juan." *Zeitschrift für Musikwissenschaft* 7 (1924–1925): 570–574.

Brainard, Ingrid. "Angiolini." In *Pipers Enzyklopädie des Musiktheaters.* Munich, 1986–.

Brown, Bruce Alan. *Gluck and the French Theatre in Vienna.* Oxford, 1991.

Croll, Gerhard. "Ein unbekanntes tragisches Ballett von Gluck." *Mitteilungen der Gesellschaft für Salzburger Landeskunde* 109 (1969): 275–277.

Einstein, Alfred. *Gluck.* Translated by Eric Blom. London and New York, 1936.

Gastoué, Amédée. "Gossec et Gluck à l'Opéra de Paris: Le ballet final d'Iphigénie en Tauride." *Revue de Musicologie* 19 (1935): 87–99.

Gerber, Rudolf. *Christoph Willibald Gluck.* 2d ed. Potsdam, 1950.

Gerber, Rudolf. "Unbekannte Instrumentalwerke von Christoph Willibald Gluck." *Die Musikforschung* 4 (1951): 305–318.

Gluck, Christoph Willibald. *The Collected Correspondence and Papers of Christoph Willibald Gluck.* Edited by Hedwig and E. H. Müller von Asow. London, 1962.

Gruber, Gernot. "I balli pantomimici viennesi di Gluck e lo stile drammatico della sua musica." *Chigiana* 29–30 (1972–1973): 508–512.

Haas, Robert. "Die Wiener Ballett-Pantomime im 18. Jahrhundert und Glucks Don Juan." *Studien zur Musikwissenschaft* 10 (1923): 6–36.

Haas, Robert. *Gluck und Durazzo im Burgtheater.* Zurich, 1925.

Haas, Robert. "Der Wiener Bühnentanz von 1740 bis 1767." *Jahrbuch der Musikbibliothek Peters* 44 (1937): 77–93.

Heartz, Daniel. "From Garrick to Gluck: The Reform of Theatre and Opera in the Mid-Eighteenth Century." *Proceedings of the Classical Association* 94 (1967–1968): 112–127.

Hopkinson, Cecil. *A Bibliography of the Printed Works of C. W. von Gluck, 1714–1787.* Rev. and enl. ed. New York, 1987.

Hortschansky, Klaus. "Unbekannte Aufführungsberichte zu Glucks Opern der Jahre 1748–1765." *Jahrbuch des Staatlichen Instituts für Musikforschung Preußischer Kulturbesitz* (1969).

Hortschansky, Klaus. *Parodie und Entlehnung im Schaffen Christoph Willibald Glucks.* Cologne, 1973.

Hussey, Dyneley. "Gluck and the Reform of the Ballet." *The Dancing Times* (December 1948): 118–119; (January 1949): 189–190.

Jersild, Jørgen. "Le ballet d'action italien au XVIIIᵉ siècle au Danemark: Versions danoises des ballets de Gluck—'Don Juan' et 'L'Orphelin de la Chine.'" *Acta Musicologica* 14 (1942): 74–94.

Khevenhüller-Metsch, Johann Josef. *Aus der Zeit Maria Theresias.* Vienna and Leipzig, 1907–.

Kinsky, Georg, ed. *Glucks Briefe an Franz Kruthoffer.* Vienna, 1927.

Liebeskind, Josef. *Ergänzungen und Nachträge zu dem Thematischen Verzeichnis der Werke von Chr. W. von Gluck von Alfred Wotquenne.* Leipzig, 1911.

Marx, Adolf Bernhard. *Gluck und die Oper* (1863). 2 vols. Hildesheim, 1970.

Testa, Alberto. "Il binomia Gluck-Angiolini e la realizzazione del balletto 'Don Juan.'" *Chigiana* 29–30 (1972–1973): 535.

Tozzi, Lorenzo. "Attorno a 'Don Juan.'" *Chigiana* 29–30 (1972–1973): 549.

Tozzi, Lorenzo. "Sémiramis." *Chigiana* 29–30 (1972–1973): 565.

Viale Ferrero, Mercedes. "Appunti di scenografia settecentesca, in margine a rappresentazioni di opere in musica di Gluck e balli di Angiolini." *Chigiana* 29–30 (1972–1973): 513.

Winter, Marian Hannah. *The Pre-Romantic Ballet.* London, 1974.

Wotquenne, Alfred. *Thematisches Verzeichnis der Werke von Chr. W. von Gluck.* Leipzig, 1904.

GERHARD CROLL
Translated from German

GLUSHKOVSKY, ADAM

GLUSHKOVSKY, ADAM (Adam Pavlovich Glushkovskii; born 1793 in Saint Petersburg, died in October 1870), dancer, choreographer, and man of letters. The name Adam Glushkovsky is inseparably linked to an important period in the history of Russian ballet. He was the first to bring ballet close to contemporary Russian literature and to the ideals of Romantic art. Through his bringing Charles-Louis Didelot's ballets to Moscow and his innovative teaching methods, Glushkovsky in no small measure contributed to the formation of a unified national school of dance.

In 1809 Glushkovsky graduated from the Saint Petersburg Ballet School, where he had studied under Ivan Valberkh and Didelot; the latter adopted the young Glushkovsky. While still a student he successfully danced the leading role in *Le Jugement de Pâris*, a Pierre Gardel ballet to Nicolas Méhul's music, staged by Louis-Antoine Duport in Saint Petersburg. After graduating Glushkovsky studied with Duport and continued to perform in Saint Petersburg. In 1812 the talented dancer was sent to Moscow as the first soloist of the city's ballet company. With a perfect physique and excellent professional training, he appeared in a variety of roles. His skills were compared in press reviews with the virtuosity of Duport himself. The critics noted, however, that the Russian dancer surpassed the famous Frenchman in pantomime. A leg injury forced Glushkovsky to give up roles calling for virtuosic technique and to concentrate instead on pantomime. Glushkovsky's most successful roles were the male leads in *Flore et Zéphire; Médée et Jason; Leon and Tamaida, or The Young Island Girl; Euthyme and Eucharis;* and *Ruslan and Ludmila, or The Downfall of Chernomor, the Evil Sorcerer;* and Vergie in *Raoul Barbe-Bleue.*

From his arrival in Moscow in 1839 Glushkovsky was also the chief choreographer of the Bolshoi Theater. He staged thirty-nine original ballets based on fairy tales, melodrama, Romantic literature, and folklore. In addition he revived and revised nineteen ballets by other choreographers, among them works by Valberkh, Jean-Baptiste Blache, Duport, Didelot, Chevalier Peicam de Bressoles (called Chevalier), Giuseppe Canziani, Salvatore Viganò, and Auguste Poireau. *Divertissements* based on scenes from folk life, battles, and other feats of Russian armies had been introduced into ballet by Valberkh, and Glushkovsky composed dances in the same vein. Their content was chiefly Russian folk dances, executed to music based on Russian folk melodies. Glushkovsky fit such song-and-dance themes into the general scheme of his ballet productions. Some of his ballets remained in the Bolshoi repertory for many years. They included *Filatka and Fedora on the Swings at Novinsk* (1815), *May Day, or A Holiday in Sokolniki* (1816), *The Triumph of the Russians, or The Military Camp at Krasnoye* (1816), and *Cossacks on the Rhine* (1817). In composing his own ballets Glushkovsky often turned to the creations of his teacher Didelot for inspiration and with care revived Didelot's ballets at the Bolshoi: *Zéphire et Flore* in 1817, *La Chaumière Hongroise, ou Les Illustres Fugitifs* in 1819, *Leon and Tamaida, or A Young Island Girl* in 1823, *Euthyme and Eucharis, or The Vanquished Shade of Libas* and *Alcestis, or The Descent of Hercules into the Underworld* in 1828, and *Karl et Lisbeth, ou Le Déserteur Malgré Lui* in 1835.

Glushkovsky was the first choreographer to translate Aleksandr Pushkin's poetry into dance. *Ruslan and Ludmila, or The Downfall of Chernomor, the Evil Sorcerer* (1821), to music by Friedrich Scholz, abounded in fantastic fairy-tale scenes and episodes of magic. The choreography retained the poem's national coloring, epic elements, and lucidity of narrative. Russian dances and ancient rites were interwoven into the fabric of the ballet and characterized the protagonists. Glushkovsky succeeded in conveying both the appeal and charm of Pushkin's heroes and the spirit and message of his tale. In 1827 at the Bolshoi, Glushkovsky staged Pushkin's *The*

Prisoner of the Caucasus, or The Bride's Shade, to music by Catterino Cavos. Glushkovsky himself danced the leading role, the Slavonic Prince Rostislav who has been taken prisoner by the warlike Circassians. The ballet had the national and romantic spirit of Pushkin's poem, and the exotic setting of the Caucasus was present as well in the choreography. *The Black Shawl, or Infidelity Avenged* (1831) was the third Pushkin ballet Glushkovsky produced. Turkish, Serbian, Moldavian, Arabian, and Bessarabian Gypsy character dances were featured, but pantomime was used to characterize the principal roles.

The ballet *Three Belts, or The Russian Cinderella* (1826), to music by Scholz, was based on Vasily Zhukovsky's eponymous tale. Round dances and fairy-tale transformations were the highlights of the production, but the leading role was played by a female singer, and poster captions were displayed to explain the action. In all of Glushkovsky's ballets the characters were strong, passionate, and relentless in their fighting spirit, and capable of self-sacrifice and martial feats. This nationalistic character was conducive to the original presentation of the Romantic repertory by the Moscow ballet in the 1830s and 1840s.

From 1812 until 1839 Glushkovsky also taught dance. The beginning of his teaching career was complicated in 1812 by the invasion of Napoleon's army. With great energy and persistence Glushkovsky managed to evacuate his school to Ples, a small town on the Volga, where he held regular classes and trained a new generation of dancers for the Moscow ballet. While preparing dancers for the contemporary repertory, Glushkovsky remained a devotee of Didelot and rigorously followed his teaching methods. Apart from his ballet accomplishments Glushkovsky was a gifted man of letters. Most of the notes he kept dealt with the art of ballet and contained his ideas about its repertory, dancing styles, and teaching methods. Pages dealing with Didelot manifest Glushkovsky's lifelong devotion to his mentor.

BIBLIOGRAPHY
Bakhrushin, Yuri. *Istoriia russkogo baleta.* 3d ed. Moscow, 1977.
Glushkovsky, Adam. *Memoirs of a Ballet Master* (1856). Translated by Yuri Slonimsky. Leningrad, 1940.
Roslavleva, Natalia. *Era of the Russian Ballet* (1966). New York, 1979.
Swift, Mary Grace. *A Loftier Flight: The Life and Accomplishments of Charles Louis Didelot.* Middletown, Conn., 1974.
Wiley, Roland John, trans. and ed. *A Century of Russian Ballet: Documents and Accounts, 1810–1910.* Oxford, 1990.

NIKOLAI I. ELYASH
Translated from Russian

GOGÓL, JERZY (born 17 November 1922 in Warsaw, died 30 April 1996 in Warsaw), Polish dancer, choreographer, and ballet director. Gogół graduated from the Warsaw Ballet School in 1937 and danced with the Warsaw Ballet until 1939. From 1945 to 1947 he was the principal dancer for the Ensemble of Song and Dance of the Polish Army. From 1948 to 1951 he studied at the Ballet Masters' Department of the State Theater Institute in Moscow, receiving his diploma with distinction.

Gogół made his choreographic debut at Bytom in 1951, with *The Fountain of Bakhchisarai* (music by Boris Asafiev). Thereafter he served as choreographer and ballet director for the opera houses at Warsaw (1954–1955), Poznań (1955–1958), Wrocław (1958–1961), and Bytom (1969–1970). He was also director of the Artistic Ensemble of the Polish Army (1962–1965), a post to which he returned in 1981. For many years he collaborated closely with the amateur dance movement.

Gogół was brought up in both the traditional Polish and contemporary Russian schools; a lover and connoisseur of classical dance, from the beginning he preferred large-scale choreographies based on classical and character styles and with strong, dramatic plots. He either choreographed traditional works in his own versions—for example, *The Sleeping Beauty* (to music by Tchaikovsky) at Poznań in 1956—or sought only general inspiration from previous versions—for example, *Giselle* at Wrocław in 1960, after Anton Dolin's version.

Despite his Russian training, Gogół's versions of Russian works—the Polish premieres of *The Fountain of Bakhchisarai* and *Romeo and Juliet* (to music by Sergei Prokofiev) at Warsaw in 1954, and of *Cinderella* (to music by Prokofiev) at Wrocław in 1959—were his independent creations. Gogół was the last active successor of the traditional school of character dances, especially Polish dances. He created various kinds of *mazur*s, *krakowiaks,* and *polonaises,* as well as large works based on national tradition, such as *Pan Twardowski* (to music by Ludomir Różycki) at Bytom in 1970.

Gogół's other productions included *The Song of the Earth* (to music by Roman Palester) at Poznań in 1958; *The Nymph of Świteź Lake* (to music by Eugeniusz Morawski-Dąbrowa) at Warsaw in 1962; and *Clementine* (to music by Piotr Perkowski) at Bytom in 1969.

BIBLIOGRAPHY
Neuer, Adam, ed. *Polish Opera and Ballet of the Twentieth Century: Operas, Ballets, Pantomimes, Miscellaneous Works.* Translated by Jerzy Zawadzki. Kraków, 1986.
Pudełek, Janina. "Jerzy Gogół." *Teatr,* no. 8 (1981).

JANINA PUDEŁEK

GOLDEN AGE, THE. Russian title: *Zolotoi Vek.* Dance work in three acts. Choreography: Vasily Vainonen, Leonid Yakobson, and Vasily Chesnakov. Music: Dmitri Shostakovich. Libretto: Aleksandr Ivanovsky. Scenery: Vera Khodasevich. First performance: 26 October 1930, State Academic Theater for Opera and Ballet, Leningrad.

Principals: Galina Ulanova (The Young Communist Girl), Olga Jordan (The Star), Boris Shavrov (The Fascist).

The Golden Age was conceived as a revue of the *suite-divertissement* type. It narrated the adventures of a Soviet football team abroad and fights between Young Communists and Fascists. The ballet was not a success despite other productions both in Kiev in 1930 and in Odessa in 1931 with different choreographers. It was soon dropped from the repertory. The score was lost and only individual musical numbers from it were performed occasionally on the variety stage.

However, the ballet was revived in 1982 by Yuri Grigorovich. The score was restored from surviving orchestral parts by a group of musicians led by Sergei Sapozhnikov, and Grigorovich with Isaak Glikman wrote an entirely new libretto, in which the previously archetypal characters were given names. Veniamin Basner and Yuri Simonov collaborated on a new musical edition in which the slow movements of Shostakovich's First and Second Piano Concertos and some of his other compositions were added to the score to intensify the lyrical motif.

The premiere of this new production was held at the Bolshoi Theater in Moscow on 30 October 1982, with decor by Simon Virsaladze. The cast included Irek Mukhamedov as Boris, Natalia Bessmertnova as Rita, Gediminas Taranda as Yashka, and Tatiana Golikova as Lyuska.

BIBLIOGRAPHY

Alovert, Nina. "The Soviet Dance Theatre of Yuri Grigorovich." *Dance Magazine* (December 1987): 39–42.

Armashevskaia, Klavdiia, and N. Vainonen. *Baletmeister Vainonen.* Moscow, 1971.

Armashevskaia, Klavdiia. "Baletmeister Vainonen." In *Sovetskii baletnyi teatr, 1917–1967*, edited by Vera Krasovskaya. Moscow, 1976.

Beaumont, Cyril W. *Complete Book of Ballets.* Rev. ed. London, 1951.

Grigorovich, Yuri, and Sania Davlekamova. *The Authorized Bolshoi Ballet Book of the Golden Age.* Translated by Tim Coey. Neptune, N.J., 1989.

Swift, Mary Grace. *The Art of the Dance in the U.S.S.R.* Notre Dame, 1968.

Vanslov, Victor V. *Balety Grigorovicha i problemy khoreografii.* 2d ed. Moscow, 1971.

Victor V. Vanslov
Translated from Russian

GOLEIZOVSKY, KASYAN (Kasian Iakovlevich Goleizovskii; born 22 February [5 March] 1892 in Moscow, died 4 May 1970 in Moscow), Russian dancer and choreographer. Goleizovsky began his dance education in Moscow, continued it at the Saint Petersburg Theater School, and completed it under Michel Fokine. Between 1909 and 1918 he danced at the Bolshoi Theater in Moscow, where he appeared in ballets by Aleksandr Gorsky and Fokine, whom he regarded as his lifelong teachers. Goleizovsky took his first steps as a choreographer outside the academic stage, at a time when Gorsky's innovations had passed their peak and the best of Fokine's ballets were being presented outside Russia. Goleizovsky and his contemporaries saw the lessons of their teachers as a tradition they were called upon to master along with that of academic ballet, and to develop their own attitude to them. His teachers passed on to Goleizovsky an appreciation of the lofty mission of a truly creative artist with a well-rounded education and a broad outlook, far removed from the isolation of academic ballet. While Gorsky and Fokine were artists of lofty subjects, Goleizovsky started out as a variety performer and creator of vaudeville-type pieces. He also wrote verse for recitation at concerts, and ballet libretti for Mikhail Mordkin (*The Legend of Aziade, The Flowers of Granada*).

In 1916 Goleizovsky opened a private school and workshop from which he began to stage dance miniatures and short ballets at Nikita Baliev's Bat Theater, the Mamonovsky Miniature Theater, and the Intimate Theater where he produced in 1916 *The Goatlegged* to music by Ilya Sats and *The Choice of a Bride* to music and a verse prologue by Mikhail Kuzmin. While Gorsky had begun his reform of academic ballet with the plot and Fokine with its structural forms, Goleizovsky, in common with his contemporaries in the other arts, began with the vocabulary by overturning the strictures of academism. In his search for a new plastique he even incorporated exaggerated social dance forms, like the fox trot and tango. His ballet miniatures continued to mark the important stages of his development during 1921 and 1922: *Prologue* and *Funeral March* to music by Nicolas Medtner, *Preludes* and *White Mass* to Scriabin, Debussy's *The Faun*, and Richard Strauss's *Salomé*. From 1922 until its demise in 1925 the studio company was called Moscow Chamber Ballet.

While the studio constituted his principal experimental workshop, Goleizovsky lent his talent to official enterprises. For a season in 1918 he headed a studio at the Bolshoi Theater School. Appearing in his productions there—*The Evolution of Dance* to music by diverse composers and *The Sonata of Death and Movement* to Scriabin's Sonata no. 10—were the young dancers Nina Podgoretskaya, Elena Ilyushchenko, and Liubov Bank, who later became his followers. When the Ministry of Enlightenment (Narkompros) in Moscow established a children's division, Goleizovsky came to teach and choreograph: *The Sandmen* (1918) to a pastiche score and *Max and Moritz* (1919) to music by Ludwig Schytte, among others. Leaving the Children's Theater in 1919, Goleizovsky spent the next couple of years trying to stage ballets at the Bolshoi Theater and the Circus, while carrying on the experimental work of his studio.

A large portion of the Russian artistic community had greeted the Revolution of 1917 above all as an opportunity to liberate the spiritual potential of the nation. Entering a new epoch the art of the early twentieth century began to undergo radical change. The theme of self-revelation and assertion of the human personality, a theme dear to Goleizovsky, was interpreted by him as free self-expression in the face of the broad opportunities that were opening up. As a choreographer Goleizovsky was fired by the challenge of following the birth and development of human emotions to the point of maturity. The successive stages of the growth of passions determined the choreographic dramaturgy of his ballets for the rest of his career. Their successful realization marked an important stage in the evolution of psychological theater in Soviet choreography.

Following the lead of Isadora Duncan, Michel Fokine, and Aleksandr Gorsky, Goleizovsky, a lyrical and highly subjective artist, always placed emphasis on revealing in visible images his own impressions of musical works. He chose emotional and lyrical scores of past composers, such as Liszt and Chopin, and contemporary composers, such as Scriabin, Rachmaninoff, and Medtner. He retained his attachment to these composers throughout his career. Goleizovsky also admired the impressionist composers, such as Debussy and Ravel.

Goleizovsky's experiments in the area of dance form were a natural extension of his searchings as a choreographer. He sought to show anew the potentialities of the human body, its emotional expressiveness and its plastique. In his quest for new physical angles he devised hand and leg gestures that began to "speak," and barely perceptible twists of the body. He placed unexpected, uncommon arrangements of human figures in space, along vertical and horizontal lines, with unusual pairings of figures. The small stages on which his chamber dances were performed was an important limiting factor. The heated arguments and discussions generated by Goleizovsky's treatment of classical form reflected the overall pattern of relation between his style and that of other epochs.

In 1924 Goleizovsky returned to the Bolshoi as a well-known choreographer. In 1925 two full-length ballets, the first results of his latest creative explorations, were premiered at the experimental theater of the Bolshoi's Filial: *Joseph the Beautiful*, to music by Sergei Vasilenko, and *Teolinda*, to music of Schubert. *Joseph the Beautiful* depicted the power of the human spirit, nourished by the traditions of antiquity and embodied in the form of ideal beauty personified by the protagonist. The image of ideal beauty was opposed by the sterile, sensuous beauty of Queen Tayakh, the wife of the despotic pharaoh, Potiphar. In *Joseph the Beautiful* Goleizovsky for the first time in the history of the Bolshoi Theater used constructivist decor, designed by Boris Erdman. The first dancer to appear as Joseph was the young Vasily Efimov, whom Goleizovsky himself judged to be unrivaled in the role. The image Efimov created anticipated a major motif that would later emerge in the art of the ballerina Galina Ulanova: the invincibility of man's inner world in the face of violence and vulgarity. [*See* Joseph the Beautiful.]

Goleizovsky did not appreciate the plots of nineteenth-century ballets, but he was careful to respect classical dance in all his experiments. He embraced not so much the academism of the late nineteenth century or the canon that had fixed the fundamentals of a classical dance, but rather the formative period, the era of lyrical romanticism. In *Teolinda* he demonstrated his command of this style, but with a touch of irony that was apparent in his handling of the plot.

GOLEIZOVSKY. The ensemble of the Bolshoi Ballet in a scene from act 2 of Goleizovsky's *Joseph the Beautiful* (1925). The monumental sets were designed by Boris Erdman in the constructivist style. (Photograph from the A. A. Bakrushin Central State Theatrical Museum, Moscow.)

In 1927 Goleizovsky unveiled a ballet on a contemporary theme, *The Whirlwind,* to music by B. Ber. It was an allegorical "poster" of socialist realism that reinterpreted many of the images of Goleizovsky's prerevolutionary ballets. The ballet was a failure, and Goleizovsky once again left the Bolshoi. He still maintained contact with its troupe of dancers through a series of concerts he mounted in 1927, 1929, and the early 1930s. The ballet *Lisztiana* (1931) carried the message of the timeless beauty of Romantic ballet. *Dionysus* (1933), to music by A. Shenshin, developed the interest in antiquity that Isadora Duncan had rekindled in Russian ballet at the turn of the century. Goleizovsky turned to antiquity in search of the harmonious essence of Dionysian festivities, as opposed to the exquisite stylizations of the early twentieth century. The ballet *Charda,* also presented in 1933, was built on a restoration of dances of the cis-Danubian Slavs and was evidence of Goleizovsky's close attention to folklore.

With the passing of time Goleizovsky's interest in folklore became a dominant element in his art. Early on in his career he had staged a variety of national dances, made a careful study of the available pictorial material, and collected and analyzed folk music. In the 1930s his wanderlust caused him to move to the various constituent republics of the Soviet Union to work as a choreographer. This enabled him to gain first-hand knowledge of local folklore, in which he saw those spiritual values that had taken centuries to consolidate in the collective mind of the peoples. One product of his sustained interest in folklore was the *Polovtsian Dances* in Borodin's opera *Prince Igor,* which he staged at the Bolshoi in 1934 and revived in 1953; the ballet was based on a medley of dances of the peoples of the East. He also created one of the first Soviet national ballets on a contemporary subject. Called *Du Gul* (Two Roses), to music by A. Lensky, this ballet, first presented in 1940 in the capital city of Tajikistan, Dushanbe, was based entirely on the idiom of Tajik and Uzbek folk dances. His production of Boris Asafiev's *The Fountain of Bakhchisarai,* first performed in Minsk in 1939, included authentic harem dances he had actually seen performed by veteran dancers in the Soviet Central Asian Republics.

In classical ballets Goleizovsky sought to create an authentic period atmosphere in each ballet and spoke sadly of his nostalgia for the disappearing beauty of the past. In an attempt to recapture some of the erstwhile glory of the French court, Goleizovsky created his own version of *The Sleeping Beauty* and presented it in Kharkov in 1935. In it he sought to meld unfettered plastique with classical dance and folk dance. Like the thrust of all creative explorations of his day, his was an imaginative search for an effective original ballet vocabulary. His interest in the personality and potential of fellow ballet artists helped Goleizovsky to discover new facets of the prodigious tal-

GOLEIZOVSKY. Vladimir Vasiliev as Kais and Natalia Bessmertnova as Leili in the original production of Goleizovsky's *Leili and Medzhnun* (1964). (Photograph by Leonid Zhdanov; courtesy of Elizabeth Souritz.)

ents of leading dancers such as Galina Ulanova, Olga Lepeshinskaya, and Maya Plisetskaya, and also of dancers from provincial theaters, constituent republics, and those appearing in variety theater and vaudeville.

In the early 1960s, when metaphorical idiom and associative thinking became a crucial factor in Soviet ballet, Goleizovsky created his Evenings of Choreographic Compositions especially for the graduating classes of the Moscow ballet school, which included Ekaterina Maximova, Vladimir Vasiliev, Elena Ryabinkina, and Natalia Bessmertnova. The ballets *Scriabiniana* (1962) and *Leili and Medzhnun* (1964), to S. Balasanian's score, completed Goleizovsky's aesthetic credo. In *Leili and Medzhnun* he used a transformed folk dance language to speak of man's continued exploration of the mysteries of his world and nature. Classical dance was blended with free plastique and folklore motifs. The static plastique of Goleizovsky's youth was replaced by a full-scale flow of dance. The role of Kais, the protagonist, was a landmark for Vladimir Vasiliev.

Goleizovsky's contributions to world choreography were acknowledged by George Balanchine and Yuri Grigorovich. His discoveries and innovations were highly influential. Goleizovsky often wrote articles for the press, and he was the author of a major study on Russian folk dances, *Obrazy russkoi narodnoi khoreografii* (The Imagery of Russian Folk Dance), published in 1964. Goleizovsky was named Merited Artist of the Belarussian SSR in 1940.

BIBLIOGRAPHY

Banes, Sally. "Goleizovsky's Ballet Manifestos." *Ballet Review* 11 (Fall 1983): 64–75.

Chernova, Natalia, and Vera Vasilyeva, comps. *Kasian Goleizovskii* (in Russian). Moscow, 1984.

Chernova, Natalia. "Kas'ian Goleizovskii i russkaia poeziia predrevoliutsionnoi pory." In *Permskii ezhegodnik–95: Khoreographiia*. Perm, 1995.

Manor, Giora. "Kasyan Goleizovsky's Russian Revolution" (parts 1–2). *Dance Magazine* (January–February 1989).

Roslavleva, Natalia. *Era of the Russian Ballet* (1966). New York, 1979.

Sheremetyevskaya, Natalia. *Tanets na estrade*. Moscow, 1985.

Souritz, Elizabeth. *Soviet Choreographers in the 1920s*. Translated by Lynn Visson. Durham, N.C., 1990.

Swift, Mary Grace. *The Art of the Dance in the U.S.S.R.* Notre Dame, 1968.

ARCHIVE. Central A. A. Bakhrushin State Theatrical Museum, Moscow.

NATALIA Y. CHERNOVA
Translated from Russian

GOLOVIN, ALEKSANDR (Aleksandr Iakovlevich Golovin; born 17 February 1863 in Moscow, died 17 April 1930 in Detskoye Selo, Russia), Russian scenery and costume designer. Golovin studied from 1881 to 1889 at the Moscow Institute of Painting, Sculpture, and Architecture, specializing first in architecture and then in painting. In 1889 he traveled to Paris, the first of several trips to western Europe. On his return, he developed a strong interest in Art Nouveau and made contact with the neonationalist colony at Abramtsevo near Moscow, which was attempting to revitalize traditional Russian arts and crafts.

In 1898 Golovin made his debut as a stage designer at the Bolshoi Theater, and in 1901 he designed Nikolai Rimsky-Korsakov's *The Maid of Pskov* there. The same year he became resident artist of the Imperial Theaters in Saint Petersburg and began to move with the *Mir iskusstva* (World of Art) group of artists and critics. In the early 1900s he contributed designs to a number of ballets, including Lev Ivanov and Marius Petipa's *Swan Lake* at the Chinese Theater in Tsarskoe Selo in 1902, Petipa's version of Arseny Koreshchenko's *The Magic Mirror* at the Maryinsky Theater in 1903, and Nikolai Legat's version of Aleksandr Glazunov's *The Seasons* at the Maryinsky in 1907.

Golovin was also active in Serge Diaghilev's enterprises abroad; in 1908, for example, he designed the sets for the Paris production of *Boris Godunov*. In 1909, with Nikolai Roerich and Dmitri Steletsky, he designed Diaghilev's production of *The Maid of Pskov*, and the following year he worked on Diaghilev's *The Firebird*, also in Paris. Golovin, a man of many talents, was equally successful as a painter of portraits of stage celebrities. He worked extensively for dramatic producers, especially for Vsevolod Meyerhold, whose 1917 production of Mikhail Lermontov's *Masquerade* he designed for Saint Petersburg's Alexandrinsky Theater. He also collaborated briefly with Ida Rubinstein on her production of the mime drama *Orpheus* in Paris in 1926.

Golovin brought to Serge Diaghilev's Paris productions of 1908 through 1910 a rich experience of scenic decoration, applying highly stylized and ornate mosaics of color to his designs. Among his distinguished ballet renderings were his sets and costumes for *The Firebird* (1910), although Diaghilev, not completely satisfied, asked Léon Bakst to redesign three of the costumes, including Golovin's splendid costume for Tamara Karsavina. Still, his swirling, exuberant backdrop for the first scene (The Impure Kingdom of Kastchei) blended well with Bakst's contributions and was much applauded by the Paris audience.

The enduring attractions of Golovin's designs were his gamut of colors and intense ornamentation, as exhibited in the more famous Paris productions and in the less familiar pieces of the mid-1910s, as well as productions such as Michel Fokine's production of Mikhail Glinka's *Jota Aragonesa* at the Maryinsky in 1916 and Pavel Petrov's *Solveig* at the Bolshoi in 1922.

BIBLIOGRAPHY

Bassekhes, Alfred. *Teatr i zhivopis Golovina*. Moscow, 1970.

Fedosova, Yelena, ed. *Alexander Golovin*. Translated by John Crowfoot. Leningrad, 1989.

Gofman, Ida, ed. *Aleksandr Golovin*. Moscow, 1981. Text partly in English.

Movshenzon, A. G., ed. *Aleksandr Iakovlevich Golovin* (in Russian). Moscow, 1960.

Pozharskaya, Militza. *Aleksandr Golovin* (in Russian). Moscow, 1990. Includes a summary and list of illustrations in English.

Souritz, Elizabeth. *Soviet Choreographers in the 1920s*. Translated by Lynn Visson. Durham, N.C., 1990.

Vidovich, Silvana de, and Gennady Chugunov, eds. *Mejerchol'd and Golovin*. Florence, 1992.

Wiley, Roland John, trans. and ed. *A Century of Russian Ballet: Documents and Accounts, 1810–1910*. Oxford, 1990.

ARCHIVES. Central A. A. Bakhrushin State Theatrical Museum, Moscow. Museum of the Maryinsky Theater of Opera and Ballet, Saint Petersburg .

JOHN E. BOWLT

GOLOVKINA, SOFIA (Sof'ia Nikolaevna Golovkina; born 13 October 1915 in Moscow), dancer and administrator. Golovkina entered the Moscow Ballet School in 1926 and studied under Aleksandr Chekrigin, Aleksandr Monakhov, and Viktor Semenov. Upon graduation in 1933 she joined the Bolshoi Ballet and danced there until 1959. Her austere, noble line and brilliant technique advanced her to a leading place in the company. During her first seven years there she danced the leading roles in *Raymonda, Swan Lake, The Sleeping Beauty,* and other ballets, but she shone in the new Soviet ballets. In these years the company was making vigorous efforts to master a modern repertory. The ideas of the time, centered on the concept of heroic labor, were expressed in Golovkina's art in a natural and truthful way; they shaped her as an artist and determined her cheerful, bold, and vigorous style. She was attracted to the heroines of Soviet ballets, particularly Svetlana in the 1939 ballet of the same name, choreographed by Nikolai Popko, Lev Pospekhin, Aleksandr Radunsky, and Dmitri Klebanov. Without departing from classical technique Golovkina showed the courage, presence of mind, and sincerity of the heroine. This heroic tone was later expressed in the roles of the French actress Mireille de Poitiers in Vasily Vainonen's *The Flames of Paris* and the Chinese dancer Tao-Hoa in Leonid Lavrovsky's *The Red Poppy,* which she performed in 1946 and 1950, respectively. In classical roles, such as Aurora, Odette-Odile, the Tsar-Maiden, Nikia, and Raymonda, Golovkina emphasized the moral integrity of her heroines, their will to struggle in defense of their freedom in love, and their human dignity.

In 1960 Golovkina was appointed principal of the Moscow Ballet School. The staff of teachers whom she guided trained many honored dancers. The prestige of the Moscow Ballet School as a first-class educational institution also grew under her leadership. Golovkina's own class graduated Natalia Bessmertnova, Nina Sorokina, Marina Leonova, Alla Mikhalchenko, Galina Stepanenko, Nadia Grasheva, and other leading soloists of the Bolshoi and other companies. In 1990 Golovkina toured the United States with sixty-five students and graduates of the Bolshoi academy, including winners of recent competitions. They gave evidence that under Golovkina's directorship the Bolshoi tradition of expansiveness in performance was being maintained. Together with Maxim Martirosian and Aleksandr Radunsky, Golovkina revived Aleksandr Gorsky's versions of *Coppélia* in 1977 and *La Fille Mal Gardée* in 1979. Golovkina was named People's Artist of the USSR in 1973, after winning the State Prize of the USSR in 1947.

BIBLIOGRAPHY

Avdeyenko, A. A. "Sofia Nikolayevna Golovkina." In *Mastera bolshogo teatra,* edited by M. A. Iakovlev. Moscow, 1976.
Chernova, Natalia. *Ot Geltser do Ulanovoi.* Moscow, 1979.
"Comments by Sophia N. Golovkina." *Dance Magazine* (November 1993): 79.
Golovkina, Sofia. *Lessons in Classical Dance.* Translated by Nigel T. Coey. London, 1991.
Horosko, Marian. "Sofia Golovkina: An Interview with the Head of the Bolshoi Dance Academy." *Dance Magazine* (November 1973): 70–72.
Horosko, Marian. "Technique Part Two: The Bolshoi School." *Dance Magazine* (July 1990): 50–51.
Horosko, Marian. "Vail's Global Workshop." *Dance Magazine* (November 1993): 76–78.
Horosko, Marian. "Vail Vaults to New Heights." *Dance Magazine* (November 1995): 79.
Inozemtseva, Galina V. "And the Lesson Continues" (in Russian). *Sovetskii balet,* no. 2 (1984).
Joel, Lydia. "Conversation with Sophia Golovkina." *Dance Magazine* (January 1961): 38–39, 65–67.

GALINA V. INOZEMTSEVA
Translated from Russian

GONCHAROVA, NATALIA (Natalia Sergeevna Goncharova; born 4 June 1881 in Ladyzhino, Russia, died 17 October 1962 in Paris), Russian-French scenery and costume designer. Although initially a student of sculpture at the Moscow Institute of Painting, Sculpture, and Architecture, in 1900 Goncharova met Mikhail Larionov, who became her lifelong companion, and she began to study painting. In 1906 Serge Diaghilev included her in his Salon d'Automne in Paris, and thereafter (1908–1910) her work appeared in the Moscow journal *Zolotoe runo* (Golden Fleece) whose followers opposed the "erudition" of the *Mir iskusstva* (World of Art) group. At this time she and Larionov exhibited their first "primitivist" works. With Larionov and other progressive artists, including Kazimir Malevich, she was involved with the avant-garde artists' groups Jack of Diamonds, Donkey's Tail, and Target (1911–1913); with the last of these she exhibited a number of cubo-futurist pictures. Between 1912 and 1914, Goncharova also embraced Larionov's rayonism.

In 1914 Goncharova exhibited with Larionov at the Galerie Paul Guillaume in Paris and designed Serge Diaghilev's production of *Le Coq d'Or,* the first of several spectacles she designed for the Ballets Russes and other companies. In 1915 she designed Aleksandr Tairov's production of Carlo Goldoni's *Il Ventaglio* at the Chamber Theater in Moscow; in 1917 she settled permanently with Larionov in Paris.

Goncharova, one of the most important Russian women artists of the twentieth century, took much of her inspiration from the indigenous art of ancient Russia, including icons, embroideries, and *lubki* (hand-colored prints). Goncharova's serious study and interpretation of the Russian decorative arts prepared the way for her folkloristic designs for Diaghilev's productions of *Le Coq d'Or* (1914) and *The Firebird* (1926) as well as for her book illustrations, such as those in the Paris edition of the *Conte de Tsar Saltan* (1922). Her recognition of the vitality of Russian and Oriental art helped to confirm the fashionable Western image of Russia as an exotic, barbaric country—one reason why her ballet sets and costumes enjoyed great success with Parisian audiences. *Les Noces* (1923) is a case in point.

GONCHAROVA. The towers, windows, and onion-shaped domes of Goncharova's mythic Russian cityscape provided a dramatic backdrop for a 1926 London revival of *The Firebird* by Diaghilev's Ballets Russes. (Photograph used by permission of the Board of Trustees of the Theatre Museum, London.)

Bronislava Nijinska, the choreographer of *Les Noces*, recalled: "I wanted all the artists to fuse in one Movement and to create a whole. In my choreography the mass of the ensemble was meant to 'speak'—[to be] able to create just as many choreographic nuances as the orchestra mass does musical ones." Goncharova tried to extend this idea of fusion and mass into her costumes, and on Diaghilev's suggestion she designed them according to the principles of the everyday work clothes that the dancers wore at rehearsals—short trousers and shirts for the men, tunics for the women. These simple garments complemented the austerity of Goncharova's set design for *Les Noces*, which Serge Grigoriev described as "a plain backcloth and wings, together with one or two central 'flats,' in which windows of varying colours were inserted to indicate changes of place." [*See* Noces, Les.]

Unfortunately, some of Goncharova's important dance projects were never realized, including, for example, the highly stylized figures for the proposed production of *Liturgie*, on which she worked with Larionov, Léonide Massine, and Diaghilev in Lausanne in 1915. In fact, in 1915 and 1916 Goncharova created designs for four major ballets—*Liturgie, España, Triana,* and *Foire Espagnole*—none of which was staged. The fact that Diaghilev's aesthetic views were becoming more progressive can be seen in his inviting Goncharova, a futurist, to collaborate on these works; with her collaboration, the first phase of the Ballet Russes ended and so, too, the artistic domination of Léon Bakst and Alexandre Benois. Indeed, in 1914, when Goncharova designed the Paris production of *Le Coq d'Or*, Michel Fokine had grave misgivings about her eligibility, but he quickly changed his mind when he saw the costumes and sets: "What great work! . . . I was amused to recall the fears and rumors." Goncharova continued to work for Diaghilev in the 1920s, collaborating with Benois on the designs for *Aurora's Wedding* (1922) and creating the experimental costumes and sets for Nijinska's *Les Noces*. Goncharova's designs for the 1926 revival of *The Firebird* have been used for many subsequent revivals, including the Royal Ballet production in 1954.

After settling in Paris, Goncharova continued to paint and to illustrate books. Her later work includes designs for Boris Romanov's *A Romantic Adventure of an Italian Ballerina and a Marquis,* mounted at Nikita Baliev's Chauve-Souris cabaret in New York in 1931.

[*For related discussion, see* Costume in Western Traditions, *overview article; and* Scenic Design.]

BIBLIOGRAPHY

Baer, Nancy Van Norman. *The Art of Enchantment: Diaghilev's Ballets Russes, 1909–1929.* San Francisco, 1988.

Bowlt, John E., ed. and trans. *Russian Art of the Avant-Garde.* Rev. and enl. ed. New York, 1988. Contains manifestos by Goncharova in English translation.

Chamot, Mary. *Goncharova: Stage Designs and Paintings.* London, 1979.

Garafola, Lynn. *Diaghilev's Ballets Russes.* New York, 1989.

Goncharova, Natalia, et al. *Les Ballets Russes: Serge de Diaghilew et la décoration théâtrale.* Paris, 1955.

Grigoriev, Serge. *The Diaghilev Ballet, 1909–1929.* Translated and edited by Vera Bowen. London, 1953.

Loguine, Tatiana. *Gontcharova et Larionov.* Paris, 1971.

Nathalie Gontcharova/Michel Larionov. Paris, 1995. Exhibition catalog, Centre Georges Pompidou.

Schouvaloff, Alexander. *Set and Costume Designs for Ballet and Theatre.* London, 1987.

Sharp, Jane A. "Primitivism, 'Neoprimitivism,' and the Art of Natal'ia Goncharova, 1907–14." Ph.D. diss., Yale University, 1992.

Tsvetaeva, Marina. *Nathalie Gontcharova, sa vie, son oeuvre.* Paris, 1990.

ARCHIVE.   Victoria and Albert Museum, London.

JOHN E. BOWLT

GOPAL, RAM (born 20 November 1912 in Bangalore), Indian dancer. Son of a Rajput father and a Burmese mother, Ram Gopal began dancing at an early age. He had thorough training in classical *bharata nāṭyam* under Meenakshisundaram Pillai of Pandanallur village and in *kathakaḷi* under the guru Kunju Kurup at Kerala Kalamandalam. He also studied *kathak* and Manipuri dance. He was the first male dancer to present classical *bharata nāṭyam* in an authentic manner in the West. Credit goes to La Meri, an American ethnic dancer who discovered him during her Indian tour.

Gopal joined La Meri in 1936 on a tour covering India, Rangoon, Malaya, Java, the Philippines, China, and Japan. In 1938 and 1939 he performed independently in Europe and America, where he was highly acclaimed. He then returned to India and opened a school of dance in Bangalore, where many great masters taught. Some of the most prominent contemporary dancers, such as Mrinalini Sarabhai, Shevanti, Kumudini Lakhia, Satyavati, Shanta Rao, and Tara Chaudhary, were students at his school. Some of them also partnered him in his dance recitals and toured abroad with his dance company.

In 1945 Gopal participated in the All India Dance Festival in Delhi and Bombay and was highly praised. Later he returned to Europe and had unprecedented success wherever he performed, paving the way for other Indian dancers to visit Europe. He represented India at the International Dance Festival in America at Jacob's Pillow in 1954 and at the Edinburgh Festival in 1956. This was followed by a successful season at the Royal Festival Hall in London. In the 1960s, after touring Europe several times, he appeared in London's Princess Theatre with a new repertory. In his *Radha Krishna,* the role of Rādhā was danced by the renowned British ballerina Alicia Markova. In 1965, Gopal participated in the Commonwealth Art Festival in London.

Ram Gopal personified the grandeur of *bharata nāṭyam,* doing justice to a tradition famous for its fascinating depth of expression and enduring vigor. In his formal harmony and aesthetic excellence, he expressed the inherent dignity of the Pandanallur school. He brought suppleness, grace, and a brilliant imagination to his interpretation of Indian classical dance. His creative compositions, such as *Dance of Garuda* and *Setting Sun,* were hailed as masterpieces.

Whereas Uday Shankar aroused initial interest in Indian dance, Ram Gopal revealed to the world its ancient tradition and its superb technique. On stage and in his private life Ram Gopal has a compelling personality. He is the author of the book *Rhythm in the Heavens* (1957),

GOPAL. A seaside portrait of Gopal in a pure-dance (*nṛtta*) pose. (Photograph from the archives at Jacob's Pillow, Becket, Massachusetts.)

based on his own life; he also revised a book on dance by Kay Ambrose. The French director Claude La Morris has made two documentary films on him, *Om Shiva* and *Nataraja*. In his later years, Ram Gopal divided his time among London, Venice, and the south of France. In 1990, he was made a Fellow of the Sangeet Natak Akademi, the national academy of dance, drama, and music in New Delhi.

BIBLIOGRAPHY

Gopal, Ram, and Serozh Dadachanji. *Indian Dancing*. London, 1951.
Gopal, Ram. "Hindu Themes Have Influenced European Ballet and Dancers" (parts 1–2). *Ballet Today* (December 1952–January 1953).
Gopal, Ram. *Rhythm in the Heavens*. London, 1957.
Gopal, Ram. "Eastern Dances for Western Dancers." *The Dancing Times* (October 1962): 16–17.
Kothari, Sunil, ed. *Bharata Natyam: Indian Classical Dance Art*. Bombay, 1979.
Misra, Susheela. *Some Dancers of India*. New Delhi, 1992.

INTERVIEW.   Ram Gopal, by Sunil Kothari on video, for the Audio/Video Archive of Sangeet Natak Akademi, New Delhi (16 March 1984); published in *Sangeet*, nos. 101–102 (July-December 1991).

SUNIL KOTHARI

GORDEYEV. As a principal dancer with the Bolshoi Ballet, Gordeyev appeared in many leading roles. Here he is seen in the title role of Grigorovich's production of *Spartacus*. (Photograph © 1979 by Jack Vartoogian; used by permission.)

GORDEYEV, VIACHESLAV (Viacheslav Mikhailovich Gordeyev; born 3 August 1948 in Moscow), Russian dancer and choreographer. Gordeyev graduated from the Moscow ballet school, where he trained under Petr Pestov, and was then admitted to the Bolshoi Ballet, where his teacher and coach was Aleksei Varlamov. He was soon given important roles in both the classical and the Yuri Grigorovich repertories. Gordeyev has been a virtuoso dancer with remarkable elevation and pirouettes. One of the famous Bolshoi duos consisted of Gordeyev and his wife, Nadezhda Pavlova. In 1973 he was awarded the first prize at the Moscow International Competition for ballet dancers.

Gordeyev started to choreograph in 1981. In 1983 he became artistic director of the Moscow company Russian Ballet. Since then, most of his works have been made for that company. His choreography consists of some thirty concert dances, one-act ballets, and some revivals of the classics. Among his original works are *Passacaglia* and *Meeting (Vstrecha)* to music by Mikhail Taraverdiev, both in 1981; *The Psaltery Player (Gusliar*, 1982), to music by Valery Kikta; *Memory (Pamiat*, 1984), to music by Boris Petrov; *Steps (Shagi*, 1985), to music by Maurice Jarre; *Animated Pictures (Ozhivshiye Kartiny*, 1986), to music by Handel, Bach, and Mozart; and *The Unexpected Maneuvers, or The Wedding with a General (Neozhidanniye Manevry ili Svadba s Generalom*, 1987), to music by Rossini.

By working for Russian Ballet, Gordeyev revealed a talent less for choreography than for administration and management. In a short time he built a company with dancers who were capable of performing the Russian classics and with a sound repertory that made successful tours abroad. When Vladimir Vasiliev took over the Bolshoi Theater in March 1995, aiming to restore the ballet and opera, tighten discipline, and build a new repertory, it was Gordeyev whom he invited to be artistic director of the Bolshoi Ballet.

BIBLIOGRAPHY

Barnes, Patricia. "Something New from Moscow." *Dance and Dancers* (February 1988): 21–23.
Greskovic, Robert. "The Bolshoi: The Picture Changes." *Ballet Review* 4.5 (1973): 35–49.
Greskovic, Robert. "Muscovy in Trenton." *Ballet Review* 16 (Spring 1988): 63–79.
Inozemtseva, Galina V. "Viacheslav Gordeev." *Sovetskii balet*, no. 4 (1988): 16–19.
Krause, Bernd. "Ballet's Third World." *Ballet International* (December 1994): 45.
Willis, Margaret E. "Russian Roulette." *Dance and Dancers* (September 1991): 8–10.

ELIZABETH SOURITZ

GORDON, DAVID (born 14 July 1936 in New York City), dancer and choreographer. David Gordon studied art at Brooklyn College and began dancing with James

GORDON. In a 1981 performance collage of various works, David Gordon was caught mid-air with his wife and longtime collaborator Valda Setterfield. (Photograph © 1981 by Stephan Driscoll; used by permission.)

Waring while still in school. He also studied dance with Merce Cunningham and composition with Waring, Louis Horst, and Robert Dunn. Gordon was part of the Judson Dance Theater and a founding member of Grand Union. He danced with Yvonne Rainer (1966–1970) and collaborated with Douglas Dunn. More recently he has collaborated with visual designer Power Boothe and video artist Dennis Diamond, and he constructed the movement for Philip Glass and Robert Coe's opera *The Photographer* (1983). He has worked closely with his wife, the dancer Valda Setterfield, since the demise of Grand Union in 1976.

Gordon is an analytic choreographer who also embraces theatrical spectacle. He is interested in the ambiguous gaps between the real and the fictional, the spontaneous and the scripted, habit and invention, and language and experience. His movement style is both casual and authoritative and often looks more like everyday behavior than dancerly motion. Like a cubist painter, he accumulates and organizes multiple views of a single phenomenon into one composition. Two of his favored choreographic techniques are repetition and variation. He is interested in mistakes and often explores them in either his variations or his themes. A paradigmatic work in the analytic vein was *One Part of the Matter* (1972), in which Setterfield performed a series of poses from Eadweard Muybridge's *The Human Figure in Motion*. (Setterfield also performed a version of this solo in *The Photographer*.)

Gordon has a predilection for quotation from dance history, popular entertainment, Hollywood myths, and even his own works as well as for ironic commentary. In *Random Breakfast* (1963), he gave instructions for making successful modern dances and imitated Judy Garland; in *Trying Times* (1983), he took on *The Merchant of Venice* and George Balanchine's *Apollo*.

Gordon's early pieces from 1960 to 1966 were all solos or duets for himself and Setterfield. After *Walks and Digressions* (1966) he stopped creating dances for five years. His works since 1971 have included duets and larger group pieces. His Pick-Up Company, formed in 1978, has existed since then in a semipermanent form.

Although his dances have incorporated talking and singing at least since 1963, since the late 1970s much of Gordon's work has been built on strong but ever-shifting patterns of movement, spoken language, and the interrelations between the two. A radical example of this is *What Happened* (1978), in which a group of women simultaneously tell a series of narratives in mimed sign language and spoken words. In various other works, Gordon establishes punning correspondences between the literal (often, kinetic) and figurative meanings of words. The collaborations with videographer Dennis Diamond (*T.V. Reel*, 1981) and designer Power Boothe (*Trying Times* and *Framework*, 1983) added a visual dimension to the patterning process.

Beginning in the 1980s, Gordon created work for several ballet companies, including American Ballet Theatre (*Field, Chair & Mountain*, 1985, and *Murder*, 1986), Dance Theatre of Harlem (*Piano Movers*, 1985), and Groupe de Recherche Chorégraphique de l'Opéra de Paris. He also choreographed for Mikhail Baryshnikov's White Oak

Dance Project and for many modern dance companies in the United States and Europe.

In the 1990s, Gordon created the multipart dance *United States*, based on images and stories from various cities in which its sections were performed, as well as works for the theater, including *The Mysteries and What's So Funny?* (1991; to music by Philip Glass, visual design by Red Grooms), which includes an appearance by Setterfield as Marcel Duchamp, and *The Family Business* (1994), of which Gordon was co-author and co-director with his son, Ain Gordon. It included performances by both Gordons and Setterfield. His videodances have been aired by the British Broadcasting Corporation and by public television in the United States. Gordon's dances, persistently changing meaning and appearance, ironically subvert impressions as fast as he projects them.

In 1994 Gordon directed *Schlemiel the First*, a klezmer musical based on short stories by Isaac Bashevis Singer, at the American Repertory Theater in Cambridge, Massachusetts, and at the American Conservatory Theater in San Francisco. Gordon also directed *The Firebugs* by Max Frisch for the Guthrie Theater, Minneapolis, in 1995. Although the experience of acting together for eight shows a week in *The Family Business* persuaded the Gordons that they no longer wished to work together as actors, Ain and David Gordon reunited as writers for *Punch and Judy Get Divorced* (with music by Edward Barnes and lyrics by Arnold Weinstein; 1996), a theme David Gordon had previously addressed in a work for television and in a dance. In 1996 the father-and-son team began work on *Silent Movie*, about the history of silent film and the rise of censorship in the United States.

BIBLIOGRAPHY

Banes, Sally. *Terpsichore in Sneakers: Post-Modern Dance*. 2d ed. Middletown, Conn., 1987. Includes a bibliography.

Croce, Arlene. "Making Work." *The New Yorker* (29 November 1982).

Dunning, Jennifer. "David Gordon's Dance Ironies." *New York Times* (12 December 1982).

Gordon, David. "It's about Time." *Drama Review* 19 (March 1975): 43–52.

Gordon, David. "The Mysteries and What's So Funny?" In *Grove New American Theater*, edited by Michael Feingold. New York, 1993.

Kaplan, Peggy Jarrell. *Portraits of Choreographers*. New York, 1988.

Ross, Janice. "Minimal Dance with a Flair: A Talk with David Gordon and Valda Setterfield." *San Francisco Bay Guardian* (3 August 1978).

Setterfield, Valda. "The Making of *Field, Chair & Mountain*." *Ballet Review* 13 (Spring 1985): 5–21.

FILM AND VIDEOTAPE. *Making Dances* (Blackwood Productions, 1979). "Beyond the Mainstream," *Dance in America* (WNET-TV, New York, 1980). *Limited Partnership 2* (KTCA-TV, Minneapolis, 1984). *Made in U.S.A.* (WNET-TV, New York, 1987). *My Folks* (BBC-TV, London, 1989). *Punch and Judy Get Divorced* (KTCA-TV, Minneapolis, 1992).

SALLY BANES

GORE, WALTER (Frederick Robert Taylor; born 8 October 1910 in Waterside, Scotland, died 16 April 1979 in Pamplona, Spain); Scottish ballet dancer, choreographer, teacher, and company director. Walter Gore was born into a family that had been associated with the theater for generations. Gore went to London at the age of fourteen and studied acting at the Italia Conti Stage School. His early London stage appearances were as a boy actor in *Where the Rainbow Ends*, *Saint Joan*, and *A Midsummer Night's Dream*. In 1925 he was engaged by Charles B. Cochran for his revue *On with the Dance*, in which Léonide Massine danced and choreographed the ballets. Massine encouraged Gore to dance and gave him lessons as well as a letter of introduction to Marie Rambert, who had opened her London school five years previously. She instantly saw Gore's potential. With her early group, the Rambert Dancers, in a 1930 season at the Lyric Theatre, Hammersmith, Gore danced Pantalon in Fokine's *Le Carnaval*, with Tamara Karsavina as Columbine and Leon Woizikowski as Harlequin.

In 1931 Gore danced in a Camargo Society season at the Cambridge Theatre, London, creating parts in Yodeling Song and Popular Song in Frederick Ashton's *Façade* and Pestilence and one of the Three Comforters in Ninette de Valois's *Job*. In the same year he joined Rambert's recently formed Ballet Club, where his early roles included a Lover in Ashton's *The Lady of Shalott* (1931), Sir Toby in Antony Tudor's *Cross-Garter'd* (1931), Cinesias in Tudor's *Lysistrata* (1932), a Lover in Ashton's *Les Masques* (1933), the Juggler in Andrée Howard's *Our Lady's Juggler* (1933), and Faust in Ashton's *Mephisto Valse* (1934).

Although he continued to dance in the Ballet Club's Sunday performances, Gore joined the Vic-Wells Ballet in 1934. His principal creations there were in two de Valois ballets: The Tinker in *The Jar* (1934) and the title role in *The Rake's Progress* (1935), in which his performance has never been surpassed. After only a year with the company, he left in 1935 to dance in West End musicals, as well as arrange dances, as he notably did in the Herbert Farjeon revue *Spread It Abroad* (1936).

Over the years, Gore developed into one of the finest British *demi-caractère* dancers. He had a unique perception of the dramatic or comic depths of the roles he danced, an insight that became apparent also in his choreography. Encouraged by Rambert, he choreographed his earliest ballets for her company at the Mercury Theatre: *Valse Finale* (1938), set to Maurice Ravel's *Valses Sentimentales* and with decor by Sophie Fedorovitch; *Paris-Soir* (1939), set to music by Francis Poulenc; and *Cap over Mill* (1940), set to a score by Stanley Bate and designed by Nadia Benois. In 1940, he created two ballets for the Oxford University Ballet Club: *Bartlemas Dances*, with music by Gustav Holst and decor by William Chappell, and *Confessional*, based on a poem by Robert Browning, set to music by Jean Sibelius, and designed by Andrée Howard. In both ballets he danced with the young Sally Gilmour, and both works were later taken into the repertory of Ballet Rambert during a season at London's Arts Theatre.

Following the outbreak of hostilities in World War II, Gore was called to active service in the Royal Navy in 1941. After many months of service, he was seriously injured when he was involved in two torpedo attacks in a single day: first on a landing craft, then on the ship that rescued him. Invalided out of the navy in 1944, he returned to Ballet Rambert. Although his dancing career was somewhat curtailed, he continued to perform for several years, often taking leading roles in works of his own creation.

In choreography, Gore found his true métier, and it was as a choreographer that he would make a major contribution to ballet. His highly individual style was seen in works that fell mainly into three categories—strongly melodramatic, sharply comic, and plotless yet evocative of a distinctive mood. His principal creations for Ballet Rambert were *Simple Symphony* (1944), *Mr. Punch* (1946), *Plaisance* (1947), *Winter Night* (1948), and *Antonia* (1949). The latter work and his final creation for Rambert—*Sweet Dancer* (1964)—were built around the remarkable dramatic qualities of his wife, Paula Hinton, who was to be a major inspiration for the rest of his career.

From the beginning of the 1950s, Gore traveled widely, creating and reviving ballets and directing companies in several countries. Between periods abroad, he returned to Britain, arranging dances in London shows, such as *The Gay Invalid* (1951) and *Wedding in Paris* (1954). Also, he created works for various companies, notably *Street Games* (1952) for the New Ballet Company; *Carte Blanche* (1953) for Sadler's Wells Theatre Ballet; and *Night and Silence* (1958) for the Edinburgh International Ballet.

Twice Gore formed and directed his own companies in England. For the Walter Gore Ballet (1953–1955), the most popular of his several creations was *Light Fantastic* (1953), set to music by Emmanuel Chabries. Among the many revivals for his London Ballet (1961–1963) was his *Eaters of Darkness*, first given as *Die im Schatten Leben* (Those Who Live in Shadows) by the Frankfurt Opera Ballet in 1958. Set to Benjamin Britten's *Variations on a Theme of Frank Bridge*, the ballet tells a dark tale of a woman unjustly committed to a lunatic asylum and driven mad by her encounters with the inmates. Also in the London Ballet's repertory was Gore's version of *The Nutcracker*, first mounted by the Ballet der Lage Landen of Holland in 1957; this production was also given by the Norwegian National Ballet and by South Africa's PACT Ballet. Both the companies Gore founded in Britain had

considerable success despite the lack of subsidy at that time.

As well as mounting over seventy ballets for many of the world's major companies, Gore founded and directed the Australian Theatre Ballet (1955–1956) in Melbourne and directed, among others, the Frankfurt Städtische Bühnen (1957–1959) and the Grupo Gulbenkian de Bailado in Lisbon (1965–1969). When he died of a heart attack in 1979, Gore was director and professor of classical dance at the Conservatorio Navarro de Musica in Pamplona, Spain.

BIBLIOGRAPHY
Beaumont, Cyril W. *Ballets of Today*. London, 1954.
Clarke, Mary. *Dancers of Mercury: The Story of Ballet Rambert*. London, 1961.
Crisp, Clement, et al., eds. *Ballet Rambert: Fifty Years and On*. Rev. and enl. ed. [Ilkley, England], 1981.
Kersley, Leo. "Choreographers of Today: Walter Gore." *Ballet Today* (April 1961): 16–19.
"Walter Gore: A Tribute in Four Parts." *Dance Research* 6 (Spring 1988): 3–29.

PETER WILLIAMS

GORHAM, KATHLEEN (born 20 December 1932 in Sydney, New South Wales, died 30 April 1983 in Gold Coast, Queensland), Australian dancer. One of Australia's most widely loved ballerinas noted for her dramatic abilities and her flashing technique, Kathleen Gorham danced for twenty years at home and in Europe. Sent to dancing and elocution classes by her family, she came to the notice of Leon Kellaway who, under his given name of Jan Kowski, had been a member of the Pavlova and Spessivtseva companies that visited Australia.

Kellaway recognized Gorham's special gifts and brought her to the notice of Edouard Borovansky, who engaged her for his company at the age of fifteen, when she was still a child in experience and physique. Later in the year the company went into recess, and Gorham joined the Ballet Rambert for the rest of its Australian tour, under the name Ann Somers.

When the Rambert company left Australia in 1949, Gorham traveled with them, joining Roland Petit's Ballets de Paris shortly after her arrival in Europe. She came back to Australia in 1951 to perform with the Borovansky Ballet but soon left again. During 1952 and 1953 she danced in London with the Sadler's Wells Theatre Ballet and in Europe with Le Grand Ballet du Marquis de Cuevas.

In 1954 she returned to Australia as Borovansky's ballerina. In that same year she was chosen by John Cranko to dance Poll in his restaging of *Pineapple Poll* for the Borovansky Ballet. She continued to dance for Borovansky and as guest artist for various European companies until she became a principal with Peggy van Praagh's Australian Ballet in 1962, where she danced a wide range of roles for four years.

These years were the culmination of her dancing career. Her versatility was displayed in *Giselle*, her style and finesse in *The Sleeping Beauty*, and her natural ability as an actress in new works, notably Robert Helpmann's *The Display*. She also danced the Moon Goddess in Helpmann's delicate Japanese-inspired ballet *Yugen*, and the title role in a revival of his violent *Elektra*. She also appeared as an actress on stage and television.

After her retirement, she opened a school in Melbourne, and was co-director of the National Theatre Ballet School in Melbourne between 1974 and 1981. She continued to teach until her death.

BIBLIOGRAPHY
Pask, Edward H. *Ballet in Australia: The Second Act, 1940–1980*. Melbourne, 1982.
Pask, Edward H. "Kathleen Gorham, 1932–1983." *Dance Australia*, no. 13 (September–November 1983): 8–12.
Potter, Michelle. "Dance Greats: Kathleen Gorham." *Dance Australia* no. 85 (August–September 1996): 33.

GEOFFREY WILLIAM HUTTON
Amended by Michelle Potter

GORSKY, ALEKSANDR (Aleksandr Alekseevich Gorskii; born 6 [18] August 1871 in Saint Petersburg, died 20 October 1924 in Moscow), Russian dancer, choreographer, and teacher. After studying at the Saint Petersburg ballet school under Nikolai Volkov, Platon Karsavin, and Marius Petipa, Gorsky danced with the company of the Maryinsky Theater from 1889 to 1900, mainly character roles in Petipa ballets: Satyr in *Les Saisons*, Harlequin in *Ruses d'Amour*, a Saracen slave in *Raymonda;* as well as performing the Chinese dance in *The Nutcracker*. Gorsky's first production was the ballet fantasy *Clorinda, the Queen of Mountain Fairies* for the 1899 graduation performance of the Saint Petersburg school, where he taught from 1896 to 1900. In the same year he was commissioned by Moscow's Bolshoi Ballet to set the production of Petipa's *The Sleeping Beauty* and the following year *Raymonda*. In 1900 he also produced his own version of *Don Quixote* there. He was appointed *régisseur* in 1901 and ballet master as well as teacher in 1902, retaining the position until his death.

Gorsky came to the Bolshoi company when it was in a state of crisis. During the late years of the nineteenth century its reputation had declined and its future path was uncertain. Gorsky began to enforce his ballet reforms on the Moscow stage. He sought to remove the conventions of academic ballet: the standard architectural form, the separation of dance and pantomime, the canonical character of dance structures (pas de deux, and so forth), and the traditional ballet costumes (tutus). He achieved an integrity of action, means of expression, and style of decor as well as a conformity to real life. These reforms reflected what was happening in Russian culture as a whole. The upsurge in public activity that had started in the mid-1890s contributed to the advancement of all arts and literature. Gorsky was also influenced by phenomena in Moscow's artistic life such as the Moscow Art Theater (as he himself later acknowledged in an interview with the newspaper *Rampa i Zhizn* [Stage and Life] on 1 June 1914) and Savva Mamontov's private opera, where special significance was attached to artistic direction and decor. During his years at the Bolshoi Gorsky totally revamped its repertory, creating new ballets and revising old ones, usually in collaboration with the designer Konstantin Korovin.

Gorsky's first fully independent work at the Bolshoi was *Gudule's Daughter* (1902), to music by Anton Simon. The production followed the events in Victor Hugo's novel *Notre-Dame de Paris* and accentuated mass episodes. Gorsky showed the lower classes with an authenticity that was unprecedented on the ballet stage: the ragged and hungry crowds, the beating of Quasimodo by hangmen, the procession of Esmeralda to the execution site. Esmeralda herself—in a torn dress, her face stained with blood and dirt, with an enormous penitential candle in her weak, childish hands—was quite unlike heroines of old ballets. The production stirred heated debates in the press, but was not long preserved in the repertory.

Gorsky staged his next original work, *Salammbô*, to music by Andrei Arends as late as 1910. In the interim he had produced a few one-act ballets (*Nur and Anitra* in 1907, to music by Aleksandr Ilyinsky; *Etudes* in 1908, to music by several composers). *Salammbô* was more traditional than *Gudule's Daughter*, although it was on an equally grand scale. The picturesque prevailed just as in Flaubert's novel, in Korovin's decor in particular, and it was just as exotic. The crowd was in the foreground: soldiers and mercenaries, beggars and slaves, priests in ritual scenes. Unfortunately, the monumental folk drama conceived by Gorsky was not supported in drama and scope by Arends's music, which was quite traditional. Gorsky had also to reckon with the performers. The role of Salammbô was intended for Ekaterina Geltser, and Mikhail Mordkin, rather than Geltser's regular partner Vasily Tikhomirov, danced the central male role of Matho. Much in the production was dictated by the ballerina's demands. A dancer with a vivid temperament, she was equally brilliant in bravura and in mime scenes. In dramatically tense scenes—the episode in Matho's tent, which Salammbô enters hating Matho and leaves as his lover, and in the scene of her parting with the dying Matho—Geltser and Gorsky reached agreement. Thanks to Geltser's performance, the central role was enlarged and dramatized and at times assumed a heroic dimension. One could believe that Salammbô would sacrifice her honor to retrieve the stolen sacred relic and would favor death when forced to renounce love. Geltser wanted classical dance, and Gorsky had to meet her halfway and stage, for example, a duet with her fiancé, Narr-Avas (Tikhomirov), in the betrothal scene. Therefore, Gorsky himself regarded *Salammbô* as a ballet not free from what he called "ballerina's tradition" and saw elements of a compromise in the production. Its stylistic integrity, which Gorsky regarded as one of the main principles of stage production, was disturbed.

Compromise was to be found in most of Gorsky's works between 1912 and 1917. They include, in addition to revivals, a few original one-act ballets. *Salammbô* was the last large-scale, full-length ballet Gorsky produced before the October Revolution. It is true that after Serge Diaghilev's "Russian Seasons" began in Paris in 1909 the one-act ballet moved to the foreground because for Michel Fokine the one-act ballet was intrinsic; its condensed form did not deprive his ballets of either their ideological message or their wide scope, as is evident in his *Petrouchka*. For Gorsky, however, renunciation of external monumentality meant abandonment of socially meaningful themes.

In the troubled years preceding the revolution, when the Russian intelligentsia anticipated a formidable change, Gorsky sought mental comfort in the idea of a healing force possessed by pristine nature: simple work and innocent love. That gave birth in 1913 to *Love Is Quick!*, a lyrical-comic genre scene set to music from Grieg's Symphonic Dances: a meeting between a fisherman survivor of a shipwreck and a shepherdess, love, betrothal, a village festival. Korovin painted an austere Norwegian landscape, with wide expanses of ocean and rocks. Gorsky showed people untouched by civilization, crude and simple as the rocks surrounding them, clumsy, slow, and bowlegged—all attributes that were contrary to images of ballet classics.

During the years of World War I the choreographer staged a series of ballets that reflected his moods. His first reaction to the war was the heroic dance "The Genius of Belgium" for Geltser, which expressed his compassion for the small country treacherously sacrificed to the interests of the stronger powers. The ballet *Eunice and Petronius* (1915), to music of Chopin, was distinctively elegiac in character. Grief merged with admiration for what man had doomed to death in his insanity. The heroes lived by love alone, ignoring all else, and died at Nero's order while enjoying the surrounding beauty and feeling no hatred for their destroyer. Stylistically, the ballet arbitrarily combined poses that recalled Isadora Duncan and the sophisticated pointe technique that was indispensable for Geltser. One of Gorsky's innovations of those years was his attempt to stage a ballet symphony, which was logically the next step after his production of ballets to con-

GORSKY. A scene from *Gudule's Daughter*, premiered at the Bolshoi Theater on 24 November 1902, with scenery and costumes by Konstantin Korovin. The heroine, Esmeralda (Sofia Fedorova), is seen here cowering in the arms of her mother, Gudule (Maria Drugasheva), as the Royal Archers arrive to arrest her and take her to the gallows. The ballet was later known as *Notre-Dame de Paris*, after Victor Hugo's novel, on which it was based. (Photograph from the A. A. Bakhrushin Central State Theatrical Museum, Moscow; courtesy of Elizabeth Souritz.)

cert music *(Etudes, Schubertiana, Love Is Quick!,* and *Eunice and Petronius)*. He selected Glazunov for *Fifth Symphony* (1916). Gorsky remained loyal to his principles: he did not think of conjuring up generalized dance images that corresponded to the music, but added a plot to produce an antique dance pastorale.

Immediately after the October Revolution, Gorsky began active work with the youth of the Bolshoi. In the summer of 1918 he staged a number of new productions at the theater of the Aquarium Garden: *A Lyrical Poem* to music by Glazunov, *Night on the Bare Mountain* to Mussorgsky, *Spanish Sketches* to Glinka's *Night in Madrid* and *Jota Aragonesa, Tamara* to Balakirev, and, most significantly, *En Blanc* to music from Tchaikovsky's Third Suite. This time Gorsky renounced plot and staged the dance to express the general mood of the music. Although this production can hardly be called a ballet symphony, it was an important precursor. On 7 November 1918 Gorsky's *Stenka Razin*, to Glazunov, was shown for the first anniversary of the October Revolution.

The first five years after the Revolution were a difficult period in the life of the Bolshoi: the civil war was in progress, followed by economic dislocation, so that funds for new productions were extremely scant and the theater was more than once threatened with closure. In those years Gorsky worked as a teacher, outside the Bolshoi in particular, and staged dances for public concerts and sometimes even for the circus. His most significant work was *The Nutcracker*, which he had conceived and started before the war, but staged only in 1919. In that production he managed to integrate both acts into common action. The heroine, who also danced to the music of the Sugar-plum Fairy, was interpreted by fifteen-year-old Valentina Kudriavtseva. Many of Gorsky's innovations were later taken up by other Soviet choreographers who staged this ballet. In 1922 Gorsky collaborated in the production of a revolutionary children's theatrical on the occasion of the fifth anniversary of the revolution: *Ever-Fresh Flowers,* to music by Boris Asafiev and other composers. His last works—*The Dance of Salomé* to Richard Strauss, *Les Petits Riens* to Mozart, and *Venusberg* from Wagner's opera *Tannhäuser,* all choreographed between 1921 and 1923—did not remain in the repertory.

However, it was not Gorsky's original productions but his revisions of classic ballets that were most performed. He turned to *La Fille Mal Gardée* at least seven times, and his 1907, 1911, 1918, and 1922 versions of *Giselle,* 1901, 1912, and 1920 versions of *Swan Lake,* and 1901, 1912,

and 1914 versions of *The Little Humpbacked Horse* are still known. He gradually revised *La Fille du Pharaon* in 1905, *Le Corsaire* in 1913, *La Bayadère* in 1917, and *Raymonda* in 1908 and 1918. As a rule, each of the subsequent versions was farther removed from the original source. In his productions of these ballets Gorsky attempted to cope with the same tasks as in his original productions. He opposed the conventions of classical ballet with the principles of veracity and realistic action, thereby revealing a consistently developed plot, dramatizing dance, and securing the authenticity of national color. In certain cases, such as *Don Quixote,* in which, as Gorsky put it in the 20 January 1902 *Saint Petersburg Gazette,* "one could observe a constant movement of masses," even though the symmetry of dance structures was disturbed the production assumed greater integrity because of its dynamism and cheerful tone.

Not infrequently, however, in his effort to perfect (as he put it) an old ballet that had been devised according to a different aesthetic, Gorsky destroyed precisely what was valuable in it. Dance subordinated to the logic of concrete acts and situations lost its abstract property. Gorsky's *Swan Lake* swans ran in a circle in confusion like a flock

GORSKY. A scene from act 1 of Gorsky's 1920 production of *Swan Lake* for the Bolshoi Ballet. (Photograph from the A. A. Bakhrushin Central State Theatrical Museum, Moscow; courtesy of Elizabeth Souritz.)

GORSKY. A scene from act 2 of Gorsky's 1922 production of *Giselle*. Margarita Kandaurova as Giselle and Lev Laschilin as Albrecht with members of the female ensemble of the Bolshoi Ballet, on stage at the Novy Theater, Moscow. The premiere of this version took place on 9 January 1922. (Photograph from the A. A. Bakhrushin Central State Theatrical Museum, Moscow; courtesy of Elizabeth Souritz.)

of frightened hens, but this dramatic realism of detail detracted from the pure and harmonious character of Lev Ivanov's production. Even more controversial was his substitution of Indian dances for the classical ensemble dance of the Shades in *La Bayadère*. In his *Giselle* of 1922 Gorsky moved far away from tradition. The first act was of an emphatically genre character (even Giselle danced in heeled shoes), while in the second act the wilis, wearing long death shrouds and thick veils, formed not a classical ensemble moving in unison but random groups: one girl lying, another sitting, a third standing, and so on. The most radical revision of *Swan Lake* was the 1920 staging, when Gorsky divided the role of Odette-Odile in two, sharply opposing positive and negative characters, and introduced a new personage, the Jester.

Gorsky's activities were of enormous significance for the Bolshoi Ballet. He managed to lead the company out of its crisis. By attempting to introduce into ballet the ideas and images of his epoch, by producing a number of picturesque and dynamic ballets, by enriching and diversifying the dance vocabulary, he reinstated the art of ballet in the eyes of audiences who had lost interest in it. He united around himself like-minded artists—Mordkin, Sofia Fedorova, Maria Reisen, Vera Koralli, Alexandra Balashova, Elena Adamovich, Valentina Kudriavtseva, and Anastasia Abramova, to name but a few. At the same time Gorsky's reforms, particularly his experiments with classic ballets, were opposed by some members of the company, especially by Tikhomirov and sometimes

Geltser. Soon after Gorsky's death his original productions were deleted from the repertory, and ballets of the classical heritage were gradually restored to their traditional versions. At the present time *Don Quixote* is the closest to Gorsky's original, while in other ballets only a few individual dances or scenes have survived.

[*See also* Bolshoi Ballet. *Many of the works mentioned herein are the subjects of independent entries.*]

BIBLIOGRAPHY

Bakhrushin, Yuri. *Aleksandr Alekseevich Gorskii.* Moscow, 1946.
Guest, Ivor. *Ballet in Leicester Square.* London, 1992.
Krasovskaya, Vera. *Russkii baletnyi teatr nachala dvadtsatogo veka,* vol. 1, *Khoreografy.* Leningrad, 1971.
Pritchard, Jane. "Alexander Gorsky." *Dance Gazette* (October 1993): 26–29.
Roslavleva, Natalia. *Era of the Russian Ballet.* London, 1966.
Scheider, I. I. "U Gorskogo." *Rampa i Zhizn* (1 June 1914).
Scholl, Tim. *From Petipa to Balanchine: Classical Revival and the Modernization of Ballet.* New York, 1994.
Souritz, Elizabeth. *Soviet Choreographers in the 1920s.* Translated by Lynn Visson. Durham, N.C., 1990.
Troziner, F. F. "Novoe v balete." *St. Petersburg Gazette* 19–20 (January 1902).

ELIZABETH SOURITZ

GOSLAR, LOTTE (born 27 February 1906 in Dresden, died 16 October 1997 in Great Barrington, Massachusetts), German-American clown and dancer. Goslar was usually characterized as a mime or as a dance-mime, but she referred to herself as a clown. For thirty years her company

GOSLAR. In her most famous creation, *Clowns and Other Fools* (1966), Goslar portrayed many moods and emotions. Here she is the picture of dismay. (Photograph by Fred Fehl; used by permission.)

was called the Lotte Goslar Pantomime Circus. It is true that her performers occasionally used the traditional trappings of clowns: bulbous noses, oversized felt feet, and long, baggy nightshirts; and occasionally, as in their opener, *Hello! Hello?*, they did behave like clowns, with handshakes mistimed and chases ending in pratfalls. Yet Goslar's work went far deeper. Hers was a theater of hope and hard-earned optimism. It was at once innocent, kindly, and wise. Its predominant radiance belied her upbringing in the bleak environs of post–World War I Germany.

Like most young German dancers of her era, Goslar had a brief encounter with the Mary Wigman School, an approach she found too grim. She also spent time in the Dresden company of former Wigman dancer Gret Palucca. Eventually, with minimal formal training, Goslar struck out on her own.

In 1933 Erika Mann, daughter of novelist Thomas Mann, along with several other young German intellectuals, put on an anti-Hitler revue called *The Peppermill*. They toured with great success outside of Germany. Goslar performed with them and then spent a year on her own in

Prague. She rejoined *The Peppermill* in 1937 for its New York debut, which turned out to be a resounding failure. But Goslar scored a personal triumph and was invited to perform on Broadway and at New York's Rainbow Room.

An invitation came in 1943 for a brief engagement at Hollywood's Turnabout Theater. The engagement lasted ten years. During that span, Goslar also choreographed productions at the Hollywood Bowl and collaborated on several films, notably *Galileo* (1946), directed by Bertolt Brecht and Charles Laughton.

Eight years later Goslar reentered the international scene with her newly formed company, the Pantomime Circus (renamed Scenes and Dances in 1985). Their repertory constantly evolved over the years, but certain of Goslar's leitmotif solos remained by audience demand. Among these were *Life of a Flower*, with Goslar as the flower lifting her wide, trusting countenance to the heavens only to be inundated by rain and defeated by a cold. In *Grandma Always Danced* Goslar tenderly and mischievously evoked the life cycle of a woman who dances from cradle to grave—and beyond. *Liebestraum* showed her as an endearing old nanny fussing over her former charge as he tries to concertize. Although Goslar was inevitably the star, she consciously created works that revealed the technical strengths of her dancers. She also challenged them with serious satire, as in *Circus Scene*, written by Bertolt Brecht as a gift for the choreographer.

BIBLIOGRAPHY

Estrada, Ric. "To Be a Clown." *Dance Magazine* (August 1968): 48.
Goslar, Lotte. "Reflections." *Mime, Mask, and Marionette* 2.1 (1979–1980).
Robertson, Michael. "Lotte Goslar, Choreographer and Clown." *Dance Magazine* (December 1980): 80–83.

DORIS HERING

GOSSELIN FAMILY, French dancers in the early nineteenth century. Geneviève Gosselin, the eldest, enjoyed the most success. Other members included her younger sister, Constance Gosselin, and brother, Louis F. Gosselin.

Geneviève Gosselin (born 1791, died 1818 in Paris). Trained at the Paris Opera Ballet School under the great teacher Jean-François Coulon, the eighteen-year-old dancer demonstrated precision, balance, and well-regulated movements at her Opera debut in August 1809. She did not, however, make enough of a mark to avoid slipping back into the anonymity of the corps de ballet, an obscurity difficult to escape owing to the depth of talent at the Opera. In 1812, however, she caught the eye of several critics, and in 1813 the audience protested loudly when she did not appear one evening; for the next three years she was one of the most popular Opera dancers, performing roles such as Flora in Charles-Louis Didelot's *Flore et Zéphire* and Psyche in the ballet of the same name. Audiences were upset again when she did not appear in 1816, but this time it was illness that prevented her from performing. She died at the age of twenty-seven.

Gosselin's rise to fame was due to the brilliance of her tours de force. At a time when it was still considered inappropriate even for male dancers to execute steps that were astonishing merely because of their difficulty, she shocked serious-minded critics and delighted audiences with her multiple pirouettes and bold movements. Indeed, it was suggested by Martainville of the *Journal de Paris* that her sudden rise to popularity was due to her mastery of one special item of technique:

> For a long time Mlle. Gosselin saw with unhappiness the perfect talent she had received from nature and the lessons of an excellent school lost in the crowd of second rate dancers, unnoticed by the public. . . . Eventually, prompted by calculation or chance, the neglected artiste raises herself more than usual *sur la pointe* of her feet, presenting an elegant figure supported, so to speak, on a toe, on a single toe-nail. Suddenly the public cries, a miracle.   (Martinville, 1813)

This very early reference to pointe work implies that other dancers were practicing the technique as well.

Gosselin's impact was powerful; she demonstrated that women could master an athletic technique and in so doing shocked many a conservative-minded critic who felt that the "weaker sex" should avoid *tours de force*. When Marie Taglioni appeared in 1827, critics immediately drew a comparison between the two dancers. "C." of *Journal des débats* recalled the

> surprising flexibility of [Gosselin's] limbs, her muscular power, which permitted her to remain suspended for a minute or two on the extremity of her foot, the lightness of her choreographic evolutions, the elegance of her figure, and finally that prodigious facility to do difficult things with that air of abandon, naturalness and softness which is the triumph of art. Mlle. Taglioni appears particularly destined to repair the loss of the excellent dancer.   (Castil-Blaze, 1827)

Constance Gosselin (born 5 January 1794, died 1829). Constance debuted at the Paris Opera in 1815. Also a pupil of Coulon, she adopted the *danse noble* style. Although not as accomplished in her chosen genre as Geneviève was in hers, she divided a successful career between Paris and London. She married the dancer-choreographer Anatole Petit and became known by the name Madame Anatole.

Louis F. Gosselin (born 24 February 1800, died 5 February 1860), dancer and ballet master. Louis began his career in 1820 at the Paris Opera. He was not much appreciated there as a dancer but fared better in London, eventually becoming assistant ballet master at Her Majesty's Theatre from 1842 to 1852. After 1852 he became chief teacher at the Paris Opera.

BIBLIOGRAPHY

Castil-Blaze. *Journal des débats* (3 August 1827).
Chapman, John V. "Auguste Vestris and the Expansion of Technique." *Dance Research Journal* 19 (Summer 1987): 11–18.
Guest, Ivor. *The Romantic Ballet in England*. London, 1972.
Guest, Ivor. *The Romantic Ballet in Paris*. 2d rev. ed. London, 1980.
Guest, Ivor. *Le ballet de l'Opéra de Paris*. Paris, 1976.
Guest, Ivor. *Jules Perrot: Master of the Romantic Ballet*. London, 1984.
Martainville, A. L. D. *Journal de Paris* (23 July 1813).

JOHN V. CHAPMAN

GRAHAM, MARTHA (born 11 May 1894 in Allegheny, Pennsylvania, died 1 April 1991 in New York City), one of the foremost American choreographers of the twentieth century and a pioneer in the modern-dance movement. Graham created a body of works innovative in structure and movement style, directed a dance company from the 1920s until her death, developed a distinctive technique for training dancers, and influenced several generations of performers and choreographers. Even dancers who have never studied with an accredited teacher of Graham

GRAHAM. *Tanagra*, the third section from *Trois Gnossiennes*, was presented at Graham's first concert at the Forty-eighth Street Theater on 18 April 1928. In this lyric dance, set to music by Erik Satie, Graham showed the influence of Ruth St. Denis in her use of drapery. (Private collection.)

technique are familiar with the principles of contraction and release that are the core of her work.

Graham and her younger sisters, Mary and Georgia, received a sedate upbringing that emphasized ladylike behavior, moral uprightness, and composure reinforced by strong lashings of the Presbyterian faith. Her father, George Graham, was a physician who specialized in nervous diseases and mental disorders. Graham later said that he impressed her with his ability to discern mental states from posture and gesture. She also recalled the sisters' theater games and the relish with which they absorbed the grandeurs of Catholic ritual through their devoted Irish housekeeper.

In 1908, Graham's mother and the three girls moved to Santa Barbara, California, supposedly because of Mary's worsening asthma. Dr. Graham visited them regularly until he felt able to leave his Pennsylvania practice. In an interview published in August 1928 in *The Dance Magazine*, Graham spoke of the liberating effect of the move: "No child can develop as a real Puritan in a semitropical climate. California swung me in the direction of paganism, although years were to pass before I was fully emancipated." The conflict between Puritanism and "pagan" sensuality was to become a crucial one for many of the dance heroines she later created.

During her school years, Graham was clearly artistic: she wrote poetry and prose, acted in class plays, and edited the yearbook when she was a senior. However, she had little dance training beyond the usual classes in social dance. She once said that her family disapproved of dancing, yet her father, at her urging, took her, in spring 1911, to see Ruth St. Denis perform three excerpts from her dance drama *Egypta* and five East Indian solos—*The Incense, Cobras, Nautch, Yogi,* and *Radha.*

St. Denis's dancing enthralled the young Graham and fired her with the idea of becoming a performer. Her parents apparently did not stand in her way; St. Denis's shrewd blend of spiritual message with physical allure may have convinced the Grahams, as it had many others, that dancing could have a moral force. When Graham finished high school in 1913, she enrolled in the Cumnock School of Expression in Los Angeles, where she studied drama, art, and literature and had some form of physical training.

In 1915, St. Denis and her husband, Ted Shawn, opened the Denishawn School in Los Angeles. Martha Graham spent part of the summer of 1916 studying there. She made what seems to have been her professional debut as one of four "Dancers with Triangles" in the Egyptian section of an elaborate Denishawn dance pageant called *Life and Afterlife in Egypt, Greece, and India*, which was performed on 29 July 1916 in the Greek Theater of the University of California in Berkeley. Graham's name, however, does not appear on the program for a San Diego

performance of the pageant in August, and she returned to Cumnock for one more year before committing herself to Denishawn.

The Denishawn curriculum was an eclectic one, to judge from a 1918 school brochure. In that year, courses were offered in basic technique, Delsarte, oriental dance, Egyptian dance, ballet, Greek dance, creative dance, music visualization, plastique, geisha, piano, French, and crafts. Piano was taught by Denishawn's musical director, Louis Horst, who years later became Graham's musical director and close associate. Although Graham was late in starting her training, Shawn took an interest in her. He entrusted the teaching of some classes to her and in *Xochitl* provided her with her first important role—that of a maiden ferociously and successfully defending her virtue from the rapacious advances of the Toltec emperor, who was intoxicated not only by her beauty but also by *pulque*, an alcoholic drink discovered by Xochitl's peasant father. The dance, a "series of barbaric pictures," according to one critic, was first performed in vaudeville engagements in 1920 and was included in the Denishawn repertory for several years. Graham's sister Georgia, later billed as Geordie, followed Martha to Denishawn, made her debut in this dance, and took over her sister's role when Martha left the company in 1923.

At the time Ted Shawn began to utilize and develop Martha Graham's evident talent, he and St. Denis were having marital difficulties and were doing some touring separately. In September 1921, Shawn set off with Graham, Charles Weidman, Betty May, and Dorothea Bowen on a national tour that ended in New York in December. Subsequent tours in 1922 and 1923, which included vaudeville engagements in England, reunited St. Denis and Shawn. On these tours, Graham danced a variety of numbers for which her dark hair, high cheekbones, and small, strong body suited her. These included *Valse Aragonese*, a Spanish solo; *Malagueña*, a duet performed with Shawn; and *Serenata Morisca*, a Moorish solo. She danced an Egyptian duet with Shawn and an Arabic one with Weidman and played a Japanese maid, a Javanese princess, and an Indian dancing girl. She also participated in Shawn's *Church Service in Dance* and a number of "music visualizations," which included Shawn's *Revolutionary Étude* and *Soaring*, choreographed by St. Denis with Doris Humphrey.

Graham attracted critical attention on these tours. A discerning reviewer for the *Omaha World Herald* wrote on 25 October 1921: "The dancing of Martha Graham has an aloofness that is almost eerie in its fascination," and went on to say that she had few of the mannerisms that marred the performing of many professional dancers.

In an essay she contributed to Oliver Sayler's *Revolt in the Arts* (Graham, 1930), Graham made harsh, if oblique, reference to Denishawn, speaking of the "weakling exoticism of a transplanted orientalism." Yet, she avowed elsewhere that her Denishawn experience provided her with a basic dance technique and a thorough grounding in theater. She admired St. Denis greatly as a performer, and it may have been from watching St. Denis that she acquired the skill in manipulating fabric that she was to develop in her own choreography, although she did say in a 1973 interview that she thought her ability was inborn (Rogosin, 1980). Traces of the Delsarte training she received at Denishawn can be discerned in some of the earliest technique classes Graham taught. Certainly the basic elements of Delsarte's system of expression would have proved useful to anyone interested in understanding the impact of emotion on the body. It was at Denishawn, too, that Graham met Horst, who was to compose scores for her, to inform her musical taste, and to guide her transition from a Denishawn soloist to a creative modern artist of originality and power. [*See* Denishawn *and the entries on Shawn, St. Denis, and Horst.*]

The transition was a gradual one. In September 1923 Graham made her Broadway debut in John Murray Anderson's *The Greenwich Village Follies*, performing Shawn's *Serenata Morisca* in a Spanish fiesta number, as well as being featured in *The Garden of Kama*, choreographed by Michio Ito (not to be confused with the Denishawn ballet of the same name).

After two years of performing in the *Follies* in New York and on tour, Graham left the show and took up teaching to support herself, commuting between the Anderson-Milton School in New York City and the newly formed Department of Dance and Dramatic Action of the Eastman School of Music in Rochester, New York. While teaching, she prepared her first independent concert, which took place at the 48th Street Theater in New York City on 18 April 1926 and featured, in addition to Graham, three of her Rochester students: Evelyn Sabin, Betty MacDonald, and Thelma Biracree.

None of the eighteen dances from this concert has survived, with the possible exception of *Three Gopi Maidens* (to music by Cyril Scott), which may have been incorporated into *Flute of Krishna*, a dance Graham put together for one of Eastman's regular weekly entertainments. *Flute* was recorded on silent film. This film, photographs, and titles of other dances on the program suggest the influence on Graham of Denishawn's exotic ballets and music visualizations. The music, played by Horst on the piano, included compositions by Robert Schumann, Franz Schubert, Johannes Brahms, Claude Debussy, Maurice Ravel, Alexander Scriabin, Erik Satie, and Horst himself. Certain works were inspired by painting and sculpture, such as *Portrait–After Beltram–Masses* (later renamed *Gypsy Portrait*), *Study in Lacquer,* and *From a XII-Century Tapestry.* *The Dance Magazine* of July 1926 affirmed that Graham had a "talent for making pictures," and the general tenor

of reviews of this and other very early concerts indicates that she was skilled as a performer and adroit at putting dances together, but not yet particularly original; her solo vignettes were not markedly different from those of Ito, Angna Enters, and other gifted soloists. It has been suggested, however, that despite the romantic prettiness, the exoticism, the Art Deco curves, and the trailing draperies, some of these dances had a simplicity and an economy that presaged Graham's later work. She did not immediately disavow them all either. *Tanagra* (from *Trois Gnossiannes*), the satiric *Deux Valses Sentimentales,* and the trio, to Scriabin's music, *Danse Languide,* were performed on a matinee program during the 1930 season of the Dance Repertory Theater, long after she had become known as an uncompromising contemporary artist.

Living in New York in the 1920s, Graham had opportunities to come into contact with all that was new in the

GRAHAM. The manipulation of fabric was an important element in many early modern dances. Typically, it was used to lyrical effect. However, in her famous solo *Lamentation*, created in 1930 and seen here in a 1935 photograph, Graham created an ingenious costume to augment the expression of grief. Throughout the dance, Graham remained seated as she struggled with a cloth tubing that encased her body. (Photograph © 1935 by Barbara Morgan; used by permission of the Barbara Morgan Archives, Hastings-on-Hudson, New York.)

GRAHAM. *Ekstasis,* one of many solos Graham created for herself in the 1930s, premiered at the Guild Theatre, New York, in 1933. (Photograph © 1935 by Barbara Morgan; used by permission of the Barbara Morgan Archives, Hastings-on-Hudson, New York.)

arts. She was also aware of developments in the German *Ausdrucktanz.* Themes of a more somber nature began to appear in her work, as in the solo *Contrition* from *Baal-Shem* (1926), but it was perhaps with the iconoclastic solo *Revolt* (1927) that Graham began to work with a starkness, angularity, and force that brought her work into line with that of modernists in the other arts. Like *Revolt,* the 1928 works *Poems of 1917* and *Immigrant* revealed the social conscience that was to be a vital part of modern dance in the 1930s.

"Like the modern painters and architects, we have stripped our medium of decorative unessentials," said Graham in 1930. In accord with this, her work had begun to be characterized by a percussive attack, an avoidance of curves, a further distillation of gesture to its essence. Like her contemporaries Humphrey and Weidman, she was not interested in impressionism or in realistic scenes. She wanted to project the contemporary American spirit through forms that would capture the heightened pace and new designs of urban, machine-age living. She

wished, too, to communicate the American pioneer spirit, to explore as sources the gestures of Native American and black cultures. And she wanted to deal in a thoroughly contemporary and abstract way with human feeling.

Graham stayed at Eastman for only one year, although she continued to teach at Anderson-Milton through 1927. In 1928 she began a long association with the Neighborhood Playhouse, teaching dance to student actors as well as to dancers. (Graham was listed on the faculty into 1966 and as a board member for more than ten years after that.) She also began to give classes on her own, training dedicated young women in order to expand her company, so that she could deal with the subject of society as well as with the individual. She presented her "Group" at the Booth Theater in New York City on 14 April 1929 in four dances: *Vision of the Apocalypse, Sketches from the People, Moment Rustica,* and *Heretic.* The last is generally considered to be her first important group work, and it was performed as late as 1994. Horst created the score out of a short Breton folk tune repeated over and over. In this terse, plain work, a solo figure in a white dress was confronted by an implacable human wall, a narrow-souled conformist society—the dancers dressed alike in long, simple dark dresses with dark nets confining their hair. Regrouping, they blocked the rebel's way, refused to consider her "statements," and finally defeated her. The soloist made her advances on the melody; on the reiterated piano chords, the women thumped their feet in denial and, in silence moved violently to each new condemnatory pose.

From 1929 to 1938, Martha Graham created twenty-one works for her all-female company and thirty-six solos for herself. Of these, the only ones performed in recent decades are *Heretic and Celebration* (1934); *Primitive Mysteries* (1931), which is considered one of her greatest group compositions; and the solos *Lamentation* (1930), *Deep Song* (1937), and *Frontier* (1935), originally the first half of *Perspectives.* During those years, certain themes recurred in her works. There were the dances that proclaimed themselves "American": *American Provincials* (1934), *Perspectives* and *Panorama* (1935), *Horizons* (1936), *American Lyric* (1937), and *American Document* (1938). There were pieces that dealt with ritual, both public and private: *Primitive Mysteries* and *Bacchanale* (1931), *Ceremonials* (1932), and *Tragic Patterns* (1933). There were dances primarily expressing the dancers' vitality and precision: *Celebration* (1934) and *Course* (1935). *Chronicle* (1936) and the solos *Imperial Gesture* (1935), *Immediate Tragedy* (1936), and *Deep Song* (1937)—three of them made around the time the Spanish Civil War broke out—dealt in eloquent, if subtle, ways with the dangers of war and the ruthlessness of fascism. [*See* American Document.]

In some of her group works Graham appeared as leader

or protagonist, and every program featured solos for her. She was hailed as a remarkable performer—intense, virtuosic, able through a wide range of dynamics to convey character, mood, and intent. Her solos varied greatly in tone—from the pointed wit of *Four Insincerities* (1929) and *Harlequinade* (1930) to the tragedy of *Lamentation* and *Deep Song;* from the stark *Danse* (1929)—an artistic credo of sorts, in which, to Arthur Honegger's music, she stood on a platform, never moving her feet, but contorting her body violently—to *Dithyrambic* (1931)—a long, ecstatic piece, set to Aaron Copland's piano work of the same name, that ranged through space and ended with a barbaric crescendo of falls.

Lamentation survived in the company's repertory, in two films of Graham, and in a 1976 *Dance in America* videotape of Peggy Lyman. In it, a woman sits on a small bench, her body encased in a long tube of blue-gray stretch jersey. To the tersely mournful sounds of Zoltán Kodály's *Piano Piece, Opus 3, Number 2,* she rocks stiffly from side to side, pressing hands, knees, and elbows against the confining fabric. At times she brings to mind the grieving women of Käthe Kollwitz's drawings or Ernst Barlach's sculpted figures (which several former Graham dancers have cited as an inspiration for the work). Yet, although the solo can be considered expressionistic, the emotion has been abstracted. Grief is presented not as an indulgence, but as the struggle of the body against itself and against the enveloping shroud.

Graham's years in her Greenwich Village studio during the Depression of the 1930s were ones of bold and iconoclastic experimenting. Shunning prettiness, lyricism, rhapsodizing, and decorativeness, Graham rejected both the ballet tradition and her Denishawn heritage. She worked at desentimentalizing the female body and redefining it in terms of rigor, power, and an alert, almost animal intensity.

The weight of the body and the pull of gravity were not to be denied; neither were they to be accepted passively. Graham's exercises often set forces within the body pulling against each other. Her many fall sequences stressed the recovery, rather than the descent. Several dancers who worked with her during this time have characterized the floor as a drumhead to strike and to rebound from. Initially, Graham made very little use of turnout: feet were planted firmly parallel to each other; when lifted, they were more often flexed than pointed. She abstracted breathing and the uneven breath that accompanies extreme physical states—laughing, panting, sobbing—into a process of contraction and release. This forceful caving in, or recoiling, and opening out in the center of the body motivated the gestures of the limbs as a whip handle impels the lash. Graham created a series of exercises, dancelike in their stylishness, done sitting on the floor; they involved rocking, twisting, revolving, and extending and folding the limbs. Variants of these exercises are still taught as part of her technique. During the

1930s, *New York Times* critic John Martin observed a gradual modulating of Graham's percussive attack, an enlarging of her vocabulary to include more curves, higher leg gestures, a variety of jumps and leaps, and, notably in *Frenetic Rhythms* (1933), a more complex use of the hands.

Graham's classwork fed her dances and vice versa. She was also inspired by the dancers with whom she worked—with the structures of their bodies as well as their particular gifts. Prominent among those joining in her company in 1929 or shortly thereafter were Mary Rivoire, Lillian Shapero, Louise Creston, Kitty Reese, Anna Sokolow, Anita Alvarez, Lily Mehlman, Sophie Maslow, May O'Donnell, and Dorothy Bird; joining in 1935 or later were Jane Dudley, Frieda Flier, Nina Fonaroff, and Marjorie Mazia. Some early company members—Martha Hill, Bonnie Bird, Bessie Schönberg, and Gertrude Shurr—embarked on influential careers in dance education soon after leaving Graham's company.

Graham's approach to music reflected her choreographic concerns. She saw America in terms of rhythmic vitality rather than melodic line. Encouraged by Horst, she shunned music that was romantic or impressionistic and began to work with contemporary music. After 1934, almost all her scores were written specifically for the dances. Horst steered her toward music that was sparse in its instrumentation and strong in its rhythms and away from the lush, the familiar, or anything that might domi-

nate the dance. Piano was usually the principal instrument, sometimes augmented by winds, brasses, or percussion; strings were frowned on: too rhapsodic. The scores Horst composed for Graham were all written to fit the dancing, reinforcing its rhythms and structure.

During the early 1930s, Graham, bent on intensifying dance and subordinating or eliminating everything else, used no sets. Her corps of barefoot women in long, simple dresses could create a living architecture that needed no enhancement beyond the modeling provided by lights. In 1935 she commissioned her first set, from sculptor Isamu Noguchi, for *Frontier*. The set, as spare and spacious as the dance, consists of a section of wood fence and, anchored to the floor behind it, a "V" of white rope extending up, out, and forward into the wings. In this celebrated solo, to music by Horst, Graham expressed the emotions of a woman discovering strength in solitude and independence, marking out her turf even as she celebrates the immensity of the space around her. In *Horizons* and *Panorama*, Graham used mobiles created for her by Alexander Calder.

These were not affluent years. Graham did some touring, both as a soloist, with Horst accompanying her on the piano, and with the Group. She made a transcontinental tour herself in 1936 and the first with the company in 1937. In 1932, she became the first dancer to receive a Guggenheim Fellowship. She continued to rely on teaching for her income. The founding of the Bennington

GRAHAM. A scene from *Deaths and Entrances* (1943), a dance inspired by the lives of the Brontë sisters. Here, Graham appears as one of the Three Sisters, with Merce Cunningham as the Poetic Beloved (center) and Erick Hawkins as the Dark Beloved (right). (Photograph © 1945 by Barbara Morgan; used by permission of the Barbara Morgan Archives, Hastings-on-Hudson, New York.)

GRAHAM. A scene from *Appalachian Spring* (1944), Graham's American frontier epic. Here, Graham as the Bride kneels before Erick Hawkins as the Husbandman; May O'Donnell as the Pioneering Woman stands at center with her hand on the post; the four Followers sit in the background. Aaron Copland composed the work's famous score, and Isamu Noguchi designed the stylized scenery. (Photograph © 1944 by Arnold Eagle; used by permission.)

School of the Dance in 1934 gave her a place to take her company for several summer weeks to teach and rehearse and present new work. [*See* Bennington School of the Dance.]

Graham's New York performances during the 1930s often consisted of a single concert, usually on a Sunday when Broadway theaters were available; Graham averaged two such "seasons" per year. However, every year from 1930 to 1937, she gave a concert at Washington Irving High School in New York City, and in 1932 she and Weidman shared a concert at the New School for Social Research, her all-female company and his all-male one providing a deliberate contrast. Like many of her contemporaries, she considered a developed political and social awareness part of a modern choreographer's equipment and often contributed works to concerts that benefited,

for example, the American League Against Fascism (1935) or the International Labor Defense (1936). In 1930 she joined Helen Tamiris, Weidman, and Humphrey at Maxine Elliot's Theater for a week of performances billed as the Dance Repertory Theater. Graham was allotted two evenings to show her works and shared three other programs. During the second Dance Repertory Theater season, at the Craig Theater in 1931, *Primitive Mysteries* received its first performance.

Graham also took part in a number of other theatrical ventures, appearing—sometimes with members of her company—in the elaborate dances that Irene Lewisohn of the Neighborhood Playhouse presented with the Cleveland Orchestra. Among those were Richard Strauss's *Ein Heldenleben* (1929) and Charles Loeffler's *A Pagan Poem* (1930), in both of which she was partnered by Weidman. Some of the work Graham undertook outside of her company may have nourished her own choreography; they also brought in money. In 1930 she gave what was acclaimed as an unforgettable performance as the Chosen Maiden in Léonide Massine's version of Igor Stravinsky's *Rite of Spring*, presented by Leopold Stokowski and the

GRAHAM. A member of the Martha Graham Dance Company from 1967 to 1985, Yuriko Kimura was a gifted interpreter of Graham's roles. She appears here as the heroine in a revival of *Errand into the Maze* (1947). (Photograph © 1978 by Max Waldman; used by permission.)

Philadelphia Orchestra. In 1931, for a production of Sophocles's *Electra*, starring Blanche Yurka, she devised movements for the small chorus, played the chorus leader, and danced three solos. In 1932 she created movement for Katharine Cornell's production of *Lucrece*, adapted from Shakespeare's poem. In 1935 she staged the crowd parts for the Phoenix Theater's performances of Archibald MacLeish's *Panic*.

In 1938 Graham entered a new phase that coincided with taking a man, Erick Hawkins, into her company. The advent of Hawkins, and Merce Cunningham the following year, fueled Graham's growing interest in theatricality and in reaching a wider audience. Up to that time she had avoided literary content, but she began to experiment with the spoken word, with role playing, and with themes involving love, desire, and emotional turbulence. She did not, however, resort to conventional narrative structure; instead, until the mid-1940s, she explored and radically adapted a variety of theatrical and literary forms. [*See the entries on Hawkins and Cunningham.*]

American Document took the minstrel show as a point of departure. The satirical *Every Soul Is a Circus* (1939) cast Graham as the frivolous Empress of the Arena, torn between a whip-cracking Ringmaster (Hawkins) and a lithe Acrobat (Cunningham) and watched by an Ideal Spectator (Jean Erdman). In *Punch and the Judy*, another light piece, Graham created a charade about the squabbles of a married couple, drawing some of her characters, images, and movement ideas from puppet plays. The 1940 *El Penitente*, inspired by rites of the Indian Christian penitential sects she had observed in the American Southwest and in Mexico, was structured as a mystery play performed with sturdy vigor and naiveté by a trio of villagers. The dancers took up simple props or added items to their costumes to indicate a change of role or state. Graham played Mary as Virgin, as Magdalene, and as Mater Dolorosa. Hawkins was the penitent, lashing himself, pulling the "death cart," and shouldering a large wooden cross. Cunningham was the benign and impassive Christ.

For these works and for *Letter to the World* (1940), *Deaths and Entrances* (1943), and *Appalachian Spring* (1944), Graham's vocabulary acquired new inflections. In 1935, she had said, "This is a time of action, not of reaction. The dance is action, not an attitude, not an interpretation" (Armitage, 1937). In the late 1930s and in the 1940s, however, she modified her stance, wishing to reveal a character's mind and heart through highly individual movements. The oppositional forces her technique made visible could be used in ways that suggested emotional ambivalence as well as the play of energy. In the dances mentioned above, she used Hawkins and Cunningham as opposites: the former as the hero—solid, dark, and masterful; the latter as the blithe youth, the ascetic, the figure of mystery or fantasy. To those of her earlier company members who adapted to her changing concerns—Maslow, Dudley, Flier, Fonaroff, Mazia and Ethel Butler—she added other dancers, notably Pearl Lang, Erdman, Yuriko, Ethel Winter, and Mark Ryder. Stylistic distinctions were made not only between characters, but also between women and men. In keeping with the increased theatricality, all the dancers had sets, most of them designed by Arch Lauterer, the resident designer at Bennington. In 1943, Jean Rosenthal began to create the lighting for the dances. [*See* Appalachian Spring; Deaths and Entrances; *and* Letter to the World.]

The 1940s were a period of extraordinary fecundity for Graham. Most of the works on which her reputation rests were made between 1940 and 1948; these masterworks were widely performed, and all were shown between 1970 and 1994. In 1944 Graham began to draw together elements that had long interested her—aspects of Greek drama, Asian theater, myth, ritual, dream. The perspectives on these were provided by psychologists such as Carl Jung and Erich Fromm and by such mythologists as Joseph Campbell and Robert Graves. Her published *Notebooks of Martha Graham* reveal the wide range of her reading.

Herodiade (1944; music by Paul Hindemith) shows stylistic, thematic, and structural concepts that were to occupy Graham for many years. These had been present in earlier dances but seem particularly clear in this duet for two women—one evidently an important personage and the other a familiar servant. Graham played a woman who, at some unspecified crossroad in her life or moment of transition between two states, reexamines her past and confronts her destiny. The audience sees the impact of thought and emotion on her body. The three structures of flat, interlocking pieces of wood, which Noguchi designed, are not decor but objects charged with meaning for the protagonist; they might be extensions of herself.

In dances such as *Cave of the Heart* (1946), *Dark Meadow* (1946), *Errand into the Maze* (1947), *Night Journey* (1947), *Judith* (1950), *Clytemnestra* (1958), and *Alcestis* (1960) Graham identified herself with many heroines of history and myth. However, she was always, too, the seeker, the questing hero (traditionally a male role in mythology) who enters the dark woods, the cave, the labyrinth, the underworld and faces what must be faced in order to emerge into a region of light. This seeker is also the artist who delves into the dark interior landscape, some feared side of his or her own nature, to arrive at illumination. In *Errand into the Maze,* for instance, the heroine forces herself to enter a terrifying place and do battle with the Creature of Fear (originally danced by Ryder), a sort of minotaur, destructive and potent, but almost unseeing, and hampered by a yoke over which his arms are always draped. [*See* Dark Meadow *and* Night Journey.]

Other characteristics began to emerge in what Leroy Leatherman (1966) termed Graham's "dance plays." One, which aided Graham in dominating the stage even when age began to limit her dancing, was the use of memory as a theatrical device. At moments of crisis the heroine, recalling her past, summons up other characters, who are seen by the audience through her eyes. This device fostered nonlinear structures related to those of cinema, cubist painting, and Eastern theater forms. The dances move fluidly between action, meditation, and ceremony. The relationship of time and space becomes an immensely flexible one; the present can precede the past or coexist with it on the stage. A character can be fragmented, as in *The Legend of Judith* (1962), when the aged Judith recalls her younger self (played by another dancer), or as in *Seraphic Dialogue* (1959), a dance in which Graham did not appear, in which a central Joan of Arc alternates danced passages with three "aspects" of herself.

Between 1944 and 1962, Noguchi designed most of Graham's sets. These usually consisted of several large, three-dimensional structures on which the dancers could perch or climb. Powerful and ambiguous, the set pieces change in appearance or significance according to how they are handled. In *Cave of the Heart,* a glittering structure of wires can be a bush for Medea to lurk under or perhaps stand for the Golden Fleece, but at the climax of the dance, she puts it on like a dress, appearing at once transfigured and pilloried by her supernatural powers. The sets Noguchi designed helped to shape Graham's vision of the stage as an "arena of the mind." They define not only zones of activity, but also symbolic provinces. For the characters, they are home bases to which they can retreat until called again into the action. Other designers Graham

GRAHAM. Paul Taylor was a soloist with the Martha Graham Dance Company from 1955 to 1962. In a role originally danced by Bertram Ross, Taylor appears here with Graham in a performance of *Clytemnestra* (1958). This ballet, with a score by Halim El-Dabh and sets by Isamu Noguchi, is Graham's only full-evening work. (Photograph from the Dance Collection, New York Public Library for the Performing Arts.)

GRAHAM. Mary Hinkson (center) performed with the Martha Graham Dance Company for twenty-one years. Here, she dances a role Graham created specifically for her in *Circe* (1963). (Photograph from the Dance Collection, New York Public Library for the Performing Arts.)

worked with—among them Ming Cho Lee, Marion Kinsella, Dani Karavan, and Leandro Locsin—had to follow to some extent the aesthetic established by Noguchi and Graham. [*See the entry on Noguchi.*]

Graham designed many of her own costumes, and even when costumes were credited to Edythe Gilfond, Graham was responsible for their conception. Many boldly echo the motifs of Noguchi's set or props with decorative zigzags or bold sunbursts of rope or gold trim. For Graham, costumes could signify a change of state or a turn of mind. In *Episodes*, Part I (1959, produced by the New York City Ballet with a second half by George Balanchine), Mary of Scotland steps out of her black dress, which remains stiffly standing, a symbol of the rigidity of ceremony. In *Night Journey*, Oedipus's mantle is integral to a solo of lust and domination: repeatedly he thrusts his arm through openings in the fabric, while wrapping it around his increasingly distended arm. [*See* Costume in Western Traditions, *article on* Modern Dance.]

Horst stopped serving as Graham's musical director in 1948, but Graham continued for most of her career to follow his rule that she should use only commissioned scores by contemporary composers. The Elizabeth Sprague Coolidge Foundation provided funds for a number of these, notably for Copland's *Appalachian Spring* and Hindemith's *Herodiade*. The Louisville Arts Council commissioned two solos and scores for their performance with the Louisville Symphony Orchestra: *Judith* (1950), with music by William Schuman, and *The Triumph of St. Joan* (1951), with music by Norman Dello Joio. Other composers Graham worked with include Mordecai Seter, Eu-

gene Lester, Halim el-Dabh, Carlos Surinach, Samuel Barber, Alan Hovhaness, and Robert Starer. These composers did not, as Horst had done, tailor a score to fit a dance. They worked from outlines, images, and time structures provided by Graham, and she choreographed to the music, with both composer and choreographer making accommodations along the way.

Graham's approach to music began to change during the 1940s. The scores she used were lusher in texture and tended not to emphasize the rhythms of the dance as strongly as had the scores of the 1930s. Stringed instruments now accorded with her aesthetic. In many of her dramatic dances from the 1940s onward, the music provides an aural landscape that heightens the emotional content of the dancing.

During the period of her "Greek" dances, Graham incorporated into her vocabulary steps derived from various forms of Asian dance—walks, crawls, and turns that could be linked to Balinese, Javanese, or Japanese sources—but used in a completely individual way. The two-dimensional look of figures from ancient art mixed with three-dimensional, spiraling falls; twisted, off-center contractions; and huge wheeling turns in a tipped-over arabesque. Graham's vocabulary gradually became more fixed; by the 1950s the creation of new movement ceased to be her primary concern as the increasing limitations of age hampered her in drawing it from her own body.

Cunningham left the company in 1945, Hawkins left in 1950 (he and Graham had married in 1948, and the rupture was both a personal and a professional one). The dancers who performed Graham's works during the 1950s and the 1960s were young in relation to Graham. The women's bodies were lighter and more flexible than those of the women in Graham's original group. Among the dancers who came into prominence during these years were Yuriko, Winter, Lang, Matt Turney, Helen McGehee, Linda Margolies (Hodes), Akiko Kanda, Robert Cohan, Stuart Hodes, Paul Taylor, David Wood, and Bertram Ross. Ross partnered Graham until her retirement from the stage in 1969.

For these dancers and others who, like them, had the finely tuned bodies and the onstage ardor Graham demanded, she created a number of works in which she did not appear. The first and probably the finest of these was *Diversion of Angels* (1948), which celebrated the ecstacy of youthful love and the appetite for living. Other company pieces included *Canticle for Innocent Comedians* (1952), *Ardent Song* (1954), and *Embattled Garden* (1958), in which she set a quartet of dancers conniving in a contemporary Eden.

The company and school enjoyed a considerable reputation. In 1952, with the aid of devoted patron Bethsabée de Rothschild, the school moved from 66 Fifth Avenue in New York City to a house on East Sixty-third Street. Students from abroad joined Americans in taking the classes taught by Graham and company members. The Bennington Festival foundered in 1941, but Graham and her company were in residence at Bennington for four more summers. She or her dancers taught from 1948 onward at the American Dance Festival at Connecticut College, in New London, where Graham was last listed as a faculty member in 1967. In 1950 a European tour was cut short because of an injury to Graham, but in 1954 the U.S. State Department sponsored another European tour and in 1955 a tour to East Asia. The latter was extremely successful; the former shocked and displeased some audiences, but also made fervent converts. These were only the first of the company's foreign tours. Graham also began to give slightly longer seasons in New York—a week was typical—also appearing with other modern-dance companies in seasons sponsored by de Rothschild in 1953 and 1955.

During the 1960s, Graham continued to make pieces featuring herself and ones in which she did not appear,

such as *Secular Games* (1962), *Part Real–Part Dream* (1965), and *Plain of Prayer* (1948). The satiric *Acrobats of God* (1960) presented her as a reluctant creator driven by a whip-cracking male, but most of her dances were more somber. She cast herself as Alcestis, Delilah, Phaedra, Judith, the Witch of Endor, Hecuba, and Heloise, with Linda Hodes as the young Judith and Noemi Lapzeson as the young Heloise. In a couple of works, parts she might once have played were given to other dancers: in *One More Gaudy Night* (1961) Winter played Cleopatra to Taylor's Antony; and *Circe* was a vehicle for Mary Hinkson. Since the days of her first company, she had sporadically allowed others to take over her roles and she continued this practice.

During the 1960s a number of young men who joined the company (Dudley Williams, William Louther, Peter Randazzo, Robert Powell, and Clive Thompson, among others) subtly influenced Graham's style. Most of the men who had entered the company during the preceding two decades were tall; Graham had emphasized their strength and their ability to convey masculine roughness and had not called on them to show a great deal of flexibility. The new male dancers of the 1960s were more lithe and, gen-

GRAHAM. Scene from Graham's 1984 production of *Le Sacre du Printemps*, set to the Stravinsky score. (Photograph © 1984 Jack Vartoogian; used by permission.)

GRAHAM. The last work Graham created was the uncharacteristically lighthearted *Maple Leaf Rag* (1990), set to music by Scott Joplin. In costumes designed by Calvin Klein, members of the company partner each other at the premiere, City Center of Music and Dance, New York. (Photograph © 1990 by Jed Downhill; used by permission.)

erally speaking, slighter in build. They and the young women they partnered inspired Graham to create new dances that showed off their physical range and virtuosity, making less distinction than before between a male style and a female one.

The last new dance in which Graham appeared was *The Lady of the House of Sleep* (1968); she last performed on 20 April 1969. Not long after her company's season at the Brooklyn Academy of Music in October 1970, she became seriously ill. The school continued without her, and in 1972 company members informally staged excerpts from her works in her studio in order to maintain continuity and keep up morale. In 1972 she resumed her role as company director and choreographer. In the past, Graham had disliked reviving works, preferring to put her energy into creating new ones. However, after her return to the company, she began to take an interest in grooming young dancers to take on her roles. During the 1970s and 1980s, Takako Asakawa, Yuriko Kimura, Janet Eilber, Elisa Monte, Lyman, Diane Gray, Phyllis Gutelius, and Christine Dakin gave excellent performances as Graham heroines. Terese Capucilli was one of the last remarkable dancers developed by Graham.

Graham continued to create for such women, and for men such as Tim Wengerd, Ross Parkes, David Hatch Walker, Peter Sparling, David Brown, and Donlin Foreman. Her style became increasingly fluid, lyric, attenuated in line, and seemingly less impelled by the center of the body. A higher incidence of ballet-trained dancers

among company members and the participation of eminent ballet performers—Rudolf Nureyev, William Carter, Mikhail Baryshnikov, and Dame Margot Fonteyn—fostered this gradual change. In 1975, the fashion designer Halston, a benefactor of Graham's company, began to create its costumes, many of which revealed the dancers' bodies to a considerable degree. Among the most well received of works Graham made during the 1970s were *Acts of Light* (1981) and *Frescoes* (1978), the latter commissioned for the dedication ceremonies of the Sackler Wing of the Metropolitan Museum of Art in New York City. This dance, dealing with the romance of Antony and Cleopatra and constructed with obvious mastery, was less harsh in both theme and movement style and more unabashedly glamorous than the works that made her reputation as a genius of the dance.

The year 1977 marked a change in Graham's policy toward music; she began to compose most of her dances to preexisting scores, as she had during her early years as a choreographer. Two—*Flute of Pan* (1978) and *Song* (1985)—were set to traditional music; others used pieces by such composers as Béla Bartók, Edgar Varèse, and George Crumb. One of Graham's most praised late works was composed to Stravinsky's *Rite of Spring* in 1984, fifty-four years after she had danced the leading role for Massine at the American premiere of the music. Her choreography for *Rite* stressed the athletic prowess of her dancers, the sexuality inherent in a fertility rite, and the terror of the chosen victim through masterfully designed formal patterns and the use of symbolic props—although a good part of the dance's success was due to Stravinsky's score.

Through the 1990s, the company continued to tour and to present seasons in New York City. The length of the seasons varied slightly: for example, thirty-two performances at the Lunt-Fontaine Theater in 1977, a week at the Metropolitan Opera House in 1978, and three weeks at the City Center Theater in 1989. A typical year involved performing and (sometimes) teaching residences, usually for half a week to a week, in American cities and universities and at summer festivals, such as those held at Jacob's Pillow and Artpark. Overseas touring was also a vital part of the schedule: just prior to her death, Graham accompanied her dancers on a fifty-five–day tour of East Asia. After her retirement, Graham herself often appeared onstage to take a bow or to regale audiences with witty and erudite speeches.

Graham created 180 works for her company, the sole repository for her dances. (Students at the Juilliard School performed *Diversion of Angels* in 1967, 1968, and 1971; the London Contemporary Dance Ensemble, a Graham-inspired company, at one time performed *El Penitente;* and for a number of years the Batsheva Dance Company of Israel performed several of Graham's works, including *Diversion of Angels, Herodiade, Cave of the Heart,* and *Embattled Garden).*

Graham was the recipient of many awards and honors in addition to the Guggenheim Fellowship of 1932: the Capezio Award (1955); the *Dance Magazine* Award (1957); honorary doctorates from Harvard (1966) and Yale and Wesleyan (both 1971); the Aspen Award (1965); the Brandeis Award (1968); New York City's Handel Medallion (1970); and the Medal of Freedom, America's highest civilian honor (1976). She was a recipient of the Kennedy Center Honor in 1979, and in 1985 she was among the first to be awarded the new National Medal of Arts in a White House ceremony. In 1984, on the stage of the Paris Opera, she was made a Chevalier de la Légion d'Honneur by President François Mitterand, and in 1985, when the company was performing in Stockholm, Princess Christina of Sweden presented her with the Carina Ari Medal. Other awards include the Samuel H. Scripps American Dance Festival Award (1981), Southern Methodist University's Algur H. Meadows Award for Excellence in the Arts (1982), Bryn Mawr College's M. Carey Thomas Prize (1983), and the Local 1 Centennial Award for dance, presented by the International Alliance of Theatrical Stage Employees in 1986.

[*See also* Modern Dance Technique.]

BIBLIOGRAPHY

Armitage, Merle, ed. *Martha Graham: The Early Years.* Los Angeles, 1937.

Ballet Review 19 (Fall 1991): 18–31. Reminiscences by Marian Seldes, May O'Donnell, Stuart Hodes, and Francis Mason.

Bliss, Paula M. "A Natural Collaboration." In *Proceedings of the Twelfth Annual Conference, Society of Dance History Scholars, Arizona State University, 17–19 February 1989,* compiled by Christena L. Schlundt. Riverside, Calif., 1989.

Dance Magazine (July 1991). Special issue on Martha Graham.

de Mille, Agnes. *Martha: The Life and Work of Martha Graham.* New York, 1991.

Dendy, Mark. "Graham without Graham." *Ballet Review* 20 (Fall 1992): 29–35.

Foster, Susan Leigh. *Reading Dancing: Bodies and Subjects in Contemporary American Dance.* Berkeley, 1986.

Gardner, Howard. "Martha Graham: Discovering the Dance of America." *Ballet Review* 22 (Spring 1994): 67–93.

Garfunkel, Trudy. *Letter to the World: The Life and Dances of Martha Graham.* Boston, 1995.

Goldberg, Marianne. "She Who Is Possessed No Longer Exists Outside: Martha Graham's *Rite of Spring." Women and Performance* 3.1 (1986): 17–27.

Graham, Martha. "Seeking an American Art of the Dance." In *Revolt in the Arts,* edited by Oliver Sayler. New York, 1930.

Graham, Martha. "A Modern Dancer's Primer for Action." In *Dance: A Basic Educational Technique,* edited by Frederick R. Rogers. New York, 1941.

Graham, Martha. *The Notebooks of Martha Graham.* New York, 1973.

Graham, Martha. *Blood Memory.* New York, 1991.

Helpern, Alice. *The Technique of Martha Graham.* Dobbs Ferry, N.Y., 1994.

Horosko, Marian, comp. *Martha Graham: The Evolution of Her Dance Theory and Training, 1926–1991.* Pennington, N.J., 1991.

Jackson, Graham. "The Roots of Heaven: Sexuality in the Work of Martha Graham." In *Dance Spectrum: Critical and Philosophical Enquiry,* edited by Diana Theodores Taplin. Waterloo, Ont., 1983.

Jowitt, Deborah. *Time and the Dancing Image.* New York, 1988.

Kendall, Elizabeth B. *Where She Danced.* New York, 1979.

Leatherman, Leroy. *Martha Graham: Portrait of The Lady as an Artist.* New York, 1966.

Lloyd, Margaret. *The Borzoi Book of Modern Dance.* New York, 1949.

Martin, John. *America Dancing.* New York, 1936.

McDonagh, Don. "A Chat with Martha Graham." *Ballet Review* 2.4 (1968): 18–28.

McDonagh, Don. *Martha Graham.* New York, 1973. The paperback edition includes complete cast lists in the chronology.

McGehee, Helen. "Working for Martha Graham." *Dance Research* 3 (Autumn 1985): 56–64.

Morgan, Barbara. *Martha Graham: Sixteen Dances in Photographs* (1941). Rev. ed. Dobbs Ferry, N.Y., 1980. The revised edition contains a list of dances through 1980.

Noguchi, Isamu. "Noguchi: Collaborating with Graham." In *Isamu Noguchi,* edited by Diane Apostolos-Cappadona and Bruce Altshuler. New York, 1994.

Oswald, Genevieve. "A Vision of Paradise: Myth and Symbol in *The Embattled Paradise." Choreography and Dance* 2.3 (1992): 27–37.

Polcari, Stephen. "Martha Graham and Abstract Expressionism." *Smithsonian Studies in American Art* 4 (Winter 1990): 3–27.

Rogosin, Elinor. *The Dance Makers: Conversations with American Choreographers.* New York, 1980.

Sears, David. "Graham Masterworks in Revival." *Ballet Review* 10.2 (1982): 25–34.

Sears, David. "Martha Graham: The Golden Thread." *Ballet Review* 14 (Fall 1986): 44–64.

Sherman, Jane. "Martha and Doris in Denishawn: A Closer Look." *Dance Chronicle* 17.2 (1994): 179–193.

Siegel, Marcia B. *The Shapes of Change: Images of American Dance.* New York, 1979.

Stodelle, Ernestine. *Deep Song: The Dance Story of Martha Graham.* New York, 1984.

FILMS AND VIDEOTAPES. *Flute of Krishna* (1926). *Lamentation* (193–), Dance Collection, New York Public Library for the Performing Arts. Excerpts from *American Lyric, American Document, Chronicle, Letter to the World,* and *Every Soul Is a Circus* in *Martha Graham and Company* (1938–1944), Dance Collection, New York Public Library for the Performing Arts. *Lamentation* (1943), a "film interpretation" by Mr. and Mrs. Simon Moselsio. Peter Glushanok, *A Dancer's World* (1957). Peter Glushanok, *Appalachian Spring* (1958). Alexander Hammid, *Night Journey* (1960). *Frontier* (1964). *El Penitente* (1964). *Primitive Mysteries* (1964), Dance Collection, New York Public Library for the Performing Arts. Dave Wilson, *Acrobats of God* (1969). Dave Wilson, *Cortege of Eagles* (1969). Dave Wilson, *Seraphic Dialogue* (1969). Merrill Brockway, "Martha Graham and Dance Company," *Dance in America* (WNET-TV, New York, 1976), with *Diversion of Angels, Lamentation, Frontier, Adorations, Cave of the Heart* (excerpt), and *Appalachian Spring.* "Martha Graham Company at Wolf Trap" (1978), with *Seraphic Dialogue, Oh Thou Desire,* and *Phaedra.* Merrill Brockway, "Clytemnestra," *Dance in America* (WNET-TV, New York, 1979). "Martha Graham: An American Original in Performance," a Nathan Kroll Production; contains *A Dancer's World* (1957) and *Appalachian Spring* (1958), both directed by Peter Glushanok, and *Night Journey* (1961), directed by Alexander Hammid.

INTERVIEWS. Bonnie Bird (1973), collection of Selma Jeanne Cohen. Ethel Butler (1977) and Jane Dudley (1979), Dance Collection, New York Public Library for the Performing Arts.

ARCHIVES. Martha Graham clipping files (1926–) and the Louis Horst Scrapbooks (1916–1948), Dance Collection, New York Public Library for the Performing Arts.

DEBORAH JOWITT

GRAHN. The first ballerina to dance on pointe on the Danish stage, Grahn is seen floating above the scenery in Jules Perrot's ballet, *Éoline, ou La Dryade.* This 1845 lithograph is by Edward Morton, after a drawing by S. M. Joy. (Dance Collection, New York Public Library for the Performing Arts)

GRAHN, LUCILE (Lucina Alexia Grahn; born 30 June 1819 in Copenhagen, died 4 April 1907 in Munich), dancer and ballet mistress. Grahn "possessed all the qualities that distinguish a *danseuse* of the highest rank," August Bournonville states in his *My Theatre Life* (1979) and continues:

> She was my pupil from her tenth to her seventeenth year and fulfilled all the expectations to which her great natural gifts entitled her. It was actually she who gave our public the first idea of what female virtuosity in dancing should be, and her noble interpretations of the Sylphide and Astrid in Valdemar created epochs in the annals of the ballet.

In fact, Grahn was not only a pupil of Bournonville. At the age of seven she had her first part as Zabi in the ballet *Danina,* directed by her teacher Pierre Larcher. Bournonville was, however, the first to recognize her extraordinary promise when he took over as ballet master of the Royal Theater in Copenhagen in 1830. On 23 September 1834, she had her official debut in a pas de deux in the opera *La Muette de Portici.* In the following year, Bournonville created the leading role of Astrid in *Valdemar* for her. She seemed to be the ideal interpreter of this pure, northern maiden—although, only a few years later, her dancing of this part, significantly altered to suit her, caused a violent break between Bournonville and his protégée.

In the meantime, *La Sylphide* was presented to the Danish public on 28 November 1836. Bournonville explains how the production came about: "I had decided not to give *La Sylphide* on the Danish stage. What changed my mind was the desire to present a very talented pupil, Lucile Grahn, who seemed made for the title role, whom I had modeled after the Taglioni ideal" (Bournonville, 1979). Bournonville had taken Grahn to Paris to see Filippo Taglioni's version. The French capital had already ushered in the age of the ballerina, and the newfound virtuosity on pointe was demonstrated by Marie Taglioni and Fanny Elssler. Grahn was the first to display these new accomplishments for a delighted Copenhagen. In

1837 she was appointed soloist and in the same year danced in Bournonville's *Don Quixote.*

Copenhagen had become too small for her, and her relationship with the ballet master was complicated. A letter from Grahn to Augusta Nielsen, written in 1854, depicts the situation: "My beloved parents sacrificed everything to make smooth my future path; aye, they almost starved in order to place all the costly gifts—silver tea and coffee pots and fruit dishes—at the feet of the Bournonville family. And when I was grown, my gratitude was demanded in another, far worse manner. The Master called these his *'bizarreries.'* I was very upset and decided to get out" (Neiiendam, 1963). So, Grahn left for Paris once more, to study and to dance. She took classes with Jean-Baptiste Barrez, and she was looking forward to her debut at the Opera when, early in October 1837, she was recalled to

GRAHN. The heroine of Jules Perrot's ballet *Catarina, ou La Fille du Bandit,* which premiered at Her Majesty's Theatre, London, in 1846, became one of Grahn's most popular roles. (Dance Collection, New York Public Library for the Performing Arts)

Copenhagen to dance in a special performance in honor of the queen.

This setback only added to her determination to dance at the Opera, and the following summer she was back in Paris: she had her formal debut on 1 August 1838 in a pas de deux in *Le Carnaval de Venise.* Théophile Gautier wrote, "Mademoiselle Lucile Grahn, the Danish dancer, is tall, slender, small-jointed, and well made and would be prettier still if she did not wear such an obstinate smile." Later in the month, after seeing her again, he told his readers that she "has much charm and natural grace but is still lacking in technique and firmness and is a little troubled by her arms, but these faults, which will disappear of themselves, are more than made up by her lightness, suppleness, and charming features."

Once more, Grahn's contract with the Royal Theater forced her to return to Copenhagen, where relations between her and the authoritative Bournonville deteriorated rapidly. In a letter directed to the Royal Theater, he had accused her of changing steps in *Valdemar* in order to display her French virtuoso style: "Astrid is no drunken bacchante nor a voluptuos *baydère* but a graceful young woman. How annoying then to see a well-thought-out composition changed into a gymnastic, equilibristic exercise by attitudes which do not belong to me, with more walking on pointe than I had prescribed and finally the intolerable squatting at each final movement!" (Neiiendam, 1963).

Grahn's last performance in Copenhagen was in the Spanish character dance *El Jaleo de Xeres* on 23 February 1839. She then left for Hamburg, but when she applied for an extension of her leave, she received a peremptory command to return at once. The price of her disobedience was dismissal, but, according to Ivor Guest (1980), this "caused her little disappointment, for it left her free to sign a three-year engagement with the Opera, commencing on June 1st, 1839, at a salary of 4,500 francs a year." The Bournonville-Grahn disputes, however, did not end with her departure from Copenhagen and subsequent rise to international fame. One ardent Grahn admirer, Count von Schulenburg, headed a demonstration against Bournonville that caused the ballet master's dismissal and a year's suspension without salary.

Grahn reappeared before the Paris public on 12 July, in a performance of Wolfgang Amadeus Mozart's *Don Giovanni,* dancing in a pas de deux by Jean Coralli. Gautier found the dance a little too vague to give scope to her grace and coquetry. Others, however, found it delightful, praising her beauty and her lightness. On 6 November 1839, Grahn appeared in Taglioni's *La Sylphide.*

Grahn's international career was making fast progress. She had her Russian debut in Saint Petersburg as Giselle on 30 January 1843 and appeared later as the Sylphide. In

Milan she danced in Bernardo Vestris's *Elda, ossia Il Patto degli Spiriti* on 26 December 1843, and in 1844 she opened her first English season at the Drury Lane. Her success caused the theater manager, Benjamin Lumley, to change his plans: instead of a pas de trois—created for Taglioni, Fanny Cerrito, and Carlotta Grisi—he decided to mount a pas de quatre, including Grahn. The performance would be at Her Majesty's Theatre, and Jules Perrot was to be choreographer. According to Lumley's instructions, "Every twinkle of each foot in every pas had to be nicely weighed in the balance, so as to give no preponderance. Each *danseuse* was to shine in her peculiar style and grace to the last stretch of perfection; but no one was to outshine the others—unless in their own individual belief" (*Reminiscences of the Opera*, London, 1864). Grahn, the youngest, danced first, and the reviews describe her allegro variation: with her "dainty semicircular hops" on pointe she was as light as "a feather in a current of wind," yet vigorous and, in her poses, astonishingly firm. This variation may have been the peak of her career.

Before and after *Pas de Quatre*, Perrot created several ballets specially for Grahn. *Éoline, ou La Dryade* (1845) showed her in a *mazurka d'extase*—according to the *Morning Post*, she united the "most graceful dance with the most soul-despairing pantomime." In *Catarina, ou La Fille du Bandit* (1846) her *pas stratégique*, in which Catarina instructs her brigands in musket drill and military evolutions, became famous. *Le Jugement de Pâris* (1846), a new *divertissement*, showed Taglioni, Cerrito, and Grahn as the goddesses. Grahn went on tour to Italy (Teatro La Fenice in Venice), Belgium, and Germany. In Germany she danced in Dresden, Leipzig, Hamburg, Hanover, and Berlin, performing *Giselle*, *La Péri*, *La Sylphide*, and *La Esmeralda*. During this tour she became somehow involved in the independence movement of 1848 of the duchies of Schleswig-Holstein. She was reported to have worn the German colors in her costume; after the Danish defeat in the Prussian war, she could never again perform in her native country.

Grahn retired from the stage in 1856, the same year that she married the opera singer Friedrich Young. From 1858 to 1861 she was ballet mistress in Leipzig. From 1869 to 1875 she took over the same function at the Munich Court Opera. There she worked with Richard Wagner on some of his opera stagings (e.g., the Bacchanale scene in *Tannhäuser*). There she met Bournonville again. He had been sent to Munich to see a performance of *Lohengrin*, an opera he was scheduled to stage in Copenhagen. In preparation for their possible meeting, he sent her a letter suggesting that, because thirty years had passed since their breakup, they might again be friends. However, Bournonville only recalls having "paid a couple of visits to the ballet school. . . . I renewed our acquaintance and

the *best* of our common memories in the most pleasant fashion."

Grahn stayed in Munich until her death. The city inherited all her goods and named a street after her. Ten years before she died she wrote down some childhood memoirs for a Danish magazine. Her portrait went all over the world—for instance, in "La Cachucha," a dance she inherited from Elssler. It is also more than probable that she was the model for the dancer, high on pointe and with a sequin heart, in Hans Christian Andersen's fairy tale "The Steadfast Tin Soldier."

BIBLIOGRAPHY

Bournonville, August. *My Theatre Life* (1848–1878). Translated by Patricia McAndrew. Middletown, Conn., 1979.
Gautier, Théophile. *Gautier on Dance*. Translated and edited by Ivor Guest. London, 1986.
Guest, Ivor. *The Romantic Ballet in England*. London, 1972.
Guest, Ivor. *The Romantic Ballet in Paris*. 2d rev. ed. London, 1980.
Guest, Ivor. *Jules Perrot: Master of the Romantic Ballet*. London, 1984.
Migel, Parmenia. *The Ballerinas: From the Court of Louis XIV to Pavlova*. New York, 1972.
Moore, Lillian. "Ballerina in Exile: The Mystery of Lucile Grahn." *Dance News* (May 1956): 10–11.
Murphy, Anne. "Age of Enchantment." *Ballet News* 3 (March 1982): 10–14.
Neiiendam, Robert. *Lucile Grahn: En skæbne i dansen*. Copenhagen, 1963.
Terry, Walter. *The King's Ballet Master*. New York, 1979.

HENRIK LUNDGREN

GRAND BALLET DU MARQUIS DE CUEVAS.

The ballet company founded by Marquis George de Cuevas in 1947 in Europe was first known as Le Grand Ballet de Monte Carlo and was connected with the principality of Monaco. When the company became autonomous in 1950, it was renamed Le Grand Ballet du Marquis de Cuevas.

The marquis was born in Santiago, Chile, in 1885, a descendant of Spanish noblemen on his father's side and of Danish on his mother's. In 1927 he married Margaret Strong Rockefeller, by whom he had two children, Maria Elisabeth Alexandra and John Dawson Alexander. A refined aesthete with a cosmopolitan background, the marquis was altogether Parisian, and a ballet enthusiast from childhood. In 1944, with the financial assistance of his wife, he founded his first company, Ballet International, in New York. Its season at the Park Theater was a financial failure, but it resulted in some remarkable creations, including Léonide Massine's *Tristan Fou*, with sets by Salvador Dali; *Constantia*, set to music by Frederic Chopin and choreographed by William Dollar; *Sebastian* by Gian-Carlo Menotti and Edward Caton; and several works by Bronislava Nijinska. This single season confirmed the reputation of the marquis in the world of ballet.

In 1947 the marquis was invited by the Société des Bains de Mer de Monte-Carlo to assume the direction of the Nouveau Ballet de Monte-Carlo, created in 1945 by Serge Lifar and Eugène Grunberg, which was now in a precarious financial situation. The marquis arrived in Monte Carlo with a group of American stars, including Rosella Hightower, André Eglevsky, Marjorie Tallchief, George Skibine, and William Dollar. They merged with the existing troupe, which included Yvette Chauviré, Zizi Jeanmaire, Youly Algaroff, and Janine Charrat. In July 1947 this company made its debut at the Vichy Opéra under the title Grand Ballet de Monte Carlo and under the direction of the marquis de Cuevas. After the debut most of the French dancers left the company, which made its Paris debut at the Alhambra music hall.

The company's initial repertory included several new ballets created in New York: *Pictures at an Exhibition* and *Brahms Variations* by Nijinska; *Constantia* and *Sebastian; Aubade* and *Romeo and Juliet* by Serge Lifar; and *La Fille Mal Gardée,* mounted by Alexandra Balachova. However, the big hit of the first season was the Black

GRAND BALLET DU MARQUIS DE CUEVAS. Marjorie Tallchief and George Skibine in Balanchine's *Concerto Barocco,* c.1948. (Photograph by Baron; used by permission of Camera Press, Ltd., London. Choreography by George Balanchine © The George Balanchine Trust.)

LE GRAND BALLET DU MARQUIS DE CUEVAS. André Eglevsky, Viola Essen, and members of the ensemble in Bronislava Nijinska's *Brahms Variations,* created in 1944 for the first season of the Marquis de Cuevas's first company, Ballet International. (Photograph by Philippe Halsman © The Halsman Estate; used by permission.)

Swan pas de deux, danced by Hightower and Eglevsky with striking virtuosity. In 1948 other works were added to the repertory, and Le Grand Ballet began international tours interspersed with lengthy seasons in Monte Carlo, where it was obligated to provide performances every year. In 1950 the marquis decided to become autonomous, renamed his troupe Le Grand Ballet du Marquis de Cuevas, and left Monte Carlo. He found two other headquarters for his company, Cannes in winter and Deauville in summer, where he prepared his Paris seasons.

It was often said that the marquis was the last Maecenas. For fifteen years, his company was subsidized exclusively from the fortune of his wife, who never intervened in its direction. He conducted business in his Paris apartment, where he met with his dancers and collaborators under the watchful eye of his secretary, Georges Lamiot, and his energetic impresario, Claude Ciraud. The marquis was very popular with the Parisian public and was always applauded as soon as he entered a theater. He enjoyed talking with the audience and habitually greeted fans and friends with a kiss, which won him the nickname "The Kissing Marquis." He clapped loudly during his ballets and shouted "Bravo" at the end. In 1953 he organized his famous Ball of the Century on Lake Chiberta, near Biarritz, to which he invited friends from all over the world; his troupe danced *Swan Lake* on a raft moored in the water.

The company danced in Paris every year, sometimes twice a year, usually at the Théâtre de l'Empire but also at the Théâtre des Champs-Élysées, the Palais de Chaillot, and the Théâtre Sarah-Bernhardt. These seasons featured new ballets and also guest ballerinas, including Tamara Toumanova, Alicia Markova, and Nathalie Krassovska. The repertory was based chiefly on the classics, including *Giselle*, act 2 of *Swan Lake, Les Sylphides,* and *La Sylphide,* with choreography by Harald Lander. In addition, there were Massine's *Gaîté Parisienne* and *Tristan Fou,* George Balanchine's *La Sonnambula* and *Concerto Barocco,* and Michel Fokine's *Le Spectre de la Rose* and *Petrouchka,* the last restaged by Bronislava Nijinska.

The company's new ballets were generally directed by two star dancers of the troupe, George Skibine and Ana Ricarda. Skibine's most popular ballets were *The Prisoner of the Caucasus,* to music by Aram Khachaturian, and *Idylle, Annabel Lee,* and *The Gray Angel.* Ana Ricarda's successes included *Doña Inés de Castro, Del Amor y de la Muerte,* and *La Tertulia.* The company had several ballet masters, including William Dollar, Nicholas Beriozoff, and Bronislava Nijinska, but the most loyal and effective master was John Taras, who also created several successful ballets, including *Dessins pour les Six* and *Piège de Lumière* (1952), with music by Jean-Michel Damase and sets and costumes by André Levasseur. This ballet was one of the triumphs of Rosella Hightower, dancing the role of an exotic butterfly, the Queen of the Morphides.

Not all the ballets produced by Le Grand Ballet were masterpieces, however. The marquis often allowed himself to be influenced by his society friends and agreed to mediocre story lines and music, but these were always redeemed by the quality of his stars and soloists.

In 1961 Rudolf Nureyev made his first appearance with a Western company in *The Sleeping Beauty*—the marquis's last gift to the people of Paris. Presented on 27 October 1960 at the Théâtre des Champs-Élysées, the sets for this

GRAND BALLET DU MARQUIS DE CUEVAS. The Awakening Scene from *The Sleeping Beauty,* staged for the company in 1960 by Robert Helpmann and Bronislava Nijinska. The set was designed by Raymundo de Larrain. (Photograph by Serge Lido; used by permission.)

sumptuous production were done by a Chilean nephew of the marquis, Raymundo de Larrain. The admirable choreography of Nijinska, and that of Robert Helpmann for act 3, were inspired by the work of Marius Petipa but displayed new vigor. (Nijinska disagreed with Larrain regarding certain details of the staging and would not allow her name to appear on the program.) The marquis, who was very ill, came to the premiere in a wheelchair. Several months later, on 22 February 1961, he died in Cannes. Under the direction of Raymundo de Larrain the troupe began a final tour but was soon dissolved. It left a great void in the world of European and, particularly, French ballet.

During its fifteen years of existence, Le Grand Ballet played a major role in the development of classical dance in France. It was the first classical company on a large scale to execute productions of major works from the classical repertory in French cities other than Paris. Its success encouraged young dancers, who often worked in the hope of becoming members of the marquis's troupe. The company was composed of dancers of every nationality—a veritable Tower of Babel—to the point that in 1958 the group was renamed the Ballet International du Marquis de Cuevas. The company toured numerous countries and gave seasons in London, New York, Barcelona, Buenos Aires, and other cities, and it appeared at most of the international festivals.

BIBLIOGRAPHY

Daguerre, Pierre. *Le Marquis de Cuevas.* Paris, 1954.
Lidova, Irène. "Un grand mécène." *Saisons de la danse,* no. 131 (February 1981): 35–38.
Lidova, Irène. "The Marquis and His Ballet." *Dance and Dancers* (July 1993): 18–20.

IRÈNE LIDOVA
Translated from French

GRANDS BALLETS CANADIENS, LES.

Based in Montreal, Quebec, Les Grands Ballets Canadiens is a classical company currently composed of about thirty-five dancers. Its repertory is notable for stylistic range—from such traditional full-length ballets as *Giselle* to modern dance works by Paul Taylor and Lar Lubovitch—and for its large proportion of original ballets. The company tours regularly within Canada and has made frequent foreign appearances, but it retains a particular affinity with the Francophone culture of its home province, Quebec. More than either of Canada's other leading ballet companies—the Royal Winnipeg Ballet and the National Ballet of Canada—Les Grands Ballets Canadiens has a reputation for artistic daring and creativity.

The company's development is inseparable from the later career of its founder, Ludmilla Chiriaeff, a Russian dancer and choreographer who was raised and trained in Germany, who relocated to Switzerland after World War

II, and who eventually emigrated to Canada and settled in Montreal in 1952. A cultured woman of great tenacity and with an almost romantic sense of personal destiny, Chiriaeff was immediately impressed by the richness and vitality of the arts in Montreal, and she determined to devote herself to the cause of ballet in Quebec, which she resolved was to be her permanent home. [*See the entry on Chiriaeff.*]

Origins and Background. The moment of Chiriaeff's arrival in the heartland of French-speaking Canada was timely. Although she had to contend with resistance from the dominant Roman Catholic church, which saw ballet as morally questionable, she found a warm welcome and enthusiastic support from a group of Canadian artists—actors, singers, musicians, composers, directors, and producers—who were then engaged in creating programs for French-language public television. Indeed, because of the lack of public support for theatrical performances, the burgeoning of cultural programs on television provided the major outlet for Canadian artists during the early 1950s. Having opened a teaching studio in Montreal, Chiriaeff soon assembled a company of dancers and from 1953 to 1957 presented it in numerous television performances for Société Radio-Canada. [*See* Television, *article on* Dance on Television in Canada.]

This company, Les Ballets Chiriaeff, made its formal public stage debut in Montreal in 1955. The next year Chiriaeff successfully presented her troupe of eighteen dancers in a program of her works during the Montreal Festival season. Impressed by the company's achievement, the city's autocratic but visionary mayor, Jean Drapeau, urged Chiriaeff to abandon her television career and to incorporate the company so that it would become eligible for municipal and provincial arts subsidies. She lost little time in following his advice, and late in 1957 Les Ballets Chiriaeff was legally reconstituted as Les Grands Ballets Canadiens.

The next year, on 12 April 1958, the new company gave its first performance at Montreal's Comédie-Canadienne. Nicholas Zvereff, a veteran of the Ballets Russes de Serge Diaghilev who had settled in Montreal, became ballet master, and Michel Perrault was appointed musical director and resident conductor. The company received small initial grants from the recently established Canada Council and from the Greater Montreal Arts Council. Funding from the government of Quebec followed the next season. Chiriaeff served not only as artistic director and principal choreographer but also as president of the company's board of directors, a post she held for the next six years.

During this period, Chiriaeff established the Académie des Grands Ballets Canadiens, a general school founded in 1958 in Montreal that was later expanded to include a professional division, the École Supérieure de Danse du Québec, founded in 1966, as well as satellite programs in

LES GRANDS BALLETS CANADIENS. Ludmilla Chiriaeff and Eric Hyrst with members of Les Ballets Chiriaeff in the television production of Chiriaeff's *Les Noces*, broadcast in 1956. Costumes were designed by Claudette Picard. (Photograph by Henri Paul; from the archives of Les Grands Ballets Canadiens; courtesy of Ludmilla Chiriaeff.)

Montreal and Quebec City. These schools were to play an important role in winning public acceptance for the company, in advancing the study of classical dancing in Quebec, and in providing a source of young Canadian dancers. [*See* Canada, *article on* Dance Education.]

Les Grands Ballets Canadiens was named almost by default, as other plausible names for the company had already been used by performing groups that had failed to survive. In 1958, when the name was announced, skeptics were swift to point out that there was nothing very grand about Les Grands Ballets. Chiriaeff, however, countered by saying that the name was a testament to her high ambitions for the new company. She always maintained that she felt a personal mission to establish the art of ballet in Quebec and to give the province a company of artistic substance and originality.

Among the first of a number of obstacles that stood in her way was the opposition of the Roman Catholic church. During colonial times, when present-day Quebec formed part of the French empire, ballet entertainments, though sporadic, were popular among the upper classes in Quebec City and Montreal. After the British conquest of Quebec City in 1759, however, and the subsequent ceding of all French territory in Canada to Britain by the Treaty of Paris in 1763, attitudes changed. The French community, consisting largely of the peasant class, turned for guidance and cultural protection to its Roman Catholic clergy, whose Jansenist leanings made them stern moralists and led them to view participation in theatrical dancing, or even observation of it, as, in the par-

lance of the church, an occasion of sin. Such religious disapproval lasted well into the 1960s, particularly in rural communities. Although foreign dance companies on tour in French Canada were tolerated, the idea of an indigenous ballet company such as Chiriaeff proposed met with vehement clerical opposition. Children were discouraged from taking classes, promotional leaflets were destroyed, and priests were even known to denounce from their pulpits an art that would have young women expose their legs on stage in classical tutus.

Chiriaeff was eventually able to conquer these prejudices by winning the aid of broad-minded clergy and by mounting a forceful educational campaign. By the mid-1960s Montreal's Catholic School Board was sending its children to company performances. The international acclaim garnered by Les Grands Ballets Canadiens during Canada's great centennial celebration and world's fair, Expo 67, and the company's subsequent tour of Europe and the United States helped further to loosen the bonds of religious prejudice. Ultimate, symbolic victory came in 1970, when the company performed Fernand Nault's *Symphony of Psalms* during Holy Week at the great church of Saint Joseph's Oratory in Montreal.

The Early Years: 1958–1964. The company's history falls conveniently into five fairly distinct phases of artistic development. During the first, from 1958 to 1964, Chiriaeff had to struggle against financial and popular odds to win acceptance for the company. Although she herself danced less frequently than she had done with Les Ballets Chiriaeff, she continued vigorously to choreograph new ballets, including a number derived from French-Canadian folklore. She also restaged several of her earlier ballets. Leading dancers during this period were Margaret Mercier, Eva von Gencsy, and Eric Hyrst, an English-born colleague from Chiriaeff's television days who also choreographed several ballets for the developing company.

Despite Chiriaeff's ambition to employ locally trained dancers, she was often obliged to hire from abroad, and some of the dancers who joined Les Grands Ballets Canadiens adopted French-sounding names in order to give the company roster a more local image. One dancer who did not was Vincent Warren, an American who joined the company in 1961. A true *danseur noble* in the classical tradition, Warren was equally adept in the contemporary repertory, and he was soon recognized as a star of the company. He was one of only a few dancers ever to be so recognized, for Chiriaeff generally discouraged the development of a star system and only rarely imported guest artists from other companies. Even today, members of the company are listed alphabetically rather than by rank in program notes.

Recognizing the commitment of the National Ballet of Canada to mounting full-scale productions of the great nineteenth-century classics, and well aware that her limited resources would not allow her to compete, Chiriaeff deliberately chose another course for Les Grands Ballets Canadiens. She aimed instead to build a more modestly scaled repertory that would offer an interesting mix of traditional and contemporary works. Popular ballets in this early period included David Lichine's *Graduation Ball,* Anton Dolin's *Pas de Quatre,* and a variety of works by Chiriaeff, Hyrst, and Brydon Paige, a young Canadian choreographer who was a protégé of Chiriaeff.

In its second year, Les Grands Ballets Canadiens began to tour. At the invitation of Ted Shawn, the company performed at the Jacob's Pillow Dance Festival in western Massachusetts in the summer of 1959, presenting a program of short works by Chiriaeff and Hyrst. These performances helped the company gain recognition in the United States and led to a second appearance at Jacob's Pillow in the summer of 1960 and to a five-week American tour during the 1960/61 season. Hometown performances at Montreal's small Comédie-Canadienne and the more prestigious Her Majesty's Theatre were supplemented with tours to smaller Quebec communities and to Canada's Maritime Provinces. The company undertook its first full-scale national tour of Canada during the 1963/64 season.

Early staff changes included the appointments in 1961 of a new musical director, Claude Poirier, a French Canadian, and a new ballet master, Edward Caton, a well-known Russian-American who had worked with numerous companies in Europe and the United States. During his brief tenure with Les Grands Ballets Canadiens, Caton's most significant contribution to the repertory was his staging of *La Fille Mal Gardée,* set to the score by Peter Ludwig Hertel. The company also hired in 1961 a resourceful new general manager, Uriel Luft. Born in Berlin of Russian and Polish parentage, the multilingual Luft did much during his twelve-year tenure to promote the company as it moved into its next phase of development.

The opening in 1963 of Montreal's large concert hall and theater, La Place des Arts, gave Les Grands Ballets Canadiens an opportunity to expand its scale of activities. This it did in 1964, when Chiriaeff invited Fernand Nault to mount a lavish production of *The Nutcracker* for the company's Christmas season. A Montrealer by birth, Nault had spent more than twenty years in the United States, as a dancer and then ballet master for American Ballet Theatre. Impressed by Chiriaeff's achievement, and sensing an unparalleled opportunity to contribute to French-Canadian culture, Nault accepted her invitation to become assistant artistic director of the company in 1965. That same year Victor Jelinek, a Czech conductor, replaced Claude Poirier as musical director, a post he held for many years, and Brydon Paige was named resident choreographer. Anton Dolin also extended his ties with Les Grands Ballets Canadiens by accepting the title of *conseiller artistique* (artistic adviser). His version of *Giselle,* staged for the company in 1967 and danced during the Expo season by the great Cuban ballerina Alicia Alonso, has been sporadically revived as a popular favorite for almost three decades.

LES GRANDS BALLETS CANADIENS. Members of Les Ballets in Eric Hyrst's *Valses Nobles et Sentimentales* (1960). Costumes were designed by Josephine Boss, scenery by Alexis Chiriaeff. (Photograph by Varkony; from the archives of Les Grands Ballets Canadiens; courtesy of Ludmilla Chiriaeff.)

LES GRANDS BALLETS CANADIENS. In Fernand Nault's 1966 production of *Carmina Burana*, the female ensemble dances to "Ecce Gratum," a hymn of joy and gratitude at the return of spring. (Photograph by Henry Koro; from the archives of Les Grands Ballets Canadiens; courtesy of Judith Karstens.)

The Nault Era: 1965–1974. It was Nault's choreography, however, that set the company's artistic tone from 1965 to 1974. Named associate artistic director in 1967, he restaged a number of his earlier works and created fourteen new ballets, many of which, through their bold theatricality, helped win the company a larger audience. [*See the entry on Nault.*] Critical reaction to Nault's choreography was often mixed, but his 1962 staging of *Carmina Burana*, remounted for Les Grands Ballets Canadiens in the 1966/67 season, won the company international attention during Expo 67 and helped secure government support for the company's first European tour in 1969. A signature piece of the company, Nault's *Carmina Burana* became part of a popular Carl Orff trilogy when John Butler's *Catulli Carmina* and Norman Walker's *Trionfo di Afrodite* were later added to the repertory.

Nault's most controversial ballet was his setting of *Tommy*, the rock opera by the British group The Who. Initially, this ballet attracted less notice than another Nault creation, *Hip and Straight*, a contest between jazz dance and ballet set to music by Montreal percussionist Paul Duplessis. Both ballets received their first performances on the same program in October 1970. Of the two, however, *Tommy* proved to be the enduring favorite with the

youthful audiences that Chiriaeff eagerly sought to attract.

During the next four seasons *Tommy* became a profitable staple of the repertory. The company performed it on four successive visits to New York City and presented it in other major U.S. cities such as Boston, Chicago, Philadelphia, and Detroit as well as in Paris in 1974. Some critics lamented the kind of pop image Les Grands Ballets acquired by its frequent performances of *Tommy*, although, in fact, the ballet did not entirely dominate the repertory. The 1971/72 season, for example, also included an all-Stravinsky program consisting of Maurice Béjart's *Firebird*, Brian Macdonald's *Jeu de Cartes*, and Nault's *Symphony of Psalms*.

Meanwhile, in 1970 Chiriaeff had established a touring offshoot of the company to act as a testing ground for younger dancers and to forward her educational goals by reaching audiences in schools and smaller communities of Quebec. This small group, Les Compagnons de la Danse, under the direction of the American choreographer Lawrence Gradus, developed its own repertory of works suitable for touring and met with considerable success until it was disbanded in 1974 because of lack of funds. It has not been revived.

The Macdonald Period: 1974–1977. That same year, 1974, Chiriaeff invited Brian Macdonald, a well-known Canadian choreographer and ballet master, to take over as artistic director of Les Grands Ballets Canadiens. Despite

LES GRANDS BALLETS CANADIENS. Led by Sonia Taverner and Richard Beaty, the full company poses in position for the polonaise in George Balanchine's *Theme and Variations,* mounted for Les Grands Ballets Canadiens in 1968. (Photograph by Henry Koro; from the archives of Les Grands Ballets Canadiens; courtesy of Ludmilla Chiriaeff. Choreography by George Balanchine © The George Balanchine Trust.)

rumors to the contrary, the change in command was amicably achieved. Both Chiriaeff and Nault were glad to pass on the responsibility of artistic direction to Macdonald, who brought to the post extensive experience with the Royal Winnipeg Ballet, the Royal Swedish Ballet, the Harkness Ballet, and the Batsheva Dance Company. Chiriaeff and Nault, who was named resident choreographer, turned their attention to the company's school, while Macdonald—whose wife, Annette av Paul, effectively became prima ballerina—set about refurbishing the company's artistic image. [*See the entry on Macdonald.*]

In this third phase of development Les Grands Ballets Canadiens responded to Macdonald's outspoken cultural nationalism by an increased commitment to Canadian arts. MacDonald sought wherever possible to employ Canadian composers, designers, and choreographers, and, like Chiriaeff before him, he sometimes turned to Canadian themes or personalities for inspiration. Thus, he restaged for the company two of his ballets set to music by the Canadian composer Harry Freedman: *The Shining People of Leonard Cohen,* created for the Royal Winnipeg Ballet in 1970, and *Romeo and Juliet,* a reworking of

a ballet made for Festival Canada Ballet in Ottawa in 1972. For two other works, *Tam Ti Delam* (1974) and *Fête Carignan* (*Hangman's Reel;* 1978), he drew on Quebec's indigenous folk music.

As a classicist by training and by instinct, Macdonald also planned a full production of *Swan Lake,* though only act 2 was ever produced. An admirer of Balanchine, Macdonald added *The Four Temperaments, Serenade,* and *Concerto Barocco* to the company's existing Balanchine repertory of *Tchaikovsky Pas de Deux, Allegro Brillante,* and *Theme and Variations.* Generally, the company's national profile became more firmly established under Macdonald. Shortly before relinquishing his directorship in 1977, he led the company on a successful ten-week Latin American tour.

Collective Direction: 1977–1989. In 1977, Macdonald was replaced as artistic director of the company by an unwieldy committee, which was soon reduced to three key figures. These were Linda Stearns, the Toronto-born ballet mistress of the company; Daniel Jackson, the American ballet master; and Colin McIntyre, a gifted, Scottish-born ballet administrator of broad theatrical experience. Stearns and Jackson had both joined the company as dancers in 1961; McIntyre had become director general of the company in 1975. Despite publicly voiced misgivings about the wisdom of collective direction, Les Grands Ballets Canadiens prospered under this unusual arrangement and soon gained a reputation as a dance company on the cutting edge of artistic creativity. McIntyre's departure in 1984 left Stearns and Jackson as joint artistic directors. When Jackson departed in 1985, Jeanne Renaud joined Stearns as co-director until the end of 1987, after which Stearns remained as sole director until early 1989.

During this turbulent period, the company's artistic profile once again changed. Macdonald, now with the title

of resident choreographer, continued to create occasional works, but the repertory was notably diversified by the addition of modern dance works. These ranged from the early Denishawn curiosity *Soaring* to José Limon's *There Is a Time* to Paul Taylor's *Aureole* and *Cloven Kingdom* and Lar Lubovitch's *Exsultate, Jubilate*. At the same time, original works by such Canadian choreographers as Linda Rabin, Judith Marcuse, Christopher House, and James Kudelka were added to the repertory.

Kudelka had already won international attention for ballets created for the National Ballet of Canada, where he danced from 1972 to 1981. His move to Les Grands Ballets Canadiens seemed, however, to mark an important turning point in his choreographic development. Able to exploit his new company's familiarity with both ballet and modern dance, Kudelka developed a personal style that seamlessly blended classical and modern idioms. His *In Paradisum* (1983) and *Alliances* (1984), both critically ac-

LES GRANDS BALLETS CANADIENS. (*left, above*) Fernand Nault's *Tommy* (1970), with Lorne Toumine, Conrad Petersen, Mannie Rowe (kneeling, as Tommy), and David Groniero. (*left, below*) John Butler's *Villon*, mounted in 1971, with Alexandre Belin (left) as the poet François Villon, Bruce Weavil as His Other Self, and Judith Karstens as his love, Innocence. (*directly below*) Lucas Hoving's *Icare*, mounted in 1972, with Guillermo Gonzales as Icarus and Manon Larin as the Sun Goddess. (Photograph at left above by André Le Coz; photograph at left below uncredited; photograph directly below by Ronald LaBelle; all from the archives of Les Grands Ballets Canadiens; courtesy of Ludmilla Chiriaeff.)

LES GRANDS BALLETS CANADIENS.
Brian Macdonald's *Double Quatuor*, made for the company in 1978, with Annette av Paul, Sylvain Senez, Jacques Drapeau, and Sylvain Lafortune. (Photograph by Melodie Garbish; used by permission.)

claimed, exemplified his strong, new choreographic voice.

The extreme eclecticism of the repertory of Les Grands Ballets Canadiens in the mid-1980s often frustrated critics' attempts to define its essential personality. Although an increasing number of the dancers came from the company school, there was no easily identifiable company style. The principal characteristics of the company were the individuality of its dancers and their ability to project a strong sense of emotional coherence in ensemble works. After the retirement of Vincent Warren and the departure of Alexandre Bélin in 1979 and the later retirement of Annette av Paul in 1984, the company sometimes suffered from a lack of maturity. By the late 1980s, however, it could boast a number of strong dancers, including Sylvain Senez, Gioconda Barbuta, Rey Dizon, and Jerilyn Dana.

As a co-director of Les Grands Ballets Canadiens, Linda Stearns had been a strong supporter of the works of Kudelka, Rabin, Marcuse, and House, and she had welcomed experiment and innovation. But during her brief tenure as sole artistic director (December 1987 to April 1989), she began the process of reshaping the repertory to reflect the company's foundation in the classical tradition. In 1988, company promotional literature still proclaimed Les Grands Ballets to be "a risk taker and trend setter," but Stearns saw the need to set this bold and admirable artistic stance within the context of an identifiable aesthetic. Eclecticism, the company had learned, has its limits both in terms of dancers' technical and stylistic range

and in the audience's ability to make sense of the company's place within the art form. There was also the pressing need to win back that part of the audience that had been alienated by the company's earlier experiments with modern dance. Stearns's additions to the repertory signalled the shift. She added, for example, not only Christopher House's *Jeux Forains* and Lar Lubovitch's *Concerto Six Twenty-Two* to the repertory but also David Bintley's neoclassical *Consort Lessons* and Enrique Martinez's staging of the three-act story-ballet *Coppélia*. The company looked quite comfortable dancing in all these works.

The return of Colin McIntyre in March 1988, as director general of Les Grands Ballets, helped the process of realignment. He would remain in the post until 1991, bringing to it not only administrative expertise but extensive international connections that enabled the company to embark on significant foreign tours. With a deep, practical knowledge of theater, McIntyre, rather like Robert Joffrey in New York, also saw a useful place in the current repertory for works created for Diaghilev's Ballets Russes in the early decades of the twentieth century. During McIntyre's two periods of service as director general, Michel Fokine's *Petrouchka*, Vaslav Nijinsky's *L'Après-midi d'un Faune*, and Léonide Massine's *Le Tricorne* were among the Diaghilev-era works given handsome productions by Les Grands Ballets Canadiens, although the company's performances of these historic works were uneven.

The Rhodes Period: 1989 to the Present. The presence of McIntyre formed an artistic bridge between

LES GRANDS BALLETS CANADIENS. Nacho Duato's *Jardi Tancat*, mounted for the company in 1991, with Andrea Boardman and Louis Robitaille. This work is set to the popular songs of María del Mar Bonet. (Photograph by David Cooper; used by permission.)

Stearns and the arrival in August 1989 of Lawrence Rhodes, her successor as artistic director of the company. Rhodes came to Montreal from a senior post at New York University following a long and distinguished career as dancer, ballet master, or director with such companies as the Joffrey Ballet, the Harkness Ballet, and the Pennsylvania Ballet. Although he had appeared frequently as a guest artist with Les Grands Ballets Canadiens, the arrival of an American director was greeted with mild suspicion by an increasingly nationalistic, French-speaking Quebec. As he took up his post, his necessary but unsettling hirings and firings also drew negative reactions from the media.

Rhodes survived this early criticism and shortly established himself as an effective if sometimes enigmatic artistic director: a mix of pragmatism, idealism, and, occasionally, apparent capriciousness. One of his early acquisitions, *The Gilded Bat* by Peter Anastos, was a vulgar trifle. In contrast, his attachment to the visceral choreographies of Jiří Kylián and Nacho Duato proved well founded, as the company performs their works with exceptional commitment and understanding. Rhodes also scored a notable coup by commissioning two impressive

works from the American choreographer Mark Morris, *Paukenschlag* (1992) and *Quincunx* (1996). Notably, however, he gradually loosened the company's allegiance to its resident choreographer, James Kudelka, and abandoned a veteran contributor to its repertory, Brian Mcdonald. At the same time, he acknowledged the company's debt to Fernand Nault with a special "hommage" program in 1990. Nault's staging of *The Nutcracker* remains a staple of the repertory and an annual holiday favorite.

While Rhodes was introducing historic works by José Limon and Kurt Jooss and commissioning new ballets by such contemporary choreographers as the American Kevin O'Day, the Danish-born Ib Andersen, and the Anglo-Canadian Mark Godden, he was criticized for failing to develop Quebec choreographers, despite the fact that most of these favor an idiom clearly unsuited to his aesthetic preferences. Only in 1996 did Rhodes add new works by Quebec's internationally acclaimed Édouard Lock, director of Montreal's La La La Human Steps, and by Jean Grand-Maître, a Montreal choreographer already successfully nurtured by the National Ballet of Canada and with a growing reputation in Europe.

Overall, however, in keeping with the history of Les Grands Ballets Canadiens, Rhodes committed himself to upholding its tradition of creativity, "within," as he describes it, "a broadly established aesthetic, one founded in ballet classicism." Even his critics concede that he sustained the company through a difficult period of retrenchment triggered by public funding cuts and that he polished it into an impressive ensemble. Although it lacks the uniformity of training and style of the much larger National Ballet of Canada, Les Grands Ballets Canadiens today delivers performances that exalt in the pure joy of movement and that clearly communicate the intentions of an impressive range of contemporary choreographers.

[*See also* Canada, *article on* Theatrical Dance, *and the entries on major figures mentioned herein.*]

BIBLIOGRAPHY

Asselin, Suzanne. "Une petite histoire des Grands Ballets Canadiens." *Reflex: Magazine de la danse* 3 (April 1983).

Citron, Paula. "The French Canadian Experience: Montreal's Les Grands Ballets Canadiens." *Dance Magazine* (April 1982): 62–69.

Crabb, Michael. "Les Grands Ballets Canadiens." *The Dancing Times* (July 1982): 744–745.

Crabb, Michael. "Les Grands Ballets Canadiens." *The Dancing Times* (March 1996): 561–563.

Everett-Green, Robert. "In Person." *The Globe and Mail* (Toronto, 25 April 1992).

Lorrain, Roland. *Les Grands Ballets Canadiens: Cette femme qui nous fit danser.* Montreal, 1973.

Officer, Jillian. *The Original Ballets Appearing in the Repertoire of Les Ballets Chiriaeff 1955–1958 and Les Grands Ballets Canadiens 1958–1980.* Waterloo, 1982.

Wyman, Max. *Dance Canada: An Illustrated History.* Vancouver, 1989.

MICHAEL CRABB

GRAND UNION was a collective of American choreographer-performers who created group improvisations from 1970 to 1976. Its shifting personnel included Becky Arnold, Trisha Brown, Barbara Dilley, Douglas Dunn, David Gordon, Nancy Lewis (Green), Steve Paxton, Yvonne Rainer, Lincoln Scott (Dong) and Valda Setterfield. Grand Union had several sources: many of the group had worked together in Judson Dance Theater; most had studied with Merce Cunningham and several had danced in his company; and five had performed with Rainer in her *Continuous Project—Altered Daily* (1969–1970), an ongoing performance that incorporated language, movement, and popular music, and changed during and between performances, manifesting in the performance itself various levels in the choreographic process (such as learning material, rehearsing, marking, and performing full-out.

At first the Grand Union presented evenings of dance with partially improvised structures, using material from *Continuous Project*. Although members of the group took turns as temporary leaders and choreographers, Grand Union was often mistakenly identified as Rainer's company. The content of the performances was not necessarily polemical, but the group was aware of its own political nature as a struggling collective working out questions of authority. In 1971, Grand Union gave three benefit performances for the Committee to Defend the Black Panthers.

By 1972, the group's members had stopped appearing in one another's dances and had developed a flexible improvisational framework for performing together. The format allowed for invention, commentary, teaching, imitation, repetition, and other modes of handling material, both verbal and physical. It also allowed any member to assume control (or to attempt to do so) for part of an evening. Any new material could be introduced, but favorite "bits" could be recycled, too. The framework was not entirely without limits; audience participation, for instance, was discouraged.

A typical Grand Union performance began before the audience entered the performance space. By the time the spectators arrived, some of the dancers might be warming up, some testing movement material from their own choreography, some engaging others in cooperative play. Gradually, clear interactions would emerge: performers imitating one another, doing variations on another's style, or entering an ongoing movement or verbal dialogue. Suddenly the entire group would coalesce into a single activity, and then break off into solos, duets, or trios. Someone would change the music and the entire scene would shift. A familiar bit—investigating the structure of dance, a doctor–patient encounter, handling objects, double entendres, quoting a well-known performance style—would be put into gear.

No two performances were exactly alike, and the moods and qualities of various evenings could utterly diverge. And yet, no matter what the surface material was, the performances were always about the logic, structure, methods, and materials of dance theater. Humor was a crucial element of Grand Union style, although in later years some critics found the group's brand of comedy esoteric.

GRAND UNION. From left to right, Barbara Dilley, Douglas Dunn (standing), David Gordon (lying), Nancy Lewis, Trisha Brown, and Steve Paxton in an improvisatory performance. (Photograph courtesy of Douglas Dunn.)

When a Grand Union performance suddenly "clicked," one was tempted to describe the sensation as theatrical magic. Yet the magic of theater was precisely what Grand Union attempted to explicate; they aimed to display the conditions that create the "magic" of performance, from choreographic structure to the psychological chemistry between performers. Grand Union demystified theater even as the group produced it.

The influence of its often witty blend of talking, dancing, handling objects, and reflexive theatrics may be seen not only in the later work of Grand Union's own members, but also in that of several generations of postmodern choreographers. Its collective organization and improvisatory daring inspired the founding of several other groups. Also, Grand Union shaped the exchange between dance and performance art in the 1970s so profoundly that its imprint could still be felt in the 1980s and 1990s.

[*See also* Improvisation.]

BIBLIOGRAPHY

Baker, Rob. "Grand Union: Taking a Chance on Dance." *Dance Magazine* (October 1973): 40–43.

Banes, Sally. *Terpsichore in Sneakers: Post-Modern Dance.* 2d. ed. Middletown, Conn., 1987. Includes a bibliography.

Foster, Susan Leigh. *Reading Dancing: Bodies and Subjects in Contemporary American Dance.* Berkeley, 1986.

Kendall, Elizabeth B. "The Grand Union: Our Gang." *Ballet Review* 5.4 (1975–1976): 44–55.

Paxton, Steve. "The Grand Union: Improvisational Dance." *Drama Review* 16 (September 1972): 128–134.

Ramsay, Margaret Hupp. *The Grand Union, 1970–1976: An Improvisational Performance Group.* New York, 1991.

SALLY BANES

GRANT. As Bryaxis, the Pirate King, in Ashton's *Daphnis and Chloe* (1951), Grant performs a vigorous jump to celebrate the capture of Chloe (Pauline Clayden), who sits trembling in fear. (Photograph by Baron; used by permission of Camera Press, Ltd., London.)

GRANT, ALEXANDER (born 22 February 1925 in Wellington, New Zealand), dancer, teacher, and director. When Grant learned a simple Russian *trepak* at the age of six, he took his first steps toward his illustrious career as the Royal Ballet's greatest *demi-caractère* dancer. Colonel W. de Basil's Ballets Russes, which he saw on one of its Australian tours, convinced him that ballet was meant to be exuberant, energetic, and highly theatrical, and over the years these qualities would color all his performances.

Grant was an experienced amateur at fifteen, when he won a Royal Academy of Dancing scholarship that finally brought him to England and the Sadler's Wells Ballet School in 1946. A few months after his arrival, he joined the Sadler's Wells Theatre Ballet on tour; by 1947 he was a soloist with the Sadler's Wells Ballet at Covent Garden, sometimes dancing the boisterous *trepak* in *The Sleeping Beauty*, at other times—owing to the postwar shortage of male dancers—thrust into the challenge of clean-lined classicism in *Symphonic Variations* and *Les Patineurs*. He even created a small role for Frederick Ashton—that of a child in the short-lived fantasy *Les Sirènes* (1946). How-

ever, it was his re-creation of the Barber in Léonide Massine's 1947 revival of *Mam'zelle Angot* that revealed his natural gift for characterization and his extraordinary potential as a *demi-caractère* dancer.

In the next ten years alone, Grant's incredible adaptability led him into more than fifty roles, ranging from the Tango and Popular Song in *Façade* and the Miller in *Le Tricorne* to Satan in *Job* and the title roles in *Petrouchka* and *The Rake's Progress*. In those same ten years, Grant took part in Frederick Ashton's *Cinderella* (1948), the first full-evening British ballet; *Don Quixote* (1950), Ninette de Valois's first creation in the Opera House; and *Clock Symphony* (1948), *Bonne-Bouche* (1952), and *Ballabile* (1950), the first original works for the company by Léonide Massine, John Cranko, and Roland Petit, respectively.

A more varied group of choreographers can scarcely be imagined; of them all, Ashton was undoubtedly the most important to Grant and the most often inspired by his remarkable talent. Their collaboration lasted thirty years, from *Les Sirènes* (1946) to *A Month in the Country* (1976). During this time, Ashton created twenty-one stage roles for Grant and one, Peter Rabbit, for the film *Tales of Bea-*

trix Potter (1971). Grant's best-remembered interpretations are probably the Jester in *Cinderella;* the Pirate King in *Daphnis and Chloe;* Tirrenio in *Ondine;* the Neapolitan dancer in *Swan Lake,* act 3; Bottom in *The Dream;* Yslaev (his last Ashton creation) in *A Month in the Country;* and Alain in *La Fille Mal Gardée,* in which he made his farewell appearance at Covent Garden in 1976.

Grant was made a Commander of the Order of the British Empire in 1965 and served as director of Ballet for All from 1971 to 1976. From 1976 to 1983 he was director of the National Ballet of Canada, where he occasionally danced Alain, Carabosse, and various mime roles. [*See* National Ballet of Canada.] After his return to Britain, Grant frequently assisted in the staging of Ashton ballets and continued to appear in mime roles with both the Royal Ballet and London Festival Ballet, with which he performed as a principal from 1985 to 1989.

BIBLIOGRAPHY

de Valois, Ninette. "Alexander Grant." *Dance Gazette* (February 1979): 9.

Newman, Barbara. *Striking a Balance: Dancers Talk about Dancing.* Rev. ed. New York, 1992.

Vaughan, David. *Frederick Ashton and His Ballets.* New York, 1977 and 1997.

Willis, Margaret E. "Russian Squats and Chinese Chequers." *Dance Now* 4 (Spring 1995): 71–76.

BARBARA NEWMAN

GRANTZOW, ADÈLE (born 16 December 1841 in Brunswick, died 7 June 1877 in Berlin), German ballet dancer. Grantzow received her early training from her father, Gustav, a ballet master, and made her first stage appearances in Brunswick as a child. Her true debut took place in Hanover in 1858. It was there that Arthur Saint-Léon saw her and was sufficiently impressed to cast her in small roles in some of the ballets he produced during his visit there. In 1864, realizing that she needed further training to perfect her technique and style, the family sent her to Paris to study under Madame Dominique (Caroline Lassiat). There, Saint-Léon saw her again, recognized her exceptional promise and recommended her for the post of prima ballerina in Moscow to succeed Praskovia Lebedeva. Grantzow made her debut in Moscow at the Bolshoi Theater in Saint-Léon's ballet *Fiammetta* on 15 [27] November 1865 and later appeared in *Météora* and *Giselle* on 29 January [9 February] 1866.

An engagement in Paris followed. She made her debut there at the Opera in *Giselle* on 11 May 1866, and was chosen by Saint-Léon to create the leading role in the new ballet he was then preparing. Unfortunately, the production of this ballet, *La Source,* was delayed, and the Russian authorities would not extend her leave to enable her to create it. As a result, the role was danced by another bal-

lerina, Guglielmina Salvioni. That winter Grantzow appeared in Saint-Léon's *The Little Humpbacked Horse* in Moscow and made her Saint Petersburg debut, at the Bolshoi Theater, in *Giselle* on 13 [25] December 1866. Returning to Paris after the Russian season, she triumphed as Naïla, the leading role in *La Source,* on 10 May 1867. She made another strong impression as Medora in the revival of Joseph Mazilier's *Le Corsaire* on 21 October 1867.

Grantzow's third Paris season, in 1868, was curtailed because of an injury. Before returning to Russia, she began to rehearse a new ballet by Saint-Léon (eventually to become *Coppélia*) that was then scheduled for production in 1869. However, upon her return to Russia that winter, Grantzow fell ill and, needing a long convalescence, had to cancel her contracted visit to Paris in 1869 and forego participation in *Coppélia.* The leading role, Swanilda, was subsequently created, in 1870, by the fledgling ballerina Giuseppina Bozzacchi.

Grantzow recovered sufficiently to resume her duties in Saint Petersburg in the 1869/70 season. She created the role of Yufei in Saint-Léon's new ballet, *The Lily,* at the Bolshoi Theater, on 11 [23] November 1869. Shortly after the premiere, Grantzow slipped and injured herself during a rehearsal, and early in 1870, while looking forward to returning to Paris, she contracted typhus.

Grantzow did not dance again until the 1870/71 season in Saint Petersburg, when she created the leading role in Marius Petipa's *Trilby* at the Bolshoi Theater, on 17 [29] January 1871. She was engaged in Saint Petersburg for the two following seasons, appearing in two of Jules Perrot's ballets that were still in the repertory, *Faust* in 1871/72 and *La Esmeralda* in 1872/73. She also created the title role in Petipa's ballet *La Camargo,* set to music by Ludwig Minkus, at the Bolshoi Theater, on 17 [29] December 1872.

In the intervals between her later Russian seasons, Grantzow began to make guest appearances in Germany. She danced at the opera house in Hanover in 1872, 1873, and 1874 and at the Royal Opera in Berlin each year from 1872 to 1876. During her last season in Berlin she created the title role in Paul Taglioni's ballet *Madeleine,* set to music by Peter Hertel and first performed on 13 March 1876.

One of the consequences of Grantzow's attack of typhus in 1870 was a persistent rash on one of her legs. In 1877 she sought treatment for this from a therapist, Friedrich Backer, who performed an operation that left her leg badly infected. She died following another operation in the Augusta Hospital in Berlin. Backer was sentenced to six months imprisonment for criminal negligence.

Grantzow's career was more than usually beset with illness and injury, which deprived her of two important creations (*Coppélia* and *La Source*) for which she had originally been selected. She was prevented from fulfilling the extraordinary promise she had shown at the time of her debut. The enthusiasm of Saint-Léon, who had discovered her, was then unbounded; he had been astounded to find such strong technique and assurance in a dancer so young and inexperienced. Grantzow was also a fine interpretive artist, able to play a wide range of roles. She was one of the finest Giselles of her generation.

BIBLIOGRAPHY

Guest, Ivor. *The Ballet of the Second Empire.* London, 1974.
Japy, George. *Adèle Granzow* (in French). Paris, 1868.
Krasovskaya, Vera. *Russkii baletnyi teatr vtoroi poloviny deviatnadtsatogo veka.* Leningrad, 1963.
Saint-Léon, Arthur. *Letters from a Ballet Master: The Correspondence of Arthur Saint-Léon.* Edited by Ivor Guest. New York, 1981.

IVOR GUEST

GREAT BRITAIN. [*To survey the dance traditions of Great Britain, this entry comprises twelve articles:*

English Traditional Dance
Scottish Folk and Traditional Dance
Welsh Folk and Traditional Dance
Manx Folk and Traditional Dance
Theatrical Dance, 1460–1660
Theatrical Dance, 1660–1772
Theatrical Dance, 1772–1850
Theatrical Dance since 1850
Modern Dance
Dance Education
Dance Research and Publication
Contemporary Criticism

The first four articles explore folk and traditional dance found in various regions of Great Britain; the following five articles focus on the history of theatrical dance; the concluding articles consider education and the history of scholarship and writing. For further discussion of theatrical dance, see entries on individual companies, choreographers, and dancers.]

English Traditional Dance

Our understanding of what constitutes folk dance in England derives from the intellectual climate prevailing at the end of the nineteenth century. Motivated by dismay at the effects of industrialization and by a romanticized nationalism, many of the intelligentsia turned to the expressive culture of the countryside to uncover, or reconstruct, their native heritage. In the country, scholars found dances performed by the laboring population that appeared to contrast with the repertory fashionable in urban and educated society. Many of the dances dated from before the nineteenth century but were disappearing as the social fabric and tastes changed. These older rural dances were gathered to form the folk dance canon of England.

The bulk of the collection was undertaken in the early 1900s by Cecil Sharp (1859–1924), whose resulting publications, *The Morris Book* (five volumes), *The Country Dance Book* (six volumes), and *The Sword Dances of Northern England* (three volumes), established the main genres of English folk dancing. His work was tied to the revival of English traditional dancing, in which dances from rural working-class culture were transmitted to an urban middle-class audience. The first revival performers in 1905 were members of the Esperance Working Girls Club, a philanthropic concern of Mary Neal, in the East End of London. Sharp and Neal worked together for a time to meet the nationwide interest in these dances. In 1909 Sharp was successful in introducing English folk dance into state education, and in 1911 he became the director of the newly founded English Folk Dance Society (which became the English Folk Dance and Song Society in 1932). This institution, with a repertory shaped mainly by Sharp and his followers, has been the prime mover behind the study and practice of English traditional dance.

Broadly speaking, the folk dances of England can be grouped into two categories: social dances performed by both sexes for recreation, and display dances in which selected performers exhibit special skills or kinetic knowledge. There is little evidence of the forms and contexts of English rural social dance before the twentieth century. The earliest dances include the jigs, hornpipe, and reel; the last is a group dance in which passages of stepping in place alternate with passages in which the dancers move through space. Most histories cite the first detailed source of English dances as *The English Dancing Master*, compiled and published by John Playford in 1651. This *aide-mémoire* of country dances, as they were termed, was compiled for an aristocratic market, but a number of other sources suggest that country dances were performed throughout English society. They were certainly popular; *The Dancing Master* went through eighteen editions by the 1720s. Country dance also enjoyed a revival in the early nineteenth century.

When Sharp began to collect social folk dances, he came across the country dances performed in a longways formation in which a line of men faced a line of women. This formation, found in Playford, was viewed in the late seventeenth and early eighteenth centuries as a distinctively English form. Sharp's later discovery of the "running set" in the southern Appalachian Mountains provided him with another clue to the evolution of the English country dance. The American dance bore similarities to formations recorded in early editions of Playford, and from this resemblance Sharp concluded (wrongly as later evidence has demonstrated) that the running set was a very early form that had been taken to America, probably by immigrants from rural England, and that it predated the dances found in Playford's London repertory.

From the eighteenth century onward, most social folk dances appear to have derived from repertories once current in upper-class and middle-class circles. The link between the gentry, the growing commercial class, and the laboring population was the dancing master. Scattered records indicate that dancing schools were established in England from the mid-seventeenth century onward, but their activity in rural regions appears to have declined by the nineteenth century. In the Lake District of northwestern England, however, the activities of dancing masters continued into the twentieth century. Oral and written sources from the early nineteenth century indicate that the profession of dancing master was often held in families and in some cases was combined with that of blacksmith or cobbler. Courses of instruction generally lasted several weeks, during which children up to thirteen years of age attended classes in a schoolroom or barn. The course concluded with a finishing ball at which the children gave a dancing exhibition, followed by general dancing for all.

The repertory of the dancing master included exhibition dances such as hornpipes, social forms such as country dances, and, later, ballroom dances. During the nineteenth century, dances popular in Paris, London, and Edinburgh were brought into the rural repertory; thus a quadrille appeared on a program for a ball in a remote community in the Lake District only ten years after its introduction in London. These new forms did not supplant the existing social dances but were often assimilated into the local manner of performance. Dancers often incorporated steps they had learned as children into new dances such as the Lancers. Hornpipes and reels, which appeared on a program for 1825, were still being performed as late as 1917.

Dancing was popular in this part of England during the nineteenth century. The finishing balls often lasted into the early hours of the morning. About three or four nights a year, special "long nights" were held that offered an extended opportunity to socialize through dancing. The construction of more village institutes around 1900 provided venues for social dancing. In the summer, if no large hall was available, dancing took place outdoors.

The nineteenth-century laboring class danced at all sorts of occasions—weddings, birthdays, christenings, harvest homes, the end of sheep-shearing, hunt balls, markets, hiring fairs (where agricultural workers were engaged by farmers) and wakes holidays, which were held to celebrate the dedication or saint's day of the parish church. Many celebrations were particular to a locality. Public inns were popular venues for dancing, and descriptions by travelers testify to the vigor and vitality of the dancers.

Throughout England, folk dance repertories appear to have included a mixture of old and fairly new. In Norfolk, longways dances coexisted with nineteenth-century couple dances, such as the polka and schottische, well into the twentieth century. Nineteenth-century group forms such as the Lancers were enjoyed at social gatherings in many parts of the countryside long after they fell out of fashion in the cities.

Sharp's focus on distinctively English social dances precluded an understanding of the historical processes by which dances were introduced, selected, and performed in rural districts. Volume 1 of his *Country Dance Book* contains exclusively longways dances, without mention of later dances that might have been included in a night's entertainment. Once Sharp had discovered Playford's *English Dancing Master*, he became interested in reconstructing earlier forms of the English country dance for revival performance. Consequently, his view was based on very limited experience of traditional dances in the northeast and in Devonshire during the late 1920s. When Maude Karpeles collected traditional dances in the northeast and Devonshire, she selected only those dances that conformed to Sharp's criteria.

This emphasis changed when Douglas Kennedy succeeded Sharp as director of the English Folk Dance and Song Society. Kennedy attempted to popularize traditional social dances, as opposed to reconstructions of Playford's dances. Further collecting after World War II revealed that the rural dance repertory did include Victorian social dances such as quadrilles. Nevertheless, standard couple dances of the nineteenth century, particularly sequence dances, whose inventors are unknown, remain somewhat neglected in collections by folk dance scholars and in the revival repertory.

A significant omission in the collections of Sharp and his contemporaries was step dancing. Characterized by a rhythmic beating on the floor, step dancing was widespread at the turn of the twentieth century, both as a display (sometimes competitive) and as a component of social dancing, notably in the Lake District and northern border country. Two basic types of solo performance exist: set step dancing, in which the dance phrases closely coincide with musical phrases (for example, each eight-bar phrase is often concluded with a recurrent two-bar pattern of movement); and improvised or "free style" step dancing, in which the music and movement are more loosely associated.

Researchers originally believed that entirely discrete traditions of step dancing had evolved in different regions. More recent study, however, has revealed that styles were more likely to have been developed by individual dancing teachers or families. For example, a style of step dancing believed to have been first practiced in Lancashire was transmitted to local fishermen in northern Norfolk by a Lancashire coastguard. Gypsies, too, are known to have acquired and transmitted steps in their travels.

GREAT BRITAIN: English Traditional Dance. Of the two types of Sword Dance, rapper is faster, more athletic, and is performed with short, flexible metal swords with handles that have a revolving pivot at one end. When the dancers weave a number of figures without releasing the swords, the result is a braid, as shown by the High Spen Blue Diamonds from County Durham. (Photograph by Derek Schofield; used by permission.)

Step dancing in England was performed by children and adults, by women and men. Step dancers tended to learn their skills young, whether in the dancing schools of the Lake District or in families, as was often the case in northern Norfolk. From the 1900s until World War II, it seems to have been common practice in some parts of Devon and East Anglia for the more proficient adults to perform for audiences at local gatherings.

Clog dancing, a form of step dancing performed in clogs, was widespread in the north of England. Special dancing clogs, lighter and more ornate than the everyday clogs, were available. A number of music hall and variety artists, including the popular Dan Leno in the late nineteenth century, included clog dancing in their stage acts. Many people knew at least the basic steps. Informal competitions took place on streetcorners or in public houses. At more formal events, prizes of cups, medals, belts, and money were offered to the best dancers. In eastern Lancashire clog dancing was taught in the local gymnasium along with wrestling and boxing. Neatness and precision were so much prized that competitions and exhibitions might require the dancer to perform on a very small portable mat, or, for aspiring professionals, on a pedestal. Formal competitions continued in northeastern England until about 1951 and were revived in the mid-1970s. Through the efforts of the Ellwood family, the traditions of teaching and performing were kept alive. The recent folk revival movement has ensured that many steps have been recorded and handed on.

The best known of England's folk dances are probably the group ceremonial versions of the Morris dance, and the Sword Dance. Traditionally performed on major holidays, usually by men dressed in special attire, these dances appear once to have been integral to community celebrations. In 1936 Joseph Needham published a geographical distribution of English ceremonial dance traditions, revised and expanded by E. C. Cawte and others in 1960. Using Needham's classifications, it is possible to identify two main types of sword dancing—longsword and rapper—and four main types of Morris—Cotswold (or south Midlands), northwest, border, and molly. Sword dancing in England is characterized by a closed circular formation in which the men hold the hilt and point of one another's swords. At certain moments in the dance, which vary with the local tradition, the swords are interwoven to form a lock that is then held aloft. Most Morris dancing is performed in two parallel lines, similar to a longways country dance, but without the progression; it is distinguished by the sticks or handkerchiefs held in the dancers' hands.

Longsword, found in Yorkshire and parts of County Durham, appears to be the older type of sword dancing. Traditionally it was performed either on Plough Monday in January or at Christmas. The dancers were generally employed in the major occupation of the area, sheep-farming on the North York Moors or mining in the industrial districts. Performances took the dancers, usually five to eight in number and often accompanied by a fool and a man dressed as a woman, to the houses of the wealthy for contributions of money and hospitality. For agricultural workers who were unemployed in winter, the activity helped to finance their enforced holiday. Some teams dragged a plow around with them; it was used to plow up the gardens of those who refused them contributions.

The folk revival has provided fresh patronage for a custom that showed signs of diminishing in the early twentieth century. Today ceremonial Sword Dance teams with strong links to an earlier tradition include those from Grenoside and Handsworth (both suburbs of the city of Sheffield), Loftus and Goathland from the North York Moors, and Flamborough on the North Sea coast.

Rapper dancing, found farther north in the Tyneside area and performed mostly by miners, is a faster and more athletic version of sword dancing. Whereas longsword dancers carry rigid wooden swords, the rapper dance is performed with short, flexible metal swords, the handles of which have a pivot and thus can revolve at one end. Usually performed by five men, the dance has tight, intricate figures, some containing somersaults, which can be interspersed with stepping. The rapper is probably an eighteenth-century variant of the longsword. Early records include evidence of teams appearing with plows, as in the longsword tradition of North Yorkshire. One such team toured the vicinity to raise money for a ball for the whole village. Early in the twentieth century, however, the rapper dance became an exhibition dance, shifting its context from performances at the houses of the gentry, in the street, or in public houses to talent contests, concerts, and competitions.

In 1919 the establishment of the North of England Tournament gave fresh impetus to the tradition of sword dancing. As in clog dancing, competition brought the dance to a new level of sophistication, although in some quarters such originality was frowned upon. The knowledge and skills of rapper dancing tended to be held in families. Today, the Royal Earsdon and High Spen Blue Diamonds teams demonstrate strong ties with earlier practitioners.

Perhaps the best-known English style of Morris dance is that of the southern Midlands region, which became the basis for the national revival of Morris dancing. The dance is performed by six men in two files, who wave handkerchiefs or clash sticks. In the early nineteenth century the dancers were accompanied by a pipe and tabor; later a fiddle, then a concertina, melodeon, and accordion variously replaced the traditional instruments.

Morris dances were traditionally performed at Whitsuntide (Pentecost), when the dancers, mostly agricultural workers, manual laborers, or craftsmen, toured the vicinity for several days, visiting pubs and the houses of the gentry. Their repertory of several Morris dances, sometimes including solo and double jigs, was rewarded by gifts of money and hospitality, which were shared among the performers and helpers, often drawn from one or two families.

This traditional patronage declined in the later nineteenth century as the transformation of popular culture gained headway; the railways took the local audience away at holiday times, attitudes hardened against performing and collection in the street, and the public drinking associated with traditional pursuits was anathema to the temperance movement. A movement known as "rational recreation" sought to change the customary leisure pursuits of the working people. Coupled with the widespread emigration of the young men who would have continued the Morris, these social pressures led to a decline in the number of Morris teams.

Urban enthusiasts traveling to the country in search of quaint English customs, as well as the national revival led by Sharp and Neal, helped to stabilize the ailing tradition at the beginning of the twentieth century, although World War I dramatically changed rural life. Today, four teams that were recorded by Sharp continue to perform on a fairly regular basis: Headington Quarry (near Oxford), Bampton and Abingdon (Oxfordshire), and Chipping Camden (Gloucestershire).

In northwestern England in the semi-industrial settlements of the late eighteenth and early nineteenth cen-

GREAT BRITAIN: English Traditional Dance. Morris dancing is distinguished by the sticks or handkerchiefs held in the dancers' hands, as shown by the parading Manley Morris Dancers from Cheshire. (Photograph by Derek Schofield; used by permission.)

turies, Morris dancing was part of the rush-bearing procession held at the annual wakes holiday in the summer. Rushes were transported in an elaborate procession to the parish church from the surrounding communities to be strewn onto the unpaved church floor. This observance was an occasion for much intercommunity rivalry; wherever financially possible, the Morris dancers tended to be numerous and ornately dressed, with accompanying bands of fifes and drums.

The dance, composed of several figures to be performed while traveling along the street and in place at the discretion of the leader, was ideally suited to slow-moving processions. Thus, when the custom of rush-bearing died out, the Morris survived for performance in new contexts such as competitions, May Day parades, and civic pageants. Although in the nineteenth century the dance was mostly performed by young men, changing tastes and circumstances led to the increased involvement of children. Today competitive girls' Morris teams are thriving; their dances have roots in the earlier men's dances but have also been strongly influenced by other forms of physical culture. Ignored by the folk revival movement, which tends to classify Morris dancing according to Sharp's criteria from the early twentieth century, this girls' form is most evident in the carnivals and special competitions of northwestern England.

Another popular revival in recent years has been what scholars call the "border Morris." In the nineteenth and early twentieth centuries, Morris dancers in the counties along the Welsh border were often composed of miners on strike or unemployed laborers. The distinctive features of this style are teams of eight dancers, stick tapping in single or double files, ordinary clothes decorated with ribbons, and Christmas performances. The dancers also blacked their faces; this custom, as well as the choice of music and instruments, may have been influenced by the Victorian enthusiasm for black minstrel shows. In some cases the sticks were replaced with percussion instruments such as the tambourine, and the performers sang popular songs as they danced. Latterly viewed as begging, the economic function of the dance died out before World War II. Today's performances, deriving from revival in the 1970s, are concerned more with recreation and aesthetics.

A similar revival of molly dancing, a ceremonial tradition mainly associated with Plough Monday in East Anglia, has occurred since the 1970s. Popular until the 1930s, it usually involved six dancers, accompanied by a man dressed up as a woman and another character to sweep the space clear for the performance. The dancers were dressed in ordinary clothes decorated with rosettes and sashes. In a departure from most other Morris traditions, their repertory was drawn from popular local social dances, which were repeated with women also dancing at a social gathering in the evening following the day's tour.

Another group of ceremonial dances are the processionals of the southwest, of which the Helston Furry Dance is the most famous. In Maytime, the custom of the nineteenth century was for men and women of the different trades and social classes to dance through the streets, houses, and gardens of Helston at different times of the day. Today, the dance operates as an annual expression of pride in community, tradition, and identity.

More unusual dance customs can be found in rural Staffordshire, where reindeer antlers are carried in the "Abbots Bromley Horn Dance" each September, and at Bacup in industrial Lancashire, where on Easter Saturday pieces of wood representing coconuts are struck rhythmically together by the Britannia Coco-Nut Dancers. Both are itinerant dance displays, performed at what was once a major community holiday. The maypole dancing popularized in schools and May Day festivals from the middle of the nineteenth century also continues today in similar contexts. Dancers move around a tall maypole, weaving intricate patterns with colored ribbons attached at the top of the pole.

Sharp's collection and dissemination of a repertory of dances viewed as alternative, more ancient, and more indigenous than those fashionable in metropolitan culture, has formed the bedrock of the folk dance movement in England. These dances, whether performed in the original manner and context or used as models for fresh inventions, have continued to provide enjoyment and a framework for expression for a significant portion of the British population.

[*For related discussion, see* European Traditional Dance *and* Folk Dance History. *See also* Clogging; Country Dance; Jig; Hornpipe; Longways; Morris Dance; Reel; Step Dancing; Sword Dance, *and the entries on* Playford *and* Sharp.]

BIBLIOGRAPHY

Buckland, Theresa Jill. "The Reindeer Antlers of the Abbots Bromley Horn Dance: A Re-Examination." *Lore and Language* 3.2 (1980): 1–8.

Buckland, Theresa Jill. "The Tunstead Mill Nutters of Rossendale, Lancashire." *Folk Music Journal* 5.2 (1986): 132–149.

Buckland, Theresa Jill. "Institutions and Ideology in the Dissemination of Morris Dances in the North West of England." *Yearbook for Traditional Music* 23 (1991): 53–67.

Cawte, E. C., et al. "A Geographical Index of the Ceremonial Dance in Great Britain." *Journal of the English Folk Dance and Song Society* 9.1 (1960): 1–41.

Cawte, E. C. "The Morris Dance in Herefordshire, Shropshire, and Worcestershire." *Journal of the English Folk Dance and Song Society* 9.4 (1963): 197–212.

Cawte, E. C. "A History of the Rapper Dance." *Folk Music Journal* 4.2 (1981): 79–116.

Chandler, Keith. *"Ribbons, Bells, and Squeaking Fiddles": The Social History of Morris Dancing in the English South Midlands, 1660–1900.* Enfield Lock, Middlesex, 1993.

Clifton, Peter, and Ann-Marie Hulme. "Solo Step Dancing within Living Memory in North Norfolk." *Traditional Dance* 1 (1982): 29–58.

Corrsin, S. D. *Sword Dancing in Central and Northern Europe: An Annotated Bibliography.* Vaughan Williams Memorial Library Leaflet, no. 21. London, 1993.

Flett, J. F., and T. M. Flett. *Traditional Step-Dancing in Lakeland.* London, 1979.

Heaney, Michael. *An Introductory Bibliography on Morris Dancing.* Vaughan Williams Memorial Library Leaflet, no. 19. 2d ed. London, 1995.

Howison, Daniel, and Bernard Bentley. "The North-West Morris: A General Survey." *Journal of the English Folk Dance and Song Society* 9.1 (1960): 42–55.

Hulme, Ann-Marie, and Peter Clifton. "Social Dancing in a Norfolk Village, 1900–1945." *Folk Music Journal* 3.4 (1978): 359–377.

Judge, Roy. "Tradition and the Plaited Maypole Dance." *Traditional Dance* 2 (1983): 1–21.

Judge, Roy. "May Day Practices in England." In *Dance: A Multicultural Perspective,* edited by Janet Adshead. Guildford, 1984.

Judge, Roy. "Mary Neal and the Espérance Morris." *Folk Music Journal* 5.5 (1989): 443–480.

Karpeles, Maud. *Twelve Traditional Country Dances.* London, 1931.

Metherell, Chris. *An Introductory Bibliography on Clog and Step Dance.* Vaughan Williams Memorial Library Leaflet, no. 22. London, 1994.

Needham, Joseph, and Arthur Peck. "Molly Dancing in East Anglia." *Journal of the English Folk Dance and Song Society* 1.2 (1933): 79–85.

Needham, Joseph. "The Geographical Distribution of English Ceremonial Dance Traditions." *Journal of the English Folk Dance and Song Society* 3.1 (1936): 1–45.

Pilling, Julian Oliver. "The Lancashire Clog Dance." *Folk Music Journal* 1.3 (1967): 158–179.

Rippon, Hugh. *Discovering English Folk Dance.* 3d ed. Princes Risborough, 1993.

Sharp, Cecil, and Herbert C. Macilwaine. *The Morris Book.* 5 vols. London, 1909–1913. 2d ed. London, 1912–1924.

Sharp, Cecil, et al. *The Country Dance Book.* 6 vols. London, 1909–1927.

Sharp, Cecil. *The Sword Dances of Northern England.* 3 vols. London, 1912–1913. 2d ed. London, 1951.

Sughrue, Cynthia, ed. *Contemporary Morris and Sword Dancing: Conference Papers.* Lore and Language, vol. 6.2. Sheffield, 1988.

ARCHIVE. Most of the new literature on English folk dance appears in a number of specific journals: *English Dance and Song, Folk Music Journal,* and *Traditional Dance.* All these plus other related literature can be found at the Vaughan Williams Memorial Library, London.

THERESA JILL BUCKLAND

Scottish Folk and Traditional Dance

The traditional dances of Scotland include both solos and dances for two, three, or more performers. Some of the solo dances, such as the "Highland Fling" and the "Sword Dance," have become internationally familiar in their standardized modern competition forms. Many of the group dances have a generic name taken from the number of dancers involved, such as twosomes, threesome reels, foursome reels, and so on; such dances have historically existed in more than one version. Styles, performance practices, and the popularity of specific dances have all varied geographically as well as historically. Scottish traditional dance draws heavily, if not exclusively, on traditional Scottish music, which itself reflects local preferences. Not all the music lends itself to dancing, but certain types of tunes that suit particular dance forms in rhythm and tempo have come to be identified with those dances. Hence there are reels, strathspeys, jigs, and hornpipes—names that refer to both types of dances and types of tunes. The fiddle was traditionally the favorite instrument indoors and the bagpipe more commonly outdoors. The repertories of both instruments have made immense contributions to Scottish dance music.

Scottish country dance is not, strictly speaking, a traditional Scottish dance form, but one whose basic structure was imported from England and assimilated, with substantial embellishment, into the Scottish cultural heritage. In this process genuine Scottish steps, music, and, to a degree, figures, all drawn from the traditional repertories of the common folk, were superimposed on the rudiments of the imported form.

Highland Dance. The crowning glory of folk dance in Scotland and the nation's most distinctive style is Highland dance. As it has been known for at least the past two hundred years, however, Highland dance is a cultivated art-dance form, which evolved from its folk origins in much the same way as did European ballet and court dance. The term *Highland* refers to the northern and western mountainous region of Scotland, which, together with the Hebridean Archipelago, formed until recent times the last stronghold in Scotland of Celtic culture and the Gaelic language that is its heart. It is from this region that the dance tradition bearing the name *Highland* emerged and came to international notice in the eighteenth century.

The most characteristic surviving social dance in this tradition is called the reel or, outside Scotland, the Scotch reel. A dance for three or four people in linear formation, it comprises eight bars of setting (dancing in place) alternating with eight bars of travel in the interweaving figure called a Reel in Scotland and more usually a Hey (or Hay) in England. The basic Reel is a figure-eight pattern.

The reel is known in two styles. One, widely favored throughout Scotland in past times, is performed to the common reel music, usually in a fast 4/4 and sometimes in 2/4 meter; such dances are sometimes called "rants" in Scotland, after a Scots word for boisterous merrymaking. The other kind of reel, associated with the Highland region of Strathspey, is more restrained and elegant. Called the Strathspey reel, or simply the strathspey, it is danced to common-time music played "Strathspey style," which is characterized by a rhythmic figure called the "Scotch snap" (a sixteenth note followed by a dotted eighth). The familiar tune of Robert Burns's *Auld Lang Syne* is a strathspey. Indeed, Burns wrote some of his best lyrics to strathspey tunes and once expressed the essence of the style as the "kindlan bauld Strathspey, lento largo in the play" (*kindlan,* "setting afire"; *bauld,* "bold"). The tempo is andante, as opposed to the allegro of the common reel. When playing for country dances or songs, musicians prefer a more legato, less syncopated line called the "slow strathspey" by the eighteenth-century fiddlers who excelled in this music. The Strathspey style of dancing is the finest flowering of Highland dance. It is to this tradition that we owe the "Highland Fling," the "Sword Dance," "Sean Triubhas" and the Strathspey reel. Observers of social dancing in Scotland in the eighteenth century marveled at the untiring vigor of the Strathspey dancers and the neatness and complexity of their footwork, likening it to the dancing they had seen in London theaters.

The Scotch reel, as it was called, was introduced mainly in its allegro form to English and European—and American—dance assemblies in the later eighteenth century and was part of the international social dance repertory throughout the nineteenth century. It was popular in the British Isles primarily in the combination of strathspey and reel, namely, the reel performed Strathspey-style followed by the same tune in the common allegro reel style. Such dances generally were called foursome reels. Another but very different reel, the "Reel of Tulloch," gained much popularity throughout the nineteenth century and sometimes replaced the common reel in the foursome. Its other name, "Breadalbane Ball Reel," hints at its probable place of origin, in Perthshire. It is first mentioned as a dance early in the century, but the vigorous pipe-reel tune from which it takes its name is found in a manuscript collection dated 1734. In this dance, four dancers stand in line as for the reel and alternate eight bars of setting with eight bars of turning (or swinging)—four bars with right arms engaged and four bars with left arms. The dancers progress to change partners every sixteen bars along the line of the dance. In the ballroom, these reels are performed by male-female couples, but in Highland society groups of men often performed them, as they did on hunting or military expeditions. The "Reel of Tulloch" ("Ruidhleadh Thulachain" in Gaelic) may originally have been a "round-the-room" dance and was known in this form in the Scots-speaking areas as the "Roon aboot Hulichan." In this version of the reel, the dancers form a circle, facing partners around the room.

The setting steps for both the "Reel of Tulloch" and the common reel are drawn from the same pool; those for the Strathspey reel are equally varied but involve more "round the leg" movements (similar to the Highland Fling "shedding" steps described below) and, as mentioned above, are more deliberate and elegant in style. The steps involved include movements similar to the *balancé, pas de basque, bourrée,* and *pied croisée* of ballet, and more traditionally Celtic steps such as shakes and rocking. The body is allowed little movement except while traveling in the Reel figure, when it must rotate so that partners pass back to back, the arms held in second position, the fingers with thumb and middle finger in contact as for snapping (from which custom this position of the fingers probably derives).

Another social dance in this tradition was a couples dance in the Strathspey style called the Strathspey minuet in the eighteenth century. No record of the execution of this dance survives except that it had the figure of the minuet and was danced in Strathspey style presumably to Strathspey reel music. Indeed one finds this dance referred to simply as a strathspey, just as later the Strathspey reel or the country-dance strathspey have come to be called strathspeys. Couples dances were called "twasomes" in Scotland, and there is reference to "twasomes" performed in the eighteenth century to various dance rhythms (rant, Scottish measure, and jig). The Highland schottische, which entered the ballroom repertory in the nineteenth century, involved strathspey steps and was performed to the Strathspey-style tunes in 2/4 rhythm familiar in Hebridean music, or to what could be called Highland Fling tunes (strathspeys in 4/4 time with accents on the first and third beats).

Two forms of the Scotch reel that survive in Cape Breton, Canada—the four-handed and eight-handed reels or, in Gaelic, *ruidhleadh beag* ("small reel") and *ruidhleadh mór* ("big reel")—were carried there by the early settlers from the Western Isles. In these, instead of the Reel figure, the dancers travel in a circle, the men moving into the center to face their partners on the periphery for the setting (in this case, hornpipe stepping,

GREAT BRITAIN: Scottish Folk and Traditional Dance. Taking a break from their spinning party, known as "a rocking," two women and their partners perform a reel in a kitchen. This engraving is by H. Robinson after A. Maclure's c.1840 painting. (Photograph courtesy of George S. Emmerson.)

GREAT BRITAIN: Scottish Folk and Traditional Dance. In dancing the reel, these dancers are using the strathspey traveling step to perform a figure known as Eight Hands Round. (Photograph courtesy of George S. Emmerson.)

such as hard-shoe trebles). In contrast to the Highland reels, which reach back several centuries, the eightsome reel, now the most widely practiced and recognized Scottish social dance, is comparatively young. It is a creation of the 1870s and involves four couples in square formation dancing to common-time reel-style tunes such as "Devil in the Kitchen."

Another popular reel, "Strip the Willow," belongs to a different tradition: it is a ballroom adaptation for four couples in longwise country-dance style of a folk dance that emulates the operations of weaving. Both this reel and another (very different) Scottish weaving folk dance collected in Canada, the "Hebridean Weaving Lilt," were originally performed with a running step, also called Strip the Willow, in a 9/8 jig rhythm. A favorite tune for this dance is the Irish "Drops of Brandy," by which name the dance itself is known in England. However, in Scotland it is now performed at social dances to a 6/8 jig. Another old surviving reel in this genre is the "Foula Reel," also danced to a jig tune.

Other reels that have been collected include "The Eight of Moidart," "The Dannsa Mór from Eigg," the "Axum Reel," the "Oxton Reel," the "Pin Reel," and "Macdonald of Sleat." In Shetland, another family of reels survives under the name *Shetland reels*. A number of pantomimic folk reels survived in the Hebrides until about the beginning of the present century, such as "Cath nan Coileach" (Combat of the Cocks), the "Reel of the Black Cocks," and others.

Reels of this kind evoke archaic Gaelic society and are likely to be of ancient lineage. [*See* Reel.]

Highland solo dances. Although reels were usually performed as social rather than display dances, the Highland tradition also produced a number of solo dances, some of which came to wider attention through competitions designed to preserve and foster them. In the early nineteenth century, sequences of Strathspey reel setting steps came to be called "Highland flings" when performed by a soloist. There is no Gaelic name for this; the term *Highland fling* first appears in the eighteenth century, with reference to a class of dance step. A Strathspey reel tune of an unusual type entitled "The Marquis of Huntly's Highland Fling" was composed by Jenkins around 1800, and a dance of that name is mentioned in 1831 and described in detail in a manuscript dated 1841 found in Aberdeen. Other specific sequences of strathspey steps were developed by dancers or dancing masters and given specific names—this or that "Highland fling"—but the details of these have not been preserved.

There were numerous Highland fling steps, with regional and popular variations in style and technique that reflected the creativity of the performers, whose only constraint was that the steps must share the common character recognizable as a "fling style," rather than any prescribed "correct" technique. The most common practice was a six-step sequence. The standardized structure, sanctioned by the Scottish Official Board of Highland Dancing

(SOBHD) in 1955, prescribed the first and last steps as the "first shedding" and the "last shedding." The remaining four steps are drawn, at the dancer's discretion, from a pool of other approved steps. "Shedding" is a kind of beat, a close movement of the working foot with the heel touching just below the knee, from calf to shin bone and back.

The SOBHD was formed to establish a standard for the Fling and other Highland dances then involved in competitive dancing. The board produced a textbook defining these steps in great detail, and to this day dancers competing under the auspices of the SOBHD are obliged to adhere to it strictly. The board has obtained control of nearly all Highland dance competitions in the British Isles and to a great extent those conducted in other countries with the exception of New Zealand, where dancers cultivate another strain of the tradition. Instead of rejoicing in this diversity, the SOBHD now seems to resent it. Such standardization greatly assists objectivity in judging competitions (a notoriously subjective process), but at the price of discarding a considerable repertory of steps and styles that have traditional legitimacy commensurate with those chosen for official sanction. Efforts are currently being made to recover the abandoned portion of the traditional dance heritage that can still be found in the recollections of past practitioners.

Solo dancing by talented dancers, both men and women, is of much older lineage than the modern competitions. In earlier times these dances were usually dramatic. The "Sean Triubhas" is clearly in this tradition: when kilts were banned by the English, Scotsmen were obliged to wear trousers; when the ban was lifted, *sean triubhas* ("old trousers") were discarded. The dance, which lends itself to bold leg movements, was probably originally done to the tune "Sean Triubhas Willichean" (Willie's Old Trousers), which is a slow rant or Scottish measure of a type sometimes called a double hornpipe in the eighteenth century. The tune that has come to be preferred for the dance, however, "Whistle o'er the Lave o' t" (also a Scottish measure), is often played Strathspey style.

The other conspicuous solo dance in the Highland tradition is a dance over crossed swords commonly called the "Sword Dance." Since only warriors wielded swords, the dance has obvious military connotations, but its performance was not traditionally restricted to military events as some Romantic writers imply. The dance is also called "Gille Calluim," after the name of the tune to which it is usually performed. This name can be translated as "boy (or servant) Columba (or Malcolm)," which suggests that the dance alludes to Saint Columba, a Christian missionary who established a great center of Christendom on the island of Iona in the sixth century, or to one of the three kings named Malcolm in medieval Scotland. Whatever the ritualistic or political origins of the symbolism of this dance, it first appears as a dance over sticks or cloths or a bonnet as part of the "cushion dance" ritual—the latter a dance that is as much English as Scottish. The cushion dance was generally called "Babbity Bowster" or "Bee Baw Babbity" in Scotland, but had many other local names and forms throughout the British Isles.

In "Babbity Bowster" the company was arranged in a circle. The first man danced around carrying a handkerchief or cushion (bolster) or bonnet, which he placed on the floor opposite the lady of his choice. Both knelt upon it and kissed; then the lady tossed the bonnet or handkerchief or cushion toward some man of her choice, who then had to pick it up and kiss the lady, and so on, until all were on the floor. The last person reversed the process by kneeling on the cloth before a selected partner, kissing as before, then leaving the ring, and so on, until all the dancers had dispersed. The cushion dance was used as a "finishing dance" at balls to end the evening. A popular version of this in some regions of Scotland was the ninesome reel, or "The Bumpkin," performed to a jig tune.

"Gille Calluim" was incorporated into the kissing reel by having each leading dancer perform a few steps over the cloth or bonnet, or over two sticks laid across it. The archaic nature of the tune, among other evidence, suggests that this dance over sticks or swords or cloths is very old, and may once have been part of a long-forgotten ritual dance. It is possible that the use of swords was a later adaptation of a custom originally unrelated to the cushion dance.

In a similar sword dance, first mentioned early in the eighteenth century, a solo dancer (male, in the warrior tradition) danced over a single sword, then brandished it in various figures; this was called "Mac an Fhorsair" (Macpherson) or sometimes the "Broadsword Exercise." Sometimes, certainly by 1800, two dancers would dance over the same sword or swords (the "Double Sword Dance"), or four dancers would perform to strathspey music over four swords arranged in the form of a cross ("Argyll Broadswords," a favorite nineteenth-century regimental dance). Other sword dances have been "collected" and published, but their history is obscure. Aside from their distant connection with cushion dances, the sword dances are all without doubt originally for men, as was a dirk dance that survived into the nineteenth century, called "Phadric MacCombish's Dirk," in which two men simulated a fight with long, straight daggers, or dirks. The dance had a death-and-resurrection motif familiar to folklorists.

Two eighteenth-century step dances known in Scotland but belonging rather to the tradition of English hornpipe stepping are "The Earl of Errol" and "The King of Sweden." The former is suspected to be the work of the celebrated Aberdeen dancing master and musician Francis Peacock. Both are now performed with soft shoes. Among Peacock's claims to celebrity is his book on dancing published in 1805, in which the very earliest details of the execution of the Scotch reel are to be found. The steps he describes are the barest rudiments of the many variations on them that were current even in his time and bear but slight resemblance to the marvelous variety of reel steps known today.

This wealth of variations on the basic steps, and the evident balletic affinities of Highland dance, probably owes something to the influence of European, and especially French Baroque, dance forms. Powerful families such as the Huntly-Gordons of Strathspey may have begun to bring French dancing masters to Scotland as early as the seventeenth century. Certainly, by the next century, the professional dancing masters of the principal towns and districts, some of them itinerant, all claimed French training. Nowhere, we are told by the English chronicler Topham, writing in 1776, was dancing so much a part of polite education as in Edinburgh. In a century that saw dance assemblies flourish all over England, this indeed was saying something. Nonetheless, many of the greatest contributors to the evolution of Highland dance into the sophisticated art form we know today continued to be now-unknown dancers in the remote regions among the mountains and islands.

Other Scottish dances in the Highland dance tradition. A number of the step dances now sometimes classified as national dances have mostly been devised within the past 150 years. These include "Hielan' Laddie," first mentioned early in the nineteenth century and formerly known in several versions, as well as "Tullochgorm," "O'er the Water to Charlie," and "Blue Bonnets," all still performed, which are attributed to Ewen

MacLachlan (died 1885), a native of South Uist who allegedly studied in France. Other dances in this category still studied, and of unknown authorship, include "Wiltu Gang tae the Barracks, Johnnie?," "Miss Forbes," "Scotch Lilt," "The Three Graces," "The Village Maid," and "Flora Macdonald's Fancy," which is now a well-established dance for women. Most of these are in jig or triple rhythm, unlike older Highland dances, which were performed to strathspey or reel tunes.

Country Reels and Country Dances. Beyond its strict use to refer to the set and step dances detailed above, the word *reel* in Scotland is also a generic term for any social dance performed by groups of people in sets or rings or lines. Most folk reels in Scotland and England belong to this category. Dances that involved more than the basic Reel figure or Hey developed in some profusion over the years, particularly in England and in the Scottish Lowland regions most exposed to northern English culture (the east coast burghs and townships), where they were sometimes called *licht* ("light") dances, as opposed to courtly dances. The *licht* dances were sprinkled with a few *bassedanses* and Italian *contrapassi*, which probably filtered down from the court. Courtly dances in Scotland, however, borrowed very little reciprocally from the native folk tradition. All the European royal courts emulated the French or Italians in dancing matters, and the Scottish court (stationed mainly at palaces in Edinburgh and the adjacent regions of Falkland, Linlithgow, and Stirling) was no exception.

Figured *licht* dances—rounds, squares, and longwise dances—which lent themselves to development through

GREAT BRITAIN: Scottish Folk and Traditional Dance. "Gille Calluim" was originally danced while negotiating a bonnet or two sticks. Now danced over two swords, the "Gille Calluim," or "Sword Dance," is included in all Highland dance competitions. (Photograph courtesy of George S. Emmerson.)

GREAT BRITAIN: Scottish Folk and Traditional Dance. Highland Dance competitions were originally organized for men only, but women have been involved in competitive dance since World War I. The jig called "Flora Macdonald's Fancy," was included to expand the repertory specifically meant for women. Here, three women perform the jig at the Gaelic College of Celtic Arts and Crafts, Saint Ann's, Nova Scotia. (Photograph courtesy of George S. Emmerson.)

the permutation of their figures and the variation of their accompanying tunes, proliferated particularly in England where, in Queen Elizabeth's time, they began to be welcomed at court and were called "country dances." By the time the Scottish and English courts were united in 1603, these dances had become important in the festivities of the upper classes and were cultivated by the court dancing masters. So highly favored became this diversion that books of country dances were published in England from about 1651, first by the Playfords, father and son, publishers to the Inns of Court, then by others until well into the nineteenth century.

Though fashions changed, the longwise dance with a progression feature, which was the basic English country dance configuration, became dominant in late seventeenth-century England and spread to the fashionable centers of Europe, including the Scottish Lowlands, as the "English country dance." The longwise configuration was made up of couples arranged in two lines facing each other, men on one side, women on the other. Usually, but not always, they would be divided into "sets" of four couples. The dance comprised a selection of figures, which required the first couple (at the top end of the set) to dance with each other and, usually, with the second and perhaps the third couple, depending on the nature of the figure. The fourth couple did not dance initially. At some point, the dance would include a figure that resulted in the first and second couples changing places—this was termed the "progression." By virtue of the progression, the next time through the dance, the first couple would repeat the same sequence of figures, engaging the third and fourth cou-

ples, with the original second couple at rest at the top of the set. The sequence was then repeated until all couples had danced at each position. The progression feature allowed each couple to dance with all the others in both a lead and a supporting role. The technique of execution was arbitrary for the most part, subject to current dancing styles, although Playford described some basic movements. When dancing country dances set to the Scottish reel tunes, Scots presumably used the setting and traveling steps of their familiar native reels. Such was the dance peculiarly called "country dance" in eighteenth-century Scotland.

The country dances in Scotland became popular in the assembly rooms (ballrooms) patronized by aristocrats and the professional classes, most notably in Edinburgh, where exposure to English court fashions was most pronounced after the union of the two crowns. The assembly rooms, some built by social clubs, became commonplace in the latter half of the eighteenth century in cities and towns throughout Scotland and England. The landed gentry from other regions visited the larger centers and carried these new fashions back home to their estates, where they were introduced to the local populations, who applied their own music, steps, and tastes to the basic country-dance format. Dancing masters traveled to these new markets and reinforced the form's growing popularity. In this way country dance evolved with a distinctive Scottish character in steps and music, which in turn became popular at the urban Scottish assemblies and then worked its way back south to London. There country dance with a strong Scottish flavor became so popular that Scottish musicians were engaged at such prominent establishments as Almack's.

Despite its considerable popularity, Scottish country dance was in decline as the twentieth century dawned, the victim of the social upheavals of the industrial revolution and the demise of the festivals of the agricultural calendar in rural areas. The form would have continued to erode except for the efforts of a small group led by Ysobel Stewart of Fasnacloich, Jean Milligan, and Michael Diack, who founded the Scottish Country Dance Society in Glasgow in 1923. The society embarked on the task of restoring and preserving the Scottish Country Dance (as it now came to be called), along with the authentic Scottish reels, which had been increasingly abused or forgotten. The Country Dance reentered the Scottish dance environment as a ballroom social dance, and it is in this format that it has been restored in Scotland and abroad. In the main, Scottish Country Dances are performed today to indigenous reel music, with many Irish importations in the same tradition, but also to jigs and common-time hornpipes of various origins, originally devised for stage dancing.

Morris Dance. Morris dancing and, to a lesser extent, ritual sword dancing, were known in medieval Scotland, at least in the principal towns. One Morris (the "Perth Glovers' Dance") survived in Perth well into the seventeenth century, but the only surviving ritual sword dance is that called "Papa Stour" in Shetland. Since the ritualistic dances and associated revelries in spring and winter were proscribed by the church and subsequently by the lay authorities after the Reformation, they have virtually disappeared.

Highland Dance Competitions. Highland Dance competitions arose from the demonstrations of dance presented as interludes in the first formal bagpipe competitions. These were organized under the auspices of the Highland Society of London, first at the Falkirk Tryste (or annual cattle fair), then in Edinburgh. The first dancers in these contests were the pipers themselves, and the earliest dances mentioned are the Scotch Reel and the Strathspey Twasome, both performed by men only. Soon prizes were offered for the dancing as well as for the piping, and the separate competitions devoted to dance that grew out of these piping contests are largely responsible for fostering and preserving the Highland dance tradition we know today. Since women did not compete publicly in the nineteenth century, only male dancers and the male aspect of the dances were developed at first. Dance competitions also played a prominent part in the Highland games from their inception in the early nineteenth century.

Although the "Reel of Tulloch" was introduced rather early, it was not until about 1840 that the "Highland Fling" was included in the competitions. The "Sword Dance" is also first noted around 1840, "Sean Triubhas" somewhat

later. These three, of course, have been the basic competition dances for the past hundred years. The dress of the competitors was originally that of the Highland regiments: kilt, plaid, hair sporran, feather bonnet, and diced (checkered) hose, which have since been augmented with an evening doublet (short jacket). Boys and girls have competed in separate divisions since children's competitions were introduced in the early twentieth century. Adult women were first allowed to compete after World War I. The dances and the dance style established by the male competitors for over a century prevailed however, and the children and adult female competitors adopted a counterfeit version of the male dress, including the kilt, and emulated their male counterparts in the execution of the dances. By the 1930s, female dominance of competitive Highland dancing was well established, although certain of the Highland games, such as Braemar and Aboyn, did not allow women to compete until the 1960s or 1970s, by which time alternative female dress had been devised, one version by the Aboyn games authorities and another by the SOBHD. The inclusion of the jig "Flora Macdonald's Fancy" (traceable to the nineteenth century) expanded the repertory to accommodate women more appropriately.

The "Irish Jig" and "Sailor's Hornpipe." Two character step dances have long been included in the fare of Scottish Highland dance schools: the "Irish Jig" and the "Sailor's Hornpipe." The competition "Irish Jig" is not a classical Irish jig but a dramatic jig in the character of an irate Irish washerwoman or male peasant, complete with *shillelagh* (a wooden club), performed to the marvelous Irish pipe jig tune "The Irish Washerwoman," with its several variations. The "Sailor's Hornpipe" is a similar dance featuring the character Jacky Tar, a folkloric sailor figure. It has been in the Scottish dance school repertory since the late eighteenth century, when "Jack ashore" was a recurrent theme in London theater entr'acte dances. Many of the tunes used for this dance (such as "Fishar's Hornpipe," "Aldridge's Hornpipe," and "Durang's Hornpipe") are named after stage dancers. Despite the similarity of this kind of common-time hornpipe tune to certain Scottish prototypes, and although the dance's original tune, "Come Ashore, Jolly Tar," is Scottish, there is nothing Scottish about the dance itself. Highland dancers find this hornpipe excellent exercise, however, good for foot and leg control, and have numbered many great exponents of the dance among them. John Durang introduced it to America. It is frequently embraced in the competitions organized by some Highland games authorities simply because so many competitive Highland dancers study it. [*See* Hornpipe.]

BIBLIOGRAPHY
Clement, Bill. *The Argyll Broadswords*. Edinburgh, 1994.
Emmerson, George S. *Rantin' Pipe and Tremblin' String: A Social History of Scottish Dance Music*. London, 1971.

Emmerson, George S. *A Social History of Scottish Dance*. London, 1972.

Emmerson, George S. *A Handbook of Traditional Scottish Dance*. Oakville, Ontario, 1995.

Emmerson, George S. *Scottish Country Dancing—An Evolutionary Triumph*. Oakville, Ontario, 1997.

Flett, J. F., and T. M. Flett. *Traditional Dancing in Scotland*. London, 1964.

Forbes, Ewan. *The Dancers of Don*. Aberdeen, 1989.

Highland Dancing: The Textbook of the Scottish Official Board of Highland Dancing. 6th ed. Glasgow, 1993.

Maclennan, D. G. *Traditional and Highland Scottish Dances* (1950–1953). Bruceton Mills, W. Va., 1988.

Peacock, Francis. *Sketches Relative to the History and Theory but More Especially to the Practice and Art of Dancing*. Aberdeen, 1805.

Pilling, F. L. *Scottish Country Dances in Diagrams*. 6th ed. London, 1994.

Williams, Isobel E. *Scottish Country Dancing*. Edinburgh, 1991.

GEORGE S. EMMERSON

Welsh Folk and Traditional Dance

The traditional dances of Wales are largely lost to posterity, because they have been suppressed by a ubiquitous puritanism for many generations and because no great folklorist did for Wales what Cecil Sharp did for England. Many countries went through puritanical regimes, but their dances survived or even flourished because the puritanism was imposed by unpopular governments. The Welsh, however, wholeheartedly converted to fundamentalist Protestantism and eschewed dancing. Thus, by the late nineteenth century there was little left of traditional dance to be discovered and collected. Hugh Mellor sought to piece together the remnants of the Welsh tradition in the 1920s, and his notations of twelve dances are almost the sum total of knowledge.

There is a Welsh processional Morris dance known as "Cadi Ha" that is reasonably well documented throughout Flintshire. The ceremony remains a May Day custom quite reminiscent of the Morris dances of Derbyshire. There are eight basic dancers who wear white shirt and trousers decorated with ribbons. They line up in two columns, one side wearing on their heads fox heads, with the skins hanging down behind, the other wearing women's hats decked with flowers. All dancers carry a colored handkerchief in each hand and wear pads of bells under their knees, to accentuate arm and leg movements. At the head of the two columns dance Bili, a fool dressed incongruously and carrying a stick with an inflated bladder attached, and Cadi, a man dressed as a woman. In front of the whole procession walks the tree bearer, a man carrying several large birch boughs hung with ribbons and shiny objects. The group procession goes down the street with the lines crossing back and forth at a signal from the lead dancer. Periodically the lines halt and cast out to reverse the set. Cadi and Bili dance down the middle improvising humorous steps and gestures. The main dancers dance back to back, and Bili and Cadi then dance back up the middle. The dancers cast inward to follow them, and the procession resumes.

The country dances of Wales are today very much like those of England and, indeed, some are known to be seventeenth- and eighteenth-century imports. The only strictly Welsh social dance that Mellor discovered was a reel taught him by Mrs. Gryfydd Richards of Llanover. This is a triple-column longways dance, composed of minor sets of a man and two women. The minor sets perform a number of country dance figures with a special straight hey as a chorus. Mrs. Richards remembered fifteen figures, but if all were danced serially with chorus, the performance would be more of an endurance test than an aesthetic enterprise. It may have been that figures were chosen from this store for any particular dance or that there were a number of reels conflated by the informant. Mrs. Richards also remembered a triple minor longways dance called "Rhif Wyth" (Figure Eight). It is quite similar to an English country dance.

All other Welsh folk dances known are based on English prototypes, modified by changing the step and adding a few idiosyncrasies to the figures. They are mostly taken from manuscripts rather than from living informants.

BIBLIOGRAPHY

Hugh Mellor, *Welsh Dance Tunes*. London, 1935.
Hugh Mellor, *Welsh Folk Dances: An Inquiry*. London 1935.

JOHN FORREST

Manx Folk and Traditional Dance

The folk dances of the Isle of Man were rescued from obscurity and almost certain extinction by Mona Douglas, who as a child began gathering the folklore of her native island. The Manx people have both social and ceremonial dances, but the two are usually distinguished from one another by context rather than by form.

The dance "Hunt the Wren" (Helg yn Dreean) clearly illustrates the relationship between social and ceremonial dance. On Saint Stephen's Day (26 December), young men and boys traditionally chased over the countryside in search of a wren. When they caught one, they made a garlanded bower for it and carried it in triumph to their village singing the song "Hunt the Wren." That night the wren was buried by torchlight with half the wren dancers dressed as men and half as women, with one extra "woman." The odd woman was called the Widow of the Wren (Ben-treoghe yn Dreean). They danced a social dance in progressive ring formation to the tune of "Hunt the Wren." At the end of each round of the dance, the men changed partners; the odd woman insinuated herself into the circle, thus forcing another out. The same dance was also used for a social dance or a game on less ceremonial occasions.

The most uniquely Manx ceremonial dance extant is "Kings of Man" (Reeaghyn-dy-Vannin), also known as the Dirk Dance. The solo male performer lays a dirk (dagger) on the ground, dances around it, picks it up, holds it at head level where he kicks it rhythmically, lays it down again, dances around it, and finally picks it up and brandishes it vigorously, making slashes over his head and body and passing it under his legs. He finishes by kneeling, holding the dirk high.

Two linked hilt-and-point sword dances are known, but there has never been notation for them, since this is an oral tradition. At the turn of the twentieth century, the White Boys Mummers performed a six-man Sword Dance and play, perhaps akin to the long-sword dance dramas of England. For a finale the swords were woven into a seat. A character called the Doctor was put on this chair, hoisted shoulder high, and chaired out. "The Salmon Leap" was a ceremonial dance carried out by the fishermen of Dalby. There were the Skipper, Mate, and Fool, plus six dancers who carried peeled hazel rods. Figures included reels of three and the forming of a circle with the hazel rods, through which the Fool leapt. To finish, the Skipper and the Mate carried the Fool on board their fishing craft, followed by the other dancers. [For general discussion, see Sword Dance.]

A progressive longways dance called "Hollantide Processional" (Hop-tu-naa) might have been danced as a village parade dance, much like the May Day processionals of Cornwall in the southern Celtic fringe of England. Hollantide (1 November) is one of the chief Manx festivals, the others being New Year's, May Day, Midsummer's Day, harvest, and Christmas. In both the eighteenth and nineteenth centuries, the Manx people danced and sang through the nights of these holidays.

The Manx social dances are much like English country dances, but they use more complicated steps. The set formations are longways, square, and round for four, six, eight, or as many as will. As is generally true of the Celtic border dances of England, these dances are energetic and exacting in their proper execution.

BIBLIOGRAPHY

Douglas, Mona. *Five Manx Folk Dances*. London, 1936.
Douglas, Mona. "Manx Folk Dances: Their Notation and Revival." *Journal of the English Folk Dance and Song Society* 3.2 (1937): 110–116.
Douglas, Mona. *Seven Manx Folk Dances* London, 1953.
Douglas, Mona. *Manx Folk-Song, Folk Dance, Folklore: Collected Writings*. Edited by Stephen Miller. Onchan, Isle of Man, 1994.

JOHN FORREST

Theatrical Dance, 1460–1660

Dance was an essential part of English town and country seasonal festivals, of disguisings and mummings, and of masques, likely introduced from Italy into Henry VIII's court in 1512. Our knowledge of the use of dance in surviving English medieval plays comes mostly from textual references; the plays seem to contain little dance, but what does appear often has a definite dramatic purpose. In *Wisdom* (c.1460–1470), the retinues of Mind, Will, and Understanding illustrate in three dances the perversions of their masters' natures; Mind declares, "This is the Devil's dance." In *The Killing of the Children* (*N. Town Plays*, c.1400–1500), women dance both an interlude to entertain the audience and in an act of worship, when they bring candles to the Christ child. These two examples were probably formal dances, but in the *Passion*, from the same cycle, the brief dance of the Jews around the crucified Christ was less structured. A dance included simply as entertainment in Henry Medwall's *Fulgens and Lucres* (c.1490–1500) may have been "a basse dance after the guise of Spain." Dance was more common in European medieval drama,

GREAT BRITAIN: Theatrical Dance, 1460-1660. Dance was an important element in the English masque and, under the leadership of writers such as Ben Jonson, designer Inigo Jones, and choreographers Jerome Herne, Thomas Giles, Mr. Bochan, and Mr. Confess, the masque reached its pinnacle during the reign of James I. This print shows Jones's designs for two fairies in Ben Jonson's *Masque of Oberon* (1611). (Devonshire Collection, Chatsworth; photograph used by permission of the Chatsworth Settlement Trustees.)

GREAT BRITAIN: Theatrical Dance, 1460–1660. Productions under Charles I became increasingly costly and were used as vehicles of political propaganda. This print shows an elaborate costume design by Jones for the King of Valentia, from the 1633 masque *The Shepherd's Paradise.* (Devonshire Collection, Chatsworth; photograph used by permission of the Chatsworth Settlement Trustees.)

where religious attitudes were more permissive than in England.

Some interludes that include dance survive from the Tudor period, notably the allegorical *Wit and Science* (c.1531–1534) by John Redford. It is thought to have been written for a court performance by the choristers of Saint Paul's, London. Wit, wanting to marry Science, is killed by Tediousness but is restored by Honest Recreation, whose followers dance a galliard with him, but he stupidly overexerts himself and falls into the lap of Idleness. In *Like Will to Like* (1568), the drunkard Haunce "danceth as evil favoured as may be devised, and in the dancing he falleth down."

In these moral interludes, dancing is an indulgence of vice; in later plays, it acquires a more positive connotation. With the rapid development of play writing that followed the building of the first permanent theater in 1576, dance became more popular both as an integrated part of a dramatic structure and as entertainment before, during, and after a performance. Court and perhaps country dances were performed in these settings. Jigs, step dances in which the performers mimed the action of the (frequently bawdy) ballads they were singing, were often performed after plays, even tragedies, and were popular until the early seventeenth century.

Perhaps a third of the plays written between 1560 and 1660 incorporate dance in various specific ways. Dance may entertain the characters within the play, as in John Lyly's *Campaspe* (c.1584); mark festivities, as in Shakespeare's *Romeo and Juliet* (c.1594); conclude a comedy like George Chapman's *Sir Giles Goosecap* (c.1602); or further the plot, as in John Webster's *The Duchess of Malfi* (c.1613). Dance may also be an aid to charms, as in Thomas Middleton's *The Witch* (c.1615). In Richard Brome's *The Antipodes* (c.1636), dance is part of a masque.

Like music, dance was a powerful symbol of harmony, and as such it was an important element in court masques, extravagant entertainments performed by men and women courtiers along with professional actors. Special choreography was devised for these shows, which frequently depicted the defeat of evil by virtue and were intended to glorify the monarch. They usually included dialogue, and dances and songs by grotesques (antimasques), as well as by the masquers; they ended with the revels, and a final song and dance. The entertainment often concluded with a banquet. The revels, which could continue for over an hour, formed an essential part of the occasion. The masquers took partners from the audience for unchoreographed social dances, beginning with pavans (often called the measures), and continuing with galliards, courantes, voltas, and similar quick dances. The masque ended when the masquers returned to the stage for their departure from the scene.

Masques reached their height during James I's reign (1603–1626); the greatest masques were written by Ben Jonson and designed by Inigo Jones. Dancing masters who choreographed the theatrical dances included Jerome Herne, Thomas Giles, Mr. Bochan, and Mr. Confess.

Short masques were sometimes incorporated in plays for dramatic purposes. In John Marston's *Antonio's Revenge* (c.1600), the anonymous *Revenger's Tragedy* (c.1608), and Middleton's *Women Beware Women* (c.1621), they provide a cover for revenge murders. To celebrate love and marriage, Shakespeare includes a simple masque in *As You Like It* (c.1599) and an elaborate one in *The Tempest* (c.1611).

Among the dramatists of this period, Shakespeare made the most consistent use of dance. Of his thirty-seven plays, certainly twelve and probably fifteen contain dance performances, which are usually related to the idea of establishing or maintaining order. In *A Midsummer Night's Dream* (c.1595), the fairies dance to keep evil away from the sleeping Titania; Titania and Oberon dance to mark their reconciliation after a quarrel; and finally they all dance and sing a carole through Theseus's palace to bless the lovers sleeping there. The bergamasque of Bottom the Weaver and his friends provides a mortal and comic contrast. In *Much Ado about Nothing* (c.1598), Shakespeare developed the plot through a dance while the characters speak (act 2, scene 1) and concludes the play with another. In his tragedies, he sometimes used dance ironically, usually to contrast death with love, joy, and marriage. Romeo, for example, does not dance, but he watches Juliet as she does. In *Macbeth* (c.1607), the witches dance to create an evil charm, and in *Timon of Athens* (c.1608), a masque of Amazons symbolizes the distortion of love and womanhood.

Shakespeare's romances make greater use of dance. In *The Winter's Tale* (c.1611), he turns the accepted masque form upside down, beginning with a feast, continuing with general dancing, then following the revels with songs and a satyrs' dance—the equivalent of an antimasque. The scene (act 4, scene 4) moves from harmony to disorder instead of from confusion to order. *The Tempest* (c.1611) includes an allegorical masque.

In *Henry VIII* (1613), dance serves as a dramatic context for the meeting of King Henry and Anne Boleyn and later as a vehicle for the vision of heavenly spirits that comforts the dying Queen Katharine.

Shakespeare and other contemporary dramatists seldom specify the kinds of dance for their plays. Nine knights in armor enter "treading a warlike almain" (allemande) in George Peele's *Arraignment of Paris* (c.1582), and in Marston's *Insatiate Countess* (c.1610), "Rogero dances a Lavolto, or a Galliard," but such directions are rare. It appears, however, that the pavan was often used in scenes where characters speak and dance simultaneously, especially when they move from one sequence of steps to another, as in John Ford's *The Broken Heart* (c.1629).

Dance continued to be an integral part of certain plays until the theaters were closed by Parliament in 1642. It was included in clandestine performances and private theatricals during the Commonwealth, but when plays were again allowed on the public stage after the Restoration in 1660, the symbolic relationship between dance and drama had been lost.

BIBLIOGRAPHY

Baskervill, Charles R. *The Elizabethan Jig and Related Song Drama.* Chicago, 1929.

Brissenden, Alan. "Jacobean Tragedy and the Dance." *Huntington Library Quarterly* 44.4 (1981): 249–262.

Brissenden, Alan. *Shakespeare and the Dance.* London, 1981.

Howard, Skiles. "Hands, Feet, and Bottoms: Decentering the Cosmic Dance in *A Midsummer Night's Dream.*" Shakespeare Quarterly 44.3 (1993): 325–342.

Meredith, Peter, and John Tailby. *The Staging of Religious Drama in Europe in the Middle Ages.* Kalamazoo, Mich., 1984.

Orgel, Stephen. *The Jonsonian Masque.* Cambridge, Mass., 1965.

Reyher, Paul. *Les masques anglais.* Paris, 1909.

Sutherland, Sarah P. *Masques in Jacobean Tragedy.* New York, 1983.

ALAN BRISSENDEN

Theatrical Dance, 1660–1772

Dance resumed its contribution to theatrical entertainment in England as soon as the theaters reopened after the restoration of Charles II in 1660. Until the turn of the century, however, there is little specific documentation of dance. When dancers began to achieve recognition as a separate category of performer, they began to attract more commentary. After about 1717, no London theater manager would have tried to mount a season without four or five performers who did nothing but dance.

GREAT BRITAIN: Theatrical Dance, 1660–1772. An etching depicting Nell Gwyn, a popular comedienne who was also known for her performance of entr'acte jigs. (Photograph used by permission of the Board of Trustees of the Victoria and Albert Museum, London.)

Even from the fragmentary evidence of these early years, we can construct a profile of dance activity. Social dances from two traditions appeared on stage. Native English dances of the kind John Playford had published in *The Dancing Master* (1651) remained a part of theatrical tradition throughout the period. In addition, Charles II brought back from exile a great enthusiasm for French court dance, and this more individual and formalized style also began to appear in the theater. After 1660 women actors and dancers replaced boys in female roles, making plays reflect daily life more closely—and controversially—than before. Playwrights felt free to call for dances by characters in their plays because they could assume that all actors had at least minimal social dancing skills.

Theatrical notices of the eighteenth century imply some continuity in this practice in such statements as, "To conclude with the original *Country Dance*" or "The Whole to conclude with a *Dance* by the Characters of the Play." We may assume that Henry Harris and Mary Betterton danced in Thomas Porter's *The Villain* (1662), because act 4 calls for a dance; we know from advertisements that David Garrick and others performed "a new Country dance call'd *Ranger's Frolic*" in *The Suspicious Husband* (4 December 1747). Dance was often featured in entr'acte entertainments, more to show off a favorite performer than to relate to the play being acted. But dance could also function as an integral part of plays and of the masque sequences in the so-called English operas. The "Zambra Dance" Dryden called for in act 3 of *The Conquest of Granada*, Part I (1670) is the visual high point of that play. The masques in such operas as *The Prophetess*, *King Arthur*, and *The Fairy Queen* in the early 1690s involved months of planning and collaboration by the best artists of the theater, including Betterton, Dryden, Henry Purcell, and the dancing master Josiah Priest.

From the Restoration onward, each theater company needed someone to supervise dances, and preferably to compose and teach them as well. John Lacy, who had trained with John Ogilby before the Civil War, served the King's Company in this capacity and was also a leading comic actor. His portrait was painted in the character of a stage dancing master, Galliard, in *The Variety*. His counterpart at the Duke's Company and later at the United Company seems to have been Josiah Priest, who apparently did not act. In the next century the position of ballet master was more likely to go to a dancer trained on the Continent than to an Englishman. Names such as Weaver and Thurmond are replaced by Nivelon, Lalauze, Dauberval, Poitier, Daigueville, and Sallé. However, single dances or even whole "Entertainments of Dancing" could be composed by anyone with an idea: the ballet master did not have to provide all the company's dances himself, and for many seasons he cannot even be positively identified.

Besides the social dance tradition, an element of *commedia dell'arte* can be documented from early in the period. In January 1669 the diarist Samuel Pepys mentions a rudimentary comic ballet by Lacy, the only part of which he liked was "Some Dutchmen come out of the mouth and tail of a Hamburgh sow." First-hand acquaintance with a master Scaramuccio dates from 1673, when Tiberio Fiorillo came to London for two seasons. Other *commedia* performers also crossed the channel from time to time. Their influence coalesced with other kinds of dance in the development of pantomime by John Rich after 1717.

GREAT BRITAIN: Theatrical Dance, 1660–1772. The 1711 frontispiece to the libretto of *Wit at Several Weapons*, a comedy by Beaumont and Fletcher. Pictures representing actual dance scenes from this period are extremely scarce. (Dance Collection, New York Public Library for the Performing Arts.)

During the Restoration, dance was sometimes the making of a career for a young actor trying to secure a position in the strictly monopolized world of London theater. Nell Gwynn's talent as a comedienne might never have had a chance to develop if she had not had confidence enough to do the entr'acte jigs that made her popular. Pepys's friend Mrs. Knepp, who was entrusted with important acting roles, was also a popular dancer; in January 1667 she made Pepys wait through a dance rehearsal before going out with him. Unfortunately, he says nothing more about the rehearsal, but the *Diary* does verify the practice of rehearsing dances for particular plays early in the period. Jo Haynes not only danced well enough to appear professionally in France, he was also able to compose dances. Since his acting was mostly limited to low comedy, this other skill made him more employable.

Such double careers continued to be possible early in the eighteenth century. Margaret Bicknell and Hester Booth (née Santlow) both began as dancers, then worked up to leading roles (usually in comedy), but continued to dance. Theirs are among the first dance attractions consistently advertised in the new daily papers (which began publishing in 1703, full ads about 1709); their partners were the company's top foreign male dancers. Theirs was, however, the last generation to move from dance to acting and retain top positions in both areas throughout a career. By the 1730s some stage dance had become entirely specialized in the major theaters, and even minor theaters employed some performers strictly as dancers, although the *commedia* and social traditions also continued.

The course of the separation is not easy to trace. As early as 1675 several male dancers came from France with the dancing master Adrien Merger de Saint-André to take part in an opera at court and were engaged to finish the season with the King's Company. To secure their services, John Lacy offered to pay four of them ten shillings a day when they performed and five shillings when they were not called. The first figure is comparable to the top salaries in the company at the time. Extravagant investment in such specialized performers was apparently not repeated until 1698, when at the behest of well-traveled patrons, theater managers again sought the superior technique of Académie-trained French performers. Claude Ballon, Marie-Thérèse Subligny, and Anthony L'Abbé were the first of many stars brought to London to dance, either for limited engagements or as principal performers and ballet masters. Their example and teaching contributed to the development of a class of performers trained only to dance.

Star dancers, particularly imported ones, were celebrated by the public and well paid by the theaters, but in managers' eyes dancers were still only accessory person-

GREAT BRITAIN: Theatrical Dance, 1660–1772. A women dancing the minuet. This engraving, by Louis Philippe Boitard, after Bartholomew Dandridge, was printed in F. Nivelon's *Rudiments of Genteel Behaviour* (London, 1737). Nivelon was known as a ballet master as well as an author. (Courtesy of Madison U. Sowell and Debra H. Sowell, Brigham Young University, Provo, Utah.)

nel. When playbills began to indicate star status by setting the names of some actors in capital letters, dancers' names still appeared in the ordinary format. Only occasionally was a choreographer's name mentioned, as Jean-Georges Noverre's was for *Les Fêtes Chinoises* in November 1755; no credit of any kind was given for music. When more space was needed on a bill, dancers' names were dropped, and often only a formula such as "With Dances proper to the Action" hints that anyone danced on a given day. The opera was even less likely than the theaters to name dancers. Native members of the corps de ballet not only suffered by comparison to superior guest dancers but were also considered more expendable than actors of comparable rank. The major theaters encouraged their employees to be loyal, and to switch from one company to another was a political risk. Most dancers of stature remained with one company for two or three multiyear contracts, or even for most of a career. John Rich's ballet master Charles Lalauze was with him for nearly thirty years. Dancers were at the mercy of changes in management, which they could not influence but which vitally affected both individual careers and the overall emphasis put on dance at a particular theater. Rich at Covent Garden al-

GREAT BRITAIN: Theatrical Dance, 1660–1772. This 1753 etching shows John Rich, an actor and theater manager who popularized pantomime in England. He was especially well known for his portrayal of Harlequin, a character from the *commedia dell'arte*. (Photograph used by permission of the Board of Trustees of the Theatre Museum, London.)

ways gave dance more attention than did the managers of Drury Lane, but after he stopped appearing as Lun (his Harlequin persona), he temporarily lost interest in both dance and pantomime. When Garrick took over Drury Lane in 1747, his attempts at upgrading dance rekindled Rich's competitive spirit. Garrick imported Noverre's *Les Fêtes Chinoises* and tried other experiments with *ballet d'action*, but he found that the public preferred imitations of Rich's familiar pantomimes.

In the last quarter of the eighteenth century, management of both theaters passed to men who, not themselves performers, were less interested in exploring the possibilities of dance as an art. Song began to replace dance as the chief entr'acte entertainment in the 1780s, and dancers were more and more relegated to spectacles such as *Alexander the Great* (1795), which used two hundred performers. Theaters imported fewer foreign dancers, improving opportunities for the best native talent, but local dancers never commanded equivalent salaries. At the same time, the opera worked to hire the best foreign dancers and advertised them heavily as attractions almost equal to singers. Residencies at the King's Theatre in the

Haymarket by Gaetan and Auguste Vestris, Lepicq, Dauberval, and Noverre established expectations that the opera season would include full-scale *ballets d'action* with international stars. The opera thus emerged as the appropriate home of an art which no longer had much visible connection with social dancing.

Country dance tunes with simple prose directions were published annually throughout the eighteenth century for the amusement of social dancers. Books of more formal dances by John Weaver, L'Abbé, Kellom Tomlinson, and others in the first third of the century recorded their instructions by means of orchesography, the newly developed dance notation, but they did not find enough audience to sustain publication. Tomlinson apparently expressed the minority view when he advocated teaching people not only to dance but also to read the notation. After 1742 the series *Comic Tunes* was published by Walsh in connection with imported stars, but the scores cannot be matched with orchesographic descriptions; the music gives only a general impression of accompaniment rather than the possibility of reconstructing specific dances.

Theaters advertised dances by descriptive titles such as *The Swedish Gardeners, The Masked Ball, Two Pierrots, A Coal Black Joke*, or *The Sportsman Deceived* more often than by technical terms such as *minuet, chaconne*, or *loure*. The titles have obvious audience appeal, but although they preserve picturesque detail, they obscure distinctions among types of dance. The three-level hierarchy set up by Weaver in 1712 and 1728—serious, grotesque, and scenical—is admittedly too general. Title alone does not tell us whether Tomlinson's *The Submission* was serious or grotesque, romantic or comic. Since he published both the tune and the dance notation in 1717, that particular dance can be reconstructed; but what of the "new Grand Warlike Dance with Moors" on 10 April 1730 at Lincoln's Inn Fields, "in which will be introduced a new *Polonese* by Poitier and Miss La Tour, with Poitier beating a Preamble on the Kettle Drums"? Apparently a group dance was interrupted by a drum prelude, which was followed by a different dance for a couple; the evidence does not tell us much more. We can deduce from the titles of most serious dances that they came from the French tradition, as might some of the grotesque subcategory Weaver called historical. Other grotesque dances, such as the many Pierrot, Scaramouche, and Harlequin variations, clearly came from the *commedia dell'arte* tradition. Those like *The Lunaticks* and *The Drunken Dutch Boor and his Frou* probably did also. A *commedia*-like song and dance interlude called *The Lamplighter* (Covent Garden, 18 March 1760) is preserved in the Folger Shakespeare Library, and the general trend of Rich's pantomimes can be discerned from their libretti. Generally, however, we have to depend on such external sources as Gregorio Lambranzi's *Neue und curieuse theatralische Tantz-Schul* (1716) for some idea of the Continental idiom brought to English performance by masters trained in Europe.

With the recognition of professional dancers came improvement in their status, but their increasing specialization also increased the distance between them and even the most capable social dancers in their audiences. Ordinary people were unwilling to make the effort required to learn and remember such technically difficult dances, however convenient the new notation might be. Although extant evidence suggests that the technique of English theatrical dancers steadily improved, audiences showed little interest in choreographers' attempts to tell any but the most formulaic stories in dance. Theater managers in the eighteenth century therefore settled for entertainment rather than innovation.

[*See also entries on the principal figures mentioned herein.*]

BIBLIOGRAPHY

Fiske, Roger. *English Theatre Music in the Eighteenth Century.* 2d ed. Oxford, 1986.

Fletcher, Ifan Kyrle, et al. *Famed for Dance: Essays on the Theory and Practice of Theatrical Dancing in England.* New York, 1960.

Goff, Moira, and Jennifer Thorp. "Dance Notations Published in England, c. 1700–1740." *Dance Research* 9 (Autumn 1991): 32–50.

Goff, Moira. "Dancing-Masters in Early Eighteenth-Century London." *Historical Dance* 3.3 (1994): 17–23.

Hilton, Wendy. *Dance of Court and Theatre: The French Noble Style, 1690–1725.* Princeton, 1981.

Lambranzi, Gregorio. *Neue und curieuse theatralische Tantz-Schul. Deliciae theatrales.* Nuremburg, 1716. Translated by Friderica Derra de Moroda as *New and Curious School of Theatrical Dancing* (London, 1928).

Milhous, Judith. "'Hasse's' Comic Tunes: Some Dancers and Dance Music on the London Stage, 1740–59." *Dance Research* 2 (Summer 1984): 41–55.

Milhous, Judith. "Dancers' Contracts at the Pantheon Opera House, 1790–1792." *Dance Research* 9 (1991): 51–75.

Milhous, Judith. "David Garrick and the Dancing Master's Apprentice." *Dance Research* 9 (Spring 1991): 13–25.

Milhous, Judith. "Vestris-mania and the Construction of Celebrity: Auguste Vestris in London, 1780–81." *Harvard Library Bulletin* n.s. 5 (Winter, 1994–1995): 30–64.

Milhous, Judith, and Robert D. Hume. "Opera Salaries in Eighteenth-Century London." *Journal of the American Musicological Society* 66 (1993): 26–83.

Price, Curtis A. "Restoration Stage Fiddlers and Their Music." *Early Music* 7 (1979).

Price, Curtis, Judith Milhous, and Robert D. Hume. *Italian Opera in Late Eighteenth-Century London.* Volume I: *The King's Theatre, Haymarket, 1778–1791.* Oxford, 1995.

Ralph, Richard. *The Life and Works of John Weaver.* London, 1985.

Tomlinson, Kellom. *Six Dances.* London, 1720.

Tomlinson, Kellom. *The Art of Dancing Explained by Reading and Figures.* 2 vols. London, 1735.

Van Lennep, William, et al., eds. *The London Stage, 1660–1800.* 5 vols. in 11. Carbondale, Ill., 1960–1968.

Weaver, John. *An Essay towards an History of Dancing.* London, 1712.

Weaver, John. *The History of the Mimes and Pantomimes.* London, 1728.

Winter, Marian Hannah. *The Pre-Romantic Ballet.* London, 1974.

JUDITH MILHOUS

Theatrical Dance, 1772–1850

From 1772, when it first offered opera audiences a full-length ballet, the King's Theatre in London was the center for ballet in Great Britain, and so it remained until after 1850. That first ballet, a production of Jean-Georges Noverre's *Admète et Alceste* (a classical myth about King Admetus who wins Alcestis by driving a chariot drawn by lions and bears), was typical of ballets of this period in its adoption of European, and especially French, styles of both production and dancing. With no school and no court tradition of ballet dancing in England, the King's Theatre was forced to seek ballet masters and performers from abroad.

From the first, ballet at the King's took two basic approaches: one in which dramatic content was the focal point, and the other in which dancing was most important. This division was common all over Europe. Ballet emphasizing drama, known as *ballet d'action*, was relatively new. Ballet emphasizing dance, the *divertissement*, was of much longer history.

The first ballet at the King's in 1772—produced by the ballet master Lépy, who had been with Noverre in Stuttgart in 1761—paved the way for *ballet d'action* in England. Another Noverre ballet, *Médée et Jason* (based upon the classical story in which Medea exacts terrible revenge upon the faithless Jason), produced by Gaëtan Vestris in 1781, was performed by Giovanna Baccelli, who demonstrated the powers of expressive interpretation. Her performance of the dying Creusa, one critic observed, "might serve as an useful lesson to our best tragedians." Until the end of the 1820s, a performer's silent acting skills were often rated more highly than dancing prowess.

Noverre spent five years as ballet master in London, from 1782 to 1794, during which he presented both *ballets d'action* and *divertissements*. His success was mixed. The 1788 season, for example, was poorly received; *Les Fêtes du Tempe*, a *divertissement*, drew the comment, "Nothing can come of nothing." The 1793 season was much more successful, highlighted as it was by the strikingly dramatic *Iphigénia in Aulide*.

Two choreographers rivaled Noverre before 1800: Sébastien Gallet (ballet master 1797/98, 1803) and the brilliant Jean Dauberval (ballet master 1784, 1791/92). Dauberval's unique talent lay in his ability to integrate dances with the story so that they actually furthered the dramatic action, an achievement that eluded other ballet masters, who usually relied on silent acting to convey the plot. *La Fille Mal Gardée* (first performed in England in 1791) and *Le Déserteur* (1784), a dramatic ballet in which the lover is saved from a firing squad at the last possible instant, were popular favorites demonstrating the potential of pastoral and sentimental themes, as well as the dramatic power of dancing. They stood in contrast to Noverre's grand historical and mythological subjects, which were taken from fashionable neoclassical sources.

Gallet was admired in London for his clear and original stories. His *Ariadne et Bacchus*, produced in 1797, was considered by one critic to be "superior to any ever before exhibited; it engaged the heart by the passion of its fable, and affords an unrivalled feast to the senses." His *Pizarre*

GREAT BRITAIN: Theatrical Dance, 1772–1850. Marie Taglioni's performances in England helped revive interest in ballet. This lithograph, after Alfred Chalon, shows her in *La Bayadère*, presented at the King's Theatre, London, in 1831. This ballet was a shortened version of Filippo Taglioni's staging of Daniel Auber's opera, *Le Dieu et la Bayadère*, which premiered in Paris in 1830. (Courtesy of Madison U. Sowell and Debra H. Sowell, Brigham Young University, Provo, Utah.)

GREAT BRITAIN: Theatrical Dance, 1772–1850. Without a court tradition of ballet or a school to train dancers, the King's Theatre, London, often sought ballet masters and dancers from abroad. Here are depicted the Italians Paolo Samengo and Amalia Brugnoli, husband and wife, as they appeared in *L'Anneau Magique* in 1832. This lithograph, printed the same year, is by Levasseur. (Courtesy of Madison U. Sowell and Debra H. Sowell, Brigham Young University, Provo, Utah.)

(1797) and *Constance et Alcidonis* (1798) won similar praises, and *L'Offrande à Terpsichore* (1797) displayed his talent for creating charming *divertissements*.

The quality of dancing varied considerably during those years. Before the First Coalition's declaration of war against France in 1793, artists moved freely from Europe to England. Madame Rossi, Mademoiselle Théodore (Dauberval's wife), Gaëtan Vestris, and Auguste Vestris were all at the King's for several seasons between 1781 and 1791. During the years of the French Revolution and First Empire, interchange was not so easy, though London did have some good dancers—Rose Didelot, Madame Hilligsberg, Mademoiselle Parisot, and Monsieur Laboire, as well as Jean-Jacques André Deshayes and Charles-Louis Didelot, the last two returning later in their careers as ballet masters.

Such dancers performed in a traditional expressive style that was slowly being eclipsed by an emphasis on virtuoso demonstrations of spins, jumps, leg extensions, and rapid footwork. Upon Parisot's retirement, one critic recorded the qualities of the traditional style that her dancing epitomized: "Her style, in fact constituted what may be called the Epic of Dancing—she elevated, she surprised, she enraptured . . . she reminded us of a superior order of beings to the character she represented." A dancer such as Armand Vestris, in contrast, sought to astonish audiences with his *tours de force*. Many observers found such an emphasis meaningless and often lacking in grace, for the feats had not been mastered. In 1825 the *Morning Herald* wrote, "too much of exhibiting the human frame in unnatural attitudes, according to the modern French school, and too much of the eternal pirouetting." After the retirement of Deshayes in 1811, there were no major dancers to perpetuate the "Epic of Dancing," though lesser artists, such as Madame Anatole, did keep old memories alive.

Technically oriented dancing favors the *divertissement* ballet, in which dancing is presented for its own sake. Yet ballet masters continued to create *ballets d'action*. The English ballet master James Harvey D'Egville, for example, created a large number of ballets in this genre—*Pigmalion* (1801), *Achille et Déidamie* (1804), and *Le Siège de Cythère* (1827; a theme that had been treated by Dauberval in 1791). It was not that he could not choreograph good dances, for D'Egville did this in *divertissements* such as *La Fête Chinoise* (1808) and *Le Bal Champêtre* (1826). He simply valued his grand dramatic ballets more. So strong were ballet masters' orientations toward dramatic action that they were accused of plagiarizing, not choreographies, but stories. D'Egville was also a teacher whose school might have given London its own ballet company if intrigue at the King's Theatre had not led to his dismissal in 1809—and if English audiences had not preferred French dancers.

During the first fifteen years of the nineteenth century, ballet was presented to a high standard at the King's and became fashionable to the point of rivaling the opera in popularity. Highlights were the Deshayes-Vestris dancing rivalry of 1809 and Didelot's seasons as ballet master from 1812 to 1814. After the 1815 financial disasters, during which two king's managers were sent to debtors' prison and British audience interest was low, ballet came to a sorry state. The appearance of Marie Taglioni between 1830 and 1847 revived British enthusiasm for ballet, which grew as more great dancers arrived—Fanny Elssler, Carlotta Grisi, and the very popular Fanny Cerrito; only

GREAT BRITAIN: Theatrical Dance, 1772–1850. Carlotta Grisi and Jules Perrot (center) in a scene from *Le Rossignol*, which premiered on 5 March 1836 at the King's Theatre, London. Published on 1 June 1836, this was the first English print to represent the pair. It was drawn and etched by T. Jones and aquatinted by George Hunt. (Courtesy of Madison U. Sowell and Debra H. Sowell, Brigham Young University, Provo, Utah.)

the very best males were tolerated—Jules Perrot, Paul Taglioni, and Arthur Saint-Léon. So popular were the female dancers that males, even the very best, were considered by many unfit to perform.

Marie Taglioni's brilliant achievement was to reintroduce the traditional emphasis on grace and elegance and to impart to her dance a sense of ease and naturalness that had not been seen before. The *Court Journal* wrote that she brought in a "new era. . . . Her dancing is the natural movement of the female form, refined into poetry." Taglioni, Elssler, Grisi, and Cerrito all possessed the ability to perform even the most difficult movements without apparent effort. This was the foundation upon which they built their unique styles.

In the 1830s and 1840s ballet masters utilized the new dance style to give expression to the fashionable themes of romance, exoticism, and adventure. Marie's father, Filippo Taglioni, although he created Romantic symbolism in ballet with *La Sylphide*, which premiered in London in 1833, failed to create another masterpiece; neither his *Sire Huon* (1834), based on Carl Maria von Weber's opera *Oberon*, nor his *Mazilia* (1835), about a tribe of women who have sworn eternal hatred to men, were impressive.

The great dancer Deshayes became a far more successful ballet master than did Taglioni. He achieved considerable popularity with ballets such as *Masaniello* (1829), *Kenilworth* (1831), *Faust* (1833), *Beniowsky* (1836), and *Le Brigand de Terracina* (1837). These works were based on themes redolent with local color, presenting monumental romantic scenic effects—the great rock chasm into which the villain plunges in *Le Brigand* and the immense staircase stretching from hell (the stage) to heaven (the flies) in *Faust*. His tales of bandits, rebels, love, tragedy, and heroic deeds were similar to those chosen by the younger Jules Perrot, who became popular during the 1840s. His ballets were still based on *ballet d'action* models, many of the dramatic roles being performed by dancers who emphasized silent acting skills.

It was Perrot who demonstrated much of the potential of the Romantic ballet. In productions such as *Giselle* (London, 1842), the new and poetic style of dancing was used to set the atmosphere of a place and to aid in telling the story. Perrot's best works were masterpieces of dramatic expression in which all elements contributed to the general effect—*Ondine* (1843), with its showpiece *pas de l'ombre* for Cerrito; *La Esmeralda* (1844); and *Lalla Rookh* (1846). A *Morning Post* review of *Ondine* observed: "In the new ballet . . . all the *pas* are interwoven with the subject, and generally all the personnages on the stage are engaged in the moving incidents of the scene—an immense improvement."

It was not only the dramatic ballet but also the *divertissement* that found a special form in the hands of Perrot. For many years the *divertissement* ballet had been out of fashion. Great female dancers performed within the context of a story ballet (though audiences devoted little attention to the ballet in their adoration of their dancing goddesses). Perrot, with some encouragement from the theater manager Benjamin Lumley, produced several dances in which there were no stories, presenting dance for the sake of dance. These showpieces for the dancers included *Pas de Quatre* (1845), performed by Taglioni, Cerrito, Grisi, and Lucile Grahn; *Le Jugement de Pâris* (1846), performed by Taglioni, Cerrito, and Grahn; *Les Éléments* (1847), performed by Cerrito, Grisi, and Rosati; and *Les Quatre Saisons* (1848) performed by Cerrito, Grisi, Carolina Rosati, and Marie Taglioni the younger. They had no pretensions to meaning over and above the beauty of pure dance. Yet for the first time people were willing to approach such *divertissements* as works of art in their own right, not just means of pleasing the senses. The *Morning Herald* commented that Perrot would have proven himself an artist if he had done no other works, and it praised the harmony and ensemble of the composition. Until this time, such an aesthetic evaluation of pure dancing was unknown.

Through its encouragement of Perrot, the dance community in London began to rival that of Paris, for the grand, prestigious Paris Opera excluded him. Shortly after the achievements of Perrot, however, London's ballet interest rapidly declined. When Taglioni, Elssler, Grisi, and Cerrito retired, no successor of equal talent appeared, and audiences once again turned to opera. In the end, London proved to be what it had always been, a capricious consumer of the art of ballet, unable to sustain interest.

[See also the entries on the principal figures mentioned herein.]

BIBLIOGRAPHY

Chaffee, George. "The Romantic Ballet in London, 1821–1858." *Dance Index* 2 (September–December 1943): 120–199.

Chapman, John V. "Ballet and the Box Office in Regency Days." *The Dancing Times* (January 1978): 208–209.

Chapman, John V. "British Ballet Criticism in London, 1785–1850." In *Dance Spectrum*, edited by Diana Theodores Taplin. Waterloo, Ont., 1982.

Chapman, John V. "The Lot of the Dancer: London, 1830–1831." In *Proceedings of the Tenth Annual Conference, Society of Dance History Scholars, University of California, Irvine, 13–15 February 1987*, compiled by Christena L. Schlundt. Riverside, Calif., 1987.

Fenner, Theodore. "Ballet in Early Nineteenth-Century London as Seen by Leigh Hunt and Henry Robertson." *Dance Chronicle* 1.2 (1978): 75–95.

Guest, Ivor. *The Romantic Ballet in England*. London, 1972.

Guest, Ivor. *Jules Perrot*. London, 1984.

Guest, Ivor. "Letters from London: Guimard's Farewell to the Stage." *Dance Chronicle* 18.2 (1995): 207–215.

Meglin, Joellen A. "Representations and Realities: Analyzing Gender Symbols in the Romantic Ballet." Ph.D.diss., Temple University, 1995.

Milhous, Judith. "Dancers' Contracts at the Pantheon Opera House, 1790–1792." *Dance Research* 9 (Autumn 1991): 51–75.

Price, Curtis A., et al. *Italian Opera in Late Eighteenth-Century London*, vol. 1, *The King's Theatre, Haymarket, 1778–1791*. London, 1995.

Schwartz, Jane D. "The Role of the Male Dancer in the Era of the Romantic Ballet, 1824–1864." Ph.D.diss., University of California, Los Angeles, 1972.

Smith, William Charles. *The Italian Opera and Contemporary Ballet in London, 1789–1820: A Record of Performances and Players*. London, 1955.

Swift, Mary Grace. *A Loftier Flight: The Life and Accomplishments of Charles Louis Didelot*. Middletown, Conn., 1974.

Van Lennep, William, et al., eds. *The London Stage, 1660–1800*. 5 vols. in 11. Carbondale, Ill., 1960–1968.

JOHN V. CHAPMAN

Theatrical Dance since 1850

During the second half of the nineteenth century in Britain, theatrical dance in the form of ballet appeared primarily in music halls. There was no native British company that was the equivalent of the state-supported ballets of Paris, Saint Petersburg, or Copenhagen. In Britain, ballet was regarded more as light entertainment than as high art, and dancers, though sometimes winning a large and devoted public, were subject to the general Victorian disapproval of performers. Women in particular had to fight the stigma of loose morals associated with the stage.

There were two music halls that produced ballets—the Empire and the Alhambra, both situated in Leicester Square in the heart of London. Here ballets formed a substantial part of a long evening of entertainment, which also included other variety acts.

The Alhambra, in which ballets were produced between 1860 and 1912, was the larger of the two music halls and maintained a large corps de ballet. Many of the corps members were English, but the featured performers had been trained abroad. A series of celebrated ballerinas came, mostly from Italy, to dance at the Alhambra, including Giovannina Pilteri (with the company in 1869–1870), Rita Sangalli (1871), Erminia Pertoldi (1874–1884), Emma Palladino (1881–1882, 1884–1887), Emma Bessone (1885–1886, 1888–1890), Lucia Cormani (1886–1890, 1893), Maria Bordin (1906–1907), and Britta Petersen from Denmark (1908–1910). One of the best known was the virtuoso Pierina Legnani (1888–1892, 1894–1897), who performed her thirty-two *fouettés* in London before introducing them, in Saint Petersburg, into Marius Petipa's *Cinderella* and *Swan Lake*.

Choreographers, too, came from abroad, including Henri Dewinne, A. Bertrand, Joseph Hansen, Eugenio Casati, Carlo Coppi, and Giovanni Pratesi. Music for the Alhambra ballets was usually composed by the theater's musical director, Georges Jacobi, who provided nearly fifty scores for the Alhambra company between 1872 and 1898. The emphasis was primarily on spectacle—lighting, technical effects, and brilliant costuming. "Transformation" scenes and water effects were very popular; in one production the audience was even sprayed with perfume. Subjects for ballets included fairy tales and children's stories (*The Sleeping Beauty, The Beauty and the Beast*, and *Ali Baba and the Forty Thieves*) as well as military triumphs and the life of the royal family. Ballets reflecting contemporary life were presented long before Serge Diaghilev took up the theme: *Up the River* (1892) took as its subject the swimmers, tennis-players, and boating parties at Henley; *Chicago* (1893) was based on the World's Fair held in that city.

The Empire's programming policy was similar to the Alhambra's but, being smaller, it could not produce spectacles quite as lavish as those of its rival. Ballets were produced at the Empire between 1884 and 1915, for much of that period (1887–1905) choreographed by Katti Lanner, daughter of the Viennese composer Joseph Lanner and a distinguished dancer earlier in her career. She was also a noteworthy teacher in London. As at the Alhambra, the themes of the Empire ballets ranged widely, from fairy tales and fantasy to modern subjects such as *The Sports of England* (1887) or *On Brighton Pier* (1894). The Empire ballets also came to be known for their lovely and varied color effects, designed by the English artist William John Pitcher, who was responsible (under the stage name C. Wilhelm) for the artistic direction and was particularly noted for his costume designs.

Most of the principal dancers in the Empire ballets had been trained abroad, but the corps de ballet was English. Pertoldi and Palladino also appeared at the Empire; its other ballerinas included Malvina Cavallazzi (1888–1899), Carlotta Brianza (1888, 1893–1894), Francesca Zanfretta (1895–1900, 1903–1909, 1914–1915), and Lydia Kyasht (1908–1913). Principal male dancers included Enrico Cecchetti (1888, 1891–1892) and Édouard Espinosa, as well as the British dancers Will Bishop (1893, 1902–1904) and Fred Farren (who also appeared at the Alhambra and choreographed ballets of his own).

The Empire dancer who had perhaps the greatest impact on the British public and the dance profession in general was Adeline Genée of Denmark, who appeared with the company between 1897 and 1909. She was a dancer of wit and delicacy, excelling in roles—such as Swanilda in *Coppélia*—that exploited her comedic abilities, deft footwork, and fine technique. After her retirement from the stage in 1914, Genée had great influence on raising and maintaining the standards of dance training in Britain. She participated in the creation of the Association of Operatic Dancing (later the Royal Academy of Dancing) and served as its president from its founding in 1920 until 1954. She was made a Dame of the British Empire in 1950 for her service to the arts. [*See the entry on Genée.*]

Genée inspired generations of English dancers. In particular, she was mentor to Phyllis Bedells (1893–1985), who became the first important native British ballerina of the twentieth century when she became *première danseuse* at the Empire in 1914. Bedells danced in musical revues as well as at the Empire, opening up the acceptance of British dancers in leading roles through both her fine dancing and her refusal to adopt a foreign stage name, as was common at that time. Like Genée, Bedells became important in efforts to raise the standard of professional dance training in Britain; she helped form the Association of Operatic Dancing and eventually became a vice-president of the Royal Academy of Dancing. [*See the entry on Bedells.*]

The arrival of Diaghilev's Ballets Russes in London (1911) marked the next and perhaps most important ad-

vance in British ballet. Between 1911 and 1929 (with the exception of 1914 to 1918, the World War I years), this company appeared frequently in London, acquiring a devoted following and providing British audiences for the first time in many years the opportunity to see a full company of male and female dancers performing at a very high level. The Ballets Russes was an example and inspiration for British dance for the rest of the century. Both of the founders of British ballet, Ninette de Valois and Marie Rambert, worked with the Ballets Russes (Rambert in 1913 and de Valois from 1923 to 1925) and learned from its policies. Furthermore, Serge Diaghilev developed two of the first international stars of British ballet—Alicia Markova and Anton Dolin—as well as employing a number of British dancers who assumed Russian names. Perhaps the best known was Lydia Sokolova, whose *Dancing for Diaghilev* is an invaluable memoir of the company.

Diaghilev brought Londoners not only their first extended look at the great nineteenth-century repertory developed in Saint Petersburg by Marius Petipa but also the most recent developments in choreography in the revolutionary ballets of Michel Fokine, Vaslav Nijinsky, Bronislava Nijinska, Léonide Massine, and George Balanchine. The Ballets Russes also popularized the influential concept of the synthesis of the arts, in which a composer worked in concert with set designer, dancers, and choreographer to create a total effect (a concept that would have

GREAT BRITAIN: Theatrical Dance since 1850. Adeline Genée (seated at center) as Swanilda, with Dorothy Craske *en travesti* as Franz and the ballet company of the Empire Theatre, in *Coppélia*, act 2, in 1908. The Empire Theatre, formally named the Empire Palace of Varieties, stood on the north side of Leicester Square and was famous for its lavish appointments and grand productions. Genée was the unrivaled star of the Empire stage from 1897 to 1908; Swanilda was her most famous role. (Photograph by Dover Street Studios, London.)

a profound impact on the creators of later British ballets). Diaghilev introduced musical scores of greater significance than had previously been used in Britain to accompany dance. Finally, such dancers as Nijinsky, Tamara Karsavina, and Lydia Lopokova were among the finest performers yet seen in Britain.

Diaghilev drew to the ballet a new audience composed of intellectuals and patrons of the other arts. Gradually, the public began to perceive dance as a serious art form. Along with Diaghilev, credit must also be given to Anna Pavlova, who eventually made London her home, appeared frequently, and employed British dancers in her own small troupe. Pavlova exerted a powerful influence on one of the greatest English choreographers, Frederick Ashton, who said that she stood in back of every one of his female roles.

Between 1910 and 1920, agitation began for the establishment of a native British ballet company equal in stature to the Ballets Russes. This movement was closely linked to the development of higher standards of dance training. The drive was in large part organized by P. J. S. Richardson, editor of the first specialist dance journal in Britain, *The Dancing Times,* and by his colleague Édouard Espinosa. They proposed the creation of a professional organization to ensure that dancers would be trained to the highest professional standards; earlier, dance students were often at the mercy of teachers who had no idea of safe or sound training techniques. Enlisting the aid of others in the dance community, including Genée and Bedells, in 1920 Richardson and Espinosa created the Association of Operatic Dancing of Great Britain, which in 1936 became the Royal Academy of Dancing. Dancers were for the first time brought together in a professional organization that served their needs and special interests and allowed them to communicate more effectively about the problems of their profession. At about the same time, a lively community of writers promoted the development of professional theatrical dance; they included Richardson himself, Arnold Haskell, Edwin Evans, and the dance historian and critic Cyril Beaumont, whose ballet bookstore in the Charing Cross Road became a center for the dissemination of dance history and criticism. [*See the entries on Beaumont, the Espinosa family, and Richardson.*]

In the 1920s and early 1930s the companies began that would eventually dominate the British dance world for the next several decades. Foremost were the Ballet Rambert, headed by Marie Rambert, and the Vic-Wells Ballet (later Sadler's Wells Ballet), headed by Ninette de Valois. [*See the entries on de Valois and Rambert.*]

De Valois and Rambert shared the goal of developing and sustaining a native British ballet. Both were inspired by Diaghilev, wished to carry on the tradition of the great nineteenth-century repertory, to develop modern choreography, and to synthesize the best from all the arts. They

GREAT BRITAIN: Theatrical Dance since 1850. Mikhail Mordkin and Anna Pavlova danced *Valse Caprice,* a pas de deux by Nikolai Legat, on their opening night in London, 18 April 1910, at the Palace Theatre. Settling in Hampstead in 1912, Pavlova adopted England as her home. (Photograph by Dover Street Studios, London; from the Dance Collection, New York Public Library for the Performing Arts.)

were cultivated and brilliant women with determined, charismatic personalities, but their differences were equally strong. De Valois's company eventually became Britain's national ballet and school, while Rambert's company, although artistically influential, followed a more precarious course.

Rambert's greatest talent lay in discovering and encouraging untried talent—in choreographers, designers, and dancers. She pushed the young Frederick Ashton to create his first ballet, *A Tragedy of Fashion* (1926), and many of his early works were created under her aegis. Antony Tudor was another Rambert discovery, as were Andrée Howard, William Chappell, and numerous other important dancers. Rambert's early championship of Petipa in a public lecture of 1930 was one of the first important public endorsements of this choreographer, then known in Britain only to a few connoisseurs.

GREAT BRITAIN: Theatrical Dance since 1850. With sumptuous sets and costumes designed by Léon Bakst, choreography by Marius Petipa and Bronislava Nijinska, and a galaxy of stars in his Ballets Russes, Serge Diaghilev presented *The Sleeping Princess* at London's Alhambra Theatre on 2 November 1921. This is a scene from the prologue, as Cattalabutte, the major-domo (at center), and members of the court bow low before the King and Queen (at right) and the cradle of the infant Princess Aurora. (Photograph by Stage Photo Company, London; from the Dance Collection, New York Public Library for the Performing Arts.)

In the beginning, Rambert's company, with a small, elite audience of intellectuals and wealthy art patrons, was considered the more stylish and avant-garde of the two companies. De Valois's group, located at the larger Sadler's Wells Theatre in the run-down, unfashionable Islington section of London, was attached, under the management of Lilian Baylis, to the existing Old Vic theater and opera companies. This umbrella organization was conceived as a people's theater—a nonprofit organization that would make great art available at affordable prices.

De Valois was, however, a more rigorously trained teacher and dancer than Rambert (she had been a soloist with the Diaghilev company), and she could choreograph works for her company as well as perform in them. In the company's first years, the bulk of the new repertory was her creation. She was also a very able administrator, and her methods and goals proved more pragmatic and durable than Rambert's. Using the models of the long-established state dance schools and companies of France, Russia, and Denmark, and a syllabus that she developed combining the best elements from her training with E-spinosa, Cecchetti, Nicholas Legat, Olga Preobrajenska, and Nijinska, de Valois set out to create a self-sustaining, self-renewing institution to train British dancers and choreographers from childhood and to provide them with a living wage and the security of a regular performance schedule when they reached maturity. The company would perform the finest works of the traditional repertory while also encouraging the creation of modern works by British choreographers and acquiring other new works from abroad.

In an inspired choice, de Valois engaged Frederick Ashton as resident choreographer in 1935. He was drawn from Ballet Rambert by the prospect of working in a reasonably stable company with a small but regular salary. De Valois also hired Nicholas Sergeyev, former *régisseur* of both the Imperial Ballet in Saint Petersburg and the Diaghilev company; exiled from Russia and living in poverty in Paris, he had brought with him notation of much of the Maryinsky repertory. During the 1930s Sergeyev mounted for the company full-length versions of *The Nutcracker, Swan Lake,* and *The Sleeping Beauty,* as well as versions of the French classics *Giselle* and *Coppélia*.

The fledgling Rambert and de Valois companies, and indeed the whole professional dance community, were strongly aided by the formation of the Camargo Society in 1930 by P. J. S. Richardson, Arnold Haskell, and Edwin Evans. Its stated purpose was to keep ballet alive in Britain after the death of Diaghilev in 1929. The organizers were determined to maintain Diaghilev's policy of creating ballets that were a true synthesis of the arts. To this end, they commissioned British composers (among them Constant Lambert, later important in the creation of the Royal Ballet) and painters to collaborate with young British choreographers.

With dancers drawn mostly from de Valois's and Rambert's groups, the Camargo Society produced performances of both old and new works. The first performance took place in London at the Cambridge Theatre on 19 October 1930. Among new works presented by the society were de Valois's *Job* and *La Création du Monde*, Ashton's *Façade*, and an early Antony Tudor work, *Adam and Eve*. Past masterworks were not neglected, either, as revivals of *Giselle*, act 2 of *Swan Lake*, and *Coppélia* were presented.

When the Camargo Society was disbanded in 1933, after two gala performances at Covent Garden, they had visibly demonstrated that ballet (previously considered the preserve of Russians) could be created and performed by British artists. The Camargo Society's funds and a number of its productions were handed over to the Vic-Wells Ballet, headed by de Valois, which was steadily growing in size and repertory, attracting increasingly enthusiastic audiences.

The 1930s saw the continuing expansion of the Vic-Wells organization, both the performing company and the "feeder" school attached to it. Initially, the Sadler's Wells company featured Alicia Markova and Anton Dolin—British performers who had been developed by Diaghilev—but in 1935 they left to form the Markova-Dolin Ballet, which toured England and Europe (1935–1938). De Valois turned to artists developed within her own school, beginning a tradition that continues to this day.

Foremost among de Valois's dancers was Margot Fonteyn, the company's principal dancer for more than thirty-five years and Ashton's "muse"; he would create many important roles for her. Fonteyn's elegant, serene, lyrical style, beautiful line, and musicality came to exemplify a particularly British style of performance. British dancers avoided both overt virtuoso display for its own sake and the space-devouring, athletic, emphatic performance style of much Russian and American dance; instead, they emphasized the beauty of more contained movement and subtle gesture. Quick, precise footwork was also seen by de Valois as a particularly British quality,

which she thought stemmed from a folk dance tradition that emphasized it. [*See the entry on Fonteyn.*]

Another important dancer of the Fonteyn generation was Robert Helpmann, who became an exemplar of another distinctive characteristic of British dance—an emphasis on dramatic expression. British dance, evolving within the context of a tradition of great playwrights and actors, encouraged and cultivated what de Valois has called "the British gift for characterization." [*See the entry on Helpmann.*]

Dance audiences and critics also judged a dancer's quality as an actor; indeed, the two skills were seen as inseparable, and a dancer, no matter how technically proficient, was not admired unless subtle and profound characterization could be created through movement and facial expression. British choreographers created ballets that demanded these skills, and British dancers were called on to create distinct, individual portrayals, even in minor roles. Equally important, they were trained to interact well with other dancers to create a unified ensemble; as a result, the emphasis on characterization did not preclude the creation of purely formalist ballets. Ashton's *Symphonic Variations* and *Scènes de Ballet*, for example, both

GREAT BRITAIN: Theatrical Dance since 1850. *The Planets*, Antony Tudor's ballet to the score by Gustav Holst, was created for Ballet Rambert in 1934. Here, Lisa Serova and John Andrewes are seen in the roles of The Mortals Born under Venus, in a 1940 performance in Oxford. (Photograph by Cyril Arapoff; from the Dance Collection, New York Public Library for the Performing Arts.)

acknowledge his debt to the classical tradition and are cornerstones of the modern British repertory. Even in abstract works, however, British dancers were expected to project mood.

Both the Rambert and Sadler's Wells companies were prominent during the 1930s, but while the Sadler's Wells company slowly but surely expanded in size and strength, the Rambert company continually had to fight for space and money. From the beginning the two companies were in close contact and often exchanged personnel. Markova, Fonteyn, and Helpmann all danced as guest artists with the Rambert company, and at Rambert's request de Valois

created *Bar aux Folies-Bergère,* based on a Manet painting, which was long a mainstay of the Rambert repertory. De Valois dedicated her first book to "Mim," Rambert's nickname.

The advent of World War II (1939–1945) and the rest of the 1940s saw both companies facing severe tests. From 1941 to 1943 the Rambert company was disbanded, but it was re-formed in March 1943 as the Ballet Rambert. It toured wartime camps and factories and also gave London seasons during the war years. In 1946 the company mounted its first full-length nineteenth-century ballet, *Giselle;* in the 1947/48 season it toured Australia and New Zealand with great success (returning, however, financially depleted).

The war also created major difficulties for the Sadler's Wells Ballet. The company lost a substantial contingent of male dancers. Nonetheless, it consolidated its position as the British national ballet in all but name by providing an important morale booster in sold-out performances in London and throughout Great Britain, often dancing during air raids. Its increasing strength and popularity were

GREAT BRITAIN: Theatrical Dance since 1850. After World War II, the Royal Opera House, Covent Garden, was reopened, and the Sadler's Wells Ballet moved in as the resident company. The first production, on 20 January 1946, was *The Sleeping Beauty,* with new sets and costumes designed by Oliver Messel and with Margot Fonteyn as Princess Aurora, the title role. Here, she is seen with Michael Somes as her partner in the final pose. (Photograph from the Dance Collection, New York Public Library for the Performing Arts.)

acknowledged after the war when, in 1946, it moved to the Royal Opera House in Covent Garden to become the resident ballet company. A smaller company, the Sadler's Wells Opera Ballet, was formed out of the larger group and remained at Sadler's Wells Theatre, where it continues today under the title of the Sadler's Wells Royal Ballet.

In 1949, the international stature of the Sadler's Wells company was acknowledged when, under the aegis of Sol Hurok, it made its first tour to the United States. There it presented a modern repertory of British ballets as well as *The Sleeping Beauty* and *Swan Lake,* its first full-length presentations of these masterworks. The American tour, repeated at regular intervals throughout the 1950s, 1960s, and 1970s, made it clear that Sadler's Wells had made London a dance center of international importance. In 1956, the company and its associated school were granted a royal charter and officially acknowledged as Britain's national ballet; they were renamed the Royal Ballet and the Royal Ballet School.

In 1963 de Valois retired as director and was succeeded by Frederick Ashton, who continued to expand the company's repertory with both his own works and other important ballets (most notably Nijinska's *Les Noces* and *Les Biches*). Under his guidance a new generation of outstanding dancers developed, including Antoinette Sibley and Anthony Dowell, and two of the company's greatest dramatic dancers, Lynn Seymour and David Wall; and the Royal Ballet corps became one of the strongest in the world. Some critics perceived, too, a new expansiveness and poetic quality in the performance style. Ashton was less concerned than de Valois with drill-like precision and absolute academic perfection of technique, although he too was firmly committed to the foundation of the *danse d'école* epitomized in the ballets of Petipa, his idol. [*See the entry on Ashton.*]

When Ashton retired in 1970 (he did not enjoy administrative work as did de Valois), he was succeeded by Kenneth MacMillan, whose career as choreographer had begun under de Valois in the 1950s and continued under Ashton's directorship. Although also firmly grounded in the *danse d'école,* MacMillan was particularly interested in the expanded vocabulary of movement found in modern dance. Influenced by his contemporaries in British film and theater, MacMillan sought to develop a more expressionistic style, with new and more varied ballet themes that moved away from idealization and explored all aspects of human psychology—especially the darker side. He developed a new kind of line for his dancers—stressing a very pliable, flexible torso—and a vocabulary of increasingly complex lifts. He found in the multi-act ballet form an opportunity to develop a complex psychological study of character.

MacMillan's detractors felt that he had distorted the classical tradition; his admirers countered that he had ex-

GREAT BRITAIN: Theatrical Dance since 1850. From the early 1930s onward, Anton Dolin and Alicia Markova enjoyed one of the most enduring partnerships in British ballet. In 1950 they were founding members of London's Festival Ballet, with which they appeared in many classical roles. Here they are seen in a pose from *The Nutcracker* pas de deux. (Photograph by Constantine Photo, Los Angeles; from the Dance Collection, New York Public Library for the Performing Arts.)

panded it, especially in pas de deux. Some American critics saw in his ascendancy a decline in the purity of the British style. However, his international influence was confirmed when his defenders within the American dance community made him a resident choreographer of American Ballet Theatre. During the 1970s and 1980s, MacMillan consolidated his reputation as the major British ballet choreographer. After resigning in 1977 from the directorship of the Royal Ballet, he remained principal choreographer for the company and a prolific and powerful force in the world of British ballet. [*See the entry on MacMillan.*]

In 1977 MacMillan was succeeded as director by Norman Morrice. A choreographer and former director of the Ballet Rambert (which in 1966 had turned entirely to contemporary dance), Morrice's succession acknowledged

GREAT BRITAIN: Theatrical Dance since 1850. John Cranko's ballet *Pineapple Poll*, based on the comic operas of W. S. Gilbert and Sir Arthur Sullivan, was a favorite with audiences during the Royal Ballet's 1958/59 tour of Australia and New Zealand. (Photograph from the Dance Collection, New York Public Library for the Performing Arts.)

the influence of London's growing modern dance community. MacMillan had expanded the repertory with works of Balanchine and Jerome Robbins, and Morrice continued this trend. He encouraged dancers from within the company, and for a time foreign guest stars were not invited to dance with the company. Under Morrice, Ninette de Valois, still influential, mounted a new production of *The Sleeping Beauty* which returned to the successful 1946 version. [See the entry on Morrice.]

In 1986 Anthony Dowell, the company's greatest *danseur noble* in the 1960s and 1970s, succeeded Morrice as company director, and a new classical emphasis appeared. David Bintley, trained at the Royal Ballet School, championed by de Valois, and acknowledging as his greatest influences Ashton and Balanchine, was made resident

choreographer. Beginning in 1980, Bintley made many ballets—both short and evening-length—for the Royal Ballet and the Sadler's Wells Royal Ballet (now the Birmingham Royal Ballet), as well as appearing as a character dancer. With the death of Ashton in 1988, MacMillan became the dean of British ballet; Bintley, designated by Ashton, was seen as his heir apparent. [See the entries on Bintley and Dowell.]

In 1991 another important phase occurred in the history of the Royal Ballet, when the smaller offshoot company, most recently known as the Sadler's Wells Royal Ballet, moved from London to Birmingham to become in effect the official company of the Midlands. It had started as a feeder company to the Royal Ballet and served as training ground for many of that group's dancers. Choreographers Kenneth MacMillan, John Cranko, and David Bintley began their careers here and continued to create works for it. Developing under the directors Ursula Moreton, Peggy van Praagh, John Field, and Peter Wright, the company had become increasingly popular in its own right, touring not only in England but to Europe, America, and Asia. The Birmingham Royal Ballet continued to perform regular seasons in London at the Sadler's Wells Theater.

Although the Sadler's Wells and Rambert companies were preeminent in Britain in the 1930s and 1940s, the renaissance of interest in classical dance at that time led to the formation of other companies of varying longevity. Of course, British dancers continued to find employment in musical comedies, revues, films, television, and Christmas pantomimes. Mona Inglesby's company, International Ballet, capitalized on the growing interest in nineteenth-century ballets and employed Nicholas Sergeyev as ballet master. He mounted *Coppélia, Swan Lake,* and *The Sleeping Beauty,* as well as works by Fokine and by British choreographers such as Andrée Howard and Inglesby herself. From 1940 until it was dissolved in 1953, the company gave annual seasons in London and toured throughout Great Britain and Northern Ireland as well as in Italy and Sicily, Spain, and Switzerland. [*See* International Ballet *and the entry on Inglesby.*]

GREAT BRITAIN: Theatrical Dance since 1850. Kenneth MacMillan's elaborate and dramatic production of *Romeo and Juliet* was an instantaneous hit when it was premiered in February 1965. Here the ensemble, led by Lord and Lady Capulet, is seen in the "Cushion Dance" from act 1. (Photograph from the Dance Collection, New York Public Library for the Performing Arts.)

London's Festival Ballet (later London Festival Ballet), founded by Markova and Dolin, gave its first London performance on 24 October 1950. Renamed the English National Ballet in 1989, it remains one of London's most active companies, touring and giving regular London seasons. It has mounted important productions of nineteenth-century and modern works, and it has been important in reviving and remounting the Diaghilev repertory under successive directors Julian Braunsweg, John Field, and Beryl Grey. Under the direction of Danish dancer Peter Schaufuss, ties to the Royal Danish Ballet have been made in a new production of Ashton's *Romeo and Juliet* (originally created for the Danish company). Under Schaufuss, too, came increasing popularity and a recognition of the company's strong links to British ballet traditions and British audiences; this was reflected in its name change to the English National Ballet, as sister company to the English National Opera, with which it alternates seasons at the London Coliseum. Both Iván Nagy and Derek Deane have served as directors. [*See* English National Ballet.]

A more recent company, London City Ballet, was founded by Harold King, emerging from a series of lunchtime performances in London in 1978. It became established as a small classical company touring throughout Britain and overseas.

GREAT BRITAIN: Theatrical Dance since 1850. Kevin Richmond with artists of English National Ballet in the "Chinese Dance" in *The Nutcracker*, mounted by Peter Schaufuss in 1986. (Photograph © by Catherine Ashmore; used by permission.)

Although British dance activity is still seen as London-based, there are important companies outside the capital. Western Theatre Ballet, established in Bristol in 1957 under Peter Darrell's direction, has evolved into the Scottish Ballet, with its permanent home in Glasgow. This company has acquired a loyal following and an important repertory of nineteenth-century and modern works. Northern Dance Theatre (renamed Northern Ballet Theatre in 1976) was founded in Manchester in 1969 for the purpose of touring the northwest of England; it too has developed a mixed repertory of classical and modern works.

[*See also* Northern Ballet Theatre; Royal Ballet; *and* Scottish Ballet.]

BIBLIOGRAPHY

Anthony, Gordon. *A Camera at the Ballet: Pioneer Dancers of the Royal Ballet*. Newton Abbot, 1975.

Beaumont, Cyril W. *Bookseller at the Ballet: Memoirs, 1891 to 1929*. London, 1975.

Benari, Naomi. *Vagabonds and Strolling Dancers: The Lives and Times of Molly Lake and Travis Kemp*. London, 1990.

Bizot, Richard. "The Turn-of-the-Century Salome Era." *Choreography and Dance* 2.3 (1992): 71–87.

Bland, Alexander. *The Royal Ballet: The First Fifty Years*. London, 1981.

Bremser, Martha, ed. *Fifty Contemporary Choreographers*. London, 1995.

Brinson, Peter. *Years of Change*. London, 1993.

Buckle, Richard. *Buckle at the Ballet*. London, 1980.

Chazin-Bennahum, Judith. *The Ballets of Antony Tudor: Studies in Psyche and Satire*. New York, 1994.

Coton, A. V. *Writings on Dance, 1938–1968*. London, 1975.

Crisp, Clement, et al., eds. *Ballet Rambert: Fifty Years and On*. Rev. and enl. ed. Ilkley, England, 1981.

de Valois, Ninette. *Invitation to the Ballet*. London, 1937.

Dolin, Anton. *Last Words: A Final Autobiography*. Edited by Kay Hunter. London, 1985.

Flitch, Crawford, et al. "English Ballet at the Turn of the Century: Three Perspectives." *Dance Research* 13 (Winter 1995): 3–46.

Garafola, Lynn. *Diaghilev's Ballets Russes*. New York, 1989.

Genné, Beth Eliot. "P.J.S. Richardson and the Birth of British Ballet." In *Proceedings of the Fifth Annual Conference, Society of Dance His-*

tory Scholars, Harvard University, 13–15 February 1982, compiled by Christena L. Schlundt. Riverside, Calif., 1982.

Genné, Beth Eliot. "Openly English: Phyllis Bedells and the Birth of British Ballet." *Dance Chronicle* 18.3 (1995): 437–451.

Guest, Ivor. *Ballet in Leicester Square.* London, 1992.

Haskell, Arnold L. *Balletomane at Large.* London, 1972.

Henshaw, David. "Black Attitudes." *Dance Theatre Journal* 8 (Spring 1991): 42–44.

Jordan, Stephanie. *Striding Out: Aspects of Contemporary and New Dance in Britain.* London, 1992.

Kane, Angela, and Jane Pritchard. "The Camargo Society" (parts 1–2). *Dance Research* 12 (Autumn 1994): 21–65; 13 (Autumn 1995).

Karsavina, Tamara. *Theatre Street.* Rev. and enl. ed. London, 1948.

Koritz, Amy. *Gendering Bodies/Performing Art: Dance and Literature in Early Twentieth-Century British Culture.* Ann Arbor, 1995.

Lloyd, Maude. "Some Recollections of the English Ballet." *Dance Research* 3 (Autumn 1984): 39–52.

Newman, Barbara. *Striking a Balance: Dancers Talk about Dancing.* Rev. ed. New York, 1992.

Nugent, Ann. "The Blurring of Distinctions: The Rise of Black Dance in England." *Dance and Dancers* (November 1990): 26–28.

Nugent, Ann. "Opening Out the Umbrella." *Dance Now* 3 (Winter 1994): 22–28.

Penman, Robert, comp. *A Catalogue of Ballet and Contemporary Dance in the BBC Television, Film, and Videotape Library, 1937–1984.* London, 1987.

Pritchard, Jane. "Dance at the Savoy" (parts 1–2). *The Dancing Times* (July–August 1993).

Richardson, Philip. "A Chronology of the Ballet in England, 1910–1945." *Ballet Annual* (1947): 115–131.

Richardson, Philip. "Classical Technique in England: Its Development under Foreign Teachers." *Ballet Annual* 2 (1948): 118–125.

Roberts, Jane B., and David Vaughan, comps. *Looking at Ballet: Ashton and Balanchine, 1926–1936.* Studies in Dance History, vol. 3.2. Pennington, N.J., 1993.

Sorley Walker, Katherine. "The Camargo Society." *Dance Chronicle* 18.1 (1995): 1–114.

Thorpe, Edward. *Kenneth MacMillan: The Man and the Ballets.* London, 1985.

Vaughan, David. *Frederick Ashton and His Ballets.* London, 1977.

White, Joan W., ed. *Twentieth-Century Dance in Britain.* London, 1985.

Woodcock, Sarah C. *The Sadler's Wells Royal Ballet.* London, 1991.

BETH ELIOT GENNÉ

Modern Dance

Modern dance took many years to gain a permanent foothold in Britain. Performances in London during the early twentieth century by Isadora Duncan, Loie Fuller, and Ruth St. Denis inspired several British dancers to explore a freer movement style, but the trend was short lived. Madge Atkinson's Natural Movement, Ruby Ginner's Revived Greek Dance, and the Margaret Morris Movement shared similar modern-dance ideals. All three enjoyed brief popularity but, as Atkinson, Ginner, and Morris began to codify systems of training and expand their network of schools, British interest came to focus on classical ballet. Thus, while Martha Graham and Doris Humphrey were pioneering modern dance in America

during the late 1920s, the thrust in Britain was to establish a native ballet tradition.

Forty years later, Graham's technique and choreography were accepted belatedly in Britain. In the interim, most of the modern-dance influences were European. Mary Wigman introduced the *Sturm und Drang* of German expressionism to British audiences in 1928. In 1934, Kurt Jooss and Sigurd Leeder set up a school at Dartington Hall, Devon. Many of Europe's most significant modern-dance exponents were based there during the late 1930s, including Rudolf Laban, who arrived in 1938. However, with the outbreak of World War II, activity at Dartington ceased. The Ballets Jooss company moved to Cambridge and became part of ENSA's (Entertainments National Service Association) touring program. After the war, Laban and Lisa Ullmann founded the Art of Movement Studio in Manchester and Leeder opened a school in London. Laban's theories of movement were adopted by industrialists and educational reformers but, despite the geographic dispersal of modern-dance influences, their impact on British choreographers was minimal.

The popularization of ballet during World War II and the subsequent "ballet boom" thwarted attempts to establish a modern-dance tradition; although the Royal Ballet and Ballet Rambert introduced choreographic workshops during the early 1950s, creativity flourished only within the context of mainstream ballet companies. Toward the end of the decade, the founding of a few smaller-scale companies helped to extend choreographic opportunities. It was within those companies that the next explorations in modernism emerged. Western Theatre Ballet choreographers such as Laverne Meyer and Clover Roope synthesized classical technique with the more torso-orientated style of modern dance. Balletmakers Limited, founded by Teresa Early in 1962, enabled young choreographers to work with contemporary music and design, to discover new structures and techniques, and, most importantly, to create dances in an environment that encouraged experimentation.

Enthusiasm for less conventional forms coincided with another important development: several classically trained dancers traveled to New York to study the modern dance techniques available there. Significantly, the style that influenced British dancers most at that time was Martha Graham's. Her technique provided the most extreme alternative to ballet, in its initiation and phrasing of movement, in its spatial design, and in its emphasis on externalizing inner experience. However, like ballet, the Graham style demands strict stylization and rigor; for many British dancers, this was part of its appeal.

Norman Morrice was one of the first British dancers to study with Graham in New York. His early choreography for Ballet Rambert—such as *Two Brothers* (1958) and *Hazana* (1959)—revealed an interest in contemporary

GREAT BRITAIN: Modern Dance. Members of the London Contemporary Dance Theatre in Robert Cohan's *Nympheas* (1976), set to music by Claude Debussy. The stage design is by Noberto Chiesa. An American and a former Graham dancer, Cohan was artistic director of the company until 1989. (Photograph by Anthony Crickmay; used by permission of the Board of Trustees of the Theatre Museum, London.)

themes, music, and design; other choreographers trained in her technique, London Contemporary Dance Theatre evolved as an essentially Graham-style company.

From 1969, both London Contemporary Dance Theatre and the school were based at The Place, a converted army drill hall that became the hothouse for Britain's most experimental choreography. One of the first students to reject the school's highly stylized training was Richard Alston, who explored such alternative techniques as *taijiquan* and release work. (The latter was introduced to Britain by Mary Fulkerson. Focusing on the body's kinetic potential, rather than on the shape–emotion orientation of the Graham technique, it provided an alternative means of initiating energy based on breath rhythm.) Alston also experimented with chance procedures, indeterminacy, and unorthodox dance–sound associations. Early works, such as *Something to Do* and *Nowhere Slowly*, were taken into London Contemporary Dance Theatre's repertory, and he went on to create four works for the company. By 1972, however, Alston wanted to pursue a more radical approach. Together with other London Contemporary Dance School-trained dancers, he formed Strider, the first independent group in Britain to receive Arts Council support. [*See the entry on Alston.*]

During its three-year existence, Strider worked as a collective. Several of its dancers—Christopher Banner, Dennis Greenwood, Nanette Hassall, Eva Karczag, Jacky Lansley, and Sally Potter—contributed choreographically. Classes in Cunningham and release techniques (the latter taught by Fulkerson during a series of residencies at Dartington) influenced their choreography. The focus was on process rather than product, and performances were often in such nonproscenium spaces as gymnasiums, art galleries, and museums. In both ideology and intent, Strider initiated some of the earliest British experiments in postmodern dance.

When Strider disbanded in 1975, Alston went to study in New York (along with Banner and Karczag, who had left England the previous year). Other Strider dancers continued to pursue postmodernist ideas in Britain: Greenwood performed in Rosemary Butcher's early group explorations, and Lansley became a founder-member of X6, a collective formed in 1976 by Royal Ballet and London Contemporary Dance School-trained dancers. Based in a warehouse in London's dockland, X6 adopted many of the ideas of the Judson movement: minimalism, improvisation, and the inclusion of multimedia elements characterized the group's work. Fulkerson and Steve Paxton taught classes. In 1977, with Lansley and Emilyn Claid as co-editors, X6 published *New Dance*, the first magazine to provide a platform for postmodern dance in Britain. Because of the magazine's influence, *new dance* in turn became the term used to describe the various experiments occurring beyond mainstream British companies.

Another group, Moving Being, focused specifically on multimedia productions. Formed by Geoff Moore in 1968, the group worked at The Place until 1972. Then, by relocating to Cardiff, Wales, Moving Being became one of the first regional satellites for experimental work. Subsequently, the Arts Council encouraged other groups to develop outside London. Cycles, based in the west Midlands, was the first to be set up in 1974; two years later another Midlands-based company, EMMA (East Midlands Mobile Arts) was formed. In 1978, Northern Arts began funding Moving Visions and, in 1980, the company moved first to Darlington and then to Newcastle in the northeast England, where it became known as the English Dance Theatre.

These smaller-scale regional companies provided performing and choreographic opportunities for the London Contemporary Dance School-trained dancers—at a time when it was the only school in Britain that prepared students for a career in modern dance. (Despite Ballet Rambert's reform in 1966, the Rambert school still concentrated on ballet training and most of its students joined classical companies.) While Strider, and subsequently X6, pursued postmodern ideas, many London Contemporary Dance School students aimed to work within a modern-dance aesthetic. Additionally, some dancers within Ballet Rambert and London Contemporary Dance Theatre wanted to explore opportunities beyond the confines of their respective repertories and touring schedules. (An indication of this was the establishment of EMMA by Gideon Avrahami and Moving Visions by Ross McKim and Sue Little. Avrahami and McKim were, respectively, former Rambert and London Contemporary Dance Theatre dancers.)

During the 1970s, experimentation and cross-fertilization flourished within small-scale dance companies, many of them benefiting from Arts Council encouragement. It was simultaneously a decade of consolidation at Ballet Rambert and London Contemporary Dance Theatre. Of the students who joined London Contemporary Dance Theatre, Siobhan Davies and Robert North emerged as the company's first associate choreographers, and each added a new dimension to the predominantly Graham-Cohan style. North's interest in popular and ethnic dance forms introduced diversity to the company's repertory. Through such works as *Gladly, Badly, Sadly, Madly* (co-choreographed with Royal Ballet dancer Lynn Seymour) and *Troy Game*, a wider audience was attracted to modern dance.

Before joining London Contemporary Dance Theatre, Davies had worked with Richard Alston. She danced in his first work, *Transit*, in 1968, which marked the beginning of a long-term association with his choreography. She worked with him again in 1976, when both were studying at Merce Cunningham's studio in New York. Upon her return to London Contemporary Dance Theatre, Davies's choreography revealed a greater emphasis on dance elements, rather than on dramatic ideas. *Sphinx* (1977) and such later works as *New Galileo* (1984) explored the formal possibilities of movement, time, and space. Davies continued to create works for the company until 1987, when she left for a second influential period in America. On returning to Britain, she formed the Siobhan Davies Company and, in 1989, became associate choreographer of the Rambert Dance Company. (Alston had been appointed artistic director in 1986 and the following year had instigated the company's name change from Ballet Rambert.) [*See the entry on Davies.*]

At various stages of their careers, Alston and Davies have combined working within mainstream modern-dance companies with choreography for independent groups. Both have created works for classical ballet companies—Alston for the Royal Ballet and the Royal Danish Ballet and Davies for the English National Ballet—and both have been responsible for introducing new designers and composers to dance.

In 1982 Alston, Davies, and the Australian dancer-choreographer Ian Spink founded Second Stride. The nucleus of the group had been formed in 1978, when Alston initiated a series of freelance projects. At that time, the group performed as Richard Alston and Dancers. Then, when Davies and Spink began to choreograph for the same group of dancers (which coincided with Alston's appointment as Ballet Rambert's resident choreographer), they became known, alternatively, as Siobhan Davies and Dancers and the Ian Spink Group.

In its first season, Second Stride presented new works alongside those created for these earlier groups. In 1983, Alston choreographed two works—*Java* and *The Brilliant and the Dark*—but these marked the end of his involvement with the group. Davies's last work for Second Stride

GREAT BRITAIN: Christopher Bruce has created many contemporary works for a variety of companies, including the Rambert Dance Company and the English National Ballet. Maximiliano Guerra and Josephine Jewkes are seen here in the English National Ballet's production of Bruce's *Symphony in Three Movements,* set to the Stravinsky score. (Photograph © Bill Cooper; used by permission.)

was in 1985. Since that time, Spink has been the group's sole artistic director and choreographer. With designer Antony McDonald and composer Orlando Gough, he has presented several large-scale productions that incorporate singing, spoken text, mime, and the manipulation of props. Though innovative, this approach led to problems in 1990: in crossing so many art forms, the group no longer attracted financial support from the Arts Council's Dance Section, and its survival became tenuous. In the following year, however, the council created a new Combined Arts section that now provides funding for multimedia work.

The dissolution of the Alston-Davies-Spink partnership was partly the result of Second Stride's evolving nondance orientation; equally significant, however, was the increasing commitment first of Alston then of Davies to mainstream dance companies. In shaping both artistic policy and repertory during the late 1980s, they became Britain's two leading exponents in formalist, cutting-edge choreography. Ironically, it was while Alston was in France, creating *Le Marteau sans Maître* for Ballet Atlantique/Regine Chopinot during autumn 1992 (his first freelance work in seven years) that the Rambert board decided to dismiss him as artistic director. Alston had introduced the Rambert dancers to Cunningham technique and, as artistic director, had revised the company's repertory radically. Cunningham's *Septet, Doubles,* and *Touchbase,* Trisha Brown's *Opal Loop,* and new works by Lucinda Childs and David Gordon were presented alongside choreography predominantly by Alston and Davies. Alston also commissioned works by some of Britain's most experimental choreographers—the first being *Swamp* in 1986, by Michael Clark, and, in 1991, *Completely Birdland,* by Laurie Booth—and reinstigated a policy of encouraging dancers from within the company to choreograph. Several workshop pieces entered the Rambert repertory during this period, the most notable by Mary Evelyn and Mark Baldwin. Alston's challenging and uncompromising policies, coinciding with recession-hit box offices, forced the board to seek a more popular replacement, however. (In hindsight, the board's agenda seems to have been even more specific: to facilitate the return of Christopher Bruce. Within weeks of the board's decision to oust Alston, it announced that Bruce would become Rambert's next artistic director.)

Following his dismissal, Alston pursued other freelance work until his appointment, in 1994, as artistic director of The Place Theatre and of the Richard Alston Dance Company. The latter had evolved from London Contemporary Dance Theatre, which, like Rambert, had encountered financial and directorial problems. London Contemporary Dance Theatre had been directed by Cohan since its inception in the late 1960s and, despite The Place's policy of

GREAT BRITAIN: Modern Dance. The DV8 Physical Theatre is known for presenting provocative works connecting physicality, drama, and politics. Here, two men become entangled in Lloyd Newson's *Dead Dreams of Monochrome Men* (1988). (Photograph © 1988 by Eleni Leoussi; used by permission.)

encouraging "in-house" dancers and choreographers, no obvious successor to him had emerged. The most likely candidates had moved on—Alston and North to Ballet Rambert (the latter as artistic director between 1981 and 1986). Other dancer-choreographers such as Micha Bergese left to direct smaller-scale companies. In 1985, a triumvirate was established: Cohan remained as artistic director, Davies was resident choreographer, and Janet Eager, Howard's former secretary, was administrative director. This proved only a temporary arrangement because Davies left two years later; in 1989, the appointment of American Dan Wagoner as artistic director was also short lived. After an interregnum, American Nancy Duncan was appointed artistic director of London Contemporary Dance Theatre in 1991, but she too resigned after only a short time.

Another upheaval came with the untimely death of Robin Howard. The Contemporary Dance Trust was re-formed, replacing the philanthropic leadership of one individual with a more businesslike management structure. One result of this was that activities at The Place became streamlined. Thus, Alston's new, smaller-scale company returned to many of the policies and practices of the fledgling London Contemporary Dance Theatre, the main aim being to rebuild from the modern-dance roots Howard and Cohan had established three decades ago.

Rambert, too, has seen a return to many of the ideas introduced during the reforms of the 1960s. Bruce enlarged the company and there is renewed emphasis on a hybrid classical-Graham style. Directorial changes at Rambert led to Davies devoting herself exclusively to her own company and, with the creation of such works as *Different Trains* (1990) and *The Glass Blew In* (1994), to producing her finest choreography. [*See* Rambert Dance Company.]

British dance in general has become more businesslike as a result of political and economic constraints. Adminis-trators and funding bodies now have a greater say, not only in the day-to-day management of companies but also in the types of repertory and projects to be developed. Inevitably, this has restricted experiment and risk taking: by the end of the 1980s, all of the companies founded during the 1970s had folded, as had *New Dance* magazine.

Surviving, however, is Dance Umbrella, initiated in 1978 by Val Bourne (at that time, an Arts Council administrator) and the dance critic Jan Murray. Dance Umbrella became Britain's first international festival for new choreography and, until the late 1980s, provided a management service for small-scale groups such as Second Stride and the solo performers Maedée Duprés, Laurie Booth, and Yolande Snaith. As an annual event, Dance Umbrella has expanded to include regional festivals in Glasgow, Leicester, and Newcastle. (Prior to Dance Umbrella, festivals had been organized by X6 and ADMA—The Association of Dance and Mime Artists—to promote the work of Britain's most experimental choreographers. Like the

GREAT BRITAIN: Modern Dance. Choreographer Lea Anderson has founded two companies, the all-female Cholmondeleys in 1984, and the all-male Featherstonehaughs in 1989. The names of the two groups are pronounced "Chumlies" and "Fanshaws," respectively. Here, Dan O'Neill and Rem Lee of the latter rush forward in Anderson's *The Bends*. (Photograph © 1995 by Chris Nash; used by permission.)

more recent Spring Loaded seasons at The Place Theatre, they were exclusively London based.)

Despite sociopolitical difficulties, Britain's dance base continues to broaden. A new strand of development during the 1980s was the emergence of choreographers from academia. Snaith, from Dartington, and graduates from the Laban Centre went on to develop their own work. Of the latter, the most successful have been Lea Anderson (founder and choreographer of two companies, all-female Cholmondeleys and all-male Featherstonehaughs) and Matthew Bourne (Adventures in Motion Pictures). Their work has been included in Spring Loaded and Dance Umbrella seasons, as has that of other innovative choreographers: Lloyd Newson (formerly of Extemporary Dance Theatre and now director-choreographer of DV8), Mark Baldwin, and Laurie Booth.

Today, modern dance in Britain competes not only with classical ballet and the more postmodernist approaches to performance, but also with an increasing multicultural awareness. Through groups such as Phoenix and Adzido, black dance is becoming increasingly popular. Also, with performances by several Indian classical dancers in Spring Loaded and Dance Umbrella seasons, British modern and contemporary dance are becoming increasingly more distinct. The melting pot simmers and new forms continue to evolve.

[*See also* London Contemporary Dance Theatre.]

BIBLIOGRAPHY

Bremser, Martha, ed. *Fifty Contemporary Choreographers*. London, 1997.

Brinson, Peter. "Modern Moves to Dance." *Dance*, no. 18 (Spring 1991): 25–29.

Clarke, Mary, and Clement Crisp. *London Contemporary Dance Theatre: The First Twenty-one Years*. London, 1989.

Dance Theatre Journal 6.3 (1988): "Tenth Dance Umbrella Anniversary Issue."

"How Britain Went Modern." *Dance and Dancers* (December 1986): 24–26.

Hunt, Marilyn. "Something in the Way Brits Move." *Ballet Review* 21 (Fall 1993): 74–78.

Jordan, Stephanie. "British Modern Dance: Early Radicalism." *Dance Research* 7 (Autumn 1989): 3–15.

Jordan, Stephanie. *Striding Out: Aspects of Contemporary and New Dance in Britain*. London, 1992.

Mackrell, Judith. "Post-Modern Dance in Britain." *Dance Research* 9 (Spring 1991): 40–57.

Mackrell, Judith. *Out of Line: The Story of British New Dance*. London, 1992.

Parry, Jann. "Dance on the Edge." *Dance Now*, 5.4 (Winter 1996–1997): 67–75.

Prestidge, Mary. "Dartington: The Dance Festival, 1978–1987." *New Dance*, no. 40 (1987): 18–19.

Pritchard, Jane, and Herman Lelie. *Rambert: A Celebration*. London, 1996. A publication of the Rambert Dance Company.

Sanders, Lorna. "Pioneers of Early Modern Dance." *Dance*, no. 16 (October 1990): 27–30.

ANGELA KANE

Dance Education

In Britain, broadly speaking, dance education—the instruction of young people in the rudiments of rhythmic movement and social or traditional dance—has been the purview of the publicly funded educational system, so it is free. Dance training—the specialized instruction of professional dancers and teachers of dance—has been available primarily through private teachers and schools. Although these two kinds of instruction have begun to merge, they are discussed separately here.

Dance education goes back at least to the sixteenth century, when dancing included the study of manners and courtesies and was an important part of the education of every upper-class Renaissance gentleman and gentlewoman. Consequently, dancing masters had considerable status in many aristocratic and noble households, and they retained a significant social influence into the nineteenth century. Among those who argued the importance of dancing in the education of young people were the scholars Francis Bacon and Erasmus during the sixteenth century, the political philosopher John Locke in the seventeenth century, and the socialist Robert Owen in the early nineteenth century.

Dance in British public education today is based on Ling's 1878 introduction of ideas about physical education. At the beginning of the twentieth century, the work of the Swedish physical educator Martina Bergman Osterberg changed British attitudes toward movement education, which led to the establishment of a number of private institutions to train teachers, mainly for girls' schools. Most of the training colleges experimented with kinesthetics and eurythmics, had links with central European ideas of dance in education (especially the ideas of Émile Jaques-Dalcroze and Rudolf Laban), and were connected with the movement for women's emancipation.

Association with Physical Education. Official government support for dance in education began with the introduction of the Syllabus of Physical Training for English and Welsh primary schools in 1909. The syllabus included English folk dance and later, the dances of Scotland, Wales, Ireland, Sweden, and other European countries. (Scottish education, although regulated separately from that of England and Wales, followed a parallel development.) Thus began the association of dance with physical education that remains a strong feature of British dance education. The natural physical training syllabi of 1919 and 1933 reaffirmed this association so that dance was subsumed under physical education in the training of teachers.

Attitudes began to change under influences from abroad, particularly from the United States and central Europe. Appearances by Isadora Duncan had an impor-

GREAT BRITAIN: Dance Education. Dame Ninette de Valois (seated) with pupils of the Sadler's Wells Ballet School, which she founded in 1947. In 1957 the Sadler's Wells Ballet and School were incorporated with the ballet company at the Royal Opera House, Covent Garden, London, to form the Royal Ballet. Since 1983 the Royal Ballet School has been directed by Dame Merle Park. (Photograph from the Dance Collection, New York Public Library for the Performing Arts.)

tant impact, introducing freer ideas that were developed in their own ways by Ruby Ginner, Madge Atkinson, and especially Margaret Morris during the first forty years of the twentieth century. By far the most important influence, however, came from central Europe through the ideas and presence of Laban, who arrived in England as a refugee from Nazi Germany in 1938. Kurt Jooss and Sigurd Leeder had arrived in England for similar reasons in 1934. These three provided an important focus for modern styles of dance performance and teaching. After World War II, Jooss returned to Germany, but Leeder remained in England for another ten years, creating through his teaching a strand of British dance education and training that remains strong. Laban's ideas, meanwhile, began to be adopted in the British public education system through vacation courses for teachers in the war years, with the official support of local education authorities and the national education inspectorate. His influence was consolidated and strengthened with the opening of the Art of Movement Studio in Manchester in 1943. Increasingly supported by the ministry of education from the end of the war, the studio became an important teacher-training center, propagating the ideas of Laban. In 1953, it moved to Addlestone, near London.

Essentially, Laban argued that dance is a liberating force, the property of everyone, with valuable community benefits. It should be open to everyone to enjoy from birth to death with consequential provision in education. In Germany, Laban was able to develop these ideas until he was forced to leave the country in 1938. In England, thereafter, his followers concentrated the ideas on children, reinforcing a child-centered educational doctrine. As a result, it is difficult to analyze and describe accurately what constituted dance education in British schools when it was adopted. The variations among titles that appeared on school timetables—modern dance, modern educational dance, movement education, art of movement—indicated some confusion. For some teachers, dance and movement were synonymous. For others, dance provided basic training for all forms of activity. For even others, it was a force to liberate expressive powers. All these interpretations existed in British schools between the late 1940s and the early 1970s. The debate was especially heated at the physical education colleges and at the Art of Movement Studio; it continues today into the era of economic recession and budget cuts.

From the 1930s to the 1960s, however, everyone agreed that the physical demands of classical ballet were inappropriate in general education. Many teachers within the public educational system also rejected the notion of rigid discipline implicit to the mastery of dance technique. A gulf developed between dance in education and professional training for theatrical dance—a gulf between the public sector and the private sector.

From the late 1960s onward, teachers on both sides began to question the reasons for the rift and to look for more challenging forms of dance education for older children. An important influence came again from the United States, through the ideas of modern dance, as disseminated in the performances and teaching methods first of Martha Graham and her company and then of Merce Cunningham and others. These were established formally in Britain in 1966, with the opening of the London School of Contemporary Dance and the 1967 formation of London Contemporary Dance Theatre. At the same time, Ballet Rambert changed its style from classical to classically based modern dance. Thus the complete dominance of classical ballet in the British theater ended, producing a new focus for both teachers and performers. Theatrical dance in Britain soon began to be seen as a resource for dance education.

Several factors influenced this rethinking. One was the introduction of graduate training for teachers. A second was the introduction of degree courses in dance studies, or in which dance was a significant option, that were separate from teacher training. A third was growing contact with the dance professions. A fourth was the introduction of professional dance residencies in British educational institutions by London Contemporary Dance Theatre in 1976. The process of rethinking that began in the late 1960s continues today. At issue are the kinds of dance that should be taught in colleges and other schools, the application of dance to a wide range of social needs through residencies, community and dance animation appointments, and the development of the art of dance in all these contexts.

The turning point seems to have been the Action Conference on Dance Education convened by the Gulbenkian Foundation in 1974, which brought leading dance educators together for the first time. The conference led to the Gulbenkian inquiry into dance education and training in Britain and laid the foundation for many of the structures that have emerged to speak for and guide the interests of a combined profession. This was followed in 1976 by the decisive intervention of the newly established, Graham-based London Contemporary Dance Theatre, introducing contemporary dance to colleges and schools. While a lack of funding threatens the schools and institutions that have helped establish British excellence and innovation in dance, the popularity of dancing, formal and informal, continues to rise among young people.

The dance animation movement has been especially important since the 1970s. Professional dancers or dance teachers, trained in community work, are appointed by local authorities and regional arts authorities to provide dance classes with performance and creative opportunities where none existed before. By 1991, more than one hundred such appointments had been made throughout the United Kingdom. The theories of Laban, classical ballet, and contemporary dance in all their variety are being reexamined, with a focus on the intellectual as well as the aesthetic aspects of dance.

These changes have come at a time when budget cuts, the result of economic recessions and conservative government philosophy, severely restrict the development of the arts in British education. Dance, as a late entrant onto the arts scene, has been particularly hard hit. Nevertheless, the foundations of dance education are now stronger and richer than seemed possible in the early 1970s.

Higher Education. In higher education, dance in Britain still lags far behind the United States, with few university dance departments. The universities of Surrey, of Kent, and of Buckingham confer dance degrees. Many more institutions offer dance as a minor subject. At universities such as Birmingham, Glasgow, and Bristol, dance is linked with music and drama; in other schools, dance is one of several options in educational, recreational, and other degree studies. Extracurricular dance activity is also popular, usually organized as a result of student or community interest. Proposals have been made to increase the amount of time devoted to the arts in teacher training, but the training of dance teachers for primary and secondary schools does not yet reflect new developments in education or the increasing popularity of dance among young people. Consequently, the private sector is an important source of training and new thinking.

In schools across England and Wales, according to the Gulbenkian Foundation and official studies, 68 percent of primary schools include "some" dance in the curriculum, often in physical education classes. Most frequently it is English country dancing, continuing a tradition from the early twentieth century; after this comes creative dance according to Laban principles; other forms are taught much less frequently than these two. The emphasis on dance varies with the region. Dance is taught most often in primary schools in inner London, the northwest, and the Midlands. Other areas tend to place less importance on dance. These trends are also borne out at the secondary level, where gender also plays a role. "Some" dance is taught in 61 percent of public secondary schools, but it is rarely taught beyond the first three years and is offered almost exclusively to girls. More boys study it in Scottish secondary schools, perhaps because of the stronger tradition of Scottish country dancing.

Generally speaking, dance has been placed at risk in public education as a result of the 1988 Education Reform Act. As a subject within physical education, it depends on individual school budgets, which are being reduced; the Department of Education has ruled that neither dance nor music should be taught, at all, to children beyond the age of fourteen.

Surveys show that young people often wish to dance more but are discouraged at the secondary level by academic pressures and parental prejudice. Their wish is reflected in the number of dance clubs meeting outside school hours and in the growing youth dance movement, of which a striking feature is the interest among boys. Youth dance usually takes the form of classes in contemporary dance, jazz dance, or some other dance type provided by local teachers or dance animators on a voluntary basis. The groups are as small as six, as large as thirty; teenage members create their own choreography and perform publicly. More than four hundred such groups exist throughout the United Kingdom. The youth dance movement spread rapidly throughout Britain following the first annual youth dance festival convened in Leicestershire in 1980. This has probably become the most compelling evidence for the educational potential of dance.

With this popularity has come increased interest in dance examinations. Although such examinations may seem at odds with ideals of creativity and self-expression, young people and their parents demand them. Examinations that offer a measure of achievement may help dance gain status and retain a place in school curricula. Consequently, one of the examination boards for the General Certificate of Education (introduced in the late 1960s) is an examination for secondary students in the history and theory of classical ballet. Later, practical examinations for the Certificate of Secondary Education tested students on the kinds of dance usually taught in schools. In the early 1980s, the London Board for the General Certificate introduced examinations covering the practice, history, and general study of dance. All these examinations, of course, are separate from grade examinations and other examinations that govern dance training in the private sector.

Private Training. Dance training, mostly private, focuses today on preparing young people for careers as performers or teachers. Candidates for classical ballet training, especially in the Royal Ballet School's junior section (ages ten to sixteen), are still recruited largely through private studios that offer ballet classes to children starting at a very young age. Contemporary dance companies generally recruit from the public educational system. Then full-time training can start at the age of sixteen, when children can leave secondary school.

Private training dates to the Renaissance and has the same roots as dance education. The first evidence of an English professional school of theatrical dance dates from 1809 at the King's Theatre in London under James Harvey d'Egville. Forty years later the impresario Benjamin Lumley attempted to form a professional company and school at the same theater, inspired by the success of his seasons of Romantic ballet, created by Jules Perrot. The government would not support him and throughout the late 1800s dance declined in popularity and respectability, first from the mainstream of general education, then from theatrical culture. Its rehabilitation in Britain began only in the early twentieth century with the

performances of the Danish ballerina Adeline Genée, Diaghilev's Ballets Russes, and the company of Anna Pavlova. From then on, private dance teaching grew comparatively quickly.

By 1904 a group of dance teachers had established what is today the Imperial Society of Teachers of Dancing, to develop and maintain their professional status and teaching standards. By the early 1920s, the society had 258 members, mostly general practitioners with a knowledge of the social dances of the day, academic ballet, and national and character dancing. In 1920, the Association of Operatic Dancing, known today as the Royal Academy of Dancing, was founded to address the specialized needs of classical ballet. The organization represented the four main schools and methods of classical training then recognized in Europe: Italian, French, Danish, and Russian. In 1922, the Cecchetti Society was established to preserve and disseminate the methods of the great dance teacher Enrico Cecchetti; it became a branch of the Imperial Society in 1924. Yet another teaching and examining body for classical ballet was established in 1930 when Édouard Espinosa, one of the founders of the Association of Operatic Dancing, set up the British Ballet Organisation, essentially expounding his own French style of the late nineteenth century. A fifth national body, the International Dance Teachers Association, was formed from a merger of smaller associations in 1967. Although there are other examining bodies, all regionally based, the national structure remains as it was when created between the two world wars.

The structure of private dance training was also more or less established between the two world wars: a relatively large number of private studios, mostly run by individual teachers; a few independent dance schools offering a full general education and incorporating classical ballet in their syllabus; the development of an apprentice system of training teachers, based on individual studios; and the formation of the first professional schools linked today with the Royal Ballet and Rambert Dance Company. Since World War II, other vocational schools have been established, most notably the London Contemporary Dance School in 1966 and the Laban Centre for Movement and Dance, reformed and enlarged since 1973. More professional methods have evolved to train teachers for the private sector, notably in the establishment of teacher-training colleges by the Imperial Society and Royal Academy of Dancing and a teacher-training course at the Royal Ballet School. The influence of foreign teachers—particularly from Russia, the United States, and central Europe—remains strong but the dance profession is now well established in Britain and is adapting foreign influences to its own character.

The Gulbenkian inquiry in 1980 attempted to estimate the size and distribution of the private dance training system. It counted about three thousand private studios, mostly run by one or two teachers and catering to young children, only a very small proportion of whom attend with any vocational aims. More than half of these studios are concentrated in London, the surrounding counties, and the southeast and southwest of England. Because the remainder are generally in the larger cities, the rural areas of Britain are poorly served. Almost all the studios teach classical ballet, although other forms, such as modern, tap, jazz, national, and Caribbean dance, are increasingly included. (The number of children served by the private sector—all fee paying and most attending once a week—is about 300,000, or about 3 percent of the total child population; only 5 percent of the pupils are boys.)

On this broad basis rests a structure of general and vocational dance education and training. General dance education in the state system continues to develop slowly. While linked still with physical education in the new national curriculum regulations of 1991, it is separating itself in practice at the school level, albeit handicapped by the results of the 1980s educational reform and the financial cuts of the Thatcher government, continued by her successors.

The biggest expansion in this period has come in community dance, which is linked with the formation of voluntary youth dance groups. There are many kinds—classical, folk dance, contemporary, jazz, Asian, Caribbean—indicating a strong dance commitment among young people. About four hundred such groups, mostly out-of-school activities, exist throughout the United Kingdom. With these has emerged a development of dance with, for, and by the elderly and disabled—again mostly under the impact of the community dance movement. The formation of dance agencies during 1991—two centers of dance development in London and four in other cities—will give extra support to public dance education, community dance, youth dance, and dance for special groups, as well as the formation of more regional dance companies.

Vocational Training. Such developments are immensely significant for vocational training, especially its recruitment. The structure of vocational training developed during the 1980s against the trend of government cuts in the arts. Today it embraces general stage schools, serving mostly the commercial sector of theater; the private dance studios, only some of whose students become professional dancers; and the specialist vocational dance schools, of which the most prominent are the Royal Ballet School, the Rambert School, the London Contemporary Dance School, and the Laban Centre for Movement and Dance. All these begin full-time professional training for students over the age of sixteen, except the Royal Ballet School, whose junior section combines a full general education with classical ballet training from the age of about ten. A number of excellent smaller schools prepare stu-

dents for careers in the theater, where the technical and choreographic demands are little different from those in the subsidized sector. Examples are the Doreen Bird College of Performing Arts at Sidcup in Kent and Laine Theatre Arts at Epsom in Surrey, both near London, and in London, the London Studio Centre. Finally, there is a developing tertiary sector embracing teacher training, including degree courses at the Laban Centre and London Contemporary Dance School and a range of specialist training such as the Laban Centre's courses in dance therapy and in community dance and movement.

The British dance profession is well aware of its weaknesses. Unqualified teachers, whose lack of training endangers young bodies, cannot legally be prevented from opening a dance studio. During the last few years, the profession has established a system of licensing comparable to other professions, such as medicine or architecture. Dancers and teachers still face low social status, isolation, low salaries, poor facilities, rising costs, and relations with the public sector that increasingly challenge the position of the private teacher. By far the greatest problem, however, is the fragmented nature of the private sector. This has given rise to an excessive number of examining bodies and examination systems, and the lack of any united voice to lobby and speak for the profession as a whole.

As a result of the Gulbenkian inquiry, national councils have been established in England, Scotland, and Wales to represent all sections of the profession. During the 1980s, the situation of these councils changed so that the Council for Dance Education and Training in London became the central point of reference, evolving a different relationship with Scottish and Welsh interests but concentrating only on education and training.

During the same period, therefore, professional companies and dancers established a national pressure group to pursue other concerns, such as injuries, touring conditions, and problems beyond the activity of the council and the dancers' union, British Actors' Equity. Called at first the National Organisation for Dance and Mime and, since 1990, Dance United Kingdom, this body and the council are discussing closer collaboration to achieve the goal of one national voice for the British profession. In 1975, the Gulbenkian Foundation established an annual international course for professional choreographers and composers, for talented young artists. Directed by choreographers of international experience and distinction (Glen Tetley, Merce Cunningham, Robert Cohan, and Christopher Bruce have held the position), and supported by a music and dance faculty of equal distinction, the course now attracts young artists from all over Europe and the British Commonwealth. It is part of a recognition of a wider, generally acknowledged need to broaden vocational training for dance, the need to produce "thinking dancers."

This need is linked, of course, with employment. Until recently, British-trained dancers, especially males, had few problems finding jobs because there were many openings in Europe. At the end of the dancers' careers, moreover, a dancers' resettlement fund, mostly for those in major subsidized companies, was able to help many prepare for new careers. Since the early 1980s, employment has been less certain because recession and government policies have eroded much of the funding base for professional dance throughout Europe. In Britain, cuts in the grant system that supported vocational training for dance have come at a time when public interest in dance is expanding, the youth dance movement is embracing both public and private sectors of dance education and training, and new dance influences from India, Africa, and the Caribbean are beginning to reflect Britain's multiracial society. These opposing trends will open a new chapter in the development of dance education and training in Britain as the twenty-first century begins. Already the trends are finding a reflection in national and local politics. Britain's Labour Party produced a policy for dance for the first time in 1992, as part of its appeal to the electorate. It is expected that other parties will soon follow suit.

BIBLIOGRAPHY

Brinson, Peter. *Dance as Education: Towards a National Dance Culture.* Falmer, 1991.

Brinson, Peter, et al. "South Asian Dance Education Forum." *Choreography and Dance* 3.1 (1992): 40–100. Proceedings of a conference on teaching South Asian dance in British schools.

Brinson, Peter. "A Culture of Mind and Body." *Dance Now* 2 (Autumn 1993): 51–59.

Glasstone, Richard. "The Royal Ballet School: A Neglected Legacy?" *Dance Now* 3 (Winter 1994): 50–53.

Guest, Ivor. *The Romantic Ballet in England.* London, 1972.

Gulbenkian Foundation. *Dance Education and Training in Britain.* London, 1980.

Kane, Angela, and Jane Pritchard. "The Camargo Society" (parts 1–2). *Dance Research* 12 (Autumn 1994): 21–65; 13 (Autumn 1995).

Ralph, Richard. "An Honours Degree for Professional Dancers." *The Dancing Times* (January 1988): 333–335.

Ralph, Richard. "New Beginnings: The Place and the London Contemporary Dance School." *Ballett International/Tanz Aktuell* (December 1995): 56–59.

Richardson, Philip. "Classical Technique in England: Its Development under Foreign Teachers." *Ballet Annual* 2 (1948): 118–125.

Smith-Autard, Jacqueline M. *The Art of Dance in Education.* London, 1994.

Sorley Walker, Katherine. "The Camargo Society." *Dance Chronicle* 18.1 (1995): 1–114.

PETER BRINSON

Dance Research and Publication

In the 1400s, English educators linked the study of dance closely with an elite education in manners and courtliness. The first book on education published in the English language in which dancing was recommended as an important accomplishment for young men was Sir Thomas Elyot's *The Governour* (1531). Roger Ascham, John Colet (founder of Saint Paul's School), and other educators all argued the same case. The Dutch humanist philosopher known as Erasmus broadened the social case in his *De civilitate morum puerilium,* published in 1530 (and translated into English in 1532 by R. Whyltington and again by R. N. M. Murray in 1963). Erasmus presented a middle-class view of manners and courtesies, replacing the Renaissance conception of the elite courtier with the ideal of the egalitarian citizen. Thus the argument was begun on behalf of dance in society. It was developed further by the political philosopher John Locke in *Some Thoughts Concerning Education* (1693), then by the social critics Joseph Addison and Richard Steele, and by the social commentator Lord Chesterfield in the 1700s. Education in Britain spread in the nineteenth century for the growing middle class; social dance remained important as part of the education of young men and women in the new public and private schools, but it gradually lost its old priority.

Parallel with this development, dancers themselves sought to explain their art. So we have from the early eighteenth century a range of work by Kellom Tomlinson, Edmund Pemberton, and John Weaver. These three were leading members of a brilliant group of English dancing masters in London at the beginning of the eighteenth century. Weaver, also the first significant English choreographer and dance scholar, was aware of the need to relate dance to the broader environment and to the new knowledge, especially the new sciences, of his day.

These three dancer-writers and others emphasized in different ways the significance of character dancing and its roots in folk dance, popular dance, and the movements of ordinary people in daily life. They emphasized, if indirectly, the interconnections of dance study with popular tradition and stage dance, which was their principal concern.

British dance scholarship is rooted in the work of its own dancers, just as dance scholarship in France and Italy is rooted in Arbeau, Caroso, de Lauze, Rameau, Noverre, and Blasis. From them, the first concerns of dance scholarship were the teaching of dance and the influence of dance upon society and general education.

Dance Research in the Twentieth Century. In England, dance scholarship did not begin to be established formally until the beginning of the twentieth century, and then through the work of private pioneers rather than dancers. Stimulus came from two directions: (1) the development of theatrical dance (influenced by Diaghilev's visiting Ballets Russes), which gave impetus to historical and aesthetic studies and to the teaching of dance; and (2) the pioneering work of Cecil Sharp and Percy Grainger on British folk dance and folk music. This ultimately gave impetus to a new anthropological strand in

British dance scholarship and had a powerful influence on music education. In turn, the combination of historical and aesthetic studies with the study of folk dance and dance anthropology raised important questions about the methodology of dance scholarship. How was nonverbal knowledge—that is, the practical element of dance—to be studied and combined with theoretical, historical, and aesthetic elements? Such problems were well known to the sciences and to many of the humanities but not to the arts, and certainly not to dance. A simple principle had to be learned and applied: dance scholarship is necessarily a partnership between the verbal and the nonverbal.

Preparation for Scholarship. Cyril Beaumont and Arnold Haskell are regarded as the early twentieth-century founders of the study of British dance history and the critical study of theatrical dance. Both began writing privately in the Diaghilev period (1910–1930). Beaumont was the painstaking historian and analyst; he left permanent reference works as well as short-lived criticism. His analysis of almost the whole repertory of his day, including *Giselle* and *Swan Lake,* remains indispensable, especially when considered in conjunction with his studies of *commedia dell'arte* and puppetry. Haskell was the more flamboyant publicist; he wrote for immediate readership and exerted immediate influence. His personal prejudices were well-known, such as his dislike of modern dance and his preference for female dancers. He was the first dance critic to be appointed to an English newspaper, and he also did the first aesthetic studies of dance in English dance literature. Alongside Beaumont and Haskell worked P. J. S. Richardson, editor of the *Dancing Times,* and music critic Edwin Evans. These four began a process lasting half a century, during which an essential literature of dance study was written and published. Without this work there would be no basis for today's more formal scholarship.

The second generation of dance scholars comprised critics, students of dance history, and the first examples of that fruitful fusion of dancer and writer in one person. The first dancer-writer was Mabel Dolmetsch, who wrote *Dances of England and France, 1450–1600* (1949/1954). Joan Wildeblood's 1952 translation of de Lauze's *Apologie de la danse* and Melusine Wood's three volumes on historical dance of the twelfth to the nineteenth centuries (1956–1964) followed. Classical dancers also began publishing, with Joan Lawson's *European Folk Dance* (1953), *Mime* (1957), *Classical Ballet* (1960), and *History of Ballet and Its Makers* (1964). The star of the dancer-writers in the 1950s and 1960s, however, was Tamara Karsavina, the great Russian ballerina, who had written *Theatre Street* (1930); she published *Ballet Technique* (1956) and *Classical Ballet: The Flow of Movement* (1962). All her works are models of clarity and beautifully written prose. *The Flow of Movement,* in particular, provides insights into the nature of dance's nonverbal communication.

Private scholars also began to publish in this field, including two contrasting personalities, Richard Buckle and Ivor Guest. Buckle brought a unique color and imagination to dance writing. His style was evident in his lively magazine *Ballet* (1939, 1946–1952), not all of whose articles or drawings were scholarly. It was reflected fully in his weekly criticism for the *Observer* and the *Sunday Times.* Buckle's work became more scholarly and influencial in his 1954 Diaghilev Exhibition at the Edinburgh Festival and in his definitive studies of the impresario Diaghilev and the dancer-choreographer Nijinsky, which were published in succeeding years. Buckle's work helped to awaken a generation of young writers, dancers, and designers to the relevance and rewards of dance scholarship. Ultimately it led to the opening in 1987 of a new permanent home for the British Theatre Museum, which had previously been located at Leighton House, Kensington.

Guest, the major British historian of nineteenth-century ballet, also played a leading role in the theater museum, principally with advice and contacts. Since 1953, Guest has written nearly thirty volumes, covering the history of the Romantic ballet in France, the United Kingdom, Russia, and the United States. His is probably the most widely read historical research of the last three decades. Guest's work is influential in its approach as well as its content. His approach to historical dance writing has been to concentrate on dance without much reference to the outside world—whose politics, industry, and social prejudices very much influence what appears on stage. The approach remains characteristic of much of British dance scholarship today.

A. V. Coton's *The New Ballet* (1947), Fernau Hall's *Modern English Ballet* (1950), and Mary Clarke's *The Sadler's Wells Ballet* (1955) and *Dancers of Mercury: The Story of Ballet Rambert* (1962) assessed achievements in dance in post–World War II Britain without Guest's detachment. *The Sadler's Wells Ballet,* in particular, remains a classic, although it has been superseded by Alexander Bland's anniversary volume, *The Royal Ballet* (1981).

Establishing Scholarship. By the early 1970s, a significant resource of British dance books and studies existed. From the 1960s, Dance Horizons, an American publishing company, reproduced a great number of historical texts, such as those of Noverre, Lambranzi, and Tomlinson, as well as twentieth-century dance writing; it has been one of the most significant influences on dance scholarship in the second half of the twentieth century. Its publications have linked dance scholarship on both sides of the Atlantic, principally by making available publications of significant post-sixteenth-century dance texts not readily available in their original form.

British publishers such as A & C Black, Pitman, and Dance Books demonstrated their confidence in the subject. Journals such as the *Dancing Times, Dance and Dancers, Dance Theatre Journal,* and *New Dance* regularly raised issues requiring scholarly inquiry. Even assembled collectively, however, the work of all the brilliant writers, both dancers and nondancers, could not be considered British dance scholarship as such. It was sporadic, scattered, uncoordinated, ideosyncratic and lacking in continuity. What was needed was a number of academic institutions prepared to devote resources to the long-term development of advanced dance study, and to coordinate with other aspects of advanced higher education.

The necessary stimulus, unexpected and remarkable for its simplicity, came from within the British educational establishment. To maintain degree standards in polytechnics and colleges of higher education, the Council for National Academic Awards (CNAA) was established by royal charter in 1964. Rapidly it became the largest single degree-awarding body in the United Kingdom, embracing two hundred thousand students in more than one hundred thirty higher-education institutions, conducting studies equivalent to those of universities. The function of the new council, however, was not just to bring polytechnics and colleges up to university standards but also to explore the validity of new degree programs. In 1974, the council began to consider degree programs in the arts, and a consensus was reached on the need for rigorously established honors courses, at all degree levels, covering drama, fine art, music, dance, photography, film and television, and many aspects of design. Some universities and polytechnics already maintained established courses in some of these subjects, but the development of dance in higher education was almost entirely new. The council, working at the college and polytechnic level, was assisted by another outside body: the United Kingdom branch of the Calouste Gulbenkian Foundation, working at the university level. The council also became linked with a significant sea change in the teaching of dance in schools. Dance education had taken its own direction in the 1940s, 1950s, and 1960s under the influence originally provided by Rudolf Laban in the 1930s. In the 1970s, Laban's theories began to be mingled fruitfully with the influences of American modern dance and applied dance education.

Degree Programs. The first British bachelor's honors degree in dance was launched at the Laban Centre for Movement and Dance in 1977, exactly fifty years after the first undergraduate dance degree course was launched in the United States. Other dance courses were developed soon at a number of British polytechnics and colleges. These courses underpinned the advanced research degree studies necessary for the development of formal dance scholarship. Two institutions in particular began the

process: the Laban Centre and the dance department at Surrey University, established by the Calouste Gulbenkian Foundation in 1981. Both have now a large group of master's and doctoral students researching a wide range of dance studies, in addition to their courses at the undergraduate and graduate levels.

In 1982 an undergraduate program for professional dancers was initiated at the University of Kent. This program, an extension of professional training offered by the London Contemporary Dance School, marked the first time the rigor of professional dance training in the studio had been recognized by a British university as equal to that of study in other disciplines. Graduate programs and research degree levels have since been added.

Throughout the 1980s, British dance scholarship also developed through other institutions in other disciplines. Margaret McGowan, professor of French at Sussex University, for example, published a long introduction to *Le Balet Comique 1582* (1982). This supplemented her *L'Art du Balet de Cour en France 1581–1643,* first published in 1963. At the Queen's University, Belfast, in Northern Ireland, the late John Blacking, professor of social anthropology, made his department a principal center in the United Kingdom for the study of dance in anthropology and ethnomusicology.

The private sector has also participated in the development of dance research. In 1982 the Society for Dance Research was established by two foundations sharing the same funding. The society immediately developed its own journal, *Dance Research,* which was edited by Richard Ralph and guided by an editorial board. Within a few years, the journal's most important functions became not only the advancement of dance studies in Britain but also the building of bridges between scholarly, sometimes rival, interests in the British and the international dance fields.

Important publications have continued, ranging from Marian Hannah Winter's *The Pre-Romantic Ballet* and Wendy Hilton's *Dance of Court and Theatre* to Robert Penman's remarkable catalog of ballet and contemporary dance (1937–1984) in the BBC Television, Film, and Videotape Library. Without a doubt, however, the most profound piece of British dance scholarship published in the 1980s was Richard Ralph's *The Life and Works of John Weaver* (1985). Working primarily at The University of Oxford, Ralph applied a rigor and detail of investigation beyond what has been normal in studies of eighteenth-century dance, uniquely illuminating a period of Augustan life. The book is also a publishing achievement in that all Weaver's written works were reproduced in facsimile of the period, with full annotation.

In 1992, the conversion of British polytechnics and some other higher-education institutions into universities marked a further significant step for British dance scholarship. Dance departments at Middlesex University, de Montfort University, Leicester University, and the Roehampton Institute joined the Laban (linked with City University in London), Surrey, and Kent in the research field.

BIBLIOGRAPHY

Beaumont, Cyril W. *Complete Book of Ballets.* London, 1937.

Blacking, John. *"A Commonsense View of All Music": Reflections on Percy Grainger's Contribution to Ethnomusicology and Music Education.* Cambridge, 1987.

Bland, Alexander. *The Royal Ballet: The First Fifty Years.* London, 1981.

Brinson, Peter, and Joan Wildeblood. *The Polite World.* London, 1965.

Brinson, Peter. *Dance as Education: Towards a National Dance Culture.* Falmer, 1991.

Brinson, Peter. *Years of Change.* London, 1993.

Buckle, Richard. *Diaghilev.* New York, 1979.

Caroso, Fabritio. *Nobiltà di dame* (1600). Translated and edited by Julia Sutton. Oxford, 1986.

Durham, K., and G. Oldham. *The Research Function of Higher Education: Conclusion and Recommendations.* Guildford, Surrey, 1982. Part of a report on the future of higher education in Britain sponsored by the Society for Research into Higher Education, University of Surrey.

Grau, Andrée, and Stephanie Jordan. "Dance Research in the United Kingdom." *Dance Research Journal* 27 (Fall 1995): 73–82.

Guest, Ivor. *Adventures of a Ballet Historian: An Unfinished Memoir.* New York, 1982.

Guest, Ivor. *Jules Perrot.* London, 1984.

Gulbenkian Foundation. *Dance Education and Training in Britain.* London, 1980.

Haskell, Arnold L. *Balletomane at Large.* London, 1972.

Hodgson, John, and Valerie Preston-Dunlop. *Rudolf Laban: An Introduction to His Work and Influence.* Plymouth, 1990.

Penman, Robert, comp. *A Catalogue of Ballet and Contemporary Dance in the BBC Television, Film, and Videotape Library, 1937–1984.* London, 1987.

Ralph, Richard. "Restoring Dance to Parnassus." *Dance Research* 1 (Spring 1983): 21–29.

Ralph, Richard. *The Life and Works of John Weaver.* London, 1985.

Ralph, Richard. "On the Light Fantastic Toe: Dance Scholarship and Academic Fashion." *Dance Chronicle* 18.2 (1995): 249–260.

Vaughan, David. *Frederick Ashton and His Ballets.* London, 1977.

World Ballet and Dance. London, 1989–.

PETER BRINSON

Contemporary Criticism

The anonymous authors of the notices that appeared in such papers as the London *Times,* the *Public Advertiser,* the *Morning Post,* and the *Illustrated London News* provide invaluable eyewitness accounts of the ballets of Jean-Georges Noverre, Charles-Louis Didelot, Jules Perrot, and the other choreographers whose works were performed in London during the period of the pre-Romantic and Romantic ballet.

Occasionally writers of serious music and drama criticism turned their attention to dance. Leigh Hunt reviewed performances at the King's Theatre from 1817 to 1819 in the Sunday *Examiner,* of which he was co-editor, and in the *Tatler* from 1830 to 1831. Henry F. Chorley's *Thirty Years' Musical Recollections* covered important ballets and dancers as well as operas and singers in the years from 1830 to 1859.

George Bernard Shaw wrote theater and music criticism in the 1880s and 1890s; his few pieces that dealt with ballet were therefore mostly about the Empire and Alhambra ballets. Although he admired several of the virtuosos who appeared there, notably Malvina Cavallazzi and Vittorio de Vincenti, his opinion was that "modern ballet . . . presents the art of dancing at the very deepest depths of degradation." Shaw disliked what he called "absolute dancing." "I have had enough of mere ballet," he wrote; "what I want now is dance drama." It is all the more disappointing that, although he is known to have attended the early London seasons of Diaghilev's Ballets Russes, Shaw wrote only about *Die Josephslegende* (Legend of Joseph) in a spirited exchange of letters with the English music critic Ernest Newman. We do not know if he believed that ballet, as he hoped it would, had "found its Wagner" in Michel Fokine. Max Beerbohm, who succeeded Shaw in 1898 as drama critic of the *Saturday Review* wrote two delicate and witty appreciations of Adeline Genée in ballets at the Empire.

In the daily press the music critic generally was given the job of covering ballet performances—often with obvious distaste. A few wrote perceptively. Nesta Macdonald, for her *Diaghilev Observed,* exhaustively researched British press coverage of his Ballets Russes and discovered that, among others, Richard Capell of the *Daily Mail* wrote with unusual insight and Ernest Newman of the London *Times* gave serious consideration to ballet.

The first issue of the *Dancing Times,* the first British periodical devoted to dance, appeared in October 1910. The founder and editor, P. J. S. Richardson (1875–1963), wrote a regular column of criticism, under the pseudonym "The Sitter-Out," until he retired in 1957. For whatever reason, he did not cover the first London performances of Diaghilev's Ballets Russes in 1911 but thereafter became their champion, as he was later of the budding British ballet. (The *Dancing Times* also published important historical articles and text translations, such as those of Noverre and Carlo Blasis, and campaigned actively for higher teaching standards.)

The experience of seeing the Russian ballet changed many people's lives; it even led some to become professional dance writers. Cyril W. Beaumont (1891–1976), who had opened an antiquarian bookshop in Charing Cross Road, London, in 1910, saw Anna Pavlova in 1911 and, the following year, the Diaghilev company. Thereafter his bookshop specialized in dance books, and Beaumont became one of the first dance historians. In his most important work, the *Complete Book of Ballets* (1937), and its several supplements, Beaumont presented detailed accounts of the major ballets of the nineteenth and twentieth centuries. He also wrote reviews for various publications, including the London *Sunday Times* from 1950 to 1959; his reviews tended to be dry and pedantic.

Arnold L. Haskell (1903–1980) was perhaps the first person outside Russia to become a professional balletomane. His interest in ballet began when he saw the Diaghilev revival of *The Sleeping Princess* in London in 1921. Through acquaintance with Alicia Markova, he gained entrée backstage when she joined the company in 1924. Haskell became what is now called a groupie or hanger-on of the Diaghilev company and especially of its successor, the Ballets Russes du Colonel W. de Basil; he chronicled his obsession in a series of books beginning with the best-selling *Balletomania* (1934). In 1930 Haskell and Richardson were among those responsible for founding the Camargo Society, an organization of great importance in the early days of British ballet. From 1935 to 1938 Haskell was ballet critic of the *Daily Telegraph*, in which capacity he continued his enthusiastic advocacy of the de Basil company. His attempts at more serious writing—early monographs on Vera Trefilova and Tamara Karsavina, a biography of Serge Diaghilev (written with Walter Nouvel), and *Ballet Panorama* (a short history)—were marred by factual errors, but *Ballet: A Complete Guide to Appreciation*, a Pelican paperback published in 1938, both acknowledged and fostered the growing popularity of the art and was another best-seller. From 1947 to 1965 Haskell was director of the Sadler's Wells (later Royal) Ballet School, a post later filled by another critic, James Monahan. Monahan, who wrote under the pseudonym James Kennedy, was ballet critic of the *Manchester Guardian* from 1935 to 1985.

Several books of intellectual value were published in the 1930s: Constant Lambert's *Music Ho!* (1934) was the work of a composer professionally involved in ballet; his analysis of the artistic tendencies of the Diaghilev period is not less illuminating for being biased. Some writers even attempted a formulation of dance aesthetics, notably the novelist Rayner Heppenstall in his opinionated but stimulating *Apology for Dancing* (1936). Adrian Stokes, the distinguished art historian, wrote *Tonight the Ballet* (1934) and *Russian Ballets* (1935); these works touch on aesthetics but are chiefly intensely personal, even poetic evocations of individual ballets.

A. V. Coton (1906–1969) was a left-wing intellectual of working-class origins whose first book, *A Prejudice for Ballet* (1938), considered aesthetic questions and was unusual in that it recognized the importance of two British choreographers, Frederick Ashton and Antony Tudor. During World War II, Coton personally edited, wrote, typed, and mimeographed *Dance Chronicle*, a review that often printed controversial opinions. *The New Ballet* (1946) was a major study of the work of Kurt Jooss. *Writings on Dance, 1938–1968* (1975), edited by Coton's widow, Lillian Haddakin, was a collection of excerpts from his books and pieces from *Dance Chronicle* and from the *Daily Telegraph*, of which Coton was dance critic from 1954 to 1969.

Just before the outbreak of World War II in 1939, the first two issues of *Ballet*, edited by Richard Buckle, appeared. It resumed publication, postwar, in January 1946 and continued until October 1952. Despite the dandyish air of much of Buckle's own writing, *Ballet* published many important critical and historical articles, as did *Dance and Dancers*, edited by Peter Williams, which first appeared in January 1950.

An important little book that appeared during World War II was P. W. Manchester's *Vic-Wells: A Ballet Progress* (1942); it was objective, sober, and prescient. Manchester also was the editor of a magazine, *Ballet Today*, from 1946 until 1951, when she immigrated to the United States to become associate editor of Anatole Chujoy's *Dance News*.

After the war dance writing proliferated in Britain. In addition to the various magazines, some daily and weekly newspapers began to publish regular dance reviews by many of the previously mentioned writers (Beaumont, Buckle, Coton, Williams) and by others, such as Clive Barnes; John Percival, who succeeded Barnes at the London *Times* when he left for the United States in 1965; Mary Clarke, editor of the *Dancing Times* and critic for the *Guardian*; Alexander Bland (a pseudonym for Nigel Gosling and his wife, former dancer Maude Lloyd), the critic for the *Observer*; and Clement Crisp, critic for the *Financial Times*.

In the 1970s and 1980s a new generation of dance writers began publishing, among them Alastair Macaulay, a guest critic for the *New Yorker* as well as a writer for the *Financial Times* and the *Dancing Times*, Jann Parry of the *Observer*, Judith Mackrell of the *Independent* and later the Guardian, and David Dougill of the London *Sunday Times*. These writers naturally showed a particular interest in the new developments in British dance, especially the emergence of British modern, and even postmodern, dance. Stephanie Jordan, who has written for the *New Statesman* and has served as director of Dance Studies at the Roehampton Institute in Surrey, published *Striding Out*, a study of contemporary dance in Britain, in 1992. In 1993 Judith Mackrell published *Out of Line*, another book on British dance.

In 1982 the Society for Dance Research was formed; it publishes a twice-yearly journal, *Dance Research*. *Dance Theatre Journal*, a quarterly, has been published by the Laban Centre since 1983. Another new quarterly, *Dance Now*, was first published in spring 1992.

BIBLIOGRAPHY

Anderson, Jack. "Balletomaniacs." *Ballet Review* 4.4 (1973).

Fenner, Theodore. "Ballet in Early Nineteenth-Century London as Seen by Leigh Hunt and Henry Robertson." *Dance Chronicle* 1.2 (1978): 75–95.

Kirstein, Lincoln. *Blast at Ballet*. New York, 1938.

Macdonald, Nesta. *Diaghilev Observed by Critics in England and the United States, 1911–1929*. New York, 1975.

DAVID VAUGHAN

GRECO, JOSÉ (Constanzo José Greco; born 23 December 1919 in Montorio-Nei-Frentani, Italy), dancer. Perhaps more than any other dancer, José Greco is responsible for bringing Spanish dance to mass audiences in the United States and Europe. Ironically—and despite early publicity to the contrary—the man nicknamed "El Chevalito de Brooklyn" is not of Spanish birth, but Italian. He came to the United States with his family when he was nine years old. They lived in New York City, where Greco attended the Leonardo da Vinci High School of Art.

GRECO. In this 1945 photograph, Greco poses with La Argentinita and Pilar López in a scene from *El Café de Chinitas*. Greco became Argentinita's partner in 1942, and after her death in 1945 danced with her sister, López. (Photograph by Alfredo Valente; from the Dance Collection, New York Public Library for the Performing Arts.)

Greco first studied Spanish dance in his teens with Helen Veola, a New York teacher who also taught his sister. He made his dancing debut in *La Traviata* and *Carmen* at the Hippodrome in New York, about 1935; during this period he also appeared at supper clubs and nightclubs. Not until late 1942, when La Argentinita invited him to become her partner, did he gain major critical notice. He learned much from this great performer, receiving particular praise for his role as the Miller in *El Amor Brujo*.

After Argentinita's death in 1945, Greco remained with her sister, Pilar López, when she revived the company as her Ballet Español. In 1947, Greco formed his own company, Ballet y Bailes de España de José Greco, with his second wife, Nila Amparo; Nila's brother Luis Olivares; and Carola Goya. In their initial seasons they toured France and Scandinavia, where they were especially popular. Within a short time the company grew to more than twenty dancers, including Lola de Ronda, who had also danced with López.

In 1951 Greco's company, with the renowned flamenco dancer La Quica, toured the United States under the auspices of Lee Shubert. They immediately gained a large following which lasted for nearly twenty years. When many Spanish companies were having trouble attracting audiences, Greco could command a crowd of ten thousand spectators at Lewisohn Stadium. Among the many dances he choreographed, perhaps the most popular was *El Cortijo*, which uses *zapateados* (heel work) to depict the rhythm of horsemen on the open plains. Unlike his mentor Argentinita, Greco worked mainly with a large company. His programs did not employ a dramatic format but instead consisted of a fast-paced sequence of eye-catching dance numbers.

In 1951, the same year that Lee Shubert brought him to the United States, Greco turned down a similar offer from Sol Hurok to tour as a small company, like those of Escudero or Argentinita. Audiences, he said, "want a spectacle, not an intimate revue" (Greco, 1977). Although some critics felt that Greco's choreography and his company's subtlety of performance suffered because of his mass-medium approach, they consistently praised Greco's own dancing as "elegant" and "sensitive."

Greco choreographed and danced with his company in a number of movies, including *Manolete* (1948), *Sombrero* (1952), *Around the World in Eighty Days* (1955), *Holiday for Lovers* (1959), *Ship of Fools* (1964), and *The Proud and the Damned* (1968). He was a frequent guest on television and variety shows in the 1950s and 1960s; he also made several records of Spanish dance music.

Greco officially retired in 1974, but he still choreographs and does lecture-demonstrations and special appearances with his third wife, Nana Lorca, who has been his partner since the late 1960s. Greco and Lorca administer two institutions devoted to furthering the study of

Spanish culture—the José Greco Foundation for the Hispanic Dance in New York, and La Campana–Centro de Arte Español in Marbella, Spain, where Greco now lives.

BIBLIOGRAPHY

Brunelleschi, Elsa. "Spanish Dancing Old and New." *Ballet* 11 (January–February 1951): 7–17.
Brunelleschi, Elsa. "Three Spanish Dancers." *Ballet Annual* 12 (1958): 109–112.
Greco, José, and Harvey Ardman. *The Gypsy in My Soul.* Garden City, N.Y., 1977.
Pohren, D. E. *Lives and Legends of Flamenco.* Madrid, 1964.
Reviews. *Dance Magazine* (July 1948); (October 1951); (November 1953); (March 1956); (August 1960); (September 1963).

JUDY FARRAR BURNS

GREECE. [*To survey the dance traditions in ancient and modern Greece, this entry comprises five articles:*

    Dance in Ancient Greece
    Dance in the Roman and Byzantine Periods
    Dance in Modern Greece
    Ritual and Carnival Dance Traditions
    Dance Research and Publication

For related discussions, see Crete, *article on* Dance in Ancient Crete; *and* Roman Empire.]

Dance in Ancient Greece

The earliest traces of Greek civilization date back to the Bronze Age. During this period, frequently called Mycenaean in honor of its wealthiest and best-known city, Mycenae, the early Greek hunting society developed into a country of rich kingdoms and palaces. The Mycenaeans borrowed heavily from the long-standing traditions of their Cretan neighbors, and recent evidence suggests that they may have conquered Crete during this time. Their prowess in war extended to Troy; archaeological evidence corroborates the Homeric account of the Mycenaeans' triumph over the Trojans sometime between 1250 and 1230 BCE.

While the archaeological evidence and the oral traditions recorded in Homer's epics reveal the heights of Mycenaean culture, the three centuries after this period are represented only sparsely in surviving texts and artifacts. Later, in the eighth through fourth centuries BCE, extant art, architecture, poetry, and prose provide a clearer picture of Greek civilization, particularly for the cities of Athens and Sparta. During this time the land of Greece was divided into separate city-states. Although differing in political organization and specific social patterns, they shared a common language and religious heritage.

The various city-states were united by conquest in 338 BCE under Phillip II of Macedon (a kingdom in northern Greece dating back to the seventh century BCE). His son Alexander the Great went on to win a vast empire, spreading Greek language and culture throughout the ancient Near and Middle East. Alexandria, the city he founded in Egypt, remained into early Christian times a center of Greek scholarship. Under the Roman Empire, Greek culture of the classical period continued to be admired and emulated, and Greece remained the language of the elite and well-educated.

Ritual Dance. The Greeks believed that dance originated in Crete when the god Zeus was born to Rhea, the earth mother. According to legend, Rhea's husband, Cronus (Time), fearing that he would be overthrown by his offspring, devoured each one at birth. After Zeus's birth, however, Rhea deceived Cronus into swallowing a stone instead of the baby and hid the child with the Curetes of Crete (some versions say the Corybantes), who danced around him, shouting and clashing their weapons to disguise his cries.

Examples of dancing divinities abound in Greek literature and art: Memory or Apollo leading the Muses; Pan and the Graces; Dionysus with a procession of satyrs or maenads. In their rituals the Greeks imitated divine examples. In earliest times, a designated leader, often the poet who had composed the text for a ritual, acted as *exarchōn* and coordinated the elements of music, verse, and dance. Usually the *exarchōn* himself participated, often as the musician. The occasions for ritual dance ranged from the celebration of the cult of a particular deity to the commemoration of important milestones—births, marriages, deaths, harvests, and athletic and military victories. Two patterns occurred most frequently in group dances: circular movement around an altar, votive symbol, or musician; and processional formations, often led by the musician or *exarchōn*. *Kōmos* (plural, *kōmoi*) was the term given to a festive procession. Some *Kōmoi* were reputed to be unruly revels; others were orderly dance-marches with music and song written for the occasion.

In general, men and women danced separately. The description of Achilles' shield in Homer's *Iliad* (18.590–605), however, seems to document a dance handed down from Crete in which young men and women danced together, holding hands. A sixth-century BCE black-figure painting on the François Vase depicts a line dance in which youths and maidens alternate. The Greek term for a dance involving both sexes was *anamix* ("mixed up").

Animal Dances. Animal dances may have been among the oldest dances in ancient Greece. The Greeks did not worship animals, but specific animals or animal qualities were associated with many deities: owls with Athena; the epithet "ox-eyed" to describe Hera; the animal disguises Zeus assumed when he wooed mortals; or the bull and the panther with Dionysus.

In secret rituals, animals often played an important role or bore symbolic significance. One such festival was the Thesmophoria, a yearly Athenian fertility ritual in honor of Demeter and Persephone. During the nocturnal rites, the women, carrying serpent-shaped images believed to have magical powers, entered caves to claim the remains of pigs—animals sacred to Demeter—left from the previous year. The carcasses were brought to the Thesmophoria altars, where feasting, playing, and dancing completed the festival.

In some animal dances the participants may have donned imitative costumes and masks. Vase paintings of dancers in costumes resembling birds, horses, or bulls suggest that the dances may have mimicked characteristic animal movements. A few comedies have a group of animals as the chorus. In Aristophanes' *Birds,* the lines following the entrance of the chorus (266ff.) describe each member parading his exotic plumage.

Dance at Dramatic Festivals. Dramatic and lyric poetry were often performed at annual festivals. The largest and best-known of these was the City Dionysia (also called the Greater Dionysia) at Athens. It began with a religious procession, called the *pompē,* culminating in songs, choral dances, and sacrifices. A revel *(kōmos)* may have concluded the first day.

The dithyramb became an annual feature of the City Dionysia in 508 BCE. Each of the ten Athenian tribes sponsored two dithyrambic choruses in the festival competition—one composed of adult male citizens, the other of boys. [*See* Dithyramb.] Each tribe appointed a wealthy citizen to act as *chorēgos* (plural, *chorēgoi*), the financial sponsor who chose and paid the poet and flutist and also paid for training and costuming the fifty-member chorus. Because the City Dionysia was a civic and religious festival honoring Dionysus, the role of *chorēgos* was considered an honor, and *chorēgoi* often vied to achieve the most spectacular effects. Even so, anecdotes survive that suggest that an occasional *chorēgos* was concerned more with hoarding his money than with supporting ritual extravaganzas.

For the festival, a poet composed an original dithyrambic song; in the earliest times he also designed the dance

GREECE: Dance in Ancient Greece. (*left*) A depiction of dancing youths on a black-figure *kalathos,* c.540–530 BCE. (*above, left*) Satyr and maenad are often paired in ancient Greek art, as seen in this red-figure *kylix* (shallow, two-handled wine cup), c.530–500 BCE. (*above, right*) Girl dancing with clappers before a youth, from a red-figure *kylix* attributed to the painter Makron, c.490 BCE. (Metropolitan Museum of Art, New York; Fletcher Fund, 1956 [no. 56.171.37]; Rogers Fund, 1922 [no. 22.139.28]; purchased by subscription, 1896 [no. 96.9.191]; photographs used by permission.)

choreography *(schēma;* plural, *schēmata),* taught the song and dance to the chorus, and even acted as *exarchōn.* [*See* Schēma.] If the poet did not do the teaching, the *chorēgos* engaged a chorus trainer *(chorodidaskalos).* The dithyrambs were performed in the circular dancing area, the orchestra, of the Theater of Dionysus. Probably the chorus circled the altar that marked the center of the dance space, but little is known of the actual dance steps or gestures. The winning tribe received a tripod (three-legged cauldron) as a prize, which was then erected upon a monument to Dionysus.

The choruses of tragedy were introduced into the Dionysia in the last quarter of the sixth century BCE. During the fifth century, three poets were chosen annually to compete for the prize for tragedy. Each wrote three tragedies and one satyr play. Some of the earliest tragedians composed their trilogies around one family or theme—as Aeschylus did in the *Oresteia*—but the lists of winning trilogies suggest that most submitted three independent plays. Like the dithyrambic poets, the earliest dramatic poets were proficient singers and dancers, and it was also customary for them to act in their own entries. Many prided themselves on their originality in creating beautiful dance movements for the chorus; by the end of the fifth century, however, the poets relegated that task to the professional chorus trainer. The tragic chorus, like the dithyramb, was financed and supervised by the *chorēgos.* The chorus members (twelve in Aeschylus's tragedies, fifteen in the later tragedies of Sophocles and Euripides) were amateurs chosen from the Athenian citizenry, in contrast to the actors, who were paid professionals. John Winkler (1990) has suggested that the chorus members were ephebes, young men of military age who had common training in military maneuvers in close-rank formations.

The chorus entered the orchestra (situated in front of the rectangular acting area) by way of the *parodos,* the side walkway that gave its name to the chorus's entrance march-song. Having arrived in the orchestra, the chorus also sang and danced odes between the dramatic episodes. The term for such a dance-song *(stasimon;* plural, *stasima)* has caused some misunderstanding. Some modern scholars assumed that the Greek root *sta-* indicates that these choruses were sung in a stationary position. More plausibly, the term may indicate that the chorus performed the ode in the orchestra rather than while entering or leaving it. The chorus sang the *exodos* while exiting the theater.

Some scholars have maintained that the chorus pantomimed the meaning of the lyrics with a system of hand gestures called *cheironomia.* [*See* Cheironomia.] This misunderstanding stems from a misinterpretation of the meaning of the Greek word in its fifth-century BCE con-

GREECE: Dance in Ancient Greece. Tanagra statuette of a girl dancing, third century BCE. Drapery, a characteristic element of classical sculpture, is effectively rendered here in terra cotta. (Metropolitan Museum of Art, New York; Rogers Fund, 1911 [11.212.20]; photograph used by permission.)

text. The term *emmeleia* also has been associated with the choral dance of tragedy, but it probably refers to a quality of the dance—noble, serious, and dignified—rather than to a definable choreographic pattern. [*See* Emmeleia.] The Roman commentators listed names of dance figures *(schēmata)* that they maintained were used in the choreography of the chorus in the Classical period; however, the intervening centuries discredit the authenticity of these lists. The most reliable indications of choreography are the odes in the dramatic texts: the lyrics often describe or suggest appropriate accompanying movement and gestures, as well as providing the metrical rhythms that accompanied the dances. Although the chorus usually did not interact directly with the actors, the *kommos,* a song of lament, was sometimes shared between actor(s) and chorus. A poignant example is the despairing song of Xerxes echoed by the chorus of Persians at the end of Aeschylus's tragedy *Persians.* The actions of grief (breast-beating, tearing of hair) may have been performed for a theatrical *kommos.*

Comedy was a late addition to the Dionysia (and an even later addition at other festivals), with the first comedy competition recorded around 486 BCE. The usual number of entries in comedy was five (reduced to three during the years of the Peloponnesian War, 431–404 BCE). As in the case of tragedy, the poets applied to the state for permission to compete in the festival. If granted support for the chorus of twenty-four, the poet wrote the play, songs, and music and then taught them to his actors and chorus. The only complete extant comedies of the fifth century are those of Aristophanes. His comic plots often satirized contemporary political, philosophical, or social situations and even burlesqued the dramatic techniques of the tragic poets. The choruses of comedy often assumed a fanciful identity, such as clouds, wasps, or birds, although human characters also appeared.

Although the comic chorus may have entered the orchestra during the *parodos* in a rectangular formation as in tragedy, the texts of the comedies suggest that there were also unorthodox and humorous entrances. As in tragedy, dance-songs occurred between scenes, but the comic dances frequently included bawdy movements and horseplay—often directly involving the actors. The *kordax* was a licentious contemporary dance reputedly incorporated into the choreography of the comic chorus. [*See* Kordax.]

Very little is known about the chorus in satyr plays. Euripides' *Cyclops* (c.423 BCE) is the only complete extant satyr play that corresponds to the genre's traditional form. The satyr play usually burlesqued a well-known legend and portrayed the major characters in a gross and obscene manner. The satyr chorus, thought to consist of twelve members, impersonated mythological goat-men, or satyrs, with the fat, drunken satyr Silenus as their leader. A dance associated with the satyr chorus was the *sikinnis*. [*See* Sikinnis.]

The chorus members of all dramatic genres wore masks and costumes that corresponded to the characters depicted. The music was supplied by a flutist who led the chorus into the orchestra. Traditionally, commentators maintain that the entrance and exit processions were made in a rectangular formation and that the chorus retained this shape while dancing in the orchestra. Xenophon's statement in *Anabasis* 5.4.12 comparing the assembled rows of military ranks to the formation of two opposing choruses supports this theory, and indeed the physical training common to all the youthful chorus members would have been their military and athletic studies. However, the orchestra was round and included a centrally placed altar, which would have inhibited the free movement of a chorus in rectangular formation. Sections of choral lyrics that describe circular or other movements (for example, the circle dance in line 968 of Aristophanes'

GREECE: Dance in Ancient Greece. Pyrrhic dances (weapon dances) are a common decoration for vases designed to hold oil, such as this black-figure (on white ground) *lekythos*, c.480 BCE. (Metropolitan Museum of Art, New York; Rogers Fund, 1906 [no.06.1021.75]; photograph used by permission.)

Thesmophoriazusae) show that the initial rectangular formation could be abandoned.

By the end of the fifth century BCE, tragic and comic choruses assumed a role secondary to that of the actors. Rather than singing and dancing lyrical passages that commented on or responded to the dramatic situation, the chorus was relegated to an increasingly incidental function. The chorus of Aristophanes' *Plutus* (his last extant comedy, produced in 388 BCE) shows its increasing insignificance: the text indicates its presence by the single word *chorou* (meaning "performance of the chorus") to explain that the chorus sang or danced something here—apparently not relevant enough to record. The chorus never regained its stature in Greek drama. In fact, by the mid-fourth century BCE, many poets wrote *embolima* (choral interludes) that had no relationship to the play and could easily be incorporated into a different drama, a practice that Aristotle heartily decried in his *Poetics* (1456a25).

Dramatic and musical performances became more and more the domain of the professional, and in the third century BCE the performers formed guilds in Athens. This professionalism extended to dance: a number of the guild members were known as chorus trainers or dancers.

Dance Training. The importance of dance in religious ritual raises the question of how and where ancient Greek dancers trained. Teaching methods differed among the city-states and also changed over time. According to evidence on educational practices of the sixth century BCE, education was a private matter; each family elected to educate its children according to its financial means. Although boys received priority (only men were considered citizens in ancient Greece), girls were by no means neglected.

In Athens, for example, boys and girls were educated separately in letters as well as in music and physical culture. Red-figure vase paintings depict girls learning to dance in groups under the supervision of a dancing mistress, who often holds a teacher's staff; sometimes a musician with castanets provides rhythmic accompaniment for the lesson. Boys had two opportunities to learn dance movements. The well-to-do received private tutelage from an athletic instructor at the *palaestra* (wrestling school). The *palaestra*, a private sports building with bathing facilities, was frequented by boys and young men in athletic training. A *gymnasium*, by contrast, was a public outdoor training ground for men, located outside the city walls, which often included a *palaestra* nearby for bathing. The athletic curriculum for Athenian boys included movement studies, precision military exercises, and athletic games, including *cheironomia* (shadow boxing), and dances performed in armor such as the *pyrrhikhē* (pyrrhic). [*See* Pyrrhic.] These movement studies were designed to develop skills and strength for combat sports and for the tactical maneuvers of actual battle, and they were executed gracefully and rhythmically to musical accompaniment. Some may have had set movement patterns. In addition, boys selected for dithyrambic choruses in the various festivals received free movement instruction. In these cases, the individual tribe of the city-state engaged a *chorodidaskalos* to instruct its contestants in a dance-song for the competition and appointed a wealthy citizen to pay the expenses.

Sparta encouraged physical education equally for boys and girls. Exercises in imitation of a certain sport or activity seem to have been a major component of the training. The *anapalē*, a dance using wrestling movements, originated in Sparta. Military songs and marching drills, as well as armed dances such as the pyrrhic, provided the youths with training for battle.

Music and dance scenes declined in the visual arts after the middle of the fifth century BCE, just as the importance of these pursuits in education continued to dwindle into Hellenistic times. From the fourth century BCE, music, dance, and athletics became the domain of specialized professionals, spectator events rather than the valued participatory activities of the previous centuries.

Dance as Entertainment. In addition to the function of dance in civic and religious ritual, physical development, and military training, the Greeks also appreciated dance as a form of entertainment and a leisure pursuit. Excerpts from Homer's *Odyssey* illustrate the importance of dance as entertainment as early as the Mycenaean Age. In each case, visitors are entertained—sometimes by participating themselves—in after-dinner activities of music, song, and dance. For example, when Odysseus's son, Telemachus, visits his uncle Menelaus, king of Sparta, he arrives during a double wedding celebration. Following the feast, a bard plays the *phorminx* (a stringed instrument) and sings while two acrobats whirl and dance among the guests (4.5–19). It is unclear whether the tumblers in this episode are slaves or freemen, professionals or amateurs; however, two other vignettes show that the guests themselves might join in. During the banquet honoring Odysseus at the court of King Alcinoös, a number of youths rise and dance in a circle while a bard plays and sings. Alcinoös then persuades his two sons, the best dancers, to show off an acrobatic ball-dance amid the ring of boys who beat time with their feet (8.256–370). In other examples, the unmannerly and presumptuous suitors of Penelope observe the decorum of the feast by enjoying dance and song after dinner (1.150–152; 1.421–424; 17.605–606; 18.304–306). All these episodes, though they occur in the context of epic storytelling, were probably based on accepted customs of the age.

This early tradition of entertainment following a banquet survived into the Classical age of Greece. Even at an encampment during a military campaign, the Greeks preserved the custom of entertaining their guests (foreign ambassadors and compatriots) with song and dance. Xenophon records an evening of campside after-dinner dances that included mimetic dance-stories, regional armed dances by the soldiers, and a pyrrhic dance by a slave girl dressed in war regalia (*Anabasis* 6.1.1–14).

In the fifth century BCE, a private feast often concluded with a drinking party featuring conversation, games, speeches, music, dances, or mime. The term *symposion* (plural, *symposia*) came to refer to both the party itself and the room where it took place. In a symposium, one person was usually selected by a throw of the dice to act as a master of ceremonies, moderating conversation and directing the order of entertainments. Wine was first poured and diluted with water, and a hymn was sung. The actual festivities varied with the party and its feast-master. Sometimes the participants were garlanded. Some drank; others demurred. Frequently the guests played a version of the popular drinking game *kottabos* (wine-throw), wherein the banqueters reclined in a circle on the floor and attempted to toss the dregs from their cups into a basin in the center.

Vivid descriptions of assorted dance entertainments at a symposium are given in the second chapter of Xenophon's dialogue *Symposium* (c.380 BCE). The host engages a man from Syracuse to bring his traveling performers (probably slaves): a girl flutist, an acrobatic dancing girl, and a boy who dances and plays the *kithara*, a kind of lyre. This group provides purely musical interludes as well as combinations of music, dance, acrobatics, and mime. The boy dances so gracefully that Socrates, one of the guests, observes that the *schēmata* make him appear all the more handsome. The girl and the boy enact a pantomimic dance representing a mythological love scene. The dancing girl's feats also include juggling hoops to flute music and executing acrobatic stunts over a hoop rimmed with upright swords.

The professionalism of the foreign troupe described in Xenophon's work suggests that the host prearranged such sophisticated entertainments for his guests. However, the participation of the banqueters was apparently not precluded: Philip, a buffoon and an observer at the feast, spontaneously burlesques the dances of the two performers, much to the delight of his companions. Nevertheless, the shift from full-fledged participation by amateurs in Homeric times to the dependence on professional performances reflected by Xenophon's work parallels the gradual de-emphasis of dance, music, and athletic education for Greek citizens in the fourth century, when these disciplines became primarily professional pursuits.

The convivial tone of Xenophon's *Symposium* contrasts sharply with the more philosophical *Symposium* of his contemporary Plato. In succeeding centuries, the symposium setting became a literary genre favored by writers attempting to emulate the style of their classical predecessors. Although some imitators concentrated on presenting high-minded philosophical discussions in the manner of Plato, others—notably Plutarch in "Quaestiones convivales" (Table Talk) in his *Moralia*, and Athenaeus in his *Deipnosophists* (Doctors at Dinner) from the first and third centuries CE—included anecdotes about antiquarian Greek and contemporary music, dance, and theatrical entertainments.

Dance Mania. The worship of certain divinities, particularly in the cults of Asiatic gods such as Dionysus and Cybele, included orgiastic or ecstatic dancing. The female devotees of Dionysus who succumbed to this dance mania were called maenads or bacchantes. Artists of classical Greece often took the dance of the maenads as a subject for vase paintings, which they represented according to certain consistent conventions. Like other devotees of Dionysus, the maenads are crowned with ivy, wear fawn skins draped over one shoulder, and wield the *thyrsus* (a wand entwined with ivy and vine leaves). To suggest the speed and wildness of their movements, the vase painters show the maenads with flying tresses and with their heads turned back over the shoulder toward the other dancers racing behind them. Intoxicated with wine and ecstatic fervor, they often dance (or run) with the arm and leg of the same side advancing together, rather than with arms and legs in opposition, to indicate the loss of equilibrium and coordination inevitably associated with the Dionysian wine-drinking rituals.

The mythological story of Euripides' *Bacchae* centers around one such instance of dance mania. When Dionysus's cousin, King Pentheus of Thebes, tries to stamp out the god's cult, Dionysus infuses the women of the city with a frenzy that drives them from their homes to the mountains to sing, dance, and partake in secret orgiastic rites. Pentheus is ultimately torn to pieces by the maenads, led by his own mother, Agave. The chorus of the play is a band of Dionysus's votaries who have followed him to Thebes from Asia Minor. The choral passages contain vivid descriptions of the revelry, and the rhythms of the poetry reflect those used in typical hymns to Dionysus.

Euripides' rendition of the Theban story, though perhaps the best known, is only one of a tradition of tales relating the incidence of dance mania throughout Greece. The stories themselves are mythological, but their proliferation probably indicates an attempt to explain actual outbreaks of this phenomenon in Greece from Mycenaean times through later periods. Certain elements of the stories are similar. Usually the victims of dance mania were women, and the inflicted frenzy was a punishment for some religious transgression. Some scholars have speculated that outbreaks of disease might have precipitated cases of dance mania, while others have suggested that the stresses of a restrictive society for Greek women might have been responsible.

Dance Prohibitions. Although the preponderance of evidence indicates that many dance forms flourished throughout ancient Greece, on occasion a city-state or an individual attempted to suppress a certain dance. For example, in the case of outbreaks of bacchic dance mania (or other wild rituals), the Greek state banned the unacceptable practices and tried to redirect the energy into more formalized and restrained ceremonies. According to Lillian Lawler (1964a), the dithyrambic competitions may have arisen from the state's effort to design alternative Dionysian rituals.

In contrast to Socrates, who extolled the virtues of dancing, the philosopher Plato advocated strict guidelines to determine which dances were appropriate for Greek citizens. Plato believed that participating in an unseemly activity would undermine a good citizen's noble character. When he outlined his ideal state, he banned all orgiastic dancing and advocated severe penalties for citizens who dared to indulge in such revelry (*Laws* 10.910b–c). Plato condemned the effects of the dances of comedy, particularly those with lewd or suggestive movements such as the *kordax* (*Laws* 7.816d–e). Plato's condemnation of the dances of comedy as morally corrupting anticipated later moral assessments of the *kordax*. In the fourth century BCE, the orator Demosthenes lambasted this dance in describing the indecencies of the court life at the court of Philip of Macedon (*Olynthiac* 2.18), and Aristotle's pupil Theophrastus described the "willfully disreputable" man as one who would dance the *kordax* when sober (*Characters* 6). Among the many Roman commentators who deplored the *kordax*, Athenaeus placed it among vulgar dances (*Deipnosophists* 14.631d).

In the epistolary books of the New Testament, the fathers of the early Christian church assailed certain pagan revels and dances, using the Greek word *kōmos* to denote these revelries in a number of passages, such as *Galatians* 5.21, *Romans* 13.13, and *1 Peter* 4.3. Often other immoral practices—idolatry, lust, or drunkenness—were enumerated alongside. In its earliest form, the *kōmos* had been a riotous, frequently bawdy street processional. Evidently, the *kōmos* retained its original character, which together with its pagan associations prompted the censure of the Christian church. Not all references to dance in the New Testament were derogatory: the parable of the prodigal son in *Luke* 15.25 ends with a feast including music and dancing. In such cases, the authors use more general Greek terms for dance.

Music for Dance. The ancient Greeks used three main types of musical instruments to accompany dance: strings, winds, and percussion. Among the stringed instruments, the *lyra* (lyre) was most important because of both its early association with the cult of Apollo and its use in the musical education of Greek youths. The *kithara*, more sophisticated than the *lyra*, was used predominantly by professionals. Epic singers played the *phorminx*, a primitive stringed instrument. All three were plucked instruments of the lyre family.

Among the many wind instruments, the *aulos* (a double-reed instrument) was most common. Often used in duets with voice or *kithara*, the *aulos* figured prominently in many Greek social or religious occasions, including processions, banquets, the Olympic games, dramatic festivals, and the rites honoring Dionysus. The *aulos* was frequently chosen to accompany dancers,

marching soldiers, or rowers. Its ancient origin has been traced to Asia Minor, and its earliest mention in literature is in Homer's *Iliad*.

Percussion instruments included forms of drum *(tympanum)*, tambourine *(rhoptron)*, bells *(kōdōn* and *seistron)*, castanets *(krotala)*, and cymbals *(kymbala)*. The *krotala* were held, a pair on each hand, and provided rhythms for dancers at dance lessons and during ceremonies in honor of Cybele or Dionysus. The *tympanum*, which women often played in Dionysian rites, consisted of a hollow cylinder with skin membranes stretched over the ends and struck with the hands.

Music, verse, and dance were interdependent art forms in the heyday of Greek culture. The poetic rhythms of the lyrics determined the musical quantities (duration of notes) of the accompanying melody. Vowels in the ancient Greek language had both pitch-accent and quantity (time

GREECE: Dance in Ancient Greece. Bronze statuette of a veiled dancer, from the Hellenistic period, early second century BCE. (Metropolitan Museum of Art, New York; Bequest of Walter C. Baker, 1971 [no.1972.118.95]; used by permission.)

value), unlike the stressed syllables of modern Greek. Thus, the syllables of a line of Greek poetry created a prosodic rhythm, with the long vowels receiving twice the time value of the short vowels. Even though no actual melodies survive from ancient Greece, the verses of choral passages do indicate the musical rhythms that accompanied the dance. [*See* Music for Dance, *article on* Western Music before 1520.]

By the end of the fifth century BCE, a number of poets (including Euripides) began to experiment with musical forms in ways that undermined the traditional correspondence between syllable and musical note. Aristophanes burlesqued these musical innovations in his comedies with an effective parody of Euripides' practice of assigning more than one musical note per syllable (*Frogs* 1314).

[*For related discussion, see* Crete, *article on* Dance in Ancient Crete. *See also* Choral Dancing; Hyporchēma; Orchestra; *and* Terpsichore.]

BIBLIOGRAPHY

Beck, Frederick A. G. *Greek Education, 450–350 B.C.* London, 1964.
Csapo, Eric, and William J. Slater. *The Context of Ancient Drama.* Ann Arbor, Mich., 1995.
Delavaud-Roux, Marie-Hélène. *Les danses armées en Grèce antique.* Aix-en-Provence, 1993.
Delavaud-Roux, Marie-Hélène. *Les danses pacifiques en Grèce antique.* Aix-en-Provence, 1994.
Dodds, E. R. Introduction and commentary to Euripides' *Bacchae.* 2d ed. Oxford, 1960.
Fryer, E. Fern. "Greek Literary Mime." Ph.D. diss., Indiana University, 1992.
Gardiner, E. Norman. *Athletics of the Ancient World.* Oxford, 1930.
Larmour, David H. "The Interrelationship of Drama and Athletics in Classical Greece." Ph.D. diss., University of Illinois, Urbana-Champaign, 1987.
Lawler, Lillian B. *The Dance in Ancient Greece.* Middletown, Conn., 1964a.
Lawler, Lillian B. *The Dance of the Ancient Greek Theatre.* Iowa City, 1964b.
Lonsdale, Steven H. *Dance and Ritual Play in Greek Religion.* Baltimore, 1993.
Michaelides, Solon. *The Music of Ancient Greece: An Encyclopaedia.* London, 1978.
Mullen, William. *Choreia: Pindar and Dance.* Princeton, 1982.
Parke, H. W. *Festivals of the Athenians.* Ithaca, N.Y., 1977.
Pickard-Cambridge, A. W. *Dithyramb, Tragedy, and Comedy.* Revised by T. B. L. Webster. 2d ed. Oxford, 1962.
Pickard-Cambridge, A. W. *The Dramatic Festivals of Athens.* Revised by John Gould and D. H. Lewis. Oxford, 1968.
Raftis, Alkis, compiler. *Proceedings of the Fifth International Conference on Dance Research, Greek Section of the International Organization of Folk Art (UNESCO–B), Athens, 4–8 September 1991.* 2 vols. Dora Stratou Theater, Athens, Greece, n. d.
Slater, William J., ed. *Dining in a Classical Context.* Ann Arbor, Mich., 1991.
Smigel, Elizabeth [Libby]. "Redefinitions of the Fifth-Century Greek Chorus Using a Methodology Applied to Aristophanes' *Thesmophoriazusae.*" Master's thesis, York University, 1982.
Sparti, Barbara. "Report on the Fifth International Conference on Dance Research: Dance and Ancient Greece." *Dance Research Journal* 24 (Spring 1992): 52–54.
Walton, J. Michael. *Greek Theatre Practice.* Rev. ed. London, 1991.
Webster, T. B. L. *The Greek Chorus.* London, 1970.
Winkler, John J., and Froma I. Zeitlin, eds. *Nothing to Do with Dionysos? Athenian Drama in Its Social Context.* Princeton, 1990.
Xenophon. *Anabasis* 5.4.12, 6.1.1–14.

LIBBY SMIGEL

Dance in the Roman and Byzantine Periods

The Roman conquest in 146 CE of the last remnants of the Greek states that had survived from the empire of Alexander the Great marked the end of Greek political independence but not the end of Greek cultural influence. Indeed, the absorption of Greece into the Roman Empire preserved and extended Hellenistic civilization; Greek remained the language of culture and education, and Greek scholars and artists flourished throughout the empire. In this context Greek dancers found themselves addressing a wider audience spread over vast territories and often incorporating many people who knew no Greek. No longer bound by the moral and aesthetic precepts of the Greek city-states, dancers turned to easy tricks to please their patrons, and their dances came to emphasize burlesque, overtly erotic, comic, and frightening elements. The unity of the classical notion of *musikē*—lyric song, dance, and instrumental music comprising one whole—was fragmented into its component parts. Song texts retained the Greek language for some time, sung as interludes by a passive chorus deprived of its integrated function in the classical drama. Music became more independent with the addition to the traditional pair of the *lyra* (lyre) and the oboelike *aulos* of several new instruments, which came to form a small orchestra.

Divested of word and melody, dance became purely pantomimic. Although mimetic dances abounded in Greek antiquity, pantomime—the solo performance of a dramatic narrative in which the dancer portrays all the characters—is the hallmark of the Greco-Roman period. Performers became famous for their ability to relate entire stories with gestures and postures. They wore masks, lavish costumes, and jewelry. Dancers became professionals of low status rather than respected artists, and dance lost its sacred public function and degenerated to mere spectacle and entertainment.

It was inevitable that the Christian church would attack this kind of dancing, especially in the theocratic Byzantine Empire. Most of what is known about dance during the Byzantine era (the fifth to the fifteenth centuries CE) comes from the prohibitions and exhortations of the Orthodox church.

Texts by the church fathers and synods (congresses of bishops) refer to dancing as demonic, blasphemous, and abominable. These ecclesiastical sources imply that stage dancing in Constantinople and other urban centers of the time was in some way obscene. Professional dancers (jugglers, circus and theater actors, prostitutes, and slaves) and mimes were often accused of living disorderly lives and pointedly ridiculing Christian rites. At the same time, rural dancing, which preserved its character as communal ritual and preserved archaic pagan elements, was not distinguished from urban dancing by the Eastern Christian Church. The persistence of ecclesiastical polemics suggests that dancing remained popular everywhere.

In spite of constant pressure from the church, successive emperors hesitated to prohibit dancing for fear of arousing public resentment. Popular dancing continued in village celebrations on saints' days, after Easter, during marriage feasts, and on birthdays. There are even reports of dancing inside the churches during Christmas. Soldiers danced during pauses in their training; charioteers danced their victories; the court danced on the emperor's birthday. After times of disaster, large public dances erupted as a way of expressing relief.

Written sources do not supply an actual description of the dances. From a multitude of scattered remarks and some paintings in churches, we can deduce that the usual pattern was a round chain dance. Sometimes the leading dancer guided the line in a sinuous pattern. Men and women danced separately, but there is mention of mixed dances. The dancers frequently held kerchiefs or veils and waved them, stamped their feet on the ground, and clapped their hands. Women dancers, especially professionals, held wooden or metal cymbals (*krotala*). A distinguishing feature of stage dancers' costumes was their shirtsleeves, which were tight down to the elbow, then very loose and long so that they could be waved to enhance the movements of the hands. The dancers or the musicians sang well-known or improvised songs. The most common instruments used for dancing were the *aulos, kithara* (a large lyre), small drum *(tympanum)*, and the *dephi*, a small frame drum, often with jingles. There is no evidence of courtly or aristocratic dances during this period.

Unlike western Europe of the Middle Ages, where political power was largely maintained by secular rulers who looked to Rome only as a religious authority, the Eastern Empire was a centralized theocratic state in which both political and religious authority emanated from Constantinople. Later, by the time of the European Renaissance, when the foundations for the modern evolution of dance were laid, Greece had become a poor province of the Ottoman Empire.

The fall of Constantinople to the Turks in 1453 marked the end of the Byzantine era. For a period of four centuries thereafter, Greek populations in the southern part of the Balkan peninsula and in Asia Minor were under Turkish rule. In general, the policy of the Ottoman Empire was one of tolerance toward the cultural autonomy of the peoples living within it. The continuity of Greek popular culture survived unbroken during this long period. Christian peoples—Greeks, Slavs, and Armenians—could freely practice their faith and consolidated their sense of national identity around their respective churches, languages, and customs.

Alone among the peoples subject to Ottoman rule, the Greeks considered themselves to be the exclusive heirs of Byzantine culture. Church hymns, which constituted the only musical education of the people aside from folk music, were (and still are) composed in traditional Byzantine style, which in turn continued ancient Greek musical forms. Since the Turks too adopted the main principles of Byzantine music, Greek music was preserved through four centuries of foreign rule. In consequence, Greek music still uses natural modal scales and is monophonic, while western European music developed polyphony and the tempered scale.

In spite of the Greek communities' wide geographic dispersion along the eastern Mediterranean coast and their proximity to countless other ethnic groups, foreign influences were minimal. Written descriptions and engravings by European travelers on their way to the Holy Land depict Greek dances of the Ottoman period that closely resemble dances practiced even today in the Greek countryside. On the whole, the fragmentary evidence confirms the continuity of Greek dancing and suggests only that the variety and richness of Greek dance were gradually reduced, with very little adoption of foreign elements.

In the Greek countryside there are villages that have always existed in economic and cultural isolation. Conquering armies frequently passed on the mainland while pirates passed along the coasts; communication was difficult even between neighboring areas or islands; the poor yield of the soil caused chronic emigration of the most dynamic elements of the population; and the absence of a local ruling class impeded cultural integration. Greek villages have consequently always been remarkably self-sufficient compared to villages in many other parts of Europe, which had constant contact with neighboring urban centers. Dances, like other traditional customs, have evolved slowly in every village and small region. Local festivities on religious occasions have preserved their ritual character as an affirmation of group identity, and the observance of ancient customs, once a defense against foreign rulers, remains as a way to preserve ties with emigrating relatives. Community dances in the village square or churchyard are one of the only occasions for a meeting of all the village's families, for open encounters between boys and girls, or for celebration amid a harsh daily life. Weddings afford such occasions on a smaller scale. Preparations and celebrations last several days or several weeks, following an elaborate pattern of prescribed customs that include dancing at specified moments.

[*For related discussion, see* Roman Empire.]

BIBLIOGRAPHY

Koukoules, Phaidon I. *Life and Culture of the Byzantines* (in Greek). Athens, 1952.

Raftis, Alkis. *The World of Greek Dance.* Translated by Alexandra Doumas. Athens, 1987.

Raftis, Alkis. "Dance in Greece." *Viltis* 49 (March–April 1991): 7–11.

Raftis, Alkis. *Enkyklopaidea tou hellinikou chorou.* Athens, 1995.

ALKIS RAFTIS

Dance in Modern Greece

Traditional dance may be defined as dance transmitted from one generation to the next by continuous immersion rather than by formal teaching, while folk dance consists of traditional dances learned within a nontraditional society for educational, performance, therapeutic, or other purposes. In this sense, traditional dancing is still widely practiced in the Greek countryside, although modernization has caused a steady decline since World War II. Young people have left the villages to find jobs in towns or abroad; roads have been opened to previously inaccessible areas; television sets have proliferated; tourists flood the coasts every summer; and discothèques sprout in the smallest towns. Customary means of entertainment have changed, while government policy toward dance has been one of marked neglect.

The Greek Civil War (1947–1949) forced a large part of the rural population to find refuge in towns, where they came to regard village life as backward. The postwar generation does not identify with the dances of its ancestors. Traditional dances have gradually become the province of folk dance groups, with a subsequent loss of feeling and increased emphasis on the spectacular.

There are about four thousand folk dance groups around the country, and about one thousand in Greek communities abroad. The Greek government does not give them financial support, but they themselves raise the funds needed for costumes and other equipment. These groups tend to base their repertory on dances from the local region for which they already have costumes. Two state-supported permanent theaters offer daily summer performances by resident companies performing dances from various regions—the Dora Stratou group in Athens, and the Nelly Dimoglou group in Rhodes. The Lyceum (Lykeion) of Greek Women, the first organization to sponsor performances of folk dances in the 1910s, has branches in all towns, each with its own dance group.

Costumes, music, and dance styles differ greatly from region to region and among Greek subcultures, sometimes even between neighboring villages. At least twenty major regions and subcultures can be distinguished, each having at least ten unique dances. This diversity results from the widespread dispersion of ethnic Greeks: Pontic Greeks, for example, lived for centuries along the northern coast of Asia Minor until they established their own villages throughout Macedonia. The most notable regions

GREECE: Dance in Modern Greece. This *ballos*, from the island of Skyros, is a couple dance in 2/4 time, in which the men circle around their spinning partners. This dance often occurs as an up-tempo break, following the open circle *syrtós*. (Photograph courtesy of Alkis Raftis, Greek Dances Theater, Athens.)

in terms of dance are Thrace, Macedonia, Epirus, the southern mainland, the Ionian islands, the Aegean islands, Crete, and Cyprus. Distinct ethnic groups that have maintained their identity despite migration are the Arvanites, Vlachs, Pomaks, Sarakatsani, and repatriated Greeks from the coasts of Asia Minor, the Black Sea, and northern Thrace.

Some dances are common to several neighboring regions, although the styles of dancing are unmistakably different, as are the related songs and music. A performing group will not present dances from another region unless it has the appropriate costumes. There is no truly panhellenic dance, although some dances have come to be widely performed.

By far the most common dance form is the *syrtós*. The name indicates a drawing action and reflects the basic motion of a line of dancers being drawn forward by the lead dancer. The term *syrtós* has been found in an ancient inscription, but there is no indication of how it was danced in antiquity. In modern Greece it has become a generic name for a dance performed in an open circle with a walklike step. The basic *syrtós* is in 2/4 meter, with a sequence of one long and two short steps to the right. The leader has freedom to improvise and to coil and uncoil the line of dancers in various patterns. One particular *syrtós*, the Kalamatianos, is in 7/8 meter (divided 3, 2, 2) and originates in the Peloponnesus. It has gradually been adopted by other regions and has come to be considered a national dance because it evokes the first part of Greece to be liberated from Turkish rule. Several similar dances are called *pēdēktos* ("hopping") to distinguish them from *syrtós*, which necessarily has a shuffling step.

Dancing face-to-face *(antikrystos)*, as in the *karsilamas*, and dancing solo (as in the *beratis*) are rare and seem to indicate the influence of the Greeks of Asia Minor. Couple dances, like the *ballos*, are an exception, presumably of Western origin. The rule for public dancing was always the solemn circular dance; improvising figures and dancing in small groups was proper only in family celebrations at home. In general, dancers move the upper part of the body very slightly, in contrast to Middle Eastern dancers; and unlike their Middle Eastern counterparts, Greek women do not dance alone in front of men.

The method of linking dancers shows only slight variety. In the most common handhold, each dancer simply holds the hands of the dancers on either side, arms down or bent at the elbows. Another handhold is crosswise, that is, between alternate dancers in the line, as seen in the *trata* of Megara or the *soústa* of Rhodes; this is mostly used in women's dances. Men sometimes hold each other's shoulders (as in the *pentozalís* of Crete or the *gaïda* of Macedonia), and they tend to stay in a straight line rather than a circle. Other holds are by the elbow (the *tsakónikos* of the Peloponnesus and the *pōgónissios* of Epirus) or by the belt (the *zōnaradikos* of Thrace).

The order in which dancers align themselves in the circular dance is of great importance, especially in the opening dance of a celebration. The most common pattern is men first according to age, followed by women, also according to age, then children. Thus, the only opportunity for a dancer to advance up the line comes when an older person can no longer dance. In some villages a married woman takes precedence in the line over an unmarried woman, regardless of age. Since holding the hand of a member of the opposite sex in public is considered improper, a problem arose as to who would be the connecting link between the men and the women. This was solved by calling on a child or an aged couple. When an entire family dances as a group, as is common in the Cycladic islands, the internal hierarchy is followed in the order of succession, sometimes causing disputes among cousins.

The first dancer in the line holds a position of honor; the dance is considered his. In some areas, after the Easter Sunday Mass, the priest leads the first dance in the churchyard or around the church as a token of benediction on the celebration. In a marriage feast the bride leads the first dance, then the bridegroom and the in-laws. Usually all participants take turns at leading the dance, each

GREECE: Dance in Modern Greece. (*left*) Traditionally, the Cyprus sickle dance was performed by harvesters as an expression of joy at having finished reaping a field. Now this dangerous dance, involving quick manipulations of two sickles near the dancer's body, is performed only in theatrical settings. The music accompanying the dance begins and ends in 2/4 time, with a 5/8 interlude in the middle. (*right*) Folk dances are often performed in suites, with specific dances occurring in a prescribed order. Here, two young women perform the second *karsilamas*, a couple dance in which the partners revolve around each other. Violin and lute accompany this dance in 7/8 time. (Photographs courtesy of Alkis Raftis, Greek Dances Theater, Athens.)

GREECE: Dance in Modern Greece. Four women in traditional costumes hold hands in "Tis Maria" (Mary's Dance). This slow, solemn dance, from the Roumlouki plain near Salonika (Thessaloníki), is performed in a complex 11/8 rhythm. The dance's title refers to the accompanying song about a girl named Mary. (Photograph courtesy of Alkis Raftis, Greek Dances Theater, Athens.)

one also asking and paying the musicians to play the tune of his choice. A woman does not lead a dance unless her father, brother, or husband asks her to do so and gives an order to the musicians. As a rule, the head of the family approaches the musicians when he wants to dance with his family or friends. Traditionally, it was considered a deliberate affront to enter into someone else's dance; many fights started this way. It was also improper for a man to ask a woman to dance unless they were engaged to marry.

In earlier times, when village people were too poor to pay a musician, girls sang as accompaniment for the Sunday afternoon dances, but big public dances on prescribed dates and marriage celebrations were always accompanied by instrumental music. The most widespread instruments in use today are the bagpipe, called *gaïda* on the mainland and *tsambouna* in the islands, where it has no drone; the three-string *lyra* (gradually being replaced by the violin); the shawm *(zourna)*, usually played by Gypsies; and the clarinet *(klarino)*, which has replaced the flute. Percussion is provided by a large drum *(daoúli)* up to one meter in diameter, a small ceramic drum *(toumbeleki)*, or a small frame drum with jingles similar to the Middle Eastern *riq (dephi)*, which is mainly a women's instrument. Most of the instrumentalists on the mainland are Gypsies, but their own musical idiom has not influenced local music as it has in other countries. Instruments were traditionally made by the musicians themselves, types and methods of construction varying widely among regions.

Of special interest are the fire-dancing rites in four Macedonian villages inhabited by Greek refugees from Kosti in northern Thrace on Saint Constantine's and Saint Helena's days, when participants dance on glowing coals until they reduce them to ashes. [See Anastárides.] Also notable are the Carnival celebrations in Naoussa, Skyros, Zakynthos, and other areas, where villagers wearing masks, bells, sheepskins, and various disguises perform ritualized mimetic and comic dances.

Urban Popular Dance. By the middle of the nineteenth century, an idiomatic form of music and dancing appeared among the lower social strata in the port cities on the Aegean Sea. In the poorer neighborhoods of cities such as Istanbul, Smyrna, Salonika, and Syra, thousands of outcasts had gathered who led a life of misery and lawlessness. They developed their own means of expression, incorporating elements from the rural tradition, Turkish culture, and the European culture of the upper classes. This genre, eventually called *rebetika*, gained increasing momentum and social acceptance to become, a century later, the international hallmark of Greek music and dance.

Originating in the *tavernas* and coffeehouses frequented by sailors, peddlers, the jobless, and petty criminals, *rebetiko* lyrics lament frustrated loves, idealize bravado, and reject bourgeois values while projecting the countervalues of a marginal social group. The music is played by string instruments, mainly the mandolin-like *bouzouki* and the smaller *baglamas*, along with violin, dulcimer *(santouri)*, and guitar. The musicians play in a neighborhood café on a stage built along one wall with a space in front of it where patrons can dance. The orchestra appears every evening (unlike traditional musicians, who used to play only on festive days and in the open air) and includes female singers who may also dance.

The *rebetiko* dance style bears the mark of its urban origin. Suitable for the small dance floors in *tavernas*, it is danced solo or by only a few dancers. Movements seem precise and calculated, with the body crouched forward and arms outstretched to maintain balance. Originally practiced almost exclusively by men, it reflects the individualism of the townsperson as opposed to the communality of large group dances in the villages. While village dancing is based on the repetition of the same steps over a long duration—a dance might last a half hour or more—*rebetiko* dances are based on incessant variation of steps for the few minutes' duration of the songs.

The most common *rebetiko* dance is the *zeybekikos*, in 9/4 meter (2, 2, 2, 3), a solo improvisational dance with movements of balanced precision that express intense concentration and self-absorption. In its original rural form it is a dance performed during Carnival by disguised characters; its name derives from a fierce tribe in Asia Minor. Equally popular is the *chasapikos* (butcher's dance) in slow 2/4 meter. The dancers hold each other's shoulders and, moving sideways to the right, take steps forward and back. It is danced by two or three men, usually close friends who have developed their own variations on the basic step. A similar dance in fast tempo and moving to the right is the *servikos*. These two dances were synthesized to create a new dance called the "Zorba dance" or *syrtaki*, in which the slow *chasapikos* modulates into the rapid *servikos*. This dance became popular around the world in the 1960s and is still the highlight of Greek fraternal balls abroad and of performances in every tourist cabaret in Greece. Other *rebetiko* dances are the *karsilamas* in 9/8 meter (2, 2, 2, 3), danced by couples, and the *tsiphteteli* ("double chord-strum"), a solo dance in 4/4 meter resembling a subdued or mock belly dance.

Until the 1950s middle-class Greeks and the media were contemptuous of *rebetika,* the music as well as the dance. When Manos Hadjidakis *(Never on Sunday)* and Mikis Theodorakis *(Zorba the Greek)* composed music for films and popular songs, adapting *rebetiko* style to modern tastes, they enjoyed immediate success in Greece and abroad and established a revival of the style, although the social conditions of its origin had disappeared. *Rebetika* has become widely adopted socially and is played on radio and television. Most *tavernas* feature modernized versions of songs and dances in this style. Young people and women as well as men dance it; patrons are encouraged to show their appreciation by breaking dishes on the dance floor.

Social Dance. After the War of Independence from Turkey (1821–1827) the liberated Greek provinces founded an independent state; other provinces joined it one after another until Greece reached its present boundaries a century later. The first Greek king, Otto, came from Bavaria, and his court introduced European couple dances to the new capital, Athens. Major Greek emigrant communities were already familiar with these dances, and the Athenian middle class gradually adopted them. European-style dances became the rule at home gatherings and celebrations in the towns, with an occasional Greek dance performed at the end. Today there are no ballrooms or competition ballroom dancing, but discothèques are very popular; there are more than one hundred in the greater Athens area, where more than one-third of the country's population live.

In Athens, besides the *tavernas* featuring *rebetiko* dance music, two dozen *tavernas* offer folk musicians from particular regions (Crete, Epirus, the islands, Pontic Macedonia, or Thrace) to draw patrons of rural origin with their families to meet fellow villagers and to dance their own dances. Major regional centers also have such gathering places; for example, in Macedonia there are *tavernas* offering Pontic dance music, and Cretan towns have *tavernas* with local music. In general, Greeks distinguish between *bouzouki tavernas* with *rebetiko* music, clarinet *tavernas* with traditional music from the mainland, and violin *tavernas* with music from the islands and the coasts.

Theatrical Dance. Stage dancing was unknown in Greece during the Turkish occupation. It was not until the middle of the nineteenth century that touring foreign groups started giving performances in the capital of the new state. At the turn of the twentieth century several

GREECE: Dance in Modern Greece. Men and women perform a *rebetiko*-style line dance as musicians play on the side. (Photograph by Jean-Louis Saiz; courtesy of Alkis Raftis, Greek Dances Theater, Athens.)

GREECE: Dance in Modern Greece. The *patinada* of Naoussa, western Macedonia, is a masked sword dance traditionally performed by groups of young men during Carnival. This white pleated skirt is characteristic not of the dance's region of origin but of the southern Greek mainland. Hundreds of coins are stitched onto the costume to created a constant jingling sound as the dancers leap and cross swords. (Photograph courtesy of Alkis Raftis, Greek Dances Theater, Athens.)

cafés chantants in Athens offered cabaret shows that included dancing numbers, always by foreign artists. The revue genre, featuring sketches of political satire and dancing, is still very popular, with half a dozen theaters in Athens.

The first notable revival of Classical Greek drama was given in the ancient theater of Delphi in 1927. It was organized by the poet Angelos Sikelianos and his wife, the American archaeologist Eva Palmer Sikelianou. They presented Aeschylus's *Prometheus Bound* and combined the event with a folk festival, exhibitions, and lectures. The Delphic Festival was repeated in 1930 with Aeschylus's *Suppliants*, also choreographed by Eva Sikelianou, who was a friend of Isadora Duncan.

In 1932 the Ethnikon Theatron (National Theater)—founded that year in Athens—presented Sophocles' *Ajax* and established an ongoing tradition of commissioning dancers and choreographers to teach movement to the chorus in Greek plays. The chorus was mainly composed of actors with some dance training and rarely of dancers. Having practically no information on the movements of the chorus in ancient drama, choreographers' approaches to the modern presentations have varied from rhythmical recitation combined with a sequence of postures to elaborate creations. Their main source of inspiration, though, remains the traditional dancing of modern Greece. In the 1927 performance of *Prometheus* at Delphi, the chorus entered the scene singing and dancing a *syrtós*. Postwar interpretations by the National Theater, the Piraïkon Theatron (Piraeus Theater) of Dimitrios Rondiris, and the Art

Theater of Karolos Kuhn have followed this line. The tendency is to move away from group recitation and archaic gestures into singing and dancing derived from the living popular tradition. Performances of ancient Greek drama, sometimes containing dance movement by the chorus, take place every summer at the ancient theaters of Athens and Epidaurus.

The state-run National Opera (Lyriki Skini) was founded in 1940 and includes a corps de ballet of forty trained dancers. Since 1960 it has been presenting ballet evenings several times a year. A smaller state-supported ballet troupe at the Theater of Northern Greece has existed since 1983 in Thessalonike. Helliniko Choreodrama, founded in 1952 under the direction of choreographer Rallou Manou and now defunct, employed the best-known Greek composers, painters, and choreographers in an effort to establish an indigenous dance theater. Other private companies were the Sismani Ballet (1955–1962), an offspring of the school of Iro Sismani, and the Experimental Ballet of Yiannis Metsis (1965–1975), which fused with the Classical Ballet Center under the direction of Renée Kammer and Leonidas de Pian (c.1974–1989).

Today there are about thirty modern dance companies in Greece, including five in Thessalonike, with the rest in Athens. Some occasionally receive financial support of a few million drachmas from the Ministry of Culture. Each company has five to fifteen dancers, paid scarcely and only for performances.

Dance Education. The first ballet school was founded in Athens by Adam Morianoff in 1929. He was followed in

1930 by Koula Pratsika, whose school became the State School of Dance Art in 1972. Several other schools were also founded before World War II. There are now about four hundred private dance schools in Greece, three-quarters of them in Athens. The total number of students is estimated at thirty-five thousand, mostly teenagers. The average student takes one-hour classes three times a week. The predominant method until 1980 was Dalcroze Eurhythmics, introduced at the Conservatory of Music by Swiss-born Marguerite Jordan as early as 1913.

About fourteen intensive schools hosting a total of approximately four hundred students follow the three-year, twenty-hours-per-week curriculum prescribed by the Ministry of Culture. Among their graduates who are presented for examination by a state board, about fifty candidates pass each year and are certified to teach dance in private schools.

Greek folk dance is frequently taught as part of physical education in high schools. It is a mandatory subject in the Physical Education departments of universities. Private schools for ballet and ballroom dance offer also some instruction of Greek folk dances, but the great majority of teenagers learn folk dances in the youth clubs that have proliferated since the 1980s in practically every neighborhood and every village.

BIBLIOGRAPHY

Butterworth, Katharine, et al. *Rebetika: Songs from the Old Greek Underworld*. Athens, 1975.

Coulentianou, Joy. *The Goat-Dance of Skyros*. Athens, 1977.

Cowan, Jane K. *Dance and the Body Politic in Northern Greece*. Princeton, 1990.

Demas, Elias S. "The Social Factors and the Folk Dance Forms in Metsovo and Melia in Epirus." *Dance Studies* 16 (1992): 9–33.

Demas, Elias S. "The Functions of Folk Dances in Epeiros and Their Relations to Contemporary Social Conditions in Hellas (Greece)." *Dance Chronicle* 19.1 (1996): 1–15.

Drandakis, Lefteris. *Improvisation in the Greek Folk Dance*. Athens, 1993.

Forty Greek Costumes from the Dora Stratou Threatre Collection. Athens, 1994.

Holden, Rickey, and Mary Vouras. *Greek Folk Dances*. Newark, N.J., 1965.

Hunt, Yvonne. *Traditional Dance in Greek Culture*. Athens, 1996.

Kakouri, Katerina I. *Dionysiaka: Aspects of the Popular Thracian Religion of Today*. Athens, 1965.

Kilpatrick, David B. *Function and Style in Pontic Dance Music*. Athens, 1980.

Loutzaki, Irene. *The Traditional Dance in Greece*. Thessalonike, 1985.

Loutzaki, Irene, ed. *The Dance in Greece*. Nauplion, 1992.

Makrakis, Basil. *Fire Dances in Greece*. Athens, 1982.

Mouzaki, Rozanna. *Greek Dances for Americans*. New York, 1981.

Petrides, Ted. *Greek Dances*. Athens, 1975.

Raftis, Alkis. *The World of Greek Dance*. Translated by Alexandra Doumas. Athens, 1987.

Raftis, Alkis. "A Call for a New Breed of Folk Dance Teachers." *Dance Studies* 14 (1990): 65–71.

Raftis, Alkis. *Choros, politismos kai koinonia*. Athens, 1992.

Raftis, Alkis. "The Legacy of Dora Stratou." *Dance Studies* 16 (1992): 35–55.

Raftis, Alkis. *Opsis tou chorou*. Athens, 1993.

Raftis, Alkis. *Enkyklopaedia tou hellinikou chorou*. Athens, 1995.

Raftis, Alkis, ed. *Proceedings of the International Congresses on Dance Research 1987–1996*, 17 vols. Athens, 1996.

Stratou, Dora. *The Greek Dances: Our Living Link with Antiquity*. Translated by Amy Mims-Argyrakis. Athens, 1966.

Stratou, Dora. "The Greek Dances." *Dance Studies* 2 (1977): 14–33.

ALKIS RAFTIS

Ritual and Carnival Dance Traditions

With two possible exceptions—the church processional round "Isaiah Dance" and the Anastenárian dance-song "Little Constantine"—no modern Greek dance can be construed as religious ritual in the narrow sense. Instead, social dances temporarily assume ritual functions when they are performed as part of a religious ceremony *(panēgyri)*. Such a dance usually is accompanied by a specific song text and is performed near the church, in the village square, or at homes as performers move around the village in procession. The dance event is a formal one, even if people may no longer believe it has an effective function in the religious or semireligious occasion with which it is linked.

For example, a popular pan-Hellenic dance type called *sta tria* in northwestern Greece appears in the central Greek village of Arachova as the *panēgyrikos*, performed on Saint George's Day (23 April); as the *kamara* in Aliverion in Euboea; as a men's dance, the *roussalia*, in Megara on Easter Monday; and as *lambre kamara* in Megara on Easter Tuesday. Another dance, *sta dyo*, is also used in ritual dance, often in a slightly modified form: it is the women's *kangelisto* in Moschopotamos, part of the "burning of the distaff" ceremony; the *kangelevto* in Ierissos (Chalkidi) on Easter Tuesday; the girls' dance *lazarinikos* in Aïani on Lazarus Saturday; and the *tranos* in Siatista on Assumption Day (15 August). The rare *dipatos choros* ("two-tier dance") used to be performed in scattered locations at important times of individual or community transition. In the *nyphiatikos choros* (bride's dance), the bride, groom, best man, and their families lead wedding guests in a pattern featuring the prevailing social dance of the locality.

Other customs that include social and ritual dancing are the celebration of Saint John's Eve (23 June), which combines bonfire jumping with a fortunetelling ritual *(klēdonas)*; the Piperia, a rainmaking rite; and the placation of Kyr' Voras (Master North Wind). The great cycles of religious festival—the Twelve Days of Christmas (especially 31 December and 1, 6, and 7 January), Carnival (Apokrea), May Day (Maēdes), and Saint Demetrios' Day (Tzamala, 26 October)—also include social dances with a temporary ritual function. These dances are performed to propitiate supernatural forces and to secure fertility. Many are solo dances of the *sta dyo* type, with jumping,

GREECE: Ritual and Carnival Dance Traditions. A Carnival goat dance from the island of Skyros. The main characters of this improvised genre are the Gheros ("old man") and the Korella ("girl"). The Gheros wears goat and sheep bells that create a racket as he chases the Korella around. (Photograph courtesy of Alkis Raftis, Greek Dances Theater, Athens.)

hip swaying, and much improvisation. Couple dances are usually done unlinked and face-to-face *(antikrystos)*. In one type of dance, the Bear, a stock character, is mimed by a man in animal costume.

These Carnival-type festivities typically involve certain elements that vary somewhat around the country. Participants may wear traditional regional costume or special costumes: shaggy capes of animal skins or, rarely, of straw; rags, bedsheets, or old clothes turned inside out; and decorations of flowers, leaves, ribbons, colored fabric, animal tails and horns, or household objects. Dancers are sometimes disguised by masks or by covering the face with flour. They often carry noisemakers such as bells, chains, or strings of coins, and may wield real or wooden swords, shepherds' crooks, or sticks.

The festivals take place in an air of revelry. There are skits including lewd songs, dialogue, and movements. Stock characters act out comic imitations of serious activities such as plowing, legal trials, weddings, deaths, and funerals. Effigies may be burned. There is general merrymaking in the village taverns.

Organized processions make the rounds of homes, performing and collecting gifts. A parade of floats with *papier-mâché* figures and heads, perhaps of Italian or southern French origin, is best exemplified in Patras but has spread to other town celebrations.

Festival dancing often takes place around bonfires, over which the men may jump during the dance. There are ribbon, pole, and hobbyhorse dances. Weddings often feature such miming dances as the Thracian *laïsios* (from *lagos,* "hare") and the well-known "Pōs to Trivoun to Piperi"

(How Pepper Is Ground). Tests of endurance may occur in men's dancing.

[*See also* Anastenárides.]

BIBLIOGRAPHY

Coulentianou, Joy. *The Goat-Dance of Skyros.* Athens, 1977.
Kakouri, Katerina I. *Dionysiaka: Aspects of the Popular Thracian Religion of Today.* Athens, 1965.
Megas, Georgios A. *Greek Calendar Customs.* 2d ed. Athens, 1963.
Petrides, Ted. "O Dipatos Choros." In *The Reports of the Third Folklore Symposium of Northern Greece.* 1979.
Petrides, Ted. "Contemporary Greek Folk Dances." In *Tourism in Greece 1982.* Athens, 1982.
Pressas, Chares. *Carnival of Patras.* Patras, 1990.
Rösler, Wolfgang, and Bernhard Zimmerman. *Carnevale e utopia nella Grecia antica.* Bari, 1991.

TED PETRIDES

Dance Research and Publication

Books on the general history of dance usually contain only a brief discussion of Greek dance during the Classical age. Their information is invariably based on a small number of scholarly works on Greek dance written in the early twentieth century. None of these studies was written by a Greek, and research on this subject was nonexistent in the 1970s and 1980s.

French scholars were the most productive, starting with a work that stirred international interest, *Essai sur l'orchestique grecque* (1895) by Maurice Emmanuel. It was immediately followed by *La danse grecque antique d'après les monuments figurés* (1896) by the same author. Other works of a similar character include *Les danses antiques grecques et romaines* by F. A. d'Ersky and *La danse grecque antique* (1930) by Louis Séchan. Finally, Germaine Prudhommeau produced her voluminous study *La danse grecque antique* (1965). The French approach was based mainly on the study of ancient vase paintings and on drawing analogies with classical ballet.

German scholarly literature relied heavily on the analysis of the meter in choral parts of the plays of the Greek dramatists. This tradition began with *Orchestra, sive de saltationibus veterum* by Ioannes Meursius (1618), *Die Tanzkunst des Euripides* by Hermann Buchholtz (1871), and *Dramatische Orchestik der Hellenen* by Christian Kirchhoff (1898). Other books include *Der Tanz bei den Griechen* by Hans Flach (1880), *Die Gymnastik und Agonistik der Hellenen* by Johann Krause (1841), *De saltationibus Graecorum capita quinque* by Kurt Latte (1913), and *Der Tanz in der Antike* by Fritz Weege (1926). For a detailed account see the article "Ancient Greek Dance in Modern Times: A Bibliography," in Greek, by Alkis Raftis (1992).

The best-known book on the ancient Greek dance was not written in Europe. *The Dance in Ancient Greece* (1964) by the American scholar Lillian Lawler is a concise and accurate introduction to ancient Greek dance, stressing its social aspects and its many forms.

No study has been made of Greek dance during the Byzantine era, so one must rely on the information contained in general books such as *Life and Culture of the Byzantines* (1952) in Greek, by Phaidon Koukoules. Thus, a historical period of about ten centuries remains largely unexplored.

Traditional Dance. In Greece, preindustrial forms of communal life have been preserved late into the twentieth century, well after they disappeared in the industrialized countries of Europe. Thus, folklorists have had an easier task collecting material; their research resembled an anthropological fieldwork until 1940.

Ethnographic interest has produced more than ten thousand books on rural customs and language, documenting the centuries-old diversity of Greek culture. The typical book of this type is written by a village native who managed to study in town and become a school teacher, lawyer, or civil servant. Upon retirement, the villager returned home and collected information about the old life from the village elders. This self-proclaimed historian then published a book on these findings at his or her own expense. Though lacking a scholarly approach, these books contain a wealth of information that is extremely difficult to collect today.

The typical folklore book contains one or two paragraphs specifically dealing with dance. Dance was felt to be of much less interest than songs, proverbs, tales, and other oral genres. Names of dances and descriptions of movements are scarce, but detailed accounts of wedding celebrations, feasts, and other activities abound. From these accounts researchers of today can extract valuable information about the moments in the life of the village when dance was indispensable, the behavior of the participants, and the general atmosphere surrounding dance. To a Greek village, dance is more ceremonial than recreational (this is still true today), so such details are integral to the dance phenomenon and very useful to students.

There is another category of books, which are essentially manuals of dance steps. The first, *Ellinikoi choroi* (Greek Dances, 1940), was written by Charalambos Sakellariou; it was followed by more than three dozen others. These works were intended primarily for students of the Physical Education Academy. The best known are *Ta dimotika tragoudia kai oi laikoi choroi tis Kyprou* (Folk Songs and Folk Dances of Cyprus, 1989) by George Averof; *Ellinikoi choroi kai dimotika tragoudia,* (Greek Dances and Folk Songs, 1932) by Argyrios Andreopoulos; *Ellinikoi choroi* (Greek Dances, 1969) by Athanassios Bikos; *Ellinikoi choroi* (Greek Dances, 1960) and *Laographia kai didaktiki ton ellinikon choron* (Folklore and the Teaching of Greek Dances, 1972) by Vassilios Pa-

pachristou; and *Ellinikoi paradosiakoi choroi* (Greek Traditional Dances, 1980) by Elias Dimas.

These books are simple collections of dances from different regions, providing for each dance a sketch of the footwork, a typical song, and notation of the music. Only Sakellariou's work has appeared in English translation.

After World War II, interest in international dance led to the publication in foreign languages of books similar to these. Among them are the following: in English, *Dances of Greece* (1948) by Domini Crosfield, *Greek Folk Dances* (1965) by Rickey Holden and Mary Vouras, *Greek Dances* (1975) by Ted Petrides, and *Greek Dances for Americans* (1981) by Rozanna Mouzaki; in German, *So Tanzt Griechenland* (1984) by Margared and Rolf Schiel; and in Swedish, *Grekiska folkdanser* (1981) by Eustathios Tatsonas and *Grekiska danser* (1978) by Eivor Underdahl.

Only in the 1980s was Greek traditional dance finally approached as an object of scientific study. The first book to be published in this context was *Function and Style in Pontic Dance Music* (1980), a doctoral dissertation by David Kilpatrick. Since then several articles have appeared dealing with the social aspects of dance, written by Ted Petrides, Rena Loutzaki, Alkis Raftis, and others. A comprehensive bibliography appeared in *The World of Greek Dance* (Greek, 1985; English, 1987) by Raftis.

Other books on Greek dance include *The Greek Dances: Our Living Link with Antiquity* (1966), *Mia paradossi, mia peripetia* (A Tradition, an Adventure, 1964), and *Ellinikoi paradossiakoi choroi* (Greek Traditional Dances, 1979), all by Dora Stratou; *The Traditional Dance in Greece* (1985), in Greek and English, by Irene Loutzaki; and *O choros stous Kountouriotes* (The Dance of the Kountouriotes, 1987) by Vangelis Liapis.

We have mentioned only books and articles that deal primarily with dance, omitting works that mention it in passing, such as publications on folk music, anthropology, or literature; however, these sometimes contain valuable information. There are also a few unpublished dissertations dealing with dance in Greece. Finally, we should mention notes on the jackets and inserts of recordings of dance music.

Research Organizations. The only organization devoted to Greek dance is the Dora Stratou Society, founded and directed for thirty years by the grand lady of Greek dance, Dora Stratou. The society has a dance and music ensemble that gives daily performances from May to September in its own theater in Athens. It also has a library and archives containing photographs, films, and field recordings. Its activities include lectures, courses for beginners, workshops on dance customs, costumes, and folk music, publication of books and records, and research. Current research projects pertain to the dance customs of villages in more than thirty localities.

The Peloponnesian Folklore Foundation is concerned mainly with folk costume, but it has an active section on folk dance headed by Irene Loutzaki. Other institutions, such as the Folklore Archive of the Academy of Athens, the Center of Asia Minor Studies, and the Lyceum of Greek Women, are active in the field of ethnography and have libraries and archives that can be useful to a researcher.

Greek universities do not currently offer a dance curriculum. Ethnography is taught as an independent subject in the literature departments of the Universities of Athens, Thessalonike, Yannina, and Thessaly, but without reference to dance ethnography, which is essential for the study of Greek dance. Anthropology is taught in the Universities of Thrace and the Aegean. Greek dance is taught in the Physical Education departments of the Universities of Athens, Thessalonike, Thrace, and Thessaly. Students can choose it as a major subject, but the instruction of dance is mainly practical, for lack of teachers with academic training in the human sciences related to dance.

Since 1987 an international conference on dance research has taken place in a different town of Greece every year. It is attended by an average of three hundred specialists from twenty-five countries and has provided great impetus for dance scholarship to both Greek and foreign practitioners. Its proceedings, in English and Greek, constitute the main contribution to the body of literature reviewed above. The state-supported Greek Dance Theater in Athens has a research library containing all publications related to Greek dance and related subjects, as well as a large collection of records and field recordings of dance music, and a wardrobe of twenty-five hundred village-made folk costumes worn by its dancers in performances.

There is no institution devoted wholly or in part to researching theatrical or historical dance. There are three periodicals on dance: *Choros* (Dance), published every three months by the Association of Dance and Eurhythmics, *En Choro* (Dancing), a monthly newspaper published since 1984, and *Paradossi kai Techni* (Tradition and Art), published every two months by the Greek Section of the International Organization of Folk Art, all three in Athens.

BIBLIOGRAPHY

Butterworth, Katharine, et al. *Rebetika: Songs from the Old Greek Underworld*. Athens, 1975.
Coulentianou, Joy. *The Goat-Dance of Skyros*. Athens, 1977.
Kakouri, Katerina I. *Dionysiaka: Aspects of the Popular Thracian Religion of Today*. Athens, 1965.
Kilpatrick, David B. *Function and Style in Pontic Dance Music*. Athens, 1980.
Makrakis, Basil. *Fire Dances in Greece*. Athens, 1982.
Mouzaki, Rozanna. *Greek Dances for Americans*. New York, 1981.
Petrides, Ted. *Greek Dances*. Athens, 1975.
Raftis, Alkis. *The World of Greek Dance*. Translated by Alexandra Doumas. Athens, 1987.
Raftis, Alkis. *Choros, politismos kai koinonia*. Athens, 1992.

ALKIS RAFTIS

GREEN, CHUCK (Charles Green; born 6 November 1918 in Fitzgerald, Georgia), American tap dancer. As a boy growing up in Georgia, Green earned his first money tapping on street corners, wearing bottletops on his bare toes to create the sound. Later with his partner, James Walker, he formed an act called Shorty and Slim and went north. There he met John Bubbles, who became his foster parent. The best in black vaudeville, Bubbles was wary of teaching his original syncopated rhythms to anyone, but Green developed a trick that caused the unsuspecting Bubbles to repeat his steps, and ultimately Bubbles took him on as a protégé. "He also liked my accent," Green later recalled. "I had such a heavy southern drawl, it made him laugh."

In 1929 Nat Nazzarro, an agent for many of the hoofers, renamed Green and Walker's act Chuck and Chuckles. Hoping to make another Buck and Bubbles (a famous vaudeville act featuring Bubbles and Ford Lee "Buck" Washington) out of Chuck and Chuckles, Nazzarro planted the duo as a kiddie act in the Buck and Bubbles routine.

Green is one of the hoofers most responsible for regenerating interest in tap dance during the late 1960s, when he took part in Leticia Jay's "Tap Happenings" at the Hotel Dixie in New York City. He has reappeared sporadically in numerous shows and clubs as a guest artist with the Copasetics and the Original Hoofers as well as in the award-winning documentary *No Maps on My Taps*, the title taken from a phrase he coined. Green's oversized feet and lilting, ambling, husky frame reminded critic Sally Banes (in a 1979 review in *Soho Weekly News*) more of an undertaker than a tap dancer. At the Word of Foot Festival in New York in 1980 Honi Coles commented, "Forget Bubbles, forget Baby Laurence, forget everyone. Chuck Green can dance to any kind of music and make it sound interesting. He comes up with such weird combinations and he never repeats the same thing twice."

Green's dancing and his stories about Chuck and Chuckles, Buck and Bubbles, Tip Tap and Toe, and other figures in jazz dance history make him one of tap's rare oral historians, one who talks about his cherished memories as poetically as he dances with his feet. After performing at George Washington University in the early 1970s, he was named the "Bach of Tap."

[*See* Tap Dance.]

BIBLIOGRAPHY

Frank, Rusty E. *Tap! The Greatest Tap Dance Stars and Their Stories, 1900–1955*. Rev. ed. New York, 1994.
Stearns, Marshall, and Jean Stearns. *Jazz Dance*. Rev. ed. New York, 1994.

FILMS. George T. Nirenberg, *No Maps on My Taps* (1979). Jolyon Wimhurst, *Masters of the Tap* (1983). *About Tap* (Direct Cinema Ltd., 1985).

JANE GOLDBERG

GREEN TABLE, THE. German Title: Der Grüne Tisch. Choreography: Kurt Jooss. Music: Friderick Cohen. Libretto: Kurt Jooss. Scenery and costumes: Hein Heckroth. First performance: 3 July 1932, Théâtre des Champs-Élysées, Folkwang Tanzbühne. Principals: Kurt Jooss (Death), Ernst Uthoff (The Standard Bearer), Walter Wurg (The Young Soldier), Lisa Czobel (The Young Girl), Elsa Kahl (The Guerilla Woman), Frieda Holst (The Old Woman), Karl Bergeest (The Profiteer).

The first International Competition for Choreographers was organized in Paris by the Archives Internationales de la Danse. Kurt Jooss, with his Folkwang Tanzbühne company, was invited from Essen to participate. *The Green Table*, created for the competition, was awarded first prize and won its creator instant renown.

The Green Table is a seminal modern ballet of social conscience. Jooss called it a *Totentanz* ("dance of death") and germinated from several seeds: in 1925 he was moved by the Dance of Death depictions in the medieval cathedral of Lübeck; in 1930–1931 he appeared in Georg Kaiser's expressionist drama *Europa*, which contained a scene of black-clad men arguing; and Jooss's political consciousness was spurred by regularly reading *Die Weltbühne*, a left-wing antiwar periodical.

The Green Table is considered the first modern political ballet, in the sense that it emerged between the two world wars as a protest against callous games of statesmen and diplomats and the suffering caused by the wars such leaders instigated. Jooss himself characterized the work as a drama of indignation and a morality play. In his advice to the dancers, he said, "You must never forget that you are performing a spiritual play, not a tangible piece of theater but a symbolic and dramatic ritual."

The ballet begins and ends with a scene of futility: seasoned statesmen-politicians deliberate around a green-covered conference table. Wearing formal attire, they appear dandyish in spite of their age. Each is caricatured by a mask that covers the head. The twisted rhetoric and sham obeisances of diplomatic intercourse soon deteriorate into physical aggression, and the scene ends abruptly with pistol shots and a sudden blackout.

In the succeeding scenes, the stage is bare and the lighting dim; spotlights follow the action. Death first appears alone, a powerful presence snuffing out life under his stamping feet and arms like scyths. War and its effects are depicted in the next six scenes. While the characters are archetypal, the women and their fate are more individually portrayed than the men. Like an insidious evil, the Profiteer moves among the victims; he is probably the only survivor. The fiercely fought battle episodes are played out with only six soldiers forming phalanxes, opposing rows, groups, and individual fights. Hovering over all, Death in his many guises is the victor, alone in a dance of triumph, until he vanishes.

THE GREEN TABLE. Otto Schuller as the Profiteer cowers before Kurt Jooss as Death. (Photograph by Gordon Anthony; used by permission of the Picture Library, Victoria and Albert Museum, London.)

The Green Table contains few realistic movements. The choreography is spare and focused—without superfluous gesture, preparation, or adornment—and it projects restrained intensity. However, it is constantly flowing, which lends it a balletic quality. The score is metrically complex; Cohen composed it in close collaboration with Jooss, binding each movement and scene.

The ballet was in the Jooss repertory exclusively until his last company disbanded. He subsequently arranged it for the Chilean National Ballet, founded by his former dancers Ernst Uthoff and Lola Botka, in 1948, later entrusting it to several other companies, including the Munich State Opera Ballet (1964) and the Joffrey Ballet (1967). *The Green Table* is recorded in Labanotation and in several films. Jooss's daughter Anna and her husband Herman Markard (who makes the masks and has improved the lighting) continue to produce the ballet.

BIBLIOGRAPHY

Blum, Odette. "*The Green Table* Project." *Dance Research Journal* 21 (Spring 1989): 38–42.

Holder, Christian. "Dancing for Jooss: Recreating the Role of Death in *The Green Table*." *Choreography and Dance* 3.2 (1993): 79–91.

Huxley, Michael. "*The Green Table*: A Dance of Death." *Ballett International* 5 (August–September 1982): 4–10.

Marinari, Silvia. "*The Green Table* by Kurt Jooss." Ph.D. diss., New York University, 1985.

Maris, Laura. "Jooss' *The Green Table* and *The Big City:* Musical Forms and Devices as Choreographic Tools." *Dance Chronicle* 19.2 (1996).

Nugent, Ann. "*The Green Table* and *Café Müller.*" *Dance Now* 1 (Autumn 1992): 34–41.

Siegel, Marcia B. "*The Green Table:* Sources of a Classic." *Dance Research Journal* 21 (Spring 1989): 15–21.

Sinclair, Janet. "*The Green Table.*" *Dance and Dancers* (July 1992): 18–21.

Walther, Suzanne K. "The Dance of Death: Description and Analysis of *The Green Table.*" *Choreography and Dance* 3.2 (1993): 53–77.

VIDEOTAPE.   *The Green Table,* performed by the Joffrey Ballet, *Dance in America* (WNET-TV, New York, 1982).

ARCHIVE.   Ann Hutchinson Guest, *The Green Table in Labanotation,* microfilm of 1939 score, Dance Collection, New York Public Library for the Performing Arts.

BENGT HÄGER

GREGORY, CYNTHIA (born 8 July 1946 in Los Angeles), American dancer. Born into a musical family, Gregory began studying ballet at the age of five with Eva Lorraine of the California Children's Ballet Company, and she later performed prominent roles with the company. In 1955 she enrolled at the studio of a former American Ballet Theatre dancer, Carmelita Maracci. She also studied with Michel Panaieff and Robert Rossellat. At the age of twelve Gregory danced in *Les Sylphides* and *The Nutcracker* with the Santa Monica Civic Ballet. The following year she received a Ford Foundation grant to work with the San Francisco Ballet; she joined that company in 1961 and was made soloist in 1964. In San Francisco Gregory met and married fellow dancer Terry Orr. The marriage was dissolved in 1976, and that year Gregory married John Hemminger, a musician and rock music promoter.

In 1965 Gregory went to New York with the San Francisco Ballet, and later that year she joined American Ballet Theatre. She was promoted to soloist in 1966 and became a principal dancer nine months later. In 1967 she danced *Swan Lake* for the first time, and the role of Odette-Odile has been closely linked with her ever since. She created roles in Eliot Feld's *At Midnight* (1967), Michael Smuin's *The Eternal Idol* and Dennis Nahat's *Brahms Quintet* (both 1969), Alvin Ailey's *The River* (1970), and Rudolf Nureyev's full-length production of *Raymonda* in 1975.

Gregory was most notably a classical ballerina of perfect proportions who danced with distinction in all the nineteenth-century classics; however, her repertory also embraced a wide variety of contemporary and dramatic works. Her versatility enabled her to succeed in ballets as diverse as George Balanchine's *Theme and Variations* and *Prodigal Son,* José Limón's *The Moor's Pavane,* Birgit Cullberg's *Miss Julie,* and Antony Tudor's *Undertow,* while her sensational use of balance, multiple pirouettes, and exem-

GREGORY. A star of American Ballet Theatre for twenty-five years, Gregory is pictured here in Victor Gsovsky's *Grand Pas Classique,* set to music by Daniel Auber. Her strength and purity of line are clearly evident. (Photograph © 1975 by Jack Vartoogian; used by permission.)

plary footwork made exciting even a work as essentially slight as *Grand Pas Classique.*

In 1974, at the invitation of Alicia Alonso, Gregory became the first American artist to dance in Communist Cuba, where she was very well received. She resigned from American Ballet Theatre in 1975 to live quietly in California. A year later she returned to the company and, but for a few brief periods, remained with it until 1991 except for a season as guest ballerina with the Cleveland Ballet. In 1976 she was featured with the dancer Ivan Nagy in the film *In a Rehearsal Room,* directed by David Hahn and with choreography by William Carter.

If there was one thing that Gregory, tall for a ballerina, lacked, it was an appropriate partner. Nevertheless, her brilliant technique, pure line, and unfailing musicality made her one of American ballet's most accomplished ballerinas. Gregory received the Dance Magazine Award in 1975. She made her farewell performance dancing Odette-Odile in *Swan Lake,* partnered by Fernando Bujones, with American Ballet Theatre on 12 June 1991. In 1993, she staged a full-length *Swan Lake* for the Monterrey Ballet in Mexico. She now lives with her third husband, Hilary Miller, and son, Lloyd, in Greenwich, Connecticut.

BIBLIOGRAPHY

Gruen, John. *The Private World of Ballet*. New York, 1975.
Gruen, John. *People Who Dance: Twenty-Two Dancers Tell Their Own Stories*. Princeton, N.J., 1988.
Hodgson, Moira. "Cynthia Gregory: In Search of Siegfried." *Dance News* (March 1975): 1–4.
Maynard, Olga. "Conversations with Cynthia Gregory." *Dance Magazine* 48 (April 1974).
Péres, Louis. *Cynthia Gregory*. Brooklyn, 1975.
Pikula, Joan. "Cynthia Gregory: Artist in Turmoil." *Dance Magazine* (February 1976): 34–35.
Terry, Walter. "American Ballet Theatre's Golden Girl: Cynthia Gregory." *Dance Magazine* (January 1973): 48–55.
Terry, Walter. "Cynthia Gregory: How She Became America's Best Ballerina." *Saturday Review* (September 1981).
Trucco, Terry. "Cynthia Gregory: Pushing to the Limit." *Dance Magazine* (June 1991): 44–51.

PATRICIA BARNES

GREGORY, JON. *See* Jazz Dance.

GREY, BERYL (Beryl Groom; born 11 June 1927 in London), English dancer and teacher. A year after joining Sadler's Wells Ballet and on her fifteenth birthday, Grey made her debut as Odette-Odile in the company's *Swan Lake*, confirming a talent of remarkable promise. Tall for a European ballerina of her time and, inevitably, immature in her approach to acting, she nevertheless revealed an exceptionally fine technique and an exciting rapport with the audience.

Grey had had her initial training with Madeline Sharp in Bromley, Kent, before going to Sadler's Wells Ballet School in 1937. There she worked with company teachers (Nicholas Sergeyev, Ninette de Valois, and Vera Volkova), later studying privately with Anna Northcote and, a very valued influence, Audrey de Vos (1947–1962).

In her early performances of *Swan Lake* and *Giselle*, Grey was partnered by David Paltenghi, an excellent cavalier. In the company tradition, she continued to dance in the corps de ballet and as a soloist. In 1942 she gave a charming interpretation of the Serving Maid in a revival of de Valois's *The Gods Go a-Begging*, also creating the technically intricate role of the Nightingale in Robert Helpmann's *The Birds* and a year later, very effectively, the scheming Duessa in Frederick Ashton's *The Quest*.

Grey's special qualities were admirably suited to the Royal Opera House, Covent Garden, where the company transferred in 1946. In the first two seasons there she danced definitive versions of the Lilac Fairy in *The Sleeping Beauty* (as well as Princess Aurora) and of Prayer in

Coppélia. She also danced Myrtha in *Giselle* and the Black Queen in de Valois's *Checkmate*, adding authority and discipline to her earlier virtues of technical and theatrical assurance. An unforgettable creation came with the Winter Fairy in Ashton's *Cinderella* (1948), in which her fluency, timing, and control in the variation were outstanding, as was her 1950 performance of the second ballerina role in Balanchine's *Ballet Imperial*. Odette-Odile, however, remained a signature performance, partnered mainly by John Field, with whom she made the first three-dimensional ballet film, *The Black Swan* (1952).

Grey left the Royal Ballet to freelance in 1957. She danced worldwide, becoming the first English ballerina to appear as guest artist in the Soviet Union, at the Kirov and Bolshoi Theaters and with the Kiev State and Tiflis (now Tbilisi) State ballets. In 1964 she was the first Western ballerina to dance with a Chinese ballet company. In 1966 she was appointed director general of the Arts Educational Trust and from 1968 to 1979 served as artistic director of the London Festival Ballet. In 1984 Grey staged *Giselle* for West Australian Ballet and in 1986 *The Sleeping Beauty* for the Royal Swedish Ballet. Her books include the autobiographical *Red Curtain Up* (1958) and *Through the Bamboo Curtain* (1965).

In 1980 Grey became became a vice president of the Royal Academy of Dancing and served on its Executive Committee from 1982 to 1989. She was chairman of the Imperial Society for Teachers of Dancing from 1984 to 1991, when she was appointed its president. She is also president of the Dance Council of Wales, an active member of the Council for Dance Education and Training, on the board of Birmingham Royal Ballet, and has been a governor of the Royal Ballet since 1993. Other offices include the Royal Ballet Benevolent Fund (Chairman of Trustees since 1992) and the Dance Teachers' Benevolent Fund (vice chairman since 1985). She has numerous honorary degrees and received the Royal Academy of Dancing's Queen Elizabeth II Coronation Award in 1996. In 1988 she was appointed a Dame of the Order of the British Empire (DBE).

BIBLIOGRAPHY

Anthony, Gordon. *Beryl Grey*. London, 1952.
Crowle, Pigeon. *Beryl Grey*. London, 1952.
Fisher, Hugh. *Beryl Grey*. London, 1955.
Gillard, David. *Beryl Grey*. London, 1977.
Newman, Barbara. *Striking a Balance: Dancers Talk about Dancing*. Rev. ed. New York, 1992.

KATHRINE SORLEY WALKER

GRIGORIEV, SERGE (Sergei Leonidovich Grigor'ev; born 5 October 1883 in Tichvin, Russia, died 28 June 1968 in London), Russian dancer, ballet director, and company administrator. Trained at the Imperial Ballet School in

Saint Petersburg, Serge Grigoriev entered the Maryinsky corps de ballet in 1900 while continuing his studies at the Imperial Theater School. A friend of Michel Fokine, whose earliest choreographic recitals he assisted, Grigoriev participated in Serge Diaghilev's 1909 Paris season as company *régisseur,* a post he held until the demise of Diaghilev's Ballets Russes in 1929.

Although administrative duties soon eclipsed Grigoriev's career as a dancer, he was a splendid mime in such roles as Shah Zeman in *Schéhérazade,* Guidon in *Le Coq d'Or,* the Russian Merchant in *La Boutique Fantasque,* and the Emperor in *Le Rossignol.* In 1912, however, he resigned from the Maryinsky to link his fortunes to Diaghilev's recently formed troupe, eventually becoming the impresario's right-hand man. That the Ballets Russes so long maintained its high artistic standard was due in no small measure to Grigoriev's prodigious memory, eye for detail, unstinting loyalty, and dedication to the task at hand. He conducted all rehearsals, except in 1916/17, when Nijinsky barred him from the second American tour, and he enjoyed a reputation for fairmindedness in his personal and professional dealings with dancers.

In 1932, Grigoriev joined Colonel Wassily de Basil's Ballets Russes de Monte Carlo in a similar capacity and for the next twenty years struggled valiantly to preserve the artistic legacy of the Diaghilev era, despite the accelerated pace of touring and personnel turnover. Retiring in 1952, he wrote *The Diaghilev Ballet, 1909–1929,* an authoritative record based on company financial documents, programs, and his own notebooks. With his wife Lubov Tchernicheva, whom he married in 1909, he staged careful revivals of *The Firebird* (1954), *Les Sylphides* (1955), *Petrouchka* (1957), and the *Polovtsian Dances* (1965) from *Prince Igor* for Britain's Royal Ballet. In 1956 he served as *régisseur* for London's Festival Ballet.

BIBLIOGRAPHY

Beaumont, Cyril W. *Bookseller at the Ballet: Memoirs, 1891 to 1929.* London, 1975.
Garafola, Lynn. *Diaghilev's Ballets Russes.* New York and Oxford, 1989.
García-Márquez, Vicente. *The Ballets Russes: Colonel de Basil's Ballets Russes de Monte Carlo, 1932–1952.* New York, 1990.
Grigoriev, Serge. *The Diaghilev Ballet, 1909–1929.* Translated and edited by Vera Bowen. London, 1953.
Sorley Walker, Kathrine. *De Basil's Ballets Russes.* New York, 1983.

ARCHIVES.   Dance Collection, New York Public Library for the Performing Arts. Dansmuseet, Stockholm. Theater Collection, Harvard University.

LYNN GARAFOLA

GRIGOROVICH, YURI (Iurii Nikolaevich Grigorovich; born 2 January 1927 in Leningrad), Russian choreographer and former director of the Bolshoi Ballet. Grigorovich graduated in 1946 from the Leningrad ballet school, where his teachers were Boris Shavrov and Aleksei Pisarev. For the next eighteen years he was a soloist with the Kirov Opera and Ballet Theater there, performing *demi-caractère* roles such as a Polovtsian Warrior in *Prince Igor* and Nurali in *The Fountain of Bakhchisarai.* His development as a choreographer was influenced by Fedor Lopukhov and Yuri Slonimsky. At first he staged dances for plays, then ballets for the children's choreographic studio of the Maxim Gorky Palace of Culture.

Grigorovich's first ballets for the Kirov, *The Stone Flower* (1957) and *Legend of Love* (1959), were important events in modern ballet. Soviet choreographers of previous generations had tended to dramatize ballet by linking it closely with its literary source. Grigorovich followed this trend, but in contrast to earlier exponents he did not allow dance to play a subsidiary role with the action developed primarily through pantomime. Instead, he placed the emphasis on dance, closely integrating choreography with music. Independent pantomime scenes are absent from Grigorovich's ballets, but elements of pantomime are incorporated into the dancing itself. Ensembles are based on the principles of symphonic music, as exemplified in the fair scenes in *The Stone Flower* and in the procession, pursuit, and visions of Mekhmene Banu in *Legend of Love.* The corps de ballet provides emotional background as a lyrical accompaniment for the dances of the soloists. Both ballets were later transferred, first to the stage of the Bolshoi Theater in Moscow and later to other Soviet cities and abroad.

Grigorovich made a further advance in *Spartacus,* which had its premiere at the Bolshoi in 1968. Instead of using the libretto of previous productions, he wrote his own and also reworked the musical score together with composer Aram Khachaturian. Here, the main actions are depicted in the juxtaposition of large choreographic scenes; for example, in the first act there are the enemy invasion, the suffering of the slaves, and the bloody entertainment of their masters. Each scene is based on a similar choreographic plan, designed on the principles of symphonic music. The scenes alternate with the danced "monologues" of the protagonists. Grigorovich himself described *Spartacus* as "a ballet for four soloists and a corps de ballet."

Ivan the Terrible, to music by Sergei Prokofiev, was staged by Grigorovich at the Bolshoi in 1975 and at the Paris Opera in 1976. Based on Russian history, it presents a psychologically complex image of the cruel tsar. In addition to ensemble and solo themes there is a leitmotif: the dance of the Bell Ringers sounding a tocsin and dancing with bell ropes in their hands. This dance varies with the character of the action, marking all the turning points in the historical destinies of the characters.

The Angara, to a score by Andrei Eshpai, is based on Aleksei Abruzov's play *The Irkutsk Story.* Produced at the

GRIGOROVICH. *The Golden Age*, a story of Soviet society in the 1920s, was created for the Bolshoi Ballet in 1982. In this scene, the heroine, Rita (Natalia Bessmertnova), tries to prevent a conflict between Yashka (Gediminas Taranda, at left) and Boris (Irek Mukhamedov, at right). (Photograph from the archives of *The Dancing Times*, London.)

Bolshoi in 1976, it tells a story of contemporary youth, raising ethical problems related to the process of personality formation and the relations between the individual and the collective. Here, classical dance is enriched with elements of folk dance, free dance, pantomime, athletics, and work movements. The choreographic image of the great Siberian river, Angara, created by the corps de ballet, is the leitmotif of the ballet, appearing alternately as the powerful force subdued by the people and as a resonator of the protagonists' emotions or an embodiment of their recollections and dreams.

Like *The Stone Flower* and *Spartacus*, *Romeo and Juliet* had been staged before, and again Grigorovich approached his task with a fresh point of view. For the first time all of Prokofiev's score was used, expanded by other music Grigorovich had found in the composer's archive. He also used the device of parallel action (simultaneous presentation of contrasting scenes). Grigorovich produced a two-act version at the Paris Opera in 1978 and a three-act version the following year at the Bolshoi.

Grigorovich's skill in reviving previously unsuccessful ballets was particularly evident in his 1982 production of *The Golden Age*, which is set at the Golden Age restaurant—a favorite haunt of surviving elements of the bourgeoisie, a den of gangsters, and an arena for young workers—where social and moral conflict are interlocked in a complex psychological drama. No other ballet by Grigorovich had such well-developed ties with realistic, everyday movement. This production, like *The Angara*, proved that the artistic principles of a classical production, forms of "symphonic" dance in particular, could be applied to choreography on a modern theme.

Grigorovich's modern ballets sought to portray vivid, larger-than-life characters and sharply dramatic conflict with moral and philosophical content. The imagery, structure, and language of his productions had innovative features but were rooted in the classical heritage. Reviving and developing forgotten traditions, they had lines of continuity to the works of Marius Petipa and other leading choreographers of the past.

Classical ballets also held an important place in Grigorovich's repertory. He revived all the Tchaikovsky ballets, not as fairy tales for children but as philosophical choreographic poems. In *The Nutcracker*, produced at the Bolshoi in 1966, the childhood scenes of the first act were danced not by pupils but by members of the corps de ballet, dancing in much more sophisticated choreography. Drosselmeyer and his dolls had grotesque features; the battle with the mice conveyed a genuine atmosphere of horror. Reinforcement of the frightening images enhanced the final triumph of good over evil.

In his production of *Swan Lake* at the Bolshoi in 1969 Grigorovich retained most of the choreography of the Petipa-Ivanov staging, but he devised a number of additional episodes. The battle between Siegfried and Rothbart was psychological, rather than physical. In the third act, Grigorovich choreographed the character dances with pointe work and invented a significant trio for Siegfried, Rothbart, and Odile.

Grigorovich staged *The Sleeping Beauty* twice at the Bolshoi. In 1963 he abridged a number of pantomime and character dance scenes, relying exlusively on classical dance. Carabosse was no longer a male mime role but was performed by a female dancer, weakening the theme of

GRIGOROVICH. *The Stone Flower,* mounted by Grigorovich at the Kirov Theater in Leningrad in 1957, was restaged in Moscow at the Bolshoi Theater in May 1959. The Bolshoi cast included Nina Timofeyeva as the Mistress of the Copper Mountain and Ekaterina Maximova as Katerina, seen here with members of the female ensemble. (Photograph reprinted from a Bolshoi Ballet souvenir program, 1959.)

good versus evil. In 1973 he preserved all of Petipa's choreography and included the scenes of the knitting maidens and Kingdom of Carabosse. The conflict of good and evil was sharpened, and the philosophical message of the ballet was enhanced.

In 1984 Grigorovich staged *Raymonda* at the Bolshoi, preserving Petipa's choreography but revising the structure of the ballet to achieve greater dramaturgical logic. In accordance with the principles of his earlier ballets he sought to convert *divertissements* into action scenes, diminishing their background effect and intensifying their dramatic significance. He enlarged choreographic scenes by blending a few isolated musical pieces to achieve an extended and integral choreographic structure. These large forms are analogous to the structure and flow of the music.

Other revivals Grigorovich produced were *Giselle* in 1987, *La Bayadère* in 1992, and *Le Corsaire* in 1994. He also staged works from the standard repertory abroad: *Giselle* in Ankara, 1979; *Swan Lake* in Rome, 1980; and *Don Quixote* in Copenhagen, 1982.

All of Grigorovich's ballets were based on his own libretti; his choreography was inseparable from the action. At the same time he built the action on the music, incarnating it in dance images. All his ballets had decor designed by Simon Virsaladze, except *La Bayadère* and *Le Corsaire,* which were produced after Virsaladze's death. In their imaginative approach, the choreographer and designer had much in common. The unity of choreography, dramaturgy, and decor accounted for much of the integrity and excellence of the ballets.

Grigorovich holds the title of People's Artist of the USSR. He won the Lenin Prize in 1970 and the State Prize of the USSR in 1977. He became a professor in the choreographic department of the Leningrad Conservatory in 1973. He has frequently presided over the jury at the International Ballet Competition in Moscow, Varna, and Helsinki. He was president of the Dance Committee of the International Theatre Institute from its founding in 1973 until 1989.

On 9 March 1995 Grigorovich resigned from the Bolshoi, citing conflict with the theater's administration. That evening the company, in sympathy with him, staged a strike and canceled the performance. After participating in the strike, his wife, Natalia Bessmertnova, also left the Bolshoi.

[*See also* Bolshoi Ballet.]

BIBLIOGRAPHY

Alovert, Nina. "Yuri Grigorovich: An Appreciation." *Dance Magazine* (July 1987): 44–47.

Alovert, Nina. "The Soviet Dance Theater of Yuri Grigorovich." *Dance Magazine* (December 1987): 39–42.

Demidov, Alexander P. *The Russian Ballet: Past and Present.* Translated by Guy Daniels. Garden City, N.Y., 1977.

Demidov, Alexander P. *Yuri Grigorovich* (in Russian). Moscow, 1987.

Greskovic, Robert. "The Grigorovich Factor and the Bolshoi." *Ballet Review* 5.2 (1975–1976): 1–10.

Jennings, Luke. "The Czar's Last Dance." *New Yorker* (27 March 1995).

Johnson, Robert. "Grigorovich Redux: Down But Not Out." *Dance Magazine* (February 1991): 70–72.

Krasovskaya, Vera. *Stati o balete.* Leningrad, 1967.

Percival, John. "Grigorovich of the Bolshoi." *Dance and Dancers* (September 1989): 10–13.

Quraishi, Ibrahim. "Grigorovich Challenged as Master of Bolshoi." *Dance Magazine* (September 1994): 18–20.

Quraishi, Ibrahim. "Grigorovich's Last Dance?" *Dance Magazine* (November 1994): 38–40.

Sedov, Yaroslav. "Yuri Grigorovich: The Hero and His Dances." *Dance Theatre Journal* 10 (Spring–Summer 1993): 23–25.

Slonimsky, Yuri. *V chest tantsa.* Moscow, 1968.

Vanslov, Victor V. *Balety Grigorovicha i problemy khoreografii.* 2d ed. Moscow, 1971.

Vanslov, Victor V. *Stati o balete: Muzykalno-esteticheskie problemy baleta.* Leningrad, 1980.

Willis, Margaret E. "Grigorovich and Bessmertnova." *Dance Magazine* (July 1995): 34.

VICTOR V. VANSLOV
Translated from Russian

GRIPENBERG, MAGGIE (Margarita Maria Gripenberg; born 11 June 1881 in Helsinki, died 28 July 1976 in Maarianhamina), Finnish modern dance pioneer. Maggie Gripenberg began performing at the turn of the twentieth century. She was largely self-taught in dance. Her family belonged to the nobility, and her father, a senator and an architect, carried the hereditary title of baron. His young daughter performed at social gatherings, school events, and charity fund-raisers, and she improvised alone and for family and friends. Dance as a career was at first unthinkable, given the high social position of her family and the low esteem in which professional dancing was then held. However, Gripenberg was increasingly expressing her artistic sensibilities through dance. She was composing and performing dances that differed from the ones traditionally seen around her. At this time she was dancing naturally, groping for an expression.

Gripenberg sang well and played the piano, eventually developing into an inspired improviser on the keyboard. Wanting to pursue the arts, in her twenties she studied painting in Helsinki (1903/04), Dresden (1904/05), and Paris (1906/07; 1908/09), with her parents' encouragement. She did, however, always yearn to dance during this time, and she performed whenever possible. While she was in Dresden in 1905, she saw Isadora Duncan perform. The event ultimately changed her life: "I saw in front of me, alive, everything that I had thought of and dreamt about in dance. I was spellbound." Gripenberg continued her art studies for a few more years, but she was miserable and unsure of her career choice. She was also unable to tell her parents of her torment.

In the fall of 1909, Gripenberg was suddenly asked by the director of the National Theater in Helsinki to become the plastique and movement teacher for the actors. To her protestations that she was not the right choice, the director simply replied, "But you are a professional dancer—everyone knows that!" (Gripenberg, 1950, p. 48). She de-

cided to accept the position but felt she had to study dance before teaching it. After working in Stockholm for three weeks with the Swedish dancer Anna Behle, she and Behle organized a study trip to Émile Jaques-Dalcroze in Geneva, for May 1910. This summer course was too short, so to finance a longer study, the two friends ventured upon a performance tour of southern Norway and Sweden. The tour proved a success, artistically and financially, and they returned to the Dalcroze Institute (now moved to Dresden, Germany) late in the fall, after the term had already started. After a couple of months Gripenberg was moved to advanced level by Jaques-Dalcroze, and she received her diploma in June 1911.

Gripenberg's official debut was at the National Theater in Helsinki on 13 November 1911. To a sold-out house, she danced barefoot (as far as is known, the first Finnish dancer to do so), in short, flowing, chiffon tunics, to the music of Weber, Chopin, Rachmaninoff, Strauss, Gluck, and Sibelius. The critics were unanimous in their praise, noting that it was a pioneering event and that a new era in dance was dawning. "After the evening's obvious success, the small baroness who danced yesterday . . . must henceforth be taken into account. She was known before, but her dancing becomes public knowledge now, and her

GRIPENBERG. A pioneer of Finnish modern dance, Maggie Gripenberg posed for the camera wearing a Grecian-style costume, c.1902. (Photograph courtesy of Saga M. Ambegaokar.)

dance, as she presented it yesterday, is art" (Hirn, 1982, pp. 101–102).

Gripenberg began a life of choreography, performance, and teaching. Her most important teaching post was to be at the Sibelius Academy, where she taught from 1914 until 1952. She also taught at the National Theater (1909 on) in her private studio, at the Swedish Theater (1934–1951), at the University of Helsinki (1938–1949), as well as at such summer sports/movement camps as Vierumäki (1938 on), Tanhuvaara and Varala (1939 on), and various other summer festivals, such as the Helsinki International Festival (1938). Mostly she taught in Scandinavia during the summers: in Denmark, at the Liss Burmester Gymnasium (1951–1958); in Sweden, at the Royal Gymnasium Central Institute in Stockholm (1955–1958), and in Göteborg (1955).

Gripenberg choreographed approximately 105 dances. Many of these were originally part of the major theatrical productions of the day; they were danced by Gripenberg, members of her group (chosen from her advanced students), and colleagues. Some notable dance performances were in plays such as Järnefelt's *Titus* (1910), Shakespeare's and Sibelius's *Myrsky* (*The Tempest*, 1929), Anski's and Pergamet-Parmet's *Dibbuk* (1934), Topelius's and Melartin's version of *Prinsessa Ruusunen* (*The Sleeping Beauty*, 1937) at the National Theater, Gluck's *Orfeus* (1926), and several different productions beginning as early as 1915 of Verdi's *Aida* and Ibsen's and Grieg's *Peer Gynt* at the National Opera. She collaborated with authors, musicians, and directors throughout her career. Raoul af Hällström later wrote, "Her performance has enormously raised the value of dance as art in the eyes of the general public. It was noticed that dance is serious art, which can accommodate deep feelings, even tragedy."

Gripenberg toured widely in Scandinavia, the Baltic countries, England from 1909, and in the United States from 1919 to 1921. Among many other honors, she was awarded first prize in choreography at the Brussels Concours International de Danse in 1939. There her Groupe Gripenberg (five women) performed *Gossip*, a humorous piece depicting female gossips in caricature—even the facial expressions were choreographed; *Percussion Instrument Étude*, a crisp, plotless dance with clean geometric lines and patterns, accompanied by the dancers on percussion instruments; and *Slavery*, based on the ideas and movement behind the "Dance of the Beggars" from the play *Dibbuk* (in which cripples and other social outcasts danced in desperate yearning for their rights). *Dibbuk* had been a masterpiece; the dance movement was shocking, grotesque, ugly by the day's standards. *Slavery* was an extension of that dance, leaving out its grotesquerie and ugliness. Wearing plain overalls, with tight kerchiefs wound about their heads, the dancers evoked everyone's striving for freedom and a better life.

In the choreographic competitions of 1945 and 1947, arranged by Les Archives Internationales de la Danse, Gripenberg was awarded third prize for her *Life Continues*, in Stockholm, and for her *Misguided*, in Copenhagen, respectively. She also received three presidential medals from the State of Finland: a medal for participating in the War for Freedom, 1939/40; the Pro Finlandia Medal awarded to outstanding artists, in 1951; and one when she became a Knight of the Order of the White Rose, in 1961.

Gripenberg's early solo work, such as *Valse triste* (c.1902), which depicted a young woman's psychological conflict before an impending death, had earned her the reputation of a charismatic and sensitive performer. A memorable partnership (1915–1921) with her handsome actor-student, Onni Gabriel Snell, brought some of the high points of her performing life. Their duets, for example *Bacchanale*, *Two Gypsies*, and *Pan and Nymph*, were often repeated several times on demand of the audience. The *Beloved* series was a sensitive coming together of two people. As far as is known, none of the duets was performed again after 1921, when Onni Gabriel (as he then preferred to be called) decided to remain in the United States.

A major contribution of Gripenberg's was "bringing rhythm to Finland." Her Dalcroze-based movement system, in parallel development with contemporary ideas in women's rhythmic gymnastics, became for many years the standard in movement education in Finland. Her choreography evolved from that learned teaching system to accommodate both her earlier movement art and the new artistic currents. Gripenberg developed from a Duncan-influenced free dancer into a modern dancer whose later work be-

GRIPENBERG. *Juoru* (Gossip), a satirical dance depicting caricatures of female rumormongers, as performed by members of the Groupe Gripenberg, c.1939. (Photograph courtesy of Saga M. Ambegaokar.)

longs somewhere between that of Kurt Jooss (whom she admired) and Doris Humphrey. Gripenberg went from lyrical music visualization, where the music was used like a map, to stylization; from soft to geometric and strong movement. She was the first to flex her foot, and she strongly disapproved of limp, droopy wrists, preferring instead stylized arms that added to the design as a whole. Hällström summed up her style: "Choreography has always been one of the strengths of Maggie Gripenberg. Her compositions are stamped by unconditional artistry. She invents original, expressive, and harmoniously clean movement phrases and groupings, with dramatic dance climaxes."

It is generally believed that Gripenberg's noble heritage enabled her to transcend social taboos—and because of her daring, dance and dancers became acceptable in Finland. Her work was the foundation for later developments in modern dance. People were likely to think, "If a baroness can dance barefoot in filmy clothes, it must be art," and they trusted their young people to study with her. As a result of this, dance gained enormously, and it also gained from Gripenberg's firm belief in the value of all kinds of dance.

Gripenberg wrote some articles on dance for a few Helsinki newspapers and magazines, including one where she spoke about the financial struggles of young dancers and encouraged the formation of the Dance Artists League in 1939. Her most important written work was her autobiography, published in Swedish, *Trollbunden av rytmen*, in Finnish, *Rytmin lumoissa*, in 1950. The title in English is *Spellbound by Rhythm*.

Gripenberg said that her life was "a celebration of three things: music, painting, and dance" and that her dance should be considered "art, that was the main thing" (Gripenberg, 1950, p. 87). She never married. She preferred to keep her personal life private, and she retired to the island of Ahvenanmaa with an old, close friend. One of the first women so honored, Gripenberg is buried at the Artists Knoll of the Old Cemetery in Helsinki.

[*See also* Finland, *article on* Theatrical Dance.]

BIBLIOGRAPHY

Ambegaokar, Saga M. "Maggie Gripenberg: A Finnish Pioneer in Modern Dance." Master's thesis, Intercampus Program in Dance History, University of California, Riverside, Calif., 1985. Includes an extensive bibliography and a list of choreographed works.

Ambegaokar, Saga M. "Maggie Gripenberg (1881–1976), a Finnish Pioneer in Modern Dance: The Early Years, and an Overview." *Proceedings of the Tenth Annual Conference, Society of Dance History Scholars*, compiled by Christena L. Schlundt. Riverside, Calif., 1987.

"Gripenberg, Maggie." In *Kuka kukin On* (Who's Who in Finland). Helsinki, 1966.

"Gripenberg, Maggie." In *Vem och Vad* (Who's Who in Finland, the Swedish language version). Helsinki, 1967.

Gripenberg, Maggie. *Rytmin lumoissa.* Helsinki, 1950.

Hällström, Raoul af. *Siivekkäät jalat.* Helsinki, 1945.

Hirn, Sven. "Våra danspedagoger och dansnöjen. Om undervissning och evenemang fore 1914." In *Svenska Literatursällskapet i Finland.* No. 505, Helsinki, 1982.

INTERVIEWS. Ritva Arvelo, Eva Hemming, Tiina Suhonen, Elli Särkkä, and Gertrud Wichman by Saga M. Ambegaokar, 1984–1985.

Saga Mirjam Vuori Ambegaokar

GRISI, CARLOTTA (Caronne Adele Josephine Marie Grisi; born 18 June 1819 in Visinada, Upper Istria, Italy, died 20 May 1899 in Saint-Jean, Genève-Petit-Saconnex, Switzerland), Italian ballet dancer. Carlotta Grisi was a daughter of Vincenzo Grisi, an employee in the public surveyor's department, and Maria Grisi née Boschetti. Through her father, Carlotta was related to the opera singers Giulia and Giuditta Grisi; her sister Ernesta also followed an operatic career before marrying the poet, novelist, critic, and scenarist Théophile Gautier.

Carlotta entered the ballet school of the Teatro alla Scala in Milan at the age of seven and received much of her early training under Claude Guillet. She gained her first stage experience in ballets by Giovanni Battista Giannini, playing such child roles as Piety in *Ipermestra* (1832) and a peasant girl in *Le Mine di Polonia*. Singled out by Auguste Lefebvre, she made such an impression in a children's *pas* he arranged that she was nicknamed "the little Heberle" after the well-known Viennese ballerina Therese Heberle.

In 1833, Grisi left Milan to accompany her sister Ernesta, who had been engaged for a touring operatic company by the impresario Alessandro Lanari. Employed as a dancer, Carlotta appeared first in Venice, then, in early 1834, at the Teatro di Apollo in Rome. In the summer of that year she arrived in Naples. There she met Jules Perrot, who was then at the height of his powers as a virtuoso dancer. Perrot was so taken with Carlotta's budding talent that he persuaded her to accept him as her teacher, making her decide to devote herself to dance, against pressure from the Grisi family to become a singer.

Having fallen in love with his young pupil, Perrot accompanied her to London, partnering her in her debut there in André Deshayes's ballet *Le Rossignol* at the King's Theatre on 12 April 1836. The couple planned to marry, and in anticipation Carlotta adopted the name Madame Perrot.

After the London season the couple returned briefly to Paris, where Grisi made her first appearance in the French capital at a benefit performance at the Théâtre Français on 30 August 1836. She made little impression, however, still having much to learn from her new mentor. From Paris the couple went to Vienna, where, at the Hofoper Perrot produced his first serious essays in choreography, beginning with *Die Nymphe und der Schmetterling*,

which was premiered on 29 September 1836. Perrot made the greater impression, although the beauty of Grisi's footwork was particularly noted. This was followed by the first ballet that Perrot created unaided, *Das Stelldichein*, a highly popular work, first seen on 23 November 1836. Grisi's appearances were cut short before the season closed, and at Auteuil, on 8 April 1837, she gave birth to a daughter, Marie-Julie, of whom Perrot was registered as the father.

Later that year Vienna welcomed the pair for a second season, and Perrot added two more works to their repertory, *Die Neapolitanischen Fischer* (10 January 1838) and *Der Kobold* (2 March 1838). They next enjoyed four successful performances in Munich before an engagement at La Scala, Milan, for the autumn 1838 season. Grisi was still remembered there as a child prodigy and was now welcomed, somewhat prematurely, by one critic, as "one of the most distinguished ballerinas of our day." Another return engagement then awaited her at the Teatro San Carlo in Naples.

Early in 1840 Perrot arranged an engagement for the two of them with Anténor Joly, manager of the Théâtre de

la Renaissance in Paris, to appear in an *opéra-ballet*, with music by Uranio Fortuna, entitled *Zingaro*. Although she had made isolated appearances in two benefit performances, it was in this work that Grisi made her true debut in Paris on 1 February 1840. Her role featured some singing, but it was as a dancer that she was primarily judged. Once again, however, Perrot received the greater share of attention; even Théophile Gautier, the critic of *La presse*, who was so soon to become Grisi's champion, was somewhat restrained when writing about her. He commented that her dancing had not seemed to him very distinctive.

Perrot, who was desperately keen on being reengaged at the Paris Opera, was hoping to negotiate an engagement for the two of them, but in spite of his gifts there was really no place for him. Grisi's family then took matters in hand and by a subterfuge arranged for Carlotta to sign a contract on her own. This was for a year beginning on 1 January 1841, at the modest salary of five thousand francs. Perrot had to accept the situation, and he arranged a pas de deux for Grisi and Lucien Petipa that was inserted into Donizetti's opera *La Favorite* for Grisi's debut on 12 February 1841.

Plans for Grisi to create her first important role in a complex narrative ballet—later to be produced as *La Jolie Fille de Gand*—were shelved at her insistence in favor of a simpler work, *Giselle*, which was specially conceived for her by the scenarist Théophile Gautier and the composer Adolphe Adam. Perrot was allowed to arrange Grisi's part, but all the credit for the choreography was given to Jean Coralli, who was in overall charge of the production and who arranged the rest of the ballet. The work was an instant success when it was first performed on 28 June 1841. [*See* Giselle.] It gave Grisi a great personal triumph, and Gautier voiced the general opinion in his review in *La presse* (5 July 1841) that she had become, overnight, a ballerina of the first order, with a style that was to be placed somewhere between the ethereal manner of Marie Taglioni and the *terre à terre* dancing of Fanny Elssler.

Giselle marked the beginning of Grisi's long friendship with Gautier as well as a change in her relationship with Perrot. Having never married, Grisi and Perrot were to separate shortly afterward, although he would continue to serve her with great devotion as a choreographer until the end of her career. [*See the entry on Perrot.*] A few months later, Grisi repeated her triumph in *Giselle* at Her Majesty's Theatre, London, where Perrot produced the ballet for the opening of the 1842 season.

The Paris Opera gave Grisi a new contract at a greatly increased salary—twelve thousand francs for 1842 and fifteen thousand for 1843, with performance fees in addition. On 22 June 1842 she appeared as Beatrix in Albert's *La Jolie Fille de Gand*, a dramatic part containing a memorable solo for her, the *pas de Diane chasseresse*. [*See* Jolie

Fille de Gand, La.] This was followed a year later, on 17 July 1843, by another important creation, the title role in Jean Coralli's *La Péri*. Hailed as a worthy successor to *Giselle*, this oriental fairy tale featured a celebrated *pas du songe* that included Grisi's spectacularly hazardous flying leap into the arms of her partner, Lucien Petipa. [*See* Péri, La.] Three months later Grisi and Petipa introduced the ballet to London during an engagement at the Theatre Royal, Drury Lane.

Grisi made further progress in her career in 1844. She signed a new contract with the Paris Opera, under which her salary was increased to twenty thousand francs a year, and she added another major creation to her repertory, not in Paris but in London, at Her Majesty's Theatre, where she was engaged to open the season. This was the title role in Perrot's new dramatic ballet *La Esmeralda*, one of his greatest works, first performed on 9 March 1844. Grisi gave a moving portrayal of the heroine of Victor Hugo's novel *Notre-Dame de Paris*, on which the ballet was based. [*See* Esmeralda, La.] During the same London season Grisi and Perrot also danced a stage version of the polka, the latest rage in the ballrooms. Set to music by Cesare Pugni, *Polka* was first performed on 11 April 1844.

A visit to London during her contractual holiday now became an annual event for Grisi, and at Her Majesty's Theatre on 12 July 1845 she took part in Perrot's extraordinary multistellar *divertissement* entitled simply *Pas de Quatre*, alongside Marie Taglioni, Fanny Cerrito, and Lucile Grahn. [*See* Pas de Quatre.]

Grisi's next creation at the Paris Opera provided her with a very different role. This was Joseph Mazilier's *Le Diable à Quatre*, first performed on 11 August 1845, a ballet based loosely on an eighteenth-century comedy in which the heroine is a basket weaver's wife who becomes a countess for a day. In it, Grisi revealed a gift for delicate comedy, being able to arouse laughter while preserving her elegance and grace. [*See* Diable à Quatre, Le.] Her next important creation in Paris was another dramatic role, in Mazilier's *Paquita*, first performed on 1 April 1846, a ballet with a Spanish setting that she and her partner Lucien Petipa introduced to London at Drury Lane shortly afterward, on 3 June 1846. [*See* Paquita.]

Grisi's contract with the Paris Opera was due to expire at the end of 1846, and she took the opportunity to insist on an interval before her new engagement (which provided for an increase in salary to twenty-four thousand francs) to enable her to dance at the Teatro di Apollo in Rome in January 1847. This proved to be an unfortunate engagement; she returned to Paris nearly a month late to face a claim for breach of contract, for which the Opera was awarded damages of ten thousand francs. As a result of the delay, the Opera had had to replace her in Jean Coralli's new ballet, *Ozaï*, which had proved to be a failure. Consequently, she was not seen in a new work in Paris that year. However, in London on 26 June 1847, at Her Majesty's Theatre, she appeared as Fire in Perrot's new all-star *divertissement*, *Les Éléments*, with Fanny Cerrito and Carolina Rosati.

Grisi's next ballet at the Opera was *Griseldis* (16 February 1848), choreographed by Mazilier to music by Adolphe Adam. It was a spectacular fantasy in which she made one of her entrances on horseback and sang a short refrain. Unluckily, the ballet's success was compromised by the revolution that broke out in Paris a few days after the premiere, causing a theatrical crisis. Her contract with the Opera had been due to terminate in January 1849 but was extended at a monthly salary of three thousand francs (as always, with bonuses) to enable her to create the leading role in a new ballet by Perrot. Preparations for this work were delayed for various reasons, first by an engagement in London, where she took the title role in Paul Taglioni's *Electra* (17 April 1849), and then, on her return to Paris, by a light attack of cholera. The new work, *La Filleule des Fées* (8 October 1849), with music by Adam

GRISI. Jules Perrot and Grisi in their pas de deux *Polka*, a staged presentation of the then-fashionable social dance, which premiered at Her Majesty's Theatre, London, in 1844. This contemporary lithographed music cover by Bouve & Sharp, after John Brandard, was printed in Boston. (Courtesy of Madison U. Sowell and Debra H. Sowell, Brigham Young University, Provo, Utah.)

and Alfred de Saint-Julien, seemed to have the ingredients for success, but it did not long survive the departure of both Grisi and Perrot from Paris.

Grisi spent the spring and summer of 1850 in London, dancing at Her Majesty's Theatre throughout the season. She appeared in two new ballets by Paul Taglioni, creating the role of the Sprite in *Les Métamorphoses* (12 March 1850) and playing Euphrosyne in the grand *divertissement Les Grâces* (2 May 1850). Grisi also made a great impression as a mime by playing the mute role of Ariel in Fromental Halévy's opera *La Tempesta* (12 June 1850).

The last phase of Grisi's career was centered in Saint Petersburg, where Perrot had been engaged as ballet master. She joined him there for the 1850/51 season at the Bolshoi Theater at a salary of 7,500 rubles, which was to be increased to 10,000 rubles by a special grant. She made her Russian debut in *Giselle* and later appeared in *La Filleule des Fées, Esmeralda, Le Diable à Quatre*, and, toward the end of the season, in a new ballet by Perrot, *The Naïad and the Fisherman*. First performed at the Bolshoi Theater on 30 January [11 February] 1851, this work had been derived from Perrot's earlier ballet, *Ondine*, but had been reworked so extensively that it was virtually a new piece.

Before her second Russian season, Grisi made what were to be her last appearances at Her Majesty's Theatre in London, appearing in only one new work, the *divertissement* that Paul Taglioni produced to reflect the influx of foreign visitors to the Great Exhibition, *Les Cosmopolites*, first performed on 15 May 1851.

The success of Grisi's first season in Russia could be measured by her increased salary (12,500 rubles) for the 1851/52 season. Perrot was absent for the early part of the season, and Joseph Mazilier was engaged as ballet master in his place. He staged two ballets that had earlier been produced in Paris, *La Jolie Fille de Gand* (26 October [6 November] 1851) and *Vert-Vert* (10 [22] January 1852), in both of which Grisi appeared.

Perrot was back in his post as ballet master for the 1852/53 season, during which Grisi created the role of Vlaida in one of his finest ballets, *The War of the Women*, first performed on 11 [23] November 1852. Toward the end of the season, she danced the title role in *Gazelda*, first performed on 13 [25] February 1853. Pugni had composed the scores for both these works.

Grisi's career was now almost at an end. Her last appearances, at the end of 1853, were in Warsaw. Rumors had it that she would be seen again at the Paris Opera, but they proved unfounded. She settled at a country property at Saint-Jean, on the outskirts of Geneva, where she spent the remaining years of her life. Grisi had a second child, Léontine, so named after its father, Prince Léon Radziwill. Grisi's retirement, during which Gautier paid her frequent visits, was comfortable and uneventful. Her daughter Léontine married the artist E. Pinchard.

The distinguishing feature of Grisi's style as a dancer was a natural spontaneity that the public found irresistible, whether she was playing a role such as Giselle, in which her interpretation was marked by a gentleness that affectingly expressed the girl's vulnerability, or a more strongly dramatic part such as Esmeralda. Her dancing always seemed effortless, but this concealed a very strong technique. Contemporary reviews make it clear that her pointe work was quite exceptionally developed for her time, and she was equal to such hazardous feats as the famous leap in *La Péri*. Her place in the history of ballet is also characterized by her lifelong friendship with the poet, scenarist, and critic Théophile Gautier, who conceived two of her best-known roles and who wrote several poems that owe their inspiration to her. Above all, she was the muse of the greatest choreographer of the Romantic ballet, Jules Perrot.

BIBLIOGRAPHY

Gautier, Théophile. *Carlotta Grisi.* Paris, 1841.

Gautier, Théophile. *Histoire de l'art dramatique en France depuis vingt-cinq ans* (1858–1859). 6 vols. Geneva, 1968.

Gautier, Théophile. *Gautier on Dance.* Translated and edited by Ivor Guest. London, 1986. French edition: *Ecrits sur la danse* (Arles, 1995).

Guest, Ivor. *The Romantic Ballet in England.* London, 1972.

Guest, Ivor. *The Ballet of the Second Empire.* London, 1974.

Guest, Ivor. *The Romantic Ballet in Paris.* 2d rev. ed. London, 1980.

Guest, Ivor. *Jules Perrot.* London, 1984.

Krasovskaya, Vera. *Russkii baletnyi teatr: Ot vozniknoveniia do serediny XIX veka.* Leningrad, 1958.

Lifar, Serge. *Giselle: Apothéose du ballet romantique.* Paris, 1942.

Lifar, Serge. *Carlotta Grisi.* Translated by Doris Langley Moore. London, 1947.

Lumley, Benjamin. *Reminiscences of the Opera.* London, 1864.

Moore, Lillian. "Carlotta Grisi." In Moore's *Artists of the Dance.* New York, 1938.

Pudełek, Janina. *Warszawski balet romantyczny, 1802–1866.* Warsaw, 1968.

Prudhommeau, Germaine. "Giselle première." *Danser* (October 1991): 35–40.

Richardson, Joanna. *Théophile Gautier: His Life and Times.* London, 1958.

Tani, Gino. "Grisi, Carlotta." In *Enciclopedia dello spettacolo.* Rome, 1954–.

IVOR GUEST

GRUCA, WITOLD (born 15 August 1927 in Kraków), Polish dancer and choreographer. Witold Gruca received his dance training at the Warsaw State Ballet School of the Wielki Theater, where he studied with Barbara Karczmarewicz, Paweł Dobiecki, and Leon Wójcikowski (also known as Woizikowski). Having begun his professional career in the corps de ballet of the Wrocław Opera in 1947, Gruca performed as a soloist with the Poznań Opera Ballet (1948–1950) and the Warsaw Opera Ballet (1951–1956). From 1956 to 1961 he toured with Barbara Bittnerówna, performing his own concert dance pieces in Poland, Great

Britain, the Soviet Union, East Germany, Romania, Czechoslovakia, Finland, and Italy. Thereafter, he returned to Poland and joined Papliński's Polish Dance Theater (1961–1962), the Warsaw Opera Ballet (1962–1965), and the Wielki Theater Ballet (1965–1978), where he eventually became a principal dancer.

As a young dancer, Gruca was frequently cast in romantic roles, in which his natural good looks served him well. In addition to his ballet training, he also studied at the Actors Studio in Kraków, and he ultimately became a dancer of great dramatic talent. He was also admired for his character roles in such works as Wójcikowski's *Till Eulenspiegel* (1950), Asaf Messerer's *Coppélia* (1974), and Frederick Ashton's *La Fille Mal Gardée* (1977).

Gruca made his debut as a choreographer with the Polish Dance Company in 1961, staging his works mainly at the Warsaw Opera (1962–1964) and at the Wielki Theater (1965–1979). His favorite form was the one-act ballet. Among his more important works are *Mandragora* (music by Karol Szymanowski) and *Love Sonnets* (music by Tadeusz Baird) in 1963; *Awaiting* (music by Augustyn Bloch), *The Nude Prince* (music by Romuald Twardowski), and *Ad Hominem* (music by Zbigniew Wiszniewski) in 1964; *Lonchiness* and *Voci* (both to music by Bloch) in 1968; *Songs of the Trouvères* (music by Baird) and *Salmo Giogioso* (music by Bloch) in 1972; *Pan Twardowski* (music by Ludomir Różycki) in 1973; *The Real Sleeping Beauty* (music by Bloch) in 1974; *Carnaval* (music by Robert Schumann) in 1975; *Kraków Wedding* (music by Karol Kurpiński and Józef Damse), *Stanisław and Anna Oświęcim* (music by Mieczyslaw Karłowicz), and *Tadeusz Baird's Third Symphony* in 1976; and *Masquerade* (music by Aram Khatchaturian) in 1979.

Gruca has produced many films and programs for Polish television and has collaborated in stage dramas. He won the Primo Premio Assoluto of the International Competition in Vercella, Italy, in 1956 and was also honored by the Polish government.

BIBLIOGRAPHY

Chynowski, Paweł, and Małgorzata Komorowska. *Witold Gruca.* Warsaw, 1975.
Lumiński, Jacek. "Warsaw and Lodz." *Ballett International* 11 (October 1988): 42–44.
Neuer, Adam, ed. *Polish Opera and Ballet of the Twentieth Century: Operas, Ballets, Pantomimes, Miscellaneous Works.* Translated by Jerzy Zawadzki. Kraków, 1986.

PAWEŁ CHYNOWSKI

GSOVSKY, TATJANA (Tat'iana Isatchenko; born 18 March 1901 in Moscow, died 29 September 1993 in Berlin), Russian-German dancer, teacher, choreographer, and ballet mistress. Tat'iana Isatchenko, daughter of the Russian actress Claudia Isatchenko, began her dance

studies at the Isadora Duncan Studio in Petrograd. After some time in classes stressing freedom of movement, she undertook the more rigorous study of ballet in classes with Laurent Novikoff, Matyatin, Vera Kirsanova, and Olga Preobrajenska. She later studied at the Dalcroze school in Dresden-Hellerau.

Uprooted in 1917 by the October Revolution, in which the Bolsheviks seized power in Petrograd, Isatchenko and her family relocated to the southern city of Krasnodar, near the Black Sea. There she became a member of the Krasnodar Experimental Theater, where she met and married the dancer Victor Gsovsky. Together they left the Soviet Union in 1925 and opened a ballet school in Berlin, which became the permanent base of her multifarious activities as ballet mistress and choreographer. The school is now the Tatjana Gsovsky Ballet School of the German Opera Berlin.

Gsovsky started to work as a choreographer for music halls, occasionally mounting ballets at German provincial opera houses, including the first productions of Carl Orff's *Catulli Carmina* (Leipzig, 1943) and Gottfried von Einem's *Princess Turandot* (Dresden, 1944). Appointed ballet mistress at the East Berlin German State Opera (1945–1952), Gsovsky made it the center of the reemerging German ballet scene after World War II. The ever-growing political frictions between East and West made her leave East Berlin and settle in West Berlin (where her school was already situated), first concentrating on a career as a freelance choreographer. In this capacity she worked repeatedly at the Teatro Colón in Buenos Aires, at the Munich State Opera, and at the Teatro alla Scala in Milan, where

TATJANA GSOVSKY. *The Idiot*, set to a score by Hans Werner Henze, was created by Gsovsky for the Berlin Ballet in 1952. Here Olga Ferri as Natassia Filipovna and Enrique Lomi as Parfion Rogoschin are seen with members of the male ensemble. (Photograph by Siegfried Enkelmann; used by permission.)

she mounted the first production of Orff's *Trionfo di Afrodite* in 1953.

In West Berlin Gsovsky began to work for what was then the Municipal Opera and for the Berlin Ballet, assembled first for the city's autumn festival in 1955. The Berlin Ballet later toured Germany and abroad until it became part of the Municipal Opera's ballet company, of which Gsovsky had been appointed ballet mistress in 1954. Eventually she became artistic director, a position she still held when the opera moved to its rebuilt former premises and became the German Opera Berlin (1961–1966). After having been officially pensioned, she continued to work as a ballet mistress and at her school, which she ran with Gert Reinholm, her former principal dancer and her successor as ballet director of the German Opera Berlin.

A choreographer of distinctly contemporary inclinations, Gsovsky never abandoned the plastic or sculptural approach, which obviously derived from her early connections with Russia's brand of modern dance. Nonetheless, she gradually assimilated the classical academic vocabulary, which enabled her to mount such classics as *The Sleeping Beauty, Swan Lake,* and (with Nicholas Beriozoff) *Raymonda.* Strongly influenced by contemporary developments in literature, music, and the arts, she preferred to collaborate with modern composers such as Boris Blacher, Hans Werner Henze, and Luigi Nono. Her ballets, often inspired by literature, concentrate mostly on the psychological aspects of the subject, as in *Hamlet* (1953) and *The Moor of Venice* (1956), both to scores by Blacher, and *The Idiot* (1952) and the García Lorca–inspired *The Red Cloak* (1954), scored by Henze and Nono respectively.

Although the actual dance content of Gsovsky's ballets was rather limited, the best of her vast output nonetheless radiated a stark modern theatricality, as in her Frankfurt adaptation of Kurt Weill's *The Seven Deadly Sins,* of which she staged the first European production after World War II, in 1960. Thus she was a highly respected figure in German intellectual circles of the 1950s and 1960s, though interest in her ballets waned with the rise of the choreographically strong ballets of the Balanchine school. As a teacher, she helped to form several generations of German dancers, including some of the best—Natasha Trofimova, Gert Reinholm, Gisela Deege, Peter van Dyk, Konstanze Vernon, and Karen von Aroldingen. Gsovsky received the German Dance Prize in 1983.

BIBLIOGRAPHY

"Ausdruckstanz and Ballet: Victor Gsovsky, Tatjana Gsovsky, Gret Palucca." *Ballett International* 10 (January 1987): 6–11.
Geitel, Klaus. "Hommage à Tatjana Gsovsky." In *Ballett 1966: Chronik und Bilanz eines Ballettjahres.* Velber bei Hannover, 1966.
Gsovsky, Tatjana, and Siegfried Enkelmann. *Ballet in Deutschland.* Berlin, 1954.
Koegler, Horst. "Twenty Years Too Soon." *Ballett International/Tanz Aktuell* 1 (January 1994): 24–27.
"Prize Awarded by the Deutscher Berufsverband für Tanzpädagogik and the Magazine *Ballett-Journal* Goes to Tatjana Gsovsky and Gret Palucca." *Ballett-Journal / Das Tanzarchiv* 31 (January–February 1983): 7.
Steinbeck, Dietrich. "Tanz . . . Tanz . . . Tanz: Tatjana Gsovsky—Ein dokumentarisches Porträt." In *Deutsche Oper Berlin, Spielzeit 1992/93, Beiträge zum Musiktheater XII,* pp. 199–217. Berlin, 1993.

HORST KOEGLER

GSOVSKY, VICTOR (Viktor Gzovskii; born 12 January 1902 in Saint Petersburg, died 14 March 1974 in Hamburg), Russian dancer, ballet master, and teacher. Gsovsky studied in Saint Petersburg with Lydia Sokolova and performed in ballets by Marius Petipa and Michel Fokine. In 1925 he was named ballet master at the Berlin Opera, and in 1928 he and his wife Tatjana Gsovsky founded a dance school that quickly became famous. Gsovsky left Germany in 1937 to become ballet master of the Markova-Dolin Company. The following year he settled in Paris and opened a school whose students included Irène Skorik, Colette Marchand, Violette Verdy, and Serge Perrault. In 1945 he restaged the second act of *Swan Lake* at the Opera, with Yvette Chauviré and Serge Peretti.

Gsovsky's spiritual, sensitive conception of romanticism flowered in *La Sylphide,* which he revived for Nina Vyroubova and Skorik in 1946 at the Ballets des Champs-Élysées; there, two years later, he put on *Mascarade* (music by Georges Bizet), *Fête Galante* (music by Claude Arrieu), and *Nocturne* (music by Mozart). In the interim he staged *Dances of Galanta* (music by Zoltán Kodály) and *Pygmalion* (music by John Field) for the Metropolitan Ballet in London. Between 1950 and 1952 he served as choreographer for the Munich Opera, where he staged numerous ballets, including *Hamlet* (music by Boris Blacher) and *Chemin de Lumière* (music by Chavadadzé) for the Grand Ballet du Marquis de Cuevas and *La Perle* (music by Pascal) for the Ballets de Paris de Roland Petit. He devoted himself increasingly to teaching, in his own studio in Paris, with the Ballet du XXe Siècle in Düsseldorf, and at the Hamburg Opera, where he passionately defended a high-toned classicism. His choreography for *Le Grand Pas Classique* (music by Daniel Auber) illustrates his saying that virtuosity was important, but that it must be linked with rigor and musicality.

Gsovsky also created the choreography for several films, including *Vautrin* and *Un seul amour* (1943), *Un revenant* (1946), and *Par ordre du Tsar* and *Cadet Rousselle* (1954).

BIBLIOGRAPHY

"Ausdruckstanz and Ballet: Victor Gsovsky, Tatjana Gsovsky, Gret Palucca." *Ballett International* 10 (January 1987): 6–11.
Chauviré, Yvette. "Hommage à Victor Gsovsky." *Saisons de la danse* (May 1974).
Hering, Doris. "'Violette Lunaire.'" *Dance Magazine* (April 1962): 38–42.

Huckenpahler, Victoria. *Ballerina: A Biography of Violette Verdy.* New York, 1978.

Peters, Kurt. "Zum Tode von Victor Gsovsky." *Das Tanzarchiv* 21 (May 1974): 407–408.

Regner, O. F. *Das Ballettbuch.* Frankfurt, 1954.

Robinson, Jacqueline. "Persons déjà aux vacances prochaines." *La danse* (April 1956).

JEANNINE DORVANE
Translated from French

GUATEMALA. The region of Mesoamerica where Guatemala is located was the homeland of the vast Maya civilization, which extended into the Yucatan Peninsula and onto the island of Cozumel. After the Spanish arrived in the early sixteenth century, the Maya were subjected to conquerers in search of precious metals and unbaptized souls. Epidemics and internecine politics weakened the Maya; by the mid-seventeenth century, only 20 percent of the Mayan population survived to work as native laborers on Spanish land grants, which produced cocoa, sugarcane, and indigo. Guatemala was the chief unit of the Audiencia de Guatemala (which included El Salvador, Honduras, Nicaragua, and Costa Rica). In 1821, New Spain, which included Mexico and the Audiencia, became independent of Spain; in 1823 the Audiencia became independent from Mexico. Today, the population of some 9 million are 54 percent Native American, 42 percent *mestizos* (mixed Native American and European), and 4 percent European; the majority are Spanish-speaking and/or Mayan-speaking Roman Catholics.

The traditional dances of Guatemala come from five sources—the Mayan, Spanish and European, colonial, African-Caribbean, and modern or Republican. The relative influence of any source or combination of sources varies from region to region. In the central and western plateau, dances of precolonial origin coexist with those of Spain and the colonial period. African-Caribbean dances are typical of the department (province) of Izabal in the northeast and near the border with Belize. Colonial dances are found in the eastern part of the country and in the Petén area. Since Guatemala achieved independence in the nineteenth century, a style of dance called *son* has emerged and spread throughout the country; it is a mixture of ethnic influences and is considered to symbolize Guatemalan national identity.

Precolonial Dance. Four major sources of information on the dances existed before European contact: the Mayan chronicle known as the *Popol Vuh,* the *Memorial de Sololá,* the *Rabinal Achí,* and pictures on Mayan ceramics. One such dance, now called "El Palo Volador," is still performed throughout Mesoamerica, particularly in El Quiché. The dance drama "Rabinal Achí" originated in Rabinal, Baja Verapaz, in north-central Guatemala. Other ancient dances, now called "El Venado" and "La Culebra,"

are performed in the western and southwestern plateau. All these dances are parts of religious rituals that have become syncretized with Roman Catholic rites; other examples include "La Paach" from San Marcos, related to the cult of corn, and the *paabanc* dances in Alta Verapaz.

Spanish and European Dances. Traditions brought from Europe, especially from Spain, are exemplified most notably by "Moros y Cristianos," (Moors and Christians), a dance drama performed in much of Latin America. In Guatemala it is presented on holidays in villages; it recounts the story of the reconquest of Spain from the Moors (North African Muslims who ruled from 711 to 1492 in the Iberian Peninsula) and was brought to the New World by sixteenth-century missionaries. "Moros y Cristianos" was adopted into the folk traditions of indigenous peoples and is now performed in the western and central plateau and in the department of Chiquimula to the east. The accompaniment is drums and whistles, and sometimes flageolets. The dance dramas "Los Doce Pares de Francia" (Twelve French Noblemen) and "Los Siete Pares de Francia" (Seven French Noblemen) have similar subjects, content, and music. Another important dance of Spanish origin is "Los Gigantes" (The Giants) danced by two male-female couples (one white, one black) representing giants; the music is provided by a single-keyboard marimba.

Colonial Dances. A broad spectrum of ritual and social dances developed as colonial society evolved in the sixteenth to nineteenth centuries. "La Conquista," a dance drama performed in western Guatemala since the sixteenth century, is of *criollo* (mixed ethnic) origin. It memorializes the Spanish conquest of Guatemala under Don Pedro de Alvarado and his native collaborator Tecún Umán and is accompanied by whistles and drums.

"Los Toritos" is widespread in Guatemala, especially in the western and central regions. It celebrates the bullfights on colonial ranches and includes such typical Spanish figures as the estate administrators and cowboys, the African herd managers, and the Mayan clown dancers costumed as monkeys. There are two major variants of "Los Toritos," the Quiché version from the west and the Cakchiquel version from the central region. The marimba was first used in Guatemala in association with this dance.

Apart from these two dances, the colonial period was characterized by imported European social dances that were first performed by the ruling classes and subsequently imitated by others. They then entered the folk tradition to become the foundation of the *son* style. In *son* one may detect the early Spanish *fandango* and *zarabanda,* the contradances and quadrilles of the seventeenth and eighteenth centuries, and the nineteenth-century minuet, mazurka, polka, waltz, and schottische.

African-Caribbean Dances. African slaves were less important in Guatemala than in some other Spanish colonial regions. The country's black population is descended largely from fugitive Caribbean slaves who settled in the northeastern part of Guatemala in the sixteenth century. In addition, the black Caribs (Garifunas), descendants of Africans and indigenous Caribs, began migrating to the mainland around the end of the eighteenth century and spread throughout coastal Guatemala, British Honduras (now Belize), and Honduras. The Garifunas perform their *wanaragua*, a street masquerade, and their *punta* dances on the feast days of Saint Isidore in May and Saint Michael the Archangel in September; any festival in their communities is an occasion for dance, accompanied by drums, bones, gourds, conch shells, and other traditional instruments. [*See* Garifuna Dance.]

Republican Dances. After Guatemala was established as a nation in 1847, a group of dances arose out of the colonial tradition. The most authentic is the *seis-ocho* ("six-eight," referring to the rhythm), which has spread all over Guatemala and has given its name to national music in general.

In addition to the *seis-ocho*, there are innumerable social dances known under the generic term *baile*. Favorites in the Petén are "La Chotona" and "El Caballito." The western region adds "Los Méxicanos," derived from "Los Toritos," and the central and northern regions have "Los Animalitos," "Los Güegüechos," "El Marinero," "La Cofradía," "Los Cinco Toros," "San Jorge," "El Costeño Grande," "Los Viejitos," and "Las Guacamayas."

The dances of Guatemala can be categorized as either religious or secular. Those performed to traditional musical instrumental accompaniment and included under the heading *son* are associated with sacred rituals, whereas the *seis-ocho* and its music are nonreligious in origin and may be performed at any type of celebration. Other popular secular dances include the fox trot, the waltz, and the *danzón* (a Cuban dance derived from the *habanera*).

[*For related discussion, see* Caribbean Region.]

BIBLIOGRAPHY

Bode, Barbara. *The Dance of the Conquest of Guatemala.* New Orleans, 1961.

Correa, Gustavo, et al. *The Native Theatre in Middle America.* New Orleans, 1961.

Departmento de Arte Folklórico Nacional. *Danzas folklóricas de Guatemala.* Guatemala, 1971.

El baile de la Conquista. Guatemala, 1981.

García Escobar, Carlos René. *Talleres, trajes y danzas tradicionales de Guatemala.* San Carlos, 1987.

García Escobar, Carlos René. *Detrás de la máscara: La danza de toritos cakchiquel en Guatemala.* Guatemala, 1989.

García Escobar, Carlos René. *El español: Danzas de moros y cristianos en Guatemala.* Guatemala, 1990.

Hanvik, Jan Michael. "Mayan Culture Is Rescued through Dance." *Dance Magazine* (November 1994): 40–44.

Juárez Toledo, J. Manuel. *La música en los rituales dedicados al maíz.* Guatemala, 1988.

Luján Muñoz, Luis. *Masks and Morerías of Guatemala.* Guatemala, 1987.

Mace, Carroll E. *Three Spanish-Quiché Dance-Dramas of Rabinal.* New Orleans, 1970.

O'Brien, Linda L. "Music in a Maya Cosmos." *World of Music* 18.3 (1976): 35–42.

Paret-Limardo de Vela, Lise. *La danza del venado en Guatemala.* Guatemala, 1973.

Rodríguez Rouanet, Francisco. *Danzas folklóricas de Guatemala.* Guatemala, 1992.

Sloat, Susanna. "Grupo Cultural Uk'Ux Pop Wuj." *Attitude* 10.4 (1994–1995): 67–68.

CELSO A. LARA FIGUEROA
Translated from Spanish

GUEDRA. *See* Morocco *and* Zar.

GUERRA, NICOLA (born 2 May 1865 in Naples, died 5 February 1942 in Cernobbio), Italian dancer, choreographer, and teacher. Guerra studied with Aniello Amaturo at the ballet school of the Teatro San Carlo in Naples. At the age of seventeen he made his debut as *primo ballerino* in Piacenza and appeared at the Teatro di Apollo in Rome. Following his successful debut at the Teatro San Carlo the next year, he received three successive engagements at the Teatro alla Scala and toured internationally, performing in Saint Petersburg, London, North America, and Paris. From 1896 to 1902 Guerra was engaged at the Vienna Opera, first as a principal dancer and then as a teacher and choreographer. Here he created such works as *Künstlerlist* (1898), to music by Franz Skofitz. During this period he also wrote *Tersicoreide* (published 1898), a collection of dance-related stories and sketches.

Guerra's greatest contribution to European ballet probably occurred during the next thirteen years (1902–1915), when he was the chief ballet master and choreographer of the Hungarian State Opera Ballet in Budapest. Guerra raised the technical and artistic level of the company, rendering it equal to that of companies in the major cities of western Europe. He also choreographed nineteen ballets for the company, most in collaboration with Hungarian composers and librettists. These works reflected his belief that ballets should be based on fantasy, legends, or folk tales and should not burden the audience with sad or ponderous themes. Guerra's residence in Hungary was terminated by the outbreak of World War I.

On his return to Italy, Guerra founded a small independent company called Pastelli Coreografici (Choreographic Pastels), which toured throughout Italy. In 1917 Jacques Rouché of the Paris Opera called Guerra to Paris to direct that company's school and to choreograph a revival of Jean-Philippe Rameau's *Castor et Pollux.* Guerra also provided choreography for *La Tragédie de Salomé* (1919), set to music by Florent Schmidt, *Artémis Troublée* (1922), to music by Paul Paray, and *Goyescos,* to music by Enrique

Granados. After the war, Guerra worked at the Opéra Comique.

In 1923 Guerra returned to Italy, but his engagement as choreographer and director of La Scala's ballet school was short-lived because of personal and artistic differences with the theater's director. Once again Guerra founded an independent company, this time a larger one, called I Nuovi Balli Italiani del Maestro Nicola Guerra. After a successful debut at Milan's Teatro Lirico, the company toured Italy, France, Spain, and Egypt. It disbanded in 1926. Guerra returned to the Paris Opera from 1927 to 1929, choreographing works such as *Le Diable dans le Beffroi* (The Devil in the Belfry), to music by Désiré-Émile Ingelbrecht, after a story by Edgar Allan Poe, and *Cyrca*, to music by Marc Delmas.

Guerra returned to Italy during the 1930/31 season to direct the ballet school of the Rome Opera and to choreograph several ballets. Once again personal differences cut short the engagement. He returned to Paris, then to Milan for a brief term as choreographer at La Scala. He finally retired to Cernobbio, where he died in 1942.

Throughout his career as a performer and teacher, Guerra clung to the traditions of nineteenth-century Italian ballet as outlined by Carlo Blasis. Guerra is credited with being "the last representative of the glorious Neapolitan choreographic school and the last artist to spread abroad the prestige of Italian ballet" (Tani and Részi, 1954). In Hungary he was decorated with the Chivalric Order of Saint Stephen, and in France he was awarded the Grand-Croix de la Légion d'Honneur.

BIBLIOGRAPHY

Caorsi, Ettore. "Un grande maestro di danza: Nicola Guerra." *Il cigno* 1 (October 1953): 70–71.

Dienes, Gedeon P. "History of the State Opera Ballet, Budapest." *Hungarian Dance News*, nos. 3–4 (1980): 3–5.

Tani, Gino, and Vályi Részi. "Guerra, Nicola." In *Enciclopedia dello spettacolo*. Rome, 1954–.

DEBRA HICKENLOOPER SOWELL

GUEST, IVOR. (born 14 April 1920 in Chislehurst, Kent), British dance historian. An internationally recognized authority on nineteenth-century ballet in France and England, Guest is best known as a specialist on the Romantic ballet. His books *The Romantic Ballet in England* (1954) and *The Romantic Ballet in Paris* (1966) are standard reference works on the period. Guest is the author of the official history of the Paris Opera Ballet, *Le Ballet de l'Opéra de Paris* (1976), and he has written definitive biographies of Fanny Cerrito, Fanny Elssler, Adeline Genée, Jules Perrot, and Virginia Zucchi. He has also translated and edited the dance reviews of Théophile Gautier, which provide important eyewitness accounts of nineteenth-century ballets and personalities.

Guest came to dance history somewhat indirectly, through an early interest in Napoleon II and the Second Empire (1847–1958). Inspired by performances of the Anglo-Polish and Sadler's Wells ballet companies, he began to explore the ballet of that era and, in 1946, published his first article on dance, "'Coppélia' 1870," in the periodical *Ballet*, to which he became a regular contributor. His first book, *Napoleon III in England* (1952), was soon followed by the two-volume *Ballet of the Second Empire* (1953, 1955). At the time of his early researches, he also studied law at Trinity College, Cambridge; in 1949 he qualified as a solicitor.

Between 1952 and 1962 Guest served as an associate editor of *Ballet Annual,* and in 1963 he became an editorial adviser to *Dancing Times*. In addition to his books he has written many articles; an extensive bibliography, compiled by Selma Landen Odom, may be found in Guest's autobiographical *Adventures of a Ballet Historian: An Unfinished Memoir* (1982). An updated bibliography, covering his works from 1982 to 1994, appears in *Dance Research* (Summer 1995), an issue published in celebration of his seventy-fifth birthday.

Through his research, Guest has also contributed to ballet performances. His discovery of the original musical score for *La Fille Mal Gardée* inspired the Royal Ballet's 1960 revival of this work, choreographed by Frederick Ashton. He served as a historical adviser to Ballet for All's *The Two Coppélias* (1969–1970) and to the British Broadcasting Corporation (BBC) television series *The Magic of Dance* (1978–1980). He has also written numerous program notes for the Royal Ballet. Guest's marriage to Ann Hutchinson, a world authority on dance notation, has also led to noteworthy collaborations, among them the reconstruction of Elssler's famous "La Cachucha" (1836).

Guest's interests include museums and exhibitions. He wrote the catalog *A Gallery of Romantic Ballet* (1965) for an exhibition at the Mercury Theatre in London, and he served as an adviser to the "Spotlight" exhibition at the Theatre Museum in London's Victoria and Albert Museum during 1980 and 1981. He was vice-chairman of the British Theatre Museum Association from 1966 until its disbandment in 1977, and he was appointed to the Theatre Museum Advisory Council in 1974. Guest has also participated in the field of dance education as a member of the executive committee of the Royal Academy of Dancing since 1965 and as its chairman since 1969. In 1992 the Royal Academy of Dancing presented him with the Queen Elizabeth II Coronation Award in tribute to his twenty-two years as chairman. His general history of ballet, *The Dancer's Heritage* (1960), is used as a textbook in British schools.

BIBLIOGRAPHY

Clarke, Mary, and Clement Crisp. "Ivor Guest: By Way of an Introduction." *Dance Research* 13 (Summer 1995): 2–6. Preface to a special issue dedicated to Ivor Guest on his seventy-fifth birthday, which includes a bibliography of Guest's work from 1982 to 1994.

Guest, Ivor. *Adventures of a Ballet Historian: An Unfinished Memoir.* New York, 1982.

SUSAN AU

GUGLIELMO EBREO DA PESARO (also known as Giovanni Ambrosio; born c.1420 in Pesaro, Italy, died after 1484), Italian dancing master, theorist, and choreographer. Relatively little is known of the private life of this respected, much sought-after instructor of "kings, of dukes, of marquesses and lords" (Mario Filelfo, *Canzon morale* [1463]; see Kinkeldey, 1929; Sparti, 1993). Guglielmo was the son of Moses of Sicily, dancing master at the court of Pesaro. He had a brother, Giuseppe Ebreo, who is mentioned as choreographer of the *bassadanza* "Partita Crudele" in the two Florentine manuscripts of Guglielmo's dance manual *De practica seu arte tripudii* (On the Practice or Art of Dancing) as well as in the manuscript of the manual held by the Dance Collection of the New York Public Library (for full information on primary sources, see the bibliography, below). Guglielmo was married twice; his second wife was the daughter of Pier Paolo di Berardi, "a good citizen of Pesaro" (Sparti, 1993, p. 31). He had a son, Pierpaolo; together, Guglielmo and Pierpaolo were dancing masters to the duke of Urbino in the 1470s.

The stages of Guglielmo's professional career emerge from the autobiographical sections in two exemplars of his manual, both held by the Bibliothèque Nationale in Paris (one of which was written under the name Giovanni Ambrosio). In both he lists a number of major festivities—weddings, entries, state visits by foreign dignitaries, Carnival celebrations—that he attended and for which he choreographed the dances, either by himself or collaborating with his teacher Domenico da Piacenza. Although no dates are given for any of these, Guglielmo mentions enough people and places to allow for the festivities' identification (Gallo, 1983; Sparti, 1993).

Guglielmo's first engagement as dancing master appears to have been at Camerino in the early 1440s. After a trip to Ferrara in May 1444 for the marriage of Leonello d'Este and Maria of Aragon, his activities were centered in Pesaro, seat of an important branch of the Sforza family. His patron there was Alessandro Sforza, for whose wedding at Camerino in 1444 he choreographed the dances. Guglielmo traveled with members of Alessandro's family and choreographed several of their nuptials, all the while maintaining close connections with Camerino. When Francesco Sforza became duke of Milan in February 1450, Guglielmo took part in the month-long festivities. This event marks the beginning of Guglielmo's increasingly close relationship with Francesco and Bianca Maria Sforza and their children, even though he remained in Alessandro's service until the prince's death in 1473.

From Pesaro, Guglielmo was frequently "on loan" (as was the custom) to other courts that requested his services (for instance, at Bologna in 1454, Imola in 1458, Urbino in 1460, Mantua in 1463, and Venice 1469; see Gallo, 1983, pp. 191–192; Sparti, 1993, pp. 22ff.) Guglielmo mentions the Venetian event, a state visit by Holy Roman Emperor Frederick III, with particular pride because on that occasion he was knighted.

Between 1450 and 1465 he seems to have divided his time equally between the Sforza courts at Milan and Pesaro. Twice during this period he collaborated with Domenico: in Forlì in 1462 and in Milan in 1455, where he created *moresche e molti balli* for the betrothal of Ippolita Sforza and Alfonso, duke of Calabria. In autumn 1465 he went to Naples for the actual wedding and remained as dancing master at the Aragonese court until the winter of 1467–1468. Among his pupils there were the princesses Leonora and Beatrice as well as the young duchess Ippolita, whose accomplishments as a dancer and choreographer he praised in an affectionate and homesick letter he wrote to her mother, Bianca Maria Sforza (cited in Motta, 1887). Shortly before his sojourn in Naples, Guglielmo had converted to Christianity and changed his name to Giovanni Ambrosio. His godparents seem to have been Bianca Maria and Duke Francesco. The later of the versions of *De pratica seu arte tripudii* held by the Bibliothèque Nationale was probably written during the Neapolitan period.

For the Carnival celebrations of February 1468 he was back in Milan. In July of that year he participated in the wedding festivities for Galeazzo Maria Sforza and Bona di Savoia. He choreographed *bel danzare* and *belle Moresche* for the wedding of Costanza of Camerino (9 August 1471) and created *vna bella liuerea de mascare* for the marriage of Roberto Malatesta and Elisabetta Montefeltro in Urbino. At this time his assistant was his son, Pierpaolo.

In autumn 1474 Guglielmo returned to Naples by special invitation to participate in the series of grand spectacles given by Ferdinand of Aragon in honor of the ambassador of Charles the Bold, duke of Burgundy. Central among these events was a masquerade in which the duke of Calabria, his brother Federigo, the Duchess Ippolita (Sforza), Leonora of Aragon, and members of the court, attired in French costumes, performed *bally francesi* that were almost certainly arranged by Guglielmo. In 1481 Guglielmo is mentioned as dancing partner and teacher of the six-year-old Isabella d'Este. The documents indicate that at the time he was in the service of the duke of Urbino.

It seems that despite all the acknowledgments of his talents as a dancer and choreographer by his contemporaries, Guglielmo ended his life in relative poverty. The date and place of his death are unknown.

Like all other fifteenth-century dance instruction books, Guglielmo's are divided into two sections: the theoretical, sometimes in the form of a dialogue between the master and his disciple, and the practical, that is, the choreographies described verbally. Only two exemplars of his work—the manuscripts in the Bibliothèque Nationale—contain music for selected *balli*. Although Guglielmo declared himself to be "a fervent disciple and fervent imitator of Domenico da Ferrara [i.e., Domenico da Piacenza]" and did, in fact, incorporate many of Domenico's concepts into his own work, his dance theory differed from that of his great teacher, especially in its emphasis on the pragmatic. As a dancing master of vast experience, Guglielmo was familiar with all the problems attendant on his art and was ready to provide solutions. His tests for the budding dancer, chapters on fashion, rules of behavior for gentlemen and ladies on the dance floor (for example, his delightful chapter addressed to "the young and virtuous lady," which appears in all the treatises), and his advice to those of his noble students who would try their hands at choreography—all these elements show him as a keen and often humorous observer of the courtly life and manners of the early Renaissance. The poet laureate Mario Filelfo praised him not only as a brilliant dancer and dancing master but as an outstanding musician (*Canzon morale*, 3d terzina; see Kinkeldey, 1929, p. 23; Sparti, 1993, p. 172); indeed, no other fifteenth-century dancing master dealt as extensively with compositional procedures, tonality, instrumentation, and the relation of movement and gesture to music as did Guglielmo.

The repertory of dances varies in size from one of Guglielmo's treatises to another; besides the two main types of *bassadanza* and *ballo*, Guglielmo recorded a few *balletti*, among which "La Malgratiosa," like Domenico's "La Sobria" and "La Mercanzia," proves that dance as drama—that is, as ballet—had in the second half of the fifteenth century found a legitimate place among courtly entertainments. In addition to his own choreographies, Guglielmo's treatises contain dances by Domenico, by Giuseppe Ebreo, by "Misser A." (who might be Antonio Cornazano), and by Lorenzo de' Medici.

PRIMARY SOURCES

De pratica seu arte tripudii. Milan, 1463. Manuscript located in Paris, Bibliothèque Nationale, f.ital.973. Translated by Barbara Sparti as *On the Practice or Art of Dancing* (Oxford, 1993).

De pratica seu arte tripudii. Naples(?), c.1471–1474. Manuscript located in Paris, Bibliothèque Nationale, f.ital.476. Translated by Barbara Sparti in *On the Practice or Art of Dancing* (Oxford, 1993).

De pratica seu arte tripudii. N.p., c.1474. Manuscript located in Siena, Biblioteca Comunale, L.V.29. Partial edition by Curzio Mazzi, "Una sconosciuta compilazione di un libro quattrocentistico di balli," *La Bibliofilia* 16 (1914–1915): 185–209.

De pratica seu arte tripudii. N.p., c.1477. Manuscript located in Modena, Biblioteca Estense (formerly Palatina), ital.82.a.J.94. Published by Giovanni Messori Roncaglia, *Della virtute et arte del danzare* (Modena, 1885).

De pratica seu arte tripudii. N.p., c.1477. Manuscript located in Florence, Biblioteca Nazionale Centrale, Magliabecchiano XIX.88. Published by Francesco Zambrini, *Trattato dell'arte del ballo* (Bologna, 1873).

De pratica seu arte tripudii. N.p., c.1480. Manuscript located in the Dance Collection, New York Public Library for the Performing Arts, *MGZMB-Res.72–254. Edited by Andrea Francalanci, "The *Copia di M° Giorgio del Guido di ballare basse danze e balletti* as Found in the New York Public Library," *Basler Jahrbuch für Historische Musikpraxis* 14 (1990): 87–179.

De pratica seu arte tripudii. N.p., 1510. Manuscript located in Florence, Biblioteca Medicea Laurenziana, Antinori 13. Published by Beatric Pescerelli, "Una sconosciuta redazione del trattato di danza di Guglielmo Ebreo," *Rivista Italiana di Musicologia* 9 (1974): 48–55.

De pratica seu arte tripudii (fragment of Book 1). N.p.,n.d. Manuscript located in Florence, Biblioteca Nazionale Centrale, Palatino 1021, f.155–156'.

Otto bassedanze di M. Guglielmo da Pesaro e di M. Domenico da Ferrara. Foligno, 1887. Published by D. M. Faloci-Pulignano from a manuscript located in Foligno, Seminario Vescovile, Biblioteca Jacobilli, D.I.42.

SECONDARY SOURCES

Becherini, Bianca. "L'Arte della danza' di Guglielmo da Pesaro." *La Scala* 84 (1956).

Brainard, Ingrid. "Die Choreographie der Hoftänze in Burgund, Frankreich und Italien im 15. Jahrhundert." Ph.D. diss., University of Göttingen, 1956.

Brainard, Ingrid. "Bassedanse, Bassadanza, and Ballo in the Fifteenth Century." In *Dance History Research: Perspectives from Related Arts and Disciplines*, edited by Joann W. Kealiinohomoku. New York, 1970.

Brainard, Ingrid. "The Role of the Dancing Master in Fifteenth-Century Courtly Society." *Fifteenth-Century Studies* 2 (1979): 21–44.

Brainard, Ingrid. "Ebreo, Guglielmo." In *The New Grove Dictionary of Music and Musicians.* London, 1980.

Brainard, Ingrid. *The Art of Courtly Dancing in the Early Renaissance.* West Newton, Mass., 1981.

Bukofzer, Manfred F. "A Polyphonic Basse Dance of the Renaissance." In Bukofzer's *Studies in Medieval and Renaissance Music.* New York, 1950.

Carter, Françoise. "Dance as a Moral Exercise." In *Guglielmo Ebreo da Pesaro e la danza nelle corti italiane del XV secolo*, edited by Maurizio Padovan. Pisa, 1990.

Castelli, Patrizia. "La kermesse degli Sforza pesaresi" and "Il moto aristotelico e la 'licita scienzia': Guglielmo Ebreo e la speculazione sulla danza nel XV secolo." In *Mesura et arte del danzare: Guglielmo Ebreo da Pesaro e la danza nelle corti italiane del XV secolo*, edited by Patrizia Castelli et al. Pesaro, 1987.

Castelli, Patrizia, et al., eds. *Mesura et arte del danzare: Guglielmo Ebreo da Pesaro e la danza nelle corti italiane del XV secolo.* Pesaro, 1987.

Cruickshank, Diana. "'In due a la fila'—'E la donna vadia innanzi.'" In *Guglielmo Ebreo da Pesaro e la danza nelle corti italiane del XV secolo*, edited by Maurizio Padovan. Pisa, 1990.

D'Ancona, Alessandro. *Le origini del teatro italiano.* 2 vols. Turin, 1891.

Daniels, Véronique. "Tempo Relationships within the Italian *Balli* of the Fifteenth Century: A Closer Look at the Notation." In *The Marriage of Music and Dance: Papers from a Conference Held at the Guildhall School of Music and Drama, London, 9th–11th August 1991.* Cambridge, 1992.

Daye, Anne. "Towards a Choreographic Description of the Fifteenth-Century Italian Bassa Danza." In *Guglielmo Ebreo da Pesaro e la danza nelle corti italiane del XV secolo*, edited by Maurizio Padovan. Pisa, 1990.

Dolmetsch, Mabel. *Dances of Spain and Italy from 1400 to 1600*. London, 1954.

Francalanci, Andrea. "Le ricostruzione delle danze del '400 italiano attraverso in metodo di studio comparato delle fonti." *La danza italiana* 3 (Autumn 1985): 55–76.

Friedhaber, Zvi, and Giora Manor. "The Jewish Dancing Master in the Renaissance in Italy, in the Jewish and Gentile Communities and at the Ducal Courts." In *Guglielmo Ebreo da Pesaro e la danza nelle corti italiane del XV secolo*, edited by Maurizio Padovan. Pisa, 1990.

Gallo, F. Alberto. "Il 'ballare lombardo,' circa 1435–1475." *Studi musicali* 8 (1979): 61–84.

Gallo, F. Alberto. "L'autobiografia artistica di Giovanni Ambrosio (Guglielmo Ebreo) da Pesaro." *Studi musicali* 12 (1983): 189–202.

Gallo, F. Alberto. "La danza negli spettacoli conviviali del secondo quattrocento." In *Spettacoli conviviali dall'antichità classica alle corti italiane del 400: Atti del VII convegno di studio, Viterbo, 27–30 maggio 1982*. Viterbo, 1983.

Gatiss, Ian. "Realizing the Music in the Fifteenth-Century Italian Dance Manuals." In *The Marriage of Music and Dance: Papers from a Conference Held at the Guildhall School of Music and Drama, London, 9th–11th August 1991*. Cambridge, 1992.

Gombosi, Otto. "About Dance and Dance Music in the Late Middle Ages." *Musical Quarterly* 27 (July 1941): 289–305.

Heartz, Daniel. "A Fifteenth-Century Ballo: *Rôti bouilli joyeux*." In *Aspects of Medieval and Renaissance Music: A Birthday Offering to Gustave Reese*, edited by Jan LaRue. New York, 1966.

Hertzmann, Erich. "Studien zur Basse danse im 15. Jahrhundert." *Zeitschrift für Musikwissenschaft* 11 (April 1929): 401–413.

Kinkeldey, Otto. "A Jewish Dancing Master of the Renaissance: Guglielmo Ebreo." In *Studies in Jewish Bibliography and Related Subjects, in Memory of Abraham Solomon Friedus*. New York, 1929.

Kinkeldey, Otto. "Dance Tunes of the Fifteenth Century." In *Instrumental Music: A Conference at Isham Memorial Library, May 4, 1957*, edited by David G. Hughes. Cambridge, Mass., 1959.

La Rocca, Patrizia. "Modelli spaziali e dispositivi coreutici nella copia parigina del trattato di Guglielmo." In *Guglielmo Ebreo da Pesaro e la danza nelle corti italiane del XV secolo*, edited by Maurizio Padovan. Pisa, 1990.

Lattes, Moses. "Intorno a Guglielmo Ebreo ed al suo 'Trattato dell'arte del ballo.'" In *Mos'e antologie israelitica*. Corfu, 1878.

Lockwood, Lewis. *Music in Renaissance Ferrara, 1400–1505*. Cambridge, Mass., 1984.

Lo Monaco, Mauro, and Sergio Vinciguerra. "Il passo doppio in Guglielmo e Domenico: Problemi di mensurazione." In *Guglielmo Ebreo da Pesaro e la danza nelle corti italiane del XV secolo*, edited by Maurizio Padovan. Pisa, 1990.

Luzio, Alessandro. *I precettori d'Isabella d'Este*. Milan, 1887.

Marrocco, W. Thomas. *Inventory of Fifteenth-Century Bassedanze, Balli, and Balletti in Italian Dance Manuals*. New York, 1981.

Mazzatinti, Giuseppe. *Inventario dei manoscritti italiani delle biblioteche di Francia*. 3 vols. Rome, 1886–1888.

McGee, Timothy J. "Dancing Masters and the Medici Court in the Fifteenth Century." *Studi musicali* 17.2 (1988): 201–224.

Melica, Ada. "Guglielmo Ebreo da Pesaro, maestro di ballo del quattrocento." *La rassegna musicale* 29.1 (1959): 51–60.

Michel, Artur. "The Earliest Dance-Manuals." *Medievalia et Humanistica* 3 (1945): 117–131.

Mingardi, Maurizio. "Gli strumenti musicali nella danza del XIV e XV secolo." In *Mesura et arte del danzare: Guglielmo Ebreo da Pesaro e la danza nelle corti italiane del XV secolo*, edited by Patrizia Castelli et al. Pesaro, 1987.

Mingardi, Maurizio. "La musica da danza italiana tra XIV e XV secolo: Raffronto e considerazioni tra il repertorio strumentale del codice London B.M.Add.29987e le intonazioni del trattati quattrocenteschi di danza." In *Guglielmo Ebreo da Pesaro e la danza nelle corti italiane del XV secolo*, edited by Maurizio Padovan. Pisa, 1990.

Motta, Emilio. "Musica alla corte degli Sforza." *Archivio storico lombardo* 14 (1887): 29–64, 278–340, 514–561.

Mullally, Robert. "The Polyphonic Theory of the *Bassa Danza* and the *Ballo*." *Music Review* 41 (1980): 1–10.

Padovan, Maurizio. "Da Dante a Leonardo: La danza italiana attraverso le fonti storiche." *La danza italiana* 3 (Autumn 1985): 5–37.

Padovan, Maurizio. "La danza nelle corti italiane del XV secolo: Arte figurativa e fonti storiche." In *Mesura et arte del danzare: Guglielmo Ebreo da Pesaro e la danza nelle corti italiane del XV secolo*, edited by Patrizia Castelli et al. Pesaro, 1987.

Padovan, Maurizio. "La danza di corte del XV secolo nei documenti iconografici di area italiana." In *Guglielmo Ebreo da Pesaro e la danza nelle corti italiane del XV secolo*, edited by Maurizio Padovan. Pisa, 1990.

Padovan, Maurizio, ed. *Guglielmo Ebreo da Pesaro e la danza nelle corti italiane del XV secolo: Atti del convegno internazionale di studi, Pesaro, 16/18 luglio 1987*. Pisa, 1990.

Pescerelli, Beatrice. "Una sconosciuta redazione del trattato di danza di Guglielmo Ebreo." *Rivista italiana di musicologia* 9 (1974): 48–55.

Pirro, André. *Histoire de la musique de la fin du XIVe siècle à la fin du XVIe*. Paris, 1940.

Pirrotta, Nino, and Elena Povoledo. *Music and Theatre from Poliziano to Monteverdi*. Translated by Karen Eales. Cambridge, 1982.

Pontremoli, Alessandro, and Patrizia La Rocca. *Il ballare lombardo: Teoria e prassi coreutica nella festa di corte del XV secolo*. Milan, 1987.

Pontremoli, Alessandro. "Estetica dell'ondeggiare ed estetica dell'aeroso: Da Domenico a Guglielmo, evoluzione di uno stile coreutico." In *Guglielmo Ebreo da Pesaro e la danza nelle corti italiane del XV secolo*, edited by Maurizio Padovan. Pisa, 1990.

Rodocanachi, Emmanuel. "La danse en Italie du XVe au XVIIIe siècle." *Revue des études historiques* 71 (1905): 569–590.

Roth, Cecil. *The Jews in the Renaissance*. Philadelphia, 1959.

Sachs, Curt. *World History of the Dance*. Translated by Bessie Schönberg. New York, 1937.

Smith, A. William, trans. and ed. *Fifteenth-Century Dance and Music: The Complete Transcribed Italian Treatises and Collections in the Tradition of Domenico da Piacenza*. 2 vols. Stuyvesant, N.Y., 1995.

Sparti, Barbara. "Stile, espressione e senso teatrale nella danza italiana del '400." *La danza italiana* 3 (Autumn 1985): 39–53.

Sparti, Barbara. "Questions Concerning the Life and Works of Guglielmo Ebreo." In *Guglielmo Ebreo da Pesaro e la danza nelle corti italiane del XV secolo*, edited by Maurizio Padovan. Pisa, 1990.

Sparti, Barbara. "How Fast Do You Want the Quadernaria? Or *Verçepe* and *Gelosia* Revisited: The Tale of the Three *Contrapassi* in Quadernaria." In *The Marriage of Music and Dance: Papers from a Conference Held at the Guildhall School of Music and Drama, London 9th–11th August 1991*. Cambridge, 1992.

Sparti, Barbara. "Rôti Bouilli: take two 'El Gioioso Fiorito.'" In *Studi musicali* 24.2 (1995): 231–261.

Tani, Gino. "Ebreo, Guglielmo." In *Enciclopedia dello spettacolo*. Rome, 1954–.

Toscanini, Walter. "Notizie e appunti sui maestri di ballo ebrei nel '400." *Il vasari* 18 (1960): 62–71.

Wilson, D. R. "'Damnes' as Described by Domenico, Cornazano, and Guglielmo." *Historical Dance* 2.6 (1988–1991): 3–8.

Wilson, D. R. "'La giloxia/Gelosia' as Described by Domenico and Guglielmo." *Historical Dance* 3.1 (1992): 3–9.

Wilson, D. R. *The Steps Used in Court Dance in Fifteenth-Century Italy.* Cambridge, 1992.

Wood, Melusine. *Some Historical Dances, Twelfth to Nineteenth Century.* London, 1952.

INGRID BRAINARD

GUILD DANCES were performed by medieval and Renaissance guilds as part of civic and religious celebrations. The guilds played a vital role in the life of European cities and towns during and for some time after the Middle Ages. Formed to protect the professional interests of their members, these unions also functioned as benevolent societies, rendering assistance to their retired members and to the disabled, widows, and orphans. Many guilds exercised considerable influence in town politics.

The strongest guilds in major cities were granted permission to hold large-scale celebrations and to organize theatrical performances and pageants. The main season for festivals was the Carnival season before Lent, culminating in Shrove Tuesday. Pentecost, more or less coincidental with the beginning of May and thus continuing the tradition of pre-Christian May celebrations, took second place; the feasts of Saint John and of patron saints came third. Another important celebration was the annual guild assembly, which usually began with attendance at Mass and ended with a banquet and a dance at night.

All major guild festivals included three types of dance activities: the progressive dances, mainly part of the "running," in which the uniformly costumed participants moved in a cortège through the streets of their city, accompanied by others dressed as fools, wild men, and whifflers, carrying emblems, and sprinkling fragrant waters over the onlookers or throwing delicacies or coins to them; the ballroom dances that took place at the stopping places of the cortège, such as inns, hostelries, private mansions, even houses of ill repute, and finally at the guild house at night; and what might be called the signature dances of the guild holding the festival, usually performed as the culmination of the activities in the city square.

No technical details of the progressive dances have survived. We may assume that simple, rhythmically executed traveling steps were used: running, skipping, and walking. As in the ballroom dances, the movement sequences of the progressive dances would have been characteristic of the time and the region; *saltarello*, *piva*, and *quadernaria* sequences in the fifteenth-century; *allemande*, *pavane*, and *tordion* sequences in the sixteenth century; and so on. During the Renaissance the bakers of Strasbourg annually performed "den morischen Tantz" (a *moresca*) from one end of their city to the other, their faces blackened, their garments adorned with ribbons and bells, carrying hoops decorated with garlands of ivy. Similar progressions are reported from the southern regions of Germany and France, the Austrian Tyrol, Italy, and elsewhere.

The high point of the artisans' pageants was the signature dance. This dance was performed exclusively by members of the guild in charge, dressed in costumes relating either to their trade or to the theme of the event and bearing appropriate accessories: butchers in sheepskins danced with small rings, representing sausages, between them; coopers carried hoops wound with fresh greenery; knifesmiths performed sword dances and mock battles in the *moresca* tradition. As late as the seventeenth century, the furriers of Breslau regularly performed a sword dance that included among its figures the rosette of swords and the decapitation motif familiar in English variations of the dance. They, too, wore bells on their garments as did the *moresca*-dancing artisans of Munich who were immortalized in Erasmus Grasser's elegant woodcarvings (*Maruschkatänzer*, 1480).

While the main festival dance, always performed outdoors, appears to have been either a line dance or a sword dance–mock battle choreography, the indoor activities consisted of social dances in which the members of the guild were joined by their wives, sweethearts, and mistresses.

Traditionally, large-scale celebrations organized by one guild were supported by others. A knifesmith's sword dance, first documented in 1386, remained for centuries as part of the Nuremberg butchers' Schembart festival. The weavers who made the cloth for the costumes from time to time joined in the butchers' festival with a garland dance, as did the cabinetmakers.

The success of any guild spectacle depended on the participation of the various musicians' guilds, minstrels, town pipers (Ger., *Stadtpfeiffer*), and trumpeters. Fifes and drums, pipe-and-tabor played for the processions; trumpeters preceded the cortège, on horseback or on foot, or were stationed at strategic places along the way; and shawm bands accompanied outdoor dances. The lute, viola da gamba, other stringed instruments, flute, and other "soft" instruments are mentioned in conjunction with the ballroom dances, the banquets, and the more intimate scenes in the plays and skits that were also part of the guild festivals.

BIBLIOGRAPHY

Baumgartner, Alois. *Der Schäfflertanz in München.* Munich, 1830.

Böhme, Franz M. *Geschichte des Tanzes in Deutschland.* 2 vols. Leipzig, 1886.

Chambers, E. K. *The Mediaeval Stage* (1903). 8th ed. Oxford, 1978.

Clune, George. *The Medieval Guild System.* Dublin, 1943.

Creizenach, Wilhelm. *Geschichte des neueren Dramas.* Halle, 1911. [5 vols, 1893–1916]

Jacquot, Jean, ed. *Les fêtes de la Renaissance.* 3 vols. Paris, 1956–1973.

Nichols, J. G. *The Fishmongers' Pageant, on Lord Mayor's Day, 1616.* London, 1844.

Nicoll, Allardyce. *Masks, Mimes, and Miracles: Studies in the Popular Theatre.* London, 1931.

Schwab, Heinrich W. "Guilds." In *The New Grove Dictionary of Music and Musicians.* London, 1980.

Shergold, N. D. *A History of the Spanish Stage from Medieval Times until the End of the Seventeenth Century.* Oxford, 1967.

Strutt, Joseph. *The Sports and Pastimes of the People of England.* 2d ed. London, 1810.

Sumberg, Samuel L. *The Nuremberg Schembart Carnival.* New York, 1941.

Toschi, Paolo. *Le origini del teatro italiano.* Turin, 1955.

Tydemann, William. *The Theatre in the Middle Ages.* Cambridge, 1978.

Withington, Robert. *English Pageantry: An Historical Outline.* 2 vols. Cambridge, Mass., 1918–1920.

INGRID BRAINARD

GUIMARD, MARIE-MADELEINE (born 27 December 1743 in Paris, died 4 May 1816 in Paris), French dancer. Guimard made her debut in 1758 as a member of the corps de ballet of the Comédie Française. She was accepted into the Opera in 1761 and made a successful appearance in *Les Caractères de la Danse.* On 9 May 1762 she replaced Marie Allard in the role of Terpsichore in *Fêtes Grecques et Romaines.* She was noticed in performances at court and in 1766 was named first *demi-caractère* dancer.

All her performances met with success, both in roles from the repertory (including *Les Éléments* and *Les Fêtes d'Hébé*) and in new roles that she stamped with her personality. On 11 December 1770, dancing the role of Creusa in Jean-Georges Noverre's *Médée et Jason* with Gaëtan Vestris and Marie Allard, she wore a dress pinned up to reveal a petticoat of a different color; this style became known as the *robe à la Guimard* and was adopted by the fashionable ladies of Paris.

In 1776 Guimard began to dance in many of Noverre's ballets, including *Apelles et Campaspe, Les Caprices de Galathée,* and *Les Petits Riens,* and in those of Maximilien Gardel, such as *Ninette à la Cour, La Chercheuse d'Esprit, Mirza et Lindor, La Rosière, L'Oracle, Le Premier Navigateur,* and *Le Déserteur.* She also appeared in several Opera *divertissements,* including *Iphigénie en Tauride, Chimène, ou Le Cid, Les Danaïdes,* and *Tarare.* In 1789 she left the Opera and married the dancer and writer Jean-Étienne Despréaux. In London that year she danced at the King's Theatre with the young Charles-Louis Didelot, appearing in several new works by Noverre, including *Annette et Lubin.* She appeared for the last time in Paris in a gala on 23 January 1796.

Edmond de Goncourt wrote that Guimard's face was "made for expressing tenderness and sensibility" and that she was of average height but extremely slender. He added that she had "the tiniest waist in France," and, less amiably, that she was "the phantom of the Graces." The sharp-tongued critic Friedrich Melchior von Grimm saw her in a pas de trois with Vestris and Gardel and described the trio as "two big dogs fighting over a bone." But her youthful appearance and vivacity made her especially

GUIMARD. An engraving by Jean-François Janinet, after André Dutertre, depicting Guimard as Mélite in Maximilien Gardel's *Le Premier Navigateur* (1785). Her stylish costume—a white muslin gown with a blue sash, her soft shoes lacking the heels typical of the day, and her loose flowing hair—anticipate the spirit of the nineteenth-century Romantic ballets. (Courtesy of Madison U. Sowell and Debra H. Sowell, Brigham Young University, Provo, Utah.)

convincing in ingenue roles, an effect she achieved in part by making her face up to resemble her own childhood portrait. She danced with grace and intelligence. She did not try to perform feats of virtuosity but was exceptionally successful in pantomime. According to Noverre, "A noble simplicity reigned in her dancing, she arranged her body tastefully, and imparted expression and feeling to her movements. . . . She had no peers in the Anacreontic ballets." The journal *Le Mercure* praised her acting, particularly her ability to play the coquette: "Through her artistry, she is always exactly who she wants to be." Grimm wrote that "She brought to the role of Ninette nuances so fine, exact, delicate, and piquant that the most ingenious poetry could not render the same characters with greater wit, delicacy, or truthfulness."

Guimard chose her costumes carefully, and her taste influenced the costumer Louis Boquet, who designed them in a refined style in which white predominated. For a role as a priestess he dressed her all in white and silver, with pearls and precious stones. As a shepherdess she wore a white dress with white panels, edged with pink chenille and decorated with flowers of every color. She was extremely proud and maintained a grand lifestyle with the support of such suitors as Monsieur de La Borde, the King's *valet de chambre*, by whom she had a daughter; Monseigneur de Jarente, bishop of Orléans; and the prince-marshall de Soubise. She had a magnificent home in the Chaussée d'Antin, designed by the architect Claude Ledoux in the form of a temple of Terpsichore. It had an entrance porch with four columns topped by a group of sculptures representing the Muses crowned by Apollo. The interior was decorated with paintings by Joseph-Marie Vien, Jacques-Louis David, and Jean-Honoré Fragonard, and it had a five-hundred-seat theater where licentious private entertainments were often presented. In 1785, when Guimard was forced to sell her home to raise money, she raffled it off.

The fervor of her admirers' devotion is expressed in an anonymous poem published in London: "For those who praise her steps, her laugh, her sensuality, a smile from Guimard amounts to immortality." She is remembered as one of the most enchanting figures of eighteenth-century dance.

BIBLIOGRAPHY

Beaumont, Cyril W. *Three French Dancers of the Eighteenth Century: Camargo, Sallé, Guimard.* London, 1934.

Chazin-Bennahum, Judith. *Dance in the Shadow of the Guillotine.* Carbondale, Ill., 1988.

Craig, Gordon. "Mademoiselle Guimard and Her Private Theatres" (1933). In *Gordon Craig on Movement and Dance*, edited by Arnold Rood. New York, 1977.

Goncourt, Edmond de. *La Guimard.* Paris, 1893.

Guest, Ivor. *The Romantic Ballet in Paris.* 2d rev. ed. London, 1980.

Guest, Ivor. "Letters from London: Guimard's Farewell to the Stage." *Dance Chronicle* 18.2 (1995): 207–215.

Migel, Parmenia. *The Ballerinas: From the Court of Louis XIV to Pavlova.* New York, 1972.

Moore, Lillian. "Marie Madeleine Guimard." In Moore's *Artists of the Dance.* New York, 1938.

Noverre, Jean-Georges. *Lettres sur les arts imitateurs en général et sur la danse en particulier.* 2 vols. Paris, 1807. Edited by Fernand Divoire as *Lettres sur la danse et les arts imitateurs* (Paris, 1952).

JEANNINE DORVANE
Translated from French

GUSEV, PETR (Petr Andreevich Gusev; born 16 [29] December 1904 in Saint Petersburg, died 30 March 1987 in Leningrad), dancer, teacher, choreographer, and critic. Gusev graduated in 1922 from the Petrograd (Saint Petersburg) Ballet School, where his primary teachers were Aleksandr Shiriaev and Vladimir Ponomarev. He danced with several ballet companies in the Soviet Union. From 1922 to 1924 he was an active member of George Balanchine's Young Ballet, and from 1922 to 1935 he danced with the Petrograd/Leningrad Opera and Ballet Theater. He made his first appearances on the stage at a time when Fedor Lopukhov, then the dance director of the Petrograd troupe, was vigorously experimenting to find new choreographic approaches. Gusev took an active part in Lopukhov's productions. A year after graduation he participated in the making of *The Magnificence of the Universe*, a dance symphony set to Beethoven's music, and was the first to dance various roles in Lopukhov's ballets: Asak in *The Ice Maiden* in 1927; the Nutcracker in the eponymous ballet and Li Shan-fu in *The Red Poppy*, both in 1929; and the Young Communist Leaguer (Komsomolets) in *Bolt* in 1932.

Under Lopukhov's tutelage Gusev became an excellent partner. One of his colleagues, Mikhail Mikhailov (1978), wrote that he was "a tall, well-proportioned man endowed with very strong muscles and inborn dexterity, and what mattered even more—courage. From the first movement the invisible currents of assurance transmitted themselves to his dancing partner, turning her at times into quite a reckless performer." In the 1920s, dancing under Lopukhov's guidance, Gusev and Olga Mungalova (whom he later married) formed a creative duo that considerably enriched the acrobatic element in virtuosic pas de deux.

From 1932 to 1935 Gusev danced in the company of Leningrad's Maly Opera Theater, where Lopukhov was again his ballet master. Gusev created the roles of Franz and the agronomist Petr in Lopukhov's premieres of *Coppélia* (1934) and *The Bright Stream* (1935), respectively. From 1935 to 1945 Gusev was a soloist with the Bolshoi Theater in Moscow, where he appeared in many roles, among them Khan Girei in *The Fountain of Bakhchisarai* in 1936, Meners in *Crimson Sails* in 1942, and Jean de Brienne and Abderakhman in *Raymonda* in 1965. The roles he created in Moscow were distinguished by thoughtful characterization, deep emotional content, and a flexible gift for impersonation. Altogether Gusev danced more than fifty solo roles, including those in classics such as *La Sylphide*, *Paquita*, *The Sleeping Beauty*, *La Fille Mal Gardée*, and *The Little Humpbacked Horse*.

While still active as a dancer Gusev displayed a bent for choreography. He started creating dances in 1924, setting them to the music of Sergei Rachmaninov, Johann Strauss, Nicolas Medtner, Johannes Brahms, Franz Liszt, Sergei Prokofiev, and Igor Stravinsky; he also composed dances for operettas and plays. In 1951 Gusev mounted his first full-length ballet, *Seven Beauties*, set to music by Kara Karaev, at the Akhundov Azerbaijani Opera and Ballet Theater in Baku (it was staged at the Maly Theater in 1953).

GUSEV. When Rostislav Zakharov mounted *The Fountain of Bakhchisarai* at the Bolshoi Theater in Moscow in 1936, Gusev created the central role of Girei, a Crimean khan. He is seen here, c.1950, as Girei, at the climactic moment of act 3, threatening his jealous wife Zarema, portrayed by Maya Pliesetskaya. Zarema, who has murdered Girei's love, the Polish princess Maria, invites death by offering her breast to his dagger. (Photograph from the Dance Collection, New York Public Library for the Performing Arts.)

From 1958 to 1960 Gusev was a guest teacher at the Peking Ballet School in China, where he was in charge of choreography and teachers' courses. For his pupils he staged the ballets *The Magic Goldfish* (1959), to music by Tzutsiang and Du Minsin, and *The Flood* (1960), by Du Minsin. In these productions Gusev succeeded in blending elements of European choreography and Chinese classical dance. The ballets embodied Gusev's principles of regard for the scenic value of dance variations and other means of expression, the use of varied production techniques, juxtaposition of devices, and the transposition of national dance idioms to the stage. While in China, Gusev also produced *Swan Lake*, *Le Corsaire*, and *Giselle*. Other ballets choreographed by Gusev include *The Ice Maiden* (1964) and *The Three Musketeers* (1966), both staged at the Novosibirsk Opera and Ballet Theater.

Gusev was most distinguished for his revival of classical masterpieces. He wrote (1963) that his objectives were "getting as close as possible to the original material and interpreting it at a new level of knowledge with a view to treating the classics in a contemporary spirit. . . . And search[ing] for the most appropriate and effective means of expression through modern performance, direction and decor at their manifold best." Gusev followed these principles in reviving *Le Corsaire* in Leningrad in 1955 and in Novosibirsk in 1962; *Giselle* in Ulan-Ude in 1978; *Harlequinade* in Leningrad in 1967 and Kiev in 1969;

Halte de Cavalerie in Leningrad in 1968; *Swan Lake* in Saratov in 1978; *The Sleeping Beauty* in Vilnius in 1981 and Warsaw in 1983; and *La Bayadère* in Sverdlovsk (Ekaterinburg) in 1984.

Gusev's main calling in life was teaching dance, working as a *répétiteur*, and studying the legacy of past masters of classical ballet. He had a phenomenal memory and an all-embracing stage vision. He established mutual understanding and trust with the dancers, imbuing them with his energy and fanatical devotion to his art. The careers of many choreographers, librettists, and dancers would have been different without his encouragement and support. He began teaching dance while still in ballet school and never gave it up. He taught at the Moscow and Leningrad ballet schools and at the Rimsky-Korsakov Conservatory in Leningrad, where he won a professorship in 1973. He conducted class in Moscow at the Bolshoi Theater and at the Stanislavsky and Nemirovich-Danchenko Musical Theater; in Leningrad at the Kirov Opera and Ballet Theater and the Maly Opera Theater; and at the Novosibirsk Opera and Ballet Theater. Gusev made a point of attending every international seminar on classical dance. He was active in promoting Russian methods of teaching ballet and was an uncompromising opponent of dilettantism or substandard dance. He instilled in his pupils a striving for perfection in technique and for well-thought-out characterization, and he usually achieved a remarkable purity of style.

Gusev was also a prolific writer on ballet theory and practice. He wrote the introductions to many works on the subject, compiled classical dance syllabi, and wrote articles describing his experiences as a ballet master and *répétiteur*. He contributed to the collection *Music and Choreography of Modern Ballet* (1974) and to books commemorating the choreographers Marius Petipa (1971) and Aleksei Yermolaev (1974), the dancer Mikhail Gabovich (1977), and the composer Kara Karaev (1978). He wrote the introductions to several books by Yuri Slonimsky—*Seven Ballet Stories* (1967), *In Honor of Dance* (1968), and *Dramaturgy of 20th Century Ballet* (1977). Many of his publications have been translated into English, French, German, Spanish, Chinese, and Japanese. Gusev was a member of the editorial boards of the Soviet encyclopedia *Ballet* and of the journal *Sovietskii Balet*, and editor of *Music and Choreography of Modern Ballet*. He was deputy chairman of the Council of Musical Theaters of the All-Russia Theatrical Society, founder and head of the Modern Ballet Research Laboratory, a permanent member of the Organizing Committee and of the Board of Adjudicators of All-Union and international ballet competitions, and vice president of the Soviet Center of the Dance Section of the International Theatre Institute.

BIBLIOGRAPHY

Chernova, Natalia. *Ot Geltser do Ulanovoi.* Moscow, 1979.

Gusev, Petr. "Choreographic Education in the USSR." In *The Soviet Ballet,* by Yuri Slonimsky et al. New York, 1947.

Gusev, Petr. "Sokhranit shedevry proshlogo." *Sovetskii balet,* no. 4 (1963).

Martin, John. "Reports from Russia." *Dance Magazine* (September 1956): 14–21, 58–64.

Mikhailov, Mikhail M. *Molodye gody leningradskogo baleta.* Leningrad, 1978.

Slonimsky, Yuri. "Maestro's Jubilee." *Sovetskaia Muzyka,* no. 12 (1964).

Souritz, Elizabeth. "A Life of New Ideas: Pyotr Gusev." *Dance Magazine* (June 1988): 32–33.

Swift, Mary Grace. *The Art of the Dance in the U.S.S.R.* Notre Dame, 1968.

Waren, Florence. "Petipa and Bournonville." *Performing Arts Journal* 2 (Winter 1978): 85–93. Report of a seminar with Gusev and Kirsten Ralov.

NIKITA DOLGUSHIN
Translated from Russian

GUYOT, MARIE-CATHERINE (fl. 1702–1752), French dancer. The name of the eighteenth-century dancer Marie-Catherine Guyot would hardly be known to us had not dance notation been developed at the peak of her career. As a result, no less than fourteen of her dances have been preserved in the Feuillet system, giving ample testimony to this dancer's prominent status at the Paris Opera. As seen through the choreography that brought her fame, Guyot seems to have had the same temperament as the great Marie Camargo, who was to succeed her: she was vivacious, spirited, quick-footed, and altogether indefatigable. Her dances—*muzettes, canaries, entrées* for bacchante or scaramouchette—all sparkled with *cabrioles, entrechats, pirouettes,* and *tours en l'air.* They were showpieces for the display of her outstanding technique.

In the opera *Tancrède* (November 1702), Marie-Catherine Guyot is listed in the corps with "La petite Prévost" (Françoise Prévost) who was to become her constant partner. By 1710 both dancers had risen to the rank of *prima ballerina* and were sharing the major roles in every production. In 1721 Guyot danced in Claude Ballon's third court ballet, *Les Éléments.* She retired from the stage in 1722, finishing the Paris Opera's season in *Thésée,* a revival of Jean-Baptiste Lully's earlier success. In April 1722 *Le Mercure de France* announced the opening of the Opera together with her retirement, "this most excellent of all the dancers who have appeared in the theater. She joined infinite grace to much nobility." According to the Parfaict brothers, she retired because of problems with her weight.

In 1725 Guyot entered a convent. Her name, however, was still inscribed in the Opera account books for the year 1752. She is said to have received a pension of one thousand livres.

BIBLIOGRAPHY

Parfaict, Claude, and François Parfaict. *Le dictionnaire des théâtres de Paris.* 2d ed. Paris, 1767.

Whitley-Bauguess, Paige. "An Eighteenth-Century Dance Reconstruction: Performance by Mlle. Guyot." *Dance Notation Journal* 5.1 (Spring 1987): 11–24.

Whitley-Baugess, Paige. "The Search for Mlle Guyot." In *Proceedings of the Eleventh Annual Conference, Society of Dance History Scholars, North Carolina School of the Arts, February 12–14, 1988,* compiled by Christena L. Schlundt. Riverside, Calif., 1988.

RÉGINE ASTIER

GYŐR BALLET. The ensemble of the Kisfaludy Theater of the city of Győr, the third professional ballet company in Hungary, was founded in 1979 by Iván Markó and a company of graduates of the State Ballet Institute in Budapest. At their graduation concert, Markó staged his first ballet, *Those Loved by the Sun* (to Carl Orff's *Carmina Burana*). This coincided with the opening of the most modern theater in Hungary in Győr, which lies midway between Budapest and Vienna. The company of fifteen members (now twenty) produced eighteen ballets in its first four years, including fourteen by Markó and four by other young choreographers. The latter included György Krámer's *Epitaph,* a beautifully structured reminiscence of a short life set to music by Richard Wagner, Antonio Vivaldi, and Carlos Chavez; and Maguy Marin's *Contrasts* (music by Béla Bartók), a parody of bureaucracy and snobbery which has added color to the Győr Ballet's palette.

Until 1991 Iván Markó dominated the stage with some twenty ballets, including two powerful mystery plays *Taboos and Fetishes* and *Totem* (1984); a biblical drama, *Jesus, the Son of Man* (1986), set to music by Franz Liszt, Iannis Xenakis, Dmitry Shostakovich; a daring persiflage of the Soviet approach to culture called *Bulgakov and the Others* (1987), set to music by various Russian composers; the drama of the man in the street titled *At the Periphery of Life* (1990); and a charming confession of the master to his pupil, *Prospero* (1987), set to music by Franz Schubert. Markó left the country in 1991 but the company has carried on under János Kiss as director.

After Markó's departure, the first faltering attempt was *Gulliver's Travels* (November 1991), choreographed by solo dancers of the company and telling of a farewell and a desire to continue. By 1992 the company seems to have recovered, as shown by the triple bill "Requiem for Life" (April 1992), with William Fomin's *Light and Shadow* (music by Mozart), Libor Vaculik's *Sea of Tears* (music by Gustav Mahler), and, later (November 1993), Robert North's *Miniatures* (music by Igor Stravinsky). Testifying to a wish to maintain the former understanding within the company, Barbara Bombicz set *Babel* (1994) to music by László Tolcsvay, as a demonstration of the anatgonism of those leading and of those led. By this time young choreographers had evolved from the ranks of the company, such as Ottó Demcsák with his *Eternal Traveler* (1992) and János Kiss with his *Monarchy, Monarchy* (1994).

The company's staff includes Judit Gombár, scenic and costume designer, and János Hani, lighting designer. The ensemble is characterized by the usual high technical standard of the dancers and by a rich variety of human messages. The company has toured extensively in Europe. [*See also the entry on Markó.*]

BIBLIOGRAPHY

Dienes, Gedeon P. "Report: Hungary." *Ballett International* 7 (September 1984): 40–43.

Dienes, Gedeon P., and Lívia Fuchs, eds. *A Színpadi tánc történeté Magyarországon.* Budapest, 1989.

Fuchs, Lívia. "The Győr Ballet Abroad." *Hungarian Dance News,* no. 1 (1987): 20–21.

Kaán, Zsuzsa. "Twentieth-Century Mystery Plays by the Győr Ballet." *Hungarian Dance News,* no. 3–4 (1984): 3–4.

Kaposi, Edit. "Hungarian Dance Forum 1980." *Hungarian Dance News,* no. 6 (1980): 1–2.

Körtvélyes, Géza, and Zsuzsa Kaán. "Rekviem az életért" I and II. *Táncművészet* 5–6 (1992): 21–22.

Körtvélyes, Géza, and Zsuzsa Kaán. "Bábel. A Győri Balett bemutatója." *Táncművészet* 1–12 (1994): 44.

Meisner, Nadine. "New Venture from Hungary." *Dance and Dancers* (August 1984): 30–31.

GEDEON P. DIENES

GYPSY DANCES. These Gypsy dancers were photographed in an outdoor setting in Granada, Spain, in 1935. (Photograph by Carl Van Vechten; used by permission of the Estate of Carl Van Vechten.)

GYPSY DANCE. Dancing among Gypsies (who call themselves *Roma, Romany,* or *Romani*) is as varied as their sedentary, nomadic, and seminomadic populations, which live throughout the Middle East, North Africa, western Asia, Europe, and the Americas. The original language of the Gypsies, Romani, belongs to the Indic branch of the Indo-European family; many regional Gypsy languages have also arisen since Gypsies began migrating from the subcontinent of India. Self-identity and language are the characteristics that tie together the diverse populations of Gypsies living within one country, but there is no intermarriage between sedentary and nomadic Gypsy groups. Gypsies tend to profess the dominant religion of the area in which they live, such as Roman Catholicism, Eastern Orthodox Christianity, or Islam.

The staged Gypsy dances in ballets, operas, and folk dance ensembles are romanticized depictions that have no relationship to dance at actual Gypsy social events. In general, Gypsies observe the same holiday celebrations as their host populations, regardless of their religious affiliation. For example, in Skopje, Macedonia, the three-day (6–8 May) Eastern Orthodox celebration for Saint George is extended two additional days by both Christian and Muslim Gypsies.

Gypsy groups, distinguished by their economic base, provide a country's host population with needed household items or services. They may be metalworkers, woodworkers, collectors and sellers of used clothing, traders in horses and cars, street cleaners, fortunetellers, or musicians. This variety in their lifestyles, religions, and trades produces a variety of dance expressions, rather than a single type of Gypsy dancing.

An analysis of data from Gypsy social dance events in Albania, Bulgaria, Canada, Chile, Egypt, Hungary, Macedonia, Romania, Russia, Serbia, Spain, and the United States discloses, however, some general similarities: simultaneous solo dances with no physical contact; arms held diagonally in front of the body at shoulder height; finger-snapping or hand-clapping; and a stepped rhythmic pattern established by the musical accompaniment common to the locale. The dancers do not sing as they dance. Otherwise, Gypsy dancing shows a diversity in form and characteristics that is related to specific geographical and social environments.

Because the Gypsies adapt themselves to the lifestyle of the population around them, they participate in the same social dances. In Los Angeles, for example, married Gypsy couples attend nightclubs or discos. Their children see popular dancing on television or in films and imitate it at home and at their own festive dance events. In southern areas of the former Yugoslavia, Gypsies participate in village festivals in which Slavic residents dance in non-partner open circle dances called *kolo*s or *oro*s.

In North America and southeastern Europe, the wedding appears to be the principal occasion for dancing. Among the Serbian and Russian Gypsies in North America, both the *baso* (solo-type dancing) and *kolo* (open circle danced in a path that progresses in a counterclockwise direction) are danced to a quick tempo, usually in 2/4 meter. During the *kolo* a flag is carried by a male or female leader, first by a member of the bride's family and then by a member of the groom's family. After the wedding veil *(diklo)* is placed on the bride's head, indicating her transference to the groom's family, the *kolo* is danced again. In Skopje, Macedonia, during the 1960s, a Muslim Gypsy wedding cycle lasted five days, during which solo dancing *(čoček)* was danced at indoor, gender-segregated all-night parties, while *oro* dancing was open to public participation outside the household. The transference of the bride to her new husband also occurred during the *oro*, when the dance leadership changed from her family to his.

In the late 1960s an international political movement arose, advocating both for greater Rom identity and the recognition of their social problems (noted at the First Congress for Rom, 1971), and this continues to influence Gypsy dance expression. Many Gypsy populations have become sensitive to their Indic roots, seeking out films from India and adapting Indian musical themes and dance movements into their music and dance. Furthermore, with encouragement by their political leaders to have greater visibility through music and dance performance, groups have been formed and encouraged to participate in European folk dance and music festivals as well as in wholly Rom festival programs.

BIBLIOGRAPHY

Dunin, Elsie Ivancich. "Čoček as a Ritual Dance among Gypsy Women." *Makedonski folklor* 6 (1973): 193–198.

Dunin, Elsie Ivancich. "Dance Change in Context of the Gypsy St. George's Day, Skopje, Yugoslavia, 1967–1977." In *Papers from the Fourth and Fifth Annual Meetings of the Gypsy Lore Society, North American Chapter*, vol. 2, edited by Joanne Grumet. New York, 1985.

Pesovár, Ernő. "The Historical Significance of the Gypsy Dance Tradition in Hungary." *Dance Studies* 11 (1987): 73–143.

Phillips, Miriam. "The 'Trained' and the 'Natural' Gypsy Flamenco Dancer." In *100 Years of Gypsy Studies*, edited by Matt T. Salo. Cheverly, Md., 1990.

ELSIE IVANCICH DUNIN

H

HAITI. In the West Indies, the Republic of Haiti occupies the western third of the Caribbean island of Hispaniola, which was discovered by the 1492 expedition of Christopher Columbus. The Dominican Republic occupies the eastern side, and both were originally part of the Spanish colonial empire of the sixteenth and seventeenth centuries, when sugar plantations were established and slaves transported from Africa as laborers. France took the island from Spain in 1697, transporting additional slaves from Africa to work the sugar and coffee plantations. In the 1780s rebellions and an ensuing class war among blacks, mulattos, and Haitians resulted in invasions by French and British troops. In 1801, the former slave Toussaint L'Ouvature conquered the entire island and abolished slavery; Haiti became the second independent nation in the Americas in 1804 (after the United States). Ruled by self-styled presidents and emperors until 1859, it lost eastern Hispaniola in 1844. Economic deprivation, dictatorship, and occasional anarchy—with a period of U.S. military occupation from 1915 to 1934—brought Haiti into the twentieth century, with the repressive rule of François ("Papa Doc") Duvalier beginning in 1957 and his son's regime from 1971 until his flight in 1986. Since that time, elections have followed that only caused more disruption, and thousands of Haitian "boat people" try to reach other Caribbean shores, including that of the United States. Today, some six million people, 95 percent of African ancestry, live within about 10,700 square miles (27,700 square kilometers), farming mainly subsistence foods—cassava, rice, and yams—as well as coffee, their main export. French and Creole, a Haitian language, are spoken, and Roman Catholicism is the national religion, with Vodun still practiced in both rural and urban areas.

Folk and Traditional Dance. Dance is the fullest expression of African cultures. Its preeminent position in African life is as apparent today as it was when the first contingent of African slaves were brought to the island of Hispaniola by the Spaniards in 1502. Today the republic of Haiti on that island is populated almost entirely by people of African ancestry. Africans use dance to express joy and grief, to reflect emotions and religious beliefs. African slaves strengthened that concept and passed it on to succeeding generations. As a result, dance today is still woven throughout Haitian life. The folklorist Harold Courlander (1960) gives insight into the role of dance in the lives of Haitian people.

> Dance touches on virtually every aspect of life in Haiti. It plays a part in the supplication of *loa, . . .* in the consecration of a *hounfor,* the installation of a *houngan* and the initiation of a cult member; in planting, harvesting and building a house.

Courlander's statement suggests why Haitian folk dance is full of excitement—it is actually extracted, to a large extent, from the rich repertory of Vodun ritual dances.

Vodun is a "danced religion," according to Alfred Métraux (1959), a French anthropologist. During a Vodun ceremony in Haiti, he observed that each dancer dances as the whim takes him without regard for his neighbors, except when two or more dancers face each other and compete in agility and improvisation. The whole art of the dance is expressed in the play of the feet, shoulders, and hips. Actually, most of the gods of the Vodun pantheon have specific dances and specific drum rhythms and songs by which they are attracted.

The dance ordinarily takes place in the peristyle of the *hounfor* (Vodun temple), the front area where public ceremonies are held. At the center of the peristyle is a pole called *poteau-mitan* ("middle pole") down which the *lwa* ("spirits") descend during the course of a ceremony to possess devotees. The dance, in fact, constitutes an attractive force to the spirits, who manifest their presence by possession of the worshipers. Almost anyone can attend a Vodun ritual dance, but not everyone is capable of being possessed. A spectator who does not belong to a Vodun congregation may nonetheless be possessed unexpectedly and start dancing to the rhythm of the spirit by whom he or she is possessed.

The most commonly performed Haitian ritual dances can be characterized by their varying functions, timing, and costume. Some are described below.

Banda. Derived from an old African dance called *chica* (Honorat, 1955), *banda* is in honor of Guede, the deity of death. *Banda* is danced by devotees who are possessed by Guede, who often appears at the end of a ceremony. It is also danced at funerals to facilitate the departure of a dead person's spirit to the other world. It symbolizes human reincarnation and mocks death. The idea is that the person who dies and is buried will germinate into a new life; therefore, there is no need for sorrow.

In this dance there is a great deal of hip-twisting and abdomen-rolling by the dancers, who are often dressed in black or in black and white, with a black hat. Some call this a Haitian "belly dance." Although it sometimes appears erotic, *banda* is not sexual exhibitionism but rather a sacred dance that ridicules death.

Spider's dance. The *lwa* Guede Zarien (Spider) belongs to Guede's family, the spirits of death and the cemetery. A devotee who is possessed by Guede Zarien imitates the movements of a spider. This spirit has his own drum beat, different from the *banda*.

Nago. The name *Nago* was applied to the Yoruba people of West Africa by the Fon people of Dahomey (Benin), whose influence is noticeable in Vodun (Herskovitz, 1971). The Nago dance is in honor of the Oggun deities, particularly Oggun Feraille, the god of war and iron. Some of the other Oggun are Oggun Balingo, Oggun Badagri, Oggun Batala, Oggun Panama, and Oggun Galone.

This dance symbolizes the determination of humans to control their destiny. The movements of the Nago dancer include a coordinated movement of the shoulders, arms, forearms, fists, and feet—reminiscent of those of a slave trying to break chains. It is in fact a war dance. The Oggun are also honored by the fast Mahi dance, in which the feet play an important role.

Zaka and juba. These two dances, closely related, are consecrated to Cousin Zaka, the peasant spirit of agriculture. This is a work dance in which the dancers mime the hardship of agricultural work, symbolizing the effort of the peasant to cultivate the soil. The *juba*, or the Martinique, is a dance of flirtation depicting the elegance and caprice of a peasant woman and the gallantry of a peasant man (Dunham, 1947). The dancers are dressed in blue for both dances.

The *juba* is derived from the *calenda* (also spelled *kalinda*), an ancient African dance very popular in Hispaniola during the period of slavery. Describing the *calenda*, Moreau de Saint-Méry, an eighteenth-century French historian born in Martinique who also lived in Haiti, wrote:

> A male and female, or several dancers divided into equal numbers of each sex, jump into the center of the circle and begin the dance, always two by two. This dance which varies consists of a very simple step in which one foot is put forward after the other. . . . The dancers replace one another without respite, and the negroes are so intoxicated with pleasure that it is necessary to force them to conclude dances of this sort, called Kalendas (1797).

Moreau de Saint-Méry's description is quite compatible with the present-day *juba*.

Yanvalou. A dance of supplication, the *yanvalou* honors Agwe, the deity of the sea, and Damballah, the snake god of fertility. In the execution of this dance the worshipers try to mime the undulating movement of a snake and the waves of the sea by moving their shoulders and upper torsos gracefully forward and back. The participants are often dressed in white during ceremonies honoring Agwe and Damballah. There are two types of *yanvalou*: *yanvalou doba*, in which the dancers bend forward, and *yanvalou debout* or *Dahomey-zepaule*, in which the dancers perform upright. The latter is often associated with another upright dance called *Vodun-zepaule*. Both dances are performed to honor all the deities of the Rada rite, who are derived from West Africa; the corresponding Petro rite comprises local (Creole) deities.

Petro. The Petro dance is the fastest Vodun ritual dance. It is symbolic of the vitality of the African slaves and their determination to set themselves free. The movements of the shoulders, arms, and feet are extremely fast. The Petro dance honors the Petro deities. One of the fastest Petro dances is the *kita* in honor of Tikita, a very powerful Vodun deity. There is also the *boumba*, not so fast as the Petro dance proper or the *kita*. During Petro

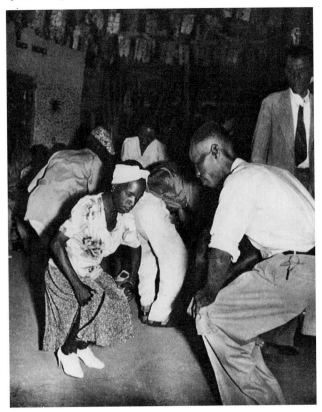

HAITI. Performers of *yanvalou doba*, a dance honoring Agwe, the deity of the sea, and Damballah, the snake god of fertility. The *yanvalou* is one of the major dances of the Rada cult. (Photograph by Pierre Verger; used by permission.)

ceremonies people often dress in red, but there is no obligation to do so.

Congo dances. The Congo rite is intermediary between Rada and Petro rites. This dance symbolizes beauty and love and honors all Congo deities. There are many types of Congo dances, including *Congo simple, Congo rond, Congo mazoone,* and *Congo paillette.* In secular presentations, Congo dancers wear shiny multicolored costumes.

Igbo. Originating in Nigeria, the Igbo dance characterizes the majestic temperament of the Igbo people, who are reputed to be very proud. This dance is for the celebration of all Igbo deities in the Vodun pantheon. The dancers perform upright with highly intricate foot movements. It is not a fast dance, but rather is full of elegance.

Secular Dance. Most Vodun dances have been secularized. Some of them are used for entertainment, especially after a *coumbite,* a communal work gathering of Haitian peasants. After a day of hard labor in the fields or building an *ajoupa* (small thatched house), the family who has been the beneficiary of the community's services provides food, drink, and music for the helpers. During *coumbite* festivities participants ordinarily perform the Congo, *yanvalou, juba, zaka,* and other ritual dances with no religious associations.

Choreographers of Haitian folk dances draw most of their materials from the rich repertory of Vodun ritual dances. *Banda,* for example, is one of the most applauded dances at any folk dance festival when it is well choreographed and executed by an excellent dancer. Famous *banda* dancers, including the late Louis Celestin—considered the king of *banda*—Emile Saint-Lot, Serge Saint-Juste, and Anthony Bayas, all immigrated to New York City and performed with the Ibo Dancers of Haiti, a folk dance group based there. The ritual dances styled by choreographers have become exciting additions to the repertory of many folk dance groups and concert companies. Katherine Dunham, the celebrated American choreographer and anthropologist, found an inexhaustible source for her dance in Vodun ritual dances. She kept a house in Haiti for decades.

Some Haitian secular dances originated in Africa, while others are derived from Europe. For example, *le bal des affranchis* ("ball of free men") is an imitation of the eighteenth century French quadrille; the *mousondi,* a battle dance, and *ti baton* or *batonie,* a stick dance, are basically African. *Tresse riban* (a maypole dance) seems to have its origins in South America, but some Haitian ethnologists argue that it is derived from the *areito* of the Arawaks who once peopled the island (Honorat, 1955).

A few secular dances are sometimes incorporated into Vodun rituals, while most of the ritual dances, as observed above, are also used secularly. In general, Vodun ritual dances and Haitian secular folk dances have undoubtedly experienced some synthesis with one another.

HAITI. Dancers in the Flag Parade, 1960. (Photograph by Pierre Verger; used by permission.)

The richness of Haitian ritual dance remains alive today through practitioners of the Vodun religion. Moreover, modern choreographers have found in it a rich repository of inspiration. Haitian ritual dance transmuted and stylized by the imagination and artistry of these choreographers has profoundly influenced African-American concert dance in the Americas and especially in the Caribbean. Modern dance and experimental or expressive dance have also been forged and shaped by many influences, and not the least of these have been the Vodun ritual dances of Haiti.

[*See also* Vodun. *For related discussion, see* Caribbean Region.]

BIBLIOGRAPHY

Aye, Molly. *Cradle of Caribbean Dance.* Baltimore, 1983.
Bastide, Roger. *African Civilization in the New World.* New York, 1971.
Courlander, Harold. *The Drum and the Hoe.* Berkeley, 1960.
Courraige, Ghislain. *La diaspora d'Haiti et l'Afrique.* Ottawa, 1974.
Dunham, Katherine. *Dances of Haiti.* Mexico City, 1947; Los Angeles, 1983.
Fouchard, Jean. *La méringue: Danse nationale d'Haiti.* Ottawa, 1973; Port-au-Prince, 1988.
Frank, Harry. *Rooming through the West Indies.* New York, 1920.
Herskovits, Melville J. *Life in a Haitian Valley.* New York, 1971.
Honorat, Michel L. *Les danses folklortiques haitiennes.* Port-au-Prince, 1955.
Jahn, Janheiz. *Mantu, the New African Culture.* New York, 1961.
Maximilien, Louis. *Le Vaudou Haitien.* Port-au-Prince, 1945.
Métraux, Alfred. *Voodoo in Haiti.* Translated by Hugo Charteris. New York, 1959.

Moreau de St.-Méry. Médéric L. E. *Description topographique, physique, politique et historique de la partie française de l'Isle de Saint-Domingue*. 2 vols. Philadelphia, 1797–1798.

Paul, Emmanuel C. *Panorama du folklore haitien*. Port-au-Prince, 1962.

Rigaud, Milo. *La tradition vaudou et le vaudou haitien*. Paris, 1953.

HENRY FRANK

HALPRIN, ANNA (Anna Shumann; born 13 July 1920 in Winnetka, Illinois), dancer, choreographer, and teacher. Halprin studied with Margaret H'Doubler at the University of Wisconsin and attended the School of Design at Harvard. She married architect Lawrence Halprin in 1940, and danced in *Sing Out, Sweet Land* (choreographed by Doris Humphrey and Charles Weidman) in 1945.

From 1948 to 1955, Halprin ran a dance studio in San Francisco with Welland Lathrop. After 1955, she established her Dancers' Workshop, an interdisciplinary group of dancers, artists, architects, musicians, and educators. Her outdoor dance deck in Marin County was the center of activity for the group from 1955 to 1957. Halprin's use of improvisation, tasks, and slow or often-repeated movements set a style for avant-garde multimedia theater on the West Coast and influenced such postmodern choreographers as Simone Forti, Yvonne Rainer, Trisha Brown, and Robert Morris, who studied at her summer workshops. Halprin's early works, such as *Birds of America* and *Flowerburger* (both 1959), were deliberate, spontaneous, joyous confusions of life and art.

Halprin's works of the 1960s, such as *Parades and Changes* (1965–1967), involved audience participation; direct confrontations with racial tensions informed such works as *Ceremony of Us* (1969) and *New Time Shuffle* (1970). As Halprin incorporated information from Gestalt therapy, body alignment work, altered states of consciousness, and the creative process (as analyzed by Lawrence Halprin), her work moved away from training artists and toward finding the artist within ordinary people. Since the late 1970s, she has organized such events as *Male and Female Rituals* (1978) and *Evolution of Consciousness through the Ages Cruise* (1979), conceived as "rituals" in which the roles of audience and performer are completely merged and learning, experiencing, and performing are united in a single process, "to apply the creative process to real life issues and to make dances with deep transforming power."

Since the early 1970s, when she was diagnosed with cancer and used a "psychokinetic visualization process" to approach its treatment holistically (in conjunction with traditional medical approaches), Halprin has given workshops for people living with cancer, HIV/AIDS, and other life-threatening diseases. *Circle the Earth* (1981) was a call for peace that has also served as a healing ritual. *Planetary Dance: A Prayer for Peace*, involving hundreds of participants, was performed in Berlin in 1995 to commemorate the fiftieth anniversary of the end of World War II.

BIBLIOGRAPHY

Anderson, Jack. "Manifold Implications: Anna Halprin." *Dance Magazine* (April 1983): 44–47.

Halprin, Anna, et al. *Collected Writings*. San Francisco, 1973.

Halprin, Anna, et al. *Second Collected Writings*. San Francisco, 1975.

Halprin, Anna. "Ages of the Avant-Garde." *Performing Arts Journal* 16 (January 1994): 44–47.

Halprin, Anna. *Moving toward Life: Five Decades of Transformational Dance*. Edited by Rachel Kaplan. Hanover, N.H., 1995.

Hartman, Rose. "Talking with Anna Halprin." *Dance Scope* 12 (Fall–Winter 1977–1978): 57–66.

Kostelanetz, Richard. *The Theatre of Mixed Means*. New York, 1968.

Schechner, Richard. "Anna Halprin: A Life in Ritual." *Drama Review* 33 (Summer 1989): 67–73.

Turner, Diane M. "Anna Halprin: An Artist and an Influence." In *Dance: Current Selected Research*, vol. 1, edited by Lynnette Y. Overby and James H. Humphrey. New York, 1989.

FILM AND VIDEOTAPE. *Lawrence and Anna Halprin: Inner Landscapes* (KQED-TV, San Francisco, 1991).

SALLY BANES

HAMBURG BALLET, also known as the Hamburg State Opera Ballet (Ballett der Hamburgischen Staatsoper). One of the first examples of German civic opera, the Hamburg Goosemarket Opera, established in 1678, offered its clients regular ballet performances. These seem to have been rather crude, despite being performed to music by such eminent composers as Jean-Baptiste Lully and Georg Telemann. When the opera house closed its doors in 1738, theater performances were given by visiting troupes, who offered ballets among their mixed bills of operas, musical plays, and drama. The ballet *Don Juan*, performed in 1769 at the Ackermannsche Komödienhaus, seems to have been the famous work by Christoph Willibald Gluck.

Not until the Hamburg municipal theater had a ballet company of its own, however, could Hamburg audiences see the standard Romantic repertory danced by such guest stars as Marie Taglioni, Lucille Grahn, Fanny Cerrito, and Fanny Elssler (who made Hamburg her residence for a few years after she retired from the stage). They were followed by Katti Lanner, who worked in Hamburg during the 1850s and 1860s. She developed into a prolific choreographer and led the Hamburg company on its first tour to Berlin in 1865, when it gave twenty performances.

For the rest of the nineteenth century, the Hamburg ballet repertory consisted of occasional performances of *Coppélia*, *Die Puppenfee*, and other works from the Vienna Hassreiter-Bauer school. Even after World War I, the company, now named the Hamburg State Opera Ballet and led by Helga Swedlund and Erika Hanka, changed little. Nor did Hamburg demonstrate any special enthusiasm for ballet in the years after World War II, when, again directed by Swedlund, the ballet company was considered mainly an adjunct to the opera. The company briefly changed direction between 1949 and 1951 under Dore Hoyer, one of the leading figures in the German modern dance movement, but this experiment proved frustrating for both the dancers and the public.

The company grew in size and ability when Rolf Liebermann was appointed general manager of the Hamburg State Opera in 1959. He collaborated with Peter van Dyk in directing the company, and although van Dyk's choreography proved unmemorable, he nevertheless built up a company capable of performing George Balanchine's ballets. In fact, the Hamburg State Opera Ballet became the first European company with a solid Balanchine reper-

tory. This approach culminated in the city's official celebration of Stravinsky's eightieth birthday in June 1962, with the composer himself in the pit conducting the company's production of *Apollo*, triple-billed with *Orpheus* and *Agon*, all choreographed by Balanchine.

When van Dyk left in 1970, standards deteriorated until John Neumeier was appointed ballet director in 1973. Since then, the company has multiplied its performances, acquired a broad and varied repertory of classics and contemporary works, gained some performing spaces outside the opera house, and considerably enlarged the affiliated ballet school. Today the Hamburg Ballet possesses a character all its own, thanks to Neumeier's dramatically oriented aesthetic sense.

Neumeier's flair for the dramatic and the original clearly shows in his unconventional stagings of some of the classics. His *Swan Lake*, for example, is set in the court of the mad King Ludwig II of Bavaria, and his *Sleeping Beauty* is dreamed by a boy in blue jeans. The panoramic view of his Mahler cycle and the thematic groupings of his mixed programs also reflect an original

HAMBURG BALLET. Scene from John Neumeier's *Bernstein-Serenade* (1993), a tribute to the music of Leonard Bernstein. At left, Ivan Liška and Janusz Mazoń leap; seated at right are Bettina Beckmann, Patrick Becker, Anders Nordström, and Gigi Hyatt. (Photograph by Holger Badekow; used by permission.)

vision. His *Giselle,* however, is staged along more traditional lines.

Many of Neumeier's works for the Hamburg Ballet have been large-scale undertakings. His staging of Bach's complete *Saint Matthew Passion* started its life in one of Hamburg's parish churches but is now performed in the opera house, and his ballets inspired by the plays of Shakespeare form a major group of works in the Hamburg repertory. These include *Romeo and Juliet,* set to the Prokofiev score; *Hamlet—Connotations,* set to music by Aaron Copeland; *West Side Story,* the musical based on the story of Romeo and Juliet, with a score by Leonard Bernstein; *Othello,* set to music by Arvo Pärt and Alfred Schnittke; and *Mozart and Themes from "As You Like It."* Other ambitious projects have been *Peer Gynt,* set to music by Schnittke, and *Odyseus,* to music by George Couroupos. The solidly Neumeier-based repertory is supplemented by a selection of ballets by John Cranko, Balanchine, Mats Ek (who staged his sensational modern production of *The Sleeping Beauty* in 1996), and a few others.

The company now gives regular workshop matinees in which Neumeier lectures on and demonstrates various aspects of his craft. During the Hamburg Ballet Days at the end of each season, the company presents a summary of its work, culminating in the Nijinsky Galas, arranged each year around a different subject. Early programs included "The Sacred Dance" (1981), "Dedicated to Igor Stravinsky" (1982), "The Romantic Dance" (1983), and "The Symphonic Dance" (1984); later programs have included "Vaslav Nijinsky at His One Hundredth Birthday" (1989), "Mozart" (1991), "To Celebrate the Twentieth Season of the Hamburg Ballet" (1993), "Fairy Tales and/or Ravel" (1994), and "Myths and Metamorphosis" (1996).

In 1990 the Hamburg State Opera opened the Ballettzentrum Hamburg–John Neumeier, a complex housing various studios for company use, the school, and a boarding school. With this strong base, the Hamburg Ballet has continued to grow. By 1996 there were eight ballet masters and *régisseurs,* eleven principal dancers, eight soloists, and a corps of thirty-eight. Besides performing regularly in Hamburg, the company now often tours abroad, having appeared in many European cities, the United States, South America, and Israel.

[*See also the entry on Neumeier.*]

BIBLIOGRAPHY

Albrecht, Christoph, ed. *Zehn Jahre John Neumeier und das Hamburger Ballett, 1973–1983.* Hamburg, 1983.
Koegler, Horst. "Balanchine als Höhepunkt: Ballett in Hamburg vor John Neumeier" and "Begehrt von New York bis Tokio: Das Hamburger Ballett unter John Neumeier." In *Die Hamburgische Staatsoper, 1945 bis 1988,* edited by Max W. Busch and Peter Dannenberg. Zurich, 1990.
Maack, Rudolf. *Tanz in Hamburg: Von Mary Wigman bis John Neumeier.* Hamburg, 1975.
Wenzel, Joachim E. *Geschichte der Hamburger Oper, 1678–1978.* Hamburg, 1978.
Willaschek, Wolfgang, ed. *Zwanzig Jahre John Neumeier und das Hamburg Ballett, 1973–1993.* Hamburg, 1993.

HORST KOEGLER

HANAKO (original name Ota Hisa; born 1868 in Gifu, Japan, died 1945), dancer and actress. Hanako was a low-ranking geisha who rode turn-of-the-century European fascination with *japonisme* to achieve wide acclaim in a series of plays climaxing in super-realistic dying scenes. Hanako trained in *nihon buyō* dance from age five and apprenticed with a traveling theater troupe for a year at age ten. She trained in dance and music in preparation for a career as a geisha, but a brief visit to Europe with a Japanese vaudeville company in 1901 led to unexpected stardom.

The slender, four-and-a-half-foot-tall dancer, who then still used her birthname, Ota Hisa, was "discovered" at a London performance by Loie Fuller, the American modern dancer and first manager of Isadora Duncan in Europe. Fuller had previously produced the large and expensive tours of *shinpa* ("new sect") performers Yakko and Kawakami in Europe. Fuller was delighted by Hanako's dainty, feminine charm and exotic passion: "She played a minor role . . . like a toddling little mouse, and she was able suddenly to transform herself with little movements which froze all the anguish of terror onto her features. She was pretty, delicate, strange." Hisa was renamed Hanako and elevated to headliner of the troupe, and Fuller rewrote each play so that it would end with Hanako performing a devastating death-scene, often a bloody hara-kiri suicide.

Fuller then wrote new *japanesque* plays to appeal to European and American audiences' appetite for the exotic. Hanako continued to tour with various companies and producers, achieving wide success throughout Europe. She retired to her sister's geisha house in Gifu in 1922 with souvenirs, including two bronze busts by Auguste Rodin for which she had posed, *Head of Death* and *A Meditating Woman.* She had a scrapbook full of ardent raves in eighteen languages. Critics had praised the savage realism of her dying scenes, although photographs betray her use of codified techniques of *kabuki* and Japanese folk dance. Like Yakko and Kawakami, Hanako's popularity seems to have owed more to Western fascination with Japanese prints and costumes "come to life" than to her innate artistic abilities.

[*See also the entry on Yakko and Kawakami.*]

BIBLIOGRAPHY

Brandon, James R., et al. "Symposium on Hanako." *Asian Theatre Journal* 5 (Spring 1988): 63–100.
Fuller, Loie. *Fifteen Years of a Dancer's Life* (1913). New York, 1978.

Keene, Donald. *Appreciations of Japanese Culture: Landscapes and Portraits.* Tokyo and New York, 1971. See pages 250–258.

Pronko, Leonard C. *Theater East and West: Towards a Total Theater.* Berkeley, 1967.

JONAH SALZ

HANAMICHI (Jpn., "flower path") is the raised walkway that is perhaps the most distinctive architectural component of the *kabuki* stage. This walkway, something over five feet (almost two meters) in width, runs at a right angle perpendicular to the edge of the stage from stage right to the rear of the auditorium, where it ends in a small room (the *toya*), which is separated from it by a decorative curtain (the *agemaku*) hung on rings. The sound of this curtain being swished aside signals the audience to prepare for an actor's entrance. At the same time, lights embedded along the side of the *hanamichi* come on to accentuate its use. Besides the main walkway, or *hon hanamichi*, a narrower, temporary walkway, or *kari hanamichi* (formerly called the *higashi no ayumi*, "eastern walkway"), may be set up on the stage-left side. Nowadays it is used only for special plays, but it was once a permanent feature (from the late 1700s to the twentieth century).

The *hanamichi* is extremely important for major exits and entrances and has numerous conventionalized uses. It creates great intimacy between audience and actor when an actor appears, moves to a position (the *shichisan*) seven-tenths the distance from the *agemaku* to the stage, and does an expressive bit before joining the others on the stage proper. At this same location is situated an elevator trap (the *suppon*)—used primarily for magical entrances and disappearances.

Although *hanamichi* means "flower path," the word *hana* also once meant "gift," and the *hanamichi* was probably created as a pathway for audiences to present gifts to their favorites. Early forms of this pathway ran on a diagonal to the center of the stage; the move to stage right came during the late eighteenth century. The secondary *hanamichi* was not used until later in the eighteenth century but was removed in the twentieth century since it took up too much of the auditorium space needed for seating.

The *hanamichi* may represent the same locale as the scene on the stage proper or an entirely different locale. It may have a dance floor placed over it or may be draped with stage cloths to simulate snow or water. Variations on this extremely versatile stage feature have appeared in the Western theater during the twentieth century.

[*See also* Kabuki Theater.]

BIBLIOGRAPHY

Ernst, Earle. *The Kabuki Theatre.* 2d ed. Honolulu, 1974.

Gunji, Masakatsu. *Kabuki.* Translated by John Bester. 2d ed. Tokyo, 1989.

SAMUEL L. LEITER

HANAYAGI SUZUSHI (born 15 August 1928 in Dojima, Osaka Prefecture, Japan), Japanese modern dancer and choreographer. Hanayagi's extensive training included obtaining the position of *shihan* ("master") in the Hanayagi school of *nihon buyō* and studying *jiuta-mai* with Takehara Han and Inoue Yachiyo, *Neuer Tanz* with Eguchi Takaya, and *nō* with Kanze Hisao. She made her debut in *nihon buyō* in 1955 and in 1961 moved to New York City, where she studied with Martha Graham, Merce Cunningham, and Anna Halprin.

In the United States, Hanayagi has performed at the Hunter Playhouse, Asia Society, the Fashion Institute of Technology, the Village Gate, and Judson Memorial Church, among other venues. In 1984 she began a collaboration with avant-garde theater director Robert Wilson, choreographing and performing in his work *The Knee Plays*, which featured music by David Byrne and which toured internationally. Hanayagi's choreography credits include *The Martyrdom of Saint Sebastian* (also with Wilson) for the Paris Opera Ballet and *Madama Butterfly* for the Opéra de la Bastille.

HANAYAGI SUZUSHI. A postmodern dancer and choreographer, Hanayagi, seen here c.1964, mixes different idioms in her work, including Japanese *nihon buyō* and American modern dance. (Photograph by Isamu Kawai; from the archives at Jacob's Pillow, Becket, Massachusetts.)

Others of her works include *Sham's Twin* (1957), *The Wall Street Journal* (1966; co-choreographed with Carla Blank), *Bitwin* (1988), and *Bitwin-2* (1992; in collaboration with videographer Yamaguchi Katsuhiro). Hanayagi's vast experience in traditional and modern genres has allowed her to employ a wide variety of movement styles and techniques in her work.

BIBLIOGRAPHY

Dunning, Jennifer. "Something about Simplicity." *Dance Magazine* (February 1977): 37–39.

Havens, Thomas R. H. "Rebellion and Expression in Contemporary Japanese Dance." In *Dance as Cultural Heritage*, vol. 1, edited by Betty True Jones. New York, 1983.

Marks, Marcia. "Suzushi Hanayagi." *Dance Magazine* (June 1963): 60.

Small, Linda. "Reflections on a Season of Ethnic Dance." *Dance Magazine* (April 1978): 79–83.

Smith, Amanda. Review. *Dance Magazine* (April 1979): 100–118.

Sorell, Walter. "Suzushi Hanayagi." *Dance News* (January 1975): 10.

Stein, Bonnie, et al. "Dance Magazine Salutes the First New York International Festival of the Arts." *Dance Magazine* (May 1988): 36–43.

HASEGAWA ROKU
Translated from Japanese

HANKA, ERIKA (born 18 June 1905 in Vinkovci, Slavonia [now Croatia], died 15 May 1958 in Vienna), Austrian dancer, choreographer, and ballet director. Erika Hanka began her work as a choreographer and ballet director of the Vienna State Opera early in the 1940s, when the classically trained ballet company was dominated by the aesthetics of German modern dance. After Hanka had tried in the early years of her directorship to combine these opposed approaches, classical ballet experienced a renaissance in central Europe, and she was able to give the ensemble a distinctive character. Hanka's ability to adapt to current dance trends may have been favored by her training, which included the study of modern dance with Gertrud Bodenwieser and Karin Schneider and of classical ballet with Irmgard Thomas.

From 1929 to 1935 Hanka worked in Düsseldorf as solo dancer and assistant to the dance masters Ruth Loeser, Harald Kreutzberg, and Aurelio Milloss. In 1935 she joined Les Ballets Jooss in Dartington Hall and toured with the company for the next three years. Jooss's influence was important for her subsequent choreographic activity. In 1938–1939 she was dance mistress at the Apollo Theater in Cologne, and in 1939–1940 she produced her first evening of dance at the City Opera House of Essen. In 1940 she moved to the Hamburg State Opera as dance mistress. Her work there included the 1941 premiere of *Titus Feuerfuchs*, set to music by Johann Strauss. She was invited to the Vienna State Opera to be the guest choreographer for Werner Egk's *Joan von Zarissa*, and in 1942 she took over the directorship of the State Opera Ballet and served as guest choreographer for Carl Orff's *Carmina Burana* at the Teatro alla Scala in Milan.

In her choreographic works Hanka endeavored to achieve a synthesis of classical vocabulary and modern forms of expression. In her sixteen years as director in Vienna she created thirty-six ballets, many with her own libretti. Her original creations set to contemporary music include *Homerische Symphonie* (1950), to music by Theodor Berger, *Der Mohr von Venedig* (The Moor of Venice; 1955), to music by Boris Blacher, and *Medusa* (1957), to music by Gottfried von Einem. Ballets with specifically Viennese subjects include *Titus Feuerfuchs* (1941), *Höllische G'schicht* (1949) to music by Johann Strauss, and *Hotel Sacher* (1957) set to music by Josef Hellmesberger and Max Schönherr. Her versions of *Don Juan* and *Die Josephslegende*, which were part of the Viennese ballet tradition, entered the repertory. She also emphasized works from the Diaghilev era, which she restaged with her own choreography. With the classic productions, which she initiated during the mid-1950s and for which Gordon Hamilton was the producer responsible, Hanka's career paralleled the development of stage dance in Central Europe. Influenced by the guest performances of leading ballet ensembles after World War II, she led the Vienna State Opera Ballet to the threshold of international status, which it crossed after her death.

BIBLIOGRAPHY

Fleissner-Moebius, Elisabeth. *Erika Hanka und das Wiener Staatsopernballett*. Frankfurt am Main, 1995.

Hanka, Erika. "Das Ballett der Wiener Staatsoper." In *Almanach der Wiener Staatsoper, 1945–1954*. Vienna, 1954.

Moore, Lillian. "Viennese Choreographer." *Dance Magazine* (September 1948): 29–31.

Oberzaucher-Schüller, Gunhild, and Alfred Oberzaucher. "Erika Hanka" (parts 1–6). *Tanzblätter* (June 1978–June 1979).

ALFRED OBERZAUCHER
Translated from German

HAN YOUNG-SOOK (born 18 October 1920 in Ch'onan, died 7 October 1989 in Seoul), Korean dancer and teacher. Han began her career in dance at the age of twelve, when she came under the tutelage of her illustrious grandfather, Han Song-jun, who was not only a master of Korean folk dance and music but also a prominent choreographer and teacher. Her formal training in dance began at thirteen, when she entered the Kyongsong Academy of Traditional Music and Dance to study with her eminent grandfather.

In 1937 Han made her first public appearance at the age of seventeen at the Pumin'gwan, the best theater in Seoul at the time, with a performance of *Sungmu* (Buddhist Monk Dance), created by her grandfather from Buddhist ceremonial dances; this was to become her trademark. Her outstanding talent and beauty so enraptured the audience that she was dubbed the "Cinderella of Dance." Her performance later served as the inspiration for the painter Idang's masterpiece, *Sungmu-do* (Portrait of a Buddhist Monk Dancer), as well as for a famous poem of the same title by Cho Chi-hun. Following the great success of her initial debut, Han accompanied her grandfather on a series of nationwide tours. In 1940 she made her Japanese debut at Hibiya Hall in Tokyo, followed by performances throughout Japan and Manchuria. In 1944 she organized her first dance company and toured the Korean countryside.

The death of her grandfather, along with the hardships of World War II and the Korean War, largely curtailed Han's dance activities until 1955, when she began to teach at the Korean Folk Arts Institute. In 1960 she was appointed head of the dance department at the Korean Musical Arts Conservatory in Seoul. She later taught at King Sejong University and other institutions of higher learning in Seoul. In 1964, as a leading member of the Sahm-Ch'un-Li Dancers and Musicians of Korea, she made her first tour of the United States under the sponsorship of the Asia Society, appearing at twenty-seven universities and culminating in two performances at Lincoln Center's Philharmonic Hall in New York. Her superb technique drew the acclaim of critics nationwide, as it did again in 1984 at the Cultural Festival of the Los Angeles Olympics, where Han performed *Sal-p'uri* (Dance of Exorcism), and at the American Dance Festival in 1986, where she performed the same dance along with *T'aep'yong-mu* (Dance of Great Peace) and the *Buddhist Monk Dance*. For the last named she was designated a Human Cultural Treasure by the Korean government in 1967, and once again in 1971 for *Hak-mu* (Crane Dance).

Ironically, Han's last performance before her death in 1989 was in front of her largest audience ever. She performed the *Dance of Exorcism* before multitudes from all over the globe who thronged Korea's 70,000-seat Olympic Stadium for the closing ceremony of the Seoul Olympic Games on the evening of 2 October 1988. Her moment in the spotlight was a fitting finale, after the Olympic flag had been lowered and the sacred flame had vanished—it was a significant conclusion to a career that spanned almost sixty years, an occasion to show the depth and beauty of Korean dance to the people of the world.

Often called the "perfect dancer," Han was adamant about preserving traditional styles and techniques and faithfully carried on the folk dance tradition handed on by her grandfather.

BIBLIOGRAPHY
Cho Dong-wha. "Dance." In *UNESCO Korean Survey*. Seoul, 1960.
Chung Byong-ho. *Korean Folk Dance*. Seoul, 1992.
Heyman, Alan C. "Dances of the Three-Thousand-League Land." *Dance Perspectives*, no. 19 (March 1964).
Heyman, Alan C. "Han Young-sook: Master of the Buddhist Monk Dance." *Korea Journal* 6.10 (1971).
Ku Hui-suh. *Ch'um Kwa Ku Saram*. Vol. 2. Translated by Lee Kyong-hee. Seoul, 1994.
"Protector of the Dance: The Story of Han Young-sook." In *The Korean Dance Academy*. Seoul, 1989.

ALAN C. HEYMAN

HARANGOZÓ, GYULA (born 19 April 1908 in Budapest, died 30 October 1974 in Budapest), Hungarian dancer, choreographer, and ballet master. As a child, Harangozó was not trained in classical dance, but he watched the performances of the Hungarian Royal Opera from the wings since his father was the theater's tailor. He also learned folk dances from Russian prisoners, and he studied the silent film comedy of Charlie Chaplin and admired the famous clown Gerard. He became an extra in the opera's ballet company, soon performing his first role, "Trepak" in Ede Brada's 1926 version of *The Nutcracker*, to the music of Petr Ilich Tchaikovsky. In 1927, he was in Albert Gaubier's version of *Le Tricorne*, to the score by Manuel de Falla; he danced the Corregidor and, as a first-class character dancer and mime, was promoted to solo dancer to perform many character roles. He did them with swift virtuosity, elastic footwork, and a pronounced talent for characterization. His best characters were Coppélius in the 1932 version of *Coppélia*, the Drunken Park-keeper in Jan Ciepliński's *Hungarian Illusions* (1932), to music by Franz Liszt, and the Prince in *The Wooden Prince* (1935), to music by Béla Bartók.

Harangozó's creative career started in 1936, with the choreography for *Scene in the Inn*, to music by Jenő Hubay, the first Hungarian national ballet. He was aiming for a style like genre painting, portraying well-articulated dramaturgy, a fast-moving dance plot, and a blend of classical ballet, character dance, and folk dance. During a scholarship to London, Harangozó became acquainted with the works of Léonide Massine and Michel Fokine, British mime traditions, and the achievements in western European dance of the late 1930s. After his return to Hungary, he staged a dynamic version of the *Polovtsian Dances* (1938) from *Prince Igor*, to music by Aleksandr Borodin, and *Salade* (1939), to music by Darius Milhaud. He also introduced the living traditions of the *commedia dell'arte* into Hungarian ballet.

Harangozó danced most character parts in his own ballets, like the Eager-Beaver in the 1949 *Mischievous Students*, to music by Ferenc Farkas, the Maecenas in the same year's *Promenade Concert*, to music by Johann Strauss, the Bailiff in the 1951 *Kerchief*, to music by Jenő Kenessey, and Mister Döbrögi in the 1960 full-evening *Matthew the Goose-Boy*, with a score by Ferenc Szabó. In Harangozó's oeuvre, there are few pieces that rely on pure classical technique, but his versions of Tchaikovsky's *Romeo and Juliet* (1939) and Nikolai Rimsky-Korsakov's *Schéhérazade* (1959) were outstanding contributions to the classical repertory.

Bartók's theatrical works have attained an important place in Harangozó's oeuvre. Having danced the original title role in *The Wooden Prince*, he later composed and danced his own two versions—one in 1939 and one in 1958; the first in a folktale-like conception, in Hungarian style, and the second emphasizing the timelessness and universal validity of the message. He choreographed to Bartók's *The Miraculous Mandarin* in 1931 and again in 1941, with each version banned after its respective dress rehearsal. In 1945 he staged a version in "eastern environment," dancing the Elderly Gentleman; his final version was staged in 1956 and this one has been shown by the company on tours abroad. It has also been revived for the repertory as of 1994.

Harangozó's recorded choreographies are *The Mischievous Students*, *Promenade Concert*, *Coppélia*, and *Polovtsian Dances*. He was ballet director of the Hungarian State Opera from 1950 to 1960 and is a posthumous life member. The Harangozó Prize for dancers is awarded in his memory.

BIBLIOGRAPHY

"Harangozó Gyula Emlékkönyv." In *A magyar táncművészet nagyjai*, edited by Eszter Szudy. Budapest, 1974.

Körtvélyes, Géza. *A modern táncművészet útján.* Budapest, 1970.

Körtvélyes, Géza. "Balett és néptánc kapcsolata Magyarországon 1945–1956." In *Tánctudományi Tanulmányok 1969–1970*, edited by Gedeon Dienes and L. Maácz. Budapest, 1970.

Körtvélyes, Géza. *The Budapest Ballet.* Budapest, 1981.

Vályi, Rózsi. *Balettok könyve.* Budapest, 1980.

ZSUZSA KŐVÁGÓ

HARKNESS BALLET. The founding of the Harkness Ballet in New York in 1964 generated great anticipation in the dance world. Writers depicted Rebekah Harkness (born 1915, died 1982), its founder, as a fairy godmother who granted her company endless wishes. The Harkness seemed to have everything: extraordinary dancers; major teachers, choreographers, composers, and designers; comfortable, even luxurious working conditions and decent pay; a patron sincerely devoted to developing modern American ballet; and, not least, the resources of two multimillion-dollar foundations. Harkness not only supported her company, she also bought a school and theater for it and founded a second company for students trained at the school.

Rebekah Harkness's commitment to ballet began in her teens, but her father forbade her to pursue a dance career. As an adult, she studied ballet daily with Leon Fokine. She also sculpted and composed music, much of it for dance; several of her works were used by the marquis de Cuevas's Grand Ballet. In 1959 she founded the Rebekah Harkness Foundation, which supported a number of dance projects, including a European tour and a New York season for Jerome Robbins's Ballets: USA, an African tour for Pearl Primus, and the summer dance festival in New York's Central Park.

In 1962 the Harkness Foundation sponsored a summer workshop at Harkness's Watch Hill, Rhode Island, estate, with the Joffrey Ballet and six choreographers, for the purpose of developing modern American ballets for the Joffrey's repertory. The works produced included Alvin Ailey's *Feast of Ashes*, Brian Macdonald's *Time out of Mind*, Fernand Nault's *Roundabout*, and Donald Saddler's *Dreams of Glory*. For the next two years the Harkness Foundation underwrote the Joffrey company, including its tours of the Middle East, the Soviet Union, and the United States, as well as a second Watch Hill summer.

In early 1964 Harkness abruptly terminated her patronage. The action effectively left Joffrey without a company, since the Harkness Foundation owned all dances produced during the previous two years, and many Joffrey dancers were under contract to the foundation as well. Harkness then committed one million dollars each from both her foundation and that of her late husband, William Hale Harkness, for the founding of the Harkness Ballet. Fourteen of the twenty-six Harkness dancers came from the Joffrey, including Lawrence Rhodes, Helgi Tomasson, Lone Isaksen, Brunilda Ruiz, Finis Jhung, Marlene Rizzo, and Margaret Mercier. The only non-Joffrey principal was Elizabeth Carroll.

If the beginning of the Harkness raised furor and cries of piracy, the company soon established its credentials through the eminent dance professionals it attracted. Harkness named George Skibine, former director of the Paris Opera Ballet, as artistic director, and Donald Saddler as assistant director. Skibine's wife Marjorie Tallchief was *prima ballerina*, and Nicholas Polajenko was *premier danseur*. During the 1964 summer session at Watch Hill, Vera Volkova, Erik Bruhn, Alexandra Danilova, and Leon Fokine taught classes (Bruhn also danced with the company as a guest dancer on its first European tour), and choreographers Brian Macdonald, Alvin Ailey, and Michael Smuin worked with the dancers. Harkness donated a special dance stage to the White House, and in September the company gave an inaugural performance there.

During the next two years the Harkness Ballet toured Europe and the United States twice (skipping New York). Critics gave high praise to the company but mixed reviews to its repertory. Well received were *Feast of Ashes* and *Time out of Mind*—from the Joffrey repertory—as well as Skibine's *Daphnis and Chloe*, Stuart Hodes's *The Abyss*, and John Butler's *After Eden*. Even during the first European tour, however, Clive Barnes (1965) pointed out that rape or seduction were the subjects of all four of the company's new dances. He also noted a double focus on traditional and modern ballet that seemed not so much eclec-

tic as "going in two directions at once." Other critics also questioned the company's overall artistic direction.

In 1967 Brian Macdonald replaced Skibine as artistic director. Skibine's more classical dances were dropped and the repertory now relied heavily on works by Macdonald and Butler. When the company finally made its long-awaited New York debut in November 1967, critics again lauded the dancers and some of the ballets—those already mentioned, as well as Butler's *Sebastian*, Macdonald's *Canto Indio*, and Rudi van Dantzig's *Monument for a Dead Boy*, with Lawrence Rhodes. Nevertheless, the critics found most of the choreography either uninspired or preoccupied with brooding or violent sex. The lavish amounts of money spent on costumes and sets (reportedly $100,000 for Macdonald's *The Firebird* alone) merely resulted in "tastelessly overproduced" dances, according to Marcia B. Siegel (1968).

The well-meaning but often excessive opulence that characterized many Harkness undertakings was evident in Harkness House, the school and home of the Harkness Ballet, which opened in 1965. The remodeled mansion's ornate decor—including a $250,000 chalice by Salvador Dali and a butterfly-encrusted elevator cage that glided past ballet murals in the elevator shaft—caused much comment. Nevertheless, Harkness House's dance education department was consistently cited for producing fine dancers. Less successful was Harkness's $5-million renovation of a Broadway theater specifically for dance in 1972–1974. Decorated on Spanish themes with imported marble and crystal, with a controversial mural of nude dancers on the proscenium by the designer Enrique Senis Oliver, the theater attracted few bookings and was sold and demolished in 1977.

In 1968 Harkness founded the Harkness Youth Dancers, a company made up of trainees at the Harkness school. The same year the Harkness Ballet reached a crisis point, with many dancers ready to walk out because of extended touring schedules and unsatisfactory repertory. At the dancers' insistence, company principal Lawrence Rhodes replaced Macdonald as artistic director; the following year, Rhodes, who continued to dance, called in Benjamin Harkarvy to co-direct. Under their leadership the Harkness began developing a more balanced repertory. Rhodes and Harkarvy brought in John Neumeier's *Stages and Reflections*, Todd Bolender's *Souvenirs*, Jerome Robbins's *New York Export: Opus Jazz*, the André Eglevsky–George

Balanchine *Sylvia Pas de Deux,* Milko Šparemblek's *L'Absence,* and several Harkarvy dances.

In March 1970, in the middle of a European tour, Harkness abruptly dissolved the Harkness Ballet, giving as the reason the financial pressure of maintaining two companies. Two months later she merged the meager remains of the Harkness Ballet with the Harkness Youth Dancers under her own directorship. The reorganized Harkness—with Ben Stevenson and later Vicente Nebrada as resident choreographers—faced the same problems as its predecessor. Its dancers, including Christopher Aponte, Tanju Tuzer, Helen Heinemann, Manola Ascensio, and Zane Wilson, were of high quality; however, most critics found its repertory inconsequential. By 1974 the company faced a deficit of $1.5 million, which Harkness refused to shoulder alone, and in 1975 it disbanded.

BIBLIOGRAPHY

Barnes, Clive. "The Opening Scene." *Dance Magazine* (April 1965):27–28.
Hering, Doris. "Passions Revisited." *Dance Magazine* (January 1968):44.
Hering, Doris. "Through the First Gate." *Dance Magazine* (March 1969):34–46.
Hodes, Stuart. "Hail Harkness!" *Ballet Review* 14 (Spring 1986):57–64.
Marks, Marcia. "Mrs. Harkness Is a Rich Woman." *Dance Magazine* (January 1970):28.
O'Connor, John J. "Another Try at the 'Inevitable' Direction." *Dance Magazine* (November 1969):65.
Rosen, Lillie. "An Interview with Lawrence Rhodes." *Attitude* 9 (Spring 1993):12–19.
Siegel, Marcia B. *Arts in Society* (Summer–Fall 1968).
Siegel, Marcia B. "Ballet Patronage: How Not to Do It" and "Noblesse Oblige." In Siegel's *At the Vanishing Point.* New York, 1972.
Unger, Craig. *Blue Blood.* New York, 1988.

INTERVIEWS.   Lawrence Rhodes, by John Gruen (1974), and Paul Sutherland, by Marilyn Hunt (1979), both held in the Dance Collection, New York Public Library for the Performing Arts.

JUDY FARRAR BURNS

HART, EVELYN (Evelyn Anne Hart; born 4 April 1956 in Toronto), Canadian ballet dancer. Evelyn Hart began concentrated dance studies in her early teens with Dorothy and Victoria Carter in London, Ontario, and studied briefly at the National Ballet School of Canada in Toronto. Her main ballet training, however, was supervised by David Moroni at the Royal Winnipeg Ballet Professional Division School. She joined the corps de ballet of the Royal Winnipeg Ballet in 1976, becoming a soloist in 1978 and a principal dancer in 1979. The following year she became the first Western dancer to win the gold medal for female soloist at the International Ballet Competition in Varna, Bulgaria. A rarely awarded certificate of exceptional artistic achievement added extra luster to this honor.

EVELYN HART. *Swan Lake* is among the classics mounted by the Royal Winnipeg Ballet to display the talents of Evelyn Hart. She is seen here as Odette in 1987. (Photograph by David Cooper; used by permission.)

During her long career with the Royal Winnipeg Ballet, Hart has danced leading roles in a majority of the works in the company's repertory. Among others, she appeared as principal dancer in *Mahler 4: Eternity Is Now* by Oscar Araiz (1974), *Four Last Songs* by Rudi van Dantzig and *Five Tangos* by Hans van Manen (both, 1980), and *Meadow Dance* by Norbert Vesak (1981). Largely to provide suitable vehicles for her marked gifts as a dramatic dancer, the company added Rudi van Dantzig's production of *Romeo and Juliet* in 1981, Peter Wright's staging of *Giselle* in 1982, and Galina Yordanova's production of *Swan Lake* in 1987.

Increasingly, throughout the 1980s, Hart sought to extend her repertory by working as a guest artist. In 1984 she made her debut as Nikia in *La Bayadère,* act 2, and as Aurora in *The Sleeping Beauty* with the National Ballet of Canada. That same year she danced a principal role in Kenneth MacMillan's *Elite Syncopations* and appeared as Odette-Odile in Peter Wright's staging of *Swan Lake* for the Sadler's Wells Royal Ballet. In 1986 she returned to the

National Ballet of Canada to dance in three works from the Balanchine repertory—*The Four Temperaments, Symphony in C,* and *Serenade*—and in 1988 she was lured to the National Ballet once again by the opportunity to dance Tatiana in John Cranko's *Onegin.* In 1990 she danced with the Bavarian State Ballet in Munich, creating the title role in Riccardo Duse's production of *Cinderella* and appearing as the ill-fated sylph in Dinna Bjørn's mounting of *La Sylphide.* Soon afterward, she joined the Munich company as a resident artist and remained on its roster until 1995.

Despite her frequent appearances with other companies, Hart has continued to appear with the Royal Winnipeg Ballet and to extend her popularity with Canadian audiences through her performances in Winnipeg and on tour. Although her regal bearing and beautiful proportions show to best advantage in purely classical works, she has been more often praised for her gentle lyricism and her innate musicality. These qualities have contributed to her brilliant interpretation of Giselle, for which she has been internationally acclaimed, and of Caroline in Antony Tudor's *Jardin aux Lilas,* which she first danced in 1991.

Hart has been featured in a number of television productions, among them *Romeo and Juliet* (1983) and *Moment of Light: The Dancing of Evelyn Hart* (1992), both televised by the Canadian Broadcasting Corporation. She also starred in the film version of Natalia Makarova's *Swan Lake,* opposite Peter Schaufuss, in 1988. Generally considered to be one of the finest ballerinas Canada has ever produced, Hart was named an Officer of the Order of Canada in 1983 and was promoted to Companion of the Order in 1994.

BIBLIOGRAPHY

Crabb, Michael. "Evelyn Hart's Giselle: The Hart of the Royal Winnipeg Ballet." *Dance Magazine* (April 1983):60–67.
Crabb, Michael. "Evelyn Hart of the RWB." *The Dancing Times* (December 1983):209–210.
Wyman, Max. "North Star: Winnipeg" Evelyn Hart Wants to Stay True to Her Roots." *Ballet News* 5 (April 1984):10–14.
Wyman, Max. *Evelyn Hart: An Intimate Portrait.* Toronto, 1991.

MICHAEL CRABB

HART, JOHN (born 4 July 1921 in London), British dancer, teacher, administrator, and director. A pupil of Judith Espinosa and then a scholarship student at the Royal Academy of Dancing, where he won the first Adeline Genée Gold Medal for male dancers, Hart joined the Vic-Wells Ballet in 1938. By 1942, when he entered the Royal Air Force, he had danced the principal male roles in all five of the company's classical revivals—*The Sleeping Princess, Swan Lake, The Nutcracker, Giselle,* and *Coppélia*—and in *Les Sylphides, Les Patineurs,* and *Les Rendezvous* as well. He was promoted to principal on his return to the company in 1946 and added such contrasting characters as the Corregidor in *Le Tricorne* and the Official in *Miracle in the Gorbals* to his already varied repertory.

A steady partner and solid, traditional actor, especially in roles like Albrecht and Prince Florimund, Hart was indispensable to the growing company. He is said to have danced nearly every leading role in the repertory of his time, graciously supporting each new generation's ballerinas from Margot Fonteyn and Pamela May before World War II to Svetlana Beriosova, Violetta Elvin, and Nadia Nerina after it. His created roles included Laertes in Robert Helpmann's *Hamlet* (1942), Orion in Frederick Ashton's *Sylvia* (1952), and the Consort to Elvin's Queen of the Waters in Ashton's *Homage to the Queen* (1953).

Hart gave his last performances, as Doctor Coppélius, in 1959, but he served the company as ballet master from 1955 to 1957, as principal of the ballet staff until 1962, and then as an assistant director until 1970. That year he became head of the dance division of the School of Performing Arts at the International University in San Diego, California, a position he held until 1979. Between 1970 and 1985 he was also artistic director of PACT Ballet in Johannesburg (1971–1975), administrator of the Royal Ballet (1975–1977), and artistic director of the San Diego Ballet (1980). In 1985 he was appointed artistic director of Ballet West in Salt Lake City, from which position he retired in 1997.

Hart has published two books of photographs: *Ballet and Camera* (1956) and *The Royal Ballet in Performance at Covent Garden* (1958). He was named a Commander of the Order of the British Empire in 1971.

BIBLIOGRAPHY

Davidson, Gladys. "John Hart." In Davidson's *Ballet Biographies.* London, 1954.
McLean, Adrienne L. "Hart of the West." *The Dancing Times* (October 1989): 40–42.

BARBARA NEWMAN

HARTONG, CORRIE (Hendrina Cornelia Hartong; born 23 February 1906 in Rotterdam, died 9 August 1991 in Rotterdam), Dutch dancer, director, and writer. Hartong studied modern dance at the Mary Wigman School in Dresden and was engaged at the Volksbühne Chemnitz (1928) and at the Wigman School in Magdenburg (1929–1931). From the time of its foundation in 1931, she directed the first subsidized Dutch dance school for amateurs and professionals, the Rotterdam Dance School, at first with Gertrud Leistikov (1931–1934) and then with Yvonne Georgi (1934–1935). From 1954 until 1963 she was sole director of this school and its offshoot for professionals, the Rotterdam Dance Academy (1954–1963).

After stepping down from the directorships in 1964, Hartong continued to teach at both schools until 1967. She was also the first director of the Centraal Dansberaad (Central Dance Council, 1967–1971). With Kit Winkel she introduced into the Netherlands the Laban system of dance education as *dansexpressie* ("dance expression"). She also took the initiative on many issues in the dance profession as one of the founders and board members of the Nederlandse Bond van Danskunstenaars (Netherlands Association of Dance Artists).

Both in Holland and abroad, Hartong was hailed as a lyrical dance soloist, leading her own company (1928–1948) in performing her choreography—seventy-five solo pieces and thirty-eight group works. She also lectured widely. Among her many publications are two introductory books on the theory and practice of dance, *Danskunst: Inleiding tot het wezen en de practijk van de dans* (The Art of Dance: Introduction to the Essence and Practice of Dance; 1955) and *Over dans gesproken* (Talking about Dance; 1982). She also published a collection of her poems, *Gedichten* (1980).

BIBLIOGRAPHY
Hartong, Corrie. *Over dans gesproken*. Rotterdam, 1982.
Hartong, Corrie. *Danse sacrée, danse profane*. Rotterdam, 1984.
Welzien, Leonore. "Corrie Hartong." *Tanzdrama*, no. 20 (1992): 10–13.

LUUK UTRECHT

HASSREITER, JOSEF (born 31 December 1845 in Vienna, died 8 February 1940 in Vienna), choreographer and ballet master. As choreographer and ballet master of the Vienna Opera, head of its ballet school, and a dance teacher in aristocratic circles, Josef Hassreiter dominated both theatrical and social dance in the capital of the Austro-Hungarian Empire for about thirty years. His works were staged or imitated at opera houses throughout the world. Son of Carl Hassreiter (1820–1870), a dancer at the Kärntnertor Theater (the old opera house), Josef probably made his debut while still a child, perhaps during Fanny Elssler's farewell season.

He began his formal ballet training at the age of nine with Gustav Carey and continued with Giovanni Golinelli. The latter, who became ballet master at the Munich Court Theater in 1864, engaged young Hassreiter as second dancer. Within two years he was promoted to *premier danseur*, a position he also held beginning in the 1868/69 season at the Württemberg Court Theater in Stuttgart under ballet master Giovanni Ambrogio (who later staged Hassreiter's *Die Puppenfee* in New York at the Metropolitan Opera).

In September 1870, Hassreiter was engaged by ballet master Carle Telle as a guest performer for the new Vienna Opera House. His debut was as the painter Henri in Pasquale Borri's *Carnevals Abenteuer in Paris* (Carnival Adventures in Paris). He also danced Albrecht in *Giselle* with Guglielmina Salvioni. Returning to live in Vienna in December because of his father's terminal illness, he was invited to become a permanent member of the Vienna Opera. As a first soloist, he performed leading roles in original ballets by Telle, Paul Taglioni, Borri, Giovanni Rota, and others as well as in Telle's adaptations of *Coppélia*, *Sylvia*, *Naila*, and *La Fille Mal Gardée*. Hassreiter became the Vienna Opera's favorite pas de deux cavalier, partnering such company ballerinas and soloists as Salvioni, Claudina Cucci (Couqui), Amalie Jaksch, Bertha Linda, and Luigia Cerale, and guest stars such as Rita Sangalli, Rosita Mauri, and Adele Grantzow. August Bournonville praised Sangalli and Hassreiter's dancing as "skillful."

In the 1880s, Hassreiter assumed character roles and added the designation "mime" to his title, which in reality was a consequence of aging. He also began to choreograph. In 1889, after the immense success of his first ballet for the Vienna Opera, *Die Puppenfee* (The Fairy Doll), Hassreiter was provisionally appointed ballet master of that house. In 1891, following Telle's retirement in 1890, he was given the full title of ballet master.

During the Hassreiter era at the Vienna Opera, which lasted officially until 1920, he headed both the ballet company and the ballet school and choreographed at least thirty-eight major works for the company and innumerable dances for operas. He also managed a private dance school inherited from his father and occasionally worked for other theaters. Hassreiter's opus includes ballets (*Rouge et Noir*, 1891; *Round about Vienna*, 1894; and *The Eighteenth Spring*, 1918), pantomimes (*Burschenleibe*, 1894; *Pierre as Guardsman*, 1897), and *divertissements* (*Pan*, 1899; *Studio of the Brothers Japonet*, 1906), as well as pieces designated "dance legends" (*The Red Shoes*, 1898), "dance pictures" (*Chopin's Dances*, 1905; *Love's Seasons*, 1911), "dance plays" (*The Judgment of Paris*, 1908; *From at Home*, 1908; *The Princess of Tragant*, 1912; *Faun and Nymph*, 1917), and "dance poems" (*Nippes*, 1911; *Gemma*, 1916).

Most of Hassreiter's major works were set to the music of ballet composers Josef Bayer, Raoul Mader, Franz Skofitz, or Heinrich Berté. He choreographed individual ballet and pantomime scores by Jules Massenet, Oskar Nedbal, and Oscar Straus; and some concert compositions by Chopin, Schubert, and Berlioz were also arranged for ballet. His libretti were often devised in collaboration with the painter Franz Gaul or with Heinrich Regel or A. M. Willner. Anton Brioschi designed much of his scenery; Gaul did the costumes.

The works performed ranged from one-act and two-act to multi-act productions, but in general Hassreiter produced shorter than program-filling works. His ballets were sometimes given on programs that followed operas.

During his tenure, programs of three short ballets came into favor, and it seems that Hassreiter, not Serge Diaghilev, instituted the balanced menu of one-act ballets. The most popular of these mixed bills consisted of Louis Frappart's *Vienna Waltzes* and two Hassreiter works, *Die Puppenfee* and *Sun and Earth*, a combination nicknamed "soup, main course, and dessert."

The form that Hassreiter and his collaborators gave their works sometimes differed from the standard formats of the classical French and Russian ballets. Sometimes they used Italian models, based on fairy tales, allegories, or dramas in which the dancing was incidental to the action and the performers consisted of two groups—dancers and mimes. Often the form of these Viennese ballets was quite original.

Hassreiter was prolific, and his work was popular with regular ballet audiences in Vienna and elsewhere. However, the significance and ultimate quality of his creations have been questioned. Adverse criticism of Hassreiter began as he grew older, especially after 1900, when the first wave of modern dancers and modernism in ballet began to excite the intelligentsia and younger critics. Gustav Mahler as director of the Vienna Opera from 1897 to 1907 became Hassreiter's nemesis when he cut the ballet company's participation in programming. Grete Wiesenthal (initially a member of Hassreiter's company, whom he considered an exotic dancer but not a classical type and who later evolved into a leading modern dancer) criticized Hassreiter as lacking imagination and inspiration but conceded that he sometimes had good dance ideas. The novelist Vicki Baum, who was raised on his ballets, called them "stupid," although she probably objected more strongly to the dramatic than to the choreographic aspects.

These criticisms were akin to those leveled against Marius Petipa and other ballet masters considered to be old-fashioned. Certainly, Hassreiter was no modernist; the extent of his mastery of academic ballet remains unknown. However, a number of authoritative contemporaries praised Hassreiter. Adeline Genée called him the most knowledgeable ballet master in Europe. Petipa, in his diary, referred respectfully to him as "the Viennese ballet master." Diaghilev and Serge Grigoriev held the Vienna ballet of the period in esteem, and Alexandre Benois praised Hassreiter ballets for their "excellent ensemble, clever lighting effects and true Austrian *Gemütlichkeit*."

That Hassreiter's works remained in the repertory of the Vienna Opera after his retirement is evidence, at least, of their entertainment value even in the days of pseudo-modernism. The 1983 revival of *Die Puppenfee* showed Hassreiter to be a highly skilled craftsman if not a great master.

Dissatisfaction with the state of late nineteenth-century ballet, even before the advent of the modern movement, was part of the reason that Hassreiter took exploratory trips to London, Paris, Brussels, Milan, and Saint Petersburg. He was disappointed by Paris (as the returning Petipa had been) but pleased by London (where Katti Lanner had instituted a Viennese tradition). Unfortunately, his observations on Saint Petersburg have not been discovered, although we know that after his visit he and Petipa corresponded about dancers.

As a teacher, Hassreiter continued to pursue Telle's goal of creating a Viennese style that was softer than the stiff Italian manner. Eventually, but not until after the empire had become a republic, two Hassreiter pupils, Else von Strohlendorf and Auguste "Gusti" Pichler, attained the rank of *prima ballerina* at the Vienna Opera, a position long held by Italian dancers from the Teatro alla Scala in Milan. One of his last pupils, Friederike "Riki" Raab, remained active in the 1990s as a coach and reconstructor. Although Hassreiter lived to be ninety-four, little use was made of his skill or knowledge during his last quarter century.

Hassreiter's social profile is as controversial as are his artistic accomplishments and influence on Viennese tradition. Was he, as portrayed in the popular press, the good-humored, resilient, bourgeois dancing master who taught beautiful dancers and powerful aristocrats or, as depicted by Vicki Baum, a bigot and brothel master?

[*See also* Puppenfee, Die.]

BIBLIOGRAPHY

Amort, Andrea. "Die Geschichte des Balletts der Wiener Staatsoper, 1918–1942." Ph.D. diss., University of Vienna, 1981.

Baum, Vicki. *It Was All Quite Different: The Memoirs of Vicki Baum.* New York, 1964.

Jackson, George. "The Weight of 3/4 Time." *Ballet Review* 2.1 (1967): 31–46.

"Josef Hassreiter." *Tanzblätter* 4 (June 1980): 11–31.

"Josef Hassreiter: Leben und Werk." *Tanz Affiche* 8 (December 1995–January 1996): 18–37.

Matzinger, Ruth. "Die Geschichte des Balletts der Wiener Hofoper, 1869–1918." Ph.D.diss., University of Vienna, 1982.

Oberzaucher-Schüller, Gunhild, and Alfred Oberzaucher. "Joseph Hassreiter." *Tanzblätter* 27 (June 1980): 11–31.

Ruziczka, Elvira. "Wiener Opernballett." *Dance News* 16.2 (1950): 11.

GEORGE JACKSON

HAUSA DANCE. A people of northern Nigeria and southern Niger, the Hausa adopted Islam from Muslim traders in the fourteenth century. Traditionally agriculturalists and craftspeople, they are the largest ethnic group of the region. Dancing *(rawa)* among the Hausa is a performance category distinct from *ki'da* (drumming, playing a stringed instrument, playing an idiophone, or playing instrumental music), *busa* (playing a wind instrument), *yaba* (praise shouting), and *wak'a* (singing). Although a great many other specialized performance categories are used by the Hausa, any event involving *rawa* also calls for some type of musical or vocal accompaniment.

The social significance and structure of Hausa dance have been strongly influenced by both Islam and the West. In pre-Islamic Hausa culture, dance was organized around a lineage's social and ritual life. Births, weddings, and other important events were marked by dancing, and each lineage had its own dances, praise epithets, and musical instruments. With the holy war *(jihad)* of 1804–1808, the Islamic reform movement of the Fulani leader 'Uthmān ibn Fūdī (Usuman Dan Fodio) banned girls' dancing and *bòorii* dances. Rooted in ancestor spirit worship, the *bòorii* is a complex dance drama combining and reflecting all facets of Hausa social, political, religious, and artistic life. 'Uthmān's tract *Nur al-'albab* (Light of the Hearts) specifically forbade men and women from dancing and singing together. Strict clerics still disapprove of dancing, but in practice most dancing is now tolerated by Islam.

Although dancing is not considered a craft *(sana'a)*, professional entertainers such as comedians and strongmen include dance in their performances. Most dancing, however, is done by nonprofessionals. Nowadays the traditional dance genres can be divided into two categories—social dances and ceremonial *bòorii* dances.

Social dances vary regionally, but general patterns of organization and style are discernible. Dancing by married men, women, and members of the older generation is considered shameful. Apart from children's dance games such as *ga'da*, social dancing is most frequently engaged in by young men and women. Dances are separated by gender, with boys primarily dancing *rawan Gane* (Gane is the third month of the Muslim calendar) and girls dancing *rawan 'yan mata* ("dancing of girls").

Dancing *rawan Gane* allows boys to criticize deviant behavior within their peer group. Like some dances popular among followers of the *anne* ancestor religion, *rawan Gane* dances, such as *taka*, are circle dances. *Rawan 'yan mata* takes place at night throughout the year. The dance is organized by the youth at designated dancing places *(filin rawa)* and provides opportunities for courtship. Young women dance to various rhythms provided by a band of drummers who are hired by the dancers. The young women usually form lines and perform dances marked by strong pelvic movements. Young men, who usually are spectators, express their interest in a girl by paying "praise shouters" to encourage her to dance.

The *bòorii* spirit-possession cult epitomizes Hausa dance. Adepts of the cult *('yan bòorii)* are described as horses *(godiya)* that spirits *(iskoki)* ride *(hawa)*. Trance is induced by means of drugs and is accompanied by passive listening to special praise tunes *(ki 'din take* or *ki 'dan zuwan aljannu)*, intensive dancing, or fast instrumental pieces *(cashiya)*. Once possessed by a spirit, adepts per-form elaborate movement patterns to symbolize characteristic activities of the particular spirit. Because the Hausa believe that spirits are fond of music and dancing, cult adepts possessed by a spirit not only act out the spirit's behavior but also dance. This phase is accompanied by special dance music for spirits *(ki 'din rawa)*. The spirits' dances are solos and display intricate, rapid footwork.

Modern Hausa dance features the imitation of Western practices, including mixed couples dances and dances such as the *tuwis* (Twist). Other dances, including the *rawan banjo*, are believed to have originated in the city of Jos and are performed by dance teams of young men and women hired by political parties. The teams travel throughout northern Nigeria, competing with one another in outdoor courtyards and at hotels. In Niger, the national youth organization Samaryaa runs cultural centers where dances are held, and Samaryaa dance teams appear on national television to popularize the ideals of self-reliance, industry, and national development.

[*See also* West Africa.]

BIBLIOGRAPHY

Ames, David W., and Anthony V. King. *Glossary of Hausa Music and Its Social Contexts*. Evanston, Ill., 1971.
Besmer, Fremont E. *Horses, Musicians, and Gods: The Hausa Cult of Possession-Trance*. Zaria, Nigeria, 1983.
Erlmann, Veit. "Trance and Music in the Hausa Bòorii Spirit Possession Cult in Niger." *Ethnomusicology* 26 (January 1982): 49–58.

VEIT ERLMANN

HAWAIIAN DANCE TRADITIONS. *See* Polynesia. *See also* Hula *and* Music for Dance, *article on* Oceanic Music.

HAWKINS, ERICK (born 23 April 1909 in Trinidad, Colorado, died 23 November 1994 in New York City), dancer and choreographer. Hawkins pioneered an independent approach to dance movement based on natural kinesthetic response; he rejected geometric classicism and emotional distortion.

In 1932 Hawkins received a bachelor of arts degree in classics from Harvard University. He then studied with Harald Kreutzberg before enrolling at the School of American Ballet, where he studied from 1934 to 1938. He later became an instructor there, while closely observing George Balanchine's style and craftsmanship.

Hawkins made his debut on 9 June 1934 in Balanchine's White Plains concert, where he performed in *Serenade*, in *Dreams*, and in *Mozartiana*. He performed in the American Ballet's *Alma Mater* and *Orpheus and Eurydice*; in *Jeux de Cartes* and *Baiser de la Fée* (during the 1937 Stravinsky

Festival); and in various Metropolitan Opera Ballet ensembles (1935).

Hawkins was a founding member of Ballet Caravan (1936–1939), and he performed in many of their works, including *Pocahontas* by Lew Christensen, and in three works by Eugene Loring, *Filling Station, Billy the Kid,* and *Yankee Clipper.* Hawkins choreographed his own first work, *Show Piece* (15 July 1937), with a plotless, circuslike structure. The popularity of this work led to its performance in 1938 on a program in which Martha Graham's company also danced.

Hawkins then studied modern dance with Martha Graham, becoming her partner in 1938, a partnership that lasted until 1950 (Graham and Hawkins were married in 1948). He created roles in *American Document, Every Soul Is a Circus, El Penitente, Letter to the World, Punch and the Judy, Deaths and Entrances, Appalachian Spring, Dark Meadow, Cave of the Heart,* and *Night Journey.* Transforming Graham's all-female company, and making dances that expressed male-female relationships, Hawkins was also allowed to introduce ballet principles to the Graham technique, to suggest aesthetic ideas (thematic, musical, and scenic), and to develop patronage.

Referring to Hawkins, Stark Young wrote in the *New Republic,* 4 May 1945: "His is an art beginning with character and manliness, a deep, ascetic, rigorous fineness of understanding and a constant search for what is clear and final." Albertina Vitak in *American Dancer,* October 1938, gave an alternative view: "[Graham] was a glowing woman instead of an abstraction of one. Hawkins made a good foil for [her]." [*See the entry on Graham.*]

While working with Graham, Hawkins maintained an independent choreographic profile, later presenting some of his works on her programs. His early modern solos *Liberty Tree* and *Yankee Bluebritches* (1940) dealt with folk themes, and *Trickster Coyote* (1941) was his first dance to use Southwest Indian imagery and masks.

Discussing Hawkins's New York solo debut (20 April 1941), Robert Sabin in *Dance Observer,* May 1941, praised his "logic and beauty of design [of] movement for its own sake." On Graham programs, his *John Brown* (1945), *Stephen Acrobat* (1947), and *The Strangler* (1948) combined spoken text with dramatic dance. If critics denounced Hawkins's daring to put his works next to Graham's, Edwin Denby of the *New York Herald-Tribune,* 17 May 1945, acknowledged that *John Brown* was seen by some as "a fine example of Japanese nō drama," adding that the gesture sequences were "reminiscent of 'primitive' American painting," thus becoming the first to suggest Hawkins's fusion of American and Asian cultures.

Hawkins broke from Graham in 1950 and returned to the kinesthetic principles that were formulated in Mabel Todd's work. Believing proper art presented normative images in which harmonic relationships were seen, he af-

HAWKINS. Seen here in a 1968 performance of his dance *Early Floating,* Hawkins demonstrates the characteristic lightness, fluidity, and sensuality for which he was noted. (Photograph courtesy of Erick Hawkins.)

firmed dance's cooperation with gravity, with decontraction, and with effortless, free-flow response. His dance was influenced by Taoist theory, which matches doing with nondoing: he saw dance in motionlessness and deeply sensed floating as well as in speed through space. Movement was centered in the *hara* (lower gut), and it naturally flowed out, tassel-like, to the extremities.

A transitional work, *openings of the (eye)* (19 January 1952), marked the formation of Hawkins's own company. This first performance collaboration with composer Lucia Dlugoszewski and sculptor Ralph Dorazio moved from dramatic to poetic metaphor. Hawkins used masks and timbre piano to proclaim his vision. The work began critical controversy over his technique; it was "anemic" to Robert Sabin (March 1952) and "strangely hypnotic" to Lois Balcom (*Dance Observer,* March 1953), who likened his "modicum of motion to the non-objective painter's canvas." A turning point came for him when the post–World War II abstract expressionism in American art achieved international acclaim, and, in 1957, Hawkins presented his duet *Here and Now with Watchers.* Louis

Horst's influential review in *Dance Observer*, January 1958, gave approval to Hawkins's direction; he welcomed the "persuasively fluid movement phrases [that] achieved a fine feeling of tenderness."

With masks and imagery inspired by Native Americans, Hawkins continued to celebrate humans and their universe. His *Eight Clear Places* (1960) celebrates natural phenomena (North Star, rain, cloud) in a ritualistic ceremony, as do *Black Lake* (1969) and *Dawn Dazzled Door* (1972). Butterfly images in *Spring Azure* (1962) and *Geography of Noon* (1964) serve as metaphors for his free-floating technique, while *Early Floating* (1962) and *Cantilever* (1963) are pure dance works unto themselves. His 1965 solo *Naked Leopard* celebrates animal innocence; Robert Sabin called it "the most extraordinary and revolutionary dance in our time, a landmark in dance history." Hawkins created works with near-nudity (*Of Love*, 1971; *Angels of the Inmost Heaven*, 1972); symphonic music (*Classic Kite Tails*, 1972; *Hurrah!* 1975); and narrative details (*Meditation on Orpheus*, 1974; *Death Is the Hunter*, 1975). Later works (*Agathlon*, 1979; *Heyoka*, 1981; *Summer-Clouds People*, 1983) return to his Native American, pure dance style, with *Plains Daybreak* (1979), according to Anna Kisselgoff of the *New York Times*, 9 February 1983, "one of [his] most subtle transpositions of American culture to the 20th-century theatre."

Hawkins received the 1979 Dance Magazine Award and, in 1983, was given an honorary Doctor of Fine Arts degree by Western Michigan University. In 1976, Kisselgoff appraised him as one of "those few dance figures who have radically changed the way we look at dance itself, changing our idea of what dance is or how it should be perceived."

BIBLIOGRAPHY

Dlugoszewski, Lucia. "Notes on New Music for the Dance." *Dance Observer* (November 1957): 133–135.

Dlugoszewski, Lucia. *"8 Clear Places."* *Ballet Review* 21 (Winter 1993): 60–65.

Hawkins, Erick. "Pure Fact in Movement, Technique, and Choreography." *Dance Observer* (November 1958): 133–134.

Hawkins, Erick. "Pure Poetry." In *The Modern Dance: Seven Statements of Belief*, edited by Selma Jeanne Cohen. Middletown, Conn., 1966.

Hawkins, Erick. *The Body Is a Clear Place and Other Statements on Dance.* Princeton, N.J., 1992.

Hawkins, Erick. "Machines versus Tools." *Ballet Review* 21 (Winter 1993): 54–59.

Hays, Joan. *Modern Dance: A Biomechanical Approach to Teaching.* St. Louis, 1981.

Kisselgoff, Anna. "Erick Hawkins: His Time Has Come." *New York Times* (17 December 1972).

Kisselgoff, Anna. "Here and Now at Whitney." *New York Times* (25 January 1976).

Kisselgoff, Anna. "Maverick of the Dance." *Harvard Magazine* (May–June 1980): 42–46.

Lorber, Richard, ed. *Erick Hawkins: Theory and Training.* New York, 1979.

Mason, Francis. "A Conversation with Erick Hawkins and Lucia Dlugoszewski." *Ballet Review* 21 (Winter 1993): 47–53.

McDonagh, Don. *Martha Graham: A Biography.* New York, 1973.

McDonagh, Don, ed. *The Complete Guide to Modern Dance.* New York, 1976.

Norton, M. L. Gordon, ed. *Five Essays on the Dance of Erick Hawkins.* New York, 1972.

Rochlein, Harvey. *Notes on Contemporary American Dance.* Baltimore, 1964.

Sabin, Robert. "What Comes after the Avant-Garde?" In *Five Essays on the Dance of Erick Hawkins*, edited by M. L. Gordon Norton. New York, 1972.

Triebe, Sheryl Popkin. "Erick Hawkins: A New Perspective." In *Dance: Current Selected Research*, vol. 3, edited by Lynnette Y. Overby and James H. Humphrey. New York, 1992.

Woodworth, Mark. "Sensing Nature's Flow: Hawkins Teaches Up a Storm." *Dance Magazine* (October 1972): 24–29.

DAVID SEARS

HAYDÉE, MARCIA (Marcia Haydée Salaverry Pereira da Silva; born 18 April 1939 in Niteroi, Brazil), ballet dancer, choreographer, and company director, active in Germany. As a young girl, Marcia Haydée began her training in ballet with Vaslav Veltchek in Rio de Janeiro. When she showed promise of being gifted, her family arranged for her to go to England to continue her studies at the Sadler's Wells Ballet School, where her principal teacher was Tatyana Leskova. While still a student, she returned to Brazil and appeared in performances at the Teatro Municipal in Rio de Janeiro. After further classes with the famed Russian teachers Lubov Egorova and Olga Preobrajenska in Paris, Haydée became a member of Le Grand Ballet du Marquis de Cuevas in 1957. She was eighteen years old. In 1961 she left the de Cuevas company to join the Stuttgart Ballet, where John Cranko had just been appointed artistic director. Named *prima ballerina* of the company the following year, in 1962, Haydée embarked upon an illustrious career that would span more than thirty years.

In Stuttgart, Haydée proved to be the ideal dancer for Cranko's choreography. Upon his death in 1973, she became a member of the company's directorate; in 1976 she was appointed artistic director. She then relinquished the title of *prima ballerina* but continued as a principal dancer of the company, with numerous guest appearances in Germany and all over the world, including numerous appearances with the Ballet du XXe Siècle and Béjart Ballet Lausanne.

Under Cranko's direction, Haydée became one of the greatest dramatic dancers of her generation. She created key roles in almost all Cranko's major works, including *Romeo and Juliet* (1962), *Onegin* (1965), *Présence* (1968), *The Taming of the Shrew* (1969), *Carmen* (1971), *Initialen R.B.M.E.* (1972), and *Traces* (1973). Ballets she created with other choreographers include Kenneth MacMillan's *Las Hermanas* (1963), *Das Lied von der Erde* (1965), and

Requiem (1977); Glen Tetley's *Voluntaries* (1973); John Neumeier's *Hamlet: Connotations* (1976), *The Lady of the Camellias* (1978), *A Streetcar Named Desire* (1983), and *Medea* (1990); and Maurice Béjart's *Divine* (1981), *Wien, Wien, Nur Du Allein* (1982), and *Chairs* (1984).

Never a classical ballerina (although she appeared in Stuttgart regularly in such classical roles as Giselle and Odette-Odile), Haydée was the prototype of the dramatic dancer, portraying blazing emotion and passion that electrified her partners (particularly Richard Cragun, principal dancer of the Stuttgart Ballet, with whom she built a remarkable partnership), her company, and her audiences. Determined to assimilate every role she tackled (although she admitted to limited enthusiasm for abstract or plotless ballets), she imprinted it with fervor and incandescence. She completely identified with the character she was portraying, thus gaining self-assurance and projecting great power and beauty.

Haydée started working as a director and choreographer with the Stuttgart Ballet's production of *The Sleeping Beauty* in 1987. In the same year she choreographed a pas

HAYDÉE. Richard Cragun and Haydée created the roles of the young lovers in John Cranko's 1962 production of *Romeo and Juliet*, staged for the Stuttgart Ballet. This 1977 studio portrait shows the noted partners embracing in a pose from the same ballet. (Photograph © 1977 by Max Waldman; used by permission.)

de deux for Richard Cragun and Birgit Keil, *Enas*, set to music by Vangelis Papathanassiou, and appeared in Neumeier's film version of *Die Kameliendame* (The Lady of the Camellias). She then directed a production of *Giselle und die Wilis* (1989), mounted especially for Birgit Keil, and choreographed *Beziehungen* (1990), set to music by Micus, and *The Planets* (1991), set to the score by Gustav Holst.

In 1993 Haydée was named director of the Ballet de Santiago de Chile, a post she held until 1995, while she continued her duties with the Stuttgart Ballet. She finished her career both as a performer and as a company director in June 1996, having become one of the most famous dancers and most honored artists in Europe. Among her awards are an Étoile d'Or (1967), a German Critics' Award (1971), the German Order of Merit, First Class (1981), an honorary doctorate from Stuttgart University (1981), a Golden Ballet Shoe award (1984), and the German Dance Prize (1989).

[*See also the entries on Cragun and Cranko.*]

BIBLIOGRAPHY

Festschrift Deutscher Tanzpreis 1989. Essen, 1989.
Gruen, John. "Stuttgart Profiles: Marcia Haydée and Richard Cragun." *Dance Magazine* (August 1975): 66–71.
Haydée, Marcia, and Telma Mekler. *Marcia Haydée: Uma vida para a dança.* Rio de Janeiro, 1994.
Kilian, Hannes. *Marcia Haydée: Porträt einer großen Tänzerin.* Sigmaringen, Germany, 1975.
Koegler, Horst. "Zum Beispiel Marcia Haydée und Richard Cragun: Über Partnerschaften im Ballet." *Jahrbuch Ballett 1987:* 45–47.
Krause, Bernd. "Interview with Marcia Haydée." *Stuttgarter Ballet Annual* 17 (1994): 4–10.
Montague, Sarah. *The Ballerina: Famous Dancers and Rising Stars of Our Time.* New York, 1980.
Woihsyk, Rainer, ed. *Marcia Haydée* (in German). Stuttgart, 1987.

HORST KOEGLER

HAYDEN, MELISSA (Mildred Herman; born 25 April 1923), Canadian-American ballet dancer, teacher, and author. Mildred Herman began studying dance at age twelve with Boris Volkoff in Toronto. She later went to New York, where she studied with many teachers—principally Anatole Vilzak and Ludmilla Schollar—and danced for six months in the corps de ballet at Radio City Music Hall. In 1945, upon joining Ballet Theatre as a member of the corps, she changed her name to Melissa Hayden at Antony Tudor's suggestion.

Hayden stayed with Ballet Theatre, becoming a soloist, until it disbanded temporarily in 1948. After working in a Broadway show, she danced with Ballet Alicia Alonso on a South American tour and then joined the New York City Ballet. Except for a brief period when she rejoined Ballet Theatre (1953–1955), she remained with the New York City Ballet until she stopped performing in 1973. She was named a principal dancer in 1955. During her career she made frequent appearances as a guest artist with the National Ballet of Canada as well as with companies in the United States and abroad. She also appeared in Charlie Chaplin's film *Limelight* (1952) and was often seen dancing on television.

With the New York City Ballet, Hayden danced a variety of roles, which her brilliant classical technique and dramatic abilities enabled her to assume. Her first important leading role was Clorinda in *The Duel*, a dramatic work that William Dollar mounted for the company in 1950. Thereafter, she created many roles in ballets choreographed by George Balanchine. Outstanding among them were one of the five ballerinas in *Divertimento No. 15* (1956), the woman in the second pas de trois of *Agon* (1957), "Liberty Bell" in the Fourth Campaign of *Stars and Stripes* (1958), the Ricercata in *Episodes* (1959), the women of the second couple in *Liebeslieder Walzer* (1960), Titania in *A Midsummer Night's Dream* (1962), and the Allegro movement of *Brahms-Schoenberg Quartet* (1966). Other roles that she created with the company included Profane Love in Frederick Ashton's *Illuminations* (1950), a principal dancer in Todd Bolender's *The Still Point* (1956), and the woman in the second couple in Jerome Robbins's *In the Night* (1970).

Hayden was also noted for her performances as the Sugarplum Fairy in *The Nutcracker*, the Girl in Robbins's *Afternoon of a Faun*, Odette in Balanchine's one-act version of *Swan Lake*, Eurydice in Balanchine's *Orpheus*, and the title role of Birgit Cullberg's *Medea*. But these are only a few of the many roles that she danced in her long, distinguished career. During her last season with the New York City Ballet in the spring of 1973, Balanchine choreographed *Cortège Hongrois*, a version of the *grand pas* from *Raymonda*, in her honor, and at its gala premiere she was presented the Handel Medallion, New York City's highest award for cultural achievement.

After her retirement from performing, Hayden joined the faculty of Skidmore College at Saratoga, New York, as artist in residence, and between 1977 and 1983 she directed her own ballet school in New York City. Since 1983 she has taught ballet at the North Carolina School of the Arts in Winston-Salem and has staged Balanchine ballets for various companies. She is the author of three books—*Melissa Hayden: Off Stage and On* (1963), *Ballet Exercises for Figure, Grace and Beauty* (1969), and *Dancer to Dancer: Advice for Today's Dancer* (1981)—and is the recipient of several honors and awards in recognition of her contributions to the arts.

BIBLIOGRAPHY

Anastos, Peter. Interview. "Melissa Hayden on Ballet, Ballets, Balanchine." *Dance Magazine* (August 1973).

Hayden, Melissa. *Melissa Hayden: Off Stage and On.* Garden City, N.Y., 1963.

Gustaitis, Rasa. *Melissa Hayden, Ballerina.* New York, 1967.

Goodman, Saul. "An Extraordinary Anniversary." *Dance Magazine* (November 1970).

Kirstein, Lincoln. "Melissa Hayden: A Tribute." *Dance Magazine* (August 1973).

Reynolds, Nancy. *Repertory in Review: Forty Years of the New York City Ballet.* New York, 1977.

Tracy, Robert, and Sharon DeLano. *Balanchine's Ballerinas: Conversations with the Muses.* New York, 1983.

FILM. Anne Belle. *Dancing for Mr. B: Six Balanchine Ballerinas* (Seahorse Films, 1981).

WILLIAM JAMES LAWSON

H'DOUBLER, MARGARET (Margaret Newell H'Doubler; born 26 April 1889 in Beloit, Kansas, died 26 March 1982 in Springfield, Missouri), American dance educator and writer. Upon completing her undergraduate work in biology, chemistry, and philosophy in 1910, H'Doubler began her career as a physical education teacher at the University of Wisconsin at Madison where she taught until her retirement in 1954. She married Wayne Claxton in 1934.

H'Doubler spent the academic year 1916–1917 in New York City doing graduate work and teaching physical education at Teachers College, Columbia University. In addition, her department chair at Wisconsin had asked her to investigate dance and develop a course for the physical education curriculum. She attended performances of Isadora Duncan and the Ballets Russes and discussed dance education with Gertrude Colby and Bird Larson. What she found most stimulating, however, was the method of music teacher Alys Bentley, who taught movement to enhance the learning of music. When H'Doubler returned to Wisconsin in the fall of 1917 she began teaching dance, and in 1918 her students organized a dance club that H'Doubler named *Orchesis*. The group was invited to perform at various institutions in the midwest and soon the Orchesis idea spread to other universities and colleges that were developing in women's physical education.

H'Doubler read widely not only in dance literature but also in education theory, aesthetics, physiology, psychology, anthropology, evolutionary theory, religion, art history, philosophy, mythology, and music. She thus brought a great breadth and depth of knowledge to the subject of dance.

H'Doubler developed a sophisticated and detailed method and philosophy of dance education based on scientific principles and the belief that each student had potential creativity and abilities that could be developed with careful nurturing. Her influence on modern dance and dance education extends beyond the thousands of students she taught in her long years at Wisconsin and in guest teaching engagements both before and after retirement; it is found also in her writings, the most notable of which are *Dance and Its Place in Education* (1925) and *Dance: A Creative Art Experience* (1940).

BIBLIOGRAPHY

Gray, Judith A. "To Want to Dance: A Biography of Margaret H'Doubler." Ph.D. diss., University of Arizona, 1978.

Moore, Ellen A. "A Recollection of Margaret H'Doubler's Class Procedure: An Environment for the Learning of Dance." *Dance Research Journal* 8.1 (1975–1976): 12–17.

NANCY LEE CHALFA RUYTER

HEINEL, ANNA (Anna Friedrike Heinel, also known as Anne-Frédérique Heinel; born 4 October 1753 in Bayreuth, died 17 March 1808 in Paris), Bavarian dancer. Heinel studied dance with Lépy and later worked with Jean-Georges Noverre, appearing in the ballets he created in Stuttgart and Vienna. In 1768 Heinel made her debut at the Paris Opera and was applauded for her precision and nobility. "You would have thought it was [Gaëtan] Vestris dancing in the disguise of a woman," wrote the critic Gaston Capon. Between 1769 and 1771 she danced for the court at Fontainebleu and Versailles in *divertissements* by Michel-Jean Bandieri de Laval, including *Zélindor, Roi des Sylphes*, *La Rosière de Salency*, *Persée* (for the wedding of the Dauphin), *Castor et Pollux*, *Aline, Reine de Golconde*, and *Les Projets de l'Amour*.

At the Opera, a scandal erupted in connection with a pas de deux in which Heinel charged that Gaëtan Vestris "kept the best for himself"; a minister ruled in favor of Heinel. She danced at the King's Theatre in London in Noverre's *Admète et Alceste*, restaged by Lépy. After a reconciliation, Heinel and Vestris appeared together at the court in a *chaconne* in *Théonis et Zélinde*. In 1774 she danced at Versailles in *Iphigénie en Aulide* and *Orphée et Euridice*, in a pas de trois with Vestris and Maximilien Gardel. At the Opera she performed in numerous *divertissements*, including works by Christoph Willibald Gluck and Niccolò Piccinni, and in various ballets, including *Médée et Jason, Apelles et Campaspe, Les Horaces*, and *Annette et Lubin*, all by Noverre, and *Ninette à la Cour* and *La Fête de Mirza* by Maximilien Gardel. Heinel danced the leading role in *Ninette à la Cour* at Versailles in 1782, after which she retired. She had become the mistress of Gaëtan Vestris; after the birth of their son Adolphe in 1791, they were married.

Heinel was much praised for her slender stature, long legs, and majestic bearing, which won her the title "queen of dance." "The most perfect model of serious dance," according to Noverre, she could seem haughty and cold and was nicknamed "the beautiful statue." In her strictly precise execution, Noverre noted that "beautiful proportions reign, and [create] an enchanting harmony of movements, marked by grace and embellished by the charm of her contours, all of which impart a heavenly air to her dance."

She was famous for the virtuosity of her pirouettes and admired for her interpretation of the tragic heroines created by Noverre—Medea, for example, or Camilla in *Les Horaces*.

BIBLIOGRAPHY

Capon, Gaston. *Les Vestris*. Paris, 1908.

Ces demoiselles de l'opéra. 2d ed. Paris, 1887.

Guest, Ivor. *The Romantic Ballet in Paris*. 2d rev. ed. London, 1980.

Lifar, Serge. *Auguste Vestris*. Paris, 1950.

Migel, Parmenia. *The Ballerinas: From the Court of Louis XIV to Pavlova*. New York, 1972.

Noverre, Jean-Georges. *Lettres sur les arts imitateurs en général et sur la danse en particulier*. 2 vols. Paris, 1807. Edited by Fernand Divoire as *Lettres sur la danse et les arts imitateurs* (Paris, 1952).

JEANNINE DORVANE
Translated from French

HELPMANN, ROBERT (Robert Murray Helpmann; born 9 April 1909 in Mount Gambier, South Australia, died 28 September 1986 in Sydney), Australian dancer; stage, film, and television actor; choreographer; and stage director. The inspiration of Anna Pavlova was widely felt by young people, but few of them actually appeared with her company. This happened to Robert Helpmann in Australia in 1926, when, at age seventeen, he joined Pavlova as a student dancer, the beginning of a career that would become internationally celebrated in the performing arts.

On both sides, Helpmann's forbears were British naval officers who settled in Australia in the eighteenth and early nineteenth centuries, but his father, James Murray Helpman (the original spelling of the name), was a leading stock auctioneer and a pioneer in wholesale meat marketing. The dramatic talent that turned professional in Helpmann's generation (his younger brother Max and sister Sheila were well-known actors in Canada and Australia) came from his mother's family; it was she, a frustrated actress, who encouraged her children to train for the theater.

Helpmann began general dancing classes with Nora Stewart in Adelaide when he was five and appeared in charity and summer shows at an early age. In 1922 he had his first acting role in Sydney in *A Message from Mars*. He was now thirteen and stayed on in Sydney to concentrate on ballet lessons. In 1926, when Pavlova appeared in Melbourne, his father arranged a student audition with her. Helpmann was accepted for the six-month Australian tour, took classes with Laurent Novikoff, and learned the repertory. At the end of that time he was asked to go overseas with the company but this met with parental opposition.

Instead of continuing in ballet, the seventeen-year-old Helpmann became a principal dancer in musicals with the important management firm J.C. Williamson Theatres

Ltd. Operettas were in vogue and during the next few years he was featured in shows such as *Frasquita, The New Moon,* and *The Merry Widow.* In December 1931 he was seen in a specialty number, "The Spider and the Fly," in the pantomime *Sinbad the Sailor* by the young English actress Margaret Rawlings and her husband Gabriel Toyne. They asked Helpmann to choreograph a curtain-raiser ballet for one of their plays and to act in their production of *The Barretts of Wimpole Street.* The ballet, *Ballet à la Russe,* was given in April 1932 and Helpmann traveled with the Toynes to Europe later in the year. In Paris he took classes with Olga Preobrajenska and Matilda Kshessinska (he would return every prewar year). He found the standard tough after a long spell of dancing in the commercial theater but profited from it. His first job in London was acting in *I Hate Men* at the experimental Gate Theatre in February 1933.

Helpmann then took up Margaret Rawlings's introduction to Ninette de Valois, who had begun to create the Vic-Wells Ballet. The two outstanding personalities were mutually impressed and he began work at Sadler's Wells Theatre by appearing in the corps de ballet of the company's new production of *Coppélia* in March 1933. By September he was sufficiently integrated to take over from Anton Dolin the important role of Satan in de Valois's *Job* and danced other leads before the end of the year.

In April 1934 Helpmann was given his first creation—the Master of Treginnis in de Valois's *The Haunted Ballroom,* with Alicia Markova. A Gothic tale with an atmospheric score by Geoffrey Toye and designs by Motley, its central scene showed the doomed man danced to death by a troupe of ghosts. The mimed prologue posited the theme and depended on the conviction with which Helpmann established the supernatural menace. Natural talent, experience in the dramatic theater, and close observation of Pavlova at work had already made him a mime of considerable ability. The concept of ballet then and for many years afterward ranked mime and characterization equally with dance technique. In London Helpmann studied dance with Nikolai Legat and mime with Tamara Karsavina. *Swan Lake* was the next step, partnering Markova in the first British production of the ballet in its entirety, in November 1934. Following Dolin, Helpmann regarded the art of presenting a ballerina in a classical pas de deux as a vital area of a leading dancer's skills. Dolin, in his book *Pas de Deux,* listed four essentials for a cavalier: strength, sureness, authority, and understanding. Helpmann added to these a stimulating element of theatrical excitement.

HELPMANN. *The Rake's Progress* was choreographed by Ninette de Valois for the Vic-Wells Ballet in 1935. Although Helpmann did not create the Rake, he danced it from 1935 onward, making it one of his greatest roles. He is seen here in a performance with members of the Sadler's Wells Ballet in the 1940s. (Photograph from the Dance Collection, New York Public Library for the Performing Arts.)

Like many ballet dancers then in England, Helpmann looked outside the profession for chances of making better money; in February 1935 he was principal dancer in the Hassard Short–directed revue *Stop Press* at the Adelphi Theatre (the London version of Irving Berlin and Moss Hart's 1933 revue *As Thousands Cheer*). He counted this time away well spent as he was dancing choreography by Charles Weidman, making a first contact with American modern dance. In his absence from the Vic-Wells Ballet, de Valois had staged a new production, *The Rake's Progress.* On his return Helpmann made this role very much his own with an unsurpassable study of Hogarth's profligate who ends his days in a madhouse. It was quickly followed by a major creation for Frederick Ashton, the Poet in *Apparitions* in February 1936.

There are many misconceptions about Helpmann as a dancer. The fact that he was not a virtuosic dancer and that the emphasis on virtuosity has become preponderant since the end of World War II has given the erroneous impression that he was barely sufficient as a *premier danseur* in the nineteenth-century ballets. Like all dancers he had strong and weak areas technically, but in the context of the time he was a typical *danseur noble.* In his solos

HELPMANN. In 1942 Helpmann choreographed and starred in *Hamlet*, with Margot Fonteyn as Ophelia. Sets and costumes were designed by Leslie Hurry. (Photograph by Tunbridge-Sedgwick, London; from the Dance Collection, New York Public Library for the performing Arts.)

he was fluent and musical, with fine *port de bras* and a keen instinct for the dynamics of movement. Additionally he was a master of traditional mime and of *grand adage*. His *Aurora (Sleeping Princess)* pas de deux with Fonteyn, for example, was a model of *haute école* classicism.

Ashton always understood his artists and in *Apparitions* he exploited Helpmann's dance characteristics as well as the increasingly popular Fonteyn-Helpmann partnership. (The quality of this conjunction has been obscured by Fonteyn's later celebrated association with Nureyev.) It had a lyrical compatibility of style and motion, of the kind achieved by Antoinette Sibley and Anthony Dowell, that made their joint presentation of *Giselle* or *Swan Lake* an exceptional artistic experience. As a *demi-caractère* dancer Helpmann matched the great Russians, presenting a gallery of superb portraits. In comedy roles he created, his range encompassed the witty elegance of the Bridegroom in *A Wedding Bouquet* in April 1937, the irrepressible Mister O'Reilly in *The Prospect before Us* in July 1940, and the uninhibited clowning of the Ugly Sister in *Cinderella* in December 1948.

Helpmann could not remain content with one specialized branch of the performing arts. Every aspect enthralled him—drama, revue, musicals, opera and operetta, cinema, radio, and television—and in time he would participate in each of them. As early as December 1937 he acted Oberon in Tyrone Guthrie's production of *A Midsummer Night's Dream*, and even during World War II when, as a key figure in British ballet he was exempted from service with the armed forces, he supplemented a full schedule by peripheral appearances in intimate revues or by choreography for musicals.

His first choreography for Sadler's Wells Ballet was *Comus* (January 1942), set to music by Purcell arranged by Constant Lambert, with designs by Oliver Messel. The same year, in May, he staged the remarkable ballet *Hamlet*, to music by Tchaikovsky, with memorable designs by Leslie Hurry. His third ballet, in November, was *The Birds*, to music by Ottorino Respighi, with designs by Chiang Yee.

HELPMANN. *Miracle in the Gorbals*, a dance drama centered on a Christ figure, was created by Helpmann in 1944. The miracle occurs when the Stranger (Helpmann) restores the Suicide (Pauline Clayden) to life. The ballet ends when the Stranger is put to death. (Photograph from the Dance Collection, New York Public Library for the Performing Arts.)

The major work of the three, *Hamlet*, has been badly served in revival both in performance and designs. In its original condition it was superb dramatic dance theater, with a closely textured and flowing development of action and great emotional impact. In its brief length it compressed not only the essential elements of the tragedy, but also many illuminating ideas from academic analyses of the play. Dramatic and literary ballet was an accepted genre in England during the 1930s and 1940s. Ballet had grown up in an atmosphere of interplay among all the relevant arts, a general application of each to all that no longer obtains, and this cultural climate exactly suited Helpmann's wide interest and ability as a man of the theater.

His next ballet, *Miracle in the Gorbals* in October 1944, to a commissioned score by Arthur Bliss, was a pioneer creation for the period, using a contemporary Glasgow slum setting designed by Edward Burra for the miracles and martyrdom of a Christ-like figure. Like all Helpmann's ballets it was artistically unified in the Diaghilev tradition. It was also ideally cast with a company who gave it passion and conviction.

In common with other creators of dramatic ballet at the time, the dance vocabulary used by Helpmann in his choreography was neither virtuosic nor showy, but guided purely by its aptness for the depiction of character and development of narrative. Where appropriate it used groupings and gestures drawn from outside classical ballet or steps from folk dance and social dance.

The end of World War II and Sadler's Wells Ballet's move to the Royal Opera House, Covent Garden, meant a time of change. Helpmann was already more deeply engaged in straight theater, having played his first Hamlet in a Guthrie production for the Old Vic in February 1944. *Adam Zero*, choreographed for Covent Garden in April 1946, with music by Bliss and designs by Roger Furse, was a large-scale theatrical conception. It aroused violent controversy, had some magnificent scenes but an overly involved scenario, and was his last ballet for many years.

In 1947 Helpmann went into play management with his friend Michael Benthall with an admired production of John Webster's *The White Devil*, in which Helpmann acted Flamineo to critical acclaim, and in 1948 he undertook his first season of Shakespeare repertory at Stratford-upon-Avon under Sir Barry Jackson's direction in the leading roles of *King John*, *The Merchant of Venice*, and *Hamlet*. Concurrently he appeared with the Sadler's Wells Ballet and saw the launching of the film *The Red Shoes*, for which he had been choreographer and leading dancer. By 1950, when Helpmann resigned from Sadler's Wells Ballet during a North American tour, he had directed his first opera, *Madama Butterfly*, at Covent Garden. From then until 1965 he directed plays and operas, acted lead-

ing roles in the United Kingdom and the United States with the Oliviers, with Katharine Hepburn at London's Old Vic Theatre, and appeared in films and on television. His capacity as a drama director was exemplified by a finely coordinated production of T. S. Eliot's *Murder in the Cathedral* (in March 1953), starring Robert Donat. One of his most striking performances was at the Edinburgh Festival in September 1954 as the Devil in Igor Stravinsky's *The Soldier's Tale*, which he choreographed.

In 1964 Peggy van Praagh, artistic director of the Australian Ballet, asked him to choreograph a ballet for the Adelaide Festival. He used the native lyrebird's courting dance as an ingredient in *The Display*, set to music by Malcolm Williamson, with designs by Sidney Nolan, and its success led to his appointment as co–artistic director of the company in 1965. In 1968 he was created Knight of the Order of the British Empire (KBE) in Queen Elizabeth II's New Year's Honours List.

HELPMANN. In Frederick Ashton's *Cinderella* (1948), Helpmann created the role of the bossy Stepsister, playing opposite Ashton as the timid Stepsister. Here, *en travesti*, Helpmann gleefully takes a "fish dive" into the arms of a suitor at the Prince's ball, in act 2. The moment is a clear reference to Marius Petipa's *grand pas de deux* at the conclusion of *The Sleeping Beauty*. (Photograph from the Dance Collection, New York Public Library for the Performing Arts.)

From then Helpmann devoted his energies to establishing the Australian Ballet internationally through important tours in North America, East Asia, and Europe. He appeared with them as Doctor Coppélius, the Ugly Sister, the Dago in *Façade*, and in the title role of Nureyev's *Don Quixote*, and he choreographed *Yugen* (1965), *Sun Music* (1968), and *Perisynthyon* (1974), also producing *The Merry Widow* (1975), choreographed by Ronald Hynd. For the Royal Ballet and Sadler's Wells Royal Ballet he was a guest in similar roles and in an immaculate new performance as the Narrator in Frederick Ashton's *A Wedding Bouquet*. He danced the Tango from Ashton's *Façade* with Fonteyn at her sixtieth birthday tribute in 1979.

After June 1976, when disagreements forced him to leave the Australian Ballet, Helpmann freelanced internationally. Among the operas he directed were Handel's *Alcina* and Gounod's *Romeo et Juliette* for the Australian Opera. He appeared in films and television, while acting commitments included *Colette* (in the United States in 1981), *Valmouth* in Chichester in 1982, and *The Cobra* in Sydney in 1983. His last performances were in ballet, as the Red King in the Australian Ballet's revival of de Valois's *Checkmate* at the Sydney Opera House in May 1986.

[*See also* Australian Ballet.]

BIBLIOGRAPHY

Anthony, Gordon. *Studies of Robert Helpmann*. London, 1946.
Brahms, Caryl. *Robert Helpmann: Choreographer*. London, 1943.
Franks, A. H. *Twentieth-Century Ballet*. London and New York, 1954.
Helpman, Mary. *The Helpman Family Story*. Adelaide, 1967.
Haskell, Arnold L. *Miracle in the Gorbals: A Study*. Edinburgh, 1946.
Salter, Elizabeth. *Helpmann: The Authorised Biography of Sir Robert Helpmann, CBE*. Sydney, 1978.
Sorley Walker, Kathrine. *Robert Helpmann*. London, 1957.

KATHRINE SORLEY WALKER

HENIE, SONJA (born 8 April 1912 in Christiania [now Oslo], Norway, died 12 October 1969 en route to Oslo), Norwegian figure skater. Henie was largely responsible for transforming figure skating into a spectator sport. At a time when tracing patterns on ice was still the primary criterion for judging skating, she brought her ballet training to the free program. She popularized skating, especially in the United States, not only through her immensely popular touring shows but also through eleven Hollywood films.

Henie was born into a wealthy and athletic family; her father was twice world cycling champion in the 1890s, and her elder brother, Leif, was a member of championship ice hockey and soccer teams. Sonja herself was at one time a top tennis player in Norway. As a small child she was taken to see Anna Pavlova, who advised her to learn ballet; accordingly, Henie's doting parents arranged lessons with Tamara Karsavina. At age five she was introduced to skating by Leif; at eleven, she was Norwegian

HENIE. The plots of most of Sonja Henie's pictures were simply excuses for big skating numbers, in which her "dancing on ice" captivated moviegoers the world over. In *Thin Ice* (1937), she appeared in this Land of Sweets scene, based on *The Nutcracker*. Her chubby cheeks, dimply smile, blond curls, pretty dress, and dainty demeanor disguised unusual strength and technical ability. (Photograph from a private collection.)

champion; at fourteen, she became world champion, a title she held for ten years, from 1927 through 1936. Henie also won an unequaled three consecutive Olympic gold medals (1928, 1932, 1936).

While she was still an amateur, her short, stylish costumes had almost as great an impact as her balletic style, though her exhibition skating frequently included her version of *The Dying Swan*, made famous by her idol, Pavlova. Henie toured extensively, performing professionally even as an amateur (the family's wealth allowed payments to be absorbed without detection), and she was, controversially, friendly with Adolf Hitler and Joseph Goebbels. These friendships would save her family's property in Norway from the occupying Nazis but would also be a factor in her country's distrust of her loyalty during World War II.

Despite her skating success and her thick Norwegian accent, Henie's ambition always was to be a movie star. After her third Olympic victory she got her wish, and in 1938 she was the number two box office draw behind Shirley Temple. Henie worked with such choreographers as Hermes Pan and Catherine Littlefield, and of her films, *Sun Valley Serenade* (1941) is generally considered to be the best.

Henie's business acumen made her one of the highest-paid performers in Hollywood. Her lavish parties were legend, and she was an avid jewel collector. With her third husband, she also became a collector of modern art. The Sonja Henie–Niels Onstad Art Center opened near Oslo in 1968, the year before Henie died of leukemia while on an airplane flying from Paris to Oslo.

BIBLIOGRAPHY

Strait, Raymond, and Leif Henie. *Queen of Ice, Queen of Shadows: The Unsuspected Life of Sonja Henie.* New York, 1985.

Welch, Paula. "Sonia Henie." *Journal of Physical Education, Recreation, and Dance* 55 (January 1984): 23–24.

FILMS. *One in a Million* (1937). *Thin Ice* (1937). *Happy Landing* (1938). *My Lucky Star* (1938). *Everything Happens at Night* (1939). *Second Fiddle* (1939). *Sun Valley Serenade* (1941). *Iceland* (1942). *Wintertime* (1943). *It's a Pleasure* (1945). *The Countess of Monte Cristo* (1948).

ROBYNN J. STILWELL

HENRY, LOUIS (Louis Stanislas Xavier Henri Bonnachon; born 7 March 1784 in Versailles, died 4 November 1836 in Milan), French dancer and choreographer. Although born in France, Louis Henry did most of his work in Italy, and he is generally identified with the Italian school of choreography. He began his career in 1792 as a very young assistant stagehand at Paris's Théâtre de la Porte-Saint-Martin, where he attracted the notice of Pierre Gardel, who sent him to the Paris Opera school to study dance under Jacques-François Deshayes and Jean-François Coulon. He made his Opera debut in 1803 in a pas de deux with Mademoiselle Clotilde, a pupil of Auguste Vestris. Although he had the height and qualities of a danseur noble, he often performed *demi-caractère* roles in ballets such as Maximilien Gardel's *Le Déserteur* and Pierre Gardel's *Achille à Scyros*.

In 1805 Henry made his debut as a choreographer with *L'Amour à Cythère*, a mythological ballet peopled by the customary Winds, Pleasures, Nymphs, and Cupids. His talent incurred the jealousy of Pierre Gardel and Louis Milon, who successfully prevented him from staging other ballets at the Opera, but undaunted, Henry found an outlet at the Porte-Saint-Martin, where he produced *Les Sauvages de la Floride* and *Les Deux Petits Savoyards* in 1807. Both ballets featured the ballerina Marie Quériau, who became his wife in 1820.

Loosely based on René de Chateaubriand's celebrated romance *Atala*, *Les Sauvages de la Floride* depicted a young prisoner of war who is rescued by his sweetheart. After an adventurous flight through the forest, the two are eventually married (unlike the frustrated protagonists of *Atala*). Henry used an unusual approach for his time in making the natives villains rather than "noble savages." *Les Deux Petits Savoyards* was a lighter work that contained a lively fairground scene, complete with magicians, peddlers, and mountebanks.

With the closing of the Porte-Saint-Martin by imperial decree shortly after the premieres of these ballets, Henry went to Italy, where he was engaged in 1808 as a principal dancer at the Teatro alla Scala in Milan. There his choreographic work was influenced by Salvatore Viganò and Gaetano Gioja, who turned him toward the highly dramatic style of Italian ballet. He soon began to work in Naples and Vienna as well as Milan. His ballets of this period include *Othello* (1808), *Robinson Crusoe* (1809), and *Pandora* (1815) in Naples, and *Wilhelm Tell* and *Atala* (1810; a revival of *Les Sauvages de la Floride*) in Vienna. In 1812 he and Salvatore Taglioni founded the royal ballet school in Naples by the order of Joachim Murat.

When the Porte-Saint-Martin reopened in 1814, Henry returned to Paris. He staged a number of works at this theater, notably *Hamlet* (1816), which was given a happy ending, and *Samson*, in which the biblical story was enlivened with hordes of dancing girls and a spectacular collapse of the temple.

Henry remained in Paris until late 1816, when he returned to Italy because of problems with the censors, who refused permission for several of his ballets. He continued to work in Milan, where he staged *Rinaldo e Armida*, based on Torquato Tasso's *Gerusalemme liberata*, and in Naples, where he first produced his Chinese ballet *Chao-Kang*. In 1822 he returned to the Porte-Saint-Martin, where he produced *Le Sacrifice Indien, ou La Veuve de Malabar*, in which an Indian widow is rescued from her husband's funeral pyre by a noble European, as well as *Agnès et Fitz-Henry*, adapted from a melodrama, and the pure dance *divertissement*, *La Fortune Vient en Dormant*, for which he also designed the stage machinery.

After more contractual problems and disputes with censors, Henry went to Vienna in 1823, where he created *Die Amazonen* for a company that included Filippo Taglioni and his daughter Marie. There in 1825 he also staged a version of *Undine*, probably inspired by Friedrich de la Motte Fouqué's popular romance, eighteen years before Jules Perrot's more famous *Ondine*. Fanny Elssler danced in Henry's *Selico, ossia Il Buon Figlio* (1826) in Naples. Although his ballet *La Silfide* (Naples, 1828) bore the same title as Filippo Taglioni's renowned masterwork (indeed, Henry's sister Elise accused Taglioni of plagiarism), their plots had little in common: in Henry's ballet the Sylphide's lover undergoes various ordeals for her sake, including a transformation into a statue, but the two are ultimately united.

Chao-Kang, restaged at the Théâtre Nautique in Paris in 1834, won great success through its lively evocation of Beijing, particularly in the closing "Festival of Lanterns." As a result, Henry was invited to stage *L'Île des Pirates* (1835) at the Opera for Elssler. The plot involved a disguised pirate chief who abducts a pair of sisters, played by Elssler and her real-life sister Thérèse. Despite a cool reception by the public and criticism for a lack of true feeling, the ballet remained in the repertory for three years and was much admired for its craftsmanship. To do Henry justice, the ballet's plot was probably imposed upon him by the Opera's administrators.

August Bournonville, who saw some of Henry's works in 1834, praised him:

> A most ingenious Frenchman, [who] had absorbed the Italian style of ballet but, by virtue of his originality, knew how to forge his own path. He employed the French style of pantomime in lyrical or idyllic subjects, and the Italian in heroic or historical ones. In this way he achieved a high degree of variety, and as he had great feeling for the picturesque, his groupings were excellent. I have learnt much from his works.

Henry then returned to Naples; during the 1828/29 season, he staged *Adelaide de Borgogna,* a historical ballet whose cast included Carlotta Grisi and Amalia Brugnoli; *Le Tre Sultane;* and *Licaone,* based on the story of Laocoön from Ovid's *Metamorphoses.* He died of cholera shortly after arriving in Milan to take up an engagement at La Scala.

Henry worked in a period of transition between the mythological and Anacreontic ballets of Gardel and the Romantic works of Taglioni and his peers. Many of his ballets were based on literary themes akin to those that inspired Romantic-era choreographers, playwrights, composers, and painters. His position as a link between the French and Italian schools of choreography merits further examination.

BIBLIOGRAPHY
Baron, Auguste A. F. *Lettres à Sophie sur la danse.* Paris, 1825.
Bournonville, August. *My Theatre Life* (1848–1878). Translated by Patricia McAndrew. Middletown, Conn., 1979.
Castil-Blaze. *La danse et les ballets depuis Bacchus jusqu'à Mademoiselle Taglioni.* Paris, 1832.
Christout, Marie-Françoise. "Henry, Louis." In *Enciclopedia dello spettacolo.* Rome, 1954–.
Guest, Ivor. *The Romantic Ballet in Paris.* 2d rev. ed. London, 1980.
Heylii, Georges d'. *Foyers et coulisses: Histoire anecdotique des théâtres de Paris.* 3 vols. Paris, 1875.
Winter, Marian Hannah. *The Pre-Romantic Ballet.* London, 1974.

ELISA VACCARINO

HENZE, HANS WERNER (born 1 July 1926 in Gütersloh), German composer. After World War II, Henze became one of the most widely performed and most versatile composers of his generation. The variety of his compositions includes operas that were staged several times both in Europe and the United States, including *Boulevard Solitude* (1951), *Elegy for Young Lovers* (1959–1961), *Der Junge Lord* (1965), *We Come to the River* (1974–1976), and *The English Cat* (1983). Early in his career, however, he wrote music for ballets, a form of dance neglected in Germany following the rise of German modern dance but reintroduced by the Allies at the end of the war.

In 1945 Henze became fascinated by the music of Igor Stravinsky, who influenced his early compositions in terms of rhythmic energy, emotional coolness, and clarity of musical forms. The Stravinskian pattern of Henze's music can be heard in his Concertino for Piano and Winds (1947) and Symphony no. 3 (1949–1950), which has been choreographed several times. Introduced to dodecaphony (atonality), Henze composed works of great coloristic refinement and strong texture, powerful in both their dramatic and their lyrical impact.

Another significant influence on Henze's compositions for dance was his visit to Hamburg in 1948, when the Sadler's Wells Ballet, headed by Margot Fonteyn, performed in Germany for the first time and he met Frederick Ashton. Henze also met Tatjana Gsovsky, ballet director and choreographer of the West Berlin State Opera, who comissioned him to compose for her group, which later became well known as the Berliner Ballet. Henze composed the ballet-pantomime *Der Idiot,* after Dostoyevsky's novel, in 1952; Gsovsky choreographed it; Ingeborg Bachmann wrote the libretto; and scenery and costumes were by Jean-Pierre Ponnelle. It premiered on 1 September 1952 at the Hebbel Theater in Berlin, with actor Klaus Kinsky as Prince Myshkin. This work made Henze the most promising ballet composer in Germany.

As early as 1950, Henze had tried to develop a ballet theater at the Wiesbaden State Opera, in collaboration with dancer Peter van Dyk as ballet director. However, the attempt to install an experimental ballet group inside the organization of one of Germany's renowned old opera houses did not succeed. Henze, who had hoped to present an alternative to the opera tradition in Germany with smaller ballets—*Ballet Variations* (1949), *Jack Pudding* (after Molière's *Georges Dandin,* 1949), *Rosa Silber* (1950), *Labyrinth* (1952), *Tancredi* (1952; a revised version was choreographed by Rudolf Nureyev and premiered on 14 May 1966 at the Vienna State Opera), and his ballet-opera *Boulevard Solitude* (1951)—ceased composing for dance and became more interested in opera. At the same time, German opera houses, which had been rebuilt after World War II, became the main promoter of contemporary music. The absence of a powerful creative choreographer in Germany beside Gsovsky was another reason for Henze's growing disinterest in ballet. In the next three decades, between 1952 and 1983, he only composed three more ballets.

Henze moved to Italy in 1953. In Rome he met Luchino Visconti, who wanted to stage a ballet for dancer Jean Babilée, using his own libretto. Henze composed the score for Visconti's production of *Maratona,* choreographed by Dick (later Dirk) Sanders, which premiered on 24 September 1957 at the Berlin State Opera, with Babilée as principal dancer.

The following year Henze created his most successful ballet, *Ondine*, composed for the Royal Ballet in London. *Undine*, as it is called in Germany, was rechoreographed for the ballet companies of Munich (choreography by Alan Carter) in 1959, West Berlin (choreography by Gsovsky) in 1959, Düsseldorf (choreography by Werner Ulbrich) in 1961, Wuppertal (choreographed by Erich Walter) in 1962, Budapest (choreographed by Imre Eck) in 1965, Wiesbaden (choreographed by Imre Keres) in 1966, Bonn (choreographed by Giuseppe Urbani) in 1968, East Berlin (choreographed by Tom Schilling) in 1970, Zurich (choreographed by Nicholas Beriozoff) in 1970, and Hamburg (choreographed by Lorca Massine) in 1972. The original Royal Ballet production (choreographed by Frederick Ashton) premiered on 27 October 1958 at the Royal Opera House at Covent Garden in London.

Ondine was Henze's first full-length ballet. He composed the second and last twenty years later: *Orpheus* was choreographed by William Forsythe and premiered on 17 March 1979 at the Stuttgart State Opera.

In the meantime, some of Henze's symphonic compositions were being danced in different choreographies under several titles. His Symphony no. 3 became *Gemini* (choreographed by Glen Tetley) and premiered on 6 April 1973 with the Australian Ballet in Sidney. In combination with his Symphony no. 1, it evolved further into *The Poppet* (choreographed by Gerald Arpino), premiered in October 1969 with the City Center Joffrey Ballet in New York. Henze's symphonic preludes for piano, orchestra, and electronic sounds, titled *Tristan*, was staged in Paris (choreographed by Glen Tetley) on 13 November 1974; in West Berlin (choreographed by Loyce Houlton) on 27 March 1979; and in Hamburg, where it formed the musical base of *Artus-Sage* (choreographed by John Neumeier), which premiered on 12 December 1982.

BIBLIOGRAPHY

Garske, Rolf. "Compositions for Dance: Hans Werner Henze." *Ballett International* 9 (November 1986): 41–43.

Henderson, Robert. "Henze, Hans Werner." In *The New Grove Dictionary of Music and Musicians*. London, 1980.

Petersen, Peter. *Hans Werner Henze*. Hamburg, 1988.

KLAUS GEITEL

HÉROLD, FERDINAND (Louis-Joseph-Ferdinand Hérold; born 28 January 1791 in Paris, died 19 January 1833 in Paris), French composer. Hérold's family settled in Paris about 1781. He first studied piano with his father, a pianist and composer, and then with Louis Adam, father of the composer Adolphe Adam. He also studied violin with Rodolphe Kreutzer, harmony with Charles-Simon Catel, and composition with Étienne-Nicolas Méhul, by whom he was greatly influenced. In 1812 he won the Prix de Rome. After a few months he settled in Naples, where he became music teacher to the daughters of the king of Naples. There he composed his first *opéra comique*, *La gioventu di Enrico*.

After a stay in Vienna, Hérold reached Paris in 1815 and obtained a position at the Théâtre Italien. From this time on Hérold was mainly a composer of *opéra comique*, although he always had difficulties in finding adequate libretti. In 1817 he had considerable success with *La Clochette*.

In 1823 Hérold made his debut as a composer at the Paris Opera with the one-act *Lasthénie;* he continued producing light works for the Opéra-Comique, achieving tremendous success with *Marie* in 1826. That same year Hérold left the Théâtre Italien and became principal chorus master at the Opera, for which during the next three years he composed occasional pieces and five scores for ballets. They included Jean-Louis Aumer's *Astolphe et Joconde* (1827), *La Somnambule* (1827), *Lydie* (1828), *La Fille Mal Gardée* (1828), and *La Belle au Bois Dormant* (1829). During this period Hérold also composed his two operatic masterpieces, *Zampa, ou La Fiancée de Mabre* (1831) and *Le Pré aux Clercs* (1832). Hérold was gravely ill by this time and died five weeks after the premiere of the latter.

Hérold was one of the geniuses of *opéra comique* in the first half of the nineteenth century, and also an important figure in the history of ballet. As early as *Astolphe et Joconde*, Hérold showed himself to be an innovator within a genre which at the time seldom rose above light arrangements of well-known melodies and dance tunes. His scores were based on musical borrowings, but he selected and used the popular material with originality. In addition to this he had a never-failing elegance of orchestration, a melodic richness, and the ability to create dramatic effects. Eugène Scribe's libretto for *La Somnambule* (later used as the basis for Vincenzo Bellini's opera *La Sonnambula*) inspired Hérold to produce a graceful, pastoral score. The style of Gioacchino Rossini had put its stamp on the music, and Hérold tried to connect the music to the drama through the use of melodic motifs. The score for *La Fille Mal Gardée* is based on the musical arrangement for Jean Dauberval's original ballet of 1789, which consists of folk melodies and popular airs. To this Hérold added two borrowings from Rossini and also composed new dances. Later, in 1837, a pas de deux for Fanny Elssler, with music taken from Gaetano Donizetti's *L'Elisir d'Amore*, was added to the Hérold score. In 1960 John Lanchbery recomposed the score for the Frederick Ashton production of the ballet. While the music for *La Fille Mal Gardée* exemplifies lively arrangement based on old *opéra comique* traditions, *La Belle au Bois Dormant* shows the first signs of the Romantic need to evoke emotion and atmosphere through the music's illustrative qualities. In this case the borrowings were taken from, among other sources, *Der Freischütz* by Carl Maria von Weber, and the music shows, if in a crude form, the first steps away from the arranged score and toward more original, dramatically penetrating music.

BIBLIOGRAPHY
Bertini, Henri. *Encyclopédie pittoresque de la musique*. 2d ed. Paris, 1835.
Clément, Félix. *Les musiciens célèbres*. 3d ed. Paris, 1878.
Fétis, François-Joseph. *Biographie universelle des musiciens*. Paris, 1875.
Guest, Ivor. *The Romantic Ballet in Paris*. 2d rev. ed. London, 1980.
Lanchbery, John, and Ivor Guest. "The Scores of *La fille mal gardée*" (parts 1–3). *Theatre Research* 3.1–3.3 (1961).
Pougin, Arthur. *Hérold*. Paris, 1966.

OLE NØRLYNG

HEY. The Hey, or Hay (Fr., *haie, haye, chaîne*; It., *bissa, catena*; Ger., *Kette*), is a serpentine dance figure or, in rare cases, a full dance. Also called a Reel, a Grand Right and Left, and a Grand Chain, the Hey involves three or more persons going in opposite directions, passing one another alternately by the right and left shoulders, with or without joining hands, until all dancers have either returned to their original places or arrived at a new place in accordance with the choreographic plan.

In a Hey for three, frequent in fifteenth- and sixteenth-century court dances and in English and Scottish country dances (reels), the dancers trace a figure eight on the floor. Heys for four usually go around in one direction: dancers 1 and 3 going in one direction, dancers 2 and 4 in the other. Heys for six or more dancers go either in a closed figure (circle, ellipse, rectangle), or in a straight line. The closed-figure type requires an even number of participants; the odd numbers, traditionally the men, face and proceed in one direction, and the even numbers, traditionally the women, face and proceed in the other direction, along two winding and intersecting paths.

The giving of hands, or "handing," during a Hey occurred in the early Renaissance but increased in frequency through the eighteenth and nineteenth centuries. For dancers of the high Renaissance, handing symbolized love, and the chain itself, besides being a means for changing partners and for intermingling participants in a dance, had a cosmological significance that was understood by all informed spectators and dancers present at a ball in the sixteenth and early seventeenth century: it symbolized the Great Chain of Being, an image of the hierarchy underlying all natural things. In Ben Jonson's masque *Pleasure Reconciled to Virtue* (1618), the chain also expressed the inseparability of pleasure, represented by the women, going in one direction, and of virtue, represented by the men, going in the other.

Choreographers of the Renaissance were fully aware of the philosophical and existential implications of the Hey and therefore used it frequently as the final figure in their dances. Whatever the implied or actual dramatic events, competitions, or love conflicts that had occurred in the preceding passages of a given choreography, the chain at the end was the sign of peace, order, and harmony restored. In later periods, entire dances were based on the chain pattern; a great variety of chains occurs in quadrilles and other ballroom dances in the nineteenth century. Heys are also frequent in folk and regional dances and in children's dance games, past and present.

[*See also* Figure Dances *and* Reel.]

BIBLIOGRAPHY
Ferrero, Edward. *The Art of Dancing*. New York, 1859.
Lovejoy, Arthur O. *The Great Chain of Being*. New York, Evanston and London, 1960.
Miller, James. "The Philosophical Background of Renaissance Dance." *York Dance Review*, no. 5 (Spring 1976): 3–15.
Sharp, Cecil J., et al. *The Country Dance Book*. 6 vols. London, 1909–1927.
Tillyard, E. M. W. *The Elizabethan World Picture*. London, 1943.
Wilson, Thomas. *An Analysis of Country Dancing*. London, 1808.

INGRID BRAINARD

HIGHTOWER, ROSELLA (born 10 January 1920 in Ardmore, Oklahoma), American dancer and teacher. Hightower was the first American ballerina to win a leading place on the European stage. Her career as a dancer is linked with that of the company of the marquis de Cuevas, of which she was the undisputed queen. An incomparable virtuoso, this Oklahoman of Native American descent danced with fascinating vitality.

Hightower was trained in Kansas City by Dorothy Perkins, a local teacher. At an early age she caught the attention of Léonide Massine, who hired her for the Ballets Russes de Monte Carlo, where she danced from 1938 to 1941. In 1941 she became a soloist with American Ballet Theatre; she danced her first *Giselle* replacing Alicia Markova when she became ill. After a season with the Original Ballet Russe, in 1947 the marquis de Cuevas hired her for his new company, the Nouveau Ballet de Monte-Carlo. At her first appearance in Paris, the public acclaimed her dynamism and easy virtuosity.

During her long career in Europe she danced the traditional repertory but also created new roles, the most famous of which were the Queen of the Morphides in *Piège de Lumière* (Light Trap) and the title role in *Doña Inés de Castro*. Her Black Swan pas de deux was a masterpiece of its genre. She was equally remarkable in *Rondo Capriccioso*, mounted by Bronislava Nijinska, and in Harald

Lander's 1953 version of *La Sylphide*. In 1960 she danced Aurora in a major production of *The Sleeping Beauty*, with staging and sets by Raymundo de Larrain.

Hightower was loyal to the de Cuevas company and rarely appeared with others. After the death of the marquis in 1962, she founded the Centre de Danse Classique in Cannes, and thereafter she rarely appeared on the stage. Her last successes included three galas given in Paris in January 1962, with Sonia Arova, Erik Bruhn, and Rudolf Nureyev. From 1969 to 1972 she directed the Marseille Opera Ballet, where she mounted a complete version of *The Sleeping Beauty*, with Margot Fonteyn and Rudolf Nureyev, as well as *Don Quixote*. In 1973 and 1974 she directed the ballet of the Grand Théâtre in Nancy, where she discovered Gheorge ("Gigi") Caciuleanu, a Romanian choreographer who succeeded her as director.

In 1981 Hightower succeeded Violette Verdy as artistic director of the Paris Opera Ballet, a position in which she remained until July 1983. She collaborated closely with Georges Hirsch, Jr., the administrator of the ballet. In 1982 she successfully mounted for the Paris Opera Ballet

HIGHTOWER. A studio portrait of Hightower and Erik Bruhn in costume for Balanchine's *Theme and Variations*, which they danced with Ballet Theatre in 1955. (Photograph by Maurice Seymour; used by permission.)

The Sleeping Beauty, inspired by the Cuevas version, at the Palais des Congrès, with sets and costumes by Bernard Daydé. In December 1982, with Georges Hirsch, she produced a new version of *The Nutcracker*. Under her direction the technical quality of the Paris Opera Ballet developed markedly. In 1985 Hightower was invited by La Scala Ballet to be artistic and ballet director; she provided the choreography (after Ivanov and Petipa) for its *Swan Lake*, with libretto, scenery, and direction by Franco Zeffirelli. In 1988, at age sixty-eight, she returned to the stage to dance François Verret's and Denise Luccioni's postmodern piece *L. et Eux, La Nuit* (L. and Them, The Night; music by Yumi Nara, Ghédalia Tazartès, and North American Indian ritual dance music). Originally created for the Festival de Châteauvallon, this short work was later presented several times by Hightower.

Hightower continued to give daily classes at the ballet academy in Cannes. In 1975 she was made a Chevalier de la Légion d'Honneur. In 1991 a mural by Mike Larsen honoring five Native American dancers from Oklahoma—Rosella Hightower, Maria and Marjorie Tallchief, Yvonne Chouteau, and Moscelyne Larkin—was dedicated at the state capitol in Oklahoma City.

BIBLIOGRAPHY

Anderson, Jack. *The One and Only: The Ballet Russe de Monte Carlo*. New York, 1981.
Baillon, Jacques, et al. *Régine Chopinot/Rosella Hightower*. Paris, 1990.
Cadieu, Martine. *Danseurs et danseuses*. Paris, 1951.
"Dossier spécial Marseille." *Pour la Danse* (April 1979): 16–32.
Gruen, John. *The Private World of Ballet*. New York, 1975.
Lemaître, Odon-Jérôme. "Rosella Hightower, ou La grande leçon." *Saisons de la danse* (November 1992): 12–13.
Lidova, Irène. "Rosella Hightower." *Saisons de la Danse* (April 1968).
Livingston, Lili Cockerille. *Trail of Fame*. Norman, Okla., 1996.
Livingston, Lili Cockerille. *American Indian Ballerinas*. Norman, Okla., 1997
Merrill, Bruce. "Rosella Hightower." *Dance Magazine* (July 1981): 54–55.

IRÈNE LIDOVA
Translated from French

HIJIKATA TATSUMI (Yoneyama Kunio; born 9 March 1928 in Akita, Japan, died 21 January 1986), *butō* performer and choreographer, creator of the *butō* form. Hijikata graduated from Akita Industrial High School and in 1952 moved to Tokyo, where he studied dance at the Ando Mitsuko Modern Dance Institute. He joined Ando's company in 1953.

Hijikata performed his first work, *Kinjiki* (Forbidden Colors), in a showcase in 1959. The piece, which used pigeons as symbols, is considered the first *butō* work, though it was structurally similar to modern dance. *Kinjiki* dealt with male homosexuality, and though its title comes from a novel by Mishima Yukio, it was based on the literary works of French writer Jean Genet. The work was criticized as antisocial.

After performing *Kinjiki*, Hijikata developed a close relationship with Mishima. In 1960, he presented nine dances in his first full-evening concert, called *Hijikata Tatsumi 650 Dance Experience no Kai* (the number 650 refers to the capacity of the theater where the work was performed, as well as to Hijikata's belief that all 650 spectators shared in the dance "experience"). On this occasion, Mishima introduced him to the novelist of sadism, Shibusawa Tatsuhiko; Hijikata choreographed a dance entitled *Sei Koshyaku (Ankoku Buyō)* (Saint Marquis [Dance of Darkness]) that same year. Also in 1960, he appeared in the movie *Heso to Genbaku* (Navel and Atomic Bomb), directed by Hosoe Eiko.

In 1961 Hijikata named his signature dance style *ankoku butō*. In 1963 he choreographed *Anma* in collaboration with the visual artist Ikeda Masuo. From this time on, Hijikata became a magnet for young, dedicated *butō* dancers. He performed solos until 1968, when his solo concert *Hijikata Tatsumi to Nihon-jin—Nikutai no Hanran* (Hijikata Tatsumi and the Japanese—Revolt of the Flesh) brought the period of *ankoku butō* to its close.

In 1970 Hijikata abandoned his male-dominated style and toured dances such as *Gibasa*, in which female dancers including Ashikawa Yoko and Kobayashi Saga played central roles. In 1972 he established the extremely influential style that has come to be known as *Hijikata butō* with his work *Shiki no Tameno 27 Ban* (27 Nights for Four Seasons), performed on twenty-seven consecutive evenings. These performances constitute one of the most important events in the history of *butō*.

After performing *Shizuka-na Ie* (Silent House) in 1973 and dancing as a guest artist for the Dai Rakudakan company, Hijikata stopped appearing on stage. He remodeled his rehearsal space into a small theater, Asbestos-kan, where he held dance concerts regularly from 1974 until 1976, when neighbors sued him for disturbing the peace. Thirteen works were presented at Asbestos-kan; Hijikata's middle period ended with the closure of the theater. Although his company went on a European tour in 1978, Hijikata stayed in Japan to direct Ōno Kazuo's *La Argentina Sho* (Admiring La Argentina).

In 1985 Hijikata became convinced that *butō*'s roots lay in *kabuki*, and he held a series of dance projects called *Tohoku Kabuki Keikaku* (Tohoku Kabuki Projects). He presented four dances in 1985, which were his last choreographed works. On 21 January 1986, at the age of fifty-seven, he died of cirrhosis and kidney cancer.

Though others participated in its genesis, Hijikata is the undisputed creator of *butō*. He had studied modern dance and flamenco, but he eagerly desired to formulate an individual style that did not originate in Western dance forms. Influenced by the sadistic literature of Mishima, Shibusawa, and Genet, he choreographed controversial dances whose themes of homosexuality, bisexuality, and disdain for the governing classes provoked conventional sensibilities. Later, he came to conceive his own *butō* style—*Hijikata butō*—based on his observations of Japanese gestures, the Japanese natural environment, and Japan's traditional entertainments. In *Hijikata butō*, bodies were transformed and beauty created as dancers achieved self-realization through exposure to physical extremity. *Butō* is unlike primitive forms in that it is not ritualistic and is not confined in rhythm or voice; it is a unique contemporary form, different from any other dance genre in the world.

[*See also* Butō.]

BIBLIOGRAPHY

Havens, Thomas R. H. "Rebellion and Expression in Contemporary Japanese Dance." In *Dance as Cultural Heritage*, vol. 1, edited by Betty True Jones. New York, 1983.

Hertzman, Lewis. "Performance." *Dance Connection* 11 (Summer 1993): 42–44.

Ichikawa, Miyabi. "Butoh: The Denial of the Body." *Ballett International* 12 (September 1989): 14–19.

Mikami Kayo. *Utsuwa to shite no shintai: Hijikata Tatsumi ankoku butō gihō e no apurōchi*. Tokyo, 1993.

Motofuji Akiko. *Hijikata Tatsumi to tomoni*. Tokyo, 1990.

Stein, Bonnie Sue. "Tatsumi Hijikata, 1929–1986." *Drama Review* 30 (Summer 1986): 126.

Stein, Bonnie Sue. "Celebrating Hijikata: A Bow to the Butoh Master." *Dance Magazine* (May 1988): 44–47.

Tanaka Min. "From *I Am an Avant-Garde Who Crawls the Earth*." *Drama Review* 30 (Summer 1986): 153–155.

Tanemura Suehiro et al. *Hijikata Tatsumi butō taiken*. Tokyo, 1993.

Ueno, Sako. "Conflict Arises over Hijikata Legacy." *Dance Magazine* (August 1992): 20–21.

Yoshioka Minoru. *Hijikata Tatsumi shō*. Tokyo, 1987.

HASEGAWA ROKU
Translated from Japanese

HILL, MARTHA (born c.1901 in East Palestine, Ohio, died 19 November 1995 in Brooklyn, New York), dance educator and administrator. Graduated from the Kellog School of Physical Education, Battle Creek, Michigan, in 1920, Hill taught gymnastics and ballet there until 1923. She then served as director of dance at Kansas State Teachers College in Emporia until 1926. Subsequently she held faculty and dance director positions at the University of Oregon, Eugene (1927–1929); the Lincoln School, Teachers College, Columbia University (1929–1930); the New York University School of Education (1930–1951); Bennington College (1932–1951); and the Juilliard School (1951–1985). Throughout the years she also served as guest teacher at numerous institutions in the United States and abroad.

Hill's leadership in dance education at New York University, Bennington, and Juilliard was crucial in shaping the development of concert dance and dance education in the United States. Particularly noteworthy was her role in the founding and direction of the summer programs in dance at Bennington (1934–1942), Mills College (1939), the University of Southern California (1946), and Connecticut College (1948–1951).

In addition to her academic background, Hill's preparation for the important role she would play in dance education included a wide range of dance studies. Ballet training under Portia Mansfield, Konstantin Kobeleff, and others was augmented by the study of Dalcroze eurhythmics, the Duncan style, and Margaret H'Doubler's approach to educational dance. Hill apparently felt the most affinity, however, for the Graham technique. Hill saw Martha Graham's first independent New York City concert in 1926 and began to study with her that year. She was a member of the Graham company from 1929 to 1931 and probably could have had a distinguished career as a performer had she not chosen instead to devote her life to dance education.

Her experience with Graham influenced Hill's developing philosophy of dance education. She was committed to the position that dance students must learn through direct contact with professional artists. Hill valued such experience in her own formative years and designed the programs she directed in accordance with that principle. For the Bennington summer programs in the 1930s, for example, she brought together a faculty of artists-in-residence that included every major figure of the developing modern dance.

Hill served on many advisory panels for the U.S. government as well as for the city of New York. She was a Fellow of the American Academy of Physical Education and received the American Dance Guild Award in 1974, the Association of American Dance Companies Award in 1975, and the New York University Presidential Citation in 1982.

Upon her retirement from Juilliard in 1985, Hill was named artistic director emerita and continued to teach a senior seminar for graduating students to discuss where they had been, where they were, and—as she told her friends—"how to go out and meet the world."

BIBLIOGRAPHY

Gunnell, Reid Jay. "Biographies of Historical Leaders in Physical, Health, and Recreation Education." Ph.D. diss., Brigham Young University, 1973.

Kisselgoff, Anna. "The Innovations of Martha Hill." *New York Times* (28 March 1982).

Kriegsman, Sali Ann. *Modern Dance in America: The Bennington Years.* Boston, 1981.

O'Donnell, Mary P. "Martha Hill." *Dance Observer* 3.4 (April 1936): 37, 44.

NANCY LEE CHALFA RUYTER

HILVERDING, FRANZ (Franz Anton Christoph Hilverding von Wewen; baptized 17 November 1710 in Vienna, died 29 May 1768 in Vienna), dancer, dancing master, and producer. Hilverding was born into a well-known Austrian theatrical family. His father, Johann Baptist, worked with marionettes, acted, and directed several theater companies. His second wife, Franz's mother, was Margarethe Rosetta, who came from a renowned family of rope dancers. After the death of Johann Baptist, Margarethe married the brilliant Viennese actor Gottfried Prehauser.

Franz probably received at least part of his schooling at the imperial court ballet and from master Alexander Philebois at the court ballet school in Vienna. He probably also studied with the ballet master Anton Coblet, whose daughter Maria Anna he married on 9 January 1729 in Vienna. The Vienna court archives show that he was a dancing master from 1731 to 1734, a court dancer in 1735, and a ballet master from 1737 onward. Hilverding was probably in Paris from about 1735 to 1737 in order to study—financially supported by an imperial scholarship—with Michel Blondy and to learn about recent artistic tendencies in French ballet. Hilverding's known choreographies, mentioned by Stefano Arteaga (1783–1788), are all ballets based on important literary works: Jean Racine's *Britannicus*, Crébillon's *Idoménée*, and Voltaire's *Alzire*. These ballets must have been composed before 1740 because, during the two years of mourning that followed the death of Emperor Charles VI (1740), all Viennese theatrical activities ceased completely. According to Hilverding's student Gaspero Angiolini (1773), Hilverding used this break to develop new theories about theatrical dancing, which he set into practice systematically after 1742.

In 1742 Hilverding also began directing the ballet at the Kärntnertor Theater, a German theater with an extensive repertory of ballet productions and pantomime, as well as ballets that were inserted into operas and spoken dramas. Hilverding gradually replaced the sturdy and stereotyped harlequinades by character dances that presented special professions (gardeners, charcoal burners, woodcutters, peasants) or ethnic groups (Gypsies, Hungarians, Dutchmen) in characteristic mime and movement and in short, appropriate actions. The music for most of these ballets seems to have been composed by Ignaz Holzbauer and Florian Deller. Hilverding's activities between 1742 and 1752 are not well documented.

After 1752, *Repertoire des théâtres de la ville de Vienne* gives a more detailed account of his work. Hilverding was then the *maître de ballet* for both Viennese court theaters. The newly embellished Burgtheater, which reopened in 1748 on the occasion of Queen Maria Theresa's birthday with *Semiramide Riconosciuta* by Christoph Willibald Gluck and ballets by Hilverding, had been placed under the management of Count Lopresti's Society of Noblemen. When this society collapsed in 1752, the Burgtheater and the Kärntnertor Theater were placed under joint court and civic administrations. In 1754 the Genoese diplomat Count Giacomo Durazzo took over the general management of all Viennese theatrical activities. Hilverding had to work for both court theaters as well as for the court theaters at the Laxenburg and Schönbrunn palaces.

From 1752 to 1758, some sixty choreographies are documented under Hilverding's name. During this time he received a court ballet master's salary of six hundred florins, with an additional two hundred florins for each dance pupil he supplied to the court theaters. The ballet masters who assisted him were Giuseppe Salamoni I, his son Giuseppe Salamoni II, Antoine-Bonaventure Pitrot from Dresden, Antoine Philebois, Karl Bernardi, Pietro Sodi (or Pierre Lodi), Philipp Gumpenhuber, and Angiolini from Florence. Among the ballets created during that time the most significant were *Pygmalion* (according to Angiolini, first produced in Vienna in 1756) and *Le Turc Généreux*, a ballet performed at the Burgtheater in April 1758 in honor of the Turkish envoy Resmi Achmed Effendi. Both these important *ballets d'action* could have been stimulated by Hilverding's experience in Paris, where he had most probably seen François Riccoboni's *Pygmalion* as well as *Le Turc Généreux* in Jean-Philippe Rameau's *Les Indes Galantes*. (Music for *Le Turc Généreux* has been found; see Dahms, 1989.)

On 3 November 1758 Hilverding received Maria Theresa's permission to leave the Viennese court service in order to accept an invitation of the Russian tsarina Elizabeth to become ballet master at her court theater. There, he was to reform and reorganize the Russian ballet. He left Vienna on 22 November 1758. His successful Russian stay, working as a choreographer, teacher, and organizer of the imperial ballet, ended in 1764. Music for most of the ten ballets recorded under his name was composed by the Viennese composer Joseph Starzer, who followed Hilverding to Saint Petersburg with the dancers Santina Zanuzzi, Giovanna Campi-Mécour, and Pierre Aubry. Vincenzo Manfredini and Dominik Springer from the Russian *troupe italienne* also provided ballet music for Hilverding. Hilverding's most significant choreographic works were created for the coronation festivities for Catherine II in late autumn 1762: the grand ballet *L'Amour et Psyché* and several ballets that were inserted in Manfredini's opera *Olimpiade* for the court theater in Moscow. Two ballets were provided for the private quarters of the tsarina in her Moscow palace: *Le Combat de l'Amour et de la Raison* and *Le Retour de la Déesse du Printemps*, both performed by amateurs from among her courtiers. In autumn 1763 Hilverding successfully restaged his Viennese *Pygmalion* in Saint Petersburg and in February 1764 produced his last Russian choreography, *Les Amours d'Acis et Galathée*. After a visit to Vienna in mid-1764, he requested his release from Russian service for reasons of health. Starzer, Zanuzzi, and his most talented Russian pupil, Timofei Bublikov, joined him in Vienna, the latter in order to continue perfecting his technique.

Hilverding returned to Vienna and met with great success. On 24 January 1765 he was head producer for the festival performance of Gluck's *Il Parnaso Confuso* and of his own ballet *Il Trionfo d'Amore*, to music by Florian Gassmann, in which Archduchess Marie Antoinette and her brothers, the archdukes Ferdinand and Maximilian, danced leading parts. These festival productions took place on the occasion of the marriage of Archduke Joseph to Maria Josepha of Bavaria in Schönbrunn. In August of the same year, on the occasion of the betrothal of Archduke Leopold in Innsbruck, Hilverding staged the ballet *Enea in Italia* with Anna Binetti and Charles Le Picq in the main roles. After the sudden death of Emperor Francis I on 28 August 1765, all theatrical activities came to an end for about a year, as they had in 1740. Hilverding, who had become lessee of the Kärntnertor Theater, received permission to reopen in spring 1766 and was extremely successful in producing his ballet *Der Triumph des Frühlings*. At about that time he began adding *von Wewen* to his name, which implies that he had been enobled. His efforts to renew interest in good literary German comedies met with little success, and financial problems and ill health forced him to resign in 1767. He died the next year, leaving his second wife and eight children in desolate financial circumstances.

Hilverding earned a place in the history of dance as a choreographer, ballet master, and teacher, and especially for having imported the pantomimic *ballet d'action* to middle and eastern Europe. In Vienna he transformed the old-fashioned stereotyped ballets into lively dramatic actions with literate and historical backgrounds. His style, which included the presentation of special professions or ethnic groups with characteristic mime and gestures, showed a striking similarity to Gregorio Lambranzi's *New and Curious School of Theatrical Dancing* (Nuremberg, 1716). Hilverding developed a new dynamic style of movement that involved the dancer's whole body but also found expression in his innovative concept of asymmetric group arrangements. The use of local costumes and colors in stage designs underlined his total-artwork concept. It seems to be justified to speak of a Hilverding or a Vienna style that developed at about the middle of the eighteenth century.

Although Hilverding's contribution to dance has been increasingly acknowledged, Jean-Georges Noverre never acknowledged his own enormous debt to his Viennese experience: he claimed to be the sole inventor and creator of the *ballet d'action*, thereby supplanting Hilverding for two hundred years.

[*See also* Austria, *article on* Theatrical Dance.]

BIBLIOGRAPHY

Angiolini, Gaspero. *Lettere di Gasparo Angiolini à Monsieur Noverre sopra i balli pantomimi.* Milan, 1773.

Arteaga, Stefano. *Le rivoluzioni del teatro musicale italiano.* 3 vols. Bologna, 1783–1788.

Branscombe, Peter. "Hilverding." In *The New Grove Dictionary of Music and Musicians.* London, 1980.

Brown, Bruce Alan. *Gluck and the French Theatre in Vienna.* Oxford, 1991.

Croll, Gerhard. "Angiolini." In *The New Grove Dictionary of Music and Musicians.* London, 1980.

Dahms, Sibylle. "Franz Hilverding, *Le Turc généreux.*" In *Pipers Enzyklopädie des Musiktheaters,* vol. 3, pp. 56–59. Munich, 1989.

Derra de Moroda, Friderica. "The Ballet-Masters Before, at the Time of, and after Noverre." *Rassegna Annuale di Studi Musicologici* 29–30 (1975).

Derra de Moroda, Friderica. "A Neglected Choreographer: Franz Anton Christoph Hilverding, 1710–1768." *The Dancing Times* (June 1968): 468–470.

Fischer, Friedrich. "Der Wanderschauspieler Johann Peter Hilverding in Salzburg." *Mitteilungen der Gesellschaft für Salzburger Landeskunde* 97 (1957); 98 (1958).

Gugitz, Gustav. "Die Familie Hilverding und ihre theatralische Sendung." *Jahrbuch des Vereins für Geschichte der Stadt Wien* 11 (1954).

Haas, Robert. "Die Wiener Ballett-Pantomime im 18. Jahrhundert und Glucks Don Juan." *Studien zur Musikwissenschaft* 10 (1923): 6–36.

Mooser, R. Aloys. *Annales de la musique et des musiciens en Russie au XVIIIe siècle.* 2 vols. Geneva, 1948–1951.

Pfannkuch, Wilhelm. "Hilverding." In *Die Musik in Geschichte und Gegenwart.* Kassel, 1949–.

Winter, Marian Hannah. *The Pre-Romantic Ballet.* London, 1974.

Zechmeister, Gustav. *Die Wiener Theater nächst der Burg und nächst dem Kärntnerthor von 1747 bis 1776.* Vienna, 1971.

ARCHIVE. Durrazzo Collection, Derra de Moroda Dance Archive, Salzburg.

SIBYLLE DAHMS
Translated from German

HINES. A leading exponent of rhythm tap, Hines is noted for his striking percussive style. He has starred in numerous nightclub acts, Broadway musicals, and Hollywood films. (Photograph from the collection of Rusty E. Frank.)

HINES, GREGORY (Gregory Oliver Hines, born 14 February 1946 in New York) tap dancer, singer, actor, director. A Tony award–winning performer, Hines revolutionized and revitalized tap in the 1980s, when it was threatened with extinction. His intensely exciting close-to-the-floor rhythm work inspired a new generation, which will propel tap dance into the twenty-first century. Hines began studying dance before the age of three, along with his older brother Maurice. Their teacher was tap master and award-winning choreographer Henry LeTang. At five, Gregory and his brother turned professional, appearing as The Hines Kids in nightclubs throughout the United States. Their father, drummer Maurice Sr., joined the act when Hines was eighteen; as Hines, Hines and Dad they worked extensively and toured internationally.

After years on the road, Hines left the act and dancing to settle temporarily in Venice, California. He eventually moved back to New York City where he was cast in *The Last Minstrel Show,* a musical that closed in Philadelphia in 1978 but launched Hines back onto the stage; a month later he was cast in the Broadway hit *Eubie* (1978), in which he received his first of four Tony nominations. Hines was also nominated for his work in *Comin' Uptown* (1979) and *Sophisticated Ladies* (1981). He was awarded the 1992 Tony for Best Actor in a Musical for his riveting portrayal in *Jelly's Last Jam.*

Hines' work in television includes an Emmy-nominated performance for *Motown Return to the Apollo;* he hosted Showtime's *Dance of the Decade* series; and he had a guest-starring role in the first season of Steven Spielberg's *Amazing Stories.* Hines hosted and tapped in the Emmy Award-winning 1989 Public Broadcasting Service (PBS) special, *Tap Dance in America,* which featured not only dance legend but the current American generation of tap artists.

Hines has performed in both dramatic and comedy films. In three of his films, his unique style of tap dancing was incorporated into the dramatic framework of the stories. The first was the 1984 film about 1920s Harlem, *The Cotton Club,* in which he appeared with his brother Maurice); the second was the 1985 adventure film about Russia, *White Nights,* in which he danced with Mikhail Baryshnikov; the third was the 1988 production *Tap,* which became the first dance musical to merge tap dancing with rock and funk. *Tap* also featured a host of tap dance legends: Sandman Sims, Bunny Briggs, Pat Rico, Henry LeTang, Harold Nicholas, Steve Condos, and Hines's co-star, Sammy Davis, Jr.

Tap master Brenda Bufalino has described Hines as taking center stage in tap's revival with his Afro-Cuban moves and his hard-hitting accents and slides. In the 1990s, Hines has continued to command the stage with his engaging tap dancing. Always one to acknowledge his mentors, Hines has said,

> When I tap dance for people, they're not just seeing me, they're seeing me *and* they're seeing Bunny Briggs—Harold and Fayard Nicholas—Gene Kelly—Sandman Sims—Baby Laurence—Steve Condos—and, of course, Henry LeTang, my teacher.   (Frank, 1994)

[*See also* Tap Dance.]

BIBLIOGRAPHY

Frank, Rusty. *TAP! The Greatest Tap Dance Stars and Their Stories 1900–1955.* Rev. ed. New York, 1994.
Stearns, Marshall, and Jean Stearns. *Jazz Dance, The Story of American Vernacular Dance.* Rev. ed. New York, 1994.

RUSTY E. FRANK

HINMAN, MARY WOOD (born 14 February 1878 in Ohio, died 4 July 1952 in Los Angeles), American educator and teacher of folk and social dance. Known for her folk dance teaching and her work to promote human understanding through pageantry, festivals, and recreation, Hinman was guided throughout her career by a keen interest in the dances of all cultures. She is said to have begun teaching dance to neighbor children in 1894 in her home in the North Shore Chicago suburb of Kenilworth. She probably had studied with Eugene Bournique and a Mister Low, who called dances in Kenilworth during her childhood, but by her own admission she had little actual training for what was to become her life's work.

Hinman's classes rapidly expanded into a successful business of dance instruction for Chicago-area society. In 1898 she coached the first Blackfriars Show at the University of Chicago, and while she continued her classes for Hyde Park students, her perspective broadened as she began a twelve-year teaching association with Hull House, where Jane Addams pioneered in the settlement of recent immigrants. Hinman was strongly influenced also by John Dewey, in whose experimental schools she developed, beginning around 1900, a graded program of gymnastic, folk, and social dancing for kindergarten through high school. From 1906 to 1919 she taught in the progressive curriculum of the Francis W. Parker School, where the young Doris Humphrey became one of her most gifted students.

At a time when few American women studied abroad, Hinman believed it was necessary to experience dances in their original context. She first concentrated on Scandinavian dances, which she studied at the Royal College at Nääs, Sweden (from which she was graduated in 1907), and by doing four months of fieldwork in the far north of that country. By 1912 she had spent several summers in Ireland and England, where she worked closely with Kimber, the Oxfordshire bricklayer and Morris dancer, as well as with folklorist Cecil Sharp, who then was actively reviving the traditional dances of England. Over the years she continued her practice of travel and study in Russia, France, Sicily, Switzerland, Germany, Hungary, the Middle and Far East, and Central and South America. Her grandniece, whom she took to see the Hopi Indian dances of the American West, remembered subsisting for a week on boiled eggs and canned pineapple: "Nothing daunted her. She would find a way to do it."

Although she was not a systematic scholar, Hinman used the approach of learning a dance thoroughly herself, taking detailed notes, and obtaining written music. She also collected costumes, photographs, and when they became available, recordings. She used what she learned not only in her teaching but also in her work with the National Playground Association and in the staging of many pageants and festivals. She was a leader in the U.S. branch of the English Folk-Dance Society and was responsible for bringing Cecil Sharp to Chicago for extensive teaching from 1915 to 1917.

As early as 1904, when her own folk dance studies had scarcely begun, she established the Hinman School of Gymnastic and Folk Dancing, with the goal of preparing young women for a new vocation, teaching dance in the public schools. Her two-year program offered folk, English country, ballroom, and interpretive dancing; pantomime, ballet, and clogging; pedagogy (with practice teaching), pageantry (or practical stage production), and "Books," a course on dance history, folk customs, the "new art," civic responsibility, and women's position in the modern world. She encouraged Lucy Duncan Hall, a 1911 graduate of her school, to study with Émile Jaques-Dalcroze at Hellerau, Germany; after becoming the first American certified to teach his method, Hall introduced eurhythmics to the Hinman school curriculum in 1913. Doris Humphrey was another graduate (in 1914) of the Hinman school who also taught there before leaving, at Hinman's suggestion, to study at Denishawn. By 1917 a total of 122 women had completed their studies at this unique school in Hyde Park.

For course materials, Hinman produced hundreds of sheets of dance directions and music; these led to her influential five-volume series *Gymnastic and Folk Dancing*, published by A. S. Barnes beginning in 1914. She described more than two hundred and fifty dances with words, music, diagrams, stick figures, and photographs; she included thoughts on teaching ("Don't talk! Do!") and what she called "dance building" with students. Four original pageant dances by Humphrey were published in these books, which went through several editions. Despite some errors and imprecisions, many of the dances that Hinman recorded still stand as a valuable record of the early collecting of traditional dances.

During World War I Hinman offered her services as a recreation leader for soldiers, both at home and abroad, through the Council of National Defense. After the war she worked for the U.S. government in Germany, and at some point after the closing of her teacher-training school in 1917, she apparently suffered severe nervous exhaustion. In the late 1920s she resumed teaching during the summers, offering a popular course at the Utah Agricultural College in Logan.

By 1930 Hinman was established in New York City, where her career took an important new turn when she helped to establish the Folk Festival Council of New York. This private service organization sponsored dances, festivals, and performances involving some forty ethnic organizations, and for it she created a popular course called "Dances of Many Peoples," which was given at the New School for Social Research beginning in 1932. Dance classes were led by representatives of the various organizations who dressed in ethnic costumes and were accompanied by traditional, usually live music. The experience was supported by folklore, maps, and bibliographies prepared by Hinman. Also during the 1930s Hinman served on the board of the New School Young Dancers Series, and she continued to encourage Humphrey, urging her to film her work.

After a career devoted to helping people through the uniquely human activity of dancing, Hinman retired in 1938 to Los Angeles, where she died fourteen years later. Her collection of folk costumes and other materials was given to the University of California, Los Angeles.

BIBLIOGRAPHY

Hinman, Mary Wood. *Gymnastic and Folk Dancing*. 5 vols. New York, 1914–1937.

Hinman, Mary Wood. "Educational Possibilities of the Dance." *Journal of Health and Physical Education* (April 1934).

Odom, Selma Landen. "Sharing the Dances of Many People: The Teaching Work of Mary Hinman." In *Proceedings of the Tenth Annual Conference, Society of Dance History Scholars, University of California, Irvine, 13–15 February 1987*, compiled by Christena L. Schlundt. Riverside, Calif., 1987.

SELMA LANDEN ODOM

HOFFMANN, REINHILD (born 1 November 1943 in Sorau, Germany), dancer, choreographer, and company director. Reinhild Hoffmann studied at the Essen Folkwang Schule. Upon graduation she joined the Folkwang Tanzstudio, where her colleagues included Pina Bausch, Susanne Linke, and Jean Cébron. She soon attracted attention with her self-choreographed solos, the most famous of which is *Solo with Sofa* (1978), with music by John Cage.

In 1978 Hoffmann was appointed artistic director of the Bremen Dance Theater, working jointly with Gerhard Bohner. From 1981 to 1986 she was in sole charge of the company. Considered one of the leading personalities in German dance theater, she works in a strictly contemporary style, preferring concrete subjects and situations with precisely worked-out dramaturgy. Imbued with a strong and even stark sense of theatricality, her productions are essentially dance-oriented, with relatively little influence from dramatic theater.

Hoffmann's important Bremen works included *Wedding* (1980, a full-length extension of Stravinsky's *Les Noces*), *Garden of Weeds* (1980, music by Gerald Barry), *Erwartung* and *Pierrot Lunaire* (1982, music by Arnold Schoenberg), *Kings and Queens* (1982, music by Peer Raaben), *Callas* (1983), *Dido and Aeneas* (1984, music by Henry Purcell), *Föhn* (1985, music collage), and *Verreist* (1986, music collage). The title *Verreist* has a double meaning, referring both to *verreisen* ("to get away") and *vereisen* ("freezing").

Hoffmann transferred to Bochum in the 1986/87 season, where she worked with her company as part of the ensemble of the Schauspielhaus through 1994–1995. Her productions include *Machandel* (1987), *Ich Schenk Mein Herz* (1989), *Zeche 1* (1992, music by Elena Chernin), and *Zeche Z* (1993, music by Chernin). She now works as a freelance choreographer.

BIBLIOGRAPHY

Bonis, Bernadette. "Reinhild Hoffmann." Interview. *Danser* (October 1990): 40–43.

Müller, Hedwig. "The Path Is the Goal." *Ballett International* 6 (April 1983): 10–19. Interview with Hoffmann.

Schlicher, Susanne. "Reinhild Hoffmann." In Schlicher's *Tanztheater*. Reinbeck, 1987.

Schmidt, Jochen. "Reinhild Hoffmann: Die Spätgeborene." In *Tanztheater in Deutschland*, pp. 123–143. Berlin, 1992.

HORST KOEGLER

HOLLYWOOD FILM MUSICALS. *See* Film Musicals, *article on* Hollywood Film Musicals.

HOLM, HANYA (Johanna Eckert; born 1893 in Worms-am-Rhein, Germany, died 3 November 1992 in New York City), German-American teacher and choreographer.

Holm is the least known of the original four pioneers of American modern dance—the others being Martha Graham, Doris Humphrey, and Charles Weidman—in part because she did not create a personal choreographic style. She was primarily a teacher and concentrated on giving dancers a thorough analytic understanding of movement, freeing them to develop their own individual vocabularies and creativity. Some of her best-known disciples were Alwin Nikolais, Valerie Bettis, Louise Kloepper, and Don Redlich.

Holm's father was a wine merchant, and her mother was an amateur scientist with several patented inventions. This early exposure to investigating how things worked was a primary influence on Holm's life.

After her secondary-school graduation in 1910, Holm entered the music-oriented institute of Émile Jaques-Dalcroze. She intended to become a professional musician, but the music visualizations she did in Dalcroze's eurhythmics (an approach to music education based on body movement) stimulated her love for dance.

In 1921 Holm saw a solo performance of Mary Wigman, then the leading modern dancer in Germany, and decided to study at her Central Institute in Dresden. Dresden during the 1920s, the golden era of expressionism, was a city alive with excitement. At the school, Holm joined a group of women who were creating a new form of dance. They explored space, energy, and time, working kinesthetically from movement starting inside the body, instead of superimposing an outward technique.

Holm explored how the natural physical forces of gravity and momentum affected movement. She conducted experiments with a pendulum: momentum carried it beyond its natural gravitational ending until the arc decreased to form figure-eight configurations, then went into a circle, and finally stood still. She discovered principles of vibratory movement accidentally when sitting on a sofa with friends and bobbing up and down in time to music. She found that the bouncing was an exchange of forces, each stimulating the other, and that it "didn't take another outside force to intrude to make it work."

Holm was the chief instructor at the Mary Wigman Central Institute from 1928 to 1931, and she was a member of Wigman's first company. The company toured Europe between 1923 and 1928 but had to disband in 1930 for financial reasons. In 1929 Holm was asked to dance the part of the Princess in Igor Stravinsky's *The Soldier's Tale;* her musical training was put to the test when she had to master the intricate rhythmic configurations. A year later she assisted Wigman in mounting a major antiwar pageant in Munich called *Das Totenmal.* This full-evening work was a total theater experience, based on a poem and score by Swiss poet Albert Talhoff. Dancers filled the stage, enveloped by a singing and speaking chorus on both sides. They used masks, fantastic costumes, and huge flags. Wigman did all the solos in the piece, and Holm supervised rehearsals and danced.

Wigman's earlier solo performance tours in the United States had been extremely successful, and there was growing interest in her avant-garde techniques. The impresario Sol Hurok, who hoped to promote a Wigman company offshoot there, offered to finance a New York school to introduce Wigman's methods. Holm volunteered to go to New York, because the undercurrent of Adolf Hitler's rise in Germany made her uncomfortable. Hurok arranged the studio and her housing, and on 26 September 1931, the day after arriving from her transatlantic voyage, Holm began teaching. It was a seven-hour day, with the clientele—a motley assortment of dance enthusiasts—changing hourly. In 1932 Hurok turned the school over to Holm, who had told him she needed five years to train a company.

Holm was interested in learning more about Americans. She traveled extensively throughout the United States, especially in the West. She taught at Mills College in Oakland, California, in 1932, and in the summer of 1933 she taught at the Perry Mansfield Dance Camp near Steamboat Springs, Colorado. The feeling of freedom and space in the United States contributed greatly to Holm's modifications of Wigman's technique. The intrinsic differences between German and American modern dance became apparent to Holm. America did not have the angst of a war-torn country that had been destroyed by bombs; Wigman's themes and mysticism had little to do with the American temperament. In 1936 Wigman gave Holm permission to change the name of her school from the Mary Wigman School to the Hanya Holm School of Dance.

In 1934 Holm was invited to teach at the prestigious summer session of the Bennington School of Dance. Other faculty included Martha Graham, Doris Humphrey, Charles Weidman, and Louis Horst. Many of the students were college physical education teachers who were interested in learning the newest techniques in modern dance to apply them in their curricula. The students also set up college tours for the major companies with whom they had studied during the summer. This touring network became known as the "gym circuit," and Holm's all-woman company was among the first and most active in taking dance to the hinterlands. Her lecture-demonstrations clearly explained to uninformed audiences how a dance was created. Concepts were illustrated through a series of études, or studies.

In 1936 Holm formed a dance company, which continued until 1944. Noted company members included Valerie Bettis, Louise Kloepper, Eve Gentry (Henrietta Greenhood), and Elizabeth Waters.

Holm's first major choreographic work, *Trend,* was commissioned by the Bennington Festival in 1937. A signature work of heroic proportions, it used a large group of dancers juxtaposed against a series of solos to depict a society being destroyed by false values. The phenomenal success of *Trend* (dance critic John Martin gave it a *New York Times* Award for being the best dance composition of the year) paved the way for other works, such as the light-hearted *Work and Play* (1938) and two works about emigration from Hitler's Germany, *Tragic Exodus* (1939) and *They Too Are Exiles* (1939). *Dance Magazine* gave *Tragic Exodus* an award for best group choreography in modern dance in 1938–1939. Also in 1939, the National Broadcasting Company telecast its first live modern dance concert. Viewers within a fifty-mile radius of New York saw Holm's *Metropolitan Daily*, a satiric look at newspapers.

Although Holm enjoyed a certain degree of success as a performer and choreographer, she was best known as a teacher. The critic Walter Terry once said that one could even become a better East Indian dancer as a result of studying with Holm, because the theory she stressed could be applied to any discipline.

HOLM. Seen here in a 1938 performance, *Trend* was created in 1937 for a large cast of women at the Bennington Festival and performed at the Vermont State Armory. Holm collaborated on her fifty-five-minute opus with set designer Arch Lauterer and composer Wallingford Riegger. (Photograph © 1994 by Barbara Morgan; used by permission of the Barbara Morgan Archives, Hastings-on-Hudson, New York.)

Holm's students enrolled in a three-year program. The curriculum included technique, anatomy, theory, dance history, pedagogy, composition, and improvisation. The composer Henry Cowell came to the studio to teach the students percussion, for the dancers were expected to provide accompaniment when they were not dancing. There were also theory classes in which students explored and analyzed the movement taught in technique class. Glen Tetley recalls, "Sometimes the dancers would do the same arm swing for two hours, for it was only after the body exhausted itself that it broke down the barriers and did the movement naturally and beautifully." Holm encouraged a lyricism in dance, a flowing quality for the torso and back. She took great care to develop articulate feet.

Holm's studio became a mecca for dancers of all disciplines, including principals from Ballet Theatre, such as Annabelle Lyon, Glen Tetley, and Bambi Linn. Holm also provided a home for the study of Labanotation, the process of notating a dance with written symbols. She was the first choreographer to copyright a dance when she submitted a Labanotated score for *Kiss Me, Kate* to the Library of Congress in March 1952.

The early Holm studio, located at 215 West Eleventh Street in New York, had much of the camaraderie of Wigman's studio in Germany. Students would spend all day working in the studio, a large space with high cathedral

ceilings and wooden floors. Holm lived above in a small apartment, and often the group would retreat upstairs at mealtime.

In class, Holm might surround herself with percussion instruments and begin a rhythm. At her nod, Louise Kloepper would begin to improvise diagonally across the floor, and the other dancers would fall in line behind her and follow. Sometimes Holm or one of the dancers started with a simple combination of steps, which the class saw once and then repeated. Gradually the combinations became more elaborate. Not a word was spoken; the idea was to be able to perform the movement by absorbing it immediately into the body.

One of Holm's most important contributions to dance theory was her use of space. She felt that inner as well as outer space could be an active part of the dance, and that it was important to visualize certain images to encourage the appropriate physical reaction. For example, Alwin Nikolais remembered one class in which Holm had the students line up and asked them to "put into our minds that we were going to run up the wall." She admonished them not to decide when they were going to do it—just to "concentrate and put it so clearly in our minds and we would do it. Sure enough, devoted students that we were, up the walls we went."

Holm also encouraged students to experience the specific feelings connected with movement in order to "taste" movement for themselves, rather than experiencing it only as an intellectual exercise. In addition, she stressed that it was important for the dancer to find his or her inner space as a point of focus and reference. She felt this would keep the movement from becoming vague or only partially executed.

In 1941 Holm's summer teaching moved from Bennington to Colorado College, where she founded an influential dance program. Until the program was discontinued in 1984, professionals and students came from every state to study with Holm. At her fortieth anniversary celebration in 1980, the trustees of the college awarded her an honorary doctorate of fine arts.

Holm choreographed not only concert dances but also movement for plays and operas. On 17 March 1941 she premiered *The Golden Fleece* at the Mansfield Theater in New York. It was a concert dance based on surrealist painter Kurt Seligmann's idea about an alchemist's prophetic dream of turning base metals into gold. The costumes, designed by Seligmann, were fantastic and imaginative but nearly impossible to move in, so the choreography became secondary to the costuming. In 1947 Holm choreographed and directed *The Insect Comedy*, a musical allegory depicting the stupidity and greed of humans as seen through the eyes of an insect.

Faced with the growing financial strain of maintaining

HOLM. Hanya Holm in her *Work and Play*, which premiered in August 1937 at the Bennington Festival, Vermont. (Photograph © 1994 by Barbara Morgan; used by permission of the Barbara Morgan Archives, Hastings-on-Hudson, New York.)

a company, Holm finally had to dissolve it in 1944. The termination of her company also marked the end of her active performing career, but this period coincided with her first Broadway success. She was given the opportunity to choreograph one of three sections of *Ballet Ballads*, a musical that premiered on 27 April 1948 at the off-Broadway Maxine Elliott's Theater. The musical, produced by the Experimental Theater, later moved uptown to the Music Box Theater. Holm's section, featuring tales of Davy Crockett, was well received for its freshness, vitality, and spirit of Americana.

Holm's success with *Ballet Ballads* led to her choreographing Cole Porter's *Kiss Me, Kate*, which premiered on 30 December 1948. Dance was an integral part of its action. According to Harold Lang, who played the male lead, "You went from spoken dialogue into dance dialogue." The dances provided the means for transition in pace, mood, and style. Another innovation was that Holm structured the rehearsals as improvisation classes, highly unusual in the high-pressure atmosphere of a Broadway musical. But Holm felt strongly about having her dancers participate in creating movement they felt comfortable doing. She was awarded a New York Drama Critics Award for best choreographer of the year.

In 1956 Holm received great acclaim for her choreography for the Broadway musical *My Fair Lady,* starring Julie Andrews and Rex Harrison. In 1960 she was nominated for a Tony award for her choreography of *Camelot,* starring Andrews and Richard Burton.

One of Holm's most unusual works was *The Golden Apple* (1954), produced at the Phoenix Theater in New York. In an innovative genre that might be termed dance opera, it set the classic stories of the *Iliad* and *Odyssey* in an American locale around the turn of the century. It was awarded a Critics' Circle Citation as the best musical of the season in 1954. Holm also choreographed *The Ballad of Baby Doe* (1956) and Christoph Willibald Gluck's *Orpheus and Eurydice* (1959) for the Vancouver Festival.

In June 1984 Holm received the Scripps Award for lifetime achievement in the world of dance. In 1985 she premiered a new work called *Capers* for the Don Redlich Dance Company, the chief repository for her work. She was awarded an honorary doctorate from Adelphi University and a citation of gratitude from Harvard University. Until 1985 Holm taught at the Juilliard School and the Louis-Nikolais studios. Her son, Klaus, is a stage designer.

[*See also* Trend.]

BIBLIOGRAPHY

Ballett International 16 (March 1993). Special issue devoted to Hanya Holm.

Choreography and Dance 2.2 (1992). Special issue on Hanya Holm edited by Marilyn Cristofori.

Cristofori, Marilyn. "Hanya Holm Resource Videotapes." *Dance Research Journal* 22 (Spring 1990): 56–57.

Fisher, Betsy. "Preserving the Solo and Duet from Hanya Holm's *Homage to Mahler.*" In *Dance Reconstructed,* edited by Barbara Palfy. New Brunswick, N.J., 1993.

Journal for Stage Directors and Choreographers 7 (Spring–Summer 1993). Issue dedicated to Hanya Holm.

Redlich, Don, and Ilene Fox. "Problems in the Process of Setting Down the Notation Score for Hanya Holm's *RATATAT!*" In *Dance Reconstructed,* edited by Barbara Palfy. New Brunswick, N.J., 1993.

Shearer, Sybil. "My Hanya Holm." *Ballet Review* 21 (Winter 1993): 4–7.

Siegel, Marcia B. "A Conversation with Hanya Holm." *Ballet Review* 9 (Spring 1981): 5–30.

Sorell, Walter. "Hanya Holm: A Vital Force.'" *Dance Magazine* (January 1957): 22–27.

Sorell, Walter. *Hanya Holm: The Biography of an Artist.* Middletown, Conn., 1969.

INTERVIEWS. Eve Gentry, Louise Kloepper, and Bernice van Gelder (Peterson), by Theresa Bowers, Oral History Research Office, Columbia University. Hanya Holm, by Murray Lewis (1979), Nikolais/Louis Studio, New York. Walter Terry, Dance Collection, New York Public Library for the Performing Arts.

VIDEOTAPE. Marilyn Cristofori, "Hanya: Portrait of a Dance Pioneer" (1984), Dance Collection, New York Public Library for the Performing Arts.

NANCY MASON HAUSER

HONG SIN-CHA (born 1 November 1940 in South Ch'oong-ch'ung Province), Korean dancer, choreographer, teacher, and author. After graduating from Sookmyung Women's University in Seoul, Hong Sin-cha, a Korean modern dancer and choreographer, left for New York at the age of twenty-five. She received a master's degree in dance education at Columbia University. She made her debut at the Dance Theatre Workshop in New York in 1973; later that year she returned to Seoul, where she introduced avant-garde dance to the Korean public.

In 1975 Hong collaborated with the eminent Korean composer and *kayagum* (twelve-stringed instrument) player Hwang Byung-ki in an experimental vocal work. She then went to India from 1976 to 1978, where she studied meditation, traditional dance *(kathak),* and singing on a grant from the Indian government. She published two translations of Indian spiritual writings in 1979 and 1980.

HONG. Scene from Hong Sin-cha's evening-length work *Isle,* which evokes the life cycle of an archetypal human community. Here, Annie-B Parson is held aloft by Gary Onsum, Christopher Caines, Henry Beer, and Christian Castren, at the Sejong Cultural Center in Seoul, South Korea, 1989. (Photograph by Cho Dae-hyung; courtesy of Christopher Caines.)

Hong returned to New York in 1981 and founded the Laughing Stone Dance Theater Company, which later performed throughout the United States, Europe, and Asia. While based in New York, Hong won numerous awards for her work with Laughing Stone, including four choreography fellowships from the National Endowment for the Arts, and grants from the New York State Council on the Arts, the New York Foundation for the Arts, the Hawaii State Foundation for Culture and the Arts, and the Asian Cultural Council, as well as a visiting scholar grant from the Fulbright Commission. *Dance of Silence*, her book of poetry (in English) and photography, was published in Japan in 1983; a collection of autobiographical essays in Korean, published in 1985, was revised and printed in English in 1993 as *Memories from Puna*. Also during this period she earned a doctorate in sacred dance from Union Graduate School in Cincinnati, Ohio.

In 1990 Laughing Stone was invited by the People's Republic of China to give the premiere of Hong's work *Pluto*, the first avant-garde dance piece ever presented in Beijing, at the arts festival of the Asian Games. At that time she was cited by Ou Jian-ping, a leading dance critic who heads the Foreign Dance Study Section at the Chinese Academy of Arts, as one of the eighteen great dancers of modern dance history, in his work *World Dance History Makers*. During the same year she was awarded the Choong-ang Grand Prize for Culture, the first such award given in the field of dance in Korea. In 1991, at the invitation of the Beijing Dance Academy, she held China's first nationwide dance workshop, attracting dancers from all over the country, and created choreography for the Guangzhou Modern Dance Company. In 1992 *Pluto* was given its New York premiere at La Mama; its Korean premiere was in 1994 at the Seoul Arts Center.

Recognized as one of Korea's most important creative artists, Hong has given modern dance new vistas through what, in her autobiographical *Mouth to Tail, the Dance World of Hong Sin-cha* (1994), she calls "the simple yet intensely frightening art of breaking out of old patterns into new awareness."

[*See also* Korea, *article on* Modern Dance.]

BIBLIOGRAPHY
Hong Shin-cha. *Dance of Silence*. New York, 1983.
Hong Shin-cha. *Mouth to Tail: The Dance World of Hong Shin-cha*. Seoul, 1994.
Pak Yong-ku. "Young Dancers Seek to Create Fresh Stage Idioms." In *Korean Art Guide*. 2d rev. ed. Seoul, 1986.

ALAN C. HEYMAN

HØNNINGEN, METTE (born 3 October 1944 in Copenhagen), Danish dancer. The Royal Danish Ballet's classical ballerina *par excellence* and one of the first in that company to master the Russian technique, Hønningen entered the ballet school of the Royal Theater in Copenhagen in 1956; she became a member of the Royal Danish Ballet in 1963 and was named a principal dancer in 1967. In 1966 she performed the leading role in the Walt Disney film *Ballerina*.

Hønningen made her debut in 1964 as the Girl in Flemming Flindt's *The Lesson*, and her company career was mostly under Flindt's direction. Her most important mentor, however, was Vera Volkova, for Flindt's emphasis on the modern repertory was somewhat at odds with her classical training. Notable performances included her role in Birgit Cullberg's *Moon Reindeer* and Odette-Odile in *Swan Lake*. In the latter work she proved herself to be one of the most outstanding classical dancers of the Danish company in the late twentieth century; her dancing was cool and precise, but at the same time she radiated the conflicting emotions of this double role: a poetic melancholy and a cold, dangerous eroticism. She danced the ballerina role in Harald Lander's *Études* to perfection and displayed a cool, proud femininity as Myrtha in *Giselle* and as the Siren in George Balanchine's *The Prodigal Son*. She also knew how to express passion and inner dramatic strength, as demonstrated by such roles as Caroline in Antony Tudor's *Jardin aux Lilas*, Lady Capulet in John Neumeier's version of *Romeo and Juliet*, and Hippolyta and Titania in Neumeier's *A Midsummer Night's Dream*.

Hønningen was never a typical Bournonville dancer, though she did add mysterious and dangerous airs to the title role in *La Sylphide* and the Troll Girl in *A Folk Tale*. Nor was she a typical Flindt dancer, but she did dance good roles in some of his ballets. Most interesting were her icy Goddess in Flindt's *The Young Man Must Marry* and her elegant Celeste in his new interpretation of August Bournonville's *The Toreador*.

In 1978, late in her career, Hønningen met Glen Tetley, a choreographer whose work allowed her to demonstrate her ability to dance in a contemporary style. She danced to acclaim in his *Greening* and *Voluntaries*, and in 1981 he created *The Firebird* for her. Similarly, in 1986 Alvin Ailey created the solo *Witness* for Hønningen. In 1992 she retired.

BIBLIOGRAPHY
Aschengreen, Erik. "Flindt, Flemming." In *Dansk biografisk leksikon*. 3d ed. Copenhagen, 1979–.
Percival, John. "Cleopatra." *Dance and Dancers* (December 1976): 24–27.

ERIK ASCHENGREEN

HOPI DANCE. For many centuries the Hopi people of northern Arizona have lived in pueblos, apartment buildings of dressed stone, with an economy dependent on dry farming. They have a rich dance culture that is justified by their cosmogony, according to which the Hopi have a sacred mission to provide moisture for the world. Ceremonies, expressed in part through dances, galvanize the energies and good thoughts of a village population to pray for moisture.

Hopi ceremonies are rites of intensification; their dance ceremonials occur regularly throughout the yearly ritual calendar. This contrasts with many non-Pueblo peoples in the Southwest, whose dance ceremonies are performed irregularly, as rites of passage.

From the winter solstice to the summer solstice, Hopi public ceremonials are performed by *katsina* dancers (plural, *katsinum;* commonly spelled *kachina*), men ritually transformed into supernatural messengers communicating between the Hopi and their deities. From the summer solstice to the winter solstice, Hopi public ceremonials are performed by members of esoteric societies to enact stylistically the conclusion of a drama that depicts the genesis of each ritual. After each solstice there is an interim period during which semisacred dances are performed in this matrilineal society by unmarried females and their patrilineal "nephews." These are sponsored by individuals who wish to express thanks for answered prayers.

Hopi dances are dignified and presented by groups with dance costumes and behavior that differ according to gender. Females wear black or dark blue handwoven, untailored dresses with wide belts. Sometimes they are barefoot, but at other times they wear moccasins with bulky leggings. While dancing, they hold their torsos upright and quiet, and they prance mincingly. Their forearms alternately move up and down, and they hold paraphernalia such as feathers or evergreen boughs.

Male dancers wear white or ochre kilts and, on their upper torsos, a variety of costumes or body paint. They usually wear moccasins. Male dancers lean forward from the hips, but their torsos are quiet. As *katsina*, they typically move in place while they lift and drop their right feet. In other dances they prance with more vigor than the women. Their leg gestures are accentuated by bells or large turtleshell rattles affixed behind their knees. Their arm gestures are more expansive and varied than women's, although they also carry paraphernalia—usually a rattle in the right hand.

Katsinum dance in single file, led in a counterclockwise direction to their dancing places. Choreography includes spirited stepping into 180-degree rotations, either in uni-

HOPI DANCE. A line of *katsina* dancers, symbolically representing spirits in human form, perform a ritual dance in Mishongnovi, Arizona, 1915. (Photograph by Robert H. Lowie; photograph from the Department of Library Services, American Museum of Natural History, New York [no. 118722]; used by permission.)

HOPI DANCE. Many dances of the Pueblo peoples of the southwestern United States, including the Hopi, involve movements that imitate animals. Here, two men perform a Snake Dance on the Hopi Reservation, Arizona, c.1900. (Photograph by H. McCormick; Photograph from the Department of Library Services, American Museum of Natural History, New York [no. 2422044]; used by permission.)

son or as a roll-off, one after the other. Women sodality members face the center of an open circle that slowly moves counterclockwise. Some semisacred dances include two or four mixed couples, who repeat complicated choreography facing each of the four cardinal directions; others are performed in "Rio Grande style," with several couples in a double file that moves counterclockwise.

Choreographic intricacies result from tricky rhythms. Theatricality arises from the orchestration of group dancers who move in unison in counterpoint, with additional performers such as drummer, choral group, and "side dancers" who execute energetic steps and illustrative gestures. Food and gifts are distributed during breaks in the dancing.

Hopi dancers achieve anonymity with masks, headdresses or bland facial expressions, and an inward focus that makes them seem oblivious to onlookers. Onlookers are psychogenic participants; each must maintain happy thoughts and a good heart for the dance to be a success.

[*For related discussion*, see Native American Dance, *article on* The Southwest.]

BIBLIOGRAPHY

Fewkes, Jesse Walter. *Hopi Katcinas.* Washington, D.C., 1903.

Kealiinohomoku, Joann W. "Dance Culture as a Microcosm of Holistic Culture." In *New Dimensions in Dance Research: Anthropology and Dance—The American Indian,* edited by Tamara Comstock. New York, 1974.

Kealiinohomoku, Joann W. *Theory and Methods for an Anthropological Study of Dance.* Bloomington, 1976.

Kealiinohomoku, Joann W. "Hopi Social Dance as a Means for Maintaining Homeostasis." *Journal of the Association of Graduate Dance Ethnologists* (1977): 1–11.

Kealiinohomoku, Joann W. "The Hopi Katsina Dance Event 'Doings.'" In *Seasons of the Kachina,* edited by Lowell John Bean. Hayward, Calif., 1989.

Titiev, Mischa. *Old Oraibi.* Cambridge, Mass., 1944.

JOANN W. KEALIINOHOMOKU

HORNPIPE. The original hornpipe dance is unique to the British Isles. It can be characterized as belonging to the step-dance tradition, which emphasizes leg actions and beating, or sounding, rhythms with the feet. In its most traditional form, it is an important source for tap dance movements.

Historically, the hornpipe appears as solo soft-shoe step dances, as clog dance, as a round dance for mixed couples, as longways country dances, as solo and duet French-style Baroque period *entrées*, and theatrical character dances, including the well-known "Sailor's Hornpipe." It has been danced in one or another of these forms by shepherds, rural villagers, aristocrats, and stage performers.

Etymology. The word *hornpipe,* or *hornpype,* is Middle English and may be derived from the Saxon or Germanic word *hoerner* ("horn"). It was first used by the English, or Anglo-Saxons, to name the dance and its accompanying music. It is also the name of a particular style of rural shepherd's reed pipe, often crafted from animal horns, with a reed mouthpiece and an inflated skin bag. There are numerous regional names for the instrument. The Irish Gaelic word, used by some traditional musicians, is *cornphíopa,* from the Latin for "horn," *cornu.* In Scotland's Lowlands the word is *stoc'n horn.* Some authorities give the Scots Gaelic term as *damhsa* (or *dannsadh*) *gradcharach* (literally, "dance of the sudden whirls"), but this term is not used by dancers. Gaelic-speaking people have generally adopted the English word *hornpipe* to describe their dances and music of this type.

Musical Forms. The most consistent characteristic of the many hornpipe dances is the musical form.

The triple-time hornpipe. Prior to the eighteenth century, hornpipes in England and Scotland were in triple meter, usually 3/2, although occasionally 6/4 or 3/4. These tunes had regular four- and eight-bar phrases, usually subdivided into two-bar units.

The peculiar jerky quality of the melody and the limping gait of the rhythm is due to frequent use of syncopation and an alternation of faster- and slower-moving rhythms. Syncopated rhythms, such as ♩♩♩♩ or ♩♩♩♩♩♩, usually occur in the second and fourth measures, and the point of arrival, usually on the third beat of the cadential measure, creates an interesting rhythmic delay. While the tempo of the half note is slow, the dance is rhythmically complex and lively.

William Stenhouse (c.1824) indicated that 3/2 hornpipes had been played in Scotland "time out of mind," and that "this particular measure originated in the borders of England and Scotland." The standard repertory of the Northumbrian small-pipes includes numerous triple-time hornpipes. The comic or jaunty verses common to Border songs such as "The Dusty Miller" and "Jockey Said to Jenny," as well as nursery tunes such as "Dance to Y'r Daddie" or "Wee Totum Fogg," illustrate the lighthearted and rhythmic character of the triple-time hornpipe.

Hornpipes appear in dance suites and theater music from the sixteenth to the mid–eighteenth century, many cast as variations over a four-measure chord pattern, I–IV–V–I, and considered uniquely English by court composers throughout Europe. The earliest printed example is "Hornepype," a keyboard composition by Hugh Aston (c.1524). This is followed by compositions of Guillaume Morlaye, Antony Holborne (in *The Cittharn Schoole*, 1597), and Thomas Robinson (in *New Citharen Lessons*, 1609).

Traditional examples from England and Scotland, as well as newly composed tunes, can be found in the instrumental lesson books of John Playford (*Musick's Delight*, 1666, and *Apollo's Banquet*, 1690), Matthew Locke (*Melothesia*, 1673), Humphrey Salter (*Genteel Companion*, 1683), and Daniel Wright (*Pleasant Humours*, 1715). Examples from a valuable collection of "original Lancashire hornpipes" by the celebrated hornpipe musician John Ravenscroft, dated 1705, were reproduced by John Hawkins in 1776. Rare copies of eighteenth-century fiddler's tune books also include traditional hornpipes.

Henry Purcell's second-most-frequent dance form is the triple-time hornpipe, which is as a result often referred to as the Purcellian hornpipe. Handel's *Water Music* contains two fully orchestrated hornpipes (nos. 9 and 12); his chorus "Now Love that everlasting boy" in act 2 of *Semele* is marked "alla hornpipe."

The duple-time hornpipe. No other class of tune was designated "hornpipe" until the appearance in the mid–eighteenth century of the common-time hornpipe, now referred to as the "Jacky Tar." It is in 4/4 or 2/4 time, with staccato eighth-note runs punctuated by stresses on the second and third beats in a bar at regular intervals. This "pom-pom" rhythm also ends the phrase, so in combination with the cadential point of arrival on the first beat, the phrase ends "pom-pom-pom." The "College Hornpipe," firmly embedded in the contemporary mind as the "Sailor's Hornpipe," is the quintessential example (see example 1).

The ancestor of this type seems to be the duple-time Scottish measure, which was referred to in Scotland as a "double hornpipe air" though never designated as such in music collections. The term *Scottish measure* first appeared in print in Playford's collection of Scots tunes (1700). Prior to this, English publications called them simply "Scots tunes," for example, "Dumbarton's Drums," "The White Cockade," and "Flooers o' Edinburgh." Purcell composed "Scotch tunes," imitating the Scottish measure, and he introduced a common-time jaunty tune called "Sailor's Dance" in *Dido and Aeneas* (1688). Thomas Arne is often credited with introducing the "new" hornpipe in his version of Purcells's *King Arthur* in 1767. Although the source and process of this shift from triple to duple time is complex, the earlier hornpipe gradually faded from use.

Dance Forms. The hornpipe has undergone great transformation over the centuries.

Pre-1650. The solo hornpipe is executed by one person, or by two or more people dancing independently and either simultaneously or consecutively. It has existed in Scotland and Wales since time immemorial and is believed to have originated as a shepherd's dance, mainly performed by men. The theory is that leg and foot dancing evolved as the shepherd played his hornpipe. From the mountainous north country, where dancers naturally developed strong leg and foot movements, the hornpipe migrated south during the reigns of Elizabeth I and James I, when Scottish dancing, particularly the male solo, was admired and cultivated by the English. English counties most associated with the hornpipe were Derbyshire, Nottinghamshire, and Lancashire.

Coexisting with the solo dance was a rustic round hornpipe for couples. The English traveler Spelman (in his *Relation of Virginia*, 1609) likened the dancing of American Indians to "our darbyshire Hornepipe, a man first, and then a woman, and so through them all, hanging in a round."

While there is no definitive evidence for the dance source, one theory associates it with a ritual harvest dance. The horn of plenty, or cornucopia, symbol of the local dieties of abundance, supplies the link to the idea of dancing to a hornpipe. A more likely association would be to springtime festivals, related to abundance but more in the sense of a fertility celebration. This would coincide with the spring shearing and lambing activities, and of course celebrations, in a rural sheep-raising community.

In the earliest literary reference, *Digby Morality of Wisdom* (c.1480), three men and three women, servants of Lechery, dance to the music of a "hornpype." Richard Barnfield's poem *Shepherds Content* (1594) shows how a shepherd "Leads his Wench a Country Horn-pipe Round / About a May-pole on a Holy-day." And Robert Greene's play *Scottish History of James IV* (1598) has the character Slipper dance a hornpipe at the end of act 2 "with a companion, boy or wench," and with buffoons at the end of act 4, scene 3. As they depart Slipper says, "Nay, but, my friends, one hornpipe further! A refluence backe, and two doubles forward! What! not one crossepoint against Sundayes?"

It is difficult to distinguish the solo from the group form in all of these references. The late sixteenth-century ballad "Our Jockye Sale Have Our Jenny" gives an account of a hornpipe at a wedding. While all are urged to dance, "and the first to break the stroke must pay the piper a penny," the leader calls out movements to individual dancers: "In with fut, Robsone! out with fut Byllynge / Torn rownde, Robyne! kepe trace Wylkyne!" The ballad's climax includes a "gambold," or tumbling flip. Whatever the relationships might be, these two early forms shared a comfortable coexistence in village life.

1650–1760. By 1680, dancing masters in England, especially Mister Isaac and Beveridge, began to create longways country dances to the distinctive syncopated 3/2 hornpipe tunes. Generally called "maggots" from the Italian *maggioletta*, meaning whim or delight, these were designed for assembly rooms, balls, and private patrons. Often named in honor of the dancing master, they can be found in John Playford's editions of *The Dancing Master* and Wright's *Compleat Collection of Celebrated Country Dances.*

Not all maggots are hornpipes, and distinguishing them from other triple-time country dances is difficult; their figuration is generally intricate. The inclusion of hornpipe steps is likely because minuet steps, and later waltz and polka steps, were used in country dances set to such tunes. Throughout the eighteenth century, "stepping" in social dancing was familiar in Scotland, and hornpipe stepping was used in country dances throughout the British Isles, although it was considered vulgar in the more select assemblies. While in vogue, a few hornpipe country dances migrated to France, generally with distorted rhythms, and were said by composer Jean-Philippe Rameau to exhibit more boisterousness and crudity than dancing finesse.

An important group of six "French-style" hornpipes, choreographed by the court master Mister Isaac and later Anthony L'Abbé, has survived in Feuillet dance notation. Five are couple dances and can be categorized as "social" dances, although the special occasions for their presentation, such as the monarch's birthday celebration, and their complex steps and rhythms indicate that they were probably performed for the enjoyment of others by high-level amateurs and professional dancers. The latest one, by L'Abbé (c.1725), is a theatrical solo for a male to the same music as the 1713 Isaac duet, *The Pastoral.*

These particular hornpipe dances use primarily the composed steps of the French ballet tradition. However, the actual step units of the dance are created by combining regular steps into a vocabulary unlike other dances of this type. Frequent use of hemiolas and other cross-rhythms also distinguishes the phrasing, and the impression is one of choreographic originality rather than definition of a specific dance type.

Here the 3/2 hornpipe rhythms are delightfully complicated by a typical hemiola pattern in the steps. For example:

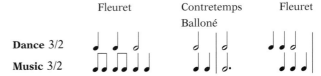

As the ballet tradition grew in the British Isles, so too the traditional step dancing evolved, including the hornpipe versions. Scottish Highland dancing extended the

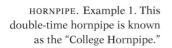

HORNPIPE. Example 1. This double-time hornpipe is known as the "College Hornpipe."

shuffles and beats of the feet to include ballet-influenced kicks, rockings, sheddings, shakes, balances, and *bourées.* Likewise, theatrical dance featured hornpipes with increasing popularity, the dancers embellishing the close stepping of the traditional form with technical and character contributions.

While any step dance, whatever its music, was often called a hornpipe, English playbills commonly distinguished the hornpipe as to the performer or character. "A Hornpipe by Tom Jones" was a specialty entertainment in the 1720s, and those plays with rural or Scottish themes often included hornpipes danced by both men and women.

Sailors' dances were familiar among other character or comic dances, but they were not associated with the hornpipe until after 1740. The dancer Yates, who frequently performed hornpipes, was suddenly billed at Drury Lane in May 1740 to perform "A Hornpipe in the Character of a Jacky Tar."

Nancy Dawson had a phenomenal success in John Rich's production of *The Beggar's Opera* in 1759 with a hornpipe entitled "By Desire," in act 3. This dance was unrelated to a sailor's character. The tune was really a jig, originally the Scottish "Who'll Come intae Ma Wee Ring," now known as "Here We Go Round the Mulberry Bush."

When David Garrick at Drury Lane enticed Dawson to move from Rich's Covent Garden Theatre in 1760, a special counter-attraction was presented by Rich. Dawson was replaced by one Mrs. Vernon, who danced to "New Hornpipe" composed by Thomas Arne. This hornpipe predates Arne's 1767 compositions, and was perhaps the first of the new generation of common-time hornpipes.

In *A Treatise on the Art of Dancing*, Giovanni Gallini reflects on the English hornpipe dances:

> They are no where so well executed. The music is extremely well adapted and the steps in general are very pleasing. Some foreign comic dancers, on coming here, apply themselves with great attention to the true study of the hornpipe, and by constant practice acquire the ability of performing it with great success in foreign countries, where it always meets with the highest applause, when masterly executed.   (Gallini, 1762)

1760–1900s. As the Royal Navy restored British glory during the mid-eighteenth century, the national security was seen to rest upon its ships, the "hearts of oak," and its sailors, "jolly tars." While hornpipes with no allusion to sailors are regularly billed, the association with the archetypal sailor Jacky Tar is clear by 1760. An interesting playbill from Drury Lane in May 1760 announced a "Hornpipe by a Sailor from *The Royal Sovereign*" (a ship of the royal fleet).

Although there is little reference to the hornpipe in the naval journals of the eighteenth century, the diary of a young Scottish woman traveling to the West Indies in 1774 tells us that "the sailors dance hornpipes and jigs from morning to night." The London dancing master G. Yates comments in 1829 *(The Ball)* on the perfection to which many English seamen can dance the hornpipe. Schoolboys destined for naval careers generally made a point of learning it, and it was included in nineteenth-century naval training.

John Durang, considered the first American dancer, was identified with the stage version of the "Sailor's Hornpipe" from his first appearance in the pantomimic dance about Jacky Tar ashore, *The Wapping Landlady*, in 1790. As early as 1780, at age twelve, Durang had learned "the correct style of dancing a hornpipe in the French stile" from the visiting French dancer Foussel, and made it his specialty. Hoffmaster, a prominent German musician in New York City, composed the music for "Durang's Hornpipe" in 1785. Durang's son Charles published what is considered to be an outline of the dance in his 1855 book, *The Ballroom Bijou.*

Each of the twenty-two steps takes one strain of the tune and the dance is at least partly decipherable by both traditional step dancers and theatrical tap dancers. The absence of nautical motifs, particularly for the upper body and arms, suggests that mimetic actions of the sailor's occupation, such as "Climbing the rigging" and "Land ahoy!" were introduced in varying degrees by different dancers throughout the nineteenth century.

Many new common-time hornpipe tunes were composed after 1760, most named after the dancers famous on English and American stages—Fisher, Aldridge, Miss Baker, Durang. The associated tunes are not traditional hornpipes but a theatrical development, just as the dances themselves were. The dance maintained its strong "stepping" influence, but the character became increasingly associated with the sailor until the "Sailor's Hornpipe," with its music taken from the "College Hornpipe" tune, became synonymous with the term *hornpipe* in the nineteenth century. The Jacky Tar hornpipe was the favorite character dance for boys at the Glasgow balls of 1864 and is still studied today in Scottish Highland dance schools to cultivate nimble foot movements and rapid changes of balance.

This mimetic character dance is far removed from the traditional hornpipe and from what was probably cultivated as the original step dance of real sailors. Hornpipe stepping continued to be essential to the country dancing master's curriculum, however, well into the nineteenth century.

In 1752, John McGill, the celebrated fiddler and southwest Scottish dancing master, wrote instructions for dancing hornpipes, jigs, and country dances. He indicated that the hornpipe contained sixteen steps. Hornpipes were danced as solos and in rows in northwest England's Westmoreland area. The dancing master taught a special step to each pupil, who regarded this as special property to be exhibited during the dance at the country assembly. There, all the dancers advanced down the room side by side in a row.

The solo stepping and the country dances coexisted in much the same way that the earlier solo and round forms once had. Welsh, Scottish, and English sources of the eighteenth and nineteenth centuries refer to hornpipes as part of the dancing at weddings, wakes, rural assemblies, and public balls. While the style of dancing was still associated with the vulgar, and considered taboo among the more formal social dance customs, the *Second Hardy Tune Book* (1811) describes country dance hornpipes as being "fashionable in London."

Hornpipe traditions continued to be cultivated among Canadian and New England settlers. Charles Durang (in his *Terpsichore*, 1847) includes among the fashionable Boston country dances the "Durang Hornpipe," to the same music as his father's celebrated solo.

The solo McGill hornpipe of 1752, John Durang's dance, and the dances cultivated in the fashionable country dance classes, can be related to both the high dance of Scotland and the stage hornpipe. But the native nineteenth-century hornpipe of the English countryside had more in common with the pure step dance that developed and remained in Ireland. At feasts, wakes, and on Saturday nights in village alehouses, men and women took turns stepping to the music of country fiddlers. Stepping shoes or light clogs were worn, and the favorite surface was the top of a large table, often soaped in Ireland. The tunes were identifiable from the audible pattern of the dancer's stepping—the mark of a good dancer—and nimble clatter was essential.

An account from nineteenth-century Nottinghamshire relates how women "would draw up their skirts short, and pull the back of the skirt forward between their legs, to show their feet and ankles." An account from the Worksop area relates how

> sometimes there would be a couple of dancers on the table. When one had gone through an arranged number of steps, he stopped, the other taking his place; and this was done so deftly that there was no break in the music whilst the change was made. The old fiddlers were hard to tire, and one "crowdy" with intervals "to wet his whistle," could keep it up for hours.

The Lancashire clog dance is probably the early Lancashire hornpipe, and the step and clog dance tradition in eastern North America evolved from this village style. The Irish hornpipe, while not indigenous, carries on this pure step-dance technique. In Ireland the hornpipe is distinguished from the jig by its duple time, and from the reel by the number of accents to the bar (the reel having one and the hornpipe two). A "single" is in 2/4 time, a ladies dance employing light shuffles and batters in an easy and graceful style. The "double" is in 4/4 time, and as a male dance exploits more difficult trebling steps with much drumming and grinding. The body and arms are kept still, and this trial of skill has been developed to competitive championship standards.

[*See also* Clogging; Jig; *and* Step Dancing.]

BIBLIOGRAPHY

Baskervill, Charles R. *The Elizabethan Jig and Related Song Drama.* Chicago, 1929.

Cohen, Selma Jeanne, ed. "There's None Like Nancy Dawson." *Dance Perspectives* 26 (Summer 1966).

Curti, Martha. "The Hornpipe in the Seventeenth Century." *Music Review* 40 (February 1979).

Dean-Smith, Margaret. "Hornpipe." In *The New Grove Dictionary of Music and Musicians.* London, 1980.

Durang, Charles. *Durang's Terpsichore.* Philadelphia, 1847.

Durang, Charles. *The Ball-Room Bijou.* Philadelphia, 1855.

Emmerson, George S. *Rantin' Pipe and Tremblin' String: A Social History of Scottish Dance Music.* London, 1971.

Emmerson, George S. *A Social History of Scottish Dance.* London, 1972.

Gallini, Giovanni. *A Treatise on the Art of Dancing.* London, 1762.

Gilchrist, Anne G. "Old Fiddlers' Tune Books of the Georgian Period." *Journal of the English Folk Dance and Song Society* 4.1 (1940): 15–22.

Marsh, Carol G. "French Court Dance in England, 1706–1740: A Study of the Sources." Ph.D. diss., City University of New York, 1985.

Moore, Lillian. "John Durang, the First American Dancer." In *Chronicles of the American Dance: From the Shakers to Martha Graham,* edited by Paul Magriel. New York, 1948.

JANIS PFORSICH

HOROSCOPE. Ballet in one act. Choreography: Frederick Ashton. Music: Constant Lambert. Libretto: Constant Lambert. Scenery and costumes: Sophie Fedorovitch. First performance: 27 January 1938, Sadler's Wells Theatre, London, Vic-Wells Ballet. Principals: Margot Fonteyn (The Young Woman), Michael Somes (The Young Man), Richard Ellis and Alan Carter (Gemini), Pamela May (The Moon).

Horoscope was one of the most important, serious, and successful collaborative works presented by the Vic-Wells Ballet in the 1930s. Lambert, who was interested in astrology, wrote the scenario, in which a man and a woman, with the Sun in the opposing signs of Leo and Virgo (who strive to keep them apart) are brought together by their mutual Moon sign, Gemini. The Sun signs were represented by two corps de ballet groups, the men the Followers of Leo and the women the Followers of Virgo.

Fonteyn, to whom the score was dedicated, was, as Ashton's muse, his choice for the woman's role. The man's was given to Somes, then being promoted to leading roles. The role of the Moon exploited May's purity of line in arabesque. The turbulent opening dance for the Followers of Leo and the final tableau, an architectural grouping of the Moon's attendants, crowned by the two lovers, reflected the continuing influence of Bronislava Nijinska on Ashton's work. But the pas de deux, as so often in his ballets, was an entirely personal creation, expressing both tenderness and passion in the lovers' interlocking *attitudes*.

Although Ashton had choreographed existing scores by Lambert (*Pomona* in 1930, *Rio Grande* in 1931), and Lambert had frequently arranged the music of other composers for Ashton, *Horoscope* was Lambert's first original composition written expressly for an Ashton ballet. The score, in nine movements, is sober without being ponderous, and most of it is eminently danceable. (Ashton found the "Saraband" overlong.) Fedorovitch had often designed for Ashton since his first ballet, *A Tragedy of Fashion*, in 1926. Her decor for *Horoscope* created an appropriate atmosphere of mystery from the very opening, with the drop curtain of the zodiac against a cloudy sky. The main setting and most of the costumes were in shades of gray, except for the red costumes for the Followers of Leo.

Although generally considered a successful work, *Horoscope* was short-lived; it was among the ballets whose scenery, costumes, and orchestral parts were abandoned in the Netherlands in the spring of 1940, when the members of the Vic-Wells Ballet had to flee before the Nazi invasion. It is the only work that was never restored to the repertory.

BIBLIOGRAPHY
Coton, A. V. *A Prejudice for Ballet*. London, 1938.
Vaughan, David. *Frederick Ashton and His Ballets*. London, 1977.

DAVID VAUGHAN

HORSCHELT FAMILY. German-Austrian family of dancers active in the late eighteenth and nineteenth centuries. Prominent members included Franz Horschelt, his daughters Karoline and Barbara, his son Friedrich, and Friedrich's son August.

Franz Horschelt (born 1760, died 1828), dancer, director, and ballet master. Franz made his name with the Koberwein theater troupe, especially as the partner of Katharina Koberwein, daughter of the troupe's director, whom Horschelt married. In 1797 Franz became director, actor, and ballet master at the theater of Count Kluszewski in Kraków, Poland. There he and his wife nurtured a family of artists: their elder daughter Karoline became a respected solo dancer at the Kärntnertor Theater in Vienna; their younger daughter Barbara (1801–1832) became a soloist in Munich, where she worked with her eldest brother, Friedrich.

Friedrich Horschelt (born 1793, died 1876), dancer, ballet master, and choreographer. Friedrich became the most famous member of the family. He began his performing career in 1810 at the Theater in der Leopoldstadt, Vienna. In 1815 he became ballet master at the Theater an der Wien. Count Ferdinand Pálffy, the theater's director, had a preference for spectacular shows, so Friedrich conceived the idea of choreographing ballets using large groups of children; he presented sixteen of these children's ballets in six years, until they were banned by imperial decree in 1821. Though imputing no blame to Friedrich, the decree responded to public concerns over the children's welfare. [*See* Viennese Kinderballett.]

In 1822 Friedrich joined the Munich Hof- und Nationaltheater, where he had the opportunity to develop his choreographic ideas with a professional ensemble. Although a few of his works revealed the influence of Jean Aumer, ballet master at the Hoftheater in Vienna during Friedrich's tenure at the Theater an der Wien, the ballets he choreographed in Munich generally developed in an original direction. In addition to his opera productions there, he choreographed twenty-four ballets, including *Portraits* and *The Mountain Goblin*, both of which used themes first essayed in his children's ballets.

His ability to draw poetry out of simple themes and to render gestures theatrically effective infused his 1823 work *Portraits*, set to music by Ignaz Moscheles. Structured as a *divertissement*, the work did not tell a story but rather depicted rustic life through character sketches: a rich tenant farmer and his family, a roguish peasant youth and pretty peasant girls, a bowlegged village barber, and an itinerant painter. This ballet survived longer than any other in the Munich repertory.

Friedrich's ability to organize space with masterfully arranged group dancing and to exploit the scenic quality of broad, billowing drapery infused his 1828 work *The Mountain Goblin*, set to music by Philipp Jakob Riotte and Friedrich Cramer. The full-length ballet, freely adapted from Johann Karl Musäu's *Rübezahl*, depicted a complicated narrative of a mountain goblin's abduction of a princess. It was revived the following year at the Kärntnertor Theater with Fanny Elssler and in 1831 at the Teatro alla Scala in Milan.

In 1829 Friedrich, along with his wife Babette Eckner (1803–1888), his sister Barbara, and five other dancers, were dismissed from the Munich theater. The public and the press vigorously protested the management's decision to allow the ballet to decline and demanded its continued support. Friedrich was called back in 1837 and over the next ten years contributed a few new ballets of his own while adapting successful Romantic ballets. His skillful leadership ensured the continuation of the troupe.

August Horschelt (born 1830, died 1887), dancer and teacher. August was the youngest of Friedrich and Babette's three sons. From 1847 to 1849 he trained in Munich and Paris. Over the next two years he gave guest performances in many cities, chiefly in the role of Albrecht in

Giselle. In 1851 he accepted a full-time engagement in Vienna, but an injury forced him to relinquish the post. After a lengthy convalescence he returned as first dancer and ballet master in Prague and in Stuttgart, where he staged the standard Romantic repertory. He married Caroline Brandstrub, a solo dancer in Darmstadt, and ultimately established himself as a teacher in Hamburg.

BIBLIOGRAPHY

Holland, Hyazinth. *Theodor Horschelt.* Bamberg, 1890.

Mlakar, Pia, and Pino Mlakar. *Unsterblicher Theatertanz: 300 Jahre Ballettgeschichte der Oper in München.* Wilhelmshaven, 1992.

PIA MLAKAR and PINO MLAKAR
Translated from German

HORSE BALLET. Part equestrian exercise, part dramatic spectacle, a horse ballet (Ger., *Rossballett, Karussell, Carossel*; Fr. *ballet de chevaux, carrousel, carroussel*) was a form of choreographed movement performed by knights on horseback that enjoyed special popularity during the seventeenth century. Claude-François Ménéstrier considered the horses' steps as "true dance figures, in harmony with the sounds and tunes which guide the horses during the ballet" (1682). The form consisted of a series of many different, more or less theatrical parts. Each of these parts had its own artistic development and continued to evolve independently of the horse ballet.

The first record of a horse ballet dates from 1606 when *Le Ballet à Cheval des Quatre Elements* was performed in Paris. In 1608 a "Ballo di persone a cavallo: La Giostra dei Venti" was staged in Florence, and in 1612 a *carrousel* was arranged at the Place Royale in Paris.

One of the first events of this kind of which we have a detailed description was *La Guerra d'Amore,* staged for Cosimo II de' Medici during the Florence Carnival season of 1615. A written description by Andrea Salvadori and engravings by Jacques Callot survive. According to these, a festive military procession marched into a huge oval that surrounded a stage. First the soldiers fought a mock battle on foot, while the riders flanked them. A feint tournament took place in which the groups formed elaborate figures, filling the elliptical space with rhythmic and geometric patterns. The foot soldiers then withdrew to the borders while the riders performed the figures of the quadrille (eight horses divided into groups of two). Finally the riders dashed out of the theater, gathering into the form of a huge tulip.

Such a performance required complex planning. Salvadori and Callot preserved sixteen figures of choreography for the foot soldiers and riders. Foot soldiers are indicated by points, riders by small ovals. Transitions between figures are shown by dotted lines.

The greatest of these feasts was *Il Mondo Festiggiante,* performed in 1661 in the Boboli Gardens of Florence on the occasion of the marriage of Cosimo III to Marguerite-Louise d'Orléans. This horse ballet was created and produced by Alessandro Carducci. The sun, the moon, the stars, and the earth (which was represented by allegorical figures of the four known continents) paid homage to the bride and bridegroom. A backdrop was constructed for the huge half-oval behind the palace, and a circle of obelisks was placed at the center. Groups of decorated coaches were surrounded by foot soldiers and a circle of riders. The terrace of the palace offered a perfect view of the huge ballet. Horse ballets were powerful symbols and the great Baroque sovereigns of France and Austria, including Louis XIV and Leopold I, vied with one another to produce the most ostentatious performances.

At the great *carroussel* of Paris in 1662, twenty groups and five hundred actors, all dressed in the same costly fashion, were guided from the Hôtel de Vendôme to an amphitheater built with posts and platforms near the Tuileries. In the procession, the king was cast as a Roman emperor, with members of the court in roles that reflected their status. Contests were organized, and on the second day there was a jousting competition. The formation comprised a combination of linear and circular patterns, with the participants creating circles and diagonal entrance lines on horseback.

The famous Viennese horse ballet, *La Contesa dell'Aria e dell'Acqua,* was performed in January 1667 on the occasion of the marriage of Leopold I to the Spanish infanta Margarita Teresa in the inner court square in Vienna. For centuries, it has been considered the greatest horse ballet in history, although, according to Hilde Haider-Pregler (1969), it was remarkable chiefly for the number of participants and the luxury of the costumes. Carducci was summoned from Florence to be producer and choreographer; Carlo Pasetti came from Ferrara to design the scenery. Only the poet Francesco Sbarra and the composers Antonion Bertali and Heinrich Schmelzer were in regular service to the Vienna court. Not surprisingly, the Viennese horse ballet showed a strong Italian influence.

The structure of the work was parallel to that of its Florentine predecessor; it had a parade of decorated coaches, a feint combat in the style of an opera, a tournament, a triumphal ceremony with the participation of the sovereign, and a dance of the horses. As in Florence, a construction at the Schweizertor provided for central structure; the square was surrounded by platforms. About fifteen hundred luxuriously dressed actors participated in the production.

After the decorated coaches representing the elements had circled the Burghof, the leading characters entered from a suspended cloud revealing the Temple of Eternity. Inside this cloud appeared a second, shining edifice; the whole construction was then lowered to the square. Led by a group of gentlemen-at-arms, grooms, trumpeters, and a "Roman Equerry," the emperor appeared, who, according to the printed program, "represents under the homage of all choirs his sublime genius, just as antiquity would have imagined him, as an earthly deity." His costume consisted almost exclusively of sapphires, emeralds, and diamonds, "the treasures of the whole world, submerged in a sea of silver." Speranza, the emperor's favorite horse, was similarly decked out.

The horse ballet was performed as the third part of the celebration. The figures were composed as follows:

1. Groups of eight rode at the side, with the emperor placed in the center group of four.
2. The center group then expanded to include six flanking riders.
3. A ring and two groups formed; four flanking riders performed the croupade (a dressage figure).
4. The ring changed to a square, and foot soldiers appeared.
5. Diagonal lines led out of the square formation.

HORSE BALLET. One of twelve etchings depicting an equestrian ballet performed at night, following a mock equestrian battle, in 1652 at an arena near the grand-ducal palace in Florence, Italy. The performance was in honor of Grand Duke Ferdinand II of Tuscany, Archduke Sigismund Frances, and Archduchess Anne of Tuscany. (Dance Collection, New York Public Library for the Performing Arts.)

6. A big ring and a small square formed with the emperor in the center.
7–11. Figures of a cup, a flower, and a figure eight formed within the ring, culminating in a double row with four horses performing the *capriole* (a leap in which the horse kicks out its hind legs).
12. A large star, composed exclusively of horses and riders, formed with the emperor in the center; four horses performed figures in front of the empress.

This splendid display also involved the participation of about two hundred professional musicians from the imperial court orchestra and other Viennese orchestras. Mythological and allegorical figures were represented by singers of the court choir.

This Viennese horse ballet epitomized the high Baroque festival with all its pomp and grandeur. It combined courtly traditions with the sumptuousness of Italian and French Renaissance feasts. Its sole purpose was to glorify the Austrian imperial court.

In the eighteenth century horse ballets lost some of the allegorical and theatrical aspects, along with the elaborate stage machinery. Events took place in indoor settings instead of city squares. An example of this is the *Frauen-Carossel* which took place at the Winter Riding School in Vienna in January 1743. It was arranged by Maria

Theresa, then archduchess of Austria. The important guests were invited to watch the quadrille ridden in the school. To allow the lower classes to see part of the spectacle, the archduchess made an extra circle at the Michaelerplatz. In March 1982, the *Frauen-Carossel* was revived during the dance festival, Tanz 82, at the Spanish Riding School of Vienna.

The *Kongress Karussell*, performed on 23 November 1814, was arranged by Emperor Francis II of Austria to mark the opening of the Vienna Congress. Present were the kings of Bavaria, Prussia, Württemberg, and Denmark, and the diplomats Péigord Talleyrand, Karl August von Hardenberg, Klemens Metternich, and Lord Castlereagh. The first part consisted of contests on horseback in which the participants galloped toward targets at which they aimed lances, darts, and pistols. All these games were ridden in quadrilles, accompanied by military music played by the best musicians of the city. The second part of the festivities consisted of a feint tournament.

Other *Karussells* took place in 1843 (in honor of Archduke Karl), 1853 (arranged by Franz Josef I for his royal guests from Prussia and Belgium), and 1880 (arranged by General Count Török). For this last event, the theme centered on the era of Emperor Maximilian I. This *Karussell* was repeated twice, and the net proceeds went to help the poor.

The last Viennese *Karussell* was performed on 21 April 1894. The subject was the wedding of Emperor Charles VI and Elisabeth Christine in which the two principals were represented by members of the contemporary high aristocracy. This event was unusual in that some civic officers and instructors of the Spanish Riding School participated. Like its predecessors, it featured quadrilles, a procession of coaches, and a feint tournament.

The performance featured 125 riders, fourteen coaches, four ordnances, and fifty pages. The *Karussell*s of the eighteenth and nineteenth centuries no longer depicted the present, but rather looked back to earlier traditions. They were performed in sixteenth-century costumes and were regarded as testaments to the longevity of the Habsburg dynasty.

The traditions of the early horse ballet are preserved at the world-famous Spanish Riding School in Vienna. Its existence was documented for the first time in 1572. According to the inscription, dating from 1735, at the court box in the riding school, its aims were "the education and exercise of the aristocratic youth and the training of horses for the art of riding and war." The famous white Lipizzaner stallions of the school are believed to have given their first public performance to music at the *Rossballett* of 1667. After the French Revolution and the Napoleonic wars, the Vienna school was the only one in Europe to train horses and riders in these advanced feats of *dressage*.

With the end of the monarchy after World War I, the survival of the school was threatened, as it was considered a relic of imperial rule. On 20 July 1920, however, the school gave a public performance to raise funds. Since then the Spanish Riding School has become an Austrian institution. Here the essential figures of the seventeenth- and eighteenth-century horse ballet can still be seen today. Groups of horses and riders perform choreographed figures in quadrille and pas de deux formations. Individual horses and riders perform leaps and acrobatic movements that require a strength and skill achieved only by years of training.

[*See* Barriera, Torneo, and Battaglia; Renaissance Fêtes and Triumphs. *For related discussion, see* Circus.]

BIBLIOGRAPHY

Gregor, Joseph. *Kulturgeschichte des Balletts*. Vienna, 1944.
Haider-Pregler, Hilde. "Das Rossballett im inneren Burghof zu Wien." *Maske und Kothurn* 15 (1969).
Handler, Hans. *Die spanische Hofreitschule zu Wien*. Vienna, 1972.
Oberzaucher-Schüller, Gunhild. "Vom 'Frauen-Carossel' Maria Theresias." In *Spanische Reitschule: Programme of "Tanz 82."* Vienna, 1982.
Sälzle, Karl. "Das Rossballett." In *Das grosse Welttheater: Die Epoche der höfischen Feste in Dokument und Deutung*, edited by Richard Allewyn and Karl Sälzle. Hamburg, 1959.
Vanuxem, Jacques. "Le Carroussel de 1612 sur la Place Royale et ses devises." In *Les fêtes de la Renaissance*, vol. 1, edited by Jean Jacquot. Paris, 1956.

RUTH SANDER

HORST, LOUIS (born 12 January 1884 in Kansas City, Missouri, died 12 January 1964 in New York), American pianist, composer, musical director, author, and editor. A major force in the development of American modern dance as a twentieth-century art form, Horst demanded high standards of excellence and considered intelligent decision making important in choreographing dance works. In his role as musical collaborator, his involvement was direct and constant. He saw the need to inject formality, discipline, and style into the work of the vigorous, expressionistic dancers who were to become the innovators of modern dance.

Horst's legacy was threefold: as a composer, he was an innovator in the creation of scores for dance works; as a dance educator, his philosophies and methods gave credibility to the field of dance; and as a critic, author, and editor, he helped support the artistic growth of dance artists by documenting this ephemeral art form with a discerning and critical eye. His genius was that of a visionary. He combined perception with tenacity in his dedication to modern dance, which lasted for almost fifty years.

Louis Horst was the son of Conrad Horst, a trumpet player, and of Carolina Nickell. His parents immigrated to the United States from Germany in 1882. Ten years later the family (including his older sister, May) moved to San Francisco, where his father joined the Symphony Society's orchestra. Horst grew up in a German-speaking household in which music was a way of life. He studied violin with John Josephs and John Marquand before completing his eight grades of public-school education; on leaving school he studied piano with Samuel Fleischman.

When he was eighteen Horst joined the musicians' union and supported himself as a pianist, specializing in ragtime in dance halls and gambling houses. He became a pit musician at the Columbia Theater, where he played violin for musical productions and piano for dramatic shows. He also worked with a concert trio and as an accompanist for violinists and singers. Horst married Bessie (Betty) Cunningham on 29 November 1909; they separated several years later.

In 1915, when the Denishawn company went to San Francisco on a Pacific Coast tour, Horst was asked to join as accompanist. Within months he became the company's musical director. The Denishawn School opened in Los Angeles that year, and Horst was named head of the music department. The school brought Horst into contact with Martha Graham in 1916, Doris Humphrey in 1917, and Charles Weidman in 1919. Together, these four were to become the dance revolutionaries of the 1920s and 1930s.

Horst had begun to analyze the relationship of music to dance with Ruth St. Denis in her "synchronic orchestra" of dancers. These experiments in musical visualization later influenced a trend toward a more abstract choreographic approach, developed more fully by Doris Humphrey. Throughout Horst's tenure at Denishawn he continued to study composition. After ten years he resigned to study composition at the conservatory in Vienna, Austria, but he was unhappy with the rigidly classical teaching there and returned to New York after nine months to join Martha Graham.

At the age of forty-three Horst began his most fertile period. His close artistic liaison with Graham began with her first New York City concert in 1926 and endured until 1948. He served as her accompanist, musical director, composer, and mentor during this seminal period of American dance history.

As Graham searched for a movement vocabulary, Horst matched her physical output with music that gave her work a modern edge and sophistication. According to Ernestine Stodelle (1964), "They dedicated themselves to the ideals underlying contemporary art: to express the inner conflicts, the dynamic rhythms and the stark realities of twentieth-century life." Graham's first choreography was challenged by the broken rhythms, unresolved dissonances, and changing dynamics in the scores by Paul Hindemith, Arthur Honegger, Zoltán Kodály, Erik Satie, Arnold Schoenberg, and Aleksandr Scriabin that accompanied her work. Modern music helped modern dance break away from the imitation common in ballet. Horst believed that physical expression in American dance needed to contain the same qualities explored by moderns in the other arts. He felt that tension and asymmetrical use of time and space in dance would parallel the new music's dissonance, mixed meter, and atonality.

Horst continued to influence future generations of choreographers by drawing from the best examples of contemporary music, theater, literature, sculpture, graphic arts, and film to deepen their understanding and scope as potential artists. These ideas grew from his experiences and collaborations with Graham.

The program for *Scène Javanaise* (1926) credits Horst as composer of a concert in Rochester, New York, given by Martha Graham and three student dancers. *Three Poems of the East* (1926) was his first composition written for Graham's choreography, followed in 1928 by *Fragments (Tragedy and Comedy)*, the first composition he finished after the choreography was completed. Horst composed *Chinese Poem* in 1928 for a solo danced by Graham. Horst and Graham spent the summer of 1930 in New Mexico, which inspired their masterpiece *Primitive Mysteries* (1931). The music, composed by Horst while Graham worked on the movement, consisted of a simple score for flute, oboe, and piano.

Chorus of Youth-Companions premiered in 1932 at the Guild Theater in New York. In 1933 *Chorus for Furies*, one section of *Tragic Patterns—Three Choric Dances for an Antique Greek Tragedy*, was presented on the opening bill of Radio City Music Hall, followed two months later by the completed work, which included *Chorus for Supplicants* and *Chorus for Maenads*. *Celebration* (1934) and *American Provincials—Act of Piety; Act of Judgment* (1934) continued to set examples of scores that supported but did not dominate the dance.

Robert Sabin (1953) wrote that Horst's main principles were "economy of instrumentation, functional relationship to the dance, harmonic appropriateness to the emotional scheme of the work, [and] rhythmic integration." The score for *Frontier* (1935), a solo that was to become a classic in American modern dance, has a clarity and simplicity that best exemplifies Horst's style. *Horizons* (1936) and *Columbiad* (1939) preceded the last Graham-Horst collaboration, *El Penitente* (1940). By this time Graham was deeply interested in creating a total dance theater.

During this musically productive period, Horst also established a precedent for the commissioning of scores from other composers for Graham's works. As her musical director, he influenced her decision to commission music by American composers Samuel Barber, Aaron Copland, Henry Cowell, David Diamond, Norman Dello Joio, Gian-Carlo Menotti, Wallingford Riegger, and many others. Although Horst's primary allegiance was to Graham, he generously served as accompanist and musical director for Helen Tamiris (1927–1930) as well as for Doris Humphrey and Charles Weidman (1927–1932), writing the scores for Weidman's *Japanese Actor 17th Century* (1928) and Humphrey's *Pleasures of Counterpoint No. 2* (1934). He also worked with Agnes de Mille, Ruth Page, Hans Wiener, Michio Ito, Adolph Bolm, Harald Kreutzberg, and others.

By 1952 Horst had written thirty scores for dance works, in later years writing pieces for Nina Fonaroff, Jean Erdman, Pearl Lang, Helen McGehee, Yuriko, and Gertrude Lippincott. He also worked on incidental music for the plays *Electra* (1932) and *Noah* (1935). From 1944 to 1950 he composed scores for five documentary films.

In 1928 Horst began to teach college-level courses on the choreographic process. He worked with actors at the Neighborhood Playhouse (where he continued to teach until his death), challenging the students' imaginations in their selection of movement within a dramatic context. Graham, also on the faculty, taught actors how to move; Horst designed studies to develop their personal vocabulary, giving them experience in using formal principles of composition with dramatic ideas. From these first years of teaching he developed his course called "Pre-Classic Dance Forms." In the 1930s he became music director for the Perry-Mansfield School of Theatre, continuing there for five summers and returning in 1946.

From 1934 to 1942, at the Bennington School of Dance in Vermont, Horst taught "Pre-Classic Dance Forms" and designed the courses "Modern Dance Forms," exploring sources for ideas in relation to the other arts, and "Music Composition for Dance." A growing number of students wanted to learn the technical skills of the leading modern dancers of the period while also finding choreographic voices of their own. Horst's "Pre-Classic Dance Forms" lent formality and discipline to the study of modern dance in its fledgling state while his second course in choreography, "Modern Dance Forms," fostered a solid philosophy that was a model of intelligence and aesthetic understanding of dance as a vital, ever-changing performing art. His students eventually held teaching positions in academic institutions throughout the United States, where these courses became part of many college programs of instruction.

Horst's popularity as a dance-composition teacher continued throughout the remainder of his life. He taught courses at Sarah Lawrence College (1932–1940), Teachers College, Columbia University (1938–1941), Mills College (1939), and Barnard College (1943; 1950–1951). He taught "Pre-Classic Dance Forms," "Modern Dance Forms," "Music for Dance," and a new course, "Group Forms" (in which students choreographed trios, quartets, and quintets) at the American Dance Festival at Connecticut College (1948–1964) and at the Juilliard School (1951–1964), institutions that became leaders in developing modern dance. His students included both traditional modern dancers and leaders of the Judson and postmodern movements.

In addition to his teaching and composition, Horst made a significant contribution to the growing public awareness of the New York concert scene. He seized every opportunity to assist lay people in understanding modern dance. In 1931 he became a member of the Dance Committee at the New School for Social Research, where he helped to inaugurate a lecture-demonstration series. From 1939 to 1942 he gave a lecture-demonstration series in dance composition at the Ninety-second Street YM-YWHA in New York. Seeing a need for a dance periodical devoted to critical review, in 1934 Horst founded *The Dance Observer*. He was its managing editor and a major contributor until his death. The magazine was devoted almost entirely to reviews and articles in support of modern dance and was dedicated to the advancement of dance as a recognized art form.

Horst's main passion was observing, nurturing, and supporting dance and its students. His personal taste in music was for Gustav Mahler and Richard Strauss, yet his dance students might hear him play a Handel saraband, a Mompou *cants magics*, or an occasional rag. As a conductor, his sensitivity to a composer's special qualities and to preserving an accurate tempo were his special gifts. His effortless wit became legendary in dance circles.

In 1955 Horst received the Capezio Award "for his unique contribution to the modern dance as composer, accompanist, teacher, critic and general force for progress." He was also awarded an honorary degree of Doctor of Humanities at Wayne State University, Ohio, in 1963. He was honored posthumously with the Creative Award of the American Academy of Physical Education on 7 May 1964.

Horst's published texts continue to be primary sources in the teaching of dance composition. *Pre-Classic Dance Forms* (1937) draws upon musical knowledge for formal principles of choreography. *Modern Dance Forms in Relation to the Other Modern Arts*, written with Caroll Russell (1961), explores content in dance by analyzing the components of modern art in movement studies that explore time, force, and space. It focuses on studies for the student in style and content, based on examples from art history and modern life.

[*Many of the figures mentioned herein are the subjects of independent entries.*]

BIBLIOGRAPHY
Dalbotten, Ted. "Louis Horst." Master's thesis, Columbia University, 1968.
Dalbotten, Ted. "The Teaching of Louis Horst." *Dance Scope* 8 (Fall–Winter 1973–1974): 26–40.
Dance Perspectives, no. 19 (1963).
Horst, Louis. *Pre-Classic Dance Forms*. New York, 1937.

Horst, Louis, with Caroll Russell. *Modern Dance Forms in Relation to the Other Modern Arts.* San Francisco, 1961.

Mazo, Joseph H. *Prime Movers: The Makers of Modern Dance in America.* New York, 1977.

McDonagh, Don. *Martha Graham: A Biography.* New York, 1973.

Pease, Esther E. "Louis Horst: His Theories of Modern Dance Composition." Ph.D. diss., University of Michigan, 1953.

Sabin, Robert. "Louis Horst and Modern Dance in America" (parts 1–4). *Dance Observer* (January–April 1953).

Sears, David, ed. "Louis Horst: A Centennial Compendium." *Ballet Review* 12 (Summer 1984): 77–98.

Soares, Janet Mansfield. "Musician Louis Horst, 1884–1964: His Influence on Concepts of Modernism in American Dance." In *Proceedings of the Twelfth Annual Conference, Society of Dance History Scholars, Arizona State University, 17–19 February 1989*, compiled by Christena L. Schlundt. Riverside, Calif., 1989.

Soares, Janet Mansfield. *Louis Horst: Musician in a Dancer's World.* Durham, N.C., 1992.

Stodelle, Ernestine. *The First Frontier: The Story of Louis Horst and the American Dance.* Cheshire, Conn., 1964.

ARCHIVES.   Dance Collection, New York Public Library for the Performing Arts, which includes in its holdings the Dalbotten and Pease manuscripts listed above.

JANET MANSFIELD SOARES

HORTON. From left to right, Esther Brown, Alvin Ailey, and Joyce Trisler in Horton's *Combata de Amor*, a Latin American style dance evoking tropical passions, set to the music of Les Baxter. Ailey and Trisler were two major choreographers to emerge from Horton's company. (Photograph by Constantine, Los Angeles; from the archives at Jacob's Pillow, Becket, Massachusetts.)

HORTON, LESTER (born 23 January 1906 in Indianapolis, Indiana, died 2 November 1953 in Los Angeles), American dancer, choreographer, teacher, and designer. In the richly creative period between the two world wars, when modern dance was coming into its own as an art form in the United States, most of the creative dance activity was centered in New York City. Horton did not follow this trend. Working alone in Los Angeles, he built an important body of work, which, along with that of his New York contemporaries, became one of the cornerstones in the development of American modern dance.

Horton grew up in Indianapolis, where his eclectic studies in dance included ballet, aesthetic dance, Denishawn, and Native-American dance. In 1929 he moved to Los Angeles, where he studied with and performed for his most influential teacher, Michio Ito. For several years Horton performed, taught classes in theatre and dance, and tried his hand at directing. He also developed his own teaching techniques, inspired by Ito and Denishawn and expanded through his gift for improvisation.

In 1932 the first group of Lester Horton Dancers appeared in a colorful repertory that included such exotic titles as *Voodoo Ceremonial* and *Allegro Barbaro*. Los Angeles critics were skeptical but encouraging. By 1934 Horton's group of handsome and polished young dancers was invited to perform in a series at the immense Shrine Auditorium. These well-attended programs drew many new students, attracted perhaps by the publicity for Horton's daringly erotic dance version of Oscar Wilde's *Salomé*. (Horton subsequently created five more versions of the theme.) One such student, the gifted Bella Lewitzky, was to enrich Horton's endeavors over the next fifteen years as the group's leading performer, as a master teacher of his technique, and as his co-choreographer. [*See the entry on Lewitzky.*]

In the especially productive period from the mid-1930s to the outbreak of World War II, Horton developed a splendid repertory for his company, moving from Native-American pageants *(Mound Builders, Rain Quest)* to dances of social and political import *(Dictator, The Mine, Terror, Ku Klux Klan)* combined with a sprinkling of satire *(Art Patrons, Flight from Reality)*. With his associate, William Bowne, Horton designed most of the highly theatrical costumes and sets, which, along with his choreography, won critical praise. The name Lester Horton was becoming synonymous with modern dance on the West Coast.

A highlight of this period was an invitation to choreograph *Le Sacre du Printemps* for the Hollywood Bowl in 1937. Bold and sensuous, Horton's *Sacre* brought considerable attention to him and to Lewitzky, who danced the leading role. In 1938 the Lester Horton Dancers appeared in San Francisco. That summer Horton

HORTON. From left to right, Carmen de Lavallade, James Truitte, and Lelia Goldoni in *Landscape of Longing*, the opening section of Horton's four-part *Another Touch of Klee*, set to a progressive jazz score by Stan Kenton. (Photograph by Constantine, Los Angeles, from the archives at Jacob's Pillow, Becket, Massachusetts.)

taught at nearby Mills College in Oakland, where he created *Conquest*, featuring Lewitzky and the young Merce Cunningham.

In the late 1930s, to provide employment for his dancers, Horton produced nightclub entertainments. Many of these works were of such high caliber that they could be used in his concert repertory. Horton lost many commercial opportunities, however, because he maintained a racially mixed company—the first in the United States. Between 1942 and 1953 he created dances for nineteen Hollywood films.

In the early 1940s Horton disbanded his concert group and devoted himself to commercial work. During this creatively fallow period he conceived of the idea of a theater-academy for dance, and with Bowne, Lewitzky, and her husband, architect Newell Reynolds, he launched plans for Dance Theater. Within months of the opening of the school in a tiny building in West Los Angeles, work began on converting the facility for evening use as a theater. Two years later, in May 1948, the first theater-academy for dance in the United States was officially opened. The program included Horton's fifth reworking of the Salomé theme and the brilliant duet *The Beloved*. Over the next two years he created eight new dances, ranging in subject matter from the Warsaw ghetto to the paintings of Paul Klee. Horton taught tirelessly. Wanting his dancers to be well-rounded artists, he required them to take classes of his design in choreography, music, costuming, stage design, and lighting.

Bowne left Dance Theater in 1949, and because of irreconcilable artistic differences with Horton, Lewitzky and

Reynolds left soon thereafter. With the help of his friend and publicist, Frank Eng, Horton reopened Dance Theater within a few months with a new repertory and a new star, Carmen de Lavallade. The next three years were the most challenging of Horton's career. He created numerous dances for the concert stage, expanded his commercial repertory, and undertook the codification of his training techniques. During this period he also created *To José Clemente Orozco*, which, like *The Beloved*, became a modern dance classic.

In March 1953 Horton's company performed at New York's Ninety-second Street YM-YWHA, where they won critical acclaim and received an invitation to perform at Jacob's Pillow. Unfortunately, Horton's many years of overwork, privation, and physical neglect were about to take their toll; eight months later, at the age of forty-seven, he succumbed to a fatal heart attack. Even thirty-five years after his death, three major dance companies that evolved from his influence were continuing to perform internationally (those of Bella Lewitzky, Joyce Trisler, and

HORTON. Lowell Smith and Cassandra Phifer in Horton's *The Beloved* (1961), staged for the Dance Theatre of Harlem in 1980. (Photograph © 1980 by Jack Vartoogian; used by permission.)

Alvin Ailey), and thousands of dance students throughout the United States were still studying his strong, clean, sensuous techniques.

BIBLIOGRAPHY

Bizot, Richard. "Lester Horton's *Salome*, 1934–1953 and After." *Dance Research Journal* 16 (Spring 1984): 35–40.

Perces, Marjorie B., et al. *The Dance Technique of Lester Horton.* Princeton, N.J., 1992.

Prevots, Naima. *Dancing in the Sun: Hollywood Choreographers, 1915–1937.* Ann Arbor, Mich., 1987.

Warren, Larry, et al. "The Dance Theater of Lester Horton." *Dance Perspectives*, no. 31 (Autumn 1967).

Warren, Larry. *Lester Horton, Modern Dance Pioneer.* New York, 1977.

LARRY WARREN

HŌSHŌ SCHOOL, one of Japan's five schools of *nō* dance-drama.

Overview. The Hōshō school claims direct descent from the Tobi-za, a fourteenth-century *sarugaku* troupe in Yamato (present-day Nara Prefecture). Because this troupe was led by Kanze-school founder Kan'ami's elder brother, who is known only by the title Hōshō-dayū ("Hōshō headmaster"), the Hōshō school is thought to represent the older of these *nō* traditions.

During the Muromachi period (1392–1490) the Hōshō troupe gave torchlit *nō* performances at Nara's Kōfuku Temple and Kasuga Shrine. As the Ashikaga shogunate fell, the Hōshō school first won the support of the Hōjō clan of Odawara, then that of Toyotomi Hideyoshi (1536–1598), and finally the patronage of the Tokugawa shogunate (1603–1867), under which it flourished. With the Meiji Restoration in 1868, Hōshō Kurō (original name Kurō Tomoharu; 1837–1917), headmaster of the school, worked with Umewaka Minoru (1828–1909) and Sakurama Banba (1835–1917) to prevent *nō* from dying out.

The seventeenth headmaster, Kurō Shigefusa (1899–1974), who also took the name Hōshō Kurō, took great pains to preserve the traditionally austere, spartan style for which the school is famous. Serious scholars no longer accept the idea that the Hōshō school developed the tradition of wearing simple, rather plain costumes and its reserved dancing style because it was poorer than other schools, which, more favored by the authorities, received gorgeous robes as gifts and vied with each other to stand out.

One of the notable aspects of the Hōshō school is its affiliated line of excellent supporting actors *(waki)*, including Hōshō Shin (1870–1944) and Hōshō Yaichi (1908–1985).

Hōshō Fusao (born 18 February 1920 in Tokyo), the son of Kurō Shigefusa, is the Hōshō school's eighteenth headmaster. Currently the leader of the Hōshō-kai troupe,

Fusao made his first stage appearance at the age of four as the child-ghost in the ever-popular *Sumidagawa* (The Sumida River), which was transformed by British composer Benjamin Britten into a musical drama entitled *Curlew River*. From his father and grandfather, Fusao inherited not only a passion for keeping the *nō* style pure but also a commitment to ensuring *nō*'s survival. Toward that end, he began traveling abroad to perform *nō* before foreign audiences in 1966, when he led a tour to the United States. That tour was followed by others—including tours to West Germany (1968) and to India (1971). In 1972 he performed at the Munich Olympics.

In 1971 Fusao was made chairman and in 1985 president of the Japan Nō Association; he is an instructor of *nō* at the Tokyo National University of Fine Arts and Music. His numerous awards include the Tokyo Performing Arts Festival Prix d'Honneur (1956) and Japan's Order of the Purple Ribbon (1989).

[*See also* Nō. *For discussion of other schools of* nō, *see* Kanze School; Kita School; Kongō School; *and* Konparu School.]

BIBLIOGRAPHY

Keene, Donald. *Nō: The Classical Theatre of Japan.* New York, 1966.

Kodansha Encyclopedia of Japan. Tokyo, 1983. See the entries "Hōshō School," "Kan'ami," "Nō," and "Sarugaku."

Komparu Kunio. *The Noh Theater: Principles and Perspectives.* Translated by Jane Corddry and Stephen Comee. New York, 1983.

Nishino Haruo and Hata Hisashi, eds. *Nō, kyōgen jiten* (Dictionary of Noh and Kyogen). 2d ed. Tokyo, 1988.

STEPHEN COMEE

HOUSE, CHRISTOPHER (Christopher Maxwell House; born 30 May 1955 in Saint John's, Newfoundland), Canadian dancer, choreographer, and director. Christopher House came late to dance, after earning a bachelor's degree in political science from the University of Ottawa in 1976. At age twenty-one, he began his studies of ballet and modern dance in Ottawa and continued at the dance department of York University in Toronto, where he attracted attention both for his dancing and for his early choreography. Upon graduating with a bachelor of fine arts degree in 1979, he immediately joined the Toronto Dance Theatre. In 1981, after the success of two early works for the company, *Toss Quintet* (1980) and *Schola Cantorum* (1981), House was appointed resident choreographer.

While continuing as one of Toronto Dance Theatre's most acclaimed performers, House produced a steady stream of new works, notably *Fleet* (1982), *Glass Houses* (1983), *Animated Shorts* (1984), *Schubert Dances* (1985), and *Handel Variations* (1987). These early dances did much to reshape the company's choreographic persona, moving the repertory away from the epic and allegorical pieces of its founding choreographers and toward compositionally formal, technically complex, and essentially abstract work. The musicality, sophistication, and broad accessibility of House's dances helped expand the company's audience and win it unprecedented international acclaim. In later works—*Fjeld* (1990), *Noli Me Tangere* (1991), *Early Departures* (1992), and *Encarnado* (1993)—House began to experiment with narrative content. His choreography became more overt in emotional content and rich in psychological nuance.

In recognition of his talent and his choreographic vision, House was appointed artistic director of the Toronto Dance Theatre in June 1994. He has enjoyed a fruitful relationship with Les Grands Ballets Canadiens both as a guest artist and as the choreographer of *Indagine Classica* (1985), *Jeux Forains* (1988), and *Agitato* (1992). His *Cafe Dances* (1993) for the National Ballet of Canada was also well received. He has taught extensively at universities and dance festivals in Canada and the United States and has won all of Canada's major choreographic awards.

BIBLIOGRAPHY
Crabb, Michael. "Reshaping a Vision." *Vandance International* (Fall 1992).
Citron, Paula. "Toronto Dance Theatre: Where the Past and Future Meet." *Dance Magazine* (March 1996).

MICHAEL CRABB

HOUSTON BALLET. Stability, both economic and artistic, characterize the Houston Ballet, one of very few regional companies in the United States that began with a founding board of directors, who then selected an artistic director. This unusual beginning was a result of the board's ability to "think big" in terms of finances and of its repeated exposure to performances by the Ballet Russe de Monte Carlo during the 1940s. Able to raise funds with comparative ease, the board members shared a dream of establishing a ballet company that would be Houston's own.

In 1955, the board established a school and selected Ballet Russe alumna Tatiana Semenova to teach and lay the foundation for a company. The task was beyond her. In 1967, another Ballet Russe alumna, Nina Popova, was made artistic director. Her vision fell short of the board's aspirations. Unpredictably, they then engaged American choreographer James Clouser, whose original works, sometimes with a Southwestern flavor, and whose use of a nonclassical vocabulary soon offended their conservative sensibilities. Finally, in 1977, they found an artistic director who shared their dream, Ben Stevenson. Since then, under his direction the ensemble has grown from twenty-eight to fifty-five dancers (whose term of contract has risen from thirty-two to forty-four weeks per year), and the company's annual budget has increased from $1 million to $11 million.

Stevenson's substantial background with the Royal Ballet and the London Festival Ballet has enabled him to set tasteful versions of the full-length ballets in the standard repertory, among them *The Nutcracker, Swan Lake, The Sleeping Beauty*, and *Coppélia*. To these he has added his own full-length treatments of *Cinderella, Romeo and Juliet, Le Papillon, Peer Gynt*, and *Alice in Wonderland*. By the late 1990s, his production of *Cinderella* was danced by twenty companies in addition to his own.

Although best known for staging full-length works, Stevenson has created many shorter works as well. One of them, *Three Preludes*, originally danced by the Harkness Youth Ballet, has also been acquired by a number of other ensembles.

Unlike those companies whose directors graduated from the New York City Ballet, the Houston Ballet has

HOUSE. Coralee McLaren and Christopher House, wearing costumes designed by Denis Joffre, in House's dance *Columbus* (1994), set to music by Michael J. Baker. The springy athleticism captured here is a trademark of House's highly musical choreography. (Photograph by Cylla von Tiedemann; used by permission.)

HOUSTON BALLET. Members of the company in Ben Stevenson's *Four Last Songs* (1980), set to the music of Richard Strauss. Scenery and costumes were designed by Matt Jacobs. (Photograph courtesy of the Houston Ballet.)

a limited number of Balanchine works. Instead, it has acquired a substantial output from leading British choreographers, among them, Frederick Ashton, Kenneth MacMillan, John Cranko, Christopher Bruce, Peter Wright, and Ronald Hynd. In keeping with the conservative nature of the company, most of its twentieth-century American choreographers are from an older generation. They include Jerome Robbins, John Butler, Paul Taylor, and Glen Tetley. A notable exception is company member Trey McIntyre.

The Houston Ballet's academy is a flourishing one, with handsome premises of its own. The company draws a majority of its dancers from the academy. Thus a healthy percentage comes from the American Southwest, a characteristic that adds openness and zest to the company's dance style and that combines effectively with the classical finesse imparted by Stevenson.

The Houston Ballet has an endowment of about $18 million, but its greatest endowment is the depth and polish of its repertory and the matching depth and versatility of its dancers. Throughout, the emphasis is on dramatic truth.

BIBLIOGRAPHY
Gladstone, Valerie. "Houston Ballet: Dance in the Heart of Texas." *Dance Magazine* (November 1994).
Hering, Doris. "What Next, Houston?" *Dance Magazine* (February 1968): 40.
Hering, Doris. "The Sweet Smell of Money." *Dance Magazine* (May 1970): 72–78.
Sandler, Ken. "Ben Stevenson and the Houston Ballet." *Ballet News* 2 (April 1981): 8.
Shelton, Suzanne. "Houston Ballet: Brainchild of a Community." *Dance Magazine* (February 1975): 48–53.
Stevenson, Larry. "Houston Ballet." *Dance Pages* 8 (Spring 1991): 22–24.

DORIS HERING

HOVING, LUCAS (Lukas Hovinga; born 5 September 1912 in Groningen), Dutch dancer, choreographer, and teacher. Best known for his long association with the Limón Dance Company and the roles created for him by José Limón, Lucas Hoving had an extensive modern dance career as a performer, teacher, and choreographer in Europe and the United States. After early dance studies in the Netherlands, he studied with Kurt Jooss at Dartington Hall in England and joined the Jooss Ballet in the late 1930s. He toured with Jooss until World War II caused the company to disband, then studied and performed with Martha Graham in New York while also performing at the Roxy Theater, until he went overseas for three years of military service.

Returning to New York in 1946, Hoving studied with Valerie Bettis and performed in Broadway shows, including *Beggar's Holiday* and *Bloomer Girl,* both choreographed by Agnes de Mille. He began working with Limón in 1949, originating roles that year in *La Malinche* and *The Moor's Pavane.* Remaining with the company until 1963, he created roles in Limón's *Concert* (1950), *Los Cuatro Soles* (1951), *Dialogues* (1951), *The Visitation* (1952), *Don Juan Fantasia* (1953), *The Traitor* (1954), *Symphony for Strings* (1955), *There Is a Time* (1956), *The Emperor Jones* (1956), *Blue Roses* (1957), *The Apostate* (1959), and *The Demon* (1963). In many of these works Limón set up a dramatic confrontation—often a moral struggle—between the tall, fair Hoving and himself.

Hoving also originated roles in Doris Humphrey's *Night Spell* (1951), *Fantasy and Fugue in C Major, Fugue in C Minor* (1952), *Ruins and Visions* (1953), *Airs and Graces* (1955), *Theater Piece Number 2* (1956), and *Dance Overture* (1957), while she was artistic director of the Limón company. He appeared in dances by Pauline Koner, including *The Visit* (1950) and *Amorous Adventures* (1951). During the 1950s Hoving collaborated with his wife, Limón dancer Lavina Nielsen, on several works.

Hoving directed and choreographed for his own troupe, Lucas Hoving and Dance Company, from 1961 to 1971. His most widely performed work is *Icarus* (1964), which has been danced by the Alvin Ailey American Dance Theater as well as by the Limón company.

Deborah Jowitt noted that especially when Hoving himself portrayed a Daedalus, the dance "suggested not only the relationship between a son and a stern, loving father, but the one existing between a young dreamer and a disillusioned one, between a poet and a practical man, between two lovers. Hoving's dance was modest, but it conveyed much" (*Village Voice,* 12 March 1970).

From 1971 to 1978 Hoving directed the Rotterdam Dance Academy and served as a dance consultant to the Dutch government. He has continued to assist the Limón Dance Company with revivals of Limón works and for a while was its artistic adviser.

Hoving moved to San Francisco in the early 1980s and remained active there, in demand as a teacher and choreographer. He returned to the stage in October 1984 to perform *Growing Up in Public,* an autobiographical solo created for him by Remy Charlip.

BIBLIOGRAPHY

McDonagh, Don, ed. *The Complete Guide to Modern Dance.* New York, 1976. The section on Hoving (pp. 185–187) includes a list of his choreographed works, 1950–1971.

Mindlin, Naomi. "José Limón's *The Moor's Pavane:* An Interview with Lucas Hoving." *Dance Research Journal* 24 (Spring 1992): 13–26.

Stahl, Norma G. "Lucas Hoving." *Dance Magazine* (August 1955): 44–45.

Zimmer, Elizabeth. "A Wizard Comes East." *Village Voice* (23 October 1984).

SUSAN REITER

HOWARD, ANDRÉE (born 3 October 1910 in London, died 18 April 1968 in London), English ballet dancer and choreographer. Howard was one of the founding choreographers of British ballet, along with Frederick Ashton, Ninette de Valois, and Antony Tudor. They created the majority of the dances for the early Rambert and Sadler's Wells companies. In her lifetime Howard made more than thirty ballets and worked for nearly every major ballet company in England.

Howard received most of her ballet training at Marie Rambert's studio in London, beginning in 1924. She also took advantage of holidays in Paris to study with the great Russian émigrée ballerinas Lubov Egorova, Olga Preobrajenska, and Vera Trefilova. She debuted in dances by Ashton and Rambert for the opera *The Fairy Queen* (23 June 1927), as one of the original members of the Ballet Club (later Ballet Rambert and since 1987 Rambert Dance Company). [*See* Rambert Dance Company.]

Although the critic Arnold Haskell cited the young Howard as a strong and charming dancer, she never became an exceptional performer. After spending six months with Colonel de Basil's Ballets Russes de Monte Carlo in 1933, she decided to become a choreographer. Through the 1930s she danced primarily in her own ballets. By the early 1940s she had retired from dancing.

While creating her first work, a recasting of Susan Salaman's *Our Lady's Juggler* (premiered on 29 October 1933), Howard also undertook to supplement the original costumes, initiating her subsidiary career as a designer, pursued intermittently throughout her life. On the tiny stage of the Mercury Theatre, Ballet Rambert's first home, Howard proved especially adept at using clever, economical designs with magical effect.

As a choreographer, Howard was masterful at uniting dance and melodrama with music, costumes, and decor to create an emotional aura. Observers often labeled her ballets feminine for the way in which they expressed the feelings of women, even though her female characters were often stereotypical and romantic. Howard's admirers characterized her special gift as sensitivity, while her detractors found her work banal. Critics often compared Howard with Tudor and Ashton, the contemporary choreographic geniuses. Like Tudor, she had a gift for expressing drama in movement without resorting to mime. Her kinship with Ashton lay in her ability to use pure dance to evoke mood and atmosphere.

Howard's best ballets from the 1930s were *Death and the Maiden* (1937) and *Lady into Fox* (1939). *Death and the Maiden,* a small, delicate work set to the slow movement from Schubert's D Minor Quartet, made its impact by virtue of its simple expressive qualities. Howard herself danced the role of the Maiden in an interpretation that, in

HOWARD. *Lady into Fox* (1939), set to music by Arthur Honegger, was based on David Garnett's novel of the same title. Sally Gilmour is seen here in the role of the Lady, which she created, with Walter Gore in the part of the Husband. Scenery and costumes were designed by Nadia Benois. (Photograph by Roger Wood; used by permission.)

the opinion of some observers, has never been equaled. The work is still performed today.

Lady into Fox was Howard's first dance based on a strong plot, an adaptation of a David Garnett novel; the ballet established her as an important choreographer. The talents of Sally Gilmour, as the Victorian wife who is transformed into a vixen, and the sets and costumes of Nadia Benois contributed greatly to the success of the work. [*See the entry on Gilmour.*]

In 1940, Howard ventured to New York with Antony Tudor, where she staged and danced in *Death and the Maiden* and *Lady into Fox* for the debut season of Ballet Theatre. Her ballets were not particularly well received, and Howard returned to London. There she began work immediately on what is generally considered her masterpiece, *La Fête Étrange*, which was premiered 23 May 1940 by the London Ballet.

La Fête Étrange was Howard's most poetic mood ballet or *ballet d'atmosphere,* based on an episode from the novel *Le grand Meaulnes.* Critics commended the blending of Howard's choreography, Sophie Fedorovitch's designs, and Gabriel Fauré's music as a triumph of Diaghilev's aesthetic, creating a potent atmosphere of winter melancholy and adolescent heartbreak. *La Fête Étrange* has been in the ballet repertory in England intermittently since its creation.

Howard's first work for the Sadler's Wells Ballet, *Le Festin de l'Araignée* premiered 20 June 1944 but was not a success. Its depiction of insect life was overly realistic, and its dances were weak.

In 1946, Howard made a neoclassical ballet, *Assembly Ball,* for the Sadler's Wells junior company, the Theatre

Ballet. *Assembly Ball* was rated merely pleasant. Many critics deemed *Mardi Gras,* also made for Sadler's Wells in 1946, to be her best work to that time, both for its choreographic invention and for its fascinating, pervading sense of evil and doom.

Through the 1940s and 1950s, Howard continued to compose both light, charming ballets and dramatic works with tragic themes. Her dances from this period include *The Sailor's Return* for Ballet Rambert (premiere, 2 June 1947); like *Lady into Fox*, this depended for its success largely on the virtuosic performance of Sally Gilmour. *A Mirror for Witches* was her second ballet for the Sadler's Wells main company (premiere, 4 March 1952); her last was *Veneziana* (premiere, 9 April 1953), a *divertissement* to music from Donizetti operas. *Veneziana*'s most outstanding feature was Sophie Fedorovitch's designs, her last before her accidental death.

From time to time during Howard's career, she returned to the stage in mime roles. In the late 1940s and early 1950s, she played the witch in *Selina,* a spoof of Romantic ballet conventions which she choreographed for Sadler's Wells in 1948. In the Royal Ballet's 1960 revival of Ashton's *Cinderella,* Howard took the role of the timid Stepsister, a character she had invented for her own ballet version for Ballet Rambert (1935). Howard's last major work, *The Tempest* (June 1964), was a contribution to the quatercentenary of Shakespeare's birth, staged for the London Dance Theatre.

BIBLIOGRAPHY

Beaumont, Cyril W. *Supplement to Complete Book of Ballets.* London, 1942.
de Zoete, Beryl. *The Thunder and the Freshness.* New York, 1963.

Franks, A. H. *Twentieth-Century Ballet.* New York, 1954.

Gilmour, Sally. "Remembering Andrée Howard." *Dance Research* 2 (Spring 1984): 48–60.

Pritchard, Jane. "The Choreography of Andrée Howard: Some Further Information." *Dance Chronicle* 15.1 (1992): 77–87.

Sorley Walker, Kathrine. "The Choreography of Andrée Howard." *Dance Chronicle* 13 (Winter 1990–1991): 265–358.

TULLIA LIMARZI

HOYER, DORE (born 12 December 1911 in Dresden, died 31 December 1967 in Berlin), German dancer. Hoyer, a headstrong and tireless advocate of German interpretive (or expressionist) dance, was a solitary person whose solitude gave her dancing a special quality. She began her dance and rhythm training at the Hellerau-Laxenburg School in Dresden in 1927, passing the examination for dance teachers. She then studied interpretive dance with Gret Palucca in Dresden. After a short engagement as a dancer in Plauen, in 1933 she appeared in her first solo dance evening in Dresden, attracting attention through the intensity of her dramatic expression. She began her career at a time when interpretive dance had long since lost its revolutionary force and was becoming an instrument for Nazi propaganda.

For a short time Hoyer worked as a ballet mistress in Oldenburg, but in 1935 she returned to Dresden and became a member of Mary Wigman's dance group; she also taught from time to time in Wigman's school. After engagements in Berlin and Graz, she took over the former Wigman School in Dresden after World War II and formed her own dance group. The performance of a group cycle, *Tänze für Käthe Kollwitz,* made the small ensemble famous. Hoyer, however, was too much a solo dancer to be able to work as a group leader, and she left to continue her work alone.

After World War II, interpretive dance in Germany declined, victim to a renaissance of classical dance. Hoyer was able to continue giving dance evenings, however, and from 1949 to 1951 she was the director of the Hamburg State Opera Ballet, but audiences found her dancing too strenuous, contemplative, and dramatic. In the 1950s she had greater success in other countries than in her native land. She gave a number of guest performances in South America and worked with the ballet of the Teatro Colón in Buenos Aires; in 1957 she made her debut with the American Dance Festival at Connecticut College. Her last major successes in Germany were a portrayal of the Victim in Mary Wigman's version of *The Rite of Spring* in Berlin in 1957 and her own choreography for the production of Arnold Schoenberg's opera *Moses und Aron* in Berlin in 1959.

In 1966 Hoyer gave her last dance evening. Having no school of her own, she fell on hard times financially, while as a dancer she was out of artistic fashion. She committed suicide in 1967.

Although much younger than Mary Wigman, Hoyer had the same intense power of expression. Her dancing was characterized by expressive, precisely calculated, tension-laden movements, with particular strengths in mime and gesture, and a profound feeling for movement symbolism; the content of her dances often involved religious and cult themes. Her most noted dances included the "Spinning Dance" from Maurice Ravel's *Boléro* (1937), the *Biblical Figures* cycles (1942), *South American Travels* (1953–1954), and *Gesichte Unserer Zeit* (1962).

BIBLIOGRAPHY

Forster, Marianne. "Reconstructing European Modern Dance: Bodenwieser, Chladek, Leeder, Kreutzberg, Hoyer." In *Dance Reconstructed,* edited by Barbara Palfy. New Brunswick, N.J., 1993.

Koegler, Horst. "Introducing Dore Hoyer." *Dance Magazine* (August 1957): 24–25.

Luley, Waltraud. "Dore Hoyer: An Attempted Portrait." *Ballett International* 11 (February 1988): 4–13.

Müller, Hedwig, et al. *Dore Hoyer: Tänzerin.* Cologne, 1992.

Peters, Kurt. *Dore Hoyer* (in German). Hamburg, 1964.

Tanzdrama 4 (1991). Issue devoted to Hoyer, with articles by Hoyer and others.

HEDWIG MÜLLER
Translated from German

HUGO, JEAN (born 19 November 1894 in Paris, died 21 June 1984 in Lunel, France), French painter and stage designer. The great-grandson of poet and writer Victor Hugo, Jean Hugo was virtually a self-taught artist; at the age of nine he began to draw and paint in watercolor as well as write poetry and essays. As a young man, he studied literature and became proficient in ancient and modern languages.

While he was studying at the University of Paris, Hugo made constant visits to the Louvre and other galleries, especially those that were exhibiting modern art. In 1917 he became acquainted with a group of artists led by Guillaume Apollinaire, and including Jean Cocteau, Erik Satie, and Georges Auric, who were revolutionizing various art forms. Through them, Hugo became friends with other artists and composers, such as Pablo Picasso, Darius Milhaud, and the painter Valentine Gross, whom he married in 1919.

Gross became an important influence on Hugo's painting, as well as on his work in the theater. Her help and encouragement first led him to create for ballet when he designed the masks and costumes in *Les Mariés de la Tour Eiffel* for Les Ballets Suédois at the Théâtre des Champs-Élysées in 1921. This fantasy by Jean Cocteau had choreography by Jean Börlin, scenery by Irène Lagut, and music by no fewer than five composers: Georges Auric, Darius Milhaud, Francis Poulenc, Germaine Tailleferre, and Arthur Honegger. Hugo's costumes had a great theatrical quality; they wittily exaggerated the fashions of 1900.

Also in 1921, Hugo designed the sets and costumes for Cocteau's choreographic production of *Roméo et Juliette* for Comte Etienne de Beaumont's Soirées de Paris. Here all was black, but white or colored calligraphic lines outlined the costumes and details in the sets. This elimination of all superfluous detail, and the use of body tights, was the beginning of a new approach to stage design, especially with regard to ballet.

Through his paintings, Hugo found a form of twentieth-century romanticism that made him one of the key figures in the development of stage design. Although he was responsible for many notable productions in France, he did not return to ballet until 1935, when he designed Bronislava Nijinska's *Les Cent Baisers* (with scenario by Boris Kochno based on Hans Christian Andersen's "The Swineherd" and music by Frédéric d'Erlanger) for Colonel de Basil's Ballets Russes at Covent Garden. The set, like Hugo's paintings, was done in simple washes, depicting a Tudor mansion surrounded by trees. Although the costumes were Tudor in style, they were slashed and simplified to give freedom of movement.

Hugo applied the same treatment to the only other major ballet he designed, Roland Petit's *Les Amours de Jupiter* for Les Ballets des Champs-Élysées in 1946. In this work, with a scenario by Kochno and music by Jacques Ibert, the five scenes for each of Jupiter's metamorphoses had the simple clarity of ancient Greek murals. Their sun-baked colors complemented the dancers, who wore all-over tights mainly in pastel shades touched with fragments of brighter color.

Although Hugo designed few ballets, his contribution to the art of ballet design is great, especially in his simplification, his use of color, and his introduction of tights, which freed the body and clarified movement.

BIBLIOGRAPHY
Cogniat, Raymond. "Jean Hugo, décorateur théâtral." *L'Œuvre: Revue internationale des arts du théâtre* 32 (1924–1925): 78–80.
Obituary. *Dance and Dancers* (September 1984).

PETER WILLIAMS

HULA. The dance known as *hula* was developed in the Hawaiian Islands by their original Polynesian settlers, who migrated there by outrigger canoes from southeastern Pacific islands beginning in the fifth century CE. Two-way voyaging continued for several centuries, during which seafarers brought domesticated animals, plant seeds and cuttings, and all the various cultural necessities for life on uninhabited islands. Other ethnic groups have come to Hawaii since the first European contact in 1778: Western (mainly British, American, and Portuguese) and Asian (mainly Chinese, Japanese, and Filipino) settlers have contributed to Hawaii's present multicultural dance culture. The hula, however, has remained largely uninfluenced by other dance traditions.

The origins of hula are shrouded in legend. One story describes the adventures of Hi'iaka, who danced to appease her fiery sibling, the volcano goddess Pele. The Hi'iaka epic provides the basis for many present-day dances.

In the pre-European period, hula was closely related to religious practices. Extant dances accompanied by the *pahu* (sharkskin-covered log drum, used in temple ceremonies) appear to be the most sacred, dedicated to the gods. As late as the early twentieth century, ritual and prayer surrounded all aspects of hula training and practice. Teachers and students were dedicated to Laka, goddess of the hula, and appropriate offerings were made regularly.

American Protestant missionaries who arrived in 1820 introduced Christianity and prevailing Western values. With the support of converted high-ranking chiefs, they denounced and banned the hula as heathen. Declining numbers of hula practitioners therefore taught and performed clandestinely through the mid-nineteenth century.

The reign of King David Kalākaua (1874–1891) was a transitional phase for Hawaiian performing arts. Over the objections of christianized Hawaiians and non-Hawaiians, known experts were gathered at his court and encouraged to practice the traditional arts. In this favorable era, hula practitioners merged Hawaiian elements of poetry, chanted vocal performance, dance movements, and costumes to create a new form, the *hula ku'i* (*ku'i* means "to combine old and new"). The *pahu* appears not to have been used in *hula ku'i*, evidently because its sacredness was respected by practitioners; the *ipu* (made from a gourd, *Lagenaria sicenaria*) was the indigenous instrument most closely associated with *hula ku'i*.

Interest in older chant-accompanied hula waned in the early twentieth century. Newer song-accompanied hula captured the attention of tourists and Hollywood film audiences, which contributed to a growing entertainment industry in Hawaii. Concessions to non-Hawaiian audiences included English-language lyrics, less allusive pictorial gestures, and sex appeal added by emphasized hip movements, removing the hula from its former religious context. Perhaps the most enduring images of hula in the 1930s and 1940s are those of dancers in cellophane skirts and seductive satin sarongs. Once again, practitioners of the older hula perpetuated it quietly in private circles.

A resurgence of ethnic pride has raised interest in pre-*ku'i* performing arts since the early 1970s. Chant-accompanied hula has been revived, and new dances are choreographed in the older style, eclipsing the song-accompanied form in popularity, especially among younger Hawaiians. Contemporary practitioners divide hula into *hula kahiko* ("ancient hula"), comprising older chant-accompanied dances, and *hula ʻauana* ("modern hula"), comprising newer song-accompanied dances. This betrays a poor understanding of the direct continuity of textual, musical, and movement elements from the old form through the *hula kuʻi* into the new form. Many texts are extant in chanted and sung versions.

Hula is now highly visible, especially in two annual competitions. At the Merrie Monarch Festival each April on the island of Hawaii, male and female groups compete in *hula kahiko* and *hula ʻauana* categories, and solo female dancers vie for the title Miss Aloha Hula. The King Kamehameha Traditional Hula and Chant Competition each June on Oahu features competitions for male, female, and mixed groups in *hula kahiko* and *hula ʻauana*. Popularity also derives from the introduction by younger choreographers of faster and flashier movement designed to maintain visual interest, since audiences (and, indeed, many dancers) no longer understand the Hawaiian-language texts.

The term *hula* refers to movement and gestures. Hula, however, cannot be performed without *mele* ("poetry"), the most important component. *Mele* are records of cultural information ranging from sacred *mele pule* (prayers) and *mele inoa* (name chants, many for chiefs) to topical *mele hoʻoipoipo* (love songs) and *mele ʻāina* (songs praising the land); the type of *mele* used is one way of classifying the dances. Allusion is greatly valued in the poetry,

and hula gestures are a secondary level of abstraction; they do not tell the entire story but rather interpret key aspects of the *mele*. The concept of hula therefore involves *mele* and its recited realization in performance (there was no concept of "music" in Hawaiian culture).

Older chant-accompanied dances may be performed in a standing or sitting position. In standing dances, performers are divided into *ʻōlapa*, who execute the dance movements, and *hoʻopaʻa*, who chant the text and provide the percussive instrumental accompaniment.

While hand and arm gestures interpret the text, named foot motifs are executed continuously as a movement ostinato. Some motifs are *kaholo* (stepping side to side), *ʻuwehe* (stepping in place, then lifting and dropping heels), and *ʻami* (circular pelvic shifts and tilts). The *kāwelu* (stepping forward and back with one foot) was introduced with the *hula kuʻi*. A close correspondence exists between foot motifs and *ipu* and *pahu* rhythmic patterns: change in one is normally simultaneous with change in the other, often at the start of a new phrase, at a narrative juncture, or in the textless interlude between verses of the *mele*. The organization of foot motifs by phrase or verse in song-accompanied *hula kuʻi* remains conceptually the same as in older hula, despite the replacement of *ipu* and *pahu* accompaniment by guitar and ukulele.

Performers in sitting dances are simultaneously musicians. They perform gestures while chanting and accompanying themselves with percussive instruments. The most commonly used instruments are the *ʻuliʻuli* (feather-decorated gourd rattle), *pūʻili* (split bamboo rattle), *ʻiliʻili*

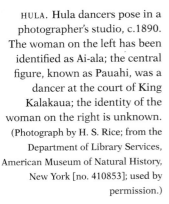

HULA. Hula dancers pose in a photographer's studio, c.1890. The woman on the left has been identified as Ai-ala; the central figure, known as Pauahi, was a dancer at the court of King Kalakaua; the identity of the woman on the right is unknown. (Photograph by H. S. Rice; from the Department of Library Services, American Museum of Natural History, New York [no. 410853]; used by permission.)

HULA. The revived interest in Hawaiian traditional arts since the 1970s has generated a number of troupes that perform hula in theatrical settings. Here, two dancers perform a *ka pa hula*. (Photograph © 1989 by Linda Vartoogian; used by permission.)

(waterworn stone pebbles, two in each hand, played in a manner similar to castanets), and *kālaʻau* (sticks).

The following proverb, used by hula practitioners, is a powerful cultural sanctioning of stylistic and choreographic differences that distinguish subtraditions of hula:

ʻAʻohe i pau ka ʻike i ka hālau hoʻokahi.
(All knowledge is not contained in only one school.)

Several major surviving subtraditions can be attributed to a handful of practitioners who maintained their knowledge into the 1960s and 1970s. They are responsible for the survival of older chant-accompanied hula into the 1980s and 1990s and are finally being accorded a recognition they have long deserved.

Iolani Luahine (1915–1978), trained by her aunt Keahi Luahine (1877–1937), earned fame as a performer of chant-accompanied hula; she was recognized in 1947 by modern dancer Ted Shawn as "an artist of world stature." She was featured in two documentary films (1960, 1976) and several television programs. She passed her knowledge to her niece, Hoakalei Kamauʻu (born 1929).

Mary Kawena Pukui (1895–1986) was trained along with her adopted sister Patience Wiggin Bacon (born 1920) by Keahi Luahine. Both were also trained by Joseph Ilalaole (1873–1965) of Puna, Hawaii. Pukui was most active as a scholar, writing three important papers on hula (reprinted in Barrère et al., 1980). Her knowledge, a rare combination of experience and scholarship, has made her one of the most significant living resources on Hawaiian culture. Pukui passed her repertory to her daughter, Pele Pukui Suganuma (1931–1979), but Bacon has been the sole practicing link to Keahi Luahine.

Eleanor Hiram Hoke (1930–1983) was trained by her adopted grandmother Keaka Kanahele (1881–1940). Hoke taught many of her traditions to Edith McKinzie, who is known today primarily as a scholar and teacher of chant. Hoke was, however, featured in one documentary teaching film (1963).

(Emily) Kauʻi Zuttermeister (1908–1994) is the primary student of Pua Haʻaheo (1886–1953), a dancer-chanter of Oahu who taught the Kauai Island repertory. Zuttermeister was the first hula master honored by the National Endowment for the Arts with the National Heritage Fellowship in 1984. Zuttermeister's traditions are being carried on by her daughter Noenoelani Zuttermeister Lewis.

Edith Kanakaʻole (1913–1979) was trained by her mother Mary Kanaele (c.1900–c.1955) in a Hawaii Island tradition of dances especially relating to the goddess Pele. Their emphatic dance style is famed for its low bent-knee stance. Kanakaʻole passed her knowledge to her daughters Pualani Kanakaʻole Kanahele and Nālani Kanakaʻole, who were honored by the National Endowment for the Arts with the National Heritage Fellowship in 1993.

In the revival of Hawaiian performing arts in the 1970s, one of the most influential figures has been Maʻiki Aiu Lake (1925–1984), whose primary teacher was Lokalia Montgomery (1903–1978), a student of Mary Kawena Pukui. Lake, a teacher of *hula ʻauana* since 1948, took the unprecedented step in 1972 of training teachers in *hula kahiko*. Within three years, thirty-nine students graduated as *kumu hula* (hula teacher); their groups dominated hula competitions in the mid-1970s until other young teachers professing *hula kahiko* appeared. The status of Lake's teachers was considerably enhanced by her institutionalized sanction, as well as by the success and popularity of their dancers. In the 1990s dance troupes are largely groups of anonymous individuals in the shadow of their teacher's reputation; from these ranks, however, will come teachers of yet another generation to perpetuate the hula.

[*See also* Music for Dance, *article on* Oceanic Music.]

BIBLIOGRAPHY

Barrère, Dorothy B. et al. *Hula: Historical Perspectives.* Honolulu, 1980.

Buck, Elizabeth. *Paradise Remade: The Politics of Culture and History in Hawaiʻi.* Philadelphia, 1993.

Kaeppler, Adrienne L. *Hula Pahu: Hawaiian Drum Dances.* Vol. 1. *Haʻa and Hula Pahu: Sacred Movements.* Honolulu, 1993.

Stillman, Amy Kuʻuleialoha. "Bibliography [of Hula]." In *The Hula*, edited by Jerry Hopkins. Honolulu, 1982.

Stillman, Amy Kuʻuleialoha. "The Hula Kuʻi: A Tradition in Hawaiian Music and Dance." Master's thesis, University of Hawaii, 1982.

Stillman, Amy Kuʻuleialoha. "Competition Hula: An Index of Mele and Hālau in the King Kamehameha Hula Competition (1982–1995) and the Merrie Monarch Hula Competition (1980–1995)." Typescript, University of Hawaii Library, 1996.

Stillman, Amy Kuʻuleialoha. "Hawaiian Hula Competitions: Event, Repertoire, Performance, Tradition." *Journal of American Folklore* 103 (forthcoming).

Takamine, Victoria Holt. "The Hula 'Āla'apapa: An Analysis of Selected Dances and a Comparison with Hula Pahu." Master's thesis, University of Hawaii, 1994.

Tatar, Elizabeth. "Annotated Bibliography [of Hawaiian Music]." In *Hawaiian Music and Musicians: An Illustrated History*, edited by George S. Kanahele. Honolulu, 1979.

Tatar, Elizabeth. *Nineteenth-Century Hawaiian Chant*. Honolulu, 1982.

Tatar, Elizabeth. *Hula Pahu: Hawaiian Drum Dances. Volume II. The Pahu: Sounds of Power*. Bishop Museum Bulletin in Anthropology 3. Honolulu: Bishop Museum Press, 1993.

FILMS. *Hula Hoʻolauleʻa* (1960). *ʻUla Nōweo* (1963). *ʻIolani Luahine: Hawaiian Dancer* (1976). *Hawaiian Rainbow* (1987). *Kumu Hula: Keepers of a Culture* (1989). *Kodak Hula Show* (1993). *Hula: The First 30 Years, Merrie Monarch Festival* (1994). *Then There Were None* (1995).

AMY KUʻULEIALOHA STILLMAN

HUMPBACKED HORSE, THE. *See* Little Humpbacked Horse, The.

HUMPHREY, DORIS (born 17 October 1885 in Oak Park, Illinois, died 29 December 1958 in New York City), dancer and one of the founders of American modern dance. Doris Humphrey decided early on a career, and from before her high school graduation until her death she was continuously active as a dancer, choreographer, company director, teacher, and theoretician. She created more than ninety solo and group dances, headed three dance companies, wrote numerous articles and an important book on dance composition, and provided the modern dance (as it was called in her day) with a steadfast example of courage, optimism, and uncompromising ideals.

Humphrey's parents, the offspring of Congregational ministers, lived on the fringes of theater and the arts. While Humphrey was growing up, her father managed a hotel for transients in downtown Chicago, where she met an assortment of entertainers who formed the clientele. Her mother, a strong-minded puritan with a musical education, supplemented the family finances by giving piano lessons and playing in small ensembles at summer resorts. Doris, the only child, was sent to the progressive Francis W. Parker school and began dance lessons there with Mary Wood Hinman, as well as taking music lessons from her mother. Hinman was noted for her openness to new pedagogical ideas, and by the time Humphrey completed her studies in Hinman's studio, she had learned interpretive, folk, clog, and some basic ballet dancing. She was assisting Hinman and giving some private classes of her own by the time she was eighteen.

Following her graduation from the Parker school in 1913, the Palace Hotel was sold, leaving her father without a job. Mrs. Humphrey decided that she and her daughter should open a dancing school to support the family, and for the next four years Doris gave highly successful classes for children and taught ballroom dance for adults, with her mother as accompanist.

Breaking away from this confining life, Doris went to study at the Denishawn school in Los Angeles during the summer of 1917. The following year, having fulfilled her teaching commitments in Oak Park, she rejoined Denishawn and left her first school permanently in the hands of Ethel Moulton, whom she had met at Denishawn. From her first association with the famous Ruth St. Denis, who had opened the Denishawn school with Ted Shawn in 1915, Humphrey wished to be a professional dancer. Her teaching and creative abilities were immediately recognized, and soon after joining the company she was assisting St. Denis as teacher, co-choreographer, and coach, as well as dancing principal roles in the repertory.

Denishawn was the first large-scale attempt to create theatrical dancing that was not dependent on the conventions of European ballet, and its repertory consisted of dramatized religious rituals and legends in what St. Denis and Shawn believed to be the styles of exotic ancient cultures, together with semi-mime characterizations and pieces of Americana suitable for the vaudeville and variety shows that provided much of the company's employment. In an effort to escape the pressures of touring, Ruth St. Denis periodically removed herself and a few dancers from the commercial circuits and worked at what she considered a more serious and aesthetic type of dancing. Called music visualizations, these dances had some of the naturalness of the widely practiced interpretive dancing, but they used the structure of the eighteenth- and nineteenth-century music to which they were set. Humphrey cut her choreographic teeth collaborating with St. Denis on note-for-note transcriptions like *Sonata Pathétique* by Beethoven and *Soaring*, with a big silk scarf; and, as sole choreographer, *Scherzo Waltz (Hoop Dance)* and *Bourrée* with music by J. S. Bach. With *Sonata Tragica* (1923) Humphrey made the first of many daring experiments: at the suggestion of St. Denis, the Edward MacDowell music was dropped after the first performances and the dance was done in silence.

After Denishawn's eighteen-month tour of the Orient in 1925 to 1926, Humphrey, together with Denishawn colleagues Charles Weidman and Pauline Lawrence, took charge of the Denishawn school in New York while the rest of the company went on another tour. This was Humphrey's first chance at independent work and by the time the company returned in the spring of 1928, she knew she could not continue to grow as an artist within the Denishawn organization. Humphrey, Weidman, and Lawrence broke with Denishawn in June after a series of bitter disagreements and gave their first concert on 28 Oc-

HUMPHREY. A scene from Humphrey's *Life of the Bee*, which premiered 31 March 1929 at the Guild Theater, New York. Humphrey choreographed her study of the social behavior of bees to silence, but it was performed to a chorus, arranged by Pauline Lawrence, of dancers hissing, humming, and buzzing offstage. (Photograph by Soichi Sunami; reprinted from Selden, 1935.)

tober 1928 at the Civic Repertory Theater in New York. With Humphrey and Weidman as choreographers, directors, and teachers and Lawrence as costume designer, accompanist, business manager and publicist, the company was continuously active for fifteen years, until March 1944. During most of this time the triumvirate also lived communally, sharing a New York apartment and a farm Weidman had acquired in New Jersey. Humphrey's husband, Charles Francis Woodford (they married on 10 June 1932), and their son, Charles Humphrey Woodford (born 8 July 1933), and José Limón, who had come to study with Humphrey-Weidman in 1928 and had quickly become a principal dancer, also lived with the trio.

The Humphrey-Weidman company was immediately recognized as a major force in the burgeoning modern dance scene. Humphrey's earliest compositions were authoritatively arranged and danced by the dedicated young company she had trained, although in fact most of the pieces were only brief studies of various movement themes she wanted to explore. For the sake of the repertory she made many pure-dance pieces during this formative period, and as a dancer she was always effective in

preclassic works like *Sarabande*, with music by Jean-Philippe Rameau and impressionistic salon pieces like *Quasi-Waltz*, set to music by Aleksandr Scriabin and *The Banshee* with music by Henry Cowell. But she was trying at the same time to work her way out of the forms with which she and the audience had grown comfortable.

Aware that her instinctive musicality could lead her to an excessive reliance on the score, Humphrey dispensed with music altogether, choreographing in silence and sometimes having music written after the dance had been completed. Wishing to free the dance from its dependence on European academicism or any other preconceived systems of the use of the body, Humphrey started with simple, nonvirtuosic movement, organizing sequences on the rise and fall of the breath. This "breath rhythm" accounted in large part for the organic look that her dance retained even after it had begun to place greater technical demands on the dancer and had been shaped by a musical superstructure.

In *Color Harmony* (1928) Humphrey also attempted for the first time to develop a compositional progression solely through group movements, by assigning each dancer a color of the spectrum and making movement that described the meeting, clashing, and finally blending of these values. She pursued this idea of group composition in *Water Study*—done in silence—where her movement source was the play of natural forces, and in *Life of the Bee* (1929), where she drew an analogy between insect behavior and the survival of groups in society. Her search for new movement and new forms without resort to any external precedents went furthest in *Drama of Motion* (1930), a large group dance in silence that used contrasting dynamics, scale, and spatial patterns as dramatic elements in their own right. Often, however, she worked for abstraction in the art sense, deriving an idea from a literal source—a quality of motion, a gesture, or a literary or musical idea, and working outward to reach more universal expressive themes.

During this period Humphrey was influenced by the German philosopher Friedrich Nietzsche's discussion in *The Birth of Tragedy* of the interplay between the Apollonian and Dionysian impulses as constituents of early Greek tragedy. Humphrey saw this dialogue of opposites as a physical drama, the lifelong conflict between stability and imbalance, the need to rest and the need to risk. She saw dance as occurring in the "arc between two deaths." Along this continuum, with stasis at one end and disintegration at the other, was an infinite possibility for exciting movement. Her movement style was based on series of swings, spirals, falls, and leaps in which the dancer could momentarily let go of his or her balance, then resume control of force, speed, and direction before the momentum was completely spent. Sometimes her technique was described as a progression of "fall and recovery." This idea took a dramatic form in *The Shakers* (1930), where the movement interplay stood for the battle between good and evil. [*See* Shakers, The.] In *Two Ecstatic Themes* (1931) she posed the physical drama of rising versus sinking—the conquest of and the surrender to gravity.

Reading Nietzsche also evoked in Humphrey an interest in Greek tragedy itself, a desire to find in this ancient form a source for meaningful contemporary drama. In *Dionysiaques* (1932), based on the sacrificial rites of the Minoan bull dancers, the group worked itself into a frenzy, until Humphrey, as the chosen victim, threw herself from Limón's shoulders into the midst of the crowd. *Orestes*, or *The Libation Bearers*, set to the choral work *Les Choéphores* of Darius Milhaud, was begun in 1931. Antedating Martha Graham's version of the Agamemnon-Clytemnestra story by a quarter of a century, *Orestes* was considered one of Humphrey's finest compositions by the dancers and witnesses of the studio showings of the work. Because of the high cost of live music, the dance was never produced onstage.

Probably another reason for Humphrey's attraction to the Greek classics was that, through formal devices, espe-cially the massed voices of the chorus, the plays transformed individual experience into symbolic acts that could instruct or inspire a whole society. Some of the most successful outside assignments Humphrey took in the early days out of economic necessity involved settings of Greek dramas. With Weidman she choreographed the Norman Bel Geddes production of *Lysistrata* (1930) and his *Iphigenia in Aulis* (1935). Humphrey-Weidman also staged the large-scale though more contemporary Neighborhood Playhouse "action interpretation" of Ernest Bloch's String Quartet (1931), directed by Irene Lewisohn.

Humphrey disliked working on any productions where dance was not the primary instrument, and she was particularly uncomfortable with the constant compromises and adjustments of the Broadway theater, although she worked on at least four shows besides *Lysistrata*. Humphrey-Weidman dances were inserted into the Shubert revue *Americana* (1932), and became the first modern dances to appear on Broadway; there were occasional forays into nightclubs, opera ballet, and "highbrow" entertainments like the Theater Guild's 1933 *School for Husbands*. Weidman was able to supplement his income and to provide jobs for company dancers in shows for several years, but Humphrey preferred to devote herself to her own choreographic investigations, earning stipends from various teaching positions in private schools and summer dance programs.

A determined independent, Humphrey nevertheless joined in every effort to promote the understanding of modern dance as a whole and gave her advice, assistance, and frequently her dances to other choreographers and teachers. The Humphrey-Weidman Company was a constituent of Dance Repertory Theater in 1930 and again in 1931, the first attempt by a coalition of modern dance companies to present their works for a season at a Broadway theater. With Martha Graham, Helen Tamiris, and, in the second season, Agnes de Mille, the coalition drew important critical attention, helping to establish the new dance—as well as their own names—in the public's mind. When the summer school at Bennington College in Vermont was started in 1934 as a training ground for the modern dance, Humphrey, Weidman, Graham, and Hanya Holm became the mainstays of the faculty. [*See* Bennington School of the Dance.]

At Bennington Humphrey premiered two parts of her groundbreaking *New Dance Trilogy: New Dance* in 1935 and *With My Red Fires* in 1936. *Theater Piece* (premiered in January 1936) was to be the first section, *With My Red Fires* the second, and *New Dance* the culminating, uplifting finale. Nothing of the size and scope of the trilogy had yet been imagined in the modern dance. Each part lasted about forty minutes. At a time when dance concerts consisted of eight or ten pieces, some only a few minutes long, there was no precedent for such demanding performance, and the trilogy was never given on a single evening. Each part, however, was a self-contained unit that could be done separately in repertory. With the satiric *Theater Piece*, the dramatic *With My Red Fires*, and the choral *New Dance*, Humphrey made a significant extended statement about individual and social relations without resort to any prior musical or literary structure.

Among other distinctions, the *New Dance Trilogy* represented Humphrey's most significant opportunity to work with large groups of dancers. Almost as soon as she began to make dances, she became fascinated with the ensemble. She thought group choreography the greatest challenge because only the group was capable of expressing the full range of dance possibilities, much as, Humphrey thought, the symphony orchestra fulfilled the highest potential of music. [*See* New Dance Trilogy.]

In its first decade the Humphrey-Weidman group fluctuated between about fifteen and twenty dancers, some of them advanced students and apprentices. In 1936 twenty-nine members of the Bennington School of the Dance choreographic workshop joined with the sixteen Humphrey-Weidman company members for the creation of *With My Red Fires*, the largest work ever presented during the nine seasons of the Bennington project. Humphrey led a second Bennington workshop in 1938, choreographing Bach's Passacaglia and Fugue in C Minor—a tremendous affirmative statement totally based on the music, with herself, Weidman, and combined company and workshop members numbering twenty-five. After this period the Humphrey-Weidman forces declined,

HUMPHREY. *The Shakers* (1930), with Humphrey (center) and the Humphrey-Weidman group. This work is a dramatic reenactment of a Shaker service, which contrasts downward shaking motions with uplifted gestures of praise. (Photograph © 1938 by Barbara Morgan; used by permission of the Barbara Morgan Archives, Hastings-on-Hudson, New York.)

HUMPHREY. In the summer of 1935 Humphrey premiered parts of her *New Dance* at Bennington, Vermont. Here, in mid-motion, are Humphrey, Charles Weidman *(right)*, and their Concert Group celebrating spatial and rhythmic counterpoint. (Photograph © by Thomas Bouchard; used by permission.)

and Humphrey had no access to large groups again until the 1950s, when she was no longer able to dance herself. *Passacaglia, New Dance*, the chorus sections of *With My Red Fires*, and many smaller works demonstrate Humphrey's commanding gifts for rhythmic and spatial counterpoint and the development of dramatic power through group movement.

During the second half of the 1930s, the Humphrey-Weidman group toured extensively in the United States. The first modern dance group to make a long tour, in January 1935, Humphrey-Weidman maintained itself for several years with cross-country trips. The dance component of the Federal Theater Project provided indirect subsidy to the company during 1936, when the dancers received stipends to prepare for a concert in June, at which the major offering was a revised version of Weidman's 1933 *Candide*. Humphrey staged two of her old dances, *Roussel Suite* and *Parade (March)*, with music by Alexander Tcherepnin, for this occasion. The Federal Theater also underwrote a revival of *With My Red Fires* in January 1938, with a reduced cast.

The necessity for constant touring and summer teaching began to take its toll on Humphrey's creative work. Aside from *Passacaglia* and the comic *Race of Life* (1938), based on cartoons of James Thurber, Humphrey produced few successful works between 1936 and 1942. She won the *Dance Magazine* award for choreography in 1937 with *To the Dance*, a curtain-raiser that she considered minor in comparison to her other more ambitious undertak-

ings. *Song of the West* (1940–1942) was an attempt to evoke three aspects of the American landscape (in sections titled "The Green Land," "Desert Gods," and "Rivers"), but although she revised it many times, it was never entirely satisfactory. *American Holiday* (1938) and *Square Dances* (1939) were short-lived attempts to use documentary material during a time of patriotic displays in all the arts.

In an effort to spend more time in New York, Humphrey-Weidman moved into its new Studio Theater on West Sixteenth Street in the fall of 1940. The renovated loft accommodated small-scale performances every weekend, showcasing the Humphrey-Weidman repertory, with children's performances and concerts by company dancers and outside groups. Humphrey's premiere at Bennington the following summer had the dual air of a celebration and a farewell. *Decade* (1941) was a survey of the achievements of Humphrey-Weidman from 1930 to 1940, with excerpts from the two directors' choreography, and the piece ended with the dancers exiting through a door representing their new quarters. In fact, however, Humphrey-Weidman had already started to crumble, and the Studio Theater was its last home.

As an institution, Humphrey-Weidman had sustained itself through a unique combination of personal loyalties and sacrifice: Humphrey's idealism and artistic reach, Weidman's affectionate charm, Lawrence's industry and persistence, and the willingness of all who surrounded them to forego conventional rewards were what made the edifice hold together in spite of its makeshift and transitory resources. Events of the early 1940s undermined and finally destroyed the enterprise.

In 1940 after teaching in a summer dance session at Mills College in California, principal dancer José Limón decided to leave the company. He spent the next two years on the West Coast doing his own choreography and dancing with May O'Donnell and other partners. Pauline Lawrence joined him and they were married in October 1941. These defections were a severe loss to the company, and with Weidman absent frequently doing theater and nightclub work, Humphrey was left to manage the school and company virtually alone. At this time she was also experiencing the first stages of a painful condition that turned out to be a disabling arthritis of the hip.

World War II decimated the ranks of the Humphrey-Weidman male dancers. Weidman was deferred from military service after a long anxious period of doubt, but most of the men were drafted. Limón returned to New York, where he was able to combine his army service with his performing career. Lawrence rejoined Humphrey at the studio, but her attentions were now partly taken up with furthering Limón's interests. Reconciled, if imperfectly for the time being, Humphrey and Limón collaborated on a program of all-Bach works at the end of 1942. For this series of studio concerts, Humphrey choreographed *Four Chorale Preludes* and *Partita in G Minor*. The company danced *Passacaglia*, and Limón performed a solo he had choreographed to the Chaconne in D Minor. The program was so successful that it was given eleven times instead of the intended three.

A few months later Humphrey made the first of a series of Hispanic-influenced pieces, *El Salón México*, for Limón. Their working relationship was to continue, while Humphrey's alliance with Weidman quietly dissolved. The last production of Humphrey-Weidman as an entity was Humphrey's *Inquest* (1944), based on a narrative of social injustice from John Ruskin's *Sesame and Lilies*. The dance told of a poor working-class family driven to starvation, despair, and suicide but held together by the stubborn pride of the mother, played by Humphrey. It was her last role, remembered as powerful and poignant by those who saw it.

After the war Limón formed his own company and paid Humphrey the singular tribute of asking her to be its artistic director. She had always lent choreographic advice and suggestions to her colleagues, and from 1946 until the end of her life she generously furnished Limón with an impeccable eye and a firm editorial hand whenever he asked for her help. By this time Humphrey was unable to move without a pronounced limp, and she could not even demonstrate her own choreographic ideas. However, their already long, intimate working relationship evidently gave her enough confidence to begin again, trusting Limón and his dancers to carry out what she imagined.

The first work Humphrey choreographed in this new set of circumstances, *Lament for Ignacio Sánchez Mejías* (1946), was based on Lorca's stirring lines about a famous bullfighter, with a score by Norman Lloyd, and, except for Limón's impassioned solos, the dance was more like a staged reading. Two women dramatically recited the poem about a splendid hero and lover who eventually meets his death in the bullring. Longtime Humphrey-Weidman dancer Letitia Ide played the Figure of Destiny, and the anguished admirer was played initially by an actress, Ellen Love. The work had an immediate and lasting success. For its premiere, a concert at Bennington College for a small audience, Humphrey also choreographed a duet based on Carl Rose cartoons from the *New Yorker* magazine. *The Story of Mankind*, for Limón and Humphrey-Weidman dancer Beatrice Seckler, was a comic look at man and his mate, striving through the ages for material and social success, until in their twentieth-century penthouse a newspaper headline announcing the arrival of the atomic age makes them revert to cowering cave-dwellers.

Humphrey quickly regained the dance initiative, and made a succession of works for the Limón company that placed her movement imagery at the service of the dancers who were now her instrument. Seckler and Ide remained only a short time, so apart from Limón himself, her collaborators were now to be dancers she had not trained herself. Instead of trying to impose a style on them, she used their own qualities. They included the small and vibrant Pauline Koner, who had already gained a reputation as a soloist and who was a frequent guest artist with Limón; and Lucas Hoving, who had left his home in Holland to dance with Kurt Jooss before settling in the United States. Humphrey always believed her work had a message of humanistic value, even when it looked the most abstract. It is a measure of her lifelong ability to adapt and extend her ideas that her choreography now became more specifically related to character and dramatic situations. Unlike Limón, however, she was not attracted to historical or literary figures as subjects for detailed descriptive essays. Her instinct for the abstract remained; her characters were always archetypes, composites, representing universal motivations and feelings. Although poems or literary ideas often propelled her into a dance, she seldom sought to transfer her source overtly to the stage.

One of her greatest works, *Day on Earth* (1947), is a perfect example of the concise way she could create abstract characters to express large and deeply affecting themes. Limón was the Everyman figure who worked, loved, suffered the loss of his loved ones, and finally died, leaving his child to carry on. Set very skillfully to Aaron Copland's Piano Sonata, the dance was the first in many years for which Humphrey used an existing piece of contemporary music instead of commissioning a score to suit her concept. Perhaps *Day on Earth* convinced her that she could conquer the temptation of literalism, because some of her best subsequent works used previously composed music. (Throughout her career she returned to Baroque and classical composers for pure-dance works.) The intimate style of *Day on Earth* proved so evocative that she made another quartet, *Night Spell* (1951), to the string quartet of Priaulx Rainier. The dance featured Limón as a dreamer, with Hoving, Betty Jones, and Ruth Currier as mysterious, threatening, and seductive creatures of his sleeping mind. [*See* Day on Earth.]

Day on Earth and *Night Spell* became staples of the Limón company's touring repertory, along with *Lament*, the folk-dance–inspired *Ritmo Jondo* (1953), with music by Carlos Surinach, commissioned by the Bethsabée de Rothschild Foundation for a season of American dance at the Alvin Theater, and an opening dance she made in 1949 for the trio of Limón, Jones, and Currier called *Invention*, to music by Norman Lloyd. In all, Humphrey choreographed thirteen works for the José Limón company, including some less successful experiments like *Corybantic* (1948), an allegory of war and peace; a fluffy *Airs and Graces* (1955), to Locatelli, and *Felipe el Loco* (1954), an ill-conceived piece based on the tragic career of the Spanish dancer who inspired Serge Diaghilev and Léonide Massine to create *Le Tricorne* (The Three-Cornered Hat). In 1953 she choreographed one of her most poetic works, *Ruins and Visions*, to Benjamin Britten's String Quartet no. 2 (op. 36). With an epigraph from Stephen Spender, the dance drew together several of her recurrent motifs: the artist, the family, the corrupting influence of war, and the redeeming potential of brotherhood.

As well as creating new works for Limón's company, Humphrey revived two of her older works, the Variations and Conclusion section from *New Dance*, and *Passacaglia*. She believed strongly in repertory as a means of familiarizing young dancers with performance material, of giving professionals a way of deepening their interpretations of works, and, perhaps not incidentally, of seeing her own creative output in a live and evolving condition. When the American Dance Festival was initiated at Connecticut College in 1948 as a sequel to the Bennington School of Dance, Humphrey and the Limón company were asked to be in residence. New London became their summer home for teaching as well as for making new dances. Humphrey had systematically used her own choreography as training pieces ever since the summer courses at the Humphrey-Weidman studio during the 1930s. At Connecticut College she started a repertory class, doing her first big student revival, *Passacaglia*, in 1951, with *The Shakers, Soaring, Water Study*, the "Desert Gods" section from *Song of the West*, and excerpts from *With My Red Fires* in subsequent years.

These student repertory productions were a forerunner of the work of the Juilliard Dance Theater, sometimes

HUMPHREY. Doris Humphrey as the possessive Matriarch in *With My Red Fires* (1936), the final part of her *New Dance Trilogy*. Considered too long and strenuous to perform together, the complete trilogy was never seen on a single evening's program, although parts of it were periodically revived. (Photograph © 1938 by Barbara Morgan; used by permission of the Barbara Morgan Archives, Hastings-on-Hudson, New York.)

HUMPHREY. During the summer of 1938 at Bennington, Vermont, Humphrey created *Passacaglia in C Minor* (1938) to music by J. S. Bach, for herself as soloist and a large cast of her students and company members. (Photograph © 1938 by Barbara Morgan; used by permission of the Barbara Morgan Archives, Hastings-on-Hudson, New York.)

called the Doris Humphrey Dancers. Humphrey joined the faculty of the newly organized dance division of the Juilliard School of Music in 1951, teaching composition and repertory. In 1955 a regular performing company was added to her responsibilities there. Limón's company had matured into one of the major modern dance groups in the country, and they were often away on tour. With a company of young preprofessionals Humphrey could not only mount her old works such as *Race of Life* (in 1956), she could also choreograph. Between 1955 and 1958 she created *The Rock and the Spring, Dawn in New York*, and *Descent into the Dream* for the Juilliard company, and began her last work, *Brandenburg Concerto No. 4* (completed from her sketches by Ruth Currier).

Doris Humphrey was not noted as a technique teacher. She was, however, an authority on dance composition. From her earliest days as a choreographer she had always felt she should understand the principles of the work she was doing. Although there was no counterpart in dance to the theory and harmony classes of music training, or to the fundamentals of form and structure taught to every budding composer, Humphrey habitually conceived of dance in terms that corresponded to such formal pedagogy. She did not know how exceptional she was in doing this. Beginning in 1927 with her first independent teaching and composing, she not only examined the elements of movement but embarked on the task of organizing her ideas into a coherent and concrete theory of dance composition, which became the basis of her classes at Juilliard, Connecticut College, and the Ninety-second Street YM-YWHA. She did not complete the presentation of this theory in book form until 1958, when, bedridden with terminal cancer, she was unable to work on anything else. *The Art of Making Dances* was published posthumously. Humphrey had been drafting it, promising it to various publishers for thirty years, and in 1949 had received a Guggenheim Fellowship to assist in its preparation.

In addition to Weidman and Limón, Humphrey helped countless other dancers to realize their choreographic ambitions. She had an exceptional generosity and lack of egocentricity with regard to other people's work, considering it a natural and necessary task to see that a younger generation of artists was well prepared to succeed her. She encouraged students and company members to experiment with their own choreography and to form small ensembles of their own. José Limón, Eleanor King, Ernestine Stodelle, and Cleo Atheneos tried out their first works as the Little Group starting in 1931, performing not only their own dances but Humphrey's and Weidman's as well. When a dancer's choreography became more assured, it was taken into the Humphrey-Weidman or Limón company repertory. In later years Humphrey served on the board of judges for the Young Choreographers' Concerts

at the Ninety-second Street Y, where she also acted as the first artistic director of a dance theater for children, the Merry-Go-Rounders.

Humphrey's partnership with Charles Weidman extended to the unusual arrangement of co-choreography in *Salutation to the Depths* (1930) and *Alcina Suite* (1934). Sections by Weidman were incorporated into Humphrey's *Roussel Suite, New Dance*, and *Theater Piece*. Humphrey frequently allowed the dancers to improvise in certain parts of a dance, for example many of the hand gestures in *The Shakers* were improvised, and in at least one instance, "Variations and Conclusion" from *New Dance*, she asked all the company members to make their own variations, from which she selected those of Limón, Seckler, Ide, and Sybil Shearer for the first performances. When a new dancer learned an existing role, she often rechoreographed it to fit the dancer better or she allowed the dancer to adapt the steps.

Humphrey used every means she could to educate the public about the modern dance and to explain and preserve her own choreographic output. She lectured frequently, developing a lecture-demonstration format to illustrate her principles, with the dancers doing classroom studies and excerpts from repertory works. She encouraged company members who had an aptitude for teaching by using them as assistants, then turning over whole jobs to them. She maintained close ties with sympathetic dance teachers around the country, especially Pauline Chellis in Boston and Eleanor Frampton in Cleveland, creating an informal network of professional interchange and support.

Gifted with a clear, simple writing style, Humphrey contributed articles to many publications; in fact, her highly developed verbal sense led her to plot her dances logically, often using combinations of words, sketches, counts, and modified musical indications to relay her needs to composers. Even when making a nonnarrative dance, she frequently wrote out a scenario, or a sort of action script, to guide her choreographic thinking. She experimented early on with movement notation but abandoned her own system when Labanotation became sufficiently developed to handle her work. More than twenty Humphrey dances have been Labanotated entirely or in part, most of them during rehearsals of Humphrey's various repertory classes in the 1950s.

For an artist with such modest financial resources, Humphrey managed to get a considerable amount of her work onto film, another means of preservation that she endorsed from the outset of her career. Footage of Humphrey's dancing exists from as far back as about 1924, and home movies taken in studios, theaters, and outdoors at Bennington and Mills Colleges have fortunately found their way into permanent archives. Professional films were also made of Humphrey's *Air for the G String* (in Hollywood), *The Shakers* (by dance photographer Thomas Bouchard), and *Lament* (by Walter Strate). Record films exist for a number of revivals directed by Humphrey as well as the original *Ruins and Visions* and other works of the Limón period.

Acknowledged from the start as a pioneer and master builder, Doris Humphrey received the Capezio Award in 1954 for "creative leadership in the modern dance and for the repertory of high distinction with which she has enriched it." Doris Humphrey had a felicitous combination of talents: an unerring sense of form and structure, an instinct for shaping the body's natural energies into arresting rhythmic and spatial sequences, and an unfailing dedication to humanistic values. A perfectionist with a relentless, single-minded passion for the work at hand, she ignored personal pain and hardship to see her work realized. After thirty years of choreographing, she had not succumbed to formulas.

Despite preeminence within the field of dance, when Humphrey was no longer able to appear before the public, interest in her work declined. She had never choreographed to replicate herself or project her own presence as a star, and she passed on the limelight to José Limón with gallantry and pleasure. It was her choreography that she wished to leave for posterity—yet today her dances make only sporadic and fleeting appearances in live repertory. This would have seemed to her the ultimate irony.

[*See also* Costume in Western Tradition, *article on* Modern Dance; Denishawn; Water Study; *and the entries on* Limón, Weidman, *and other principal figures mentioned herein.*]

BIBLIOGRAPHY

Dance Notation Bureau. *Doris Humphrey: The Collected Works.* 2 vols. New York, 1978–1992. Labanotation scores.
Dils, Ann. "Performance Practice and Humphrey Reconstruction." In *Dance Reconstructed*, edited by Barbara Palfy. New Brunswick, N.J., 1993.
Dils, Anne. *Re-conceptualizing Dance:* Reconstructing the Dances of Doris Humphrey. New York University, 1993. Unpublished Ph.D. dissertation.
"Doris Humphrey-A Centennial Celebration (1995)." *Dance Research Journal* 28/2 (Fall 1996): 1–74. Collected conference papers.
Hofmeister, Eleni Bookis. "Balanchine and Humphrey: Comparing *Serenade* and *Passacaglia.*" *Choreography and Dance* 3.3 (1993): 13–30.
Humphrey, Doris. *The Art of Making Dances.* New York, 1959.
Humphrey, Doris. *Doris Humphrey, an Artist First: An Autobiography.* Edited by Selma Jeanne Cohen. Middletown, Conn., 1977.
Jordan, Stephanie. Music as a Structural Basis in the Choreography of Doris Humphrey. University of London, Goldsmith's College, 1986. Unpublished Ph.D. dissertation.
Kaye, Meli Davis. "Doris Humphrey at Green Mansions, 1947." *Dance Chronicle* 18.3 (1995): 405–418.
King, Eleanor. *Transformations: The Humphrey-Weidman Era.* Brooklyn, 1978.
Kriegsman, Sali Ann. *Modern Dance in America: The Bennington years.* Boston, 1981.
Lloyd, Margaret. *The Borzoi Book of Modern Dance.* New York, 1949.
Martin, John. *The Modern Dance.* New York, 1933.
Selden, Elizabeth. *The Dancer's Quest: Essays on the Aesthetic of the Contemporary Dance.* Berkeley, 1935.
Sherman, Jane. "Martha and Doris in Denishawn: A Closer Look." *Dance Chronicle* 17.2 (1994): 179–193.
Sherman, Jane. "Doris Humphrey Centennial: Fall and Recovery." *Dance Magazine* (October 1995): 56–59.
Siegel, Marcia B. *The Shapes of Change: Images of American Dance.* New York, 1979.
Siegel, Marcia B. *Days on Earth: The Dance of Doris Humphrey.* New Haven, 1987.
Stodelle, Ernestine. *The Dance Technique of Doris Humphrey and Its Creative Potential.* Princeton, 1978.
Wentink, Andrew Mark. "The Doris Humphrey Collection: An Introduction and Guide." *Bulletin of the New York Public Library* 77 (Autumn 1973): 80–1142.

ARCHIVES.   The Dance Collection of the New York Public Library for the Performing Arts has extensive holdings on Doris Humphrey: scrapbooks, photographs, films, and audiotapes covering her work and the Humphrey-Weidman Company, as well as three major collections of letters to and from Humphrey. Additional material is held in the José Limón and Pauline Lawrence Limón Collections, New York Public Library for the Performing Arts.

MARCIA B. SIEGEL

HUNGARIAN STATE FOLK ENSEMBLE.

After World War II great enthusiasm for folk dance festivals swept Hungary. At the national summit festival in Gyula in 1947, for example, more than five hundred amateur ensembles performed, proving the vitality of folk dance on stage. This encouraged the formation of many major professional and amateur folk dance companies in the late 1940s.

The Állami Népi Együttes (State Folk Ensemble), the official folk art company of the Hungarian People's Republic, was formed in 1949 under the direction of Miklós Rábai (1921–1974); its first production premiered on 4 April 1951. The ensemble consisted of three sections, a choir, an orchestra, and a dance group; this triple structure allowed for frequent joint productions. Initially, the group's organization and program followed the Soviet model of large, overstaged, and thematic numbers, with huge Gypsy orchestras as accompaniment.

Although choral literature has played a substantial role in the modern development of Hungarian art music (especially the works of Béla Bartók, Zoltán Kodály, and their followers), contemporary Hungarian composers have seldom written works exclusively for the type of orchestra used by the ensemble, necessitating mixed productions using both choir and orchestra. The orchestra, however, readily performs nineteenth-century *verbunkos* music and other arrangements (such as Franz Liszt's rhapsodies) that use this instrumental style.

Between 1950 and 1974, the ensemble created a specific Hungarian style of theatrical folk dance. Dances of various regions, types, and dates were used with a minimum of scenery. Epic and dramatic dance plays drawing material from folk tales, ballads, and historic events were choreographed, mostly by Rábai and his pupil Dezső Létai; examples include *Wedding at Ecser* and *Evening in the Spinnery*.

The 1980s saw a change in direction when Sándor Tímár, an expert in Hungarian dance folklore, became both artistic director and choreographer. Using the fruits of two decades (1950–1970) of Hungarian dance research, Tímár brought new color to the ensemble's repertory by drawing on the traditions and characteristics of small peasant orchestras as well as those of more archaic music and dance traditions, authentically interpreted. The en-

HUNGARIAN STATE FOLK ENSEMBLE. This publicity photograph shows a men's open circle dance. Traditional Hungarian dances for men are often fast-paced and highly virtuosic. (Photograph from the Dance Collection, New York Public Library for the Performing Arts.)

semble has toured the world extensively under Tímár's direction.

Otherwise, the Hungarian folk dance movement remained static until the early 1970s, when a new generation of artists emerged. On 6 May 1972, the first public *táncház* ("dance house") opened in Budapest, soon followed by many others throughout the country. The new movement used authentic material—steps, music, dress, and research-based choreographies—onstage. With the presence of these recreational institutions (since the early 1990s, dozens more have opened), many young people were introduced to folk dance and its beauty as a performing art. A new populism thus emerged, and a new generation rediscovered a part of its history, culture, and identity.

Hungary now has dozens of first-class amateur folk dance companies and several professional ones, including Állami, Duna, Budapest, Honvéd, and Népszinház companies. National yearly competitions award gold, silver, and bronze medals and offer outstanding dancers the titles Young Master of Folk Art and Master of Folk Art. In ama-

teur competitions, women can receive the Golden Pearl and men the Golden Spur awards. Professional dancers and choreographers are presented with various state prizes (the Liszt, Erkel, Kossuth, and Outstanding Performer or Ensemble). In 1980, the Amateur Folk Dance Federation (ANOT) and the Professional Workshop were formed; both cater to the needs of groups and dance enthusiasts.

[*See* Hungary, *article on* Traditional and Popular Dance.]

BIBLIOGRAPHY

Dance Ensemble of Budapest, 1958–1978. Budapest, 1978.
Kürti, László. "The New Hungarian State Folk Ensemble in America." *Arabesque* 9 (March–April 1984): 12–13.
Vadasi, Tibor. "Thirty Years of the Hungarian State Folk Ensemble." *Hungarian Dance News,* no. 3–4 (1981): 7.

LÁSZLÓ KÜRTI

HUNGARY. [*To survey the dance traditions of Hungary, this entry comprises seven articles:*

Traditional and Popular Dance
Theatrical Dance before World War II
Theatrical Dance since World War II
Modern Dance
Dance Education
Folk Dance Research and Publication
Theatrical Dance Research and Publication

For further discussion of theatrical dance, see the entries on individual companies, choreographers, and dancers.]

Traditional and Popular Dance

Magyar (ethnic Hungarian) dances and customs are complex owing to local geographical and cultural differences. Located in central Europe just to the west of the Carpathian Mountains, the region was part of the Roman provinces of Dacia and Pannonia. It was later occupied by Germanic tribes, the Huns, the Avars, and then by the Magyars of Central Asia in the ninth century, who profoundly shaped the history of Hungary. As a kingdom, Hungary fell to Ottoman and then Austrian Habsburg domination, but its resistence resulted in the dual monarchy called the Austro-Hungarian Empire from 1867 until the end of World War I. After World War II, Hungary joined the Soviet bloc as a people's republic. The 1990 election resulted in the withdrawal of Soviet troops and the attempt to join the free-market economy.

The term for "folk dance" *(néptánc)* is used here to refer to indigenous peasant dances. Researchers have found that ethnographically distinct regions and their dances do not correspond to modern political divisions, and that cultural influences from both Asia and Europe have been important in shaping a unique dance tradition within the Carpathian Basin. Characterized by irregular, improvised solos and couple dances, tight performing space (known as "dancing on a plate"), and competitive and virtuoso men's dances, this cultural tradition differs markedly from the organized and set performances of both western European couple dances and Balkan communal circle and chain dances.

Early History. The origin of the Hungarians provides some clues to the origins of their folk dances. The Magyar language belongs to the Finno-Ugric branch of the Uralic family of languages; its closest relations are languages spoken along the Ob River of north-central Russia, and those ethnic groups provide evidence for their earliest dance development. Present-day Hungarians have more in common with their longtime Slovak, Ukrainian, Romanian, Croatian, and Gypsy neighbors than they do with their own ancient linguistic kin. Almost nothing is known about the dances of the ancestral Ugric people who came west into the Carpathian Basin in large numbers around 896 CE. Certainly the verb *táncolni* ("to dance") is of medieval origin, yet older native terms—*lejteni, lépni, járni,* and *szökni*—were also used then. Derivatives of these terms still occur in terms for dance movements.

Christianity was accepted in Hungary during the reign of Stephen I (997–1038), who became Saint Stephen. Few medieval laws and religious codes seem to have prohibited dancing; the few restrictions that did exist were associated with previous pagan practices, such as dancing at funerals and cemeteries. For example, the decision of the Forty-sixth Synod, held in Buda in 1279, ordered priests to prohibit dancing in cemeteries and churches.

The first consistent references to dance are found in fifteenth- and sixteenth-century Hungarian literature. Two interrelated dance genres were mentioned: the *hajdútánc* ("heyduck") and the *ungaresca* (Italian for "Hungarian dance"). Little is known, however, of these early dance steps, formations, rhythms, and performance styles, although the *heiducken dantz, balletto ungero,* and *ungarescha* were fashionable in court balls and mummeries throughout Europe. The *hajdútánc* belongs originally to cattle-drivers and seems to have been a type of improvised martial dance to bagpipes, performed with sword, hatchet, or stick in hand.

The development of an international cattle trade certainly helped to disseminate the heyduck beyond the Carpathian region. Hungarian dance styles spread throughout Europe via trade, royal marriages, pilgrimages, professional musicians, and vagrant students, who also brought back foreign dances and musical styles. The musical tablatures of Paix, Nömiger, Phalése, Mainerio, and others also show that the *hajdútánc* and *ungaresca* were performed to the same melodies and rhythms.

Types and Regional Variations. Like folk songs, ballads, tales, traditions, and handicrafts, Hungarian dances have been classified by historical type as either "old style" or "new style." (Hungarian scholars often use "style," "layer," and "type" interchangeably when referring to historical categories.) Each style indicates a specific cultural complex, an intersection of socioeconomic class and historical period. Hungarian folklorists' attention has been directed mostly toward identifying dances by typology; the classic work that laid the foundations for such research was György Martin's *Research and Classification of Dance Motifs* (*Motivumkutatás, motivumrendszerezés,* 1964). By analyzing the total number of dance steps found in the Sárköz region, Martin identified five major dance types: *ugrós* ("jumping"), *karikázó* (women's circle dance), *verbunkos,* and two forms of the *csárdás*—slow and fast.

HUNGARY: Traditional and Popular Dance. A scene from *Wedding at Ecser,* a dramatic dance play choreographed for the Hungarian State Folk Ensemble. Between 1950 and 1970, ensemble founder and director Miklós Rábai and his pupil Dezső Létai created numerous theatrical choreographies based on folk tales, ballads, and historical events. (Photograph by Ferencné Bartal; reprinted by permission from Varjasi and Horváth, 1956, p. 159.)

Subsequent scholars have examined other regions and delineated major dance types according to morphology, music, linguistics, and other formal properties. Within the two historical types, old and new, are nine dance families—six in the old style and three in the new. About thirty major dance types follow, many with generic and local variations.

Modern History. By the beginning of the eighteenth century, Hungarian society was undergoing rapid transformation. Socioeconomic ties had been cut with the Ottoman Empire and established with the Habsburg Empire. A new cultural complex was emerging, and with it came new national dance forms—the *verbunkos* and the *csárdás,* a popular couple dance. According to contemporary evidence, the name *verbunkos* (also *verbung* or *verdung*) was derived from the German verb *werben* ("to recruit") and was indicative of the military outlook that permeated Hungarian society. This folk dance became firmly established with the formation of Hungary's permanent army in 1715; period sources describe how officers led drinking bouts and shouted dance instructions at young recruits while music played incessantly. This practice still can be seen in extant derivatives of the *verbunkos,* including the circle versions of the Rábaköz region, the

recruiting skit of the Great Plain region, and the *borica* of the Barcaság area.

The story of the *csárdás* (Eng., *czardas;* literally, "dance of the inn") is intriguing because it was the middle and upper classes who brought it to national popularity during the 1830s and 1840s. In the dance's most common form, a couple dance, partners face each other in a waist-shoulder hold and sidestep to folk or popular songs in 4/4 time. Other popular urban middle-class parlor dances created and developed by dance masters since the mid-nineteenth century included the *körmagyar, palotás,* and *sortánc.* Hungarian peasant dances were also adapted into ballroom forms. [*See* Czardas.]

Daniel Speer, a Silesian traveler, noted that Hungarian dances were similar to Western dances but more orderly and charming. In his *Mémoires historiques* (Amsterdam, 1736), Abbé Reverend, the ambassador of France's King Louis XIV, described the dances as similar to French *branles* and *contredanses.* In *Travels in Lower Hungary* (London, 1818), the English traveler Richard Bright described a performance by students:

> Presently about a dozen lads, dressed in their Hungarian leathern jackets and pantaloons, with boots and large fur caps, came in marching . . . and with them came the piper. Each had a large stick in his hand, and they immediately began a national dance, in which they sometimes moved in a circle, sometimes flourished their sticks triumphantly in the air, threw them upon the ground, then picked them up again; struck their boots with their open hands; clapped their heels together, making loud clattering noise; then came towards the middle, with their sticks across, or pointed in varied directions, and maintained a succession of spirited manoeuvres.

Ballroom dances of the late nineteenth and early twentieth centuries—that is, urban middle-class dances—were the most recent additions to the peasant dance tradition. Two specific categories dominated: the eastern European (for example, the polka and waltz) and the western European (the one-step, seven-step, tango, and fox trot). All were introduced by various means—by soldiers, immigrants, dancing masters, and migrant workers.

To this day, the *verbunkos* and the *csárdás* remain the most popular types of dance. Three related *csárdás* types dominate: the couple *csárdás* proper; a trio dance known as *hármascsárdás* in the central dialect and *szászka* ("Saxon dance") in the Transylvanian district of Mozőség; and the circle *csárdás,* a group dance using the same kind of music and steps. The trio may have originated in Renaissance court dance; for example, one contemporary version of an Italian *bassadanza* required one man and two women. The *csárdás's* enormous popularity can be seen as much outside the Carpathian Basin as within its borders: the medium-tempo *tropotianka* followed by the faster *csárdás* in the Uz Valley east of the Carpathians in

HUNGARY: Traditional and Popular Dance. Members of the Hungarian State Folk Ensemble in the stage presentation *At the Vintage.* (Photograph by Ferencné Bartal; reprinted by permission from Varjasi and Horváth, 1956, p. 50.)

Ukraine; as a couple dance, the *csárdás* is popular in the Dubrovnik region, on the Dalmatian coast.

The *verbunkos* also has solo, couple, and group or circle variations. Improvised solo versions can be found throughout the country but are most common in the northern part of the Great Plain region; the versions of Szatmár and Nyireség are especially colorful. Only a few forms of couple dances can be found, although women are allowed to participate in versions recorded in the northern areas as well as in Transylvania. Circle types perhaps have the most historical depth and are common in the western regions but rare in the Great Plain. Known as *karéj* and *körverbunkos,* these dances contrast with the individual and improvised solo versions in having highly organized but simple steps and a dance leader who directs the performance.

Known by the generic term *karikázó,* women's circle dances are old-style in origin. During Lent, when Christians are forbidden to dance, only women's circle dances were performed without music. Many of the versions with verses have magical meanings, and regional variations are considerable. The women's circle dances of Transylvania are the simplest, with sidestepping and turning, basket handholding in front or back, and, usually, simultaneous performance with the *legényes* type of men's dances. These women's dances have only one part, without singing, although *csujogatás* (shouted rhymes) are common. Other women's circle dances usually have two or three parts; slow, *lépő* (stepping); medium, *csárdás* (double-stepping);

HUNGARY: Traditional and Popular Dance. Known as *karikázó*, women's circle dances are old-style in origin and are found in many versions. Members of the Hungarian State Folk Ensemble perform *Dances of the Three Jumps*, while accompanying themselves by singing. (Photograph by Ferencné Bartal; reprinted by permission from Varjasi and Horváth, 1956.)

and fast, *futó* (running). Women's dances of the western-central and northern-central regions belong in this category; in other regions, this form disappeared long ago. In addition, there are such variations as the *kerekecske* of Dunafalva in the Sárköz region, which has five separate parts; and the *karikatánc* of Magyarbőd in the northeastern Hegyköz area, with four distinct parts, one of them the so-called "shoulder dance." A relative of the Hungarian women's circle dance, the *karička*, is popular in the dance traditions of both the Slovak region and in Ukraine just east of the Carpathians.

Staff dances constitute another intriguing family. Present forms are of three major types: the *kanásztánc* ("swineherd dance"), the *botoló* ("stick dance"), and the *seprütánc* ("broom dance"). Variations on the last are performed with hats, eggs, bottles, and other objects. The formal and musical characteristics of these dances show them to be related to the fifteenth- and sixteenth-century *hajdútánc* and *ungaresca* complexes, which were also per-

formed by pastoral, seminomadic people. The interrelation of the two complexes also is seen in the staff dances' formal characteristics, instruments, music, rhythmic patterns, and individual performances. The dances may also be related to earlier weapons dances. Generally, staff dances are performed only at certain occasions (for example, work dances and weddings) and by only a few outstanding dancers. Couple forms of the stick dances are also popular; Gypsies in the Carpathian Basin are exceptionally good performers.

The music used in the *ugrós*, or jumping dances, is almost identical to that used in the staff dances, to which they are closely related. Several major forms exist, all with many regional variations in Hungary: the *ugrós* proper, which is common in both the western and central regions; the *mars* ("marching"), most popular in the Alföld region, where it is used as a wedding procession dance; the *dus*, a close relative of the *mars*, in the Rábaköz region; and the *oláhos* (Romanian dance) in the southern part of Transdanubia and most of the Great Plain. Solo, couple, and group forms are all popular in Hungary. The general tempo is quarter note (♩) = 116–138; the major dance motifs use eighth notes, while quarter notes dominate the motifs of the new-style dances.

The *legényes* (bachelors' dances) form the most complex dance family, an amalgam of Transylvanian men's dances known for their intricacy and difficulty. The simplest *legényes* are the *silladri* of Bukovina and the *féloláhos* ("half-Romanian") of Csik. Another subtype, the *sűrű* ("fast"), is popular in most regions and has many variations. Performances are energetic, fast, and highly eccentric, expressing masculinity and competitiveness. Women do not perform these dances in public; instead, they perform their circle dance while the men perform *legényes*. The women meanwhile shout rhymes, some of which are almost obscene. Regional variations in patterns of movement sequences are important; four distinct dance motifs are possible for one melody, for example. Romanian communities in Transylvania perform a similar bachelors' dance, although the patterns of motifs and phrases are distinctly different.

In the Mezőség area, the fast bachelor dance is paired with a slower version known as *ritka* ("rare," "thin," or "sparse"). Although both versions are similar in steps and performance styles, they differ significantly in tempo—♩ = 130–150 and ♩ = 70–90, respectively. The *lassú,* another type of bachelor dance, is found in both the Küküllő region and the Mezőség area. Its main features are its specific dance melodies, some of which are sung, dance motifs in quarter notes (this contrasts with the fast and slow versions in which the motifs are always in eighths), and irregular sequencing of dance steps. The variations between the two regions also are significant. In the Küküllő area of Transylvania, the dance is performed by older men and is known as *szegégyes* ("poorish"), *öreges*, or *véneké* (both, "dance of the elderly"). This dance is performed only by special request, usually as a solo, and never in connection with other dances. In the Mezőség, the dance is called *lassú magyar,* mainly in the communities of Válaszút (Rašcruci in Romanian) and Bonchida (Bontida). This dance is paired with the fast version and performed both in groups and solo.

The final type of Transylvanian bachelors' dance is the *verbunkos.* Despite the name, this is not the same as the new-style *verbunkos*, even though new-style music is sometimes used. The formal and kinetic elements of the Transylvanian *verbunkos* closely resemble those of the bachelors' dances. One unique form, the *székelyverbunkos* of the Küküllő area, is part of the regular dance set and is performed with partners; men and women face one another and perform intricate and difficult footwork.

Old-style dances include those performed for such special occasions as work gatherings, magical events, significant calendar dates, and rites of passage. A fundamental distinction must be made between general dances that are used at ritual occasions and those that are inherently ritualistic. In the Kalotaszeg region, the bachelors' dance is performed outside immediately after a church wedding ceremony but is not a specific ritual dance. The *menyasszonyporkolás* ("burning," or "smoking, of the young bride") of the Palóc area, however, can be considered a proper ritual; in this special circle dance, the bride must jump over burning logs.

Magical dances are remnants of the distant past. Among the few extant are the Galga region's *Carneval danes,* which uses high jumping to ensure the growth of wheat. Other dances are used for special occasions in the cycle of peasant life, including harvest dances, which are popular in most regions. Work dances use mime movements to imitate specific work acts; examples are the *kaszástánc* ("scythe dance"), which imitates hay reaping, and the *baltástánc* ("hatchet dance"), which mimics woodcutting. There are also craft or guild dances, the

HUNGARY: Traditional and Popular Dance. Members of the Hungarian State Folk Ensemble perform a "spur dance" characteristic of County Békés in southern Hungary. Many traditional dances performed by men display a competitive athleticism. (Photograph by Ferencné Bartal; reprinted by permission from Varjasi and Horváth, 1956.)

most famous being the *bodnártánc* ("coopers' dance") of Erdőbénye. With their complex meanings and magical and ritual purposes, several other pantomimic dances—for example, the "Dance of the Outlaw Vendel Bene," the "Dance of the Uninvited Turks," and the "Dance of the Shepherd Lamenting the Loss of His Sheep"—could be classified as magical, work, or guild dances.

Old-style couple dances are the last family in the classification system used here. Their origins reach at least as far back as the Renaissance, if not earlier. Their slow, reserved tempo and quiet performance to old-style folk music distinguish them from new-style couple dances. Many of these can be found in the Hungarian dance traditions of Transylvania, because of that region's relative historical and geographical isolation and the strong interethnic ties among its various groups of people. The slow-stepping couple dances and medium-tempo turning dances of the Mezőség, Székelyföld, and Gyimes belong in this category. Curiously, no dance can be tied to a specific historical era. Among the Slovenes in the Zilja Valley of Carinthia, however, the "Matjažev Rejc" (King Matthias) couple dance chronicles King Matthias's heroic fight against the invading Ottoman Turks and thus hints at the existence of other, lost historic dances with Hungarian themes. Circle and chain dances may also date to at least the Middle Ages, if not earlier.

The differences between old-style and new-style dances may be more marked in some areas, such as Transylvania, than in others. As new-style dances flourished since 1700, elements of the two styles mixed and fused; in the process, the newer and more "modern" elements often won out. Currently, the *csárdás* is the only dance popular throughout the Carpathian Basin and in Hungarian communities abroad.

Revivalism: Folk Dance Onstage. Hungarian folk dance, in whole or in part, found favor in court repertories for centuries. Although specific information is scant, professional entertainers known as *joculators*, *igrics*, or *regős* were the first professionals in medieval Hungary to dance at balls, festivals, and rituals.

More information on the use of staged folk dance is available beginning in the early nineteenth century. As nationalistic sentiment increased, dance masters became popular among both the aristocracy and the aspiring middle class. Among these teachers were Lajos Szabó Szöllősi (1804–1884), Sándor Veszter (1810–1864), Sándor Lakatos (1819–1889), and Mihály Havi (1815–1880). Szöllősi was the most successful. In 1839, with the help of Gypsy violinist Márk Rózsavölgyi, he composed *Körmagyar* (Hungarian Circle), a reference to the Circle of Opposition, a political movement opposed to Habsburg rule. The dance was an instant success; in 1842 a contemporary noted that it was "being learned by two hundred couples in aristocratic circles." The *csárdás* too was adopted by the upper classes, who imitated the peasantry to counterbalance the predominance of French and Austrian dances.

In 1848, Sándor Veszter created an entire peasant wedding celebration for the stage of the new National Theater. With his friend Mihály Havi, Veszter even gathered an orchestra and dance ensemble to tour the rest of Europe performing Hungarian folk plays and dances. In the 1860s, following the restoration of the Hungarian constitution, the upper-class balls of Heves, Gömör, and Borsod counties became popular for their solely Hungarian dance bills, despite the presence of Austrian military garrisons.

The Hungarian Royal Opera House later staged several folk ballets, often using regional costumes and dances, choreographed by the Italian ballet master Luigi Mazzantini (1857–1921). In 1896, during the Millennarian Exhibit in Budapest, organizer and ethnographer János Jankó had peasant villagers perform their dances for an international audience.

Reawakening nationalist sentiments after World War I led to increasing numbers of local festivals, regional and national cultural programs, and harvest and folklore festivals throughout the country, with people dressing in traditional costumes and dancing all day long. The aristocratic *palotás* ("parlor dance") was performed by a women's gymnastic group under the direction of Edit Weber Elekes in 1928 at the Olympic Games in Amsterdam. Meanwhile, the Royal Opera, led by Ede Brada (1879–1955) and Gyula Harangozó (1908–1974), acquired a folk character, with many ballet evenings featuring regional traditions in both music and dance. In 1929 Béla Paulini (1881–1945) successfully staged Zoltán Kodály's folk musical *János Háry*, using peasant performers from the village of Csákvár. In the same year, a modern company led by Olga Szentpál (1895–1957) turned for the first time to folk customs and dances to perform folk ballads with modernist interpretations.

Hungarian populism, a strongly democratic political movement, developed in the 1930s to create unity and ethnic Hungarian identity among populations both inside and outside the country. Its national movement, the Gyöngyösbokréta (Pearly Bouquet), brought hundreds of peasant dance groups to perform in Budapest each year between 1931 and 1944, reviving traditional dances throughout Hungary and saving them from extinction. During the feast of Saint Stephen on 20 August, peasant groups performed on the open-air stages of Budapest's parks. Many of these groups later traveled the countryside and even to major cities of western Europe, exhibiting their local dances, customs, and dress.

A similar movement spread dance through the Hungarian communities of Transylvania. Under the direction of Jenő Szentimrei, approximately fifty dancers from five villages in Kalotaszeg staged a series of performances of a folk ballad, as *Csáki Biró Lánya* (The Daughter of Judge Csáki). Many local customs and dances were incorporated in this lavish folk play.

In the late 1930s, István Molnár (1908–1987) left his modern dance career in Paris to return to Hungary, where he began to collect folk dances and perform them with the Muharay folk ensemble. He developed his own teaching technique using strenuous folk dance movements to train able dancers. The Molnár technique's effectiveness was not recognized until much later.

[*See also* Hungarian State Folk Ensemble *and the entry on Molnár.*]

BIBLIOGRAPHY

Andrásfalvy, Bertalan. "Párbajszerű táncainkról." *Ethnographia* 74 (1963): 55–83.

Balassa, Iván, and Gyula Ortutay. *Hungarian Ethnography and Folklore.* Budapest, 1985.

Belényessy, Márta. *Kultúra és tánc a bukovinai székelyeknél.* Budapest, 1958.

Cardaro, Janice. "Hungarian Panel Discussion." *UCLA Journal of Dance Ethnology* 18 (1994): 37–50.

Felföldi, László. "A finnugor népek Néptánckutatásáról." *Tánctudományi tanulmányok* (1986–1987): 291–312.

Felföldi, László, ed. *Martin György emlékezete.* Budapest, 1993.

Kallós, Zoltán, and György Martin. "A gyimesi csángók táncélete és táncai." *Tánctudományi tanulmányok* (1969–1970): 195–254.

Kaposi, Edit, and Ernő Pesovár, eds. *The Art of Dance in Hungary.* Translated by Lili Halápy. Budapest, 1985.

Karácsony, Zoltán. "Egy régies szóalak (fittyent-pittyent) története és elterjedése." *Tánctudományi tanulmányok* (1992–1993): 130–138.

Könczei, Csilla. "Motivumépitkezési elvek a hétfalusi borica táncban." *Tánctudományi tanulmányok* (1988–1989): 145–170.

Kürti, László. "The Bachelors' Dance of Transylvania." *Arabesque* 8 (March–April 1983): 8–15.

Kürti, László. "The Ungaresca and Heyduck Music and Dance Tradition of Renaissance Europe." *Sixteenth-Century Journal* 14 (Spring 1983): 63–104.

Kürti, László. "Juhmérés és henderikázás Magyarlónán." *Ethnographia* 98.2–4 (1987): 385–393.

Kürti, László. "Language, Symbol, and Dance: An Analysis of Historicity in Movement and Meaning." *Shaman* 2.1 (1994): 3–60.

Lugossy, Emma, and Sándor Gönyey. *Magyar népi táncok.* Budapest, 1947.

Martin, György, and Ernő Pesovár. "A Structural Analysis of the Hungarian Folk Dance." *Acta Ethnographica Academiae Scientiarum Hungaricae* 10.1–2 (1961): 1–40.

Martin, György. "Determination of the Motif Types in Dance Folklore." *Acta Ethnographica Academiae Scientiarum Hungaricae* 12 (1963): 162–210.

Martin, György. *Motivumkutatás, motivumrendszerezés.* Budapest, 1964.

Martin, György. *Magyar tánctipusok és táncdialektusok.* 3 vols. Budapest, 1970–1972.

Martin, György. *A Magyar körtánc és Európai rokonsága.* Budapest, 1979.

Martin, György. "A Survey of the Hungarian Folk Dance Research." *Dance Studies* 6 (1982): 9–45.

Martin, György. "Tánc és társadalom: A történeti táncnévadás tipusai itthon és Európában." In *Történeti antropológia*, edited by Tamás Hofer. Budapest, 1984.

Martin, György, ed. *International Monograph on Folk Dance*, vol. 1, *Hungary, France.* Budapest, 1986.

Mintz, Elissa, and Bennett Feld. "Hungarian Tanchaz Dancing." *Viltis* 51 (June–August 1992): 14–15.

Molnár, István. *Magyar tánchagyományok.* Budapest, 1947.

Pávai, István. *Az erdélyi és moldvai Magyarság népi tánczenéje.* Budapest, 1993.

Pesovár, Ernő. "Küzdő karakterű páros táncaink." *Népi kultúra–népi társadalom* 9 (1977): 329–356.

Pesovár, Ernő. *A Magyar nép táncélete.* Budapest, 1978.

Pesovár, Ferenc. *Juhait kereső pásztor.* Székesfehévár, 1983.

Peters, Kurt. "Die höchste Stufe choreographischer Kunst: Zum Volkstanz-Festival nach Ungarn." *Ballett-Journal/Das Tanzarchiv* 31 (October 1983): 68–73.

Rearick, Elizabeth C. *Dances of the Hungarians.* New York, 1939.

Réthei Prikkel, Márián. *A Magyarság táncai.* Budapest, 1924.

Reynolds, William C. "Improvisation in Hungarian Folk Dance: Towards a Generative Grammar of European Folk Dance." *Acta Ethnographica Hungarica* 39 (1994).

Vályi, Rószi. *A táncművészet története.* Budapest, 1969.

Varjasi, Rezso, and Vine Horváth. *Hungarian Rhapsody: The Hungarian State Folk Ensemble.* Budapest, 1956.

Viski, Károly. *Hungarian Dances.* Translated by Sydney H. Sweetland. London, 1937.

Wilson, Tink, and Eva Kiss. "An Interview with László Dioszegi." *Viltis* 48 (January–February 1990): 12–13.

LÁSZLÓ KÜRTI

Theatrical Dance before World War II

Ballet in Hungary was first seen in the princely courts of the Esterházy family at Ezterháza (now Fertőd, Hungary) and at Kismarton (now Eisenstadt, Austria), where dancers from the Vienna Opera and other companies performed in spectacular dramatic and musical productions to entertain aristocratic and royal guests. In the summer of 1772, Jean-Georges Noverre's troupe from the Vienna court theater performed his *Le Jugement de Pâris* at Ezterháza, featuring the talented young Marguerita Dolphine as Venus. When Prince Esterházy's court moved to Kismarton in 1794, the luxurious opening ceremonies included dances by Salvatore Viganò and his wife Maria Medina, who also danced in *Pygmalion* there in 1797.

Amateur dancers had performed earlier in the so-called school dramas, and dance societies were formed early in the nineteenth century to perform national and folk dances with technical distinction in Hungary as in England, France, and Italy. The National Theater opened in Pest in 1837; in 1839, *La Fille Mal Gardée* was "adapted" to a set of dances compiled by János Kolossánszky. This was followed by several guest performances, including some by Fanny Elssler and her partner Gustave Carey in the summer of 1844; they performed a pas de deux from *Giselle*, and Elssler danced her *cachucha*. In fall 1846, Arthur Saint-Léon staged and danced *Ondine, ou La Naïade* with Fanny Cerrito, followed by a month-long dance potpourri. In 1847, Augusta Maywood and Pasquale Borri appeared in *Giselle* and Frederico Campilli staged *Paquita* by Antonio Guerra and Joseph Mazilier. This began the forty-year domination of the Vienna Ballet in Hungary, interrupted only for two years during the War of Independence (1848–1849); during this period, Sándor Veszter and Lajos Kilányi staged ballets with Hungarian themes.

In 1850 a committee of aristocrats took over management of the National Theater. They banned "pedestrian" spectators even from the galleries and began to reform the ballet by inviting foreign dancers to appear, including Lucile Grahn (to dance *La Péri* and other works), Pepita da Oliva, and Paul and Marie Taglioni. Cerrito and Elssler undoubtedly scored the biggest successes, although the latter was criticized for her love of money. Grahn was praised for the mime scenes in Jules Perrot's ballets and for using Hungarian dancers in addition to her foreign partner. Oliva was criticized for being sexually provocative, and the Taglionis were found to be cool and unexpressive.

The most important event in national dance was the engagement of Emilia Aranyváry, first solo dancer at the Théâtre Lyrique of Paris and the greatest Hungarian ballerina of the century. Between 1854 and 1859, she was admired by both audiences and critics for her dancing in many ballets, including *Esmeralda*, *La Péri*, and *Giselle*. One critic later wrote, "When she left, ballet stopped being an autonomous art." For two decades after her departure, no ballet premiered at the National Theater of Pest.

Budapest Opera Ballet. The cities of Buda and Pest were united in 1872. In 1884, the Royal Opera House opened in Budapest, an achievement of great political and cultural significance, which testified to a certain Hungarian national independence within the Austro-Hungarian Empire. This event, however, did not change the course of ballet's development in Hungary. Campilli was still ballet master and transferred the ballets he had composed in the late 1870s—among them, *Coppélia* and *Sylvia*—to the opera stage, where they were performed by a seventy-member company with one male dancer, Enrico Pini.

The survival of Viennese taste was evidenced by several hundred performances of Josef Hassreiter's *Die Puppenfee*, which premiered in Budapest in 1888 and continued until the 1930s. In constant but unequal competition with Vienna, preparations for the coming Millennium, which celebrated Hungary's conquest by the Magyars in 896 CE, increased demands for the presentation of ballets with Hungarian plots set to music by Hungarian composers. The best of these was *Viora* (1891), which won acclaim as the first "national dance play." Its music was by Károly Szabados, and its plot was derived from *Fairy of the Tarn* by the Hungarian novelist Mór Jókai. The choreographer Luigi Mazzantini traveled to Transylvania to study Hungarian dances and brought back Székler (Transylvanian Hungarian) boys to perform the *borica* on stage.

The first guests in the Hungarian Royal Opera House were dancers from Saint Petersburg's ballet company in 1899, who appeared again in 1901. Their high technical standards and artistic expression overwhelmed the public, critics, and management, and cries went up that the Budapest Opera Ballet company's own standards should be raised. To that end, ballet master Nicola Guerra and solo dancer Ede Brada were engaged in 1902. Guerra was given double duty, to stage new ballets and to raise the company to a higher technical level. In his thirteen years there, he reformed the opera's corps de ballet and trained such solo artists as Brada, Emilia Nirschy, Anna Pallay, and Ferenc Nádasi; the last later transmitted his training to subsequent generations of dancers. Guerra's best ballet was *The Dwarf Grenadier* (music by Adolf Szikla), which had one hundred performances between 1903 and 1934; it featured village youngsters who simulated bodily defects to avoid being recruited. The production's success resulted mostly from the unity of dance and music, a clever exploitation of farcical situations, and, significantly, males dancing male roles.

In 1912, the Ballets Russes de Serge Diaghilev visited Budapest with its avant-garde repertory. As a result, the opera's directors commissioned Guerra to stage a modern ballet to Ludwig van Beethoven's score for *The Creatures of Prometheus*. As a fervent exponent of academic ballet, however, Guerra was unequal to the task and the result was a stylistic incongruity.

Following Guerra's departure, the ballet declined until 1924 under Otto Zobisch, who was not successful in mixing classical and modern ballets. In 1917 the opera decided to stage Béla Bartók's *The Wooden Prince*, but the choreography had to be done by solo dancers Brada and Pallay and librettist Béla Balázs. In 1919, politically and socially repressive regime prohibited the arts from evolving along progressive lines, and ballet was straitjacketed by a return to academic traditionalism.

The first big, successful production following World War I was *Little Princess Hollyhock* (choreography by Ede Brada; music by Rezső Máder), which used a folklore-inspired plot but succeeded largely because of its lavish sets and costumes. Although similar ballets, such as Brada's *Butterfly Love* and *Prince Argyle*, used monotonous dances and syrupy plots with some success, others were stylistically unsuitable and failed. Between 1925 and 1935, director Miklós Radnai made several attempts to raise the level of Hungarian ballet. Brada's 1926 production of *Petrouchka*, however, was conceived in an academic style that could not express the music's dramatic force.

The year 1927 brought several important guest performances. Anna Pavlova's company gave five recitals in March, and Diaghilev's Ballets Russes appeared again. This time, the director's invitations to modern choreographers brought better results. A. Gaubier staged *Le Tricorne* with the young dancer Gyula Harangozó. The Rudolf Kölling company from Berlin staged *Schéhérazade* as a classical ballet but in German expressionist style.

The third guest, Jan Ciepliński of Poland, became a permanent choreographer for the company in 1930 and was given the dual task of staging ballets in the style of the Ballets Russes and creating a Hungarian national ballet. From Diaghilev's repertory Ciepliński took *Die Josephslegende*, and from Jean Börlin's Ballets Suédois he took *La Boîte à Joujoux*. Despite his foreign origin, Ciepliński did his best to meet the demand for national ballets; the most noteworthy was his 1933 production of *Hungarian Dreams* (music by Franz Liszt), based on studies in Hungarian folk dance. To lay the foundation of national ballet more firmly, Hungarian-born Aurelio Milloss was invited to stage and dance *Petrouchka* in 1933 and then to choreograph *Kurut's Tale* (music by Zoltán Kodály) in 1935. Ciepliński also rechoreographed *The Wooden Prince* in 1935; the revival's success was largely attributed to the ultrafashionable sets by Zoltán Fülöp and Gusztáv Oláh, Harangozó's excellent performance in the title role, and the music itself. [*See the entries on Ciepliński and Milloss.*]

In the second half of the 1930s, a truly Hungarian national ballet was born and attained international standards thanks to the convergent activities of three great artists: the choreographer Harangozó, the teacher Nádasi, and the stage designer Oláh, who also acted as librettist and ballet director. On 6 December 1936, Harangozó's first choreographic work, *Scene in the Inn*, set to music by Jenő Hubay, premiered with Fülöp's sets. Having studied Hungarian folk dance, Harangozó succeeded in the production by combining the dancing and mime scenes into a dynamic one-act ballet, thus launching the dance play genre in a national folkloric style.

In 1938 Harangozó re-created the *Polovtsian Dances* from *Prince Igor* and *La Salade* for the Budapest company, but without copying the original productions. The power and conciseness of the *Polovtsian Dances* led one British critic to remark that the production was "better than the original." Two other events of importance in Harangozó's early period were the creation of dances to two Bartók compositions that had been conceived for the dance stage. In November 1939, Harangozó revived *The Wooden Prince* in the Bartókian spirit and felt it his duty to choreograph *The Miraculous Mandarin;* the production was banned after its premiere in 1941, resulting in a serious depression not only to Harangozó's creative energy but also to Hungarian ballet.

Harangozó's successes in this period cannot be imagined without Nádasi's contributions as ballet master beginning in 1937. An exponent of Enrico Cecchetti's classical methods yet also open to modern trends, Nádasi began to train dance artists in technical skills that equalled any in Europe. Some of the best dancers of the period—Harangozó, Bella Bordy, Melinda Ottrubay, Karola Szalay, Ilona Vera, Ferenc Kőszegi, Zoltán Sallay, and Károly Zsedényi—used his methods in their exercises. Among Nádasi's younger pupils were Dóra Csinády, Nóra Kovács, Gabriella Lakatos, Vera Pásztor, Zsuzsa Kun, Klotild Ugray, István Rabovsky, Ernő Vashegyi, and Viktor Fülöp. [*See the entries on Harangozó and Nádasi.*]

BIBLIOGRAPHY

Dienes, Gedeon P. "History of the State Opera Ballet, Budapest." *Hungarian Dance News*, nos. 1–3 (1978); no. 1 (1979); nos. 3–4 (1980); nos. 1–2 (1981).

Dienes, Gedeon P., and Lívia Fuchs, eds. *A Színpadi tánc Történeté Magyarországon.* Budapest, 1989.

Gelencsér, Ágnes. "Balettmüvészetünk az Opera-házban, 1884–1919." *Tánctudományi tanulmányok* (1982–1983).

Kaposi, Edit, and Ernő Pesovár, eds. *The Art of Dance in Hungary.* Translated by Lili Halápy. Budapest, 1985.

Kaposi, Edit, and Zsuzsa Kövágó, eds. *Válogatás a korabeli sajtöböl és a táncarchívum gyüjteményeiböl*, vol. 1, *Antológia a hazai tánciroda-lomböl, 1884–1914.* Budapest, 1987.

Koegler, Horst. "Budapest" and "Szeged." In *The Concise Oxford Dictionary of Ballet.* New York, 1977.

Körtvélyes, Géza. "Balettmüvészetünk az Opera-házban, 1919–1945." *Tánctudományi tanulmányok* (1982–1983).

Vályi, Rózsi, ed. *A magyar balett történetéböl.* Budapest, 1956.

Vályi, Rózsi. *Balettek könyve* (1959). Budapest, 1980.

GEDEON P. DIENES and GÉZA KÖRTVÉLYES

Theatrical Dance since World War II

Following World War II, Gyula Harangozó began his second creative period with a series of Hungarian-inspired ballets—*The Miraculous Mandarin* (1945), *Mischievous Students* (1949), and *Kerchief* (1951). Choreographed to music by Ferenc Farkas and Gusztáv Oláh's libretto from a Mór Jókai short story, *Mischievous Students* depicts students, teachers, horseherders, and stallkeepers at a fair; the work has a wide array of humorous shadings and gags and a diversity of Hungarian folk dance elements. A three-act ballet, *Kerchief* is an enlarged version of *Scene in the Inn* (1936), with a more realistic rendering of a Gypsy camp using both Hungarian and Gypsy folk dance elements. Both ballets remained in the repertory for many years.

Other Harangozó creations in this period were rooted in foreign traditions, including *Le Tricorne* (1947) and *Coppélia* (1953). In the former, he used Manuel de Falla's wild rhythms and the spirit of the Spanish folk tale to ridicule the three-cornered hat as a symbol of power. The three-act *Coppélia* was a typical Harangozó ballet as he humanized the evil magician by transforming him into a pottering jack-of-all-trades who performs no miracles but does play tricks.

Not until 1956 did Harangozó re-create *The Miraculous Mandarin* according to Béla Bartók's original conception.

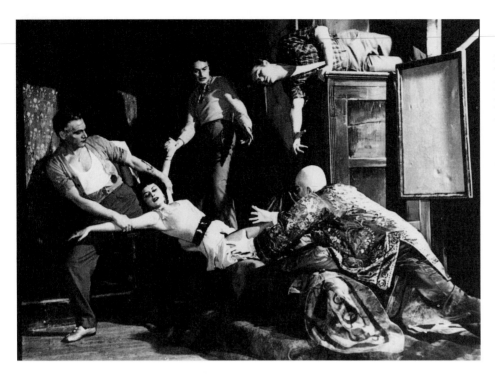

HUNGARY: Theatrical Dance since World War II. A scene from the Hungarian Opera Ballet's 1956 production of *The Miraculous Mandarin*, choreographed by Gyula Harangozó. This lurid one-act ballet, with a score by Béla Bartók, is about three pimps who force a prostitute to steal from her customers and eventually kill a wealthy Chinese man. Here, Gabriella Lakatos appears as the Girl, Ernő Vashegyi as the Mandarin, and Andor Gál, Imre Eck, and Zoltán Sallay as the Ruffians. (Photograph by László Tóth; from Magyar Távirati Iroda Photo Archives, Budapest; courtesy of Gedeon P. Dienes.)

In this period, he concluded his series of modern dramatic ballets with *Schéhérazade* and his full-evening Hungarian works with *Mattie the Gooseboy* (1960); the latter was inspired by a folk tale of vengeance by a poor lad unjustly beaten by his landlord. In the 1960s many of Harangozó's ballets were revived as living testimony to the birth and first great period of Hungarian ballet.

During Harangozó's long tenure, the Budapest Opera Ballet also invited many other choreographers. Aurelio Milloss revived *The Creatures of Prometheus* in 1942, the same year in which he staged Ferenc Nádasi's one-act *Sylvia*, which also was couched in noble classicism. Jan Ciepliński was engaged again and produced five new works, including *Boléro*, which remained a public favorite. From 1946 to 1948, Ciepliński produced several ballets in Budapest, among them *Divertimento*, to music by the Hungarian composer and dance critic Sándor Jemnitz; this was the first abstract ballet on the opera's stage. This period also saw the opera ballet's only Western import in 1948—an evening of Janine Charrat's ballets, including Maurice Ravel's *Introduction et Allegro* and Igor Stravinsky's *Jeu de Cartes*.

In the 1950s, the era of full-evening Soviet ballets, a promising Hungarian talent, Ernő Vashegyi, choreographed his first works. *Petrouchka* (1949) and *The Wooden Prince* (1952) testified to his great musicality and deep sense of neoclassicism. To music by Jenő Kenessey, he produced *Bihari's Song* (1954); in this work, the plot's turning points are conceived in theatricalized folk dance style.

Throughout this postwar period of growth and development, choreographers were attracted to Bartók's music, even though the scores he wrote expressly for the stage tended to fare less well there than did his nonprogrammatic compositions. The latter tended to have simpler rhythmic structures that lent themselves better to choreographic interpretation. The scores of both *The Wooden Prince* and *The Miraculous Mandarin* are extremely complex, although the former sums up the features of Bartók's earlier works while the latter is the product of his experimental years. The music of the *Prince* creates a quiet atmosphere and has great harmonic beauty; the *Mandarin* is more direct and disturbing in capturing city noises. Both plots are symbolic. The apparently simple story of a conceited princess who nearly loses a fine husband by falling in love with an elegant puppet is an allegory of the dissolution of the individual in the universe. In the *Mandarin*, ruffians use a prostitute to lure a victim to their den, although he will not die until he can hold the girl in his arms; death lies in the satisfaction of desire.

The most successful ballets using Bartók's music have been plotless. Outstanding among them are Imre Eck's choreographies for *Music for Strings, Percussion, and Celesta, Concerto,* and *Divertimento,* and Harangozó's to *Dance Suite.* Choreographers outside Hungary have also done well with such scores. [*See the entry on Bartók.*]

From the mid-1930s on, a corps of scenic and costume designers within the opera's ballet company became coauthors of ballet choreography. Gusztáv Oláh had the greatest impact on the Hungarian ballet stage from the 1920s until his death in 1956; he was not only a capable designer able to work in diverse artistic styles, but also a librettist and then ballet director from the mid-1940s on. Zoltán Fülöp, Oláh's pupil and colleague, created many ballet sets between 1928 and 1968 in cooperation with costume designer Tivadar Márk. Since 1950, Gábor Forray has been a worthy follower of the company's stylistic traditions.

Soviet ballet's achievements made themselves felt in Hungary in 1950 with Petr Ilich Tchaikovsky's *The Nutcracker* and Boris Asafiev's *The Flames of Paris*, both choreographed by Vasily Vainonen. The two productions opened up both the great classics and Soviet ballet dramas to the Hungarian stage. The Budapest company could perform at a level equal to Soviet companies because of ballet master Nádasi's fifteen years of instruction to his dancers and Vainonen's and Armashevskaya's recruitment, which increased the company from sixty to one hundred dancers. The Soviets also introduced Agrippina Vaganova's method, which allowed the State Ballet Institute to produce such dancers as Adél Orosz, Jacqueline Menyhárt, Vera Szumrák, Ferenc Havas, and Viktor Róna.

In the early 1960s, a new generation of choreographers put works on the stage. After his *Csongor and Tünde* (1959), Imre Eck staged five more ballets with the opera company, including Stravinsky's *Le Sacre du Printemps* and Bartók's *Music for Strings, Percussion, and Celesta* (1965). Sándor Barkóczy used neoclassical idioms in *Classical Symphony* (1966), set to music by Prokofiev, and Bartók's *Dance Suite* (1968), among others.

László Seregi's choreography dominated the opera ballet's stage in the 1970s and early 1980s. After several successful creations in the folk dance idiom and dance interludes in operas, he conceived a production of *Spartacus* that combined Harangozó's realism, Soviet traditions, and a variety of styles from classical to naturalistic. Its success earned him a commission to rechoreograph the two Bartók ballets, *The Wooden Prince* and *The Miraculous Mandarin,* to commemorate the twenty-fifth anniversary of the composer's death (Forray and Márk designed the sets for all three ballets). Seregi used the entire score for the *Prince* in a combination of neoclassicism and modern dance; unlike earlier versions, the puppet aggressively courts and then jilts the princess. Seregi's *Mandarin* was closer to its forerunners except in costuming: the Mandarin wore a skin-colored leotard to symbolize general human qualities. In 1981 Seregi rechoreographed the two Bartók works again. In this version of the *Prince*, he emphasized the folk tale and the sets with large groups. In the *Mandarin,* he intensified the protagonist's Asian character and the dramatic power of closed space in the ruffians' den.

Following his parodistic *Sylvia,* which was done in *fin-de-siècle* style, Seregi produced the two-act *The Cedar Tree* (1975), a sequence of dance scenes conceived as surrealistic visions of the tragic life of Tivadar Csontváry Kosztka, the great Hungarian painter of the twentieth century. In

HUNGARY: Theatrical Dance since World War II. László Seregi's first major production for the Hungarian Opera Ballet was his version of *Spartacus,* set to the Khachaturian score. Seen here with the company in act 2, Viktor Fülöp created the role of Spartacus at the ballet's premiere in Budapest in 1968. Gábor Forray designed the scenery, and Tivadar Márk created the revealing costumes. (Photograph from Magyar Távirati Iroda Photo Archives, Budapest; courtesy of Gedeon P. Dienes.)

the late 1970s, Seregi turned to smaller forms. His *Chamber Music 1* (1976) is a virtuosic neoclassical tale of rivalry between two ballerinas. *Serenade* is a symphonic ballet, and *On the Town* is a jazzy Broadway-style pastiche (both 1976, music by Leonard Bernstein).

An evening of ballets by Hungarian composers in 1978 included Seregi's *Variations on a Nursery Song*, which used flashback to recall happy and tragic moments in life, as well as Antal Fodor's *Eighth Eclogue* (music compiled by Iván Székely), which symbolically rendered the poem of the same title by Miklós Radnóti into a dialogue about humanity and the meaning of human tragedy.

Fodor came from Eck's modern-dance workshop in Pécs, where he already had shown his musicality and penchant for neoclassicism. After *Victim* (music by Sándor Szokolay), his first work for the Budapest Opera Ballet, he turned again to the symphonic genre with Bach's *Violin Concerto in E Major* (1974), using classical steps with elements of modern dance. This probably has been Fodor's most mature and successful work. His *Metamorphoses* to Claudio Monteverdi's *Orfeo* offered an oratorical dance play; he followed this in 1977 with an "Evening with Fodor," which included Ravel's *Boléro*. Later works displayed his wide-ranging interests, from the good humor of *Via la Vita* to the deep psychological conflict of *Polymorphia* (both, 1979). In *Próba* (which means both "rehearsal" and "trial") in 1982, he cries out against the fate of the persecuted by relating the rehearsals for a passion play to the dramas that occur in a contemporary ballet company; he accomplished this by coupling Gábor Presser's rock music with passages from Johann Sebastian Bach's *Passion*.

Among the outstanding dancers of the Budapest company in the 1970s were Mária Kékesi, Katalin Csarnóy, Márta Metzger, Lilla Pártay, Ildikó Pongor, Edit Szabadi, Imre Dózsa, Sándor Erdélyi, and Gábor Kevehàzi. Dancers Gyula Harangozó, Jr., Jenő Lőcsei, and György Szakály became the principal interpreters of Seregi's and Fodor's creations as well as those by modern foreign choreographers. Most of these dancers studied both in Hungary and the Soviet Union, and many have performed as guest artists with major European companies.

A repertory already enriched by the introduction of the great classics and Soviet realism of the 1950s continued to broaden public tastes until the mid-1970s, particularly with revivals and the premiere of *The Creation of the World* by Natalia Kasatkina and Vladimir Vasiliev in 1976. The company was open to other influences, including modern Western trends, which began with Frederick Ashton's *La Fille Mal Gardée* in 1971; this was followed by Bournonville's *La Sylphide*; Harald Lander's *Études*; several Maurice Béjart ballets (*The Firebird, Opus 5, Le Sacre du Printemps*, and *Would This Be Death?*); a 1977 evening of George Balanchine's works (including *Serenade, Apollo,*

and *Symphony in C*) and a 1979 production of Balanchine's *Agon*; Alvin Ailey's *The River*; an evening of Alberto Méndez works, including *Plasmasis, Dolls, The River and the Forest,* and *Spring*; Hans van Manen's *Adagio Hammerklavier*; Rudi van Dantzig's *Monument for a Dead Boy*; Toer van Schayk's *Forsaken Garden*; Jiří Kylián's *Symphony in D Major* (music by Franz Joseph Haydn) and *Nuages* (music by Claude Debussy), both in 1984; and Oleg Vinogradov's *Cinderella* (1984).

During the 1980s, some of the company's young dancers, Ivánka Sámdor, Teodora Bán, Lilla Pártay, Aranka Hegyesi, Gábor Kevehàzi, and Péter László, began their own choreographic experimentations in what was to become the Chamber Ballet of the Hungarian State Opera. In 1986, the year devoted to Franz Liszt's music, the opera management staged a night of their works which included László Pethő's *Death Wedding*, Lilla Pártay's *Funérailles*, Péter László's *Divertissement*, and Gabor Kevehàzi's *Struggle*. Two Soviet revivals and a new work, Vladimir Vasiliev's *Macbeth* (music by Konstatin Molchanov) demonstrated a new choreographic trend from Moscow. In an evening devoted to Hungarian-born choreographer Aurelio Milloss, *Estri* and *The Miraculous Mandarin* were performed in 1990. One of the most important events was László Seregi's *Romeo and Juliet* (which admittedly reflected Zeffirelli's visual impact). This began a Shakespeare renaissance on the Hungarian dance stage. To his *A Midsummer Night's Dream* (music by Felix Mendelssohn, 1989), Seregi added *The Taming of the Shrew* (music by Károly Goldmark, 1994) to complete his Shakespeare triptych. As a result, young choreographers were further influenced by literature. Lilla Partay created her *Anna Karenina* (to music by Tchaikovsky, 1991) and *The Moor of Venice* (to music by Schubert, 1994) and Péter László, another young dancer, choreographed *Derby* (music by György Vukán, 1989).

The social changes in the early 1990s impacted on the maintenance of the theater and the economics of programming. Endeavors were made to stage performances in cooperation with the opera and private funds. As a result, Gábor Kevehàzi choreographed *Cristoforo* (music by Béla Szakcs Lakatos, 1992) to celebrate the five hundredth anniversary of the discovery of America. Rudolf Nureyev performed the role of the Angel. It was his last stage performance. To commemorate this event, the EuroDance Foundation started the Budapest International Ballet Competition in his memory. The first was held in 1994; the second was held in 1996. Of major importance during the 1990s was Robert North's *Death and the Maiden* (music by Schubert, 1990) and the continuation of the annual summer gala, World Stars in the Opera. Here outstanding performers show the recent achievements in dance to Budapest audiences. A change in opinion regarding the importance of ballet in the opera is reflected in the presentation of full-evening ballets, such as Viktor Róna's *Sleeping Beauty* (1991) and Youri Vámos's *Swan Lake* (1995). In September 1996 a unique series was organized by the EuroDance Foundation and the Hungarian State Opera. For seven evenings, the Festival of Mandarins featured fifteen Hungarian and foreign choreographic versions of Béla Bartók's composition, *The Miraculous Mandarin*. György Szakály was director between 1992–1995 and Gyula Harangozó, Jr., has held the post since 1996.

The Budapest Opera Ballet first began to perform abroad in the 1950s, beginning in Romania, Czechoslovakia, and Poland. Harangozó's *The Miraculous Mandarin* opened a European tour in Turin, Italy, in 1961. Productions of both the *Mandarin* and *The Wooden Prince* won the Golden Star Prize at the 1963 International Dance Festival in Paris; successful appearances followed at the Edinburgh Festival (1963, 1973, and 1983) and in Moscow (1965 and 1971) and were significant moments among almost six hundred guest performances abroad.

Ballets have been produced sporadically at the Metropolitan Operetta Theater as interludes under the direction of Ágnes Roboz and Hedvig Hidas. Choreographer Richárd Bogár produced *West Side Story,* among other ballets, and Éva Gáczy has choreographed popular productions of children's fairy tales, including Sergei Prokofiev's *Cinderella.* Between 1987 and 1991 the ensemble was led by Lilla Pártay who enhanced the technical and artistic standards of the dancers. Partay also produced "Dance in the Realm of Music," which included works by herself, Gábor Keveházi, and Zoltán Imre. László Pethő has led the ensemble since 1992 and has engaged choreographers best suited to the ensemble such as László Seregi, Ferenc Novák, Zoltán Imre, József Gajdos, Andrea Ladányi, and György Krámer.

In addition to the big companies, a general revival in interest in ballet can be attested by the presence of provincial dance groups such as the Miskolc National Theater where the head of the ensemble, István Majoros, has staged versions of *The Nutcracker* and *The Fountain of Bakhchisarai.* In the Csokonai Theater of Debrecen, György Nagy has engaged guest choreographers, most recently György Szakály who produced *The Death of a Faun* (music by Debussy, 1996). The Veszprém Dance Workshop operates under choreographers Katalin Lorinc and György Krámer.

International Activities. Hungary actively participates in the international dance scene. In addition to the many companies and performers who appear abroad, experts are exchanged annually under cultural agreements with other countries. In 1973, Gedeon P. Dienes became a founding member of the Dance Committee of the International Theater Institute, serving on its board for more than a decade. Conferences with foreign participants are

HUNGARY: Theatrical Dance since World War II. The Szeged National Theater's 1967 production of *La Création du Monde,* choreographed by Zoltán Imre to the score by Darius Milhaud. Here, Imre appears with Andrea Lászay. (Photograph by József Siflis; courtesy of Gedeon P. Dienes.)

frequently held in Hungary. Since 1979, the Interballet festivals have been held every four years with the participation of foreign companies, which show their work of the previous five years. From the early 1990s, it has alternated with the Interfolkdance festival. Both festivals are organized by the Dance Forum (Tibor Galambos, artistic director) and feature the widest possible range of dance forms. Contemporary dance companies are included in the Budapest Autumn Festival held in October and the Spring Festival held in April features works in classical style.

[*See also* Ballet Sopiane; Győr Ballet; Szeged Contemporary Ballet; *and the entries on Eck, Kun, Markó, Molnár, Róna, and Seregi.*]

BIBLIOGRAPHY

Dienes, Gedeon P. "Hungary: World Survey." *The Dancing Times* (August 1963).

Dienes, Gedeon P. "Dance Art in Hungary." In *The Hungarian Theatre Today*, edited by György Lengyel. Budapest, 1983.

Dienes, Gedeon P. "Report: Hungary." *Ballet International* 7 (September 1984).

Dienes, Gedeon P., and Lívia Fuchs, eds. *A Színpadi tánc történeté Magyarországon*. Budapest, 1989.

Fuchs, Lívai. "Coming Back to Past Traditions." *Ballett International* 16 (April 1993): 32–33.

Gelencsér, Ágnes. "A Contemporary Ballet Institute: Interview with Imre Dózsa." *Hungarian Ballet News*, no. 3–4 (1982): 4–5.

Kaposi, Edit, and Ernő Pesovár, eds. *The Art of Dance in Hungary*. Translated by Lili Halápy. Budapest, 1985.

Kargl, Silvia. "Made in Hungary." *Ballet International/Tanz Aktuell* (November 1995): 54–55.

Koegler, Horst. "The Hungarian State Ballet at the Budapest Opera House." *Dance and Dancers* (August 1973): 52–56.

Körtvélyes, Géza. "A magyar balettművészet tizenöt." *Tánctudományi tanulmányok* (1961–1962): 11–24. Includes a summary in French, "Quinze années de ballet hongrois."

Körtvélyes, Géza, and György Lőrinc. *The Budapest Ballet: The Ballet Ensemble of the Hungarian State Opera House*. 2 vols. Translated by Gedeon P. Dienes and Éva Rácz. Budapest, 1971–1981.

Körtvélyes, Géza. "Korszerű tendenciák a magyar táncművészetben." *Tánctudományi tanulmányok* (1978–1979).

Manhercz, Károly, ed. *Hungarian State Ballet Institute*. Budapest, 1981.

Percival, John. "The Inspiration from Traditions of the Hungarian National Ballet in Budapest." *Dance and Dancers* (April 1977): 27–31.

Peters, Kurt. "Interbalett '79 in Budapest." *Das Tanzarchiv* 27 (April 1979): 183–194.

Staud, Géza, ed. *A Budapesti Operaház 100 éve*. Budapest, 1984.

Vitányi, Iván. "Uj törekvések a magyar balettművészetben." *Tánctudományi tanulmányok* (1969–1970).

GEDEON P. DIENES and ZSUZSA KŐVÁGÓ

Modern Dance

Modern dance in Hungary has had a short but significant history, which began after Isadora Duncan first danced for theater audiences in Budapest in April 1902 and then toured the country to tremendous acclaim. Alice Madzsar, following study with Bess Mensendieck in Berlin and Lofthus in Norway, began her instruction in 1912; at this time Valéria Dienes showed "free movements of the human body" to her friends in Budapest. Dienes had studied philosophy under Henri Bergson and trained in "Greek gymnastics" with Raymond Duncan's Parisian colony. Both Madzsar and Dienes relied on the aesthetics of the human body, primarily the female, although Madzsar was interested in physical and mental health and Dienes in the scientific analysis and artistic expression of human movement. Dienes's first public performance was in the spring of 1917; with her young women pupils, barefoot and dressed in chitons, dancing joy and sorrow, Dienes made dozens of appearances until 1919.

Olga Szentpál became the third significant exponent of modern dance, which came to be called "art of movement" (from the German *Bewegungskunst*). After studying at Émile Jaques-Dalcroze's school in Hellerau, Germany, Szentpál opened her own school in Budapest in 1919. With her husband Mariusz Rabinovszky, an art historian and critic, she evolved her own system of instruction which went beyond the Dalcrozean concept of *rythmicienne*. Her system consisted of four principal parts: the morphology of artistic movement, function theory to analyze movement, composition theory, and expression theory, the last two examining the deeper problems of artistic performance. She classified dance styles according to four major functions: elevated (as in ballet), streaming, contrasting (for example, Indian classical dance), and steady. She described the system in 1928 in *Tánc, a mozgásmüvészet konyve* (Dance: A Book of the Art of Movement). Following her single solo recital in 1923, Szentpál composed dances for the Budapest Opera Ballet and the National Theater. She organized her own dance group in 1925 to interpret her choreography, including the folklore-inspired *Julie, Fair Girl* by Béla Bartók (1930), Modest Mussorgsky's *David* (1931), and Jenő Zádor's *The Mechanical Man* (1935). She discontinued her art-of-movement activities in the late 1940s to devote herself to folk dance research.

Other art-of-movement representatives came somewhat later. One was Lili Kállai, who opened her school in 1920 to teach a combination of Dalcrozean movement with many other Western influences. In 1928 she organized a dance group that continued until 1950. Sári Berczik danced in her own recitals beginning in 1922 and ran a school in artistic gymnastics between 1932 and 1948; the form has since won international recognition as a competitive event.

Art-of-movement schools flourished between the mid-1920s and the early 1940s. Alice Madzsar, undertook an anatomical analysis of human movement, paying attention to conscious energy consumption, muscular tension and release, and breathing. She published her method for improving women's health and beauty in 1926 in Budapest (it was published as *La culture physique de la femme moderne* in Paris, 1936). Her school's productions were also influenced by social problems faced by the workers' movement, which resulted in her first collaborations with the modern poet Ödön Palasovszky. Her own works, such as *Fetters* (1930) and *Contemporary Suite* (1933), shared these concerns; the latter production was banned by the police for its antiwar character. In 1937 her school was closed, although her pupils continued their activities until the German occupation of Hungary.

Valéria Dienes studied human movement by analyzing space, time, force, and expression. These studies yielded an analysis of space within the body's reach, rhythmics based on Greek prosody and the natural pulsation of life, dynamics based on energy entering and leaving the body, and symbolism. She called her system *orchestics* (from

Greek *orkheomai*, "I move"). Dienes produced her first dance play, *Waiting for the Dawn*, in 1925. She became interested in modern religious and historical mystery plays and worked with composer Lajos Bárdos to write, choreograph, and produce several of her own works, including *The Eight Beatitudes* (1926); *Road of the Child* (1934), which featured almost a thousand participants; and *Patrona Hungariae* (1938). She used both classical and modern music and even poems. After choreographing the pantomime *The Princess Who Never Laughed*, set to music by György Kósa, she choreographed several of her own verse plays for children, including *Sleeping Beauty* (1933) and *Cinderella*. After closing her school in 1944, she devoted her time to publishing her system. [*See the entry on Dienes.*]

All art-of-movement schools closed in the late 1940s when modern dance was branded "bourgeois survival" and banned from the stage and from education.

In the mid-1980s, after nearly a half century, modern dance trends enjoyed a revival. Contemporary dance companies began to form in the late 1980s and included Company of the General Disasters (1984), The Artus Company (founded by Gábor Goda in 1985), individual companies founded by Gyula Berger and Yvette Bozsik, Orchestics Movement Theater (headed by Mária Tatai since 1987), the Central Europe Dance Theater (organized by Csaba Szögi in 1989), Company Sarbo (1990), Andaxinház (1990), Trance Dance (organized by Péter Gerzson-Kovács in 1991), and Dream Team (1991). During the early 1990s, several festivals and competitions were organized including the Dance Festival, the Spring Festival, and Dance Parade.

These artists represent different trends in modern dance. The work of Yvette Bozsik, first dancer and choreographer for the Company of General Disasters, is characterized by minimalism, subdued tension, and repetition in static situations, as shown by her *Zone of Silence* (1992), *The Lady* (1994), and *The Miraculous Mandarin* (1995). Dancer and teacher Ivan Angelus is a central figure in organizing dance events. The Central Europe Dance Theater has, perhaps, the richest repertory with works by choreographers Csaba Szögi and Istvan Enekes, including *Pictures from a Cry* (1986) and *Satan's Ball* (1993). Coming from a folk dance background, Péter Gerzson-Kovács founded Trance Dance to show the magic power of rites, as in *Astral Years* (1993). The Orchestic Movement Theater is developing the Duncan-Dienes style along a very individual line and its works include *Antique Feast* (1987) and *Hommage à Meredith Monk* (1994). As a challenge to daily politics, Gábor Goda revives ancient Hungarian myths in an enigmatic and grotesque style. Gyula Berger, a fervent follower of pure dance, acts as manager, administrator, and choreographer of his own company and exploits the rhythmic and dynamic possibilities of movement as evidenced in his *Roaming* (1992) or *Body Language* (1995).

Other modern dancers, including Iván Angelus, Gyula Berger, Katalin Lőrinc, Yvette Bozsik, Ákos Hargitai, among others, appear individually or with newly organized companies in sites such as the Petőfi Hall, the Skéné Theater, the Merlin Theater, and the Mu Theater. Most of these dancers are united in the Kortárs Tánc Szinház Egyesület (Society for Contemporary Dance Theater). A large number of schools and courses on contemporary forms of dance have emerged, for example, Ivan Angelus's Creative Movement Studio and Budapest Dance School, the postgraduate course for art of movement pedagogues at the Imre Hajnal University of Health Sciences (organized by the new Society for Movement Culture), and the Talentum School for young dancers.

BIBLIOGRAPHY

Dienes, Gedeon P. "Isadora Duncan in Hungary." In *Proceedings of the Tenth Annual Conference, Society of Dance History Scholars, University of California, Irvine, 13–15 February 1987*, compiled by Christena L. Schlundt. Riverside, Calif., 1987.

Dienes, Gedeon P. "Budapest: Kamaraszinház." *Táncművészet* (November–December 1991): 35.

Dienes, Gedeon P. "Cro-Artés Meredith Monk. Kortárs orkesztika fekete-fehérben." *Táncművészet* (November–December 1994): 52.

Fuchs, Lívia. "Modern Hungarian Dance." *Ballet International* 14 (December 1991): 40–41.

Gradinger, Malve. "Innovation Out of the Tradition." *Ballett International/Tanz Aktuell* 4 (April 1995): 47–49.

Haselberger, Gabriele. "Artus Turul." *Tanz Affiche* 6 (August–September 1993): 30.

Kaán, Zsuzsa. "A humorban nem ismernek tréfát. Artus Tánc és Ugró Szinház. *Táncművészet* (November–December 1992): 36.

Lőrinc, Kartalin. "Magyar posztmodernek." *Táncművészet* 6–7 (1991): 47–49.

Maácz, László. "Egy kiáltás képei." *Táncművészet* (June 1989): 2–7.

M(ajor), R(ita). "Legyen nekünk modern tánc." *Táncművészet* (January 1991): 29.

Várszegi, Tibor, ed. *Fordulatok. Hungarian Theatres 1992.* 2 vols. Budapest, 1992.

Várszegi, Tibor, ed. *Féluton, Contemporary Theatre and Dance in Hungary.* Budapest, 1994. Text in Hungarian and English.

Verrièle, Philippe. "Danses hongroises, l'accent français." *Saisons de la danse*, no. 247 (June 1993): 39–40.

Willis, Margaret E. "Spring in Budapest." *The Dancing Times* (June 1995): 909–911.

GEDEON P. DIENES

Dance Education

The State Ballet Institute (Állami Balett Intézet) in Budapest was founded in 1950 as the first training institute for the higher education of dancers and teachers in Hungary. The institute's nine-year training course fused the Vaganova method (developed by Agrippina Vaganova) with the systems of instruction used by the former ballet school of the Budapest Opera and by Ferenc Nádasi's private school, which had opened in 1937. The new method was formalized in *Methodik des klassischen Tanzes,* published with text by Zsuzsa Merényi in Leipzig, East Germany, in 1964, with later editions in 1972, 1974, 1978, and 1981.

Among the subjects taught at the institute are classical ballet, pas de deux, historical social dances, character dance, acting, Hungarian and foreign folk dances, acrobatics, fencing, kinetography (dance notation), solfège, and piano. Second-year pupils take part in the opera's graduation ballet productions, which have been performed almost every year since 1954. The secondary school's curriculum includes history of dance, music, and arts. The final year's curriculum comprises philosophy, aesthetics, world literature and drama, and modern dance history, among other subjects.

Beginning in 1968, teachers have been assisted by the "Methodical Cabinet" and by guest instructors such as Olga Lepeshinskaya (1963–1964) and Anatoly Yelyagin (1973–1975). The number of successful annual auditions is thirty to forty, with ten to fifteen graduates a year. Most graduates find employment with professional ballet companies such as the Budapest Opera Ballet, the Ballet Sopianae, and the Győr Ballet, as well as at the Szeged Theater and the Operetta Theater in Budapest.

A training program for forty professional folk dancers began in 1971 with a four-year curriculum; a second class started in 1975, a third in 1979, and a fourth in 1983. Important, though temporary, training courses have included those for teachers of dance (1950–1951, 20 graduates), ballet (1956–1959, 134 graduates), and social dance (1967–1969, 60 graduates). An additional three-year course to train ballet teachers began in 1974 and had 33 graduates in 1977; the course has been repeated every three or four years since then.

The institute also supervises amateur ballet courses, dance art for the four-year secondary schools at Pécs and Szeged, and, since 1974, an elementary school for dancing at Dunaújváros. The institute's directors have been György Lőrinc (1950–1961), Hedvig Hidas (1961–1972), Zsuzsa Kun (1972–1979), and Imre Dózsa (1979 to the present).

BIBLIOGRAPHY

Kaposi, Edit. "Experiments in Dance Education in Hungary." *Hungarian Dance News,* no. 1–2 (1983): 5–6.

Kaposi, Edit. "Dance Teacher Training." In *The Art of Dancing in Hungary,* edited by Edit Kaposi and Ernő Pesovár. Translated by Lili Halápy. Budapest, 1985.

Lőrinc, György, et al. *A balettmüvészet felé.* Budapest, 1961.

Manhercz, Károly, ed. *Hungarian State Ballet Institute.* Budapest, 1981.

Merényi, Zsuzsa L. "The Teaching of Dance." In *The Art of Dance in Hungary,* edited by Edit Kaposi and Ernő Pesovár. Translated by Lili Halápy. Budapest, 1985.

Staud, Géza, ed. *A Budapesti Operaház 100 éve.* Budapest, 1984.

GÉZA KÖRTVÉLYES

Folk Dance Research and Publication

The Hungarian Ethnographic Society was founded in 1899 and began publishing its journal *Ethnographia* a year later. Established by the intellectuals of a country celebrating a millennium of statehood, the journal reflected feverish activity in its areas of interest. Among early articles, the most notable include S. Borbélys's account of the dances of the Aranyosszék region of Transylvania; Sándor Pintér's detailed description of Palóc dances; Gyula Káldy's monograph on historical dances; Antal Horger's analysis of the *borica,* a midwinter ritual dance from the Barcaság area of Transylvania; G. Gárdonyi's comments on the funeral dances; D. Balásy's monograph on Székelyföld dances; and János Seprődi's article on dances from the village of Kibéd, also in Transylvania. In the years 1905 and 1906 a minor scholarly battle was waged: one group claimed that the *hajdútánc* ("heyduck") dance was of Hungarian origin, and another that it was of Slavic origin. Only much later could folklorists determine that the heyduck is common throughout the Carpathian Basin.

It was not until the publication of Márián Réthei Prikkel's *Magyarság táncai* (Dances of the Hungarians; 1924) that the study of folk dance gained a place among scholarly pursuits. Réthei carried out field research and classified dances according to historical and regional characteristics. In addition to the wealth of data it provided, Réthei's work is important for two reasons: first, it made a fundamental connection between language, music, and dance; and second, it recognized that animal movement was not dance. As Réthei wrote in 1924, "Rhythmical, structured and defined movements of the human body could be called dance."

Scholars from such established academic disciplines as folklore, ethnomusicology, and ethnography also contributed to the emerging field of dance research. In 1926, when he used a 16-millimeter silent camera to film regional dances in the Kaposvár area, Sándor Gönyey became the first Hungarian ethnographer to film folk dances. In 1937 Károly Viski, president of the Ethnographic Society, published his classic work *Hungarian Dances,* the first comprehensive survey of the subject published in English. In the same year, a dance section appeared in the fourth volume of the *Ethnography of the Hungarians* by Sándor Gönyey and László Lajtha, an ethnomusicologist; this monumental undertaking classifies dances into six major groups—women's rounds, men's solos, herdsmen's dances, stick dances, couple dances, and ritual dances. Although there are musicological and historical bases for these categories, István Molnár's *Magyar tánchagyományok* (1947) proposed a more thoughtful classification of dances based on movement categories. Molnár used ten years of field experience and dozens of film clips to divide dances scientifically into four movement groups. Except for a few isolated efforts, such as Ákos Szendrey's 1936 study of symbolic dance forms and Elizabeth C. Rearick's *Dances of the Hungarians* (1939), it was Molnár's essay that determined the direction of the scientific study of dance in Hungary.

Hungarian School. Immediately after World War II, Hungary became part of the Soviet bloc, and scientific and cultural institutions were reorganized and centralized. The Hungarian Dance Federation, founded in 1949, and the Institute for Popular Culture directed dance research until 1965. At this time, with the help of Zoltán Kodály, the new Folk Dance Research Department was established at the Institute of Musicology, under the auspices of the Hungarian Academy of Sciences. This department probably possesses today's most extensive film, photo, and manuscript archives of Hungarian and eastern European dances. Other important collections are found at the Ethnographic Museum in Budapest, the Ethnographic Institute, the Hungarian State Folk Ensemble, and other regional centers of folk dance activity.

Following in Molnár's footsteps, researchers became more and more concerned with the process of recording and notating dances. Intensive training was necessary in such fields as Labanotation, filming techniques, interviewing, and archival research. Use of these skills became the trademark of folklorists studying dance in Hungary and neighboring countries.

To document dances of previously neglected Hungarian communities, from the 1950s many field trips were conducted in Romania, Yugoslavia, and Czechoslovakia. Dialectology, the geographical division of dances, and typology have been major concerns since that decade, when a new group of researchers came to the scene, including György Martin, the Pesovár brothers, Ernő and Ferenc, and Ágoston Lányi. As Martin wrote in 1970–1972, the spatial or synchronic division of Hungarian dances serves several purposes. One is the grouping of diverse but interrelated dances into larger, homogeneous units; another is the identification of characteristic patterns in dance genres and traditions developed in varying cultural circumstances.

Regionality and historical development of dances thus received extensive treatment. Here folklorists were aided by the historical division of folk music into old and new styles—those before and after the eighteenth century, a model borrowed from the ethnomusicologist Béla Bartók. Detailed studies trace the development of couple dances to the Renaissance, and the connection between herdsmen's dances and staff dances to the historic *hajdútánc-ungaresca* complex. Other studies chart the influence of historical dances, such as the *moresca* of the fifteenth century and the Polish polonaise, on Hungary's indigenous dances.

The best-known approaches developed by the Hungarian school are probably its structural and morphological analyses of folk dance. The studies of Emma Lugossy, Lányi, Martin, and Pesovár began establishing a system to reveal and analyze the major units of dance and elements of dance movements. The *motif,* also known as *figura, pont,* and *fogás* in folk taxonomy, was recognized as the smallest meaningful, structured, repetitive, and recognizable unit that can be isolated in eastern European dance. Such studies were important in determining formal characteristics and movement patterns in major dance types.

In the 1970s, a revival movement arose among choreographers and teachers who felt the need for more research and the collection of original materials; consequently many important collections were published at that time. Scientific analyses and historical and artistic studies have been published in the journals *Tánctudományi tanulmányok, Táncművészet, Ethnographia,* and other institutional periodicals. In the early 1980s, the Hungarian school of dance folklore was seriously affected by the passing of several of its pioneers (Martin, Ferenc Pesovár, and Lányi). It took a few years to reorganize and replenish the Folk Dance Research Department of the Institute of Musicology. The legacy of its pioneers remains strong at the school, however, and future work will bear their distinctive marks.

Between 1948 and 1988 the socialist state provided adequate financial support for scholarly work and for promotion of the art of folk dancing in its traditional milieu and onstage. With the collapse of state socialism in 1990, however, funding for the arts has been considerably reduced. This has forced companies and institutions to limit their activities, affecting folk dance research and publishing negatively, and producing a situation comparable to that of the United States and western Europe. Nonetheless, true to the spirit of the pioneers, research and the collecting of folk dance at the Folk Dance Research Department continues undiminished despite the lack of state funding.

LÁSZLÓ KÜRTI

Theatrical Dance Research and Publication

Research into the history and theory of theatrical dance in Hungary was scarce before World War II. Hungarian-language publications in Budapest, such as those of Emilia Nirschy, Melinda Ottrubay, Olga Szentpál and Máriusz Rabinovszky, Emil Haraszti (*History of Dance,* 1937), S. F. Varga (*Introduction to Dance Literature,* 1939), and K. Szalay (*Dance in Fine Arts,* 1941), were the first books on theatrical dance. After the war, between 1951 and 1958, the monthly *Táncművészet* (Dance Art), edited by Zsuzsa Ortutay, helped dance criticism develop. This journal and a research team led by Rózsi Vályi were the centers of dance literature and research. The research team produced the first overview of ballet history in Hungary *A magyar balett történetébol* (The History of Hungarian Ballet, edited by Vályi, 1956). Vályi's other books include *Balettek könyue* (The Book of Ballet 1959, 1980) and *A táncmüvészet története* (The History of Dance Art, 1969).

After 1956, publication activities were assumed by the Scientific Section of the Association of Hungarian Dance Artists (AHDA). Géza Körtvélyes published scholarly studies in book form—*On the Path of Modern Dance Art* (1970), and *The Budapest Ballet* (with György Lórinc, 1971 and 1981), both with sections by Gedeon P. Dienes. Iván Vitányi wrote *A tánc* (The Dance, 1963) and other studies. Dienes wrote "A Pécsi Balett reperteárjanak: Koreográfiai elemzé se." (Ballet Sopianae: A Choreographic Analysis, 1969), "Dance" in *Minerva Encyclopedia* (1973), "Hungary: World Survey" in *The Dancing Times* (August 1963), and "Report: Hungary" in *Ballett International* (September 1984). Mária Szentpál published a number of works on kinetography and taught several courses in Labanotation. Ágnes Gelencsér wrote several studies on Hungarian ballet and many reviews.

Since 1976, a monthly called *Táncmüvészet*, first edited by László Maácz, and, since 1990, by Zsuzsa Kaán, has been published. Professional criticism by Körtvélyes, Maácz, and Gelencsér has appeared since 1964 in the daily *Magyar Nemzet*. AHDA has published the following journals on a regular basis: *Tánctudományi Tanulmányok* (Studies in the Science of Dance), published every second year since 1956 and the only regular publication to have survived the 1990s; *Táncmüvészeti értesítő* (Bulletin on the Art of Dancing), published between 1953 and 1976; *Táncmüvészeti dokumentumok* (Documents in the Art of Dancing), published annually since 1976; and *Külföldi szemle* (Information from Abroad), published three or four times a year since 1959. The bimonthly *Hungarian Dance News* was edited by Edit Kaposi and Gedeon P. Dienes between 1976 and 1989; the annual *Dance–Information–Danse*, the bulletin of dance activities of the ITI Dance Committee Board put out by the ITI Information Center in Budapest, was also edited by Dienes between 1977 and 1985.

Other writers and critics include Anna Pór, Zsuzsa Kaán, and Livia Fuchs. Horst Koegler's *Ballet Encyclopedia* was translated and edited by Körtvélyes and published with additional Hungarian material in 1977. Members of the Scientific Section (replaced since 1991 by the Hungarian Society of Choreology) have contributed to many international encyclopedias.

In addition, AHDA has been commissioning translations of such important foreign works as Jean-Georges Noverre's *Letters*, Michel Fokine's *Against the Current*, and Agrippina Vaganova's *Method*. Other translations have included Curt Sachs's *World History of the Dance*, Liubov Roslavleva's *Era of the Russian Ballet*, and selections from texts on such topics as the history of English ballet and modern dance.

Dienes has compiled and edited *EDRIN 1992* (European Dance Research Information Network) containing institutions and individuals engaged in dance research and documentation in thirty-five European countries. The publication is currently being enlarged and updated under the title *EUDRID* (European Dance Research Information Directory) and will be mounted on the World Wide Web.

Hungary is an active participant in the international dance world. In addition to the many guest performances made by Hungarian companies and individual dancers on all continents, experts are exchanged annually under cultural agreements with Russia, Poland, Germany, Czechoslavakia, and other countries, and scientific conferences are held with foreign participants.

GEDEON P. DIENES and GÉZA KÖRTVÉLYES

HUROK, SOL (Solomon Izrailevich Iurok; born 9 April 1888 in Pogar, Ukraine, died 5 March 1974 in New York City), American impresario. Hurok's life reads as a classic American success story. The son of a hardware merchant, Hurok at age seventeen was sent to Kharkov, Ukraine, to learn the hardware business, but instead he set out for the United States via Poland. He arrived in the United States in May 1906 with the equivalent of $1.50 in his pocket. After living briefly in Philadelphia, he moved to New York, where he began his managerial career by arranging concerts for labor organizations and workers' groups in Brooklyn. In 1911 Hurok established the Van Hugo Musical Society and presented violinist Efrem Zimbalist at Carnegie Hall. He followed this with a highly successful series of Sunday concerts at the enormous Hippodrome theater, offering quality musical attractions at affordable prices. Over the years, Hurok's roster of musical artists included Fedor Chaliapin, Mischa Elman, Marian Anderson, Andrés Segovia, Isaac Stern, Arthur Rubinstein, the Vienna Boys Choir, Van Cliburn, and Maria Callas. Among the theatrical groups he sponsored were the Comédie Française, the Old Vic, the D'Oyly Carte company, and the Azumi Kabuki company.

Although Hurok's first love was music, it was not long before he began to present dance attractions as well. In 1916, producer Charles Dillingham introduced Hurok to Anna Pavlova, who became the first of the many dance artists he would manage in his career. Hurok admitted his preference for ballet, but the list of dancers and dance companies that appeared under the banner "S. Hurok Presents" represented a variety of dance styles. That list is a veritable honor roll of dance, and it includes Loie Fuller, Mary Wigman, Michel Fokine and Vera Fokina, Isadora Duncan, the Irma Duncan Dancers, Vicente Escudero,

Uday Shankar, Trudi Schoop, La Argentinita, Martha Graham, Ballet Theatre, Katherine Dunham, Alicia Markova and Anton Dolin, André Eglevsky, Margot Fonteyn and Rudolf Nureyev, the Paris Opera Ballet, the Sadler's Wells Ballet, Roland Petit, Agnes de Mille Dance Theater, Antonio's Ballet Espagnol, the Moiseyev Dance Company, the Beryozka Russian Folk Ballet, the Bolshoi Ballet, the Polish State Folk Ballet, the Roberto Iglesias company, the Bayanihan Philippine Dance Company, the Georgian State Dance Company, the Kirov Ballet, Ballet Folklórico de México, the Royal Danish Ballet, the Royal Winnipeg Ballet, the Romanian Folk Ballet, the Stuttgart Ballet, the Australian Ballet, the Ukrainian Folk Company, the National Ballet of Canada, and the various Ballet Russe companies.

Although he had no artistic training himself, Hurok's love of dance, paired with his intuitive sense of what the public would enjoy, made Hurok Concerts, Inc., a multimillion dollar business while at the same time creating an enthusiastic dance audience in the United States. In addition to encouraging the acceptance of dance, particularly ballet, Hurok's exchanges with Soviet artists were instrumental as a prelude to more formal cultural ties between the Soviet Union and the United States.

Hurok published two volumes of memoirs: *Impresario* (1946) and *S. Hurok Presents* (1953), and his story was adapted for the screen in the 1953 film *Tonight We Sing*. Among the many honors awarded him were a Handel Medallion of the City of New York, appointment as a Commander of the British Empire, and election as an Officier de la Légion d'Honneur.

BIBLIOGRAPHY
Anderson, Jack. *The One and Only: The Ballet Russe de Monte Carlo.* New York, 1981.
Dorris, George. "The Legacy of Hurok." *Ballet Review* 5.1 (1975–1976): 78–88.
García-Márquez, Vicente. *The Ballets Russes: Colonel de Basil's Ballets Russes de Monte Carlo, 1932–1952.* New York, 1990.
Hurok, Sol. *Impresario.* New York, 1946.
Hurok, Sol. *S. Hurok Presents: A Memoir of the Dance World.* New York, 1953.
Robinson, Harlow. *The Last Impresario: The Life, Times, and Legacy of Sol Hurok.* New York, 1994.

THOMAS CONNORS

HUSAIN, GHULAM (known as Maharaj Ghulam Husain Kathak; also known as Maharaj; born 1905 in Calcutta, India), Pakistani dancer and teacher. Maharaj is considered an institution in Pakistan, where he taught *kathak* for more than forty years. He was born to a traditional Muslim family; his father, Maulvi Tasadduq Hussain, an officer in East Bengal Railways, and his mother, Salima Bibi, wanted him to acquire higher education in some prestigious field, but he was always more inclined toward the arts and left home in adolescence to pursue them. He spent several years studying painting under Rabindranath Tagore, music under Nawab Munawwar Sultan of Mysore, and acting under Agha Hashar Kashmiri. In 1935 he became a disciple of Acchan Maharaj, a pioneer of the Lucknow school of *kathak*, to which he dedicated the rest of his life. After training for about seven years, Maharaj established himself as a brilliant dancer and was subsequently given the title Maharaj of Kathak.

When Pakistan came into being in 1947, Maharaj moved to Dhaka and then to Karachi. He started teaching small private classes. Since then his popularity has grown tremendously: he now teaches not only in Lahore, but also regularly in Islamabad and Karachi, in private homes as well as at cultural institutions. The institution at which he has taught the longest is the government-run Alhamra Arts Council in Lahore, where he has been holding classes for more than twenty years. Recently Maharaj received the Pride of Performance award from the government of Pakistan in recognition of his longstanding commitment to teaching dance.

It is significant that in a country where dance is often considered synonymous with vulgarity, a dance teacher's efforts should be rewarded with a prestigious award from the government and with permanent employment as dance teacher at an eminent government-run cultural institute. Maharaj's age is one source of his status, but just as important is his personality. Now in his nineties, Maharaj is an elegant man, tall and well-built, with sharp features and long white hair, who complements his appearance with long, flowing robes, ample jewelry, and a shining silver walking stick. In the dusty basement classroom at Alhamra, he sits majestically on traditional floor cushions, surrounded by his musicians and admiring students who are ever ready to fetch his slippers, tea, and betel nuts. Many do not depart until they have asked for his leave and touched his feet with respect, a custom generally considered Hindu and out of place in Pakistan. In the evenings Maharaj holds court at his residence in Anarkali; he has created a mystic aura around him and claims to belong to a Sufi order, the Qadiriyah.

Maharaj has trained some of Pakistan's most famous dancers, such as Nighat Chowdhry, Fasih-ur Rahman, and Nahid Siddiqui. Although almost all Pakistani dancers seek further training in India, Maharaj provides an excellent grounding in *kathak*. He has done so for generations of students, most of whom describe him as a generous, loving teacher—so much so that some of his students have studied under him for years without paying any fees.

BIBLIOGRAPHY
Khan, Rina Saeed. "Dancing to His Own Tune." *Friday Times* (Lahore) (5–9 September 1992).

INTERVIEW. Ghulam Husain, by Shayma Saiyid and Navaid Rashid (Lahore, January 1995).

SHAYMA SAIYID

HUS FAMILY, French family of dancers, ballet masters, choreographers, and teachers in the late eighteenth to early nineteenth centuries. Notable members were the father, Auguste Hus; his two adopted sons, Eugène and Pierre; and Pierre's son, Auguste.

Auguste Hus (born 1735, died after 1781), dancer and choreographer. Auguste danced with the Paris Opera from 1756 to 1760, presented his ballets at the Théâtre de la Foire, and was hired as a choreographer with the Comédie Française (1759–1760). Jean-Georges Noverre mentioned the success of his *La Mort d'Orphée* and praised his heroic inspiration. It was probably Auguste, under the name of Jean-Baptiste Hus, who won applause in Lyon in 1761 for *La Mort d'Orphée* and *Mars et Vénus Surpris par Vulcain*. A dancer and choreographer in Turin and later in Lyon, he danced several *divertissements* at the Comédie Italienne in Paris in 1779. In 1780, in partnership with Félix Gaillard, he was awarded the concession for the Lyon Opera, where he directed *Les Quatre Fils Aymon*, revived Noverre's *Les Amours d'Enée et de Didon* (1781), and created *La Rose et le Bouton*. The "Parisian" licentiousness of the last shocked the public so much that it led to his departure and probably to the end of his career.

Eugène Hus (Pierre-Louis Stapleton; born 1758 in Brussels, died 1823), dancer, choreographer, and ballet master. Auguste's adopted son, Eugène, followed him at the Lyon Opera, where in 1784 he presented *Le Ballon*, inspired by the ballooning feats of Montgolfier brothers. As assistant to Jean Dauberval in Bordeaux, he mounted two of Auguste's ballets, *Les Quatre fils Aymon* and *La Mort d'Orphée*. In 1786 he danced at the Paris Opera without much success and created *Le Coq de Village*, undoubtedly inspired by Maximilien Gardel, and *Le Nid d'Amours*. Becoming an assistant ballet master in 1793, he directed *Les Muses, ou Le Triomphe d'Apollon*. He then returned to Bordeaux, where he staged Pierre Gardel's *La Dansomanie* and *L'Apothéose de Flore* (1806) and *Le Siège de Cythère* (1806). He presented Dauberval's *La Fille Mal Gardée* at the Théâtre de la Porte-Saint-Martin (Paris, 1803), where he replaced Jean-Louis Aumer as ballet master until the theater closed in 1807; there he created *La Joute, ou Les Amours d'Été* and *Les Illustres Fugitifs*. He went on to the Théâtre de la Monnaie in Brussels, where he was director in 1815, ballet master in 1817, and assistant (1819–1822) to Jean-Antoine Petipa, director of the Conservatoire de Danse.

Pierre Hus (also known as Pietro Hus; *fl.* 1790–1820), director and choreographer. Auguste's brother, Pierre, carved out a career in Italy and by 1812 he was director of the ballet school and choreographer at the Teatro San Carlo in Naples. He restaged Maximilien Gardel's *Ninette à la Cour* in 1815, and created several ballets, including *Télémaque dans l'Île de Calypso* in 1820, in collaboration with Louis-Antoine Duport.

Auguste Hus (*fl.* 1820–1850), dancer, choreographer, and director. Pierre's son, Auguste, danced in Padua (1827), Trieste (1838–1839), and Genoa (1846–1847). As a choreographer, he presented *Apollon et Daphné* (1839), *Le Château de Kenilworth* (1840), *Le Devoir et l'Amour* (1842), and Salvatore Viganò's *Les Créatures de Prométhée* (1843) at the Kärntnertor Theater in Vienna. For the Teatro alla Scala in Milan he created *Le Naufrage de la Méduse* (1841), *Luisa Strozzi* (1843), and *Gustave III* (1846). As director of La Scala's ballet school, where he taught with his wife Savina Galavresi, his pupils included Caterina Beretta and Guglielmina Salvioni.

BIBLIOGRAPHY

Almanach des spectacles de Paris, ou Calendrier historique et chronologique des théâtres. Paris, 1790–1815.
Campardon, Émile. *L'Académie Royale de Musique au XVIIIᵉ siècle.* 2 vols. Paris, 1884.
Chazin-Bennahum, Judith. "Wine, Women, and Song: Anacreon's Triple Threat to French Eighteenth-Century Ballet." *Dance Research* 5 (Spring 1987): 55–64.
Chazin-Bennahum, Judith. *Dance in the Shadow of the Guillotine.* Carbondale, Ill., 1988.
Isnardon, Jacques. *Le théâtre de la Monnaie.* Brussels, 1890.
Swift, Mary Grace. *A Loftier Flight: The Life and Accomplishments of Charles Louis Didelot.* Middletown, Conn., 1974.
Vallas, Léon. *Un siècle de musique et de théâtre à Lyon, 1688–1789.* Lyon, 1932.

ARCHIVE.   Walter Toscanini Collection of Research Materials in Dance, New York Public Library for the Performing Arts.

JEANNINE DORVANE
Translated from French

HUTCHINSON, ANN (Ann Hutchinson Guest; born 3 November 1918 in New York), American dancer and dance notator. Hutchinson is known chiefly for her work in movement analysis and notation. Her dance training began in 1936 at the Jooss-Leeder School at Dartington Hall, England. Following the outbreak of war in 1939 she returned to New York, where she studied both ballet and modern dance with the leading teachers of the time. She also familiarized herself with such diverse genres as tap, ballroom, folk, Spanish, and Hindu dance. In the 1940s Hutchinson performed with the Welland Lathrop Company and also danced in some Broadway musicals, including *One Touch of Venus*, *Billion Dollar Baby*, *Finian's Rainbow*, and *Kiss Me, Kate*.

Hutchinson returned to London in 1947 and worked closely with Rudolf Laban. It was she who coined the term *Labanotation*, and perhaps her greatest contribution has been the theoretical development of that system. She found new ways of looking at movement, developed the symbology to express these, and helped to define the field of movement analysis.

Hutchinson is a prodigious thinker, writer, teacher, and organizer. Her book *Labanotation*, published in 1954, was the first Labanotation text in English and has become the standard work for students. She has written dozens of articles and many books on notation and has created numerous games, wall charts, and other aids for teaching notation to children as they are learning to dance.

Hutchinson is a practitioner as well as a theoretician. She has notated many major choreographic works, including eight by George Balanchine, four by Kurt Jooss, and others by Marius Petipa, Lev Ivanov, Léonide Massine, Ted Shawn, Antony Tudor, Hanya Holm, Doris Humphrey, Jerome Robbins, and Eugene Loring.

Referring to the crucial importance of notation for the preservation of dance, John Martin wrote in the *New York Times* that notation could save the present richly creative period from passing into the limbo of illiteracy. Martin added that Doris Humphrey once remarked, when she saw one of her own compositions on paper, *"New Dance* is no longer legend; it is history."

Because Hutchinson is familiar with more than fifty systems of notation and has studied twenty-two systems intensively, she has been able to transcribe works from earlier forms to Labanotation and teach them to contemporary companies. One such project is "La Cachucha," a popular nineteenth-century dance originally performed by Fanny Elssler; another is Arthur Saint-Léon's pas de six from *La Vivandière.*

Besides her theoretical and practical contributions to dance notation, Hutchinson has been a tireless advocate. In 1940 she was one of the founders of the Dance Notation Bureau in New York, the center of notation activities in the United States. As its president until 1961, she was a prime mover in successfully promoting the use of Labanotation by dance companies, universities, and scholars.

After moving to London in 1961, Hutchinson founded the Language of Dance Centre in 1967, which became a hub for notation teaching, reference, and research. It maintained a library of notated materials and published both a newsletter called *Action! Recording!* and a forum for practitioners called *The Labanotator.*

In September 1985 many of these activities were taken over by the newly formed Labanotation Institute, housed at the University of Surrey. This freed Hutchinson to concentrate her energies on writing, on teaching, and on the Language of Dance teaching method that she developed.

In 1959 Hutchinson was a founding member of the International Council of Kinetography Laban, the theoretical body that unifies the symbol language Labanotation and initiates and oversees new developments.

Hutchinson has been the recipient of three Rockefeller Foundation grants for research and the writing of Labanotation textbooks. She received an honorary doctorate from Marygrove College in Detroit, Michigan, in 1977, and one from Ohio State University ten years later.

In 1987 Hutchinson inaugurated the Language of Dance series of publications, which included major new scores, such as *Nijinsky's "Faune" Restored,* and books dealing with specific issues encountered in the use of advanced Labanotation.

BIBLIOGRAPHY

Chujoy, Anatole, and P. W. Manchester, eds. *The Dance Encyclopedia.* Rev. and enl. ed. New York, 1967. See the following entries: "Hutchinson, Ann," "History of Dance Notation," "Laban Dance Notation System," and "Dance Notation Bureau."
Guest, Ann Hutchinson. *Labanotation* (1954). 3d rev. ed. New York, 1977.
Guest, Ann Hutchinson. *Fanny Elssler's Cachucha.* London, 1981.
Guest, Ann Hutchinson. *Your Move: A New Approach to the Study of Movement and Dance.* 2 vols. New York, 1983.
Guest, Ann Hutchinson. *Dance Notation: The Process of Recording Movement on Paper.* New York, 1984.
Guest, Ann Hutchinson. *Choreographies: A Comparison of Dance Notation Systems from the Fifteenth Century to the Present.* New York, 1989.
Guest, Ann Hutchinson. *"La Vivandière" Pas de Six.* Lavsanne, 1994.
Guest, Ann Hutchinson. *A History of the Development of the Laban Notation System.* New York, 1995.
                                            BERNICE M. ROSEN

HYND, RONALD (Ronald Hens; born 22 April 1931 in London), British ballet dancer, choreographer, and company director. After early training with Marie Rambert, Ronald Hynd joined Ballet Rambert in 1949 and danced many principal roles. In 1951, he joined the Sadler's Wells Ballet (later the Royal Ballet) and was appointed soloist in 1954. During his eighteen years with the company he danced principal roles in all the classics as well as a wide variety of dramatic parts. As a dancer he had a commanding presence and an innate sense of drama.

While he was still dancing with the Royal Ballet, he was urged by Leslie Edwards, director of the Royal Ballet Choreographic Group, to create a work for one of the group's occasional workshop performances. His first choreographic attempt was a scene from Igor Stravinsky's *Le Baiser de la Fée* in 1967; the complete ballet was first given in the following year by the Dutch National Ballet and was later revived for the Munich Ballet and London Festival Ballet. For the same group in 1969, he created *Pasiphaë,* which led to his first association with composer Douglas Young and prompted Beryl Grey to commission a work from Hynd for the London Festival Ballet. The resulting *Dvořák Variations* (1970) started a collaboration with Peter Docherty, who subsequently designed most of his ballets.

Apart from two periods (1970–1973 and 1984–1986) as director of the Bavarian State Ballet in Munich, which allowed him to create his most adventurous works—*The Telephone* (1972), based on Jean Cocteau's *La Voix Humaine,* and the controversial *Ludwig: Fragments of a Puzzle* (1986), set to a score by Young—Hynd has worked as a freelance choreographer. He has been in steady demand for his ability to create entertaining narrative ballets fulfilling audiences' demands for full-evening works. The first of these was *The Merry Widow*, made for the Australian Ballet in 1975, with music by Franz Lehár and a scenario and staging by Robert Helpmann. This was followed by *Rosalinda* (1978), set to music by Johann Strauss, for South Africa's PACT Ballet; *Papillons* (1979), set to music by Jacques Offenbach, for the Houston Ballet; and *The Hunchback of Notre Dame* (1988), set to music by Hector Berlioz, also for the Houston Ballet. In addition to these works (for all of which John Lanchbery arranged the music), Hynd mounted new productions of *The Nutcracker* (1976) and *Coppélia* (1985) for London Festival Ballet.

Hynd's one-act works have covered more varied subject matter. *Orient/Occident* (1975; Tokyo Ballet), set to music by Iannis Xenakis, concerned Marco Polo's travels; *Fanfare für Tänzer* (1985; Bavarian State Opera Ballet), set to music by Leoš Janáček, deals with the Holocaust. His narrative works include the dramatic *Charlotte Brontë* (1974; Royal Ballet Touring Section), to music by Young; *The Sanguine Fan* (1976; London Festival Ballet), to music by Sir Edward Elgar; and the comic *Les Liaisons Amoureuses* (1989; Northern Ballet Theatre), set to music by Jacques Offenbach as arranged by Carl Davis. His version of *The Seasons* (1981; Houston Ballet), set to Aleksandr Glazunov's familiar score, was simply a *divertissement*. He has also choreographed for films, television, operas, musicals, and John Curry's ice ballet.

BIBLIOGRAPHY
Hynd, Ronald. "The Battle of Munich." *Dance and Dancers* (June 1973): 38–41.
Stuart, Otis. "To Humanize the Classics." *Ballett International* 7 (August 1984): 10–15. Interview with Hynd.

PETER WILLIAMS and JANE PRITCHARD

HYPORCHĒMA. The *hyporchēma* (plural, *hyporchēmata*) was a lively choral dance-song of ancient Greece. It is difficult to determine the exact origin and form of this dance because of conflicting and confusing accounts through the centuries. The ancient Greeks believed that the *hyporchēma* originated in Crete and was an integral part of the worship of the Great Mother and her son Crete. The Dorian Greeks apparently borrowed the Cretan form of the dance and adapted it for their ceremonies honoring Apollo. Ancient sources agree that the dance of the *hyporchēma* was characterized by vigorous movement, a rapid tempo, and expressiveness.

It is possible that the metrical structure of the lyrics distinguished the *hyporchēma* from other types of choral ode. The Alexandrian scholars of the third century BCE designated certain odes of Pindar and Bacchylides (c.480–450 BCE) as hyporchematic, and one commentator termed a certain cretic (long–short–long) type of poetic meter *pous hyporchēmatikos* ("hyporchematic foot").

The unusual quality of the *hyporchēmata* lay in the relationship of the song to the dance when performed. The Roman commentator Lucian (*On the Dance* 16) and the Greek Athenaeus (*Deipnosophists* 1.15e) both indicate that a chorus of singers may have sung the lyrics while a separate chorus danced, rather than the usual arrangement in which a single chorus danced while singing the ode.

At one time the *hyporchēma* was thought to be a song with dance performed by the Greek dramatic chorus. This view arose from a misinterpretation of Aristotle's division of choral odes in tragedy into the *parodos* (the processional entrance song) and the *stasimon* (the song delivered in the orchestra space in the theater). Some later ancient grammarians speculated incorrectly that the term *stasimon* (plural, *stasima*) might have evolved from a Greek word meaning "stationary" and that such choruses were therefore sung without dancing. The conflict between this conclusion and the words of choral odes in surviving dramas, which often indicate dance movements, prompted some Byzantine commentators to form a third category, the *hyporchēma*, to cover the problematic choruses. To these commentators, a *hyporchēma* was simply a song accompanied by dancing. The *hyporchēma*, however, in its technical sense—a particular type of lyric poetry distinguished by its metrical form, in performance by two choruses (one singing, one dancing)—could not have been contained in dramatic poetry, although a dramatic choral ode may have been reminiscent of hyporchematic style.

[*For related discussion, see* Choral Dancing; Dithyramb; *and* Sikinnis. *See also* Greece, *article on* Dance in Ancient Greece.]

BIBLIOGRAPHY
Dale, A. M. "Stasimon and Hyporcheme." In *Collected Papers*. Edited by T. B. L. Webster and E. G. Turner. London, 1969.
Lawler, Lillian B. "The Dance in Ancient Crete." In *Studies Presented to David Moore Robinson on His Seventieth Birthday*, vol. 1, edited by George E. Mylonas. St. Louis, 1951.
Mullen, William. *Choreia: Pindar and Dance*. Princeton, 1982.
Webster, T. B. L. *The Greek Chorus*. London, 1970.

LIBBY SMIGEL

HYRST, ERIC (Eric Hertzell; born 4 April 1927 in London, died 31 January 1996 in Montreal), ballet dancer and choreographer. While still a boy, Eric Hyrst began to take acting and dancing lessons at the Italia Conti Stage School in London. Enrolled in the Sadler's Wells Ballet

School when he was nine years old, he made such rapid progress that he was accepted into the Sadler's Wells Ballet in 1943, at the tender age of fifteen. Continuing his studies in classes with Nicholas Sergeyev and Vera Volkova, he was promoted to soloist at sixteen, and in 1946, at age eighteen, he made his debut as *premier danseur* with the newly formed Sadler's Wells Theatre Ballet, partnering the Soviet ballerina Violetta Prokhorova (later Elvin) in *Les Sylphides*. The following year, 1947, he was named a principal dancer in the even more newly formed Metropolitan Ballet, where he remained until the company was disbanded, for financial reasons, three years later.

Despite its short life and shaky finances, the Metropolitan Ballet provided Hyrst with the opportunity to dance leading roles in many classic works of the ballet repertory as well as in the works of such contemporary choreographers as Nicholas Beriozoff and John Taras. It also provided him with the challenge of partnering such ballerinas as Sonia Arova, Nadia Nerina, and Svetlana Beriosova and with the congenial company of such dancers as Celia Franca, Erik Bruhn, David Adams, and Poul Gnatt, all of whom appeared with the company at various times. Upon its demise in 1949, Hyrst formed his own company for a single London season, after which he left England and spent the remainder of his life abroad.

Journeying first to the United States, he joined the New York City Ballet in 1950 and remained with this company until 1952, when he left to dance in a South American tour with Ballet Alicia Alonso. Traveling next to Canada, he spent a season with the Royal Winnipeg Ballet and finally, in October 1953, settled in Montreal, where he joined Les Ballets Chiriaeff as a principal dancer. Working closely with the founder of this company, Ludmilla Chiriaeff, Hyrst helped her transform it into Les Grands Ballets Canadiens, the major dance company of Francophone Canada. [*See* Grands Ballets Canadiens, Les.]

For eleven years, Hyrst served Les Ballets Chiriaeff and Les Grands Ballets Canadiens as *premier danseur*, choreographer, and artistic adviser. He danced leading roles in classics from the standard repertory; in many of Chiriaeff's works, notably *Kaléidoscope* (1954), *Les Noces* (1956), and *Suite Canadienne* (1957); and in works of his own creation. Among the many ballets he choreographed in Montreal are *Drawn Blinds* (1954), to music by Frank Bridge; *Labyrinthe* (1954), a capsule version of *Romeo and Juliet*, to Tchaikovsky music; *Variations sur un Thème de Haydn* (1955), to the familiar Brahms piano solo; *Première Classique* (1958), to music by Tchaikovsky; *Sea Gallows* (1959), to music by Michel Perrault; and *Valses Nobles et Sentimentales* (1960), to Ravel's orchestral score. *Première Classique* was choreographed especially for the Canadian ballerina Margaret Mercier and was presented at the

HYRST. Margaret Mercier and Eric Hyrst in his setting of the Black Swan pas de deux, 1959, with Les Grands Ballets Canadiens. (Photograph by Gaby; courtesy of Ludmilla Chiriaeff.)

American debut of Les Grands Ballets Canadiens at Jacob's Pillow in the summer of 1959.

Hyrst left the company in 1964 and set himself up as a teacher, first at L'Atelier, a school he established with his wife, Dianne de Saint Pierre, and then at a school he shared with Camille Malashenko. While teaching, he continued to perform as a guest artist and to choreograph occasional works for Les Grands Ballets Canadiens. In 1972 he once again attempted to found his own company, the Metropolitan Ballet of Canada, but it failed.

Discouraged, and divorced, Hyrst left Canada in 1974 and returned to the United States. After a brief stint at the Wisconsin Conservatory of Music, he became the artistic director of the Kansas City Ballet and then of the Springfield (Missouri) Civic Ballet. For these companies, he restaged such classics as *Giselle* and *The Nutcracker* and produced many of his own works, including a modern *Hamlet* and the deeply moving *Crucinom*, depicting the crucifixion and resurrection of Christ. In 1980 Hyrst left the Midwest and, with his second wife, Diane Gaumond, founded the State Ballet of Oregon in the city of Medford. In only a few years, he had established this company as a vital cultural force in southern Oregon and northern California, presenting a repertory of both classical and contemporary ballets and featuring works choreographed by himself.

A dancer of enviable technical prowess as a young man, Hyrst quickly and justly achieved fame as a performing artist. In later years his artistic visions were realized in a prolific stream of choreography. Working in a wide range of styles, he created more than 180 original dances in a career that spanned more than forty years.

BIBLIOGRAPHY

Tembeck, Iro. *Dancing in Montreal: Seeds of a Choreographic History.* Studies in Dance History, vol. 5.2. Madison, Wis., 1994.

Wyman, Max. *Dance Canada: An Illustrated History.* Vancouver and Toronto, 1989.

FILM AND VIDEOTAPE.   *The Swan Lake Story,* J.A.T.F. Productions (1988); features Hyrst's production of *Swan Lake* for the State Ballet of Oregon. "Two for Ballet," New Classic Films (1990), a documentary series narrated by David Vaughan, on six original works choreographed by Hyrst to music by Webster Young.

CLAUDE CONYERS

I

IAKOBSON, LEONID. *See* Yakobson, Leonid.

ICARE. Choreography: Serge Lifar. Music: Serge Lifar (rhythms) and Georges Szyfer (orchestration). Scenery and costumes: Paul Larthe. First performance: 9 July 1935, Théâtre de l'Opéra, Paris Opera Ballet. Principal dancer: Serge Lifar (Icarus).

Serge Lifar created *Icare* in response to criticism of his 1935 book, *Le manifeste du chorégraphe*, and to demonstrate the autonomy and primacy of dance independent of score and scenery. The heroic subject allowed him to symbolize the dancer's flight and to evoke the daring of modern man eager to explore unknown regions. In the secrecy of a private studio, Lifar worked out in dance the rhythms subsequently orchestrated by Arthur Honegger. (Honegger was under exclusive contract to Ida Rubinstein, so he had to allow credit for the orchestration to be taken by Szyfer, the orchestra conductor.) After rejecting extravagant designs by Salvador Dali, Lifar utilized neoclassical sets and costumes by Larthe; designs by Pablo Picasso were used in a 1962 revival by Attilio Labis at the Opera.

The rhythms were determined by the choreography, classical ballet uninfluenced by the school of Isadora Duncan. A staccato dance of boys and girls is followed by a despairing Daedalus crumbling under his enormous wings. The radiant Icarus bursts forth with repeated *entrechats* and joyful leaps. His father communicates his passion to Icarus, teaching him the flight of the arrow and the bird, and the new equilibrium required by the artificial wings, in a sequence featuring pirouettes, *développés*, and *grands jetés*. Icarus collects himself, then with a prodigious leap he disappears from the stage, followed by the eyes of the crowd. A wing comes falling down. The broken hero, falling from the loft, attempts a final jump, then crashes to earth, with one leg pointed toward heaven.

Both the critics and the public applauded the exceptional plastic beauty of the poses, the precision of the transitions, and the ballet's sense of tragedy. Paul Valéry praised Lifar for "constructing an entire ballet based on rhythm alone, making an abstract poem of some sort to which his body gives body."

BIBLIOGRAPHY
Beaumont, Cyril W. *Supplement to Complete Book of Ballets.* London, 1942.
Laurent, Jean, and Julie Sazonova. *Serge Lifar, rénovateur du ballet français.* Paris, 1960.
Lifar, Serge. *Le manifeste du chorégraphe.* Paris, 1935.
Lifar, Serge. *Au service de la danse.* Paris, 1958.

MARIE-FRANÇOISE CHRISTOUT
Translated from French

ICE DANCING. Although the term has been applied to everything from Sonja Henie's skating to ice hockey, ice dancing is technically a competitive discipline within the sport of figure skating. It combines figure skating's original emphasis on the tracing of patterns on ice with the body movements and rhythms of ballroom dancing.

The two aspects of ice dancing were perhaps first combined in the 1813 treatise *Le vrai patineur, ou Principes sur l'art de patiner avec grâce* by J. Garcin, and several British clubs promoted tests of combined figure skating during the early nineteenth century, but the modern form of ice dancing was introduced in Vienna in 1868 by American skater Jackson Haines. For decades, Vienna and Britain vied for domination of the sport, but by the 1930s the dance-based Viennese-Haines style and the figure-based British style had merged. The first world championship was held in 1952 and the first Olympic championship in 1976, although its inclusion in the Games has always been a point of contention for the International Olympic Committee because of the subjective judging of the event.

Ice dancing competitions have three sections: two compulsory dances (worth 10 percent each in the overall score), an original dance (30 percent), and a free dance (50 percent). Compulsory dances are closest to the origins of the sport: each couple must evoke a specific ballroom dance to music selected by the International Skating Union (ISU) while also tracing a set pattern on the ice. Each year two of four dance groups are selected: Viennese Waltz, Yankee Polka, and Blues; Westminster Waltz, Paso Doble, and Rumba; Starlight Waltz, Kilian, and Tango Romantica; and Ravensburger Waltz, Quickstep, and Argentine Tango. One dance from each of the two chosen categories is danced at each competition. (Before 1989 competitions had three compulsory dances.)

ICE DANCING. Jackson Haines in an exhibition of figure skating on the Neva River, Saint Petersburg, 1865. A few years later, on 16 January 1868, he appeared at the Vienna Skating Club, where he was billed as "the celebrated American Ice Dancer." Skating to waltzes by Johann Strauss the younger, he was a smash hit. The first to treat skating as an art form, Haines had a profound effect on skating in Europe and North America. (Reprinted from Sheffield and Woodward, 1980, p. 36.)

The original dance is created by the dancers or their choreographer but must conform to the rhythm, tempo, and character of a dance specified each year. The original dance is a 1991 amendment to the original set pattern (OSP) dance, in which each couple would present, in effect, a compulsory dance of their own design.

The rules in ice dancing are rigid yet frequently change. These qualities constitute an attempt by the ISU to keep ice dancing distinctly different from pairs skating, with its side-by-side skating, multirevolution spins, and acrobatic lifts and throws. The difference between the two skating disciplines is most evident in the four-minute free dance, which prohibits extended separations between the partners, spins of more than one revolution, and lifts in which the man's arms rise above his shoulders.

As in all figure skating disciplines, competitors are given two sets of marks out of a perfect 6.0 in each section: one for technical merit (the only mark in compulsories) and one for artistic impression. The distinction between the two marks in ice dancing, however, is very fine, as technical merit includes difficulty, variety, cleanness, and sureness; and artistic impression includes choreography and its relationship to the music, utilization of the performance area, ease of movement, carriage, and originality.

Jean Westwood and Lawrence Demmy won the first world championships in 1952, and British partnerships dominated the sport for almost two decades until the rise of the Soviets, led by Ludmila Pakhomova and Aleksandr Gorschkov, who became the first Olympic champions. The British drew heavily on their ballroom tradition, whereas the Soviets followed the balletic tradition of a charismatic woman presented by her unobtrusive partner. Although the Soviets Irina Moiseeva and Andrei Minenkov brought a thematic unity and dramatic style to the free dance, they were quickly outstripped by British partners Jayne Torvill and Christopher Dean, world champions from 1981 through 1984 and 1984 Olympic champions. The technical perfection of the British team was allied with Dean's explosive growth as a choreographer, the increasing influence of theatrical dance on their programs, and their genuine charisma as a couple to create the most popular and influential ice dancing team in history. Torvill and Dean brought to the sport a modern dance aesthetic and an unprecedented equality between partners. As professionals, they mounted their own ice shows, and Dean also began to choreograph for other skaters, most notably the French Canadians Paul and Isabelle Duchesnay, world champions in 1991. [See Torvill and Dean.]

After Torvill and Dean left amateur competition, style became increasingly polarized between the dramatic/theatrical and the classic/ballroom. The former was exemplified by both the 1988 Olympic champions Natalia Bestemianova and Andrei Bukin, who attracted as many detractors as fans for their flamboyant, almost hysterical programs, and the Duchesnays; the latter was exemplified by Marina Klimova and Sergei Ponomarenko, 1992 Olympic champions, and Maia Usova and Aleksandr Zhulin, 1993 world champions.

Many of the rules changes of the 1980s were explicitly or implicitly aimed at reducing Dean's impact. Some of his most distinctive traits as a choreographer, such as guiding a partner by the leg or skate, were deemed illegal, and music was restricted to that with a recognizable dance beat. The professional competitions that proliferated throughout the decade, however, allowed for the parallel development of the sport without such restrictions, and during the early 1990s the balletically inclined team of Natalia Annenko and Genrikh Sritensky, who had never won a medal as amateurs, regularly defeated former world champions in professional competitions.

The fall of the Soviet Union in the early 1990s coincided with a major upheaval in the rules of figure skating, and this confluence led former Soviets to train in the West, Westerners to train with ex-Soviet coaches, and former professionals to return to amateur, or "eligible," competition. Exemplifying all these trends was Gorsha Sur, who defected while on tour with The Russian All-Stars, coached and choreographed in the United States, and competed professionally with American champion Renée Roca; in 1993 they became the first East-West and the first professional team to compete in the world champi-

ICE DANCING. Jayne Torvill and Christopher Dean in the opening moments of their most famous number, *Boléro* (1984), set to the music of Maurice Ravel. Their perfect score for artistic impression in this dance helped them win a gold medal at the 1984 Olympic Games. By 1995, they estimated that they had performed it more than fifteen hundred times. (Photograph courtesy of Torvill and Dean.)

ICE DANCING. John Curry, a 1976 Olympic gold medalist in "singles skating," was noted for the choreography of his numbers as well as his superb execution. He formed a professional company, Theatre of Skating, with a repertory of works created by leading choreographers from the dance world. He is seen here with Lorna Brown in *Scenes from Childhood* (c.1977), set by Peter Darrell to music by Robert Schumann. (Photograph by Keith Money; reprinted from Keith Money, *John Curry*, New York, 1978.)

onships. Torvill and Dean also returned to eligible competition, winning a controversial bronze medal at the 1994 Olympics. The suspicion that the judges marked professionals more severely than amateurs cast doubt on the viability of merging the two classifications. Audiences, however, embraced the new developments in record numbers: in 1994 ice skating became the second most popular sport on American television.

[*See also the entries on John Curry and Sonja Henie.*]

BIBLIOGRAPHY
Copley-Graves, Lynn. *Figure Skating History: The Evolution of Dance on Ice.* Columbus, Ohio, 1992.
Hennessey, John. *Torvill and Dean.* London, 1994.
Hilton, Christopher. *Torvill and Dean.* London, 1994.
Sheffield, Robert, and Richard Woodward. *The Ice Skating Book.* New York, 1980.

VIDEOTAPES.   *Path to Perfection* (1984). *Fire and Ice* (1986). *An Ice-Dancing Seminar* (1990). *Torvill & Dean and the Russian All-Stars* (1990). *Blade-Runners* (1991). *The Best of Torvill & Dean* (1994), which includes *Path to Perfection, Fire and Ice,* and the 1994 British National Championships. *1994 Winter Olympics Figure Skating Competition and Exhibition Highlights Gift Set* (1994).

ARCHIVE.   The IceStage Archive in Minneapolis, Minnesota, contains the Roy Blakey collection of theatrical skating memorabilia, compiled during his fifty years' association with professional skating.

ROBYNN J. STILWELL

ICELAND. [*To survey the dance traditions of Iceland, this entry comprises two articles. The first article discusses the history of traditional dance; the second explores the development of theatrical dance.*]

Traditional Dance

Dance was part of the culture the first settlers in Iceland brought from Scandinavia (mainly from Norway) and Ireland in the ninth and tenth centuries CE. Dancing and dance games are mentioned in the Norse sagas *(Fornaldarsögum Nordurlanda)* and in the Icelandic sagas of the eleventh through fourteenth centuries.

Early Dance. A historical document from around 1200 mentions courtship dances in which a man and woman sang alternately to each other; a bishop attempted in vain to suppress this kind of dance. In 1255 a priest was censured for taking part in a dance festivity.

Arngrimur Jonsson, in his *Crimogaea* (1609), described various dances and dance games of his own and earlier times. He mentioned *kvaedadansleikir* ("song dances"), *staticule*, and the *vikivaki* or *hringdans*; in the last, men and women danced and sang alternately. Many dance games were also noted. Eggert Olafsson in 1772 described *vikivaki* as a song dance in which men and women held hands while singing; they rocked forward and back, stepping onto the right foot. In addition to the song dances, there were early dances done to musical accompaniment; they seem to have been called *slagur*.

Vikivaki was still a living tradition in western Iceland in 1902, when it was recorded by Helgi Valtysson. Both the melody and the song text of this dance, known as Olafur liljurós, are known from older sources. The first figure of the dance is a typical *branle double* with a clear *branle* sway-and-turn. The second part of each verse is danced with the regular six-beat *vikivaki* step: step-together-step beginning on the left foot, and a step on the right for counts five and six. The circle continuously moves to the left. The basic step, also known as the *branle simple* or Faeroese step, is danced to various meters, including 4/4 and uneven meters. Another variation of the *vikivaki* step, the *branle simple*, has vigorous stamping and a low kick with the left foot. It was recorded in the Westfjords shortly after 1900 and was known by elderly people as late as 1977.

In these circle dances the dancers hold hands in a closed circle and move in unison. The content of the song's lyrics is not mimed in the movements, but the mood of the lyrics can be expressed through slight movements of the joined arms and by the character or forcefulness of the simple steps. Narrative events can also be reflected by changes in the smoothness or vigor of the dancing.

The name *vikivaki* was also used for the dance event, more usually termed *gledi*. By the time of the writer Jon' Arnason (c.1860) the *gledir* were no longer held, but a few older people could remember them. These festivities occurred the evenings prior to religious holidays in churches or large farms, even though church officials made many attempts through the centuries to control or prohibit dancing. Public opposition to the church's edicts died out gradually in the eighteenth century, however, and the last such festival was finally terminated around 1790. The suppression of the ancient song dances was made easier for the authorities by the growing popularity of imported social dances brought by travelers and foreign merchants.

Dance Games. Many traditional *dansleikar* ("dance games") are recorded. One of the best known is the *hringbrot* ("breaking the circle"), a kind of farandole danced in an open or closed circle. In 1808 Magnus Stephensen described it as the only national dance still performed in Iceland. The accompaniment is led by three singers; however, the dancers do not sing. Unlike the circle dance songs, which usually tell stories, *hringbrot* songs give instructions to the dancers. The *hringbrot* has no set pattern of steps but uses basic steps such as running, skipping, or walking. It is performed in an open or closed circle or in a line or facing lines. The dancers are linked by holding hands or by holding garters or woven belts between them. During the dance one person tries to break the circle by moving under and out of the dancers' arms while holding the adjacent dancers' hands and drawing them along. Elements of the *hringbrot* appear in other kinds of dances, including the weaving dance, Icelandic march, and children's games.

In some variations of the *hringbrot* the dancers moved in elaborate patterns as they turned and wove under one another's linked arms. There are early references to it as a men's dance, but other writers say it was performed by both sexes; for example, a thirteenth-century saga mentions a variation of *slagur* called *faldafeykir*, a fast dance in which the women's high headdresses fell off.

Many other dance games were described by Olafur Davidsson (1896). All are miming dances to sung texts that prescribe the action. The largest category are wedding or courtship games in which dancers find a partner and sometimes participate in a mock wedding ceremony. There was a frightening dance performed by a man costumed as a giantess; in another, a troll woman comically solicited a mate for her daughter. In a dance similar to the hobby-horse performances elsewhere in Europe, a man wore an elaborate rig representing a horse. The hart (deer) dance was apparently derived from a fertility ritual, and the *finngalkn* ("monster") dance may have been related to pre-Christian shamanism.

The dance games may be seen as a primitive form of dance drama. In 1967 Sigridur Valgeirsdóttir first reconstructed many of the documented dance games for presentation at Iceland's national theater.

Imported Social Dances. The first couple dance known in Iceland, the waltz, was introduced in the 1780s from Denmark. At this time the old circle dances were in decline. Earlier, contradances also came into the country, primarily from England, which had much contact with Iceland through fishing and other commerce.

The first contradance mentioned in Icelandic literature is the reel, which was danced before 1800. Visitors to Iceland in 1809 and 1810 mentioned seeing the reel, waltz, English country dances, and indigenous song dances. A letter requesting dance music in 1836 mentions contradances, waltzes, the galop, the Molinowski, and the *cotillon*.

Only a few contradances from this period have survived. The weaver's dance (*vefarinn* or *vefaradans*) was a contradance popular all over Iceland, where it was usually performed to singing by the participants. In the late twentieth century it survived in rural areas in eight or nine variants. A contradance called the *aframraell* ("forward reel") was recorded in 1977 in the Westfjords region.

The fact that contradances did not develop as highly in Iceland as in other Nordic countries can be explained by their need for instrumental musical accompaniment. The melodies were not readily adapted to the Icelandic singing tradition; however, the couple dances that soon surpassed contradances in popularity could be performed to singing or lilting of simple melodies if instruments were not available.

The *cotillon* and *polonaise* were also danced in the nineteenth century and contributed to the development of the Icelandic march. The *française* (quadrille) was danced, as was the Lancers, especially at urban gatherings. The most popular of this group was the *ecossaise* or English reel, but it has not survived.

Today the most popular old-time dance is the Icelandic reel, a simple dance different in structure from the reels of Scotland and Scandinavia. It is believed to have originated from English country dances or old Scottish reels. Another group dance still performed is the Icelandic march, which includes movements from the *polonaise* and figures from the *cotillon*, performed in a sequence which may last one-half to one hour. About fifty Icelandic march figures have been recorded by dance researchers.

During the course of the nineteenth century European couple dances were imported one after another and replaced almost all the group dances. Most important were the waltz, galop, mazurka, polka, *Wienerkreutz* (known as *vinarkruss*), schottische, *hoppsi*, and clap dances. These couple dances were popular throughout Iceland until World War II, and in country districts many were recorded after 1970 and are still danced on special occasions.

Contexts for Dance. Dancing in Iceland has always been mainly an indoor activity, except at some summer festivals. After the large dance festivals or *gledir* were banned in the eighteenth century, dancing lived on at family social gatherings in homes and farm buildings. A hall for dancing was built in Reykjavik shortly after 1800, but during the nineteenth century only a few larger towns had such facilities.

Around the turn of the twentieth century organizations began to build halls in rural communities for dancing and other activities. Strict rules of conduct governed the community-hall dances. After several decades dancing began to be part of evening entertainment at restaurants as well, and its social context came to resemble that of the rest of Europe.

Dance Music. *Vikivaki* and other song dances are accompanied by the singing of the dancers themselves; the verses are rendered by a soloist, and the repeat phrases and refrains by all the dancers. In *dans* and dance games, three or more people outside the dance usually sing the verse and the refrain.

Folk dances today, other than *vikivaki*, are usually accompanied by instrumental music played by an accordion or a small ensemble. In the early nineteenth century violin, mouth-organ, flute, and harmonium (a type of organ) were often used. Many old dance tunes have been collected, published, and recorded, and composers continue to produce new melodies for folk dances (old time dances).

Revival. In 1930 Helgi Valtýsson published a collection of of *vikivaki*. In 1951 the folklorist Sigridur Valgeirsdóttir established Tjoddansafelag Reykjavikur (Folk Dance Society of Reykjavik). Its aim was to collect and preserve Icelandic dance, music, dance poetry, and costume and to perform the dances in an authentic manner. In 1994, the organization also published 144 dances by Sigridur Valgeirdóttir and Minerva Jonsdóttir in Labanotation.

Today there are a number of clubs which give opportunities to participate in traditional dancing to anyone who wishes to attend. Some schools and folk dance societies offer courses, and ballroom dancing schools may also include some folk dancing. Song dances, dance games, and contradances are performed mainly by clubs and on special occasions, or in theatrical settings. The enthusiasts are amateurs from all age groups and all walks of life.

Research and Publication. After indigenous Icelandic song dances and dance games had almost died out in the eighteenth century, a few scholars became interested in gathering information about these folk traditions. In 1839 Hid Islenska Bokmenntafelag (the Icelandic Literature Society) sent out a questionnaire to clergymen all over the country, but these longtime enemies of dance provided few indications of the popularity and nature of dance in their parishes.

The first serious attempt to study traditional dances and their poetry was made by Jon Sigurdsson (1811–1879). His work was continued and eventually published by Olafur Davidsson in the book *Vikivakar og vikivakakvaedi* (Vikivaki and Poems for Vikivaki; 1894). This excellent collection prevented the loss of much important information.

Literary historians and philologists have paid some attention to medieval dance as it figures in the literature of that time. Notable are the works of Olafur Briem (1946), Jon Samsonarson (1964), and Vesteinn Olason (1979). Because Icelandic dances were performed to singing, the texts of the dance poems often contain suggestions of what the characteristics and structures of the dances may have been.

The major collection of Icelandic folk music was made by Bjarni Thorsteinsson (1906–1909). It includes many dance songs.

Helgi Valtysson began work on collecting and reviving *vikivaki* in 1902. He taught these dances to youth organizations for many years, publishing a book on them in 1930.

Modern research on traditional dance began shortly after 1950 with the work of Sigridur Valgeirsdóttir on *vikivaki* and the revival of song dances. Her early collections were published in 1959. She used documentary references and fragmentary descriptions to reconstruct circle dances, *hringbrot*, and dance games for participatory and theatrical performance. Most recently, two full-evening performances of song dances were presented at the National Theater in January 1995.

Working with Minerva Jonsdóttir, a specialist in dance notation, Sigridur Valgeirsdóttir began in 1958 to record old-time couple dances in Labanotation. The results were finally published in two volumes in 1994, along with the history, music, and texts accompanying the dances.

Dance is not presently included in Icelandic university curricula, and little financial support is available for dance research. This field thus remains the province of a few dedicated enthusiasts.

BIBLIOGRAPHY

Arngrimur Jonsson. *Crimogæa: Thættir úr sögu Islands* (1609). Translated by Jakob Benediktsson. Reykjavik, 1985.
Björn Bjarnason, ed. *Sturlungasaga.* Vol. 1. Reykjavik, 1908.
Björn Halldorsson. *Lexicon islandico-latino-danicum.* Copenhagen, 1814.
Björn Thorsteinsson. *Islensk Thjodlög.* Copenhagen, 1906–1909.
Dansbok II. Reykjavik, 1914.
Eggert Ólafsson. *Ferdabok Eggerts Olafssonar og Bjarna Palssonar: Um ferdir theirra a Islandi, 1752–1757.* Reykjavik, 1943.
Grimur Thomsen. *Um vikivaka.* Reykjavik, 1879.
Gudni Jonsson. *Islenskir sagnathættir og thjodsögur.* Reykjavik, 1948.
Gudni Jonsson, ed. *Fornaldarsögur Nordurlanda III.* Reykjavik, 1950.
Gunnlaugur Leifsson. *Saga Jons biskups helga Ögmundssonar, Biskupasögur II. og III.* Edited by Gudni Jonsson. Reykjavik, 1950.
Helgi Valtýsson. *Vikivakar og söngleikir.* Reykjavik, 1930.
Holland, Hebry. *Dagbok i Islandsferd* (1910). Translated by Steindor Steindorsson fra Hlödum. Reykjavik, 1960.
Jón Arnason. *Vikivakar.* Reykjavik, 1860.
Jón Samsonarson. *Kvædi og dansleikir.* 2 vols. Reykjavik, 1964.
Magnus Stephenson. *Island i Det Attendete Aarhundrede.* Copenhagen, 1808.
Olafur Briem. *Dansar.* Reykjavik, 1946.
Olafur Davidsson. *Islenskir vikivakar og vikivakakvædi.* Copenhagen, 1894.
Pall Eggert Ólafsson. *Islenskar æviskrar.* Reykjavik, 1948–1952.
Peterson, Paul. *Danse album.* Copenhagen, 1884.
Quirey, Belinda. *May I Have the Pleasure? The Story of Popular Dancing.* London, 1976.
Sigridur Valgeirsdóttir. *Thjoddansar I.* Reykjavik, 1959.
Sigridur Valgeirsdóttir and Minerva Jonsdóttir. *Nu tökum vid marsinn.* Reykjavik, 1980.
Sigridur Valgeirsdóttir. "Korleis gammaldansformerne kom til Noreden." In *Gammeldans i Norden.* Throndheim, 1988.
Sigridur Valgeirsdóttir and Minerva Jonsdóttir. *Gammeldans i Norden.* Throndheim, 1988.
Sigridur Valgeirsdóttir and Minerva Jonsdóttir. *Gomlu dansarnir i tvar aldir.* 3 vols. Reykjavik, 1994.
Thurston, Ólason. *Sagnadansar.* Reykjavik, 1979.

SIGRIDUR VALGEIRSDÓTTIR

Theatrical Dance

When they came under Danish control, Icelanders were forced to convert from Roman Catholicism to Lutheranism (in the mid-sixteenth century); dancing was then prohibited and it remained proscribed for centuries. For that reason no theatrical dance tradition exists in Iceland. Not until the eighteenth century was dancing reintroduced, in the form of social dancing.

Because of Iceland's isolation as an island colony (a republic since 1944) in the North Atlantic near the Arctic Circle, ballet did not arrive until the 1930s, when Asta Nordmann, an Icelander, opened a ballroom dancing and ballet school after having been overseas to study. Once a year she staged and produced recitals and performances for her students, dancing some difficult numbers herself. For many years she choreographed short dance pieces for stage productions at the theater in Reykjavik, the capital, and at that time the only professional theater in Iceland. These productions ostensively mark the beginning of Iceland's theatrical dance.

The National Theater opened in April 1950. The size of its stage and its technical facilities has enabled it to present large ballet productions. In 1952, the theater opened its ballet school, which concentrates on every aspect of theatrical dance. Whereas visiting ballet companies come from overseas and perform the classical works, dance students at the National Theater school primarily perform short pieces, classical works as well as folk ballets based on Icelandic literature. Most are set to the music of Icelandic composers and staged and choreographed by various teachers brought from overseas to head the ballet school. Good training has produced such fine dancers as Helgi Tomasson, who was a principal dancer with the New York City Ballet from 1970 to 1985; later, he became artistic director of the San Francisco Ballet.

The professional Icelandic Dance Company was formed in 1973. Initially the group comprised ten dancers, was supported by the government, and was attached to the National Theater. Since then, the company has staged several ballet productions a year and the dancers have participated in plays, operas, and musicals such as *Oklahoma!* and *Guys and Dolls*. Although they are classically trained, company dancers learn many styles, including folk dance.

Englishman Alan Carter, who formed the Icelandic Dance Company and selected its first dancers, based some of his ballets on modern techniques, using contemporary music and sound effects. Before departing in 1975, Carter staged *Coppélia*. Next, Natalia Conus came from the Soviet Union and introduced the dancers to the style and technique taught at the Bolshoi school in Moscow. In 1977 Yuri Chatal from the United States produced *The Nutcracker* as well as some works of his own. Anton Dolin staged his *Pas de Quatre* in 1978 and *Giselle* in 1982. In 1983, the company acquired Birgit Cullberg's *Miss Julie*; Jochen Ulrich from Germany created *Blindisleikur* (Blind Man's Bluff) to music by Icelandic composer Jón Ásgeirsson, who also wrote the libretto.

Because it is the policy of the company to build from within, the Icelandic Dance Company encourages dancers to choreograph and teach, with the goal of developing an Icelandic tradition. Ballet mistress Nanna Ólafsdóttir, formerly a dancer with the company, had studied in Leningrad and taught the Kirov style and technique. In 1985, she staged her own version of *Daphnis et Chloé*, the first full-length ballet by an Icelander. Other Icelandic choreographers are Ingibjörg Björnsdóttir, whose *Requiem* was staged in 1983, and Hlíf Svavarsdóttir, whose *Amalgam* and *Duende* were performed in 1986.

BIBLIOGRAPHY

Ólafur Ólafsson. "The Future Looks Brighter." *Ballett International* 13 (April 1990): 26.

Ólafur Ólafsson. "Keeping the Dream Alive." *Ballett International* 14 (July–August 1991): 44–45.

Ólafur Ólafsson. "Almost Like Starting over Again." *Ballett International* 16 (February 1993): 32–33.

ÖRN GUDMUNDSSON

ICHIKAWA DANJŪRŌ, name used by twelve generations of *kabuki* actors. The line is considered *kabuki*'s most prestigious.

Ichikawa Danjūrō I (born 1660 in Edo [Tokyo], died 17 February 1704 in Edo) borrowed the role of the legendary superhero Sakata Kintoki from the violent Kinpira puppet theater for his 1673 debut under the name of Ichikawa Ebizō I. Thus was founded the style of *aragoto* ("rough business"), the bravura acting associated with Edo theatricals. His red-painted face evolved into the formalized *aragoto* makeup called *kumadori,* and his heroic manner in such plays as *Shibaraku* was revered by the Edo townsmen, for whom he seemed almost a lesser deity.

A religious man, he was called by the actor's nickname *(yago)* Naritaya because of his devotion to the *aragoto*-like god Fudō, enshrined at Narita, whom he often played in the theater. He was the first *kabuki* actor to take a haiku poet's pen name, and under the playwright's name of Mimasuya Hyōgo, he wrote more than fifty plays in which he himself starred (for each art one takes another "artistic" name). *Aragoto* was only one of Danjūrō I's specialties; his artistry also extended to romantic acting in the *wagoto* manner preferred in the Kamigata (Kyoto-Osaka) area. In 1704, he was stabbed to death by another actor for reasons never fully determined.

Ichikawa Danjūrō II (born 11 October 1689 in Edo, died 24 September 1758 in Edo), the son of Danjūrō I, debuted as Ichikawa Kuzō I and then became Danjūrō II in 1704. He first gained acclaim in 1710, when he played the pitchman-like role of a seller of moxa (an herb used in Asian medicine). In 1713, he played the earliest version of the great character of Sukeroku, for which role he mixed elements of the *aragoto* and *wagoto* styles. Danjūrō II perfected *aragoto* and was the first actor to transfer many great puppet plays to Edo *kabuki* from Kyoto-Osaka, where they had been created. In 1735, he conceded his name to his young son, who became Danjūrō III, while he became Ichikawa Ebizō II. Around this time, he earned the incredible salary of two thousand ryō (according to one source, about $500,000 in present-day terms).

Ichikawa Danjūrō III (born 1721 in Edo, died 27 February 1742 in Edo), the son of one of Danjūrō I's disciples, was adopted by Danjūrō II and held the names Ichikawa Tokuben and Ichikawa Shogorō before becoming Danjūrō III. He died before he could attain greatness.

Ichikawa Danjūrō IV (born 1711 in Edo, died 25 February 1778 in Edo) was the illegitimate son of Danjūrō II. At three, he was adopted by Matsumoto Kōshirō I and debuted as Matsumoto Yazō. He played mainly female *(onnagata)* roles, rare for a Danjūrō, but was versatile enough to play male roles as well. After holding the name Matsumoto Kōshirō II, he became Danjūrō IV in 1754. He gave the Danjūrō name to his son in 1770, reverting to Kōshirō II and then switching to Ichikawa Ebizō III in 1772. He ran an actors' practice group at his home, where he taught young actors about theater and other subjects. Considered a progressive, Danjūrō IV mixed with every class of society, realizing that an actor's key to character portrayal is the accurate observation of human beings.

Ichikawa Danjūrō V (born August 1741 in Edo, died 30 October 1806 in Edo), the son of Danjūrō IV, began his career as Matsumoto Kōshiro III. He was the dominant actor of the late eighteenth century and like his father a talented *onnagata*, although he primarily acted male roles *(tachiyaku)*. Much of his youth was spent in hedonistic pursuits; still, he progressed at his own pace and acceded to the name of Danjūrō V in 1770. This eccentric player retired in 1796, when still vigorous, and became a hermit under the name Ichikawa Hakuen I, but he made several returns to the stage before his death.

Ichikawa Danjūrō VI (born 1778 in Edo, died 13 May 1799 in Edo), possibly the illegitimate son of Danjūrō V, died young. He debuted as Ichikawa Ebizō IV and took the name Danjūrō VI at thirteen, becoming an Edo favorite and playing a succession of great roles, gaining special renown as Gongorō in *Shibaraku*.

Ichikawa Danjūrō VII (born 1791 in Edo, died 23 March 1859 in Edo) was one of the greatest actors in *kabuki* history. He was the son of a samurai retainer and Danjūrō V's daughter. Danjūrō VI adopted him, and he became Danjūrō VII in 1800, at age nine. He lived lavishly, had three wives and three concubines, and fathered seven children. In 1832, the actor, reputed for his conceit, surprised many by giving his name to his son and taking the name Ichikawa Ebizō VI for himself. His early career was unspectacular, but he developed into a marvelously versatile artist, capable of playing as many as ten roles—male and female—in a single play. He brought deeper realism to his family's *aragoto* style than did any of his predecessors. Among his famous accomplishments was the *Kabuki Jūhachiban*, a compilation of the plays he considered the line's greatest accomplishments. This greatly strengthened the family's prestige and led other acting lines to make similar compilations. One of the plays, written at Danjūrō VII's suggestion, was the innovative dance-drama *Kanjinchō*, the most often revived *kabuki* play. It was the first *kabuki* adaptation of a *nō* play that attempted to recreate the essential quality of a *nō* performance.

The sumptuary laws of the 1840s had forced the removal of Japan's playhouses to a segregated district and an enactment of prohibitions against excessive stage display. The authorities made an example of Danjūrō VII (Ebizō VI) and banished him from Edo in 1840. He temporarily changed his name and moved to Kamigata to begin a new career. Seven years later, he was pardoned and returned in triumph to the Edo stage, where he strove to pay off his large debts. The suicide of his young son was a powerful blow. In 1852, he shaved his head as if to retire into the priesthood. But the stage was too much in his blood and he returned to it often until his death.

Ichikawa Danjūrō VIII (born 5 October 1823 in Edo, died 6 August 1854 in Osaka), the son of Danjūrō VII, began his career as Ichikawa Ebizō V but was given the name Danjūrō VIII by his father in 1832. The city of Edo treated him as its pet—partly for his reputation as a devoted son—and he treated Edo to several outstanding productions of his family's *aragoto*, as well as to young-lover roles, for which his exceptional good looks made him perfect. Some say he was the most popular actor in *kabuki* history, particularly with female fans. He was plagued by private demons, however, and his weaknesses were aggravated by his youthful successes. In 1854, he was performing with his father in Osaka when he killed himself by slashing his wrists, possibly because of crushing debts. Many memorial volumes and death pictures devoted to him were published.

Ichikawa Danjūrō IX (born 1839 in Edo, died 13 September 1903 in Chigasaki, Kanagawa Prefecture), the fifth son of Danjūrō VII, was adopted by the actor-manager Kawarazaki Gonnosuke VI, who provided him with a then-extraordinary upbringing, in which his training included various areas of classical Japanese art and learning (such as the tea ceremony), Chinese literature, painting, and calligraphy. He debuted as Kawarazaki Chōjūrō, changing to Kawarazaki Gonjūrō I in 1852. His early career was overshadowed by that of his enormously popular elder brother, but the latter's suicide, followed by the death of another brother, propelled the seventeen-year-old into prominence as the only remaining natural son of Danjūrō VII of whom greatness might be expected. His fortunes looked dismal when his adoptive family's theater, the Kawarazaki-za, was destroyed in the earthquake of 1865. In 1869, after his adoptive father was murdered, he became Kawarazaki Gonnosuke VIII. He specialized in *tachiyaku* but occasionally played *onnagata*.

In 1869 he became an actor-manager *(zagashira)* at the Ichimura-za. This was a year after the Meiji Restoration, and Gonnosuke VIII found the times receptive to new, Western-influenced ideas. He revived the Kawarazaki-za for a brief time in 1874 and staged history plays *(jidaimono)* that attempted great realism. He returned to the Ichikawa family, assuming the name of Danjūrō IX that same year (1874). Danjūrō IX joined the reformers in attempting to remake the often vulgar, fantastical *kabuki* into a respectably modern form of theater. He sought increasingly realistic, psychological acting and historically authentic productions, a style called "living history" *(katsureki)*. The public, however, was not impressed by the dull dramaturgy, and he eventually, if reluctantly, returned to more conventional presentations. He was one of the three stars invited in 1887 to perform for the first public viewing of *kabuki* by the imperial family, an event of great significance in raising the social status of *kabuki* actors. In 1888, Danjūrō IX became *zagashira* at the Kabuki-za, Japan's prestigious new playhouse. He and Onoe Kikugorō V acted there together in many of the old plays and dances, and classic *kabuki* witnessed a glorious revival. Danjūrō IX established his own play anthology, the *Shin Kabuki Jūhachiban,* containing more than thirty plays.

Ichikawa Danjūrō X (born 31 May 1882 in Tokyo, died 1 February 1956 in Tokyo), the husband of Danjūrō IX's daughter, was given the name Danjūrō X posthumously, largely because of his efforts to preserve the family tradition. Known for most of his career as Ichikawa Sanshō V, he trained for the stage relatively late and never became a satisfactory actor, but his revivals of forgotten *kabuki jūhachiban* plays were important to the Danjūrō line's position.

Ichikawa Danjūrō XI (born 6 January 1909 in Tokyo, died 10 November 1965 in Tokyo) was the son of the great actor-dancer Matsumoto Kōshirō VII, an avid student of Danjūrō IX, and the elder brother of Matsumoto Kōshirō VIII and Onoe Shōroku II. He debuted as Matsumoto Kotarō and in 1915 became Matsumoto Kintarō. He did not show much promise in his youth, but he was diligent about improving his craft. He, his brother (the future Kōshirō VIII), and the future Morita Kanya XIV formed a trial performance group, giving demonstrations of their work to invited audiences. In 1929, Kintarō became Ichikawa Komazō V, demonstrating an informal alliance with the Ichikawas. He worked so hard to deserve the name that he collapsed, requiring four years to resume his career. When he returned, only minor roles were offered to him. In 1936, he joined the idealistic new Tōhō Gekidan troupe, splitting from the Shōchiku company. His father disinherited him. After three unrewarding years, he returned to Shōchiku and was reinstated by his father. Komazō V was adopted into the family of Sanshō V in 1940, taking the name Ebizō IX.

In 1943, he was drafted, but illness led to his release from the armed forces and he performed throughout the war years. Ebizō IX's career was propelled in 1946 when he starred as Sukeroku, supported by several superstars. Audiences packed the Tokyo Gekijō to see his inspired performance. Many feel that this was the turning point in postwar *kabuki.* The handsome star was soon recognized as the leading player of romantic heroes. His fame grew enormously in 1952, when he starred as Prince Genji in *Genji Monogatari.* His acting deepened and the variety of his roles increased. In 1962, he was granted the name of Ichikawa Danjūrō XI. His death three years later was a terrible blow to *kabuki.* Danjūrō XI was known for his stage charm, powerful voice, and acting brilliance, but he was neither versatile nor an excellent dancer. His greatest roles included Yosaburō in *Kirare Yosa,* Sukeroku, Benkei in *Kanjinchō,* Narukami in *Narukami,* Yuranosuke in *Chūshingura,* and Matsuomaru in *Terakoya.*

Ichikawa Danjūrō XII (born 6 August 1946 in Tokyo), Danjūrō XI's son, debuted as Ichikawa Natsuo but became

ICHIKAWA DANJŪRŌ. A leading *kabuki* actor in the postwar era, Ichikawa Danjūrō XI achieved recognition for his portrayals of romantic heros. He appears here as Matsuō in the drama *Terakoya.* (Photograph courtesy of Samuel L. Leiter.)

Ichikawa Shinnosuke in 1958. He, Onoe Kikunosuke (later Onoe Kikugorō VII), and Onoe Tatsunosuke were known as the "three Sukes" and were responsible for a boom in *kabuki*'s popularity when they played together in the late 1950s. A large-eyed, handsome, dynamic actor who majored in art at Tokyo University, he is one of the most widely liked contemporary stars. In 1969 he became Ebizō X. The following year, he formed a blockbuster combination with the *onnagata* Bandō Tamasaburō V, costarring in *Narukami* and *Toribeyama Shinjū.* The name of Ichikawa Danjūrō XII was conferred on him in 1985.

He excels not only in *aragoto* characters but also in the portrayal of young lovers such as Yosaburō in *Kirare Yosa,* Naojirō in *Naozamurai,* and Kanpei in *Chūshingura.* He has also done well in major *jidaimono* roles such as Moritsuna in *Moritsuna Jinya* and Kumagai in *Kumagai Jinya*. Danjūrō XII has also appeared in *shinpa* plays, modern dramas, films, and television and has performed abroad on a number of occasions.

[*See also* Japanese Traditional Schools *and* Kabuki Theater.]

BIBLIOGRAPHY

Akasaka Jiseki, ed. *Kabuki haiyū daihyakka*. Tokyo, 1993.
Fujita Hiroshi. *Kabuki handobukku*. Tokyo, 1994.
Engekikai 43.2 (1985). Special issue: Ichikawa Danjūrō XII.
Engekikai 52.2 (1993). Special issue: *kabuki* actors' directory.
Ihara Toshio. *Danjūrō no shibai*. Tokyo, 1934.
Kanazawa Yasutaka. *Ichikawa Danjūrō*. Tokyo, 1962.
Kominz, Laurence. "Ichikawa Danjūrō V and the Golden Age of Kabuki." In *The Floating World Revisited*, edited by Donald Jenkins. Honolulu, 1994.
Leiter, Samuel L. "Ichikawa Danjūrō XI: A Life in Kabuki." *Educational Theatre Journal* (October 1977):310–319.
Nishiyama Matsunosuke. *Ichikawa Danjūrō*. Tokyo, 1965.
Nojima Jusaburō. *Kabuki jinmei jiten*. Tokyo, 1988.
Toita Yasuji, ed. *Kabuki kanshō nyūmon*. 3d ed., rev. Tokyo, 1994.
Usui Kenzō. *Ebizō Kara Danjūrō E*. Tokyo, 1985.

SAMUEL L. LEITER

ICHIKAWA ENNOSUKE, name used by three generations of *kabuki* actor-dancers.

Ichikawa Ennosuke I (born 21 July 1855 in Edo [Tokyo], died 1922 in Tokyo), the son of a fight-scene choreographer *(tateshi)*, debuted in 1859 as Ichimura Chōmatsu and held the names Bandō Utasuke, Yamazaki Ennosuke, and Matsuo Ennosuke before becoming Ichikawa Ennosuke I in 1890. In 1910 he took the name Ichikawa Danshirō II.

This popular actor was a specialist in dance and plays taken from the puppet theater, the role of Shunkan in *Heike Nyogo no Shima* being his greatest. He was also a specialist in the acrobatic and special-effects tradition called *keren*, which he handed on to his descendants. Much of his career was spent in the minor theaters called *koshibai*, traditionally looked down upon by the major-theater actors. He was excommunicated for years from the family of his master, Ichikawa Danjūrō IX, for this breach of etiquette, although he was eventually forgiven and was influential in the ultimate abandonment of official and nonofficial discrimination against *koshibai* actors.

Ichikawa Ennosuke II (born 21 May 1888 in Tokyo, died 12 June 1963 in Tokyo), the eldest of Ennosuke's four important actor sons, debuted as Ichikawa Danko in 1892, became Ichikawa Ennosuke II in 1910, and took the name Ichikawa En'o I in 1962, giving the name Ennosuke III to his grandson. Extremely progressive, he joined the

ICHIKAWA ENNOSUKE. An internationally renowned performer, Ichikawa Ennosuke III helped to revive popular interest in *kabuki* in the 1980s. In 1974 he struck this pose as Nango Rikimaru in the drama *Bentenkozō*. (Photograph courtesy of Samuel L. Leiter.)

Jiyu Gekijō (Free Theater) troupe to explore modern drama and, in 1919, traveled abroad, picking up influences that he brought to the "new dance" *(shin buyō)* movement. His Haruaki Kai group produced many excellent new-dance plays, including *Mushi* and *Koma*. In the 1950s, he was *kabuki*'s senior actor and president of the Japan Actors' Association. In 1955, he became Japan's first postwar theatrical envoy and performed in China.

Ichikawa Ennosuke III (born 9 December 1939 in Tokyo) debuted as Ichikawa Danko III in 1946. His childhood was focused more on education than on performing, and in 1961 he began attending Keio University, ultimately becoming the first *kabuki* actor to complete a college education. Both his grandfather and his father (Ichikawa Danshirō III, born 1913) died in 1963, which plunged the young actor into hardship as none of the companies would accept him, forcing him to travel his own road. Since 1966, he has led a study group called Haruaki Kai and is today the leader of his own Ichikawa Ennosuke troupe. He directs the troupe's productions and co-stars in them with his brother, Ichikawa Danshirō IV (born 1946). His company toured abroad in 1977, 1985, 1987, and 1991, making him one of the internationally best-known *kabuki* stars, a distinction that was furthered when in 1984 he directed the opera *Coq d'Or* in Paris.

In Japan, he directs not only his own company's productions but also commercial musicals. He is a perpetual explorer of new territory and is largely responsible for the 1980s explosion of interest in *kabuki*, especially through his spectacular "super-*kabuki*" productions, such as the enormously popular *Yamato Takeru* of 1986. It ran for six months and was revived in 1988 for another four months, playing to more than half a million spectators during its two showings. Beginning with his revival in 1968 of *Taiheiki Chūshin Kōshaku*, he has tirelessly resuscitated forgotten old plays, making them work for modern audiences. A revolutionary in the spirit of his forebears, he is devoted to the idea of rediscovering the energy, rhythm, and wonder that he believes *kabuki* had in the days before the reforms of the Meiji era (1868–1912). His advocacy of "story, speed, and spectacle" and his flashy techniques, however, are not appreciated by conservative connoisseurs.

Ennosuke III is an extremely versatile actor, playing every type of male and female role and specializing in quick-change and *keren* acting. In 1968, when he produced *Yoshitsune Senbon Zakura*, starring as the fox-Tadanobu, he reintroduced the technique of aerial flight on wires *(chūnori)* into the climactic scene, and this became a hallmark of his work. His powerful voice, great versatility, boundless energy, and enthusiasm for experiment place him at the top of today's theater.

Ennosuke III has collected the best productions of his grandfather into the family repertories, known as *En'o Jūshu* (En'o's Ten) and *Omodokaya Jūshu* (The Omodokaya [the family's *yagō*, "shop name"] Ten), to which he has added his own *Ennosuke Jūhachiban* (Ennosuke's Eighteen). Critics consider his five best productions to be *Yoshitsune Senbon Zakura*, *Yamato Takeru*, the Kotsuyose no Iwafuji scene from *Kagamiyama Kokyō no Nishikie*, *Date no Jūyaku* (in which he plays ten roles), and *Oguri Hangan*. His best dance pieces include *Kurozuka* and *Kokaji*.

[*See also* Japanese Traditional Schools *and* Kabuki Theater.]

BIBLIOGRAPHY

Akasaka Jiseki, ed. *Kabuki haiyū daihyakka.* Tokyo, 1993.
Bach, Faith. "The Contributions of the Omodokaya to Kabuki." Ph.D. diss., Oxford University, 1991.
Engekikai 52.2 (1993). Special issue: *kabuki* actors' directory.
Fujita Hiroshi. *Kabuki handobukku.* Tokyo, 1994.
Ichikawa Ennosuke III. *Ennosuke kabuki kōza.* Tokyo, 1984.
Leiter, Samuel L. "*Keren:* Spectacle and Trickery in Kabuki Acting." *Educational Theatre Journal* (May 1976):175–188.
Leiter, Samuel L. "Ichikawa Ennosuke III: Japan's Most Versatile Actor." In *The Grand Kabuki: National Theatre of Japan* (souvenir program). New York, 1977.
Leiter, Samuel L. *Kabuki Encyclopedia: An English-Language Adaptation of "Kabuki Jiten."* Westport, Conn., 1979.
Toita Yasuji, ed. *Kabuki kanshō nyūmon.* 3d ed., rev. Tokyo, 1994.

SAMUEL L. LEITER

IDEOKINESIS. *See* Body Therapies, *article on* Ideokinesis.

IDZIKOWSKI, STANISLAS (Stanisław Idzikowski; born 1894 in Warsaw, died 12 February 1977 in London), Polish dancer, ballet master, and teacher. Trained from the age of ten at the ballet school of Warsaw's Wielki Theater, Idzikowski later studied with Auguste Berger and Enrico Cecchetti. In 1911, at age seventeen, he made his English debut partnering Phyllis Bedells in the musical comedy *New York* at the Empire Theatre in London. In 1912, he appeared with Anna Pavlova's company in *La Fille Mal Gardée* at the Palace Theatre, and shortly thereafter, he joined Theodore Koslov's Imperial Russian Ballet. In 1914, Idzikowski opened a school in London, and the following year he and his longtime partner, the British dancer Wanda Evina (Evelyn Iles), were invited to join the Ballets Russes de Serge Diaghilev.

Between 1915 and 1923, Idzikowski was a leading dancer with the Diaghilev company, celebrated for his technical virtuosity as well as the variety of comic roles he created in Léonide Massine's *Les Femmes de Bonne Humeur* (Battista; 1917), *Le Tricorne* (The Dandy; 1919), *La Boutique Fantasque* (The Snob; 1919), and *Pulcinella* (Coviello; 1920). Despite his diminutive stature, he successfully appropriated Vaslav Nijinsky's roles in *Le Carnaval, Les Sylphides, Petrouchka,* and *Le Spectre de la Rose,* as well as the Bluebird pas de deux from *The Sleeping Beauty.* As Battista, wrote Cyril W. Beaumont, Idzikowski "conjures up a delicious miniature of the gay, care-free life in the Venice beloved of Goldoni and Cassanova. All his movements, all his gestures radiate an effervescent humour" (Beaumont, 1926).

In 1922, Idzikowski created the role of the Cat in Bronislava Nijinska's *Le Renard* and, certainly of more lasting importance, collaborated with Beaumont in writing a manual of classical dancing according to the principles of his teacher Cecchetti (Beaumont and Idzikowski, 1922). In 1924, he appeared with his frequent partner Lydia Lopokova at the London Coliseum and in Comte Étienne de Beaumont's Soirées de Paris. He rejoined Diaghilev in

1925, creating one of his finest interpretations in George Balanchine's *Jack-in-the-Box* (1926), but he left again to form his short-lived Russian Ballet (1928–1931). In 1933, Idzikowski appeared as a guest artist with the Vic-Wells Ballet, partnering Alicia Markova in the Bluebird pas de deux, *Le Spectre de la Rose*, Frederick Ashton's *Les Rendezvous*, and *Le Carnaval*, which he and Evina staged. In the early 1940s he served as ballet master to Mona Inglesby's International Ballet. Private teaching and classes at the Royal Academy of Dancing absorbed his later years.

BIBLIOGRAPHY

Beaumont, Cyril W., and Stanislas Idzikowski. *A Manual of the Theory and Practice of Classical Theatrical Dancing: Cecchetti Method.* London, 1922. Includes a preface by Enrico Cecchetti.
Beaumont, Cyril W. *The Art of Stanislas Idzikowski.* London, 1926.
Beaumont, Cyril W. "A Tribute to Wanda Evina." *The Dancing Times* (February 1967): 248.
Howlett, Jasper. "Stanislas Idzikowski: An Appreciation." *The Dancing Times* (April 1944): 306–307.
Manchester, P. W. *Vic-Wells: A Ballet Progress.* London, 1942.

INTERVIEW. Stanislas Idzikowski, by John Gruen, Oral History Archives, Dance Collection, New York Public Library for the Performing Arts.

LYNN GARAFOLA

ILLUMINATIONS. Ballet in one act. Choreography: Frederick Ashton. Music: Benjamin Britten. Scenery and costumes: Cecil Beaton. First performance: 2 March 1950, City Center of Music and Drama, New York, New York City Ballet. Principals: Nicholas Magallanes (The Poet), Tanaquil Le Clercq (Sacred Love), Melissa Hayden (Profane Love).

In *Illuminations* Frederick Ashton made a work markedly unlike his other ballets and unlike others in the repertory of the New York City Ballet. Prepared in collaboration with Lincoln Kirstein and Cecil Beaton, it was based on the poet Arthur Rimbaud's life and work and set to Benjamin Britten's suite of songs to texts from Rimbaud's volume *Les illuminations*. The program note described the ballet as "a sequence of danced pictures *(tableaux dansants)*, or charades, in which images suggested by Rimbaud's poems and symbolic incidents from his violent life are interwoven on the musical pattern."

The notion of charades is present in the device of having the ballet performed by a troupe of ragged Pierrots, suggesting Rimbaud's view of the world as a rundown sideshow. At the same time, the hero is an artist—the Poet—surrounded by figures and symbolic events. There are specific references to incidents in Rimbaud's life. Ashton's choreography, however, is primarily a response to Britten's music and to the individual poems in the score. Ashton rarely attempted to match specific verbal image with dance image. Instead, he developed choreographic images of comparably intense construction.

ILLUMINATIONS. Members of the original cast: Tanaquil Le Clercq as Sacred Love, Nicholas Magallanes as the Poet, and Melissa Hayden as Profane Love. Of many innovations in choreography and costume in this ballet, one of the most effective was the absence of a shoe. The bare left foot of Profane Love was shockingly sensual. (Photograph by Cecil Beaton; used by permission of Sotheby's of Bond Street, London.)

Sections of the music called "Fanfare," "Phrase," and "Interlude" are brief solos for the Poet, suggesting that the ballet's other scenes are his visions, depicted or imagined. Other sections—"Dreamtown," "Royalty," "Anarchy," and "Sideshow"—portray societies alien to the Poet. After a monarchic procession in "Royalty," in "Anarchy" Ashton takes his most liberal departure from the words' literal meaning and follows the music's violence to present not Rimbaud's turbulent seascape but a civic riot in which the Poet disrupts the ceremony, pushing over the King and taking his crown. The scene's disturbance builds, finding a choreographic development at the song's climax: to the coloratura on the word *tourbillons* ("whirlwinds"), two men spin in *pirouettes sautés*.

The Poet's most personal imaginings are the recurrent ballerina figures of Sacred Love and Profane Love. Sacred Love appears costumed as a queen in "Royalty"; later the Poet sees her reappear with four partners in "Being Beauteous." This episode, a sustained poetic essay in supported adagio, is in contrast to the Poet's sexual dealings with Profane Love. At the end of "Sideshow," in which the Poet is ostracized by the crowd, Profane Love directs the gunshot that wounds his arm. In "Farewell" the wounded Poet abandons society in pursuit of Sacred Love, who is carried across the rear stage in arching lifts. In the ballet's closing image the Poet is silhouetted and transfigured by blazing sunlight.

The ballet made periodic returns to the New York City Ballet repertory until the 1970s. In 1980 it was revived for the Joffrey Ballet. In 1981 Ashton supervised a revival for the Royal Ballet, dedicating it to Beaton's memory and making minor changes; Ashley Page, Jennifer Penney, and Genesia Rosato led the cast.

BIBLIOGRAPHY
Aloff, Mindy. "Frederick Ashton's *Illuminations.*" *Dance Magazine* (November 1980): 71–75.
Buckle, Richard. *Buckle at the Ballet*. London, 1980.
Chujoy, Anatole. *The New York City Ballet*. New York, 1953.
Goodwin, Noël. "Britten and the Ballet." *Dance and Dancers* (February 1982): 12–13.
Jowitt, Deborah. *The Dance in Mind*. Boston, 1985.
Kirstein, Lincoln. *Thirty Years: The New York City Ballet*. New York, 1978.
Macaulay, Alastair. "New Clarity?" *The Dancing Times* (February 1982): 328–331.
Reynolds, Nancy. *Repertory in Review: Forty Years of the New York City Ballet*. New York, 1977.
Vaughan, David. *Frederick Ashton and His Ballets*. London, 1977.
ALASTAIR MACAULAY

IMPEKOVEN, NIDDY (born 2 November 1904 in Berlin), German dancer. Impekoven was one of those special figures who arose on the periphery of German interpretive (or expressionist) dance. Soon after beginning her training at the age of six, she made her debut in 1910 as a classical dancer at a Berlin charity performance. Her childish charm and imagination immediately fascinated the audience. Pressured by parental ambition, as she later wrote, the prodigy continued her training, making appearances as both dancer and actress. From 1914 until her move to Munich in 1917, she worked with the Frankfurt ballet master Heinrich Kröller, who sought to combine classical tradition with modern trends. After a period of study at the Bieberstein Castle School for Classical Gymnastics, Impekoven worked with Kröller to design her first solo program, which included *Der Gefangene Vogel* (The Caged Bird), *Das Leben der Blume* (The Life of Flowers), *Schalk* (Rascal), and *Puppentänzen* (Doll Dances), stylized character studies that she introduced with great success in 1918 at Berlin's Theater unter den Linden. Her first dance evening led to tours throughout Europe. She danced chiefly to classical music, and her repertory included humorous sketches such as *Münchner Kaffeewärmer* (Munich Coffeepot) as well as classically based short ballets (*Harlekin* and *Pizzicato*).

In her childlike lightheartedness—which aroused the enthusiasm of audiences all over Europe in the 1920s and guaranteed sold-out theaters for weeks at a time—Impekoven was a typical representative of the rising genre of concert dance. Her style, composed from various techniques ranging from classical ballet to free eurythmic dance composition and pantomime, well typified the artistic trends in Germany that gave rise to interpretive dance. Her manner of representation, a combination of childlike sweetness and an almost magical delicacy and grace, could render both cheerful and poignant narratives, but it was less suitable for portraying the anguish and struggle common in German expressionist dance.

BIBLIOGRAPHY
Impekoven, Niddy. *Werdegang*. Dresden, 1922.
Impekoven, Niddy. *Die Geschichte eines Wunderkindes*. Zurich, 1955.
HEDWIG MÜLLER
Translated from German

IMPROVISATION. Dance improvisation can be defined as the spontaneous exploration of human movement possibilities. It is an important element in performance dance, as well as in ritual, social, educational, and therapeutic dance.

Improvisation has been widely misunderstood and unappreciated in the western theatrical tradition. Its use in performance is valued in many traditions—in Asia, India, Africa, the Middle East (*raqs al-sharqi*), and Spain (flamenco)—where creative ability is considered an important element of a performer's skill. Although the complete history of its use in the West is difficult to trace, in general, creative ability became separate from performing

IMPROVISATION. Jon Gibson plays the tenor sax as Simone Forti (standing) and Lauri Nagel (kneeling) engage in a movement improvisation. This performance was part of the second annual Improvisation Festival in 1993. (Photograph © 1993 by Anja Hitzenberger; used by permission.)

ability. Since 1960s, there has been an increase in interest in improvisational performance.

Identifying Improvisation. Only the performer can know which aspects of his or her work are truly improvised and which are planned. Unless the members of the audience are informed that a performance is improvisational, they cannot know for sure. Its intentional use in performance should not be confused with its unintentional use—for example, in response to an emergency situation such as a memory lapse, accident, or injury.

The intentional use of improvisation in performance can be understood best when viewed as existing on a spectrum ranging from the dancer's interpretation of set material at one end to completely free improvisation at the other. No material can be completely set; each performance will be different. By contrast, no material can be completely open or unset; the performance will be subject to the patterns of response and training the performer brings to it. Between extremes of set interpretation and unset improvisations exists a wide range of structured improvisations with varying kinds and degrees of set and unset materials.

Variable elements might include the overall shape of the dance; its specific timing, spacing, vocabulary, and qualities; the amount of prestructuring and rehearsal it involves; the source of the decision-making authority (one person or several, constant or changing); the relationship of the participants to each other and to the audience; the dancer's relationship to the environment; and the use of and interaction with music, text, costumes, and props. Solo improvisation, which requires skill in both perform-

ing and creating, is distinct from group improvisation, which requires the ability to communicate and, usually, a common movement vocabulary.

History of Improvisation. Dance in the Renaissance valued improvisation, as did the music and theater (*commedia dell'arte*) of the time. Although subsequent historical documents have yet to be adequately scrutinized and, in the case of dance, might be particularly elusive, it is probable that interest in improvisation diminished as interest in the development of set choreography increased.

For several centuries improvisation in the West seems to have been largely a matter of interpretive artistry, a choreographic tool (e.g., Carlo Blasis advised choreographers to use it), and a response to accident (e.g., Marie Camargo is said to have made her debut improvising a dance to replace an injured soloist; however, whether she used something she already knew or created something extempore is unknown). The Russian ballerina Olga Preobrajenska provided a rare example of virtuosic improvisational skill. She was known for her ability to improvise encores based on the choreography she had been given to dance, much in the manner of the improvised cadenza in Baroque music.

Against the background of new theories of human development that were rooted in the nineteenth century—such as those of Sigmund Freud, Charles Darwin, and John Dewey—improvisation became increasingly important as an educational and therapeutic tool in the twentieth. Educators like Bird Larson, who worked with children, and Margaret H'Doubler, who pioneered dance in the university, incorporated improvisation into their training programs. Self-expression was encouraged by the use of music and evocative images and themes. Although this use of improvisation led many to associate all improvisation with amateurism, it nonetheless provided a foundation for later developments in performance improvisation.

Meanwhile, great dancers of interpretive genius, such as Anna Pavlova and Ruth St. Denis, were reputed never to have given the same performance twice. Their gift for creating the illusion of spontaneity may, in fact, have been in part that the spontaneity was real. Pavlova admitted that she liked to take interpretive liberties with material—but only if she owned the choreography because she felt it would be disrespectful to tamper with someone else's work. Her approach may also explain why her choreographic materials were criticized for their mediocrity, while her performances were praised for their magic.

Although Isadora Duncan is widely reputed to have improvised in performance, the point still is being debated. It is clear that at least some of her material was set, and it is probable that some people who labeled her work improvisational did so because its style and seeming free form were different from what they knew. However, it is also possible that she departed from set material when inspired to do so—spontaneously responding to a favorite piece of music or a familiar idea in a new way.

Mary Wigman and Rudolf Laban. At about the same time, two very influential figures—Mary Wigman and Rudolf Laban—were beginning their work together in central Europe. Both used improvisation extensively in the training process and in preparing material. Although Wigman was adamant about its value as a means to an end, but not as an end to itself, Laban sometimes used improvisation in performances by his movement choirs, providing loose structures that sometimes included untrained dancers.

Between them they developed an approach to the training of improvisation and a respect for improvisation that has been the legacy of an expanding network of artistic descendants throughout Europe, the United States, and Japan: for example, Hanya Holm, Truda Kaschmann, Alwin Nikolais, Murray Louis, Phyllis Lamhut, Dorothy Vislocky, Beverly Schmidt, Barbara Mettler, and Don Redlich. The Wigman-Laban approach still influences improvisational activity in dance today. Largely analytical and abstract, their approach, which focuses on the exploration of body parts in isolation or on space, time, or effort-shape qualities also employs images as motivations for movement. The approach is used to sensitize dancers to their own impulses and to each other.

Alwin Nikolais and Murray Louis. Among later choreographers who use improvisation in performance are Alwin Nikolais and Murray Louis, whose companies give improvisational lecture-demonstrations. As early as 1958, Nikolais, who at the time had a company of skilled performers who had been working together and with improvisation for several years, created *Mirrors*. In it, the overall structure of the dance was set, but the dancers were free to improvise within the style of each section. Later pieces, such as *Tower* (1965) and *Crucible* (1985), continued to provide an overall framework for the dance, time cues or tasks to accomplish, and a style of approach and then left specific movements to the dancers. Louis sometimes allowed for improvisational material in the transitions between one section of a work to the next to accommodate variations in spacing and timing.

The turning point in the use of improvisation in performance came in the early 1960s, against the background of experimentation and rebellion that permeated all the arts and other activities of the time. Emphasis on spontaneity, the overlapping of art forms (looking to theatrical and musical improvisational activity), process as an acceptable part of performance, the influence of Eastern improvisational forms, and a drug culture that provided a model of free associative thought all created an environment conducive to the development of improvisational dance.

Anna Halprin, Robert Ellis Dunn, and Students. Two people who were largely responsible for encouraging the spread of improvisational dance were Anna Halprin and Robert Ellis Dunn. Halprin (who had studied with H'Doubler and Mettler) was working in California with improvisational workshops that later evolved into performances. She was especially concerned with group process, tasks, ritual, stream of consciousness, and interaction with the environment. Dunn conducted a composition workshop in New York from 1960 to 1962 in which he introduced the use of scores and challenged many prior attitudes toward developing material. Halprin's work was introduced to Dunn's workshop by Simone Forti, Trisha Brown, and Yvonne Rainer, who had recently studied with her. It would be the seedbed of the Judson Dance Theater choreographic activities that followed. [*See* Judson Dance Theater.]

Forti, who first worked with Halprin in 1956, focused her continuing commitment to improvisational structures on task approaches, such as in *See-Saw* and *Huddle*, and on childlike movements, animal movements, and circular patterns. She later coined the phrase "dance as artsport" to describe the sports- or gamelike nature of many improvisational structures. In those structures rules or limits were set up and the players were challenged to demonstrate their skills within them, as well as to challenge the limits themselves. Forti's collaborations with various improvising musicians typified the relationships a number of performers, especially soloists, established with musicians.

Brown was especially interested in game structures. Her early solo *Trillium* (1962) had a minimal structure involving lying, sitting, standing, and levitating. Her later group works emphasized the importance of structures and of rehearsals to allow for the adequate exploration of those structures. Her introduction of text to dance, which she did not exploit as fully as others, allowed her the option of having dancers call out cues as a way of varying material in performance.

Rainer found herself becoming less interested in making distinctions between process and performance and in exerting control over the precise sequence of events or the precise manner of performance. She explored improvisation in sections of *Terrain* (1963); in *Continuous Project— Altered Daily* (1970), she allowed a variety of materials at various levels of preset clarity, including surprises—that is, material introduced without the previous knowledge of all performers. Casual behavior and rehearsal behavior, both of which have spontaneous aspects, were allowed. Bizarre images, such as "macrobiotic foodist" and "W. C. Fields" were used to prompt activity.

Improvisational Groups and Forms. Rainer's increasing interest in such issues led her to instigate the formation of the Grand Union in 1970, an improvisational group that became well known and broke important ground. The personalities and styles of its changing personnel played a major role in its character. Material was

IMPROVISATION. The performance improvisations of the Grand Union were permeated with a profound sense of play. At this moment, an unseen partner manipulates Trisha Brown (left) as David Gordon, in boots and a silly hat, observes the proceedings. (Photograph © 1975 by Johan Elbers; used by permission.)

not rehearsed or planned before each performance, although some material did carry over from one performance to the next or become ongoing leitmotifs to vary. The performers allowed themselves the full range of ways to relate to each other—copying, varying, doing something associated (either connected or contrasting), and ignoring. Their explorations were not limited purely to movement but included text and a great deal of self-reflective commentary on their processes. [*See* Grand Union.]

The Judson participants experimented with a vast range of improvisational forms, and several of their concerts were devoted solely to improvisational structures. A number of the Judson choreographers, such as Elaine Summers, Deborah Hay, and Sally Gross, as well as such Grand Union members as Barbara Dilley Lloyd and Nancy Lewis, continued to experiment.

Some of the performers had been members of the Merce Cunningham company. Despite the general impression of many audience members, Cunningham rarely incorporated improvisation in his work, the exception being an unusual early solo, *Fast Blues* (1946) with jazz drummer Baby Dodds, a single Event (Cunningham's signature evening-length college format), and sections of *Story* (1963) that allowed the dancers some options for the origination of material. His most open works, such as *Field Dances* (1963) and *Scramble* (1967), tended to be in the form called *indeterminate structures* in which the actual material was set, but in which performers were given options of selection, order, timing, and spacing. Although the rest of his material was rigorously set, his use of chance procedures and his collaboration with John Cage encouraged new ways of looking at performance possibilities.

Steve Paxton, a former Cunningham company member who was also very active in Judson and Grand Union, performed highly skilled improvisational solos, often in collaboration with percussionist David Moss. Paxton is largely responsible for the evolution of the immensely popular and influential form called *contact improvisation*, which dates its official beginning to 1972 but grew out of several of his ongoing concerns. Contact improvisation is primarily a duet form (the most basic unit of social interaction) that emphasizes the qualities of mutual trust and interdependence by requiring ongoing contact between the two participants (with little use of the hands and eyes, traditionally the most basic forms of social contact). It has a relaxed, sustained, athletic quality and a noncompetitive nature. Although nontheatricality was one of its founding premises, contact improvisation has become a spectator activity. Groups evolved that perform contact work alone, such as Freelance and ReUnion, and others that use contact as a base, such as Mangrove and Channel Z. Contact improvisation has created a worldwide network of participants and a successful publication, *Contact Quarterly*, that addresses other aspects of improvisation as well. [*See the entry on Paxton.*]

A number of other choreographers explored approaches to group improvisation. In some of her early works, such as *Medley* (1969) and *Dancing in the Streets . . .* (1969), Twyla Tharp had performers respond to audience activities and mimic their actions. Daniel Nagrin's *Workgroup* (1971–1974) evolved a number of structures focusing primarily on traditional dance movement and vocabulary and using extensive rehearsal to guarantee a high level of performance. Art Bauman looked to theatrical and musical improvisational models for his pieces, including one at the Museum of Modern Art in New York City and one in the Washington Cathedral in Washington, D.C. *Dances for Women* (1973) applied the jazz device of varying a well-known melodic line by taking choreographed phrases from works of well-known early modern dancers such as Doris Humphrey and Martha Graham and having several women vary them in a performance. Richard Bull has been creating group structures since 1967, including *Making and Doing* (1970). It requires the performers to memorize everything they improvised in the first half of the work and repeat it exactly as the second half of the work. In 1983 John Bernd organized a group called Screws Loose with as disparate a membership as he could find and had them perform without rehearsal.

A number of soloists, some of whom have also done group works, have been successful with a wide variety of structures. Margaret Beals sometimes asks audience members for word cues (in the manner of many theatrical improvisational groups) and then improvises little vignettes, often with text, in response to such cues as "ripe raspberry" and "wet newspaper." Kenneth King uses text extensively in solos like *Wordraid*, in which he moves at high speed as he recites complex and humorous tongue twisters. His group pieces, such as *World Trade*, often use a Cunningham vocabulary and a grid structure in space as a way of organizing sections of material within a larger philosophical framework.

In her many rigorously structured solo and group works, Dana Reitz demonstrates the potential for improvisation to allow the exploration of infinitely subtle nuances between gestures and their variations. The Japanese dancer Tanaka Min explores nuance at the seemingly microscopic level in his solo "bodyweather" experiments: he makes infinitesimal responses to both inner and outer impulses. He is one of many dancers from the Japanese *butō* tradition who often incorporate improvisation into their performances. Mark Morris, known more for choreography than improvisation, has looked to improvisation in Indian dance as a model for keeping solo material interesting in *Orangasayee* (1984). In 1987, inspired by the tra-

IMPROVISATION. Performances of contact improvisation often occur in informal settings. Here, Steve Paxton (standing) suspends Danny Lepkoff inches from the floor. At left, a man seems ready to join the duet. (Photograph © 1997 by Beatriz Schiller; used by permission.)

dition of the solo improvisational performances of major Baroque composers, Morris premiered an improvised solo to music by Domenico Scarlatti (Sonata in D, K491), which was danced differently and newly titled at each subsequent performance.

African-American Dance. The African-American dance tradition—rooted in an oral tradition of storytelling—deserves special mention because of its ongoing use of improvisation in jazz, social dance, tap dance, and more recently in break dancing and the rap song all of which have been an important source and inspiration for improvising dancers. Great tap masters such as Honi Coles, Cookie Cook, Chuck Green, and Gregory Hines have demonstrated extraordinarily complex and subtle rhythmic explorations. Challenge matches between solo tappers show the virtue of competition to push performers to their maximum achievement. The young virtuoso Savion Glover has displayed his virtuosity on the Broadway stage in *Bring in 'da Noise, Bring in 'da Funk.*

As has been indicated, jazz has been an important model for improvising dancers. Although the term *jazz dance* more often applies to a style and vocabulary of movement than to the use of improvisation, a number of performers have worked improvisationally to jazz, including Judith Dunn, in her collaborations with jazz musician Bill Dixon, and Dianne McIntyre in her group works. More recently groups like the Jazz Tap Ensemble have drawn on both jazz and tap traditions to create choreographed and improvised works. David Parsons, a modern dancer who performed with the Paul Taylor Dance Company, created a work, *Step into My Dream* (1994), for his own company with jazz pianist and composer Billy Taylor, which had improvised sections using a highly virtuosic and athletic modern dance technique.

A number of young black choreographers have incorporated an awareness of their heritage into a continuing exploration of other improvisational approaches. Bill T. Jones has performed brilliant autobiographical solos, often with text, that are notable for their wide-ranging and virtuosic movement vocabulary. Blondell Cummings has also performed improvisational solos, including *The Ladies and Me* (1979), set to recordings of female blues singers. Ishmael Houston-Jones and Fred Holland collaborated on *Cowboys, Dreams and Ladders* (1984), a story work about black cowboys and childhood. Jowale Willa Jo Zollar has created a number of group works for her company, the Urban Bush Women, which use improvisation to address feminist and racial issues.

Ballet. Until recently, ballet has done little to exploit the possibilities of improvisation. Interpretive liberties most often are taken with dramatic material, such as the mad scene in *Giselle*. Some performers are, however, able to play with phrasing or the embellishment of a step in skillful ways that do not subvert the intentions of the work. Suzanne Farrell was acknowledged for the spontaneity of her interpretations in performance of works by George Balanchine. Ballet choreographers vary widely in their use of improvisation in the preparation of material, some drawing more than others on material created by or suited to the performers. Some works, such as Glen Tetley's *Voluntaries* (1973) and Eliot Feld's *Impromptu* (1976), were inspired by qualities often associated with improvisation, such as spontaneity and apparent free form.

There have been a few rare experiments, such as Richard Tanner's *Eatin' Rain in Space* (1979), an "enormously risky free-form" duet (*Dance Magazine*, November 1982) for Mikhail Baryshnikov and Heather Watts to music by jazz pianist Cecil Taylor. As Baryshnikov has explored more modern dance territory with his company, the White Oak Dance Project, he has discreetly ventured into improvisational terrain in works by Twyla Tharp, Mark Morris (*Ten Suggestions*, 1991), and Dana Reitz. The iconoclastic, American-born ballet choreographer William Forsythe has pushed the ballet vocabulary and the use of improvisation to new limits in any number of works for his companies in Germany.

As modern dance technique and ballet technique have begun to merge, the vocabularies of improvisational dance performances have become more virtuosic and complex. Many institutions including those associated with the Wigman-Laban line of training and with the contact improvisation network are encouraging the development of interest and skill in improvisation. Public School 122 holds weekly "open-movement" sessions in which dancers are encouraged to jam freely. The School for Movement Research has sponsored workshops and provocative forums as well as performances. The Naropa Institute integrates Eastern principles and practice with Western improvisational activity. Other groups and schools throughout the world are both active and innovative with improvisation festivals lasting a week or more occurring regularly in major modern dance capitals.

Performance tradition in India places a high value on improvisational skill, largely the domain of the virtuosic soloist. The complex interaction of improvising musicians and the improvising dancer is one of the pleasures of watching a performance. Improvisation divides into two principle areas—gestural and rhythmic. *Abhinaya*, the gestural interpretation of poetry and song or of famous stories, was the special strength of the *bharata nāṭyam* artist Balasaraswati. She also codified the traditional form of a *bharata nāṭyam* performance and defined the areas in which improvisation occurred achieving its height in the complex section called *varṇam*. Complex rhythmic improvisation, danced with bare feet and ankle bells, and incorporating various types of stamps and taps of the foot, is present in all the classical forms of Indian dance but is most highly developed in the *kathak* style of North India. Sometimes soloists will challenge each other or their musicians with complex rhythmic lines to be mimicked or embellished. Traditional rhythmic patterns may be passed from teacher to student as a starting point for improvisation.

The flamenco dance of Spain is also traditionally improvised although many performers today choreograph their material. Spontaneous invention was prized in performances at the family and tavern gatherings that nourished and sustained this form.

[*See also the entries on the principal figures mentioned herein.*]

BIBLIOGRAPHY

Banes, Sally. *Terpsichore in Sneakers: Post-Modern Dance.* Boston, 1980.
Banes, Sally. *Democracy's Body: Judson Dance Theater, 1962–64.* Ann Arbor, Mich., 1983.
Contact Quarterly. Northampton, Mass., 1976–.

Livet, Anne, ed. *Contemporary Dance.* New York, 1978.

McDonagh, Don, ed. *The Complete Guide to Modern Dance.* New York, 1976.

Nagrin, Daniel. *Dance and the Specific Image: Improvisation.* Pittsburgh, 1994.

Novack, Cynthia J. *Sharing the Dance: Contact Improvisation and American Culture.* Madison, Wis., 1990.

Stearns, Marshall, and Jean Stearns. *Jazz Dance.* Rev. ed. New York, 1994.

KATY MATHESON

INBAL DANCE THEATRE was founded in 1950 in Tel Aviv, Israel, by Sara Levi-Tanai, who became its artistic director and chief choreographer. The company's name, *Inbal*, means the "tongue of a bell" in Hebrew. Of Yemenite-Jewish ancestry, Levi-Tanai met with groups of new immigrants from Yemen soon after Israel's declaration of independence in 1948 and thus became familiar with their distinctive traditional dance style. She began to create her own choreography for original modern dramatic works based on those traditional Yemenite stylistic elements.

Originally, Inbal was supported by the cultural department of Israel's trade unions (the Histadrut) and the America-Israel Culture Fund (then called the Normal Fund). In 1952 the fund invited Jerome Robbins to make a survey of dance in Israel. In his report he stressed Inbal's artistic potential and the great artistic merit of Levi-Tanai's choreography. He was instrumental in inviting the dancer and choreographer Anna Sokolow to instruct the Inbal dancers in modern technique.

In 1957 the impresario Sol Hurok invited Inbal to tour the United States. Audiences and critics were equally impressed by Inbal's originality—a fusion of dance, poetry, and music sung and played live by the dancers themselves; the performance was "total theater" long before that term became common. Dance critic John Martin, in the *New York Times* on 7 January 1958, found Inbal "irresistible" and remarked that its "biblical dramas remind one of Greek tragedy." Inbal toured the United States again in 1959 and in 1962 took part in the World Theatre Festival in Paris. The company also toured in Australia, Southeast Asia, most of Europe, and Latin America.

The thematic material for Inbal's dances drew on biblical and contemporary Israeli sources as well as traditional Jewish material. The movement language Levi-Tanai created for Inbal is based on the typical Yemenite dance step, the *da'assa*—the rather introverted and lyrical hand gestures of the male dancers who entertain guests at weddings. Their clowning dances are improvised, often using typical *demi-plié* and up-and-down movement, prompting Robbins to coin the term *Yemenite-Gothic* to describe Inbal's style.

From its foundation until 1972, all the works performed by Inbal were choreographed by Sara Levi-Tanai. Since then, other choreographers have been invited to work with the group, among them Margalit Oved (Inbal's former star performer), Rena Sharett, Oshra Elkayam, Anna Sokolow, and Kei Takei.

Among the important works choreographed for Inbal by Levi-Tanai are the following: *Yemenite Wedding* (1956); *The Story of Ruth* (1961), with music by Ovadia Tuvia and sets by Danni Karavan; *Jacob in Horan* (1973), with music by Jossi Mar-Haim and sets by David Sharir; and *Song of Songs* (1982), with music by Levi-Tanai and sets by Moshe Sternfield. In 1991, Sara Levi-Tanai was unceremoniously removed from the position of artistic director and forced to retire. Rena Sharett was nominated as her successor, but in the two years she held the post no new work of any importance was created. The company faced disbanding.

In 1994 the former star performer of Inbal, Margalit Oved, returned to Israel after having worked since the

INBAL DANCE THEATRE. Sara Levi-Tanai, founder and choreographer of Inbal, was often inspired by Jewish liturgy and Yemenite cultural traditions. Here, members of the company create a communal tableau in her *Wild Rose* (1980). (Photograph from the Israel Dance Library Archive, Tel Aviv; courtesy of Giora Manor.)

1960s in California, and was appointed artistic director of Inbal. For two seasons she rehearsed and created a program consisting of her own works, as well as some by her son, Barak Marschall; she left the company under a cloud. In order to rescue the company from disbanding, Israel's Ministry for the Arts decided to change the status of the company to that of a multicultural folklore arts center. The new management asked the veteran Inbal dancers to re-create some of Sara Levi-Tanai's masterpieces, which had not been performed for many years. It was the first time that Sara Levi-Tanai gave permission to reconstruct her choreographies. In July 1996 the reconstructed *Story of Ruth* and *Song of Songs* were presented to the public with great success.

[*See* Israel, *overview article; and the entry on Levi-Tanai.*]

BIBLIOGRAPHY

Eshel, Ruth. *Dancing with the Dream.* Tel Aviv, 1991.

Hering, Doris. "Inbal Dance Theatre of Israel." *Dance Magazine* (February 1958): 90–91; (January 1960): 81.

Ingber, Judith Brin. "Inbal Dance Theatre." *Dance Magazine* (November 1973): 66–69.

Joel, Lydia. "Sara Levi-Tanai: Dreamer and Doer." *Dance Magazine* (January 1960): 16–17.

Manchester, P. W. "Inbal, Dance Theatre of Israel." *Dance News* (February 1958): 9.

Manor, Giora. *Inbal: Quest for a Movement-Language.* Tel Aviv, 1975.

Margolin, Yaron. "Dances from the Olympus: The 'Landscape Dances' of Sara Levi-Tanai." *Israel Dance* (1989–1990): 11–19.

Terry, Walter. "Woman's Vision Reshapes Ancient Heritage." *New York Herald Tribune* (5 January 1958).

GIORA MANOR

INDES GALANTES, LES. *Opéra-ballet* with a prologue and two *entrées.* Choreography: Louis Dupré. Music: Jean-Philippe Rameau. Libretto: Louis Fuzelier. Sets: Giovanni-Niccolò Servandoni. First performance: 23 August 1735, Théâtre de l'Académie de Musique, Paris. Principals: David Dumoulin, Louis Dupré, M. le Breton, M. Javellier, Marie Sallé.

Although *Les Indes Galantes* was originally created with two *entrées,* *Le Turc Généreux* and *Les Incas du Pérou,* a third, *Les Fleurs,* was added on 25 August 1735 and a fourth, *Les Sauvages,* was added on 10 March 1736, giving the opera the structure it has today. As a genre, the *opéra-ballet* was enhanced by these additions, since each *entrée* offered an independent action. They also gave dance an important place in the work, and the subjects of the *entrées* demonstrated a fondness for local color. In *Les Indes Galantes,* the spectator was taken to Turkey, Peru, Persia, and finally North America. The enthusiasm for the exotic at that time undoubtedly justified this choice. In calling his libretto a "heroic ballet," Fuzelier also wanted to give it a noble and imposing character, by utilizing in the first two *entrées* natural catastrophes, a tempest and an earthquake, which inspired Rameau with impressive descriptive musical possibilities.

The heroic taste was also evident in the prologue, in which allegorical figures are used to announce that the European nations of France, Italy, Poland, and Spain are abandoning love affairs for war. The lovers take refuge "in the various climes of the Indies." Several dances describe this action, particularly a kind of pantomime performed by the lovers who follow Bellone.

The first *entrée, Le Turc Généreux,* takes place in the gardens of the Pasha Osman, who is enamoured of his Provençal slave, Emilie. Because she is in love with Valéry, the Pasha gives her up. During the *divertissement,* Provençal dancers dance two *rigaudons* and two *tambourins,* the purpose of which is to reveal the southern charm of these characters.

In *Les Incas du Pérou,* Don Carlos, a Spanish officer, is in love with Phani, an Inca princess. He succeeds in freeing her from the grip of Huascar, the high priest. During the magnificent Festival of the Sun, the dancing evokes the great mystery of the Inca cult in an *air* and a very beautiful *loure.*

The *entrée Les Fleurs* (which was added at the third performance and revised after the eighth), takes place in Persia, where the princes Tacmas and Ali satisfy their amorous desires by exchanging their slaves. The "Ballet des Fleurs," which ends the act, presents an entire choreographic action in a description of the fate of the flowers in a garden devastated by a storm.

Finally, in *Les Sauvages,* the last *entrée* to be added, the Indian woman Zima refuses the hand of Damon, a Frenchman, and Don Alvar, a Spaniard, in order to marry Adario, chief of the Indians. They join with their European conquerors in celebrating peace in a *divertissement;* after the famous "Danse du Grand Calumet de la Paix" (the inspiration for which came to Rameau from the sight of two Louisiana Indians at the Théâtre Italien), two *menuets* and a monumental *chaconne* end the opera on a sumptous note.

Featuring most of the Opera's leading performers, led by the tenor Pierre Jelyotte, the work was a great success and was revived several times until 1761. In the twentieth century, *Les Fleurs* was revived at the Opéra Comique on 30 May 1925 with choreography by Jeanne Chaslas and Maurice Frigara. The entire work was given a spectacular revival at the Paris Opera on 18 June 1952 under the direction of Maurice Lehmann. Albert Aveline choreographed the prologue and the first *entrée,* Serge Lifar the second and fourth *entrées,* and Harald Lander the third. Virtually every member of the company appeared in this enormously successful production, which remained in the repertory until 1965 and has inspired a number of other productions since then.

[*See also the entry on Rameau.*]

BIBLIOGRAPHY

Girdlestone, Cuthbert. *Jean-Philippe Rameau: His Life and Work.* Rev. ed. New York, 1969.

Langellier-Bellevue, Richard. "Le concept d'exotisme chez Rameau." In *La vie musicale en France sous les rois Bourbons, 2. sér.: Recherches sur la musique française* 21 (1983): 158–160.

Rameau: Les Indes galantes. L'Avant-Scène Opéra, no. 46. Paris, 1982.

JÉRÔME DE LA GORCE
Translated from French

INDIA. [*To survey the dance traditions of India, this entry comprises six articles:*

History of Indian Dance
Philosophy of Indian Dance
Epic Sources of Indian Dance
The Rādhā-Kṛṣṇa Theme in Indian Dance
New Directions in Indian Dance
Dance Research and Publication

The first article explores origins, gestures, costumes and makeup, classifications of Indian dance forms, and the importance of patronage; the second focuses on the unity and continuity within the diversity of Indian dance; the third and fourth articles consider literary and mythic themes in Indian dance; the fifth discusses innovation and experimentation within classical genres and the development of the modern dance movement; the concluding article provides a brief history of scholarship and writing.]

History of Indian Dance

Many elements and their interactions have produced the major living forms of traditional dance in India. In addition to social, economic, and political factors, the geography of the subcontinent has played an important part.

The Indian subcontinent extends southward from the Himalayas to the Indian Ocean; it is bounded on the west by the Arabian Sea and on the east by the Bay of Bengal. Eastward and northward lie sea routes to Indochina and to China.

From the northwest, wave after wave of migration and conquest entered the subcontinent, bringing new ethnic stocks and cultural influences that became part of the immense mosaic that is pan-Indian culture. Neither significant conquest nor migration has come from the east.

Peoples of Central Asian and East Asian ethnic stocks have long occupied the hill areas of India's Himalayan border. These peoples are variously influenced by contact with Tibeto-Mongolian culture and with Indian culture, and some have maintained their own distinct tribal cultures. Farther south in the eastern, northern, and central plains of Madhya Pradesh, Orissa, and Bihar are numerous tribal peoples with distinct cultures, living in tiny enclaves and speaking their own languages, essentially apart not only from urban culture but often from nearby Hindu or Muslim villages as well.

Still farther south, the Vindhya Mountains form a partial barrier between northern and southern India. The Western and Eastern Ghats, long ranges of hills, border most of the southern portion of the peninsula. These mountains and hills have tended to isolate southern India from the influence of northern invaders and immigrants. In South India live the Dravidian-speaking peoples whose languages are unrelated to the Indo-European languages except in the matter of vocabulary adopted from Sanskrit. The latter language family includes both Sanskrit and the majority of North Indian languages. Difference in language is a reliable indicator of other variations, those of dress, customs, food, and—predictably—dance.

Dance and Cultural History. The Aryan peoples who began entering the Indian subcontinent around the second millennium BCE came from Central Asia. In India they encountered both city-dwellers and forest-dwellers. They themselves were nomadic herdsmen, warriors, and priests, with a complex literary and ritual culture. The religion and other major facets of the civilization of these invaders spread gradually throughout the subcontinent. They succeeded in uniting many ethnic and linguistic groups under an integrated high culture, but this did not eliminate the rich diversity and variety that still constitute a significant aspect of India's cultural landscape.

This cultural landscape is complex, and its performing arts traditions are equally so. The documented dance and theater history of the subcontinent begins at least as early as the first centuries of the Christian era. The antiquity of Indian dance is often claimed to date to the period of the Vedas, the sacred scriptures of Hinduism, and to prehistoric artifacts, but the more realistic and substantial historical evidence really begins with the final compilation of the *Nāṭyaśāstra* of Bharata, a treatise probably composed between the second and fourth centuries CE. This period has left rich visual evidence of dance, such as bas-reliefs at Barhut and Sanchi from the first and second centuries BCE, and at Amaravati from the first to third centuries CE. The early dances pictured in bas relief give evidence of significant changes after the third century CE, and again after the fifth century. Regional variations in form and style are discernible, as well as details of choreographic design. By the later medieval period, we see a multiplicity of regional styles in art, including the pictorial representation of dance. This period witnessed the rise of vernacular literatures and the development of regional variations on shared materials taken largely from the epic works of the *Rāmāyaṇa* and the *Mahābhārata*, as well as the later Purāṇas (collections of traditional tales). While Sanskrit literature remained the major literary source, between the tenth and fifteenth centuries the epics as well as many

Purāṇas were rendered into vernacular versions.

In the pre-Muslim period before the tenth century, a rather arbitrary date, India's older classical performing art forms had reached their apogee; some scholars would say they had already begun to decline. The great Hindu empires of the North had begun to dissolve into hundreds of smaller kingdoms and principalities, and the power of the imperial Cholas in the South was beginning a slow decline. By the tenth century most of the major works on dramaturgical theory, including dance, music, and theater architecture, had been written. However, through the thirteenth and fourteenth centuries, and even as late as the eighteenth, scholarly treatises on the performing arts continued to be written in both Sanskrit and the vernacular languages.

The decline of the older classical Sanskritic tradition was already well under way by the time Muslim armies cut across North India at the close of the thirteenth century. Muslim power subsequently began to consolidate and expand to the south. By the close of the fourteenth century, the Vijayanagara Empire had emerged to form a bastion against further Muslim penetration of the Deccan and the regions farther south; however, for a brief period Muslim armies had cut deep into the South and sacked and destroyed many of the temples, which were centers of culture and patronage for the arts. During the rule of the Vijayanagara emperors and their patronage of Hindu cultural institutions, the major development of most present forms of South Indian dance and dance drama began; they reached maturity in the turbulent eighteenth and nineteenth centuries.

The contributions of Muslim culture to the arts of North India in general, and to classical dance in North and central India, were most potent from the sixteenth century through the eighteenth. Drawing on preexisting Hindu artistic traditions and elements of Persian, Arabic, and Turkic performing arts traditions, a series of transformations over two or three centuries produced new art forms of great beauty in poetry, music, and dance.

The period of the thirteenth to sixteenth centuries is an important era in the development and systematization of classical music in India. This era saw the emergence of the northern school, or Hindusthani classical music, and the southern or Karnatic school, two related but distinct major traditions. The traditions of dance in North and South India are also related but distinct.

The coming of the British in the 1600s and the influences of the West on dance in India can be understood only after examining the traditional forms. This involves the relationships of dance with Hinduism and with other art forms; the classification of dance genres; thematic material for the performing arts; aesthetic theories of theatrical performance; and patronage and the place of performing artists within Indian society.

INDIA: History of Indian Dance. A dancing figure depicted in a railing pillar bas-relief (red sandstone, second century BCE), from a *stūpa*—a dome-shaped Buddhist monument—at Barhut, central India. (Asutosh Museum of Indian Art, Calcutta; photograph used by permission.)

Sources of Dance. The *Nāṭyaśāstra* of Bharata, the oldest and most voluminous of the Sanskrit texts on theater, begins with the story of the divine origins of drama, of which dance is an important part. This charming tale has tended to shape attitudes toward dance and theater over

INDIA: History of Indian Dance. A sandstone relief depicting an *apsarā*, one of the celestial nymphs who dance in the waters of Indra's heaven, with a small female attendant at left; from Rajasthan, twelfth or thirteenth century. (Metropolitan Museum of Art, New York; Gift of Mrs. John D. Rockefeller, Jr., 1942 [42.25.18]; photograph used by permission.)

the centuries. It may be instructive, however, to attempt to discover the actual origins of these performing arts. [*See* Nāṭyaśāstra.]

Two possible sources of Indian dance and drama are ritual performance and martial arts. Rituals in which drama is integral are performed in several regions of India. Particularly in South India, there are religious rituals in which several arts are combined. These rituals, performed in evocation and propitiation of various deities, play a major role in temple festival celebrations. One is Tiyyāṭiyāṭṭam, "the drama of the Tiyyāṭis," a high-ranking caste belonging to temple-dwelling service communities in Kerala state. Their ceremonies usually occur in a cycle of as many as forty-one nights of performance. Various tantric rituals are performed in connection with an elaborate painting made on the ground with colored powders; the space is decorated with flowers and leaves, lamps and food; and several musicians perform alternately throughout the ritual. A story is sung describing the birth and exploits of the deity Ayyappan. Then the story is enacted through choreographed movement, a system of gestural

language, and stylized mime. Finally, an elaborate dance is performed in which the dancer becomes possessed by the deity and brings the ritual to a climax by uttering oracles from the god. The audience of devotees participates as well, showing devotion at particular junctures in the ceremony and again at the climax, when they receive blessings and sanctified offerings from the shaman celebrant. In this ritual and many similar ones, the elements of dance and theater are a vital, functioning part. In many other rituals, dance may be added as an embellishment pleasing to the gods but not indispensable. Traditional dramas such as *kathakaḷi* and *yakṣagāna* are often included in temple ceremonies and festivals but are not a necessary part of the actual central act of worship.

It is quite possible that the more elaborately developed forms of dance and theater evolved from the obligatory performances of ritual. In ritual forms such as Tiyyāṭiyāṭṭam, the element of choreographic movement taken from the martial arts tradition is clearly present. The shaman carries a sword in honor of the deity, who is both a warrior and a hunter. Other highly developed genres of dance drama, such as *kathakaḷi*, have special physical training that is known to have developed from the martial arts tradition. The main *kathakaḷi* actors in former times were always drawn from the Nayar community, a military caste who became actors and farmers when there was no war to pursue. The Mayurbhanj *chhau* and the Seraikella *chhau* both incorporate military exercises, including practice with sword and target, in the training of their actor–dancers. Epic dramas demand gymnastics and facility with weapons, or with miming their use, in order to portray the battles that are almost always a feature of their plots. [*See* Chhau.]

In the *Nāṭyaśāstra*, the deity Brahmā is said to have created a "fifth Veda" on the subject of theater by taking elements from the four sacred Vedas. He is said to have taken recitation from the *Ṛgveda*, consisting essentially of hymns for use in Vedic sacrifice; music from the *Sāmaveda*, comprising many of the hymns from the *Ṛgveda* arranged for liturgical purposes; histrionic representation from the *Yajurveda*, which includes instructions for the priest who performs the sacrifice; and the emotional moods and their expression from the *Atharvaveda*, which contains magical spells for a variety of purposes. Thus the essence of the most sacred texts of Hinduism, intended for only the upper levels of the social hierarchy, underwent a mystical transformation and was made available through the medium of theater to all the people (Ghosh, 1951, pp. 2–4).

The Upavedas are ancillary works attached to specific Vedic texts. The *Gāndharvaveda* on the science of music is attached to the *Sāmaveda;* the *Dhanurveda*, on archery, is attached to the *Yajurveda*, reinforcing the connection between movement in dance and theater on the one hand

and movement in the martial arts on the other. The detailed instructions for the casting of spells found in the *Atharvaveda* clarify the theory that emotional moods were taken by Brahmā from that source. In the casting of spells, the priest-magician must portray the appropriate mood; like a performer on stage, he must in fact recreate and project the emotional state required in order to assure the success of his work.

Thus, the relationships of theater and dance with the Vedas and Upavedas have given a logical as well as a symbolic basis to the continual integration of religion and art in India. In India, myth becomes reality to a surprising degree.

Dance, along with architecture, sculpture, and painting, has been extensively employed by Hinduism, and to a lesser degree by Buddhism and Jainism. Dance has always been used in ritual celebrations; it was also used in the past in daily temple rituals in many areas of southern India. Furthermore, the thematic material for both dance and theater is strongly related to Hinduism; the myths and legends of gods and heroes constitute a major vehicle of communicating the values of the religion to the mass of the people. In addition, traditional dancers and actors commonly observe rituals of worship before lessons, rehearsals, and performances, incorporating the dance or dance-drama performance into a kind of ongoing self-dedication.

The figure of the god Śiva (Shiva) as Nāṭarāja, king of actors or dancers, the cosmic dancer, is surely unique among the great religions of the world: a major deity who fulfills his function of creation and destruction through dance. Śiva's divine dance is said to represent his five major activities—creation, protection, destruction, giving rest, and salvation.

Not only is dance closely related to religion, it also has definite interrelationships with the other arts of India. A text of the late classical period (fifth to seventh centuries CE), the *Viṣṇudharmottara Purāṇa*, makes this clear. It tells of a king who, wishing to learn the art of sculpture, questions a sage, who replies that the king must learn first the art of painting. But before he can learn painting, he must learn the art of dance. Before that, he must learn instrumental music, and before that, vocal music. But first he must learn poetic composition and also the art of prose.

INDIA: History of Indian Dance. *Śiva Nāṭarāja*, bronze, from Tamil Nadu, early Chola dynasty, c.1000 CE. Śiva as Nāṭarāja (Lord of the Dance) is depicted here in his most famous pose. Trampling the body of Apasmāra, the dwarf demon who personifies ignorance and forgetfulness, Śiva dances within the orb of the sun, represented as a ring of flames *(tiruvāśi)*. His upper right hand holds a *ḍamaru* (miniature hourglass drum), symbolizing creation; his upper left a flame, signifying destruction. The lower right hand makes a gesture of protection; the lower left a sign of liberation (salvation). The matted locks streaming from his head symbolize the sacred river Ganges. (Metropolitan Museum of Art, New York; Harris Brisbane Dick Fund, 1964 [no. 64.251]; photograph used by permission.)

Without a knowledge of all the arts, their effects cannot be fully understood nor their aesthetic purpose achieved (Kramrisch, 1928, pp. 2–5, 31–32).

In classical dance and dance drama we can clearly see the interdependence of the arts. The relationships of time, measurement, tone, color, volume, and space in the various arts, and their reflexive development and interplay, are implied in the sage's reply to the king. In painting and sculpture, as in dance, there are corresponding manipulations of volumes, the disposition of figures in space, and weight, density, and tension. Indeed, the vocabulary of attitudes, gestures, and dramatic expressions developed by dancers is also applicable to painting and sculpture. The dynamics of rhythmic structures, systems of measurement, and temporal and spatial relationships, apply to all the arts; the dimensions of time and interval, and the perception of space, are shared concepts. The arts in India, in both dance and dance drama, are ideally combined into a single harmonious whole.

Classification of Dance Genres. There are many different kinds of dance in India. In order to gain some idea of the scope and variety of these, it is useful to discuss their classification.

The usual broad division into classical and folk dance presents certain difficulties in the Indian context. The English word *classical* is used principally as a translation of the Sanskrit *śāstrīya* and indicates that a dance tradition has a relatively highly developed technique and theory of movement that relate to theoretical texts of the earlier period, known generally as *śāstras* (such as the *Nāṭyaśāstra* of Bharata). The folk or rural category in the Indian tradition is called *deśi*, provincial or rural. Both *śāstrīya* (sometimes called *mārga*) and *deśi* modes are present to varying degrees even in some genres usually called classical.

The terms *participational* and *presentational*, useful in many dance contexts, do not quite solve our problem in India. There are numerous folk and tribal dances in India that are both participational and presentational—for example, the many folk dances performed at the temple festivals or at the homes of patrons to entertain the host and his guests, after weeks of rehearsals conducted by a professional. There are, of course, other folk and tribal dances that are purely participational.

There are also forms of dance that have a strictly ritual function and that are difficult to classify as either *śāstrīya/mārga* or *deśi*. An example is the dance of the Tiyyāṭi Nambyār shaman, who becomes possessed in the course of the performance. In structure and movement concept, the dances of the Tiyyāṭi Nambyār shaman appear to be classical, but their relationship with literature on the theory and technique of dance is minimal.

Another approach to classification is on the basis of thematic material. In dance drama, and to a great extent in dance as well, a sung poetic text forms the basis of the

INDIA: History of Indian Dance. Ram Gopal, c.1960, as Śiva Tripurāntaka (Destroyer of Three Cities). This pose, signifying drawing a bow *(ālīdha sthāna)*, is commonly seen both in *bharata nāṭyam* and in sculpture. The Tripurāntaka episode is a founding myth of Indian dance drama: Śiva does a victory dance after destroying the three cities of the Asuras with a single flaming arrow. When Brahmā creates a drama on this theme for the festival of Indra, Śiva remembers his dance and commands a disciple to teach dance to Bharata (author of the *Nāṭyaśāstra*). Dance and drama have been inseparable in Indian theater ever since. (Photograph by Houston Rogers; used by permission of the Board of Trustees of the Theatre Museum, London.)

performance. The thematic material for these texts comes largely from the epics and Purāṇas, which provide an endless source of stories and hundreds of characters. According to Bharata's *Nāṭyaśāstra*, myth and legend are to be the themes of drama; furthermore, the drama "will give guidance to the people of the future in all their actions" (Ghosh, 1951, pp. 3–4). Certainly these myths and legends provide a practical vehicle for Hinduism among the great mass of the people. The conscious purpose of traditional theater and dance is not only to amaze, delight, and entertain with technical and aesthetic brilliance, or to relate a moving or exciting story, but to bring alive traditional ethical and moral values. The purpose, ultimately didactic, is achieved through endlessly entertaining dance and theater.

INDIA: History of Indian Dance. *Ananda Sivaram in a meditative pose from* kathakaḷi. *Traditionally performed by men,* kathakaḷi *is a dance drama based on episodes in the Hindu epics. It originated in the state of Kerala in the seventeenth century.* (Photograph from the archives at Jacob's Pillow, Becket, Massachusetts.)

In considering thematic material and its sources as a possible basis for classification, we find that many dance-drama genres rely heavily on the heroic tales from the epics for their plots and characters; these may be classified as epic dance-theater genres. Other genres, particularly of solo dance, have been classified as devotional dance-theater genres because their focus is on themes underlaid by the concept of devotion to deity. Some dance-drama genres also fall into the latter category.

Devotional movements have been known in India from at least the seventh century, when singer-saints (Ālvārs and Nāyanārs) in South India composed thousands of verses of praise and devotion to the gods. These devotional songs and the religious movement of which they were a part led eventually to the composition of the *Bhāgavata Purāṇa*, relating the story of Kṛṣṇa in great detail and giving impetus to later devotional movements from the twelfth to the sixteenth century, the majority also centered on Kṛṣṇa.

Although there are compositions for dance and theater of a devotional nature dedicated to Śiva, Subrahmaṇya, Rāma, and other deities, the most common focus of sung, danced, and enacted poetic compositions is Kṛṣṇa. The devotional dance-drama forms portray Kṛṣṇa in a variety of situations but usually concentrate on his life as a child and young man, growing up among the cowherds. In solo dance, Kṛṣṇa is often referred to as the beloved; he is portrayed as a young man, flirting with the milkmaids, especially with his favorite Rādhā. But his lighthearted play has a deeper mystical significance, and the longing of the dancer as devotee for union with the godhead is equated with love on the earthly plane. This concept has led to flights of creativity and a special beauty of conception.

Theme and Interpretation. In traditional dance and theater, the fact that the thematic material is familiar and the techniques polished conventions open the possibilities of greater refinement both technically and aesthetically. It is not what the artist does but the inspired manner in which he or she does it, and the level of technical brilliance. Such constant reworking of embellishments and refinements on familiar themes might in the West be regarded as artistically decadent: not so in Asia. The discipline of form is regarded as essential, and the flowering of the mature actor-dancer as master interpreter and subtle innovator, often after the age of fifty or sixty, is considered the quintessence of the performer's art.

Another aspect of dance and dance drama in India that lends freshness to universally known plots and themes is the use of interpolation and improvisation. Interpolations abound in both dance and dance-drama genres. In the latter, the interpolated material sometimes far outweighs the basic text and is often the part of the performance most relished by the audience. An extreme example is *kūṭiyāṭṭam*, the Sanskrit drama form of Kerala state, in which the interpolations, delightful examples of dance, mime, and acting, may extend a single act of a drama over many nights of performance. In some genres the interpolated material tends to follow set patterns; in others, especially in solo dance genres such as *bharata nāṭyam*, the distinguished artist is expected to improvise most of the interpolations. In fact, the aesthetic perceptions which the artist brings to these improvised interpolations are the major criteria by which he or she is judged.

Theories of Performance. A number of theoretical concepts have informed Indian dance at least from the time of Bharata's *Nāṭyaśāstra* and still find practical application today. The application of these theories may vary greatly among genres, but the theories themselves remain unchanged. Among these concepts is the theory of *nāṭyadharmī*, or the way of the theater, and *lokadharmī*, or the way of the world, the naturalistic mode (Ghosh, 1951, pp. 245–247, 437).

Nāṭyadharmī, the highly stylized or conventionalized mode, is the more prevalent manner of presentation in India's traditional dance drama, as it is in traditional Indian sculpture and painting. This high degree of stylization extends to the makeup and costumes of the characters. The fact that the theme often is centered on deities and heroes, demons and demigods, may account for this conventionalized approach; in many dance dramas, however, the female characters tend to be the most realistically portrayed. Solo female dance genres such as *bharata nāṭyam* and *mōhiniāṭṭam*, tend toward more naturalistic dress and makeup; when the dancer becomes essentially an actress, interpreting a sung text through gesture and pantomime, the portrayal also approaches realism.

Other theoretical concepts that have persisted throughout the long history of dance in India are the presentational techniques of the four *abhinaya*s, and the nine basic emotional states, or *bhāva*s, with their corresponding "essences," or *rasa*s.

There are four *abhinaya*s. *Āṅgikābhinaya*, the technique of movement, includes movement of the body and limbs, both pantomime and dance, and also movements of the head and facial expression. *Vācikābhinaya* relates to the element of sound, including all types of vocal sound as well as instrumental music. *Sāttvikābhinaya* has been interpreted as acting through involuntary actions such as perspiration, change of color, trembling, or loss of consciousness, and also as the complete concentration of the actor as he projects an emotional state. *Āhāryābhinaya* includes decor and stage properties as well as costumes and makeup. Perhaps it was the Indian predilection for breaking down any entity into its component parts that led to this division; whatever the reasons, the result has been a high degree of refinement of each element, and the careful blending of these elements into a harmonious whole.

The use of gesture in Indian dance is one of the more important facets of *āṅgikābhinaya*. Most genres of traditional dance and theater use some system of codified gestures. There has been much speculation on the reasons for the prevalence of codified systems of gesture in Indian dance and theater. One reason may be the great number of different languages spoken in India; gesture might be understood when the spoken word was not, if a dance troupe were on tour far from their home. It has also been said that gesture is more potent than the spoken word. The use of gestures as mnemonic devices in learning and reciting the Vedas may have led gradually to the use of gesture for other purposes. Gesture used in connection with the Vedas is for the purpose of clarifying the text and preventing ambiguities; the gestures correspond to particular phonemes and their rhythmic pronunciation and not to the meaning of words, although some of the hand positions themselves are the same as those used in dance and theatre (Howard, 1977). As gesture is used in tantric *pūjā*, gestures represent lexical meanings and in many cases are identical in form and meaning to gestures used in dance. [*See* Mudrā.]

Vācikābhinaya relates to the melody and rhythmic pattern of the accompaniment as well as to the actor-dancer's singing or speaking. The *rāga*s, or melodic patterns, of Indian music are thought to correspond to some particular emotional moods; *tāla*s, or rhythmic patterns, along with *kāla*s, or tempi, are also related to emotional moods or dramatic situations. In addition, Indian composers have used particular vowel and consonant sounds with a view to the intended emotional response. The musical instruments used for accompaniment of dance and dance drama are specific to particular genres, and musicians are trained specifically to accompany one genre. As a result, the musicians may know the repertory almost as well as the dancers do and can follow to perfection every nuance of expression, as well as the dancer-actor's improvisations.

Sāttvikābhinaya is ambiguous in that its definition in the *Nāṭyaśāstra* can be interpreted in two different ways. If perspiration, horripilation, trembling, weeping, fainting, and other responses are a part of *sāttvikābhinaya*,

INDIA: History of Indian Dance. Elaborate costumes and makeup are worn by many characters in *kathakaḷi* dance dramas. Traditionally, heroic characters wear a *cuṭṭi*, a frame made of rice paste and paper that curves first inward, then outward at the cheek, and then inward again to meet in a diminishing, bladelike curve at the chin. (Photograph © 1984 by Jack Vartoogian; used by permission.)

these states or actions are portrayed in traditional Indian dance and theater through stylized conventional movements. Even change of skin color could sometimes be achieved by traditional actors, using a technique to suffuse the capillaries with blood to produce a dark red color, expressing rage or physical distress. On the other hand, the *Nāṭyaśāstra* states that *sāttvikābhinaya* can be accomplished only through complete concentration of the mind and that it is the true expression of emotion. One occasionally sees a dancer or actor express emotional mood not through movement of any kind but only through intense concentration; it is a rare experience, and an unforgettable one.

In *āhāryābhinaya*, the use of costume, make-up, decor, and stage properties, a high degree of stylization is commonly found. The elegant and effective use of forms and colors to denote a character's inner nature is a facet of *āhāryābhinaya* that not only makes the presentation more interesting visually but also uses the symbolism of color to enhance emotional mood. The designs and colors used in costumes and makeup for performances within temple precincts often serve to integrate the performer into the traditional architectural setting. The use of actual decor is minimal; the performer describes—through gesture, pantomime, speech, or some combination of these—the setting for the scene. The figure of the performer is extremely ornate; possibly the lack of decor as such has led to the development of highly decorative costume.

The eight basic emotional states of Indian theory as enumerated in the *Nāṭyaśāstra* are called *bhāvas*; they are felt, portrayed, and projected by the actor. The eight corresponding emotional moods perceived and enjoyed by the audience are called *rasas*. A ninth *bhāva* and a ninth *rasa*, added in later theoretical texts, are related to peace and tranquility. There are also numerous transitory states related to the sustained *bhāvas* and *rasas*. This theory might be applied to dance and theater everywhere in the world, but it was in India, and at a very early date, that it was first systematically stated.

Social Context. Whatever the excellence of any performing art, it cannot exist without patronage. To understand the patronage of the performing arts in India, we must first examine traditional attitudes toward the arts and artists.

The fact that scholars and theoreticians found the performing arts worthy of their attention from a very early period is a significant indication of attitudes toward dance and dance drama. These attitudes, however, were not the sole forces governing the relationships of dance and dancers to society in general. Rather, these interactions are a product of India's caste system and the practice of developing traditions of art within specific communities, and indeed within families. These schools of art descend through teacher-to-disciple lineages.

Since dancers traditionally tended to belong to specific communities within the caste system and to follow the art as their sole means of livelihood, amateur performers were rare in most parts of India (except for folk dance) until recently. The castes from which dancers and musicians were drawn, like those supplying sculptors and

INDIA: History of Indian Dance. Two men from South Kanara, in the southwestern state of Karnataka, perform *yakṣagāna*, a dance drama enacting stories from the Hindu epics. Elaborate headdresses are typical of this genre. (Photograph from the archives of The Asia Society, New York.)

painters, were comparatively low on the ancient, systematic scale of ritual purity and social status. There were exceptions, however: some forms of music and also of dance drama were the province of the brahmans, the priestly caste at the top of the hierarchy. Most of these dance dramas were performed exclusively by males. The performing communities of brahmans were lower on the scale than, for example, those brahmans whose special duties involved the learning and teaching of the Vedas or other ancient texts. Even the communities of dancers, however, were usually of sufficient ritual purity to be allowed to perform within temple precincts. In Orissa, for example, female temple dancers (*māhārī*s) actually performed before the sanctum, while boys impersonating female dancers (*gōtipūa*s) performed in less exalted surroundings in the outer precincts. The actor-dancers of *kūṭiyāṭṭam* Sanskrit drama in Kerala who perform in specially built theaters within the temple grounds are lower-ranked brahmans, according to some authorities; according to others, they are highest among the Kerala Ambalavāsis, or temple servants. The actresses and musicians of *kūṭiyāṭṭam* are of the next highest rank. [*See* Kūṭiyāṭṭam.]

In general, however, dancers and actor-dancers were held in low esteem, even though their art was closely linked to religion. The fact that female dancers attached to the temples as *devadāsī*s were often also courtesans reinforced this attitude. [*See* Devadāsī.] Until very recently, when many attitudes began to change, no "woman of good family" would have thought of learning to dance, not only for reasons of status, but also because in the traditional Hindu view of life, one does not follow another's *dharma*, or ritual and social duty.

Although the temples were traditionally the chief patrons for the *devadāsī*s of South India, and often for other arts as well, the structure and variety of patronage systems varied greatly and usually reflected local or regional aspects of the traditional social structure. In one form of traditional patronage, a group of artist families and their patrons were of the same ritual and social level; in other cases, the patrons were of a slightly higher level. Traditional patrons often supported performing artists throughout the season, in some cases for generations, even to the present day. In rare cases a single patron—a temple authority, royal personage, or merchant prince—has been the principal or even exclusive patron of a particular family of artists, or even a group of such families. Patronage in the past involved not only annual monetary payment for the artists' services, but also payment in kind (clothing, grain, or goods). In the case of royal or temple institutional patronage, the bestowal of land and domicile, education, and other benefits was part of the ongoing agreement between the patron and artists. The relationship was also one of master and servant, which in the traditional context carried mutual responsibilities.

The source of patronage indicated the context of the performance. Relatively exclusive performances were the ideal, in which family, class and social rank prescribed the composition of the audience. Performances in temples or in the open air before religious shrines allowed a wider range of society to attend in the village. Such public performances were usually the gift of a patron to the community, which reinforced the patron's social and ritual position.

The counterpart of the essentially elite patronage pattern of the classical performing traditions was found in connection with the folk or tribal performance of dance or ritual drama as part of seasonal ceremonies or lifecycle rites. Today, as a result of the decline of patronage, performers often canvass the villagers from house to house, seeking donations or performing services for pay to support their performance at a coming festival. Parallel to these essentially local patterns is that of the itinerant professional performers, both classical artists as well as more humble bands of tumblers, magicians, and actor-dancers, who travel established circuits through the performing season—usually the long dry season after the harvest, when most South Asian festivals take place.

INDIA: History of Indian Dance. *A performer of* kūṭiyāṭṭam, *one of the oldest continuous theater traditions in India. Practiced exclusively in the central and south-central region of Kerala by a small community of temple servants, this genre utilizes a vocabulary of more than six hundred hand gestures. A full-scale performance may last from five to thirty-five days.* (Photograph from the Dance Collection, New York Public Library for the Performing Arts.)

Colonial and Modern Eras. Traditional dance is sometimes popularly believed to have evolved within essentially traditional societies and to be crystallized and repeated without change, incapable of relevance to contemporary society, uncreative, and unoriginal. Another view holds that, since a traditional genre of dance often encompasses many variations and also embraces great creative and improvisational possibilities, there is no single authentic type, and one may use or abuse traditional dance without any obligation to artistic integrity or respect. Both views are too extreme and subjective.

Certainly the many kinds of dance and dance drama in India have evolved and changed through the centuries, although those most closely connected with temple ritual have probably changed least. In the past, the innovations and creative transformations were wrought by masters of the art; only recently has change tended to come from outside, often in response to socioeconomic and technological changes.

The British colonial period had a profound effect on India's arts, as on all facets of the society. Patronage of the arts became principally the province of a new rising middle class, greatly influenced by nineteenth-century British morality. This social group rejected the ancient institution of the courtesan class, which also included many dancers and musicians. The classical female dance arts survived, however, under the patronage of the temples and a small traditionalist elite, and in the much reduced courts of a few princely states. The exclusively male dance traditions—*bhāgavata meḷa nāṭakam, yakṣagāna, satria, chhau, kathakaḷi,* and others—were afflicted by a dislocation of patronage and the indifference and even embarrassment of many early modern Indians about their own heritage. [*See* Kathakaḷi *and* Yakṣagāna.]

The suppression of female solo dance eventually evoked a reaction in the case of *bharata nāṭyam.* A number of urban intellectuals took up this art as a symbol of India's growing nationalism. They bestowed upon it the name *bharata nāṭyam* (it was formerly called *dāsiāṭṭam, sadir nāṭyam,* and other names) and proclaimed it an ancient form of dance. (*Bharata nāṭyam* is undoubtedly rooted in a very old tradition, but it was recodified and largely recreated at the end of the eighteenth century by four brothers of the Pillai community from Tanjore.) Suddenly, by the mid-twentieth century, its study and performance became a popular pastime for the daughters of wealthy upper-class families, establishing a pattern that persists to the present. Among very traditional families, these young women tended to give one or two performances, then leave dancing to marry and raise a family. Few professional or semiprofessional female dancers in India continue to perform after marriage. This pattern spread to

INDIA: History of Indian Dance. Shanta Rao is an expert in several styles of classical Indian dance and is noted for her innovative costume designs. (*left*) Here, she performs a movement from *bharata nāṭyam,* a classical style of South India. (*right*) She dances *mōhiniāṭṭam,* a genre developed by women in the Kerala region, combining elements of the traditionally male *kathakaḷi* with the rhythms of *bharata nāṭyam.* (Photographs from the archives at Jacob's Pillow, Becket, Massachusetts.)

other forms of dance, and urban intellectuals, ambitious young dancers who wanted to be identified with the movement to rediscover lost treasures of dance, proclaimed the great antiquity of their finds. The controversy over which form of dance was the most ancient continued in certain circles for some time. [*See* Bharata Nāṭyam.]

At one end of the spectrum today is the traditional teacher-student relationship, an institution still an integral part of conservative Hindu and Muslim societies. The student learns thoroughly not only the basic dance technique, but also the traditional repertory, including the texts and music. Ultimately he or she can perform the musical and choreographic masterworks, mostly of the eighteenth and nineteenth centuries. At the other extreme of the spectrum is the urban-bred dancer, educated in a system based largely on Western concepts of education, living in a modern technological society. The dance world is influenced by the cinema, with images of success, by tours, by elaborately staged presentation and theatrical effects, and now by growing television exposure. All of these factors orient the choices confronting the dancer or the teacher-choreographer who attempts to create within the scope of Indian dance and music but with an awareness of contemporary developments, most often based on European concepts. The ideal is to bring creative imagination, originality, and sociocultural relevance to newly created or recreated works.

In India, contemporary dance, in the Western sense, is rare; there are, however eclectic adaptations of classical or folk techniques. The cinema has been influential in setting the models of taste and technical production for currently popular experiments with traditional dance. Many of the professional dancers are also film stars. [*See* Film Musicals, *article on* Bollywood Film Musicals.]

Despite all the feverish innovation revolving about today's dance performance, there are several traditional genres of dance and theater that have endured for centuries. A few can even claim historical continuity over a millennium or more. The ephemeral performing arts are today the most vulnerable cultural artifacts in the vast, rich, and complex texture of India. Preserving, studying, analyzing, and understanding those artifacts and the processes of evolution, creativity, variation, and change can be invaluable in sharing India's civilization.

[*See also* Kathak; Kṛṣṇāṭṭam; Manipur; Mōhiniāṭṭam; Nāṭyaśāstra; Nautch; Oḍissi; Rās Līlā; Sikkim; Tamasha; Teyyam; *and* Yoga.]

BIBLIOGRAPHY

Ambrose, Kay. *Classical Dances and Costumes of India.* 2d ed. Revised by Ram Gopal. New York, 1983.
Anand, Mulk Raj, ed. *Classical and Folk Dances of India.* Bombay, 1963.
Banerjee, Sures Chandra. *A Companion to Indian Music and Dance.* Delhi, 1990.
Basham, A. L. *The Wonder That Was India.* New ed. New York, 1963.
Brown, W. Norman, ed. *India, Pakistan, Ceylon.* Ithaca, N. Y., 1951.
Coorlawala, Uttara Asha. "Ruth St. Denis and India's Dance Renaissance." *Dance Chronicle* 15.2 (1992): 123–152.
Dimock, Edward C. *The Place of the Hidden Moon: Erotic Mysticism in the Vaiṣṇavasahajiyā Cult of Bengal.* Chicago, 1966.
Gargi, Balwant. *Theatre in India.* New York, 1962.
Gargi, Balwant. *Folk Theater of India.* Seattle, 1966.
Gaston, Anne-Marie. *Śiva in Dance, Myth, and Iconography.* Delhi, 1982.
Ghosh, M. M., ed. and trans. *The Nāṭyaśāstra Ascribed to Bharata-Muni.* 2 vols. Calcutta, 1951–1961.
Ghosh, M. M., ed. and trans. *Nandikeśvara's Abhinayadarpanam.* 2d ed. Calcutta, 1957.
Haas, George C. O., ed. and trans. *The Daśarūpa.* Delhi, 1962.
Howard, Wayne. *Sāmavedic Chant.* New Haven, 1977.
Khokar, Mohan. *The Splendours of Indian Dance.* Rev. ed. New Delhi, 1988.
Kliger, George, ed. *Bharata Nāṭyam in Cultural Perspective.* Manohar, 1993.
Kramrisch, Stella. *The Vishnudharmottara,* part 3, *A Treatise on Indian Painting and Image-Making.* 2d ed., rev. and enl. Calcutta, 1928.
Krishna Rao, U. S., and U. K. Chandrabhaga Devi. *A Panorama of Indian Dances.* Delhi, 1993.
Lobet, Marcel, et al. "The Living Dance." *World Theatre* 6 (Autumn 1957): 166–223.
Richmond, Farley, et al., eds. *Indian Theatre: Traditions of Performance.* Honolulu, 1990.
Samson, Leela. *Rhythm in Joy: Classical Indian Dance Traditions.* New Delhi, 1987.
Sanyal, Snehalata. "The Fifties in India." *World Theatre* 11 (Autumn 1962): 279–287.
Sarada, S. *Kalakshetra-Rukmini Devi: Reminiscences.* Madras, 1985.
Shah, Pankaj. *Performing Arts of Kerala.* Edited by Mallika Sarabhai. Ahmedabad, 1994.
Singer, Milton B., ed. *Krishna: Myths, Rites, and Attitudes.* Honolulu, 1966.
Varadpande, M. L. *History of Indian Theatre.* New Delhi, 1987.
Vatsyayan, Kapila. *Classical Indian Dance in Literature and the Arts.* New Delhi, 1968.
Vatsyayan, Kapila. *Indian Classical Dance.* 2d ed. New Delhi, 1992.
Wood, Leona. "The Twilight of the Maharajas." *Arabesque* 19.1 (1993): 8–12.

FILMS.   *Art and Ritual in South India: The Worship of the Deity Ayyappan* (1975), and *Kūṭiyāṭṭam: Sanskrit Drama in the Temples of Kerala* (1974), both available from the Ethnic Arts Center, Santa Rosa, California (also on videotape).

CLIFFORD REIS JONES

Philosophy of Indian Dance

Amid the apparent diversity of Indian dance, a common worldview gives all the forms a basic unity and continuity. According to Indian thought, the universe is eternal yet in constant flux, the parts merely emanations of the whole. Everything is constantly being born, growing, and dying. All matter is composed of the five basic elements of fire, water, earth, space, and sky; humans are but a part of nature, responding to it rather than dominating it. Like plants or animals, humans develop from a seed in the womb, grow to maturity, and in turn produce the seeds of new life. So the cycle continues without beginning or end.

The distinctiveness of being human lies in inner consciousness, the understanding that every part of our being (body, mind, and spirit) reflects the nature of the cosmos. At the center of the universe and the human spirit is a still point like the hub of a wheel with consciousness expanding outward like the spokes in concentric circles, but held together within the boundaries of the universe.

This cosmology is first explained in the earliest Indian texts, known as the Vedas. Subsequent philosophic texts called the Upaniṣads give the concept its theoretical foundation. Finally, the Brāhmaṇas or ritual texts describe the exact rituals (yajña, usually translated as sacrifice) that give concrete form to the abstract principles. In the Upaniṣads the cosmos is described in metaphors as the hub and spokes of a wheel; in the Brāhmaṇas the cosmos is symbolized physically by every sound, word, gesture, and object of the ritual. The ritual performance involves the whole community. The Upaniṣads introduce the philosophic concept of yoga as the gathering inward of all energies, both physical and mental, so revelation can take place; the Brāhmaṇas describe the ritual acts of the yajña: how to design a consecrated space by establishing a center within an enclosure and lighting fires in each of three altars, one shaped like a square, one like a circle, and one like a semicircle. These ritual acts symbolize the sacrifice of parts of the body, which must take place over a prescribed number of hours or days. The purpose of both experiences—the inner yoga and the outer yajña—is to achieve harmony, equilibrium, and tranquillity.

These concepts and rituals recognize the human capacity for both introspection and growth. At the same time both the introspection of yoga and the concrete ritual of yajña are important not by themselves but only within the framework of the whole. Life and death are part of the same continuum. According to Indian philosophy, all life grows out of the formless (arūpa) ground of the cosmos, develops into the many forms (rūpa) of life, and returns in the end to that which is beyond form (pararūpa). All these concepts are fundamental to the Indian theory of aesthetics, as is the notion that the individual soul (ātman) is constantly aspiring to merge with the universal (brahman, the Supreme Being). The direction is from physical to metaphysical, from the senses to the spirit in a continuous progression.

Indian Theory of Aesthetics. An Indian theory of aesthetics is first referred to in Bharata's *Nāṭyaśāstra* (c. 1000 BCE). The purpose of this treatise was to lay down the rules for the kind of total artistic performance through which the audience might achieve a state of supreme joy or release from the world of illusion; the theory is implicit rather than spelled out.

Known popularly as *rasa* (religious or artistic essence), this theory envisages a three-part process: first, the vision of the artist; second, the content, form, and technique of artistic expression; and third, the evocation of a similar aesthetic experience in the audience. The artist's inner vision resembles that state of mystical bliss called *brāhmānanda;* it is an experience of the whole, the universal where the individual ego and subjective emotion are transcended, the distinctions of physical time and space are erased, and the finite and infinite merge. The artist's state of concentration can be described by the word *yoga,* the release from pain and pleasure in this life. It is said that at that moment, the artist sees the white light of luminosity in his or her inward eye. The artist's problem, then, is to convey this experience, this essence *(rasa)* to the audience through sound, word, gesture, movement, mass, line, color, symbols, and dynamic images. The work of art serves as the bridge from the formless, through the many forms, to that which is beyond form.

Naturally, such art cannot deal with the unique individual, but only with the universal and symbolic. The form and content of these works of art—whether a small icon, a brief dance or song, or a great architectural monument like a temple or stupa—find their counterparts in the symbols and acts of the ritual sacrifice and in the many forms of speculative thought. Every part of the work is related to the whole, and the energies flow out from the central hub. The characters in such art become archetypes and the emotions impersonal and general. There are nine dominant *rasas* or *bhāvas* (moods or emotions): eroticism (*śṛṅgāra*), pathos or compassion (*karuṇā*), heroism (*vīra*), fierceness (*raudra*), laughter (*hāsya*), fear (*bhaya*), disgust (*vibhatsa*), wonder (*adbhuta*), and tranquillity (*śānta*).

In addition, there are the transient emotions, like minute shades of color, called the *sañchāri bhāvas.* For example, love can be expressed by passion or jealousy and may pass through phases of separation and yearning, culminating in union. These two kinds of emotion are presented through the archetypal characters of gods and humans in drama, dance, music, poetry, sculpture, and painting. Whatever the language of the art (speech, sound, gesture, mass, line, color), its smallest unit corresponds to a single state of emotion. When combined, as the notes of a song or the gestures of the human body, these forms merge into a work of art with its distinctive shape, color, or taste, which evokes the state of joy in the audience as it did in the artist. The three steps in the process are called *rasānubhāva* (experience of *rasa*), *rasābhivyakti* (expression of *rasa*), and *rasoutapati* (evocation of *rasa*). Inspired by the Upaniṣads, Yeats summed up the theory of Indian art in a line: "How can we know the dancer from the dance?" Indeed, the dancer becomes the vehicle for transmitting the emotion to the spectator.

In the tenth century, the Kashmiri philosopher Abhinavagupta spelled out the theory that Bharata only implied:

> Artistic creation is the direct or unconventionalized expression of a feeling of passion "generalized," that is, freed from distinctions in time or space and therefore from individual relationships and practical interests, through an inner force of the artistic or creative intuition within the artist. This state of consciousness (rasa) embodied in the poem is transferred to the actor, the dancer, the reciter, and to the spectator.

These statements, made nearly one thousand years ago, remain pertinent today for a proper understanding, appreciation, and appraisal of Indian art, especially dance and music, which have enjoyed a remarkable continuity in their traditional forms.

Since artistic experience was regarded as an instrument and discipline vital for the uplifting of the individual toward the universal self, both artist and spectator made a special effort to use the experience for achieving a state of harmony. The language employed by the performer for this purpose was symbolic rather than realistic, revealing the truth and beauty of life by suggestion. And the spectator had to be trained to understand the symbols before communication could take place.

The terms used for the spectator in Sanskrit sum up this view: *sahṛdaya* (one of attuned heart) and *rasika* (one who experiences *rasa*). Art evokes in the spectator certain states of consciousness that already existed in his or her soul. So, like the creative artist, trained spectators are capable of experiencing the emotion that frees them from the limitations of time and space.

Because of the continuity between past and present in classical Indian performing arts, both performer and spectator believe in the importance of such arts as a means of experiencing the universal and are willing to undergo the necessary and exacting preparations for these performances.

For example, in classical Indian dance, the performer must learn to use his or her body in a manner that symbolizes the universal self. The dancer, therefore, uses every design in space, every instance of muscular tension and release, and every gesture of hand and eye to convey to the audience this universal self rather than a particular subjective emotion. Just as the dancer's body becomes the vehicle for communicating universal feelings, so the spectator responds to these impersonal feelings rather than the personal experience of the artist. All these classical Indian art forms are based on the worldview and theory of aesthetics originally enunciated in the Vedic texts, and the highest fulfillment of art comes when the mystical unseen spirit permeates the whole community.

Since the pleasure of witnessing these classical dances comes from recognizing the unfolding of something latent rather than from encountering something unusual and highly individual, the demands made upon the spectator are different from those required for an appreciation of Western dance. The themes recurring in much of the classical dance of India are highly literary in character, drawing upon the same sources of Indian legend, mythology, and epic poetry as the other classical arts. The positions and stances that the Indian dancer assumes can be recognized in the chiseled poses of Indian sculpture and iconography; the gestures are symbolic and are derived from the ancient rituals specified in the Brāhmaṇas; the music and rhythmic patterns of the dance are the classical *rāga*s and *tāla*s.

In pure dance sequences, called *nṛtta*, the body may form a single geometric design, such as a triangle in *bharata nāṭyam* (in South India), a square in *kathakaḷi* (from Kerala), a figure eight in Manipuri (from Manipur), a line in *kathak* (in North India). Floor space may also be covered in the same rigidly structured design. The navel becomes the symbol of the cosmic center, and all movement flows outward from it and returns to it in a fixed pose. Just as in the traditional rituals, time and space may be consecrated.

In the mime or expressive dance sections (*nṛtya*), a line of poetry is set to music and rendered within a metrical cycle (*tāla*) in order to recreate one of the dominant emotions: those like love, valor, or pathos with their variations and improvisations are intended to evoke in the spectator an experience of joy and release. Specific characters and themes are important not in themselves but only as aids in evoking the dominant mood. The dance is composed of the interplay between stasis and dynamics.

To the uninitiated spectator this highly symbolic dance form may seem repetitious and full of bewildering complexity. The appreciation for such dance requires a knowledge and training that goes beyond the mere visual experience to an understanding of meaning and technique. These demands merely increase the initiated spectator's delight in the performance. The thrill of recognition arises partly from the spectator's experience of emotional states and forms already familiar from works of poetry, music, architecture, and sculpture. However, since the content and the formal elements are only part of the total design and are, in fact, tools of expression in attaining a higher state, a sensitive though uninitiated spectator who is not looking for specific meaning or story may be transported to that elevated state of joy or bliss that transcends the world of appearances.

There is an organic unity connecting the Indian worldview, the aesthetic theory, and the performance with its many layers of meaning and expression. By giving up the limited sense of self, the artist is enabled to create a greater realm of life in art and to expand the consciousness of both performer and spectator into the universal self. Those who experience this enlarged consciousness return to the ordinary world with a heightened sense of harmony and tranquillity.

[*For related discussion, see* Aesthetics, *article on* Asian Dance Aesthetics.]

BIBLIOGRAPHY

Bose, Mandakranta. *Movement and Mimesis: The Idea of Dance in the Sanskritic Tradition.* Dordrecht, 1991.

Ghosh, M. M., ed. and trans. *Nandikeśvara's Abhinayadarpanam.* 2d ed. Calcutta, 1957.

Ghosh, M. M., ed. and trans. *The Nātyaśāstra Ascribed to Bharata-Muni.* 2 vols. Calcutta, 1951–1961.

Iyer, Alessandra. "A Fresh Look at *nrtta*." *Dance Research* 11 (Autumn 1993): 3–15.

Kramrisch, Stella. *The Vishnudharmottara, part 3, A Treatise on Indian Painting and Image-Making.* 2d ed., rev. and enl. Calcutta, 1928.

Lidova, Natalia. *Drama and Ritual of Early Hinduism.* New Delhi, 1994.

Tarlekar, G. H. *Studies in the Natyasastra: With Special Reference to the Sanskrit Drama in Performance.* Delhi, 1975.

Vatsyayan, Kapila. *Classical Indian Dance in Literature and the Arts.* New Delhi, 1968.

Vatsyayan, Kapila. *The Square and the Circle of the Indian Arts.* New Delhi, 1983.

Vatsyayan, Kapila. *Bhārata and the Nātyaśāstra.* New Delhi, 1996.

KAPILA VATSYAYAN

Epic Sources of Indian Dance

Epic tales of heroes of the past were important in ancient India in royal sacrificial ritual, part of which involved the telling of such stories. Thus these tales of war and heroism were put into the hands of the priesthood, who probably somewhat altered their character and interpolated the long passages on theology, morals, and statecraft. Some scholars believe that the epics were originally secular in nature, but in their present form the deities of Hinduism figure prominently throughout. The legends that form the basis of many dances of India are found in its two great epics, the *Mahābhārata* and the *Rāmāyaṇa*, as well as in the Purāṇas, or collections of "the old stories."

Mahābhārata. Especially in those dance-drama forms in which heroism and prowess on the field of battle are important elements of the thematic material, tales from the *Mahābhārata* are of prime importance. *Kathakaḷi* in Kerala State, *yakṣagāna* in Karnataka, and *terukkūttu* in Tamil Nadu are examples of this type of heroic dance drama. Almost all forms of dance and dance drama in India do, however, draw upon this epic at least occasionally for thematic material.

The *Mahābhārata* is the longest epic poem in any language, consisting of some ninety thousand verses arranged in eighteen sections, or *parvan*s. It is credited to

the sage Vyāsa, and the story is that the elephant-headed deity, Gaṇapati, wrote it down as Vyāsa dictated.

The main story of the *Mahābhārata* takes place in North India and concerns the great war between the Pāṇḍavas and their cousins, the Kauravas. Originally it was probably the story of a local feud, but no doubt as it was told and retold, it was much elaborated.

The *Mahābhārata* relates the strife over the disputed throne of the Kurus. The blind Dhrtarāṣtra of the Kauravas was the legitimate heir to the throne, but custom rendered a blind king unacceptable, and so his brother Pāṇḍu was crowned. When Pāṇḍu later retired to the forest, renouncing the throne, Dhrtarāṣtra reigned, since Pāṇḍu's sons (the Pāṇḍavas) were still but children. They were taken to live in the capital so as to be educated along with Dhrtarāṣtra's one hundred sons. When Yudhiṣthira, the eldest of the Pāṇḍavas, reached majority, he was legally entitled to the throne. The sons of Dhrtarāṣtra, however, formulated a number of plots against the lives of their cousins, because Duryodhana, the eldest, coveted the throne for himself. Finally, after a particularly sinister plot against them had failed, the five Pāṇḍavas left the capital and wandered from one court to another. In the kingdom of the Pañcālas they met Kṛṣṇa (Krishna), who was their uncle and who also became their staunch friend.

Dhrtarāṣtra eventually gave up the throne and divided the kingdom between the Pāṇḍavas and his own sons, the Kauravas. Angry at this turn of events, Duryodhana invited Yudhiṣthira to a gambling match in which Duryodhana won from Yudhiṣthira all that he had, including the five Pāṇḍavas' joint wife, Draupadī. Finally a compromise was agreed to: the Pāṇḍavas were to go into exile for thirteen years, the last year of which was to be spent incognito. At the end of that time they were to regain their half of the kingdom. When Duryodhana did not keep his bargain, the Pāṇḍavas prepared for war. At the end of eighteen days of battle, only the Pāṇḍavas and Kṛṣṇa remained alive, leaving Yudhiṣthira the undisputed ruler. When he finally gave up the throne, after many years of peaceful rule, he installed in his place Parikṣit, grandson of his brother Arjuna.

Many episodes were added gradually to the *Mahābhārata* over the years. These interpolations, as well as the main story, constitute a major source of thematic material for the arts in India.

Rāmāyaṇa. The *Rāmāyaṇa*, the other of the two great Indian epics, is much shorter than the *Mahābhārata*, and most of its few interpolations are didactic in nature. It consists of seven books, but the first and last are thought to be later additions. The author is traditionally believed to be the poet Vālmīki, and certainly it seems to have had but one author, unlike the *Mahābhārata*, which is a compilation. It is believed that the *Rāmāyaṇa* in its present form dates from about the beginning of the common era, although there are many earlier versions.

The story centers around the figure of Rāma, the son of King Daśaratha of Kosala. At an archery contest held in the court of King Janaka of Mithilā, Rāma won the hand of Sītā, daughter of the king. When King Daśaratha felt he was too old to rule the kingdom, he decided to give up his throne and named his son Rāma as heir. At this juncture, however, one of Daśaratha's three wives, Kaikeyī, reminded the king that he had promised her a boon many years before, and she now demanded that he keep his promise. She wanted her own son, Bharata, to become the king, and she also insisted that Rāma be exiled from the kingdom. Both Daśaratha and Bharata were dismayed by her demand, but Rāma himself insisted upon going into voluntary exile in order to fulfill his father's promise. Sītā and Rāma's brother Lakṣmaṇa accompanied Rāma into exile. Lakṣmaṇa destroyed many of the demons who attempted to disrupt the sacrifices of the holy ascetics who dwelt in seclusion in the forest.

One day a demon appeared in disguise, magically taking the form of a beautiful woman. She was Śūrpaṇakhā, sister of Rāvaṇa, ruler of a kingdom of demons. Spurned by both Rāma and Lakṣmaṇa, she resumed her true form and attacked them, upon which Lakṣmaṇa severely wounded her. She left in a rage, vowing vengeance. Her brother, the arrogant and dangerous Rāvaṇa, retaliated by kidnapping Sītā. Rāma was utterly despondent until he met with Hanumān, a warrior, and later with Sugrīva, a chieftain, both belonging to the monkey tribe.

Sugrīva agreed to aid in the search for Sītā by sending out his monkey army to the far corners of the earth. The brave and trustworthy Hanumān, who had become devoted to Rāma, eventually found Sītā in Rāvaṇa's kingdom of Laṅkā (modern Sri Lanka). Deaf to Rāvaṇa's pleas and enticements, Sītā dwelt in a grove of *aśoka* trees in the palace grounds, despondent and guarded by Rāvaṇa's demon henchmen. Hanumān contrived to speak with Sītā, and she was rescued.

However, because Sītā had dwelt on another man's premises, far away from her husband, the people could be expected to doubt her purity. Although Rāma himself had no such doubts, as a righteous king he had no choice but to repudiate her. She voluntarily entered the fire as a test of her purity, but Agni, the god of fire, delivered her unharmed, testifying to her innocence. Rāma and all his followers, with Sītā and Lakṣmaṇa, then journeyed to Ayodhyā, capital of Kosala, where Bharata, who had been ruling only as regent during Rāma's absence, returned the kingdom to Rāma amid great rejoicing.

Both Rāma and Sītā are seen as embodiments of virtue. Sītā represents the perfect Hindu wife. Not only is she unshakably constant and chaste, but she remains cheerful under all circumstances and wants nothing more than to serve her lord. Rāma is the ultimate Hindu hero, representing an unswerving devotion to *dharma,* or duty.

The story of the *Rāmāyaṇa* has endured in India for many centuries and has enjoyed wide popularity in Southeast Asia as well. It has provided the theme for numerous Sanskrit dramas in India, each playwright lending his own personal vision to the plot, sometimes with fairly substantial variations.

Eight plays on the theme of the *Rāmāyaṇa* were known as *rāmanāṭṭam* in Kerala; this was the forerunner of the dance drama form *kathakaḷi.* Many other traditional forms of dance and theater also draw upon the *Rāmāyaṇa* for thematic material. The Rām Līlā pageants and processions presented in northern India, particularly in Banaras and New Delhi, are based on the *Rāmāyaṇa* theme, and today many more modern vernacular presentations may also be seen in the various regions of India as well as in Indonesia.

Purāṇas. The word *purāṇa* means "belonging to ancient times," or "ancient tale or legend." There are eighteen chief Purāṇas, of which the most important are the *Viṣṇu Purāṇa,* the *Bhāgavata Purāṇa,* the *Agni Purāṇa,* the *Bhaviṣya Purāṇa,* and the *Vāyu Purāṇa.* In addition to mythological material, the Purāṇas contain instruction in ritual observances and details of the legal code. The most important aspect of the Purāṇas from the standpoint of dance and dance drama is the use of their many myths and legends as thematic material. Myths involving the god Viṣṇu (Vishnu) and especially Kṛṣṇa (Krishna), one of the ten *avatāra*s or incarnations of that deity, are popular as thematic material. The principal sources for these myths are the *Viṣṇu Purāṇa* and the *Bhāgavata Purāṇa.*

The *Viṣṇu Purāṇa* appeared around the sixth century; stories of Kṛṣṇa are contained in its fifth book. The *Bhāgavata Purāṇa* is believed to have been written in southern India around the ninth century; it tells the story of Kṛṣṇa's life in great detail in its tenth book. The highly appealing stories of Kṛṣṇa as a child and as a young man growing up among the cowherds—from time to time defeating the demons sent to destroy him by his cousin, the wicked King Kaṃsa, at other times in amorous play with the *gopī*s, or milkmaids—provide an endless source of material for interpretation and elaboration. The relationship of Kṛṣṇa with the *gopī*s has lent itself to a mystical interpretation; the longing of the *gopī*s to be united with Kṛṣṇa is symbolic of the yearning of the human soul for union with the divine.

Both the *Bhāgavata Purāṇa* and the *Viṣṇu Purāṇa* contain the stories of other *avatāra*s of Viṣṇu as well as stories of Kṛṣṇa. *Avatāra*s such as Narasiṃha and Vāmana figure in many of the plots of dance drama forms, but the stories of Kṛṣṇa are by far the most prevalent. Vaiṣṇava as well as Śaiva devotional cults today continue to use Puranic source material as a central basis for visual and aural communication through the performing arts, expressing and reinforcing the traditional integration of religion, philosophy, and the arts so characteristic of Indian culture.

BIBLIOGRAPHY

Basham, A. L. *The Wonder That Was India*. New ed. New York, 1963.
Burnouf, Eugène, et al., trans. *Bhâgavata Purâña*. 5 vols. Paris, 1840–1898.
Griffith, Ralph T. H., ed. and trans. *The Ramayan*. 3d ed. Varanasi, 1963.
Narasimhan, Chakravarti V., trans. *Mahābhārata*. New York, 1965.
Rajagopalachari, C., trans. *Mahabharata*. 6th ed. Bombay, 1958.
Rajagopalachari, C., trans. *Ramayana*. 6th ed. Bombay, 1968.
Wilson, H. H., ed. and trans. *The Vishñu Purâña*. 5 vols. London, 1864–1870.

CLIFFORD REIS JONES

The Rādhā-Kṛṣṇa Theme in Indian Dance

Rādhā-Kṛṣṇa is a popular theme in many contemporary Vaiṣṇava styles of Indian dance. Although the Hindu god Kṛṣṇa (Krishna) belongs to ancient India, the Rādhā-Kṛṣṇa theme flowered in medieval India.

The figure of Kṛṣṇa emerges first in the section of the *Mahābhārata* known as the *Bhagavad Gītā* as teacher and preceptor of the prince Arjuna. In an appendix to this epic, the *Harivaṃśa*, ("genealogy of Hari," i.e. Kṛṣṇa) another aspect of the same god is vividly described. Here he dances with many women in a circular dance called the *hallisaka*. In the *Bhāgavata Purāṇa* (from approximately the ninth or tenth century CE), Kṛṣṇa's early childhood and the miraculous feats of his adolescence are described. The tenth book contains an extensive account of the circular dance called *rāsa*, in which Kṛṣṇa dances with several milkmaids, or cowherdesses, called *gopī*s. Rādhā is not mentioned by name, but one line briefly alludes to Kṛṣṇa's disappearance in the woods with a special *gopī*. Similar descriptions of the *rāsa* dance and Kṛṣṇa's divine "sport" *(līlā)* are found in the *Viṣṇu Purāṇa* and other Purāṇic texts.

Various poems composed independently around the seventh and eighth centuries CE mention the name of Rādhā. The combined form as Rādhā-Kṛṣṇa is developed in a Sanskrit work called the *Gīta Govinda*, attributed to the poet Jayadeva (twelfth century CE). In this work Rādhā emerges as a full-fledged character. Through twelve cantos, the love story of Rādhā and Kṛṣṇa is vividly portrayed, highlighting the classic Vaiṣṇava themes of separation, yearning, and union. The poem begins as Kṛṣṇa's father Nanda commands Rādhā to escort the young god through thick woods as dark clouds gather. Here, through allusion, one learns of the passionate love that develops between the two. Following a description of the ten incarnations of Viṣṇu (Vishnu) as fish, tortoise, boar, man-lion, dwarf, the hero Paraśurāma, Rāma of the *Rāmāyaṇa*, Kṛṣṇa, the Buddha, and ultimately the future incarnation Kalki, the poem returns to Kṛṣṇa and Rādhā.

Now separated, Rādhā yearns for Kṛṣṇa and recalls their first meeting. Her girlfriend describes to her Kṛṣṇa's dance in the springtime with many women. Rādhā's jealousy mounts, and Kṛṣṇa's repentance for his wantonness intensifies; many cantos give poignant descriptions of the separate yearning of the two. Finally Kṛṣṇa appears in the early dawn, suppliant and humble. Rādhā, unrelenting, rebukes him, but as he departs she weeps and collapses in tears. Rādhā's friend brings about the reconciliation delicately, first persuading Kṛṣṇa and then Rādhā. Rādhā enters Kṛṣṇa's bower, where he awaits her; their reunion concludes the poem.

The traditions of Indian dance prevalent in various regions of India include dance numbers based on the closely related themes of Kṛṣṇa and Rādhā-Kṛṣṇa. The circular dance called *rāsa*, usually featuring one man in the center of a circle formed by many women, represents the eternal play of the god with the world. Kṛṣṇa is the god, the women are human; he is whole, they are parts. From this fundamental symbolism developed many variations of circular dances, all emphasizing interlocking, pairings, pirouettes, and incessant revolutions. In kinetic terms, the principal movement is rotation (pirouettes) along the circumference of a circle. From a slow tempo, the dance invariably speeds up to culminate in a crescendo of clapping and ceaseless movement. There is a notable absence of mime or interpretation of poetry through gesture.

Within this generic form, many variations appear. Some of the variations are danced by men, as for example the *rāsa* dance of Gujarat. Others, like the *garba*, are danced only by women, while yet others are mixed dances performed by men and women. The male partner in the circle is considered an allusion to Kṛṣṇa, who duplicates himself for each *gopī*. The symbolism of the shared myth provides enjoyment for performer and audience alike. The dances are popular because of the myth rather than the intricacy of the kinetic form.

In contrast to the Kṛṣṇa theme, the Rādhā-Kṛṣṇa theme provides opportunities for the interpretation through mime and gesture of poetry set to music. At the metaphysical level, it symbolizes the yearning of the human and the divine, the individual soul separated from and united to the omniscient. The principle of this theme is not the one and many, but one and one, the godhood and human. The two are considered indispensable to each other, for separately, both divinity and humanity are incomplete. Sometimes the two themes coalesce, as in the dances of Manipur and the dance plays of Mathura.

The Rādhā-Kṛṣṇa theme naturally lends itself to duets, but the greatest interpretations are in the solo numbers of different classical styles. In the *bharata nāṭyam* of South India, the theme is incorporated in the poetic musical composition called *padam*. These short lyrics were specially composed for the dance in the fifteenth to eighteenth centuries. Many were the creations of the saint-poet-musicians. The poems delineate the yearning and suffering of Rādhā as a youthful, eager girl, expectant and waiting, as a courageous beloved who braves thunder and rain to keep a tryst with her lover, as a jealous woman who decries his infidelity, as the quarrelsome one, or as one who is coaxed and persuaded to receive him. Singly or sequentially presented, each of the phases of yearning, separation, and union provide scope to the dancer to present the dominant mood of hope, expectancy, disappointment, jealousy, anger, or repentance, all within the all-encompassing emotion of love. The dancer is both narrator and actor; her mime presents the diverse heroine types known to Indian aesthetic theories. The excellence of a dancer lies in her ability to improvise and elaborate on the poetic line. The character of Kṛṣṇa is not presented; rather, the solo dancer suggests his presence through gestures and mime. [*See* Bharata Nāṭyam.]

Medieval poetry composed in Brajbhasha (a form of Hindi) is replete with descriptions of Rādhā and Kṛṣṇa. This poetry, along with that of Binadin, a great poet-musician-dancer of the nineteenth century, inspires the dancer to present the human longing for the divine. Like poetry, dance and mime move concurrently on multiple planes, the sensuous and the mystical, the profane and the sacred. The dancer's challenge is to communicate these levels simultaneously. Improvisations and variations, almost parallel to poetic metaphor and imagery, are essential. The imagination of the dancer builds upon a line, a phrase, or a word, and it evokes a world of human emotion through the love of Rādhā and Kṛṣṇa.

In Oḍissi (a dance style from Orissa, in eastern India), the original Sanskrit text of the *Gīta Govinda*, the fountainhead of the Rādhā-Kṛṣṇa theme, is more frequently employed than elsewhere. The verses of the poem constitute the foundation on which movement is created. It is essentially a solo dance performed by a female or male dancer, traditionally held within the precincts of a temple. The performance begins with the portrayal of Viṣṇu in his ten incarnations. Thereafter, the dancer selects either a full canto or even a single verse or line to interpret through mime, which is interspersed with pure dance movement. The themes of estrangement and desertion, reproach, reconciliation, and the final consummation are portrayed with extreme subtlety and delicacy. The singer plays an important role, because it is the poetry set to specific melodic patterns that provides the basis for the dancer's movement. The original poem itself indicates both melodic patterns (*rāga*s) and metrical structures (*tāla*s), which are normally followed by the drummer: the cumulative effect is a richly textured orchestration of word, sound, melody, rhythm, and movement. Two favorite verses are those describing the springtime dance of

INDIA: The Rādhā-Kṛṣṇa Theme in Indian Dance. A Seraikella *chhau*-style performance depicting Kṛṣṇa, the blue-skinned eighth avatar (incarnation) of Viṣṇu, and Rādhā, his favorite playmate, as portrayed by Gopal Dubey (left) and Neeta. (Photograph © 1996 by Jack Vartoogian; used by permission.)

Kṛṣṇa with the *gopī*s and the moment of Kṛṣṇa's approaching Rādhā at dawn when she reproaches him and he slinks away. Juxtaposed sequentially, they provide contrast and balance to a single recital lasting over two or three hours. [*See* Oḍissi.]

Recently, choreographers and dancers have attempted to compose full-length dance dramas, employing a large cast of dancers and using two principals as Rādhā and Kṛṣṇa. Such dance dramas have been presented on modern stages in *bharata nāṭyam*, *kathak*, and Oḍissi.

However, the tradition of presenting the Rādhā-Kṛṣṇa theme as a theatrical spectacle with dialogues, sung arias, and dances has also been prevalent in India from the sixteenth century. It cannot be established conclusively whether or not the two were concurrent or whether the solo dance interpretation evolved out of total theatrical performance.

Foremost among such theatrical dances are the *rās līlā* of Mathura and Vrindavan in northern India, and the *rās līlā* of Manipur in the extreme northeastern part of India. Both are inspired by the literary sources of the *Bhāgavata Purāṇa* and the *Gīta Govinda*. Here the two coalesce, as the dramatic dance performance presents both the dance of Kṛṣṇa and the *gopī*s and the love of Rādhā and Kṛṣṇa. Always performed in conjunction with temple ritual at specific seasons, they mark the annual calendar. In spring the *Vasant Rāsa* is performed and in autumn the grand *Mahārāsa*, both on full-moon nights under open skies. Between these is another dance that coincides with the rainy season and two others that can be performed on any occasion. In Mathura and Vrindavan, only young boys take part; in Manipur only young girls perform the dance. The *rās līlā* of Mathura and Vrindavan traveled to Manipur in the eighteenth century, and it was transformed into a dramatic dance of great lyrical beauty. [*See* Rās Līlā.]

The Rādhā-Kṛṣṇa theme has survived in India through many centuries, and flourished today because of its conception of God in human form. God seeks the individual human soul (represented by the *gopī*s), as much as the human individual ego seeks God. The deserted Rādhā symbolizes the proud, lonely path of human beings and their inability to recognize God even when he stands before them. The messenger symbolizes the awakened consciousness, which brings the two together. The union or consummation is fulfillment, but the rhythm of life continues only in differentiation, so the two must again be separated. Rādhā entreats Kṛṣṇa in the last canto of the *Gīta Govinda* to adorn her with the music of the universe, the auspiciousness of the waters, the fragrance of the earth, and the color of the vegetation. The spiritual message couched in the passionate poetry of love holds the imagination of the performers and spectators. In the countryside more than in city theaters, the artistic presentation of this theme is an eagerly awaited event.

BIBLIOGRAPHY
Sarada, S. "Krishna Theme in Music and Dance." In *Readings on Indian Music*. Trivandum, India, 1979.
Varadpande, M. L. *Krishna Theatre in India*. New Delhi, 1982.
Vatsyayan, Kapila. *Classical Indian Dance in Literature and the Arts*. New Delhi, 1968.
Vatsyayan, Kapila. *Mewari Gita Govinda*. New Delhi, 1987.
Vatsyayan, Kapila. *Indian Classical Dance*. 2d ed. New Delhi, 1992.

KAPILA VATSYAYAN

New Directions in Indian Dance

A renaissance of classical Indian dance came with the advent of Uday Shankar and of intellectuals and poets such as Rabindranath Tagore, who introduced dance to the curriculum of his Vishwa Bharati-Shantiniketan. The poet Vallathol established Kerala Kala Mandalam in Kerala to teach *kathakaḷi* dance; Rukmini Devi founded Kalakshetra in Tamil Nadu on the eastern coast of southern India; and Madame Menaka started an institute near Bombay at Khandala on the western coast. Many other schools followed, and classical dance spread from them to attain great popularity among the masses. [*See the entry on Shankar.*]

When India became independent in 1947, the new government established academies and centers for dance, music, and drama. Along with classical dance, the Indian modern dance movement embarked on innovations and experimentation. Uday Shankar had already developed a unique style and had choreographed such works as *Labour and Machinery*, dealing with the exploitation of labor by capital and the struggle for freedom. His associates, including Narendra Sharma, Sachin Shankar, and Shanti Bardhan, followed his example in choreographing works that did not rely only on mythological themes but wove in the problems of contemporary life; thus, the Bengal famine found expression in the ballet *Bhookh*, by Sadhana Bose.

Classically trained dancers discovered other indigenous genres, such as *chhau*, as well as martial-arts traditions such as Kerala's *kalaripayattu* and Manipur's *thang-ta*. They also began to explore the related physical disciplines of yoga.

As they became aware of this vast range of traditions, imaginative dancers began to incorporate them into new dance vocabularies. Modern Indian dance thus came into being, continuing the efforts of Uday Shankar and the ideas of Tagore. Tagore himself wrote three dance dramas—*Chitrangada*, *Chandalika*, and *Shyama*—in which Manipuri, *kathakaḷi*, and other dance genres were employed, resulting in a new genre known as Rabindrik. This style has expanded to admit Oḍissi, *kathak*, and movements from the martial arts and yoga. The result may be seen in the choreography of Manjusri Chaki-Sircar in her version of *Chandalika*, produced under the title *Tomari Matir Kanya*. [*See the entry on Chaki-Sircar.*]

Innovation and experimentation also took place within the classical genres of *bharata nāṭyam*, *kathak*, Manipuri, *kathakaḷi*, Oḍissi, Kuchipudi, and *mōhiniāṭṭam*, resulting in a shift in theme and content as well as in movement vocabulary. In *bharata nāṭyam*, Mrinalini Sarabhai has addressed the themes of dowry, death, and suicide; Chandralekha has used the theme of the female creative principle with images of Indian women that focus on energy, both raw and refined as is evident in her work, *Stree*. The latter choreographer extended dance vocabulary by integrating the physical disciplines of martial arts and yoga with *bharata nāṭyam* and has choreographed several works. Daksha Sheth combined Mayurbhanj *chhau* dance with the martial arts of Kerala in her work *Yajna*. Kumudini Lakhia and Birju Maharaj set *kathak* movements in a novel manner in a group of works. In dances such as *Atah Kim* and *Dhabkar*, Lakhia has attempted to give basic *kathak* movement a new look; in works such as *Lilangika*, Maharaj used movements of different body parts in a novel configuration. Themes of conservation and the environment were set in Manipuri dance in Chao Tombi's *Sangai* and *Loktak Lake*, while Priyagopal Rajkumar used the same style with folktale themes. R. K. Singhjit Singh has used martial arts such as *thang-ta* in his dance dramas. Biblical themes and a dance drama based on *Faust* have been attempted in a *kathakaḷi* context, with traditional costumes and makeup. [*See the entries on Chandralekha, Lakhia, Maharaj, and Sarabhai.*]

A number of dancers of the younger generation have also studied Western modern dance. Uttara Asha Coorlawala trained with Martha Graham, the Dance Theatre of Harlem, and the Juilliard School, and she pioneered the integration of modern dance with the strict traditions of *bharata nāṭyam* and yoga to create Indian contemporary dance. She also introduced Astad Deboo and Bharat Sharma to modern dance. Astad Deboo studied with Pina Bausch and took part in workshops with Murray Louis; Deboo evolved his own style, creating such works as *Drug Addict* and *Death*. Bharat Sharma trained with Alwin Nikolais and used the Indian technique he had learned from his father, Narendra Sharma, in his choreography for *Swapnakosha*, portraying the dream of a monk.

Not only in India, but also where Indians have settled in the United States, Canada, and Great Britain, Indian dancers have experimented with and explored many styles of dance in attempts to fuse new techniques with their own traditions. Their works are now part of the Indian dance scene, side by side with classical and folk dances.

BIBLIOGRAPHY

Bharucha, Rustom. *Chandralekha: Woman, Dance, Resistance.* New Delhi, 1995.
Dove, Simon. "'Navanritya': New Dance." *Ballett International* 13 (November 1990): 24–27.
Fernando, Sonali. "Vivarta." *Dance Now* 1 (Summer 1992): 63–65.
Fisher, Jennifer. "New Directions in South Asian Dance." *Vandance International* 21 (Spring 1993): 4–7.
Khan, Naseem. "Changing Concepts versus Traditional Forms." *Dance Now* 2 (Summer 1993): 72–74.
Kothari, Sunil. "New Directions in Indian Dance." *Dance Connection* 11 (April–May 1993): 41–42.
National Centre for the Performing Arts XIII (June 1984). Special issue on East-West Dance Encounter, held in Bombay, 22–29 January 1984.
New Directions in Indian Dance: International Dance Festival and Conference, February 10 to 15, 1993, Toronto, Canada. Toronto, 1993.
Rubidge, Sarah. "Modern Movement and Traditional Tales." *Dance Theatre Journal* 10 (Spring–Summer 1993): 32–37.
Schmidt, Jochen. "Divine Law versus the Body: The Laborious Rebirth of Indian Dance." *Ballett International/Tanz Aktuell* (August–September 1994): 70–75.
Segal, Lewis. "India Dances around the Avant-Garde." *High Performance*, no. 54 (Summer 1991): 19–23.
Sloat, Susanna. "Deepti Gupta's *Quanta*." *Attitude* 11 (Summer 1995): 62–63.
Vatsyayan, Kapila. "The Future of Dance Scholarship in India." *Dance Chronicle* 18.3 (1995): 485–490.

SUNIL KOTHARI

Dance Research and Publication

Some of the oldest writings on dance in the Indian subcontinent are contained in the *Nāṭyaśāstra,* one of the longest extant Sanskrit texts. Said to date from about the second to the fourth centuries CE, the text is usually ascribed to Bharata but is undoubtedly a compilation written at various times. Its subject matter is principally drama, but, because Indians conceive of dance as an integral component of drama, the text contains extensive information about dance. In addition to theory, the *Nāṭyaśāstra* describes body poses and movements, hand positions and gestures and their meanings, and the correct portrayal of emotional moods through movement and mime. Much of the descriptive material, however, is difficult to interpret and to apply accurately in reconstructing movement sequences.

The Tamil epic *Silappadikāram*, written by Prince Ilanko Adikal in about the second century CE, contains a great deal of material on dance. A prominent figure in the *Silappadikāram* is a courtesan-dancer, descriptions of whose dancing imply the presence of an indigenous dance tradition distinct from the Sanskrit tradition. Further, the epic indicates the contexts within which many types of folk dance were performed, provides song texts that accompanied some of the dances, and describes the cultural background in which courtesan-dancers flourished. Although the technical information provided by Adikal about dance movements is difficult or impossible to understand today, he did make a contribution by describing at least one environment of southern Indian dance in the second century.

Many Sanskrit treatises were written after the *Nāṭyaśāstra* and the *Silappadikāram*. Following the model created by the *Nāṭyaśāstra*, most treat dance only insofar as it contributed to theater. Among these works are the *Daśarūpa*, written in the late tenth century; the *Bhavaprakāśana*, written in the twelfth century (Yadugiri Yatiraja and K. S. Ramaswami Shastri, eds., 1929); the *Abhinayadarpaṇa*, dating from the fifth to thirteenth centuries (Manomohan Ghosh, ed. and trans., *Nandikesvara's Abhinayadarpanam*, 1957); and the *Bhāratārṇavaḥ*, dating from the seventh to fifteenth centuries (K. Vasudeva Sastri, ed. and trans., *Bharatarnavah Nandikesvaraviracitah*, 1957). Additionally, vernacular texts on dance written in various regions documented local dance forms.

Scholarly publications began to deal specifically with dance much more recently, in the mid-1900s. The *Madras Music Academy Journal* is the most academically oriented periodical that prints articles about dance. The *Quarterly Journal of the National Centre for the Performing Arts* also publishes articles on dance and theater, ranging from the intellectual to the popular. The same is true of *Sangeet Natak*—published by the government-supported Sangeet Natak Akademi—a journal that deals extensively with dance and other performing arts. Regional academies also publish journals including articles on dance, usually written in the regional languages and varying widely in level of scholarship.

In the 1950s *Marg*, an arts periodical, published a series of issues containing highly informative articles on dance.

These were collected in a single volume published in 1963, *Classical and Folk Dances of India,* edited by Mulk Raj Anand. Additional articles on dance have appeared in subsequent individual issues.

In Kerala, a state on India's southwestern coast, *Matribhumi,* a Malayalam-language weekly, formerly included in-depth, scholarly articles on sacred rituals that involved the performing arts. Since the early 1970s, however, the character of the weekly has shifted from an academic focus to a popular one.

The *Illustrated Weekly* and the *Times of India Annual* frequently contain articles on dance, which tend to be popular. Subject matter includes reviews of recent performances, brief historical accounts, and descriptions of performances in remote villages.

Most journals contain photographs that vary in the quality of both reproduction and content. Authors are often historians, Sanskritists, musicians, actor-dancers, dancers, or intellectuals of various professions, not necessarily from academic circles. Articles may focus on such topics as historical background from inscriptions or from early Sanskrit texts; various aspects of a traditional dance form; a rarely presented scene from a Sanskrit play in *kūtiyāttam;* makeup and costume for a traditional dance or dance-drama genre; a famous composer, musician, or dancer; or dance and theater as discussed in Sanskrit texts.

Dance reviews are published in many newspapers, particularly the *Hindu* (Madras); these reviews generally lavish abundant and indiscriminate praise on performers. Authors usually remain unnamed or are identified simply as "dance critic."

Financial assistance for dance publications comes from the National Centre for the Performing Arts and from the Sangeet Natak Akademi. Such organizations as the Bharatiya Lok Kala Mandal, Kalavikash Kendra, and Bhulabhai Memorial Institute, as well as the Department of Culture within the government's Ministry of Education, give scholarships and grants for research and for the study of dance. The Jawaharlal Nehru Memorial Foundation also supports research.

The government sponsors performances, seminars, workshops, and exhibitions through the Sangeet Natak Akademi, which also provides grants to students at state-supported schools and sometimes at private schools. Additionally, the academy presents awards to dancers and other artists, in recognition of distinguished achievements and contributions. Each of these awards consists of both a title and a monetary gift.

Most book-length writing about Indian dance treats multiple genres, though not in great depth and sometimes with questionable accuracy. Those few books that deal with only one dance or dance-drama genre are usually more useful. K. P. S. Menon has written a very detailed

work on *kathakaḷi* history in Malayalam (*Kathakalirangam,* 1957), as well as two volumes of performance manuals for selected *kathakaḷi* plays (*Kathakaliyattaprakaram,* 1963 and 1966) and a number of shorter works on *kathakaḷi.* These manuals do not describe technique but rather present the plays scene by scene, with the text and interpolations, indicating through a system of symbols the appropriate types of movements to be used. Kapila Vatsyayan has authored numerous articles on aesthetics. She has also written books and articles on the interrelationships of the arts (*Classical Indian Dance in Literature and the Arts,* 1968), classical dance *(Indian Classical Dance,* 1974), and folk dance (*Traditions of Indian Folk Dance,* 1976). Her subject matter has covered a wider range than that of any other dance author.

Because of the extensive use of the English language in the urban centers of India, many Indian authors write in English; hence, the works of some indigenous authors are readily accessible to English-speaking researchers. A 1973 bibliography of relevant source materials in English, Judy Van Zile's *Dance in India: An Annotated Guide to Source Materials,* included almost 800 entries by both Indian and non-Indian writers.

The most prolific Indian writers on the subject of dance are Kapila Vatsyayan, K. P. S. Menon, the late V. Raghavan (principally on dance and theater in Sanskrit literature), Manomohan Ghosh (including translations of Sanskrit texts on dance and theater), Mohan Khokar (particularly on the sociocultural context of *bharata nāṭyam,* Bhāgavata Mela, and Kuchipudi), Sunil Kothari, K. Kunjunni Raja (on indigenous Kerala forms), and Mulk Raj Anand (editor of the *Marg* series on dance).

JUDY VAN ZILE and BETTY TRUE JONES

INDONESIA [*To discuss the dance traditions found throughout the Malay Archipelago, this entry comprises ten articles:*

The introductory article explores the range of Indonesian dance from the formality of the royal courts to the rituals associated with animist practices, common choreographic elements, and musical accompaniment; the companion articles focus on five geographic areas of Indonesia where dance has flourished. The concluding article explores the historical and contemporary sources for the study of Indonesian dance. For related discussion in a broader context, see Asian Dance Traditions.]

An Overview

Indonesian dance today is an expression of diverse cultures, vividly reflecting thousands of years of indigenous creation and a syncretic integration of outside influences. With two hundred million citizens, Indonesia is the world's fourth most populous nation, an archipelago with thirteen thousand islands that include at least four hundred volcanos and stretch across the equator for three thousand miles from the Indian Ocean to the Pacific, from the Asian subcontinent to Australia. The ecology ranges from the densely populated islands of Java and Bali with their terraced rice fields, to the rainforests of Irian Jaya and Kalimantan, thinly populated with groups that up until recent decades have been described as Stone Age cultures. The tropical monsoon climate alternates between a rainy season and a hotter dry season. Preceding and throughout this millennium Indonesia's coastal areas have actively traded with merchant ships from China and Arab countries followed by Portugal, Spain, Great Britain, and the Netherlands. Trade routes were already long established before Marco Polo's visit, during which he was overwhelmed by the abundance of gold in Borneo (Kalimantan). The Moluccas (Maluku), known as the Spice Islands, played a major role in world history. Most of what is now the nation of Indonesia (excepting East Timor, which was under Portuguese rule) was under the control of the Dutch East Indies Company from 1602 until 1799. Indonesia continued to be ruled by the Netherlands until Japanese occupation during World War II, which was followed by a revolution against the Dutch (who had resumed control after the Japanese defeat). The nationalist leaders Sukarno and Hatta proclaimed Indonesia's independence in 1945 and sovereignty was negotiated in 1949. Since the attempted coup in 1965, with the resulting anti-Communist purge and seizure of political control by the military, Suharto has remained president for three decades of what is euphemistically referred to as "Guided Democracy."

On the more than one thousand inhabited islands of Indonesia there are about three hundred distinct ethnic groups, most of them speaking languages of the Malayo-Polynesian family, with contemporary communities practicing Islamic, Hindu, Christian, Buddhist, and animist beliefs. The form and spirit of their dances varies widely. Choreography ranges from an expression of the stylized formality of the Hindu-Javanese royal courts to animal- and nature-inspired movements arising from fertility, exorcism, and funeral rites associated with animist practices.

The best-known dance traditions, those of Bali and Central Java, evidence the strong Hindu and Buddhist influences from India, which began around 200 CE, with the establishment of the first Hindu-Javanese kingdom of Taruma about 400 CE in West Java (Sunda). The major period of Hindu-Javanese culture was in Central Java from the seventh until the tenth century, under the rule of the rival Sailendra and Mataram dynasties, Buddhist and Śaiva, respectively. The Sailendra dynasty, established at Palembang in Sumatra as a kingdom named Sriwijaya, was a center for Tantric Buddhist learning from the seventh until the thirteenth century CE, with students who traveled from India and China. The island of Sumatra was gradually won over by mystical Sufi missionaries and traders, who spread the word of Islam beginning at the end of the thirteenth century. In East Java, a series of Hindu-Javanese kingdoms reigned from the tenth until the sixteenth centuries, with the last, Majapahit, controlling and influencing the culture of a greater area of the archipelago, and especially that of Bali. In the sixteenth century, an Islamic kingdom reestablished Mataram in Central Java, and held power until the eighteenth century, when the Dutch established economic and political control, dividing the conquered kingdom between Surakarta and Jogjakarta. Though 90 percent of Indonesia is now Muslim, Bali has remained Hindu, with a syncretic amalgam of Buddhism and animism.

One can see experimental forms, contemporary social dance, modern dance, ballet and break dancing in urban Jakarta and other rapidly modernizing cities, which lead the rest of the country toward industrialization, international media consumption, and commercialization. A great many Indonesian dancers have toured the world and entertained, in their own country, international audiences of tourists since the 1920s. This inspired the development of modern dance genres such as *kebiar* and *kécak* in Bali in the 1920s, as well as *séndratari* in central Java in the 1960s. Today's innovative Indonesian choreographers and dancers have studied and taught at dance schools and festivals around the world, soaking up modernist influences. But a strong sense of national artistic identity has allowed them to incorporate some of the ideas of contemporary international dance while maintaining many of the aesthetic characteristics of Indonesian arts and culture. The modern influence has so far consisted less in the importation of dance techniques and choreographic forms from Europe and America, than in the liberation of some artists to compose, improvise, recombine, and juxtapose more freely from a wider range of Indonesian themes and references.

Living human cultures of the tropical rainforest such as the Dayak of Kalimantan (Indonesian Borneo) and the Asmat and Dani of Irian Jaya form a link with the ancient past, even as they undergo rapid change due to their conversion from traditional animism to Christianity, and as Indonesia's international trade activities overtake their environment with timber cutting, oil drilling, and mining. In the choreography of the Kenyah Dayaks one sees distinct indigenous elements that still characterize Indonesian dance in general: a sense of gravitation toward the earth, extended arms often with elbows bending in angular positions, wrists bent back, swivelling steps on the balls of the feet, cross-steps with the heel leading and subtle neck movements. These descendants of the early Austronesian migrants, who came to Indonesia tens of thousands of years ago, were less influenced by the historical forces shaping Java, Bali, and most of Sumatra and Sulawesi (Celebes) as well as other islands, until the outside world penetrated their cultures during the latter half of the twentieth century.

In her *Art in Indonesia* (1967), Claire Holt elucidates a broad, generalized range of choreographic elements shared by most dances of Indonesia, and her study is highly recommended for further reading. She describes how many dances involve

> sitting, kneeling, crouching and half-crouching positions. When upright, a dancer often lowers his body on pliant knees. Progress in space is largely accomplished in a variety of measured steps, with little running and virtually no hopping, leaping, or skipping. . . . Conspicuous by its absence is spinning or whirling of the body around its own axis. Sinuous undulations of the body, as for instance in the Polynesian hula dances, are absent too. Back bends are rare as are other acrobatic features.

Dealing with temporal elements, Holt writes,

> The tempo of dances is more often slow or moderate than rapid. Dance gestures in many areas tend to weave between rather than coincide with the accents of musical beats. In speed, the Balinese are exceptional as, for instance, in the scintillating rapidity of the *legong* dances performed by little girls.

In terms of spatial elements,

> Dancers as a rule do not traverse wide space while in motion. In many cases they remain practically in one place. There may be grandiose formations of many rows or large circles, but the space within which each participant moves at any given moment is limited.

The hands are a vital means of expression, with finger positions an essential aspect of characterization. Costume, including headdress, is a major means of defining a dance and establishing character, whether it be an elegant and brightly painted crown, a headscarf, feathers, or flowers in the hair. Most dances are specific to either males or females, with the exception of some courtship and recreational dances, in which both may dance together; even then, bodily contact between males and females is not seen in traditional forms. Dance-theater often involves performers of both sexes, although, in the past, female roles were generally performed by male dancers. In both Java and Bali, female dancer-actors have even assumed the roles of male characters for various dance-theater genres.

The best known musical ensembles are the gamelans of Java and Bali, consisting of bronze gongs, knobbed gong-chimes, metallophones, double-headed drums, bamboo flutes, and bowed lutes. Wooden and bamboo xylophones are also used in various instrumental contexts. In Sumatra, ensembles of frame drums reflect Islamic influence, as does the wooden lute of the *gambus* ensemble, which also includes clarinet, accordian, flute, and violin. Among Kenyah and Modang groups, drums, plucked lutes, and gongs are used for various dances.

Indonesia's national slogan, "Bhinneka Tunggal Ika" (Unity in Diversity), is a Hindu-Javanese phrase dating back at least to the fourteenth century. As current an issue as ever, the nationalist aspiration is described as valuing the rich cultural diversity of Indonesia while recognizing shared interests and commonalities.

BIBLIOGRAPHY

Anderson, Benedict R. O'G. *Mythology and the Tolerance of the Javanese.* Ithaca, N.Y., 1965.

Artaud, Antoniu. *The Theater and Its Double.* New York, 1958.

Bandem, I Madé, and Fredrik DeBoer. *Balinese Dance in Transition: Kaja and Kelod.* 2d ed. New York, 1995.

Becker, A.L. "Text Building, Epistemology, and Aesthetics in Javanese Shadow Theater." In *The Imagination of Reality: Essays in Southeast Asian Coherence Systems,* edited by Aram A. Yengoyan and A. L. Becker. Norwood, N.J., 1979.

Becker, Judith. *Traditional Music in Modern Java: Gamelan in a Changing Society.* Honolulu, 1980.

Becker, Judith, and Alan Feinstein, eds. *Karawitan: Source Readings in Javanese Gamelan and Vocal Music.* 3 vols. Ann Arbor, Mich., 1988.

Becker, Judith. *Gamelan Stories: Tantrism, Islam and Aesthetics in Central Java.* Tempe, Ariz., 1993.

Belo, Jane, ed. *Traditional Balinese Culture.* New York, 1970.

Brakel-Papenhuijzen, Clara. *The Bedhaya Court Dances of Central Java.* Leiden, 1972.

Brandon, James R. *On Thrones of Gold: Three Javanese Shadow Plays.* Cambridge, Mass., 1970.

Coomaraswamy, Ananda K. *History of Indian and Indonesian Art.* New York, 1927.

Covarrubias, Miguel. *Island of Bali.* New York, 1956.

de Zoete, Beryl, and Walter Spies. *Dance and Drama in Bali* (1938). New ed. New York, 1973.

Dibia, I Wayan. "Arja: A Sung Dance Drama of Bali; A Study of Change and Transformation." Ph.D. diss., University of California, Los Angeles.

Fontein, Jan. *The Sculpture of Indonesia.* Washington, D.C., 1990.

Herbst, Edward. "Intrinsic Aesthetics in Balinese Artistic and Spiritual Practice." *Asian Music* 13.1 (1981): 43–52.

Herbst, Edward. *Voices in Bali: Energies and Perceptions in Vocal Music and Dance Theater.* Hanover and London, 1997.

Hitchcock, Michael, and Lucy Norris. *Bali, the Imaginary Museum: The Photographs of Walter Spies and Beryl de Zoete.* New York, 1995.

Holt, Claire. *Art in Indonesia: Continuities and Change.* Ithaca, N.Y., 1967.

Hood, Mantle, *The Evolution of Javanese Gamelan.* 3 vols. New York, 1980.

Hood, Mantle, et al. "Indonesia." In *The New Grove Dictionary of Music and Musicians*. London, 1980.

Hood, Mantle, "The Enduring Tradition: Music and Theater in Java and Bali." In *Indonesia*, edited by Ruth McVey, pp. 438–560. New Haven, 1983.

Keeler, Ward. *Javanese Shadow Plays, Favanese Selves*. Princeton, 1987.

Kunst, Jaap. *Music in Java*. 2 vols. Translated by Emile van Loo. 3d ed. The Hague, 1973.

Lindsay, Jennifer. "Klasik, Kitch or Contemporary: A Study of the Javanese Performing Arts." Ph.D. diss., University of Sydney, 1985.

McPhee, Colin. *Music in Bali*. New Haven, 1966.

McPhee, Colin. "Dance in Bali." In *Traditional Balinese Culture*, edited by Jane Belo, pp. 290–321. New York, 1970.

Murgiyanto, Sal. "Four Indonesian Choreographers: Dance in a Changing Perspective." Ph.D. diss., New York University, 1990.

Olsin-Windecker, Hilary. "Characterization in Classical Yogyanese Dance." In *Dance as Cultural Heritage*, vol. 1, edited by Betty True Jones. New York, 1983.

Peacock, James L. *Rites of Modernization: Symbolic and Social Aspects of Indonesian Proletarian Drama*. Chicago, 1968.

Pucci, Idanna. *Bhima Swarga: The Balinese Journey of the Soul*. Boston, 1992.

Sumarsam. *Gamelan: Cultural Interaction and Musical Development in Central Java*. Chicago, 1995.

Vickers, Adrian. *Bali: A Paradise Created*. Singapore, 1989.

Vickers, Adrian. *Being Modern in Bali: Image and Change*. New Haven, 1996.

Wolters, O. W. *History, Culture, and Region in Southeast Asian Perspective*. Singapore, 1982.

Zoetmulder, P. J. *Kalangwan: A Survey of Old Javanese Literature*. The Hague, 1974.

Zurbuchen, Mary S. *The Language of Balinese Shadow Theater*. Princeton, 1987.

EDWARD HERBST

Balinese Dance Traditions

The island of Bali, which lies just off the eastern tip of Java, is very small (just 2,000 square miles) but has a rich dance tradition. In Balinese culture one can see evidence of indigenous features affected by outside influences, which in turn have been continually transmuted into new forms here.

Trade relations between India and Indonesia were established as early as the first century CE. During the following centuries Hindu and Buddhist influences strongly shaped Indonesia's already highly developed civilization. Bali was especially affected by the great cultural achievements of the Hindu Majapahit empire of East Java during the thirteenth and fourteenth centuries. When Islam spread across Java, Hindu-Javanese nobility began to migrate to Bali in increasing numbers. By the final collapse of Majapahit in 1478, many nobles and high-caste families had established new domains in Bali with their attendant craftsmen, militia, priests, and artists. This influx had a great impact on the development of dance in Bali.

Twentieth-century Bali has thousands of temples and numerous rites of fertility and passage, ancestor worship, exorcism, purification and propitiation; public ceremonies most generally occur with the aid of music and dance. In some, such as *sang hyang* trance rituals or the dance drama of Rangda and the Barong, deities act or speak through the dancers. In others, such as women's *rejang*, *topéng pajegan* (mask play), and ritual shadow-puppet plays *(wayang lemah)*, performance is a direct form of religious offering, intended to propitiate or otherwise influence deities, ancestral spirits, and other supernatural beings. Other dramatic forms may serve as entertainment for deities and human worshipers, accompanying ceremonies but not central to the function of the spiritual activities.

Some performances have no connection with religious events, but worship is an aspect of all music and dance. Any performance, whether in a temple courtyard or on a hotel stage in front of tourists, is preceded by ceremonial offerings (*banten* and *caru segehan*) and a prayer *(sanggah taksu)* for inspiration.

A performance area may be set up within a temple, in a family compound, by the side of a road, in a village square, or in any suitable place that can accommodate a dance space roughly eighteen by thirty feet in size with room for an audience. The performance space is oriented according to the cosmological principle of *kaja-kelod*, the north-south, mountain-sea axis. Most dances require a curtain *(langsé)* for entrances and exits. This is suspended from two bamboo poles sunk into the ground. The dance floor may be newly swept dirt, a layer of straw mats, or an elevated proscenium stage, which has been used in some formal and commercial venues since the 1960s. The traditional performance space is demarcated with bamboo poles *(taring)* decorated with leaves and flowers.

In Balinese dance theater a performer is expected to communicate character, mood, and dramatic action through gesture, stylized facial expressions, vocalization, mime, and dance. The delicate positions of the hands are reminiscent of Indian *mudrā*s; the quivering of the hands, the exacting articulation of the limbs, the isolation of parts of the body, and the rather fixed posture of hips and back indicate a restraint and sense of shape that are specifically Balinese. Refined *(alus)* character types move with a serene, graceful quality, their eyes half-closed, lips smiling sweetly, and speaking voices high and lyrical. A strong *(keras)* character displays bold, intense movements, wide-open eyes, frowning mouth, and a deep and percussive voice filled with emotion.

The literary sources of the plays include the Indian epics *Rāmāyaṇa* and *Mahābhārata*, the Javanese *Panji* cycle, Chinese and Malayan love stories, and Balinese historical chronicles. Elements of all are incorporated into a variety of standard format, of stylized characterization, choreography, and plot development. The dialogue, song, and comical antics are generally not fixed in rehearsal and feature spontaneity and sudden inspiration.

Dancers are very tightly bound in their costumes, which generally consist of many separate pieces. Some of the standard elements of male costume are a velvet jacket; a wide, colorful cloak with elaborate motifs painted in gold, which is wrapped under the armpits and draped down to the knees; leggings, often intricately sewn with silver thread or painted in gold designs, reaching from knee to ankle; and trousers, which are always white. Fastened

around the neck and hanging over the shoulders and chest is the *bapang*, a piece of velvet decorated with beads and silver thread and stuffed for thickness. A dagger *(keris)* is usually worn fastened on the performer's back in a position that allows him to draw it from its sheath.

Female costumes often include a more delicate *bapang*, a folded skirt painted in gold designs which covers the legs to the ankles, and a train trailing behind. A narrow cloth strip is wound many times around the torso, tightly binding it from breast to hips; decorative wrist and arm bands of leather or cloth are worn over a close-fitting blouse.

In dramatic performances, male and female characters are distinguished by their headdresses *(gelungan)*, elaborately designed constructions of gold-painted leather on a basketry frame. The *gelungan*, which is treated in a sacral manner—as are masks—immediately identifies the char-

INDONESIA: Balinese Dance Traditions. *Jogéd* performance at the village of Batuan. The young girl, called the *jogéd*, begins the dance with a *légong*-style solo. A man from the audience then joins in for an improvisatory duet, called the *ngibing*, which involves a playful mirroring of gestures. (Photograph by Walter Spies/Beryl de Zoete; reprinted from Hitchcock and Norris, 1995, fig. 222.)

acter's status and rank through its stylized shape and design.

The basic components of the musical gamelan ensemble are metallophones, gongs, gong-chimes, cymbals, drums, and flutes. The typically five-tone ensemble, which spans a range up to five octaves, produces striking, often rhapsodic melodic ornamentation while constantly providing the dancers with precise, emphatic, complex rhythmic motifs, which often shift. Whether a dance has a set choreography, is improvised on the basis of practiced gestures, or is unconsciously performed in trance, the music is always necessary as a support, pivotal point, and reflection of the dancers' activity. [See Gamelan.]

Social Dance. *Jogéd bumbung* is the only style of Balinese social dance a visitor to Bali is likely to see today, although several other varieties were popular into the early twentieth century. *Bumbung* means "bamboo tube" and refers to the four xylophones which accompany this dance. The music for *jogéd bumbung*, in *sléndro* tuning, is also popular as background music in hotels and tourist restaurants.

The dance is generally performed by about six girls, performing one by one. There is a brief entrance dance in which the performer does a simplified version of *légong* movement, after which she solicits a dance partner from the audience. The duet which ensues, called *ngibing*, is the main feature of *jogéd*. The dancer is referred to as *ibing*, or *jogéd*.

While some basic elements of *légong* are employed, the accent is on the swaying of the hips, coy gestures with the fan, alluring smiles, and a provocative, sexy appeal uncharacteristic of most Balinese dance forms. In the *ngibing* there are certain stylized conventions, although the audience participants are not bound to them, being free to improvise, parody, or stop at any time. The movement of the man involves rolling hips, shoulders held high, extended arms, and swaying head, with sudden shifts of gaze. The *jogéd* and man may circle each other or face each other at a distance, trying to mirror each other's gestures. The attitude usually meant to be conveyed is that of somewhat restrained erotic enticement. As they approach each other, the dance turns into a version of the classic *pengipuk* movement of courtship and love-making. The dancers gaze into each other's eyes from very close as they shift their heads from side to side *(engotan)*, mirroring each other's extended arm movements as if embracing without touching. The man may playfully attempt to steal a real kiss, which is always resisted by the *jogéd;* this is a definite cue for the *jogéd* to complete the round of the dance. She may dance with several partners before another member of the troupe enters to replace her.

Related dances still performed occasionally in a few villages are *leko, jogéd pingitan, gudegan,* and *tonkohan.* All include an opening dance in the *légong* style.

Gandrung was a dance performed until the 1930s by boys who had been trained in *nandir,* a male version of *légong.* In the *ngibing* sequence, male audience members danced flirtatiously with the boy, the crowd often working up to a frenzy. This context allowed adult males to display erotic feelings toward the boy dancers and gave some well-known *godogan* dancers fanatically devoted followings.

Some historical connections have been drawn between the entire family of *jogéd* dances and prostitution during the nineteenth century. Princes had their own troupes of *jogéd* dancers, who might sometimes be concubines as well. The *jogéd* performed for royal guests and in village events, where they received money for dancing *ngibing* with audience participants; it has been said that dancers provided sexual favors as well. The courtly forms of *jogéd* were accompanied by the *gamelan semar pegulingan,* rather than the more common *jogéd bumbung* ensemble.

Another dance form which appears to be linked to some ancient social dance tradition can still be found in the Bali Aga village of Tenganan. *Abuang kalah* is danced annually by unmarried young men and women to the accompaniment of the sacred *gamelan selundeng,* an archaic iron-keyed metallophone ensemble. The dancers dress in very formal attire; girls wear gold flowers in their hair and their unique *gringsing* cloth; each boy wears an old-fashioned skirt and cape, with a *keris* dagger fastened against his back. Males and females face each other in rows, and each pair, or a few pairs at a time, take turns dancing in mirror fashion. The movements consist of very simple arm gestures which show a wide range of dance skill, from awkward to meditative and graceful.

Génggong denotes both a musical genre and an almost extinct dance style, named for the musical instrument unique to these contexts. The *génggong* instrument itself is a jew's-harp made from sugarpalm wood, played by groups of boys or men to the accompaniment of *arja*-style *geguntangan* percussion. Generally performed as a light evening diversion, this ensemble has become popular as background music in hotels, restaurants, and tourist spots.

In the 1930s, a dance style evolved in the villages of Batuan and Sanur, based on the music of *Génggong* just as Bedaulu was experimenting with the *kécak* chorus. Members of the group took turns interpreting the movements and qualities of butterflies, frogs, and other animals, as well as such elements of nature as the breeze passing through rustling leaves. In a freer, nonrepresentational manner, they might also improvise, playing off the rhythms and melodies of the lively, ethereal music. During this period a play evolved in the village of Batuan, based on the story of a frog who marries a princess. Accompanied by the *génggong* ensemble, the story, *Godogan,* is enacted using choreography and masks unique to the

INDONESIA: Balinese Dance Traditions. I Nyoman Kakul was a much admired performer and instructor of several classical genres, including *gambuh, arja, baris,* and *topéng.* Here, he is seen instructing his granddaughters at his home in the village of Batuan. Many of Kakul's descendents perform with the *gambuh* ensemble named after him, called Sanggar Tari Nyoman Kakul. (Photograph by Edward Herbst; used by permission.)

genre, sometimes joined by standard *topéng* mask characters. *Godogan* continues to be popular tourist entertainment.

Dance Education. Training in the performing arts became institutionalized only in the latter half of the twentieth century as government schools came into being, but most training and performances still occur in the villages. K.O.K.A.R. (Konservatori Karawitan Indonesia Bali) is the high school of traditional performing arts, and S.T.S.I. (Sekolah Tinggi Seni Indonesia) is the national college of performing arts in Bali. In some ways, the tourist industry has replaced the Balinese nobility as the patron of artistic activities, although aesthetic criteria and influence vary immensely between the two audiences.

The idea of a professional performing artist does not fit the traditional Balinese cultural context, with the exception of the *dalang* (shadow-puppeteer). Performances are most often given as religious offerings or community service, although a nominal payment is made when performers play in a village other than their own. As a result

of tourism, the number of commercial troupes has increased significantly in recent decades, and now many performers derive their main income from their artistic activity.

Dance or music specialists who train a performance group from a village other than their own are usually paid in kind or in services. For basic income and material sustenance, performers, like everyone else, work as rice farmers, craftsmen, chauffeurs, schoolteachers, and so on.

Training and rehearsing are generally sporadic, preceding specific ceremonies or events. Older dancers instruct the younger ones, who are familiar with the basic form and technique from having watched the dance over the years but need instruction in the specific roles they are to portray. Once the dancer has internalized and integrated movement, voice, facial expression or use of the mask, he or she can begin to embody the character *(masolah).* Balinese language does not differentiate between dancer and actor, because a performer *(pragina)* must be both.

For group ceremonial dances such as *rejang,* participants learn by following more skilled dancers during the actual ritual. When young dancers are being trained for a performance role, they may take intensive lessons from an individual master teacher from their own or another village. The students are literally molded into shape by the guiding hands of the teacher, who sometimes gently and sometimes forcefully wrenches their bodies into position. The student is expected to begin performing as soon as the basic form is attained and then to learn by doing. The blessing the dancer receives by performing in ceremonies is an integral part of the educational process.

BIBLIOGRAPHY

Bandem, I Madé. "*Panji* Characterization in the *Gambuh* Dance Drama." Master's thesis, University of California, Los Angeles, 1972.

Bandem, I Madé, and Fredrik Eugene DeBoer. *Balinese Dance in Transition: Kaja and Kelod.* 2d ed. New York, 1995.

Bateson, Gregory, and Margaret Mead. *Balinese Character: A Photographic Analysis.* New York, 1942.

Belo, Jane. *Trance in Bali.* New York, 1960.

Belo, Jane, ed. *Traditional Balinese Culture.* New York, 1970.

Covarrubias, Miguel. *Island of Bali.* New York, 1956.

Daniel, Ana. *Bali: Behind the Mask.* New York, 1981.

de Zoete, Beryl, and Walter Spies. *Dance and Drama in Bali* (1938). New ed. New York, 1973.

Dibia, I Wayan. "Arja: A Sung Dance-Drama of Bali; a Study of Change and Transformation." Ph.D. diss., University of California, Los Angeles, 1992.

Emigh, John. "Playing with the Past: Visitation and Illusion in the Mask Theater of Bali." *Drama Review* 23 (June 1979).

Geertz, Hildred. "A Theatre of Cruelty: The Contexts of a Topéng Performance." In *State and Society in Bali,* edited by Hildred Geertz. Leiden, 1991.

Herbst, Edward. *Voices in Bali: Energies and Perceptions in Vocal Music and Dance Theater.* Hanover and London, 1997.

Hitchcock, Michael, and Lucy Norris. *Bali, the Imaginary Museum: The Photographs of Walter Spies and Beryl de Zoete.* New York, 1995.

Hobart, Angela. *Dancing Shadows of Bali.* London, 1987.

Holt, Claire. *Art in Indonesia: Continuities and Change*. Ithaca, N.Y., 1967.

Hood, Mantle, et al. "Indonesia." In the New Grove Dictionary of Music and Musicians. London, 1980.

Kakul, I Nyoman. "Jelantik Goes to Blambangan." *Drama Review* 23 (June 1979): 11–36.

Lendra, I Wayan. "Bali and Grotowski: Some Parallels in the Training Process." *Drama Review* 35 (1991): 113–128.

McPhee, Colin. *A House in Bali*. New York, 1946.

McPhee, Colin. *Music in Bali*. New Haven, 1966.

Murgiyanto, Sal. "Four Indonesian Choreographers: Dance in a Changing Perspective." Ph.D. diss., New York University, 1990.

Ramseyer, Urs. *The Art and Culture of Bali*. Oxford, 1977.

Young, Elizabeth F. "Topeng in Bali: Change and Continuity in a Traditional Drama Genre." Ph.D. diss., University of California, San Diego, 1980.

Zoetmulder, P. J. *Kalangwan: A Survey of Old Javanese Literature*. The Hague, 1974.

EDWARD HERBST

Balinese Ceremonial Dance

Many varieties of group ceremonial dance are performed by members of Balinese temple congregations as an offering to the deities being honored during a particular festival or ritual. These dances performed for deities can generally be distinguished from dances such as *sang hyang*, which are considered to be performed by or with deities. Even in these group temple dances, however, it is not unusual for individuals to enter a trance state *(kerauhan)*, or *nadi*, indicating the temporary presence of a deity or spirit within the dancer. As ritual offerings, these dances are obligatory for particular ceremonies, and every family in the village or temple association is required to have one or more family members participate.

Rejang is perhaps the slowest and most stately of these processional dances; it is usually performed by females of all ages. In some of the Bali Aga villages, such as Tenganan and Asak, *rejang* is danced only by unmarried girls in elaborate costume, including a gold-leaf headdress and a colorful train which falls between the dancer's legs and trails behind. In most other villages it is performed within the temple by female dancers of all ages, usually costumed in less elaborate but still ceremonial dress; Often a fan *(képét)* and a long sash *(anteng)* tied around the waist are the only required elements of the costume, as they are incorporated into the choreography.

The dance is characterized by continuously flowing movement and gradual shifts of weight from one leg to the other, followed by a sinking into the knees or stretching upward. *Rejang* is not highly synchronized with the accompanying gamelan music, but at intervals in the melody the fan flutters, and the sash is slowly lifted by an extended arm and then gently flipped back. Older woman may impart a floating, meditative quality to their dance, while adolescents are more self-conscious under the watchful eyes of their young male counterparts, who stand on the sidelines or play in the gamelan.

In the village of Batuan, *rejang* is performed throughout the rainy season just outside the community temple. During this season of illness the dance has some exorcistic function. In some mountain villages, such as Batur, *gamelan gong gedé* provides the music, while in Tenganan and Asak, the ancient iron-keyed *selundéng* is played for such ceremonial dances. In other villages, the long, ethereal melodic phrases are played on whichever gamelan is on hand, such as *gamelan gong* or *semar pegulingan*.

In *rejang*, the dance itself serves as a religious offering; *gabor*, however, often incorporates a material offering, perhaps a bowl of flowers, carried by each dancer. *Gabor* is also performed by both girls and women, but in closer coordination with the gamelan, particularly the drum *(kendang)*. The basic walk is similar to that of *rejang*, but the dance is livelier and more complex in its patterns and requires special training.

Memendet is performed by dancers in pairs, holding offerings and ritual vessels. The performers vary from village to village: it may be done by males and females joining in a long procession, or by only males in a simple version of *baris*, accompanied by *baris*-style music.

In the Bali Aga villages there are several versions of *mabuang*, a ritual libation dance. The *mabuang kalah* involves unmarried boys and girls arranged across from each other in long rows. Each boy is paired with a girl, they join in a simple and restrained series of gestures, accompanied by the iron-keyed *gamelan selundéng*.

Religious ritual and martial exercise are brought together in ritual *baris*, a male group dance. In the *Kidung Sunda*, an East Javanese historical poem dated to 1550, it is written that seven versions of *bebarisan* were performed at the cremation ceremonies of King Hayam Wuruk. *Baris* literally means "row" or "line" and refers to the most characteristic formation of dancers, who carry heirloom weapons such as the *keris* (dagger), *presi* (shield), *jojor* (lance), or *tumbak* (spear). The dancers' formations traditionally exhibited the splendor of a king's warriors, often described as bodyguards for the deities being honored at the ceremony. The styles of *baris* vary widely, and some mountain villages claim sixteen or twenty unique versions. The largest display of ritual *baris* may be seen at yearly ceremonies for the two great temples, Pura Besakih and Pura Batur.

The *baris* costume uses the standard *prada* gold-leaf floral designs painted on cloth, but it is unique in its headdress, which is triangular and covered with shimmering pieces of mother-of-pearl fixed on tiny springs. Another feature specific to *baris* (and *jauk*) is *awiran*, numerous brightly painted strips of cloth hanging loosely around the body. The dancer's *awiran* and vibrating *gelungan* headdress have a specific role in the choreography. As the *baris* dancer jumps or spins, the costume sways, shimmers, and rustles from side to side. *Baris* is also characterized by martial poses, as if in the midst of combat or lying in wait, ready to spring into action. Flicking eye movements *(seledét)* and shifting glances *(dedeling)* convey impressions from serenity to ferocity or mortal fear. Usually accompanied by the ceremonial *gamelan gong gede*, *baris* is heightened by occasional unison shouts and calls from the dancers.

Baris tumbak is performed by as many as sixty men carrying ten-foot spears. *Baris presi* is danced by groups of six using painted leather shields. *Baris jojor* is danced with spears, while *baris omang* and *baris dadap* utilize decorative shields made from the wood of the magical *dadap* tree. *Baris cina*, performed only in the southern coastal village of Sanur, is a frenetic, wild variety using swords and riding whips, while *baris kekupu* incorporates fans (in Tenganan) or wings (in Lebah) to imitate the movements of butterflies. Performed as a nonceremonial dance by four small boys, the last was developed, or revived, during the 1930s in Lebah, Badung, a village also known for its *légong*.

The term *baris gedé* (great *baris*) is used generically for any group ceremonial *baris*. In some locales it denotes a specific style.

Baris pendent is often performed by four to six boys, or by grown men, sometimes in alternation with *rejang* within the temple. Each dancer holds a bowl of flower offerings *(banten)* in one hand as the group goes through a somewhat elaborate sequence of movements. Among the numerous additional styles are *baris cerek koak* (a quail-like bird), *baris bajra* (mace weapon), *baris bedil* (gun), *baris lutung* (monkey), *baris poléng* (checker-painted lance), and *baris panah* (using bow and arrow). [*See* Baris.]

INDONESIA: Balinese Ceremonial Dance. *Rejang*, a processional dance, performed by women and girls in the village of Tenganan. Linked by their sashes, the dancers move in unison with each age group forming a separate line. (Photograph by Walter Spies/Beryl de Zoete; reprinted from Hitchcock and Norris, 1995, fig. 123.)

An entirely different genre of ritual dance involves direct communication with deities or spirits for the purpose of purification or exorcism during the rainy season or other spiritually unclean *(sebel)* times. In these dances a trance state *(kerauhan)* is the main element. The dance is not merely an offering; it is actually performed by sacred nonhuman personages who have the power to enter dancers and appease local malevolent forces, which may be demonic spirits *(buta-kala)* or human practitioners of black magic *(pengiwa)*. The best-known of these *sang hyang* (revered divinity) dances is *sang hyang dedari*, performed by two preadolescent girls possessed by Widyadari (heavenly nymphs). As the girls sit within the temple waiting to enter the trance state, incense is lit and a *pemangku* priest recites prayers while a chorus of women sing a "smoking melody" *(gending penudusan)* in the style of *kidung* liturgical song. Once the divine presences have descended into the dancers' bodies, they may convey messages of ritual significance, such as cures for illnesses and recipes for spiritual purification. Traditionally, a male *cak* chorus replaces the women's *kidung* once the girls have become possessed. To this complex fabric of percussive vocal sound, the dance begins, often leading to a test of the trance-state in which the girls jump on red-hot embers. Following this, the girls are carried out from the inner temple courtyard, often to the road, in a dance accompanied by a *gamelan pelégongan* or some equivalent.

The young *sang hyang* dancers traditionally chosen from among the village youths are not performers. Their innate gift is the ability to enter the trance state, not to dance. Once within the ritual, however, the possessed dancers often perform difficult choreography in close synchronization, as if the pair had been rehearsed by a careful teacher. They may be lifted onto the shoulders of men, where they stand and sway. Their movements traditionally reflect the world of nature: *kidang rebut muring* imitates a deer disturbed by biting flies; *ngelayak* suggests a branch bending under the weight of many flowers; *sayar soyor* suggests trees swaying in the wind, and *capung mandus*, a bathing dragonfly. These movements are said to be indigenous dance gestures and the basis for more complex dance forms such as *légong*. In turn, *légong* choreography has influenced *sang hyang* movement. In addition to *légong*, the dancers may decide to perform in other styles, such as *baris* or roles of the *Calonarang* magic drama. When the girls are tired of performing, they are carried back inside the temple, where a *pemangku* priest officiates with his *mantra*, holy water, and offerings to the departing divinities.

Sang hyang jaran is a trance dance traditionally performed by a temple priest or chosen boys as part of a ritual exorcism. It involves riding a hobby-horse, accompa-

INDONESIA: Balinese Ceremonial Dance. A row of men carry long spears in a performance of *baris tumbak* in Sukawana. (Photograph by Edward Herbst; used by permission.)

nied by a *cak* chorus, and stepping on glowing cinders. Several varieties of *sang hyang* have been popular as tourist performances since the 1930s. Although performers may enter a trance or semitrance state during these daily or weekly performances, it is more common for the state to be portrayed rather than experienced. The success of a commercial *sang hyang jaran* dancer is often related more to having callused feet from rice-farming than to a psychic disposition.

Berutuk is a rite now unique to the mountain village of Trunyan on the shore of Lake Batur, one of several Bali Aga villages retaining many ancient, pre-Hindu traditions. The *berutuk* ritual is enacted by unmarried young men at irregular intervals to honor His Lordship Déwa Ratu Gedé, the deity of the temple Pura Pancering Jagat (Navel of the World). *Berutuk* is a rite of initiation for boys as well as a rite of origin for the whole village. Men

INDONESIA: *Balinese Ceremonial Dance.* This *berutuk* figure, from the mountain village of Trunyan, is animated by a performer wearing two large banana-leaf skirts, one around his neck and the other around his waist. Wielding two long whips, he strikes at those who come near. (Photograph by Walter Spies/Beryl de Zoete; reprinted from Hitchcock and Norris, 1995, fig. 164.)

cannot officially marry and enter the village council until they have participated in the *berutuk* ceremony. At the same time, the event is said to enact the story of the village's origin when, because of hostility from surrounding villages, the men of Trunyan had to abduct their wives.

For forty-two days preceding the actual rite the young men stay in a village across the lake, learning special prayers and gathering banana leaves for their *berutuk* costumes. After paying respects to the sun deity Bhatara Surya, they visit the underground shrine and statue of Déwa Ratu Gedé and then emerge as *berutuk*s. The banana leaves have been dried and strung into two huge, bushy skirts, one hung from the neck and the other from the waist. The *berutuk*s also wear sacred masks of a king and queen, a prime minister, and the queen's brother. Each *berutuk* has a ten-foot-long fiber whip which he brandishes and cracks throughout the rite. All the others are divided between male (brown and red) and female (white and yellow) masked characters. They all circle the shrine, cracking their whips menacingly, but some villagers take the risk of running up and grabbing a banana leaf from a *berutuk*. Although this provides an element of play, these leaves are believed to possess protective spiritual power.

The king and queen perform a dance enacting the courtship of male and female wild woodfowl. The other *berutuk*s remain on guard, using their whips to keep spectators back. As the queen begins to evade the king, a stylized chase ensues, concluding when the queen throws herself into the lake. The king follows suit, as do the remaining *berutuk*s. As the young men splash about, enjoying their cool bath after a strenuous day, they remove their costumes and masks, which are laid out to dry by village elders.

BIBLIOGRAPHY

Bandem, I Madé. "*Panji* Characterization in the *Gambuh* Dance Drama." Master's thesis, University of California, Los Angeles, 1972.

Bandem, I Madé, and Frederik de Boer. *Balinese Dance in Transition: Kaja and Kelod.* 2d ed. New York, 1995.

Bandem, N. L. N. Swasthi Wijaya. "Dramatari Calonarange Di Singapadu." Master's thesis, Akademi Seni Tari Indonesia, 1982.

Belo, Jane. *Trance in Bali.* New York, 1960.

Belo, Jane, ed. *Traditional Balinese Culture.* New York, 1970.

Covarrubias, Miguel. *Island of Bali.* New York, 1937, 1956.

Daniel, Ana. *Bali: Behind the Mask.* New York, 1981.

de Zoete, Beryl and Walter Spies. *Dance and Drama in Bali* (1938). New ed., New York, 1973.

Eiseman, Fred B. *Bali: Sekala and Niskala.* 2 vols. Berkeley, 1989.

Emigh, John. "Playing with the Past: Visitation and Illustion in the Mask Theater of Bali." *Drama Review* 23 (June 1979): 11–36.

Geertz, Hildred. "A Theatre of Cruelty: The Contexts of a Topéng Performance." In *State and Society of Bali*, edited by Hildred Geertz, pp. 165–198. Leiden, 1991.

Herbst, Edward. *Voices in Bali: Energies and Perceptions in Vocal Music and Dance Theater.* Hanover and London, 1997.

Holt, Claire. *Art in Indonesia, Continuities and Change.* Ithaca, N.Y., 1967.

Hood, Mantle. "The Enduring Tradition: Music and Theater in Java and Bali." In *Indonesia*, edited by Ruth McVey, pp. 438–560. New Haven, 1983.

Hough, Brett. *Contemporary Balinese Dance Spectacles as a National Ritual.* Monash University, Centre of Southeastern Asian Studies, Working Paper no. 74. Clayton, 1992.

Kakul, I Nyoman. "Jelantik Goes to Blambangan." *Drama Review* 23 (1979): 11–36.

Lange, Roderyk. "Galungan in Bali: A Religious Event." *Dance Studies* 15 (1991): 9–67.

Lansing, J. Stephen. *The Three Worlds of Bali.* New York, 1983.

Lendra, I Wayan. "Bali and Grotowski; Some Parallels in the Training Process." In *Drama Review* 35 (Winter 1991): 113–128.

McPhee, Colin. "Dance in Bali." In *Traditional Balinese Culture*, edited by Jane Belo, pp. 290–321. New York, 1970.

Siegel, Marcia B. "Liminality in Balinese Dance." *Drama Review* 35 (Winter 1991): 84–91.

Young, Elizabeth Florence. "Topéng in Bali: Change and Continuity in a Traditional Drama Genre." Ph.D. diss., University of California, San Diego, 1980.

EDWARD HERBST

Balinese Dance Theater

The diverse genres of Balinese dance theater may highlight historical intrigue, romance, comic antics, or magical transformation, or combine any of these elements in myriad ways.

Gambuh. This is the most explicit source of the gestures, choreography, characterization, and narrative elements found in other forms of dance theater. Similarly, *gamelan gambuh* music has been a continual resource for other gamelan styles, which adapt modes, melodies, and musical structure from its repertory. Although seldom seen today, *gambuh* continues to have fundamental influence on almost all Balinese dance theater. The village of Batuan still maintains at least two active *gambuh* ensembles, and Sekolah Tinggi Seni Indonesia, the government performing arts dance academy, has helped revive the waning style of Pedungan village.

Gambuh depicts the pomp, intrigue, and formal manners of the Hindu Javanese Majapahit courts, which influenced Bali most strongly from 1343 until the early sixteenth century. *Gambuh* is still a stately and elaborate genre performed at ceremonies of the royal courts *(puri)*, as well as at some *odalan* temple festivals.

The stories are derived from the *Malat* literature of sixteenth-century East Java, especially the tales of Prince Panji and Princess Candra Kirana, whose romance is continually thwarted by intrigues, obstacles, and adventures. Although other stories can be used, they still adhere to the stock characterizations and standard plot development derived from the Panji cycle. In *gambuh* pageantry and style are somewhat more important than story line. In the past, performances were around four hours in length; a story could be serialized over several days if a large ceremony such as a royal funeral warranted it. Nowadays two-hour performances are more common. In former times *gambuh* ensembles were all-male, but now many roles are performed by girls and young women. The cast can be very large, because each character of rank is preceded and accompanied by his or her own heralds and attendants.

INDONESIA: Balinese Dance Theater. Although *gambuh*, a dance drama depicting characters from the Hindu Javanese Majapahit courts, is the source of much Balinese theater, it is rarely performed today. (*left*) In this scene from a *gambuh* play, the *patih* (prime minister) character receives two *arya* (warrior princes). (*above*) Although in former times *gambuh* was performed exclusively by men, now women play some roles. Here, Ni Nyoman Ganti appears in the role of the *condong* (female court attendant) in a performance at Batuan. (Photograph at right by Walter Spies/Beryl de Zoete; reprinted from Hitchcock and Norris, 1995, fig. 187. Photograph above by Edward Herbst; used by permission.)

INDONESIA: Balinese Dance Theater. *Arja* is a nineteenth-century opera genre derived from the classical *gambuh* dance drama. Here, a *mantri*, a refined hero character from an *arja* play, sings in a loud, wailing voice, lamenting his lost love. (Photograph by Walter Spies/Beryl de Zoete; reprinted from Hitchcock and Norris, 1995, fig. 211.)

Preceding a king are the attendants Demang and Temunggung, outlandish and comical ministers with a *keras* ("strong") style. Their dance shows skilled and stylized characterization of clumsiness and overzealousness. They circle each other merrily, exchanging coarse vocal outbursts of challenge, encouragement, and self-satisfied laughter. The *arya*, the four warrior princes to whom Demang and Temunggung pay respect, are serious and strong. Their walk has a wide gait and prolonged stances, in which one foot or another is lifted high while the supporting leg conveys the power of gravity. The old prime minister (*patih tua*) arrives next, moving and speaking in a refined *manis* style, showing the burden of old age. When the king or prince finally appears, we see the fullest characterization of the *alus* or *manis* male, refined and "sweet." His voice is high, its pitch rising and falling in a sliding, somewhat whining manner, in contrast to the percussive *keras* outbursts of stronger characters. His movement is slow and gradual, punctuated by light, delicate ac-

cents as he walks with a graceful, narrow, winding gait. He is joined by his two servants, Semar and Togog, or Turas, who parody and joke as they interpret the classical Kawi (an obsolete dialect) dialogue of the principal characters into common Balinese for the audience's benefit.

A similar formal entrance is provided for the princess (*putri*), who is ushered in by her maidservant (*condong*) and four ladies-in-waiting, called *kakan-kakan*. The *putri's* dance is restrained and delicate, the epitome of the *manis* style. The dance of the *condong* is energetic and suggestive of *légong*, as are the complex symmetrical patterns of the *kakan-kakan*, all rising, bending, and sinking in synchronization with accents and sudden cadences of the gamelan music. Through these characters we see the compositional roots of *légong*.

The last of the major entrances involves the principal antagonist king (*prabu*) and his large retinue. They are of the *keras* style, strong and strident. The structure of *gambuh* performance is a prototype for other dance dramas, invariably adapted with great freedom to new dramatic contexts. Scenes of meeting (*pengunem*) of main characters, love (*pengipuk*), weeping (*tangisan*), fighting (*pesiat*), and departure (*pangkat*) all have specific musical pieces and poetry, varying also from character to character.

Gamelan gambuh is most distinctive for its chorus of three-foot-long bamboo flutes (*suling*), which impart a soaring, ethereal quality as their sound carries over a light fabric of bronze percussion instruments. The two relatively small drums (*kendang*) provide a tight rhythmic link with the dancers through the elaborate choreographic patterns, as the flutes shift among five modes to connect with the dancers' singing. A bowed lute (*rebab*) with a plaintive sound is the only other melodic instrument employed. A vocalist (*juru tandak*) sits with the musicians, offering occasional narration and song and helping to create the mood for each scene.

Arja. In *arja*, the greatest stylistic emphasis is on the singing, while the narrative is notable for its reliance on romance, dramatic twists, and surprises. Stories may be drawn from the classical Javanese *Malat* literature used in *gambuh*, excerpts from the Kawi *Mahābhārata*, indigenous tales of love and adventure such as *Jayaprana*, or Chinese romantic intrigues such as *Sampik*. Whatever episode is chosen for a performance, roles are developed from *arja's* own set of stock characters, with their own stylized movement, speech, singing, and personalities. Among these characters are the delicate and despairing heroine (*galuh*); her comical lady-in-waiting (*condong* or *inia*); the refined king or prince (*mantri*); a strong-willed queen-mother (*limbur*); her odd, comical attendant, (*désak*); and the zany, ugly princess, Liku, who with the *limbur's* encouragement often competes with the *galuh* for the hero's love. The attendants to the hero, who supply much of the comic antics and story through-line, are two brothers, Punta and Wijil—unmasked versions of *topéng*'s *panasar* and *kartala;* one pompous and overzealous, the other lazy and wisecracking. As the *galuh* must strive against the *liku,* the *mantri* is often set against a coarse male rival, the *mantri buduh.* This "crazy prince" has his own Punta and Wijil attendants, modeled after *wayang* shadow-puppet theater's outrageous Délem and Sangut.

Arja relies on its performers' acting and singing abilities to move its audience to tears or laughter. The song-poem style is *sekar alit,* generally referred to as *tembang arja,* or *arja* songs. Great improvisational skill is prized, particularly with regard to the use of *tembang.* Actors sometimes quote extensively from Balinese texts *(geguritan)* composed in *sekar alit* meter, but much of the story and dialogue is composed spontaneously by the performers, while adhering to strict poetic and melodic rules. Each stock character have a particular stylized way of phrasing songs, melodically and rhythmically, in order to evoke contrasting emotions. The performer is also expected to coordinate each song phrase with a sequence of dance as well as with the instrumental music structure. While the bamboo flute follows and improvises from the dancer's songs the two small drums articulate all gestures and dance sequences, sensitive to sudden cadences and tempo shifts.

Traditional *arja* music is played by the *gamelan gaguntangan* ensemble, named for the bamboo slit-gong which is used instead of bronze gongs. Since the early 1960s, however, the popular *gong kebiar* ensemble has all but replaced the subtle and distinctive *gaguntangan.*

Arja is an early twentieth-century offshoot of the classical *gambuh* theater and employed an all-male cast until the 1920s. At the same time that female performers were brought into *arja, topéng* mask theater was beginning to open up to female performers and *arja* influence, as evidenced by a new genre, *prémbon.* At present, all roles are performed by females, except Punta, Wijil, other comic characters, and a coarse prime minister *(patih).*

In 1958 the government radio station, Radio Republik Indonesia, began broadcasting *arja* on Sunday mornings. The project was facilitated by bringing together many of the most skilled performers from numerous villages, assuring a consistently high level of singing and storytelling. By touring throughout the island in the early 1970s, this all-Bali RRI ensemble introduced a media-inspired star system which has dominated the world of *arja* until the present. Although abridged performances are becoming common, "*arja* RRI" often maintains the practice of starting live performances at about eleven at night and continuing until dawn.

Kécak. Perhaps the best-known of all Balinese dance theater forms, *kécak* or *cak* is actually a recent development performed almost exclusively as a commercial tourist entertainment. It has been called the "Monkey Chant" or "Monkey Dance" in tourist phraseology since the 1930s, when this new dance genre began using the *Rāmāyaṇa* as its main dramatic theme, and the *cak* chorus became associated specifically with the monkey army of Anoman (Hanumān). The secular genre began in the villages of Bedaulu and Bona, where male choral ensembles were already accustomed to accompanying local *sang hyang* ritual trance dances. Groups sprang up in other villages, and it is impossible to trace exactly who is responsible for particular aspects of present-day *cak.* Experiments

INDONESIA: Balinese Dance Theater. Scene from the popular *kécak,* or "Monkey Dance", at Singapadu, Bali. Forming concentric circles around a singer-narrator figure, the large *cak* chorus—named for the wave of "cak" sounds it produces—performs movements in mass unison, including a stretching out of the arms and a trembling of the hands. (Photograph © 1989 by Linda Vartoogian; used by permission.)

began with using the *cak* chorus as a focal point, while dancers adapted *baris* or various stylized animal movements to the musical form. Encouraged by European friends, they began to use episodes out of the *Rāmāyaṇa*, such as the abduction of Sita, the fight between the brothers Subali and Sugriwa, or the entire story from Sita's abduction to the death of Rawana.

The *cak* chorus retains musical elements of the *sang hyang* trance ritual, which is considered by the Balinese to be a primal indigenous form. As the music was adapted from ritual to entertainment, a more elaborate structure evolved, and the size of the chorus expanded to 30 to 150 performers. The "chakke-chak" sound resembling the chatter of monkeys is one of many vocables (such as "tik-tik" or "chuk-chuk") used to suggest the voices of frogs, crickets, and other animals, as well as the wind, ocean waves, and other natural phenomena. As is typical of Balinese music, the rhythmic fabric is woven from an interlocking of small phrases within an eight- or sixteen-beat gong cycle. The sound "cak" is repeated in phrases of three, five, and seven, some singers following the pulse and others filling in between, just anticipating each pulse. Other singers improvise, creating a constantly shifting undercurrent, much as the drums do in instrumental gamelan music. Other sounds are vocal imitations of gamelan instruments, with the characteristic pulsating tones of colotomic instruments ("sir-r-r" for gongs and "pur-r-r" for smaller *kempul*

gongs). Vocables without lexical meaning are interspersed with phrases of Balinese solfeggio—*nding, ndong, ndéng, ndung, ndang*—as well as occasional disjointed words and phrases. The "chak-ke-chak" rhythms are used for the livelier segments, while long, winding melodic phrases accompany slower action.

The *cak* ensemble sits in loosely-arranged concentric circles; all are dressed simply and are bare-chested. A solo singer–narrator *(juru tandak* or *dalang)* sits amid the chorus, speaking for some characters and singing classical Kawi poetry. In some contemporary *cak* performances, *wayang wong*-style storytellers *(panakawan)* fulfill a similar role.

A torch is placed in the center of the chorus, an area large enough to accommodate all the dramatic action of the story. In the early days of *cak,* characters would rise from the chorus, clad as simply as everyone else, perform their roles, and then sink back into the mass of singers. Since 1965, under the influence of the popular *Sendratari Rāmāyaṇa,* characters are generally costumed, some are masked, and entrances and exits are made from outside the circle. Another influence of *Sendratari* is that instead of depicting a single episode, *cak* now often dramatizes the entire epic, from Rāma's banishment to Rawana's death.

The movements of the chorus are synchronized to reflect every rhythm and mood of the music. Slow swaying of the upper torso and head, trembling of hands and out-

INDONESIA: Balinese Dance Theater. Performers of *jangér,* a hybrid dance drama, enacting an episode from the *Mahābhārata.* The dancer at left portrays a heavenly nymph trying to rouse the hero Arjuna from his meditation. (Photograph by Walter Spies / Beryl de Zoete; reprinted from Hitchcock and Norris, 1995, fig. 213.)

stretched arms, and animated shifting of gaze in unison, convey a powerful group dynamic.

Jangér. A hybrid genre, *jangér* has experienced waves of popularity interspersed with periods of neglect since its inception in North Bali early in the twentieth century. The word *jangér* has been translated both as "infatuation" and "humming." The form involves boys and girls in an interaction which in some ways resembles very old social and ritual dance styles. Under the influence of Javanese *stambul* and Western theater styles, however, *jangér* incorporated realistic scene backdrops and Western male costumes—beret, tennis shoes, short trousers, knee socks, neckties, large epaulettes, and so on. The girls' costumes are traditional, basically keeping to the *légong* style. Musical accompaniment is provided by the *gendér wayang* ensemble with additional percussion instruments, including a wide drum (*rebana* or *tambur*) of Arab origin.

The boys are referred to as *kecak* and their songs and movement utilize *kécak* elements. The choreography departs from *kécak* and traditional *baris gedé* in the direction of contemporary military salutes, gymnastic exercises, and marches, as well as jabs and punches derived from the martial arts. The *cak*-style chorus is interspersed with comic nonsense syllables as well as "si do re si do," taken from Western solfeggio.

The *kécak* group alternates with the female performers, whose dance is based on traditional *rajang* and whose music is straightforward folk song set to *gendér* accompaniment. The mood of the performance jumps from the sweet, relaxed style of the girls to the frenetic gestures and calls of the boys. After about thirty minutes this interaction may be followed by a story performed in typical *arja* or *prembon* style.

Basur. The term *Basur* refers to both a character and his story, as well as to the performance genre itself. Although very closely related to *arja*, *Basur* has its own peculiar characterizations, which include the transformation of the man Basur into the demonic Rangda. This makes it something of a male counterpart to the *Calonarang* drama. The *arja* musical ensemble is used, along with *tembang* poetry, but the *Basur* songs have their own distinctive melodies. The theme of *Basur* is an indigenous love story, and the combination of the romantic element with the supernatural aspects of black magic make it a very compelling drama for Balinese audiences.

Cupak. Like *Basur*, *Cupak* denotes a character, his story, and a performance genre. Though stylistically similar to both *arja* and *gambuh*, *Cupak* is now most often performed in a *jangér* context. The story is Balinese, although it is set in the East Javanese court of Daha. Actually, Balinese drama often uses "Daha" as a generalized name for any royal court of the distant past.

The story contrasts the extreme caricature of the boastful, gluttonous, cowardly Cupak with his younger brother Grantang, who is refined and handsome. The narrative involves adventures which lead the brothers to Princess Mustika Ing Daha, who has been kidnapped by the ogre Detya Menarung. The king has promised that whoever rescues his daughter can marry her and succeed him on the throne. Although it is Grantang who saves the princess, Cupak tries to take credit. Eventually, in a royal tournament to test their combat prowess and strength, Grantang prevails and wins the hand of Mustika Ing Daha.

Perhaps the chief allure of *Cupak* is the wild and excessive comedy staged by Cupak and his attendants. The most outrageous and memorable scene involves a gluttonous feast during which Cupak eagerly consumes endless amounts of food and drink. The performer may go into trance at this point, possessed by the spirit of a pig, *sang hyang celeng*. The *wayang* shadow-puppet version of *Cupak* is an unusual and powerful theatrical genre which very few *dalang*s have in their repertory because of its magical aspects.

[*See also* Baris; Gamelan; Kebiar; Légong; Wayang; *and the entries on Kakul and Mario.*]

BIBLIOGRAPHY

Bandem, I Madé. "*Panji* Characterization in the *Gambuh* Dance Drama." Master's thesis, University of California, Los Angeles, 1972.

Bandem, I Madé, and Frederik de Boer. *Balinese Dance in Transition: Kaja and Kelod*. 2d ed. New York, 1995.

Covarrubias, Miguel. *Island of Bali*. New York, 1937, 1956.

Daniel, Ana. *Bali: Behind the Mask*. New York, 1981.

de Zoete, Beryl and Walter Spies. *Dance and Drama in Bali* (1938). New ed., New York, 1973.

Dibia, I Wayan. "Arja: A Sung Dance-Drama of Bali; a Study of Change and Transformation." Ph. D. diss., University of California, Los Angeles, 1992.

Emigh, John. "Playing with the Past: Visitation and Illusion in the Mask Theater of Bali." *Drama Review* 23 (June 1979): 11–36.

Geertz, Clifford. "Deep Play: Notes on the Balinese Cockfight." In Geertz's *The Interpretation of Cultures*. New York, 1973.

Geertz, Hildred. "A Theatre of Cruelty: The Contexts of a Topéng Performance." In *State and Society of Bali*, edited by Hildred Geertz, pp. 165–198. Leiden, 1991.

Herbst, Edward. *Voices in Bali: Energies and Perceptions in Vocal Music and Dance Theater*. Hanover and London, 1997.

Hobart, Angela. *Dancing Shadows of Bali*. London, 1987.

Holt, Claire. *Art in Indonesia, Continuities and Change*. Ithaca, N.Y., 1967.

Hood, Mantle. "The Enduring Tradition: Music and Theater in Java and Bali." In *Indonesia*, edited by Ruth McVey, pp. 438–560. New Haven, 1983.

Kakul, I Nyoman. "Jelantik Goes to Blambangan." *Drama Review* 23 (1979): 11–36.

Lendra, I Wayan. "Bali and Grotowski; Some Parallels in the Training Process." In *Drama Review* 35 (Winter 1991): 113–128.

McPhee, Colin. *A House in Bali*. New York, 1946.

McPhee, Colin. "Children and Music in Bali." In *Childhood in Contemporary Cultures*, edited by Margaret Mead and Martha Wolfenstein. Chicago, 1955.

McPhee, Colin. *Music in Bali*. New Haven, 1966.

McPhee, Colin. "Dance in Bali." In *Traditional Balinese Culture*, edited by Jane Belo, pp. 290–321. New York, 1970.

Robson, S. O. *Wañbañ Wideya, A Javanese Pañji Romance*. The Hague, 1971.

Sugriwa, I Gusti Bagus. *Ilmu Pedalangan/Pewayangan*. Denpasar, 1963.

Sumandhi, I Nyoman. "Gending Iringan Wayang Kulit Bali." In *Pakem wayang parwa Bali*, pp. 3–10. Denpasar, 1978.

Vickers, Adrian, ed. *Being Modern in Bali: Image and Change*. New Haven, 1996.

Wallis, Richard. "The Voice as a Mode of Cultural Expression in Bali." Ph.D. diss., University of Michigan, 1980.

Yayasan Pewayangan daerah Bali. *Pakem Wayang Kulit Bali*. Denpasar, 1978.

Zurbuchen, Mary S. *The Language of Balinese Shadow Theater*. Princeton, 1987.

EDWARD HERBST

Balinese Mask Dance Theater

In Bali, masks are the defining feature of several dance theater genres.

Topéng.   The genre of mask theater called *topéng* is based on the chronicles *(babad)* of the Balinese royal families, their battles and intrigues. Although a few stories,

INDONESIA: Balinese Mask Dance Theater. The comic *topéng* character Gusti Pande, one of King Pemajun's prime ministers. In this scene, he wears an ornate costume to impress the king, but this later gets him into trouble. (Photograph by Walter Spies/Beryl de Zoete; reprinted from Hitchcock and Norris, 1995, fig. 202.)

such as *Arya Damar, Rangga Lawé,* and *Ken Arok,* deal with purely Javanese subjects, it is through *topéng* that the exploits of Bali's descendants of the Majapahit dynasty (1293–1520) are dramatized and honored. The word *topéng* is derived from *tup,* "to cover," and denotes something (carved wood, *kayu pulé*) pressed against the face. The earliest text referring to masked dance in Bali is a copperplate charter, *Praçasti Bebetin* (896 CE), but no description of dance exists from that period. The oldest *topéng* masks may be found at the temple Pura Penataran Topéng in Blahbatu. According to accompanying *lontar* writings, the masks were acquired when King Dalem Batu Renggong sent an expedition to invade the East Javanese kingdom of Blambangan in the late sixteenth century. About a century later a descendant of the king's war minister, Patih Jelantik, composed a dance drama using the captured masks. Chronicles tell how the mask dramas were performed every six months for the palace's temple festivals, first in Klungkung and later at Gelgel, until the Jelantik family was forced to flee to the outlying area of Blahbatu, where their descendants and masks remain to this day. The masks, like those still used in West and Central Java, have a mouthpiece which is held by the dancer's teeth. All other Balinese masks *(tapel)* use an elastic band rather than a mouthpiece to secure the mask to the dancer's head.

From these prototypes Balinese mask-carvers and dancers increased the thematic repertory to include the full range of *Babad Dalem,* or *Usana Bali,* dealing with the genealogical histories of its royal families. Refined *alus* masks are usually white or light yellow. Ministers may be any shade of red or brown and may have either refined or coarse features—such as bulging eyes—depending on their character. Comic characters *(panasar, kartala,* and *bondrés)* may be blue, green, yellow, or any other color that suits the type. Queens or princesses are sometimes included, their complexion being the same as that of the refined king.

Masks, like other features of dramatic characterization, are thought of in terms of stock roles. A particular mask may be used to portray any one of a wide range of historical characters as long as the character type is appropriate. An actor-dancer meditates on the masks in his personal collection and develops a unique spiritual relationship with specific masks and stock characters. Although an adept *topéng* performer is expected to be able to perform many roles, there is some specialization. One performer may be respected for his depiction of the refined prince or king, another for the strong minister, and still others as either *panasar* or *kartala* comic storytellers. The ability to bring a mask alive is the prime skill of the *topéng* performer, and the technique of wearing a mask is the most subtle level of the dance. Headpieces vary according to each character's rank, but the rest of the *topéng* costume is the same for all characters throughout the play.

The graceful dance of Dalem in some ways resembles *gambuh*'s *patih,* but there is a mask-derived intention of directness and simplicity. His bends and turns are gentle and his feet relatively light on the ground. Dalem keeps his feet close together, sometimes delicately crossing one foot over the other as he walks; in contrast, the stance of Patih is wide and his weight rooted solidly to the ground. His steps are higher, deliberate and bold, derived from *gambuh*'s *arya* or *prabu. Topéng* choreographic style varies considerably among villages and regions, and Balinese tend to appreciate particular aesthetic approaches and reject others. Batuan and Singapadu have drawn from *gambuh* for their *topéng* style, while Mas, though influenced by *gambuh,* reflects its *wayang wong* and *wayang* traditions. Much of the *topéng* in the Badung area is said to show influences from *légong* and *kebiar.* [*See* Kebiar *and* Légong.]

Unlike *gambuh* and most female dances, *topéng* requires a spontaneous relationship between dancer and gamelan, in which the musicians must watch for sudden cues from the dancer. He may signal a subtle accent, a more strident walk, a lunge, or an exit. He may gesture for the music to stop altogether while he makes a few extemporaneous comments, announces an entrance, or sings praise. As in other dramatic forms, there are standard musical pieces for each type of character and specific songs for their entrances.

Topéng, like *gambuh,* is a favorite of older men interested in the literary arts of history, poetry, and philosophy. The *panasar* must be able to take the barest facts of a given historical account and expand it through the use of poetry, song, and comic antics, into a two- or three-hour drama. More than in *gambuh* plays, where elaborate choreography often subordinates the plot, the narrative element in *topéng* is central. Because *topéng* is expected to be particularly reflective of the *désa-kala-patra,* or place-time-context of performance, the audience looks for relevance as well as a transcendent aesthetic experience. A story may deal with some audience members' ancestors or the history of their community, while others may find relevance in the improvised digressions on contemporary life—comical, philosophical, or both. [*For discussion of* gambuh, *see article on* Balinese Dance Theater, *above.*]

Before the story begins, there are usually a few introductory *penglembar* dances to create a mood of interest and awe in the audience, as well as to establish a link with the spiritual world of the masks. The most common characters portrayed are an old man (*orang tua*), often a retired minister; a strong, younger minister (*patih*), sometimes rather comical; and a refined king, Dalem, or a *jauk* (discussed below).

INDONESIA: Balinese Mask Dance Theater. The *topéng* dramas from Mas reflect an influence of *wayang,* the Balinese shadow-puppet theater, and *wayang wong,* a related genre performed by human actors. In this scene from a *wayang topéng* play in Mas, the refined King and Queen characters wear *manis* ("sweet") white masks. (Photograph by Walter Spies/Beryl de Zoete; reprinted from Hitchcock and Norris, 1995, fig. 201.)

The two half-masked comic storytellers (*panasar* and *kartala*), may also be referred to as *panasar kelihan* ("older brother") and *panasar cenikan* (the "smaller" one), or collectively as *panakawan.* They are generally servants to the protagonist king or minister; a rival may have his own pair of servants. The *panasar* and *kartala* explain, interpret, and joke about the dramatic situation as the plot unfolds. The chief dramatic characters have full masks, so their mode of expression is dance and mime. The *panasar* and *kartala* speak for these characters, and just as a dancer must form a creative bond with the spiritual entity (*taksu*) of a mask, the *penasar* or *kartala* should also form such a bond as he provides a voice for that character. The language of kings in *topéng* is Kawi, classical Old Javanese; a flowery High Balinese is spoken to kings by lower-ranking characters. Both are highly stylized in performance, with a distinct sense of rhythm and intonation which takes on the quality of melody. Snatches (*tandak* or *cecantungan*) of Kawi or Malat (Middle Javanese) poetry are sung to describe a character or enhance the mood of a scene. In addition, modern colloquial Balinese is spoken between the Panakawan in order to explicate the dramatic situation for the audience as well as to translate each statement delivered in the less familiar language varieties.

Additional half-mask comic characters, called *bondrés*, usually represent common villagers, but sometimes personages such as a Brahmin priest (*pedanda*). These *bondrés* enter late in the story, either to bring the plot down to an earthy level or to create a play within the play, referred to as carangan (branch). This *carangan* may well completely obscure the central plot for a substantial segment of the performance.

Topéng pajegan is a ritual genre that may be performed in the inner yard (*jeroan pura*) of a temple during an *odalan* festival, or in a consecrated area at the home of a family taking part in an important ceremony, such as cremation or other death rites. In *topéng pajegan* a single performer enacts the entire play, including all dance and storytelling roles. Such a performance may last from one to three hours, depending on the performer's skill as well as the requirements and scheduling of the larger ceremony. One unique feature of *topéng pajegan* is a long-haired, grinning, buck-toothed character who comes out once the story is completed. Referred to as *sidha karya* ("he who completes the work"), he may be given offerings, of rice, flowers, Chinese *képéng* coins, and holy water by a priest; he may otherwise go through the ritual of blessing the offerings himself, reciting prayers, *mantra*, and performing sacred hand gestures (*mudrā*) as the gamelan plays and the audience looks on. He then sprinkles the audience with the blessed water and rice and tosses a few blessed *képéng* coins on the ground, for which waiting children scramble. More often this character is known as *pengejukan*, referring to his common practice of grabbing a child from the audience, taking him up in his arms and carrying him around before rewarding him with a *képéng* coin.

Topéng is usually performed by an ensemble of three to five actor-dancers. Another variety, *prémbon*, developed early in the twentieth century, employs nonmasked female dancers to portray female or refined male roles. With an increase in romantic themes and the resulting addition of *arja* theater's sweet, melodic *tembang* songs, *prémbon* has become the most popular form of *topéng*, especially with female audiences. Performances do not generally exceed four hours.

The standard musical accompaniment for *topéng* is *gamelan gong*, and the dance phrasing and vocal style are based on that genre. However, almost any other gamelan can be used, depending on the availability of local ensembles.

Barong. During the holiday season of Galungan one sees magical beasts called *barong* roaming the roads of Bali, from the hill villages down to the seacoast or up toward the mountains. For the ten days from Galungan until Kuningan, processional *gamelan batél* ensembles accompany their *barong* from village to village. A *barong* belongs to a particular temple congregation, where it is kept throughout the year and given offerings on various ritual occasions. Varieties include tiger (*barong macan*), wild boar (*bangkal*), lion (*singha*), elephant (*gaja*), cow (*lembu*), and dog (*asu*).

The large *barong* costume is animated by two dancers. The front dancer holds the mask (*tapel*), which usually has movable jaws allowing the mask to snap and chatter. The basket-like body frame is woven from bamboo and covered, in its simplest form, with cloth painted in stripes, spots, or decorative floral designs, depending on the nature of the creature portrayed. The colorful carved wood mask is the source of the *barong*'s spiritual power (*tenget*); the tail is often touched by children for fun and good luck.

Perhaps every village in Bali has a *barong* costume of some kind. Members of the *barong*'s temple congregation take it out at Galungan time. The *barong* is carried along the roads and paths from village to village, stopping occasionally to perform a dance which may bestow blessings and protection from spiritual ills. Small amounts of money are collected for the maintenance of the *barong* and its required religious offerings.

The most magnificent and popular form is the *barong kékét* or *két* with a stylized lion-like face. This is not referred to as a lion but as Banaspati Raja (King of the Forest); however, the resemblance and historical connection suggest the Chinese lion dance, which spread to many East Asian cultures from China during the Tang dynasty of the seventh to tenth centuries CE. The *barong* is, however, distinctly and uniquely Balinese in performance style and spiritual significance. The mask suggests another historical connection, in its resemblance to Śiva's monstrous manifestation, Kirttimukha, originating with Tantric Śaivism in India.

The coat of the *barong két* is usually made from the bleached fibers of the sugar or *braksok* palm; at times, the feathers of black crows, pigeons, white herons, or peacocks have been used. The coat is also covered with elaborate ornamentations of perforated gold-painted leather inlaid with patterned designs of mirror-like mica chips. A long black beard hangs from his bright red-and-white face.

The dance style of *barong két* alternates strong martial poses and walks with playful animal gestures. The position of the feet changes between turned-out, as in *baris*, and turned-in (pigeon-toed). One comic aspect is his fascination and play with the two or four umbrellas (*pajeng*) positioned to his left and right. Coordination between the front and rear dancer is crucial: they must work together to execute a single gesture or set of steps within a circumscribed rhythmic and melodic phrasing. The front dancer initiates a sequence of movements which cue the rear dancer, whose sequence completes the musical cadence, or *angsel*. The importance of the *kendang* drum here is paramount in responding to every twitch, shift of gaze, and approaching cadence, which is often sudden and unexpected. The musical style is usually that of *baris*, following the *gilak-bapang-gilak* format, basically strident, then subdued and pensive, and then strident again. The *gamelan bebarongan* is similar to the delicate *pelégongan*, using, among other instruments, light cymbals and the distinctive *kentong* gong-chime for mid-phrase punctuation.

The ritual context of the wandering *barong* is not limited to the Galungan season. If an epidemic or disaster occurs, a *barong* may be brought out to exorcise the village of malevolent *buta-kala* spirits and demons. In some villages a *barong két* may be brought out at the full moon for an all-night tour of surrounding villages.

Barong landung are sacred personages very different from the numerous animal varieties of *barong*. This husband and wife, each ten feet tall and animated by a single performer, also roam the countryside during the Galungan holiday season. The mask of Jero Gedé (Big Man) has a black complexion, long hair, and fangs, while Jero Luh (Female Person) suggests Chinese features, pale or yellow in color. Jero Gedé suggests to some an ancient Indian or Dravidian, personage, but many stories identify him as Jero Gedé Mecaling, the tusked giant originally from the neighboring island of Nusa Penida. A story tells how the tusked giant came over to Bali with his attendant demons (*omang* or *jauk*) of every color. While Jero Gedé Mecaling waited on the beach, the *omang* group went inland to destroy. The local people built a *barong* in Jero Gedé's likeness, as well as all kinds of *omang*, which succeeded in scaring the demons away. Ever since, this has been one way of ridding an area of illness and malevolent spirits.

The personalities of the *barong landung* are comical and in many ways endearing. They are occasionally accompanied by three children, who are somewhat shorter and resemble *jauk* or *télék*. They are followed by a small *gamelan batél* ensemble as they walk from place to place. They stop now and then to perform a sequence of songs *(tembang)* and comic dialogue, often dealing with domestic life and sexual humor as well as a little good-natured bickering. Like other *barong*, the *barong landung* belong to a temple and receive offerings at recurring *odalan* celebrations.

Jauk. The mask characters called *jauk* were at one time closely associated with ritual *barong két* dances on such occasions as Galungan and Tumpek Landep, the ritual day honoring sharp objects such as weapons. A variety of dramatic contexts were employed in which a *barong két* and a *jauk* group interacted, sometimes as adversaries and other times as friends. A group of female *jauk luh*, *télék*, or *sandaran* might also enter into a dramatic situation with their male counterparts, as friends or enemies

INDONESIA: Balinese Mask Dance Theater. Jero Gedé (Big Man) and Jero Luh (Female Person) are ten feet tall, husband-and-wife *barong landung* figures. Parading through the streets during the holiday season, these characters make comic displays of affection. (Photograph by Walter Spies/Beryl de Zoete; reprinted from Hitchcock and Norris, 1995, fig. 167.)

according to the story or choreographic idea. The varieties of *jauk* characterization have dwindled during the twentieth century; earlier, episodes from such sources as the *Mahābhārata* were enacted by a full range of *jauk* characters, both refined and coarse, with the help of the standard *panasar* and *kartala* storytellers.

Nowadays the male *jauk* has a red, pink or white mask with large, protruding eyes, a row of shining mother-of-pearl teeth, and a good deal of facial hair, often including a beard. The appearance is part demonic, part human, but quite otherworldly. The mood is comic at times, especially when the dancer improvises a sequence of playful movements in direct interaction with the gamelan's drummer. The *jauk's* unique *gelungan* headdress is a tall, gold-painted, pagoda-like structure resembling in shape a Buddhist *stupa*. His gloved hands are highlighted by long, transparent fingernails made of buffalo horn, set on the ends of hairy fingers. The female *jauk télék* resembles the *sang hyang légong* masks of Ketéwel village, almond-eyed,

INDONESIA: Balinese Mask Dance Theater. The witchlike figure of Rangda. (Photograph by Walter Spies / Beryl de Zoete; reprinted from Hitchcock and Norris, 1995, fig. 36.)

INDONESIA: Balinese Mask Dance Theater. *(above)* Flanked by attendants with parasols, Barong Két emerges from the temple gates. This protective magical beast battles the evil Rangda in the *Calonarang* drama. *(below)* In this scene, the young witch Devi Krishna has assumed the guise of Rangda (left) and faces off with the Patih (Prime Minister) who appears in the guise of the Barong (right). His defenders, the *keris* (dagger) dancers, crouch in the background. (Photographs by Walter Spies / Beryl de Zoete; reprinted from Hitchcock and Norris, 1995, figs. 153 and 181.)

light in color, and refined in features. Still other varieties are said to be somewhere between male and female.

Jauk is often presented in pure dance contexts, such as the *penglembar* dances preceeding *topéng* performances as well as revue-style presentations for tourists. Current *jauk* characterization is generally *keras* (coarse and strong), although varieties of the sweet and refined *jauk manis* still exist. The choreographic style of *jauk* is similar to that of *baris,* while the use of the mask is similar to *topéng. Jauk télék* or *sandaran* dance with *képét* fans; their strikingly simple, refined movements combine aspects of male and female dance styles. The traditional ensemble which accompanies *jauk* is the same as for *barong két*—the sweet and rather ethereal *gamelan bebarongan.*

Calonarang. There are a great many stories in which Barong Két may play a role; he is most often pitted against the character Rangda. But the mask of Rangda (the widow) may be used in many other contexts without a *barong,* as a manifestation of any deity in a wrathful, monstrous state, such as Çiwa in *Semaradana,* Rawana in the *Rāmāyaṇa,* Basur in his magical transformation, or Durga, goddess of death and wife of Çiwa. The most prominant contemporary dramatic genre in which Barong Két and Rangda both participate is *Calonarang*, which enacts the story of the widow of Girah.

The sacred mask, with its intense, protruding eyes and huge white teeth and fangs, suggests a fearsome personage. White goat hair falls from the head to the ground, covering the entire back of the costume. Her long buffalo-horn fingernails are attached to gloves, also covered with hair.

Calonarang is a semihistorical story that takes place in the eleventh-century East Javanese kingdom of Kahuripan. It was only around 1900 that the present dance-drama form of *Calonarang* was first performed, drawing elements from diverse sources such as Rangda and Barong ritual, *gambuh*, and *arja*. *Calonarang* has a role in counteracting and neutralizing (or in some sense appeasing) the work of local practitioners of black magic, and at times of illness and spiritual trouble it is performed near the graveyard, or at *odalan* temple festivals at the Pura Dalem, the temple of the dead.

A *Calonarang* performance often begins with dances of *barong két, baris, jauk*, or *télék*. The play itself generally begins with the Condong, maidservant to Ratna Menggali, the daughter of Calonarang. The Condong's dance is similar to that of *arja*, but the singing is in *tandak* style, following the gamelan melody rather than standard *tembang* poetry form. She soliloquizes in stylized long, sweeping phrases, explaining that no one will marry the beautiful Ratna Menggali because of the evil sorcery of her mother. The Daughter enters, singing delicate *tandak* phrases and dancing in the style of a *putri*, the princess in *arja* and *gambuh*. She asks the Condong why no one has proposed marriage to her, and the servant suggests she ask her mother. The *sisya* then enter, four to six girls who are disciples of the witch, similar in movement to the *kakan-kakan* of *gambuh* but with more twists, turns, and searching, ethereal arm movements. As they finish their dance, the *sisya* sit in two rows and await Calonarang. Usually portrayed by a man, Calonarang enters leaning on a cane, walking slowly and speaking in a hoarse, unearthly voice. She describes to her daughter and disciples the magic they will perform, spreading disease and death to punish the people of the area for ostracizing Ratna Menggali.

After these characters exit, Punta and Wijil, comic servants to King Erlangga, enter. They discuss the fact that the countryside is full of *léyak* (evil spirits) and that something must be done about Calonarang. They await the King, whose strong movements resemble the *prabu* of *gambuh*, as he sings a determined, loud *tandak*. He summons his Minister (*pandung*), who is instructed to go to Girah with a special *keris* in order to kill Calonarang. There is much loud yelling of commands and strident pledges of support, fast wide circles of movement alternating with slow, high, majestic steps.

Now we see the *sisya* in the graveyard, performing a unique dance that replaces many standard female movements with suggestive bends and twists accentuating the buttocks and breasts—gestures indicating their bodily transformation into animal-like *léyak*. The witch arrives as Rangda, shrieking and laughing, and in-

INDONESIA: Balinese Mask Dance Theater. In trance, the *keris* dancers rush forward to attack Rangda. She defends herself by casting a spell, causing the men to fall back and stab their own chests. (Photograph by Walter Spies/Beryl de Zoete; reprinted from Hitchcock and Norris, 1995, fig. 158.)

INDONESIA: Balinese Mask Dance Theater. The *keris* dancers driving Rangda away. A fallen attacker lies in trance on the ground. (Photograph by Walter Spies/Beryl de Zoete; reprinted from Hitchcock and Norris, 1995, fig. 158)

structs the *sisya* to go out and spread disease and destruction.

The main comic scene follows, in which *bondrés* (common villager characters), with slapstick rather than dance, use all the themes of illness, *léyak,* and sorcery. Rangda's assistant, PangPang or Celuluk, arrives to haunt the villagers. With a grotesque mask featuring movable jaw, balding head, long fingernails, and huge sagging breasts, PangPang conveys both menace and humor. After terrifying the *bondrés,* PangPang is in turn chased away by them in a hilarious fight.

Next the Pandung arrives at the shack of Calonarang (now Rangda), and with the vacillating moral support of his servants, he attacks the witch with his *keris.* After violent pushing, stabbing, and kicking, Rangda chases the Pandung away. In the literary version of the story, the Pandung is reduced to ashes by fire emanating from Rangda.

If the Rangda performer has by this time gone into a trance state, he may run around frantically, challenging the local *léyak* population to a fight. The play often ends at this point, and the performer is subdued, his mask is removed, and holy water sprinkled on him by a priest (*pemangku*). At other times, the Barong enters as a minister to King Erlangga and does battle with Rangda. The barong is subdued by Rangda's magic cloth, whereupon his enraged assistants, dressed as ordinary villagers, attack Rangda with their *keris;* but because of her magic spells, each of these villagers turns his *keris* against himself, pressing the dagger to his chest. After they collapse in exhaustion or are subdued by people from the sidelines, the barong enters again and the men are brought out of their trance with holy water, the balance restored.

Many versions of the *Calonarang* story exist, and the literary text offers a different plot than that described here. In that version, King Erlangga calls upon the ascetic holy man Mpu Bharada for a plan to destroy the witch. Mpu Bharada sends his handsome son, Bahula, to court Ratna Menggali, and as they are making love Bahula inquires about the source of the witch's magic. Ratna Menggali gives him her mother's book of magic formulas, which he brings to his father. Once Mpu Bharada knows Calonarang's spells, he has the power to defeat her. When the holy man finally confronts her, a heated argument and test of power ensues. Eventually, she surrenders and is shown the way to heaven. Whichever version is used in performance, it never includes the defeat of Rangda, because the humble purpose of the rite is to appease or subdue evil only temporarily.

BIBLIOGRAPHY

Bandem, I Madé. "*Panji* Characterization in the *Gambuh* Dance Drama." Master's thesis, University of California, Los Angeles, 1972.

Bandem, I Madé, and Frederik de Boer. *Balinese Dance in Transition: Kaja and Kelod.* 2d ed. New York, 1995.

Bandem, N. L. N. Swasthi Wijaya. "Dramatari Calonarange Di Singapadu." Master's thesis, Akademi Seni Tari Indonesia, 1982.

Belo, Jane. *Trance in Bali.* New York, 1960.

Belo, Jane, ed. *Traditional Balinese Culture.* New York, 1970.

Covarrubias, Miguel. *Island of Bali.* New York, 1956.

Daniel, Ana. *Bali: Behind the Mask.* New York, 1981.

de Zoete, Beryl and Walter Spies. *Dance and Drama in Bali* (1938). New ed., New York, 1973.

Dibia, I Wayan. "Arja: A Sung Dance-Drama of Bali; a Study of Change and Transformation." Ph.D. diss., University of California, Los Angeles, 1992.

Emigh, John. "Playing with the Past: Visitation and Illustion in the Mask Theater of Bali." *Drama Review* 23 (June 1979): 11–36.

Geertz, Hildred. "A Theatre of Cruelty: The Contexts of a Topéng Performance." In *State and Society of Bali,* edited by Hildred Geertz, pp. 165–198. Leiden, 1991.

Herbst, Edward. *Voices in Bali: Energies and Perceptions in Vocal Music and Dance Theater.* Hanover and London, 1997.

Holt, Claire. *Art in Indonesia, Continuities and Change.* Ithaca, N.Y., 1967.

Kakul, I Nyoman. "Jelantik Goes to Blambangan." *Drama Review* 23 (1979): 11–36.

Lendra, I Wayan. "Bali and Grotowski; Some Parallels in the Training Process." In *Drama Review* 35 (Winter 1991): 113–128.

McPhee, Colin. "Children and Music in Bali." In *Childhood in Contemporary Cultures,* edited by Margaret Mead and Martha Wolfenstein. Chicago, 1955.

McPhee, Colin. *Music in Bali.* New Haven, 1966.

McPhee, Colin. "Dance in Bali." In *Traditional Balinese Culture,* edited by Jane Belo, pp. 290–321. New York, 1970.

Napier, A. David. *Maska, Transformatin and Paradox.* Berkeley, 1984.

Ramseyer, Urs. *The Art and Culture of Bali.* Oxford, 1977.

Robson, S. O. *Wañbañ Wideya, A Javanese Pañji Romance.* The Hague, 1971.

Robson, S. O. "The Kawi Classics in Bali." In *Bijdragen tot de Taal-, Land-en Volkenkunde* 128 (1972).

Wallis, Richard. "The Voice as a Mode of Cultural Expression in Bali." Ph.D. diss., University of Michigan, 1980.

Zurbuchen, Mary S. "Internal Translation in Balinese Poetry." In *Writing on the Tongue,* edited by A. L. Becker. Ann Arbor, Mich., 1989.

EDWARD HERBST

Javanese Dance Traditions

Java and Bali are the two centers of Indonesian dance and dance theater. Java has become a center of art and cultural development largely because it has long been the center of political authority in Indonesia.

Historical Overview. About 400 CE, Hindu rulers established the kingdom of Tarumanagara in West Java. Other Hindu kingdoms were later established, including Old Mataram (Central Java, eighth to tenth century), Kahuripan (East Java, tenth to eleventh century), Kediri (East Java, eleventh to thirteenth century), Majapahit (East Java, thirteenth to fourteenth century), and Pajajaran (West Java, fourteenth century). Dance theater, which is an important part of Hindu religious ceremony, entered Javanese culture during this period, as did the *Rāmāyaṇa* and *Mahābhārata* epics of India. These Hindu influences later spread to Bali.

The Islamic period in Java began with the establishment of the Demak and Pajang kingdoms in the early sixteenth century in Central Java, followed by Cirebon and Banten in West Java. The kingdom of Mataram (Central Java), founded at the end of the sixteenth century, lasted until the early twentieth century. Under Islamic rule, dance and dance theater lost their religious function but were still practiced in the royal court as entertainment. From Islamic culture the Javanese performing arts adapted the *Menak* cycle, the story of Wong Agung Menak, or Amir Hamzah, uncle of the prophet Muḥammad.

In 1596 Dutch explorers came to Java searching for the "Spice Islands." Eventually they colonized not only Java but the whole Indonesian archipelago. In 1755 they divided the Mataram kingdom into the kingdoms of Surakarta and Jogjakarta. Although these kingdoms were divided again in 1757 and 1811, respectively, and the Republic of Indonesia was established in 1945, traditional Javanese dance is still divided into the Surakarta and Jogjakarta styles.

Javanese Court Dances. By the time Hindu influence was felt in Java, Javanese art and culture had developed to the point that the new elements enriched rather than replaced the existing Javanese forms. The aesthetic of Javanese dance thus remains distinct from the Indian aesthetic. For example, foot-stamping and rhythmical elements are very important in Indian dance, whereas Javanese dance emphasizes refinement and subtlety of movement. Ideal heroes such as Arjuna and Rāma are expressed with strong, forceful movement in Indian dance, but the Javanese dance them in the refined mode.

Like all Javanese dances, Javanese court dances can be divided into male and female dances. Male dance may be in the refined mode (*putra alus*) or in the strong or forceful mode (*putra gagah*). This classification developed when the *wayang wong* dance drama emerged in the eighteenth century. Javanese court dances include the female *bedaya* and *srimpi*, the male *wireng*, and their combinations, *beksan*, *pethilan*, and others.

Bedaya. A court dance performed by nine female relatives of the ruler or by specially chosen ladies-in-waiting, *bedaya* compositions have a story line, but the dancers do not have character roles or recite dialogue. They are normally serene and restrained: the expression of the face and eyes does not change; emotions are expressed by body stance and gestures of the arms, hands, and head, in conjunction with narratives, songs, and gamelan music.

The *bedaya* dancer's basic stance is formed with slightly bent knees and both feet turned out so that the thighs always face front. The dancer moves from one place to another with the soles of the feet always in contact with the ground. There is no running or leaping; to move faster, the dancers trips on tiptoe (*srisig*) or shifts both feet sideways.

INDONESIA: Javanese Dance Traditions. The demon-king Ravana, a character in *wayang wong* plays at the Dalem Pujokusuman, Jogjakarta. Taking a wide, deep stance, this dancer exemplifies the strong male character type (*putra gagah*). (Photograph by Jukka O. Miettinen; used by permission.)

Hand movements have great importance. The usual movement of the hand or hands is in the shape of a spiral. The arms are kept low, as if something were being carried under them. *Bedaya* should convey qualities of patience, calm, and harmony; its ideal movements suggest a swaying palm tree.

All nine *bedaya* dancers dress alike, wearing a trailing batik skirt that confines the body from waist to ankle and a long scarf tied tightly at the front of the hip so that both ends hang loosely to the ankle. The scarf can be used to intensify or accentuate dance movements; the ends may be flicked in time with the gong or held with both hands as the dancer does the *srisig* movement. Sometimes the scarf is used as a weapon or as a link between dancers, who usually make no physical contact.

Bedaya is composed of movement phrases called *sekarans*. Although the names of some *sekarans* refer to movements of animals, such as the eagle (*nggruda*), peacock (*merak kesimpir*), or crow (*gagak linchak*), the movements are so stylized and abstractly symbolic that they are not comprehensible to outsiders.

INDONESIA: Javanese Dance Traditions. *Bedaya* dancers at the sultan's palace in Jogjakarta. With origins in the sixteenth century, this refined ceremonial dance for nine female dancers is one of the oldest extant dance traditions in Java. (Photograph © 1989 by Linda Vartoogian; used by permission.)

The nine *bedaya* dancers are named Endel, Pembatak or Batak, Endel Weton, Gulu, Dada, Buncit, Apit Ngajeng, Apit Wingking, and Apit Meneng. The traditional opening position of *bedaya* dancers is represented diagrammatically as

```
        7    3
1       2    4    5    6
        8    9
```

Kanjeng Gusti Pangeran Hario Hadiwijaya claims that this basic arrangement is the same as the arrangement of small statues on the altar of Gurdwara in Tamil-Chetty temples in Sumatra and Singapore.

Bedaya is believed to be among the oldest dance traditions in Java. Of the many *bedaya*s staged in the courts of Surakarta and Jogjakarta, the most sacred is Surakarta's *Bedaya Ketawang*. Generally performed only once a year, it commemorates the anniversary of the ruler's accession to the throne. It originated during the reign of Sultan Agung of Mataram (1613–1645) and depicts the sacred relationship between Panembahan Senopati, founder of the Mataram dynasty, and the goddess of the South Sea, Kanjeng Ratu Kidul. After the Mataram kingdom was split, King Hamengku Buwana II of Jogjakarta composed the *Bedaya Semang*, which is no longer performed but resembled the *Bedaya Ketawang*.

*Bedaya*s in the court of Surakarta are usually named after the gamelan melody *(gending)* that accompanies them; in the court of Jogjakarta, they are sometimes named after their story themes. *Bedaya Bedah Mediun* depicts the suppression of the rebellion of the regent of Mediun by the kingdom of Mataram; *Bedaya Sayembara Sinta* depicts the meeting and marriage of Prince Rāma and Princess Sinta.

Traditionally, *bedaya* composition consists of two parts. The first is pure dance, and the second tells a story. The floor patterns *(rakit)*, structure of the dance, placement of the dancers, and the structure of the musical accompaniment are formal, following a set pattern. The *bedaya* is thus more than a dramatic story; it is a unified presentation of dance and music. In the *Bedaya Ketawang*, for example, the dramatic scene can only be interpreted, according to the writer Hadiwijaya, when "toward the conclusion of the dance, only two dancers remain standing and, in their dance, seem to court and pour out their passionate love to each other, and it might symbolize Kanjeng Ratu Kidul's love for Ingkang Sinuwun Panembahan Senopati."

Except for the sacred *Bedaya Ketawang*, many *bedaya*s are now taught to students outside the court. Many choreographers now compose new dance dramas using *bedaya* movement phrases and the ensemble of nine female dancers.

Srimpi. A second category of court dance is performed by four female dancers related to the ruler, usually in honor of visiting royalty. Created by Prince Mangkunagara I (1757–1795), the *Srimpi Anglirmendung* from Surakarta was originally a small *bedaya* performed by seven dancers, later reduced to four. In Yogyakarta tradition, the four dancers symbolize the four winds. One *srimpi* from Jogjakarta has five female dancers—*Srimpi Renggawati*, which describes Princess Renggawati catching a white bird that is the animal form of her ideal king, Anglingdarma.

Many other *srimpi* compositions were created by noblemen to commemorate important events. *Srimpi* compositions are usually named for the gamelan melody accompanying them.

Bedaya and *srimpi* are alike in many ways, and even the average Javanese finds it difficult to distinguish them. Neither has dialogue; neither has contrast and dynamic as understood in the West. Even the transitions of the gamelan melody and the dance movements usually occur very slowly. The basic stance, progress in space, and arm and hand movements are basically the same in *bedaya* and *srimpi*, and both are so symbolic and refined that they have little meaning to outsiders.

Nevertheless, every *bedaya* and *srimpi* composition has its characteristic movement phrase, and there is a significant difference between the attitude required of the *srimpi* or *bedaya* dancer. According to Pangeran Suryobrongto of Jogjakarta, a *bedaya* dancer should be steady and tranquil, with the character of a noble; her gaze should penetrate deeply. In contrast, a *srimpi* dancer must express inner brightness in a sophisticated manner without smiling. Her gaze is neither penetrating nor wandering, and she should be attractive without being flirtatious or unstable.

In Jogjakarta the *srimpi* dance is choreographed in pairs; two girls play the role of one character, and the other two play another character. Some Jogjanese *srimpi*s have themes from the Islamic period, such as the battle between Princess Sirtupelaeli and Princess Sudarawerti in the *Menak* story. Two couples in *srimpi* engage in a struggle that represents the eternal struggle of *loroloroning atunggil* (the unity of two contrasting elements in life). One never defeats the other because both elements are necessary: day and night, man and woman.

Bedaya and *srimpi* were originally performed at the front of a noble house in a large open pavilion with four grand pillars. *Bedaya*, with its nine dancers, has more possible spatial arrangements than *srimpi* does, but *srimpi*, with its four dancers, has other choreographic possibilities because of the nature of the space defined by the four pillars.

Wireng. A third genre of court dance is *wireng* (from *wira*, "courageous"), a term used only in the Surakarta court. This traditional martial dance may have originated in a weapons dance of the pre-Hindu period.

Most *wireng* compositions are performed by male dancers in either refined or forceful mode. The less popular female *wireng* was created later. *Wireng* usually depicts combat between couples using such weapons as *keris* (dagger), sword, short stick, lance, or bow and arrow. The dancers have the same dance vocabulary and structure, and they dance in a pair or in symmetrical pairs of two, four, or eight. *Wireng* compositions have no story or dialogue. The fighting scenes are done to the rhythm of a characteristic gamelan melody.

Wireng can be in a refined mode (*wireng alus*) or a forceful mode (*wireng gagah*). *Dhadhap Alus* and *Jemparing Ageng* are refined *wireng*s created during the reign of Susuhunan Paku Buwana II (1727–1749). The former is danced by four refined male dancers holding small shields (*dhadhap*) in their left hands and daggers (*keris*) in their

right hands. The second is danced by male dancers using bows and arrows.

Some *wireng gagah* are *Lawung Ageng*, created by Panembahan Senopati and danced by four athletic males using long lances (*lawung*); and from the same period, *Tameng Towok*, danced by two forceful males using shields and short spears. *Tameng Towok* inspired Susuhunan Paku Buwana II to create the *Wireng Tameng Gleleng* (*gleleng* means "arrogant gait"), danced by four forceful males using shields and daggers.

One of the most famous *wireng*s is *Bondoboyo* (Pacifying Danger) from the lesser court Paku Alaman in Jogjakarta. Created by Sri Paku Alam II (1829–1858), the dance depicts a military exercise and is performed by four forceful males using sabers and shields. A similar dance is *Bondoyudo* (Fighting Hand to Hand) from the court of Mangkunagaran in Surakarta; the dancers use shields and short sticks as their weapons.

Pethilan. A fourth court genre is *pethilan* ("fragment"), which depicts part of a larger story such as the *Mahābhārata*, *Rāmāyaṇa*, or *Panji* epics. *Pethilan*, known in both Surakarta and Jogjakarta, can be a solo, duet, or quartet dance; it can also be danced in pairs, or it may be a multiact drama performed by a greater number of dancers. *Pethilan* can employ two different modes or even combine male and female characters. The dancers wear different costumes appropriate for the characters being danced. Some *pethilan*s are also performed with dialogue and singing.

Examples of solo *pethilan* in Surakarta style are *Gatutkaca Gandrung*, which depicts Gatutkaca, the son of Bima, falling in love with Arjuna's daughter Pregiwa, and *Klono Topéng*, which depicts the *Panji* story of King Klono falling in love with Sekarataji. The latter is performed by a dancer wearing a mask (*topéng*).

Some *pethilan* are duets which developed from *wireng*. The dancers wear identical costumes but are understood to be specific characters. *Wireng Dhadhap Karnotinanding*, for example, depicts the fight between Arjuna and his cousin Karna, who use shields and daggers as their weapons. Other *pethilan*s in duet are *Gatutkaca Antasena*, which depicts the fight between the two sons of Bima (from the *Mahābhārata*) and is danced in strong male style; *Anoman Indrajit*, the fight between the white ape Anoman (Rāma's warrior) and the son of Rahwana (from the *Rāmāyaṇa*), in strong male style; and *Abimanyu Chakil*, the fight between the son of Arjuna and the ogre Chakil (from the *Mahābhārata*). An extended version of the last, called *Kusumayuda* (The Flowering Battle), has five dancers: Abimanyu (refined); Chakil (rough); Gatutkaca (forceful); and two ogres (rough). The first of its two acts features a fight between Abimanyu and Chakil, and the second a fight between Gatutkaca and the two ogres.

Beksan. The name of this genre of court dance is also the High Javanese word for "dance" and encompasses a broader range of dances than either *wireng* or *pethilan*. In Jogjakarta *beksan* refers to solo, duets, quartets, and pair dances. The most popular *beksan*s in Jogjakarta style are the *Beksan Golek* (solo female) and the *Klono Topéng* (solo male). The dances called *wireng* in Surakarta are called *beksan* in Jogjakarta. *Bedaya, srimpi, wireng,* and *pethilan* are sometimes also called *beksan bedaya, beksan srimpi, beksan wireng,* and *beksan pethilan.*

Javanese Dance Theater. The dance theater or dance drama of Java is a distinct art form whose major categories are *wayang wong, largendriya,* and *wayang topeng.*

Wayang wong. The first of these, *wayang wong,* is derived from shadow-puppet theater. *Wayang* is a flat, carved leather puppet mounted on rods and displayed behind the lighted screen of the shadow play, but the word has been extended to mean a dramatic performance with either puppet or human actors.

Wayang is thought to have originated from a form of the ancestor worship in which people made images of ancestors from stone, wood, or animal skins. The images evolved into flat puppets that were believed to call forth and to be entered by ancestral spirits during shadow-puppet plays.

With time *wayang* became the independent art form *pedalangan,* which fuses plastic arts, puppetry, literature, singing, and Javanese music. The term *pedalangan* is derived from *dalang,* who, according to the *Javanese-English Dictionary,* is "the central performer of a leather puppet shadow play, who leads the musicians, narrates, sings, and speaks the dialogue while manipulating the puppets."

During the Hindu-Javanese period, the two epics *Mahābhārata* and *Rāmāyaṇa* contributed themes for the shadow plays. The Javanese then developed *wayang wong,* a dance drama with dialogue, singing, and dancing, accompanied by a gamelan orchestra. Because *wayang wong* has human actors instead of puppets, the *dalang* only narrates, sings, and leads the musicians.

In Jogjakarta *wayang wong* was developed by Sultan Hamengku Buwana I (1755–1792). The first performance held in the court used the play *Gondowerdoyo,* an episode from the *Mahābhārata.* In Surakarta *wayang wong* was developed by Prince Mankunagara I (1757–1795); the first performance in his court was of *Wijanarka,* also an episode from the *Mahābhārata. Wayang wong* dance drama expanded with adaptations from the Hindu epics, leading to the further development of the characterization and aesthetic ideal of Javanese dance.

In Surakarta, the categories of female and refined male dance were divided into *oyi* or *luruh,* with soft speech and subtle movement, and *mbranyak,* which is talkative and has faster movements. An intermediate dance category,

INDONESIA: Javanese Dance Traditions. Susetyo Hario Putro portrays Bathara Guru, in a performance of the *wayang wong* drama *The Meditations of Arjuna* in Jogjakarta. (Photograph © 1989 by Linda Vartoogian; used by permission.)

madyataya, emerged; its style falls between the refined and strong male styles. Strong male dance was divided into three subcategories, *kambeng, kalangkinantang,* and *bapang.* This elaboration in the characterization and movement categories of dance was accompanied by changes in dialogue, music, and dance costumes.

In Jogjakarta *wayang wong* reached its peak during the reign of Sultan Hamengku Buwana VIII (1921–1939). The performance was staged with fifteen episodes, mostly from the *Mahābhārata.* Productions of *Jayasemedi* and *Sri Suwela* (1923), and *Somba Sebit* and *Suciptahening Mintaraga* (1925), each used eight hundred artists and lasted four days. With the establishment of the dance academy Krida Beksan Wirama in 1918, many court dances and *wayang wong* began to be taught to students outside the royal court.

In Surakarta *wayang wong* reached its peak during the reign of Sri Mangkunagara VII (1915–1944), who selected the performers, designed the costumes, and choreographed and directed the performances himself. In Jogjakarta female characters in *wayang wong* were danced by young boys, while in Surakarta women were allowed to dance refined and strong male characters as well as female characters.

Surakarta *wayang wong* spread beyond the court when Susuhunan Paku Buwana X established the Sri Wedari park with a proscenium theater where *wayang wong* is performed six days a week. The founding of a *wayang wong* group was well accepted by the common people and stimulated the founding of many companies that perform commercially as resident groups in big cities or as traveling troupes moving from one city to another. Among these companies were Sri Wanito and Ngesti Pandowo in Semarang and Sri Wandowo in Surabaya.

The newest and most unusual of all Javanese court dance dramas is probably *wayang wong golek menak*, which originated in 1941 when Sultan Hamengku Buwana IX of Jogjakarta decided to create a dance drama in the style of *wayang golek* (a theater of three-dimensional wooden puppets, with the puppeteer as the main actor). The sultan appointed a team headed by Kanjeng Raden Tumenggung Purbaningrat, with Panji Tamaprawira, Sasraprawira, Atmanetya, Kuswaraga, and Kintakamardawa

INDONESIA: Javanese Dance Traditions. Three-dimensional, wooden *wayang golek* puppets. This popular genre, which has a strong tradition in West Java, is said to have been invented in the late sixteenth century by a Javanese Muslim ruler. The *dalang* (puppeteer) often remains visible to the audience as he uses one hand to manipulate the rod making the puppet's head turn and the other hand to control its arms. (Photograph © 1989 by Jack Vartoogian; used by permission.)

as members. The team explored and developed the movement of the puppets to find new movement vocabularies but maintained the characterization used in *wayang wong:* gentle movement for female and refined male roles, and strong movement for male roles.

As in *wayang golek*, the repertory of *wayang wong golek menak* consists of plays based on stories about Amir Hamzah (an uncle of the prophet Muḥammad), whose adventures are related in the Javanese book *Serat Menak*. At first *Menak* stories were performed not as elaborate dance dramas but only as *beksan menak*, dances depicting fights between two *Menak* characters, such as Marmoyo and Raja Jibarya or Sirtupelaeli and Sudarawerti. These basic dance movements and compositions later developed into the elaborate dance dramas known today as *wayang wong golek menak*, in which the dancers also speak the dialogue and sometimes sing. The most popular episode in *wayang wong golek menak* is *Menak Chino*, the story of Dewi Adaninggar, daughter of the Chinese emperor Hong Dede, who is madly in love with the handsome and courageous Wong Agung Menak Jayengrana, or Amir Hamzah.

Beksan golek menak must not be confused with *beksan golek*, a Javanese dance for girls created by Prince Mangkubumi of Jogjakarta and originally performed as an epilogue of a *langendriya* dance drama in the second half of the nineteenth century.

Langendriya. The second major category of Javanese dance drama is *langendriya* (from *langen*, "entertainment," and *driya*, "heart"). The dialogue is sung, and the story presented is *Damarwulan*, a historical romance

INDONESIA: Javanese Dance Traditions. Two performers of *wayang wong golek menak*, a dance drama derived from the *wayang golek* puppet theater. In this genre, first presented in 1941, human actors characterize the movements of wooden rod-puppets. (Photograph © 1989 by Linda Vartoogian; used by permission.)

about the struggle of Queen Ratu Ayu Kencanawungu of Majapahit to suppress the rebellion of Menakjingga, the regent of Blambangan.

Langendriya was created in Surakarta by Raden Mas Hario Tondokusumo. It was presented to Prince Mangkunagara IV (1853–1881) and became the favored entertainment of the court. In Jogjakarta, *langendriya* appeared in 1876, choreographed by Raden Tumenggung Purwadiningrat and Crown Prince Mangkubumi.

Langendriya was originally performed in a squatting position, although in Surakarta it has been performed in the standing position since becoming established at the court. Previously, Surakarta *langendriya* was performed only by female dancers, while in Jogjakarta all the dancers were male. Today, *langendriya* is performed by male and female dancers in both places.

Other Surakarta operas were subsequently composed. *Langen Pranasmara* was created by Raden Mas Hario Tondokusumo during the reign of Susuhunan Paku Buwana IX (1861–1893). It is performed by women dancers and tells the *Panji* love story of Raden Panji Inukertapati, the crown prince of Jenggala, and Dewi Chandrakirana or Dewi Sekartaji of the kingdom of Kediri. *Langen Asmara*, composed by Prince Prabuwijaya, son of King Paku

Buwana IX, also has women dancers but tells the story of Wong Agung Menak.

In Jogjakarta in 1895, Kanjeng Pangeran Hario Yudonegoro III created the dance opera *Langen Mandra Wanara*, literally "a beautiful entertainment in the form of ape dancing." It tells the *Rāmāyaṇa* story in which the ape king Sugriwa and his ape armies help Rāma fight Rahwana to recover Rāma's wife Sītā. *Langen Mandra Wanara* is performed in a squatting position. Unlike *langendriya*, which could only be performed for and by royalty, *Langen Mandra Wanara* was performed and well received in many villages in Jogjakarta.

These dance operas experienced a decline in the 1930s because the court circles in both Jogjakarta and Surakarta preferred *wayang wong*.

Wayang topéng. The third major category of Javanese dance drama is *wayang topéng* (*topéng* means "mask"). The *Panji* story is the usual *wayang topéng* theme, but a few of the dramas, such as *Topéng Madura* in East Java, use themes from the *Mahābhārata*. Three of most popular *Panji* episodes are *Jaka Semawung*, *Jaka Penjaring*, and *Jaka Bluwo*. A *topéng* performance requires about forty masks.

Like the shadow play, *wayang topéng* originated from ancestor worship. During the Kediri period (1045–1222) there was a masked dance drama, *wayang wang*, based on the *Mahābhārata* or *Rāmāyaṇa*; it is considered by many scholars to be the oldest dance drama in Java. According to Javanese tradition, however, *wayang topéng* was created by Sunan Kalijaga, one of the nine miracle-working apostles of Islam in Java.

In some places *wayang topéng* is called *topéng dalang*, because in the past a masked dancer was also a *dalang* or puppeteer of the shadow play. It was also customary in villages to celebrate a wedding ceremony with a *topéng* performance during the day and a shadow play at night. In the Klaten area and in the villages of Jogjakarta, performers still function as both masked dancers and *dalang*.

Topéng barangan, or strolling *topéng*, hired by nobility is performed in the courtyard or in a small area in front of the main hall. *Topéng* dance is presented in the main hall only if it is being performed by the nobility themselves. *Topéng barangan* is usually held during the day.

In the past, Javanese *topéng barangan* had four or five dancers and five musicians. The duration of the performance would depend on the amount of money the performers received or collected from the audience.

In the early twentieth century, Krida Beksa Wirama in Jogjakarta brought together many masked dancers from the villages, and out of this encounter they composed new masked dances. In Surakarta, Raden Mas Hario Tondokusumo, creator of *langendriya* and *langen pranasmara*, was known as an expert *klono topéng* dancer; he learned and rechoreographed *klono topéng* from an episode in the folk masked dance drama.

In Surakarta masks are held by gripping between the teeth a small piece of leather projecting from the inside of the mask's mouth. In Jogjakarta masks are tied to the headdresses of the dancers. The clowns, who speak their own dialogue, wear special masks without lower jaws.

Wayang topéng is also found in Malang and Madura, East Java, where it always employs a narrative theme. There are seven to ten male dancers and twenty-five to thirty masks in a full episode. The dialogue, except for the clowns', is spoken in an East Java dialect by the *dalang*. The gamelan is also played in East Java style.

In Malang, *topéng* is usually performed outdoors. One side of the stage has a cloth backdrop that separates the stage from the dressing room. A gamelan ensemble is arranged at the other side. The *Panji* episodes popular in Malang are *Asmoro Bangun Topo*, *Sayemboro Sodo Lanang*, and *Patih Kudonorowongso;* episodes from the *Mahābhārata* are also performed at times.

[*See also* Asian Martial Arts; Gamelan; *and* Pencak.]

BIBLIOGRAPHY

Ang, Swee-Lin. "The Training of Female Court Dancers in Yogyakarta." *UCLA Journal of Dance Ethnology* 17 (1993): 52–57.
Bandem, I Madé, and Sal Murgiganto. *Teater Daerah Indonesia.* Jogjakarta, 1996.
Banjaran Majapahit. Surabaya, 1993. In English and Indonesian.
Brakel-Papenhuijzen, Clara. *The Bedhaya Court Dances of Central Java.* Leiden, 1992.
Brinner, Benjamon E. "Cultural Matrices and the Shaping of Innovation in Central Javanese Performing Arts." *Ethnomusicology* 39 (Fall 1995): 433–456.
Damais, Aji, ed. *Festival Jakarta 78.* Program published by the Arts Council of Jakarta, 1978.
Ensiklopedi musik dan tari daerah Jawa Barat. Semarang, 1979.
Ensiklopedi musik dan tari daerah Jawa Tengah. Semarang, 1977.
Foley, Kathy. "My Bodies: The Performer in West Java." *Drama Review* 34 (Summer 1990): 62–80.
Hadiwidjojo, K. G. P. H. *Bedaya ketawang.* Jakarta, 1981.
Hazeau, G. A. J. *Bijdrage tot de kennis van het javaansche toneel.* Leiden, 1897.
Kunst, Jaap. *Music in Java: Its History, Its Theory, and Its Technique.* 2 vols. The Hague, 1949.
Morrison, Mirriam J. "Women's Dance and Tradition in Jogjakarta." In *Asian and Pacific Dance: Selected Papers from the 1974 CORD-SEM Conference.* edited by Adrienne L. Kaeppler, New York, 1977.
Murgiyanto, Sal. "Hasta Sawanda: Eight Basic Principles of the Javanese Court Dance." Unpubl. ms., 1978.
Murgiyanto, Sal, and A. M. Munardi. *Topeng Malang.* Jakarta, 1980.
Murgiyanto, Sal, and A. M. Munardi. *Seblang Dan Gandrung.* Jakarta, 1980.
Murgiyanto, Sal, and I. Made Bandem. *Teater Daerah: Sebuah Pengantar.* Jakarta, 1982.
Murgiyanto, Sal. "Basic Principles of Javanese Court Dance." *Dance Research Annual* 15 (1983): 179–184.
Murgiyanto, Sal. *Ketika cahaya merah memudar.* Jakarta, 1993.
Murgiyanto, Sal "Schnittpunkt der Kulturen." *Tanz Affiche* 7 (February–March 1994): 12–14.
Olsin-Windecker, Hilary. "Characterization in Classical Yogyanese Dance." In *Dance as Cultural Heritage*, vol. 1, edited by Betty True Jones. New York, 1983.
Pigeaud, Theodoor. *Javaansche Volkvertoningen.* Jakarta, 1938.
Raffles, Thomas Stamford. *The History of Java.* 2 vols. London, 1817.
Soedarsono. "Classical Javanese Dance." In *Dance in Africa, Asia, and the Pacific*, edited by Judy van Zile. New York, 1976.
Soedarsono. *Wayang Wong: The State Ritual Dance Drama in the Court of Yogyakarta.* Jogjakarta, 1984.
Suharto, Ben. *Tayub.* Jogjakarta, 1980.
Suryaatmadja, R. I. Mamam. *Topeng Cirebon.* Bandung, 1980.
Tirtaamidjaja, Nusjirwan. "A Bedaya Ketawang Dance Performance at the Court of Surakarta." *Indonesia* 1 (April 1967).
Van Ness, Edward C., and Shita Prawirohardjo. *Javanese Wayang Kulit: An Introduction.* Singapore, 1979.

SAL MURGIYANTO

Sumatran Dance Traditions

The diversified dance tradition of Sumatra is as rich as that of Java, though Sumatran dance shows more Islamic influence. The four major ethnic groups in Sumatra are the Aceh (Achehnese), Malay, Batak, and Minangkabau, all of whom have characteristic dances.

The Aceh in northern Sumatra are famous for their tradition of *pantun bersambut*, recitations of four-line poems accompanied by rhythmic movements. This tradition has given birth to many Aceh dances, such as *seduati*, *saman*, *leuweut*, *likok pulo*, *gerimpheng*, and *meusekat*.

The most popular of these dances, *seudati*, is found throughout the Aceh region. It is a group dance performed by eight males in two rows of four. The dancer in the front row at the audience's middle left is called *syekh*, the leader. He commands his dancers to move, change positions, or change the tempo by singing, clapping, smacking his hands on his chest, or snapping his fingers. Two singers *(anouk syahis)* recite and sing to accompany the dance. Many Aceh group dances are presented as a contest. Similar dances, such as *meusekat* and *pho*, are sometimes performed by females.

The greatest concentration of Malays is along the coast of eastern Sumatra. The Malays' traditional dances usually portray a sacrificial ceremony related to work activities such as collecting honey, fishing, or threshing rice. The dances are accompanied by a bamboo flute, a double-headed drum, and readings of sacred verses by the shaman *(pawang)*.

The most important Malay dance is *ronggeng* or *tandak*, a social dance performed by a woman who entertains males in the audience by dancing with them. Originally the dance was performed without any prescribed structure, having no formal introduction or ending. *Ronggeng* was then incorporated to develop a dance in pairs performed at many occasions in the courts. This new dance includes three basic *rentaks* (rhythmic drum motifs that establish specific dance motifs): *rentak senandung, sentak mak inang,* and *rentak iagu dua.* Based on these three *rentaks,* intricate dance steps and variations were elaborated.

In the 1950s, the Sauti created the dance *serampang dua belas.* It is accompanied by violin or accordion, two Malay drums (one large, one small), and a small gong called *chanang* also popular in other parts of Indonesia.

The Batak people, who occupy the interior of the north-central Sumatran plateau, have distinctive dances that are entirely different from those of the lowland Malays and Aceh. In the nineteenth century many Bataks converted to Christianity or Islam, but the people have not abandoned ties to their clans *(marga).* A priest-healer usually leads other villagers in dances that celebrate the marriage and blood ties of the clan.

Among the Bataks' dances is the *hoda-hoda,* the horse dance, associated with death rites. At Huta Siampipira it is performed by three men in a line, one behind another. Those at each end wear masks of dark wood. Another

dance, the *tor-tor* or *boru,* provides an opportunity for young people to become acquainted. It is arranged by a clan. The girl members of the clan commence the dance; boys from other clans join in, dancing around the girls without touching them. Rules that once excluded boys from the girls' clan have now become less rigid.

The dances of the Minangkabau people of western Sumatra have been strongly influenced by Islam. This can be seen in the *indang* dance, in which seven men dance in a row while playing tambourines, an instrument brought to the archipelago by Islamic invaders and used to accompany chanted praises to Allah. Six of the *indang* dancers hold small tambourines *(rapa'is),* and the seventh holds a large one *(rebana).*

An indigenous Minangkabau dance is the *pencak randai* genre. *Pencak-silat* (the martial art of Indonesia) provides the basic movements of all Minangkabau dances. *Randai* is performed by a procession of men to the sound of a drum, tambourines, small gongs, a bamboo flute, and a thin-voiced reed instrument *(pupuik). Randai* is a rhythmic expression of manly grace and vitality, used to teach village youths about the customs and values of the family.

Another dance that uses *pencak* movements is *tari piri-ang,* the plate dance. It is performed by several men, each carrying two plates larger than the spread of his outstretched fingers. On the middle finger the dancer wears a

INDONESIA: Sumatran Dance Traditions. Members of the Romplis Mude company performing *saman,* a traditional dance of the Aceh people of northern Sumatra. (Photograph © 1991 by Jack Vartoogian; used by permission.)

INDONESIA:Sumatran Dance Traditions. Two scenes of a Tobo Batak dance depicting a local legend in the village of Simanindo, Samosir Island, North Sumatra. (Photographs courtesy of Joyce Berry and Elizabeth Jeneid.)

special hard ring that is clicked rhythmically against the plate.

[*See also* Pencak.]

BIBLIOGRAPHY

Holt, Claire. "Batak Dances." *Indonesia* 12 (October 1971).
Holt, Claire. "Dances of Minangkabau." *Indonesia* 14 (October 1973).
Pekan Seni 1976. Jakarta, 1976.

SAL MURGIYANTO

Sundanese Dance Traditions

Today *Sunda* denotes an ethnic group in West Java who speaks the Sundanese language. According to Paramita R. Abdurachman, however *Sunda* once referred to several kingdoms on the northern coast and in the mountainous region Parahyangan (abode of the gods) of West Java.

With the beginning of Indian cultural influence, dance in West Java developed a style of its own, called the West Java or Sunda style. The Hindu-Indonesian kingdoms of Cirebon and Banten were converted to Islam in the early sixteenth century, chiefly because of the influence of the Islamic kingdom of Demak in Central Java. Especially during the Mataram period, the cultural influence of Central Java on these two kingdoms was great, as is evident in the West Java styles of *wayang, gamelan, topéng,* and *bedaya* performance.

Banten collapsed much earlier than Cirebon, where a dance tradition was successfully maintained. Nevertheless, because there were no West Javanese ruling princes to patronize dance during the colonial period, dance here did not develop to the same degree as in the princely courts of Surakarta and Jogjakarta.

Bedaya in the court of Kanoman (Cirebon), according to the writer Soedarsono, was performed by six women and presented dance plays based on the *Menak* stories of the Islamic period. In Cirebon this dance was also called *sinding* (from the word *sinden,* "singing"), because the *bedaya* performers sang as they danced.

In the past, mask dances were often performed by the court, but today the villagers in Cirebon favor *topéng* performances. Before the twentieth century, dance in West Java involved mostly common people, but in the 1920s the *menak* ("nobility") began to take interest in the development of the art.

Masked Dance and Masked Dance Drama. Like the people of Central Java, the Cirebonese believe that *wayang topéng* was created by Sunan Kalijaga. The first person to be trained by Sunan was Pangeran Bagusan, who is believed to be the ancestor of the *dalang topéng*s in many villages of Cirebon. Even today many Cirebonese mask dancers regard Bagusan's grave as a holy place which they visit in order to pray for his mercy.

Although Sunan Kalijaga used *topéng* to propagate Islam, *topéng*'s relation to ancestor worship has not vanished completely. In Cirebon today, *topéng* is still performed as homage to ancestors at their tombs.

In Cirebon the individual characters and the plays used in *topéng* are the same as in Central and East Java, where they almost certainly originated. Unique to Cirebon, however, are the manner of presentation, the liveliness of the dances, and the dramatic atmosphere engendered by the low tones of the Cirebon gamelan as it follows the movements of the dancers.

Topéng performance in Cirebon is divided into the small-scale *topéng babakan* and the large-scale *wayang topéng. Topéng babakan* is not usually danced in its entirety but only in scenes using five or six masks. Its structure is simpler than that of *wayang topéng* and can also be used by strolling *topéng* ensembles. The dancers (or sometimes a single main dancer of the group) begin each scene sitting on the wooden box in which they keep the masks. Each character is usually danced first without the mask, which is wrapped in a piece of cloth and held in the right hand.

The first of the five *topéng babakan* scenes is the Panji dance. Brilliant in its simplicity, it is extremely refined and is contrasted with vigorous musical accompaniment. The Panji hero wears a smooth white mask symbolizing his self-control in the midst of a chaotic world.

The Pamindo (second) scene also uses a white mask. Its movements are smooth but more accentuated and faster, characterizing a young gentleman who has not yet reached maturity.

The third scene is called *rumyang* or *parumyangan* and has many variations in Cirebon. In Gegesik, this dance does not even exist, whereas in Cileuweung and Mayung it is usually performed last, after the *Klana* dance. The *rumyang* character wears a pink mask throughout the dance.

Tumenggung is the fourth scene. The character wears a pink or brown mask with a long nose and big round eyes, and his movements are strong, vigorous, and decisive. Tumenggung is usually followed by the clown *(bodor)* dance, which serves as an interlude. Tumenggung is to become King Bawarna's son-in-law on the condition that he defeat Jinggananom from Jongjola, who has formed his own government and ceased to pay tribute to King Bawarna.

The fifth scene, Klana, depicts the giant King Klana, who uses a red mask signifying a greedy, angry, rude personality. He has no self-control. His supernatural powers have made him arrogant and greedy, and his desires drive him crazy.

The five main mask dances (except the *bodor* Jinggananom) are sometimes performed by a single dancer. *Topéng babakan* is accompanied by *gamelan pelog* and is usually performed from 9:00 in the morning to 3:00 in the afternoon.

Wayang Topéng or Wayang Wong. This genre is preferred by rich villagers who disdain to hire a small-scale *topéng* performance. A large-scale *topéng* performance uses the *Damarwulan, Mahābārata,* or *Panji* stories used in *wayang* (shadow puppet plays). It also uses human actors, or *wong.* Large-scale *topéng* is therefore called *wayang topéng* or *wayang wong,* especially in Cirebon, where the dance uses twenty to thirty masks and is accompanied by *gamelan slendro.* The Jaka Bluwo episode from the *Panji* cycle is one of the most popular plays in Cirebonese *wayang wong.*

A complete performance of *wayang topéng* can take a

INDONESIA: Sundanese Dance Traditions. (*above*) Keni Arja as Pamindo in a scene from a *topéng* play performed at Plumbon, a village near Cirebon in Sunda, West Java. (*opposite*) In this scene, Sandrut Bin Sarwiti appears in the role of the *bodor* ("clown"). The performer Sujana Arja is seated at right. (Photograph above © 1989 by Linda Vartoogian; photograph opposite © 1989 by Jack Vartoogian; both used by permission.)

whole day. *Wayang wong* are performed less often than *topéng babakan* because of their much greater expense. The influence of Central Javanese and East Javanese *topéng* is found not only in Cirebon but also in the folk traditions of Jakarta and Karawang.

Women's Dances. *Ronggeng* is a dance performed by a woman for the purpose of entertainment. A statue at the Dieng temple and reliefs at the Borobudur and the Prambanan temples indicate that *ronggeng* existed as early as the eighth or ninth century.

In Ciamis there is *ronggeng gunung,* in which a female dancer *(ronggeng)* starts the performance by singing while an audience gathers. Later the *ronggeng* dances with men from the audience. The accompaniment of the *ronggeng* dance is very simple: a small drum *(kulanter),* a gong, a *rebab* (a two-string gamelan cello), and a set of three inverted bronze bowls *(ketuk tilu).*

In his *History of Java,* Thomas Stamford Raffles mentioned that *ronggeng* performances of the nineteenth century were sometimes danced by one woman but often by several women. While dancing, the women also sang. Noblemen attending a *ronggeng* performance usually joined the dancing.

Ronggeng is the predecessor of the *ketuk tilu* and *tayub* dances, in which one or more women dancers entertain men from the audience by dancing with them. The *ketuk tilu* uses several women dancers and is named for the musical instrument that sets the rhythm of the dance. A full performance consists of four segments. In the first, called *tatalu*, the gamelan is played to gather an audience, which will automatically form an open arena *(kalangan)*. Next, in *jajangkungan*, *ronggeng* dancers introduce themselves by walking around the *kalangan*, which has a three-branched oil lamp at the center. During *wawayangan*, *ronggeng*s sing one after another and to a dance similar to the Sudanese *wayang wong* as they select men from the audience to be their partners. Finally, all the *ronggengs* dance in pairs with the men, whose dance movements are

based on the Sundanese martial art *pencak*. Today the most popular *ketuk tilu* is the *jaipongan*, a version of which is presented in many Jakarta nightclubs.

Tayub is a variation of *ronggeng* dance popular among the nobility of West Java. As in *ketuk tilu*, a woman dancer accompanies male guests in a wedding party or other celebration. But whereas *ketuk tilu* is performed outdoors with simple musical instruments and spontaneous dance movements, *tayub* is always performed indoors accompanied by a full *gamelan slendro* or *pelog* and has standardized movements. The woman dancer is also called *sinden* (female vocalist) because she sings while dancing.

After the opening gamelan melodies, one or more persons, on behalf of the host, dances toward the most distinguished guest. One of the dancers presents the honored guest with a dagger and a dance scarf to hold as he begins the *tayub* by dancing with the *ronggeng*. A second honored guest is then invited to dance with the *ronggeng*. He may dance escorted by another male guest if he wishes; these

escorts are called *nairan*. Each guest usually dances to his favorite melody and after concluding his dance returns the dagger and scarf to the host. He puts some money in a designated place and may also tip the *ronggeng*.

Tayub is known throughout Java. The dance movements and accompaniment are relatively formal and standardized among the nobility but rough and sometimes rude among the common people.

In Central and East Java the term *ronggeng* is no longer used; the woman dancer is usually called *ledek* or *taledek*. In the eastern part of East Java one finds a dance similar to *tayub* called *gandrung banyuwangi*.

Ibing Kursus. This style of dance, also called *tari kursus*, emerged in West Java in the 1920s. At that time many noble families in the Priangan region, who had long hired Cirebonese *topéng barangan* performances and were acquainted with the *tayub*, combined the two into a new dance. This new style was taught in the *peguron*, or informal school, established in many nobles' houses.

Unlike the relatively free and spontaneous *tayub*, *tari kursus* is standardized and is taught systematically. It reached its peak from 1930 to 1945, when almost every region in West Java had its own *peguron*. The most famous was Wirahma Sari, under the direction of Raden Sambas Wirakusumah.

The basic categories of *ibing kursus* are *lenyepan* or *leyepan*, with refined movement and slow tempo; *nyatria*, with refined movement and faster tempo, sometimes called *gawil; monggawa*, with strong, forceful movement and medium tempo; and *ngalana*, with forceful, dynamic movement and fast tempo. These categories have characterizations similar to those of *wayang* (shadow play) and Cirebonese *topéng*.

The *tari kursus* movement vocabulary was used by many dance teachers, including Raden Cece Somantri, Raden Sambas Wirakusumah, and Raden Maman Suriaatmaja, to create Sundanese female dance. *Tari kursus* was also used in choreographing the Sundanese *wayang wong* dance drama which emerged later and other new forms of Sundanese dance and dance drama. The *ibing kursus* has become the most popular Sundanese dance today.

Dance Education. Javanese and Sundanese dance and dance theater are now taught widely in many private studios and studios sponsored by local communities. The Ministry of Education and Culture of the Republic of Indonesia has opened many formal performing arts schools in different regions. There are high schools for traditional performing arts in Surabaya (East Java), Surakarta and Jogjakarta (Central Java), and Bandung (West Java). On the university level, there are dance academies in Jogjakarta and Bandung and *karawitan* academies in Surakarta and at the Jakarta Institute of Arts.

SAL MURGIYANTO

Dance Traditions of the Outlying Islands

The major outlying regions of Indonesia are Kalimantan, Sulawesi, Irian Jaya, and Nusa Tenggara, which includes Lombok and Timor. Because these regions are more remote from India and the Malayasian peninsula than are Sumatra and Java, they have been less influenced by Hindu and Islamic culture and have maintained indigenous dance forms to a greater degree. Where these regions were reached by Hindu or Islamic influence, the dance traditions are likely to have elements also found in Sumatra and Java. For example, the strongly Islamic dance *zapin* of Sumatra's eastern coast is also found with slight variations in Kalimantan. *Rodat*, a dance using the Islamic tambourine, is found not only in Sumatra but also in Nusa Tenggara and western Kalimantan.

To the degree that alien religions, including Christianity, have achieved a foothold, indigenous Indonesian beliefs, in which ancestor worship is central, have dwindled if not disappeared altogether. But in places where these alien religions have less influence or have failed to penetrate, rites are still held to invoke ancestral spirits or deities by dancing and singing.

The rites of ancestor worship are presided over by a male or female medium, referred to in the interior of Kalimantan as *balian* or *belian*, in Minahasa (northern Sulawesi) as *walian*, in southern Sulawesi as *bissu*, in the Batak lands as *sibasso*, and in Lombok as *pakon*. In these areas, dancing is integral to the medium's ritual.

To maintain relationships with their dead, the Asmat people in the interior of Irian Jaya erect a huge wooden ancestral statue in front of the men's house. The ritual dance *bis pokmbui* must be performed when the statue is erected. Boys and girls, men and women, children and adults all participate in the dance, accompanied by the sound of the *tifa*, a small drum.

In central Sulawesi people carry out the ritual war dance *rego* to secure the victory of their heroes going to battle. Similar war dances found in Nusa Tenggara are the *toda gu, maekat*, and *kataga*.

In central Kalimantan people perform the *kanjan halu* for the fertility of the soil. In southern Sulawesi they express their gratitude and joy after a bountiful harvest by performing the *ratte puyo*.

There are social group dances on occasions such as weddings, rice harvests, and festivals in many parts of Indonesia. *Mapia, yosim*, and *pancar* are the best-known social dances in Irian Jaya. The Dayak people in Kalimantan have the *manasai*, in which men and women alternately dance in a circle. In Timor, the social group dance is called *biddu*.

Originating from the Maluku and Minahasa is the *lenso*, or handkerchief dance. This social dance requires men and women to move about in couples without coming into physical contact; while dancing, each person holds a handkerchief in his or her hand.

When a social dance is performed by couples of opposite sexes, the most prominent male guest is often invited to dance by the eldest hostess. Professional female dancers who—like the *ronggeng* of northern Sumatra and West Java, the *taledek* of central Java, and the *jogéd* of Bali—dance with males in the audiences are also found in southern Sulawesi (where they are called *pejoge*), southern Sumatra *(pelandok)*, and Lombok *(gandrung)*. This genre of dance is very much on the decline.

Although they are part of sacred ceremonies, dances may also serve as recreation and entertainment. Where indigenous Indonesian beliefs have been supplanted by Islam, Christianity, or the effects of modern life, secular functions of dance predominate. Where conditions are favorable, secular dances may develop into an art in themselves, practiced for their beauty alone. For example, the ritual *belian dadas* of central Kalimantan priestesses survives mostly as a form of entertainment, having undergone modernization in technique, costumes, and musical accompaniment. Similarly, the *maengket* dance from Minahasa, performed by men and women in a circular formation, was in the past a magical and religious rite. It has now become a form of entertainment and has been altered many times, although it is still claimed that the dance is a manifestation of the people's cheerfulness, gratitude to God, and hope for a good rice harvest.

BIBLIOGRAPHY

Ensiklopedi musik dan tari daerah Irian Jaya. Jayapura, 1980.
Ensiklopedi musik dan tari daerah Sulawesi Utara. Manado, 1978.
Grund, Francoise. "Un archipel aux portes de l'Asie: Les Moluques, iles de danses." *Danser* (March 1992): 26–29.
Halilintar, Lathief. *Tari-tarian daerah Bugis.* Jogjakarta, 1983.
Holt, Claire. *Dance Quest in Celebes.* Paris, 1939.
Nadjamuddin, Munasiah. *Tari tradisional Sulawesi Selatan.* Ujung Pandang, 1982.
Sapada, Andi Nuhani. *Tari kreasi baru Sulawesi Selantan.* Ujung Pandang, 1975.

SAL MURGIYANTO

Dance Research and Publication

There are no extant manuscripts treating dance in depth during very early times in Indonesia. Among the earliest sources mentioning dance is *Sumanasantaka* (Death by Means of the Sumanasa Flower), dating from twelfth-century Java, which makes passing mention of a performance of dance drama. Passing references are also found in *Nagarakertagama* (The Kingdom Ordered According to Holy Tradition), from fourteenth-century Java, in which the court poet Prapanca describes a masked play; and *Calon Arang*, from fifteenth- or sixteenth-century Java and Bali, which is set in the eleventh century and describes the dancing of demons and ghosts.

Tales of the *Panji* cycle, set in twelfth-century Java, often include dance descriptions. The historical accuracy of these stories, however, is questionable; they were written after 1600 and probably reflect contemporary activities, either accurately or in idealized form.

Many court manuscripts of Java and Bali include dance scenes as part of the setting of palace life. Examples are *Serat Ranggalawe* (Story of Ranggalawe), written in fourteenth-century Java; *Serat Pranacitra–Rara Mendut* (Story of Pranacitra and Rara Mendut), seventeenth-century Java; *Babad Giyanti* (History of the Division of the Kingdom), eighteenth-century Java; and *Babad Dalem* (Court Chronicles), eighteenth- and nineteenth-century Bali. Additionally, manuscripts containing notations for palace dances performed from the eighteenth century on may be found in the libraries of the four courts of Java—Jogjakarta, Surakarta, Mangkunagaran, and Paku Alaman. These documents in Javanese script include a few diagrams but are difficult to use for accurate dance reconstruction. Cornell University houses microfilms of the Surakarta and Mangkunagaran court manuscripts.

Serat Centhini (The Book of Centhini), dating from nineteenth-century Java, is an encyclopedia of Javanese subjects. It contains a wealth of information about itinerant dancers and social dancing.

Scholarly periodicals in indigenous languages began only recently. *Adat Istiadat dan Tjerita Rakjat* (Customs, Traditions, and Folklore), published in Indonesian during the 1960s, occasionally included articles on Javanese dance. Another Indonesian-language periodical, *Analisis Kebudayaan* (Analysis of Culture), published three times a year since 1980, contains occasional articles on dance and has devoted several issues entirely to it. Black-and-white photographs are included in this publication, but their quality is only fair. *Semi Pertunjukan Indonesia*, published since 1990, also occasionally includes articles on Indonesian dance.

The popular Indonesian weeklies *Tempo*, *Topik*, and *Gatra* print reviews of new dance pieces and interviews with dancers and choreographers.

Several periodicals in Western languages provide important information, and Dutch publications are also valuable for both the content and quality of their photographic materials. Noteworthy is *Nederlandsch Indie Oud en Nieuw* (Netherlands Indies Old and New), published from 1916 to 1937, which contained numerous articles on dance of all types from many islands.

Djawa (Java), published from 1921 to 1940, had regular features written by both native and Dutch authors on Javanese court and folk dances, with an ethnographic focus. Its excellent black-and-white photographs are useful for research.

Significant English-language periodicals are *Indonesia* and *Review of Indonesian and Malayan Affairs*, both of which contain excellent black-and-white photographs accompanying occasional articles by Indonesians and foreigners.

The German-language *Internationale Archiv für Ethnographie* occasionally publishes scholarly ethnographic articles on dance, with many excellent photographs and color illustrations. Several complete issues of this publication are devoted to dance, for example, volume 14 (1901) on masked genres. A valuable source for writings prior to the twentieth century is G. J. Nieuwenhuis's bibliography of Indonesian dance in volume 23 (1916). Although this bibliography does not include full citations for entries, its sources, arranged by island, constitute a useful starting point for research.

A great deal of research has been done on religion, particularly in Bali, and many related publications include discussions of dance; see, for example, Jane Belo's *Bali: Rangda and Barong* (1949) and *Bali: Temple Festival* (1953) and her edited volume *Traditional Balinese Culture* (1970). Anthropologists have also written on dance and provide the only sources available for remote regions. Examples include Gregory Bateson and Margaret Mead's *Balinese Character* (1942), B. A. G. Vroklage's *Ethnographie der Belu in Zentral-Timor* (1953) and P. Voorhoeve's *De Dans met de Bedjan* (1940). Surprisingly, ethnomusicologists—except for Colin McPhee in his *Music in Bali* (1966)—have not dealt with dance to any great extent in spite of the close relationship between dance and music. They have, however, notated the music and texts for dances; see, for example, Jaap Kunst's *Music in Java* (1949), with an expanded version published in 1973.

Research on the plastic arts often includes information about textiles used in dance costumes, the carving of masks for dance, and the relationship of puppets to dance. Such works are usually lavishly illustrated, often including photographs of dancers in costume. Particularly noteworthy is Claire Holt's *Art in Indonesia* (1967), which contains useful information specifically about dance.

Some historical works, such as Thomas Raffles's *The History of Java* (1817), include descriptions of dance.

A number of organizations support research, sponsor performances of traditional and new dance, conduct seminars and lectures, and contribute to publishing. These include Departemen Pendidikan dan Kabudayaan/Direktorat Jendral Kebudayaan (Department of Education and Culture/Directorate General of Culture), Dewan Kesenian (Arts Council, with local chapters), Proyek Pengkajian Kebudayaan Nusantara–Javanologi (Project for the Study of Indonesian Culture–Javanology), and Institut Seni Indonesia (Indonesian Arts Institute).

A secondary-level system comprising Sekolah Menengah Karawitan Indonesia, Konservatori Tari Indonesia, and Konservatori Karawitan Indonesia (Indonesian Arts High School, Indonesian Dance Conservatory, and Indonesian Music Conservatory) provides programs in traditional music and dance throughout Indonesia. In addition to sponsoring performances of traditional art forms, it publishes monographs. At the university level, Akademi Seni Tari Indonesia (Indonesian Dance Academy), a government-run institution with branches in Yogyakarta and Bandung (Java), Denpasar (Bali), and Padang Panjang (Sumatra), sponsors performances of traditional and contemporary dance, holds lectures and seminars, and requires theses for both bachelor's and master's degrees. A similar institution, Akademi Seni Karawitan Indonesia and Lembaga Pusat Kesenian Jawa (Indonesian Music Academy and Central Institute for Javanese Arts) is located in Surakarta, Java.

The government is actively involved in supporting dance, primarily through the activities of the department of education. Wijayakusuma Awards, comparable to the national treasure status awarded in other countries, are presented to selected artists. Teams are sponsored to conduct research on traditional culture in various areas, and their findings are published. The government also sponsors annual choreographic competitions in Jakarta and runs Indonesia's television stations, which frequently broadcast performances of dances from all regions of Indonesia.

Dutch and foreign writings tend to be mainly ethnographic and anthropological, well documented and well photographed, and published in journal or book form. Indonesian writings, in contrast, are mainly historical, descriptive, and analytical and vary in documentation. Generally, they are poorly printed and available in limited quantities or are unavailable outside the geographic area with which they deal. Graduate theses usually remain unpublished and are difficult to obtain unless one is enrolled in the school from which they originated.

Current publications are mostly articles and essays in a variety of magazines and journals. There are a few books, usually collections from several contributors; see, for example, *Mengenal Tari Klasik Gaya Yogyakarta* (Getting to Know Classical Jogjanese Dance), edited by Fred Wibowo (1981).

What little criticism appears usually deals with performances of mixed styles or Western dance. Comparisons between regional dance forms are more common.

In addition to government sources, Universitas Gajah Mada publishes some books on dance, and Gunung Agung has issued several books on dance in English. The most notable foreign publishers are G. Kolff and Company (before the 1950s) and Cornell University Press.

Among the most prolific writers are I Madé Bandem (*Kaja and Kelod: Balinese Dance in Transition*, 1981, with Fredrik Eugene de Boer); Claire Holt (*Dance Quest in Celebes*, 1939); Theodore Bernard van Lelyveld (*De

Javaansche Danskunst, Art of Javanese Dance, 1931; Theodore G. Th. Pigeaud (*Javaanse Volksvertoningen, Javanese Folk Performances*, 1938, and *Java in the 14th Century: A Study in Cultural History*, 5 volumes, 1960–1963); Soedarsono (*Djawa dan Bali: Dua pusat perkembangan drama tari tradisionil di Indonesia* [Java and Bali: Two Centers of Development of Traditional Dramatic Dance in Indonesia], 1972; *Mengenal Tari-tarian Rakyat di Daerah Istimewa Yogyakarta* [Getting to Know Folk Dances in the Special Region of Jogjakarkta], 1976; *Bebarapa Faktor Penyebab Kemunduran Wayang Wong Gaya Yogyakarta* [Several Factors Causing the Decline of Jogjakarta-Style *Wayang Wong*], 1979–1980; and *Wayang Wong in the Yogyakarta Kraton: History, Ritual Aspects, Literary Aspects, and Characterization*, 1984); Ben Suharto (*Langen Mandra Wanara di Daerah Istimewa Yogyakarta* [*Langen Mandra Wanara* in the Special Region of Jogjakarta], 1979, and *Tayub: Pengamatan dari segi tari pergaulan serta kaitannya dengan unsur upacara kesuburan* [*Tayub:* Observations on Social Dance Aspects and Connections with Elements of Fertility Rites], 1980); G. B. P. H. Suryobrongto (*Tari Klasik Gaya Yogyakarta* [Classical Jogjakarta-Style Dance], 1976); and Beryl de Zoete and Walter Spies (*Dance and Drama in Bali*, 1938). Articles by Sal Murgiyanto and Edi Sedyawati appear frequently in periodicals mentioned previously.

Although Indonesia contains thirteen thousand islands, dance writings have dealt primarily with Java and Bali; Sumatra and Sulawesi have been dealt with only in recent times. This focus undoubtedly resulted from the lack of court scribes on other islands and the concentrated interest of the Dutch in Java and Bali. A contributor to balancing the geographic focus is a twelve-volume series, *Republik Indonesia*, published in 1953 by Kementerian Penerangan (Ministry of Information). Each volume treats a major cultural area of Indonesia and includes a chapter on dance. The text is in Indonesian.

Another valuable source of information is programs from dance schools, which often include histories of the dances performed. During the 1920s the Java Institute printed elaborate booklets in Dutch, with excellent photographs. Similar booklets, in Dutch or Javanese, were printed by Jogjakarta Palace from the 1920s to the 1930s.

Indonesia has captured the fancy of many filmmakers, and researchers have used film to document their subjects of study. A great deal of valuable research material is contained on celluloid. Among early films is Margaret Mead and Gregory Bateson's *Trance and Dance in Bali* (1938). Also in 1938, Claire Holt assisted Rolf de Maré from the Paris Archives Internationales de la Danse in documenting dance, particularly from Bali, Sumatra, Nias, and Sulawesi (formerly known as Celebes). Some of Holt's materials are now available at the Dansmuseet in Stockholm, Sweden, and at the Dance Collection of the New York

Public Library in New York City. The latter collection also houses some of the earliest films about dance, including those of Tassilo Adam, official ethnologist of the Governor General of the Dutch East Indies, who documented dance in the context of court life. Some films are now available commercially, such as the *Miracle of Bali* series, which contains a great deal of dance in its three films.

SAL MURGIYANTO and GARRETT KAM

INDRANI (Indrani Bajpai Rahman; born 19 September 1930 in Madras), Indian dancer. The only child of the well-known dancer and teacher Ragini Devi (an American, born Esther Sherman) and Ramlal B. Bajpai of Nagpur, Indrani was five years old when her mother began teaching her Indian dance. Indrani was soon ready to perform small roles with her mother's company. In 1947

INDRANI. A versatile performer, Indrani has popularized such lesser-known forms of Indian dance dramas as *mōhiniāṭṭam*, Kuchipudi, and Oḍissi. She is seen here in an Oḍissi pose representing Kṛṣṇa. The gesture of her left hand symbolizes his flute; her right hand, representing a cow, indicates that he is a cowherd. (Photograph from the Dance Collection, New York Public Library for the Performing Arts.)

Chokkalingam Pillai became her master in the Pandanallur style of *bharata nāṭyam*. He accompanied her, his most prominent disciple, on tours throughout India.

Later Indrani began expanding her repertory with lesser-known genres of classical dance. Srimati Chinnammumma of Kerala Kalamandalam taught her *mōhiniāṭṭam*, the "dance of the divine temptress"; Korada Narasimha Rao was her teacher in Kuchipudi technique; and Guru Deba Prasad Das taught her Oḍissi dance, which she presented on a professional stage for the first time in 1957. Indrani did much to educate Indian audiences about these genres and was the first to incorporate them in concert tours abroad. Emulating her mother's pioneering zeal, Indrani expanded appreciation for the broad range of India's classical dance. In her many international tours she often included promising dancers of other styles, encouraging them in establishing their careers.

Indrani's success may be attributed to her personal charm, graciousness, stamina, and dedication in her performance, as well as to the tasteful presentations of her varied programs. These qualities have made her an ideal choice for tours sponsored by the Indian government. She has performed before many heads of state and was among the first group of Indian artists sent to Russia and China.

Indrani's awards and honors include the Padma Sri from the government of India; the Sahitya Kala Parishad, Delhi State; the Nritya Vilas Sangeet Peet, Bombay; the Natya Kala Bhushanam, India Institute of Fine Arts, Madras; the key to the city of New York; and a written tribute from Galina Ulanova.

Indrani maintains residences in both New Delhi and New York. She has taught at The Juilliard School of Dance, New York University, and Brooklyn College, and she has devised a notation system for students and teachers. She is married to Habib Rahman, former chief architect of India; they have a son, Ram, a photographer and graphic artist, and a daughter, Sukanya, a professional solo dancer who also joins her mother in concert and on tour.

BIBLIOGRAPHY

Hanna, Judith Lynne. "Touched by the Timeless Female Creator and Destroyer: Indrani Dances Kuchipudi." In Hanna's *The Performer-Audience Connection*. Austin, 1983.

Hering, Doris. "Indrani and Company." *Dance Magazine* (February 1962): 61–62.

Indrani. "Classical and Creative Dance in India." *Natya* 7 (December 1963): 73–76.

Ragini Devi. *Dance Dialects of India*. 2d rev. ed. Delhi, 1990.

Small, Linda. "Reflections on a Season of Ethnic Dance." *Dance Magazine* (April 1978): 79–83.

VIDEOTAPE.   "Indrani and Her Classical Dancers and Musicians of India" (WGBH-TV, Boston, 1975).

LUISE ELCANESS SCRIPPS

INGLESBY, MONA (Mona Kimberly; born 1918 in London), English ballet dancer, choreographer, and company director. Mona Inglesby studied with many of the leading ballet teachers in England and France during the 1930s, including Margaret Craske, Marie Rambert, Lubov Egorova, Nicholas Legat, Matilda Kshessinska, Judith Espinosa, and Nicholas Sergeyev. At an early age she danced principal roles at Rambert's Ballet Club, in such works as Ninette de Valois's *Bar aux Folies-Bergère*, Michel Fokine's *Le Carnaval*, Andrée Howard's *The Mermaid*, and Antony Tudor's *Lysistrata*. She created the roles of La Môme Fromage and a Can-Can Dancer in *Bar aux Folies-Bergère* (1934) and later took the leading part of La Goulue; in *Le Carnaval* she danced the lively role of Papillon, originally created by Bronislava Nijinska. In 1939 she appeared in the London season of the Ballets Russes de Colonel W. de Basil, which, as it was performing at the Royal Opera House, Covent Garden, was billed in English as the Covent Garden Russian Ballet.

In the late 1930s, Inglesby also began to try her hand at choreography. Her first ballet was *Endymion*, set to music by Moritz Moszkowski. With designs by Sophie Fedorovitch, it was presented at a charity gala at the Cambridge Theatre, London, in 1938. Her next work was *Amoras*. Set to music by Edward Elgar and designed by William Chappell, it was given at the same theater in 1940.

At the beginning of World War II, Inglesby gave up dancing for a time and enlisted as an ambulance driver. However, she soon realized that she could better serve the war effort through dancing. In those days, the British public, especially those on national service, were finding that ballet provided an especially effective antidote to the horrors of war. Inglesby therefore decided to start a company of her own, with the primary purpose of taking classical ballet to a vast, new audience. With the financial support of her family she founded the International Ballet in the winter of 1940, becoming its director, chief choreographer, and principal ballerina.

From its first season in the spring of 1941 until her retirement in 1953, Inglesby successfully guided the International Ballet through many London seasons and on extensive tours of Great Britain and continental Europe. She was *prima ballerina* throughout the life of the company, dancing most of the principal roles in the repertory. As Odette-Odile in *Swan Lake* or Princess Aurora in *The Sleeping Beauty*, she exhibited an impeccable technique, but she was at her best in *demi-caractère* parts such as Swanilda in *Coppélia*.

As chief choreographer, Iglesby mounted her earlier works, *Endymion* and *Amoras*, for the company and added *Planetomania*, with music by Norman Demuth and designs by Doris Zinkeisen, in 1941. In 1943 she provided the choreography for Leslie French's production of *Every-*

man, set to music by Richard Strauss and with designs by Rex Whistler. In addition to these works, she assisted in the production of many other ballets in the company's repertory.

[*See also* International Ballet.]

BIBLIOGRAPHY

Franks, A. H. "The Inglesby Legend." *Ballet Annual* 4 (1950): 104–109.

Handley-Taylor, Geoffrey. *Mona Inglesby, Ballerina and Choreographer.* London, 1947.

Inglesby, Mona. "From the Cradle of British Ballet." *Dance Now* 4 (Spring 1995): 35–45.

Peter Williams

INSTRUCTION BOOKS. *See* Technical Manuals.

INTERMEDIO. The Italian *intermedio* (plural, *intermedi, intermedii*) or *intermezzo* of the fifteenth, the sixteenth, and the early seventeenth centuries was a lavishly staged and richly costumed theatrical interlude of music, dance, and pantomime presented with elaborate stage effects. These entertainments, usually inserted between acts of plays, also enlivened the great balls known as *veglie* ("vigils"). The dances used in the *intermedi* were called *balli, brandi, moresche* or *morescas* (dramatic or stage dances, not Morris dances in the modern sense), *mattacini* (mock battle dances similar to the "Bouffons" in Thoinot Arbeau's *Orchésographie,* published in 1588), and the *galliardes* and other existing ballroom dances, such as the *barriera.*

The term *intermedio* comes originally from the Low Latin *intromissum,* meaning "the third or middle course of a banquet." *Tramessi* (or *entremets*) came to mean any extra presentations at a banquet, including the fanciful constructions that were brought into the hall to amuse guests between courses. As they became more elaborate, these *tramessi* came to resemble parade floats, complete with musicians and dancers.

Gradually the *intermedi* moved from the banquet hall to the theater, where they came to be regarded as integral to any theatrical event, whether play, pastoral, comedy, or sacred drama. In the closing days of the fifteenth century, Isabella d'Este complained in a letter that, "At 23:30 began the comedy of the *Bacchae,* which was so long and wearisome, and lacking inserted dances [*Balli intramezzi*] . . . only two *moresche* were interpolated [*tramezzati*]" (D'Ancona, 1891, p. 385).

In Italy the *intermedio* was used between the acts of plays to suspend the action and thus create the illusion of time passing. But the rapid scene changes, spectacular and intricate machinery, and sumptuous costumes of the *intermedi* so dazzled spectators that in 1565 the poet

Il Lasca wrote, "Formerly, they were wont to perform the intermedii to serve the drama; but now one gives the play for the sake of the intermedii." In 1608 *The Judgment of Paris* was presented in Florence; it received scant attention in the letters and reports of envoys, but its *intermedi* were minutely described, especially the final dance in the sixth *intermedio, The Temple of Peace*: "From the two apertures on the sides, issued forth two clouds full of Gentle Breezes and Zephyrs, who, prettily dressed, and hand in hand, moved in a circular dance, to the great astonishment of the spectators, as it was something never before attempted in the air" (*Descrittione delle Feste,* p. 49; quoted in Welsford, 1927, *The Court Masque,* p. 239; also cited in both Solerti and Nagler but without the full Italian quote).

The spectacular dance effects were not limited to rounds danced on clouds hovering in midair. D'Ancona (1891) quotes Isabella d'Este writing from Ferrara to her husband, Francesco II Gonzaga, about the *intermedi* during the performance of the *Eunoco*: "At the fourth [act intermedio] was performed a *moresca* by XII persons, carrying torches approximately four *braccie* [about eight feet] in length, lit at each end, which was a great and wondrous sight, because of the dexterity of those who wielded them one against the other, with movements of great beauty, and in time to the music, without injury to anyone."

In 1617 an evening *veglia* was held in Florence to celebrate the wedding of Francesco III Gonzaga and Caterina de' Medici. According to a contemporary account, in addition to dancing in which all the guests took part, the evening's entertainment included an enactment of the *Liberation of Tirreno and Arnea* and its *intermedi*: a *balletto* in which the grand duke and grand duchess danced amid their lords and ladies; a mock combat with squadrons of cavaliers, which "hastened by with such quickness and beauty, that it was universally commended, since due to good rehearsal, that boredom which the length of similar combats is wont to cause was avoided"; and a final dance, "a *ballo* of forty cavaliers and forty ladies, in which all those of the Tourney took part (which number included the combatants, Lords, and Pages who had served). And although the great number [of participants] led one to fear major confusion, in any case there was not so much as to diminish the delight and admiration, since the *ballo* was to the music of the *barriera* which is customarily danced, and according to the same rules" (Solerti, 1905, pp. 121–124, footnote).

Thus, although it is not listed as an *intermedio* dance in the source books, the *barriera* is the *intermedio balletto* with the most extant versions: two in each of Fabritio Caroso's books, *Il ballarino* (folio 77 and the reverse of folio 277) and *Nobiltà di dame* (p. 139 and p. 190), and one in Cesare Negri's *Le gratie d'amore* (p. 122). Two other choreographies for dances performed in *intermedi* survive. The first, from 1589, is the final dance composed and choreographed by Emilio de' Cavalieri in the sixth *intermedio* of *La Pellegrina*, staged to celebrate the wedding of Christine of Lorraine and Ferdinand de' Medici, grand duke of Tuscany. The music for this dance became popular throughout Europe as the "Grand Duke's Air" or "Aria di Fiorenza"; a version of the music with a *balletto* dedicated to Christine of Lorraine is included among Caroso's choreographies in his book *Nobiltà di dame* (1600).

In Cavalieri's choreography, most of the intricately staged dancing, with its geometrical spatial patterns, was for seven dancers, three men and four women. They performed steps as described in the books of Caroso and Negri, including variations in *galliarde* and *canario* styles. Three renowned singers sang and danced while accompanying themselves on guitars and a tambourine, and twenty singers danced in the final section of the *ballo*. The

instructions for Cavalieri's *Gran Ballo* (also known as *Ballo del Gran Duca, Aria di Fiorenza, Laura Soave, La Fiorentina,* and *Aria Gran' Duc*) in the *Rappresentazione di Anima, et di Corpo* (1600), set forth in the preface written by Alessandro Guidotti, could apply equally well to the choreography for the wedding celebrations of 1589:

> These dances, or *moresche,* if they are made to appear outside the common usage will be prettier and more novel: for example, use the *moresca* for a combat dance, & the *Ballo* as a jesting game, as in the Pastoral of *Fileno* in which three satyrs come to do battle and use the occasion to sing while fighting and dancing to a *moresca* air . . . Let it not be said that one should not do a figured [that is, formally patterned] dance at the end, on a suitable occasion. But note well that the *Ballo* should have those who are dancing in it also singing, and where possible they should have [musical] instruments in hand, which they should play.

Detailed instructions for the dance include "braidings and interweavings by all the couples" and the use of four dancers who should "exquisitely dance a jumped *ballo* with caprioles, & without singing." The dancers were to continue varying the *ballo* in all the verses, dancing "one time a *Gagliardo,* another a *Canario,* & another the *Cor-*

INTERMEDIO. At the 1589 wedding of Christine of Lorraine and Ferdinand de' Medici, Girolamo Bargagli's comedy *La Pellegrina* was performed with six *intermedi.* This engraving by Agostino Carracci, after Bernardo Buontalenti's designs, shows the first *intermedio, The Harmony of the Spheres.* (Courtauld Institute of Art, London; used by permission.)

rente . . . And let the *Ballo* be choreographed by the best master to be found."

The other extant *intermedio* dance was choreographed by Negri as a *brando* for four shepherds and four nymphs in the final *intermedio* of the pastoral *L'Armenia,* presented in Milan in 1599 during the visit of the Infanta Isabella of Spain and Archduke Albert of Austria. Like the *Gran Ballo* by Cavalieri, it uses both simple and complex steps from the ballroom repertory in *gagliardo, canario,* and duple-time variations. As in Cavalieri's *Gran Ballo,* Negri's dancers form intricate patterns in pairs, lines, and half-moons, and they exchange places, calling out "Hays" and interweaving passages.

[*See also* Ballo and Balletto; Italy, *article on* Theatrical Dance before 1800; Matachins; Moresca; Renaissance Dance Technique. *For related discussion, see* Ballet de Cour, *article on* Ballet de Cour, 1560–1670; France, *article on* Theatrical Dance, 1581–1789; *and* Masque and Antimasque.]

BIBLIOGRAPHY

Arbeau, Thoinot. *Orchesography* (1589). Translated by Mary Stewart Evans. New York, 1948.

Caroso, Fabritio. *Il ballarino* (1581). New York, 1967.

Caroso, Fabritio. *Nobiltà di dame* (1600). Translated and edited by Julia Sutton. Oxford, 1986.

D'Ancona, Alessandro. *Le origini del teatro italiano.* Vol. 2. Turin, 1891.

Nagler, A. M. *Theatre Festivals of the Medici, 1539–1637.* New Haven, 1964.

Negri, Cesare. *Le gratie d'amore* (1602). Bologna, 1969.

Solerti, Angelo. *Musica, ballo e drammatica alla corte medicea dal 1600 al 1637.* Florence, 1905.

Walker, D. P., ed. *Musique des intermèdes de "La Pellegrina."* Paris, 1963.

Welsford, Enid. *The Court Masque.* Cambridge, 1927.

ANGENE FEVES

INTERMEZZO. *See* Intermedio.

INTERNATIONAL BALLET. A large-scale English company that gave many London seasons from 1941 to 1953, the International Ballet also toured extensively throughout Britain and continental Europe, presenting a repertory consisting mainly of full-length classics. The company was founded and directed by its principal ballerina, Mona Inglesby, who was originally motivated by a desire to bring classical ballet to a war-weary British public. [*See the entry on* Inglesby.]

Begun in the winter of 1940, the International Ballet rehearsed through the worst period of the London blitz and opened its first season at the Alhambra Theatre, Glasgow, on 19 May 1941. After a provincial tour, the company gave its first London season, at the Lyric Theatre, Shaftsbury

Avenue, later that year. At that time, the repertory consisted of one-act works: Michel Fokine's *Les Sylphides* and *Le Carnaval;* act 2 of *Swan Lake;* and *Aurora's Wedding,* a suite of dances from *The Sleeping Beauty,* staged by Stanislas Idzikowski. The modern repertory included Harold Turner's *Fête Bohème* (music by Antonin Dvořák, designs by William Chappell) and three works by Inglesby: *Endymion* (music by Moritz Moszkowski, designs by Sophie Fedorovitch), *Amoras* (music by Edward Elgar, designs by William Chappell), and *Planetomania* (music by Norman Demuth, designs by Doris Zinkeisen). In addition to Inglesby, the principal dancers included Nina Tarakanova, Harold Turner, Rovi Pavinoff, Leo Kersley, Celia Franca, and a young woman named Moira Shearer, then unknown to the ballet public.

One of the most important aspects of the company was the involvement, from the start, of Nicholas Sergeyev as *régisseur* and director of the associated International Ballet School, which opened in 1943. Having been a soloist, ballet master, and director from 1904 to 1918 at the Maryinsky Theater in Saint Petersburg, Sergeyev had a complete knowledge of the standard full-length classics, some of which, by means of Stepanov notation, he had mounted for western European companies. His first revival for International Ballet was act 2 of *Swan Lake;* in 1947, he mounted the whole four-act work in a version generally considered to be the nearest to the original Maryinsky production of 1895. Other classical revivals from the Maryinsky repertory included *Giselle* in 1942, Marius Petipa's version of *Coppélia* in 1944, excerpts from Petipa's *The Sleeping Beauty* in 1945, and the full-length ballet in 1948.

Although the classics dominated the International Ballet's repertory, particularly in the later years, a number of one-act works were created for the company. In 1942, Andrée Howard choreographed Inglesby's production of *Twelfth Night* (music by Edvard Grieg, designs by Zinkeisen). In 1943, Inglesby herself choreographed Leslie French's production of *Everyman* (music by Richard Strauss, design by Rex Whistler), while in 1946 French choreographed her production of *The Masque of Comus* (music by Handel, designs by Zinkeisen). In 1948, Dorothy Stevenson created *Sea Legend* (music by Esther Rofe, designs by John Bainbridge). In the 1949/50 season, Julian Algo choreographed and designed *Visions* (music by Modest Mussorgsky). In the same period, Léonide Massine revived two of his most popular works: *Gaieté Parisienne* and *Capriccio Espagnol.*

If the repertory was not, on the whole, particularly imaginative, the real importance of the International Ballet lay in its success in fulfilling Mona Inglesby's ambition: to bring ballet to new audiences and to increasing national interest in the classics. Although the company gave several seasons in central London, it also pioneered the

INTERNATIONAL BALLET. Nicholas Sergeyev staged *Swan Lake* for the company in 1947. Here, Mona Inglesby and Jack Spurgeon are seen in the Black Swan pas de deux. As Odile, the Black Swan, dances with Prince Siegfried, the image of Odette, the White Swan, hovers over the heads of the ensemble seated at left. (Photograph by Frank Sharman; used by permission.)

use of new venues, including the vast cinemas that then existed in the London suburbs, such as the Davis Theatre, Croydon, and the Gaumont State Cinema, Kilburn, and throughout England's provincial cities. Whenever possible, the company gave special performances for children, accompanied by lectures and demonstrations in schools. In 1951 it was the first dance company to appear on the concert stage of the Royal Festival Hall. The company also had considerable success on its European tours.

Inglesby was *prima ballerina* of the International Ballet throughout its lifetime, dancing most of the principal roles in the repertory. She was admired for her command of classical technique but was most charming in *demi-caractère* parts such as Swanilda in *Coppélia*. Frequent changes among the company dancers (originally only twenty-one, expanding to about one hundred) resulted in uneven quality. Occasionally there were distinguished guests, such as Nana Gollner and Paul Petroff in 1947 and Yurek Shabelevsky in 1951, who remained for a season. The character dancer Harcourt Algeranoff joined the company in 1944 as soloist and teacher at the school; his wife, Claudie Algeranova, became one of the company's ballerinas. Other principals included Domini Callaghan, Herida May, Michel de Lutry, Ernest Hewitt, Ann Suren, Errol Addison, Peter White, Hélène Armfelt, Maurice Béjart, Bridget Kelly (Espinosa), and Milorad Miskovitch. When Inglesby retired from dancing in 1953, the company disbanded.

BIBLIOGRAPHY

Davies, Richard. "Should Auld Acquaintance." *Dance and Dancers* (February 1983): 21–24.

Franks, A. H. "The Inglesby Legend." *Ballet Annual* 4 (1950): 104–109.

Handley-Taylor, Geoffrey. *Mona Inglesby, Ballerina and Choreographer.* London, 1947.

Haskell, Arnold L. "Ballet in Britain, 1934–1944." *Dance Index* (October 1945): 164–184.

Inglesby, Mona. "From the Cradle of British Ballet." *Dance Now* 4 (Spring 1995): 35–45.

Raffé, W. G. "The International Ballet of London." *Dance Magazine* (March 1948): 12–17.

PETER WILLIAMS

INVITATION, THE. Choreography: Kenneth MacMillan. Music: Matyas Seiber. Scenery and costumes: Nicholas Georgiadis. First performance: 10 November 1960, New Theatre, Oxford, England, Royal Ballet. Principals: Lynn Seymour (The Girl), Christopher Gable (Her Cousin), Anne Heaton (The Wife), Desmond Doyle (The Husband).

A work of great power, *The Invitation* marked MacMillan's first important excursion into the territory of sexual encounter and psychological tension that he would eventually explore so thoroughly. Based on two novels, Colette's *The Ripening Seed* and Beatriz Guido's *House of the Angel*, the ballet is a dramatic narrative of love, lust, and the loss of innocence.

In an unnamed Latin country at the turn of the century, a young girl, her male cousin, and an unhappily married older couple are among the guests at a weekend house party. The two adolescents flirt with each other shyly, ignorant of passion and mindful of the strict social conventions that surround them, until the lighthearted revelry of a children's party engages them and then separates them.

Later, lured and flattered by the older woman's attention, the boy is easily, perhaps willingly, seduced by her. Her disillusioned husband, encouraged and teased playfully by the young girl, pursues her doggedly; when she rejects his embrace, he rapes her. Terrified and humiliated by the assault, she seeks her cousin's tenderness for comfort, but his touch instantly revolts her and she rejects him too. Brutally stripped of innocence, purity, and trust, she faces a future that seems suddenly bleak and loveless.

MacMillan created a remarkable dance language for this ballet—explicit but not sensational, delicately shaded with emotion but not sentimental, clear and legible but not pedantic. The characters' behavior emerges naturally from the expressive range of movement, and the poetic beauty of the dance images, especially in the various pas de deux, reveals every nuance of motivation and feeling.

As he developed this violent and sensual language over the years, particularly in *Romeo and Juliet*, *Anastasia*, and *Mayerling*, MacMillan also cemented his creative association with Lynn Seymour, whose searing portrayal of the girl launched her reputation as the greatest English dance-actress of her generation.

BIBLIOGRAPHY
Barnes, Clive, et al. "The Invitation." *Dance and Dancers* (February 1961): 6–13.
Currie, Jean. "The Invitation." *The Dancing Times* (January 1961): 223–225.
Thorpe, Edward. *Kenneth MacMillan: The Man and the Ballets*. London, 1985.

BARBARA NEWMAN

THE INVITATION. Desmond Doyle (The Husband) and Lynn Seymour (The Girl) were members of the original cast, forming one of the two couples involved in a tale of double seduction and loss of innocence. (Photograph by Houston Rogers; used by permission of the Board of Trustees of the Theatre Museum, London.)

IRAN. As the locale for one of the oldest continuing cultural, linguistic, and ethnic entities, Iran provides archaeological evidence for dance portrayed on Mesopotamean pottery dated to 5000 BCE (Zoka', 1978). Evidence for continuing choreographic activity is documented in the historical writings of foreigners, from biblical times to ancient Greece to the Persian and Ottoman empires. Iconographic artworks showing dance also exist, such as silver objects from the Sasanian period (224–650 CE) and Persian miniatures from the twelfth century. Iran is, and most likely has always been, a place of immense ethnic and linguistic diversity, a continental crossroad open to influences from a wide variety of cultural sources. Its dance traditions reflect this diversity.

Two basic types of dance are performed throughout the Iranian cultural sphere and, indeed, throughout the Middle East generally. The first type is regional folk dancing, which is most often performed, but not exclusively so, in groups; the second is solo improvised dancing.

Regional Folk Dances. In the folk dances of the northern and western regions of this vast cultural region—which includes Georgia, Armenia, Daghestan, Azerbaijan, Kurdistan, and Luristan—the dancers are often linked by various hand holds. The performance of these dances in line, semicircular and/or circle formations forms the eastern terminus of the "belt" whose western terminus is in Europe. In the northwestern region of the Iranian cultural sphere, such patterned line and circle dances constitute the most common form of choreographic expression (Hasanov, 1988; Lisitsian, 1958, 1972). By contrast, in the eastern and southern districts—such as Khorasan, Fars, the Persian Gulf region, Baluchistan, Afghanistan, and Turkmenia—the regional dances are performed in groups. The dancers do not touch one another and often carry scarfs or other objects with which to embellish their movements. In the southern area, some scope for improvisation is possible because of the relative freedom of the body; however, the dancers conceive of themselves as part of a group that moves together. These dances are most often associated with the countryside, even though they may sometimes be seen in urban areas, particularly the line and circle dances. Because of the many participants associated with these dances, the dances are commonly associated with outdoor performances. Briefly, these dances are characterized by regional specificity of style and short, patterned, choreographic phrases repeated and embellished with variations—in contrast to the solo improvised dance, which is based entirely on improvisation and solo performance.

Some of these Iranian regional dances, particularly those performed in lines and circles, can be seen at various communal events in Europe and the United States, where communities of Azerbaijanis, Kurds, Assyrians (Aramaic-speaking Chaldeans), and Armenians now live.

Solo Improvised Dance. The second type of dance, solo improvised dancing, is more often associated with urban life than the regional dances performed in rural village and tribal areas. Solos are performed in a strikingly

IRAN. With his arms and head hidden, this modern-day street entertainer performs a belly dance, manipulating the face painted on his abdomen to the delight of his young audience and a cameraman, at left. (Photograph from the collection of Metin And.)

uniform manner, demonstrating the aesthetic and creative impulses that pervade this vast region. Such dancing can be seen from Tiflis in Georgia east to the border-region of China, from Khiva in Uzbekistan to Shiraz in southwestern Iran—as well as in the Iranian diaspora, especially southern California. The solo dancing is potentially limitless in its improvisational creativity, but it remains within its own stylistic framework. Solo improvisational dancing, although rarely performed by more than one at a time, often reached great technical and physical mastery; in Iran, the professional performer (Per., *motreb*) also often acted, sang, played an instrument, and executed feats of athletic dexterity. Such acrobatics included handstands, cartwheels, balancing the body in the air while holding onto a dagger planted in the floor, writing someone's name with flour on the floor, or balancing lighted candles or tea glasses filled with hot tea. Sometimes a dancer would become associated with a particular skill and bear a nickname derived from it. Commonly, the dancers performed with such objects as clappers or finger cymbals, with which they accented the musical rhythms. In Iranian dance, the performance of beautiful and intricate hand and arm gestures is highly prized and forms the major focus of interest in this dance tradition. An unusual feature of this dance is the manipulation of eyebrows, lips, and other facial features in witty or sensual gestures, which makes this dance tradition unique in the Middle East.

Historically, from 1796 to 1925, there existed male and female troupes of entertainers; in the male troupes, young boys often donned female garb. These troupes toured both urban and rural settings. Comic elements and sexually suggestive movements by the dancers, particularly the males, were described by many European visitors who were shocked by them. While the best-known and most beautiful and skillful performers might reach the shah's court or the homes of the wealthy, small itinerant troupes could be seen in villages and poor urban districts throughout the country, particularly during celebrations for the Iranian new year (Per., *Nawrūz*), beginning on the first day of spring, as late as the mid-twentieth century.

The solo dance forms the basis of the movement practices of the indigenous men's and women's improvised comic theater (Beza'i, 1965; Safa-Isfahani, 1980; Shay, 1995b). In the cities this dance is the major form of choreographic expression, with some individuals attaining the technical ability of professional performers. However, the fear of being labeled *motreb*, or worse, can still serve as a deterrent to many from performing in any but the most intimate social surroundings.

As in much of the Asian world, the historical association of professional dancers with prostitution is probably the major cause of the opprobrium expressed by conservative Islamic authorities. Since the Iranian Revolution of

IRAN. A posed portrait of two Persian sword dancers and a referee (center) that was used for promotional material at the Columbian Exposition held in 1893 in Chicago. This martial arts–related entertainment was performed to the accompaniment of drum and pipe music. A contemporary report indicates that this sword dance was not a popular event at the exposition. Some visitors appreciated the colorful costumes of these performers but considered their music and dance unpleasant and monotonous. (Photograph courtesy of Elizabeth Artemis Mourat.)

1979, this type of dance has been banned in the Islamic Republic of Iran; its performance can result in severe punishment.

Patterned Movement Practices. Performed in Iran on a large scale are certain purposeful patterned rhythmic activities. These occur in religious or spiritual contexts, on the one hand, and largely as martial arts on the other—as well as a blend of the two, such as the *zūrkhānah*. These movement activities cannot—in strict spiritual Islamic contexts—be labeled "dance." (For further discussion of these practices, see Shay, 1995a).

[*See also* Islam and Dance; *and* Kurdish Dance.]

BIBLIOGRAPHY
Beza'i, Behzad. *Namayesh dar Iran.* Tehran, 1965.
Bolukbashi, Ali. "Namayesh-ha-ye Shadi-avar-e Zananeh-ye Tehran." *Honar va Mardom*, no. 27 (1964).
'Enjavi-Shirazi, Sa'id Abolqasem. *Bazi-ha-ye namayeshi.* Tehran, 1973.
Friend, Robyn C. "Modern Persian Dance." In *Encyclopaedia Iranica.* Costa Mesa, Calif., 1994.
Hamada, Geoffrey M. "Dance and Islam: The Bojnurdi Kurds of Northeastern Iran." Master's thesis, University of California, Los Angeles, 1978.
Hasanov, Kamal. *Azerbaijan gedim folklor ragslari.* Baku, 1988.
Khaleqi, Ruhallah. *Sar gozashteh musiqi Iran.* Tehran, 1974. See volume 1, pages 465–486.
Lisitsian, Srbui. *Starinnye plyaski i teatrlinye predstvleniia Armianskogo naroda.* 2 vols. Yerevan, 1958–1972.
Rezvani, Madjid K. *Le théâtre et la danse en Iran.* Paris, 1962.
Safa-Isfahani, Kaveh. "Iranian Culture: Symbolic Representations of Sexuality in Dramatic Games." *Signs* 6.1 (1980).
Shay, Anthony V. "Dance and Non-Dance: Patterned Movement in Iran and Islam." *Iranian Studies* 28 (Winter–Spring 1995a): 61–78.
Shay, Anthony V. "*Bazi-ha-ye namayeshi:* Iranian Women's Theatrical Plays." *Dance Research Journal* 27 (Fall 1995b): 16–24.
Zoka', Yahya. "Tarikh-e raqs dar Iran" (parts 1–4). *Honar va Mardom*, nos. 188–192 (1978).

ANTHONY V. SHAY

IRELAND. [*To survey traditional and theatrical dance in Ireland, this entry comprises two articles: the first article provides an overview of traditional dance; the second focuses on the history of theatrical dance.*]

Traditional Dance

Ireland is an island that consists of thirty-two counties, twenty-six of which make up the Irish Republic (Eire); the remaining six counties, called Northern Ireland, are part of the United Kingdom. The Irish people are Celts, and their language is Gaelic, although English is the language spoken commonly today. The rich folk dance tradition of Ireland comprises solo step dances, set dances (similar to country dances), *céilí* dances, and various social dances.

IRELAND: Traditional Dance. Couples dancing at a crossroads in county Wicklow, Ireland, c.1930. In many folk traditions, crossroads have spiritual significance and are associated with the meeting of the opposing forces of good and evil. (Photograph courtesy of the National Council for the Traditional Arts, Silver Spring, Maryland.)

Dancing masters were first mentioned in *A Tour in Ireland, 1776–1779,* by Arthur Young, who wrote, "Dancing is very general among the poor people. . . . Dancing masters of their own rank travel through the country from cabbin [house] to cabbin, with a piper or blind fiddler; and the pay is six pence a quarter." Each dancing master had his own territory and taught at each location in rotation for six weeks at a time, instructing young rural people in winter, often in a barn or farmhouse. The dancing masters systematized the solo step dances known today as the reel, jig, light jig, slip jig, and hornpipe, as well as the *céilí* dances and the traditional solo set dances, such as the Blackbird and the Saint Patrick's Day.

Besides the dance schools, the Irish danced at weddings, "patterns" (patrons' days), fairs, holy days, and Sunday gatherings, as well as on annual festivals such as saints' days and harvest. The dances were primarily communal, including jigs, minuets, and country dances; step dancers might also perform between the communal dances. Dancing masters displayed their art here to attract students; some danced on a small platform or barrel, and it was said that a good step dancer could perform on a space six inches square.

There was conflict over dancing between Roman Catholic church authorities and the rural communities. Dancing on religious occasions was condemned from church pulpits, as it was considered unruly behavior, and parish priests were asked to suppress it. In some parishes dancing masters had to have the permission of a local priest to conduct a school.

During the nineteenth and early twentieth centuries, sets and half sets were performed at all informal dance events in rural Ireland, including house and crossroads dances, patterns, pilgrimages, fairs, weddings, harvest festivals, and feast days. Impromptu performances of step dances might also occur. The set dances are believed to have been derived from the French quadrilles introduced by Irish soldiers returning from the Napoleonic Wars. Dancing masters adapted the quadrilles to local abilities and traditional Irish music, and regional styles became differentiated. Throughout this period, Irish dancing was integral to the social lives of the rural people and was integrated with other aspects of Irish culture (e.g., music, singing, and storytelling).

In 1936 the Public Dance Halls Act was passed, and all public dances had to be licensed. Consequently rural dances at home, a primary social event in winter, declined. They were replaced by events at the larger parish halls, and some older dances were supplanted by newer ones, such as the waltz and polka.

The Gaelic League (Conradh na Gaeilge) had been established in 1893, with a desire to resurrect a sense of national identity. Although primarily concerned with the Irish language, the Gaelic League promoted other aspects of traditional culture, including dancing. It held its first *céilí* not in Ireland but in London, on 30 October 1897; there were sets and waltzes to Irish music, singing, and step dancing. The *céilí* spread to Ireland and to Irish emigrant communities worldwide, becoming a popular venue at which Irish people could express their common identity and solidarity. It was later decided that the sets and waltzes of foreign origin should be replaced by Irish dances, such as the Eight-hand Reel, Sixteen-hand Reel, and High Cauled Cap; these were invented by the dancing masters who had combined steps from the quadrilles with Irish stepping.

Today *céilí* dancing is still held under the auspices of the Gaelic League, either in competitions or as a social event. The dances are relatively easy to perform and are done by young and old. The most popular *céilí* dances are "The Waltz of Limerick," "The Siege of Ennis," and "The Haymakers' Jig." A revival of set dancing in the 1980s led to set dances also being included in many *céilithe* (plural of *céilí*), both in Ireland and abroad. The most popular set dances are the Caledonian, the Plain, the Lancers, Sliabh Luachra, the Baile Mhuirne Reel, the Baile Mhuirne Jig, and the Kerry Set.

The Gaelic League promoted step dancing at festivals *(feiseanna)* and field days *(aeraíochtaí)* at which step-dance competitions were held concurrently with those in music, singing, and sports. Beginning in the 1920s, schools of step dance were founded in the cities and towns of Ireland to provide regular tuition. Teachers obtained recognition and students obtained success in competitions, so these became the focus of step dancing.

In March 1931 the Irish Dancing Commission (An Coimisiún le Rincí Gaelacha) was established under the auspices of the Gaelic League to administer step-dance competitions, training, and standards. Qualifying examinations for teachers and judges were developed. Three booklets produced in 1939, 1943, and 1969 remain the key textbooks for all Irish step-dance teachers and judges. An independent group, the Organisation for Irish Dance (An Cómhgháil le Rincí Gaelacha), emerged in 1969. Both organizations now have their own registered teachers and judges and hold competitions exclusively for their own members. Today registered schools of Irish step dance exist not only in Ireland but also in England, Scotland, Wales, the United States, Canada, Australia, and New Zealand.

Progressive competitions are held at local, regional, national, and international levels. They are divided by dance type, age group, and standard. The principal types are the reel, jig, and hornpipe. Soft laced pumps are worn when dancing the reel, slip jig, light jig, and single jig, which are thus known as "light shoe dances"; hard shoes are worn for the jig, hornpipe, treble reel, and solo set dances. The dances themselves are choreographed by the teachers and taught by imitation; there are identifiable and innovative movements used from year to year. The Coimisiún's control has led to a uniformity of style among Irish step dancers worldwide, but to the loss of regional styles and regional step dances.

There are also competitions for *céilí* dances and a new category, dance drama, introduced by the Coimisiún at the world championships in 1970. This is a choreography competition in which music, decor, and costume are combined with dance to illustrate an aspect of Irish culture, such as a historical event, a social custom, or a traditional story. The *céilí* dance competitions consist of particular dances selected and documented by the Coimisiún in *Ar*

IRELAND: Traditional Dance. This soft-shoe step dancer displays an admirable carriage of the arms, which are held in a relaxed manner at the sides of her body. The extreme height of her jump shows the characteristic exaggeration of competitive step dancing in relation to the *sean-nós*, or traditional, style. (Photograph courtesy of the National Council for the Traditional Arts, Silver Spring, Maryland.)

Rinncidhe Foírne; other regional *céilí* dances are disallowed.

In the solo step dances the dancer's torso is held upright, with the hands held loosely at the sides and the emphasis laid on footwork. Hands are, however, used for the creation of figures in the *céilí* dances and in the dance dramas.

Costumes have become more elaborate during the course of the twentieth century. Today women wear embroidered dresses and decorative shawls adorned with motifs from Celtic art. Men wear kilts with shirt, tie, jacket, and shawl.

Another change that has occurred in the past century is a decrease in the age at which step dances are learned; today the students and competitors are mostly under age

IRELAND: Traditional Dance. Donny Golden, one of the foremost teachers and performers of Irish step dancing in the United States, with his sister, Barbara Golden, c.1985. (Photograph courtesy of the Smithsonian Institution, Washington, D.C.)

eighteen. The older step dances were earthy in style and were performed in a confined space, but with younger performers and the larger space of the hall and stage, the steps became more airborne, the leg gestures higher, and traveling movements increased. In addition, more men now perform the older style whereas more young women perform the contemporary style.

Improvisation was traditionally important in step dances, but because competition is so important today, the dancers perform what they have been taught. Older dancers, particularly those who have retired from competing, may still improvise, but this is not commonly seen.

The musical accompaniment for traditional dance at first depended on what was available. During the eighteenth and nineteenth centuries the fiddle and *uillean* pipes (a kind of bagpipes) were popular, and the melodian or button-row accordion became widely used in the twentieth. Any combination and number of traditional Irish instruments has generally been acceptable. Most of the music for classes and competitions today is recorded, but social and concert dances often feature live music. Irish step dance is no longer integral to the lives of rural people. The city and big towns have become the centers for step dancing, where it is taught separately from other aspects of Irish culture (e.g., music and singing).

A theatrical venue for Irish dancing was established in 1974 when Siamsa Tire, the National Folk Theatre, was founded; in its productions step-dance motifs are adapted to dramatic contexts. *River Dance,* performed at the 1994 Eurovision Song Contest, showed Irish step dance freed from the characteristic controlled torso and combined with movements from flamenco and tap dance. This event provided the first professional Irish step dance touring troupe.

In 1978 the Irish Ballet performed *The Playboy of the Western World,* based on a play by J. M. Synge and choreographed by Joan Denise Moriarty; it employed step-dance motifs in a ballet context. More recently the Irish-American step dancer Liam Harney collaborated on a work for the New York City Ballet.

Research and Publication: Traditional Dance. Little was done to preserve traditional Irish dance through documentation. The first attempt was *A Handbook of Irish Dances* (1902 and subsequent editions) by J. G. O'Keeffe and Art O'Brien; however, it did not utilize a system of notation. This was also true of other early publications, including Sheehan (1902), Burchenal (1925), O'Rafferty (1934), and the booklets published by An Coimisiún le Rincí Gaelacha (1939, 1943, 1969).

Early folklorists (O'Keeffe and O'Brien, 1902; O'Neill, 1910, 1913; O'Rafferty, 1953; and Lawson, 1955) mentioned the names of dances but did not describe them. Most were interested in the origins of the dances rather than their actual performance.

Between 1983 and 1986 Catherine E. Foley studied step dances in North Kerry, utilizing the technique of participant observation to learn from elderly step dancers. She also made video and audio recordings of both performances and reminiscences, tracing step dances in the region back to 1775 and examining their development in a sociohistorical framework. Her dissertation (1988) is a contextual and structural analysis of Irish step dance and includes Labanotated dances and music notation. Foley's recordings are archived at Muckross House Folk Museum, Killarney.

One dance post now exists in an Irish university. The post, in ethnochoreology, has been established at the Irish World Music Centre of the University of Limerick. Begun in 1996, it is a master's degree course, with application to Irish traditional dance, and taught by Foley. The Arts Council has supported Foley's work, but it does not fund the step-dance organizations; other genres of dance, such as ballet and modern dance, have sometimes received such government support.

[*For related discussion, see also* Jig; Reel; *and* Step Dancing.]

BIBLIOGRAPHY

An Coimisiún le Rincí Gaelacha. *Ar Rinncidhe Foírne: Thirty Popular Figure Dances.* 3 vols. Dublin, 1939–1969.

Breathnach, Breandán. *Dancing in Ireland.* Miltown-Malbay, Ireland, 1983.

Burchenal, Elizabeth, ed. *Rince na h-Eireann: National Dances of Ireland.* New York, 1925.

Foley, Catherine. "Irish Traditional Step-Dance in North Kerry: A Contextual and Structural Analysis." Ph.D. dissertation, Laban Centre, London, 1988.

Foley, Catherine. "Irish Traditional Step-Dance in Cork." *Traditional Dance* 5–6 (1988): 159–174.

Lawson, Joan. *European Folk Dance: Its National and Musical Characteristics.* London, 1955.

Murphy, Pat. *Toss the Feathers: Irish Set Dancing.* Cork, 1995.

O'Keeffe, J. G., and Art O'Brien. *A Handbook of Irish Dances.* 6th ed. Dublin, 1944.

O'Neill, Rosemary. "Irish Traditional Dance in the Twentieth Century." *Traditional Dance* 5–6 (1988): 27–52.

O'Rafferty, Peadar. *The Irish Folk Dance Book.* 2 vols. London, 1934–1950.

Rimmer, Joan. "Carole, Rondeau, and Branle in Ireland, 1300–1800." *Dance Research* 7 (Spring 1989): 20–46.

Sheehan, J. J. *A Guide to Irish Dancing.* London, 1902.

Young, Arthur. *A Tour in Ireland.* 2 vols. 2d ed. London, 1780.

RECORDINGS. *Irish Dance Music,* J. J. Carty, Accordion, 2 vols. (CL 501–502). *Moving Cloud* (Green Linnet Records, GLCD 1150). *Music for the Sets,* vol. 1, *Round the House;* vol. 2, *Mind the Dresser;* vol. 3, *Pay the Piper;* vol. 4, *Call the Tune.* Sharon Shannon (Solid Records, ROCD 8).

CATHERINE FOLEY

Theatrical Dance

The late nineteenth century in Ireland saw the cultural renaissance known as the Irish Literary Revival, led by William Butler Yeats, Lady Augusta Gregory, George Moore, and Edward Martyn. Yeats was a great admirer of Gordon Craig and was influenced by Craig's theories of movement and light. Craig designed the costumes and screens for Yeats's play *The Hour Glass,* presented at the Abbey Theatre, Dublin, in January 1911. Dance imagery is vivid in many of Yeats's poems, and in his plays dance is an integral element of the action and symbolism.

In 1926, Yeats invited the Irish-born dancer Ninette de Valois to come to Dublin and help him restage his *Four Plays for Dancers.* This marked the beginning of an eight-year collaboration at the Abbey Theatre and its small annex, the Peacock Theatre. These plays—*The Dreaming of the Bones, The Only Jealousy of Emer, At the Hawk's Well,* and *Calvary*—were written between 1917 and 1920 and reflect Yeats's interest in Japanese *nō* drama. The most notable of the Abbey productions came in 1929, *Fighting the Waves,* with music by George Antheil. This was a prose version of *The Only Jealousy of Emer,* rewritten to use a large ensemble of dancers. De Valois created the role of the Woman of the Sidhe.

In 1934 de Valois created the role of the Queen in Yeats's *The King of the Great Clock Tower,* revised the following year as *A Full Moon in March.* The roles of the Queen and the Woman of the Sidhe were rewritten by Yeats so that de Valois could perform both roles in dance and mime, wearing masks. Yeats described *The King of the Great Clock Tower* as "the most successful of my dance plays" and dedicated it to de Valois, "asking pardon for covering her expressive face with a mask." The play is replete with dance imagery and has two solos to the accompaniment of drum and gong.

A number of other dance concerts were staged at the Abbey during the 1920s and 1930s, including *Bluebeard,* a ballet poem by Mary Davenport, and *The Drinking Horn,* to music by Arthur Duff. Jill Gregory, who was later associated with de Valois in the Vic-Wells (later the Royal) Ballet, was in the first cast of *The Drinking Horn.* De Valois also founded the Abbey School of Ballet in 1927; it was directed by one of her students, Vivienne Bennett. The school did not survive when de Valois gave up her association with the Abbey to concentrate on the Vic-Wells Ballet in London.

After the departure of de Valois, little happened in the Irish dance world until 1945, when Joan Denise Moriarty (who had studied with Madame Espinosa and Marie Rambert) returned to her native Cork to open a ballet school. She also founded the Cork Ballet Company, a group of amateur dancers; it gave its first performance in

1947. Into the 1960s, Dublin saw a succession of visiting companies—the Royal Ballet, London Festival Ballet, and Bolshoi Ballet—which stimulated the formation of new Irish companies. Moriarty founded the Irish Theatre Ballet in 1959, but it collapsed in 1964 owing to lack of funds. In 1961 the National Ballet was founded with Patricia Ryan as artistic director and with Nadine Nicolaeva Legat, Léonide Massine, and de Valois as patrons. The company performed *Giselle, Swan Lake,* and *Les Sylphides* but folded in 1963.

Although the Arts Council of Ireland had been established in 1951, it was more than twenty years before it gave funding to any dance company. In 1973 Moriarty was given a grant by the Arts Council to establish a professional company. The Irish Ballet Company, now the Irish National Ballet, with de Valois as patron, gave its inaugural performance at the Cork Opera House in January 1974. The company's success at last put professional ballet on a secure basis in Ireland. It performs regularly at the Cork Opera House but is restoring a nineteenth-century rotunda as its permanent home. The company also has an annual season at the Abbey Theatre in Dublin, as well as performing for the Dublin Grand Opera Society and the Wexford Festival. It undertakes frequent tours of the rest of Ireland and visited Yugoslavia in 1977.

In 1978 Moriarty created *The Playboy of the Western World,* based on the play by J. M. Synge. The music was composed by Sean O'Riada and arranged by The Chieftains, a group of traditional Irish musicians. This was one of the company's most popular works and was later performed in London and New York. Moriarty followed this in 1981 with *The Táin,* based on the early Irish saga *Táin bó Cuailnge,* with music by Aloys Fleischmann. The Israeli dancer and choreographer Domy Reiter-Soffer served as artistic adviser to the company in the 1980s and created many works for it, including *Paradise Gained, Pomes Penyeach* (based on poems by James Joyce), *Shadow Reach, Loveraker, Women,* and *Yerma.* The company also has works by Marius Petipa, August Bournonville, Anton Dolin, and Peter Darrell in its repertory.

The Dublin City Ballet, also funded by the Irish Arts Council, was founded by Louis O'Sullivan and presented its first program in 1979. Paula Hinton staged Walter Gore's *Eaters of Darkness* in 1980 and *Les Sylphides* in 1982. John Gilpin and Anton Dolin produced *Giselle* in 1980, with decor by William Chappell. Other choreographers who have worked with the company include Terez Nelson, Anne Courtney, Lynda Davis, Miro Zolan, Babil Gandara, and Donald Vluegels. The Dublin City Ballet School was opened in 1981, but it is separate and autonomous from the company.

A number of smaller companies have made an impact in recent years. The Dublin Contemporary Dance Theater was established in 1977 by Joan Davis; it teaches Graham, Cunningham, and Limón techniques. It has received small grants from the Arts Council and occasionally performs at the Peacock Theatre. In Limerick, John and Jean Regan founded the Mid-West Ballet Workshop; this led in October 1981 to the formation of Theatre Omnibus, a small mime group. Theatre Omnibus performs in schools and workshops and has also appeared at the Edinburgh Festival and in New York.

BIBLIOGRAPHY

Brinson, Peter. *The Dancer and the Dance: Developing Theatre Dance in Ireland.* Dublin, 1985.
Casey, Betty. *International Folk Dancing U.S.A.* Garden City, N.Y., 1981.
de Valois, Ninette. *Come Dance with Me: A Memoir, 1898–1956.* Cleveland, 1957.
de Valois, Ninette. *Step by Step: The Formation of an Establishment.* London, 1977.
Finneran, Richard J., et al., eds. *Letters to W. B. Yeats.* New York, 1977.
O'Rafferty, Peadar, and Gerald O'Rafferty. *Dances of Ireland.* London, 1953.
Robinson, Lennox. *Ireland's Abbey Theater: A History, 1899–1951.* London, 1951.
Swift, Carolyn. "Dance in Ireland." *Ireland Today* (March 1983).
Yeats, William Butler. *Explorations.* New York, 1962.
Yeats, William Butler. *The Varorium Edition of the Plays of W. B. Yeats.* Edited by Russell K. Alspach. New York, 1966.
Yeats, William Butler. *Selected Plays.* Edited by A. Norman Jeffares. London, 1974.

DEIRDRE MCMAHON

IRIAN JAYA. *See* Indonesia, *article on* Dance Traditions of the Outlying Islands.

IROQUOIS DANCE. *See* Native American Dance, *overview article and article on* Northeast Woodlands.

IRVING, ROBERT (Robert Augustine Irving; born 28 August 1913 in Winchester, England, died 13 September 1991 in Winchester), English conductor considered by many to have been the finest ballet conductor of the twentieth century. Irving's father, Robert Graham Irving, was a schoolmaster at Winchester. The younger Irving attended Winchester before going to New College, Oxford, where he studied music with Sir Hugh Allen. From 1934 to 1936 he was also enrolled at the Royal College of Music in London, where his teachers included Malcolm Sargent and Constant Lambert, whom he called the "greatest influence on my future course." Having earlier studied the piano and cello, Irving began conducting at Oxford, leading the Oxford University Music Club in a performance of Jean-Philippe Rameau's *Castor et Pollux.* In 1936 he worked under Albert Coates as a *répétiteur* at Covent Garden, but he returned to Winchester as music master (1936–1940) and occasionally gave piano recitals in London.

During World War II Irving served with the Royal Artillery (1941), then switched to the Royal Air Force (Coastal Command), serving as a navigator. He was twice awarded the Distinguished Flying Cross. From 1945 to 1948 he was associate conductor of the British Broadcasting Corporation Scottish Orchestra in Glasgow, gaining experience in a large and varied repertory.

When Constant Lambert stepped down as musical director of Sadler's Wells Ballet in 1948, Irving was invited by David Webster to become the company's principal conductor, and he served in that capacity from 1949 to 1958. Bringing undeniable authority, a firm yet flexible beat, an understanding of musical architecture, and an instinctive feel for dance rhythms and pacing, he raised dance accompaniment to a consistently high level in a theater where other musicians considered ballet music to be inferior. He was much admired on the company's tours abroad, especially in North America.

Although not primarily a composer, Irving wrote the score for the film *Floodtide* (1949) and incidental music for Katharine Hepburn's New York production of *As You Like It* (1949). He also arranged Aleksandr Glazunov's music for Frederick Ashton's ballet *Birthday Offering* (1956) and in 1967 composed the score for Jacques d'Amboise's *Prologue*, based on the Fitzwilliam Virginal Book, a collection of seventeenth-century English music.

Irving had worked with the New York City Ballet during its first London visit in 1950. On the retirement of Leon Barzin as music director in 1958, he became principal conductor of the New York City Ballet Orchestra and was named music director in 1969. Encouraged by George Balanchine, with whom he worked on a wide variety of complex modern scores, including works by Igor Stravinsky, Anton Webern, Charles Ives, and Iannis Xenakis, Irving made the orchestra one of New York's finest ensembles. During the 1972 Stravinsky Festival the orchestra played seven challenging programs in eight days to wide musical acclaim. Irving also provided notable support for the Ravel Festival in 1975, the Tchaikovsky Festival in 1981, and the second Stravinsky Festival in 1982. Balanchine said that "Most ballet conductors are like ringmasters. But I could not do a *Movements* or a *Violin Concerto* without Irving. They wait for, they announce the ballerina. With our orchestra, if you don't like what you see, you can close your eyes and still hear a good concert."

After meeting Martha Graham when she collaborated with Balanchine on *Episodes* in 1959, Irving conducted for her 1960 New York season and worked with her regularly in the early 1960s and again in the mid-1970s. He conducted for the Graham company's appearances at the Edinburgh Festival and in London in 1963. "He puts music under the dancer's feet," Graham said. It was she who presented him with the Capezio Award in 1975. In 1984 he received the *Dance Magazine* Lifetime Achievement Award.

As a pianist, Irving was often one of the onstage musicians in Balanchine's ballet *Liebeslieder Walzer*, to music by Johannes Brahms. As a guest conductor, he worked with many companies, especially those with strong Balanchine connections, such as the Boston Ballet, the Geneva Ballet, and the Paris Opera Ballet. Between 1978 and 1983 he returned to the Royal Ballet four times as guest conductor, especially for *The Sleeping Beauty*.

Irving's abilities were appreciated beyond the ballet. He conducted concerts with many orchestras, including the London Philharmonic Orchestra, the Royal Philharmonic, the Philharmonia, the New York Philharmonic, the National Symphony, the Toronto Symphony, the Detroit Symphony, and the City Center Gilbert and Sullivan Company. For two summers (1976 and 1977) he also worked with the School of Orchestral Studies in Saratoga, New York.

As Don McDonagh once noted, "Irving is a conductor who respects the composer's intent and can take the leeway granted to him by the musical notations without overstepping the legitimate bounds of interpretation. In effect he shows consideration for everyone in the art and the art itself."

BIBLIOGRAPHY

Irving, Robert. "Of Ballet Conducting et al." *Music Journal* (October 1960).

Irving, Robert. "The Conductor Speaks." *Dance and Dancers* (March 1963).

Irving, Robert. "Conducting for Dance." *Dance Chronicle* 15.1 (1992).

McDonagh, Don. "On the Podium: Robert Irving." *Dance Magazine* (February 1965).

Mueller, John, and Don McDonagh. "Making Musical Dance." *Ballet Review* 13 (Winter 1986): 23–44.

INTERVIEW.   Robert Irving, by Tobi Tobias (1976), Oral History Archives, Dance Collection, New York Public Library for the Performing Arts.

GEORGE DORRIS

ISAAC, MISTER (born c.1640, died c.1720), English dancing master and choreographer. Isaac was the leading English social dancing master from the end of the seventeenth century until his death. With Thomas Caverley he established an English style of dancing and gained acceptance for it as an important feature of English recreational life and social education.

Isaac's origins and even his full name remain obscure. Available evidence suggests that he was probably English, trained by John Ogilby (Master of the Revels in Dublin and author of *The Entertainment of His Most Excellent Majestie Charles II in His Passage through the City of Lon-*

don to His Coronation), probably in the early 1660s. This training in the dance traditions of Stuart court culture might explain Isaac's later involvement in the production at Whitehall of John Crowne's court masque *Calisto* (February 1675), in which, according to the formal records of the production, he headed the English dancers. There were however several actors and dancers of the same name active in France at about this time, including a Monsieur Isac who was reputed to be one of the best dancing masters in Paris in 1652, and the dancer Isaac who performed with Adrien Merger de Saint-André in the comic ballet *Le Bourgeois Gentilhomme* in 1670 and who may or may not have been the dancer later to appear (again with Saint-André) in England in *Calisto*. The structure and style of Isaac's later notated dances, however, suggest very strongly that he was not French, even if the prevailing fashion in London was to address the most prestigious dancing masters as if they were.

Isaac was effectively court dancing master to the last Stuart monarchs, from Charles II to Queen Anne—the appointment was not official, and members of the royal family made their own arrangements with the master of their choice. In the last quarter of the century, Isaac's pupils could gain access to court through him and sometimes looked to him preferment at court. Records from 1684 show that an English dancing master named Isaac visited France to teach country dances to the ladies of the court, which suggests that his royal connections were by then well established.

Under England's William III (ruled 1689–1702), Isaac was responsible for composing the special dances for the monarch's Birthnight Ball—a brilliant occasion at court. Isaac became particularly close to Queen Anne (ruled 1702–1714), whom he taught when she was a young princess. She was very fond of dancing and made a great impression at the Birthnight Ball of 1696 as the dancer of the final piece. She continued to dance, long after she had become troubled by gout. During her reign, Isaac usually composed a single dance for each birthnight ball that was given special prominence. These ball dances may have been performed by courtiers or by professional dancers. There is evidence that some of these dances were performed again by the same professionals, within a few days, on the public stage.

In 1706, Isaac's *A Collection of Ball Dances Perform'd at Court* was published by John Weaver, who used the system of notation that Pierre Beauchamp and Raoul-Auger Feuillet had developed in France and which Feuillet had published in 1700 as *Chorégraphie*. (Weaver translated this work into English at Isaac's suggestion and published it in 1706 as *Orchesography*, with a dedication to Isaac.) Isaac was a responsible leader in his profession, who supported Caverley and Weaver in their attempt to raise standards among dancing masters by regulating and explaining their art. [*See* Feuillet Notation *and the entries on* Caverley *and* Weaver.]

Isaac's dances, available singly as well as in Weaver's collection, were frequently reissued. The purpose and chronology of Isaac's birthnight dances, apparently made to celebrate the monarch's birthday each year, is somewhat problematic, however, since some of the dances seem to survive only as later reissues of the notation published by the music firm of John Walsh, who averred that they were birthnight dances even when they may not have been. Moreover it is not possible to assign definite dates to the dances collected in 1706 that had been created during the previous decade or earlier: "The Britannia," "The Favorite" ("A Chaconne"), "The Rigadoon," "The Richmond," "The Rondeau," and "The Spanheim." Apparent dates of publication, according to extant title pages, of Isaac's other dances are "The Princess" and "The Union" (1707); "The Salterella" (1708); "The Royal Portuguez" (1709); "The Royal Galliarde" (1710); "The Rigadoon Royal" (1711); "The Royall" ("The Royall Anne") (1712); "The Pastoral" (1713); and "The Godolphin" (1714). The dates of "The Northumberland" and "The Gloucester" are uncertain. Isaac's "The Friendship" (1715) and "The Morris" (1716) were published after the death of Queen Anne.

Isaac's "A Chaconne" was printed in Edmund Pemberton's *Essay for the Further Improvement of Dancing* (1711). John Playford published "The Maggott" ("Isaac's Maggott") in the 1703 edition of *The Dancing Master*, and the dance also appears in Dezais's *Recüeil de Nouvelles Contredanses* (Paris, 1712) as "Les Folies d'Isac."

Isaac wisely cultivated a natural and unaffected manner of movement that was well adapted to the music, was not coquettish, and sought to set off the natural charms of youth. John Evelyn described the effect on his daughter Mary, one of Isaac's outstanding pupils:

> Her carriage had "an aire of spritefull modestie, not easily to be described: Nothing of haughty, nothing affected, but natural and easy."
> (*Diary*, 14 March 1685)

In *The Tatler*, Isaac's students were described as moving "with such an agreeable freedom, that you would believe their gesture was the necessary effect of the music, and not the product of skill and practice." John Essex referred to Isaac's own "Easy Address and graceful Deportment, which always appeared without Affectation" (*The Dancing-Master: or, The Art of Dancing Explained*, 1728).

Little is known of Isaac's private life. A reference among the papers of Dr. Charles Burney suggests that the eminent violinist Matthew Dubourg (1703–1767) was his illegitimate son. Louis Goupy's portrait of Isaac, as engraved by George White, although undated, is extant. The original is unknown but a reproduction may be seen on page 12 of Richard Ralph's *Life and Works of John Weaver* (London, 1985).

BIBLIOGRAPHY

DeBeer, E. S., ed. *The Diary of John Evelyn*. Oxford, 1955.

Goff, Moira, and Jennifer Thorp. "Dance Notations Published in England, c. 1700–1740." *Dance Research* 9 (Autumn 1991): 32–50.

Goff, Moira. "Dancing-Masters in Early Eighteenth-Century London." *Historical Dance* 3.3 (1994): 17–23.

Marsh, Carol. "French Court Dance in England, 1706–1740: A Study of the Sources." Ph.D. diss., City University of New York, 1985.

Rader, Patricia Weeks. "Harlequin and Hussar: Hester Santlow's Dancing Career in London, 1706–1733." Master's thesis, City University of New York, 1992.

Ralph, Richard. *Life and Works of John Weaver*. London, 1985.

Thorp, Jennifer, and Ken Pierce. "Taste and Ingenuity." *Historical Dance* 3.3 (1994): 3–16.

Thorp, Jennifer. "Style or Stylus? Mr Isaac's Dance Notators in the Early Eighteenth Century." In *On Common Ground, Proceedings of the Dolmetsch Historical Dance Society Conference, February 1996*.

Thorp, Jennifer. "John Walsh, Entrepreneur or Poacher: The Publication of Dance Notations 1705–c.1730." *Handbook for Studies in Eighteenth-Century English Music* 8 (1996).

RICHARD RALPH and JENNIFER THORP

ISHII KAORU (born 7 July 1932 in Tokyo), Japanese modern dancer and choreographer. Ishii studied modern dance with Ishii Baku and ballet with the Russian dancer Asaf Messerer. She became a soloist with the Ishii Baku Dance Company in 1955. Her interest in choreography grew, and she presented her first dance, *Face, Face, Face*, at the age of twenty-four. In 1964, after graduating from the Juilliard School in New York City, she founded TMG, which was renamed Tokyo Dance Theater in 1991; she has served as the company's artistic director since its founding.

Ishii's company first toured Europe and the United States in 1977; among other overseas appearances were performances in Poland in 1980 and in six U.S. cities in 1991. Ishii has also choreographed for the Poznan Ballet in Poznan, Poland.

Samusara (1969), one of her early works, was based on the main character of Franz Kafka's 1915 short story "The Metamorphosis"—a man who wakes to find himself transformed into a giant insect. Performed in a small underground theater, it was praised for its "abnormal," mysterious beauty. *Récit—Chapter 5* (1974) dealt with women's incomprehensible behavior. Other dances have been visualizations of musical scores, including *The Rite of Spring* (to Igor Stravinsky's score) in 1970, *Symphonie Fantastique* (to Hector Berlioz's score) in 1974, and *Vita* (based on Carl Orff's *Carmina Burana*) in 1989. In 1981, Ishii performed *Mandara-Uta 2* in a large stone garden in Tokyo designed by sculptor Isamu Noguchi; *Mandara-Uta 3*, in 1982, was presented in collaboration with composer Takahashi Yuji. The latter dance was developed from Japanese habitual gestures and was accompanied by music combining voice and simple folk instruments.

Since the late 1980s, Ishii has investigated themes that have included the destruction of human beings and the loss of the natural environment—the subjects of *The Last Seven Days* (1987) and *Wither* (1992). Takahashi composed the music for both these dances. The music for *Wither 2* (1993) was composed by Ishii Maki. Hamada Koji, a performance artist, collaborated on the stunning set design for both *Wither* dances.

ARCHIVE.   The Dance Collection, New York Public Library for the Performing Arts, contains clippings for the Tokyo Modern Dance Group.

HASEGAWA ROKU
Translated from Japanese

ISLAM AND DANCE. Over the centuries, Islamic literature has identified three forms of dance: sacred (mystical), secular (art), and folk. Of the three, sacred dance has received most of the attention from scholars and theologians; of particular interest has been the sacred dance of Islam's mystical orders, known as Sufis (the mystics or dervishes).

Secular (art) dance, as practiced in the courts of rulers or in the houses of aristocrats, was banned by the theologians, who claimed that it was unlawful because of its licentious aspects. Art dance received some attention in the Middle Ages, but folk dance, when it was mentioned, was usually tolerated only for its special function in personal and community ceremonies, because it was associated with the most sophisticated forms of entertainment.

Sacred (Mystical) Dance. Islamic classical mysticism is known as Sufism, derived from the Arabic word for wool *(ṣūf)*. The term was originally applied to certain ascetics who wore clothes of coarse wool as a sign of penitence, of worldly renunciation. The Arabic terms *faqīr* and *darwish*, both meaning "pauper," are also related to this asceticism.

The first instances of organized Islamic mysticism appeared in the eighth century CE (mid-second century of Islam). By the fifteenth century (mid-ninth century of Islam), the basic tenets of mysticism were established, and it had gained a considerable following. Sufis are organized in congregations affiliated with orders that have adopted the name of a patron or a founder. No female order exists, but some convents were reserved for women in association with certain of the male orders.

This mystical movement developed complex rituals and spiritual exercises designed to send adherents into religious ecstasy and mystical union with God. The ritual is usually called *dhikr* ("remembrance"), which is the glorifying of God with ritual phrases. The musical and dancing portion of the ritual is known as *samāʿ* ("listening"), and it is regarded as sacred.

Both *samāʿ* and *dhikr* can be combined in one meeting (however, not all orders practice music and dancing, and

ISLAM AND DANCE. A Mughal painting depicting a Sufi ritual dance, from the reign of Jahāngīr, emperor of India from 1605 to 1627. (Metropolitan Museum of Art, New York; Purchase, Rogers Fund and the Kevorkian Foundation Gift, 1955 [55.121.10.18]; photograph used by permission.)

their emotion by dance. The dance uproots a man's foot, which is stuck in the terrestrial mud, and transports him upward into the celestial sphere. Such an explanation has been used to justify and validate this mystical dance in the face of strong opposition from Sunni Muslims and even from some Sufi leaders. Of particular note in Sufi ceremony is the *mukabele*. Certain non-Sufi trance dances also merit attention.

Sufi Dancing. In its simplest form, Sufi dancing is a swaying movement performed collectively by adherents who stand in a line or circle. To an occasional drum beat or cymbal clash, a chanter uses his modulating voice to lead the dancers. Shoulder to shoulder, they sway to and fro, vigorously move their hands up and down, clap their hands occasionally, repeat fixed phrases, and breathe ever more deeply.

The most sophisticated and spectacular form of the dance is that of the Mawlawīyah (also known as Mawlawī or Mevlevi), named for Mawlānā ("our master") Jalāl al-Dīn Rūmī (died 1273), the founder of the order and the greatest mystic poet in Persian literature. (This is known in the West as the dance of the whirling dervishes.) Tradition recounts that Rūmī was in profound sorrow after the death of his teacher, Shams al-Dīn Sabzawārī of Tabriz (Shams-i Tabrīzī), whom he admired deeply. To express his pain, he danced for many days and nights, becoming an earthly metaphor for the spinning heavens above. Music and dance were then performed by Rūmī's followers, both as ritual and as a means of achieving inner harmony.

One of the most important of the Mevlevi ceremonies is known as *mukabele;* every detail is regulated. Ensembles of singers and instrumentalists sit apart, according to their ranks, to perform the various sections of the ceremony, of which dance is the most important.

On a huge octagonal platform near the shaykh sponsoring the ceremony stand the *semazen* (dancers) and the *semazen bashi* (leader). Each wears a high cap that symbolizes a tomb and a white robe that symbolizes a shroud; the robe is covered by a black mantle. A ritual prayer is read, praise to the Prophet *(na'at sharif)* is sung, and a flute player improvises a tune; the dancers then walk around the platform three times. After they throw off their black mantles, the leader asks permission from the shaykh to dance. One after the other, the dancers kiss the shaykh's hand and begin the performance.

Each dancer spreads out his arms, holding his right hand upward and his left downward, while leaning his head to the right. The right side is said to receive divine energy, while the left side is said to be connected with the profane world. In this posture, each dancer begins to whirl, letting his white robe float out away from his body. Following the leader's directions, the dancers orient themselves in one of two orbits in the dance enclosure. While

the nature of the dance varies from order to order). When dancing is involved, it is always combined with singing and musical instruments. Although dancing is often an essential element of the *samā'*, descriptive texts define it in general terms—sometimes simply mentioning that adherents dance and sometimes commenting only on the dance's symbolism.

The mystics' ecstatic dance is said to demonstrate their infinite love of God. It is used in Sufi ritual to awaken the spirit immersed in the slumber of ignorance and to make it stand and dance like the dead, who will rise at the resurrection's trumpet call. Human spirits, whose origin is the superior world, recall their homeland in hearing the music; they shake the cage of their bodies and manifest whirling slowly around their own axes, the dancers complete a large circle; an older dancer usually whirls in place in the center. The ceremony includes three or four dance phases separated by musical interludes and characterized by a variety of rhythms and tempos.

Other Trance Dances. Whereas the *mukabele* ceremony is deeply spiritual dance, certain marginal groups with only a remote relationship to classical Sufism engage in highly frenetic trance dances. The extravagant practices performed by exhibitionist dervishes who dance in the marketplace, undress in public, sit on hot coals, swallow glass, or engage in acts of self-mutilation, are considered a heretical perversion of *sama*ᶜ.

One such fringe group is that of the Ḥamadisha of Morocco, who practice healing and exorcism. Their healing ceremony, known as *ḥadra*, has two parts: hot and cold. The hot part is performed collectively, in a line, and is the louder and faster of the two; the cold is quieter and is danced only solo. The *ḥadra* is designed to lead the performers, including the patient, into a trance and to satisfy certain spirits. The particular spirits are usually alluded to by the melodies played by the oboelike *ghayṭa*. The dancers line up opposite the musicians and form the outer boundary of the dance area. They sharply swing chest and head back and forth as they spring up and down with agility, vigorously stamping their feet. At the cold part, a few individuals and the patient perform in the center of the ring formed by most of the dancers. A wilder dance begins in an increasingly frenetic fashion until a trance state is achieved, which is said to occur when each dancer has heard his or her special spirit.

Medieval Art Dance. Unlike the field of music, the medieval art dance has not had much attention from contemporary Islamic scholars. From the scarce documentation, it can be said that a form of sophisticated art dance existed, based on codified rules that required both talent and a long period of training; when it is mentioned, it is always associated with the art of music, which was also a recreational activity of prospering medieval urban aristocratic society.

The lack of literary discussion and description of dance probably resulted from two prevailing attitudes: (1) that dance was a secondary, or an inferior, art and (2) the puritanical, rigid Muslim attitude that *raqṣ* ("dance") was no more than an amusement, a frivolity, or a libertine activity connected with women.

In his monumental treatise on music, the philosopher Abū Naṣr al-Fārābī (died 850) mentions dance briefly, along with drumming, handclapping, and mime. He considers dance, drumming, and handclapping as secondary and subordinate to the art of playing melodic instruments and singing, which are the highest art. Mime was considered the lowest art. Almost seven centuries later, the six-

teenth-century Ottoman encyclopedist and biographer Tashköprüzāde delineated three branches for the "science" of music: instrumental music (and only that of melodic instruments), *raqṣ*, and mime (or coquetry).

The nature of medieval dance can be seen pictured—in miniatures, on pottery, in wall paintings, and the like. One of the earliest and most interesting examples is an automaton that was described and illustrated in the *Book of Knowledge of Ingenious Mechanical Devices* by the Iraqi author Shams al-Dīn ibn al-Jazarī in the twelfth century. The automaton consisted of three slave girls: two stood on a balcony, one with a flute to her mouth and the other with a frame drum hanging from her neck; the third girl stood on a platform above the balcony and held a baton in each hand while balancing on a ball.

The automaton dance depicted probably corresponds to the *raqṣ al-kurra* ("dance of the ball") mentioned in one of the earliest and most extensive texts on art dance, *Meadows of Gold and Mines of Gems*, by the historian Abu al-Ḥasan al-Masᶜūdī (died 956). Following a discourse on music and its origins, al-Masᶜūdī describes the relationship between dance and rhythm and the three basic qualifications required of the dancer: (1) natural grace, amiability, and a sense of rhythm; (2) a body well-proportioned, strong, light, flexible, and able to master every dance movement; (3) a mastery of the dance repertory and all the attendant choreographies.

[*See also* Middle East *and the entries on countries of the Islamic world.*]

BIBLIOGRAPHY

Abdullah, A. "Dancing East of Suez." *The Dancing Times* (June 1938): 274–278; (July 1938): 400–403.

Chottin, Alexis. *Corpus de musique marocaine*. Paris, 1931.

Chottin, Alexis. *Tableau de la musique marocaine*. Paris, 1939.

Christensen, Dieter. "Tanzlieder der Hakkari-Kurden: Eine materialkritische studie." *Jahrbuch für Musikalischevolks und Völkerkunde* 1 (1963): 11–47.

Crapanzano, Vincent. *The Hamadsha: A Study in Moroccan Ethnopsychiatry*. Berkeley, 1973.

Hickmann, Hans. "Quelques considérations sur la danse et la musique de danse dans l'Égypte pharaonique." *Cahiers d'histoire égyptienne* 5 (1953).

Hickmann, Hans. "La danse aux miroirs." *Bulletin de l'Institut d'Égypte* 37 (1954–1955).

Holt, George E. "The Two Great Moorish Religious Dances." *National Geographic* 22 (1911): 776.

Macdonald, D. B. "Emotional Religion in Islam as Affected by Music and Singing." *Journal of the Royal Asiatic Society* (1901): 195–252; (1902): 1–28.

Meier, Fritz. "Der Derwishtanz: Versuch eines Überblicks." *Asiatische Studien* 8 (1954): 107–136.

Molé, Marijan. "La danse extatique en Islam." In *Les danses sacrées*, edited by Jean Cazeneuve. Paris, 1963.

Murray, Margaret A. "Ancient and Modern Ritual Dances in the Near East." *Folklore* 66 (1955): 401.

Random, Michel. *Mawlana Djalâl-ud-Dîn Rûmi: Le soufisme et la danse*. Tunis, 1980.

Rezvani, Madjid K. *Le théâtre et la danse en Iran*. Paris, 1962.

Rouget, Gilbert. *La musique et la transe*. Paris, 1980.

Serjeant, R. B., ed. *Prose and Poetry from Ḥaḍramawt*. London, 1951. See pages 17–50.

Shiloah, Amnon. "Réflexions sur la danse artistique musulmane au Moyen-Âge." *Cahiers de civilisation médiévale* 6 (October–November (1962): 463–474.

Shiloah, Amnon. "Ibn Hindu: Le médecin et la musique." *Israel Oriental Studies* 2 (1972): 447–462.

Shiloah, Amnon. *The Theory of Music in Arabic Writings*. Munich, 1979.

AMNON SHILOAH

ISRAEL. [*To survey dance traditions in Israel, this entry comprises two articles. The first article provides a general overview; the second explores ethnic dance.*]

An Overview

Israel lies on the eastern side of the Mediterranean sea; as a modern country it was established in 1948 by the United Nations. Within its tiny borders are some remarkable facts: the lowest point on earth—the Dead Sea; one of the oldest capitals of the world—Jerusalem—holy to Judaism, Christianity, and Islam; and the land where the ancient Israelites established monotheism. King David made Jerusalem his capital around 1000 BCE. The ancient civilizations of Egypt, Assyria, Babylonia, Greece, and Rome have fought over this land corridor linking Africa, Asia, and Europe. In 70 CE, Rome conquered the Israelites, renaming the land Palestine. Almost all the Jews went into captivity, known as the Diaspora, changing their lives completely from citizens of an independent nation with a temple-based religion to one with teachers or rabbis who inspired them and helped to keep alive the messianic idea that Jews would some day return to the land.

In the Middle East, battles continued over the centuries involving the Byzantine Empire, the Muslim caliphs, the Christian Crusaders, the Mamluks, the Ottoman Turks, and finally the British Empire. Modern-day Israel was populated in large part through migrations of persecuted Jews: in the 1930s, German Jews; in the 1940s, Holocaust survivors; in the 1950s, refugees from the Arab world; and since the 1970s, Russian Jews. The institutions of the modern Jewish state were largely created by voluntary immigrants from eastern Europe who arrived in Palestine during the first quarter of the twentieth century to farm the land cooperatively (creating kibbutzim) and to build new cities such as Tel Aviv.

Traditional Dance. Dance was a common expression of the ancient Israelites as described in the Bible, integral to both the identities of individuals and the nation. When Miriam led the women in dance after the Hebrew tribes fled slavery in Egypt and crossed the Red Sea (*Exodus*

15.20), it embodied the whole nation's freedom, whereas King David's ecstatic solo in the streets of Jerusalem (*2 Samuel* 6.14–16) demonstrated his individual joy. The ritual that developed in the Temple in Jerusalem included processions and choreographed pageantry for the holidays. Hebrew literature is rich in dance description, beginning in the Torah (the Five Books of Moses) and included in the later commentaries—the Mishnah and the Talmud. In the Mishnah (*Taʿanit* 4.8), there are descriptions of the bucolic dances of young women in the vineyards on the holiday of Tu be-Av, the feast of love. In the Talmud, dancing is prescribed for weddings (*Ketubbot* 17a), where all Jews are commanded to dance to make the new couple happy. *Responsa* literature by rabbis to their communities also describes dance practices.

Even after the Jews were exiled by the Romans in 70 CE, dance continued as part of prayer, during the annual cycle of holidays (especially at Purim and Simḥat Torah), and at celebrations. Dance figured in such individual life-passage celebrations as weddings, circumcisions, and *bar mitzvah*s, even when host communities in the Diaspora frowned on dance. A remarkable variety of Jewish dances developed as exiled Jews moved from land to land. The Jewish world in diaspora became a mosaic of communities at first influenced by the diverse locales of Greco-Roman Christendom, in emerging Islamic society, and even in Africa and Asia. The dispersal resulted in two major spheres of Jewish life by the Middle Ages, known as Ashkenazic Judaism and Sephardic Judaism, each with its own cultural expression and dance traditions. The Ashkenazic tradition includes Jews from communities based in central and eastern Europe, with descendants mainly in Israel, Europe, and the Americas; the Sephardic tradition includes Jews from medieval Spain who were exiled in 1492 to communities centered mainly around the Mediterranean Sea. The Sephardic rubric also includes Jews called the "eastern communities," or in Hebrew, ʿadot ha-mizraḥ—those living in areas once dominated by the Babylonians (Iran, Iraq, Kurdistan), those from Africa (North Africa, Ethiopia), and those from Yemen. Their descendants live mainly in Israel, the Americas, the Middle East, and Asia.

Differences in dance practice between Sephardic and Ashkenazic Jews are described in letters exchanged between rabbis and their communities over the generations, in the rabbinic literature known as the *responsa*. For example, dancing was permitted during the Sabbath among Sephardic Jews but allowed only at the conclusion of the Sabbath among Ashkenazic Jews. Rabbi Shelomoh ben Avraham Adret (c.1235–1310) complained in his *responsa* that it was a bad habit for boys to dance in the streets accompanied by musical instruments on the Sabbath. Dancing at weddings also proved to be an area of difference between Sephardic and Ashkenazic communities. The great

Rabbi Mosheh ben Maimon, known as Maimonides (1135–1204), complained in his *responsa* that a Jewish bride in Egypt executed a sword dance, as was the habit in Muslim society when entertaining wedding guests of both sexes. Ashkenazic Jews, starting in twelfth-century Germany, used a special *Tanzhaus* (Ger., Yid., "dance house") or large halls to accommodate communal dancing at weddings. An entire repertory of wedding dances known as the *Mitsvah Tanz* developed in those halls with a special dance leader, the *badhan*, organizing the dances. The Ashkenazic rabbi Ya'aqov ha-Levi Molin (1360–1427) complained in his *responsa* that certain *mitsvah* dances included men and women dancing together. He considered that lascivious, even if each partner held a corner of a kerchief to keep them separated at a modest distance.

Intricate wedding dances are part of the traditions of Yemenite Jews. These are mainly improvised male dances, although special women's dances do occur before a wedding at the ritual bath *(miqveh)*, at the henna cere-mony in which the hands and feet of the bride and groom are died red, during processions before the wedding, and at the actual wedding ceremony. Vast differences developed in wedding-dance traditions within the widespread Sephardic tradition, such as the practice of dancing with trays of sweets and a saddle from Kurdistan; dancing with broken pieces of a drinking glass, arms held straight out from the body, from Salonika in Greece; and the lyrical belly and hip dancing from Morocco. Whether Ashkenazic or Sephardic, Jews follow their tradition that everyone in the community dances to ensure the joy of the bride and groom.

Several Jewish dancing masters became famous in Italy beginning in the fifteenth century, Guglielmo Ebreo da Pesaro being the best known. Most Renaissance Jewish communities in central and eastern Europe had dancing masters who became prominent functionaries, a post that carried such privileges as the right to dance with female partners as long as their hands were gloved, to prevent touching bare skin. When the ducal court of Renaissance Europe used dance extensively in their secular and their holiday celebrations, they often hired Jewish dancing masters for lessons and choreography.

ISRAEL: An Overview. Dancers on the streets of Jerusalem celebrate Israel's first independence day in 1949. (Photograph courtesy of Judith Brin Ingber.)

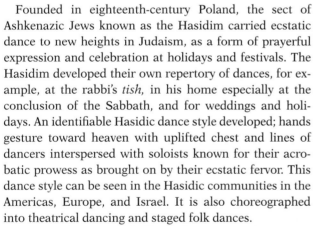

ISRAEL: An Overview. (*above*) This photograph from the 1940s shows men and women of the Palmach, Israel's first defense group, dancing shoulder to shoulder in the hora. (*right*) Young women from a kibbutz performing a line dance at the Dalia Festival in 1951. The use of a handkerchief to link hands harks back to the Jewish wedding dances from eastern Europe known as *Mitzvah Tanz.* The costumes seen here won second prize at the festival for the most original Israeli dance dress. (Photographs courtesy of Judith Brin Ingber.)

Founded in eighteenth-century Poland, the sect of Ashkenazic Jews known as the Hasidim carried ecstatic dance to new heights in Judaism, as a form of prayerful expression and celebration at holidays and festivals. The Hasidim developed their own repertory of dances, for example, at the rabbi's *tish,* in his home especially at the conclusion of the Sabbath, and for weddings and holidays. An identifiable Hasidic dance style developed; hands gesture toward heaven with uplifted chest and lines of dancers interspersed with soloists known for their acrobatic prowess as brought on by their ecstatic fervor. This dance style can be seen in the Hasidic communities in the Americas, Europe, and Israel. It is also choreographed into theatrical dancing and staged folk dances.

During the second half of the nineteenth century, Sephardic and Ashkenazic Jews began sporadic waves of immigration to return to Erets Yisra'el (the Land of Israel—the area of the ancient Hebrew kingdoms), at that time within the Ottoman Empire. The newcomers founded agricultural settlements, farming cooperatives (kibbutzim), and new towns such as Tel Aviv, and they revitalized ancient cities, including Jerusalem. Some who arrived in the 1880s brought with them a circle dance from Romania called the hora, which became symbolic of the energetic new society. Each dancer stood shoulder to shoulder with the next, each a symbolic link in a tight, vibrant, egalitarian circle. The dance changed as more new-

comers arrived, and by the second wave of immigration (1904–1914), the shoulder-to-shoulder hold became hand clasps, expanding to a more open circle; sometimes, concentric circles of dancers moved one inside the other. The hora, which now symbolizes the State of Israel, involves a driving discord between the vigorous 4/4 musical rhythm and the 6/4 dance phrase of two clockwise steps followed by a jump, kick, jump kick. Ashkenazic Jews also brought other favorite folk dances from Europe, including the *krakowiak,* the *sher,* the *cherkessia,* the polka, and the polonaise, the last adapted by kibbutz members who call it a rondo and use it to start off many festive communal gatherings.

Theatrical Dance. The third wave of immigration to Palestine (1919–1923) brought some creative European Jews trained in theatrical dance. Baruch Agadati and Rina Nikova were outstanding among them. Agadati was known mainly as a solo performer of the modern expressionist style; Nikova was a Russian-trained classical ballet dancer who became a company director.

Agadati (born 1895 in Odessa, died 1976 in Tel Aviv) originally went to Jerusalem to study painting during Ottoman rule. With the 1914 outbreak of World War I, he soon returned to Odessa, where he joined the city opera ballet. He began researching Jewish dance and choreographing solos for himself, portraying Jewish types in, for example, *Melaveh Malka,* which depicted four rabbis and their different responses to the Sabbath. After returning to Tel Aviv when the war was over, in 1919 he presented the first modern dance recital there at the Eden cinema. The religious community criticized his dance *Morning Prayer*, in which he appeared cloaked in the traditional *tallit* (prayer shawl). His dances depicted the colorful personalities he had met, Yemenite and Persian Jews as well as local Arabs. In 1925 Agadati toured Europe with great success; Diaghilev's Ballets Russes designer Natalia Goncharova created costumes for his solo performances in Paris. By the 1930s, Agadati had branched out from solo work to larger projects, which included initiating Tel Aviv's popular Purim street celebration, the 'Adlayada'. His dance "Hora Agadati" became a classic Israeli folk dance. Agadati was one of the first to mix his own steps with Middle Eastern syncopated rhythms and Arab-influenced *debka* (Ar., *dabkah*) stamping.

Nikova (born 1898 in Russia, died 1974 in Jerusalem) arrived in Palestine in 1924 and opened a ballet studio in Tel Aviv. She soon began choreographing ballets on biblical themes and formed a company, the Biblical Ballet. Classical ballet was at the heart of her style, but she also taught her dancers to improvise. By 1933 she had seven Yemenite Jewish women dancers in her company, with Rachel Nadav one of the stars. Nikova realized that the Yemenite dance style suited her biblical subjects much better than *danse d'école*. In 1937, Baron Maurice de Rothschild sponsored an extensive British and European tour for the company; it continued until 1947. Nikova then taught in Jerusalem until her death.

Yardena Cohen (born c.1910 in Bat Galim Palestine, now Israel) grew up in an established Haifa family and was sent to Europe to study dance with Gret Palucca. Returning home in the mid-1930s, Cohen began choreographing solo concerts for herself and her Sephardic musicians. Because she wished to capture her country's authentic sights and sounds, for her solo programs, she used such props as straw mats, ceramic pitchers, fish nets, tambourines, and a one-headed clay drum. In 1937 she won the Tel Aviv Municipality competition for the use of the most authentic Israeli dance sources. An outlet for her talents were the kibbutzim, who asked her to stage their festivities with her original dances, many of which became folk dance classics, although she resented their being excerpted from her pageants. Cohen ran a studio in Haifa for about fifty years. Some of her students were Shalom Hermon, later a renowned folk dance creator himself, noted for the Debka Dayagim, for creating the Haifa Independence Day dance parades, and for becoming matriculation dance-education advisor to Israel's Ministry of Culture and Education; other of her dancers were Roni Segal, Yehudah Maor, and Yaron Margolin.

Gertrud Kraus (born 1903 in Vienna, died 1977 in Tel Aviv) was to become the most important dance personality in Erets Yisra'el in the 1930s and 1940s. She first visited Palestine on a solo tour in 1931 and again in 1933. In 1935 she decided to settle in Tel Aviv, bringing with her a strong repertory of expressionist solo and company works from her renowned European career, such as *Songs of the Ghetto*. She opened a studio and formed a modern troupe, at first consisting mainly of young European-born dancers, including Hilde Kesten and Naomi Aleskovsky. Kraus's dramatic and contemporary-looking dances enlivened Palestine Folk Opera performances in the 1940s. Her group also performed in Tel Aviv with the Palestine Orchestra, founded in 1936 by the internationally renowned conductor Arturo Toscanini and virtuoso violinist Bronislaw Huberman.

Although Kraus had little financial support, she gathered around her such artists as composer Marc Lavry and set and costume designer Anatol Gurevitch, and she main-

ISRAEL: An Overview. Baruch Agadati, c.1927, wearing a costume of his own design in one of his many solos. (Photograph from the Israel Dance Library Archive, Tel Aviv; courtesy of Giora Manor.)

tained performances through 1951. In that year she founded the short-lived Israel Ballet Theatre. At her invitation the American choreographer Talley Beatty created a dance about Israel's struggle for survival called *Fire in the Hills*. Dancers in the new company included Arie Kalev, Yonatan Karmon, Naomi Aleskovsky, Nira Paz, Hilde Kesten, and Rina Shaham, all of whom became prominent in Israel's fledgling modern dance movement. Kraus's company disbanded after one season, but she continued to teach and remained the most influential personality in modern dance in Israel. In 1968 she was awarded the prestigious government award, the Israel Prize. She was appointed professor in the dance department of the Rubin Academy of Music and Dance in Jerusalem, which each year awards a prize in her memory to a young choreographer. [*See the entry on Kraus.*]

In the 1930s and 1940s, a unique dance phenomenon occurred—the revitalization of an ancient people's community dance culture. Living outside Erets Yisra'el for

ISRAEL: An Overview. Viennese-born Gertrud Kraus became one of Israel's most influential choreographers. Here, Hilde Kesten and Vera Goldman appear in her characteristically expressionist work *The Poet's Dream* (1938), set to music by Franz Schubert. In 1988, this dance was reconstructed by former Kraus dancer Naomi Aleskovsky. (Photograph from the Israel Dance Library Archive, Tel Aviv; courtesy of Giora Manor.)

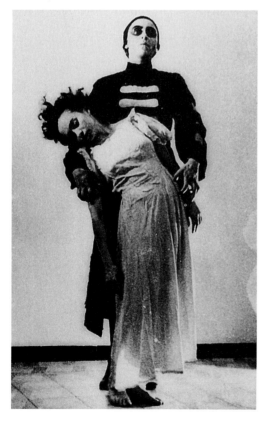

centuries, the majority of Jews had become accustomed to celebrating the spring Passover holiday, the summer Shavuʿot holiday, and the autumn Sukkot holiday with few of their biblical agricultural dance components. With the return to the land and its cycle of planting and harvest, Israel's kibbutzim rejoiced at each new crop in a traditional Jewish way—with dances of celebration for the whole community. Some of the kibbutzim had members with theatrical dance training from Europe, such as Lea Bergstein; others hired such artists as Yardena Cohen, whose dance pageants were so successful that they spoke to all Israelis, not just those living on a kibbutz. These new dances supplied Israelis with replacements for the social dances imported from Europe and for the folk dances that were considered foreign to the emerging Jewish life. After 1948, as the first generation of children born in the State of Israel began to mature, the new society searched for authentic cultural material to call its own.

The seminal figure in what became the Israeli folk-dance movement was Gert Kaufmann, later known as Gurit Kadman (born 1897 in Leipzig, Germany, died 1987 in Tel Aviv). She maintained that "for people who fervently wished to have dances of our own in our lifetime, there was no other choice" than to break with the traditional view that folk dance takes generations to create. Within a generation she had created the first Israeli folk dance company, Ha-Poel (The Worker), which toured Europe in 1947. Like the Jewish dancing masters of Renaissance Europe, she roamed the countryside, but in Israel, instilling excitement, spreading the new dances, and creating celebratory contexts for the people. With her charismatic leadership, she originated festivals, contests, companies of ethnic dancers from the various Jewish communities, and a network of Israeli folk dance companies; she published literature about Israeli folk dance, produced films, and trained a brigade of teachers and folk dance leaders. She got government backing to sustain her activities and the support of the countrywide Histadrut labor union. Tirtza Hodes followed Kadman as director of the Histadrut folk dance department. Kadman received the Israel Prize in 1981. [*See the entry on Kadman.*]

In 1944, while World War II raged and Nazi Germany was destroying European Jewry, Kadman created the Dalia Folk Dance Festival at Kibbutz Dalia, where she had been invited to stage a Shavuʿot celebration. That festival and all the subsequent Dalias she directed in 1947, 1951, and 1955 were catalysts for the Israeli folk dance movement, when new dances were introduced. The festivals became a pilgrimage for Israelis to acknowledge the spirit and vitality of their new country. At the final Dalia Festival in 1968, sixty thousand spectators celebrated Israel's twentieth anniversary.

Many of the early creators of Israeli folk dance were professional dancers who immigrated in the 1930s from central Europe, students of expressionist dance artists. Lea Bergstein (born 1902 in Galicia, died 1989 at Kibbutz Ramat Yoḥanan) danced in the companies of Vera Skoronel and Gertrud Kraus before moving to the Galilee in northern Israel. With composer Matityahu Shelem, she created an annual cycle of festivals that became the tradition at Kibbutz Ramat Yoḥanan, though her dances were taught and danced far beyond her kibbutz realm.

Others trained in the German expressionist dance style contributed to the development of Israel's theatrical dance with performances and studio training: Shoshana and Yehudit Ornstein; Devora Bertonov from Kurt Jooss's company; and Katia Michaeli, Tehilla Roessler, and Ilse Dublon, trained by Mary Wigman. Dublon also worked in the folk dance movement and is credited with the folk dance classic *Mayim Mayim* (Water, Water), created when water was discovered at Kibbutz Naʿan. Bartonov received the Israel Prize in dance in 1971, in recognition of her performance, teaching, and dance writing.

Rivka Sturman (born 1905 in Leipzig), one of Israel's most prolific and successful folk dance creators, emigrated from Germany in 1929, where she had studied dance with Jutta Klamt. Sturman was inspired to create Israeli dances only when her own children learned German folk dances and songs at Kibbutz ʿEin-Harod for lack of Israeli ones; she incorporated the steps and rhythms of both Yemenite Jewish and the neighboring Arab dances into her own dances, which were acclaimed at every Dalia Festival. Some of her classic dances are *Zemer Atik*, *Kuma Eha*, and *Dodi Li*.

Folk dance festivals were held at Zemach in the Galilee once the Dalia Festivals ended. In 1988, to honor Israel's fortieth anniversary, a new festival was held in the Galilee town of Carmiel. Directed by Yonatan Karmon (born 1931 in Romania), a veteran Dalia dancer, the Carmiel Dance Festival takes place yearly. Karmon expanded the scope of the festival, which now includes dance companies in all styles of ethnic, folk, modern, and ballet, as well as companies from abroad. In the twenty years between Dalia and Carmiel, Karmon had created his own companies, Alumim and The Grand Music Hall of Israel, which have performed in New York, on Broadway, and in several other cities in the United States, Europe, and South America. Karmon also worked at the Olympia Theater in Paris. He began his own theatrical dance training with Kraus. Shalom Hermon, the innovative folk dance creator headed the folk dance curriculum in Israeli public schools for all grade levels. Israeli-born dancers who have become creators in the folk dance movement include the Inbal star Moshiko Halevy, Yakov Levy, Viki Cohen, Yoav

ISRAEL: An Overview. A scene from the Batsheva Dance Company's 1965 production of *The Embattled Garden*, with Moshe Efrati and Linda Hodes. Originally created by Martha Graham in 1958, this study of Adam, Eve, Lilith, and the Serpent became a cornerstone of the company's repertory. (Photograph by Jaacov Agor; used by permission; from the Israel Dance Library Archive, Tel Aviv; courtesy of Giora Manor.)

Ashriel, Eliyahu Gamliel, Shlomo Maman, Smulik Govari, and Gadi Biton.

The period following the independence of Israel in 1948 brought about fundamental changes in the country's dance life, mainly resulting from the end of central European expressionist influence and the advent of American dance influence. Several American-born dancers influenced by Martha Graham went to settle, teach, and perform in Israel, including Rena Shaham and Rena Gluck. Israeli-born dancers soon went to New York to study at the Juilliard School and at the Martha Graham studio; Hassia Agron-Levy was the first. Mirali Sharon attended the Alwin Nikolais school.

A most important development in Israeli dance occurred when thousands of Yemenite Jews were airlifted to the new country soon after independence. Sara Levi-Tanai, born into the small Yemenite community in Jerusalem, sealed her destiny when she met a group of

Yemenite youngsters, newcomers to Israel. Levi-Tanai, already known as a folk dance creator at the Dalia Festivals and the composer of some of Israel's favorite folk songs, developed into a choreographer and company director. The youngsters became the dancer-singers of her Inbal Yemenite Dance Theater. Like Rina Nikova, Levi-Tanai set about learning Yemenite steps from her dancers. She created masterpieces, such as *Yemenite Wedding*, using Yemenite Jewish folk traditions for choreography. In 1954, Jerome Robbins was asked to assess the Israeli dance situation for a Jewish-American funding agency. He identified Inbal as the most worthwhile and innovative. He arranged for the American dancer and choreographer Anna Sokolow to teach modern dance technique to Inbal and introduced the troupe to the impresario Sol Hurok. By 1958, Hurok was sponsoring Inbal and its nineteen dancers on tours in the United States, Europe, and England. The company continued to tour the world but by the 1970s had lost support at home. In 1991 Sara Levi-Tanai was ousted from her position as director and choreographer. After several attempts to find a replacement, Margalit Oved became artistic director. Although Oved was one of the original Inbal dancers and had gained fame during her twenty years in Los Angeles, she resigned after just one season. The company is now mandated to become a center for the preservation of folklore material, though Sara Levi-Tanei's works continue to be performed. [*See the entry on Levi-Tanai.*]

Sokolow returned yearly to teach at Inbal and gathered a group of young modern dancers around her, including Ze'eva Cohen, for seasons from 1962 to 1964. Sokolow's Israeli company, The Lyric Theater, performed some of her best-known works, such as *Rooms* and *Dreams*. When Sokolow returned to the United States, many of the dancers became the founding members of the Batsheva Dance Company.

Batsheva was especially important to modern dance in Israel. The premiere performance was in December 1964. Baroness Batsheva de Rothschild, who left America to live in Israel, decided there was a need for a modern dance company with professional salaries, full-scale sets and costumes, and thorough modern training. Rothschild sent several young dancers to New York to study, mainly at the Martha Graham school, where Rothschild had been the benefactress. Graham agreed to be the new company's artistic advisor. Several of Graham's dancers—Robert Cohan, Jane Dudley, and Linda Hodes—came to work with Batsheva, to direct, to teach, or to choreograph. The Israeli company members included Rina Schoenfeld, and Rena Gluck, Moshe Efrati, and Ehud Ben-David, powerful dancers well versed in the Graham canon who became international stars.

There followed a period in which many of the world's great choreographers came to Tel Aviv to work with the Batsheva Dance Company, among them Jerome Robbins, José Limón, John Cranko, and Kurt Jooss. Moshe Efrati, one of Batsheva's original dancers, left the company in 1967. He continued to choreograph for it before he established his own group, Kol Demama, in 1975. Efrati began experimenting with hearing-impaired dancers, perfecting a method using vibrations on the floorboards of the stage to communicate rhythm. His company continues to perform his works, although there are few hearing-impaired dancers in it today. In 1996, Efrati won the prestigious Israel Prize for his dance work. Other Batsheva dancers also became choreographers and teachers, including Oshra Elkayam.

During the early 1970s, the Batsheva Dance Company earned acclaim in the United States, Europe, and Asia. However, in 1974, the Baroness withdrew her support for the company that bears her name. In 1967 she had founded a second Israeli company, the Bat-Dor Dance Company, to provide a basis for her protégé Jeannette Ordman to dance and to develop a company with a more balletic base. As with the Batsheva Dance Company, many choreographers from abroad built the repertory, and many of the same people choreographed for both companies—while Israelis Domi Reiter-Soffer, Mirali Sharon, Siki Kol, and others were also given opportunities to choreograph. Reiter-Soffer, like many Israeli dancers, had already made his name abroad in the British Isles and Australia and had choreographed for the Dance Theatre of Harlem.

In 1974 the Batsheva Dance Company became a publicly supported company through Israel's Ministry of Culture and Education. Artistic directors—all invited artists from abroad—came and went, and the company lost its Graham repertory to become stylistically adrift. New impetus was given to Batsheva in the 1980s by a young generation of choreographers, including Mark Morris, Daniel Ezralow, and the native Israeli choreographer Ohad Naharin. Batsheva's identity crisis was finally resolved in 1990 when Naharin became its artistic director. He had started with the company but had gone on to work with the Martha Graham and the Maurice Béjart companies and to do his own work in New York. He has since made Batsheva a company almost exclusively for his own works. Its extensive tours within Israel and abroad are met with much acclaim. [*See the entry on Naharin.*]

In 1970 another modern-dance company that was to become central in the dance life of Israel was founded by a group of kibbutz members who were dancers. In 1974, Yehudit Arnon became the artistic director of the Kibbutz Contemporary Dance Company situated in the northern region at Kibbutz Ga'aton. The special atmosphere of this company, whose members live in collective settlements, has attracted many well-known choreographers such as Jiří Kylián and Mats Ek. The company has traveled throughout the world, presenting mainly the works of its resident choreographer, Rami Be‘er.

In the 1980s, as established companies seemed to falter, several independent choreographers experimented in dance theater: Ruth Ziv-Eyal, Oshra Elkayam, Yaron Margolin, and Ruth Eshel. Rina Shoenfeld, acclaimed Batsheva soloist known for her Graham interpretations, created solo and group works and continued to be an active figure in Israel's dance scene. In 1988, the Bat-Dor Dance Company had to curtail its activities when its producer, Batsheva de Rothschild, could no longer underwrite its

expenditures. Other setbacks occurred, including the partial destruction by fire of the company's studios and theater. A reduced company was soon augmented by dancers who emigrated from the former Soviet Union. Domy Reiter-Soffer, Gheorge ("Gigi") Caciuleanu, and many Dutch choreographers have been working with the company.

For the 1988/89 season, a new center for dance, the Suzanne Dellal Center, was established in Tel Aviv's old picturesque neighborhood. The Batsheva Dance Company as well as the Inbal Dance Theater were finally allotted modest quarters in a permanent arrangement of buildings housing studios, offices, and three performance spaces in reconstructed school buildings. The first director of the Suzanne Dellal Center was former Batsheva and Rambert Dance Company dancer Yair Vardi. The center has provided space and support for experimental and nonestablishment dance; it has also become a showcase for the government-funded Gevanim Hadashim Bemahol (New Variations in Dance) and Haramat Masach (Lift the Curtain) for young choreographers, the biannual International Choreographic Competition, and the annual Mia Arbatova Classical Ballet Competition (named after the esteemed ballet teacher).

Among those whose works have been shown at Suzanne Dellal are Nir Ben-Gal and his wife Liat Dror, who began their joint choreographies and dance-theater works with the Kibbutz Contemporary Dance Company. Since 1992 they have run their own group, which often tours abroad.

ISRAEL: An Overview. (*above*) A scene from *Mythical Hunters*, created by Glen Tetley for the newly formed Batsheva Dance Company in 1965. (*right*) A dramatic moment from *Jacob in Horan* (1973), created by Sara Levi-Tanai for Inbal Dance Theatre, a company she founded in 1950. (Photograph above by Jaacov Agor; photograph at right by Mula & Haramaty, Tel Aviv; both used by permission; from the Israel Dance Library Archive, Tel Aviv; courtesy of Giora Manor.)

Ido Tadmor, a former dancer at Bat-Dor, Batsheva, and the American Lar Lubovitch Dance Company, also has a new group associated with the Suzanne Dellal Center. Others whose work has been seen there are Amir Kolben and Noa Dar. Kolben had worked in Jerusalem with Meira Eliash-Chain in a promising dance venture, Tamar-Jerusalem, which lasted for three seasons in the 1980s.

Jerusalem, Israel's capital, has never held a central position in the dance world. The Jerusalem Ensemble, which performed works by Anna Sokolow and Flora Cushman, and Yaron Margolin's company were theater-dance companies active in Jerusalem in the 1980s. The Israel Festival, held in Jerusalem, is one of the main venues for visiting dance companies. A new opera house opened in Tel Aviv in 1994 that also serves as a stage for foreign dance companies.

Although ballet students in Israel had less of an outlet than modern dance students, ballet teachers began arriving in the 1920s. Ballet students in the 1940s and 1950s studied with Haifa's Valentine Archipova or with Tel Aviv's Mia Arbatova, a former dancer for Michel Fokine's Riga company. Israeli ballet dancers had no choice but to look for work abroad. Among these were Berta Yampolski and Hillel Markman, who danced in European companies for several years. In 1968, they returned and started a company with five dancers. From this modest beginning their company, the Israel Ballet, developed with repertory by Balanchine and mainly by Yampolski.

A special contribution to dance research is Noa Eshkol's movement-notation system, which she devised with Avraham Wachman in the 1950s. Today, it is used by many scientists as well as dancers all over the world. Her former student Amos Hetz heads the movement department at the Rubin Academy of Music and Dance in Jerusalem. He teaches the Eshkol-Wachman method and he produces

ISRAEL: An Overview. A number of choreographers have staged works for the Bat-Dor Dance Company, founded by Batsheva de Rothschild in 1967 under the direction of Jeannette Ordman. Here, men from the company arch backward in Gene Hill Sagan's *And After . . .* (1974). The set was designed by Dani Karavan. (Photograph by Mula & Haramaty, Tel Aviv; used by permission; from the Israel Dance Library Archive, Tel Aviv; courtesy of Giora Manor.)

ISRAEL: An Overview. Ido Tadmor, one of the new generation of Israeli choreographers, in his *Solo* (1995). (Photograph by Gadi Dagon; used by permission; from the Israel Dance Library Archive, Tel Aviv; courtesy of Giora Manor.)

BIBLIOGRAPHY

Cohen, Yardena. *Betof u'bemahol.* Tel Aviv, 1963.
Eshel, Ruth. *Lirkod im hahalom.* Tel Aviv, 1991.
Friedhaber, Zvi. *Hamahol b'am Yisrael.* Tel Aviv, 1984.
Friedhaber, Zvi. *Em vekala.* Haifa, 1989.
Goren, Yoram. *Sadot lavshu mahol.* Ramat-Yohanan, 1983.
Ingber, Judith Brin. "Shorashim: The Roots of Israeli Folk Dance." *Dance Perspectives*, no. 59 (Autumn 1974).
Ingber, Judith Brin. *Victory Dances: The Life of Fred Berk.* Tel Aviv, 1985.
Ingber, Judith Brin, ed. "Dancing into Marriage: Jewish Wedding Dances." *Dance Research Journal* 17 (Fall 1985); 18 (Spring 1986).
Ingber, Judith Brin. "The Priestesses." *Dance Chronicle* 18.3 (1995): 453–465.
Israel Dance Annual. Tel Aviv, 1975–1990.
Kadman, Gurit. *Am roked.* Tel Aviv, 1969.
Mahol Be Yisrael (Israel Dance Quarterly). Haifa, 1993–.
Manor, Giora. *Inbal: Quest for a Movement-Language.* Tel Aviv, 1975.
Manor, Giora. *Hayey hamahol shel Gertrud Kraus.* Tel Aviv, 1977.
Manor, Giora, ed. *Agadati: The Pioneer of Modern Dance in Israel.* Tel Aviv, 1986.
Sharett, Rena. *Kumah eha.* Tel Aviv, 1988.
Sowden, Dora. *Bat Dor: A Tribute to Jeannette Ordman.* Tel Aviv, 1990.
Warren, Larry. *Anna Sokolow: The Rebellious Spirit.* Princeton, 1991.
JUDITH BRIN INGBER and GIORA MANOR

Ethnic Dance

The dances of the ethnic communities within Israel may be divided into three main categories: (1) those created by particular Jewish communities in the Diaspora and brought with them to Israel (e.g., European Hasidim; Yemenites); (2) those adopted and preserved by Jewish communities from the peoples among whom they dwelt in the Diaspora (e.g., the Circassian dances from Russia; those of Bukhara and Georgia; the dances of Kurdistan;

ISRAEL: Ethnic Dance. The men's dances of the Yemenite Jews are accompanied by songs from the *diwan*, a collection of paraliturgical Arabic poetry. Here, one man leads another in the *shira* dance, based on poetry in the *diwan*. (Photograph by Eckhard Joite; courtesy of Naomi Bahat-Ratzon and Avner Bahat.)

annual seasons of dance performances based on this system. He has developed the system for stage performance known as "chamber dance."

Dance education is widespread in Israel. Private and municipal studios are active in most towns, and regional dance centers, based mainly in kibbutzim, supply much of the young talent for the professional companies. There are several high schools for the arts that also maintain dance departments. In the public high schools dance theory as well as dance practice are optional subjects offered for matriculation certificates upon graduation. Israeli folk dance has also been integrated into the public school curriculum for all grades. The Rubin Academy of Music and Dance, located in Jerusalem, offers a bachelor of arts degree in dance. The dance program is directed by Rena Gluck, former Batsheva star. The physical education department of the Kibbutz Teachers Seminary in Tel Aviv, directed by Naomi Bahat, is the only other institution to bestow a bachelor of arts degree in dance.

In 1975, the Israel Dance Library was initiated by American patrons, including Anne Wilson Wangh. It is situated in the Tel Aviv Municipal Library at Beit Ariela and serves some two thousand students and teachers annually. Another resource, the *Israel Dance Annual* was begun in 1975 by Judith Brin Ingber and Giora Manor. It was replaced in 1993 by the *Israel Dance Quarterly*, edited jointly by Giora Manor and Ruth Eshel. Since 1988, *Rokdim* (Dancing), a magazine of Israeli folk dance, has been edited by Yaron Meishar.

[*See also* Inbal Dance Theatre.]

ISRAEL: Ethnic Dance. In this henna ceremony, performed at a wedding, two Yemenite Jewish women dance and balance objects atop their heads. (Photograph by Naftali Hilger; courtesy Naomi Bahat-Ratzon and Avner Bahat.)

those of North Africa and Ethiopia); and (3) those of the Palestinian Arabs of Israel.

The dominant ethnic dances in Israel are those of the first category. Except at weddings, the public place to see Hasidic dancing in Israel is on the holiday of Lag ba-'Omer at Meiron in the Galilee, when Hasidim gather to celebrate.

The dances of the Yemenite Jews differ greatly from those of the Hasidim. The presence of Jews in Yemen may date back to the destruction of the First Jerusalem Temple in 587 BCE, when Jews fled the conquering Babylonians. They lived in Yemen for centuries, establishing there several different communities. They began their return to Israel in the 1880s by caravan, which corresponds with the First 'Aliyyah, or wave of emigrants, from Europe. From 1948 to 1950, when the new State of Israel began to rescue beleaguered Jews worldwide, the remaining Yemenite community was airlifted almost in its entirety to Israel.

Yemenite Jewish dance is always accompanied by song and percussion on domestic vessels (e.g., metal cans, brass plates) but never by musical instruments. It is said that because Yemenite Jews are still mourning the destruction of the Temple, they will not play on instruments. Nevertheless, their drumming and singing are skillful and developed.

In communities of Jews from the northern Yemenite district of Haidan, men and women dance together in lines, both sexes wearing almost identical dress. In communities from Habban and Ḥaḍramawt in southern Yemen, the men wear tight-fitting skirts and perform a turbulent dance.

Curiously, Yemenite Jews are ambivalent in their attitude toward dancers. On the one hand, dancers are regarded with affection, even admiration, if they perform

skillfully and give their audiences good entertainment. On the other, dancing itself is not considered the most honorable of occupations, and the rabbis tend to view dancers as somewhat frivolous members of society. It is also, however, a *mitsvah* ("commandment") that all Jews dance at weddings in order to entertain the groom and bride, and even the rabbis take part in a restrained and decorous manner.

The main dance in the Yemenite repertory comes from central Yemen, from the region of the capital city, San'a. In that region men and women dance separately, performing chamber dances confined to a limited area in the main room of an ordinary house. The space is referred to as the *diwan;* this is also the term used for the collection of paraliturgical poetry written in Hebrew, Arabic, and Aramaic that is sung by men.

Yemenite men's dances are accompanied by the songs preserved in the *diwan.* Singers, seated near the dancers, accompany themselves by beating the rhythms on metal cans. There are no professional dancers among the Yemenite Jews, but there are dancers whose special talents are recognized and upon whom audiences call to perform. Yemenite Jews learn these dances from childhood by watching and imitating their elders. Little boys are often seen trying out the steps and body movements alongside the older men.

The number of male dancers is two or four, and their short dance steps are taken over short distances—they usually dance in pairs, one of them leading the other by means of eye or hand signals. Their feet perform a regular dance pattern, while the upper part of the body effects a more improvisatory series of movements. The dance follows the text of the song, particularly its form and meter. The musical meter is alternately binary and ternary—the transition from one to the other depending on the song's text. The beat is varied, usually proceeding from slow to fast (*accelerando*). Musical and poetic meter are related in a somewhat complex manner.

Some of the hand and torso movements are connected with the chironomic motions that go with the study of the biblical cantillation symbols: the right hand is especially entrusted with a complete system of agreed-upon signs and gestures, to aid in memorizing the melodic fragments and their combination in the traditional change. Yemenite boys begin at age three to read books of the Torah, so all these gestures become part of male body vocabulary.

The dance is incorporated, then, in a three-part event that is also poetic and musical; it serves, with the poetry it accompanies, as the centerpiece. The first part is the *nashid*, a slow introduction in free meter, with neither percussion nor dancing—a formalized invitation to dance is enacted and the dancer, first rejecting the invitation, finally "succumbs" and agrees to perform. The second part is the *shira,* a poetic piece sung and accompanied by the dancers drumming on a large metal can. Finally comes the *hallel,* an anticlimactic piece, in which the dancers join the singers and with them sing a hymn of praise to God, to the guest of honor, and to all those present.

Yemenite women accompany their dancing with songs in their own gender-specific Yemeni-Arabic vernacular. The songs relate to the women's life in the community and in the family—to the pleasures and hardships that are their lot—and they are handed down orally. The women accompany their singing and dancing by tapping their fingertips on the *sahn,* a brass plate held vertically. One of the best known of the Yemenite women's dances is the sedate *da'asa,* which has a 7/8 measure and consists of swaying the torso and hips gently forward and backward. The women dance together at weddings, especially at the henna ceremony—before and after the bride's hands are smeared with the red pigment (symbolizing life and health).

Yemenite dance has strongly influenced the theatrical art dance of Israel, mainly by choreographers with a Yemenite background, like Sara Levi-Tanai and her world-renowned Inbal Dance Theater and her disciple Margalit Oved, but also by non-Yemenite artists. Yemenite dance has strongly influenced the newly developing folk dance of Israel as well.

Another category of ethnic dance comes from the Muslim countries of the Middle East and Africa, in which some Jews lived for centuries. As executed today in Israel, some of these are not straightforward folk dances but are instead stage-managed presentations that demand considerable physical prowess and professional dance training. Included in this category are the lyrical Bukharan dance of the Kurdish Jews and the very vigorous dance of the Circassians (non-Jews from the Caucasus Mountains who live in Israel). In Kurdish dance, responsive singing alternates between two soloists or a soloist and a group of dancers, typically accompanied by a drum *(dohla)* and a reed instrument *(zurna).* The dances are performed in an open circle; the arms of the dancers are tightly linked while their legs move in energetic stamping patterns.

An emerging trend in Israel is for reviving some traditional customs and celebrations that immigrants abandoned when they first assimilated into Israeli culture. Kurdish Jews, for example, have revived the Seheraneh celebration that includes much of their dance tradition. Moroccan Jews have revived their spring festival, following Passover, called the Mimunah, which includes dance. Also being revived are the *hillulot,* the Hasidic pilgrimages, to the graves of renowned rabbis, where dancing is an important part of the celebration.

Instrumental in this change has been the Israel Ethnic Dance Project, begun in 1971 by Gurit Kadman. It combines the efforts of the Folk Dance Department of the Histadrut (trades union), of Hebrew University, and of Israel's Ministry of Education and Culture. The project revived the Maimuna, which it documented with information from the Moroccan community's elderly and published its research. It also created folk dance troupes based on the authentic dances of Kurdistani Jews, as well as those from

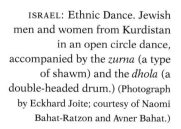

ISRAEL: Ethnic Dance. Jewish men and women from Kurdistan in an open circle dance, accompanied by the *zurna* (a type of shawm) and the *dhola* (a double-headed drum.) (Photograph by Eckhard Joite; courtesy of Naomi Bahat-Ratzon and Avner Bahat.)

India, Yemen, and other countries—all with distinctive dance repertories.

The *lehaka*, the ethnic performing ensemble, is an innovative ethnic dance development that reflects Israel's pride in its cultural diversity. Ensembles demonstrate the dance traditions of the various ethnic communities, both Jewish and non-Jewish, frequently ensuring a dance presence at local, national, and even international ethnic festivals and events. Ensembles also allow the young people of a particular ethnic community the opportunity to learn and perform the dances of their elders, a natural progression that had ceased. Young dancers and the *lehaka* directors are aided by the *lehaka* network, frequently sponsored by government agencies.

Another important category of ethnic dance is performed by Palestinians, Israel's Arab population. While their dances differ slightly from place to place and from group to group (villagers, townsfolk, nomadic bedouin, Druze), they are basically the same throughout the country, and in most respects they are similar to the dances of Arab societies in neighboring countries. They are performed as part of family and communal celebrations, and men and women usually dance separately.

There are two main types of Arab men's dances: the *dabkah* and the *saff*, or *sahge*. The *dabkah* is a lively affair whose outstanding feature is the often complex rhythmic movement of the feet. A group of eight to twelve young men arrange themselves in an open circle and hold on to each other in any of three characteristic ways: by holding hands, by gripping each other's belts, or by resting their hands on their neighbors' shoulders. The group has a leader who may either take first place in the line, waving a kerchief (tradition has it that he once brandished a sword), or take up a position opposite the line, rousing his companions' enthusiasm by calling to them, by singing, or

by his own emphatic dance movements. The musical accompaniment is provided by a *nay* (a Persian and Arab flute), which improvises on set melodic phrases, by a *durbakka* (a pitcher-type drum), and by the rhythmic shouts and singing of a soloist or of the entire group. The energetic foot stamping serves as a counterpoint to the musical accompaniment. The dancers move in a circle around the musicians, and the audience participates by clapping hands, shouting cries of encouragement, and, on some more excited occasions, firing rifles into the air. There are several versions of the *dabkah* but all share these characteristics.

The *saff*, or *sahge*, is a procession dance that advances slowly in a long line. Most of the Arab men present at a celebration take part, whether young or old—sometimes numbering dozens. The *saff* is a far simpler dance than the *dabkah* and is often performed as part of nuptials, to conduct the bridegroom on his wedding day from the home of his family to that of his bride or to the house in which the newlyweds are to settle. On such an occasion the dancers may traverse several miles and dance for several hours with occasional rest breaks. The dance, however, may be performed for its own sake; the dancers, in a long, arc-shaped line, will move around the village square, following a circular route that repeats itself endlessly. Within the line, the many dancers arrange themselves by village or neighborhood. Each group has its own leader, who spurs his group on to greater efforts. In doing so, he improvises his steps more freely than those of the rest of his group. The dance movements are simple: the legs execute walking steps forward, while the hands move rhythmically and clap at regular intervals. The musical accompaniment is vocal and provided by a soloist (the *sha'er*), to whom the dancers respond in song. The dance is divided into two periods: in the first, the soloist improvises in free rhythm and the dancers, standing still, sing their responses to him; in the second, the solo singing is more measured and the dancers move forward in line, continuing their responses.

Arab women have simpler dances than the men have. For example, they form a circle to surround a bride on the eve of her wedding; then executing a plain walking-step, they accompany themselves by repeatedly singing a short refrain.

Different types of ethnic dance are important in contemporary Israel. There is dance that is an integral part of family and community life, based on the traditional precepts of the specific ethnic group (even if some change has taken place in the new, more modern environment); urban folk dancing is based on original models (e.g., on the hora or on Yemenite "pop") or on ideas assembled from several original models (e.g., modern Hasidic dances); and new dances or artworks created by Israeli choreographers and/or dance instructors are usually for a perfor-

ISRAEL: Ethnic Dance. Druzes from Galilee performing the *dabkah*, a popular men's line dance. (Photograph by Avner Bahat; used by permission.)

mance program or an event, which then may become part of the Israeli folk dance tradition.

BIBLIOGRAPHY

Avraham, L., and Naomi Bahat-Ratzon. "Song and Dance as Means of Expression of the Inner World of the Jewish Women in Yemen" (in Hebrew). In *Bat-Teman/Daughter of Yemen*, edited by Shalom Seri. Tel Aviv, 1993.

Bahat-Ratzon, Naomi. "Le Saff: Procession dansée dans les cérémonies du mariage druze." *Orbis Musicae*, no. 5 (1975–1976).

Bahat-Ratzon, Naomi. "Is the Hora an Israeli Dance?" *Israel Dance* (1977): 9–15.

Bahat-Ratzon, Naomi. "The Debka: A Traditional Dance of Unity and Relaxation." *Israel Dance* (1978–1979): 9–14.

Bahat-Ratzon, Naomi, and Avner Bahat. "Traditional Scriptural Reading Hand Movements as a Source of Dance of Yemenite Jews." *Israel Dance* (1980): 22–24.

Bahat-Ratzon, Naomi. "The Status of the Dancer in the Jewish-Yemenite Tradition." *Israel Dance* (1982): 9–12.

Bahat-Ratzon, Naomi, and Avner Bahat. "Music and Dance of Yemenite Jews in Israel: One Hundred Years of Activity and Research" (in Hebrew). In *Se'i Yona: Yemenite Jews in Israel*, edited by Shalom Seri. Tel Aviv, 1984.

Bahat-Ratzon, Naomi, and Avner Bahat. *Saperi Tama*. Tel Aviv, 1995.

Eshel, Ruth. "Shoulder Dances: Dance Traditions of the Ethiopian Jews." *Israel Dance*, no. 2 (September 1993): 68–71.

Eshkol, Noa, et al. *Folk Dances of Israel: The Yemenite Dance—142 Steps*. Tel Aviv, 1972.

Friedhaber, Zvi. "Dance Customs among Bukharan Jews" (in Hebrew). *Jewish Dance Archive*, no. 5 (1976).

Friedhaber, Zvi. "Dramatization in Chassidic Dances." *Israel Dance* (1983): 5–8.

Goren, Ayalah. "The Ethnic Dance in Israel." *Jewish Folklore and Ethnology Newsletter* 8.3–4 (1986).

Squires, Pamela. "Dance and Music of Iraqi Kurdish Jews in Israel." Master's thesis, University of California, Los Angeles, 1975.

Staub, Shalom. "The Yemenite Jewish Dance: An Anthropological Perspective." Master's thesis, Wesleyan University, 1978.

RECORDINGS. *Hassidic Tunes of Dancing and Rejoicing* (RCA, 1976). *The Yemenite Jews* UNESCO Collection, Auvides D8024, 1980). *Yemenite Jewish Songs from the Diwan* (AMTI [Anthology of Musical Traditions in Israel], Jewish Music Research Center, Hebrew University, 1982). *Ahavat Hadasa* (Beth Hatefutsoth Records 9001, 1990). *Neve Midbar, Jewish Yemenite Women's Songs* (Beth Hatefutsoth Records, BTR 9503, 1995).

NAOMI BAHAT-RATZON and AVNER BAHAT

ISTOMINA, AVDOTIA (Avdot'ia Il'inichna Istomina; born 6 [17] January 1799 in Saint Petersburg, Russia; died 26 July [8 August] 1848 in Saint Petersburg), dancer. Istomina was the favorite ballerina of the poet Aleksandr Pushkin, who saw her as the ideal exponent of the Russian school of dance. She was the inspiration for Pushkin's remarkable poetic definition of ballet as "flight informed by the dancer's soul." Istomina was only six years old when she began attending the Imperial Theater School in Saint Petersburg, where her teachers were Evgenia Sazonova, Charles-Louis Didelot, and especially Evgenia

Kolosova—then reigning ballerina and Didelot's surrogate as master teacher—who influenced her dancing style and artistic manner. Istomina graduated in 1816, but her performing career had begun when she was only eight. Didelot particularly favored her, introducing her to every aspect of a professional career and to the latest performing techniques.

Istomina made her formal debut as Galatea in Didelot's *Acis and Galatea* on 30 August 1816 and became an instant idol of the public. Her elevation and graceful line made her indispensable for principal roles in Anacreontic ballets, especially Flora in Didelot's *Zéphire et Flore*, which she performed two years later and thereafter retained in her repertory. Pimen Arapov, a contemporary chronicler of Russian theatrical life, left this thumbnail sketch:

> Of medium height and pleasing visage, Istomina was slender, shapely, and had fiery black eyes with beautiful long eyelashes that lent her face a unique quality. She had well-shaped, strong legs, total aplomb on the stage, and at the same time grace, lightness, and astonishing speed. Her pirouettes and elevation were breathtaking.

The numerous roles Istomina created revealed her multifaceted talent. In comedy her portrayals were noted for gaiety, playfulness, wit, and a touch of mischief. Examples include Lise in *La Fille Mal Gardée*, Susanne in Didelot's *Don Carlos and Rosalba*, and another Susanne in Auguste Poireau's *Almaviva et Rosine, ou Le Tuteur Dupé*. She gave memorable performances in various *divertissements* and pantomimes, creating dynamic characters capable of heroism, such as Louisa in *La Héroine Villageoise*, choreographed by Chevalier Peicam de Bressoles (called Chevalier) and Ivan Valberkh, and as another Louisa in Valberkh's *Le Déserteur* (after Dauberval). But she could equally well portray attractive, graceful characters, romantic girls trembling at first love, such as Zetulba in Didelot's *The Caliph of Baghdad, or The Youthful Adventures of Harun al-Rashid* and Laura in his *Laura and Henry*. She danced Isora in Didelot's *Raoul Barbe-Bleue* (after Valberkh) and the title role in Giuseppe Canziani's *Inès de Castro*, which called for subtle miming, dramatic temperament, and good acting. Her appearances in other Didelot ballets—Eucharis in *Euthyme and Eucharis, or The Vanquished Shade of Libas*, Cora in *Cora and Alonzo, or The Virgin of the Sun*, and Thisbe in *Pyramus and Thisbe*—established her reputation as a fine tragic actress. She was an adept character dancer of Polish, Russian, Italian, Serbian, and Oriental dances.

Istomina proved to be a natural actress; vaudevilles and comedies were created especially for her, for which she showed ingenuity and aptness with dialogue. Her first appearance in a drama was as Zephyretta in Aleksandr Shakhovsky's vaudeville *Phoenix, or The Morning of a Journalist*. Audiences and critics alike acclaimed her dramatic acting and beautiful singing voice. In another vaudeville by the same author, *A Traveling Dancer-Actress, or The Three Sister-Brides,* she played several roles in distinctly different styles, exhibiting her flexibility and range.

The apex of Istomina's career was in ballets based on Pushkin's works. Her Circassian Girl in Didelot's *The Prisoner of the Caucasus, or The Bride's Shade* (1823) was a real mountain girl with an authentic gait and Oriental plastique. Istomina achieved complete fusion with Pushkin's character when she magnanimously granted freedom to the man she loved and to her rival. As Ludmila in Didelot and Poireau after Glushkovsky's *Ruslan and Ludmila, or The Downfall of Chernomor, the Evil Sorcerer* (1824), Istomina emerged as a regal Russian beauty, recalling the Russian princesses of fairy tale and legend. Taking her characterization from Pushkin, she displayed courage, pride, devotion, loyalty, and defiance. Istomina's last original role before her retirement from the stage in 1836 was Tsaritsa Sumbeka in Jean-Baptiste Blache's *Sumbeka, or The Subjugation of the Kazan Kingdom* (after Didelot; 1832).

Istomina represented the dawn of the Russian ballet. The unique qualities of her talent—a natural, unaffected manner, a soulful spontaneity of movement, winsome sincerity—breathed life into the traditional classical ballet and became hallmarks of the Russian style.

BIBLIOGRAPHY

Elyash, Nikolai. *Avdotia Istomina* (in Russian). Leningrad, 1971.
Karsavina, Tamara. *Theatre Street.* Rev. and enl. ed. London, 1948.
Krasovskaya, Vera. *Russkii baletnyi teatr: Ot vozniknoveniia do serediny XIX veka.* Leningrad, 1958.
Migel, Parmenia. *The Ballerinas: From the Court of Louis XIV to Pavlova.* New York, 1972.
Schmidt, Paul. "Pushkin and Istomina: Ballet in Nineteenth-Century Russia." *Dance Research Journal* 20 (Winter 1988):3–7.
Swift, Mary Grace. *A Loftier Flight: The Life and Accomplishments of Charles Louis Didelot.* Middletown, Conn., 1974.

NIKOLAI I. ELYASH
Translated from Russian

ITALY. [*To survey the dance traditions of Italy, this entry comprises five articles:*

For further discussion of court dance, see Social Dance, *article on* Court and Social Dance before 1800; *for further discussion of theatrical dance, see the entries on individual companies, choreographers, and dancers.*]

Dance Traditions before 1800

The earliest known culture of the Italian Peninsula was that of the Etruscans, a people of obscure origin who established themselves in west-central Italy in the eighth century BCE. Their dance heritage remains mostly unknown, but the material remains of their culture—frescoes, sculptures, tomb decoration, and vases—are rich in iconography, including dance motifs. Although kinetic elements cannot be deduced with certainty from the tomb paintings of the sixth and fifth centuries BCE, much can be understood from them about the role of dance in Etruscan culture. Dance appears to have been an integral part of religious ceremonies, military and political celebrations, and games and festivities accompanying salient life experiences.

The main actors in these events were probably from a nucleus of professionals called, by later writers, *histriones* ("actors") or *ludiones* ("players"), eclectic artists who were dancers, mimes, jugglers, actors, and musicians and who probably specialized in one or another of the genres. Their repertory included armed dances (*tityristae*), satyric dances (*satyristae*), masked dances, religious and funeral representations, comical-satirical pantomimes, and instrumental music. These arts influenced the spectacles of ancient Rome—the Latin-speaking civilization to the southwest of Tuscany that expanded militarily to rule Europe and the Near East—which inherited a taste for circus games from their Etruscan neighbors.

The existence of Etruscan games and contests is attested by frescoes in the Tomb of the Augurs and the Tomb of the Olympic Games in Tarquinia, both dating from the early sixth century BCE. The murals in the Tomb of the Olympic Games also show a series of scenes in what appears to be a variety show, culminating in a scene of dancers, which seems to be the finale of the show. A number of painted vessels found in other well-preserved tombs near Tarquinia and Chiusi are decorated with dancing scenes, such as the war dances depicted on the Secchiello di Chiusi and the Falerio Vase. Probably the oldest of the painted vases showing Etruscan dance is the Bucacce Vase of Bisenzio, on which three light dancers and three dark dancers—male and female—hold each other's hands. Artifacts such as these make it clear that the Etruscans were a cultivated and refined people, with a pronounced love of music, dancing and feasting, pomp and ceremony, dress and show. The Romans, who conquered Etruria in the third century BCE, were the successors to the Etruscan heritage.

Although influenced by Etruscan culture in many ways, ancient Rome was unique in the matter of dance. Because of the austere and militaristic spirit on which Roman power was based, the Romans have generally appeared to have been averse to dance. Nevertheless, especially in their earliest period, the Romans did have dances. Collective dances were performed by men belonging to certain occupational guilds and were held on the occasion of the sowing season for the blessing and purification of the fields, an example being the dance of the Arval Brothers (Collegium Fratrum Arvalium), a fraternity of Roman priests devoted to the goddess Dia. Another priestly brotherhood, the Salii (lit., "jumpers, leapers"), consisted of colleges of dancer-priests devoted to the war god, Mars. They performed armed dances that involved the striking of javelins against sacred shields and that was characterized by a triple beat of the feet, from which the Latin word *tripudium*, which defined that dance, was derived. It was performed by a soloist, the *praesul*, and two choirs—old men and young men. This dance was remembered by Lucian of Samosata (second century CE) as the most majestic of all the Roman dances. [*See* Tripudium.]

The austere character of Roman dance changed with their conquest of Greece, which exposed the invaders to a refined civilization. Of the high spirituality that permeated the dances of the Greek world, however, Rome adopted only the most superficial aspects. The sacred maenads who had been devoted to the Greek cult of Dionysus soon became the unrestrained Roman bacchantes who danced during the licentious days and nights of such major festival seasons as the Lupercalia and Saturnalia. [*See* Roman Empire.]

During the slow and inexorable decline of the Roman Empire, the emerging Christian church—strengthened by Emperor Constantine's edict of 313 CE—took a strong stand against the increasingly lewd and violent character of Roman theater. Although pagans and paganism felt fierce condemnation from the church, this element remained a part of popular culture, especially in the theater, where it found an avenue for its expression. Assimilation of the pagan world into Christian religion and culture was the only way for Christians to enforce their views and to resolve the conflict. Once Christians replaced the old legends and myths with stories from the Bible and the lives of the saints, the theater would be rehabilitated.

Dance, too, was stripped of any licentious element and became a part of the liturgy along with hymns, psalms, and canticles. A prelate took on the role of *praesul*, once played by a priest of the ancient Salii, and the chorus became the area of the church used for the orchestra. One modern scholar, Renato Torniai, a Jesuit priest, maintains that the terms *praesul* and *chorus* had a metaphysical connotation and did not refer to dance (Torniai, 1952). He recognizes, however, that dance may have been performed in churches and that the early church councils' prohibitions of dance may have referred to the location rather than to the activity *per se*. [*See* Christianity and Dance, *article on* Early Christian Views.]

The church's opposition became stronger when various forms of expression later became freer, allowing some nonreligious elements, for example, in the Feste dei Folli (Feast of Fools), which was held shortly after Christmas. Ecclesiastical authorities repeatedly condemned the immoderateness of these celebrations, since they involved the temporary upsetting of the social hierarchy and culminated in the election of an *episcopello* (a mock bishop)—an obvious attempt to lampoon church dignitaries. The festival clearly incorporated elements of pagan celebrations, the Roman Saturnalia in particular. Toward the end of the fifteenth century, the church managed to ban the Feste dei Folli altogether, but the feast survived in a more secular version.

In the complex and contradictory relationship between the church and dance, a crucial role was played by jesters, singers, dancers, mimes, actors, and jugglers. During the Middle Ages, they moved from court to court and from town to town, and from a dramatic viewpoint, represented a link of continuity with the *histriones*. Their art, which largely relied on visual impact and the seductive use of the body, brought strong ecclesiastical opposition, precisely because of the sensuous participation demanded of the spectators. The jesters connected popular elements with some aristocratic ones and were thus responsible for an essential contribution to early European theatrical tradition. [*See* Medieval Dance.] Among the forms of theater they presented were the *contrasto*, a dramatic action often centered on the theme of courtship, and the *ballata*, where verse, music, and dance were fused into a whole. And while the jesters gradually gave up their traveling habits to settle in royal courts under the protection of powerful patrons, the church did incorporate some aspects of their artistic stock.

In the thirteenth century, an innovative wave forced society to attempt to blend secular culture with Christian dogma. The Franciscans were powerful mediators of this movement at a time when the Latin language was being replaced by local vernaculars. This process found expression in hymns and sacred drama. Plastic compositions, an outstanding component of traditional nativity scenes, and the *tableaux vivants* that accompanied the *trionfi* (spectacular parades and shows) highlighted the most important public celebrations. The problem of the approach to religion was the dominant theme of Europe's medieval society, and this inevitably affected the art of dance, stimulating the rise of various forms, notably the procession of the flagellants. [*See* Christianity and Dance, *article on* Medieval Views.]

The more relaxed atmosphere that emerged during the thirteenth century became manifest with the advent of humanism in the fourteenth and the spread of the "sweetness of life" ideal in the courts. The *memento mori* in sermons, literary sources, and representations of macabre dances in earlier centuries was soon forgotten. With the loosening of restraints brought about by the Renaissance, all forms of creative expression of the human spirit, especially music, drama, and dance, experienced a revival.

The fifteenth century took its dances from the *ballonchi, tresche, rigoletti, ruote, ridde,* as well as from the *moresche, mattaccini,* and court dances. With the changed outlook, which placed human beings at the center of the universe, dance became of the means for the harmonious development of the psychological and physical aspects of the human personality. Dance masters of the fifteenth century were well aware of this attitude when they combined the technical and stylistic rules of dance with the rules of deportment and manners. Their manuscripts, which have survived, describe *bassedanze* (Italian for "low dances"; in French, *bassedanses*) and the balls in fashion during that period. [*See* Bassedanse.]

Dance was recognized by dance masters only its court form—however much it owed to the rhythms, melodies, and choreography of popular dances—which were stylistically altered for performance at court. *Pive, saltarelli,* and *chiaranzane* spread throughout the courts, alongside the highest form of court dancing, the *bassadanza.* The original contributions of the court dance were attention to its stylistic execution; the "air" that was supposed to permeate the dancer's every movement, including the pauses, and the emphasis placed on the dance's exquisitely artistic quality. [*See* Renaissance Dance Technique.]

Although most dance masters of the time are now forgotten, fifteenth-century dance treatises testify and describe the *ballare lombardo* (Lombard dancing), inspired by humanistic ideals, on which both social and spectacular dances were founded. It is important to mention here the *ballicti,* as defined by Antonio Cornazano, author of *Il libro dell'arte del danzare* (The Book on the Art of Dancing; 1455); these were "composizioni di diverse misure" (compositions of different measures): the *bassadanza, quaternaria, saltarello,* and *piva.* In this form, the dramatic, figurative, and decorative intuitions of the dance masters were most successfully rendered. Among those whose names have survived to our day, Domenico da Piacenza (or da Ferrara) and Guglielmo Ebreo da Pesaro (also known as Giovanni Ambrosio) are the most famous, and we also have their writings. [*See the entries on Cornazano, Domenico, and Guglielmo.*]

Like Cornazano, Guglielmo declares himself to be Domenico's dedicated disciple and includes his master's choreography in his *De pratica seu arte tripudii* (On the Practice or Art of Dancing; 1463). Guglielmo stands as a model for his time both in his life and works, and his merits were widely recognized and admired. A member of a family of artists (his brother Giuseppe opened a professional dance school in Florence in 1467), he compiled the most complete body of dance music for the fifteenth century, recorded in the various versions of his treatise. He also favored spreading the art of dance to the most important courts of his time.

In these aristocratic circles, where the arts were fostered and encouraged, performances known as *intermedi* flourished. Held in the courts, these lyrical, allegorical, pantomimed, and musical performances characteristically revolved around a unifying theme. [*See* Intermedio.] A unifying theme was also typical of choreographic feasts, like the one staged in 1473 in the Piazza Santi Apostoli in Rome by Cardinal Riario, on the occasion of the triumph of Eleanor of Aragon. For this grand occasion, *Il Ballo d'Ercole* was performed, containing a variety of dance forms. Among them was a *moresca,* a mock battle between Christians and Moors that, in the late fifteenth century, was the most popular of the pantomimed dances in court performances. In the sixteenth and seventeenth centuries, the *moresca,* by then a term referring to different dances, only some of which were reminiscent of the original armed character, developed into a fundamental part of the *intermedi* and one of the elements of the *opera in musica.* [*See* Moresca.]

The various performances and celebrations that characterized festivals and feasts at Italian courts strengthened the power of the nobles, whose self-glorification was typically expressed through classical myth. [*See* Renaissance Fêtes and Triumphs.] Toward the end of the fifteenth century, the importance of dance in court life, as well as in the education of young noblemen, was reduced. Doubtless the masters felt that they had to give dance the dignity of other art forms, following the lead of painting. The fifteenth century became the crucial one for the origins of ballet. [*See* Ballet Technique, History of.]

For Italian society, the sixteenth century brought a new political equilibrium, which influenced the relationships between the social classes. Thriving on their newly acquired social status, the merchant and middle classes aspired to the mores of the aristocracy. The "high dances," such as the *gagliarda,* favored by the ascendent bourgeoisie, consequently began to prevail over the "low dances" traditionally practiced at court. The high dances were the object of extensive contemporaneous studies, including Lutio Compasso's *Ballo della gagliarda* (1560), Prospero Lutij's *Opera bellissima nella quale si contengono molte partite, et passeggi di gagliarda* (1589), and Livio Lupi's *Libro di gagliarda, tordiglione, passo e mezzo, canari e passeggi* (1607). Such works as Giovanni della Casa's *Il galateo* (Code of Manners; 1559) further show that the dances were restricted by a rigid formal etiquette. Extensive dance manuals by Fabritio Caroso and Cesare Negri strongly emphasized the rules of court etiquette, with detailed technical and stylistic descriptions; they also have a copious repertory of social and spectacular dances, such as the *brando,* with the relevant music. [*See the entries on Caroso and Negri.*]

The work of the Italian dance masters of the sixteenth century endowed us with a unified choreographic language that contains the rudiments of academic technique, including the virtuosity of the *capriole intrecciate* and the *salto tondo.* The homogeneity of style that the masters achieved in this period was made possible largely by the work of Caroso, who left an explicit and conscious reflection on the fundamental principles of composition. In his *Nobiltà di dame* (1600), a revised edition of *Il ballarino* (1581), he restyles some choreographies according to principles of symmetry, balance, and order.

The popularity of Italian style in Europe was clearly

documented by Cesare Negri, a sixteenth-century dance master. In *Le gratie d'amore* (1602), he lists many successful and talented artists. Among them were those, such as his own master Pompeo Diobono, who gave their distinctive contribution to what became the flourishing ballet of the French court. The French sovereigns had surrounded themselves with the most famous artists in order to magnify their own power. Thus, they encouraged and supported the talent of many Italians, such as Baldassare da Belgiojoso (Balthazar de Beaujoyeulx), author of the famous *Balet Comique de la Royne* (1581). [*See* Ballet de Cour.]

Cultural exchanges with other countries, France and Spain in particular, brought about mutual influences, including some in the field of dance (as shown by the Spanish color of the *canario*), although at the time the Spanish, French, and Italian dance styles were kept separate. The Italian style, as codified by several treatises, appeared between 1559 and the 1630s. By then firmly consolidated, it remained extremely popular in the seventeenth century. Toward the mid-sixteenth century, the French style also became commonly accepted and admired in Italy along with the work of professional dancers, who had emerged with the opening of public playhouses.

ITALY: Dance Traditions before 1800. This etching by Jacques Callot depicts a float designed by Giulio Parigi for a celebration honoring the prince of Urbino's arrival in Florence in 1616. Pulled by oxen wearing stag skins, this car bears the figure of Thetis, perched high atop a shell, and attendant sea creatures, including sirens, nereids, and tritons. Eight "giants" walking on foot represent the major seas of the world. (Dance Collection, New York Public Library for the Performing Arts.)

In the meantime, the art of dance was cultivated both in the academies—their experiments contributing to the rise of melodrama—and in the Jesuit schools, above all in the Collegio Romano. The Jesuits used dance in their theatrical productions, in forms that suited religious performances with edifying purposes; they aimed at artistic expression with seamless continuity from word to dance, since they recognized not only the pedagogical power but also the rhetorical possibilities of dance. Emanuele Tesauro, in his *Cannocchiale Aristotelico* (1670), defined dance as a metaphor, which, through gesture and movement, expresses subjective feelings and objective human actions. According to Tesauro, who owed his intellectual formation to Jesuit instruction, it is from metaphor that "the marvel" derives, since through its ingenious images one can "express the inexpressible and see the unseeable."

In the early seventeenth century, the Italian courts were in decline. Very few were still independent of the Papal States or from foreign powers, especially Spain. This situation, however, did not immediately affect Italian court dance, which in various instances kept its splendor and capacity for renewal.

Such was the case with the Medici court in Florence, where in 1637 Agnioli Ricci presented *Le Nozze degli Dei* (The Wedding of the Gods), his fabulous dance drama created for the wedding of Ferdinand II, grand duke of Tuscany. [*See* Nozze degli Dei, Le.] Ricci also staged there *abbattimenti*, performances of a kind of "figurative joust" in which horseback riders executed dance patterns. Combined with melodrama in the *opera-torneo* ("jousting opera"), the *balletti a cavallo* ("riding dances," or "horse ballets") by Ricci himself, Alfonso Ruggieri di Sanseverino, and Alessandro Carducci confirm the Medici role in spectacles. [*See* Horse Ballet.]

Florence was also the home of Bernardo Buontalenti, designer of splendid sets and costumes for such productions as the six *intermedi* performed during intervals in Girolamo Bargaghli's comedy *La Pellegrina* (The Pilgrim; 1589), at a time when *intermedi* were soon to acquire an independent and unified form. Giovanni Bardi was the librettist, and the score resulted from several musicians who gathered around him in the renowned Camerata Fiorentina. Among them was Emilio de' Cavalieri, described as a *leggiadrissimo danzatore* ("very graceful dancer") and remembered chiefly as the author of the famous *Rappresentazione di Anima e Corpo* (Representation of Soul and Body; 1600), staged in Rome at the Oratorio dei Filippini.

No less active was the court of Savoy, a duchy on the northwestern border of Italy with France and Switzerland, which often succeeded in emulating French magnificence. This resulted because of the work of the poet and choreographer Marquis Ludovico d'Aglié, uncle of the celebrated Comte d'Aglié (Filippo San Martino). Besides ex-

celling as a diplomat and a soldier, he was an applauded producer of ballets with historical, epic, mythological, and fantastic backgrounds. Praised by Claude-François Ménestrier, his fame as a choreographer spread to France with the representations of the *Ballet des Montagnards* in 1631. His *Il Gridelino, o Ballet du Grisdelin* was restaged in Paris upon the request of Anne of Austria after its premiere in Turin in 1653.

A different but no less important case was that of Claudio Monteverdi, who gave life to dramatic ballets such as *Il Ballo delle Ingrate* (Mantua, 1608), using the verse of Ottavio Rinuccini, and *Il Combattimento di Tancredi e Clorinda* (Venice, 1624), a madrigal danced to the words of Torquato Tasso's epic poem *Gerusalemme liberata*. The text of the latter work specifies that the roles of Tancredi and Clorinda be shared by dancers and singers.

The further development of musical theater demanded a linking figure that could blend the various forms of performance, and this was extensively described around 1630 in *Il corago*, presumably written by Pierfrancesco Rinuccini, Ottavio's son. As the opera theater developed into a private enterprise, a phenomenon that began in 1637 with the staging of *Andromeda* by Benedetto Ferrari at the Teatro San Cassiano in Venice, the *balli* gradually became a recurrent feature of the show. Performed by professional dancers, whose style differed greatly from the French noble style, theatrical *balli* were generally placed at the end of acts or in the entr'actes, both in the serious opera and in the later comic opera; more and more they were losing contact with the main action of the musical drama, if not becoming altogether independent. The subjects of these *balli* belonged to the most varied genres: serious, comic, allegorical, pastoral, martial, and exotic.

The Italian style was characterized by a strong pantomimed component and by a conspicuous liveliness in rhythmic and acrobatic dance—clear evidence of its kinship with the *commedia dell'arte*. Even before the famed eighteenth-century dispute between Gaspero Angiolini and Jean-Georges Noverre about the *ballet d'action*, the Italians seemed to have been looking for a synthesis between mime and dance. Their seventeenth-century *balli* were thus founded on that "unstable balance" caused by the dialectic fluctuation between realism and abstraction, as so keenly described by theater critic André Levinson in the 1920s (see Levinson, 1991). Although profoundly marked by the aesthetics of the "marvellous," dance theater in the seventeenth century did not disdain to use details, especially with comic and burlesque subjects. In seventeenth-century characterizations, however, exotic characters and fantastic apparitions were many, as were dances of animals and animated objects. Gregorio Lambranzi, in his two-part treatise *Nuovo e curiosa scuola de' balli teatrali*, published in Nuremberg in 1716 as *Neue und curieuse theatralische Tanz-Schul,* deals both with scenes taken from the *commedia dell'arte* and with the exotic characters, both in the 1600s and early 1700s.

If the precious testimony of Lambranzi's work—containing 101 etched plates with musical examples and relevant captions—comes from publication in Nuremberg, from Venice comes the only instance known to date of Italian dance in notation, complete with its own music. This work records three *balli,* none lacking in spectacular qualities, all notated in the Beauchamps-Feuillet system by Sebastiano Gobbis. Composed for the wedding of Loredana Duodo to Antonio Grimani, which was celebrated in Venice on 6 May 1726, these three *balli* were performed by Gaetano Grossatesta, a dancer and choreographer from Modena. He was featured in the most important theaters of northern Italy in the first half of the eighteenth century.

In Naples, a major treatise was published in 1728 that centered on social dances as "temperate and noble exercise," suitable to royalty. The author, who declares himself a disciple of Pierre Beauchamps and Guillaume-Louis Pecour, is Giambattista Dufort, who worked at the Teatro San Bartolomeo in Naples and at the Collegio Ducale in Parma. He dedicated his *Trattato del ballo nobile* (Treatise on the Noble Ball) to the gentlewomen and gentlemen of Naples. His text shows many resemblances with Raoul-Auger Feuillet's *Choréographie, ou L'art de décrire la danse* (Paris, 1700) and Pierre Rameau's *Le maître á danser* (Paris, 1725), although the early contributions of Italian and Spanish dance to the development of artistic dance is also explicitly mentioned. The work clearly states the existing supremacy of French dance and a particular preference for the *menuet,* an aristocratic form *par excellence,* which in the book occupies a much larger space than that given to the *contredanse.*

Some fifty years after the publication of Dufort's treatise, a second important treatise, by Gennaro Magri, was also published in Naples. In Magri's *Trattato teorico-prattico di ballo* (1779), the favor of the *menuet* and the *contredanse* is completely revised. In this work the *menuet* appears to be in decline against the growing popularity with the middle class of the *contradanza* (as it was then spelled), of which the author notates an extensive repertory both as a *ballo* and as a theatrical dance.

It is noteworthy that the consolidated tradition of the *mezzo carattere* (Fr., *demi-caractère*) and the "grotesque" style of dance is recorded by Magri in the very years when Noverre's influence was particularly strong in Naples, especially through Charles Le Picq. Magri's treatise is in fact the only specific work of the second half of the eighteenth century that has a theoretical didactic character; it is a precious document that testifies to the line of the Italian school. Magri was a major representative of the grotesque style, as both a dancer and a choreographer, in some of

the most important Italian cities as well as in Vienna. His work therefore offers new perspectives on the various genres of theatrical dance in the 1800s and on Italian performing style—then virtuosic, acrobatic, and rich in mimed characterizations.

In France, Louis XIV had promoted the rise of dance by establishing the Académie Royale de Danse in 1661. Passage from the *ballet de cour* to *comédie-ballet* and *tragédie lyrique*—achieved mainly by the dancer-choreographer-composer Giovanni Battista Lulli (1632–1687)—further popularized dance in France. Known in France as Jean-Baptiste Lully, he composed many operas in which he made the ballet an essential part.

Meanwhile, in Italy during the seventeenth and eighteenth centuries, the nobility attempted to become a diplomatic oligarchy, with a sumptuous ceremonial it could not afford without financial partnerships and speculations. This resulted both in the financing of court spectacles and in a proliferation of theaters for the public. Although unable to compete with the magnificence of court dances, the theaters favored the stabilization and regulation of stage life.

Apart from the above-mentioned artists, in the eighteenth century a number of dancers emerged, often belonging to theatrical dynasties, who went beyond national borders, spreading the rich Italian choreographic tradition throughout Europe. Outstanding among them is Francesco Quilanti, as well as the above-mentioned Grossatesta, and Antonio Rinaldi il Fassano, especially active in the 1720s and 1730s. In Saint Petersburg in 1735 Fassano produced ballets and worked in the first ballet school established in Russia, by Tsarina Anna Ivanovna. Among Italy's professional female dancers, Barbara Campanini became famous for her virtuosity and her expressive gifts. Toward midcentury several Italian choreographers were renowned, such as Giuseppe Salomini "di Vienna" and his two sons Giuseppe and Francesco as well as Giovanni Battista Guidetti and Gaspero Angiolini.

Both Giuseppe Salomoni and Gaspero Angiolini represented the Austro-Italian line that was derived from Franz Anton Hilverding. Only recently have dance historians acknowledged the greater importance and value of Angiolini in his feud with Noverre, the author of the renowned *Lettres sur la danse et sur les ballets* (1760), and the role their quarrel had in the Italian cultural debate of the time (Tozzi, 1972; Hansell, 1988).

During the second half of the eighteenth century, especially in the decade 1766 to 1776, a lively debate had developed in cultural circles, centered more on the theory of dance from an aesthetic point of view than on an analysis of technique. Dance, and theatrical dance especially, were the objects of unprecedented attention in those years when the entries of the great *Encyclopédie* (1751–1772), edited by Denis Diderot, sanctioned the cultural and artistic dignity of this form of expression. Starting from observations concerning the relationship between opera and dance, the various contributions extended to the definition of the very nature of dance in its various expressive forms. Most Italian intellectuals considered the dance section in operas only slightly related to the main action of the work, a viewpoint that encouraged the separation of ballet from opera.

The necessity for clarity and for dramatic consistency in narrative dance soon emerged, and many pointed out that, among theatrical genres, comic dance had achieved a better formal balance than had serious dance. At least one voice was ahead of its time in the controversy about the expressiveness of mime: in *La musica imitativa e i balli pantomimi* (1800), Matteo Borsa claimed for theatrical dance the right to exist on its own, saying "dance imitates nothing but itself." At the beginning of the century, Pier Jacopo Martello, in *Della tragedia antica e moderna* (1715), had elaborated his views on Italian, French, and Spanish styles; much later, Pietro and Alessandro Verri's *Carteggio . . . dal 1766 al 1797* offered observations on taste and on some productions. In London, Giovanni Andrea Gallini, in *A Treatise on the Art of Dancing* (1762), defended the expressive strength and eloquence of mimic language "diffused through the whole body, the face especially included."

Not long thereafter, however, the barbs of Ange Goudar in his *Osservazioni sopra la musica ed il ballo* (1773) exposed the flaws of pantomimed dance. Goudar attacked the confused points made in dance programs, since the use of libretti especially composed for dance had by then become widespread, offering extensive stage directions and role interpretations. He preferred simple actions and comic or realistic subjects to those inspired by ancient history and myth, and he valued the Italian *grotteschi* more than Noverre's *danseurs nobles*. The preference held by many artists at that time for a dance theater with a tragic slant was perhaps a necessary stage in the expressive search for a legitimate dance vehicle. In this respect the dance theories presented by Angiolini and Noverre, respectively, represented the two opposing positions that participated in the same ongoing process for innovation and reform. [*See the entries on Angiolini and Noverre.*]

In Italy the two views were popularized not only by these two major masters of the *ballet d'action* but also by the activity of numerous dancers who performed both Angiolini's and Noverre's works. Later they reproduced some of the ballets onstage or created their own versions, using the same subject matter. Domenico Rossi, for example, was one of the interpreters at the premiere of Angiolini's *Orpheus and Eurydice* in Vienna in 1762. Rossi later translated into Italian and published Noverre's fifteen letters of his first edition of *Lettres sur la danse et sur les ballets* (Naples, 1778). In 1805 it was still possible to compare di-

rectly the different solutions worked out by the two famous rivals in *ballet d'action*, when Pietro Angiolini restaged for the Teatro alla Scala in Milan both his uncle Gaspero's *Suleiman II* and Noverre's *Adèle de Ponthieu*.

The traveling lifestyle of dancers was a key factor in the various suggestions for theatrical dance. Turin, with its continuous exchanges with the French ballet world, was able to offer the choreographies of Gaetano Vestris, Jean Dauberval, Pierre Alouard, and Jean-Antoine Terrades. Milan had sided with Angiolini, while Naples, traditionally with Noverre, adopted Charles Le Picq, Noverre's most devout pupil between 1773 and 1782. Venice kept a balance between the two schools. On the whole, this variety gradually strengthened Italian dance and enabled Italy, enlivened by the process, to make great contributions to European dance. Vincenzo Galeotti's invaluable role in the development of Danish dance is but one example. Galeotti created the oldest ballet in the Copenhagen repertory, *The Whims of Cupid and the Ballet Master*, staged in 1786. In Saint Petersburg, Giuseppe Canziani succeded Gaspero Angiolini as choreographer. There, he taught for several years at the Imperial Theater School, beginning in 1784.

Toward the end of the eighteenth century, many dynasties of dancers had emerged, to continue working in the following century. Among them the Viganòs are particularly outstanding, especially Onorato and his son Salvatore. Salvatore may even outshine one of Italy's greatest choreographers, Francesco Clerico. Experimentation in pantomimed dance during the late eighteenth century was perfected in the early decades of the nineteenth by choreodramatic solutions, for which Salvatore Viganò was the most important representative.

BIBLIOGRAPHY

Alm, Irene. "Theatrical Dance in Venetian Opera." In *L'arte della danza ai tempi di Claudio Monteverdi*, edited by Angelo Chiarle, pp. 95–111. Turin, 1996.

Angiolini, Gaspero. *Riflessioni sopra l'uso dei programmi nei balli pantomimi*. Milan, 1775.

Basso, Alberto, ed. *Musica in scena: Storia dello spettacolo musicale*, vol. 5, *L'arte della danza e del balletto*. Turin, 1995.

Bragaglia, Anton Giulio. *Danze popolari italiane*. Rome, 1950.

Brainard, Ingrid. *The Art of Courtly Dancing in the Early Renaissance*. West Newton, Mass., 1981.

Cahusac, Louis de. *La danse ancienne et moderne: Traité historique de la danse*. 3 vols. The Hague, 1754.

Calendoli, Giovanni. *Storia universale della danza*. Milan, 1985.

Carrieri, Raffaele. *La danze in Italia, 1500–1900*. 2d ed. Milan, 1955.

Celi, Claudia. "Talhor tacere un tempo e starlo morto . . .: Il moto in potenza e in atto." In *Guglielmo Ebreo da Pesaro e la danza nelle corti italiane del XV secolo*, edited by Maurizio Padovan. Pisa, 1990.

Celi, Claudia. "I balletti di corte del Seicento: Tensioni e poetiche di un equilibrio instabile." In *L'arte della danza ai tempi di Claudio Monteverdi*, edited by Angelo Chiarle, pp. 275–281. Turin, 1996.

Celi, Claudia, and Andrea Toschi. "Signor Rossi's Riddles: An Annotated Chronology of Domenico Rossi (ca. 1745–post 1821)." *Cairon* 2 (1997).

Centro di Studi sul Teatro Medioevale e Rinascimentale. *Il contributo dei giullari alla drammaturgia italiana delle origini.* Rome 1978.

Centro di Studi sul Teatro Medioevale e Rinascimentale. *Spettacoli conviviali dall'antichità classica alle corti italiane del'400.* Viterbo, 1983.

La danza italiana 3 (Autumn 1985). Monographic issue on fifteenth-century Italian dance; includes an extensive bibliography.

D'Aronco, Gianfranco. *Storia della danza popolare e d'arte, con particolare riferimento all'Italia.* Florence, 1962.

Domenico da Piacenza. *De arte saltandi et choreas ducendi* (1455). Translated by A. William Smith as *Fifteenth Century Dance and Music.* Stuyvesant, N.Y., 1995.

Gatti, Carlo. *Il Teatro alla Scala nella storia e nell'arte, 1778–1963.* 2 vols. 2d ed. Milan, 1964.

Giordano, Gloria. "A Venetian Festa in Feuillet Notation." In *Dance to Honour Kings: Sources for Courtly and Theatrical Dramatic Entertainments, 1690–1740.* London, 1997.

Hall, John F., ed. *Etruscan Italy: Etruscan Influences on the Civilizations of Italy from Antiquity to the Modern Era.* Provo, Utah, 1996.

Hansell, Kathleen Kuzmick. "Il ballo teatrale e l'opera italiana." In *Storia dell'opera italiana,* vol. 5., pp. 175–306. Turin, 1988. Includes a detailed bibliography.

Johnstone, Mary A. *The Dance in Etruria: A Comparative Study.* Florence, 1956.

Levinson, André. *André Levinson on Dance: Writings from Paris in the Twenties.* Edited by Joan Acocella and Lynn Garafola. Middletown, Conn., 1991.

Massaro, Maria Nevilla. "Il ballo pantomimo al Teatro Nuovo di Padova, 1751–1830." *Acta musicologica* 57.2 (1985): 215–275.

Padovan, Maurizio, ed. *La danza in Europa fra Rinascimento e Barocco.* Rome, 1995.

Pontremoli, Alessandro. *La danza negli spettacoli dal Medioevo alla fine del Seicento.* In *Musica in scena: Storia dello spettacolo musicale,* edited by Alberto Basso, vol. 5, pp. 3–36. Turin, 1995.

Pontremoli, Alessandro, and Patrizia La Rocca. *La danza a Venezia nel Rinascimento.* Vicenza, 1993.

Reyna, Ferdinando. *Des origines du ballet.* Paris, 1955.

Rossi, Luigi. *Storia del balletto.* Rev. ed. Bologna, 1972.

Sasportes, José. "Noverre in Italia." *La danza italiana* 2 (Spring 1985): 39–66.

Sasportes, José. "La danza 1737–1900." In *Il Teatro di San Carlo,* vol. 1, pp. 365–396. Naples, 1987.

Sparti, Barbara. "The Function and Status of Dance in the Fifteenth-Century Italian Courts." *Dance Research* 14.1 (summer 1996): 42–61.

Tani, Gino. "Italia: Balletto." In *Enciclopedia dello spettacolo.* Rome, 1954–.

Testa, Alberto. *I grandi balletti.* Rome, 1991.

Testa, Alberto. *Storia della danza e del balletto.* Rev. ed. Rome, 1994.

Tani, Gino. *Storia della danza dalle origini ai nostri giorni.* 3 vols. Florence, 1983.

Torniai, Renato. *La danza sacra.* Rome, 1952.

Tozzi, Lorenzo. *Il balletto pantomimo del Settecento: Gaspare Angiolini.* Aquila, 1972.

Tozzi, Lorenzo. "Musica e balli al regio di Torino, 1748–1762." *La danza italiana* 2 (Spring 1985): 5–21.

Tozzi, Lorenzo. "Il balletto in Italia: Il Settecento." In *Musica in scena: Storia dello spettacolo musicale,* edited by Alberto Basso, vol. 5., pp. 39–87. Turin, 1995.

Winter, Marian Hannah. *The Pre-Romantic Ballet.* London, 1974.

CLAUDIA CELI
Translated from Italian

Theatrical Dance, 1801–1940

The early ballet reached its zenith in Italy with the choreodrama (drama in dance) of Salvatore Viganò, who rivaled Jean-Georges Noverre in the *ballet d'action.* Viganò synthesized the contrasting and divergent styles of Noverre and Gaspero Angiolini by transforming the pantomime ballet into a danced drama with integrated music, story, and action. In essence, dance in all its variation and artistry replaced pantomime; there were both "expressive" and "ornamental" dances, usually with classical Greco-Roman themes.

In 1801 Viganò collaborated with Beethoven on the ballet *Die Geschöpfe des Prometheus* (he had studied music and was himself a composer). In 1813 he added his own music to that of Mozart and Haydn for another ballet, *Prometeo.* The scenographer Alessandro Sanquirico was his frequent collaborator. Viganò's followers, Gaetano Gioja among them, managed only feeble imitations of his techniques.

Meanwhile, Carlo Blasis (1795–1878) was strengthening Italian dance technique. In 1837 at the Teatro alla Scala in Milan, Blasis and his wife, Annunciata Ramaccini, established and conducted the supplementary training course in the theater's dance school. Through his efforts Italian classical technique evolved and became the mainstay of early Romantic ballet. In the tradition of Italian dance masters of the eighteenth century, Blasis also traveled to Russia to teach.

Romantic ballet's adoption of dancing on pointe altered the history of theatrical dance. The technique made dancers seem lighter, almost detached from the earth, an effect enhanced by the white tutu. The resulting aesthetic effects naturally lent themselves to Romantic stories of love. The first dance master fully to appreciate this new technique was Filippo Taglioni, who used it to emphasize the poetic grace of his daughter Marie. Although Marie Taglioni was not the first to dance on pointe, in *La Sylphide* (1832) she danced the role of a restless spirit with such lightness that the technique gained new attention from dance masters throughout Europe.

Another Italian master, Giovanni (Jean) Coralli, also achieved prominence with his creation of *Giselle* in 1841. Coralli's wife, Teresa, won great acclaim as a soloist in Vienna.

The best-known dance master of the period, however, was Enrico Cecchetti, who was taught by Giovanni Lepri, himself a student of Blasis. The Cecchetti method of instruction and dance became known and emulated throughout Europe, especially in Britain, and was embraced with particular fervor by Russian dancers. Serge Diaghilev, for example, asked Cecchetti to give his Saint Petersburg and Moscow dancers advanced training, and Cecchetti became Anna Pavlova's private teacher. He was responsible in large part for the success of Diaghilev's company.

A certain decadence began to set in with the post-Romantic period. The late nineteenth century, the so-called Positivist era, exalted progress, the glory of the motherland, and the Industrial Revolution. Dance masters and others talked of a new form of ballet that would use the mechanics of Baroque ballet and the imposing stagings of the choreodrama. The music written, however, was not equal to such a form; the choreography tended to use mass groupings; and the ostentatious sets did little more than stimulate the public's superficial taste. Choreographer Luigi Manzotti was a specialist in this genre; his most important collaborator was the musician Romualdo Marenco. *Excelsior* (1881) was the most popular of their efforts.

While western Europe debated between superficiality and substance, Diaghilev was transforming his Ballets Russes into something no longer recognizable to Italian ballet critics. The company's tour of Rome, Milan, Turin,

ITALY: Theatrical Dance, 1801–1940. Epitomizing the ethereal grace of the Romantic ballerina, Marie Taglioni transformed pointe work from a technical feat into an expression of lyricism. This engraving depicts her balancing effortlessly on the tips of her toes in *La Sylphide*. (Dance Collection, New York Public Library for the Performing Arts.)

ITALY: Theatrical Dance, 1801–1940. Enrico Cecchetti as the Satyr in Luigi Manzotti's ballet spectacle *Amor*, which premiered at the Teatro alla Scala, Milan, in 1886. (Photograph from the Dance Collection, New York Public Library for the Performing Arts.)

Florence, and Naples went almost unnoticed by the public. Italian musicologists were largely responsible because of their inability to appreciate this new ballet style. In general, the new refinements in choreography, music, sets, and costumes were judged to be the products of a remote artistic elite. Most Italians remained devoted to the ballet of the nineteenth century, superficial and escapist. This devotion hampered the development of modern ballet in Italy for many years.

[*For further information, see the entries on the principal figures and theatrical works mentioned herein.*]

BIBLIOGRAPHY
Beaumont, Cyril W., and Stanislas Idzikowski. *A Manual of the Theory and Practice of Classical Theatrical Dancing: Cecchetti Method.* London, 1922.
Bentivoglio, Leonetta. *La danza moderna.* New ed. Milan, 1982.
Cagli, Bruno, and Agostino Ziino, eds. *Il Teatro di San Carlo, 1737–1987,* vol. 2, *L'opera, il ballo.* Naples, 1987.
Carrieri, Raffaele. *La danza in Italia, 1500–1900.* 2d ed. Milan, 1955.
Celi, Claudia. "Il balletto in Italia: Il Ottocento," *In Musica in scena: Storia dello spettacolo musicale,* edited by Alberto Basso, vol. 5, pp. 89–138. Turin, 1995.

Doglio, Vittoria, and Elisa Vaccarino. *L'Italia in ballo*. Rome, 1993.

Felici, Stelio, ed. *Il balletto e l'opera di Aurelio M. Milloss, al Maggio Musicale Fiorentino*. Florence, 1977.

Guatterini, Marinella, and Michele Porzio. *Milloss, Busoni e Scelsi: Neoclassico, danza e musica nell'Italia del Novecento*. Milan, 1992.

Guest, Ivor. *The Divine Virginia: A Biography of Virginia Zucchi*. New York, 1977.

Guest, Ivor. "L'Italia e il balletto romantico." *La danza italiana* 8–9 (Winter 1990): 7–15.

Ivaldi, Fabio A. "Michele Canzio e le scene per i balli al Carlo Felice di Genova (1838–1850)." In *Creature di Prometeo: Il ballo teatrale dal divertimento al dramma in Venezia*, Fondazione Giorgio Cini Studi di Musica Veneta 23, pp. 287–304. Venice, 1996.

Jürgensen, Knud Arne. "Sulle tracce della Silfide italiana." *La rivista illustrata del Museo Teatrale alla Scala* 1.4 (Autumn 1989): 18–39.

Jürgensen, Knud Arne. *The Verdi Ballets*. Parma, 1995.

Lawson, Joan. "Masters of the Ballet of the Nineteenth Century" (parts 1–6). *The Dancing Times* (November 1939–April 1940).

Livio, Antoine. "Ballet: A European Institution." *Ballett International* 11 (August–September 1988): 12–21.

Lo Iacono, Concetta. "Minima choreutica: Fasti e dissesti de ballo italiano sul declino dell'Ottocento." In *Musica senza aggettivi: Studi per Fedele d'Amico*, pp. 391–421. Florence, 1991.

Meglin, Joellen A. "Representations and Realities: Analyzing Gender Symbols in the Romantic Ballet." Ph.D. diss., Temple University, 1995.

Milloss, Aurelio M. "La lezione di Salvatore Viganò." In *La danza italiana* 1 (Autumn 1984): 7–19.

Mostra del bicentenario della Scala di Milano, Palazzo Reale. Milan, 1978.

Noverre, Jean-Georges. *Lettres sur la danse et sur les ballets*. Stuttgart and Lyon, 1760. Translated by Cyril W. Beaumont as *Letters on Dancing and Ballets* (London, 1930).

Ottolenghi, Vittoria. *I casi della danza*. Rome, 1981.

Pasi, Mario. *La danza e il balletto*. Milan, 1983.

Poesio, Giannandrea. "The Story of the Fighting Dancers." *Dance Research* 8.1 (Spring 1990): 28–36.

Poesio, Giannandrea. "In maestro Giovanni Lepri e la sua scuola fiorentina." *Chorégraphie* 1 (Spring 1993): 68–75.

Poesio, Giannandrea. "Cecchetti: The Influence of Tradition." In *Dance History*, 2nd ed., edited by Janet Adshead Lansdale and June Layson, pp. 117–131. London and New York (1994).

Rossi, Luigi. *Storia del balletto*. 3d ed., rev. Bologna, 1972.

Raimondi, Ezio, ed. *Il sogno del coreodramma: Salvatore Viganò, poeta muto*. Bologna, 1984.

Ruffin, Elena. "Il ballo teatrale a Venezia nel secolo XIX." *La danza italiana* 5/6 (Autumn 1987): 151–179.

Ruffin, Elena. "Il ruolo del ballo nelle vicende del romanticismo a Venezia." *La danza italiana* 8/9 (Winter 1990): 27–44.

Runchy, Geraldine. "The Significance of the Italian Ballet." *Carroccio* 33 (1931): 317–322.

Sasportes, José. "Virtuosismo e spettacolarità: La risposte italiane alla decadenza del balletto romantico." In *Tornando a Stiffelio*, edited by Giovanni Morelli. Florence, 1987.

Schwartz, Jane D. "The Role of the Male Dancer in the Era of the Romantic Ballet, 1824–1864." Ph.D. diss., University of California, Los Angeles, 1972.

Secondo, Giovannio, and Alberto Testa, eds. *Mostra del libro e del documento di danza, 1581/1975*. Turin, 1975.

Siniscalco, Carmine, ed. *Fifty Years of Opera and Ballet in Italy*. Rome, 1956.

Tani, Gino. *Storia della danza dalle origini ai nostri giorni*. 3 vols. Florence, 1983.

Testa, Alberto, ed. *Due secoli di ballo alla Scala, 1778–1975*. Milan, 1975.

Testa, Alberto. *Giselle*. Rome, 1980.

Testa, Alberto. *Romeo e Giulietta*. Rome, 1981.

Testa, Alberto. *Don Chisciotte*. Rome, 1982.

Testa, Alberto, et al. *Il balletto nel Novecento*. Turin, 1983.

Testa, Alberto. *Storia della danza e del balletto*. New ed. Rome, 1994.

Testa, Alberto. "Una testimonianza viva: La coreografia in Italia fra le due guerre." *Chorégraphie* 7 (Spring 1996).

Testa, Alberto. "Una testimonianza via: La coreografia in Italia durante la seconda guerra mondiale e nell'immediato dopo guerra." *Chorégraphie* 8 (Autumn 1996).

ALBERTO TESTA
Translated from Italian

Theatrical Dance since 1940

After the profound upheaval of World War II, there was a slow renaissance of dance in Italy, and subsequently a revival of specifically Italian dance. Dance had been almost completely crushed by Fascism, allowed to survive only at the Accademia Nazionale di Danza on the Aventine Hill, where Jia Ruskaja was allowed to conduct classes to tem-

ITALY: Theatrical Dance since 1940. Carla Fracci is, unquestionably, Italy's *prima ballerina* of the twentieth century. She is seen here in the title role of *La Sylphide*, staged by Harald Lander for the 1961/62 season of La Scala Ballet. (Photograph by Erio Piccagliani for the Teatro alla Scala, Milan; used by permission.)

per the bodies and spirits of future Italian wives and mothers. Only a few prominent artists, critics, and artistic directors were able to keep dance alive during those dark decades by surreptitiously reintroducing the world of the Ballets Russes.

Among the artists, the main protagonist of the ballet scene during the Fascist period was Aurelio Milloss, but his achievements were noted only by the cultural and social elite and never really found a following among the larger public. [*See the entry on Milloss.*] The war and the German occupation produced a blank slate: it was necessary to start from scratch, to recycle the tatters of a now uncertain patrimony, and to reinvent the very idea of the dance performance. Italians succeeded by means of a series of internal and external events.

Two invaluable stimuli came from the United States. One was a warm and festive wave of musical films, which for years had been banned from Italian screens. The other was the tours of American Ballet Theatre (1950) and the New York City Ballet (1953 and 1955), which introduced

Italian intellectuals to the idea that dance too was an art and that, like others, it was capable of expressing the temper of the times. Enlightened Italian artistic directors, such as Mario Labroca of the Teatro La Fenice in Venice, gave dance prominence, and following their example, other musical directors opened the doors of their institutions to dance. The renowned Accademia Filarmonica Romana had begun to host dance performances as early as the end of 1947 (with Harald Kreutzberg's recital), as a part of its concert season. But the real force behind the rise of dance in Italy was given by the festivals in Nervi (1955) and Spoleto (1958). For the first time, these prestigious summer festivals, one backed by Mario Porcile and the other invented and managed by Gian-Carlo Menotti, drew a large public that was being introduced to dance for the first time.

Over the next twenty-five years the decentralization of political power made the Italian regions more important in the artistic domain. Festivals and special summer and winter seasons multiplied, making it possible to take the best dance companies, particularly foreign ones, to large cities, towns, and resorts.

Among the many events that contributed to the spreading of dance in Italy, mention should be made of the enormous Danza '75, a festival that took place in Venice in 1975, hosting scores of companies from all over the

ITALY: Theatrical Dance since 1940. La Scala Ballet in scene 3 of *Le Donne di Buon Umore* (The Good-Humored Ladies), choreographed by Luciana Novaro in 1961, with scenery and costumes designed by Pier Luigi Pizzi. Carla Fracci as Mariuccia can be seen posing at right front. (Photograph by Erio Piccagliani for the Teatro alla Scala, Milan; used by permission.)

ITALY: Theatrical Dance since 1940. (*top*) Gabriella Tessitore as Farfella and Luigi Martelletta as Prince Djalma in *Le Papillon*, staged by Pierre Lacotte, after Marie Taglioni, for the Rome Opera Ballet in the late 1970s. (*bottom*) Lucia Truglia and Stefano Teresi as the young lovers Lise and Hermann in Roland Petit's *La Dame de Pique* (The Queen of Spades), staged for the Rome Opera Ballet c.1980. (Photographs from the Dance Collection, New York Public Library for the Performing Arts.)

world. Later, seasons sponsored by La Fenice in Venice culminated in 1985 in an entire month of old and new works by Tanztheater Wuppertal under the direction of Pina Bausch. Another factor that contributed to Italy's growing interest in dance was television. This was accomplished not only by the broadcasting of masterworks of ballet and international dance, as in the *Maratona d'estate* (Summer Marathon) of Network 1, which offered two solid months of dance shows, but also by a gradual improvement in the quality of choreography and interpretation in popular music and vaudeville shows. For example, in the 1960s and 1970s Italian television brought its audience Herbert Ross and Hermes Pan, as well as the Italian Gina Landi, a choreographer of remarkable imagination and quality.

Last but not least among the factors that contributed to the reestablishment and even reinvention of dance and the dancing profession in Italy was the rise of the ballerina Carla Fracci. Fracci—who in 1985 celebrated her thirtieth year of professional activity—was instrumental in promoting dance in Italy, first at La Scala, where she became *prima ballerina*, and then throughout Italy as a guest star in other theaters and also as star of her own company. [*See the entry on Fracci.*]

In the meantime, most Italian dance companies managed a subordinate and difficult existence within the opera houses. Of the thirteen major houses, only three had their own ballet schools: the Teatro alla Scala in Milan, the Teatro dell'Opera in Rome, and the Teatro San Carlo in Naples. The rise of foreign dance in Italy, promoted by scores of festivals and theaters (including the opera houses themselves), was not accompanied by a comparable blossoming of Italian companies. All-dance programs were limited to two or three a year; the teachers were not of high quality; and the choice of programs was entrusted to musical directors, most of whom were ignorant of the culture and problems of dance.

Most of the opera houses, instead of yielding to the public's growing interest in dance by presenting an equal number of opera and dance performances, continued to offer little ballet. Among the exceptions were Paolo Grassi, superintendent of La Scala in Milan, and Massimo Bogianckino, the artistic director of the Teatro dell'Opera in Rome, who worked with energy and conviction toward the goal of making dance a more prominent part of the repertories of their theaters.

Nonetheless, by 1990 many established dance companies had been eliminated or badly reduced, notably in Turin, Genoa, Venice, and Bologna, where only foreign companies are invited to perform. Only at La Scala in Milan, the Teatro dell'Opera in Rome, the Teatro San Carlo in Naples, the Teatro Massimo in Palermo, and, to a certain degree, the Teatro Verdi in Trieste, were there well-established companies. In recent years the fortunes of the Rome Opera Ballet have declined, but the company is now under the direction of Mario Pistoni, and the future seems brighter. The ballet companies of the Teatro San Carlo, directed by Roberto Fascilla, and the Teatro Comunale in Florence, directed by Evgeny Polyakov, also provide programs that draw substantial audiences.

Still the richest and healthiest of all the Italian opera houses is La Scala, where Carla Fracci has reigned as *prima ballerina* for so many years. The current director of La Scala Ballet is another famous Italian ballerina, Elisabetta Terabust, who spent most of her performing career as an artist with the London Festival Ballet. [*See* Scala Ballet *and the entry on* Terabust.] Another healthy dance company is Aterballetto, based in Reggio Emilia. Directed by Amedeo Amodio, it offers a varied repertory of works to a consortium of theaters in the cities of Emilia-Romagna. [*See* Aterballetto *and the entry on* Amodio.]

Over the years, there have been many short-lived private companies, born out of private schools and subsidized by the government for short seasons, usually during the summer. Most such companies have been unable to give performances at a truly professional level, as pupils of the schools, with various levels of expertise, are required to provide support for a few prestigious guest stars from the opera ballet companies. Private companies presenting a repertory of modern and contemporary works have a greater chance of success.

Despite economic recession and various and contradictory difficulties, theatrical dance is alive and well in Italy, and in some cities is even flourishing. Although schools are inadequate and theater managements hostile, dozens of new talents miraculously continue to emerge as the years go by. Young Italian dancers are, for the most part, forced to look abroad for the richness and quality of work that they do not find in Italy. Still, some do find work in their homeland, if not in the ballet companies of major opera houses then in companies presenting contemporary dance, in popular theater, or on television.

BIBLIOGRAPHY

Bentivoglio, Leonetta. "The Changeless and the Changing." *Tanz International* 2 (January 1991): 30–35.

Doglio, Vittoria, and Elisa Vaccarino. *L'Italia in ballo.* Rome, 1993.

Fagiolo, Marcello, et al. *Cinquant'anni del Teatro dell'Opera.* Rome, 1978.

Ottolenghi, Vittoria. *I casi della danza.* Rome, 1981.

Rossi, Luigi. *Storia del balletto.* Rev. ed. Milan, 1967.

Rossi, Luigi. *Il ballo alla Scala, 1778–1970.* Milan, 1972.

Siniscalco, Carmine, ed. *Fifty Years of Opera and Ballet in Italy.* Rome, 1956.

Testa, Alberto, et al. *Il balletto nel novecento.* Turin, 1983.

Testa, Alberto. *Discorso sulla danza e sul balletto.* 3d ed. Rome, 1981.

Turnbull, Ann Veronica. "Carolyn Carlson's Years at Il Teatro la Fenice, Venice, Italy, 1980–84: A Unique Experiment on the Italian Dance Scene." In *Proceedings of the Fifteenth Annual Conference, Society of Dance History Scholars, University of California, Riverside, 14–15 February 1992,* compiled by Christena L. Schlundt. Riverside, Calif., 1992.

Vaccarino, Elisa. *Altre scene, altre danze: Vent'anni di balletto contemporaneo.* Turin, 1991.

Venticinque anni di balletto a Nervi. Genoa, 1980.

Volpi, Gianna. *Spoleto Story.* Milan, 1982.

VITTORIA OTTOLENGHI
Translated from Italian

Classical Dance Education

With the great tradition of the Italian masters (Carlo Blasis, Giovanni Lepri, and Enrico Cecchetti, who was considered the "master of masters") having run its course, concern has been frequently voiced about the difficult situation in which the teaching of dance now finds itself in a country that was one of its cradles.

In the 1940s Jia Ruskaja, with the help of the Fascist regime, founded the Accademia Nazionale di Danza, which until 1951 continued to turn out dancers trained according to her teaching methods, which were directly influenced by the personal styles of Isadora Duncan and Anna Pavlova. This excessive centralization provoked an opposite reaction. Since 1974, access to teaching has been liberalized following a ruling by the Constitutional Court based on Article 33 of the Italian constitution, which states, "Arts and sciences shall be freely pursued, and the teaching thereof shall be freely available." Now all that is required to open a dancing school in Italy in compliance with standards of health, hygiene, and morals, without the state inquiring into the quality of the instruction offered.

There is still no professional registry: there are, however, two associations. The first is the Associazione Nazionale Insegnanti Danza (ANID), an association of certified teachers long directed by Bianca Gallizia, who, in close collaboration with the Italian National Academy, emphasized since 1957 the need to bring the profession up to date. The second is the Associazione Nazionale Liberi Insegnanti Danza (ANLID), an attempt to promote freedom of instruction and to combat monopoly, has since 1982 been attracting both certified and uncertified teachers.

In addition to the Accademia Nazionale, under the leadership of Giuliana Penzi from 1970 and Lia Calizza since 1990, there are three major schools. That at the Teatro alla Scala in Milan, now directed by Elisabetta Terabust, trained Carla Fracci and Luciana Savignano; it was closed in 1917 until Arturo Toscanini got it reopened under the direction of Enrico Cecchetti in 1921. The second major school is at the Teatro dell'Opera in Rome, directed by Walter Zappolini from 1973, then by Elisabetta Terabust, and now by Mario Pistoni. The third school, at the Teatro San Carlo in Naples, formerly directed by Bianca Gallizia, who studied under Cecchetti, is now directed by Roberto Fascilla.

Of the numerous private schools, only a few are noteworthy, primarily because of their famous founders. Sara Acquarone, Susanna Egri, and Marika Besobrasova established schools in Turin; the school of Liliana Cosi and the specialized Aterballetto school are in Reggio Emilia; that of Luciana De Fanti in Venice; that of Mara Fusco in Naples; and that of Cristina Bozzolini in Florence. Rome has schools directed by Giuseppe Urbani, Ugo dell'Ara, Giuseppe Carbone, and Renato Grecof.

Recently many schools have been offering courses with foreign and guest teachers. Some of these are no more than "lesson packages"; others are directed by ballet dancers still performing at their local opera houses. Some summer festivals, such as those at Nervi in Liguria and at Vignale Monferrato in Piedmont, also offer long, specialized courses in a complete range of disciplines.

BIBLIOGRAPHY

Beaumont, Cyril W., and Stanislas Idzikowski. *A Manual of the Theory and Practice of Classical Theatrical Dancing: Cecchetti Method*. London, 1922. Published in Italian in 1984–1989.

Blasis, Carlo. *An Elementary Treatise upon the Theory and Practice of the Art of Dancing* (1820). Translated by Mary Stewart Evans. New York, 1944.

Blasis, Carlo. *The Code of Terpsichore: A Practical and Historical Treatise on the Ballet, Dancing, and Pantomime*. London, 1828.

Cecchetti, Grazioso. *Manuale completo di danza classica: Metodo Cecchetti*. Rome, 1995–.

Cecchini, Egilda. *Invito alla danza classica: Secondo il metodo Basarova-Miei della scuola russa contemporanea, in uso al Teatro Bolscioi di Mosca*. 2d ed. Milan, 1974.

Doglio, Vittoria, and Elisa Vaccarino. *L'Italia in ballo*. Rome, 1993.

Ferrari, Donatella. *Agenda della danza*. Rome, 1981.

Fusco, Mara. *Metodo Vaganova*. Rome, 1981.

Fusco, Mara, and Francesco Falcone. *Danza e metodo: La scuola napoletana di Mara Fusco*. Rome, 1990.

Guatterini, Marinella. "Regola o libertà?" *Balletto*, nos. 8–9 (1982).

Lojodice, Leda. *La danza come un gioco*. Rome, 1984.

Otinelli, Marcella. *Come nasce una danzatrice*. Rome, 1970.

Ottolenghi, Vittoria. *I casi della danza*. Rome, 1981.

Pappacena, Flavia. *Tecnica della danza classica*, vol. 1, *La coordinazione*. Rome, 1985.

Pappacena, Flavia. *Tecnica della danza classica*. Vol. 2. *L'impostazione*. Rome, 1986.

Pappacena, Flavia. *Tecnica della danza classica*. Vol. 3. *Il ritmo*. Rome, 1988.

Rossi, Luigi. *Enrico Cecchetti, il maestro dei maestri*. Vercelli, 1978.

Ruskaja, Jia. *La danza come un modo di essere*. Milan, 1928.

Ruskaja, Jia. *Teoria e scrittura della danza*. Rome, 1970.

Viti, Elena. *Avvio alla danza*. Rome, 1989.

ELISA VACCARINO

Dance Research and Publication

Italy's rich heritage of traditional, courtly, and theatrical dances is universally recognized. Also well known is Italy's important contribution at the origins of ballet with the treatises written by the dancing masters of the fifteenth century. Subsequently, innumerable critical and aesthetic reflections by artists and men of letters were written and published, providing descriptions of dances, dancing, and dancers as well as assessments of their greater or lesser correspondence to the taste of the times. For this vast corpus of publications, and for studies relative to folk dance published in the past, the reader is referred to the bibliographies of entries on dances, topics, and figures in Italian history located elsewhere in this encyclopedia.

This survey focuses on recent scholarly publications and research, part of which is still under way. However, as this is not the place for a detailed and exhaustive listing of everything that has been published in recent decades, this article is confined to the exemplification of work representing currently active fields of research. At the same time, an outline will be given of the general framework within which scholars operate, with a brief account of the institutions that are directly charged by the state with public instruction and research, not overlooking what has been done out of personal initiative by single scholars and by nongovernmental institutions and organizations.

Basic references for the topic of this article are Barbara Sparti and Patrizia Veroli's "Dance Research in Italy," *Dance Research Journal* 27.2 (Fall 1995); the *Annuario italiano della danza*, edited by Anita Bucchi, with advice from dance consultant Concetta Lo Iacono (Rome, 1996); and my own essay "Dance Scholarship in Italy," in *Documentation: Dance Scholarship Today* (Berlin, 1989), the proceedings of a conference held in Essen, 10–15 June 1988. The reader is particularly referred to the *Annuario italiano della danza*, jointly published by CIDIM (Comitato Nazionale Italiano Musica) and IALS (Istituto Addestramento Lavoratori Spettacolo), for ampler treatment and data on specific subjects.

Unquestionably rich, the documents of various nature preserved in Italian libraries, archives, and collections have been only partially investigated, and it would be difficult even to estimate the quantity of material directly or indirectly pertaining to dance. The last years have witnessed the discovery of previously unknown precious sources. A manuscript containing a fragment of the treatise by Guglielmo Ebreo, for example, was discovered by A. William Smith, on which see "Una fonte sconosciuta della danza italiana del Quattrocento," in *Guglielmo Ebreo da Pesaro e la danza nelle corti italiane del XV secolo,* edited by Maurizio Padovan (Pisa, 1990). Other treasures are the Montefiascone codex containing ornamented fifteenth-century dances, on which see Barbara Sparti, "Rôti Bouilli: Take Two 'El Gioioso fiorito,'" *Studi Musicali* 24.2 (1995), and the Feuillet notation of three *balli* by Gaetano Grossatesta in a Venetian manuscript discovered by Michela Ferracin and studied by Gloria Giordano, on which see Giordano's "A Venetian Festa in Feuillet Notation," in *Dance to Honour Kings: Sources for Courtly and Theatrical Dramatic Entertainments, 1690–1740* (London, 1997), proceedings of a 1996 conference held at King's College, Cambridge.

A better assessment and evaluation of this patrimony of dance research will require some form of systematic cataloging and data collection, and a move in this direction has been the publication of several catalogs of archival funds and theater chronologies that contain explicit reference to data and material pertaining to dance. *Le fonti musicali in Italia,* published yearly by CIDIM jointly with SIdM (Società Italiana di Musicologia), is one of the reference points for music archival research, and there is a project of printing along with it a companion journal, *Le fonti della danza.*

The necessity to find common ground in order to unite forces is felt diffusely also outside the sector of scholarly research. In response to this need, the *Annuario italiano della danza* has made easily available to a wide audience, far beyond the circle of specialized professionals, a wealth of data and information on institutions, associations, and unions; production and training centers, means of distribution and promotion, and centers of research and documentation as well as specialized periodicals, dance sections in newspapers, and dance programs on television and radio networks.

One outcome of the effort to jump over fences and get beyond traditional disputes was the 1996 convention on the "Stati Generali della Danza," hosted by AIAD (Associazione Italiana Attività di Danza) jointly with AGIS (Associazione Generale Italiana dello Spettacolo), with the aim of bringing together all the existing forces to exert pressure on the national parliament and obtain a legislative reform of dance activities in the sectors of production, training, and teaching. On that occasion, the need was reasserted of legal protection of the quality of teaching, to be ensured by a certificate, but at the same respecting Italy's constitutionally guaranteed freedom of artistic expression and teaching. A coverage of legislative themes pertaining to dance is given by the monthly *Danza Sì,* founded in 1991 by Francesca Bernabini and Rafaello Luciani. Devoted to all aspects of dance-related legislation and administration, it gives up-to-date information on scholarships and grants awarded by national and local governments, on the management of dance schools and companies, and on technical facilities at existing theaters. It follows closely the activity of the Italian parliament and the state of advancement of reform projects in the dance sector.

While pointing out this recent tendency to merge efforts, one cannot omit to mention the crisis experienced in Italy after the transitory "dance boom" of the 1970s and 1980s (see Claudia Celi, "Dance Scholarship in Italy" [1989], already cited). Those decades saw a decided emergence of ballet and dance, characterized by an increased audience for performances and an outcropping of greater and lesser events, festivals and galas, particularly in the summer months. This in turn caused newspapers to devote more space to specialized criticism, breaking the previous habit of entrusting music critics with the coverage of dance events. Also, Radiotelevisione Italiana (RAI), the national state television network, in those years devoted more time to dance, featuring it also in prime time. All this space in the media has now progressively contracted, paralleling a general crisis in the world of live performance, and a certain decrease in interest by the audience.

Notwithstanding this, the legacy of those decades is not entirely lost, as is evidenced for example by the greater attention by state schools to initiating pupils in the practice and appreciation of the performing arts, within the reformed programs of the compulsory school cycle (from six to fourteen years of age) and the programs of some experimental high schools. A positive outcome of this has been the increased demand by university students for courses and degrees in subjects related to dance or movement. This demand has been positively answered by some university departments, and the result has been the supervision of several dissertations covering a wide range of subjects in Italian literature, history, theater history, music history, ethnomusicology or art history, as well as dance therapy, rehabilitation, and psychology. While no regularly active, dance-specific course exists presently in Italian universities, many have been the instances when artists or dance scholars have been invited to hold conferences and to teach courses. Still, the overall offer from universities remains inadequate; only the DAMS (Department of Studies in Performing Arts) at the Università di Bologna has managed to actuate a systematic and regular approach to dance-related disciplines, appointing in the 1992/93 academic year Professor Eugenia Casini Ropa to hold temporarily the teaching of "History of Mime and Dance" in addition to her tenured chair of history of spectacle.

The only state institution specifically devoted to dance training strictly correlated with theoretical study is the Accademia Nazionale di Danza. Established by decree as an independent state institution in 1948, the Accademia was initially directed by Jia Ruskaja (pseudonym of Eugenia Borisenko), and one of its aims under her directorship was to train a qualified body of teachers. Subsequently, under the direction of Giuliana Penzi, who collaborated with Ruskaja from the beginning in creating the school, the Accademia sought a stronger contact with the world of theatrical professional dance and opened its courses to both sexes (at the beginning the students were all girls). In order to facilitate the two-sided preparation, the Accademia houses a branch of a middle school (for pupils eleven to fourteen years old). In 1976, instead of the former *liceo classico*, a *liceo sperimentale coreutico* was annexed to the Accademia. Besides the regular eight-year course for choral dancers, the overall structure of the Accademia provides for advanced specialized courses with a final diploma for soloists, teachers, and choreographers, and an introductory teaching course that grants a certificate. Pupils in these last courses are required, during their final examination, to present a dissertation written under a teacher's supervision.

Under the new national work contract for Italian state schools and academies, the teachers of the Accademia Nazionale di Danza have obtained official recognition for their research activity. Requirements for periodic career advancement can be met by research projects that are approved by the governing bodies of the Accademia; this should ensure greater visibility to the longstanding engagement in research and publication by a number of teachers.

Connected to the Accademia is the Opera della Accademia Nazionale di Danza, a nonprofit organization to which was bequeathed Ruskaja's estate. The mandate of the Opera dell'Accademia is to encourage and strengthen the artistic and cultural activities of the Accademia, including performances by pupils. In pursuance of its mandate the Opera dell'Accademia organizes lectures, meetings, and training courses for teachers; it also manages a documentation center. In 1993 the Opera dell'Accademia resumed its publishing activity with the annual *Incontri con la danza*, edited by Elena Grillo.

An adhesion to the basic tenet that is at the origin of the Accademia Nazionale di Danza—namely, the necessary connection between theory and practice—can be found in the systematic approach pursued by the biannual *Chorégraphie: Studi e ricerche sulla danza*, founded in 1993 by Flavia Pappacena, who also serves as editor. In fact, the editor and most of the members of the editorial board are teachers of the Accademia, but the journal, printed in Italian with abstracts in English, avails itself of Italian and foreign collaborators coming from various specializations and experiences. The structure provides for three deeply interrelated sections: the first, more devoted to didactical issues, features regular columns for subjects as dance terminology, dance training methodology, and dance medicine; the second features scholarly essays that cover a wide spectrum of subjects relative to dance, also in relation to other arts as music, stage design, literature, cinema, and to dance legislation and regulations; the third section is devoted to information on scholarly conferences, publications, exhibitions and seminars. The journal up to now has focused in particular on nineteenth-century ballet, and on the technical and stylistic development of the "Italian school." Since 1995, *Chorégraphie* has also published extra issues in a monographic series, in which in 1997 appeared the *Inediti teorico-tecnici* by Enrico Cecchetti.

Specifically devoted to historical essays that underline the contribution by Italy to dance as an art is *La danza italiana*, founded in 1984. The programmatic introduction to the first issue, written by the founder José Sasportes, stated in part:

> The birth of *La danza italiana* derives from . . . the lack of a history of dance in Italy [and from] the belief that the history of dance in Europe, as today emerges from texts, is incomplete and distorted just because of an imperfect knowledge of what has been Italian dance.

Including its initial issue in the autumn of 1984, seven issues appeared before publication was suspended in 1990, including three monographic ones: *Il Quattrocento* (Autumn 1985), *La danza a Venezia* (Autumn 1987), and *Il ballo romantico in Italia* (Winter 1990). The published issues contain essays, by scholars from many countries, that investigate both the Italian ballet productions and the activity of Italian artists abroad, covering many different historical periods, and unpublished texts, such as "Due nuove lettere sulla controversia tra Noverre e Angiolini" in the spring 1989 issue. Particular emphasis was placed on the relation between dance and word, from the very first issue that significantly featured Sasportes's essay "La parola contro il corpo ovvero il melodramma nemico del ballo." At the time of this writing (1996), a project of starting a new series of *La danza italiana* is in an advanced stage.

In a sense, Sasportes's initial appeal for a history of dance in Italy has been answered with the publication of an ample section on Italian dance written by Alessandro Pontremoli (fifteenth–seventeenth centuries), Lorenzo Tozzi (eighteenth century), Claudia Celi (nineteenth century), and Alberto Testa (twentieth century) in a comprehensive major work: the fifth volume, devoted to dance, of *Musica in scena: Storia dello spettacolo musicale*, edited by Alberto Basso (Turin, 1995). To this volume, entitled *L'arte della danza e del balletto*, have contributed other Italian and foreign scholars; particularly well documented are the essays by Francesca Falcone ("Il ruolo della Danimarca," "La Svezia e gli altri Paesi candinavi"), Concetta Lo Iacono ("Il balletto in Russia"), and Patrizia Veroli ("Le compagnie di Djagilev e di Börlin").

Choreola, founded in 1990 by Giuseppe Michele Gala, is devoted to ethnochoreutics and in particular to traditional Italian dance, without disregarding contacts and contaminations with the world of "cultivated" dance. Its aim is to offer a space for scholarly research (essays are printed in Italian with abstracts in English, French, and Spanish) and at the same time to be a vehicle for diffusing to a wider audience the knowledge of a repertory that is in danger of becoming extinct. Two monographic issues on the Italian *canzone a ballo* have been published (3/4, Autumn-Winter 1991, and 7/8, Autumn-Winter 1992), while other issues present many different contributions by researchers in this sector. The publisher of *Choreola* featured *Un incontro di culture: La tarantella per pianoforte* by Marcello Cofini in the companion book series I Quaderni della Taranta. Also *Culture musicali: Quaderni di etnomusicologia,* founded in 1982 by Diego Carpitella as the journal of the Società Italiana di Etnomusicologia, has devoted considerable space to traditional dance: in 1985 a double issue was entirely devoted to dance.

The Associazione Italiana per la Musica e la Danza Antiche, which publishes the quarterly *Quattrocentoquindici 415,* regularly informing on early dance and music performances, festivals, and courses, also published *La danza in Europa fra Rinascimento e Barocco,* edited by Maurizio Padovan (Rome, 1995) in the series Monografie di Musica Antica.

If the Centro FLOG Tradizioni Popolari in Florence, with its collection of ethnic dance video and sound recordings, is a reference point for ethnochoreutic studies, an analogous role for ballet and dance is played by the Alberto Testa collection of about two thousand books on choreography kept by the Centro per la Danza Documentazione e Ricerca sponsored by the municipality of Turin, and the Fondazione Giorgio Cini in Venice, which keeps the Milloss Collection of books, documents, and letters, on which see Patrizia Veroli, "The Aurel Milloss Collection at the Giorgio Cini Foundation in Venice," *Cairon* 2 (1996). Sponsored by local governments and connected with the center for periodicals at the University of Maryland, the Centro Internazionale di Ricerca sui Periodici Musicali (CIRPeM) in Parma makes available to scholars a catalog of theatrical and musical periodicals from the second half of the eighteenth century up to 1945, listing in the indexes many names of choreographers and dancers. Soon expected is the opening to the public of the Andrea Francalanci collection of books and and research material, bequeathed to the Morris Music Library in Florence (Biblioteca Berenson).

A growing awareness of the role of dance in Italy led to several international conferences that were entirely devoted to dance. Published proceedings of such conferences include *Guglielmo Ebreo da Pesaro e la danza nelle corti italiane del XV secolo in Pesaro,* edited by Maurizio Padovan (Pisa, 1990); *L'arte della danza ai tempi di Claudio Monteverdi in Turin,* edited by Angelo Chiarle (Turin

1996); and *Creature di Prometeo: Il ballo teatrale dal divertimento al dramma in Venezia,* Fondazione Giorgio Cini Studi di Musica Veneta 23 (Venice, 1996). Several other important cultural conferences reserved a special session for dance, as for example the SIdM conference Le Relazioni Musicali tra Francia e Italia nel XVI Secolo held in Mondovì in 1994 (proceedings forthcoming).

Essays on dance also appear in such theater history journals and publications as *Teatro e storia* or *Biblioteca teatrale.* Among recently published books and essays on dance and mime by theater historians are *La danza e l'agitprop* by Eugenia Casini Ropa (Bologna, 1988), *Alle origini della danza moderna,* edited by Eugenia Casini Ropa (Bologna, 1990), *Teatro e spettacolo fra Oriente e Occidente* by Nicola Savarese (Bari, 1992), and "Tra scienza dell'uomo e scienza dell'attore" by Luciano Mariti, which serves as the introduction to *Lettere intorno alla mimica* by Johann Jakob Engel (Rome, 1993), a facsimile reprint of the nineteenth-century Italian edition of Engel's *Ideen zu einer Mimik.*

Attention to dance by musicologists has steadily continued, as testified for example by the conferences and publications sponsored by SIdM, some already cited, among which is the *Storia dell'opera italiana,* edited by Lorenzo Bianconi and Giorgio Pestelli (Turin, 1988) that includes the fundamental essay "Il ballo teatrale e l'opera italiana" by Kathleen Kuzmick Hansell. To Hansell is also due the reevaluation of the figure and the activity of the choreographer Gaetano Gioja ("Gaetano Gioia, il ballo teatrale e l'opera del primo Ottocento," in *Creature di Prometeo,* already cited). Musical institutions have published monographs on dance, such as the Istituto Nazionale di Studi Verdiani with *The Verdi Ballets* by Knud Arne Jürgensen, edited by Pierluigi Petrobelli and Fabrizio Della Seta (Parma, 1995), and the Fondazione Rossini with *"Di sì felice innesto": Rossini, la danza e il ballo teatrale in Italia,* edited by Paolo Fabbri (Pesaro, 1996). Essays and reviews on dance often appear in scholarly journals devoted to music, as for example in *Nuova rivista musicale italiana, Rivista italiana di musicologia, Studi musicali,* and *Il saggiatore musicale.* Among the publications pertaining to both music and dance are the scores of six *balli* by Giacomo Brighenti, Gaspero Angiolini, and Onorato Viganò printed in facsimile in *Balli teatrali a Venezia (1746–1859)* (Milan, 1994), which also contains an introduction by Sasportes, "Invito allo studio di due secoli di danza teatrale a Venezia (1746–1859)," and a "Catalogo generale cronologico dei balli teatrali a Venezia dal 1746 al 1859" by Elena Ruffin and Giovanna Trentin.

This interest in dance by scholars of other disciplines has favored the popularization and the penetration of dance themes in a wider audience than the circle of dance lovers and professionals for whom such specialized newsmagazines as *TuttoDanza* (founded in 1976), *Balletto oggi* (founded in 1980), *Danza & danza* (founded in 1986), and *Ballando* (founded in 1994) are published. Regular dance sections appear in many other periodicals such as for *La rivista illustrata del Museo Teatrale alla Scala*.

A particular response from the public of dancers was stimulated by publications on dance practice or training methodology. This kind of publication has probably enjoyed a wider penetration in the world of dancers than the handbooks on history of dance, the dictionaries, the monographs on famous ballets, choreographers, and performers, or the repertories of ballets, to which the publishers Di Giacomo Editore and Gremese Editore have regularly devoted themselves. Among dance methods, a particular interest by researchers has been awakened by the recent discovery and publication of the book written and illustrated by Grazioso Cecchetti, the son of the famous dancer and teacher Enrico, *Manuale completo di danza classica: Metodo Enrico Cecchetti*, edited by Flavia Pappacena (Rome, 1995–1997). English and French editions of this work are forthcoming.

Having drawn, in an inevitably brief outline, the picture of dance research and publication in Italy, a complex situation in unstable equilibrium, one must also note a few works that—because of their original perspective, their citations of new sources, or their attention in epitomizing previous literature in a critical form—represent benchmarks for the growth of dance research in Italy or that are essential reference texts.

For fifteenth-century Italian dance a comprehensive survey is *Il ballare lombardo* by Alessandro Pontremoli and Patrizia La Rocca (Milan, 1987). To Barbara Sparti is owed the English translation, with ample introduction and commentary, of Guglielmo Ebreo's treatise *De pratica seu arte tripudii* and to Andrea Francalanci the transcription of the Giorgio/Guglielmo Codex in the Dance Collection of the New York Public Library of the Performing Arts (*Basler Jahrbuch für historische Musikpraxis* 14 [1990]). The catalog of the exhibition that accompanied the Guglielmo Ebreo conference was edited by Patrizia Castelli, Maurizio Mingardi, and Maurizio Padovan as *Mesura et arte del danzare . . .* (Pesaro, 1987).

Among the recent publications relative to sixteenth-century dance are the introduction by Sparti to the facsimile reprint of *Ballo della gagliarda* by Lutio Compasso (Freiburg, 1995) and *La danza a Venezia nel Rinascimento* by Alessandro Pontremoli and Patrizia La Rocca (Vicenza, 1993).

Sparti's "'Baroque or Not Baroque–Is That the Question?': Dance in Seventeenth-Century Italy," in the already-cited *L'arte della danza ai tempi di Claudio Monteverdi*, contains a thorough survey of seventeenth-century dance-relevant sources. The same conference proceedings contain the paper "Theatrical Dance in Venetian Opera, 1637—1660" by Irene Alm, also author of "Operatic Ball-room Scenes and the Arrival of French Social Dance in Venice" (in the proceedings of the 1994 Mondovì conference, already cited). Other important publications for this period include the modern edition of the anonymous treatise *Il corago* (c.1628–1637), edited by Paolo Fabbri and Angelo Pompilio (Florence, 1983); "La sirena e l'angelo: La danza barocca a Roma tra meraviglia ed edificazione morale," *La danza italiana* 4 (Spring 1986), and "La danza nelle scuole gesuitiche" (in the Mondovì proceedings) by Alessandra Sardoni.

For the eighteenth century, many essays have been published in *La danza italiana*, including "Noverre in Italia" by Sasportes and "Musica e balli al regio di Torino (1748–1762)" by Lorenzo Tozzi, both in the spring 1985 issue, and "Dove gli eroi vanno a morir ballando, ovvero la danza a Roma nel Settecento" by Elisabetta Mori, in the spring 1986 issue.

Research in eighteenth- and nineteenth-century Italian dance has brought to a better appraisal of the activity in Italy and abroad of Italian dancers and choreographers. Examples are *Il balletto pantomimo del Settecento: Gaspare Angiolini* by Lorenzo Tozzi (Aquila, 1972); "Signor Rossi's Riddles: An Annotated Chronology of Domenico Rossi (ca. 1745–post 1821)" by Claudia Celi and Andrea Toschi, in *Cairon* 2 (1996); "Francesco Clerico, il poeta del ballo pantomimo" by Giovanna Trentin, in *La danza italiana* 5/6 (Autumn 1987); *Il sogno del coreodramma: Salvatore Viganò, poeta muto*, edited by Ezio Raimondi (Bologna, 1984); "Alla ri-scoperta di Giovanni Galzerani," by Rita Zambon, in *Chorégraphie* 5 and 6 (1995); "Salvatore Taglioni re di Napoli," in *La danza italiana* 8/9 (Winter 1990); "Il maestro Giovanni Lepri e la sua scuola fiorentina" by Giannandrea Poesio, in *Chorégraphie* 1 (Spring 1993); "Cecchetti: The Influence of Tradition" by Giannandrea Poesio, in *Dance History*, edited by Janet Adshead Lansdale and June Layson, 2d edition (London, 1994); and "La carne, la vita e il diavolo: I libretti dei balli di Virginia Zucchi." by Concetta Lo Iacono, in *La danza italiana* 4 (Spring 1986).

For the Italian versions of the first famous Romantic ballet, see "Sulle tracce della Silfide italiana" by Knud Arne Jürgensen, in *La rivista illustrata del Museo Teatrale alla Scala* 1.4 (Autumn 1989). In the winter 1990 issue of *La danza italiana* on Italian Romantic ballet are, among others, two contributions that single out two Italian cities and their relations with ballet: "Il ruolo del ballo nelle vicende del romanticismo a Venezia" by Elena Ruffin and "L'arivamento de la gran maravija der ballo: Il ballo a Roma dal 1845 al 1854" by Claudia Celi (English translation to be published in Studies in Dance History in 1997). In the same issue the essay by Andrea Toschi ("Un esperimento di catalogazione elettronica dei balletti dell'Ottocento") advocates the adoption of uniform formats and standards (see also, by the same author, "Verso una catalogazione unica dei libretti di danza italiani dell'Ottocento," in *Le fonti musicali in Italia* 7 (1993).

On the situation of Italian ballet at the end of the nineteenth century, see "L'imaginaire de la danse dans le théâtre italien à l'époque Umberto I" by Concetta Lo Iacono, in *Cairon* 2 (1996), and "Minima choreutica: Fasti e dissesti del ballo italiano sul declino dell'Ottocento" in *Musica senza aggettivi*, edited by Agostino Ziino (Florence, 1991).

Research papers on nineteenth-century ballroom dancing have been published in *Danza e società*, founded in 1992 by Fabio Mollica, also author of *La danza di società nell'Italia dell'800* (Bologna, 1995).

On dance in the twentieth century, see "Nicola Guerra maestro e coreografo nella Parigi degli anni '20" by Francesca Falcone, in *Chorégraphie* 9 (1997), and *I Sakharoff: Un mito della danza fra teatro e avanguardie artistiche*, edited by Patrizia Veroli (Bologna, 1991). Veroli is also the author of *Milloss: Un maestro della coreografia tra espressionismo e classicità* (Lucca, 1996), an extensive and richly documented biography.

Coreografie contemporanee, edited by Laura Delfini (Roma 1996), a collection of data on productions by Italian contemporary choreographers, has made even more evident the need to organize in a systematic and critical framework the Italian productions of the last decades. *La musa dello schermo freddo: Videodanza, computer e robot* by Elisa Vaccarino (Genoa, 1996) is devoted to the impact on dance of new technologies, a field of research not yet much explored in Italy.

For notation, see "La 'Terpsi-choro-graphie' di J.-E. Despréaux (1813): La trasformazione della notazione coreutica fra il XVIII e il XX secolo" by Flavia Pappacena, in *Chorégraphie* 7 (Spring 1996), and the works published by A.N.T.A.M. (Associazione Nazionale Trascrizione e Analisi del Movimento).

About issues relative to dance legislation, school regulations, and copyright, see Nadia Scafidi's "La danza nelle istituzioni scolastiche governative nell'Italia dell'Ottocento," in *Chorégraphie* 3 and 4 (1994), and "La Scuola di Ballo del Teatro alla Scala: L'ordinamento legislativo e didattico nel XIX secolo," in *Chorégraphie* 7 and 8 (1996). See also, by Concetta Lo Iacono, "Manzotti & Marenco: Il diritto di due autori," in *Nuova rivista musicale italiana* 21.3 (July–September 1987).

After more than forty years from the publication of the *Enciclopedia dello spettacolo* (1954–), still a reference point, a sort of ideal continuity is discernible between the pioneering efforts of artists and intellectuals as Aurelio Milloss, Gino Tani, and Fedele D'Amico and today's research.

CLAUDIA CELI
Translated from Italian

ITO, MICHIO (born 13 April 1892 in Tokyo, died 6 November 1961 in Tokyo), Japanese exponent of American modern dance. Michio Ito developed a free natural style combining Eastern and Western techniques in musical interpretations that he termed *dance poems*. Like a lyric poem, each expresses an idea and is wrought about a mood, which is a part of the idea, embodies the idea, or is embodied by the idea.

Ito was exposed to Western influences from childhood. His father, the architect Tamekichi Ito, educated at the University of Washington in Seattle and a friend of Frank Lloyd Wright, introduced earthquake-proof construction to Japan; as a convert to Christianity, he built Tokyo's first church in order to have a church wedding. Michio's mother, Kimiye Iijima, was no less enamored of Western ways.

As a small child, Michio Ito evinced a talent for music, enthusiastically studying piano and, later, voice. After secondary school he appeared in a German opera in 1911 with his teacher, Tamaki Miura, at the Imperial Theater, Tokyo. (Ito had also studied Japanese classical drama and dance.) Later in 1911 he went to Paris to study singing but was disillusioned by the incongruities of European opera. When he saw dancer Vaslav Nijinsky, however, interpreting the music of Weber (June 1911), he became so excited that after the performance he walked the streets all night in a pouring rain. Despite his admiration, Ito felt that Nijinsky's interpretation, good as it was, was hampered by ballet technique. When Ito saw Isadora Duncan dance a few months later, he became convinced that her style was more attuned to interpreting the European composers he had come to love in Japan. With these thoughts in mind, he entered the Jaques-Dalcroze Institute at Hellerau, Germany, in 1912. Here, in addition to music and rhythmic movement, he studied stage design and lighting under the great innovators Adolphe Appia and Alexander von Salzmann.

At the outbreak of World War I, Ito fled to London, where he remained for two years. As in Paris, he again found himself a member of an artistic coterie. Persuaded by a painter friend, he performed a dance at Herbert Asquith's birthday party in September 1914 and, as a consequence, was taken up by London society, performing at many charitable benefits. On 10 May 1915 he made his professional debut at the Coliseum Theatre with a program of dances that, judging from the criticism, already possessed a style remarkable for its economy and strength. Later that summer, he assisted Ezra Pound in editing Ernest Fenollosa's *nō* manuscripts, and he joined Pound and William Butler Yeats in the production of *At The Hawk's Well*, Yeats's *nō*-style play (performed April 1916). He created the Hawk's dance for it, directed the movement of the other actors, and helped Edmund Dulac design and execute the costumes and masks, persuading him to inject an Egyptian flavor into both. Since his Parisian days, when he haunted the Louvre, Egyptian art had exerted a strong influence on Ito. In later dance compositions he took for his own the balance, rhythmic vigor, and energy of figures carved on Egyptian monuments.

In 1916, he signed a three-year contract with Oliver Morosco to appear in New York. When he discovered that he was to dance in a "sex" musical, he released the producer from the contract. Ito's next twelve years were spent in New York City. He continued to develop his own style, using a technique based on ten arm gestures in various combinations with respect to plane, angle to body, hand position, context, and rhythm. His dances therefore presented a seemingly endless variety. Costume and lighting were skillfully contrived to reinforce meaning and visual effect.

Ito was also engaged in other forms of artistic theater, variously as director, scenic director, and choreographer for such plays as: *Bushido* (Washington Square Players, 1916); *The Three Strings of Samisen* (Provincetown Players, 1919); *The Faithful* (Theatre Guild, 1919); *Emperor Jones* (Provincetown Players, 1920), with lighting effects by Ito; *Arabesque* (Herndon, 1925); *Goat Song* (Theatre Guild, 1926); and *Turandot* (Habima Players, 1929). Ito also worked for musical revues; for the *Greenwich Village Follies* (1919–1923), he provided "What's in a Name" (1920) and "The Garden of Kama" (1923, in which Martha Graham appeared). His highly acclaimed *Michio Itow's Pinwheel Revel* (1922) marked the professional debuts of Angna Enters and Busby Berkeley. He was also involved with *Cherry Blossoms* (1927); *The Mikado* (1927); *Madama Butterfly* and other productions of the American Opera Company (1928); and Stravinsky's *The Soldier's Tale* (1928). Throughout those years he gave classes in his system of dance, numbering among his pupils Pauline Koner, Angna Enters, Nimura, Eleanor Painter, Ruth St. Denis, Doris Niles, and Clare Boothe Luce. When he moved to California in 1929, Lester Horton, Benjamin Zemach, and Sally Rand joined his classes.

In January 1929, Michio Ito left New York on a recital tour that ended three months later in Los Angeles. He remained in Los Angeles until 1942. In California he choreographed large symphonic works. On 20 September 1929, he presented two hundred dancers, with symphony orchestra and choruses, in the Pasadena Rose Bowl, interpreting music by Tchaikovsky, Grieg, and Dvořák, the different groups of dancers carrying the different musical themes. He presented this type of dance with even greater success in the Hollywood Bowl: *Prince Igor* (1930) and *Etenraku* and *Blue Danube* (1937). In the Redlands Bowl, he presented *Orpheus* (1936). Ito also served as dance or scenic director for a number of motion pictures noted for their artistry: *No, No, Nanette* (1930); *Madame Butterfly*

ITO. Seen here in a Chinese-style costume, the Japanese-born Ito combined Eastern and Western genres in his uniquely personal dances. (Photograph by Henningsen; from the Dance Collection, New York Public Library for the Performing Arts.)

(1933); *She* (1935); and *Booloo* (1938). His first experience in this medium, however, had been in New York, as the model for the pierrot-like clown in a cartoon series titled *Out of the Inkwell*.

After the outbreak of World War II, Ito was deported in 1942 as an enemy alien and resided henceforth in Tokyo. From 1946 to 1948 he was director of Tokyo's Ernie Pyle Theater, producing revues for the U.S. occupation troops in Japan. Later he directed opera and was a producer and adviser for Nippon Television. He was commissioned to organize the 1964 Olympic Games and, though he died before the games opened, his plans were carried out. At the time of his death, Ito maintained a dance studio in Tokyo, where he taught and presented pupils in recital. His dances strike responsive chords in almost all spectators through a use of universal symbolism expressed by strong, incisive gesture in a symmetry of continuous movement that is at one with the music.

BIBLIOGRAPHY

Caldwell, Helen. *Michio Ito: The Dancer and His Dances*. Berkeley, 1977.

Cowell, Mary-Jean, and Satoru Shimazaki. "East and West in the Work of Michio Ito." *Dance Research Journal* 26 (Fall 1994):11–23.

Fujita Fujio. *Itō Michio sekai o mau.* Tokyo, 1992.

Gauville, Hervé. "Michio Ito danse 'At the Hawk's Well.'" *Empreintes*, no. 3 (June 1978):12–17.

Ito, Michio. "Omoide o Katuru: Takanoya." *Hikaku Bunka* 2 (1956).

Ito, Michio. *Utsukushi naru Kyoshitsu.* Tokyo, 1956.

Kisselgoff, Anna. "An All-But Forgotten Pioneer of American Modern Dance." *New York Times* (26 February 1978).

Kisselgoff, Anna. "Dance: Michio Ito Salute." *New York Times* (4 October 1979).

Prevots, Naima. *Dancing in the Sun: Hollywood Choreographers, 1915–1937.* Ann Arbor, Mich., 1987.

ARCHIVE. Dance Collection, New York Public Library for the Performing Arts.

HELEN CALDWELL

IVANOV, LEV (Lev Ivanovich Ivanov; born 18 February [2 March] 1834, died 11 [24] December 1901 in Saint Petersburg), dancer, choreographer, and teacher. It was not until many years after his death that Lev Ivanov was recognized as "the soul" of Russian ballet of the late nineteenth century. Ivanov was the assistant and modest shadow of Marius Petipa and the second ballet master of the Maryinsky Theater in Saint Petersburg. Contemporaries overlooked Ivanov's talent in part because he displayed it only late in his career, when he was influenced by Tchaikovsky's music, and in part because as a choreographer his preferences and tastes were ahead of his time. Ivanov's entire career may be seen as a steady progression toward his choreography of *Swan Lake*.

Lev Ivanov was one of several children of Thio Adamova, a single parent, and spent several years in an orphanage. His father, a kind and fairly well-educated merchant, introduced Lev to the theater at an early age. The first performance the boy saw consisted of several one-act plays and a short ballet, *Don Juan*, probably one of Jean-Baptiste Blache's ballets with music by Hippolyte Sonnet (1832, revived in 1840). The boy liked the ballet so much that he decided to become a dancer. He was sent to the Imperial Theater School, where he studied under some of the best professionals of the day: Aleksandr Pimenov, Pierre-Frédéric Malavergne, Émile Gredlu, Jean-Antoine Petipa. In the 1840s the pupils were allowed to watch the rehearsals of Jules Perrot, whom Ivanov later described as "the most talented of choreographers." On 7 June 1850 Jean Petipa presented Ivanov to the public in Blache's *Le Ballet des Meuniers*, in which he danced in the classical pas de deux. From then on Ivanov, still a student, appeared in *divertissement* ensembles.

Dancer. On 20 March 1852 Ivanov was admitted to the ballet troupe of Saint Petersburg's Bolshoi Theater, where Jules Perrot, Marius Petipa, and Christian Johansson were the *premiers danseurs*. Each of them was unrivaled in his particular type of role, and it seemed that Ivanov had little chance to excel. However, two ballerinas, Elena Andreyanova and Tatiana Smirnova, noticed the young man's talents. On 22 February 1853 Andreyanova revived for a benefit performance Charles Didelot's ballet *La Chaumière Hongroise*, to a new music score by Konstantin Liadov, and chose Ivanov for the role of the young peasant Ulrich. Ivanov later wrote in his memoirs, "Seeing me in the class, Smirnova once asked me why I never danced on the stage separate *pas* but always as part of the corps de ballet. Well, I could only reply that I danced only what they allowed me to dance. Then she offered me to partner her for the grand pas de deux of the ballet *La Fille Mal Gardée* in her future benefit." The benefit took place on 3 November 1853, and Ivanov lived up to expectations. In September 1854 he was given the title role in *Le Ballet des Meuniers*. Vasilko Petrov wrote in his review on 19 September in *Peterburgskaia gazeta*: "Lev Ivanov danced so well that it seems to me that in all fairness only Mr. Johansson could have performed this pas with greater clarity of line and spontaneity."

Four years later Ivanov was made a *premier danseur*. As a stand-in for Marius Petipa, who fell ill on 18 November 1858, the day *La Vivandière* was to be presented, Ivanov, without preparation, appeared as the postilion Hans, the heroine's beloved. He then stepped in for Petipa as Phoebus in Jules Perrot's *La Esmeralda*. After that, roles in other Perrot ballets followed in quick succession, but their sheer variety indicated that Ivanov, with his musicality and rare professional memory, was seen not as a highly original actor but as a docile stand-in for other *premiers danseurs*. Ivanov replaced the lyrical Christian Johansson in the role of Valentine in *Faust* and the character dancer and mime Feliks Kshessinsky in the role of the romantic villain Claude Frollo in *La Esmeralda*. Toward the end of his career he replaced Timofei Stukolkin in the grotesque role of the old man Coppélius in Arthur Saint-Léon's *Coppélia*. Ivanov was engaged in nearly every ballet in the repertory. Beginning on 14 February 1858 he also taught dance to the two junior classes for girls at the Imperial Theater School. Nevertheless, in 1860, having been in the theater for ten years, Ivanov was still little recognized and poorly paid. In fact, his entire earnings in the theater and the school were less than Marius Petipa received for just his lessons. At first his poverty-stricken existence did not unduly worry him. He was proud of his ability to perform any role because he loved anything to do with music and dancing. Moreover, he tried his hand at composing music and choreography.

Ivanov dedicated his works in both genres to Vera Liadova (1839–1870), who was accepted in 1858 straight from school into the ballet troupe of the Bolshoi Theater. The young beauty responded to his love, and in December 1858 Ivanov applied for a marriage license. The marriage

IVANOV. A versatile performer, Lev Ivanov danced leading roles in many productions of the Bolshoi Theater in Saint Petersburg. He appears here as Conrad, a pirate, the principal male role in *Le Corsaire*. (Photograph from the Dance Collection, New York Public Library for the Performing Arts.)

proved unhappy. Unlike Ivanov, Liadova was energetic, ambitious, and dissatisfied with her position as principal character dancer of the Saint Petersburg ballet. In 1866 she performed in several vaudevilles on the stage of the Aleksandrinsky Theater, but her career was to reach incredible heights when French operetta established itself in Saint Petersburg. On 18 October 1868 Liadova played the title role in the premiere of Jacques Offenbach's *La Belle Hélène* and met with unprecedented success. In the synthetic genre of the operetta, ballet training was an advantage: Liadova drew stormy applause in the "variety" items with duets and the can-can. A new repertory was devised especially for her. On 18 July 1869 Ivanov made an official request that Liadova be issued a "separate residence permit in her name." A year later, Liadova died. Seven years later Ivanov married the dancer Varvara Malchugina.

In the 1860s and 1870s Ivanov took the leading roles in the ballets of Saint-Léon and Marius Petipa, which formed the repertory of the Bolshoi Theater in Saint Petersburg. In Saint-Léon's ballets he appeared as Sternhold in *Fiammetta* (1864), Petro in *Le Poisson d'Or* (1867), John Barker in *Météora* (1867), and Khanchung in *The Lily* (1869). In the ballets of Petipa his main roles were Ernest in *Florida* (1866), Gyges in *King Candaule* (1868), Wilhelm in *Trilby* (1870), and Solor in *La Bayadère* (1877). These

roles were limited to pantomime because the ballerina would be partnered by a *danseur noble,* a role usually filled by Pavel Gerdt, who was well proportioned, dapper, and elegant. He gradually supplanted Ivanov, who ceased training and began to drink too much. Toward the end of the 1880s critics were already writing about Ivanov as if his career were over. On 3 January 1893 he performed onstage for the last time—a Spanish dance with Marie Petipa—for a benefit performance. Ekaterina Vazem, his contemporary, recalled: "Ivanov was a first-rate classical dance soloist, artistically complete and highly experienced. His dancing was serene, correct, and a pleasure to watch. He was also a good partner for any ballerina. He loved to perform in the character genre as well; he was spectacular and graceful. [As a mime] he was always in the right place, impressive and sufficiently expressive, but out of his extensive repertory nothing particularly striking has made any lasting impression on my memory. His talent shone with an even light, so to speak, without the occasional flash" (*Zapiski baleriny Sankt-Peterburgskogo Bolshogo teatra,* 1937, pp. 116–117). His temperament was somewhat similar. Moreover, Ivanov realized that it was this aspect of his nature that suited the masterful Petipa.

Ballet Master. Petipa had appointed Ivanov *régisseur* of the Saint Petersburg ballet troupe in 1882. "I never counted on being either a *régisseur* or a ballet master, knowing how very placid and weak my character was," Ivanov confessed. But placidity and mildness of character were the reasons he became a choreographer. The position of *régisseur* called for administrative ability, something Ivanov did not possess, and he loosened discipline among the company members so much that in 1885 he was demoted to the post of second ballet master. He remained "completely satisfied because the position of *régisseur* is very disquieting. Being a ballet master may not be particularly less burdensome; still, it's far better." Petipa was also satisfied with an assistant who took on any assignment without demur and made no claims to independence. Moreover, Ivanov possessed a remarkable memory: "Monsieur Ivanov is a walking reference book who is always called on when old ballets are being revived," the critic Nikolai Bezobrazov wrote in *Russkaia gazeta* on 6 October 1887. In the summer months Ivanov composed small ballets and *divertissements* for stage performances in the Kamenyi-Ostrov Theater in Saint Petersburg and the suburban theater at the spa Krasnoe Selo. In winter Petipa sent him to Moscow to produce the Saint Petersburg ballets and also entrusted him with the dances performed in operas.

Influence of music. His work as an opera ballet master had important consequences. The music of the great composers stimulated Ivanov's imagination and was often echoed in his compositions. This was the case in 1890 when he composed the *Polovtsian Dances* for the premiere of Aleksandr Borodin's opera *Prince Igor*. It is customary to ascribe the revolution in character dancing to the *Polovtsian Dances* Fokine choreographed for the opera in Paris in 1909, but the character dancer Aleksandr Shiriaev, who performed the solo dance with a bow in Ivanov's production, maintained that "Fokine only reinforced, revitalized, emphasized, and embellished with various details the motifs of the dances composed by Lev Ivanov" (*Iz vospominaniy artista Maryinskogo teatra*, 1941, p. 91). Critics of the premiere of *Prince Igor* were unanimous in their praise of the *Polovtsian Dances*, although no one mentioned Ivanov. However, his musical ability was legendary. Shiriaev claimed that after the composer Anton Rubinstein had finished playing the music of his ballet *La Vigne* and left the rehearsal hall, "Ivanov went to the piano and, playing by ear, reproduced almost the whole score." Ivanov himself composed music for dancing: mostly mazurkas and Hungarian czardas, and, less frequently, music for classical dances. In 1878 the ballerina Evgenia Sokolova, appearing as the Tsar-Maiden in *The Little Humpbacked Horse*, danced a "new variation composed for her by the ballet master M. Petipa to the music by the composer, dancer, and amateur musician Lev Ivanov," said *Peterburgskaia gazeta* on 8 December 1878.

Ivanov's imagination as a choreographer depended entirely on the music: it determined the essence of the ballet's image and form, and the success or failure of a performance was directly proportional to the quality of the music. On 24 March 1887 Petipa entrusted him with the production of the one-act ballet *The Enchanted Forest* for the Imperial Theater School's graduation performance. The subject of the ballet was a modification of a romantic theme: a storm overtakes a Hungarian girl in a forest; the wood spirit attempts to turn her into a dryad but her betrothed arrives in time to rescue her. Riccardo Drigo's music, fresh and completely versatile, suggested a combination of fantasy and folklore. Ivanov embodied its forms in the classical dance of the dryads and the spirited peasant ensembles. The audience and the press acclaimed this ballet, and the management included it in the repertory of the Maryinsky Theater.

On 4 October 1887 there was the premiere of the three-act fantastic ballet *The Tulip of Haarlem*. The poster advertising the ballet indicated that it was composed by L. Ivanov with music by Boris Schell, and that the dance was produced by M. Petipa and L. Ivanov. Some critics were of the opinion that the dancing was entirely of Ivanov's making. Ivanov's plot repeated the familiar outline of Romantic ballets: in a field of bewitched girls who have been turned into tulips, the hero seeks out his beloved and with a kiss frees her from the spell. Several years later Ivanov came across a similar theme in *Swan*

IVANOV. As the dancing master Milon in Petipa's *L'Ordre du Roi* (1886), Ivanov posed with a *pochette*, a characteristic instrument played by French dancing masters. (Photograph from the Dance Collection, New York Public Library for the Performing Arts.)

Lake, only this time Tchaikovsky transformed the hackneyed situations, characters, and feelings. The uneven music score of *The Tulip of Haarlem* inhibited Ivanov's imagination, and his choreography drew differing appraisals. The classical ensembles were the most successful. Aleksandr Pleshcheyev wrote in the 6 October *Peterburgskaia gazeta*

> Of the many dances and groups, the one that stands out is the second act in which the poetic *scène de séduction* catches the eye . . . distinguishing itself by its freshness and having little in common with similar scenes from other ballets. The dances of the Butterflies are beautifully produced.

The novelty in Ivanov's choreography lay in the rejection of symmetry in the placement of dancers, in the transparency of the dance pattern, and in the tonal freedom of the dance vocabulary within the established canon.

Despite his activities in Saint Petersburg, Ivanov's main work was still in Krasnoe Selo, a town whose theater audience consisted of officers and lovers of ballet who had come from the capital. The theater's repertory was dominated by vaudevilles, *divertissements*, and short ballets, but the performers were the best that Saint Petersburg's theaters could offer. In 1888 Ivanov composed and set to the music of various composers the one-act ballet *The Beauty of Seville*, which ran for several seasons. In 1890 the corps de ballet dancer Alexandre Friedman composed for Ivanov the music for the ballet *Cupid's Prank*. The scenario recalled the Anacreontic works of choreographers from various periods and, probably without the knowledge of the authors, almost exactly repeated Gaëtan Vestris's 1773 ballet *Endymion*. But Ivanov's Diana and her nymphs were dressed in tutus, and the technique of their dancing obeyed the rules of late nineteenth-century academism. In 1891 Ivanov, again with Friedman's collaboration, produced the one-act ballet *The Boatmen's Festival*, also in the genre of theatrical *divertissement*.

The Nutcracker. By this time Ivanov had a large family, three children by the first marriage and three from the second. He was on the verge of destitution and his personal archives are full of requests for financial assistance. In the theater he drudged along. However, on 24 July 1892 *Peterburgskaia gazeta* announced a new ballet, *The Nutcracker*, by Petipa, and when the aging Petipa fell ill, Ivanov took over as choreographer. The possibilities for using his own initiative were limited: according to press reports he had to devise the dances "with advice and directions" given by Petipa. At the same time, the scenario by the director of the Imperial Theaters, Ivan Vsevolozhsky, and Petipa was at odds with Tchaikovsky's music, failing to develop the theme of childhood's naive discovery of the world. The boy characters of the first act, coming to life in the second, only touched upon this theme, while the music, in the words of Boris Asafiev, did convey the move from childhood to youth (B.V. Asafiev, *Izbrannye trudy*, vol. 4, 1955, pp. 107–109). This theme blossomed and asserted itself in the grand pas de deux of the second act for the Prince and the Sugarplum Fairy.

Although Ivanov could not fully exploit the grandiose revelations in the music of *The Nutcracker*, he achieved a good deal, undoubtedly relying on the discoveries made by Petipa in his realization of the symphonic music of *The Sleeping Beauty*. The attitudes of the two choreographers to Tchaikovsky's music differed: Petipa actively co-authored the musical and choreographic forms; Ivanov bowed obediently to the composer and in the best mo-

IVANOV. Seen here in a Kirov Ballet revival, the *Polovtsian Dances* from *Prince Igor* were originally choreographed by Ivanov for the second act of Aleksandr Borodin's opera, premiering 23 October 1890. This production marked the first time Ivanov set a ballet to the music of a Russian nationalist composer. The success of Michel Fokine's restaging of the *Polovtsian Dances*, presented by Diaghilev's company in Paris in 1909, has tended to overshadow the original production. (Photograph from the Dance Collection, New York Public Library for the Performing Arts.)

ments of his unequal production lost himself in the music, drawing from its depths the calm, pure movements of the dancing. This was because Petipa had met the composer and already knew the forms and situations of the ballet to come. It was precisely in the music that Ivanov found the source that stirred his imagination; the creative process for Ivanov began when Petipa's was already complete. Following in Petipa's footsteps with varying degrees of success, but without his refined humor, Ivanov devised the children's and adults' dances and the numbers with the mechanical toys in the scenes with the Christmas tree; in the battle scenes he filled the large stage with regiments of students as soldiers and mice. In the second act, Kingdom of Sweets, he conscientiously staged the *divertissements,* and in the grand pas de deux he clearly brought to mind Aurora's dance with her suitors in *The Sleeping Beauty.*

Ivanov reveled in the "Waltz of the Snowflakes" (the finale of the first act), which was performed by eight women soloists and fifty corps de ballet dancers dressed in identical white tutus strewn with small balls of fluff. Their heads were decorated with crowns branching off into rays and covered with snowflakes. Each dancer held an "ice" wand in her hand with a quivering bunch of "flakes." When Ivanov's production was replaced in 1922 with another, the dance was verbally preserved by the dance scholar and critic Akim Volynsky:

[There is the] barely perceptible glitter of the frostlike dust, the shapes and patterns of the snow crystals, the ornaments and arabesques of the frostlike movements. The flakes fall from above gently and moistly. This creates a sense of being inevitably attached to the earth. Three round dances cut the stage with zigzags, forming various figures: small stars, circles, dashing lines—both parallel and crisscrossing. Some of the dancers form a large and long cross, with an internal circle formed by other snowflakes. In front of them, facing the audience, eight winter sylphs dance in a waltz rhythm, executing swift but gentle *pas de basques.* The circle turns in one direction, but the cross goes to the other side.

(*Zhizn skusstva,* 20 February 1923)

The "Waltz of the Snowflakes," similar to that of the fairies in the prologue to Petipa's *The Sleeping Beauty,* created a fantastic image of nature. While Petipa showed its flowering and teeming life, Ivanov showed its winter slumber. In *The Sleeping Beauty* everything was built on a kaleidoscope of sounds and colors; in *The Nutcracker* the monotonous circling of snowflakes developed the lullaby theme. The novelty of this dance lay in its simplicity, in the pensive length of the phrases and the bright leisureliness of the tempo. The dance scene went beyond the confines of the subject and, having thus freed the choreographer from canonical methods, cleared the path toward musical-symphonic action.

Petipa's illness was lengthy, so that in September 1893 it was Ivanov who restaged Petipa's ballet *L'Offrande à l'Amour,* devising the dances anew. On 5 December 1893 the premiere of the ballet *Cinderella* took place. Petipa worked out a detailed plan for the dance scenes and entrusted the production of the first and third acts to Enrico

IVANOV. In Ivanov's original production of *The Nutcracker,* the eight soloists in the "Valse des Flocons de Niege" (Waltz of the Snowflakes), the finale of act 1, carried "ice" wands and wore snowflake headdresses. This ballet, with a score by Tchaikovsky and a scenario devised by Petipa after stories by E. T. A. Hoffmann, premiered on 6 December 1892 at the Maryinsky Theater. Innumerable versions of *The Nutcracker* have since been staged all over the world. (Photograph from the Dance Collection, New York Public Library for the Performing Arts.)

Cecchetti and the second act to Ivanov. In the grand *pas d'action* of this act Pierina Legnani, who appeared as Cinderella, demonstrated for the first time in Russia the technique of the thirty-two *fouettés,* and this act alone was preserved until 1900. On 28 July 1894 the ballet *Le Réveil de Flore* was part of the Peterhof (summer palace) theater's gala performance. The program read, "Anacreontic ballet in one act, composed by M. Petipa and L. Ivanov. Music by R. Drigo. Dances and *mise-en-scène* by choreographer M. Petipa." Petipa jealously stressed his authorship because five months earlier, on 17 February, Ivanov had staged the second act of *Swan Lake* at a memorial concert dedicated to Tchaikovsky.

Swan Lake. When composing *Swan Lake* in 1876 Tchaikovsky had not been constrained by the competent assistance of the choreographer. This determined the originality of the musical form, which meant that Ivanov was freed from the necessity of adhering to the norms and formulas laid down by Petipa. Ivanov was carried away by a theme in each of his works and he raised his treatment of each theme to the level of poetic generalization. The search for new means of artistic expression was not an end in itself for Ivanov, but neither did strict classical form seem to be the only possibility. In *Swan Lake* he blurred the outlines of this form, subordinating it to the truth of psychological states, and thus put forward the very problem of a new perception and portrayal of the world that the writer Anton Chekhov, the artist Isaak Levitan, and the composer Petr Tchaikovsky had raised in their works.

The second act of *Swan Lake* continued and was in a sense the climax of the Romantic tradition of nineteenth-century ballet, but it also looked toward the twentieth century. Like the Shades in Petipa's *La Bayadère,* the Swans in the *entrée* descend toward the footlights, multiplying in a zigzag motion the movement of the first arabesque. But this arabesque loses its customary outlines. An outstretched arm rises above the head, which leans toward the shoulder, while the other is slightly drawn back and dropped: the silhouettes of the dancers assume a mournful pensiveness. The corps de ballet's movements are broken up by pauses, while the arms rising and falling in a smooth motion maintain the lyric flow of the dance. The *sissonne* jump from the right leg to an arabesque at the first downbeat of the measure, the indecisive mincing of the feet, and another jump from the other leg at the next downbeat all convey the questioning quality in the motion of the dance, which is constructed on disturbing, broken sighs. The Swans first gather together in close circles, then fly apart in a falling, scattering pattern. The motif of hope and expectation, inherent in the works of many poets, artists, and musicians of the day, shows through the second act of the ballet. In the corps de ballet's waltz, this theme acquires a nuance that suggests peace and quiet. Eight small girl stu-

IVANOV. Act 2 of *The Nutcracker* takes place in the Land of the Sweets. Among the original *divertissements,* Ivanov created one for "La Mère Gigogne et les Polichinelles," which was performed by a Mr. Yakovlev, *en travesti,* and children from the Imperial Theater School. La Mère is the French equivalent of The Old Woman Who Lived in a Shoe (i.e., a woman with many children). This *divertissement* is today often called "Mother Ginger and Her Children." (Photograph from the Dance Collection, New York Public Library for the Performing Arts.)

dents, as Cygnets, are added to the thirty-two dancers. They advance to the proscenium with a *balancé* movement and, repeating the jumps in arabesque, appear to be learning to fly from their seniors.

When the main characters meet, Benno (Siegfried's sword bearer) is present, but his participation in the partnering does not intrude on the intimate confessions in the pas de deux. With the harp's first chords Odette runs around Siegfried and, having fluttered her "wings," sinks to the ground in a highly dramatic pose. (This pose would become the emblem of Russian choreography at the turn of the century; in concluding his concert dance *The Dying Swan* with it, Fokine intensified its self-restraint and aloofness.) Ivanov's pose was filled with a sense of trustful peace. In the fluid movements of the adagio the melody of the orchestra is given a plastique, first fading then soaring

IVANOV. The "Dance of the Little Swans" in act 2 of *Swan Lake* is one of Ivanov's signature pieces of choreography. Arms interlaced, the four Cygnets zig-zag across the stage, executing brisk and precise footwork and little jumps. The quartet pictured here is from the Sadler's Wells Ballet, c.1955. (Photograph from the Dance Collection, New York Public Library for the Performing Arts.)

up to the high notes. The impetuous pirouettes and the sudden flights of the dancer with the support of her partner take on a metaphoric meaning: Siegfried both helps Odette's flight and anxiously restrains her. The rush of feeling accompanies the sense of calm. The dance ends. Having laid her head on Siegfried's shoulder and rested her hand on his, Odette departs in pensive silence. The Swans join in the story and swim in arabesques at the orchestra strings' pizzicato and the staccato of the woodwind section. The flock sways rhythmically on the lake's surface. The dance begins afresh from a high, tense note. Falling silent once again, it ends not with an effectively placed period but with the drawn-out sigh of an arabesque.

After the scherzo episode with the four cygnet soloists and the mournful waltz of the other four soloists comes Odette's solo variation. Siegfried becomes silent witness to this poetic monologue. He withdraws to the wings like many a prince in a fairy-tale ballet. But Odette dances as though Siegfried could see and experience it. Ivanov here entered into the sheer poetry of Tchaikovsky's music, visibly conveying both its external motion and its emotional saturation. Odette's dance expressed not one particular feeling but a confused mixture of feelings: the human soul persistently and vainly endeavoring to exert its will.

The general coda follows Petipa's symphonic devices and gives them a new coloring. Ivanov paid due regard to the emotional subtext of the music and embodied it in the disturbing pattern of the coda. The Swans, gathered together in small flocks, break the horizontality of their lines by rising on pointe and throwing up their hands. The groups of four soloists fan out across the stage in various directions. The ballerina cuts across it diagonally in the confused nuances of her motif movement. The valedictory embrace and arabesque is a signal for the Swans' departure. Continuing Odette's gesture, the line of Swans runs around the stage then hides in the same wings whence it had first appeared. Behind the Swans, slowly and with a floating movement on pointe, Odette withdraws.

On 15 January 1895, *Swan Lake* was shown in its entirety with Ivanov's second act. Petipa produced the first and third acts; the fourth he entrusted to Ivanov, thus recognizing the merit of his work. The difference in the styles of the two choreographers determined the eclectic nature of the whole. The first act developed in the traditional manner, and the pas de trois of the Friends of the Prince, although excellent, nevertheless gave the impression of being an introductory concert item. At the ball in the third act the *divertissement* of various character dances was preparation for the *pas d'action* by Odile, Siegfried, the sorcerer Rothbart, and Benno. In place of this dance Petipa soon composed Odile and Siegfried's pas de deux, brilliantly setting off Ivanov's Odette, with her elegiac arabesques, against Odile, the bird of prey, with her resilient and commanding attitudes. His skill triumphed in the *fouetté*, which was no longer a technical stunt but the culmination in the depiction of cunning temptation: the swift repetition of the dancer's spins put the finishing touches to Odile's character. In the last scene of Tchaikovsky's ballet the motif of moral guilt comes tragically to the fore. This kind of guilt seeks to punish itself and find expiation in punishment. The scenario of the Saint Petersburg production offered a happy ending; its banal optimism disturbed Ivanov. The waltz—in which the black Swans, by cutting through the lines of white Swans, intensify the intonations of sorrow and anxiety— rose above the level of the ordinary. The Romantic motif of discord between dream and reality, highly relevant to Ivanov's own life, stood out clearly for all to see but disappeared at the end. The press regarded *Swan Lake* as a run-of-the-mill premiere and responded with irrelevant praise or senseless reproaches. Five years later, on 6 December 1899, *Peterburgskaia gazeta* informed its readers that at Ivanov's benefit performance Pierina Legnani presented him with a gold pendant bearing the inscription "De la part d'Odette." The first performer of this role was grateful to the choreographer for creating her best role.

Last works. In 1896 Ivanov composed the one-act ballet *Acis and Galatea*, to music by Andrei Kadlets. In 1897 he went to Warsaw, where he produced Petipa's ballets *Le Marché des Innocents* and *La Halte de la Cavalerie* as well as his own *The Magic Flute*. On 9 November the premiere of his three-act ballet *The Mikado's Daughter* took place at the Maryinsky Theater; the libretto was by the ballet *régisseur* Vladimir Langammer and the music by Vasily Wrangell. The legend of the Japanese princess who was abducted by a dragon and saved by her betrothed had recurred in many ballets. But the composer, whose main

works were drawing-room love songs, provided music that did not contain the natural dancing element evident in Pugni's and Minkus's music. Music of this kind did not stir Ivanov's imagination. The ballet closed after only a few performances.

Ivanov returned to his duties as a reviver of the old repertory and composer of *divertissement* dances at Krasnoe Selo. But he was to produce one more major work. In 1900 posters stated that on 11 October a new dance, "Czardas," to music by Liszt, would be included in the *divertissement* of the next performance of the ballet *The Little Humpbacked Horse*. On 12 October *Peterburgskaia gazeta* reported: "The 'Czardas' is produced by L. I. Ivanov, whose name was omitted from the poster. The production of this dance is as original as it is beautiful. The choreographer has skillfully adapted the dances and various steps to a tempo which unexpectedly alternates between fast and slow. This 'Czardas,' one of the most beautiful charac-

IVANOV. *Swan Lake* is undoubtedly Ivanov's greatest legacy. The first complete version outside Russia was staged by Nicholas Sergeyev for the Vic-Wells Ballet in 1934. That production is the basis for all later productions in Great Britain and many other Western countries. The formation pictured here is the finale of the *grand pas des cygnes* in act 2 of a Royal Ballet production, with Anthony Dowell and Georgina Parkinson as the principals. (Photograph by Houston Rogers; used by permission of the Board of Trustees of the Theatre Museum, London.)

ter dances ever staged, was hugely successful last night." The article continued by referring to the "Czardas" as "a complete choreographic poem." Turning next to Liszt's Second Rhapsody, Ivanov enriched ballet's repertory by adapting the music of a major composer who had never intended it for this purpose. Yet Ivanov had not shrunk from a perfectly legitimate theatricalization of a Hungarian dance. Such theatricalization corresponded to Liszt's treatment of national motifs, to its attractive, histrionic nature and its brilliant and elegantly elevated style. The spontaneous quality of the dance motifs, seemingly intent on going beyond the limits imposed by the composer, and the gyrations of the rhythms, regulated by an expert hand, were both embodied in the movement. Ivanov was continuing his search for the image-based arrangement of the music that he had begun with the Polovtsian Dances.

In April 1900, long before the appearance of *The Rhapsody*, the newspapers informed their readers that the production of the ballet score *Egyptian Nights*, by Anton Arensky, had been entrusted to Ivanov. According to the newspapers' repeated assertions, the rehearsals were over and the ballet was ready for performance. In the spring of 1901 they even referred to it as one of those performances designated for Peterhof. But Ivanov's production did not see the light of day. The young dancer Michel Fokine might well have been engaged in this production; in 1908 his ballet *Une Nuit d'Égypte* was shown at the Maryinsky Theater and in 1909, under the title *Cléopâtre*, in the first Saison Russe of Diaghilev's Ballets Russes at the Théâtre du Châtelet in Paris. Ivanov naturally interpreted his Egypt within the rules of the academic stage of the nineteenth century, whereas Fokine proceeded from the stylization of Egyptian visual art, which excluded direct continuity. A more general continuity existed in the closeness of the two choreographers' Polovtsian Dances, in the similarity between *The Dying Swan* by Fokine and Ivanov's Swans, and, finally, in the fact that both (Fokine more consciously than Ivanov) preferred symphonic music already composed and found the sources of their dance imagery in such music.

On 2 December 1901 there was the premiere of Léo Delibes's ballet *Sylvia* in Saint Petersburg, with choreography by Ivanov and Pavel Gerdt. But Ivanov had already been seriously ill for many months, and his contribution to the production was marginal. The ballet was not successful. When Ivanov died the obituaries listed his ballets but did not mention *Swan Lake*, although he was eventually recognized as the chief choreographer of this ballet, which incarnated Tchaikovsky's music and stood as a monument to Russian and world ballet of the nineteenth century. As the critic of *Peterburgskaia gazeta* wrote on 1 January 1901, "Ballet of the nineteenth century ended last night, December 31, with *Swan Lake*. One cannot think of a more fitting end."

[*See also* Nutcracker, The, *article on* Productions in Russia; Swan Lake, *article on* Productions in Russia.]

BIBLIOGRAPHY
Beaumont, Cyril W. "Lev Ivanov." In Beaumont's *The Ballet Called "Swan Lake."* London, 1952.
Krasovskaya, Vera. *Russkii baletnyi teatr vtoroi poloviny deviatnadtsatogo veka.* Leningrad, 1963.
Krasovskaya, Vera. *Istoriia russkogo baleta.* Leningrad, 1978.
Lawson, Joan. "Masters of the Ballet of the Nineteenth Century" (parts 1–6). *The Dancing Times* (November 1939–April 1940).
Roslavleva, Natalia. *Era of the Russian Ballet* (1966). New York, 1979.
Slonimsky, Yuri. *Mastera baleta.* Leningrad, 1937.
Slonimsky, Yuri. *P. I. Chaikovskii i baletnyi teatr ego vremeni.* Moscow, 1956.
Slonimsky, Yuri. "Writings on Lev Ivanov." Translated and edited by Anatole Chujoy. *Dance Perspectives*, no. 2 (Spring 1959).
Wiley, Roland John. *Tchaikovsky's Ballets.* Oxford, 1985.
Wiley, Roland John, trans. and ed. *A Century of Russian Ballet: Documents and Accounts, 1810–1910.* Oxford, 1990.
Wiley, Roland John. *The Life and Ballets of Lev Ivanov.* Oxford, 1997.

VERA M. KRASOVSKAYA
Translated from Russian

IZMAILOVA, GALIYA (Galiia Baiazetovna Izmailova; born 12 [25] February 1923 in Tomsk, Russian Soviet Federated Socialist Republic), dancer and choreographer. Izmailova graduated in 1941 from the School of Ballet in Tashkent, where she studied under Usta Alim Kamilov, Tamara Khanum, Evgenia Obukhova, Valentina Viltsak, and Pavel Yorkin. Upon graduation she joined the ballet company of the Uzbek State Theater of Opera and Ballet (now known as the Novoi State Academic Theater of Uzbekistan) as a soloist. In 1943 she began to appear in variety concerts dancing Uzbek dances, later adding other oriental dances to her repertory. Izmailova developed two separate careers, one as a concert performer of national dances and another as an accomplished stage artist. Her singular talent was best revealed in ballet productions from the national repertory, in which a harmonious blend of classical choreography with Uzbek or Indian material spawned a new form of stage dance. From the early 1940s onward she had leading roles in Fedor Lopukhov and Kamilov's *Ak-Bilyak* and Yorkin and Kamilov's *The Ballerina* as well as in classics such as *Coppélia, Don Quixote, The Fountain of Bakhchisarai, The Red Poppy*, and *Spartacus*.

Rendering the exquisitely refined ornamentation of the poses and movements of oriental dances, Izmailova searched for elements with which to create new forms of stage dance. In 1959 she choreographed *The Kashmir Legend* to music by Georgi Mushel, and in 1969 *The Love Charm* to music by Mukhtar Ashrafi. For concerts she created and performed plotless choreographic miniatures, employing various forms of national dances supplemented by elements of classical dance. Among the best were the Ferghan and Bukhar dances, the Lyazgi, *The Em-*

broideress (an Indian classical dance in the style of *bharata nāṭyam*), a Korean sword dance, and dances of the Punjab and Java.

In 1969 Izmailova received a degree in directing from the Tashkent Institute of Theatrical Arts, where she had been working as a choreographer since 1959. In 1977 she became ballet mistress at the Novoi Theater. Among the ballet scores she has staged are Ikram Akbarov's *Leili and Medzhnun* (1968) and Arif Melikov's *Legend of Love* (1979). Izmailova was named a People's Artist of the USSR in 1962, after having received a State Prize in 1950.

BIBLIOGRAPHY

Ashrafi, Mukhtar. *The Amulet of Love* (in English). Tashkent, 1969.

Avdeeva, Lubov. *Galiia Izmailova*. Tashkent, 1975.

Coton, A. V., et al. "A Symposium: The Russian Dancers in London." *Ballet Annual* 9 (1955):75–82.

Gray, Laurel Victoria. "From the Steppes of Central Asia, to the Mountains of the Caucasus." *Arabesque* 11 (May–June (1985):10–11.

Karasyova, Nina. "Galia Ismailova: First Classical Ballerina of Uzbekistan." *Ballet Today* (May–June 1963):17.

LUBOV AVDEEVA
Translated from Russian

J

JACKSON, LAURENCE. *See* Baby Laurence.

JACOBSON, LEONID. *See* Yakobson, Leonid.

JACOB'S PILLOW. An eighteenth-century farm in Becket, Massachusetts, purchased by Ted Shawn in 1930, became the home of the summertime Jacob's Pillow Dance Festival and school. The name refers to a large boulder on the property, which is situated near a mountain pass once called Jacob's Ladder. In the 1950s and early 1960s, "the Pillow" was the only summer showcase that combined programs of ballet, modern dance, and ethnic dance, and since then it has continued to be one of the major dance festivals in the United States.

At first Shawn planned to use the Berkshire farm as a quiet rehearsal retreat, but this was not to be. In 1931 the last group of Denishawn dancers rehearsed there before their final tour. In 1932–1933 Shawn taught a class at Springfield College for men only. Inspired by the enthusiastic response, he formed an all-male company to prove that dancing was an honorable and viable profession for men. The Men Dancers gave a trial performance in May 1933 in Boston and from then until 1940 toured to great success: more than one thousand performances in 750 cities.

The first public performance at Jacob's Pillow took place in July 1933, when Shawn was urged to give lecture-demonstrations with his all-male company during summer rehearsals. The first audience of forty-five was served tea, heard Shawn talk, and watched technical demonstrations as well as finished works. In 1934 the barn studio was enlarged, and eventually two performances a week were given. The men did most of the labor on the farm, building, planting, and caring for the grounds. Movements based on this work were often incorporated into the dances Shawn devised. Many of the farm buildings remain on the property and are used as cabins and a dining hall.

When the men's group disbanded, Shawn leased Jacob's Pillow to dance educator Mary Washington Ball for use as a school. In the summer of 1940 she started the first performance series to incorporate a wide variety of dance styles. The following summer, after Ball's plans to buy the Pillow fell through, the property was leased to Alicia Markova and Anton Dolin. They taught and performed with members of Ballet Theatre (now American Ballet Theatre), including Antony Tudor, Lucia Chase, Nora Kaye, and Agnes de Mille.

Later in 1941 a group of Berkshire residents formed a corporation to buy Jacob's Pillow; as part of the negotiations they hired Shawn to direct the festival and the school, which he called the University of the Dance. A theater was planned by Joseph Franz, architect of the Music Shed at nearby Tanglewood, and construction began in November 1941. In spite of the difficulties caused by U.S. entry into World War II, the Ted Shawn Theatre, the first theater in the United States to be designed exclusively for dance, opened on 9 July 1942. At present the theater seats 618. Franz also designed the distinctive, three-foot-high weather vane that sits atop the building; the weather-vane design was based on a photograph of Barton Mumaw, lead dancer of Shawn's men's group.

Over the next twenty-five years the Jacob's Pillow Dance Festival earned a reputation as the nation's most unusual dance festival, presenting all kinds of dance and upholding Shawn's firm belief that "the art of the Dance is too big to be encompassed by any one system, school or style. On the contrary, the Dance includes every way that men of all races in every period of the world's history have moved rhythmically to express themselves." This philosophy became the foundation of his eclectic policy: a typical program on each bill during the season would include ballet and modern and ethnic dance or mime. Artists appearing during this time, for example, included Alexandra Danilova, Frederic Franklin, Erik Bruhn, Alicia Alonso, Edward Villella, Patricia McBride, José Limón, Alvin Ailey, Carmen de Lavallade, Pearl Lang, Pauline Koner, Balasaraswati (U.S. debut), Carola Goya, and Lotte Goslar.

An important aspect of the Pillow was Shawn's activity as an impresario. Many companies made their U.S. debuts under his aegis: the National Ballet of Canada in 1953, the Celtic Ballet of Scotland in 1954, Ten Leading Dancers of the Royal Danish Ballet in 1955, Ballet Rambert and Les Grands Ballets Canadiens in 1959, and the Netherlands Dance Theater in 1965. Many solo artists also performed and more than three hundred world premieres were presented during Shawn's tenure.

In the late 1960s, with the advent of growing government support for dance, air conditioning in theaters, and a boom in dance, the Pillow's unique status waned. Shawn died in January 1972 and was replaced in quick succession by John Christian (1972), Walter Terry (1973), Charles Reinhart (1974), and Norman Walker (1975–1979). Throughout the seventies the varied Pillow format was kept. Of special note were the first appearance at the Pillow of Dame Margot Fonteyn in 1973 and the debut of a new company, Soloists of the Royal Danish Ballet, in 1976.

In 1979 Liz Thompson was named artistic director, and two years later she became executive director. Under Thompson's leadership the Pillow began to seek new directions for the school and festival. She dropped the three-part program, emphasized single companies, and offered special encouragement to young choreographers. An outdoor platform was built for additional performances, and the school established special jazz dance and ballet modules. In addition, a jazz music series was estab-

JACOB'S PILLOW. This open-air portrait of Barton Mumaw inspired Joseph Franz's design for the weather vane that sits atop the Ted Shawn Theatre. (Photograph by Shapiro Studio, Pittsfield, Massachusetts; from the archives at Jacob's Pillow, Becket, Massachusetts.)

lished. Thompson also balanced the Pillow's budget, which passed the $1 million mark in 1985.

In 1984 attendance at the festival was listed at 33,162 and the first capital campaign to overhaul the rustic plant and grounds was announced. As directed by the Pillow board and Thompson, the campaign's challenge was to maintain the Pillow's rugged strength, bucolic charm, and sense of history while providing an even more responsive environment for the future needs of dance, dancers, and dance audiences. This mandate has continued. Many renovations have been made but always in keeping with the original farmlike setting. In 1990 a studio theater seating 160 was created to showcase small dance groups and performance artists who need a working space before an audience. This facility complements the artist-in-residence program started by Thompson in 1983, which allows choreographers and companies to work for several weeks at a time in a hassle-free environment. A nearby farmhouse purchased in 1991 is used to house artists and companies for rehearsals even during the off-season months. The Ted Shawn Theatre was renovated in 1992 as part of an ongoing project of renewal and care of the original buildings.

In 1990 Thompson left the Pillow. She was succeeded by Samuel A. Miller, her managing director, who continued to present, preserve, and nourish dance. A visitor's center was established to show art and artifacts of dance, from photographs to costumes. Miller expanded the Pillow's reach, sponsoring yearlong projects such as the Philadelphia Project at the University of the Arts and the Jacob's Pillow Men Dancers company, which toured for two years (1991–1993) nationally and also to Russia and Holland. The Pillow also sponsors an improvisation workshop at Bennington College during the summer.

In 1995 Sali Ann Kriegsman was appointed executive director. In 1996 Jacob's Pillow received a grant from the National Initiative to Preserve American Dance. As a result of the grant, a reading room in the visitors' center will make the Pillow's archive of films, videos, programs, and photographs accessible to the public.

[*See also the entry on Shawn.*]

BIBLIOGRAPHY

Fay, Anthony. "The Festival of '42: A History Making Summer at Jacob's Pillow." *Dance Magazine* (July 1976): 61–65.

Jowitt, Deborah. "Bountiful Harvests at the Dance Farm." *Dance Magazine* (July 1992): 46–50.

Poulin, Jari. "Dancing with Ted Shawn: Pillow Days." *Dance Magazine* (July 1995): 46–48.

[Shawn, Ted]. *The Story of Jacob's Pillow.* N.p., n.d.

Shawn, Ted, and Gray Poole. *One Thousand and One Night Stands.* Garden City, N.Y., 1960.

Underwood, Sharry T. "Pillow Talk." *Dance Magazine* (July 1989): 28–31.

ARCHIVE.   Jacob's Pillow, Becket, Massachusetts.

KITTY CUNNINGHAM

JAMAICA. A West Indies island republic of some 3 million people lying south of Cuba and west of Haiti in the Caribbean Sea, Jamaica has a traditional economy based on sugar plantations and mining. Sighted by the 1494 expedition of Christopher Columbus, it was settled by the Spanish in 1509. The Arawak people, who had lived there for thousands of years, fought the Spanish, fled, and died in great numbers from epidemics. Britain captured the island in 1655, and it became a part of the British Empire in 1670. In the 1700s, slaves from Africa were transported as laborers. After Jamaica's 1838 abolition of slavery, the sugar market declined, leading to economic harship, civil unrest, and British government suppression of local autonomy. Rebellions by Jamaican blacks then occurred periodically because of their poverty and Britain's racial policies. In 1944 the vote was granted to all adults; from 1958 to 1962 Jamaica was part of the West Indies Federation; in 1962 it became an independent member of the British Commonwealth. Today a large majority of Jamaicans are well-educated, speak English and Creole English (a dialect), and are Protestants. More than 90 percent are of African ancestry; the rest are Europeans, East Indians, Chinese, and Lebanese.

Traditional Dance. In Jamaica the traditional dances developed out of sixteenth- to eighteenth-century encounters between Europeans—who came as explorers, planters, indentured servants, administrators, and adventurers—and Africans who were brought to work the plantations. Colliding cultures cross-fertilized to produce the quadrille (both "ballroom" style and the more rustic "campstyle"), maypole, schottische, and Jonkonnu (the John Canoe). These have undoubted European antecedents but were definitely shaped by the African majority, who also created other dances, many of them embedded in religious ritual or used for recreation on festive occasions. Jonkonnu, the most widespread festival dance play, is a Yuletide event dating back to slavery, when bands of masqueraders paraded the streets with dancing characters making pointed social comments and recalling significant events. [See Jonkonnu Festival.]

Eighteenth- and nineteenth-century European chroniclers found the dancing of the African-Jamaicans barbaric and lascivious. There developed a class-oriented division into two forms of Jamaican dance—one for the white upper classes, and another for those of mixed (Creole) origin, who were strongly influenced by African movement patterns, rhythms, and customs. The latter type of dance became a survival tool for the marginalized majority, through organic links with religion, in the worship of forbidden but persistent gods who were beyond the control of the masters.

The Jamaican dance heritage includes such enduring forms as the African-Jamaican dances *kumina; pukkumina* (also known as *pocomania*); *etu,* a Yoruba-influ-

JAMAICA. Two men performing Bruckin' Party, a dance that originated in the nineteenth century, during Jamaica's early post-emancipation period. (Photograph from the archives of the National Dance Theatre Company of Jamaica, Kingston; courtesy of Rex Nettleford.)

enced secularized dance play; *tambu,* a flirtatious couple dance; *goombay,* a fast acrobatic dance often associated with spirit possession and healing; *gerreh* (or *calembe*), an acrobatic dance involving a dancer with feet astride two bamboo poles, borne aloft at knee level by two people carrying the poles horizontally, while the dancer simulates walking to the drum rhythm; *dinki-mini,* lively dances performed to cheer the bereaved at a mourning ritual; Bruckin' Party, a competition dance originally performed to commemorate the emancipation of the slaves in 1838; *warrick,* a stick-fighting dance; Zion revivalism, a set of religious dances involving the stamping out of rhythmic spirit messages; Rastafarian dance, an urban dance genre with African roots; and East Indian *hosay,* a dance performed during mourning celebrations for Islamic martyrs. Later dance movements associated with the reggae

JAMAICA. Members of the National Dance Theatre Company of Jamaica in *Interconnexions* (1984), choreographed by Rex Nettleford. This African-influenced work was performed to a varied selection of music, including Handel's "Hallelujah Chorus" from *The Messiah* and South African spirituals and folk songs. (Photograph by Denis Valentine; used by permission; from the archives of the National Dance Theatre Company of Jamaica, Kingston; courtesy of Rex Nettleford.)

and dance-hall music of the 1970s, 1980s, and 1990s hark back to ancestral traditional forms, especially in the circular movements of the pelvis (called *dance-hall*) and the undulating movement of the upper back *(bogle)*.

Theatrical Dance. Jamaican folk dances have long influenced theatrical dance, as have Hollywood films, vaudeville, and modern dance. Classical ballet emerged in the 1920s among the white upper class, developing independently of traditional sources until the 1950s, when the surge of nationalism overtook all artistic and cultural endeavors. The work between 1939 and 1946 of Hazel Johnston, a London-trained Jamaican of means and artistic vision, is a landmark in Jamaican dance art, which she kept alive by maintaining high standards of presentation and sustained training. From her studios emerged Ivy Baxter, known as the mother of Jamaican creative dance, and the ballet teachers Fay Simpson, Punky and Betty Rowe, and Barbara Fonseca, who introduced the British Royal Academy of Dancing examinations to Jamaica alongside training given by Anatole and May Soohih in Russian ballet.

Influence from the United States produced in Kingston, the capital, the tap dancer Kid Harold and cabaret and variety artists such as Daisy Riley, Rudolph ("Sarsaparilla") Williams, and La Ciba Somani in the late 1940s, while Rex Nettleford staged dances for the popular Worm Chambers Group in Montego Bay. Berto Pasuka and Harold Holness migrated to Britain and won fame as dance artists in the 1950s, as dancer Clive Thompson and choreographer Garth Fagan were to do in the United States in the 1970s and 1980s.

Modern dance began to gain popularity in Jamaica under Ivy Baxter, who fused what she learned at the Sigurd Leeder School in London with Jamaican traditional dance forms in her pioneering Creative Dance Group (IBCDG) from 1950. She created the first full-length Jamaican work, *Rat Passage* (1954) to music by her pupil Eddy Thomas, who later taught modern dance after studying with Martha Graham in New York. Eyrick Darby, an alumnus of Jacob's Pillow, was an earlier influence. Dance also gained impetus from summer schools held at the University of the West Indies with American-trained teachers, including Neville Black and Lavinia Williams. Further stimulus came from Jamaican pantomimes (musicals) produced annually beginning in 1940 by the Little Theatre Movement. The 1962 pantomime, *Banana Boy*, directed and choreographed by Rex Nettleford, was a turning point in the integration of dance into pantomusicals.

From all this emerged the National Dance Theatre Company of Jamaica (NDTC), instituted at the time of Jamaica's independence in August 1962. The company is a voluntary group of dancers, singers, musicians, and technicians engaged in forging a distinctive dance theater genre, through experimentation with traditional Caribbean lore fused with contemporary modern dance and ballet idioms. Its repertory reflects a unique vocabulary and style realized through staged rituals, dance dramas, abstract studies, and Creole pantomimes. Its principal choreographer and artistic director since 1967 has been Rex Nettleford, who co-directed with Eddy Thomas from 1962 to 1967. Other seminal contributors have been choreographers Sheila Barnett, Bert Rose, and Barbara Requa; performers Yvonne daCosta, Barry Moncrieffe, Monica McGowan, Bridget Spaulding, Pansy Hassan,

Noelle Chutkan, Patsy Ricketts, and Melanie Graham; musical director Marjorie Whylie; vocal soloist Joyce Lalor; lighting designer George Carter; photographer Maria LaYacona; and administrator Verona Ashman.

The repertory of the National Dance Theatre Company clusters into several thematic areas. There is social commentary, as in *Two Drums for Babylon* (1964) and *Court of Jah* (1975), both inspired by the Rastafari movement. The central role of women in Jamaican society is expressed in *Ni—Woman of Destiny* (1976), a tribute to a Maroon (escaped slave) warrior heroine. African influences dominate *African Scenario* (1962), *Drumscore* (1979), *Interconnexions* (1984), and *Praise Songs* (1989), an exploration of

polyrhythms. Caribbean religious themes are exemplified by *Pocomania* (1963), *Kumina* (1971), and *Myal* (1974), *Gerrehbenta* (1983), based on authentic rituals involving ancestral spirits. Jamaican history and legend feature in *Legend of Lovers' Leap* (1962) and in *I Not I* (1977), which chronicles the creolization of Jamaica through its dances. Plantation culture has been explored in works such as *Plantation Revelry* (1963) and *The Crossing* (1978). Abstract works based on a variety of modern dance and African-Caribbean styles have also had a place in the company since its inception.

The National Dance Theatre Company has toured internationally, appearing in several countries of North and South America, as well as in Britain, Finland, Germany, the former Soviet Union, Australia, and the Caribbean Archipelago. It has also inspired the formation of similar companies in the Commonwealth states of the Caribbean (Barbados, Bahamas, Dominica, and Guyana).

By the 1990s many dance groups had emerged in Jamaica, pledged to expand the work done by the National Dance Theatre Company and such earlier ensembles as the Jayteens Dance Workshop (led by Joyce Campbell), the Jamaica Dance Company (founded by Eddy Thomas after he retired from the company), and the community-based Harbour View Dance Centre run by Alma Mock Yen. Out of the last group came L'Antoinette Stines, who in 1982 established the L'Antoinette Caribbean American Dance Company (L'adco). A year before that came the Movements Dance Company under the direction of Monica Campbell and others who worked in the short-lived Jamaica Dance Company. In 1989 the Company Dance The-

JAMAICA. The varied repertory of the National Dance Theatre Company of Jamaica includes several modern works with dramatic themes. (*right*) In this scene from the company's production of *Edna M*, a tribute to the late Jamaican artist Edna Manley, three women pose as statues. (*above*) A soul-searching duet from the the dance drama *O Come All Ye Faithful* (1993). (Photograph above by Denis Valentine; used by permission; both photographs from the archives of the National Dance Theatre Company of Jamaica, Kingston; courtesy of Rex Nettleford.)

atre was founded by Tony Wilson, a National Dance Theatre Company alumnus and choreographer. This was followed by the formal launching in 1994 of the Stella Maris Dance Ensemble, directed by Monica Lawrence, a National Dance Theatre Company principal dancer and choreographer. Both Wilson and Lawrence have produced full-evening dance dramas—one based on a popular Jamaican legend (*The White Witch of Rose Hall*) and the other on a modern novel about ghetto life in Kingston by Harvard sociologist Orlando Patterson (*The Children of Sisyphus*).

After forty years of exploration and experimentation, Jamaican dance can be seen to manifest a distinctive vocabulary, technique, and style within Caribbean dance theater. Thus Nettleford, in a *Dancing Times* essay of May 1990, could confidently write:

> The technical discoveries are strong in terms of the way Caribbean people move whether in ritual, for recreation, or in reaction to everyday concerns; whether in jumping for joy, crawling with fear, writhing in pain, standing frozen in fear, or shimmying with anger. None of such locomotor responses are peculiarly black or Caribbean, but the Caribbean people do express these emotions in body language that betray a way of releasing energy and a vocabulary of "dance" that is distinctively different from other cultures.
>
> A rigid back centred on a firm pelvis is bound to make designs different from a supple undulating spine synchronised into a contraction-release signature of an equally supple pelvis. Therein lies one important difference.
>
> The setting up of polyrhythms through simultaneous isolations in the body in axial splendour and the syncopated con-touring of designs in the release of energy and the progression from point to point are signatures of cultural significance that speak to African continuities in the heritage of the region. Europe's heritage also persists albeit in newly reconnected forms, alongside long adapted, versions of *jeté*, *fouetté*, arabesque, attitude, *pas de bourrée*, *pas de basque*, *sissone* and so on, as can be found in the Jamaican quadrille with its heel-and-toe polkas, or in the Haitian contre-danse with its elegant balance and waltz steps which admittedly finally break out into earthy gyrations.
>
> As I have said elsewhere there is a logic and inner consistency in the way Caribbean people move which gives to the commonplace crawl, hop, skip, jump and walk distinctive aesthetic significance.
>
> The emphasis on weight in the negotiation of and the shaping of many a movement-pattern find kindred association with the fall-recovery, tension-relaxation complexes of some schools of American modern dance as does the contraction-release complex usually identified as a Martha Graham invention but organic to all African dance which predates Modern Dance by a few centuries. Movement is moulded more often than attenuated. It is as though the material being worked on is clay rather than steel. Arms flow like rivers and torsos undulate like the outlines of rolling hills or the ebb-flow of the surrounding sea. There are technical foundations in the preparation of the body as instrument of dance expression.

This has become not only the hallmark of Jamaican dance theater but also a catalyst for community dance, dance research, and dance education.

All three of these areas fall within the nation's cultural policy. The Jamaica Cultural Development Commission fosters community dance through annual arts festivals.

JAMAICA. The Jamaican Cultural Development Commission sponsors dance festivals that include competitions for young people. These grade-school girls won a silver medal at one such event for their performance of a ring game. (Photograph by Austin Ferguson; used by permission; from the archives of the National Dance Theatre Company of Jamaica, Kingston; courtesy of Rex Nettleford.)

The dance competitions attract thousands of schoolchildren, adults, and traditional dancers, under the direction of veteran dancer Joyce Campbell. Dance research forms part of the program of the African-Caribbean Institute, a division of the Institute of Jamaica. It was given impetus by the field investigations of Cheryl Ryman (after study in Ghana) and Sheila Barnett (trained in the Laban method). Barnett, assisted by Barbara Requa and Bert Rose, initially developed the curriculum of the Jamaica School of Dance, founded in 1970 and now a part of the nation's Cultural Training Centre (later the Edna Manley College of Visual and Performing Arts). Courses offered in the training of teacher-performers and community cultural agents include technique (Caribbean traditional, modern, and ballet), choreography, educational dance, teaching methods, dance history, and Caribbean studies. Private studios teach ballet, modern dance, or both; small performing groups periodically spring to life and attract new audiences.

Continuing interest in Jamaican and wider Caribbean cultural forms is also revitalizing traditional dance in rural Jamaica and stimulating contemporary popular dance among urban youth.

[*See also* Caribbean Region.]

JAMISON. Alvin Ailey created *Cry* for Jamison in 1972 as a solo homage to black women. In this work, seen here in a 1976 performance, Jamison demonstrated the strength, clarity, and dramatic presence that won her international recognition. (Photograph © 1976 by Max Waldman; used by permission.)

BIBLIOGRAPHY

Barnett, Sheila. "Jonkonnu and the Creolisation Process: A Study in Cultural Dynamics." Master's thesis, Antioch International University, 1977.

Barnett, Sheila. "Jonkonnu-Pitchy Patchy." *Jamaica Journal* (March 1979).

Baxter, Ivy. *The Arts of an Island: The Development of the Culture and of the Folk and Creative Arts in Jamaica.* Metuchen, N.J., 1970.

Beckwith, Martha W. *Black Roadways: A Study of Jamaican Folklife.* New York, 1969.

Carty, Hilary S. *Folk Dances of Jamaica.* London, 1988.

Gladstone, Valerie. "National Dance Theatre of Jamaica." *Dance Magazine* (July 1993): 32–35.

Nettleford, Rex. *Roots and Rhythms.* London, 1969.

Nettleford, Rex. *Caribbean Cultural Identity: The Case of Jamaica.* Los Angeles, 1979.

Nettleford, Rex. *Dance Jamaica: Cultural Definition and Artistic Discovery—The NDTC, 1962–83.* New York, 1985.

Nettleford, Rex. "Afro-Caribbean Dance." *The Dancing Times* (May 1990): 1–8.

Ryman, Cheryl. "The Jamaican Heritage in Dance." *Jamaica Journal* (June 1980).

Stewart, John. *An Account of Jamaica and Its Inhabitants.* London, 1803.

Wynter, Sylvia. "Jonkonnu in Jamaica." *Jamaica Journal* (June 1970).

REX NETTLEFORD

JAMISON, JUDITH (born 10 May 1943 in Philadelphia, Pennsylvania), American dancer, choreographer, and director. Jamison began her dance studies at the age of six under the tutelage of dance pioneer Marion Cuyjet at the Judimar School of Dance in Philadelphia. She subsequently studied with Antony Tudor, John Hines, Delores Browne, Maria Swoboda, John Jones, and Joan Kerr. After attending Fisk University as a psychology major, she enrolled at the Philadelphia Dance Academy (now the University of the Arts), where Agnes de Mille discovered her and brought her to New York to dance in *The Four Marys* for American Ballet Theatre's twenty-fifth anniversary on 23 March 1965. Shortly after, at an audition for Donald McKayle, she caught the eye of Alvin Ailey, who subsequently asked her to join his company. She stayed with the company for fifteen years, including a short period in 1966 when the Alvin Ailey American Dance Theater joined with the Harkness Ballet in Barcelona.

Ailey and Jamison suited each other perfectly, and theirs became an inspiring partnership. Her dancing, a combination of strength, clarity, and poetry, was heightened by her flawless technique and dramatic stage presence. Her early work for Ailey included "House of the Rising Sun" in *Blues Suite* and "Fix Me, Jesus," "The Day Is Past and Gone," and "Rocka My Soul" in *Revelations*. She dazzled audiences as the "umbrella woman" in *Revelations* and in the first character solo Ailey created for her in *Masekela Langage*. She created memorable statements in the works of other choreographers in the Ailey repertory, including those of Talley Beatty, John Butler, Lucas Hoving, Louis Falco, and Ulysses Dove.

In 1972 Ailey choreographed for Jamison his celebrated solo *Cry*, as a birthday present for his mother; he dedicated it to "Black women everywhere, especially our mothers." *Cry* brought Jamison critical recognition as well as international celebrity. Clive Barnes called it "Judith Jamison's triumph" in his review in the *New York Times*. That year Jamison received the *Dance Magazine* Award. Ailey continued to create works for her, including *Pas de Duke*, in which she was partnered by Mikhail Baryshnikov for *Ailey Celebrates Ellington* in 1976; in 1981 he choreographed *Spell*, a *pièce d'occasion* in which she was partnered by Alexander Godunov.

In 1976 Jamison danced with Kevin Haigen in John Neumeier's *Die Josephslegende* for the Hamburg State Opera Ballet. Maurice Béjart choreographed *Le Spectre de la Rose* for Jamison and Patrice Touron with his Ballet du XXᵉ Siècle.

In 1980 Jamison left the Alvin Ailey American Dance Theater and soon after starred in the Broadway show *Sophisticated Ladies*. Her first company, The Jamison Project, premiered at the Joyce Theatre in New York on 15 November 1988; *Divining*, her 1984 ballet for the Ailey company, was shown. The following year Alvin Ailey died, and on 20 December 1989 Jamison was appointed artistic director of the Alvin Ailey American Dance Theater. Under her aegis works by Billy Wilson, Elisa Monte, Lar Lubovitch, and Jawole Willa Jo Zollar have been added to the repertory.

Her choreography includes *Divining* (1984), *Just Call Me Dance* (1984), *Time Out* (1986), *Time In* (1986), *Into the Life* (1987), *Tease* (1988), *Forgotten Time* (1989), *Rift* (1991), *Hymn* (1993) with libretto by Anna Deveare Smith, and *Riverside* (1995).

[*See also* Alvin Ailey American Dance Theater.]

BIBLIOGRAPHY

Jamison, Judith. *Dancing Spirit: An Autobiography*. New York, 1993.
Lyle, Cynthia. *Dancers on Dancing*. New York, 1977.
Maynard, Olga. *Judith Jamison: Aspects of a Dancer*. Garden City, N.Y., 1982.

HOWARD S. KAPLAN

JAPAN. [*To survey the dance traditions of Japan, this entry comprises six entries:*

The first article explores past and present dance forms; the second focuses on kagura *and* dengaku; *the third discusses folk dances known as* minzoku buyō *and highlights several dances associated with festivals; the fourth and fifth articles consider the development of theatrical dance; the sixth provides a brief history of scholarship and writing. For related discussion in a broader context, see* Asian Dance Traditions, *overview article. For discussion of more specific topics, see* Aesthetics, *article on* Asian Dance Aesthetics; Asian Martial Arts; Costume in Asian Traditions; Mask and Makeup, *article on* Asian Traditions; *and* Music for Dance, *article on* Asian Music.]

An Overview

Japan's rich variety of past and present dance forms reflects profoundly different religious and social phases of cultural history. The oldest recorded dances, the *kagura* described in the *Kojiki* (Chronicles) at the beginning of the eighth century, mirror a society recently developed from a nomadic tribal organization into a cluster of agricultural clans, ruled by shamans, under the supremacy of the ancestors of the present imperial dynasty. In their beginnings, *kagura* are described as shamanic rituals of possession, and they were seminal for the development of the basic circular and up-and-down movements common to many of the Japanese dance genres. Similarly, the rhythmical stamping of the feet and the lifting of both hands into the air, in a beckoning motion, probably originated in ancient rituals meant to invite the gods to be present among the participants. Historians also see in *kagura* the origin of geometrical floor patterns, in which dancers move from the center toward the cardinal points, and of the strong directionality, both linear and circular, of Japanese dance. Moreover, the belief that props held by *kagura* performers were temporary receptacles inhabited by the deity presiding over the dance is probably the source of the importance attached, even today, to fans and other hand props in many traditional Japanese dance forms.

The generic term *kagura* now refers to an astonishing variety of Shintō ceremonies, shrine theatricals, and colorful dances performed throughout Japan. These range from the highly formal *mikagura* performed at the Imperial Palace in Tokyo to the richly picturesque *satokagura* of numberless small village shrines. In a number of *kagura* the initial ceremonial section still reflects ancient Shintō worship. Often, however, *kagura* nowadays are merely adaptations of popular theatricals followed by colorful processions and folk dances that reflect a variety of local traditions. But such popular forms still preserve *kagura*'s original character of a communal honoring of the deity. There is no emphasis on revealing body forms or creating erotic tension between the sexes. The costumes, which totally conceal the body, as well as the dance patterns, which aim solely at the beauty of pure movement, are usually the same for female and male dancers. [*See* Kagura.] This places *kagura* in contrast with most Western folk dances, which have entirely lost their religious meaning and now focus solely on social concerns such as wooing.

JAPAN: Dance Traditions. *Bugaku,* the dances of the Japanese imperial court, arrived in Japan via Korea and China in the sixth century, becoming an established tradition by the eighth century. *(above)* A hand scroll depicting *bugaku* dancers, from the Tokugawa period, c.1800. *(right)* This *bugaku* performer of the Osaka Garyokai company performs a characteristically slow, stately movement. (Above: Metropolitan Museum of Art, New York; Seymour Fund, 1957 [57.52.2]; photograph used by permission. Right: photograph from the archives of The Asia Society, New York.)

Traditionally, *kagura* have been performed by the *miko,* usually female (in the past they were sometimes also male) professional shaman-dancers in the service of Shintō shrines. In the old Japanese sources the *miko* appear as direct descendants of the goddess Ame-no-Uzume. The *miko* dances performed at the major centers of worship today, however, preserve little trace of the trance-inducing movements of the ancient shamans. On the contrary, they show the marked influence of the fluent, elegant, slow motions of *bugaku* (court dances of nonmilitary origin), and they often follow choreographic patterns established—not without Western influence—in the nineteenth century by Tomita Makiko.

The introduction of Buddhism to Japan during the sixth and seventh centuries deeply transformed Japanese culture, adding new dimensions to dance. *Gigaku,* the Buddhist-inspired ceremonial and entertainment dances that were imported into Japan from mainland Asia at about this time, introduced the important Japanese performance tradition of using sophisticated masks and brightly colored silk costumes—in contrast to the unmasked and simple white garb of the older Shintō tradition. *Gigaku* processional and pantomimic performances reached a peak of prestige and popularity during the first half of the eighth century, reflecting the rapid diffusion of Buddhist culture throughout Japan. When new forms supplanted *gigaku* as official court entertainment, *gigaku* gradually faded away, leaving its traces in the masked pro-

cessions and pantomimes performed today in remote mountain temples. [*See* Gigaku.]

Meanwhile, the sophisticated splendor of life at the imperial palace in Kyoto during the Heian period (794–1185) found expression in *bugaku* dance and *gagaku* mu-

JAPAN: An Overview. Dancers of the Japanese imperial court in a performance of *bugaku*. This ceremonial genre is characterized by symmetry, a slow pace, and the refined attention of the four dancers. The spears and shields that the dancers wield here indicate one of *bugaku's* military-style dances. (Photograph by Phillip Bloom; from the Dance Collection, New York Public Library for the Performing Arts.)

sic. Components of what ultimately became *bugaku* reached Japan in waves from different parts of China and Korea and reflected traditions of even more remote lands, opening Japanese dance to a variety of highly refined influences. Although the subject matter of these traditions, Buddhist and non-Buddhist, was sometimes alien to the experience of the Japanese, the forms and the pace of *bugaku* either corresponded or were adapted to the preferences of the elite society confined within the golden precincts of the imperial-court compounds. The creative vitality of early *bugaku* soon gave way to a formalized conservatism, which reflected the court's increasing loss of contact with the vital forces that were shaping deep social and cultural changes outside the palace walls.

Besides introducing the Japanese to the wonders of colors, masks, and rhythms from countries as far away as India, Tibet, and Mongolia, *bugaku* also brought to Japanese performing arts the structural elements of beginning, middle, and end (or introduction, development, and finale), which later became essential elements of *nō*. Moreover, *bugaku* introduced into Japanese dance a concern for using body movement and musical rhythms to express the harmonies of the celestial spheres. The forceful, symmetrical, emotionally detached movements were meant to express the vast, solemn force that gives birth to all movement and to celebrate the way in which human behavior

can conform to the order and rhythm of this universal, primeval source. [*See* Bugaku *and* Gagaku.]

The development of the medieval dance forms that by the middle of the fourteenth century gave birth to *nō*, took place during a long, bloody period of continuous civil war, which brought about the collapse of imperial court authority and shifted real power into the hands of the military, or samurai, class. During this period, folk entertainment became more and more popular. The performers of the popular arts originally came mostly from the lower classes; eventually, however, they became part of the establishment of powerful Buddhist temples, serving a dual function as entertainers and as performers of ceremonies to which religious connotations were in a de facto manner attached. The families of the best performers succeeded in working their way up the social ladder and developing dramatic religious dances of the highest quality and inventiveness, eventually gaining the admiration of the new, powerful supreme leader of the country, the shogun.

The final transformation of the new dance art was accomplished by Kan'ami and his great son, Zeami. The imperial court continued to support *bugaku* as its official entertainment, but the court of the real ruler of Japan, the shogun, and the courts of the powerful feudal lords patronized *nō*, which became the expression of samurai culture. The samurai class and the court of the shogun, in particular, were strongly influenced by Buddhist spirituality, particularly that of Zen and other sects, which stressed the importance of individual enlightenment achieved through meditation and the practice of austere discipline—an appealing set of practical precepts for military people who were always confronting the danger of violent death. The frequent appearance of ghosts in *nō* dance drama testifies to their preoccupation with the afterlife and to their fascination with the revenge wrought by the angry spirits of heroes killed in battle. *Nō*'s powerful blend of Buddhist aesthetics and Shintō–shamanic themes and structures brought to it not only a sublime recognition of the transitoriness of beauty but also a sense of awe at violent outbursts of the primal passions of revenge and anger and an immense sadness in the face of the human condition. Through *nō*, its highest artistic expression, Samurai culture contributed sophisticated playwriting and original, stylized choreography to the performing arts of Japan. *Nō* continues to be performed, essentially unchanged, to the present time.

Nō has also produced masks that rank among the most beautiful in world theater, some of the most magnificent costumes ever used in dance, a stage that still commands admiration for its simplicity and impressive functionality as a dance floor, and, in Zeami's and Konparu Zenchiku's treatises on the "secret tradition" of *nō*, intriguing theoretical speculation on performance and the training of performers. [*See* Nō *and the entries on Kan'ami, Konparu; and Zeami.*]

At the beginning of the seventeenth century, the shogun Tokugawa Ieyasu succeeded in bringing unity and peace to Japan, unleashing an extraordinary energy and joy in dance that led to the formation of *kabuki*. The ultraconservative Tokugawa regime of the Edo period (1603–1868) assured the political supremacy of the samurai class, but it could not stop the profound shift of economic power from the military aristocracy to the burgeoning middle class of the new large cities. The townspeople created a new culture, which used the theater as an important vehicle of expression. *Kabuki* had broad appeal; it was geared to please the large numbers who frequented the red-light districts of the big cities.

The first *kabuki* dancer, Okuni, modernized the structure of *nō* plays, choosing for her main roles not the ghosts of famous heroes of the past but the recently deceased idols of the masses. The sensual appeal of the prostitutes' *kabuki* and the boys' *kabuki* that followed in the wake of Okuni's creation of the genre established the importance of the erotic element in this form of dance drama. The full development of *kabuki* occurred when the *onnagata*, the male performers of female roles, rose to the position of the form's peerless masters. *Kabuki* dance became the quintessential symbol of the *ukiyo*, "the floating world" of the urban demimondes of the Tokugawa period, so masterfully described by the novelist Ihara Saikaku and depicted by the masters of woodblock prints. *Kabuki* brought to Japanese dance theater a tone of immediacy, of open erotic appeal, and of gaudy and eccentric theatricality. With its long, complicated, melodramatic plots and its use of heavy makeup, stage machinery, lighting tricks, and ingenious set design, *kabuki* is a dance theater of broad appeal, geared to please large sectors of big-city populations. Performed in large theaters for profit, it is

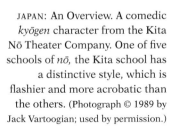

JAPAN: An Overview. A comedic *kyōgen* character from the Kita Nō Theater Company. One of five schools of *nō*, the Kita school has a distinctive style, which is flashier and more acrobatic than the others. (Photograph © 1989 by Jack Vartoogian; used by permission.)

rightly considered the first fully commercial theater of Japan. [*See* Kabuki Theater *and the entry on Okuni.*]

The sweeping impact of the official reopening of Japan after the Meiji restoration in 1868, and the ensuing race toward modernization and Westernization, also prepared the way for a new era in dance. The upper level of Japanese society, at first as a courtesy to foreign diplomatic representatives, introduced the Western custom of social dancing in male-female pairs. A deepening of interest in and the systematic teaching of Western music prepared Japanese audiences for the introduction of Western forms

of theatrical dance and spurred a number of attempts to modify traditional forms. Characteristic of this epoch of transition, which lasted through the first two decades of the twentieth century, were several attempts to modernize *kabuki*. Especially worthy of mention are the mainly theoretical achievements of the foremost pioneer of modern theater and dance in Japan, Tsubouchi Shoyo, and the work of the dancer Fujime Shizue (also known as Fujikake Shizuki and Fujikake Shizue). Tsubouchi advocated a new style of dance drama based on *kabuki* but incorporated the teachings of the great Western artists. Fujime started the important "new dance" movement (*shin buyō*), asserting the right of female artists to perform in the highest and most sophisticated of theatrical forms, thus breaking the male monopoly that had relegated women to a secondary role as geisha entertainers.

A great many schools of traditional dance flourish in Japan today. Most are related to *kabuki*—for example, the Fujima school, which holds an eminent position in *kabuki*

JAPAN: An Overview. Ichikawa Danjūrō XII in *Kanjinchō* (The Subscription List; 1840), perhaps the most frequently performed *kabuki* drama. Developed by the renegade priestess Okuni in the seventeenth century, *kabuki* was originally performed by women and was associated with prostitution. After women were banned from performing *kabuki* in 1629, the genre was transformed into the all-male drama featuring *onnagata*, or female impersonators, and is today the most popular classical form in Japan. (Photograph © 1985 by Jack Vartoogian; used by permission.)

choreography, and the Hanayagi school, which in its many branches probably counts the greatest number of performers. Many schools took their names and styles from *kabuki* actors; others derived their styles from folk music and dance presented under the patronage of the imperial court. Of great importance in the last several centuries has been the *iemoto* (headmaster) system, which has determined and preserved with strict discipline the characteristics of each group and created a mystique of respect for and dependence on the *iemoto* responsible for keeping the school's secrets and the traditions. The *iemoto* system assures the prestige of the dancers allowed to assume the name of a famous master and to present themselves as official members of a group of national standing. There is conflict however, between the rigid conservativism of the *iemoto*-dominated dance world and of individual artists who feel the need to assert a personal creativity.

Western-style ballet developed in Japan after 1900 at the Imperial Theater under the leadership of the European ballet master Giovanni V. Rossi. Soon a few Japanese ballet groups were formed, but they were not popular for many decades, because Japanese audiences then found it difficult to appreciate Western symbols and stylization. After almost disappearing during World War II, ballet had an unexpected postwar revival because of the U.S. occupation, its sociocultural and educational policies, and some successful performances by several important Western stars.

A similar pattern has occurred in modern dance, which received an enormous boost from the Martha Graham Company's visit to Japan in 1954. Since then, Japan has produced many important modern dancers; some have trained abroad, but all have brought discipline and a special, exquisite sensitivity to their craft. In recent years, performers and choreographers belonging to the dance movement known as *butō* have earned international acclaim. *Butō* ingeniously synthesizes intense discipline and concentration with spectacular acrobatics. The white-painted bodies and the slow, intense movements of *butō* dancers are reminiscent of *nō*, but *butō* has gone far beyond traditional Japanese dance, creating an East–West encounter of striking effect.

[*For related discussion, see* Bon Odori; Bunraku; Būto; Geisha Dance; Kyōgen; *and* Shimai. *See also* Ainu Dance Traditions *and* Okinawa.]

BIBLIOGRAPHY

Ashihara, Hidesato. *Japanese Dance*. Tokyo, 1965.
Barth, Johannes. *Japans Schaukunst im Wandel der Zeiten*. Wiesbaden, 1972.
Bethe, Monica and Brazell, Karen. *Dance in Nō Theatre*. 3 vols. Ithaca, N.Y., 1982.
Gunji, Masakatsu. *Buyo: The Classical Dance*. Tokyo, 1970.
Klein, Susan B. *Ankoku Butoh: The Premodern and Postmodern Influence on the Dance of Utter Darkness*. Ithaca, N.Y., 1988.
Komparu, Kunio. *The Noh Theatre: Principles and Perspectives*. New York and Tokyo, 1983.
Ortolani, Benito. *The Japanese Theatre: From Shamanistic Ritual to Contemporary Pluralism*. Rev. ed. Princeton, 1995.
Togi, Masataro. *Gagaku: Court Music and Dance*. New York and Tokyo, 1971.
Wolz, Carl. *Bugaku: Japanese Court Dance*. Providence, 1971.
Wolz, Carl. "Dance in the Noh Theatre." *World of Music* (1975).

BENITO ORTOLANI

Ritual Dance

Ritual or sacred elements form a major part of three important categories of Japanese traditional dance as defined by the folklorist Honda Yasuji: *kagura, dengaku,* and *furyū*. This article treats *kagura* and *dengaku*, dances for shrine attendants and professional troupes, respectively. [*For discussion of* furyū, *communal dances, see the article on* Folk Dance, *below*.] Because ritual dance has tended to include or to become entertainment, definitions have not always remained clear cut; *kagura* and *dengaku* may today be found on the same program given by the same performers.

Kagura. The first dances recorded in Japanese sources, *kagura* were used in the shamanistic rites of Shintō ("The Way of the Gods"), the polytheistic aboriginal Japanese religion whose elements include animistic beliefs, the cult of the emperor, and a veneration of nature and fertility. The mythical origins of *kagura* can be traced to the dance of the goddess Ame-no-Uzume before the heavenly cave where the sun goddess, Amaterasu, had concealed herself, plunging the world into darkness. Alone or in combination with later Confucian or Buddhist influences (which came from China and Korea), Shintō has pervaded Japan's performing arts since earliest times.

The word *kagura* probably comes from a euphonious contraction of *kam[u]kura*, "seat of the deity." In ancient times the powerful spirit *(kami)* invoked for the dance was thought to preside over or take part in the performance. Originally, the god was thought to dwell in a sturdy pillar; later, the god was believed to possess the shaman (usually a medium at a shrine, called a *miko*) by entering one of the ceremonial objects *(torimono)*—a tree branch, a paper pendant, a sword—that the shaman held during a trance dance. The shaman's magical gestures were intended either to invoke the spirits or to seek repose for the spirits.

The most commonly used Japanese words for dance, *mai* and *odori*, are also linked to these primeval trance dances. *Mai* comes from *mawaru*—"to rotate" or "to spin"—because female shamans circled round and round as a trance-inducing technique. *Odori* comes from *odoru*, "to leap" or "to jump," referring to the jumping technique used by male shamans for the same purpose.

JAPAN: Ritual Dance. *A performer of* kagura, *the Shintō dance-ritual with origins in the eighth century that is traditionally performed at shrines.* (Photograph from the archives of The Asia Society, New York.)

Today, the term *kagura* is used to describe a wide variety of dances performed at different places all over Japan. Some dances still reflect their shamanistic origins; others show the influence of later theatrical forms such as *nō,* *kabuki,* and *kyōgen,* or even of Western styles of dance. As a result of these influences, today many *kagura* performances consist of two parts: first, a sequence of rituals of purification and conjuration of spirits with hymns to the gods; and, second, an entertainment for the spirits that have been invoked. The ritual section of the dance has often remained basically unchanged over the centuries, whereas the entertainment part tends to follow contemporary trends.

An example of this combination of sacred and secular is found in a program of the Yamabashi Kagura group performed in the northeastern part of Honshu, Japan's main island. The opening group of dances and the closing *shishimai,* or lion dance, are considered ritual dance by both performers and audience, while the other dances that dominate the second half of the program, which are chosen by the evening's host, are thought of as entertainment. In this case, the core of sacred dances undoubtedly formed the original repertory of the group, which later incorporated or composed a variety of entertainment dances.

Kagura are divided into two major classifications: *mikagura,* those performed at the imperial court, and *satokagura,* or "village *kagura,*" which category includes all other types. The *mikagura* are performed each year for the emperor in his role as the high priest of Shintō worship. Essentially, the ritual represents a shortened, though largely unchanged, version of the eleventh-century courtly liturgy, which is composed of solemn, slow dances and hymns. The ceremony is always performed at night in an open courtyard of the Imperial Palace before the shrine dedicated to Amaterasu, the ancestor of the emperor.

One group of *satokagura,* the *miko kagura,* are performed by the *miko* of today—the white-and-orange-clad Shintō shrine maidens. Despite the traditional trappings, many of these *kagura* reflect modern and Western elements introduced into Japan in the nineteenth century.

Most of the rich variety of *satokagura,* however, embody local traditions and are performed by local dancers and musicians. There are three major traditions of *satokagura;* the first two are associated with the geographical locales that give them their names. The Izumo tradition, which centers on the ritual of changing the straw mat in the dwelling of the local god, is the origin of the two-part *kagura* tradition (sacred ritual and fashionable entertainment); from Izumo this form was diffused throughout Japan. The Ise tradition, centered on the ritual of boiling water and sprinkling it over the shrine's sacred premises and the worshipers, is marked by dances employing *torimono* hand props and traditional masks. The third tradition, called the *shishi* ("lion") tradition, focuses on dances that use lion masks and incorporate acrobatics, magic acts, and dance plays derived from *nō* and *kyōgen.* [*See* Kagura; Shishimai.]

Dengaku. The other form of traditional ritual dance, *dengaku* ("field music"), developed out of the rituals and rhythms of rice planting. In medieval times, this kind of dance and the related genres of *sangaku* ("scattered music") and *sarugaku* ("monkey music") were, in their less sophisticated forms, performed as popular entertainments at the shrines, sponsored by the aristocracy and clergy. *Dengaku* included skits, magic acts, and acrobatics as well as dance. Later, troupes became associated with particular shrines and, in the fourteenth century, *nō* was born from a synthesis of *dengaku* and *sarugaku* performed as entertainment for the samurai class. [*See* Nō.]

Specific Dances. The characteristics of *kagura* and *dengaku* can best be seen through descriptions of specific dances representing each type.

Flower Festival. Performed in about twenty localities in Aichi Prefecture on various dates between 2 December and 18 January, the Flower Festival is classified as Ise *kagura* by folklorist Honda Yasuji. According to the tradition of the villages of Donyu and Misawa, the festival takes its name from the exiled emperor Kazan-in (the first of the Chinese characters with which his name is written means "flower") and is offered for the repose of his soul. In the popular mind, however, the festival is associated with the flowering of the rice crop.

A dance floor made of earth is prepared in the entrance-way to the house that is chosen to be the community's "flower place" for that year's festival. In the center of the dance floor, a large caldron of water boils through the night. A variety of vigorous dances accompanied by flute and drum music and performed by groups of young men punctuate the festival, which begins with a ritual invoking the local deities. The first dances of the evening are performed without masks; later, masked figures appear. The dances performed without masks include *jigatame no mai* ("preparing the ground"), danced by thirteen- to eighteen-year-olds; *mitsumai* ("dance for three"), danced by twelve- to eighteen-year-olds; *yotsumai* ("dance for four"), by twenty- to twenty-six-year-olds; *hana no mai* ("flower dance"), by six- and seven-year-olds; and *ichi no mai* ("shamanic dance"). *Ichi no mai* is distinguished by energetic jumping that is said to preserve the movements of the ancient shamans. *Yubayashi no mai* ("excitement over boiling water") is a masked dance. Toward the end of the night, boys scatter the spectators by sprinkling them with boiling water from the caldron for the purpose of purification. As morning approaches, a performer wearing a lion mask and several wearing devil masks appear. The masked figures and the spectators mill about in a mood of elation, and the carefully executed traditional steps give way to spontaneous movements. At dawn, order and tranquillity are restored when two other masked dancers—the Spirit of Fire and the Spirit of Water—enter to terminate the festival.

Fan Festival. The *dengaku odori* ("dance of *dengaku*") is one among many events during the Fan Festival (Ōgi Matsuri) that takes place on 14 July in Wakayama Prefecture. The celebration, which is dedicated to the deity of the magnificent waterfall of Nachi, opens with a spectacular meeting of two groups of young men, one group carrying massive flaming torches and the other twelve lofty poles decorated with fans. This invocation to the god is followed by a daylong festival.

Performed on a temporary stage, the dance of *dengaku* resembles a performance depicted on scrolls of the later Heian period (794–1185). The performances were discontinued shortly after the Meiji Restoration of 1868, but the dance remained in the memory of one flutist, who helped reconstruct it some five decades later. The dance is per-

formed by a troupe of young men who accompany themselves with instruments: four with waist drums, two with shoulder drums, one on a flute, and four with the *bin-sasara*. This last instrument, especially associated with rice planting, consists of many small pieces of wood strung together; when the string that joins them is flipped dexterously by the dancers' hands, it makes a crackling sound. Twenty stately dances that take a little over forty minutes to perform make up the repertory. The dancers' style of movement, their rhythms, and their geometric floor patterns are suggested by some of the dances' titles, which translate into English as "Saw Teeth," "Lining up Shoulders," "The Waterwheel," "Leading the Horse," "Double-Beat," and "Eight-Beat."

BIBLIOGRAPHY
Gunji Masakatsu. *Buyo: The Classical Dance.* New York, 1970.
Hoff, Frank. *Song, Dance, Storytelling: Aspects of the Performing Arts in Japan.* Ithaca, N.Y., 1984.
Honda Yasuji, ed. *Festivals of Japan.* Tokyo, 1972.
Immoos, Thomas. *Japanisches Theater.* Zürich, 1975.
Ortolani, Benito. *The Japanese Theatre: From Shamanistic Ritual to Contemporary Pluralism.* Rev. ed. Princeton, 1995.
BENITO ORTOLANI AND GUNJI MASAKATSU

Folk Dance

A Japanese expression, *minzoku buyō* (*buyō* is one of several Japanese words for "dance," can be translated as "folk dance." The term *kyōdo buyō* ("countryside dance") was popular earlier in the century. In Japan, folk dance has always been performed in ritual or religious contexts (Honda, 1974). The recreational purpose is secondary. Men and women do not touch hands while dancing, though independent groups of men and women may dance and/or sing responsively.

It is useful to classify Japanese folk dance according to the major divisions in Honda's Yasuji system of Japanese folk performance: dance in *kagura* (rites for prolonging life), in *dengaku* (rites related to agriculture), and in *furyū* (rites to drive away malevolent spirits through dance and colorful costuming that includes objects carried by or attached to the body of the dancer). Although participation in many types of *minzoku buyō* is restricted to certain groups according to age or gender, some types of *furyū*, such as *bon odori* (dance performed at the time of the *bon*, the annual festival in mid- to late summer that marks the return of the dead), are performed by men and women, young and old, and are perhaps closest to the Western idea of folk dance.

Innumerable dances performed in countless places throughout Japan constitute a rich treasure of folk dance. It is misleading to think that each originated in the community where it is now performed. The process by which dances came to be performed where they are now found

JAPAN: Folk Dance. Like many folk dance forms, *odori* is now often performed in theatrical contexts. Here, an *odori* performer in an exquisite costume rises on his toes and spreads his arms. (Photograph © 1976 by Johan Elbers; used by permission.)

can be significant (Yamaji, 1979): (1) some became folk dances when local people went off and learned dances performed elsewhere or when local authorities invited outside performers to come and dance; (2) some were taught by professionals or by religious groups traveling throughout the country; (3) some are the dances that originated in one locale but were transposed to another when performers from one part of the country settled in another community.

Examples of the first type include many *bon* dances learned in the period after 1600. Economic growth prompted local communities' interest in what lay beyond them. Travel was popular. *Bon* dances are sometimes still identified locally as having been learned when a traveler went on a pilgrimage to the Ise Shrine, say, or when an ancestor went sightseeing to the capital. Similarly, in the second half of the nineteenth century, many communities built local theaters and invited *kabuki* actors or *bunraku* puppeteers to perform. Still earlier, local authorities imported entire festivals—the Gion festival of Kyoto was transferred to many places in the countryside in this way.

The well-known Ayakomai (of Kashiwazaki City in Niigata Prefecture) exemplifies the second process by which dance found a new home. One of the several groups of performers traveling in the countryside during the late sixteenth and early seventeenth centuries was forced to spend a winter in this community and taught local people the lovely dances, which suggest the choreography and costuming of early *kabuki*. In many cases associations of young people learned dances. This is how the popular lion dance *(shishi odori)* has survived so widely.

The growing affluence of rural communities toward the end of the Edo period (1600–1868) encouraged some, for their own prestige, to rescue dances that might otherwise have been lost. The increasing political and economic stability of certain communities was paralleled by a decline in the economic base of traveling troupes of performers, leading some of these groups to restrict their travel to a small area centered on a local family base. With the onset of hard times, this community inherited the art.

The choreography of certain *bon* dances was learned from *kabuki* actors invited as teachers into a community. Itinerant ascetics known as *yamabushi* taught other types of dance. In this way, dances that had been part of the great nationwide tradition of *furyū* in the late Muromachi period (1392–1573) acquired new local identities as part of the life of specific communities.

Bugaku is an example of the third process by which dance became folk dance. *Bugaku* was first introduced and taught through the patronage of state and Buddhist institutions. In an earlier period *bugaku* was performed by professionals in festivals at local temples within a national network. When political change weakened the centralized state and the position of former patrons, local people performed the dances instead.

In 1979, the Japanese government designated fifty performance traditions as Important Intangible Folk Cultural Properties *(juyo mukei minzoku bunkazai)*; fifteen of these were *furyū* dances. The following paragraphs discuss three of these dances to illustrate issues already raised and to exemplify principal types of *furyū* (in each case, the place of performance is given using the Japanese order, from largest to smallest geographical unit).

Taue Odori (Miyagi Prefecture, Natori-gun, Akyumachi, Baba). Performed during the New Year season, *taue odori* ("dance of transplanting") was originally a way of praying in advance for a successful rice crop (rice is actually planted several months later) through dances based on and named after agricultural work. The older custom, still followed, is to invite dancers to perform at individual homes, in which temporary stages are sometimes built, but nowadays performances are also held in a public auditorium. Management of the festival belongs to an association of young people (in their twenties). Today, the dancers, called *saotome* (the word for the women who do the work of transplanting rice), are girls from fifteen to twenty years of age, though in the past they were boys costumed as girls. Besides the eight to ten female dancers, the performers include two boys (fifteen or sixteen years old), called *yajuro*, who deliver a formal greeting *(kojo)* before the first dance and announce each of the dances that follow, and two other boys (seventeen to eighteen years old) who play hand-bells called *suzu-furi*. All the boys encourage the dancers with their onstage movements and rhythms. Two flutes, a large drum, and singers provide musical accompaniment.

The village of Akyu, which sits on a main transportation route, was often visited by traveling troupes of dancers, and it appears that *taue odori* was performed there by the end of the seventeenth century. Groups from some ten different sections of Akyu once performed; now fewer do. The same style of dance is found elsewhere in Miyagi Prefecture. At two places, tradition records that dances were imported from Kyoto: one tradition indicates that *taue odori* arrived during the Genroku period (1688–1703), the other, that it was first performed during the Tempo period (1830–1843).

In a traditional *taue odori* performance, performers gather in the young people's association. Before a Buddhist altar they dance three or four dances, then march out in procession to flute accompaniment. Other musicians join them as they reach the dance site. As the performance proper begins, the dancers line up in rows, with the *yajuro* and *suzu-furi* players at the end of the front row. The *suzu-furi* players begin to move rhythmically, then the *yajuro* recite the formal greeting.

The repertory has two sets of dances: first the *taue odori* proper (ten dances) and then a set of six "entertainment" dances. Dances are of the *kouta odori* type: each is accompanied by old songs, some from the seventeenth century or earlier. Dancers hold various objects—folding fans, rigid fans, bells—in their hands while dancing. During *taiko-taue* ("drum-transplanting"), a large drum is placed in the middle of the stage and the dancers beat it as they move. They wear flower hats during the first set but remove these and otherwise adjust their costumes for the second set of "entertainment" dances.

Shiraishi Bon Dance (Ikayama Prefecture, Kasoaka City, Shiraishi Island). *Bon* dance is the most widespread of countryside dance types. The *bon* dance performed at Shiraishi (on 13 or 14 August or thereabouts) retains features of *bon* dance from the late seventeenth century. Shiraishi, an island in the Inland Sea, was once an important cultural center. One of the most important battles of the civil war between the Minamoto and Heike clans took place nearby in the late twelfth century, and shortly afterward a monument was erected to honor the dead of both sides. The *bon* dance, too, is said to have originated as an offering for their repose.

The dance can also be performed as a prayer for rain. During the *bon* festival, however, dancers visit families in which someone has died during the previous year and dance in an open area before the house. The dancers then proceed to the beach, where two towers are set up. A drummer takes up a position on one of the towers, and a singer *(ondo-tori)* on the other. They perform throughout

JAPAN: Folk Dance. Performers of *Oni Kenbei* (Demon Sword Dance) at City Center of Music and Drama, New York. (Photograph © 1993 by Jack Vartoogian; used by permission.)

the night, as dancers, young and old, men and women, circle about under the moon. Steps and costumes used at *bon* dances elsewhere in Japan have mostly been standardized, but here each of the four groups of dancers is differently costumed and uses different steps. Such diversity was once common, as can be seen from pictorial evidence of the early Edo period. Dancers' movements were taught here by *kabuki* actors in the late seventeenth century, when the dance was extremely popular.

Throughout the performance, the *ondo-tori* sings long ballads, called *kudoki*, that commemorate the dead. Songs based on stories from the puppet theater *(joruri)* are also sung. The dancers, whose faces are concealed under deep plaited-straw hats, suggest wraiths crossing from the other world. Their vocal refrains, skillfully inserted into the pauses of the *ondo-tori*'s song, resound like a sign of ghostly delight in the dance.

Nenbutsu Dance of Taki Tenmangu Shrine (Kagawa Prefecture, Ayauta-gun, Ryonancho, Takimiya). This dance combines diverse elements: it is performed to placate a vengeful spirit, to pray for rain, to give thanks after rain, and to invoke the Buddha's name. Once performed beside ponds and reservoirs or at the shrines of local divinities and dragon gods during times of drought, it is now offered at the festival of the Taki Tenmangu shrine, on 25 July. The shrine is dedicated to Sugawara Michizane, a wrongfully exiled courtier who after his death became a vengeful spirit and was later venerated as a thunder and rain deity. Several stories purport to explain the origin of the dance. One tells of a time of drought in the year 888, when the historical Michizane was the governor of Sanuki (present-day Kagawa Prefecture). Compassion for the suffering of his people led him into the mountains to pray for rain. His gesture worked, and on 25 July rain began to fall—and continued for three days and nights; the relieved inhabitants gathered at the governor's estate to dance. Another story says that after Michizane's death a monk of the Taki shrine read a thousand sutras and originated the *nenbutsu* dance for the repose of Michizane's soul. A third story reports that the famous Buddhist priest Honen, exiled to Sanuki in 1207, invented the dance to accompany the recitation of the six syllables of the *nenbutsu* prayer as a means of proselytizing.

Twenty-two villages in two districts of Kagawa Prefecture have been organized into four groups; each year, one of these groups makes the dance offering at the Taki Tenmangu shrine. A procession of 120 or more people moves from smaller shrines and dancing places before reaching the Taki Tenmangu shrine. The procession goes once around the shrine before entering. Once within, the main dance begins.

[*See also* Bon Odori; Bugaku; *and* Costume in Asian Traditions; *for discussion of the lion dance, see* Shishimai.]

BIBLIOGRAPHY

Hoff, Frank. "Bon odori," "Dengaku," "Folk Performing Arts," "Furyū," and "Kagura." In *Kodansha Encyclopedia of Japan*. Tokyo and New York, 1983.
Honda Yasuji. *Dengaku/Furyū*. Vol. 1. Tokyo, 1967.
Honda Yasuji. *Katarimono/Furyū*. Vol. 2. Tokyo, 1970.
Honda Yasuji. "Nihon no minzoku buyō." In Honda's *Nihon no matsuri to geinō*. Tokyo, 1974.
Honda Yasuji. "Minzoku geinō gaisetsu." In Honda's *Minzoku geinō no kenkyū*. Tokyo, 1983.
Ikema Hiroyuki. *Folk Dance of Japan*. Tokyo, 1981.
Kelly, William. "Japanese No-Noh: The Crosstalk of Public Culture in a Rural Festivity." *Public Culture* 2.2 (1990): 65–81.
Minzoku geinō kenkyū bunken mokuroku. Engeki gaku, 17. Tokyo, 1976.
Nihon minzoku geinō jiten. Tokyo, 1976.
Nihon rekishi to geinō, vol. 5, *Odoru hitobito: Minshū shūkyō no tenkai*; vol. 9, *Gōsha to ryūkō: Furyū to bon-odori*. Tokyo, 1991. Both volumes are accompanied by hour-long videotapes.
Ortolani, Benito. *The Japanese Theatre: From Shamanistic Ritual to Contemporary Pluralism*. Rev. ed. Princeton, 1995.
Thornbury, Barbara E. "From Festival Setting to Center Stage." *Asian Theatre Journal* 10 (Fall 1993): 163–178.
Thornbury, Barbara E. "Behind the Mask: Community and Performance in Japan's Folk Performing Arts." *Asian Theatre Journal* 12 (Spring 1995): 143–163.
Yamaji Kōzō. "Minzoku geinō no denpa to ninaite." In *Geinō*, edited by Yasuji Honda. Kōza Nihon no minzoku, 8. Tokyo, 1979.

FRANK HOFF

Ballet

The ballet arrived in Japan with ballet master Giovanni V. Rossi in 1912. Rossi, a former dancer at the Empire Theatre in London, is thought to have been ballet master of Her Majesty's Theatre when a Japanese impresario engaged him for the newly opened Imperial Theater in Tokyo (Teikoku Gekijo, a private enterprise). As resident choreographer and ballet teacher there, he staged several ballets and operettas with considerable success, but, because both forms were so novel to Japanese audiences, they failed to become popular. Discouraged, Rossi left for the United States in 1918. Interestingly, the performers he left behind formed the first generation of modern dancers in Japan.

The next important event in Japanese ballet was the arrival in 1922 of Anna Pavlova and her company, which toured all over Japan and scored a huge success. The interest in classical ballet raised by the tour resulted in the opening of a ballet school by the immigrant Russian sisters Eliana and Nadezhda Pavlova. Although neither was a fully qualified ballet teacher, the first generation of Japanese classical dancers was trained under their guidance.

Among these, Azuma Yusaku (1910–1971) showed a keen interest in the Western ballet movement. With the help of the dance critic Ashihara Eiryo (1907–1981), who had spent several years in Europe, Azuma did extensive research and succeeded in mastering a considerable range of classical technique based on the Cecchetti method. Azuma's studies were augmented by his partnering of a Russian dancer, Olga Sapphire (1912–1982). Sapphire, a graduate of the Leningrad Ballet School, settled in Tokyo and married a Japanese diplomat. Azuma and Sapphire danced her version of Russian ballet at Nihon Gekijo, a variety theater, between 1936 and 1938, and in 1941 Azuma staged his version of *Les Sylphides* and *L'Après-midi d'un Faune* with some *divertissements*. This was the first ballet performance in Japan that followed the Western repertory. Azuma continued to stage ballets—including *Le Spectre de la Rose*, *Giselle*, and *Seventh Symphony*—until World War II halted almost all theatrical activity in Japan.

After the war, from 1946 to 1949, as the first Tokyo Ballet Company, a group of Tokyo's foremost dancers and choreographers joined together to stage *Swan Lake*, *Giselle*, and *Coppélia*. Komaki Masahide (1914–), who had danced in Shanghai, China, with a company of Russian expatriates, returned to Japan, where he founded his Komaki Ballet company. In 1946, he staged a full-length *Swan Lake*. Almost all the classically trained dancers in Tokyo joined forces for this production, which played to full houses for a month. This was followed by other productions, including *Le Spectre de la Rose* and *L'Après-midi d'un Faune*. Komaki also brought important foreign dancers to Japan, including Sonia Arova, who staged and danced in a full-length *Sleeping Beauty*, as well as Margot Fonteyn, Michael Somes, and Nora Kaye. With Komaki, the "ballet boom" had begun: small ballet studios opened all over Japan, and visiting foreign companies such as the New York City Ballet, the Bolshoi Ballet, and the Kirov Ballet, regularly had month-long runs in Tokyo (today, by contrast, a ten-performance run is the most that can be expected).

Although the ballet studios flourished and visiting companies were successful, the boom soon waned, and resident companies could no longer attract large audiences. Bored with banal productions, Japanese balletomanes began to recognize the gulf between the quality of Japanese and overseas companies. The need for competent ballet teachers was apparent.

In 1960, the arrival of two prominent teachers from the Bolshoi School, Sulamith Messerer and Aleksei Varlamov, was a turning point for Japanese ballet. They stayed until 1963, establishing the Tchaikovsky Memorial Ballet School in 1961 (with a performing company known as the Tokyo Ballet since the 1970s but formed in 1964 by Tadatsugu Sasaki, then a young impresario), reeducating the older generation, and training the promising younger dancers at the Tokyo Ballet School. Following them, many Russians, including Galina Ulanova and Vakhtang Chabukiani, taught there. Their presence, together with

JAPAN: Ballet. Morishita Yoko, one of Japan's leading ballerinas, appearing with the Matsuyama Ballet of Tokyo. (Photograph by Jack Vartoogian; used by permission.)

frequent tours of Japan by major Soviet troupes, brought Japanese ballet under strong Russian influence. The popularity of full-length ballets is one result. The technical standards of Japanese ballet improved greatly, producing international stars such as Morishita Yoko, Ohara Noriko (of the Scottish Ballet), Fukugawa Hideo, Kumakawa Tetsuya (Royal Ballet), Yoshida Miyako (Birmingham Royal Ballet), and Horiuchi Gen (New York City Ballet). These are the exceptionally talented few, however, and almost all dancers who remain in Japan still find their opportunities for development restricted.

Although more than a dozen ballet companies exist in Tokyo, none meets the highest Western standards. Because they give only a few performances a year, their chances to improve their artistry and performance technique are limited. Companies currently active in Japan include the Tokyo Ballet, Tokyo City Ballet, Matsuyama Ballet, Asami Maki Ballet, Tani Ballet, and Kaitani Ballet.

BIBLIOGRAPHY
Ashihara, Eiryō. *The Japanese Dance.* 2d ed. Tokyo, 1965.
Hirai, Takane. "External Influences in the Transformation of Japanese Dance." In *Culture Embodied*, edited by Michael Moerman et al., Senri Ethnological Studies, no. 27. Osaka, 1990.

Houseal, Joseph. "Toward a Japanese Ballet." *Ballet Review* 17 (Fall 1989): 38–52.

Japan Centre, International Theatre Institute. *Theatre in Japan 1994.* Tokyo, 1995.

Kennedy, Gilles. "Escaping from the Swans." *Ballett International* 13 (January 1990): 111–115.

Komaki Masahide. *Hareta sora ni—: Buyōka no ase no naka kara.* Tokyo, 1984.

Morishita Yoko. *Barerina no jōnetsu.* Tokyo, 1984.

Ortolani, Benito. *The Japanese Theatre: From Shamanistic Ritual to Contemporary Pluralism.* Rev. ed. Princeton, 1995.

Shimizu Masao. *Purima tanjō, Morishita Yōko.* Tokyo, 1982.

Shimizu Tetsutarō and Morishita Yoko. *Baree no sekai: Odoru, tsukuru, kitaeru.* Tokyo, 1983.

USUI KENJI

Modern Dance

Giovanni V. Rossi, the ballet master who introduced ballet to Japan as resident choreographer of the Imperial Theater in Tokyo from 1912 to 1918, was also indirectly responsible for the beginnings of Japanese modern dance. Among his students were Ishii Baku and Takada Seiko (1900–1977), both of whom were to play important roles in the development of modern dance in Japan.

There are four different styles of Japanese modern dance, each having a separate origin. The first grew out of

JAPAN: Modern Dance. Saeko Ichinohe is a modern dancer and choreographer who uses elements of traditional Japanese dance in her choreography. (Photograph from the archives of The Asia Society, New York.)

Western rationalism, which during the early twentieth century exerted a strong influence on Japanese culture, including dance. Modern dance assumed a leading place in Japan's performing arts, for a time eclipsing the wild dramaturgy of *kabuki* dance-drama, as dance and theater professionals sought to establish a new art form.

Ishii Baku was a primary proponent of this "rationalist school." Because Ishii did not wish simply to reproduce the classical ballet technique he had learned from Rossi, he strove to attain rational construction by developing his own methods and choreography. Though his works were based on European ideas, his technique was his own creation. In 1922, Ishii toured Europe, performing in Germany, Poland, Czechoslovakia, and other countries, where he danced his works *Melancholy* (to music by Edvard Grieg) and *Lonely Shadow* (to music by Yamada Kosaku). Another choreographer with similar concerns, Takada Masao, also traveled to Europe, appearing in London and Paris in 1923.

The second style was represented by Fujime (or Fujikage) Shizue, a geisha born in Niigata, who founded the Toin Kai troupe in 1917. Collaborating with writers, painters, and composers, she sought to create a new dance form that, while based on *kabuki* techniques, broke free of traditional works. Unlike Ishii, who danced in Western costume, Fujikage's group performed in kimonos—the traditional garb of *kabuki*—because of the close relationship between this type of dress and the *kabuki*-style movements her work employed. Fujikage traveled to Europe in 1928 for a highly successful concert in Paris. After returning to Japan, she choreographed constructivist pieces such as *Construction 231* (to music by Arthur Honegger). Another work, *Commune Warrior,* based on Russian writer Ilya Ehrenburg's 1941 *Padenie Parizha* (Fall of Paris), was set to the music of "La Marsellaise" and clearly influenced by Isadora Duncan. Another choreographer of this genre was Gojo Tamami.

The third Japanese modern dance style was strongly influenced by the expressionism and constructivism of German modern dance. Among representatives of this style were Eguchi Takaya (1900–1977), who studied with Takada Masao (1895–1929) in Japan and subsequently went to Germany to study with Mary Wigman; Kuni Masami and Shigyo Masatoshi also studied with Wigman, and Tsuda Nobutoshi studied with Max Terpis. During this period, many Japanese modern dancers studied in Germany not only because they were attracted to the new dance forms originating there but because the close political relations between Germany and Japan fostered cultural interchange.

The fourth style originated in the years after World War II, when both ballet and modern dance experienced a boom in popularity in Japan. This time the creative source was the United States; a visit to Japan by the

Martha Graham Company in 1954 provided a jolt that activated modern Japanese dance theater, as did tours—arranged by the U.S. State Department—by the José Limón, Alvin Ailey, Merce Cunningham, and Paul Taylor companies. Many among the younger generation of Japanese modern dancers—including Kanda Akiko, Kimura Yuriko, and Asakawa Takako—traveled to the United States to learn American modern dance.

These four groups still form the core of modern dance in Japan today. (Dancers from all but the second group—that based on traditional *kabuki* movement—belong to the Contemporary Dance Association.) Once these forms had been established, however, still newer forms began to develop, among them the genre known as *butō* (introduced in the early 1960s) and avant-garde dance influenced by American postmodern dance.

Butō, which had its genesis in works by Hijikata Tatsumi, Ōno Kazuo, and Kasai Akira, has been enthusiastically received around the world. Along with American postmodern dance and the German expressionist dance style exemplified by Pina Bausch, *butō* has been widely recognized as one of the preeminent trends in world dance theater during the late twentieth century. Among the visual elements incorporated in many *butō* works are white-painted bodies and the use of tragic facial expressions; monstrous self-degradation is often portrayed. A second generation of *butō* dancers has added more bizarre elements and even greater spectacle.

Another recent development has been Japanese postmodern dance, which was initiated in close conjunction with the same idiom in America. Some Japanese postmodern choreographers have been influenced by Eastern thought—especially the denial of mind-body duality—but some have drawn more closely from the work of American choreographers such as Yvonne Rainer and other members of the so-called Judson school. Among dancers representing the postmodern trend in Japanese dance are Atsugi Bonjin, Tanaka Min, Kasami Yasuko, Kato Miyako, Ebara Tomoko, Tano Hideko, and Teshigawara Saburō.

[*See also* Butō *and the entries on the principal figures mentioned herein.*]

BIBLIOGRAPHY

Durland, Steven. "Contemporary Art in Japan." *High Performance* (Summer 1990): 22–31.

Durland, Steven. "The Future Is Now." *High Performance*, no. 50 (Summer 1990): 32–37.

Havens, Thomas R. H. "Rebellion and Expression in Contemporary Japanese Dance." In *Dance as Cultural Heritage*, vol. 1, edited by Betty True Jones. New York, 1983.

Hirai, Takane. "External Influences in the Transformation of Japanese Dance." In *Culture Embodied*, edited by Michael Moerman et al. Senri Ethnological Studies, no. 27. Osaka, 1990.

Hosokawa, Eriko, and Chiyoe Matsumoto. "The Theories of Modern Dance and Its Related Fields." In *Hong Kong International Dance Conference*. Hong Kong, 1990.

Japan Centre, International Theatre Institute. *Theatre in Japan 1994.* Tokyo, 1995.

Kam'bayashi, Sumio. "Modern Dance in Japan." *Impulse* (1965): 29–47.

Klein, Susan B. *Ankoku Butō: The Premodern and Postmodern Influences on the Dance of Utter Darkness.* Ithaca, N.Y., 1988.

Mieko Fuji Dance Works. Tokyo, 1976.

Ortolani, Benito. *The Japanese Theatre: From Shamanistic Ritual to Contemporary Pluralism.* Rev. ed. Princeton, 1995.

Tomoe Shizune & Hakutobo. Tokyo, 1991.

Tsuki wa suigin: Teshigawara Saburō no buyō. Tokyo, 1988.

Viala, Jean, and Nourit Masson-Sekine. *Butoh: Shades of Darkness.* Tokyo, 1988.

Wakamatsu, Miki, and Miyabi Ichikawa. "The Modern Situation and the Traits of Japanese Dancers." In *Hong Kong International Dance Conference*. Hong Kong, 1990.

MIYABI ICHIKAWA

Dance Research and Publication

Writing on the art of dance has a long history in Japan. The *Kojiki* (Chronicles), written in 712 CE, and one of the earliest Japanese writings about dance, relates the origin of Japanese dance in the myth of the goddess Ame-no-Uzume. This anonymous work describes the spiritual origin of the performing arts and reflects the religious connections of many of Japan's dance, music, and drama forms.

Three historical works—*Kyokunsho* (1231), *Taigensho* (1510–1512), and *Gakkaroku* (1690)—provide verbal notations of music and dance sequences of the *gagaku* and *bugaku* tradition. In 1867, sections of these texts were combined into the *Samai fu* (Left Dance Record) and *Umai fu* (Right Dance Record), corresponding to two of the major classifications of dances in the *bugaku* repertory. In the past, because they had not been published formally, these texts were available only to group leaders and teachers.

The most important primary sources on *nō* are those by Zeami (1363–1443), the playwright, theoretician, and performer who is considered the father of *nō*. His *Kadensho* (Way of the Flower, 1400–1402) and *Kyakuraika* (Return of the Flower, 1433) are the major sources of the theory that forms the basis of *nō* techniques and aesthetics. Another important source relating to *nō* is Nose Asaji's *Nogaku genryu-ko* (1938), a monumental work exploring early performance genres that undoubtedly contributed to the formalization of *nō* in Zeami's time.

The *Yakusha rongo* (Actor's Analects), by Hachimonjiya Jisho, provides accounts by *kabuki* actors of the late seventeenth and early eighteenth centuries. Much factual information about *kabuki* is also contained in *Kabuki hyobanki* (A Record of Kabuki Performers), which has been published almost annually since the late 1700s. Its brief reviews include names of actors who performed during the period represented and the roles they played, as well as the names of troupes active at the time.

Most Japanese scholarly journals that deal with dance focus on specific genres. Examples include periodicals on *bugaku*, *nō*, *kabuki*, and *nihon buyō*. A notable exception is *Buyōgaku* (Choreologia), which has been published annually since 1978 and which treats both traditional and modern dance forms as well as dance in education. *Buyōgaku's* bibliographies are valuable for researchers.

More popular in nature, but also significant for research, is *Hogaku to buyō* (Japanese Music and Dance). This monthly, which began publication in 1950, contains essays, reviews, and calendars of events. Quarterly issues feature special topics, and most contributors to the journal are performers. *Engekikai* (The World of Theater) is a popular monthly, begun in 1943, that treats many theatrical arts and also publishes selected issues on individual genres. Additionally, it announces and documents current events in the performance world.

Dansu waku (Dance Work) contains in-depth articles on modern dance. It also includes interviews with people involved with dance, articles on avant-garde trends, and many photographs. The magazine *Tes*, which includes many photographs, documents both modern dance and ballet, particularly current performances.

On Stage, a popular Japanese weekly newspaper, informs readers of current happenings in many genres, as do *Pia* (a biweekly begun in 1972) and *Cityroad* (a monthly begun in 1971). Additionally, the major genres and theaters publish their own newsletters publicizing ongoing events. Folk dance is treated primarily in *Matsuri* (Festival) and *Minzoku geino* (Folk Performing Arts).

Because the performing arts are so closely related in Japan, many references to dance may be found in music and drama publications. An active group of writers and photographers interested in the folk performing arts provide a steady stream of information on folk forms.

Grants are offered to researchers by the Japan Foundation, and conferences on the folk arts are organized by Nihon Minzoku Geino Kai (Japanese Folk Performing Arts Association). Although they do not offer major programs in dance, several Japanese universities—including Tokyo Gaikokugo Daigaku, Musashino Joshi Daigaku, and Waseda Daigaku—support performing arts study groups and do some publishing.

The National Theater of Japan in Tokyo maintains both a library and a research department, and the recently built National Nō Theater, also in Tokyo, will undoubtedly follow a similar framework, though maintaining a focus on the genre of *nō*.

The Imperial Household Agency supports court musicians and dancers, and major Shintō shrines in various locations assist performing artists.

To date, studies on Japanese dance have focused on one of four major areas: (1) defining and describing *kata* (forms) in the various dance styles; (2) developing ethnographies that deal particularly with the religious content of plays and folk materials (and therefore provide more information on the contexts in which dance is found than they do on movement); (3) characterizing individual styles and their conventions in the manner of a guide for audiences; and (4) documenting histories of particular styles.

A number of publishers in both Japan and the United States work to make dance materials available. In Japan, these include Heinbonsha, Hokuseido, Kodansha, Kokusai Bunka Shinkokai (Japanese Cultural Society), and Tankosha. The American publishers Charles E. Tuttle and Weatherhill both frequently collaborate with Japanese publishers to issue dance texts. Additionally, several university presses publish works on Japanese dance—most prominently, the presses of the University of California, Columbia University, Cornell University, the University of Hawaii, the University of Michigan, and Tokyo University. These sources publish the works of both Japanese and non-Japanese authors.

Honda Yasuji, particularly noted for developing a classification system of folk performing arts (documented in his *Nihon minzoku geino jiten*, 1976), has been one of the most important writers in the area of folk dance (in, for example, *Zuroku Nihon no minzoku geino*, 1960; *Minzoku geino saiboroku*, 1971; *Geino ronsan*, 1976; and *Minzoku geino no kenkyu*, 1983). Kawatake Shigetoshi is the leading scholar of *kabuki* (in, for example, *Nihon engeki zuroku*, 1956; *Nihon engeki zenshi*, 1959; and *Geino jiten*, 1970). Gunji Masakatsu is best known for his work on *kabuki* and *nihon buyō* (in, for example, *Kabuki*, 1969; *Jishibai to minzoku*, 1971; and *Nihon buyō jiten*, 1977). Hattori Yukio has published widely on *kabuki* (for example, *Kabuki seiritsu no kenkyu*, 1968; *Kabuki no kozo*, 1970; and *Kabuki no genzo*, 1974). Ashihara Eiryo has published extensively on many types of dance and other performing arts (for example, *The Japanese Dance*, 1965).

Other exceptional works on Japanese dance are *Nihon buyō soran* (General Introduction to Japanese Dance (Nihon Buyō Kyokai, ed. 1952), and Tsuneo Ishifuku's *Buyō no rekishi* (A History of Dance in Japan, 1974).

Non-Japanese writers who have made significant contributions to the literature include Frank Hoff (in, for example, *A Theatre of Metaphor: A Study of the Japanese No Form*, 1965; *The Life-Structure of Noh: An English Version of Yokomichi Mario's Analysis of the Structure of Noh*, 1973; and *Song, Dance, Storytelling: Aspects of the Performing Arts in Japan*, 1978) and Carl Wolz, who provided an extensive study on *bugaku*, including Labanotation scores for basic movements and several dances (*Bugaku: Japanese Court Dance*, 1971).

Dance reviews appear regularly in Japan, in major newspapers, covering traditional Japanese dance, ballet, and modern dance.

MICHIKO UENO-HERR and CARL WOLZ

JAPANESE TRADITIONAL SCHOOLS (Jpn., *buyō no ryūha*). There are more than 150 schools or styles of traditional Japanese dance *(buyō)* that exist both in *kabuki* and in the world of *kabuki*-related dance outside the theater. Many nontheatrical people study Japanese dance both in Japan and abroad, but all licensed teachers of traditional dance in Japan belong to one or another of the traditional schools, or to one of their branches. Some of the schools have close relationships with *kabuki* and may be headed by an actor, whose headmastership is termed *iemoto* or *sōke*. Occasionally, the actor uses one stage name for acting work and another for dance concerts: for example, the *kabuki* actor Onoe Shōroku II used the name Fujima Kan'emon IV as a dancer.

Some schools were created by actors, others by choreographers *(furitsukeshi)*, while others sprang from Edo-era (1603–1868) individuals who performed under various powerful patrons, such as daimyos and shoguns or, in the Kyoto-Osaka region (Kamigata), even the imperial court. A number of other schools arose early in the twentieth century during the period when classical dance was being reinvigorated as part of the "new dance" *(shin buyō)* movement. The constant splintering of groups under ambitious new leaders continues to this day, and differences among the schools are not always obvious. This article looks only at the main theater-related schools. Non-theater-related schools do not differ in significant ways from those described.

Choreographers first appeared in *kabuki* in the second quarter of the seventeenth century, when *kabuki* was performed only by adolescents *(wakashu kabuki)*. From such early sources sprang the Shigayama Ryū, begun by the Genroku-era (1688–1703) choreographer Shigayama Mansaku (dates unknown), but made important by the contributions of the late eighteenth-century star Nakamura Nakazō I (1736–1790) and now the oldest school in existence, although it has lost its close theatrical ties. The popular dances *Seki no To* and *Shitadashi Sanbasō* are associated with this school.

The most powerful school of *kabuki* dance today is the Fujima Ryū, which consists of two main branches. An earlier branch, the Kanbei, was founded by the choreographer Fujima Kanbei (died 1769). Its most famous choreographer was Fujima Kanbei III (died 1821), whose creations included *Shiokumi* and *Sanbasō*. This branch died out in 1878.

When Fujima Kanbei III temporarily became Kanjūrō I in 1798, he began a separate line under that name, but the line is counted from the appearance of Kanjūrō II (1796–1840), who created such still-performed dances as *Yasuna*, *Komori*, *Tomo Yakko*, and *Kasane*. The line's theatrical connections were later weakened, but the theater reclaimed the name with Kanjūrō VI (born 1900) in 1927.

The other important Fujima branch is the Kan'emon.

Fujima Kan'emon II (1840–1915) was one of the greatest choreographers of the Meiji era (1868–1912), creating such dances as *Kagamijishi* and *Onatsu Kyōran*. The actors Matsumoto Kōshirō VII (1870–1945), Onoe Shōroku II (1913–1989), and Onoe Tatsunosuke I (1946–1987) as dancers used the names Kan'emon III, Kan'emon IV, and Kan'emon V, respectively.

The Hanayagi Ryū, founded in the nineteenth century, is the most prestigious *kabuki* school founded by a nonacting choreographer. This was Nishikawa Yoshijirō (1821–1902), who was a disciple of Nishikawa Senzō IV, and who began the school in 1849 after leaving the Nishikawa Ryū during a time of internal conflict. He took the name Hanayagi Yoshijirō and later changed to Hanayagi Jūsuke I, which name he made famous. He worked closely with playwright Kawatake Mokuami. Among his representative works are *Dontsuku*, *Kioi Jishi*, *Renjishi*, *Tsuri Onna*, *Modori Bashi*, *Tsuchigumo*, *Funa Benkei*, *Hagoromo*, and *Sannin Katawa*.

Hanayagi Jūsuke II (1892–1970) became a leader in the "new dance" *(shin buyō)* movement after founding, in 1923, the Hanayagi Buyō Kenkyū Kai (Hanayagi Association for the Study of Classical Dance), which was responsible for making great inroads in the study and performance of both classical and new works. He was succeeded by Hanayagi Jūsuke III (born 1936).

The Nishikawa Ryū, founded by the musician Nishikawa Senzō I (?–1756), was responsible for the choreography of the great dance drama *Kanjinchō*, created by Nishikawa Senzō IV (1792–1845), who also staged *Munekiyo*, *Osome*, and *Mitsu Men Komori*. Earlier, Nishikawa Senzō II (1797–1845) had choreographed a number of important dances, including *Modori Kago*. The contributions of Nishikawa Senzō V (?–1860) included *Ayatsuri Sanbasō* and *Noriaibune*.

Among other important *kabuki*-related schools are the Bandō Ryū, associated with the acting line of Bandō Mitsugorō; the Ichikawa Ryū, made famous by actors in the Ichikawa Danjūrō line; the Matsumoto Ryū, dominated by actors in the Matsumoto Kōshirō line; the Nakamura Ryū, headed by actors associated with the Nakamura family and divided into three main branches; the Ichiyama Ryū, whose once-powerful theater connections have dwindled; the Wakayagi Ryū; the Onoe Ryū; the Saruwaka Ryū; and the Tachibana Ryū.

[*For general discussion, see* Kabuki Theater. *See also* Azuma Tokuho, Kataoka Takao, Matsumoto Kōshirō, *and the entries under the following* kabuki *lineages and family names:* Bandō, Fujima, Ichikawa, Onoe, *and* Nakamura.]

BIBLIOGRAPHY

"Buyō no ryūha to omo na kakeizu." In *Buyō meisaku jiten*. Tokyo, 1986.

Leiter, Samuel L. *Kabuki Encyclopedia: An English-Language Adaptation of "Kabuki Jiten."* Westport, Conn., 1979.

Masakatsu, Gunji. *Buyo: The Classical Dance.* Translated by Don Kenny. New York, 1970.

SAMUEL L. LEITER

JAQUES-DALCROZE, ÉMILE (Émile-Henri Jaques; born 6 July 1865 in Vienna, died 1 July 1950 in Geneva), Swiss composer, teacher, and developer of eurhythmics. Jaques-Dalcroze was the son of Jules and Julie Jaques, French-Swiss living in Vienna, where Jules represented clock-making interests. Descendants of pastors and musicians, Jules and Julie Jaques introduced Émile and his younger sister Hélène to concerts, opera, and theater, and the children took piano lessons. In 1875 the family moved to Geneva, where Émile studied at the famous *collège* founded by John Calvin and concluded his academic education after one year at the Université de Genève.

From 1877 to 1883 Jaques-Dalcroze studied at the Conservatoire de Musique de Genève, where he received the final certificate and several awards. In 1881 he was elected to the Belles-Lettres, the student society that first published his songs. He took roles in the society's theatrical productions and, for a time, considered a career in the theater. From 1884 to 1890 he spent long periods in Paris and Vienna, studying diction with Talbot (Denis Stanislas Montalant) and music with Gabriel Fauré, Albert Lavignac, Antoine François Marmontel, Mathis Lussy, Hermann Grädener, Adolf Prosniz, Robert Fuchs, and Anton Bruckner. In 1886/87 he worked as assistant conductor at the Théâtre des Nouveautés in Algiers. North African music stimulated his interest in the connections between human movement and rhythm.

During his early twenties, when Jaques-Dalcroze began to compose seriously, a publisher suggested that he change his name to avoid confusion with a French composer famous for his polkas. With the consent of his school friend Raymond Valcroze, he invented the name Dalcroze and added it to his surname. Jaques-Dalcroze was later made the legal name of his immediate family. In 1899 he married Maria-Anna Starace, an Italian concert singer known as Nina Faliero; they had one son, Gabriel-Émile, born in 1909. The extensive oeuvre of Jaques-Dalcroze included works for orchestra, chamber orchestra, and piano; music dramas, operas, choral works, and some seventeen hundred songs; and many teaching manuals that included musical examples and short compositions.

In 1892 Jaques-Dalcroze was named professor of harmony in the upper division of the Conservatoire de Musique de Genève, where he taught until 1910. He reorganized the teaching of *solfège* (sight singing and ear training), producing his first pedagogical work in 1894. During the 1890s he searched for better ways to help his students attain accurate hearing and spontaneous physical response, abilities that he believed were essential to the development of musicianship. His first attempts to use movement led him to compose many charming children's gesture songs, including pantomimes and games such as making statues or playing trains, which became popular in recitals and concerts throughout French Switzerland.

The Dalcroze method emerged and achieved widespread use in the early twentieth century. An approach to music education based on whole body movement, it was a seedbed of new ideas about how to move and how to make music with the original instrument, the human body. Working from the fundamental activities of listening, singing, breathing, walking, and beating time, Jaques-Dalcroze and his early students eventually explored more adventurous possibilities of connecting music and movement. Lunging, skipping, pulling a partner, carrying an imaginary weight, or making a canon all called for timing, strength, greater shifts of the body in space, imaginative motivation, awareness of form, and cooperation with other people. The "rhythmic gymnastics," as Jaques-Dalcroze first called this movement work, combined with *solfège* and improvisation to offer a rich and well-rounded initiation into music.

The Conservatoire de Musique was slow to recognize the value of what Jaques-Dalcroze and his bloomer-clad young students were doing in the special classes he set up to advance his experiments. But he persevered, building on his knowledge as a musician, which included extensive conducting, and his excellent powers to observe clearly the efforts of other people. Moreover, he could draw on his schoolboy's study of formal gymnastics and drill, as well as his considerable background in the theater. In Paris he had studied breathing and the use of the voice, along with the concepts introduced by François Delsarte, the mid-nineteenth century master, who tried to correlate the various emotions with their physical manifestations in posture, attitude, and gesture. As did other innovators at the turn of the century, Jaques-Dalcroze forbade his students to wear corsets and instructed them in breathing and strength-building exercises. He studied anatomy, physiology, and psychology to base his method on the most current thinking in those fields.

Many exercises in the method were based on walking, which Jaques-Dalcroze considered to be the natural break down of time into equal parts. For example, students might be told to walk around the room, following the music that he improvised at the keyboard, responding directly to the beat and to changes in speed and dynamics. Students would thus become aware of how they had to adjust the length of their steps and how they needed to control their use of energy and body weight to respond to the music. In some walking exercises they practiced quick reactions, such as starting or stopping on command; in others they would start walking at a given tempo and then, on command or in response to a musical cue, change to walking twice as fast or twice as slow.

Another basic practice was called the walking or stepping of rhythmic patterns. The teacher would play a musical example. After listening carefully, the students would immediately repeat it, matching their steps exactly to the duration and sequence of notes they perceived. Alternatively, they could "echo" the pattern by moving in the teacher's silences, or they could follow in canon, making one pattern while simultaneously listening to the teacher's music for the next one. Typical exercises often involved singing as well as listening and moving so that patterns and whole phrases might be sung and stepped together.

Students developed the sense of measure or bar time by enlarging the standard arm gestures of conducting. They would stand with arms lifted straight overhead, then bring them down, firmly extending the elbows, for the downbeat on the count of "one," and so on. Experienced students could beat regular bar time with their arms while stepping rhythms of great complexity.

Jaques-Dalcroze considered breathing a natural source of dynamics and phrasing. He developed hundreds of exercises to help students feel the variety that could be achieved through shaping the flow and energy of breathing. He used other concepts to encourage the sense of phrasing, such as contrasting muscular force (light and heavy steps), using real or imagined resistance (stretching an elastic), or simply taking turns moving with a partner or in groups (alternating voices, movement versus stillness). This work with expressive activities led to "realizations" of more complex forms, such as inventions, fugues, and rondos. For these, the movement might fuse the stepping of patterns with almost any sort of expressive body attitude or gesture. A student might even create "plastic counterpoint," or movement independent of, but related to, the music.

In the growth of his method, Jaques-Dalcroze recognized the dance innovations of his contemporaries Loie Fuller, Isadora Duncan, and Grete Wiesenthal and her sisters, whose work both inspired and confirmed his own between 1900 and 1910. Surviving photographs and the teaching notes of this period show that his movement expanded from relatively modest walking, conducting, and Delsartian pantomimes to embrace the more dynamic and free action of the new dance. Like Duncan, Jaques-Dalcroze wanted to investigate the basic movements of walking, lunging, running, skipping, and jumping. Using music and the human body as their source, Jaques-Dalcroze and his students also discovered many new choreographic possibilities.

Jaques-Dalcroze popularized his method through lecture-demonstrations in Switzerland and other European countries and by publishing the several volumes of directions and music that made up the *Méthode Jaques-*

JAQUES-DALCROZE. The Dalcroze method (also called eurhythmics) became a widespread approach to movement education in the early twentieth century. Exercises emphasized such qualities as rhythmic awareness, the flow of breath, and group cooperation. These two women demonstrate a Dalcroze pulling exercise. (Photograph by White Studio, New York; from the Dance Collection, New York Public Library for the Performing Arts.)

Dalcroze (1906), which appeared in both French and German editions. A widening circle of teachers and professional students filled his summer courses in subsequent years. These people were interested in not only music and education but also physical training, dance, and theater.

From 1910 to 1914 Jaques-Dalcroze directed the Bildungsanstalt Jaques-Dalcroze, the training college built to support his work by Wolf and Harald Dohrn in the new garden city of Hellerau, near Dresden, Germany. Hundreds of students were attracted to this forward-looking school, which offered an extensive curriculum. The core courses in the Jaques-Dalcroze method included *solfège*, rhythmic gymnastics, keyboard improvisation, and *plastique*, or advanced music-movement study. The program was augmented by courses in music theory and practice, Swedish gymnastics, dance, and anatomy.

In the unique experimental atmosphere of Hellerau, Jaques-Dalcroze and the young faculty he had trained defined a theory of human movement based on time, space, and energy. Through experience and observation, they explored the use of body weight, the articulation of the joints, and the effects of muscular force. They developed a vocabulary of simple gestures and movements to be used as points of departure for creative studies. Their movement notation involved identifying points on horizontal and vertical planes with reference to the human body at high, middle, or low levels. The work of this intense period of discovery was documented in the 1916 edition of

JAQUES-DALCROZE. Dancers at the Geneva Festival in July 1914. The simple gestures and harmonic spatial motifs seen here are characteristic of Jaques-Dalcroze's choreography. (Photograph reprinted from Jaques-Dalcroze, *The Eurhythmics of Jaques-Dalcroze*, London, 1917.)

the *Méthode Jaques-Dalcroze* and in *Exercices de plastique animée*, published the same year.

People from all over the world attended or read about the Hellerau school festivals, in which lecture-demonstrations preceded student productions. Most notable among these was Christoph Willibald Gluck's *Orpheus*, presented in 1912 and 1913 according to the new movement principles of Jaques-Dalcroze in the austere architectural spaces designed by the stage reformer Adolphe Appia. The famous Hellerau studio theater was a large rectangular hall with walls made of stretched cloth panels. The advanced lighting surrounding these walls could be dimmed or brightened with great precision and subtlety, thus effecting a kind of music of light. Modular steps and platforms formed the settings for what many writers acclaimed as a whole new synthesis of music, movement,

and design. Photographs show that the student choruses essentially performed this work in practice dress: the then-radical leotard was used for the Furies, who filled the stage with their flailing arm motions, and the Blessed Spirits wore the brightly colored kimono-style robes worn between classes by the students at Hellerau. Among those who visited the school during its brief history were Prince Serge Wolkonsky, who convinced Serge Diaghilev and Vaslav Nijinsky to visit, Anna Pavlova, George Bernard Shaw, Harley Granville-Barker, Max Reinhardt, Darius Milhaud, and Paul Claudel, whose play *L'Annonce Faite à Marie* received its German premiere there in 1913. Upton Sinclair set the first chapter of his Lanny Budd novel *World's End* at Hellerau.

Among the faculty and students of Hellerau who became prominent in dance were Suzanne Perrottet, Marie Rambert, Mary Wigman, Valeria Kratina, Elsa Findlay, Michio Ito, and Beryl de Zoete. Many others helped to spread the Jaques-Dalcroze method by teaching in conservatories and schools throughout Europe and North America, while some followed careers in music, theater, physical education, and therapy for the blind and handicapped. In England the method became known as *eurhythmics*, meaning good or right rhythm; this term is still widely used to identify the Dalcroze method.

World War I ended Jaques-Dalcroze's association with the Hellerau school, although the school continued there under different direction with students such as Rosalia Chladek, Yvonne Georgi, and Hanya Holm. In 1925 the school was moved to a castle near Vienna and renamed the Hellerau-Laxenburg School. Rosalia Chladek served as director from 1930 until the school had to close in 1938, the beginning of the German occupation of Austria.

In 1915 Jaques-Dalcroze established his own school in Geneva, the Institut Jaques-Dalcroze, where he taught until shortly before his death. The institute, now state-supported, flourishes as an international center of the Dalcroze approach to music education. Professional training programs are offered in a number of other countries as well. Thousands have used and extended the Dalcroze method, which has widely influenced the teaching of Western music and dance.

The importance of Jaques-Dalcroze was not simply that he developed a new understanding of the sources of music and movement in the human body. For nearly sixty years he was an inspiring, imaginative master whose musicianship and personality helped to form many outstanding teachers and artists. Beyond the circle of his students and associates, his ideas have stimulated a broad public, particularly through his books *Rhythm, Music and Education* (1921) and *Eurhythmics, Art and Education* (1930). Other dancers who had contact with the method include Ruth St. Denis, Doris Humphrey, Bessie Schönberg, Louise

Soelberg, Martha Hill, Ninette de Valois, and, more recently, Meredith Monk.

[*See also entries on the principal figures mentioned herein.*]

BIBLIOGRAPHY

Bachmann, Marie-Laure. *Dalcroze Today: An Education through and into Music.* Translated by David Parlett. Oxford, 1991.

Brunet-Lecomte, Hélène. *Jaques-Dalcroze: Sa vie, son oeuvre.* Geneva, 1950.

Jaques-Dalcroze, Émile, et al. *The Eurhythmics of Jaques-Dalcroze.* London and Boston, 1912.

Martin, Frank, et al. *Émile Jaques Dalcroze: L'homme, le compositeur, le créateur de la rythmique.* Neuchâtel, 1965.

Odom, Selma Landen. "Choreographing *Orpheus*: Hellerau 1913 and Warwick 1991." In *Dance Reconstructed*, edited by Barbara Palfy. New Brunswick, N.J., 1993.

Spector, Irwin. *Rhythm and Life: The Work of Émile Jaques-Dalcroze.* Stuyvesant, N.Y., 1990.

SELMA LANDEN ODOM

JARDIN AUX LILAS. Ballet in one act. Choreography: Antony Tudor. Music: Ernest Chausson. Libretto: Antony Tudor. Scenery and costumes: Hugh Stevenson. First performance: 26 January 1936, Mercury Theatre, London, Ballet Rambert. Principals: Maude Lloyd (Caroline), Hugh Laing (Her Lover), Antony Tudor (The Man She Must Marry), Peggy van Praagh (An Episode in His Past).

In *Jardin aux Lilas* Tudor created a new genre, the psychological ballet. The essence of the story is suggested by the descriptions of the four principal characters. Caroline's marriage, we are given to understand, is one of convenience. The action of the ballet takes place at an evening garden party, at which she will say goodbye to her friends and particularly to the man she really loves. Also among the guests is her fiancé's discarded mistress. The attempts of Caroline and Her Lover to snatch a few moments together, and of the other woman to be alone with the man who no longer loves her, are continually foiled by interruptions from the other guests. When Caroline finally has to leave, on the arm of her husband-to-be, she does so without having been able to take the fond farewell she had so dearly hoped for.

Originally Tudor had wanted to make a ballet based on a short story by Finnish author Aino Kallas in which a rich landowner wishes to exercise his *droit de seigneur* on the eve of the marriage of a young peasant couple. Although the bride assents to the assignation, she goes armed with a knife. Tudor soon abandoned that plot line and looked for another. The idea for *Jardin aux Lilas* suggested itself in a painting that Stevenson showed him. He started to work with the *Ballade* of Gabriel Fauré but finding it unsuitable chose instead Chausson's *Poème*, which fits the action so perfectly that it might have been written for the purpose.

As much as it is a ballet about unrequited love, *Jardin aux Lilas* is also about the necessity for people in a certain social milieu and situation to suppress their emotions. The dancers' very carriage reveals that "artificial upper-class constraint" that dance critic Edwin Denby called "the theme and the pathos" of the ballet. Tudor realized that the slightest gesture may be expressive of a character's thoughts and feelings. The most audacious moment occurs at the music's climax, when the characters come together in a frozen group, from which Caroline alone steps forward and moves slowly in a circle—her interior monologue made visible.

Jardin aux Lilas was the first of Tudor's ballets to be presented in the inaugural season of Ballet Theatre, on 15 January 1940, with Viola Essen as Caroline, Karen Conrad as the other woman, and Laing and Tudor in their original roles. The ballet has since been revived by many companies, including the New York City Ballet in 1951, the Royal Ballet in 1968, and the Paris Opera Ballet in 1985.

JARDIN AUX LILAS. Nora Kaye (Caroline), Antony Tudor (The Man She Must Marry), Alicia Alonso (An Episode in His Past), and Hugh Laing (Her Lover), in the Ballet Theatre production, c.1944. (Photograph from the Dance Collection, New York Public Library for the Performing Arts.)

BIBLIOGRAPHY

Barnes, Clive. "Ballet Perspectives: *Jardin aux Lilas.*" Dance and Dancers (June 1959): 18–19.

Chazin-Bennahum, Judith. *The Ballets of Antony Tudor: Studies in Psyche and Satire.* New York and Oxford. 1994.

Perlmutter, Donna. *Shadowplay: Antony Tudor's Life in Dance.* London, 1991.

DAVID VAUGHAN

JAVA. *See* Indonesia, *article on* Javanese Dance Traditions. *For discussion in a broader context, see* Asian Dance Traditions.

JAZZ DANCE. As the United States became a melting pot for many cultures, nations, and peoples, American jazz dance resulted from the assimilation of many cultures, techniques, and dance styles—all set to the pulse of the city. Dancer and choreographer Jack Cole was often quoted as having called it "urban folk dance," and Louis Horst (1961) defined jazz as "the trademark of the city." The subject matter is life, with realistic characters and situations brought to expression by contemporary music. Jazz dance has an immediacy of communication, an energy and dynamic power—sometimes highly charged and sometimes subtle—that implies more than is shown. It projects direct communication, a sense of humor, and a feeling of suspense and surprise, provocative and shocking. A highly personal form, jazz dance is more concerned with individual expression than with tradition; its basis is feeling.

Rhythm is basic for all jazz dance, which can incorporate several simultaneous rhythms, syncopation (with the accent on the offbeat), and the pause, creating a charged state of rhythm and energy. The feet are either parallel or turned out slightly in a natural manner, and the dancers use isolated movements in various parts of the body, such as shifts and rotations of the rib cage, shoulders, pelvis, and head, as well as successions of movement through the torso—the torso, then, rarely moves in one piece. Strength emanates from the front of the pelvis, which is drawn in and made shallow. Moving at a low level achieves an earthy quality and a distinctive use of space. Movement can be performed on the flat foot, if it is primitive-based, or it can develop through the foot, with quick footwork on the high half-toe in low *plié.*

Jazz dance grew out of popular dance types of the early twentieth century and spread, in various forms, to nightclubs, the Broadway stage, films, and television. Theatrical jazz dance probably started in 1936, when ballet master George Balanchine choreographed the "Slaughter on Tenth Avenue" dance sequence for the Broadway musical *On Your Toes.* Balanchine was assisted by tap dancer Herbie Harper, who introduced black rhythm dancing to blend with the ballet. About this time, Jack Cole was adding jazz rhythms to authentic Hindu dance for his variety act. With a background in modern dance at Denishawn, he created a technique derived from Doris Humphrey and Charles Weidman, with innovations based on Indian, Spanish, and Latin American styles, all brought together with American swing music. During the 1940s, Cole's work in film musicals, both as performer and choreographer, was outstanding. In 1944, at the studios of Columbia Pictures in Hollywood, he organized the Dance Workshop, a dance group that performed in nightclubs and theaters until 1948, with choreography borrowed from Harlem, Asia, and the Caribbean. Many early jazz dance teachers, as well as prominent performers and choreographers of the musical theater, were influenced by Cole's work.

JAZZ DANCE. The dances of Katherine Dunham, which combined Afro-Caribbean styles with modern and ballet idioms, were enormously influential in the development of American jazz dance. Here, Dunham appears with Vanoye Aikens, a member of her company, in the dance number "Blues." (Photograph by Vandamm Studio, New York; from the Dance Collection, New York Public Library for the Performing Arts.)

Jerome Robbins became another influential figure in theatrical jazz dance. In 1945, more than a decade before Robbins would create the choreography for Leonard Bernstein's musical *West Side Story* (1957) Louis Biancolli, writing in the *New York World Telegram and Sun*, described Robbins's dances in Bernstein's *On the Town* as the "rich new blend of classic technique, jive, tap, and what is unctuously called adagio."

Also during this period, Katherine Dunham and her dancers were appearing in films and on Broadway. The Dunham technique combined classical ballet with central European, Caribbean, and African elements. By the 1950s her school in New York City had trained dancers and teachers proficient in primitive, Afro-Cuban, Haitian, and other ethnic dance types. Perhaps the best-known, most influential teacher was Syvilla Fort. Accompanied by one or more drummers on congas and bongos, her students would move to the rhythm in step patterns across the floor on the diagonal, with movements isolated in the shoulders, rib cage, hips, and pelvis. By the end of class, the tempo would build to an almost frenzied pitch, sending the dancers into flying leaps across the room.

Two other major forces emerged in New York City to bring the jazz craze into the dance studio. In 1953, in a small, crowded studio in the old Roseland Building on Broadway, Jon Gregory, who had created dance sequences for stage and film musicals, was conducting stimulating, exciting classes of the caliber of a Broadway show. Gregory's distinctive style of movement, dictated by his six-foot-four-inch frame, made professional dancers flock to his classes. He did not teach a particular technique; his two- and three-hour classes, accompanied by records of the current jazz favorites—Stan Kenton, Tommy Dorsey, Artie Shaw, and Duke Ellington—began with a series of arm gestures to "Night Train," followed by a few movement transitions across the floor. In less than fifteen minutes the class would be doing the prechoreographed combinations that were Gregory's trademark; these included spectacular leaps, knee drops, and falls that burst out of unorthodox spins. The repetition of such combinations developed strength and stamina. Although his work was sensuous and provocative, these qualities were achieved through action in the knees, as Gregory allowed no pelvic movements in his combinations. Unfortunately his personal style went uncredited in the popular media for years.

While New Orleans-born and Chicago-bred Peter Gennaro was dancing the "Steam Heat" number with Jack Cole dancers Carol Haney and Buzz Miller in the musical *Pajama Game* (choreographed by Bob Fosse, 1954), Gennaro was also holding classes in a rehearsal studio. They began with a warm-up at the *barre*, including *pliés* and various ballet-based leg exercises. These were developed

JAZZ DANCE. Bob Fosse's choreography featured turned-in legs, hunched shoulders, and eccentric arm movements. Here, Buzz Miller and Peter Gennaro appear in rehearsal for the "Steam Heat" number in the Broadway musical *The Pajama Game* (1954), choreographed by Fosse. (Photograph from the Dance Collection, New York Public Library for the Performing Arts.)

into jazz movements by adding deep knee bends, changing the rotation of the legs, and varying the rhythms. Next followed across-the-floor combinations. Gennaro's style was light, quick, loose, and flexible, with articulate, rhythmically accurate footwork and legwork. A jazz pianist provided the accompaniment.

Through the early 1950s, the term *jazz* was shied away from for dance classes, unless the teacher was working on those specific steps that had been popularized in ballrooms during the first half of the century. Instead, classes might be called "free-style," musical comedy, Afro-Cuban, or primitive. New York City jazz classes began when dancers and choreographers actually working in Broadway shows brought the movement of those dances into the studio, devising warm-up exercises and stretches to prepare the body for jazz dance's specific demands. Dance per se was not taught; the class was more of a jam session where professionals got together and danced, following their "leader."

The key events that led to formalized jazz classes occurred in 1955. Jon Gregory had left New York to become dance director at Twentieth Century–Fox and to choreograph in Las Vegas; Peter Gennaro was beginning to work with Jerome Robbins as co-choreographer for *West Side Story*. Matt Mattox, a Jack Cole dancer, arrived in New York and started teaching a Cole-based class at the June Taylor School. Mattox's class, which was accompanied by a single bongo drummer, started with floor stretches, then moved to center-floor isolations, and on to improvised combinations. His strict and disciplined classes featured his own clean, strong technique of sometimes percussive, sometimes fluent, liquidlike movement.

Also in 1955, a short-lived Broadway musical brought West Coast dancer Eugene Louis (Luigi) Facciuto to New York. Luigi had a distinctive style that emphasized the line of the body, with arms lifted, chest high, and head thrown back. (He developed this style after an automobile accident had left the muscles in half his face paralyzed.) Accompanied by a solo drummer on snare, bass drum, and cymbals, dancers in Luigi's classes began with standing center-floor stretches and *port de bras* incorporating the whole body, followed by floor stretches (sitting, lying, and kneeling), *pliés*, and kick-outs. His warm-up included highly stylized, continuously flowing movements that developed the technique and style for the combinations that followed—from slow blues to lyrical to fast Latin movements. Luigi's classes, along with those of Matt Mattox, dominated the field over the next decade.

By the 1960s, Robbins's *West Side Story* choreography had made its impact throughout the United States, and at dance-teacher conventions jazz teachers were hired to bring the new dance style to the hinterlands. The movement spread, and soon every local dance studio, community center, and weight-reducing salon had added jazz classes to its schedule. In the 1970s, even college dance departments began adding jazz dance to the curriculum.

Whether jazz dance should be viewed as the disciplined dance of the musical theater or the dances popularized in twentieth-century commercial ballrooms (Savoy, Palladium, Roseland) remains a matter of dispute. In the early studio days, dancers were told to "forget technique—just dance." Today the serious jazz dancer is highly efficient and very likely accomplished in ballet and modern dance, with additional training in tap, ethnic forms, and even acrobatics. However jazz dance is defined, its essence will always be rhythmic movement based on feeling and improvisation, set to jazz music, inspired by an urban setting.

[*See also entries on the principal figures mentioned herein.*]

BIBLIOGRAPHY

Buckle, Richard, ed. *Katherine Dunham: Her Dancers, Singers, and Musicians*. London, 1949.

Giordano, Gus, ed. *Anthology of American Jazz Dance*. Evanston, Ill., 1977.

Horst, Louis, with Caroll Russell. *Modern Dance Forms in Relation to the Other Modern Arts*. San Francisco, 1961.

Mahoney, Billie. *Vocabulary of Jack Cole*. New York, 1976. Contains notated scores.

Mahoney, Billie. "Jazz Dance." In *The Dance Catalog*, edited by Nancy Reynolds. New York, 1979.

Munstermann, Uta F. *Jazz Dance and Jazz Gymnastics*. New York, 1978.

Stearns, Marshall, and Jean Stearns. *Jazz Dance*. New York, 1968.

BILLIE MAHONEY

JEANMAIRE, ZIZI (Renée Jeanmaire; born 29 April 1924 in Paris), French dancer. After beginning her career as a classical ballerina, Zizi Jeanmaire turned to singing and ultimately became a music-hall star. A student of the École de Danse of the Paris Opera, Jeanmaire did not have the patience to climb the ladder of the professional ballet hierarchy, so she left to carve out an independent career. In 1944 she appeared in a recital at the Salle Pleyel with Roger Fenonjois. Her attractiveness, brilliant dancing, and typically Parisian coquettishness brought her to the attention of the public.

In December 1944 Jeanmaire enjoyed success in the Soirées de la Danse ("dance evenings") organized by Irène

JEANMAIRE. As Roxanne in Petit's *Cyrano de Bergerac* (1959), with Petit in the title role. Created for the Ballets de Paris de Roland Petit, this three-act work was set to music by Marius Constant. The costumes were designed by Yves Saint-Laurent. (Photograph by Serge Lido; used by permission.)

Lidova at the Théâtre Sarah-Bernhardt, where she danced the Rose Adagio from *The Sleeping Beauty*. In 1946 she followed Serge Lifar to the Nouveau Ballet de Monte Carlo, where she demonstrated her talent in Francis Poulenc's *Aubade*, with Vladimir Skouratoff. Her dance master, Boris Kniasseff, mounted *Piccoli* for her, and she danced it in London with de Basil's Ballet Russe de Monte Carlo.

Her career began in earnest in 1948, when she became one of the stars of the Ballets de Paris, recently established by Roland Petit (whom Jeanmaire later married), and particularly in 1949, with the creation of his version of *Carmen*, a ballet that shaped her future. It took her to New York, to Hollywood—where she appeared in several films—and then back to Broadway to dance the title role in *The Girl in the Pink Tights*. She made her debut as a singer in the ballet *La Croqueuse de Diamants*. Major revues at the Alhambra in Paris in 1961 and 1963 brought her great popularity, and she took her most successful number, *Mon Truc en Plumes*, on a world tour. In 1970 she and Roland Petit assumed the management of the Casino de Paris, where she became the sole star. In 1975 she appeared at the Paris Opera, where Petit mounted for her the *Symphonie Fantastique*, to the music of Hector Berlioz. An accident to her leg prevented her from dancing, but by 1979 she was back at work, this time with the Ballet de Marseille, Petit's new company, in *La Chauve-souris* (The Bat), a role she later danced in New York and in a film made for French television.

In January 1985 Jeanmaire appeared in a revue, *Hollywood Paradise*, at the Théâtre des Champs-Élysées. In 1988 she performed at the Opéra-Comique in Paris a new piece, *Java Forever*, with Eric Vu-An as her partner. She returned in 1991 with the Ballet de Marseille, dancing the part of the fairy Carabosse in Petit's modern production of *The Sleeping Beauty*. In 1996, Jeanmaire made a brilliant return to the stage in a show dedicated to the singer Gainsbourgh, at the Palais des Sports, at the Marigny Theatre, and on tour.

BIBLIOGRAPHY

Croce, Arlene. *Going to the Dance*. New York, 1982.

Diénis, Jean-Claude. "Zizi Jeanmaire." *Danser* (January 1985): 20–23.

"Dossier spécial Marseille." *Pour la Danse* (April 1979): 16–32.

Lidova, Irène. *Dix-sept visages de la danse française*. Paris, 1953.

Lidova, Irène. *Roland Petit*. Paris, 1956.

Lidova, Irène. "Zizi Jeanmaire." *Saisons de la Danse* (January 1975).

Lidova, Irène. "Mes rencontres: Zizi Jeanmaire." *Ballet 2000* (Summer 1996).

Vaughan, David. "Shop Talk with Roland Petit and Zizi." *Dance and Dancers* (May 1958): 42–43, 80–82.

IRÈNE LIDOVA
Translated from French

JETÉS. *See* Ballet Technique, *article on* Jumping Movements.

JEUNE HOMME ET LA MORT, LE. Ballet in one act. Choreography: Roland Petit. Music: Johann Sebastian Bach. Libretto: Jean Cocteau. Scenery: Georges Wakhevitch. First performance: 25 June 1946, Théâtre des Champs-Élysées, Paris, Ballets des Champs-Élysées. Principals: Nathalie Philippart (Death), Jean Babilée (The Young Man).

The entire production of *Le Jeune Homme et la Mort* (The Young Man and Death) bore the strong imprint of Jean Babilée, the dancer for whom Roland Petit created this masterpiece of postwar French ballet. The program notes synopsize the story as follows:

> The young man is waiting for a young woman who does not love him. She arrives, he pleads with her, she insults him and leaves. He hangs himself. The room disappears. Death comes, and tears off her mask; it is the girl. She puts the mask on the young man, then leads him over the rooftops.

The action took place in an attic room with a beamed ceiling, which became transformed into a vision of the rooftops of Paris, with the Eiffel Tower shining in the background. Jean Cocteau originally asked Roland Petit to set the choreography to jazz rhythms, but at the last minute he substituted Bach's Passacaglia in C Minor. The choreography was based on realistic, expressive movements.

The work was performed with stunning intensity and power by Babilée and his future wife, Nathalie Philippart. *Le Jeune Homme et la Mort* had a profound effect on Babilée's entire career. He performed it with equal success at the Teatro alla Scala in Milan and with American Ballet Theatre in New York. His last appearance was in 1989 when he was sixty-six years old, for a revival in Paris.

Petit had revived the ballet in 1966, but most later performers did not bring out the full significance of the work. It was performed for television by Rudolf Nureyev and Zizi Jeanmaire, and also by Mikhail Baryshnikov. In 1983 Petit presented the ballet at the Piccola Scala in Milan, with Luigi Bonino and Luciana Savignano in the leading roles. The same year, Patrick Dupond danced the role of the Young Man during the American tour of Petit's Ballet National de Marseille. The Paris Opera Ballet performed it on a program with Petit's version of *Carmen* in 1990.

[*See also the entry on Petit.*]

BIBLIOGRAPHY

Aschengreen, Erik. *Jean Cocteau and the Dance*. Translated by Patricia McAndrew and Per Avsum. Copenhagen, 1986.

Beaumont, Cyril W. *Ballets of Today*. London, 1954.

Mannoni, Gérard. *Roland Petit: Un chorégraphe et ses peintres*. Paris, 1990.

Ries, Frank W. D. "Postwar Paris: *Le Jeune Homme et la Mort*." In Ries's *The Dance Theatre of Jean Cocteau*. Ann Arbor, 1986.

IRÈNE LIDOVA
Translated from French

JEWISH DANCE TRADITIONS. Historical sources and documents about the Hebrew tribes in biblical times mention dance but do not include details about dance or actual dance steps. Postbiblical sources do, however, include rich descriptions of the social function of dancing in later Hebrew communities as a tradition accompanying celebration. Such celebration continues throughout Jewish history. Descriptions exist from as early as the Roman period (the years before the destruction of the Second Jerusalem Temple in 70 CE), and continue, especially in the Jewish communities dispersed to Mesopotamia during the Talmudic period (third–fifth centuries), into the *responsa* literature in the Middle Ages and until today. The Talmud is the collected literature of Jewish civil and religious law; the *responsa* literature began in the Middle Ages as letters from rabbis to their congregations and communities as answers to questions about what was proper Jewish conduct in all areas of life. The two editions of the Talmud (one from Babylonia and one from Jerusalem), as well as the *responsa*, include descriptions of dances, dancers, and the circumstances in which dancing took place.

Most of the descriptions in the Talmud deal with dance as connected to the rituals performed in the First Temple (Solomon's Temple), which fell to the Babylonians in 586 BCE, and in the Second Temple, which fell to the Romans in 70 CE, and into dance in celebration of Jewish festivals. The festivals are connected with the agricultural cycle: Qatair ha-ʿOmer, the harvest of the first field crops in the spring, on the eve of Passover; ha-Bikkurim, the summer offering of the cycle's first fruits, Tu be-Av, the summer feast on the fifteenth of the month of Av; and Simḥat Beit ha-Shoʾevah, the autumn rejoicing of the waters.

The Talmud also describes dance during Sukkot, the autumn pilgrimage holiday to Jerusalem (a festival also called the Feast of Booths). The congregants would gather in the women's court of the Temple and celebrate through the night. The energetic torch dance performed by Rabban Shimʿon ben Gamliʾel is described there; the rabbi stood on the steps leading from the women's court to the main Temple area, juggling flaming torches and performing in order to keep the people awake. Children added to the excitement by beating drums and cymbals, and the *shofar* (the ceremonial horn) was blown. It is stated that the crowd often imitated the rabbi's acrobatics. The earliest mention of separating men from women while dancing, a feature of Jewish dance often mentioned in later documents, is described first in the Talmud.

In the Talmud are found relevant details about dances performed during other holidays, the reasons for them, and who performed them. Several reasons are given for why dancing is prohibited on the Sabbath (the day of rest). Then too the bucolic vineyard dances on the fifteenth day of Av are described, as well as the wider objectives of dance and the attire of the dancing women: "The daughters of Israel go out into the vineyards and dance . . . those men who do not have a wife go there" (Mishnah *Taʿanit* 4.8, 31.1). This festival, called Tu be-Av was very popular, and when the Jews were exiled following the Babylonian conquest, their loss was expressed in the biblical *Book of Lamentations:* "Her virgins lamented because they ceased dancing on the fifteenth of Av and Yom Kippur, tenth day of the month of Tishrei, when they used to dance." Today Yom Kippur is of a very solemn nature, for fasting and contrition.

When the Jews were exiled to Babylon, their agricultural life ended as did such occasions for dance. Instead they became centered around festive family events. Some very simple forms of ancient Temple ritual movement became part of the synagogue service, in particular body swaying (forward and back) during prayer.

Another type of dance mentioned in the *responsa* deals with traditions at weddings. These customs evolved differently in the dispersed Jewish communities of the Diaspora after the Roman conquest. Before the period of Roman domination, it was considered a *mitsvah*, a commandment of Jewish life, for everyone to dance before the bride and groom, ensuring their happiness. Learned scholars competed with each other in the dancing to entertain the couple. The ecstasy was so great, it is reported in the Talmud, that one Rav Aḥaʾ lifted the bride and danced with her perched on his shoulders. This behavior resulted in a Talmudic discussion of how one should dance before the bride (Babylonian Talmud, *Ketubbot* 16.2, 17.1).

In the case of divorce, if a woman lost or mislaid the all-important wedding contract *(ketubbah)* and could not present it to the court of religious law during the divorce hearing, the Talmud allowed that if she could produce witnesses to testify that she "was danced before as a bride," the validity of her marriage would be proven (*Ketubbot* 16.2).

In the post-Talmudic period, the *responsa* literature provides considerable evidence for dancing. From the beginning of the Middle Ages onward there are more and more admonitions and prohibitions regarding men and women dancing together and of women dancing in front of a male audience. Special festival houses *(beit hillulei)* were set apart from regular living quarters for rejoicing and dance. In the Ashkenazic (central and eastern European) Jewish communities, the *Tanzhaus* ("dance house") developed just for wedding celebrations. It acquired great importance from the twelfth through the seventeenth centuries. Whether it was the long tradition in Jewish life for the community to dance at weddings or whether a ghettoized life stimulated the development of a communal dance house is unclear. Having a special place to hold wedding dances, however, contributed to the development of the role of master of ceremonies, the *badḥan* (the dance master or dance leader). References to the dance house, the dances therein, and the dance leader conducting the festivities abound in the *responsa* literature. From the responses of Rabbi Mosheh ben Naḥman (1194–1270), known as Nahmanides, it is evident the dances practiced by gentiles infiltrated the *Tanzhaus*. Nahmanides also wrote that he had observed, in his travels to Egypt, that there a Jewish bride would execute a sword dance (as was the Muslim custom), and that she entertained wedding guests of both sexes together (which was not the Muslim custom).

The *Tanzhaus* acquired great importance in the social life of the Jewish towns *(shtetls)*, and wedding dances developed in elaborate ways. In the eleventh century it is reported that the bride and groom were put on pedestals and that the guests danced around these stages. Rabbi Yaʿaqov ha-Levi Molin (c.1360–1427) was the first to mention the *mitsvah* that Jews were commanded to perform at weddings. Some *mitsvah* dances included mixed dancing, and Rabbi Meʾir ben Barukh of Rothenburg (1215–1293) threatened to excommunicate anyone "perpetrating such an offense." In other communities the wedding dances caused class distinction; it became obligatory for the dancer to wear a special girdle or belt elaborately embroidered with costly ornaments. Those unable to afford this were prevented from participating in the *mitsvah* dance.

Jews living in medieval Spain enjoyed a much less restricted life than those in central Europe. The Iberian Peninsula was, from 711 until 1492, under the rule of the Moors (Muslims from North Africa), except in the areas conquered by Christians. The Sephardic Spanish Jews initially took part in gentile life, so Jewish dance was introduced into secular life. Under some Muslim and Christian rulers of Spain, Jewish female dancers performed at social gatherings of the Jewish middle class. In Toledo, in a special dance, the dancers fastened toy wooden horses to their bosoms. The Jewish courtier Todros ben Yehudah ha-Levi (1243–1279) described Jewish maidens dancing with young Christian aristocrats during the reign of King Alfonso of Castile.

Young Jewish boys were reprimanded in a *responsa* by Rabbi Shelomoh ben Avraham Adret (c. 1235–1310) because he frowned on their dancing in the streets accompanied by musical instruments, especially on the Sabbath. Sephardic rabbis also record that Shelomoh ben Hazen, a learned Jewish physician, instructed gentile dancers in a formal dance that was executed in the cathedral at Saragossa.

Toward the end of the fourteenth century, the *responsa* literature records two dances popular among the Sephardim: the *danza generale* (not elaborated on) and the *danza de la muerte* ("dance of death"), which apparently originated in a drama about the bubonic plague (Black Death). The dance took many forms and was much danced by the Jews. When Spain was reconquered by the Catholic monarchy of Ferdinand and Isabella in 1492, the Sephardim were expelled from the Iberian Peninsula; they went to Holland, France, Italy, the Balkans, North Africa, and other provinces of the Ottoman Empire, as well as to the Portuguese, French, and Dutch colonies in the Americas. Their dancing continued, and so did the "dance of death." Centuries later it may even have influenced a Jewish sect in eastern Europe, the Hasidim, who dance the *Tehias Hamesim*, in which two friends fight and one falls dead, but is revived by his remorseful friend. This dance, also known as the "resurrection dance," is still performed.

In Renaissance Italy, the dance master had become important even beyond the Jewish community. The best known was Guglielmo Ebreo da Pesaro, also known as Johannis Ambrosio or William the Hebrew (born 1420). He was so famous for pageants and dance instruction that his sponsors, the Sforzas, sent him to Milan to teach the ruling family there. His skill was no doubt honed in the Jewish communities of Italy, where the dance master staged weddings and other festivities. These talents were used in turn by the ducal courts in their grand stagings at pageants, feasts, and weddings. Thus Guglielmo staged the Sforza family wedding pageant in Milan in 1475. [*See the entry on Guglielmo Ebreo.*]

In the *responsa*, the rabbis granted permission to the dance master to hold the hands of Jewish women in the community while dancing if he wore gloves. Otherwise, only fathers or brothers were allowed to dance hand in hand with their daughters or sisters. A husband was allowed to hold his wife's hand. An exception was made for boys to dance hand in hand with girls, because it was necessary for the youngsters to become acquainted with the opposite sex before betrothal. Dance became an integral part of the social education, in Jewish as well as gentile society, through the dance master.

There was mixed dancing on Jewish holidays and on the Sabbath, which the rabbis tried to suppress, but with little success. Some rabbis turned a blind eye so as not to drive what they considered to be "sinful activity" underground. They did however lift their ban on mixed dancing during the Purim feast, which coincides with the Christian season of Carnival. The ancient Purim story of the *Book of Esther* describes Queen Esther of Persia thwarting the plot of Haman, the wicked vizier, to destroy the Jews; it was enacted in a dance drama by performers wearing masks (men even wore female apparel). A document from the archives of the Jewish community of Padua, Italy, from the first half of the sixteenth century, reports that the Purim festivities lasted about three weeks and included staged performances with dancing. The Purim performers

JEWISH DANCE TRADITIONS. The Bible relates several instances of ancient Israelite dancing. *Exodus* 15.20-21 tells of the prophetess Miriam leading women in a celebratory dance after crossing the Red Sea. This illustration, from a fourteenth-century Spanish Haggadah, depicts the scene. (British Museum, London.)

became known as the *Purimspielers*. They used all the theater arts to tell the Purim story, going from house to house and from community to community.

On the holiday of Simḥat Torah, the joy of receiving the Five Books of Moses is expressed. Jews traditionally hold the Torah scrolls and dance with them in the synagogues in processionals called *haqqafot* in Hebrew. The great eighteenth-century interpreter of Jewish law, Eliyyahu ben Shelomoh Zalman, known as the Vilna Ga'on, stated that it is appropriate to dance with the Torah scroll because he could remember even old men indulging in dance for the greater glory of the holy Torah.

During the sixteenth and seventeenth centuries, the descendants of the Sephardic Jews of the Iberian Peninsula settled in countries surrounding the Mediterranean Sea. Secular dancing in those communities was encountered on holidays, arranged by a master of ceremonies. One of his duties was to provide female partners for the male dancers, and even married women participated in the dance. At the same time, some rabbis wished to keep the sacred traditions intact, and they objected to the infiltration of customs from the surrounding culture, which included mixed dancing and maidens entertaining wedding guests by dancing in front of mixed company.

The dance customs of the Jews who had remained in Palestine, as discovered by the first wave of Sephardim to arrive there in the sixteenth century, were of a different character. In Palestine, dance was part of the religious ambience and had never been secular. The first Jewish communities to return to the Holy Land were mainly from North Africa; in the seventeenth to nineteenth centuries, Ashkenazim, many of whom were mystics who settled in the holy cities of Jerusalem, Safed, and Tiberias, introduced rhythmic movement into prayer (called *davening*) and the act of Torah study. In the synagogue they swayed vigorously forward and back as they *daven*ed, reciting the text.

These rhythmical elements of prayer influenced the development of dance in many Jewish communities of central and eastern Europe, especially in the emerging Hasidic community, which had begun following the teachings of Rabbi Yisra'el ben Eliʿezer (c.1700–1760), known as the Baʿal Shem Tov. The highest form of prayer, he taught, not only moves the soul but sets the limbs in motion. Disciples gathered around the Baʿal Shem and other Hasidic rabbis to follow their teachings using song and dance. Each of these different Hasidic groups—such as the Lubavitchers, Bobovers, Satmars, and others—has its own distinctive ways of celebrating with dance. All, however, separate the men from the women in distinct dance repertories and customs. The men favor dances of individual exhibition for skill, strength, and stamina. Improvisation is especially evident in their solos. The women make use of unison in group dances. As in most Jewish communities, dance is part of the stages that precede the wedding—the legal betrothal, the signing of the marriage contract, the dressing of the bride, the procession to the wedding canopy (*ḥuppah*)—and the stages that follow—the bride walking around the groom under the *ḥuppah*, the withdrawal of the bride and groom into privacy (*yiḥud*), and the wedding banquet. It is at the concluding wedding banquet where most of the dancing takes place. The *badḥan* would orchestrate and lead the various *mitsvah* dances for everyone present, including the bride. A kerchief or a scarf was often used to separate the men from the women, with each sex holding an opposing corner of the cloth. The *badḥan* would also entertain the guests with impromptu, rhymed verses about personalities in the community. Records of the *badḥan*'s sometimes bawdy satires exist, as do price lists showing the cost of each dance to be played by the *klezmorim* (European Jewish folk musicians).

Hasidic music and dance had been influenced by European dances in the surrounding communities, as they were later in Israel and the United States. The dances are performed at Hasidic weddings and at other functions at the courts of Hasidic rabbis. Since the establishment of the State of Israel in 1948, at the celebration of the spring festival of Lag ba-ʿOmer, for example, such dances as the Arab *dabkah* are performed, and Middle Eastern melodies as well as newly composed Israeli songs are sung and played—the influence, after almost five hundred years of immigration, of certain stylistic elements that originate in the dance and music of Israel's neighbors. Lag ba-ʿOmer has developed into an elaborate yearly event; Hasidim from all over Israel gather at the grave of Rabbi Shimʿon bar Yoḥai (the founder of Jewish mysticism, the Kabbalah) in Meiron on the eve of the holiday. Mindful of the ancient dances of Simḥat Beit ha-Shoʾevah, torch and fire dances have been reintroduced. At the gravesite, the three types of Hasidic men's dances are performed: circular dances, participated in by many, including several variations of progression and several ways of holding hands; solos and same-sex dances for two; and acrobatic dances done for the entertainment of the spectators. These are all basically improvisatory, and although the dancers are amateurs, some are very specialized and accomplished artists in this form of exhibition dance. Certain families have recorded a special proficiency in executing a specific dance, which was passed from one generation to the next. At Meiron, the Hasidim come to enact the ceremony marking a Hasidic boy's first haircut at the age of three in which only the earlocks are left long. In conjunction with this festivity a pillar-of-fire ritual is held during the night with dancing, then again at dawn, and then during the day. After the haircutting, the boys are also included in the dancing. During this ceremony the virtuosic bottle dance *(Flashtanz)*, which involves balancing bottles in elaborate ways; the *Stocktanz* ("rod dance," or "staff dance"); and the "resurrection of the dead" dance, as well as other improvisatory solo dances, are all performed.

Eighteenth- and nineteenth-century Hasidic dance influenced Ashkenazic Jewish communities in eastern Europe to such an extent that Hasidic dance forms can be found in non-Hasidic contexts, where it developed into a purely social activity, even alien to the original spirit of rejoicing before the Lord.

The Jewish people have danced in every locale and epoch—to celebrate life, their beliefs, and the major community events. The ceremonies and dances developed as Jews went from a nomadic people to an enslaved and exiled people to a community living in their own ancient kingdoms. They continued to develop during the Diaspora, whether in Europe, the Middle East, Asia, Africa, or the Americas. Today Jewish dance is choreographed and performed in theatrical presentations, musical theater, and film versions.

Fred Berk (1911–1980) emigrated from Austria to the United States in 1941, fleeing Nazism. With his wife, Katja Delakova, he formed a school and a company of young dancers in New York, the Jewish Dance Guild. The couple toured extensively in programs evoking Jewish life in Europe before World War II, and they featured folk motifs from Israel. In 1952, Berk began his annual Israel Folk Dance Festival, sponsored by the American Zionist Youth Foundation, which also published Berk's books and manuals. He taught for many years at the Ninety-second Street YM-YWHA in New York City, choreographing for their Hebraica Dancers as well as for the Merry-Go-Rounders. [*See the entry on Berk.*]

Americans of Jewish descent have made significant contributions to theatrical dance as well. Among them are Sophie Maslow, whose *The Village I Knew* (1950) depicted scenes of Jewish life as portrayed in the stories of Sholem Aleichem, and Eliot Feld, whose *Tzaddik* and *Sephardic Song* (both, 1974) vividly evoke the Jewish heritage. Then, too, Jerome Robbins's choreography for the musical *Fiddler on the Roof* (1964) was also based on stories by Sholem Aleichem and set to the music of Sheldon Harnick and Jerry Bock; its use of Jewish dance tunes and motifs enhances the musical play, which takes place in a late nineteenth-century Russian *shtetl* and demonstrates the importance of "tradition."

[*See also* Israel.]

BIBLIOGRAPHY

Adams, Doug, and Diane Apostolos-Cappadona, eds. *Dance as Religious Studies*. New York, 1990.
Berk, Fred, ed. *The Chasidic Dance*. New York, 1975.
Friedhaber, Zvi. "The 'Instructor' of Folk Dance" (in Hebrew). *Folklore Research Center Studies* 1 (1970): 275–279. Includes an English summary, pages 99–100.
Friedhaber, Zvi. "Jewish Folk Dance Customs as Reflected in the Memorial Literature of the Jewish Communities" (in Hebrew). In *Proceedings of the Fifth World Congress of Jewish Studies (1969)*. Jerusalem, 1972. Includes an English summary, pages 293–294.
Friedhaber, Zvi. "Dance in Judaism in the Middle Ages and the Renaissance." In *Physical Education and Sport in Jewish History and Culture: Proceedings of an International Seminar, July 1981*, edited by Uriel Simri. Netanya, Israel, 1981.
Friedhaber, Zvi. "The Dance in Sephardic Jewish Communities as Reflected in Their Response Literature" (in Hebrew). In *The Sephardi and Oriental Jewish Heritage: Studies*, edited by Issachar Ben-Ami. Jerusalem, 1982. Includes an English summary, pages vii–ix.
Friedhaber, Zvi. "The Dance with the Separating Kerchief." *Dance Research Journal* 17–18 (Fall 1985–Spring 1986): 65–69.
Friedhaber, Zvi. "Dramatization in Chassidic Dances." *Israel Dance* (1983): 5–8.
Jewish Folklore and Ethnology Newsletter 4.1–2 (1981); 8.3–4 (1986).
Rivkind, Isaac. *Klezmorim: Jewish Folk Musicians* (in Hebrew). New York, 1960. See pages 28–35.

Roth, Cecil. *The Jews in the Renaissance.* Philadelphia 1959. See pages
    221–304, 309–361.
Zoder, Raimund. "Judentanze." *Jahrbuch für Volkshederforschung*
    (1930): 122–139.

ZVI FRIEDHABER

JHAVERI SISTERS. An Indian dance group, the
Jhaveri Sisters included Nayana Jhaveri (born 12 May
1927 in Bombay; died 7 February 1985); Ranjana Jhaveri
(born 7 August 1930 in Bombay); Suverana Jhaveri (born
14 April 1935 in Bombay); and Darshana Jhaveri (born 9
January 1939 in Bombay). The Jhaveri Sisters were
trained in classical Manipuri dances from an early age by
the renowned master Guru Bipin Singh. Performing as a
group, the sisters became synonymous with this genre

JHAVERI SISTERS. Darshana, Ranjana, and Nayana, three of the
four Jhaveri Sisters, in *Holī* (Playing with Colors), a Manipuri-
style dance. During the Hindu festival of Holī, brightly colored
confetti and powdered pigment are tossed in the air. (Photograph
from the Dance Collection, New York Public Library for the Performing
Arts.)

over a long career of more than four decades. Guru Bipin
Singh and the Jhaveri Sisters were instrumental in popu-
larizing classical Manipuri dance throughout India and
abroad with their aesthetic and theatrically polished presentations. Retaining the basic spirit of Manipuri, Guru
Bipin Singh directed and choreographed traditional numbers for performance on the proscenium stage in metropolitan centers. By condensing the night-long dance dramas, such as the cycle of the various *rās līlā*s, he
introduced urban audiences to the devotional dances of
Manipuri.

The Jhaveri Sisters presented such dance dramas as *Jai
Somnath, Usha,* and *Rajnartaki* in the late 1940s and early
1950s in Bombay. Later they worked toward developing a
repertory suitable for stage presentation from the vast
corpus of traditional Manipuri dance and dance drama.
Guru Bipin Singh choreographed several solo dances inspired by solos from the *rās līlā*s; he also explored the
Vaiṣṇava literary and oral traditions of both Manipur and
West Bengal. The solos, duets, and group dances, polished
like a diamond, dazzled audiences.

Nayana Jhaveri was honored with the Central Sangeet
Natak Akademi award for her contribution to Manipuri
dance and for making it accessible to the rest of India.
Several other honors and awards have been received by
the Jhaveri Sisters, individually and collectively. The three
surviving sisters train Manipuri dancers at centers in
Bombay, Calcutta, and Imphal. The youngest, Darshana
Jhaveri, in collaboration with Guru Bipin Singh, has published several books in English and Hindi on various aspects of Manipuri dance and music. The sisters, who have
performed all over the world, continue performing, training, researching, and choreographing new dances within
the traditional parameters from their base in Bombay.

BIBLIOGRAPHY
Doshi, Saryu, ed. *Dances of Manipur: The Classical Tradition.* Bombay,
    1987.
Jhaveri, Darsana, and Kalavati Devi. *Maṇipūrī tāla prakāśa.* Varanasi,
    1990. In English and Hindi.
Marg 14 (September 1961). Special issue on Manipuri dances, edited
    by Mulk Raj Anand.
Sloat, Susanna. "Jhaveri Sisters Manipuri Dance Troupe." *Attitude* 10
    (Winter 1994): 50.

SUNIL KOTHARI

JIDAIMONO is a classification of plays in *kabuki* theater that deal with Japanese history prior to the Tokugawa
shogunate of the Edo period (1603–1868). The other main
category of *kabuki* plays, *sewamono,* deals with the life of
townsmen during the Edo period.

The characters in *jidaimono* are drawn from the samurai (aristocratic warrior) or imperial classes. The relation
between *jidaimono* and historical fact is tenuous (even
more than, for example, in Shakespeare's histories). Be-

cause of legal restrictions, Japanese writers dealt with historical fact still within living memory by fancy and indirection. History plays were often thinly disguised presentations of well-known occurrences, with characters' names sufficiently modified to evade the law. The best example is *Chūshingura* (1748), which portrays the revenge taken by forty-seven masterless samurai on the man guilty of causing their lord's demise; the playwright placed these relatively recent events several centuries earlier, in the Ashikaga period (1392–1573). *Jidaimono* playwrights did not attempt historical accuracy until the late nineteenth century, when a class of plays called *katsureki geki* ("plays of living history") was created under the impact of Western ideas.

Jidaimono are classified according to the specific historical cycle they cover or, in a more general way, as *ōchōmono*, *jidaimono* proper, and *oiemono*. *Ōchōmono* (court plays) are set in the Nara (696–794) and Heian (794–1185) periods and recount events at the imperial court. *Jidaimono* plays proper deal with events of the thirteenth through sixteenth centuries. The conflict between the Taira and Minamoto families is crucial to many of these plays. *Oiemono* ("family-feud plays") dramatize intrafamilial disputes, often over succession rights, in the households of powerful daimyos. Because commoners often figure importantly in the *oiemono* category, these plays are sometimes called *jidai-sewamono*. To these categories may be added the *katsureki* plays mentioned above.

The acting in *jidaimono* is *kabuki*'s most formal and stately; costumes and makeup tend to be more exaggerated and stylized than in other genres, and the pace is generally rather slow.

Kabuki derives the bulk of its history plays from *bunraku* (puppet theater), and the acting of the puppets has had an enormous influence on the way the living actors play their roles.

[*See also* Kabuki Theater.]

SAMUEL L. LEITER

JIG is a general term for a fast solo dance of Anglo-Irish origin that has been in use in English since at least the beginning of the seventeenth century. Since that time many dance styles have evolved that were called jigs, and this evolution continues today. These many styles of dance are generally solo performances, usually calling for showmanship and virtuosity on the part of the performer. Sometimes two or more dancers will perform jigs simultaneously, creating a competitive spirit.

The term *jig* is also used for one of the predominant forms of traditional dance music, specifically those tunes in which each beat of music is subdivided into three parts. These tunes are today notated in 6/8 or 9/8 time, although until the late eighteenth century 6/4 or 9/4 time signatures

were common. Jig dances are sometimes, but not necessarily, performed to jig-time tunes.

More confusion arises because the term has also been applied to dance and performance in other contexts. In the Elizabethan theater, for example, a short farcical entr'acte or postlude evolved that was called a "jig" or "jigg." This Elizabethan jig involved several characters in a comical music and dance performance. The practice of presenting such jigs with virtually all types of plays spread from England to northern Europe in the first half of the seventeenth century. Beyond the occasional inclusion of a virtuoso solo dance, these jigs seem to have had little in common with the folk jig of the period.

The French *gigue* (or Italian *giga*) became a standard movement in Baroque dance suites. Although the word may have come from the English *jig*, it was used there to indicate a musical meter, not a particular dance form.

In England, the jig has been a part of the Morris dance since at least 1600, when William Kempe danced his famous jig in Morris dance costume from London to Norwich. Jigs are still part of this old dance tradition in the Oxford area, where they are danced either by a single dancer or by two dancers alternately as a contrast to the predominant six-man Morris dances. In a few instances, Morris jigs continued to be danced after other elements of the Morris dance tradition had disappeared. Since the 1960s, a revival of Oxfordshire and Gloucestershire Morris dancing has resulted in its reappearance, complete with jigs, throughout much of the English-speaking world.

The jig is also related to the English hornpipe dance. Moving to a slow, broken-rhythm 2/4 time, the hornpipe has remained distinct from the jig, although the two dances frequently share steps.

In Ireland, jigs are danced only to jig-time music, notated in 6/8 or 9/8. A similar dance to common-time music is called a reel. Although essentially a virtuoso solo dance, the Irish jig often includes interaction between three or more dancers as well as independent step dancing.

Jigs have been danced in the Americas since the first arrival of European settlers. The style began to diverge from the European sources early, when jig dancers began to imitate the dancing of African slaves. An Englishman, Andrew Burnaby, observed this in Virginia as early as 1759:

> Towards the close of an evening, when the company are pretty well tired with country dances, it is usual to dance jiggs; a practice originally borrowed, I am informed, from the Negroes. These dances are without any method of regularity: a gentleman and a lady stand up, and dance about the room, one of them retiring, the other pursuing, then perhaps meeting, in an irregular fantastical manner. (Burnaby, 1775)

The other early influences on jig dance in the New World stem from the dance traditions of the dominant

JIG. Although most jigs are solo dances, the Irish jig often included interaction with other dancers. Here, in an engraving after Wrightson, two customers in a bawdy tavern dance a jig to a fiddler's tune. (Reprinted from Lily Grove, *Dancing*, London, 1895.)

immigrant groups: Dutch, British, French, Iberian, Scandinavian, and German. Nineteenth-century influences included the minstrel dance routines, especially clog dances, and the other show dances, such as the buck-and-wing and sand dancing. The jig became an essential part of the stage Irishman act in the popular theater and later in vaudeville; it was also a standard dance in minstrel shows, after it was made famous by Juba (William Henry Lane) in the 1840s.

In some parts of the United States, jig dance steps are customarily incorporated into square dances, and this practice led to the creation of competitive teams that dance jig steps while executing patterned dance figures. Originating in the western part of North Carolina, these teams call themselves clog dancers; clogging is now danced throughout the United States. A comparable dance movement exists in Canada, based on indigenous jig dance steps. The music for jig, flatfoot, buck, or clog dancing is almost entirely in 2/4 reel or hoedown time; 6/8 jig tunes are no longer used in North America to accompany step dancing.

Although it has been common practice since the 1700s to give country dances (also called, by the French, *contredanses*) titles such as "No-body's Jig," "Haymaker's Jig," or "Chorus Jig," these dances are not jigs. They simply draw on the association in the dancers' minds of the jig as a lively and challenging dance. Even the tunes are not necessarily in jig time.

In other instances, some aspect of jig dancing actually has influenced another dance form, as in the use of jig steps in the rapper sword dances of northern England. The stationary step dancing that is performed at intervals by all the dancers in the set is referred to as "jigging" by most traditional dancers, although none of them would describe the stepping as "dancing a jig."

[*See also* Clogging; Hornpipe; Morris Dance; *and* Sword Dance. *For discussion of the jig in an eighteenth-century court version, see* Gigue.]

BIBLIOGRAPHY

Baskervill, Charles R. *The Elizabethan Jig and Related Song Drama.* Chicago, 1929.

Breathnach, Breandán. *Folk Music and Dances of Ireland.* Rev. ed. Dublin, 1977.

Burnaby, Andrew. *Travels through the Middle Settlements in North-America in the Years 1759 and 1760.* 2d ed. London, 1775.

Sharp, Cecil J., and Herbert C. Macilwaine. *The Morris Book.* 5 vols. London, 1909–1913. 2d ed. London, 1912–1924.

JAMES E. MORRISON

JITTERBUG. *See* Lindy Hop. *See also* United States of America, *articles on* African-American Concert Dance Traditions *and* African-American Social Dance Traditions.

JIVE. *See* Ballroom Dance Competition; Lindy Hop; *and* Social Dance; *article on* Twentieth-Century Social Dance to 1960.

JOB. Masque for dancing in eight scenes. Choreography: Ninette de Valois. Music: Ralph Vaughan Williams. Libretto: Geoffrey Keynes. Scenery and costumes: Gwendolen Raverat. First performance: 5 July 1931, Cambridge Theatre, London, Camargo Society. Principals: Anton Dolin (Satan), Stanley Judson (Elihu).

Keynes, the authority on the life and work of William Blake, based his libretto on Blake's illustrations for the *Book of Job;* these were also the source of Raverat's designs. The eight scenes depict the trials and temptations visited on Job by Satan in his attempt to usurp the authority of God, Job's rebellion and repentance, and Satan's defeat. Keynes, having solicited the collaboration first of Raverat and then of Vaughan Williams, had first submitted his scenario to Serge Diaghilev, accompanied by reproductions of Blake's illustrations. Diaghilev had rejected the proposal (though it has been noted that he then went on to produce a ballet on a biblical subject, George Balanchine's *The Prodigal Son*).

De Valois's production for the Camargo Society followed the composer's stipulation that there should be no pointe work; her choreography is in a "free" style that shows some influence of central European modern dance. Many of the groupings are derived from Blake; much of the piece has a static quality, particularly in the case of the title role—Job is a passive character whose movement is limited to a few not very effectual gestures. The most important dance roles are those of Satan, powerfully portrayed in the original production by Dolin, and Elihu, whose beauty was strikingly embodied by Judson.

Job went into the repertory of the Vic-Wells Ballet at the Old Vic on 22 September 1931; Robert Helpmann succeeded Dolin. *Job* was revived by the Sadler's Wells Ballet at the Royal Opera House, Covent Garden, London, on 20 May 1948, with new designs by John Piper that more richly evoked Blake than had Raverat's. As one of the most important achievements of British ballet, *Job* has been frequently revived. Another 1931 version, choreographed by Ted Shawn, was presented by the Denishawn dancers at the College of the City of New York's Lewisohn Stadium, on 24 August. In 1992 the British choreographer David Bintley choreographed a new version for the San Francisco Ballet (Opera House, San Francisco, 23 April 1992) with designs by Hayden Griffin.

BIBLIOGRAPHY

Beaumont, Cyril W. *Complete Book of Ballets*. London, 1937.
de Valois, Ninette. *Come Dance with Me*. Cleveland, 1957.

DAVID VAUGHAN

JOFFREY, ROBERT (Abdulla Jaffa Anver Bey Khan; born 24 December 1930 in Seattle, died 25 March 1988 in New York City), ballet dancer, teacher, choreographer, and company director. The son of an Afghan father and an Italian mother, Joffrey took up dance as a child to improve an asthmatic condition. At twelve he began serious study with Mary Ann Wells in Seattle and performed locally in his teens, giving a solo recital of his own choreography in 1948. Later that year, he moved to New York, where he studied with Alexandra Fedorova at the School

of American Ballet, and also at the Gertrude Schurr–May O'Donnell studio.

Joffrey made his professional debut as a soloist with Ballets de Paris de Roland Petit during its 1949/50 New York season. He appeared as a soloist with May O'Donnell's company in 1953.

From the beginning of his career, Joffrey was a teacher as well as a dancer. He was already on the faculties of the American Ballet Theatre School and the High School of Performing Arts in 1953 when he opened his own studio, the American Ballet Center, which continues to be the official school of the Joffrey Ballet.

Joffrey choreographed his first professional ballets in 1952: *Scaramouche* for his students at Performing Arts, and *Persephone* for the Choreographers' Workshop, a privately sponsored showcase. These ballets and a third work, *Umpateedle*, were performed at the Jacob's Pillow Dance Festival in 1952 and 1953 under the auspices of the Workshop. In 1954 and 1955, Joffrey presented his own small troupe of dancers at the Ninety-second Street YM-YWHA in New York, dancing his newest ballets—*Pas des Déesses, Le Bal Masqué, Harpsicord Concerto*, and *Pierrot Lunaire*. Also in 1955, Joffrey staged *Pas des Déesses* and a revised version of *Persephone* with music by Vivaldi for Ballet Rambert in London.

JOFFERY. Prodded by Lillian Moore, a great scholar of Romantic ballet, and inspired by Alfred Chalon's famous lithograph of Arthur Saint-Léon, Marie Taglioni, Lucile Grahn, and Fanny Cerrito in Jules Perrot's *Le Jugement de Pâris* (1846), Joffrey created *Pas des Déesses* (Dance of the Goddesses) in 1954. It became one of his most popular works. Here are Brunhilda Ruiz (as Cerrito), Glen Tetley (as Saint-Léon), Dianne Consoer (as Grahn), and Beatrice Tompkins (as Taglioni), who danced numerous performances on the first tour of the Robert Joffrey Theater Dancers in 1956. (Photograph from the Dance Collection, New York Public Library for the Performing Arts.)

In the fall of 1956, six dancers went on tour with a repertory of four Joffrey ballets, and his company was born. It was first called the Robert Joffrey Ballet Concert, later the Robert Joffrey Ballet, and now the Joffrey Ballet. For the first ten years of his troupe's existence, Joffrey kept his dancers working and his enterprise solvent by teaching and taking on various choreographic assignments for opera, theater, and television. He was resident choreographer of the New York City Opera from 1957 to 1962 and continued to make ballets for its company periodically through the early 1970s.

Joffrey choreographed only occasionally after 1966, the year his company began to have regular New York seasons. He left the task of creating most of the Joffrey's new ballets to his associate Gerald Arpino, supplementing the Arpino repertory with commissions from other contemporary choreographers and revivals of twentieth-century masterpieces.

From the late 1950s until his death Joffrey taught at numerous regional ballet festivals sponsored by the National Association for Regional Ballet. He also served as co-chairman of the International Council of the USA International Ballet Competition, as a member of the Dance Panel of the National Endowment for the Arts, and (with Yuri Grigorovich of the Soviet Union) as co-president of the International Dance Section of the International Theatre Institute.

[*See also* Joffrey Ballet.]

BIBLIOGRAPHY

Anawalt, Sasha. *The Joffrey Ballet: Robert Joffrey and the Making of an American Dance Company.* New York, 1996.

Dorris, George. "The Choreography of Robert Joffrey: A Preliminary Checklist." *Dance Chronicle* 12.1 (1989): 105–139.

Dorris, George. "The Choreography of Robert Joffrey: A Supplement." *Dance Chronicle* 12.3 (1989): 383–385.

Gruen, John. *The Private World of Ballet.* New York, 1975.

Joffrey, Robert. "Past and Present: The Vital Connections." In *Visions: Ballet and Its Future,* edited by Michael Crabb. Toronto, 1978.

Whitney, Mary. "Viva Joffrey." *Ballet News* 3 (October 1981): 30–34.

TULLIA LIMARZI

JOFFREY BALLET. The Joffrey Ballet's most distinctive feature has traditionally been its repertory composed of contemporary choreography (primarily by its director Gerald Arpino) and revivals of important twentieth-century ballets. The Joffrey does not dance the standard nineteenth-century repertory, although it has occasionally mounted full-length story ballets.

The first dance troupe to perform under the Joffrey name was the Robert Joffrey Ballet Concert, an outgrowth of the American Ballet Center, the studio Robert Joffrey founded in 1953, which continues to be the official school of the Joffrey company. The Ballet Concert gave performances of Joffrey's choreography in May 1954 and March 1955 at the Kaufmann Auditorium of the Ninety-second Street YM-YWHA in New York. The first performance included the premieres of *Pas des Déesses* and *Le Bal Masqué;* the second, *Harpsichord Concerto* and *Pierrot Lunaire.*

In the fall of 1956, Gerald Arpino, Dianne Consoer, Brunilda Ruiz, Glen Tetley, Beatrice Tompkins, and John Wilson (then known collectively as the Robert Joffrey Theater Dancers) went on tour with a repertory of Joffrey ballets. (Joffrey himself stayed behind to run the school.) They traveled through eleven states in a borrowed station wagon, performing twenty-three one-night stands. The company's frequent affectionate references to these humble origins are an important clue to its self-image as a hardy, adventurous troupe bringing ballet to America, often in the face of adversity.

For nearly ten years the annual tours, which grew longer each season, gave the company continuity and regular opportunities to perform its repertory. In its first decade, between tours, the troupe took on various assignments to keep it both visible and solvent, including performances at summer arts festivals and stints in opera for NBC television and with the New York City Opera.

From 1962 to 1964, Joffrey's company functioned under the patronage of the Rebekah Harkness Foundation. Grants underwrote summer workshops in 1962 and 1963 at the home of Rebekah Harkness Kean at Watch Hill, Rhode Island. There, specially commissioned ballets were created, and for the first time, Robert Joffrey was able to pay his dancers to rehearse.

Sponsored by Harkness, the Joffrey Ballet gave two performances for invited audiences at the New York Fashion Institute of Technology, 28 and 30 September 1962, featuring the six ballets created at the summer workshop: Gerald Arpino's *Incubus,* Joffrey's *Gamelan,* Brian Macdonald's *Time out of Mind,* Alvin Ailey's *Feast of Ashes,* Donald Saddler's *Dreams of Glory,* and Fernand Nault's *Roundabout.* The company's leading soloists included Lisa Bradley, Elizabeth Carroll, Richard Gain, Lone Isaksen, Finis Jhung, Nels Jorgensen, Vicente Nebrada, Lawrence Rhodes, Brunilda Ruiz, Paul Sutherland, and Helgi Tomasson.

The Fashion Institute performances were only the second time Joffrey's company had danced in New York (the first was in a public performance at the Brooklyn Academy of Music in March 1958). Nonetheless, by the fall of 1962 the Robert Joffrey Ballet, as the company was then known, had visited nearly four hundred cities in the United States and performed in forty-eight states. The troupe, now around twenty dancers who traveled with a small orchestra, had an active repertory of twenty-one works, only three of which were by Joffrey. On the strength of this national reputation and with Harkness

Foundation backing, the company embarked on a State Department tour of seven countries in the Near and Far East in October 1962.

Following the 1963 summer workshop at Watch Hill, Joffrey's dancers shared the stage with American Ballet Theatre and the New York City Ballet on 4 September 1963 in a gala performance, part of the Harkness Ballet Festival at the Delacorte Theater in New York's Central Park. The Joffrey segment of the program consisted of Arpino's *Partita for Four,* Macdonald's *Time out of Mind,* and the New York premiere of Arpino's *Sea Shadow,* newly created at Watch Hill.

On 1 October the Joffrey company made its first White House appearance, for President John F. Kennedy. Soon after, the dancers departed for a ten-week tour of the Soviet Union, where their contemporary, youthful style was warmly received, for the most part, by the ballet establishment and audiences alike. A second trip to the Soviet Union in 1974 was a similar success.

Following the company's next U.S. tour, which ended in March 1964, the Harkness Foundation proposed changing the terms of its sponsorship. Rebekah Harkness Kean wanted to rename the troupe the Harkness Ballet, while retaining Joffrey as director. Joffrey, not assured that he would have final control over the company's artistic policies, withdrew from the partnership.

The separation from Harkness cost Joffrey the ballets that had been commissioned through the Harkness Foundation and many of his dancers, who were under contract to Harkness. [*See* Harkness Ballet.] A temporary disbanding of the company ensued, but by the fall of 1964, the Ford Foundation had given Joffrey the resources to continue his work: a grant of $155,000, with the stipulation that another $120,000 be raised through private donations. A reorganized Joffrey company made its debut at the Jacob's Pillow Dance Festival in the summer of 1965, and gave its first official New York season that September at the Delacorte Theater.

The following spring, Joffrey produced his first season at the City Center Fifty-fifth Street Theater. This appearance prompted the City Center board to make the company its resident ballet troupe, filling the void left when the New York City Ballet moved to Lincoln Center. The Robert Joffrey Ballet was rechristened the City Center Joffrey Ballet (in October 1976, the name became simply the Joffrey Ballet) and it presented most of its New York seasons there.

In 1979 a financial crisis brought the Joffrey to the brink of bankruptcy, forcing it to suspend operations for six months. Saved from extinction by a grant from the National Endowment for the Arts, the Joffrey moved toward building a stronger base of financial support from private sources. In 1983, the Joffrey also became the resident bal-

JOFFREY BALLET. Set to music by Emmanuel Chabrier, Joffrey's *Le Bal* (The Ball) was on the first program of the Robert Joffrey Theater Dancers, given 2 October 1956 at State Teachers College in Frostburg, Maryland. This photograph, taken in 1957, when the company was called the Robert Joffrey Theater Ballet, shows five members of the original cast: Gerald Arpino, Beatrice Tompkins, Ivan Allan (in Glen Tetley's original place), Dianne Consoer, John Wilson, and Brunhilda Ruiz. (Photograph from the Dance Collection, New York Public Library for the Performing Arts.)

let company of the Los Angeles Music Center, the first American dance troupe to make its home at performing arts centers on both coasts.

As the Joffrey Ballet came into its own as a major force in American ballet, its distinctive identity was taking shape. Reacting against the traveling ballet companies he had seen as a youth, Joffrey was determined to eschew the pseudo-Russian aesthetic and maintain an American repertory. But he also dreamed of putting on the great European ballets, such as *The Green Table* and *Petrouchka,* which had enchanted him in childhood. This resolve was strengthened by Marie Rambert, who captivated him with her reminiscences of the Diaghilev era.

For the repertory he envisioned, Joffrey wanted and needed dancers who could adapt to many styles. The company's own early ballets were already diverse: Joffrey's *Pas de Déesses,* a *divertissement* in the Romantic style for three ballerinas and a male dancer representing Marie Taglioni, Lucile Grahn, Fanny Cerrito, and Arthur Saint-Léon; Macdonald's *Time out of Mind,* an orgy of predatory sex; Ailey's *Feast of Ashes,* a dramatic work based on Federico García Lorca's play *The House of Bernarda Alba,* with much modern dance movement; and Arpino's *The Palace,* a pastiche of vintage vaudeville. In its first decade the Joffrey also danced the works of Balanchine and Bournonville, Fernand Nault's staging of *La Fille Mal Gardée,* and the pas de deux from *Giselle.*

JOFFREY BALLET. Using a score by Toshirō Mayuzumi, Gerald Arpino created *Olympics* for the company in 1966. Inspired by ideals of athletic performance in Classical Greece, it was danced by an all-male cast. (Photograph from the Dance Collection, New York Public Library for the Performing Arts.)

In the early 1960s, Joffrey relinquished his role as the company's chief choreographer to Gerald Arpino. A principal dancer since the days of the YMHA concerts, Arpino began to choreograph in 1961, and his ballets *Sea Shadow* and *Ropes* entered the Joffrey repertory in January 1962. After that time Joffrey left the shaping of the contemporary face of the company primarily to Arpino. Joffrey considered *Viva Vivaldi!* (1965), *Trinity* (1970), and *Suite Saint-Säens* (1978), all by Arpino, to be his company's signature ballets.

Arpino became a controversial choreographer. His champions maintained he was extraordinarily versatile and clever. They cited his knack for putting difficult steps together imaginatively, his exhilarating sense of theater, the emotional abandon of his works, and his ability to create ballets in many styles, from the strictly neoclassical to those that incorporated jazz and popular dance idioms. They extolled the way he produced yearly premieres that challenged dancers and kept audiences coming back.

His critics, while they sometimes acknowledged that Arpino was a serviceable and inventive choreographer,

claimed he was seldom a truly creative one; rather, they felt he catered to a sensation-hungry audience with dances that were rousing but shallow. They sometimes called his spectacular ballets vulgar, and his blatantly erotic ones tasteless. The choreographic excitement of an Arpino ballet, said his detractors, came not from deft handling of the classical vocabulary but from acrobatic tricks. Even though he often used easily accessible scores, either lushly melodic or rousing and vibrant, he was accused of being an unmusical choreographer, of fitting dance and music together unharmoniously.

Many of Arpino's ballets, although essentially plotless, have dramatic undercurrents—the psychological symbolism of *Ropes* (1961), the philosophical metaphor of *The Clowns* (1968), or the ritualistic tribal ceremony of *Sacred*

JOFFREY BALLET. Arpino's works were the mainstay of the repertory throughout the 1960s, providing numerous roles tailored to the talents of the company's leading dancers. (*top left*) Trinette Singleton and Gregory Huffman in *Viva Vivaldi!* (1965). (*top right*) Ann Marie De Angelo and Luis Fuente in *Fanfarita* (1968). (*bottom left*) Lisa Bradley and John Jones in *Nightwings* (1966). (*bottom right*) Erika Goodman and Frank Bays in *Cello Concerto* (1967). (Photographs from the Dance Collection, New York Public Library for the Performing Arts.)

Grove on Mount Tamalpais (1972). By the 1980s, Arpino was producing mostly abstract ballets, each new one sleeker than the last. From the company's earliest days Joffrey dancers were noted for their polished, athletic style and their youthful enthusiasm. Under Arpino's tutelage they moved to the forefront of the dancer-as-superathlete trend in American ballet.

By the Joffrey's first season at City Center in spring 1966, Arpino's ballets dominated the repertory. The sea-son's two big successes were *Olympics* and *Viva Vivaldi! Olympics*, created for the male strength of the company, featured manly gymnastic feats. *Viva Vivaldi*, made to celebrate the rebirth of the company after the dispute with Harkness, was a bravura display piece with a Spanish flavor, led by Robert Blankshine, Trinnette Singleton, and Luis Fuente.

The period from the late 1960s into the mid-1970s was one of startling contrasts for the Joffrey Ballet. As

JOFFREY BALLET. Arpino's pantomine-ballet *The Clowns* (1968) was danced to a score commissioned from Hershey Kay, a twelve-tone, serial-form piece with electronic sound effects. Costumes were designed by Edith Lutyens Bel Geddes, and special effects (bomb explosions, helium balloons) were created by Vernon Lobb and Kip Coburn. A group of clowns enacted a parable of human duality, exhibiting both the urge to destroy and the will to survive. The central figure, a tearstained boy-clown, was movingly portrayed by Robert Blankshine (at right front, with dark hair), who became a pop star, briefly, as a result. (Photograph from the Dance Collection, New York Public Library for the Performing Arts.)

Arpino continued to add new works to the repertory, many of them reflecting the influence of the youth cult and protest movement of that time, Joffrey began gathering his treasures from the past. His first major recension was *The Green Table*, staged in 1967 by Ernst Uthoff and Ulla Söderbaum under the supervision of the choreographer, Kurt Jooss. Maximiliano Zomosa was outstanding in the role of Death, and Michael Uthoff re-created the role of the Standard Bearer, which his father Ernst had originated. Joffrey and Jooss also collaborated to revive Jooss's *Big City* in 1975 and his *Pavane on the Death of an Infanta* and *A Ball in Old Vienna* in 1976.

In 1969, the Joffrey Ballet acquired *Façade*, its first Frederick Ashton ballet. The company went on to stage six others, including *Les Patineurs* in 1977, *A Wedding Bouquet* in 1978, and *Illuminations* in 1980.

Also in 1969, Robert Joffrey undertook the first of his Diaghilev revivals, Léonide Massine's *Le Tricorne* (The Three-Cornered Hat), staged by the choreographer. Joffrey brought *Petrouchka* into the repertory in 1972. A painstaking restoration, Joffrey's *Petrouchka*, staged by Yurek Lazowski, bypassed several revisions to return as closely as possible to the choreography of Michel Fokine and the original Alexandre Benois designs. The first Joffrey cast featured Edward Verso as Petrouchka, Erika Goodman as the Ballerina, and Christian Holder as the Moor.

The following year Joffrey and Massine scrupulously brought back to life the collaborative work by Massine, Erik Satie, and Pablo Picasso, *Parade*, which had not been seen in a full-length authentic version since the 1920s. Gary Chryst played the Chinese Conjurer, Donna Cowen the Little American Girl, and Eileen Brady and Gregory Huffman the Acrobats.

In 1976 Robert Joffrey revived an important rarity, the pas de six from *La Vivandière*, an 1848 *divertissement*, which was re-created from Arthur Saint-Léon's newly discovered notation by Ann Hutchinson Guest. A notable if ephemeral experiment was the 1980 revival of *Relâche*, which had been a *succès de scandale* for Les Ballets Suédois in 1924. Moses Pendleton replaced Jean Börlin's lost choreography while retaining the original Satie score, the René Clair film *Entr'acte*, and the Francis Picabia scenario.

Joffrey also revived a number of important ballets of American origin during this period. These were Jerome Robbins's *Moves* (1967), *New York Export: Opus Jazz* (1969), and *Interplay* (1972), Agnes de Mille's *Rodeo* (1976), and Antony Tudor's *Offenbach in the Underworld* (1975).

While Robert Joffrey was pursuing a course of careful restoration of lost or rarely seen masterworks, his company also acquired faddish novelties. Although they attracted new audiences to ballet, many of these works were minor and disposable. Some of the company's commissions, however, resulted in truly inventive work, notably from Twyla Tharp in the 1970s and Laura Dean in the 1980s.

In the fall of 1967 Joffrey created *Astarte,* a multimedia extravaganza with a rock score that reflected the hippie era. The movement, an erotic pas de deux for Zomosa and Singleton, was performed in an environment of psychedelic colors, blinding lights, ear-piercing sounds, and a background film of distorted, fantastic images based on the live action.

The following year Arpino made spectacular use of pop-art effects, particularly plastic balloons and mobiles, in *The Clowns,* a parable about nuclear war told through the antics of Pierrot-like characters. Like *Astarte, The Clowns* put theatricality and stagecraft above dance values.

Trinity, Arpino's ultimate tribute to youth, came in 1970. Inspired by the company's residence at the University of California at Berkeley, it featured Gary Chryst, Christian Holder, and Rebecca Wright in leading roles. *Trinity* combined images of flower children, love-ins, and peace rallies, but it was devoid of dated trappings. Its lasting appeal lies in the exuberant dancing—a hybrid of ballet, jazz, and pop—that rides on the strong, driving beat of a rock score.

In 1973 Joffrey made a daring artistic move when he asked modern dancer Twyla Tharp to choreograph for him. *Deuce Coupe,* with a Beach Boys score and a backdrop painted on the spot by graffiti artists, was as trendy and pop as *Trinity* and *Astarte.* Tharp's achievement, however, was genuinely contemporary as she transferred the unconventional dynamics, patterns, and postures of her style to the Joffrey dancers, with her own company joining in. Tharp refashioned the ballet into *Deuce Coupe II* for the Joffrey dancers alone in 1975. The success of

JOFFREY BALLET. Frederick Ashton's *A Wedding Bouquet,* staged for the company by Christopher Newton in 1978, was one of several Ashton works that entered the repertory, following *Façade* in 1969, *The Dream* in 1973, *Monotones I & II* in 1974, and *Jazz Calendar* and *Les Patineurs* in 1977. Here, Gary Chryst as the Bridegroom supports Beatrice Rodriguez as Julia, his former mistress, who has gone mad with grief and has collapsed in the midst of the nuptial celebration. (Photograph © 1978 by Jack Vartoogian; used by permission.)

Deuce Coupe led to Tharp's production of *As Time Goes By,* a witty ballet to music by Haydn, in the fall of 1973.

In the late 1970s and 1980s the Joffrey Ballet became less preoccupied with youth-oriented themes but continued its pattern of presenting newly commissioned ballets (at least one per season by Arpino) and revivals.

In 1976, the Joffrey Ballet was the first company to be featured on the television series *Dance in America*—an apt distinction in light of the troupe's avowed populism. In 1981 the company appeared again on the public television series, collaborating with Rudolf Nureyev in a tribute to Nijinsky. They danced *Le Spectre de La Rose, Petrouchka,* and *L'Après-midi d'un Faune,* re-creating a special program they had given with Nureyev in New York and on tour during their financial crisis in 1979. (That program

was one of the few instances in which the Joffrey, always a true ensemble company, had danced with a guest star.) The Joffrey's third *Dance in America* appearance in 1982 was a tribute to Kurt Jooss, featuring *The Green Table* in its entirety.

In 1980 Joffrey again made a daring move when he asked postmodern choreographer Laura Dean to make *Night* for the company. Dean's *Fire* followed in 1982, and *Force Field* in 1986. During this period Joffrey also began staging the works of young choreographers from the world of ballet, among them Jiří Kylián, William Forsythe, and James Kudelka, to diversify the company's contemporary side.

Joffrey decided during this time that his dancers should perform full-length ballets regularly. In keeping with his earlier goals, he looked not to the nineteenth century but to contemporary works that could be staged by either the choreographer or members of his original cast. Thus Joffrey produced John Cranko's *Taming of the Shrew* in 1981, Cranko's *Romeo and Juliet* in 1985, and Ashton's *La Fille Mal Gardée* in 1986. The last Diaghilev revival supervised by Robert Joffrey was a landmark re-creation of Vaslav Nijinsky's lost ballet *Le Sacre du Printemps.* It was staged

JOFFREY BALLET. The re-creation and preservation of historic works was one of Joffrey's goals. In 1980, Moses Pendleton, assisted by Philip Holland, mounted a version of Jean Börlin's Dadaist fantasy *Relâche,* first given by Les Ballets Suédois in 1924. Santo Loquasto reproduced Francis Picabia's original designs for scenery and costumes. Here, a pantless Gregory Huffman is seen at dress (undress?) rehearsal. (Photograph © 1980 by Jack Vartoogian; used by permission.)

by Millicent Hodson and designed by Kenneth Archer after Nijinsky and Nikolai Roerich.

Joffrey fell seriously ill in 1986, and by 1987 could take no part in the realization of a long-held dream, the staging of Petipa and Ivanov's *The Nutcracker*. Based on the Ballets Russes de Monte Carlo version but set in nineteenth-century America, the production was staged by George Verdak and Scott Barnard, with choreography by Arpino for the snow scene and Waltz of the Flowers. Joffrey's last public appearance was a weak but emotional curtain call at the production's New York premiere in December 1987. Joffrey died on 25 March 1988.

Later that year the company gave the premiere of Hodson and Archer's reconstruction of Balanchine's *Cotillon*, a work from 1932 not seen since 1946. October 1989 saw the troupe's last repertory season at City Center; financial and administrative turmoil engulfed the Joffrey a few months later on the eve of its May 1990 season at the Los Angeles Music Center. A debt to the dancers' union for unpaid health insurance premiums came to light, and a faction of the board acted to remove Arpino as director. He responded by resigning and withdrawing his ballets from the repertory. By the end of the month the board had reinstated Arpino, but a number of its members, some among the most crucial to the company's financial viability, departed. Also, the Music Center ended its arrangement with the Joffrey.

The company retrenched, reducing rehearsal weeks and eliminating its costly New York fall season. The Joffrey did dance at the New York State Theater in spring 1991, bringing *Empyrean Dances*, a world premiere by twenty-three-year-old Edward Stierle, a virtuoso dancer with a talent for crafting ballets. Stierle died of AIDS a few days after the premiere; a biography detailing his illness, Diane Solway's *A Dance against Time*, revealed, as had long been believed, that Robert Joffrey had died of AIDS as well.

Arpino himself no longer choreographed. However, he endeavored to maintain the company's profile, commissioning many new ballets by young choreographers and mounting a reconstruction of Massine's 1933 ballet *Les Présages* in 1992.

As financial problems worsened, the Joffrey found it difficult to maintain payments guaranteed to the dancers for salaries and benefits. Arpino decided to maximize the company's "pop" image for box office impact. The rock musician known as Prince (and by other names) was introduced to the company, and he offered to make his music available, without charge, for a ballet. The finished work, *Billboards*, which premiered in 1992, had four sections, each by a different choreographer. The opening section, by Laura Dean, was a relatively classical group dance in characteristic Dean style. The other three sections, by Charles Moulton, Margo Sappington, and Peter Pucci, featured much slithering and gyrating, bikinis under see-through bodysuits, and an aura of male-female combat and competitiveness.

There was no doubt the Joffrey Ballet had changed since its founder's death. Critically the best that could be said was that the work might be accessible enough to attract a mass audience. Though the Joffrey still presented some repertory programs, most of its bookings consisted of only *Billboards*, or mostly *Billboards*. Box office was strong, but the piece proved unable to "save" the company or pull it out of debt. The company had lacked a strong board of directors and solid executive management since the crisis of 1990. Its base in New York had also frayed—the Joffrey returned to City Center only for a week of *Nutcracker* in 1991, and, without regular appearances anywhere in the city, had lost its New York profile as well as its Los Angeles identity. Though *Billboards* drew great media attention, and was televised in excerpt, it could not compensate for these basic problems.

In January 1995, unable to pay its dancers, the Joffrey suspended operations. To resolve its debts, the Joffrey Ballet dissolved as a legal entity in July 1995, reaching agreement with its creditors; it owed the dancers' union close to $1 million. A new entity, Arpino Ballet Chicago, Inc., was established to implement the bankruptcy; it was succeeded by another new organization, Joffrey Ballet Chicago. The Joffrey had decided to retreat from the crowded New York dance scene, to seek a new base and source of funding in Chicago.

The original Joffrey Ballet's rights to perform the works of Balanchine, Ashton, Tharp, and other choreographers died with it, and Joffrey Ballet Chicago faced the problem of negotiating for rights not with Balanchine and Ashton themselves—who during their lifetimes had simply given Robert Joffrey permission to perform their ballets—but with their estate trusts, which charged large fees. Tharp was notorious for demanding extremely high royalties for permission to perform her works. As a result of these circumstances, Joffrey Ballet Chicago based its repertory on Arpino's ballets, new commissions, and a few older masterpieces such as *La Vivandière*, in the public domain, and Kurt Jooss's *The Green Table*.

[*Many of the works herein are the subjects of independent entries.*]

BIBLIOGRAPHY

Albig, Pegeen H. "A History of the Robert Joffrey Ballet." 2 vols. Ph.D. diss., Florida State University, 1979.

Anawalt, Sasha. "No Compromise: Gerald Arpino and Joffrey Ballet." *Dance Magazine* (May 1992): 40–47.

Finkel, Anita. "The Hand of Fate." *New Dance Review* 2 (April–June 1990): 1–8.

Finkel, Anita. "Reversal of Fortune." *Dance International* 23 (Fall 1995): 14–17.

Solway, Diane. *A Dance against Time: The Brief, Brilliant Life of a Joffrey Dancer*. New York, 1994.

Whitney, Mary. *The Joffrey Ballet XXV: Celebrating Twenty-Five Years of the Joffrey Ballet from A to Z.* New York, 1981.

Whitney, Mary. "Viva Joffrey." *Ballet News* 3 (October 1981): 30–34.

TULLIA LIMARZI and ANITA FINKEL

JOHANSSON, CHRISTIAN (Per Christian Johansson; Khristian Petrovich Johansson; born 8 [20] May 1817 in Stockholm, died 12 [25] December 1903 in Saint Petersburg), dancer and teacher. Johansson entered the ballet school of the Royal Theater in Stockholm in 1829. After making his stage debut at the Royal Opera in 1836 he went to Copenhagen, where he studied on and off with August Bournonville until 1839. In 1838 at the Royal Theater in Stockholm Johansson staged Bournonville's *Soldier and Peasant* under the title of *Hemkomsten*. The following year he danced in Saint Petersburg. In 1841 he partnered Marie Taglioni for her guest performances in Stockholm, but that same year he left for Saint Petersburg, never to visit Sweden again. Johansson's letters clearly express his gratitude to Bournonville, his "beloved teacher." From the letters it becomes clear that Johansson found the atmosphere of the Stockholm Ballet decidedly unpleasant. Above all he regarded the ballet master, Anders Selinder, as completely incompetent, and in fact Selinder did fail to use Johansson's talent.

Johansson's Russian stage debut came in 1841 at the Bolshoi Theater in Saint Petersburg; together with Elena Andreyanova, who became his permanent partner, he danced in Filippo Taglioni's *La Gitana*. Contemporary critics were impressed by the dancer's lightness and elasticity of movement, his mastery of jumps, pirouettes, and turns, and the eloquence of his artistic manner. At the same time, however, they noted his tendency to grandiloquent poses and exaggerated turnout, unusual in the Russian school of ballet, and also his insufficient attention to conveying actions and feelings by mute gesture. Johansson worked endless hours to improve his dancing technique and studied acting, particularly under Jules Perrot. His deepened understanding of the Russian school of choreography had a marked effect on his performing style and elevated him into the elite of Russian classical ballet dancers.

On the Russian stage Johansson danced with Marie Taglioni in 1842 and with Fanny Elssler in 1850 and 1851. His vast repertory of roles included Alvar in Filippo Taglioni's interpretation of *Gerta, la Reine des Elfrides;* Akbar in Taglioni's *Daia, ou Les Portuguais aux Indes;* Achmet in Jean Coralli's *La Péri;* Albert in Coralli and Perrot's version of *Giselle;* Colin in *La Fille Mal Gardée*, choreographed by Jean Dauberval; François in *Pâquerette* and the principal role in *The Little Humpbacked Horse*, both choreographed by Arthur Saint-Léon; Altamirano in Saint-Léon's version of *Jovita, ou Les Boucaniers Mexicains,* Alvarez in Perrot's *Délire d'un Peintre;* Salvatore Rosa in Perrot and Pugni's *Catarina, ou La Fille du Bandit;* Gringoire in Perrot's *La Esmeralda;* Valentine in Perrot's production of *Faust;* Rajah Dugmanta in *La Bayadère,* choreographed by Marius Petipa; and Bozko in Petipa's version of *Roxane, la Belle de Montenegro.* Johansson performed onstage for the last time in 1883.

Johansson taught at the Saint Petersburg theater school from 1860 (officially from 1863) until the end of his life. Over the course of many years before becoming a teacher he studied in detail the Russian methods of teaching dance. The system that Johansson devised synthesized the best that Russian and Western ballet had to offer and borrowed from traditions going back to Bournonville, Auguste Vestris, the French Romantic ballet of Filippo Taglioni and Perrot, and the Russian school of classical dance. He condemned gratuitous virtuosity, regarding technique as a means to artistic expression through faultless academic form. With his students he used a highly individualized approach that revealed what each of them could do differently and neutralized particular physical inadequacies. Possessing a boundless imagination in composing lively studies and combinations that gradually increased in difficulty, he also encouraged and stimulated his students to invent new dance movements. He retained his fine dancing form until old age and taught his understudies by demonstration.

Thanks to his methods Johansson groomed a great number of brilliant ballet dancers, including Pavel Gerdt, Nikolai and Sergei Legat, Praskovia Lebedeva, Matilda Kshessinska, Marie Petipa, Olga Preobrajenska, Anna Pavlova, Tamara Karsavina, and Ekaterina Geltser. In 1892 he gave advanced lessons to Pierina Legnani, and in 1898 and 1899 his classes were attended by Michel Fokine. Marius Petipa, who had become deeply interested in Johansson's teaching methods, visited his class and fixed in his mind choreographic combinations that he later drew on in his ballets. Johansson the ballet teacher and Petipa the choreographer were bound by a shared philosophy and similarity of artistic desires. Together they created an integrated aesthetic system of theory and execution that dominated Russian ballet until the beginning of the twentieth century.

Johansson's daughter, Anna Christianovna (1860–1917), was an artist at the Maryinsky Theater from 1878 to 1898, teaching ballet there upon her retirement from the stage.

BIBLIOGRAPHY

Gregory, John. *The Legat Saga.* 2d ed. London, 1993.

Guest, Ivor. *Jules Perrot: Master of the Romantic Ballet.* London, 1984.

Johansson, Christian. "Letters from Johansson" (parts 1–6). Translated by Lulli Svedin, with commentary by John Gregory. *The Dancing Times* (February–July 1986).

Karsavina, Tamara. "Family Album 2: Christian Petrovich Johansson." *The Dancing Times* (July 1964): 516–517.

Krasovskaya, Vera. *Russkii baletnyi teatr nachala dvadtsatogo veka*, vol. 2, *Tantsovshchiki*. Leningrad, 1972.

Legat, Nikolai. "Twenty Years with Marius Petipa and Christian Johansson." *The Dancing Times* (April 1931): 11–14.

Legat, Nikolai. "'The Class of Perfection' of the Imperial Ballet School." *The Dancing Times* (July 1931): 324–327.

Lilliestam, Åke. "Christian Johansson och hans brev till August Bournonville." *Personhistorisk Tidskrift* 1–2 (1973).

Roslavleva, Natalia. *Era of the Russian Ballet* (1966). New York, 1979.

VALERY A. KULAKOV
Translated from Russian

JOHANSSON, RONNY

JOHANSSON, RONNY (Ronny Irene Johansson; born 26 July 1891 in Riga, Latvia, died 8 April 1979 in Stockholm), Swedish dancer and teacher. Born of a Swedish father and a Scottish mother, Johansson arrived in Stockholm in 1913 to start her studies. Clotilde von Derp recommended further studies in Germany, including ballet and gymnastics. Johansson's ballet teachers included Heinrich Kröller and his wife; she also studied with the sports trainer Leppjé.

Johansson toured Europe from 1918 to 1925 as a solo dancer, occasionally sharing performances with the exotic dancer Sent M'ahesa. She developed a personal technique and style far from the expressionism epitomized by Mary Wigman. Her dances were light, witty, and humorous, often using character and ballroom steps. The titles of the dances she created at this time include *Allegro Energico*, *Polka*, *Waltz*, *Mazurka*, and *Gavotte Joyeuse*. In later years her style became more serious and more involved with social themes. The suite *Ett Dygn* (Day and Night; 1938) included the sections "Play at Dawn," "The Toil of the Day," "Dance in the Twilight," and "Voices at Night." Johansson developed her technique to suit the needs of these thoughtful dances, drawing less on ballet and folk dance steps and devising movements in a freer style.

In 1926 Johansson went to the United States to perform, primarily at colleges and universities. While there she was also employed as a choreographer at the Eastman Theatre in Rochester, New York, and she danced with the Adolph Bolm Company, where she was allowed to perform her own dances. She was also employed at the Denishawn school.

In the United States Johansson started teaching and gave lecture-demonstrations. Her training method, which included special floor exercises, was immediately accepted as revolutionary and inspired Martha Graham and others. Ruth St. Denis wrote about her in the August 1928 issue of *Dance Magazine*, "She has an illusive and most individual sense of humor and poetry. . . . She has actually added new gestures to the slowly growing dictionary of the dance."

Johansson went back to Sweden in 1928 and opened a school in Stockholm, but she returned several times to the United States. In Sweden she continued her lecture-demonstrations, analyzing her system. In 1939 she founded the Swedish Dance Teachers Association in order to unite the interests of classical and modern teachers. She became a teacher at the Royal Dramatic Theater in 1942 and was considered a unique expert on period theater and movement. Johansson was much appreciated as an adviser long after her retirement in 1966. In 1964 she was awarded the Swedish State Lifetime Award for Outstanding Artistry.

BIBLIOGRAPHY

Martin, John. "Movement: Some Basic Principles as Seen in Ronny Johansson's Art." *New York Times* (13 February 1938).

Thiess, Frank. *Der Tanz als Kunstwerk*. Munich, 1920.

LULLI SVEDIN

JOHN CANOE FESTIVAL

JOHN CANOE FESTIVAL. *See* Jonkonnu Festival.

JOHNS, JASPER

JOHNS, JASPER (born 15 May 1930 in Augusta, Georgia), American artist and dance collaborator. Although Johns's primary involvement in the theater was as artistic adviser for the Merce Cunningham Dance Company, beginning in 1967, he had in 1955 designed costumes for James Waring's *Little Kootch Piece* and in 1957 worked with Robert Rauschenberg on Paul Taylor's *The Tower* and *Seven New Dances*. He also assisted Rauschenberg on most of his designs for Cunningham from about 1954 to 1960.

Johns often does many renditions of the familiar, ready-made images he selects. In his targets and in his numbers paintings (begun in the mid-1950s), for example, the different versions may involve variations in color or material as well as the addition of items to the initial structure. For example, *Numbers*, from 1964, hangs in the New York State Theater at Lincoln Center in New York City; it contains an impression of Cunningham's foot: "I didn't feel that my work belonged in the theater and I felt that his did; I thought his foot should get through the door" (Klosty, 1986).

Along these lines in his performance-related pieces, Johns continues to rework ordinary things in the context in which they will be perceived. For *Homage to David Tudor*, with Jean Tinguely, Niki de Saint-Phalle, and Rauschenberg (Paris, 1961), Johns contributed two pieces: *Floral Design*, a target made of flowers, and *Entr'acte*, a painting shown at intermission. Writer Michael Crichton (1977) suggests that the target may have served as a stand-in for Johns, who was disinclined to perform. It may also have been an allusion to the practice of sending flowers to performers or, because flowers last at most a few days, a representation of the momentariness of performance. *Entr'acte* may also have been a reference to René Clair's film *Entr'acte*, part of the ballet *Relâche* (1924).

During his tenure as the Cunningham company's artistic adviser, Johns engaged distinguished artists as designers—Frank Stella for *Scramble* in 1967, Andy Warhol for *RainForest* in 1968, Robert Morris for *Canfield* in 1969, and Bruce Nauman for *Tread* in 1970. Marcel Duchamp agreed to let Johns design a set based on his *Large Glass* for the dance *Walkaround Time* (1968; film, 1973). The set comprised seven clear plastic boxes: two were hanging and the rest were moved around the stage by the dancers, altogether effecting an ever-changing montage. Conceptually, this seems connected to Johns's use of the encaustic technique in painting, in which he builds up elements on a surface. This approach recalls John Cage's layering of sound and Cunningham's simultaneous dispersal of independent dance sequences.

In 1980 Johns painted two versions of *Dancers on a Plane*. On the bottom of one, Johns played with the letters in the name Merce Cunningham and in the title Dancers on a Plane by placing some of them backward and out of sequence and starting some words in the middle. The design forces the viewer into multidirectional readings from one side or the other of the picture plane—another possible reference to some of Cunningham's compositional concerns. In Johns's *The Seasons* (1985–1986), images evolve through time, regrouping as organically as the cycle he is representing. In these works, as in so many, by unanchoring situations from their ordinary and expected context, recycling the familiar and even the personal, Johns achieves—in the words on "good writing" of the poet William Carlos Williams—"the continual and violent refreshing of the idea," the image, and the event.

BIBLIOGRAPHY
Adam, Judy, ed. *Dancers on a Plane: Cage, Cunningham, Johns*. New York, 1990.
Crichton, Michael. *Jasper Johns*. New York, 1977.
Francis, Richard. *Jasper Johns*. New York, 1984.
Klosty, James, ed. *Merce Cunningham*. New ed. New York, 1986.
Sylvester, David. *Jasper Johns: Drawings, 1954–1984*. New York, 1974.

ARCHIVE.   Leo Castelli Gallery, New York.

MELISSA HARRIS

JOLIE FILLE DE GAND, LA. Ballet in three acts and nine scenes. Choreography: Monsieur Albert. Music: Adolphe Adam. Libretto: Jules Henri Vernoy de Saint-Georges. Scenery: Pierre Ciceri, Humanité Philastre, and Charles Cambon. Costumes: Paul Lormier. First performance: 22 June 1842, Théâtre de l'Académie Royale de Musique, Paris. Principals: Carlotta Grisi (Beatrix), Lucien Petipa (Benedict), Monsieur Albert (Marquis de San Lucar).

La Jolie Fille de Gand was derived from the successful melodrama *Victorine, ou La Nuit Porte Conseil* (1831). An earlier ballet with a similar plot was Salvatore Taglioni's *Edwige, o Il Sogno* (Naples, 1839). In *La Jolie Fille de Gand*, Beatrix, who is engaged to marry her cousin Benedict, becomes the mistress of the Marquis, only to find herself embroiled in a life of jealousy, bloodshed, and remorse. Awakening, she realizes that it was only a nightmare and prepares to marry Benedict.

Under the title *La Rosière de Gand*, the ballet was first proposed at the Paris Opera in 1840 as a vehicle for Pauline Leroux, who fell ill. Carlotta Grisi was asked to replace Leroux after her triumph in *Giselle* (1841). The 1842 production was the Paris Opera's most expensive to date. The music and choreography were of a high standard, particularly the *pas de deux de carillon*, danced by Grisi and Lucien Petipa to a melody played on little bells. Grisi's *pas de Diane chasseresse*, the high point of the ballet, was commemorated in Eugène Lejeune's print *Les Trois Grâces*, along with Marie Taglioni's Sylphide and Fanny Elssler's *cachucha*.

Similar moralizing dream ballets were Filippo Izzo's *Un Sogno* (1855) and Pinzuti Agrippa's *Un Sogno d'Ines* (1865), both produced in Naples. In 1966 Jack Carter created *Beatrix*, using Vernoy de Saint-George's libretto and Adolphe Adam's music, for the Festival Ballet, London.

BIBLIOGRAPHY
Beaumont, Cyril W. *Complete Book of Ballets*. London, 1937.
Chaffee, George. "Three or Four Graces: A Centenary Salvo." *Dance Index* 3 (September–November 1944): 136–211.
Guest, Ivor. "La Jolie Fille de Gand." *The Dancing Times* 56 (August 1966): 573–575.
Guest, Ivor. *The Romantic Ballet in Paris*. 2d rev. ed. London, 1980.

SUSAN AU

JONES, BILL T. (William Tass Jones; born 15 February 1952 in Bunnell, Florida), dancer, choreographer, and artistic director of the Bill T. Jones / Arnie Zane Dance Company. Jones was the tenth of twelve children, eight of them boys, of Augustus and Estella Jones. His father, a migrant farm worker, shuttled the family around the American South before settling in upstate New York, about forty miles (65 kilometers) south of Rochester in Wayland, a community of about ten thousand people, where the Jones family became one of two African-American families. In high school, Jones was introduced to the theater, playing Marcellus Washburn in a student production of *The Music Man*.

He entered the State University of New York at Binghamton in 1970, where he began his dance training during the spring of his freshman year. In college, Jones studied experimental movement with Kei Takei, contact improvisation with Lois Welk, Humphrey-Weidman technique, Cecchetti ballet, West African and Afro-Caribbean dance, Graham technique, and Hawkins's "free-flow."

While in college, Jones met Arnie Zane (1948–1988), who became his companion and collaborator for seventeen years. They began their long choreographic collaboration in 1971. In 1973, with Welk, Zane, and Jill Becker, Jones co-founded the American Dance Asylum. From the mid-1970s until 1981, Jones choreographed and toured the world, dancing both as a soloist and with Zane in provocative, same-sex duets. In 1982, the pair formed the Bill T. Jones / Arnie Zane Dance Company, recruiting a troupe of individualistic and nontraditional performers who represented different body sizes, shapes, and colors. Jones has created over forty works for his company.

In 1988, Jones lost his life partner Arnie Zane to AIDS, and Jones has been HIV-positive since about 1985. Jones's personal sense of alienation from society and the politics of race, sexual orientation, and AIDS has informed his work consistently. Jones, a choreographic *provocateur*, presents his ideas about identity, art, race, sexuality, nudity, power, censorship, homophobia, and AIDS-as-chemical-warfare with a streetwise, in-your-face attitude. His position on these issues is apparent in such seminal and thought-provoking works as *Secret Pastures* (1984), *D-Man in the Waters* (1989), and *Last Supper at Uncle Tom's Cabin / The Promised Land* (1990), which was documented by the British Broadcasting Corporation and aired as part of the U.S. Public Broadcasting Service (PBS) series *Dance in America*. His controversial multimedia production *Still / Here* (1994)—created in workshops with the participation of terminally ill people—confronted audiences with issues of loss, death, survival, and hope. Decried by some critics who labeled it "victim art," the dance nevertheless was chosen to open the Bill Moyers series for PBS, *Healing and the Arts*.

Jones has received many commissions from dance companies, including the Alvin Ailey American Dance Theater, the Lyon Opera Ballet, the Berlin Opera Ballet, and the Boston Ballet. In 1990, he choreographed Sir Michael Tippet's opera *New Year* for the Houston Grand Opera. He conceived, co-directed, and choreographed *Mother of Three Sons*, presented by the New York City Opera, among others, and he directed *Lost in the Stars* for the Boston Lyric Opera. In 1994, he was appointed resident choreographer of the Lyon Opera Ballet.

Jones has received the Creative Artists Public Service Award in Choreography (1979); three National Endowment for the Arts Choreographic Fellowships (1980–1982); a MacArthur Fellowship (1994); the Dorothy B. Chandler Performing Arts Award for his innovative contributions to the performing arts (1991); two "Bessie" awards (1986 with Mr. Zane, and 1989); and the *Dance Magazine* Award (1993).

In the summer of 1995, he premiered a collaboration

BILL T. JONES. A controversial choreographer, Jones is also a consummate craftsman. He appears here (right) with Arthur Aviles in his *Forsythia* (1989). (Photograph © 1989 by Jack Vartoogian; used by permission.)

with jazz great Max Roach and author Toni Morrison, commissioned by *Serious Fun* at Lincoln Center. In 1995 he collaborated with Trisha Brown and with Laurie Anderson in 1996. His autobiography, *Last Night on Earth* (1995), was published by Pantheon.

BIBLIOGRAPHY

Gates, Henry Louis, Jr. "The Body Politic of Bill T. Jones." *The New Yorker* (28 November 1994).

Jones, Bill T. *Last Night on Earth*. New York, 1995.

Sarandon, Susan. "Up in Arms: Bill T. Jones Gives It Up for Susan Sarandon." *QW Magazine* (October 1992).

Tracy, Robert. "Full Circle." *Dance Magazine* (October 1992):38–41.

Zimmer, Elizabeth, and Susan Quasha, eds. *Body against Body: The Dance and Other Collaborations of Bill T. Jones and Arnie Zane*. New York, 1989.

ROBERT TRACY

JONES, INIGO (born 1573 in London, died 21 June 1652 in London), British architect, painter, and stage designer. Historical assessment of Inigo Jones demands superlatives. Clearly the greatest British architect of the early seventeenth century, he was also the first British architect of international stature since medieval times, the first to absorb Renaissance architectural precepts from the Continent and introduce them into his native land, and the first fully professional architect to work in Britain. In addition, he was a talented painter and draftsman, an ingenious designer of stage scenery and machinery, a connoisseur, a European traveler, and altogether a central fixture in the culturally sophisticated and cosmopolitan Stuart court.

Jones was a true Renaissance man, the intellectual equal of court literati as well as a master of the visual arts.

His earliest surviving sketches are costume designs for Queen Anne's *Masque of Blackness,* performed on Twelfth Night in 1605. As a creator of masques, he was assured of close association with British royalty until the fall of Charles I in 1649. Until 1631 Jones's primary collaborator in these court entertainments was Ben Jonson, and by 1641 Jones had helped present more than fifty masques, plays, tournaments, weddings, funerals, and other court ceremonies. The masques in particular were demonstrations of Stuart legitimacy and supremacy. With the demise of Charles I, Jones, too, lost power and influence; a parliamentary broadside of 1645 referred to him as the "Contriver of Scenes for the Queen's Dancing Barne." [*See* Masque and Antimasque.]

The many surviving drawings for the expensive performances that Jones designed show less stylistic innovation than do his well-known buildings: the Queen's House, Greenwich (1616–1619, 1630–1635); the Queen's Chapel, Saint James's Palace, London (1617–1618); and the Banqueting House at Whitehall Palace (1619–1622), residence of the Stuart court. Nevertheless his masques demonstrated great vitality, technical ingenuity, and symbolic power. In figure drawing he clearly was influenced by Parmigianino, Jacques Callot, and Il Guercino; for stage scenery he borrowed heavily from Sebastiano Serlio and especially from Alfonso and Giulio Parigi, whose late sixteenth-century works for the Florentine Medici had appeared in a book of engravings.

Given that members of the royal court participated in many of the performances, the hall of the Banqueting House, where most of the productions were composed, could be seen as the symbolic nexus of the entire realm. Spacious without encumbrances, it could accommodate not only scenery, performers, and audiences but also the large-scale revels and other dances that made up a large part of the masque. Although most of these dances were typical allemandes and courantes, for the later masques Jones contrived elaborate spectacles, such as scene 5 of the 1640 production of Sir William Davenant's *Salmacida Spolia,* which included an aerial ballet of dancers descending from clouds.

BIBLIOGRAPHY

Colvin, Howard. "Jones, Inigo." In *A Biographical Dictionary of British Architects, 1600–1840.* 3d ed. New Haven, 1995.

Harris, John, et al. *The King's Arcadia: Inigo Jones and the Stuart Court.* London, 1973.

Jones-Davies, Marie-Thérèse. *Inigo Jones, Ben Jonson et le masque.* Paris, 1967.

Lees-Milne, James. *The Age of Inigo Jones.* London, 1953.

Orgel, Stephen, and Roy Strong. *Inigo Jones: The Theatre of the Stuart Court.* 2 vols. Berkeley, 1973.

Peacock, John. *The Stage Designs of Inigo Jones.* Cambridge, 1995.

Strong, Roy. *Festival Designs by Inigo Jones.* Washington, D.C., 1967.

Summerson, John. *Inigo Jones.* Harmondsworth, 1966.

GERALD L. CARR

INIGO JONES. A design for Divine Beauty, a role played by Queen Henrietta Maria, from Jones's 1632 masque *Tempe Restored.* Masque costumes from this era reflected contemporary court dress. (Devonshire Collection, Chatsworth; photograph used by permission of the Chatsworth Settlement Trustees.)

JONES, MARILYN (born 17 February 1940 in Newcastle, New South Wales), Australian dancer. Jones is widely regarded as one of the finest classical ballerinas Australia has produced. As a performer, Jones was noted at home and abroad for her consummate technique and her exceptional blend of line with fluidity. After winning a scholarship offered by a popular women's magazine, she entered the Royal Ballet School in 1956. Her natural elegance and talent were soon noticed, and after nine months, she joined the corps de ballet of the Royal Ballet and with the company visited the United States in 1957. Edouard Borovansky persuaded her to return to Australia to join his company as a soloist in 1959. After the company disbanded she returned to Europe, and danced first with the London Festival Ballet and then as *prima ballerina* of Le Grand Ballet du Marquis de Cuevas.

In 1962 Peggy van Praagh invited her to join the Australian Ballet where she danced the leading roles in *The Sleeping Beauty* and in John Cranko's *The Lady and the Fool*, a part that she repeated later with great success. As *prima ballerina* she danced all the great classical ballets, including *Swan Lake, Giselle,* and Rudolf Nureyev's version of *Raymonda*. She also showed a lively flair for comedy in Frederick Ashton's version of *La Fille Mal Gardée* and other roles. Tall and technically accomplished, her dancing deepened in feeling as she matured. For almost ten years she was partnered by Garth Welch, whom she married but later divorced.

Jones continued in the company until her early retirement in 1971, with a break in 1963 when she returned to the London Festival Ballet as a guest artist. In 1978 she again returned to the Australian Ballet as a principal dancer, extending her repertory to include such works as Cranko's *Romeo and Juliet,* John Butler's commissioned *Night Encounter,* Ashton's *The Dream,* Barry Moreland's *Sacred Space,* Ronald Hynd's *The Merry Widow,* and Jerome Robbins's *Afternoon of a Faun.*

From 1979 to early 1982 Jones was artistic director of the Australian Ballet, and was responsible for introducing much new work, including a number of full-length ballets such as *The Hunchback of Notre Dame* (Bruce Wells) and *The Three Musketeers* (André Prokovsky). The company presented a tribute to Borovansky at her request. During this period, she also established a second performing group—the Dancers of the Australian Ballet, later simply called the Dancers Company. Her directorship of the Australian Ballet was not without its problems. The repertory she introduced did not always receive critical acclaim and during her term of office the dancers went on strike. It was a devisive time.

After her retirement as artistic director of the Australian Ballet in 1982, Jones pursued a career as a teacher, and has been a frequent guest artist with the Australian Ballet, Sydney Dance Company, the Queensland Ballet, and the West Australian Ballet. In 1990 she founded the Australian Institute of Classical Dance, an organization whose major aim is the establishment of an Australian dance syllabus. Since 1995 she has been director of the National Theatre Ballet School in Melbourne. Her two sons, Stanton and Damian Welch, now dance with the Australian Ballet; Stanton is also establishing a career as a choreographer.

BIBLIOGRAPHY
Baum, Caroline. *Artists of the Australian Ballet.* Sydney, 1989.
Laughlin, Patricia. *Marilyn Jones: A Brilliance All Her Own.* Melbourne, 1978.
Laughlin, Patricia. "Marilyn Jones Talks about the Dancers Company." *Dance Australia,* no. 1 (September–November 1980): 14–16.
Laughlin, Patricia. "AICD: Teachers Unite." *Dance Australia,* no. 58 (February–March 1992): 45–47.
Laughlin, Patricia. "Dance Greats: Marilyn Jones." *Dance Australia* no. 85 (August–September 1996): 26–30.

INTERVIEW.   Marilyn Jones, by Michelle Potter (September 1990) National Library of Australia, Canberra (TRC 2629).

MICHELLE POTTER
Based on material submitted by
Geoffrey William Hutton

JONKONNU FESTIVAL. In Jamaica today the term *Jonkonnu* denotes an exclusively male ensemble of costumed dancers, who most often perform at Christmas and on important state occasions. This type of street masquerade has existed since at least the beginning of the eighteenth century. Jonkonnu troupes paraded the streets at Christmas and gave performances, originally before colonial great houses and later in front of the residences or offices of people important in the life of the community. Today many troupes do not perform on the streets, but they maintain visibility by hiring out to organizations for a set fee. Jamaican Jonkonnu is linked to other Caribbean festivals. Variations of this folk festival have been integrated with other Christmas celebrations.

Jonkonnu troupes are typically organized by neighborhood. The performers wear wire screen masks, headwraps and headdresses, and a costume; they mime named characters from a standard but flexible cast. The troupes parade, gathering an appreciative audience, and traditionally proceed to the center of patronage or authority in the neighborhood, where an actual danced performance takes place. Increasingly, these performances occur onstage as part of a larger organized national or local festival.

The performance itself begins with the "break out" (the central section of any performance), in which characters interact in narrative mimes, comic bits, or stick fights. After the break out, the performers receive donations and reassemble in procession to move to their next stop. The repertory of characters in any troupe varies considerably, although certain core characters routinely appear. The individual troupes' performances are structurally the same, but the quality of motion and the identity of the characters and the costumes vary.

In Jamaica there are two types of Jonkonnu troupes— root, and the fancy dress (masquerade). A typical procession of a fancy dress troupe begins with the Courtiers followed by the King and the Queen, perhaps preceded by

JONKONNU. Stock characters of the Jonkonnu Festival. Descended from West African rituals brought to Jamaica by slaves, this street masquerade has been performed during Christmastime since the late eighteenth century. (Photograph by Maria LaYacona; used by permission; from the archives of the National Dance Theatre Company of Jamaica, Kingston; courtesy of Rex Nettleford.)

the Flower Girl. Sailor Boy runs around outside the line, wielding a whip to keep the audience back; Babu, the East Indian cowherd with a long cattle prod, may accompany him. Pitchy Patchy, dressed in rags, runs around outside the procession; like Sailor Boy and Babu, he is more exuberant than the courtly entourage. The Courtiers perform steps in a contained fashion, emphasizing movements that are straight up and down and to the side, with hip swings that cause their short skirts to flare out.

In root Jonkonnu, the Courtiers are replaced by the Native Americans and the Warriors. The former are more expressive than the Warriors, who are forceful but dignified. The Native Americans perform the same steps as the Courtiers, but with a different rhythm, with a more pulsating movement of the hips and hands, and with more syncopation expressed by the feet and knees. Other troupe members include the Whore Girl, who raises her skirts to titillate the audience, and Belly Woman, who shakes her belly to the beat. A Cowhead may confront the crowd, charging and butting to keep people back. Horsehead shakes his buttocks and kicks while running at people, also to help clear the performance space.

Although individual characters may perform specific steps, the repertory of movement patterns is standardized enough to suggest a vernacular vocabulary of danced steps shared by generations of performers. Jonkonnu music is usually provided by a bass drum, a repeater drum, and a fife.

[*See also* Jamaica.]

BIBLIOGRAPHY

Barnett, Sheila. "Jonkonnu and the Creolisation Process: A Study in Cultural Dynamics." Master's thesis, Antioch International University, 1977.

Barnett, Sheila. "Jonkonnu-Pitchy Patchy." *Jamaica Journal* (March 1979).

Bettelheim, Judith. "The Jonkonnu Festival: Its Relation to Caribbean and African Masquerades." *Jamaica Journal* 10 (1976).

Bettelheim, Judith. "The Afro-Jamaican Jonkonnu Festival." Ph.D. diss., Yale University, 1979.

Nunley, John W., and Judith Bettelheim. *Caribbean Festival Arts.* Saint Louis, 1988.

Wynter, Sylvia. "Jonkonnu in Jamaica." *Jamaica Journal* (June 1970).

JUDITH BETTELHEIM

JOOSS, KURT (born 12 January 1901 in Wasseralfingen, died 22 May 1979 in Heilbronn, Germany), modern dancer and choreographer. The German-born (later British) dancer and choreographer grew up in a musical home. His father, owner of an estate, was a keen producer of amateur theatricals, and his mother was a trained opera singer. In 1919, Jooss began his studies at the music conservatory in Stuttgart. His first dance teacher, Grete Heid, suggested him to Rudolf Laban, with whom he soon became associated. His first stage appearance, in the *Tannhaüser* Bacchanale, as choreographed by Laban, was at the Mannheim Opera.

By 1921, Jooss was dancing important roles in Laban's *Die Geblendeten* and *Himmel und Erde* (later called *Oben und Unten*). In 1922, Aino Siimola joined the Laban school; she later became one of the best interpreters of the Jooss choreography and his wife. Jooss spent four years in Stuttgart, Mannheim, and Hamburg as a leading dancer with Laban and, during that period, choreographed *Königstanz* (without music), *Cyklop* to the *Allegro Barbaro* by Béla Bartók, and some others. Jooss met Sigurd Leeder in 1924 and brought him to the Tanzbühne Laban, where they both contributed to the notation system that Laban was developing (Labanotation, in particular the vertical staff). Later in 1924, Jooss left Laban to accept the position of ballet master at the Münster Opera.

Jooss's dance group in Münster, Die Neue Tanzbühne, was joined by Aino Siimola, Sigurd Leeder, Frieda Holst, Jens Keith, Elsa Kahl, Edgar Frank, Yvonne Georgi, and Hein Heckroth, as well as Kahl's husband, the composer-pianist Fritz A. Cohen. In 1924, Jooss choreographed for

JOOSS. In the 1920s, both Rudolf Laban, Jooss's teacher, and the choreographer Mary Wigman utilized the expressive effects of masks in their works. Jooss did so in *Seltsames Septett* (Strange Septet), seen here in a 1928 performance by members of the Essen Folkwang Tanztheater company, and in his later, most famous work, *The Green Table* (1932). (Photograph from the Dance Collection, New York Public Library for the Performing Arts.)

his group *Ein Persisches Märchen*, to music by Egon Wellesz, and in 1925, *Der Dämon*, to music by Paul Hindemith, and his first four-act work, *Die Brautfahrt*, to music by Jean-Philippe Rameau and François Couperin, which toured widely in a program with *Larven* (accompanied by "noises" made by Jooss). His 1926 *Tragödie*, a full-evening ballet, was directly inspired by his break with Laban. The music was unwritten and was improvised by Jooss at each performance.

In these early works, some of the characteristics of Jooss, the choreographer, were established. For example, he disliked in-the-round stages and choreographed only for the proscenium stage. Furthermore, in his concern for the public he wanted to convey clear and understandable stories; thus the form as well as the movements were dictated by the narrative. The Jooss themes were often deeply moral and poetic, but the Jooss sense of humor—mostly good-natured, sometimes scathing—provided contrast. Abstract ballet was alien to him; all movements had to be meaningful, not merely decorative or aesthetic. Deeply musical, he worked with complicated rhythmical patterns, which made the fabric of his choreography extremely tight.

Until 1924, Jooss had studied only with Laban, and although he was also proficient in the various prevalent modern techniques, enlarged by his own inventions, he felt the need to broaden his scope. He and Leeder therefore went to Paris in the winter of 1926/27 and studied classical ballet with Lubov Egorova. In his short stay, Jooss acquired enough sense of classical ballet style to understand that only by knowing classical dance as well as modern dance could dance in all its variety be seen as part of a continuum.

In September 1925, Jooss and Leeder had started a school in Münster based on the principles of Laban. It was called Westfälische Akademie für Bewegung, Sprache, und Musik, and all the pupils had to learn dance, the playing of various instruments, singing, and declamation. The school lasted until 1927.

In 1927, Jooss moved to Essen and became dance director of the Folkwang Schule. In the same building complex that housed the dance school, art and crafts classes were also offered.

Jooss soon organized the second Dancers Congress (the first had been the previous year in Magdeburg), which was held in July 1928. Most of the leading central European dancers attended. Laban, who for the first time presented his dance notation in public, was the dominating pacesetter, and Mary Wigman was the leading artist. From the time of the congress, however, Jooss began to emerge as a new spiritual leader, yet all his life he emphasized that he had been Laban's student; and he credited Laban rather more than was due with the development of modern dance. Laban had been a begetter of ideas, while Jooss was a choreographer and pragmatic developer of a philosophy of dance.

At the 1928 Dancers Congress, Jooss suggested in a speech that classical technique was necessary even for modern dancers. This raised violent opposition. Nevertheless, in his school Jooss included a ballet class twice a week in addition to the daily modern classes. An old knee injury led Jooss to turn over the directorship of the school to Sigurd Leeder and to concentrate on choreography. Leeder was to become the most important teacher in European modern dance, the promulgator of the Jooss-Leeder style.

After the 1928 Dancers Congress, Jooss formed the Folkwang Tanztheater company with students of the school Rudolf Pescht and Ernst Uthoff, dancers from the opera, and with Siimola, Leeder, Kahl, and Cohen, who were later joined by Lola Botka, Lisa Czobel, Karl Bergeest, and Heinz Rosen. The first important creation was *Drosselbart* (1929), to music by Wolfgang Amadeus Mozart, a full-evening's dance drama, in four acts, based on the Grimms' fairy tale. In style it combined the modern and the Baroque styles. For the first time Jooss used a scenery change with the curtain open, which was later to have great impact in *Big City* (1932). In 1929, Jooss also choreographed *Pavane for a Dead Infanta* to music of Maurice Ravel, as a fiftieth birthday present for Laban, and *Zimmer Nr. 13* as well, publicizing his long collaboration with composer Fritz Cohen, his friend and accompanist.

JOOSS. Caricatures of statesmen arguing in *The Green Table* (1932), Jooss's signature work. The year it was created, this antiwar ballet won first prize in a competition for new choreography organized by Swedish impresario Rolf de Maré. (Photograph from the Dance Collection, New York Public Library for the Performing Arts.)

JOOSS. A choreographer with a strong moral conscience, Jooss often expressed social concerns in his work. *Big City* (1932), depicted here, critiqued the rift between urban rich and poor. (Photograph from the Dance Collection, New York Public Library for the Performing Arts.)

In autumn 1929, the official Central School of Laban moved to Essen, with Jooss as director and Laban as visiting examiner several times a year. Toward the end of 1929, Serge Diaghilev died; his company, the avant-garde Ballets Russes, soon dispersed. Like other modern choreographers, Jooss took up some of its repertory, retaining the music and libretto but creating completely different choreography and scenography.

In 1930, Jooss was engaged by the Essen Opera to direct its ballet company, which was then merged with his own group to form the Folkwang Tanzbühne. At the same time the Berlin State Opera offered Jooss the directorship of their ballet. Jooss, preferring the greater independence he had in Essen, arranged for Laban to get the post. As further proof of their reconciliation, Jooss restaged Laban's five-act ballet *Gaukelei* in 1930 (he also used a newly devised choreography, a common practice at the time). His *Prodigal Son* (1931), to music by Sergei Prokofiev and scenography by Heckroth was filled with a warm and simple serenity, very different from George Balanchine's 1929 version. [*See* Prodigal Son, The.].

Jooss and Aino Siimola married in 1929. She applied her intelligence and clear artistic judgment to her husband's choreography, helping to perfect it with her subtle suggestions. Their unusually happy and harmonious marriage produced two daughters: Anna became a dancer, teacher, and later a ballet master, who faithfully bestowed her parents' knowledge and her father's masterpieces on new generations of dancers; the younger child, Christina, did not follow a stage career.

In 1932, Jooss took part in the first international competition for new choreography, of the Archives Internationales de la Danse in Paris, which was arranged by Rolf de Maré. *The Green Table* won first prize and Jooss won international acclaim. Unknown outside his own country until then, Jooss became world famous overnight. *The Green Table* was his signature, to become an indispensable and publicly demanded item in his repertory. What makes *The Green Table* special, even among the Jooss works, is its statement—the abomination of war. Created in vehement protest, this pacifist sermon has continued to move spectators. Jooss gave a new dignity to dance by opening it to the serious presentation of social and political problems.

The 1932 competition also initiated his use of reduced musical accompaniment. A full orchestra was available for the participants, but Fritz Cohen, foreseeing difficulty in getting sufficient rehearsal time, had scored *The Green Table* for two pianos. This proved not only ample, even for large theaters, but also inexpensive, an expediency for what became a regularly touring company. [*See* Green Table, The.]

After the competition, the Jooss company toured in Germany and abroad. In January 1933, the National So-

JOOSS. In 1931, Jooss choreographed his first version of *The Prodigal Son,* to the Prokofiev score, casting Rudolf Pescht in the title role and himself in the role of the Father. In 1933, he restaged it with new music by Fritz Cohen. This photograph, taken in Stockholm, shows Pescht as the Prodigal Son, most likely in the later version of the ballet. (Photograph by Riwkin, Stockholm; from the Dance Collection, New York Public Library for the Performing Arts.)

cialists (Nazis) began ruling Germany under Adolf Hitler, and they tried to take advantage of the company's fame. Jooss was offered privileges on condition that the name of composer Fritz Cohen, who was part Jewish, be replaced on performance programs with Anonymous, and that Cohen and two Jewish dancers be dismissed. Jooss, opposed to all that Nazism stood for, made his position clear to party representatives. He soon received a warning from a friend that the authorities were going to arrest him. Overnight, Jooss, his artists, and all their theatrical baggage crossed the border into the Netherlands. In autumn 1933, the Essen Folkwang Tanzbühne became Les Ballets Jooss, an itinerant company in exile.

In 1932 Jooss had created two major pieces, *Big City* and *A Ball in Old Vienna.* The realistic approach he had begun in *Drosselbart* was furthered in *Big City,* a scathing drama on the polarity between upper- and lower-class town life. With the utmost economy of movement and duration—the story is compressed into a dozen minutes—Jooss tells an intense but universal tale of human tragedy. His compositional invention of keeping the curtain open during scene changes was also developed. The audience, almost without realizing how it came about, suddenly found itself confronted with a new scene, which lent a dreamlike, almost surrealistic, quality to the realistic narrative. *Big City* was first danced to a concert piece by Alexandre Tansman; in 1935 the composer created a new score for the Jooss choreography.

A Ball in Old Vienna, to music by the early nineteenth-century Viennese composer Joseph Lanner, revealed a different aspect of the Jooss character—his good-natured, relaxed, and subtle sense of humor. Jooss was a fine ballroom dancer and was particularly fond of the waltz. He used this knowledge for *A Ball in Old Vienna,* which seemed to be a light entertainment but was actually a repository for all known forms of the waltz.

In 1933 Jooss choreographed *Seven Heroes,* to music by the seventeenth-century English composer Henry Purcell as arranged by Cohen (revised 1937), a light comedy. He also revived *The Prodigal Son,* with new music by Cohen, a revised libretto, and new choreography. Both these ballets have remained popular.

Les Ballets Jooss—with Uthoff, Pescht, Leeder, Siimola, Kahl, Botka, Holst, Czobel, Bergeest, Frank, and Rosen—toured New York from October to December 1933, then went to Paris and through Europe from January to June 1934. While the company was performing in the Netherlands, Belgium, and Poland, Jooss accepted an engagement by Ida Rubinstein to choreograph the world premiere in Paris of Stravinsky's *Perséphone,* with music by Igor Stravinsky and libretto by André Gide. Jooss had to follow Rubinstein's directions more than he liked but was well remunerated. He rejoined his company in Norway, and their tour ended in Sweden. Then Les Ballets Jooss disbanded and most of the dancers went back to German or Swiss theaters.

Jooss found a home for his school at Dartington Hall in England, an extraordinary cultural institution. It reopened as the Jooss–Leeder School of Dance in summer 1934, with five teachers brought from Essen. The school drew pupils from around the world and became the flagship of Dartington Hall, joined by other émigrés from Nazi domination, such as Laban, who managed to escape from Germany on the pretext of lecturing in Paris. To the emerging English ballet, the presence of a teeming center of modern ideas and a superior, experienced, foreign dance company was a challenge. The Jooss influence, probably greater than realized, is evident, for example, in the ballets of Ninette de Valois.

Only Cohen, Kahl, Pescht, Leeder, and the young Noëlle de Mosa followed the Joosses to Dartington, where they made up the core of the new Ballets Jooss. Siimola had stopped dancing, but there were new people trained by Jooss and Leeder. Foremost among them was Hans Züllig, who emerged as one of the great dancers of his generation. Later to join were Ulla Söderbaum and Rolf Alexander, pupils in the school, as well as Gabor Cossa, Maria Fedro, Erika Hanka, and later still Lucas Hoving and Gert

Malmgren. Uthoff and Botka came back. This Ballets Jooss began performing in autumn 1935 with two major pieces newly added, *Ballade* and *The Mirror.*

Ballade was based on a French *chanson* about love intrigues at a Baroque court. The rhythmically intricate music was specially composed by the Dalcroze pupil John Colman, and the choreography, ornamental and elegant, was unusual for Jooss.

The Mirror, to music by Cohen, was a sequel to *The Green Table,* done in the same compact compositional method. It depicted postwar devastation and its effect on people's lives. When in 1939 World War II broke out, Jooss felt that *The Mirror* no longer had a purpose and discontinued it.

Early in 1939, at Stratford-on-Avon, Jooss presented *A Spring Tale,* to music by Cohen. His full-length *Chronica*—thematically a social commentary but stylistically evocative of Botticelli—premiered a month later in Cambridge. After a tour of England, at the end of 1939 the company left for a previously contracted tour of North and South America. It lasted over two arduous years. During the war years, Jooss was kept from joining his company in America; as a German, he was interned in England in 1940. Several prominent English cultural personages, and especially his wife, intervened energetically and obtained his release—but he found no work despite his artistic reputation. Not until 1947, after nearly fifteen years' residency, was he made a British citizen.

During the 1940s, Les Ballets Jooss for the first time produced pieces by choreographers other than Jooss: Agnes de Mille's *Drums Sound in Hackensack* (1941) to music by Cohen, performed only in the United States; Leeder's *Sailor's Fancy* (1943); and Züllig's *Le Bosquet* (1945), to music by Jean-Philippe Rameau.

In February 1942, the company was disbanded in New York, having given 1,625 performances in ten years. Some of the members stayed in the United States; Uthoff, Botka, and Pescht formed a company in Chile. Others returned to England to join Jooss, Züllig, de Mosa, Söderbaum, and Alexander in a new company—the third of the name Ballets Jooss—which found a home theater in Cambridge.

After nearly four years of involuntary silence, broken only by the commission in 1942 from Sadler's Wells Theatre to produce two Mozart operas, *The Marriage of Figaro* and *The Magic Flute,* Jooss had a new ballet ready in February 1943. *Company at the Manor,* set to music by Beethoven, was a warmhearted comedy depicting early nineteenth-century life in England. In 1944 he created *Pandora.* Instead of his customary clarity of message, Jooss created visions of future dangers for humanity that eerily presaged the atomic bomb only a year later. *Pandora* was not liked by the public or even by its dancers, yet in retrospect it was a remarkably visionary statement.

This third Jooss company toured England, the United States, and Scandinavia, ending in Paris in summer 1947. It triumphed everywhere, but the company was exhausted. Jooss and Leeder had been dancing extensively, in addition to their other duties, and the core members craved a year's rest. In August, the company was disbanded temporarily; it never regained its unique position in the international dance world.

Leeder opened his own dance school in London, and Jooss spent an inactive winter in London, then joined his former dancers who had stayed in Chile. For their thriving company he choreographed *Juventud* (1948), to music by George Frideric Handel; later in England it was called *Song of Youth.* It was more abstract than his previous ballets and dealt with human emotions. Jooss was asked to stay in Chile but thought it unfair to his colleagues to do so; Argentina and Uruguay also invited him to settle and form state-supported national ballet companies. Then an offer came from Essen that promised him his old position at the Folkwang Schule and a large subsidy for a new company. After some hesitation, he accepted and worked

JOOSS. The choreographer in his *A Spring Tale* (1939), a fairy-tale ballet set to a score by Fritz Cohen. (Photograph from the Dance Collection, New York Public Library for the Performing Arts.)

JOOSS. Noëlle de Mosa, a core member of Les Ballets Jooss, in *Chronica* (1939). (Photograph from the Dance Collection, New York Public Library for the Performing Arts.)

for two years to reestablish the school, with Züllig as his assistant.

The fourth Jooss company, the Folkwang Tanztheater, started in 1951 after a year of rehearsal. New works were *Colombinade* by Jooss, in the *commedia dell'arte* style, and *Fantasie* by Züllig, a contrast in refinement. *The Green Table* was revived. The company toured in the Netherlands and extensively in Germany—the first time since 1933 that Germany had seen a Jooss company.

In 1952 Jooss made two new ballets. His *Weg im Nebel* (Journey in the Fog) treated the tribulations resulting from war, an enlargement of ideas implied in *The Green Table* but here built on his own war experiences. The four scenes included the loneliness of exile; the claustrophobia of internment; the shadow of bereavement; and the restlessness of attempted rehabilitation. It ended, however, in a celebration of life. *Nachtzug* (Night Train) had a witty plot about people dreaming during a train journey, drawn from his memories of England.

Touring widely, his company was welcomed and Jooss hailed as a genius everywhere but in Essen. The Oberbürgermeister had decided that the Folkwang Tanztheater had its principal exposure abroad so therefore was no concern of his municipality. Financial support was soon withdrawn, and no other town in Germany came to the rescue. The Jooss company was once again disbanded.

Some of the dancers went to the Chilean ballet. Jooss remained in Essen and entered the most financially difficult period of his life. In 1954, while sharing responsibilities of the school in Essen with Züllig, he accepted an appointment as ballet director at the opera house in Düsseldorf. There he did new versions of his *Perséphone* and *Pulcinella* but was denied artistic authority over decisions on repertory and production; in 1956 he left. Eventually, in 1963 in Essen, he received professorial status and remained head of the dance school until he retired in 1968.

In 1962 he formed his fifth company, Folkwang Tanzstudio, with Pina Bausch, Jean Cébron, and graduates of the school. [*See* Folkwang Tanzstudio.] Some important commissions that Jooss fulfilled during this period were productions for the Schwetzingen Festival of Purcell's early operas, *The Fairy Queen* in 1959 and *Dido and Aeneas* in 1966, as well as Rameau's opera-ballet *Castor and Pollux* (1962), and for the 1968 Salzburg Festival, Emilio de' Cavalieri's sixteenth-century *La Rappresentazione di Anima e di Corpo*.

For the first time, Jooss in 1964, mounted *The Green Table* with a company not his own, the Munich Opera Ballet. He later produced it for the Dutch National Ballet in Amsterdam, the Joffrey Ballet in New York, and the Cullberg Ballet in Stockholm.

After his wife's death in 1971, Jooss retired to live in Bavaria; however, he traveled and lectured extensively. He was artistic adviser and guest teacher at the state-run dance school in Stockholm, where he choreographed to music by Handel *Dixit Dominus*, a solo for the Indian dancer Lilavati. In the 1970s Jooss was frequently asked to choreograph but usually refused. He considered the choreography for the Cavalieri piece at the Salzburg Festival—in particular the middle section, with its Dance of Death—his last significant work. Jooss died in Germany, after an automobile accident, on 22 May 1979.

Of his many works, the few that are still extant are performed by dance companies worldwide, produced by his daughter Anna Markard-Jooss with her husband Herman Markard as scenographer. The ballets live through their compositional strength, sometimes carried to austerity. As Jooss himself stated, "Not a step that the drama does not demand or that the form [does not] require. The compositional form is as important as the theme, if not more so."

[*See also the entries on Laban and Leeder.*]

BIBLIOGRAPHY

Adamson, Andy, and Clare Lidbury, eds. *Kurt Jooss*. Birmingham, 1994.

Coton, A. V. *The New Ballet: Kurt Jooss and His Ork.* London, 1946.

Hodgins, Paul. *Relationships between Score and Choreography in Twentieth-Century Dance.* Lewiston, N.Y., 1992.

Holder, Christian. "Dancing for Jooss." *Choreography and Dance* 3.2 (1993): 79–91.
Jooss, Kurt. "The Dance of the Future." *The Dancing Times* (August 1933): 453–455.
Markard, Anna. "Kurt Jooss and His Work." *Ballet Review* 10 (Spring 1982): 15–67.
Markard, Anna, and Hermann Markard. *Jooss.* Cologne, 1985.
Walther, Suzanne K. "Kurt Jooss: The Evolution of an Artist." *Choreography and Dance* 3.2 (1993): 7–24.
Walther, Suzanne K. *The Dance of Death: Kurt Jooss and the Weimar Years.* Chur, Switzerland, 1994.

VIDEOTAPE. *The Green Table*, performed by the Joffrey Ballet, *Dance in America* (WNET-TV, New York, 1982).

BENGT HÄGER

JOSEPHSLEGENDE, DIE. French title: *La Légende de Joseph.* Ballet in one act. Choreography: Michel Fokine. Music: Richard Strauss. Libretto: Count Harry Kessler and Hugo von Hofmannsthal. Scenery: José Maria Sert. Costumes: Léon Bakst and Alexandre Benois. First performance: 14 May 1914, Théâtre National de l'Opéra, Paris, Ballets Russes de Serge Diaghilev. Principals: Léonide Massine (Joseph), Maria Kuznetsova (Potiphar's Wife), Vera Fokina (The Shulamite Woman), Alexis Bulgakov (Potiphar).

The plan for *Die Josephslegende* came into being in connection with the first appearance by the Ballets Russes at the Vienna Hofoperntheater in February and March 1912. In Vienna, Diaghilev became acquainted with Hugo von Hofmannsthal, who proposed a discussion with Richard Strauss concerning a composition to be choreographed and danced by Vaslav Nijinsky. In collaboration with Count Harry Kessler, Hofmannsthal prepared a libretto, basing it on the biblical story. Joseph, a naive and chaste shepherd boy, rejects the lascivious approaches of Potiphar's Wife. In the end, Joseph is taken up to God by an angel, while Potiphar's Wife strangles herself with her pearl necklace.

According to Alexandre Benois's plan, the setting would be a Venetian doge's court in the style of Paolo Veronese, around 1530. Because of the excessive scenery, the librettists limited themselves to only one danced role, that of Joseph, while Potiphar's Wife was conceived as a mime role. With Nijinsky's departure from the company in 1913, Michel Fokine did the choreography while the company was on tour, but not even he could convert the sumptuous spectacle into a dance success. Joseph was danced by the very young, still technically weak Léonide Massine. After the Paris premiere, several performances were given in London, with Tamara Karsavina as the Shulamite Woman and Maria Carmi in the mime role of Potiphar's Wife. Then *Die Josephslegende* disappeared from the repertory of the Ballets Russes.

In 1920, Strauss asked the Berlin State Opera to try to restage his ballet. Heinrich Kröller created a primarily pantomime version in a purist setting by Emil Pirchan on 4 February 1921, which was repeated on 19 August at the Munich State Opera. This version received its first performance at the Vienna State Opera on 18 March 1922, under Strauss's direction. Performances in Prague and Leipzig followed.

Die Josephslegende became a significant and continuing part of the Vienna State Opera Ballet's repertory. New productions of Kröller's version were created by Margarete Wallmann on 28 October 1936 and Willy Fränzl on 9 February 1943. Erika Hanka created an expressive choreography, which made more use of dancing, for the Vienna State Opera Ballet at the Theater an der Wien on 17 September 1949, revived on 27 March 1956 at the home theater. John Neumeier was the first to rework the libretto and to create a purely dance version of the work, with staging by Ernst Fuchs and starring Judith Jamison and Kevin Haigen, which had its premiere at the Vienna State Opera on 11 February 1977.

Other productions have been choreographed: by George Balanchine, in 1931 for the Royal Theater, Copenhagen; by Wallmann for the Teatro Colón in Buenos Aires in 1938; by Heinz Rosen in 1958 for the Munich State Opera and in the same year by Antony Tudor for the Teatro Colón. In 1992 there were two productions, one by Bernd Roger Bienert for the Zurich Opera and one by Heinz Spoerli for the Düsseldorf-Duisberg Ballet.

BIBLIOGRAPHY

Amort, Andrea. "Die Geschichte des Balletts der Wiener Staatsoper, 1918–1942." Ph.D. diss., University of Vienna, 1981.
Ballette von John Neumeier. Munich, 1980.
Buckle, Richard. *Diaghilev.* New York, 1979.
Manor, Giora. "The Bible as Dance." *Dance Magazine* (December 1978):55–86.

ANDREA AMORT
Translated from German

JOSEPH THE BEAUTIFUL. Russian title: *Iosef Prekrasny.* Ballet in two acts, five scenes. Choreography: Kasyan Goleizovsky. Music: Sergei Vasilenko. Scenery and costumes: Boris Erdman. First performance: 3 March 1925, Experimental Theater, Moscow, Bolshoi Ballet. Principals: Vasily Efimov (Joseph), Lubov Bank (Queen Tayakh), Aleksei Bulgakov (Pharaoh Potiphar).

Goleizovsky was invited to stage *Joseph the Beautiful* at the Bolshoi after he had made his mark as a bold experimenter, having produced in the space of several years a series of short ballets and concert pieces for various dance and ballet companies, including his own troupe, Moscow Chamber Ballet. *Joseph the Beautiful*, which was an extension of what Goleizovsky had done outside the academic theaters, crowned his choreographic explorations, elevating them to a higher artistic plane. Goleizovsky based the libretto on the biblical story of the young shepherd,

Joseph, who was sold into slavery by his own brothers. At the court of Pharaoh Potiphar, Joseph attracted the attention of Queen Tayakh but refused to respond to her amorous overtures. The vindictive Tayakh retaliated by accusing him of encroaching on her honor. Upon learning this, an enraged Pharaoh ordered Joseph executed. This story appealed to Goleizovsky because of its stark contrasts between lofty, inspired spirituality and brute force (act 1), despotism, and arbitrary rule (act 2).

Act 1 contains a characterization of the poetic youth (his variation with the reed pipe opens the ballet) and of the serene world in which he grew up (the bucolic dance of girls and youths and a ritual Jewish dance, among others). The idyll is rudely interrupted by the arrival of a traders' caravan, followed by the perfidious attack on Joseph by his brothers, who then sell him to the traders. In act 2 the dances performed by Pharaoh's retinue to celebrate his might and invincibility are ornamental and devoid of individuality. In this sterile world Joseph, despite his suffering and his downtrodden status, is the only living person with a rich inner sensibility, and this makes him free even in captivity.

Erdman created constructivist designs and stage sets for the ballet, which contained no concrete indication of the place of action (the Hills of Canaan) but did evoke the correct period atmosphere. The stage construction for the first act was an installation of several small platforms, straight and inclined, placed at different levels but articulated and joined with bridges. In one of the dances the participants formed a garland of standing, sitting, and recumbent figures spreading low over the floor, extending from the lower to the higher parts of the structure and twining along the slopes. The dancers held hands to form the coils of the garland and to emphasize the spiritual unity of a free people. In the second act the structure on the stage was also made up of platforms and ramps forming a monumental pyramid. Atop the pyramid stood the mighty figure of Pharaoh, a tall tiara on his head, his arms spread like the wings of a giant bird of prey. This represented a repressed world, where everything is strictly regimented and lifeless and where any manifestation of individuality is brutally suppressed. Groups of Pharaoh's courtiers, slaves, warriors, and women harpists formed a strictly symmetrical ornament, petrified in solemn immobility. The dull uniformity of a profusion of similar shapes and forms was designed to show that any internal contradictions were ruled out.

The creative alliance between the choreographer and the designer conferred on the ballet a well-thought-out production design, logical composition, and stylistic purity. Goleizovsky used free dance movements that were sufficiently complex to demand from the dancers a high standard of excellence in classical technique. Movement combinations and the organization of the dancers into sculptural groups exhibited an exceptional variety and diversity. The groups moved following a strict rhythmic pattern. One pose would flow into another to form a new dance pattern. Everything was carefully prearranged: each turn of the head, position of the hands, and angle of extended legs. There were neither purely classical nor purely ethnographic dances in *Joseph the Beautiful*. Goleizovsky, Vasilenko, and Erdman made no attempt to achieve ethnographic authenticity either in the choreog-

JOSEPH THE BEAUTIFUL. A scene from act 1, showing the Egyptians subduing a rebellious slave. The ballet caused controversy not only for its unrestrained eroticism but also for its purely constructivist aesthetic. (Photograph from the A.A. Bakhrushin Central State Theatrical Museum, Moscow; courtesy of Elizabeth Souritz.)

raphy or in the costumes. Only details suggested national motifs in the dances. In the costumes such motifs unexpectedly became an eccentric device in the style of the 1920s. The women's wigs, with their straight hair and bangs, recalled both Egyptian drawings and fashionable hairstyles. The clothing used asymmetry: a clasp on one side, a bodice set on one shoulder, a lace twining around only one leg. The ornaments were also asymmetrically arranged to create unexpected shifts and contrast spots. This served to emphasize the dynamism of color and form, which was characteristic of urbanist art of the twentieth century rather than the art of ancient Egypt.

Joseph the Beautiful generated a good deal of bitter controversy within the Bolshoi Theater company. While the younger dancers hailed it as a welcome innovation that opened up new vistas for development, the adherents of ballet academism agitated against it. When, under their pressure, alterations began to be introduced into the ballet (e.g., barefoot dancing was banned and all the members of the cast were ordered to wear standard ballet tights) the conflict erupted and went down in the annals of the Bolshoi Ballet as the "youth rebellion." More than seventy young members of the company signed a protest, contesting in particular the credentials of the conservative Vasily Tikhomirov to head the company. Eventually the academists won out; by the end of the 1920s a return to the more traditional forms in art was a universal trend. *Joseph the Beautiful* marked the peak of Goleizovsky's achievements at the Bolshoi Theater but was quickly dropped from the repertory. Goleizovsky staged *Joseph the Beautiful* in Odessa in 1926 and also in Kharkov in 1928.

BIBLIOGRAPHY

Chernova, Natalia, and Vera Vasilyeva, comps. *Kasian Goleizovskii.* Moscow, 1984.

Lawson, Joan. "A Short History of the Soviet Ballet, 1917–1943." *Dance Index* 2 (June–July 1943): 77–96.

Manor, Giora. "Kasyan Goleizovsky's Russian Revolution" (parts 1–2). *Dance Magazine* (January–February 1989).

Manor, Giora. "Goleizovsky's *Joseph the Beautiful:* A Modern Ballet before Its Time." *Choreography and Dance* 2.3 (1992): 63–70.

Souritz, Elizabeth. *Soviet Choreographers in the 1920s.* Translated by Lynn Visson. Durham, N.C., 1990.

ELIZABETH SOURITZ

JUBA, MASTER (William Henry Lane; born c.1825 in Rhode Island, died c.1852 in London), originator of American tap dance. Although *juba* was an honorary title awarded to fine minstrel dancers, in tap dance history the name "Master Juba" refers specifically to this extraordinary black artist, whose early contributions to tap dance were seminal in the development of the form. Born a freeman, Lane spent his young adolescence in Manhattan's Five Points neighborhood, where he mastered traditional Irish jig and clog dancing and then developed his own legendary style. Some historians believe that Lane was the young dancer described by Charles Dickens in his *Travels in America* (1841).

A renowned champion of important minstrel dance contests, Lane performed with four prominent, early minstrel companies, a potent testament to his artistic brilliance, as blacks were not normally allowed to perform with whites on the stage. In 1848 he traveled with Pell's Ethiopian Serenaders to England, where he took London by storm. English critics, well versed in traditional jig and clog dancing, noted that Juba did not just recycle those dances, but that he danced in a manner never before seen, presenting rhythms never before heard. By blending the techniques of jig and clog dancing with powerful African-American percussions and performance styles, Lane had perfected a dance hybrid that would quickly evolve into American tap dance.

Finding Europe to be a more welcoming place for himself and his art, Lane became one of the first expatriate black dancers. He married an English woman and did not return to the United States. Although Lane died while still a young man, his excellence and influence were so profound that he is acknowledged as the earliest-named father of American tap dance.

BIBLIOGRAPHY

Emery, Lynne Fauley. *Black Dance from 1619 to Today.* 2d rev. ed. Princeton, 1988.

Nathan, Hans. *Dan Emmett and the Rise of Early Negro Minstrelsy.* Norman, Okla., 1962.

Stearns, Marshall, and Jean Stearns. *Jazz Dance.* Rev. ed. New York, 1994.

Winter, Marian Hannah. "Juba and American Minstrelsy." In *Chronicles of the American Dance: From the Shakers to Martha Graham,* edited by Paul Magriel. New York, 1948.

SALLY R. SOMMER

JUDSON DANCE THEATER. A cooperative for avant-garde choreography, the Judson Dance Theater began in the summer of 1962, when a group of young choreographers presented, at Judson Memorial Church in Greenwich Village, a concert of dances composed for Robert Dunn's choreography class. Dunn had taken a course in experimental music theory taught by John Cage and was invited by Cage to teach a choreography class along the same lines at the Merce Cunningham studio in the Living Theater building.

A Concert of Dance, presented on 6 July 1962, was open to the public free of charge and lasted for several hours, with twenty-three dances by fourteen choreographers. Though some were members of Cunningham's company and several more studied at his studio, these choreographers were not all dancers by training. Some were visual artists, composers, and filmmakers; the interdisciplinary nature of Judson Dance Theater would continue to be a striking feature of the cooperative.

In the autumn of 1962 the group formed a workshop to show choreography privately for criticism and publicly in concerts. The workshop met weekly, first at Yvonne Rainer's studio and then at the Judson Church. Over the course of the next two years, nearly two hundred dances were given by the Judson Dance Theater, as the group called itself by April 1963, either at the church itself or under the group's auspices in other locations.

Influences on the Judson Dance Theater include Cunningham, Cage, Anna Halprin, James Waring, Simone Forti, and other avant-garde choreographers of the 1950s, as well as other artistic movements, such as Fluxus and happenings. After the cooperative unofficially disbanded in the summer of 1964, more work was presented by Waring and his dancers (including Toby Armour, Deborah Lee, Charles Stanley, Gretchen MacLane, Joan Baker, and

Eddie Barton), as well as by original members of the workshop (including Yvonne Rainer, Steve Paxton, David Gordon, Deborah Hay, Arlene Rothlein, Carolee Schneemann, Trisha Brown, Elaine Summers, and Sally Gross) and a second generation of Judson choreographers (including Meredith Monk, Kenneth King, and Phoebe Neville).

The choreographers of the Judson Dance Theater radically questioned established dance aesthetics, both in their dances and in the weekly workshop discussions. They rejected the conventions of both ballet and modern dance. They not only carried out experiments that called for a new theory of dance but also initiated political changes in the dance world and discovered methods of working collaboratively with musicians, designers, and one another. Attracting a grassroots audience of Greenwich Village artists and intellectuals, the Judson Dance Theater flourished as a popular center of radical experimentation.

The Judson aesthetic was never monolithic; it was deliberately undefined and unrestricted. However, eventually a number of specific themes and styles arose, just as several choreographers emerged as the most productive

JUDSON DANCE THEATER. An environmental sculpture by Charles Ross forms the context for *A Collaborative Event*, performed in the sanctuary of Judson Memorial Church, New York, on 11 November 1963. (Photograph © 1963 by Peter Moore; used by permission.)

and influential. A commitment to democratic methods and to the collective process led to choreographic strategies that metaphorically stood for freedom: improvisation, spontaneous determination, and chance. The highly refined historical consciousness of the choreographic process also led to the making of reflexive dances that, through satire, movement quotation, and verbal commentary, raised questions about dance in the dances themselves. Questions of technique and its perfection were less important than formal problems for both practical and theoretical reasons: well-trained dancers were not always available, but also, these choreographers were committed to a democratic embrace of ordinary bodies in their dances.

Perhaps the most important legacy of Judson Dance Theater was the attitude that anything might be looked at as a dance—not only the activities of a dancer but also those of a visual artist, a musician, or everyday people. This redefinition of dance was strongly articulated in Jill Johnston's dance reviews in the *Village Voice*.

Three strands of what would later be called postmodern dance grew out of Judson Dance Theater's initial, permissive stage. One strand was the analytic, reductive work (by such choreographers as Rainer, Paxton, Robert Morris, and Lucinda Childs) that tested theories of dance as an innovative modern art. A second strand was a theatri-

cal, baroque, often humorous style (by Gordon, Rothlein, and Fred Herko); a third was multimedia work (by Summers, Judith Dunn, and Philip Corner).

BIBLIOGRAPHY
Ballet Review 1.6 (1967). Judson issue.
Banes, Sally. *Democracy's Body: Judson Dance Theater, 1962–64.* Ann Arbor, Mich., 1983.
Carmines, Al. "In the Congregation of Art: The Judson Dance Theatre." *Dance Scope* (Fall–Winter 1967–1968): 25–31.
Dunn, Robert. "Judson Days." *Contact Quarterly* 14 (Winter 1989): 9–13.
Johnston, Jill. "The New American Modern Dance." In *The New American Arts,* edited by Richard Kostelanetz. New York, 1967.
Johnston, Jill. *Marmalade Me.* New York, 1971.
McDonagh, Don. *The Rise and Fall and Rise of Modern Dance.* Rev. ed. Pennington, N.J., 1990.
Paxton, Steve. "Performance and Reconstruction of Judson." *Contact Quarterly* 7 (Spring/Summer 1982): 56–58.
Perron, Wendy, et al. *Judson Dance Theater, 1962–1966.* Bennington, Vt., 1981.
Rainer, Yvonne. *Work, 1961–1973.* Halifax, N.S., 1974.
Schneemann, Carolee. *More Than Meat Joy.* New Paltz, N.Y., 1979.
Siegel, Marcia B. "The Death of Some Alternatives." *Ballet Review* 10 (Fall 1982): 76–80.

SALLY BANES

JUMPS. *For discussion of jumps and leaps in ballet, see-* Ballet Technique, *article on* Jumping Movements.

K

KABUKI THEATER. The Japanese word *kabuki* is now written with Chinese characters meaning "song-dance-skill," but in Japan it originally bore the connotation of something shocking, deviant, or offbeat. Until the late nineteenth century, *kabuki* was written with the characters for "song-dance-prostitute," because of its close association with the pleasure quarters. *Kabuki* is Japan's most popular classical theater form, although its status in the twentieth century has been consistently threatened by mass-media entertainment and rapid cultural change. The major center for *kabuki* is Tokyo, but it may also be seen, if less regularly, in such cities as Kyoto and Osaka. Rural performances are also given by semiprofessionals and amateurs.

History. When *kabuki* was created, at the beginning of the seventeenth century, the predominant performance forms in Japan were *nō* and *kyōgen;* they were produced for and enjoyed by the samurai ruling class. *Kabuki* emerged to serve the needs of the common people in growing urban centers: Edo (now Tokyo), Osaka, and Kyoto were then, as now, the chief production centers. In 1603, the foundations for early *kabuki* were established when a renegade female attendant of the Izumo Shrine named Okuni gained widespread notoriety for herself and her mainly female company doing personalized interpretations of popular contemporary dances called *furyū odori*. Dramatic and comedic elements were soon added; Okuni's early performances were held mainly in dry riverbeds, where makeshift theaters were erected. [*See the entry on Okuni.*]

Kabuki was a product of the Tokugawa shogunate of the Edo period (1603–1867), a period known by the name of the feudal military dictatorship that ruled Japan and which, from 1639 to 1853, kept the nation isolated from all but the most inconsequential outside influence.

Early *kabuki* had several stages. At first it was primarily *onna kabuki*, an accomplishment of female prostitute troupes who used its sensual dances and erotic scenes to advertise their services. Then, in 1629, when women were banned from performing *kabuki*—because of the disruptive audience behavior that was provoked—it became *wakashu kabuki*, young men's *kabuki*, and their appeal, too, was essentially erotic. Only in 1652, when the government forbade performances until *kyōgen* (a farce play) be-

came a performance basis and actors shaved off their alluring, youthful forelocks did *kabuki* begin to make serious artistic progress.

Chief among the new playwrights whose literary skills helped deepen *kabuki*'s thematic and stylistic qualities was Chikamatsu Monzaemon (1653–1724), best known for his contributions to the emerging rival performance form, *bunraku*, puppet theater. Outstanding actors soon specialized in *kabuki*, and their skill and technique became the basis for acting methods still seen today. In Edo, the capital, Ichikawa Danjūrō I (1660–1704) founded both a family line and a specialized *kabuki* dramatic form—the superhuman, exaggerated, heroic theatrical style called *aragoto* (meaning "rough business"). Sakata Tōjūrō (1647–1709) of the Kyoto-Osaka area exemplified a subtle, more realistic style known as *wagoto*. The prohibition against women onstage led to the development of the *onnagata* (female impersonator); an important early *onnagata* was Yoshizawa Ayame (1673–1729), who wrote a valuable treatise on the subject. [*See* Onnagata.]

During the eighteenth century, a process of artistic give and take existed between *kabuki* and the puppet theater; a significant number of *kabuki*'s greatest plays were adapted from puppet theater originals (puppet theater, peaked in the eighteenth century). The most famous example is *Chūshingura* (1748) by Takeda Izumo, Miyoshi Shōraku, and Namiki Sōsuke. The two principal dramatic genres of "history play" *(jidaimono)* and "realistic play of daily life" *(sewamono)* emerged around this time, to form a trio with the dance-play genre called *shosagoto* or *buyō geki*. [*See* Jidaimono.] In the nineteenth century, the influence of *nō* and *kyōgen* was strongly felt, and *kabuki* began to adapt plays from these forms. *Kanjinchō* (1840), perhaps *kabuki*'s most often performed dance play, was the first.

Theater. In the first century and a half of *kabuki*, the architectural features that evolved remained to form one of its most distinguishing aspects. These included elevator traps for actors and sets, the revolving stage, and the runway through the audience (the *hanamichi*). Situated on the stage right side of the house, the *hanamichi* was originally paired with a narrower one on stage left, but the use of two runways is only seen today in special revivals. The runway is used for all major exits and entrances. It is of-

KABUKI THEATER. (*above*) The love scene from the *kabuki* drama *Naozamurai*, with Ichikawa Danjūrō XII (seated) as Naozamurai and Onoe Kikugorō VII (standing) as Michitose. (*below*) A closer view of the young lovers. Danjuro XII excels in romantic leads and has made Naozamurai one of his most famous roles. Kiguroro VII, seen here as an *onnagata*, is equally admired for his performances in both male and female roles. (Photographs courtesy of Samuel L. Leiter.)

ten the locale of important processions, and important pieces of acting are performed at a spot on it seven-tenths the distance from the rear of the theater to the stage. An elevator trap is also found at this spot, used for magical entrances and disappearances. [*See* Hanamichi.]

Kabuki playwrights belonged to the staff of a specific theater. They wrote about various themes, including the travails of lovers, divided loyalties, filial piety, and revenge—but social and political topics could only be dealt with by implication; legal pressures forced playwrights to historicize tales dealing with the samurai class and to disguise the names of samurai characters. For their plots, writers might only draw freely from a number of fixed "worlds" *(sekai)* of recognizable characters and backgrounds.

The early nineteenth century, a period of social decadence in Japan, was reflected in plays that became preoccupied with ghosts, murders, robberies, the world of the demimonde, and trick production techniques. A major development was the emphasis on multiple role-playing by a star who might, through quick changes, perform many widely disparate roles—male and female, old and young—in the same piece.

Kabuki's last great playwright was Kawatake Mokuami (1816–1893), whose career overlaps the final days of the Tokugawa shogunate and the following era, the Meiji (1868–1912), during which the emperor was restored to power and Japan responded to new contacts with the West. New Japanese theater forms did arise reflecting Western influence—but *kabuki* virtually froze in its tracks. Some plays of the Meiji era achieved an interesting blend of conventional *kabuki* and Western realism.

Performance Techniques. *Kabuki* thrives on its traditional techniques of performance, called *kata*, and theatergoers take pleasure in discerning the differences in interpretation of the classical *kata*, as demonstrated by leading actors. Actor training is intense and ongoing; *kabuki* actors are born into or adopted into the profession; they begin training in early childhood. An actor bears a name with a number that marks his place in the family hierarchy, so great respect is shown for the artistic legacy of the family. Actors learn a variety of vocal methods, musical instruments, and dance styles. Much of their training is through continual observation of others.

Actors usually specialize in certain role types, yet some take pride in their versatility at playing many types. Principal male types include good men *(tachiyaku)*, evil men *(katakiyaku)*, and comic men *(dōkegata* or *sanmaime)*; females include young women *(wakaonnagata)*, middle-aged women *(kashagata)*, and old women *(fuke oyama)*. Each character has a traditional costume and makeup. The most unusual makeups belong to heros of the *aragoto* style. These characters wear colorful lines painted on their faces to emphasize their dramatic expressions; this makeup, which has various symbolic associations, is called *kumadori*.

Costumes *(ishō)* offer the viewer an array of gorgeous patterns, fabrics, and colors. They range from the highly stylized to the realistic and, for the most part, resemble those worn during the years of the Tokugawa shogunate. The main element is the kimono, for men and women, but the variations in usage are endless. Costumes reveal social class, sex, age, and various character qualities. Several striking techniques for quick onstage costume changes are used, most notably the *hikinuki*, whereby a stage assistant whisks away an entire outer garment to reveal another underneath. A dance like the hour-and-a-half

Musume Dōjōji (Maiden of Dojoji) makes extensive use of this method. Wigs are of great importance to *kabuki*, and one can tell by the style of the wig much about its wearer.

Actors are aided in their performances by a black robed-and-hooded assistant called the *kurogo* or *kurombo*. When the piece is a dance, the assistant is usually dressed in formal kimono and is called the *kōken*. The *kōken*, unlike the *kurogo*, makes no attempt to emphasize his invisibility by hiding behind props or actors. Each hands the actor or dancer props, takes them away when they are not being used, adjusts costumes and wigs, and even prompts when necessary.

Kabuki acting ranges from the fantastical to the illusionistic. The actor may engage in symbolic movements or behave in a relatively realistic fashion. The basis for all *kabuki* movement is dance, which is appropriate for a form owing its origins to a dancer. All Japanese classical theater forms began in dance, and unlike their Western counterparts, never forgot this heritage. The beginnings of Japanese theater are traditionally observed in the mythical dance of the goddess Ame-no-Uzume, who did some lively erotic stepping on an overturned tub to lure another deity out of a cave. Japanese dance went through numerous manifestations, a great many still observed, before culminating in the most wide practiced of classical Japanese dance arts, that seen in *kabuki*.

Dance. Kabuki dance is formally known as *nihon buyō* (Japanese dance) or *kabuki buyō*. The word *buyō* is written with characters for two other vital dance words, *mai* and *odori*. *Mai* is generally used to refer to pre-*kabuki* classical dance movements, such as those used in *nō*; it implies a circular or rotational style using a sliding step. *Odori*, more commonly used in connection with *kabuki* dance, suggests a light, leaping or jumping method. *Mai* and *odori*, along with the wide range of mime called *furi*, constitute the foundation of *nihon buyō*.

Within the broad heading of *nihon buyō* as applied specifically to *kabuki* are works that are pure dance and others that are dance dramas. Pure dance pieces are generally called *buyō* and include *Kagamijishi* (Mirror Lion) and *Fujimusume* (Wisteria Maiden). Dance dramas are usually called *buyō geki* or *shosagoto* (*keigoto* in the Kyoto-Osaka area). More specifically, *buyō geki* refers to dance plays provided with a *shamisen* (3-stringed musical instrument) and a chanter for narrative accompaniment (*jōruri*). The major *jōruri* styles are *tokiwazu*, *kiyomoto*, and *gidayū bushi*. *Jōruri* styles emphasize narrative content. *Nagauta*, another very important musical genre used in dance, is more lyrical in content. [*See* Nagauta.]

In addition to dances seen as independent program pieces, dance is often incorporated within the structure of a dramatic play. Dance passages that are clearly marked off from conventionally realistic acting are seen at moments of heightened emotion; they are classified according to the specific dramaturgic purposes they fulfill. There is, for example, the lamentation dance (*kudoki*), as presented in *Shunkan*, or the travel dance (*michiyuki*), as presented in the double suicide plays of Chikamatsu. Related to these are the mimed sequences that are dance based, varying from play to play in their degree of musicality and complexity. Among these are the pantomime scenes (*danmari*), *hanamichi* entrances (*de*), battle scenes

KABUKI THEATER. This scene from *Bentenkozō* shows a gang of five dashing bandits lined up in gorgeous costumes at the bank of the Inase River. Each delivers a boastful speech of self-identification before the group, battling with umbrellas only, engages in a stylized fight scene (*tachimawari*) with policemen. (Photograph courtesy of Samuel L. Leiter.)

KABUKI THEATER. Nakamura Ganjirō II as Chiyo (left) and Kataoka Nizaemon XIII as Genzō in *Terakoya*. (Photograph courtesy of Samuel L. Leiter.)

(tachimawari), bounding exits *(roppō)*, and rhythmic poses *(mie)*.

Japanese dance pieces are classified according to various criteria. *Kabuki* has many dance genres. A dance may be classified by its type of musical accompaniment *(nagauta, jōruri,* etc.); its subject matter (works about the legend of the maiden at Dōjō Temple are *dōjōjimono* and those about lions are *shakkyōmono*); its theatrical mode (pieces borrowed from the *nō* or *kyōgen* theaters and staged in a manner resembling their sources are *matsubamemono*, the "pine-tree background" dances); its unique techniques (*hengemono* are transformation dances with multiple role changes by a star performer; once they allowed up to twelve characters but now usually show only one of the originals in a separate piece); or its general background (*kyōranmono* depict characters who have gone mad, *michiyukimono* show travelers to an important destination), and so on.

Kabuki dance pieces are usually performed on special dance platforms *(shosa butai)* that are placed over the stage floor. These facilitate the conventional sliding foot movements with their smooth surfaces, and the hollow structure allows the frequent foot-stamping movements to resonate well. The dancer almost always wears *tabi* socks; sandals or other footwear are rarely worn. The female dances ordinarily present gently waving hand movements, accentuated by the long kimono sleeves, with gliding foot movements, the knees pressed closely together, and the feet in a mildly pigeon-toed position. The male dances often present vigorous arm movements and foot stamping. Most dances are solo specialties, some employ duets, and a few have group choreography. Solo dances are confined within a very small area of the stage, thereby intensifying the impact of the performer.

Kabuki dance is ruled by strict traditions, which are supervised by various "schools" *(ryū)* led by headmasters known as *iemoto*. The most well known of the numerous schools and branches are the Bandō, Fujima, Hanayagi, Ichikawa, Nakamura, Nishikawa, Saruwaka, and Tachibana. [*See* Japanese Traditional Schools.]

Music. Music is important to *kabuki* dance, and it plays a pervasive role in *kabuki* works without dance as well. An enormous number of musical techniques have been developed to accompany dramatic acting. Much of this music is played from an offstage room at stage right, called the *geza. Geza* music can be both atmospheric or literal—as, for example, when it imitates the sound of waves, bells, or rain. In many instances the musicians appear on stage, formally dressed; this is most evident in dance pieces where an entire orchestra may be seen seated in rows on platforms covered in red.

The Present. Kabuki is studied today for its literary qualities, but for most of its history it was appreciated chiefly for its theatrical values. Its focus has remained on the actor, a master of vocal, physical, and emotional arts, who is among the world's most well-trained of performing artists. He has at his disposal an arsenal of techniques that allow him to perform in an eclectic variety of styles. He can play either with recognizable realism or with highly suggestive and abstract mime. His use of the fan typifies this diversity of approaches: in ordinary use, the fan can be employed to cool his brow or shade his eyes; used symbolically, it can be the rising moon, a sake bottle, a bow from which an arrow springs, a sword, a flowing river.

Kabuki is valued in Japan as opera is valued in the West. It is loved rabidly by a dwindling body of fans, but most other Japanese merely pay it lip service as an important cultural artifact that does not speak to their immediate concerns. When a great star appears today with unique talents and personal attributes, such as the female impersonator Bandō Tamasaburō V, the form attracts many newly interested spectators. [*See the entry on Bandō Tamasaburō.*] This is not unlike the stimulus an opera star, like Luciano Pavarotti, can have on his art. Like opera, *kabuki* is very expensive to produce, and admission prices are generally very high. A top orchestra seat in 1995 cost about $160. World interest in *kabuki* has grown in the post–World War II years, however, guaranteeing it an international fame and increased understanding; it is sure to survive for many years to come.

[*For further general discussion, see* Asian Dance Traditions, *overview article;* Costume in Asian Traditions; Japan, *overview article;* Mask and Makeup, *article on* Asian Traditions; *and* Music for Dance, *article on* Asian

Traditions. *For stylized combat in* kabuki, *see* Asian Martial Arts. *See also entries on Azuma Tokuho, Kataoka Takao, and Matsumoto Kōshirō and the entries under the following lineages and family names: Bandō, Fujima, Ichikawa, Onoe, and Nakamura.*]

BIBLIOGRAPHY

Arnott, Peter D. *The Theatres of Japan.* London, 1969.

Bowers, Faubion. *Japanese Theatre.* New York, 1952.

Brandon, James R., trans. *Kabuki: Five Classic Plays.* Cambridge, Mass., 1975.

Brandon, James R., et al. *Studies in Kabuki: Its Acting, Music, and Historical Context.* Honolulu, 1978.

Cavaye, Ronald. *Kabuki: A Pocket Guide.* Rutland, Vt., 1993.

Dunn, Charles J., and Bunzo Torigoe, trans. and eds. *The Actors' Analects.* New York, 1969.

Ernst, Earle. *The Kabuki Theatre.* New York, 1956.

Halford, Aubrey S., and Giovanna M. Halford. *The Kabuki Handbook.* Rutland, Vt., 1956.

Kincaid, Zoë. *Kabuki: The Popular Stage in Japan.* New York, 1925.

Leiter, Samuel L., trans. and comp. *The Art of Kabuki: Famous Plays in Performance.* Westport, Conn., 1979.

Leiter, Samuel L. *Kabuki Encyclopedia: An English-Language Adaptation of "Kabuki Jiten."* Westport, Conn., 1979.

Malm, William P. *Nagauta: The Heart of Kabuki Music.* Rutland, Vt., 1964.

Masakatsu, Gunji. *Kabuki.* Translated by John Bester. 2d ed. Tokyo, 1985.

Masakatsu, Gunji. *Buyo: The Classical Dance.* Translated by Don Kenny. New York, 1970.

Masakatsu, Gunji. *The Kabuki Guide.* Translated by Christopher Holmes. Tokyo, 1987.

Pronko, Leonard C. *Guide to Japanese Drama.* 2d ed. Boston, 1984.

Scott, A. C. *The Kabuki Theatre of Japan.* New York, 1955.

Shaver, Ruth M. *Kabuki Costume.* Rutland, Vt., 1966.

Toita Yasuji. *Kabuki: The Popular Stage.* New York, 1971.

SAMUEL L. LEITER

KADMAN, GURIT (also known as Gert Kaufmann; born 3 March 1897 in Leipzig, died 20 March 1987 in Jerusalem), folklorist. Kadman galvanized both Israelis and their institutions to create a native folk dance genre. Although criticized for breaking tradition, in which folk dance evolves over time, Kadman maintained that "for people who fervently wished to have dances of our own in our lifetime, there was no other choice."

She first collected folklore as a member of the German youth movement Wandervogel. In 1920 she and her husband moved to a kibbutz in Ottoman Palestine, then to Tel Aviv. She taught gymnastics and dance in schools and kibbutzim and in 1931 organized the Teachers Association for Physical Culture. In 1944 Kadman was invited by Kibbutz Dalia to create a Shavu'ot harvest festival. Convinced of the importance of a national folk dance movement, she used the occasion to gather two hundred folk dancers. They gave a gala performance, directed by Kadman, which became known as the Dalia Festival. She also directed the Dalia Festivals of 1947 and 1951, each time requiring new dances and thereby providing a stage, stimulus, and direction for their development.

In 1945 Kadman established the Israel Folk Dance Committee of the Histadrut (the national labor organization) and wrote most of its manuals and main history of folk dance (*Am roked,* 1969). She directed Ha-Poel, the first Israeli folk dance company, which she took to tour Europe in 1947. Always an innovator, she taught dance to the army, used radio for national folk dance instruction, and stimulated folk dance curricula through Israel's Ministry of Culture and Education.

Interested in preserving Jewish ethnic dance, she filmed Jewish immigrants from elsewhere in the Middle East and from North Africa when they arrived in Israel to settle. In 1972 she initiated the Israel Ethnic Dance Project in collaboration with the Ministry of Culture and Education, the folklore department of the Hebrew University of Jerusalem, and the Histadrut. The project revived Jewish Kurdish dance in particular. On 7 May 1981 Kadman received the prestigious Israel Prize for her contribution to the creation of Israeli folk dance. Her daughter, Ayalah Goren, is also an Israeli folk dance leader, researcher, and producer of performances and folk dance festivals. Since Kadman's death, she has become revered in Israel and her work has gained in stature.

BIBLIOGRAPHY

Friedhaber, Zvi. *Kadman—Em vekalah* (Kadman: Mother and Bride). Haifa, 1989.

Kadman, Gurit. *Am roked.* Jerusalem, 1969.

Kadman, Gurit, and Pamela Squires, eds. *Five Kurdish Dances.* Tel Aviv, 1977.

Kadman, Gurit. *Rikudi edot be-Yisrael.* Givatayim, 1982.

Kaufmann, Gert, comp. *Palestine Folkdance Series.* Nos. 1–6. Tel Aviv, 1945–1947.

Rikud etni be-Yisrael. Israel Ethnic Dance Project, vols. 1–3. Jerusalem, 1977–1979.

FILMS. Gurit Kadman, *The Dances of Israel's Ethnic Groups* (1951, 1962, 1969).

JUDITH BRIN INGBER

KAGURA. The first dances recorded in Japanese sources, *kagura* originally constituted a substantial part of the shamanistic ritual of ancient Shintō worship. Today, the word *kagura* is used for many radically different kinds of dance performed throughout Japan.

Shintō, the aboriginal Japanese religious system, is composed of syncretized beliefs, institutions, and rituals that had developed in ancient, pre-Buddhist Japan from animism, polytheism, the cult of the emperor, and the worship of nature and fertility. From Japan's prehistory to the present, Shintō—alone or in combination with Confucian and Buddhist influences from China and Korea—has permeated the Japanese performing arts.

The term *kagura* is probably a euphonious contraction of *kam[u]kura* (the seat of the deity), referring to the place—in ancient times, a sturdy pillar—in which the powerful spirit *(kami)* dwells and from which it presides over or takes part in the performance. Later, the possessing god was believed to reside temporarily in the *torimono*—the objects (tree branches, paper pendants, swords) held by the *miko,* the shaman, during her or his trance dance.

Some of the *kagura* performed today still reflect a shamanistic origin, while others originated in and drew their form from later dance-drama genres such as *nō, kyōgen,* and *kabuki* or even from Western music and dance. Many *kagura* consist of two parts: first, a sequence of rituals of purification, conjuration of the gods, and hymns; second, an entertainment performed for the conjured spirits. While the first part of a *kagura* performance has often remained unchanged over centuries, the second part sometimes follows trends in contemporary entertainment.

There are two kinds of *kagura: mikagura* and *satokagura. Mikagura* are performed annually by court musicians *(gakunin)* at the Imperial Palace in the presence of the emperor, who functions as the high priest of Shintō worship. Today's *mikagura* represent a shortened though not essentially altered version of the courtly Shintō liturgy of the eleventh century; they consist of solemn, slow dances and hymns performed at night within the precincts of the Imperial Palace in an open courtyard before the Kashikodokoro, a shrine dedicated to the goddess Amaterasu.

All other *kagura* are referred to as *satokagura* (village *kagura*). These present an immense variety of (mostly) folk dances that follow local traditions and are performed by local talent. The three major traditions of *kagura* are the Izumo tradition, the Ise tradition, and the *shishi* tradition; the first two of these take their names from the geographical locales with which they are identified.

The Izumo tradition centers on the ritual of changing the straw mat in the abode of the local god. The division of the *kagura* performance into two parts (sacred ritual and fashionable entertainment) originated at Izumo and from there diffused all over Japan; a set of nineteenth-century plays that reenact ancient Shintō myths also developed at Izumo and has been widely diffused.

The Ise tradition centers on the ritual of boiling water *(yūdate)* and sprinkling it on the cult premises and spectators for the purpose of purification. *Kagura* from the Ise tradition are also known for their use of *torimono* hand props and masks.

The *shishi* (lion) tradition comprises dances that use lion masks and that include acrobatics and magic acts. In many cases, *kagura* performances in the *shishi* tradition include dance-plays derived from *nō* and *kyōgen.* At Shintō shrines today, many of the elegant, slow-paced dances performed by the white-and-orange-clad shrine maidens (today's *miko* are all female) incorporate choreographic elements introduced during Japan's period of modernization and Westernization, since the mid-nineteenth century.

[*See also* Japan, *article on* Ritual Dance; *and* Shishimai.]

KAGURA. The *yamabushi kagura* (also called *bangaku, gongenmai,* and *shishimai*) was developed by *yamabushi,* wandering ascetics who practiced an indigenous form of mountain worship. They performed rituals, sword dances, and masked dramas in local shrines and farmhouses. Here, in a theatrical setting, dancer Takashi Sasaki performs a *yamabushi kagura* called *The Dance of the Mountain Goddess.* (Photograph © by Jack Vartoogian; used by permission.)

BIBLIOGRAPHY

Blacker, Carmen. *The Catalpa Bow: A Study of Shamanistic Practices in Japan.* London, 1975.

Endress, Gerhild. "Kagura." In *Japan-Handbuch,* edited by Horst Hammitzsch. 2d ed. Wiesbaden, 1984.

Hoff, Frank. *Song, Dance, Storytelling: Aspects of the Performing Arts in Japan.* Ithaca, N.Y., 1978.

Honda Yasuji, ed. *Festivals of Japan.* Tokyo, 1972.

Immoos, Thomas. *Japanisches Theater.* Zürich, 1975.

Ortolani, Benito. *The Japanese Theatre: From Shamanistic Ritual to Contemporary Pluralism.* Rev. ed. Princeton, 1995.

Sadler, A. W. "*Okagura:* Field Notes on the Festival Drama in Modern Tokyo." *Asian Folklore Studies* 29 (1970).

Yoshinobu Inoura. *A History of Japanese Theater,* vol. 1, *Noh and Kyogen.* Yokohama, 1971.

BENITO ORTOLANI

KAIN, KAREN (born 28 March 1951 in Hamilton, Ontario), Canadian ballet dancer. Trained at the National Ballet School in Toronto from 1962 to 1969, Karen Kain joined the National Ballet of Canada on graduation, becoming a principal dancer two years later, in 1971. She rapidly established herself as a leading ballerina and became widely known across Canada, even to non-balletgoers. At the 1973 International Ballet Competition in Moscow, she won the silver medal for female soloist and, with fellow company member Frank Augustyn, the gold medal (first prize) for pas de deux. Her partnership with Augustyn proved enduringly popular with audiences, although she subsequently danced with many other partners.

Kain was a strong, tall dancer of great versatility, equally at home in classical roles and in contemporary ballets. Her extensive repertory included most of the leading ballerina roles in the classics, notably Aurora in *The Sleeping Beauty* and Odette-Odile in *Swan Lake.* Her marked gift for comedy, aided by an attractive and expressive face, was well shown as Lise in Frederick Ashton's *La Fille Mal Gardée* and as Swanilda in *Coppélia.* In the latter role she appeared in Roland Petit's production for the Ballet National de Marseille in 1975 as well as in Erik Bruhn's more traditional staging for the National Ballet of Canada in 1976.

During the 1970s, Kain's international reputation was established by her many guest appearances in Great Britain, Australia, and the United States, often with Rudolf Nureyev as partner. Roland Petit invited her as a frequent guest of his Ballet National de Marseille, creating for her not only the role of Swanilda in his *Coppélia* but the role of Albertine in *Les Intermittences du Coeur* (1974). She also created the title role in Petit's *Nana* (1976) with the Paris Opera Ballet and several roles in original ballets made for the National Ballet of Canada by Ann Ditchburn and Constantin Patsalas. In 1977 she and Augustyn appeared as guest artists in *Giselle* with the Bol-

KAIN. Striking beauty, dramatic intensity, musical sensitivity, and a strong classical technique were among the assets that Kain brought to her portrayal of Giselle. She is seen here in act 2, in a mid-1970s performance with the National Ballet of Canada. (Photograph from the Dance Collection, New York Public Library for the Performing Arts.)

shoi Ballet in Moscow and with ballet troupes in other cities in the Soviet Union.

Despite the wide acclaim and international celebrity Kain acquired during the 1970s, by 1980 she appeared to have reached an artistic plateau. She even considered quitting dance. However, by making herself a pliable and inspirational muse for choreographers—John Neumeier, Eliot Feld, Glen Tetley, and James Kudelka, among others—Kain continued to build a large repertory of created roles and, in the process, matured into an artist of exceptional dramatic and expressive power. Although her technique remained impressive well into her forties, Kain judiciously and successively chose to relinquish the major ballerina roles probably sooner than was necessary and instead concentrated on shorter ballets and on works created especially for her. As a result, the luster of her reputation remained untarnished. Ironically, by devoting herself almost exclusively to her home company at a time when its international touring to major dance capitals diminished, this rich period of her career received less widespread recognition than it deserved.

In 1994, James Kudelka created *The Actress* for Kain, a work that, while not specifically biographical, had obvious references to her career and that appeared to be a summary of its varied achievements. The following year, Kain announced her impending retirement, to take effect in October 1997 at the conclusion of an extensive cross-Canada farewell tour.

In recognition of her distinguished career, Kain has received numerous honors and awards. She was named a Companion of the Order of Canada in 1976, and she holds honorary doctoral degrees from York University, McMaster University, Trent University, and the University of British Columbia.

BIBLIOGRAPHY

Darling, Christopher, and John Fraser. *Kain and Augustyn.* Toronto, 1977.

Kain, Karen, with Stephen Godfrey and Penelope Reed Doob. *Movement Never Lies: An Autobiography.* Toronto, 1994.

Neufeld, James. *Power to Rise: The Story of the National Ballet of Canada.* Toronto, 1996.

Street, David, and David Mason. *Karen Kain: Lady of Dance.* Toronto, 1978.

Tobias, Tobi. "Karen Kain." *Dance Magazine* (May 1978): 50–55.

FILM AND VIDEOTAPE. Kain, partnered by Augustyn, appears in two ballets captured on videotape: *Giselle* (CBC-TV, 1976) and *La Fille Mal Gardée* (CBC-TV, 1979). She is the subject of *Karen Kain Superspecial* (CBC-TV, 1979), and she appears in *100th Anniversary of the Met* (PBS-TV, 1983), a special event televised from the Metropolian Opera House in New York, and in *Making Ballet* (CBC-TV, 1995).

MICHAEL CRABB

KAKUL. The renowned Indonesian performer I Nyoman Kakul is seen here in the role of Dalem, a refined king (*raja*), in a *topéng* performance in his home village of Batuan, Bali. (Photograph by Edward Herbst; used by permission.)

KAKUL, I NYOMAN (born 1905 in Bali, died 2 August 1982), Indonesian dancer, actor, and teacher. Born into a rice-farming family in the village of Batuan, I Nyoman Kakul at about the age of thirteen began performing *gandrung* and sacred *barong ngelawang* with roving village dance troupes. He specialized in the *barong bangkal* (boar) and *celeng* (pig), the costumes of which are made of woven coconut leaves and animated by two dancers. *Gandrung* involved a solo male dancer performing in a style related to *légong.* He also performed *arja telu,* an early, unadorned form of *arja* dance drama performed by only three dancer-actors, who would rove their own and neighboring villages for informal presentations. While involved in these itinerant dance genres, Kakul studied *gambuh* dance theater with I Dewa Ketut Gedit and Ida Bagus Kakiang Turuh. He next learned the male dance form *baris* from Anak Agung Gede Raka of Batuan; after having studied only about a month, the young Nyoman Kakul was being sought after as a performer of *baris* in Batuan and the nearby village of Sukawati. He was soon teaching *baris* as well. He studied *topéng* mask dance with Ida Pedanda, the Brahmana priest of Batuan, and *Jauk* with the Raja (traditional ruler) of Sukawati.

Nyoman Kakul has recounted that as he grew into adulthood, he was eager to have a wife and family, but worried about his uncertain livelihood. Once he had married Ni Made Suken and had two children, he sought out jobs and labored intensely, selling firewood, coconut oil, and rice, but still not making ends meet. He worked with a cart and ox, selling goods such as betelnut, sweet potatoes, and sugar cane. After his third child was born, Kakul was asked to teach *baris* at the royal residences and the palace in the district of Klungkung and Bangli, where he became an illustrious teacher with numerous notable dance students. He went on to teach *baris* and *arja* in other regions, including about three years in the district of Pangi, and continued to dance as a member of the various ensembles he taught. Teaching a dance-drama genre such as *arja, gambuh, Calonarang,* or *wayang wong* could entail training all the dancers in both male and female roles, dialogue, dramaturgy and plot development, song, stylized speech, and vocal characterization.

One of Kakul's many strengths was his ability to articulate and teach how the spirit of each specific dramatic character could be embodied through a unity of gestural movement and vocal characterization. He taught in the district of Bangli for about two years, staying until the village's dancers had been trained sufficiently to go out and perform in other villages. In the mountain village of Dawan he also taught *arja* for one to two years, again staying until the village group was skilled enough to stage their own performances. His fifth child, a girl, was born in Batuan at this time and named Dawan. Kakul moved farther east to teach *baris* at the palace of Karangasem, and then back west to Gianyar, where he continued to teach *baris* in the palaces and villages.

Highly prized by Balinese audiences was the *jiwa* ("spirit") manifested in Kakul's dance. He was initiated to perform certain priestly functions as a *mangku topéng*, and his solo performances of ceremonial *topéng pajegan* (accompanied by gamelan orchestra) were often electrifying three-hour *tours de force*. Changing back and forth from one masked character to another, he could create comic scenes full of intrigue and hilarity. His personal collection of *topéng* performance masks included some that he carved himself as well as spiritually endowed masks bestowed upon him by rajas and Brahmana priests.

In his own village of Batuan, the *Calonarang* group he taught included many of his children and grandchildren. The *gambuh* ensemble he founded in the early 1970s also included three generations of his family. Today, however, almost all of his performing descendants are with the *gambuh* group named after him, Sanggar Tari Nyoman Kakul.

Nyoman Kakul performed on John Coast's 1952–1953 tour, The Dancers and Musicians of Peliatan, traveling to the United States, Canada, Germany, France, and England. He later joined an ensemble of dancers from Bedulu on a tour of Czechoslovakia, the U.S.S.R., Holland, and India. During the 1960s and 1970s he taught many foreigners as well as dance students and faculty from arts academies in Java and Bali. For several years he taught at KOKAR, the high school conservatory of traditional performing arts in the city of Denpasar. He was honored with numerous awards, most notably the Piagam Seni for highest artistic achievement, from the president of the Republic of Indonesia; yet even into his later years, Nyoman Kakul considered his occupation to be that of farmer.

BIBLIOGRAPHY

Bandem, I Madé. "*Panji* Characterization in the *Gambuh* Dance Drama." Master's thesis, University of California, Los Angeles, 1972.

Bandem, I Madé, and Fredrik Eugene DeBoer. *Kaja and Kelod: Balinese Dance in Transition.* Kuala Lumpur, 1981.

Bandem, N. L. N. Swasthi Wijaya. "Dramatari Calonarang Di Singapadu." Master's thesis, Akademi Seni Tari Indonesia, 1982.

Daniel, Ana. *Bali: Behind the Mask.* New York, 1981.

Dibia, I Wayan. "Arja: A Sung Dance-Drama of Bali." Ph.D. diss., University of California, Los Angeles, 1992.

Emigh, John. "Playing with the Past: Visitation and Illusion in the Mask Theater of Bali." *Drama Review* 23 (June 1979).

Geertz, Hildred. "A Theatre of Cruelty: The Contexts of a Topéng Performance." In *State and Society in Bali,* edited by Hildred Geertz. Leiden, 1991.

Herbst, Edward. "Voices in Bali: Energy and Perceptions in Vocal Music and Dance Theater. Hanover, N. H., 1997.

Kakul, I Nyoman. "Jelantik Goes to Blambangan." *Drama Review* 23 (June 1979): 11–36.

Kanthor, I Ketut. Personal communication, 1995.

Sura, I Wayan. Personal communication, 1995.

Young, Elizabeth F. "Topeng in Bali: Change and Continuity in a Traditional Drama Genre." Ph.D. diss., University of California, San Diego, 1980.

Zoete, Beryl de, and Walter Spies. *Dance and Drama in Bali.* London, 1938.

EDWARD HERBST

KALIMANTAN. *See,* Indonesia, *article on* Dance Traditions of the Outlying Islands.

KALLINIKOS. The term *kallinikos,* meaning "fair victor" in classical Greek, was a cultic epithet for the deified hero Heracles. According to legend, Heracles succeeded in performing many labors and trials and was regarded as the originator of the Olympic games. The cult of Heracles the Fair Victor and Serpent-Slayer included a ritual dance involving males dressing in women's costume; therefore, the dancing youths wearing female attire on a black-figure cylix in the collection of the Museo Municipale in Corneto, Italy, may represent the *kallinikos* dance.

The term *kallinikos* came to be applied to the mortal winners of military or athletic contests and to the songs and dances commemorating those victories. The Greek lyric poet Archilochus (active c.650 BCE) composed a victory ode in honor of Heracles (frag. 119) that was used thereafter at victory celebrations for which no special song had been written. Scholars believe that this song had a refrain of the line *tenella kallinikos,* the former word being an imitation of the sound of lyre accompaniment. A century later the lyric poets Pindar (Olympian Odes) and Bacchylides frequently used the word *kallinikos* in their songs to commemorate athletic victories.

In the fifth century BCE the Greek dramatists incorporated the *kallinikos* into songs and dances for the chorus at appropriate moments of victory. The chorus announced the dance or song by name. In some cases the dance retained its original association with Heracles, as in lines 681 and 785 of Euripides' *Heracles Mainomena* (The Madness of Heracles), where the chorus sang and danced a cult hymn in honor of Heracles. In other plays the chorus celebrated different victories: in Euripides' *Bacchae* (1153–1164) the chorus danced a *kallinikos* to celebrate Dionysus's triumph over King Pentheus. In Aristophanes' comedies, the serious *tenella kallinikos* refrain is mimicked in celebration of less laudatory victories, such as drinking contests or the acquisition of a wife (as in *Acharnians* 1227–1234 and *Birds* 1763–1765).

[*See also* Greece, *article on* Dance in Ancient Greece.]

BIBLIOGRAPHY

Lawler, Lillian B. "Orchēsis Kallinikos." *Transactions and Proceedings of the American Philological Association* 79 (1948): 254–267.

LIBBY SMIGEL

KAMIZAWA KAZUO (born 26 June 1929), Japanese modern dancer and choreographer. While in college, Kamizawa became involved in directing and acting in theatrical productions. He studied modern dance with Homura Yasuyuki in Osaka from 1949 to 1953, but it was seeing Kuni Masami's *Kami no Kyujitsu* that led Kamizawa to decide to make choreography his career. Like Kuni, Kamizawa studied the works of Rudolf Laban, whose movement theory became the fundamental basis of his style.

He opened the Kamizawa Modern Dance Institute in 1962. In his first concert, held at Osaka Midou in February of that year, he danced *Tragodia* (or *Song of Goat Tragedy*) and *Scrapped Ship*. Other works include *Mountain Trainers* (1986) and *Kagai* (1993). Kamizawa's dances combine Eastern and Western techniques; their beauty results from his deep knowledge of Japanese dance, literature, and spiritual traditions. Every year since 1990, Kamizawa has performed a piece accompanied by a group of Sho Myo Buddhist monks, who chant sutras as he dances. Kamizawa's troupe has toured in the United States (1986, 1991) and performed in Malaysia for the World Dance Alliance in 1994. He is a professor of dance at Kinki University in Nara.

BIBLIOGRAPHY

Bestland, Sandra. "The Kamizawa Workshop." *Contact Quarterly* 17 (Winter 1992): 10–12.

Jennings, Bernadine. "The Asia Society Presents . . ." *Attitude* 4.2 (1987): 23–24.

Kamizawa Modern Dance Ensemble. Nara City, Japan, 1986. English and Japanese.

Stuart, Otis. "Kamizawa Modern Dance Ensemble." *Dance Magazine* (October 1985): 25.

ARCHIVES.   Dance Collection, New York Public Library for the Performing Arts.

HASEGAWA ROKU
Translated from Japanese

KAN'AMI (original name unknown; performing name, Kanze Saburō Kiyotsugu; born 1333 in Yamato, present-day Nara Prefecture, Japan, died 19 May 1384 in Suruga Province, Japan),   *nō* actor and playwright; father of Zeami; founder of the Kanze school of *nō*. Thought by many to have been a nephew of Kusunoki Masashige (1294–1336), a supporter of the Southern Court (and thus an enemy of the Ashikaga shogunate), Kan'ami was adopted by Yamada-tayū, son of Mino-tayū and leader of the Yamada *sarugaku* troupe. He was therefore the younger brother of Hōshō-dayū, who became leader of the Tobi troupe. Early on, Kan'ami became a member of the Yūzaki-za, a troupe connected with the Tō-no-mine and Kōfukuji temples and Kasuga Shrine and one of the four main troupes comprising Yamato *sarugaku*. He studied dancing and acting with the great *dengaku* (an older dance-drama genre) actor Itchū (died c.1370); he also studied the popular dance form known as *kusemai* (literally, "rhythmic dance") with the legendary Kaga-province dancer Otozuru and injected them into his own art to create a new form—*nō*.

Naming his troupe Kanze, after the bodhisattva Kanzeon (Skt., Avalokiteśvara), the deity worshiped at the nearby Hase Temple, Kan'ami traveled far beyond the Yamato region performing his art and learning various singing and dancing techniques from other famous actors of the day.

In 1374 he performed before the Shogun with his twelve-year-old son, Zeami, at Kyoto's Imagumano Shrine. The shogun immediately became an enthusiastic patron of their art, and both father and son enjoyed special privileges and received great support from the court. This marked the first time that a shogun had ever viewed what had been looked down on as a plebeian art. (The Buddhist name Kan'ami was posthumously given to the performer by the shogun.)

Many feel that Kan'ami's greatest contribution to the development of *nō* as a performing art was his incorporation of elements of *kusemai* dance, which employed lively music with a strong, rhythm pattern, during which the entertainer performed a rather long dance with symbolic and complicated choreography. *Kusemai* now survives as the *kuse*, a climactic dance in many *nō* plays. The narrative nature of the long song to which it is danced allows greater complexity of plot than did earlier dramatic conventions. Many celebrated masterpieces of the *nō* repertory are attributed to Kan'ami, including *Matsukaze* (Wind in the Pines), *Sotoba Komachi* (Komachi and the Gravestone), and *Motomezuka* (The Sought-for Tomb).

It is thought that, until Kan'ami, *nō* plays revolved only around the *shite* (protagonist), but Kan'ami often reworked older plays, infusing them with more dramatic realism and loftier diction. *Sotoba Komachi* contains a lively theological debate between doctrine-bound priests and the one-hundred-year-old courtesan and poet Ono no Komachi, who emerges the victor. *Eguchi*, about a poet-priest who visits a high-ranking prostitute (actually a manifestation of the bodhisattva Fugen [Skt., Samantabhadra]) in the riverside town of Eguchi, reaches a poetic elegance rarely matched by later playwrights.

The plays attributed to Kan'ami mark him as a dramatic innovator of great importance in the development of *nō*. His vision of dance as an essential part of *nō* drama was unprecedented, but because he left behind no documents at all, our information about him is mainly derived from Zeami's praise-filled writings. Kan'ami, always a consummate artist, died following a performance at Sengen Shrine, dedicated to the goddess of, and located at the foot of, Mount Fuji.

[*See also* Kanze School; Nō; *and the entries on Otozuru and Zeami.*]

BIBLIOGRAPHY

Dōmoto Masaki. *Zeami akutingu mesōdo*. Tokyo, 1987.
Keene, Donald. *Nō: The Classical Theatre of Japan*. New York, 1966.
Kodansha Encyclopedia of Japan. Tokyo, 1983. See the entries "Dance, Traditional," "Dengaku," "Kan'ami," "Kusemai," "Nō," "Sarugaku," and "Zeami."
Komparu Kunio. *The Noh Theater: Principles and Perspectives*. Translated by Jane Corddry and Stephen Comee. New York, 1983.
Nishino Haruo and Hata Hisashi, eds. *Nō, kyōgen jiten* (Dictionary of Noh and Kyogen). 2d ed. Tokyo, 1988.
O'Neill, P. G. *Early Nō Drama*. London, 1958.
Zeami. *On the Art of the Nō Drama: The Major Treatises of Zeami*. Translated by J. Thomas Rimer and Yamazaki Masakazu. Princeton, 1984.

STEPHEN COMEE

KANDYAN DANCE. An ancient chronicle, the *Mahavamsa*, states that when the culture hero Vijeya landed in Sri Lanka (Ceylon) in 543 BCE, he heard the sounds of music and dancing from a wedding ceremony. Dance is still of paramount importance in Sri Lankan (Sinhala) arts. There are three main styles: the Kandyan dance of the hill country, known as *uda rata natum;* the low country dance of the southern plains, known as *pahatha rata natum;* and *sabaragamuwa* dance, or *sabaragamuwa natum.*

Kandyan dance takes its name from Kandy, the last royal capital of Ceylon, which is situated about sixty miles (140 kilometers) from the modern capital at Colombo. This genre is today considered the classical dance of Sri Lanka. In Sanskrit terminology it is considered pure dance *(nṛtta);* it features a highly developed system of *tāla* (rhythm), provided by cymbals called *thālampataa*. There are five distinct types: the *ves, naiyandi, uddekki, pantheru,* and *vannams.*

Ves Dance. *Ves* dance, the most popular, originated from an ancient purification ritual, the Kohomba Yakuma or Kohomba Kankariya. The dance was propitiatory, never secular, and performed only by males. The elaborate *ves* costume, particularly the headgear, is considered sacred and is believed to belong to the deity Kohomba. [*See* Kohomba Kankariya *and* Ves Dance.]

Only toward the end of the nineteenth century were *ves* dancers first invited to perform outside the precincts of the Kankariya Temple at the annual Kandy Perahera festival. Today the elaborately costumed *ves* dancer epitomizes Kandyan dance. [*See* Kandy Perahera.]

Naiyandi Dance. Dancers in Naiyandi costume perform during the initial preparations of the Kohomba Kankariya festival, during the lighting of the lamps and the preparation of foods for the demons. The dancer wears a white cloth and white turban, beadwork decorations on his chest, a waistband, rows of beads around his neck, silver chains, brass shoulder plates, anklets, and jingles. This is a graceful dance, also performed in Maha Viṣṇu (Vishnu) and Kataraga Devales temples on ceremonial occasions.

Uddekki Dance. *Uddekki* is a very prestigious dance. Its name comes from the *uddekki*, a small lacquered hand drum in the shape of an hourglass, about seven and a half inches (18 centimeters) high, believed to have been given to people by the gods. The two drumskins are believed to have been given by the Moon god, the strings by the god Natha, the ring by the god Iswara, and the sound by Viṣṇu; the instrument is said to have been constructed according to the instructions of Sakra and was played in the heavenly palace of the gods. It is a very difficult instrument to play. The dancer sings as he plays, tightening the strings to obtain variations of pitch.

Pantheru Dance. The *pantheruwa* is an instrument dedicated to the goddess Pattini. It resembles a tambourine (without the skin) and has small cymbals attached at intervals around its circumference. The dance is said to have originated in the days of Prince Siddhartha, who became Buddha. The gods were believed to use this instrument to celebrate victories in war, and Sinhala kings employed *pantheru* dancers to celebrate victories in the battlefield. The costume is similar to that of the *uddekki* dancer, but the *pantheru* dancer wears no beaded jacket and substitutes a silk handkerchief at the waist for the elaborate frills of the *uddekki* dancer.

Vannams. The word *vannam* comes from the Sinhala word *varnana* (descriptive praise). Ancient Sinhala texts refer to a considerable number of *vannams* that were only sung; later they were adapted to solo dances, each expressing a dominant idea. History reveals that the Kandyan king Sri Weeraparakrama Narendrasinghe gave considerable encouragement to dance and music. In his

Kavikara Maduwa (a decorated dance arena) there were song and poetry contests.

It is said that the *kavi* (poetry sung to music) for the eighteen principal *vannam*s were composed by an old sage named Ganithalankara, with the help of a Buddhist priest from the Kandy temple. The *vannam*s were inspired by nature, history, legend, folk religion, folk art, and sacred lore, and each is composed and interpreted in a certain mood *(rasaya)* or expression of sentiment. The eighteen classical *vannam*s are *gajaga* ("elephant"), *thuranga* ("horse"), *mayura* ("peacock"), *gahaka* ("conch shell"), *uranga* ("crawling animals"), *mussaladi* ("hare"), *ukkussa* ("eagle"), *vyrodi* ("precious stone"), *hanuma* ("monkey"), *savula* ("cock"), *sinharaja* ("lion"), *naga* ("cobra"), *kirala* ("red-wattled lapwing"), *eeradi* ("arrow"), *Surapathi* (in praise of the goddess Surapathi), *Ganapathi* (in praise of the god Ganapathi), *uduhara* (expressing the pomp and majesty of the king), and *assadhrusa* (extolling the merit of Buddha). To these were added *samanala* ("butterfly"), *bo* (the sacred *bo* tree at Anuradhapura, a sapling of the original *bo* tree under which Buddha attained enlightenment), and *hansa vannama* ("swan"). The *vannama* dance tradition has seven components.

KANDYAN DANCE. A musician plays the *gete-bere* (a type of cylinder drum) to accompany a classical dance performed by Sicille Kotelawala. (Photograph from the archives of The Asia Society, New York.)

Accompaniment. The *vannama* tradition is to sing *thanama*, a note of the melody to each syllable. *Thitha*, the beat indicated with the cymbals, gives the rhythmic timing. Other elements include *kaviya*, the poem vocalized by the dancer; *beramatraya*, the rhythm of the drum; *kasthirama*, the finale of the first movement of the dance; and *seerumaruwa*, the movement in preparation for the *addawwa*, the finale of rhythmic body and foot movements, the last embellishment.

The drum is an integral part of Kandyan dance, and sanctity is associated with drums and drumbeats. The notes of the basic drum scale, *tha-ji-thoh-nun*, are salutations to Buddha, the gods, the master *(gurunnanse)* or the preceptor, and the audience, respectively.

The most important drum for Kandyan dance is the *gete-bere* (*gete* means "boss"); it is also called *magul-bere* (ceremonial drum) since it is used for all festive and ceremonial occasions throughout the country. It is believed to have been constructed under the directions of the Maha Brahma, the supreme god. The cylinder is scooped out of a single block of wood twenty-seven inches (67 centimeters) long. The skins are monkey skin on the right and oxhide on the left, to give very different tones. The braces are made of deerskin and are adjusted to give the desired tension in tuning. The drum is slung around the waist of the drummer and is played with both hands. The *davula* and the *thammattama* are other drums that are also used in temple ceremonies, rituals, and road pageants, called *pereheras*. With the patronage of the Sinhala royalty, Kandyan dance has flourished over the years as an institution vital to the socio-religious life of the people of Sri Lanka.

[*See also* Costume in Asian Traditions; Mask and Makeup, *article on* Asian Traditions; *and* Tovil.]

BIBLIOGRAPHY

Amunugana, Sarath. *Notes on Sinhala Culture.* Colombo, 1980.

Bowers, Faubion. *Theatre in the East: A Survey of Asian Dance and Drama.* New York, 1956.

de Zoete, Beryl. *Dance and Magic Drama in Ceylon.* London, 1957.

Disanayaka, Mudiyanse. *Udarata santikarma saha gami natya sampradaya.* Colombo, 1990.

Gunasinghe, Siri. *Masks of Ceylon.* Colombo, 1962.

Kotelawala, Sicille P. C. *The Classical Dance of Sri Lanka.* New York, 1974.

Makulloluwa, W. B. *Dances of Sri Lanka.* Colombo, 1976.

Molamure, Arthur. "The Outlook for Kandyan Dancing." In *Some Aspects of Traditional Sinhalese Culture,* edited by Ralph Pieris. Peradeniya, 1956.

Nevill, Hugh. "Sinhalese Folklore." *Journal of the Royal Asiatic Society, Ceylon Branch* 14 (1971): 58–90.

Pertold, Otaker. *Ceremonial Dances of the Sinhalese* (1930). Colombo, 1973.

Raghavan, M. D. *Dances of the Sinhalese.* Colombo, 1968.

Reed, Susan A. "The Transformation of Ritual and Dance in Sri Lanka: Kohomba Kankariya and the Kandyan Dance." Ph.D. diss., Brown University, 1991.

Sarachchandra, Ediriweera R. *The Folk Drama of Ceylon.* 2d ed. Colombo, 1966.

Sedaraman, J. I. *Nrtya ratnakaraya.* Colombo, 1992.

Sedaraman, J. I., et al. *Udarata natum kalava.* Colombo, 1992.

Seneviratna, Anuradha. *Traditional Dance of Sri Lanka.* Colombo, 1984.

Seneviratne, H. L. *Rituals of the Kandyan State.* Cambridge, 1978.

ARCHIVE. Of special interest to the student of Kandyan dance are the Palm Leaf Manuscripts held in the National Museum, Colombo: Bera Davul Tammattam Adiye Upata (82, v.16), Davul Up- ata (82, v.21), and Udakki Upata (82, v.1, v.5).

SICILLE P. C. KOTELAWALA

KANDY PERAHERA. In the picturesque hills of the Central Province of Sri Lanka lies Kandy, the last capital of the kings. Here, an annual national festival of great magnitude and magnificence, the Kandy Perahera, com- bines religious, cultural, and historical aspects. It is also known as the Dalada Maligawa Perahera; *perahera* signi- fies "a procession," and *Dalada Maligawa* means "Temple of the Sacred Tooth."

The history of this festival dates back to the fourth cen- tury CE, when King Kithsiri Megawanna received from In- dia the Sacred Tooth, a relic of Buddha, and placed it in a casket lodged in an edifice built in the third century BCE by King Devanampiyatissa, who made Buddhism the na- tional religion of Sri Lanka. This relic became the symbol of monarchy and was venerated to invoke blessings on the king and his people. A king-elect had to pay homage to this shrine before being crowned.

The *Mahavamsa,* an ancient chronicle, records that King Kithsiri decreed that the sacred tooth be taken around his capital city of Anuradhapura once a year in a great festival. This decree was faithfully adhered to by succeeding kings, as the fifth-century Chinese traveler Faxian confirmed. Once Anuradhapura was replaced as the capital by Polonnaruwa and then by the regional cap- ital Kandy, it is doubtful whether the procession contin- ued to be held annually.

The Esala Perahera, as we know it today—which com- bines the Buddhist rite with the four Hindu *devale peraheras* —was inaugurated in 1775 by King Kithsiri Raja-singha. At that time the Sacred Tooth relic was carried at the head of the *devale* processions, but today it is replaced by a dupli- cate of the casket, which contains a few lesser relics.

The Esala Perahera is held in the lunar month of July–August. On the day following the new moon in July, an *esala* tree is cut and *kap* planted as a vow that the *pera- hera* will be held. Owing to an overlay of Hindu influ- ences, the processions now are confined for five days within the precincts of the four Hindu *devale*s, or temples. On the fifth night, the four *perahera*s emerge into the

KANDY PERAHERA. Ves Dance, one the most typical of the Sinhala classical dances, is performed by a procession of dancers at the Kandy Perahera. Wearing a traditional costume, Heen Baba here demonstrates a solo *ves* dance. (Photograph from the archives of The Asia Society, New York.)

street and combine with the Maligawa Perahera at the en- trance to the Maligawa. The Randoli Perahera, which is the main one, is named after the *randoli,* the golden palanquins in which the queen and the monarch's concu- bines formerly brought up the rear, adding luster to the pageant. The four golden palanquins now represent the four *devales.*

Ancient protocol is strictly adhered to, and the relics are taken along a prescribed route with customary fanfare. The heads of the temple, clad in traditional ornate cos- tumes, take their places in the procession according to their official status. The Maligawa Perahera is led by whip crackers and flag bearers, followed by the Peramunarala, the official who rides on the first elephant. In ancient times, he carried the mandate from the king to hold the *perahera;* today, this is replaced by a register of the Mali- gawa lands, with the tenants and the services owed by them. He is followed by drummers playing martial music. Then follows the Kariyakorale, who is responsible for all the ceremonies and is next in rank to the Diyawadane Ni- lame, the lay custodian of the Sacred Tooth.

Dressed in a magnificent costume, the Nilame places the casket on the howdah on the back of the Temple Tusker, a majestic elephant. Richly caparisoned, it moves to the rhythm of the music, walking on a white cloth (*pavada*), which is spread for it as a mark of respect to the relics.

The procession is flanked by dancers of several traditional schools: *ves* dancers, wearing elaborate headdresses and breastplates of multicolored beads; *uddekki* dancers; *pantheru* dancers; and *naiyandi* dancers, who perform in the Viṣṇu (Vishnu) and Kataragama *devales*.

This awe-inspiring procession, with more than a hundred elephants, wends its way through the streets for five nights. It concludes with a day *perahera* and a ceremony in the Mahaveli River. The *perahera* then breaks up, and each *devale* procession goes back to its respective *devale*.

[*For articles on other dance traditions in Sri Lanka, see* Kandyan Dance; Kohomba Kankariya; Tovil; *and* Ves Dance. *See also* Costume in Asian Traditions *and* Mask and Makeup, *article on* Asian Traditions.]

BIBLIOGRAPHY

Amunugana, Sarath. *Notes on Sinhala Culture.* Colombo, 1980.
Bowers, Faubion. *Theatre in the East: A Survey of Asian Dance and Drama.* New York, 1956.
de Zoete, Beryl. *Dance and Magic Drama in Ceylon.* London, 1957.
Disanayaka, Mudiyanse. *Udarata santikarma saha gami natya sampradaya.* Colombo, 1990.
Gunasinghe, Siri. *Masks of Ceylon.* Colombo, 1962.
Kotelawala, Sicille P. C. *The Classical Dance of Sri Lanka.* New York, 1974.
Makulloluwa, W. B. *Dances of Sri Lanka.* Colombo, 1976.
Nevill, Hugh. "Sinhalese Folklore." *Journal of the Royal Asiatic Society, Ceylon Branch* 14 (1971): 58–90.
Pertold, Otaker. *Ceremonial Dances of the Sinhalese* (1930). Colombo, 1973.
Raghavan, M. D. *Dances of the Sinhalese.* Colombo, 1968.
Sarachchandra, Ediriweera R. *The Folk Drama of Ceylon.* 2d ed. Colombo, 1966.
Sedaraman, J. I. *Nrtya ratnakaraya.* Colombo, 1992.
Sedaraman, J. I., et al. *Udarata natum kalava.* Colombo, 1992.
Seneviratna, Anuradha. *Traditional Dance of Sri Lanka.* Colombo, 1984.

SICILLE P. C. KOTELAWALA

KANZE SCHOOL, one of Japan's five schools of *nō* dance-drama.

An Overview. Famous for its lyrical chanting, elegant dance, and colorful style of acting, the Kanze school is directly descended from the Yūzaki-za troupe, from which Kan'ami (1333–1384) broke away. Kan'ami founded the Kanze troupe, which flourished under the shogun Ashikaga Yoshimitsu (1358–1408) but waned under the rulers who followed, especially Toyotomi Hideyoshi (1537–1598), who favored the Konparu troupe. [*See the entry on* Kan'ami.] During the Edo period (1603–1868), the Kanze school was favored by the Tokugawa shogunate and became the foremost of the five *nō* schools. [*See* Nō.]

In 1752, the tenth Tokugawa shogun, Ieharu, granted permission to Kanze Oribe Kiyohisa (1729?–1782), younger brother of the fifteenth headmaster, Sakon Motoakira (1722–1774), to establish the Tetsunojō branch family. After the Meiji Restoration (1868), Kanze Kiyotaka, the twenty-second headmaster, left Tokyo with the exiled shogun. In the absence of the main Kanze school, Umewaka Minoru I (1828–1909), headmaster of a branch school, along with Hōshō Kurō (1837–1917) and Sakurama Banba (1835–1917), managed to prevent *nō* from disappearing—literally saving the art. Kanze Kiyokazu (b. 1959) now serves as the twenty-sixth headmaster of the school.

Among the most celebrated of twentieth-century Kanze-school performers have been the brothers Kanze Hisao, Kanze Hideo, and Kanze Tetsunojō VIII, all grandsons of the legendary Kanze Kasetsu (Tetsunojō VI, 1884–1959) and sons of the great Kanze Gasetsu (Tetsunojō VII, 1898–1988). All achieved renown for the excellence of their acting, dancing, and chanting—characterized by quiet lyricism (Hisao), originality of expression (Hideo), and inner strength (Tetsunojō).

[*See also the entry on* Umewaka Makio.]

BIBLIOGRAPHY

"Kanze School" and "Nō." In *Kodansha Encyclopedia of Japan.* Tokyo, 1983.
Nishino Haruo and Hata Hisashi, eds. *Nō, kyōgen jiten* (Dictionary of Noh and Kyogen). 2d ed. Tokyo, 1988.

STEPHEN COMEE

Kanze Hisao (born 12 November 1925 in Tokyo, died 7 December 1978 in Tokyo) was the leading *nō* actor of his generation. Hisao was a performer and theorist of unparalleled profundity; his experiments both within and outside the *nō* world won him a devoted following in Japan and Europe among *nō* cognoscenti and theater professionals.

Hisao, the eldest son of Kanze Gasetsu (Tetsunojō VII), and his younger brothers Hideo and Shizuo (now Tetsunojō VIII) received training from their grandfather, the honored Kanze Kasetsu. Hisao debuted at the age of three in the play *Shōjō*, and his first appearance in a lead role came at age seven. Hisao's sharp, resonant voice and beautiful physical form led to his early recognition as a leader among his generation of *nō* performers.

Joining a *nō* study group in 1946, Hisao came to believe, through a close reading of Zeami's theories of *nō* dramaturgy, that *nō* had grown overly codified during its years of protection by the shoguns. He thought that contemporary actors had to shed the weight of empty formality in favor of a more direct and forceful style for *nō* to recreate its potential as profound entertainment in modern Japan.

Although Hisao felt inhibited by the constraints of the Kanze school organization, he, unlike his younger brother Hideo (who left the *nō* world for a time), determined to pursue two paths simultaneously—he would infuse orthodox *nō* with his own innovative interpretations and at the same time go beyond the exclusive *nō* world to explore Japanese and world music, dance, and theater. In his way, he managed to pursue creative experimentation without imperiling *nō*'s dignity and aesthetic.

Hisao put his ideas into action with the Nō Renaissance Kai, founded in 1950 with *nō* actors of the Kanze, Kita, and Konparu schools studying and performing together in an unprecedented alliance. In 1953 he founded the Hana no Kai (Flower Group) with his brothers Hideo and Shizuo (later Tetsunojo VIII) and the Nomura brothers to research the world of *nō*. With affiliated scholars, the group examined technique to discover ways of moving modern audiences with their classical *nō* repertory. In

1955, Hisao and Nomura Mansaku performed the dance play *Pierrot Lunaire* to music by Arnold Schoenberg, and in 1957 Hisao acted in Igor Stravinsky's *The Soldier's Tale (L'Histoire du Soldat)*.

In his lifelong quest for *nō*'s essential properties, Hisao sought further inspiration abroad. In 1954 he was a member of the first *nō* troupe invited to the Venice International Theater Festival, led by Kita Roppeita XV. In 1962 he received a grant from the French government to study in Paris for six months, and under the influence of Jean-Louis Barrault he studied the organization of theater companies and theater production. He was profoundly affected by Barrault's recognition of *nō* as a theater of dramatic power that, like classical Greek theater, grapples with issues of life and death and of human fate in the universe.

In 1967 he performed *Takahime* (The Hawk Princess), a *nō* adaptation of W. B. Yeats's "play for dancers," *At the Hawk's Well*. The adaptation was repeated in numerous incarnations as a workshop for experiments in vocalization, choral arrangements, and balancing roles. These were produced by Mei no Kai (The Underworld Troupe, 1971–1977) with actors from different schools of *nō* and other theatrical and musical genres. Hisao also appeared

KANZE SCHOOL. After four hundred years of oblivion, the *nō* drama *Daihannya* (The Sutra of Great Wisdom) was revived by the Kanze school in 1983. Hosho Kan (center) appeared as the priest Xuanzang in a 1993 performance in the forecourt of the Temple of Dendur, Metropolitan Museum of Art, New York. (Photograph © 1993 by Jack Vartoogian; used by permission.)

in the company's first production, Sophocles' *Oedipus the King* (1970), as well as in productions of Aeschylus' *Agamemnon* (1972), Samuel Beckett's *Waiting for Godot* (1973), and Seneca's *Medea* (1975). In 1974 he portrayed Menelaus in Suzuki Tadashi's Waseda Shōgekijō (Small Theatre) production of Euripides' *The Trojan Women* and in 1978 played Dionysus in that company's production of Euripides' *Bacchae*.

Hisao's experiments within *nō* were subtle but radical. Possessing remarkable technical skills, he "destroyed" his natural voice to create a "true voice" that was rougher and more direct. Combining a deep knowledge of Zeami with gleanings from modern theorists such as Bertolt Brecht, Jerzy Grotowski, and especially Konstantin Stanislavsky, Hisao sought the psychological meaning behind the ritualized gestures of *nō*. Infusing *nō*'s gestures with his own personality, he would create new movement patterns, attempting to interpret a play differently each time he performed it. Although criticized by some as appealing only to an elite audience already familiar with *nō*'s conventions, Hisao believed that only through stripping away unnecessary conventions and attempting subtle reinterpretations could he bring a truly modern *nō* into existence.

Despite his "princely" status as heir to a leading branch family within the largest *nō* school, Hisao was unconcerned with the authority of financial rewards of his position. In 1965 he was designated Bearer of an Important Intangible Cultural Asset and inducted into the Nō Theater Association, but he declined the honors, citing the possibility of corruption. The legacy of his extensive writings continues to influence the direction of contemporary *nō*. His untimely death from cancer at age fifty-three deprived Japan of the "second Zeami." Some critics felt that, had he lived longer, he might have rewritten Zeami's fifteenth-century classic on *nō*, *Fushi kaden* (Transmission of the Style and the Flower), for the modern world.

BIBLIOGRAPHY

Harris, Albert J., Jr. "This Radical Noh: A Study of Two Productions by Kanze Hisao and Kanze Hideo." Ph.D. diss., Ohio State University, 1973.

Kanze Hisao. *Kokoro yori, kokoro ni tsutauru hana*. Tokyo, 1979.

Kanze Hisao. *Collected Writings (Chōsakushū)*. 4 vols. Tokyo, 1980.

Kanze Hisao. "Life with the Nō Mask." Translated by Don Kenny in *Nō/Kyōgen Masks and Performance*, compiled by Rebecca Teele. Claremont, Calif., 1984.

JONAH SALZ

Kanze Hideo (born 3 August 1927 in Tokyo), though a celebrated *nō* actor, has throughout his career questioned the relevance of the restrictive classical style and repertory of *nō*. The second son of Kanze Gasetsu (Tetsunojo VII), Hideo has been the black sheep of the Kanze school, directing and acting in modern plays and seeking *nō*'s essence in experiments with other performance genres.

Hideo trained under his father and grandfather, Kanze Kasetsu, making his stage debut at the age of four. His intensive training continued until he was twenty-two. He was expected to follow in the esteemed Kanze line, but in 1949 he disrupted *nō*'s system of exclusive schools by being adopted into a Kita school family (where he took the name Goto Hideo) so that he could study with the greatest actor of his day, Kita Roppeita XIV (1874–1971). This rare opportunity permitted him to compare the differences in texts and movement patterns between the two schools, which he assumed were caused by mistakes passed down by rote through the centuries. Dissatisfied with *nō*'s conservatism and feudal economic organization, Hideo withdrew from the *nō* world in 1958 to begin a remarkable career as a *shingeki* (modern, Western-style theater) actor and director.

Believing that all art contains the seeds of its own destruction, Hideo set about to "destroy" *nō* in order to build something new, to reestablish the communication with the audience that he believed had been lost in modern *nō*. Exploring the full range of performative expression, Hideo collaborated with artists, musicians, opera singers, filmmakers, and theater performers. He was a founding member of the Young People's Art Theater Seigen (1959–1966), an antiestablishment troupe, and then joined the Free Theater. He appeared in films by Kaneto Shindo, directed such modern plays as Samuel Beckett's *Waiting for Godot* (1973) and Bertolt Brecht's *The Good Woman of Szechuan* (1977), and participated in avant-garde workshops with Jerzy Grotowski in Poland in 1978 and 1980.

As a member of Mei no Kai, Hideo performed with his brother Hisao and the Nomura brothers and with modern-theater actors and actresses in *nō*-influenced versions of W. B. Yeats's play *At the Hawk's Well* (entitled *Takahime* [The Hawk Princess], 1970) and of *Oedipus the King* (1971), *Agamemnon* (1972), and *Medea* (1975). Despite the gaps in style between the *nō* and *shingeki* actors, the Kanze brothers and many critics considered these productions to be important first steps linking the separate vertical strata of modern Japanese theater genres.

Following Hisao's death in 1979, Hideo returned to *nō*, establishing Hashi no Kai (Bridge Group) to continue intergenre exchange: acting in and directing "revived *nō*," "new *nō*," *nō*-based experiments with flamenco dance and electronic music, and "nōpera" directed by flower-arrangement master and film director Teshigahara Hiroshi. Hideo continues to speak out against the *nō* school-system's stranglehold on creativity and the need for *nō* actors continually to question the place of their art in contemporary Japan.

Kanze Hideo combines the expansive, expressive energies of modern theater with the internal, suppressed energies of *nō*. His performances, influenced by his study of Konstantin Stanislavsky's theory of acting and his decades of *shingeki* experience, are more improvisatory and emotional than Hisao's were. Through his deep contact with other genres and schools, Hideo has been able to grasp the essential techniques and spirit of modern *nō*.

BIBLIOGRAPHY

Goodman, David. "Noh—Business and Art: An Interview with Kanze Hideo." *Drama Review* 15 (Spring 1971): 185–192.

Harris, Albert J., Jr. "This Radical Noh: A Study of Two Productions by Kanze Hisao and Kanze Hideo." Ph.D. diss., Ohio State University, 1973.

Kanze Hideo, ed. *Dentō to gendai*, no. 3, *Nō to Kyōgen*. Tokyo, 1970.

JONAH SALZ

Kanze Tetsunojō VIII (Kanze Shizuo; born 5 January 1931 in Tokyo), the fourth son of Kanze Gasetsu and the younger brother of Kanze Hisao and Kanze Hideo, is the eighth headmaster of the Tetsunojō branch of the Kanze school and the leader of the Tessen-kai troupe. He made his debut appearance as a professional *nō* actor at the age of three and has developed his art to such a degree that the silent beauty of his dancing, the restrained strength of his acting, and the lyricism of his chanting have made him extremely popular.

Tetsunojō exerted much effort to revive nearly forgotten *nō* works, such as *Mitsuyama* and *Tōgan Boto*. With his brothers he formed and was active in the Sarugaku-no-za, a group devoted to perfecting the art of *nō* through study of the writings of Zeami and the performance of a number of experimental works, attempting to extend the limits of *nō* as dance and as theater. Working for the revitalization and transformation of *nō* into a modern art, the three brothers investigated and performed contemporary *nō* plays as well as adaptations of ancient Greek plays and modern dramas.

Tetsunojō has helped to spread the art of *nō* internationally by accepting a number of foreigners as amateur students and traveling extensively with his son, Akeo (b. 1956), performing *nō* abroad, especially in the United States and Australia. He has received numerous awards, including the Minister of Education's Prize (1991–1992) and the Japan Art Academy Prize (1991–1992). In April 1995 he was designated a Living National Treasure by the Japanese government.

BIBLIOGRAPHY

Keene, Donald. *Nō: The Classical Theatre of Japan*. New York, 1966.

Kodansha Encyclopedia of Japan. Tokyo, 1983. See the entries "Kanze School" and "Nō."

Komparu Kunio. *The Noh Theater: Principles and Perspectives*. Translated by Jane Corddry and Stephen Comee. New York, 1983.

Nishino Haruo and Hata Hisashi, eds. *Nō, kyōgen jiten* (Dictionary of Noh and Kyogen). 2d ed. Tokyo, 1988. See entries "Kanze School" and "Kanze Tetsunojō."

STEPHEN COMEE

KANZE SCHOOL. Kanze Tetsunojō VIII as the Goddess of Mount Kazuraki preparing to perform the special "Dance of Yamato" in the *nō* drama *Kazuraki*. (Photograph by Morita Toshirō; used by permission; courtesy of Stephen Comee.)

KARINSKA, BARBARA (Varvara Ivanovna Zhmoudska; born 3 October 1888 in Kharkov, Russia, died 18 October 1983 in New York City), costume designer known as Karinska. Trained in embroidery in Russia, Karinska immigrated to Paris in 1923, where she survived by selling handiwork until discovering her true *métier* as a costumer. She constructed her first ballet costumes for the 1932 debut season of the Ballets Russes de Monte Carlo, which included George Balanchine's *Cotillon* (Christian Bérard, designer) *La Concurrence* (André Derain, designer), and *Le Bourgeois Gentilhomme* (Alexandre Benois, designer). The following year she again worked with Balanchine, executing costumes for his short-lived troupe Les Ballets 1933. Other important painter-designers—Henri Matisse, Pablo Picasso, Marc Chagall, Eugene Berman—soon discovered in her the rare combination of craftsmanship, imagination, and taste that allowed the innovative and essentially painterly concepts represented in their costume sketches to be realized in the plastic three-dimensionality of fabric on the dancer's body.

In 1936 and 1937 Karinska constructed costumes for Frederick Ashton's *Apparitions* (Cecil Beaton, designer) and *Harlequin in the Street* (Derain, designer), as well as costumes for musical revues in London. In 1939 she arrived in New York City and constructed costumes for *Too Many Girls,* the first of many Broadway musicals she

KARINSKA. Peter Martins and Suzanne Farrell pose in costumes designed by Karinska for Balanchine's production of *The Nutcracker.* Details of her craftsmanship can be seen in the gusset in the sleeve of Martins's tunic, which permitted him to raise his arm without disturbing the line of the tunic; in the bouffant shape of Farrell's tutu; and in the appliquéd decorations that embellish both costumes. (Photograph from the Dance Collection, New York Public Library for the Performing Arts.)

would work on, as well as Léonide Massine's *Bacchanale,* based on suggestions by Salvador Dali. In 1941 she costumed dancers for *Princess Aurora* after designs by Léon Bakst (the first of her many assignments for American Ballet Theatre).

Karinska was invited to Hollywood in 1944 by Raoul Pêne du Bois to execute some of his designs for the film *Lady in the Dark;* afterward she constructed or designed for several other films, including *Gaslight* (1944), *Frenchman's Creek* (1944), and *Kismet* (1955), all notable for their elaborate wardrobes. In 1948 she shared with Dorothy Jeakins the Academy Award given for Best Costume Design for a Color Film—for *Joan of Arc.*

When Ballet Society (precursor to the New York City Ballet) was founded in 1946, Karinska once again worked with Balanchine and established an artistic collaboration that lasted throughout the remainder of her life. Encouraged by him, she began to design as well as construct costumes for his ballets, beginning in 1949 with *Bourrée Fantasque.* This was followed by forty-seven other works over a period of twenty-eight years, including *Serenade, Symphony in C, La Valse, Metamorphoses, The Nutcracker, Jewels, Chaconne,* and her last designs, before falling ill in 1977, for *Vienna Waltzes.* For Balanchine's more abstract works, for which no designer was listed, Karinska provided the simple practice tunics, tights, and leotards that became part of his stylistic signature. These were proportioned and fitted as expertly as the elaborately constructed tutus for which she was famous. Karinska also designed for Jacques d'Amboise and John Taras at the New York City Ballet, and she constructed costumes for Broadway theater, the Metropolitan Opera, Teatro alla Scala in Milan, Le Grand Ballet du Marquis de Cuevas, Ballets des Champs-Élysées, Ballets Russes de Monte Carlo, and American Ballet Theatre—until 1964, when she assigned her shop exclusively to the New York City Ballet.

Karinska's costumes enhanced dancers' proportions and displayed, uninterrupted, the long body lines so essential to legibility in Balanchine's work. Theater critic Walter Terry wrote of Karinska, "She does not clothe a body nor simply dress it. Rather does she address herself to the task of making the garment part of dancing itself, whether it is a tunic which caresses the body, a costume *(Western Symphony)* which promises rollicking ribaldry or a gown *(Liebeslieder Walzer)* which extends the melody of movement out from the body into space." In their extended collaboration, Karinska's talents—her refined taste in decoration, her extraordinary craftsmanship, and in particular her understanding of balletic metaphor—achieved perfect confluence with Balanchine's genius; her designs became organic extensions of his choreographic form.

[*For related discussion, see* Costume in Western Traditions, *overview article.*]

BIBLIOGRAPHY

Bentley, Toni. *Costumes by Karinska.* New York, 1995.

García-Márquez, Vicente. *The Ballets Russes: Colonel de Basil's Ballets Russes de Monte Carlo, 1932–1952.* New York, 1990.

Kirstein, Lincoln. *The New York City Ballet.* New York, 1973.

Kisselgoff, Anna. Obituary. *New York Times* (19 October 1983).

Notable Names in the American Theatre. Rev. ed. Clifton, N.J., 1976.

Reynolds, Nancy. *Repertory in Review: Forty Years of the New York City Ballet.* New York, 1977.

Rigdon, Walter. *The Biographical Encyclopaedia and Who's Who of American Theatre.* New York, 1966.

Rubin, Joan A. "Costumes by Karinska." *Dance Magazine* (June 1967): 49.

MALCOLM MCCORMICK

KARSAVINA, TAMARA (Tamara Platonovna Karsavina; born 9 March 1885 in Saint Petersburg, died 26 May 1978 in Beaconsfield, England), Russian-British ballerina, teacher, and writer. Karsavina's father, Platon Karsavin, was a first dancer and mime with the Maryinsky Theater in Saint Petersburg. She and her brother, Lev, grew up in an apartment overlooking a canal that curves around to join the River Fontanko, in a happy and artistic family environment. Early on, she displayed a voracious appetite for reading, which led her later to devour the works of Aleksandr Pushkin and Mikhail Lermontov. Encouraged by her mother, Tamara took dancing lessons with a retired dancer, Madame Joukova, and showed such aptitude that her father overcame his initial opposition to a dancing career and gave her lessons himself. On 26 August 1894 Karsavina auditioned for the Imperial Theater School, was accepted, and after a period of probation became a boarder. Her teachers included Pavel Gerdt, Christian Johansson, Enrico Cecchetti, Evgenia Sokolova, and Nikolai Legat. She also worked with Aleksandr Gorsky and Fedor Koslov. To Gerdt in particular she acknowledged an enormous debt: he taught pantomime in addition to dance technique and once showed her—prophetically, as it transpired—how to hold a rose. (Her schooldays are enchantingly described in her autobiography, *Theatre Street.*)

Karsavina appeared as a student on the Maryinsky stage and was quickly spotted by Grand Duke Vladimir, who boomed, "She will beat them all in time." She made her official debut on 1 May 1902 in *Javotte.* In 1907 she had her first great success as Medora in *Le Corsaire;* dancing a big role in a full-length ballet, Karsavina felt she had at last fulfilled herself. She was highly praised, notably by Valerian Svetlov, who was to become both mentor and friend. Although her progress was gradual, Karsavina was always among the top dancers in the Maryinsky company, alongside Anna Pavlova, Julia Sedova, and Vera Trefilova. Sedova befriended her, and she became a protégée of the all-powerful Matilda Kshessinska.

The most important influence upon Karsavina's artistic development, however, was that of Michel Fokine. She

KARSAVINA. The Ballerina in *Petrouchka* (1911) was one of many roles Karsavina created for Diaghilev's Ballets Russes. (Photograph from the Dance Collection, New York Public Library for the Performing Arts.)

and Fokine seriously discussed the future of their chosen art, and she supported him when, at the time of the October Revolution of 1905, he led a delegation of dancers demanding a reformed constitution. She was in sympathy with the "new ballet" he wished to create, a repertory that would be concerned with dramatic truth in both choreography and design.

Karsavina heard with interest Fokine's reports of Serge Diaghilev's plans to take a Russian ballet company to Paris. When Diaghilev invited her to join his enterprise she gladly accepted, although she remained a member of the Maryinsky company until she left Russia for good in 1918. Her repertory in Saint Petersburg included *The Awakening of Flora, The Little Humpbacked Horse, Swan Lake, Le Corsaire, The Sleeping Beauty, Giselle, Raymonda,* and *La Bayadère.* On 15 May 1918, she danced on the Maryinsky stage for the last time, in *La Bayadère,* before leaving for England with her second husband, H. J. Bruce, and their small son, Nikita. (She had been married previously to Vasily Moukhin.)

Although never celebrated as a virtuoso dancer, Karsavina's exceptional artistry was admired in Russia by critics

With Vaslav Nijinsky, Karsavina posed in costume for *Le Spectre de la Rose* (1911). This is one of a series of now-famous photographs by Bert. (Photograph from the Dance Collection, New York Public Library for the Performing Arts.)

and balletgoers alike. In the West her fame was most-closely associated with the artistic innovations of Diaghilev's Ballets Russes, although she also danced classic roles with the Diaghilev Company (her Giselle, in particular, was acclaimed for its Romantic beauty). A deep bond of sympathy, affection, and understanding grew between Diaghilev and Karsavina. She understood the greatness of his work, and she remained for the next twenty years his favorite artist.

Fokine found in Karsavina the ideal interpreter of his ballets. He appreciated not only her youthful beauty but also her intelligence, expressive grace, and dramatic powers. Karsavina was later to create important roles in ballets by choreographers as different as Vaslav Nijinsky *(Jeux)*, Léonide Massine *(Le Tricorne, Pulcinella)*, and Bronislava Nijinska and George Balanchine *(Roméo et Juliette)*, but essentially she was a Fokine dancer. In *Les Syl-*

phides, Cléôpatre, Le Carnaval, and then *The Firebird* (her first created role), she became synonymous with his ideals. For the second Diaghilev season in Paris, Fokine created for her the Doll in *Petrouchka,* the cruel imperious Thamar, the Queen in *Le Coq d'Or,* the voluptuous Zobéïde in *Schéhérazade,* and the Young Girl in *Le Spectre de la Rose,* in which she fully shared Nijinsky's triumph.

In 1919 Karsavina rejoined Diaghilev in London to create the role of the Miller's Wife in *Le Tricorne* and Pimpinella in *Pulcinella.* She undertook various concert tours but continued to return to Diaghilev from time to time, dancing with his last protégé, Serge Lifar, in *Roméo et Juliette* in 1926 and also appearing in his company in London during the last season of 1929.

Karsavina retired from the stage in 1931 after giving some guest appearances to help the infant Ballet Rambert (Marie Rambert had been a friend since early Diaghilev days). Frederick Ashton wrote,

> When she danced with us we watched her every movement, admired her discipline, her exquisite manners, her humanity and her approach to the public; we loved and respected her as she moved among us, an exiled queen from a bigger and more glorious world.   (Quoted in Vaughan, 1977, p. 46)

From the outbreak of World War II, Karsavina and her husband lived in London. There she enjoyed a quiet home life, although she was ready to help and coach when needed. She taught Margot Fonteyn *Le Spectre de la Rose* in 1942 and coached Fonteyn and Michael Somes in *The Firebird* in 1954. She helped devise a special syllabus for the teacher-training course of the Royal Academy of Dancing, of which she was a vice president, and she broadcast and lectured on memories of Diaghilev and on the art of mime. She also wrote many articles on ballet technique. Karsavina's last great contribution to ballet was to teach Lise's mime scene in *La Fille Mal Gardée* to Frederick Ashton, who incorporated it into his version.

After her husband died in 1951, Karsavina continued to live in their Hampstead house until increasing infirmity forced her to move, in 1974, to a nursing home near her son and his family. She died in 1978. Her eightieth birthday was celebrated in Hampstead (Fonteyn and Rudolf Nureyev, who adored her, were there) and her ninetieth in a hall in Beaconsfield, when Ashton and John Gielgud sang her praises.

Karsavina was a beloved ballerina. After her early Paris triumphs, crowned heads were at her feet but, as she assured Richard Buckle, "I was virtuous." Her sensibility, charm, wit, and deep culture, so easily and naturally borne, endeared her to everyone. She was drawn or painted by John Singer Sargent, Glyn Philpot, Valentin Serov, Léon Bakst, Jean Cocteau, Jacques-Émile Blanche, Randolphe Schwabe, Wilfred de Glehn, and Mstislav Dobujinsky, among others. Robert Brussel wrote in the pages of *Le Figaro* during one of the Paris seasons, "Karsavina's beauty is perfect, incomparable. . . . And when the dark, dark eyes open in the dead whiteness of her face, how delicious is the vision of poetry and grace she evokes."

[*See also* Ballets Russes de Serge Diaghilev.]

BIBLIOGRAPHY

Bruce, H. J. *Silken Dalliance*. London, 1946.

Bruce, H. J. *Thirty Dozen Moons*. London, 1949.

Clarke, Mary. "Tamara Karsavina." In Clarke's *Six Great Dancers*. London, 1957.

Garafola, Lynn. *Diaghilev's Ballets Russes*. New York, 1989.

Inglesby, Mona. "From the Cradle of British Ballet." *Dance Now* 4 (Spring 1995): 35–45.

Karsavina, Tamara. *Theatre Street*. Rev. and enl. ed. London, 1948.

Karsavina, Tamara. *Ballet Technique*. London, 1956.

Karsavina, Tamara. *Classical Ballet: The Flow of Movement*. London, 1962.

Lifar, Serge. *The Three Graces: Anna Pavlova, Tamara Karsavina, Olga Spessivtzeva*. Translated by Gerard Hopkins. London, 1959.

Moore, Lillian. "Tamara Karsavina." In Moore's *Artists of the Dance*. New York, 1938.

Sorley Walker, Kathrine. "The Karsavina Syllabus." *Dance Now* 4 (Summer 1995): 48–54.

Vaughan, David, *Frederick Ashton and His Ballets*. New York, 1977.

Wildman, Carl. "Conversation with Karsavina." *The Dancing Times* (June 1965): 458–463.

Williams, Peter. "Celebrating Karsavina, 1885–1978." *Dance Gazette* (July 1985): 28–31.

MARY CLARKE

KARSTENS, GERDA (born 9 July 1903 in Copenhagen, died 13 June 1988 in Copenhagen), Danish dancer. Although Karstens was named a principal dancer of the Royal Danish Ballet when the company's grade system changed in 1942, she is remembered principally as the ballet's appointed character dancer, a title created especially for her in 1935. Her dancing career lasted from the 1930s well into the 1950s. When foreign critics "discovered" the Royal Danish Ballet after World War II, they celebrated Karstens as a superb artist whose character dancing and highly cultivated mime technique helped to guarantee the Danish ballet its place among the leading international ballet companies.

Karstens entered the ballet school of the Royal Theater in Copenhagen in 1910 and made her debut a decade later in Emilie Walbom's *Times Past*. Not until 1931, however, in Harald Lander's Argentine ballet *Gaucho*, did she reveal the tremendous power that came to characterize her portrayals. The Danish national repertory provided Karstens with many opportunities, and it needed her talent. Most powerful and important was her characterization of the evil Witch in August Bournonville's *La Sylphide*. She was also comical as the bourgeois Trutje in Bournonville's *Kermesse in Bruges* and as the Quaker in Vincenzo Galeotti's *The Whims of Cupid and the Ballet Master*. As Grand-

mother December in Børge Ralov's Hans Christian Andersen ballet *Twelve with the Mail Coach* in 1942, she also showed that she could be mild and sweet.

The modern Danish choreographers Birger Bartholin, Lander, Ralov, and Nini Theilade capitalized on Karstens's gift for memorable and economical characterization. The frightening inner power she brought to the Wickedness in Lander's *Bird Fønix* in 1946 and the witty Mother and the grotesque Teacher she created in Lander's *The Land of Milk and Honey* in 1942 reflected a wide artistic range. In the international repertory Karstens covered roles from the Mother in *Giselle* to the funny, spinsterish Principal in David Lichine's *Graduation Ball*.

To acquire a deeper understanding of dramatic action, Karstens studied at the acting school in the Royal Theater. She performed a few roles in plays but did not work toward an acting career. After retiring from the Royal Danish Ballet in 1956, she danced a few more times; her last appearance was in 1979 in Flemming Flindt's *The Triumph of Death*.

BIBLIOGRAPHY

Hering, Doris. "The Royal Danish Ballet and Copenhagen." *Dance Magazine* (July 1956): 14–19.

Kragh-Jacobsen, Svend, and Torben Krogh, eds. *Den Kongelige Danske Ballet*. Copenhagen, 1952.

ERIK ASCHENGREEN

KASAI AKIRA (born 25 November 1943 in Tsu City, Mie Prefecture, Japan), choreographer and *butō* performer; one of the originators of the *butō* form. After receiving a bachelor's degree in economics from Meiji University, Kasai began ballet and modern dance classes, studying the Mary Wigman technique. He met Ōno Kazuo and Hijikata Tatsumi in 1963 and 1964, respectively, and he danced in Hijikata's *Rose Colored Dance* in 1965.

In 1966 Kasai collaborated with Ōno and the writer Mishima Yukio on *Crucified Virgin Mary*. He played an active role in the development of *butō* with his performances *Invitation to Butō* (1967), *Chigo no Soshi* (1968), and *Tannhaüser* (1969). In 1971, he founded a training center, Tenshi-kan (Angel House), for what he called *seirei butō* (Holy Ghost *butō*). With works such as *Seven Seals* (1973) and *Denju no Mon* (1974), he won equal popularity as Hijikata.

In 1979, Kasai went to Germany to study at the school of eurythmics in Stuttgart. In 1985, he returned to Japan with a eurythmics teaching certificate and opened a four-year school of eurythmics in Kokbunji, near Tokyo, where he became head teacher. For the next few years Kasai rarely performed, but resumed his career as a *butō* choreographer and performer in 1994 with his work *Seraphita*.

Kasai's earlier interest was in literature, particularly the theme of androgyny. His dance work of the 1970s was characterized by an emphasis on improvisation. Later, Kasai became interested in mysticism and began incorporating themes from the mystical traditions of Japan, the Middle East, and Germany into his *butō* pieces. It was therefore not a change but a natural development when he came to include eurythmics, the movement method advocated by German anthroposophist Rudolf Steiner, into his dance. Works performed since his return onstage incorporate eurythmics structures.

Kasai is also an author, having published two books: *Tenshi-ron* (The Theory of Angels, 1972) and *Seirei Butō* (1977).

[*See also* Butō.]

BIBLIOGRAPHY

Regitz, Hartmut. "Tempeltanz im Schneckenhaus: Akira Kasais Auftritt in Stuttgart." *Ballett-Journal/Das Tanzarchiv* 29 (March 1981): 22.

Stein, Bonnie Sue. "Celebrating Hijikata: A Bow to the Butoh Master." *Dance Magazine* (May 1988): 44–47.

Ulrich, Allan. "San Francisco Butoh Festival." *Dance International* 23 (Fall 1995): 43.

ARCHIVE.   Dance Collection, New York Public Library for the Performing Arts.

HASEGAWA ROKU
Translated from Japanese

KATAOKA TAKAO (born 3 March 1944 in Osaka), *kabuki* actor-dancer. This extremely popular player of leading male roles *(tachiyaku)* is one of three sons of *kabuki* star Kataoka Nizaemon XIII (1903–1993) and like his father an heir to the traditions of the Kyoto-Osaka (Kamigata) region, in which romantic heroes are played in the gentle, almost feminine *wagoto* style, as opposed to the more masculine style of Tokyo (which Takao has also mastered).

Takao, who debuted in Osaka in 1949, presents the rare case of a *kabuki* actor who not only uses his private name as a stage name but has retained it throughout his career. He has been designated, however, to become Kataoka Nizaemon XV in 1997. Raised in Osaka during the 1950s, when Kamigata *kabuki* was in decline, Takao did not receive the public attention accorded Tokyo's young hopefuls. In 1962, however, when his father created his own company in an effort to revive Kamigata *kabuki*, Takao—beginning with the role of Yohei in *Onna Goroshi Abura no Jigoku*—came into his own in one classic role after another. His innate talent and excellent training were supplemented by the three essentials of a romantic star: good looks, a good physique, and an excellent voice.

In 1970, he became a Tokyo idol when he was featured in the Young Stars' Kabuki at the Shinbashi Enbujō, where he was paired as leading man opposite the brilliant female impersonator *(onnagata)* Bandō Tamasaburō V (born 1950). Since both were unusually tall and slender for *kabuki* actors, they made a dazzling stage picture that enraptured fans, especially in their hit revival of *Sakura Hime Azuma Bunshō*, in which Takao played both Seigen and Gonsuke. They then co-starred in a series of old plays. Takao rose to even greater heights when he played three major roles in a 1980 revival of *Chūshingura* at Tokyo's Kabuki Theater.

Among the many other roles associated with him are Kajiwara in *Ishikiri Kajiwara*, Togashi in *Kanjincho*, Tsunatoyo in *Genroku Chūshingura*, the title role in *Sukeroku*, and Seishin in *Izayoi Seishin*. His height makes him especially suitable for the heroes of period plays *(jidaimono)*. Moreover, he has also displayed considerable skill playing villains *(katakiyaku)*, such as Iwafuji in *Kagamiyama*. In addition to *kabuki*, Takao's career has encompassed movies and television, and the stage genres of *shin kabuki* and *shinpa*. For all his skills as a dancer, he has never been truly outstanding in this area, although he has steadily improved, as demonstrated by his performance as Ukyō in the dance comedy *Migawari Zazen*. Illness forced him off the stage in 1993, but fans were relieved when he recovered and returned to acting in 1994. His eldest son performs as Kataoka Takatarō, and his daughter, Shio Kazako, performs with the all-women Takarazuka troupe.

[*See also* Japanese Traditional Dance *and* Kabuki Theater.]

BIBLIOGRAPHY

Akasaka Jiseki, ed. *Kabuki haiyū daihyakka.* Tokyo, 1993.

Engekikai 52.2 (1993). Special issue: *kabuki* actors' directory.

Fujita Hiroshi. *Kabuki handobukku.* Tokyo, 1994.

Toita Yasuji, ed. *Kabuki kanshō nyūmon.* 3d ed., rev. Tokyo, 1994.

SAMUEL L. LEITER

KATHAK. A classical dance genre of North India, *kathak* derives its name from *kathakar*, traditional storytellers who also recited the sagas of contemporary heroes and commented on current events. Ancient literature is full of references to these bards, who were also singers and dancers. They were sometimes attached to families, temples, or courts, and they were sometimes itinerant pilgrims, rather like wandering minstrels. Frequent drama and dance recitals were held on festive occasions in villages of western and central India. The *kathakar*s recounted legends revolving around the gods and goddesses of Hindu mythology, or the lives, loves, and heroic exploits of local heroes, to a spontaneously gathered audience in village courtyards, temple grounds, or the courts of native kings. They took their themes from medieval poetry composed in the vernacular languages, Braj, Avadhi, and Maithali. *Kathak* is not mentioned in the *Nāṭyaśāstra* as one of the four dance genres prevalent in ancient India. Works such as the *Nāṭyaratnakośa*, compiled in the fifteenth century, indicate that the dance form is at least that old; miniature paintings of the thirteenth and fourteenth centuries give some evidence of what appears to be *kathak* style. Related traditions of the *bhakti* poet-saints, however, point to even earlier origins. *Kathak* originally seems to have been a free-flowing, almost folk style, not evolved from the strict rules laid down in the *Nāṭyaśāstra*, but more or less spontaneous. In addition, it seems to have been a solo performance by a male artist, who spoke, sang, danced, and narrated the story all by himself. The medieval poet-saints sang and danced with devotional fervor in Vrindavan, sacred abode of the god Kṛṣṇa (Krishna) in his childhood and adolescence.

In time, dance moved to the courts of the Muslim rulers who had invaded India around the tenth century. As they gradually settled in India and looked for forms of entertainment that would suit their more secular tastes, dance acquired an urbane form reflecting its courtly environment. The dancers' art, aimed at pleasing their royal patrons, gained in grace, elegance, and sophistication. There was also interaction between the two religions of Hinduism and Islam, which influenced each other in dance, music, and painting.

Eventually the technique of this court style, the predecessor of present-day *kathak*, abandoned some of the characteristic features of the earlier styles, such as the wide turnout of the knees and the *tribhaṅga* (thrice-bent) position seen frequently in Hindu sculptures of gods, goddesses, dancers, and musicians. In this posture the head and the hip are cocked to one side, and the torso inclined to the other, so that the body forms a kind of S curve. Instead, the evolving *kathak* acquired an erect stance, flowing rather than chiseled, lines, and multiple pirouettes, or *chakkars*, probably influenced by the whirling of the Sufi dervishes, members of a Muslim religious order. The rhythmic aspect of dance also became important, and dances took on more intricate patterns. The weaving of different metrical patterns, sometimes superimposing a different rhythmic variation over the basic measure, became a distinctive feature of this style, which with its subtle nuances and delicate details came to resemble the miniature paintings of the period. Technical virtuosity was stressed, displayed in lightning footwork, dazzling turns (as many as one hundred), and remarkable feats with the ankle bells, such as sounding only a single bell at a time.

The *kathak* style includes both rhythmic and expressive dance. As is usual with Indian dance, a song of prayer to a deity, in this style called *vandana*, ceremonially begins and concludes a performance. The first dance in a *kathak* performance is the *thāt*, in which the body stance is displayed along with some basic footwork and movements of the eyes, eyebrows, and sometimes torso. The *thāt* is followed by the *āmad, tora, tukra,* and *paran.* In these

dances, the basic dance units are combined into continuous rhythmic pieces of varying lengths, which are then concluded with the *tihai*, repeated three times. Sometimes the *tora*s and *tukra*s themselves are repeated three times, in which case they are called *chakkardar. Paran*s combine rhythmic vocables with descriptive words, usually in praise of a deity, especially Kṛṣṇa.

The *paran*s are followed by *gat-bhav*s, which tell a story or depict a mood. *Gat-bhav*s have little footwork and only an occasional turn, usually done to separate one story from another. Their expressive aspect depends a great deal on the dancer's facial expressions. The gestures are simple and do not follow any complicated or codified vocabulary. The facial expressions are also natural and spontaneous; the eyes and eyebrows are used in a delicate and suggestive manner.

The *kathak* program is concluded with the *tatkar*, in which the dancer's command of the footwork is displayed to perfection. The hands remain inactive, and the entire emphasis is on the feet tapping out the rhythm, from a slow to a very fast tempo. Counterrhythms are woven against the basic rhythm, and sometimes there is a *savāl-*

KATHAK. Sitara Devi, a well-known *kathak* dancer. (Photograph from the archives of The Asia Society, New York.)

javāb (question-answer), in which the dancer and drummer vie with each other in a gradually mounting crescendo of rhythmic brilliance.

The rhythmic cycles of *kathak* are played on the *tabla-bayan*, a two-drum ensemble, or the *pakhavaj*, a double-barreled drum. The drummer, or *tabalchi*, is the most important member of the orchestra, and rapport between him and the dancer is essential. Also in the orchestra is a player of the *sarangi* (a stringed instrument) or harmonium (a later, British addition), who continuously repeats one line, in a *rāga* (melodic mode) in the Hindustani, or northern Indian style, while the dancer and the drummer create new dance patterns. A singer sings the occasional song, usually in Brajbhasha, a medieval form of the northern Indian language Hindi. The sitar, another stringed instrument, may also be in the orchestra.

The costumes also acknowledge their debt to the two religions and cultures influencing *kathak* style in their design, fabric, and ornamentation. Hindu themes call for the *ghaghra*, a wide, pleated skirt; the *choli*, a blouse covering only the chest and leaving the midriff bare; and the *odhni*, a veil draped gracefully over them. The Muslim or Mughal themes are depicted in tight-fitting pajamas called *churidar*s, a diaphanous long jacket, and a little waistcoat cut away from the front and hooked only below the chest. Again, a veil is thrown over this, and sometimes a jeweled cap is worn over the head at a provocative angle. The jewels sparkling on the dancer are also drawn from both cultures.

[*See also* Asian Dance Traditions, *overview article; and* Costume in Asian Traditions. *For general discussion see* India, *article on* History of Indian Dance. *See also the entries on* Anwar, Durgalal, Husain, Lakhia, Maharaj, Sen, Sharma, Siddiqui, *and* Sitara Devi.]

BIBLIOGRAPHY

Hall, Fernau. "Maharaj and Indian Classics." *Daily Telegraph* (22 September 1981).

Khokar, Mohan. "Lucknow Gharana." *Marg* 12.4 (1959).

Kothari, Sunil. *Kathak: Indian Classical Dance Art.* New Delhi, 1989.

Massey, Reginald, and Jamila Massey. *The Dances of India: A General Survey and Dancer's Guide.* London, 1989.

Ragini Devi. *Dance Dialects of India.* 2d rev. ed. Delhi, 1990.

Samson, Leela. *Rhythm in Joy: Classical Indian Dance Traditions.* New Delhi, 1987.

Saxena, Sushil Kumar. *Swinging Syllables: Aesthetics of Kathak Dance.* New Delhi, 1991.

Shah, Purnima. "Farmayishi Poetics of Kathak." *UCLA Journal of Dance Ethnology* 18 (1994): 1–7.

RITHA DEVI

KATHAKALI. The Indian dance drama *kathakali* (literally "story-play") originated around the seventeenth century in the state of Kerala on India's southwestern coast. Performed by men, *kathakali* takes its themes from the Hindu epics and Purāṇas (collections of traditional stories). There is a high degree of stylization in all facets of the art—acting, dance and stage movement, costume, and makeup.

Kathakali is performed in association with temple festivals in an open courtyard within or near the temple precincts, or for domestic celebrations in the courtyard of the patron family. It is most often performed during the dry season, from December to early June. The performance is lit by a large oil lamp of burnished bronze placed at downstage center, and it is accompanied by two singers standing upstage and two drummers at stage right. Also indispensable to the performance is a stool, which in the course of the drama may elevate a performer to indicate that the character is flying through the air, or it may represent the lion-throne of a king, a mountain, or a log in the forest. A curtain *(tiraśśīla)* held up by two assistants divides one scene from the next and reveals the characters at the appropriate moment. No further stage equipment is required.

Kathakali has its roots in much older traditions, particularly in the techniques of military training exercises, in the dances of the shaman–priests who perform in many ancient rituals still found in Kerala, and in the only surviving tradition of Sanskrit drama, known as *kūṭiyāṭṭam*. The latter dates from at least as early as the ninth century. [*See* Kuṭiyāṭṭam.]

In the sixteenth century the first literary composition in the Malayalam language of Kerala was written by Tuñcan Ezhuttacchan; until that time Sanskrit had been the predominant language of literature. This composition was based on the *Rāmāyaṇa;* its great popularity seems to have inspired the Raja of Kottarakkara (1555–1605) to write eight plays on the same theme. Although the staging of these plays, which were known as *rāmanāṭṭan*, was not very highly developed, the new form of dance drama quickly gained favor, especially among the nobility. Four plays on themes from the *Mahābhārata*, written by a prince of Kottayam (1645–1716), greatly increased interest in this dramatic art. The poetry was of higher quality than in earlier plays, and the epic characters were portrayed as having some human qualities rather than as stereotypical legendary figures.

The principal patrons in the early period were the Tamburans or Rajas and Nayar chieftains, belonging to the upper levels of the ruling aristocracy; they were soon joined by Nambutiri brahmans. Although from an early period a variety of castes and communities produced performing artists, the actors were principally Nayars, dependents of the ruling families or of wealthy landowners. The military ethos of Kerala's Nayar warrior class, famous for their prowess in battle, found expression particularly in stories based on the *Mahābhārata*, with battle scenes and the triumph of the hero forming the climax of the performance. It has been said that heroism *(vīra)* is the pervading mood of *kathakaḷi,* and few plays in the repertory would refute this.

Many more texts for *kathakaḷi* plays were written, and the techniques of presentation continued to develop. In the mid-eighteenth century, Kaplingad Nambutiri, a performer, teacher, and artistic director of his own troupe, effected changes that brought the art much closer to its present form. He established canons of perfection that are still observed and new techniques of staging that set the future tone of *kathakaḷi.*

In the early years of the twentieth century, however, *kathakaḷi* and other indigenous arts of Kerala suffered a decline. In 1930 Kerala's famous poet, Mahākavi Vallattol Narayana Menon, and Manakkulam Mukunda Raja Tamburan, at great effort and expense, established the Kerala Kalamandalam, a school to preserve and maintain the traditional arts. They engaged the finest teachers available, among them Pattiykkantoti Ramunni Menon, the leading exponent of the Kalluvazhiciṭṭa, or central Kerala style of acting. In 1941 financial pressures made it necessary to turn the school over to the Raja of Cochin, and Vallattol was appointed director. Today Kalamandalam receives grants from the government of India through the Sangeet Natak Akademi, and also from the government of Kerala state. There are other excellent schools of *kathakaḷi* in Kerala, such as the school attached to the P. K. Warrier Arya Vaidya Shala in Kottakkal.

Kathakaḷi is performed today, as in the past, for religious and domestic celebrations, but another element has been added. Many towns and cities of Kerala have *kathakaḷi* clubs whose members arrange monthly performances. In recent years *kathakaḷi* troupes have made performance tours in the West as well as in Japan, Southeast Asia, and the Middle East.

The performance of the drama is largely regulated by the poetic text, or *āṭṭakatha.* There are many structural variations in the presentation of the approximately thirty plays in the repertory, but a basic pattern may be discerned.

The actor or actors are concealed by a curtain as the scene opens with a four-line verse or *śloka,* sung without a strict rhythmic pattern. The *śloka* is written in the third person and describes the scene and situation. The curtain is removed as a passage of drumming leads to the *padam,* written in the first person as if the actor were speaking. The *padam* consists of *pallavi, anupallavi,* and usually three or four *caraṇas;* the *caraṇas* follow the same melodic pattern, while the *pallavi* and *anupallavi* each has a distinct melody. Each line, or part of a line, of a *padam* is sung two or three times to enable the actor to complete the gestures or *mudrās* that interpret the words, using a highly codified system of gestural language. Each *mudrā* may involve two or more of twenty-four basic hand poses

KATHAKAḶI. It is customary for *kathakali* dancers to oil their bodies for practice sessions. This dancer, from the Kerala Kalamandalam, demonstrates a characteristic *kathakali* pose, turning his toes in and bearing the weight on the outer edge of his supporting foot. (Photograph by Andrew Arnault; from the archives of The Asia Society, New York.)

and is accompanied by choreographic movements of the arms, body, feet, and legs, as well as appropriate facial expression. A *kalāśam* or passage of dance follows each line of the *padam.* The *padam* is followed by an interpolated passage *(āṭṭam* or *iḷakiyāṭṭam)* that serves to fill out the story line, shown in *mudrās* but accompanied only by percussion with no singing. The sequence of verse, *padam* with *kalāśams,* and *āṭṭam* is then repeated, usually by another character in the scene. [*See* Mudrā.]

In addition to the brief interpolated passages at the end of almost every *padam,* there are longer and more structured interpolations that may be used in any story for which they are appropriate. Many of these are descriptive; others relate episodes from the epics or Purāṇas. The actor may also improvise an interpolation or may use improvisatory material within one of the standardized interpolations.

The characters fall into typological categories, although there may be small adjustments according to an individual role. The heroic or divine character uses *pacca* or "green" makeup, with a stylized black design for eyes and eyebrows and matte red-orange for the mouth. A design associated with devotees of Viṣṇu (Vishnu) adorns his forehead. He wears a *cuṭṭi,* a frame made of rice paste and paper that begins at the upper cheekbone, curves first inward and then outward at the cheek, and then inward again in a diminishing, blade-like curve to the chin, where the two sides meet. For a *katti* character, whose admirable qualities are in conflict with his rapacious and arrogant nature, the makeup involves red, black, and white designs on a green base and knoblike protuberances on nose and forehead. The villainous character wears *cukkunnattāṭi* makeup, predominantly red with black and white designs, a red beard, fringes of paper attached to the face with rice paste, and protuberances on nose and forehead. Hanumān's makeup, called *veḷḷattāṭi,* emphasizes his simian nature. The *kaṭuttattāṭi* makeup of the aboriginal hunter is predominantly black, with red and white accents. The most naturalistic class of characters, called *minukku,* includes females, *brāhmaṇas,* sages, messengers, and charioteers. There are also other character types. The costumes are colorful, as stylized as the makeup and extremely ornate.

The *rāga*s, or melodic modes, and the *tāla*s, or rhythmic patterns, used in *kathakali* are related to Karnatic music but belong to a special genre. The leading singer plays the *cēṁmalam,* a gong held in the left hand and struck with a curved stick held in the right; the second singer plays the *ilattāḷam,* very large hand cymbals with which he reinforces the beat of the *cēṁmalam.* One percussionist plays the *śuddha maddaḷam,* a barrel-shaped drum about a meter in length and made of jackwood. The drumhead on the right is of ox hide and that on the left of buffalo hide. The *ceṇṭa,* the other principal drum used in *kathakali,* is a cylindrical drum, less than a meter in length, made of jackwood and with two heads of cowhide. The *ceṇṭa* is tuned by means of tension cords passed through loops or rings. A third drum, used especially for female characters, is the *iṭekka,* a double-headed, hourglass-shaped pressure drum about 30 to 35 centimeters in length. The *śaṅkha,* or conch shell, is also sounded at dramatic or portentous moments.

This brief description cannot, unfortunately, convey the dramatic power, the elegance and richness, or the harmonious blending of visual and audial elements that characterize a *kathakali* performance.

[*See also* Asian Dance Traditions, *overview article;* Costume in Asian Traditions; India, *articles on* History of Indian Dance *and* Epic Sources of Indian Dance; Mask and Makeup, *article on* Asian Traditions; *and the entries on* Ragini Devi *and Rao.*]

BIBLIOGRAPHY

Barba, Eugenio. "The Steps on the River Bank." *Drama Review* 38 (Winter 1994): 107–119.

KATHAKALI. Performers from the Kerala Kalamandalam in the *kathakali* dance drama *Dussasana Vadhan* (The Annihilation of Dussasana). The Kerala Kalamandalam is a prestigious school founded in the 1930s to preserve the traditional arts. (Photograph © 1985 by Jack Vartoogian; used by permission.)

Bharatha Iyer, K. *Kathakali: The Sacred Dance-Drama of Malabar.* London, 1955.

Daugherty, Diane, and Marlene Pitkow. "Who Wears the Skirts in Kathakali?" *Drama Review* 35 (Summer 1991): 138–155.

George, David E. R. *India, Three Ritual Dance Dramas: Raslila, Katakali, Nagamandala.* Cambridge, 1986.

Jones, Clifford Reis, and Betty True Jones. *Kathakali: Introduction to the Dance-Drama of Kerala.* New York, 1970.

Nair, D. Appukuttan, and K. Ayyappa Panikar, eds. *Kathakali: The Art of the Non-Worldly.* Bombay, 1993.

Ragini Devi. *Dance Dialects of India.* 2d rev. ed. Delhi, 1990.

Samson, Leela. *Rhythm in Joy: Classical Indian Dance Traditions.* New Delhi, 1987.

Shah, Pankaj. *Performing Arts of Kerala.* Edited by Mallika Sarabhai. Ahmedabad, 1994.

Zarrilli, Phillip B. *The Kathakali Complex: Actor, Performance, and Structure.* New Delhi, 1984.

FILMS.   *God with a Green Face* (American Society for Eastern Arts and the California Institute of Arts, 1971. David A. Bolland, *Masque of Malabar* (1974).

RECORDING.   *The Music of Kathakali: The Dance-Drama of Kerala* (American Society for Eastern Arts, 1972), with liner notes by Clifford Reis Jones and Betty True Jones.

CLIFFORD REIS JONES

KAWAKAMI. *See* Yakko and Kawakami.

KAYE, NORA (Nora Koreff; born 17 January 1920 in New York City, died 28 February 1987 in Los Angeles), American dancer and associate director of American Ballet Theatre. Nora Kaye, principal dancer for most of her career with Ballet Theatre, created a special title of "dramatic ballerina." She stirred audiences by the power of motivated movement. Kaye was a method dancer according to the Stanislavsky method of character analysis. In her essay in *American Ballet Theatre* by Charles Payne (1980), she wrote that in his coaching and training, Michel Fokine, one of her principal teachers, stressed knowing how the body expressed feelings. She noted that Antony Tudor, her chief mentor, "worked through the mind. Mental events dictated what the character would be like as a person and how she would move." These influences made Kaye a "thinking dancer."

In tune with the Freudian interpretations of the times, she often played the frustrated female in such ballets as *Pillar of Fire, Fall River Legend, Facsimile,* and *A Streetcar Named Desire.* She was also a skillful actress in romantic roles in *Romeo and Juliet, Gift of the Magi,* and *Winter's Eve.* She gave a powerful performance in *The Cage* and was hilarious in *Gala Performance.* Well-formed and attractive, Kaye had the necessary strong technique, virtuosity, clarity of attack, and authoritative presence for clas-

KAYE. With Nicholas Magallanes as the Second Intruder, Kaye created the role of the Novice in Jerome Robbins's insect-inspired ballet *The Cage,* choreographed for the New York City Ballet in 1951. The music was by Igor Stravinsky; lighting was set by Jean Rosenthal; and the costumes were designed by Ruth Sobotka. Outside the Tudor repertory, the Novice was Kaye's greatest achievement. (Photograph from the Dance Collection, New York Public Library for the Performing Arts.)

sical ballet, although her lack of complete turnout flawed her line.

Kaye studied dance with Fokine, Margaret Curtis (at the Metropolitan Opera Ballet School), Anatole Vilzak, Ludmilla Schollar, and the School of American Ballet. Her first performances were with children, directed by Rosina Galli in opera ballets. In 1935, when George Balanchine was ballet master, Kaye became a member of the Metropolitan Opera corps de ballet. Next she appeared in the Broadway musicals *Great Lady* and *Stars in Your Eyes,* and she then joined the ballet at Radio City Music Hall. In January 1940 she appeared in the first season of Ballet Theatre, dancing in the ensemble and *coryphée* roles. In 1942 she was acclaimed for her creation of the leading role in Tudor's *Pillar of Fire* and was recognized as a leading ballerina. From then on, she danced leading classical and dramatic roles, creating many of them. She specialized in Tudor ballets, such as *Jardin aux Lilas, Gala Performance,* and *Romeo and Juliet.* She danced in Léonide Massine's *La Boutique Fantasque, Mlle. Angot,* and others, and in George Balanchine's *Apollo* and *Waltz Academy.*

With Ballet Theatre she danced the classics: *Swan Lake, Giselle, Princess Aurora, Pas de Quatre,* and others. She created roles in Michael Kidd's *On Stage!* and *Graziana,* choreographed by John Taras.

From 1951 to 1954 Kaye danced with New York City Ballet. She created the leading roles in Tudor's *La Gloire* and Jerome Robbins's *The Cage* and *Ballade* and danced in several Balanchine ballets. She returned to Ballet Theatre in 1954 and danced in *A Streetcar Named Desire,* choreographed by Valerie Bettis, Tudor's *Offenbach in the Underworld,* and in 1957 in Kenneth MacMillan's *Winter's Eve* and *Journey.* She also created roles in Herbert Ross's *Paean, Tristan, Concerto,* and *Dialogues.*

Kaye danced abroad many times, beginning with Ballet Theatre's 1946 appearance in London. In the summers of 1954, 1955, and 1956, she toured Japan with Paul Szilard, including *Giselle* in her repertory. With Ross she participated in several seasons of the Spoleto Festival of Two Worlds (1959 and 1960). In 1960 Kaye headed the Ballet of Two Worlds, a Ross-directed group that toured Europe. For this project Ross choreographed *Within the Grove,* based on *Rashomon,* with Kaye creating the leading role. After this tour Kaye retired from dancing and in the next years assisted Ross in the direction of musicals on Broadway and in Europe and in making Hollywood films. She played a major role in producing the Ross-directed films *The Turning Point* (1978) and *Nijinsky* (1980), both involving ballet.

From 1977 to 1983 Kaye was an associate director of American Ballet Theatre, and after that she served the company in an advisory capacity until her death. Her last work was as co-producer with Ross on the film *Dancers,* made in Italy in 1986 and 1987.

BIBLIOGRAPHY

The Herbert and Nora Kaye Ross Collection. Los Angeles, 1988.
Kaye, Nora. "Nora Kaye Talks about Working with Antony Tudor." In *Proceedings of the Eighth Annual Conference, Society of Dance History Scholars, University of New Mexico, 15–17 February 1985,* compiled by Christena L. Schlundt. Riverside, Calif., 1985.
Newman, Barbara. *Striking a Balance: Dancers Talk about Dancing.* Rev. ed. New York, 1992.
Payne, Charles, et al. *American Ballet Theatre.* New York, 1977.
Reynolds, Nancy. *Repertory in Review: Forty Years of the New York City Ballet.* New York, 1977.
Taras, John. "Nora Kaye: A Tribute." *Ballet Review* 14 (Winter 1987): 36–48.

FILMS.   Amateur 16 mm silent films converted to video are held in the Dance Collection, New York Public Library for the Performing Arts, and the San Francisco Dance Archives.

ANN BARZEL

KAZAKHSTAN. The largest state in Central Asia, after Russia to its north, Kazakhstan is bounded by China on the east; Kyrgyzstan, Tajikistan, Uzbekistan, and Turk-menistan on the south; and the Caspian Sea on the west. The earliest known inhabitants of the region were a branch of the Kyrgyz, of Turkic origin. While under Mongol domination from the thirteenth century onward, Kazakhstan became a Muslim nation; however, a long-standing tribal and family hierarchy system has had a greater influence on Kazakh society. Russia gradually took over the area during the mid-eighteenth to mid-nineteenth century, and in 1936 Kazakhstan joined the USSR as a constituent republic. It became an independent state when the USSR dissolved in 1991.

Folk Dance. Kazakhstan is a land with a rich tradition of music and song; dance has also long existed in the everyday life of the people and it expresses their national identity. Traditional dances have taken many forms: representations of hunting scenes, such as a golden eagle hunting a hare *(koyan-berkut);* competitive dances *(utys bi);* humorous and satirical dances; imitations of animal movements, such as a jumping goat *(orteke),* a galloping steed *(tepenkok),* and a clumsy bear *(ayu-bi);* work dances like those of carpet weavers *(ormek-bi);* dance games; dances accompanied by singing and storytelling; and imitations of ritual folk healers *(bakhsy).* Dances were taught by one generation to the next. In the patriarchal feudal society, each clan had its own professional master, who was in the retinue of the khan as a jester to amuse the people.

Kazakh dance, reflecting the life and customs of nomadic cattle-breeders and the nature of vast prairie lands, embodied a variety of tastes and ideals. The dances expressed the traits of the Kazakh—bravery, emotion, and optimism—and were typified by a vivid style of performance, flexibility and sharp movements of the shoulders, tension and muscular concentration of the body, and an agility that enabled the dancer to perform intricate acrobatics. Another typical feature was a combination of expressiveness and inventiveness that was especially manifest in dance competitions. The dancers' mastery of improvisation kept the dance vocabulary varied and mobile.

The folk dances in existence long before the advent of ballet influenced the development of ballet. The characteristic features of folk dance—such as the richness of emotion, energy and swiftness of male dancing, and soft yet noble movements of female dancing—were adopted into theatrical dance.

Theatrical Dance. Professional ballet was born in Kazakhstan in the 1930s when amateur theaters, followed by professional theatrical companies, were established all over the state. The interest in folk dance of leading figures in the musical theater largely contributed to the effort to master the art of classical ballet. In 1933 a music studio was opened by the Kazakh drama theater to train singers and dancers. A ballet company formed at the studio began to learn classical dance. In the first production by the studio, *Aiman-Sholpan,* based on Mukhtar Auezov's eponymous play, the spectators saw familiar scenes of equestrian contests and falcon hunts translated into the language of dance. In 1934 the studio was designated the State Musical Theater. In its productions—*Shuga, Kyzzhibek, Er-Tagryn, Zhalbyr,* to music arranged by Evgeny Brusilovsky—Kazakh theatrical dance was further developed. The choreographer Aleksandr Aleksandrov carefully preserved the finest examples of folk dance but made them more balletic. The ballet costume was reformed. The dancers, among whom were Shara Zhenkulova, Sania Absoliamova, Bibian Seifutdinova, Kamysh Karabolinova, Gainula Ismailov, Bulat Beibosynov, and Nursula Tapalova, grew more skilled so that creative potential expanded through the 1930s and 1940s. Aleksandrov founded a ballet school in 1934 and was its first teacher. His creative work affirmed the new trend in Kazakh ballet: the synthesis of national originality and classical technique.

In 1936 the musical theater became an opera and ballet theater called the Abai Ballet Theater. The first ballets presented on its stage were *Coppélia, Swan Lake,* and a Kazakh ballet, *Kalkaman and Mamyr,* created by Leonid Zhukov to music by Vasily Velikanov. In 1940 the Kazakh ballet *Koktem* (Spring) was staged by the choreographer Aleksandr Chekrygin to music by Ivan Nadirov. In the 1940s the increased skill of the company enabled the theater to produce a number of standard and Soviet classics with choreography by Lev Kramarevsky, Vakhtang Chabukiani, Yuri Kovalev, and Galina Ulanova. On 18 June 1942 Ulanova made her debut on the Kazakh stage, ultimately dancing the roles of Odette in *Swan Lake,* Maria in *The Fountain of Bakhchisarai,* and Giselle. She also performed concert pieces in the so-called night concerts, which were held after hours to benefit the armed forces.

In 1950 the choreographer Mikhail Moiseyev produced the Kazakh ballet *Kambar and Nazym* to music by Velikanov, and restaged *Doctor Oh-It-Hurts, The Red Poppy,* and *The Sleeping Beauty.* In the 1960s the first Kazakh choreographers to be educated at the Lunacharsky Theater Technicum in Moscow, Daurent Abirov and Zaur Raibayev, started to work on the Kazakh stage. Abirov produced *Youth* to music by Mikhail Chulaki; *Esmeralda; Shurale; The Path of Friendship* to music by Lev Stepanov, Evgeny Manayev, and Nurgisa Tlendiev; *Old Man Khottabych* to music by Aleksandr Zatsepin; a new version of Velikanov's *Kambar and Nazym; Kozy Korpen and Bayan-Slu* to music by Brusilovsky; and *Akkanat* (White Wings) to music by Gaziza Zhubanova. Raibayev created the original ballets *The Legend of the White Bird,* Zhubanova's *Hiroshima,* Tchaikovsky's *Francesca da Rimini,* Ravel's *Bolero, Chin Tomyur and Makhrum* to music by Kuddus

Kuzhamiarov, and *Frescoes* to music by Timor Mynbaev. In its productions on national themes the Abai Ballet Theater relied as always on the wealth of indigenous folk art, while absorbing the achievements of Russian repertory and aesthetic principles by offering ballets originally staged at the Bolshoi Theater in Moscow. The Kazakh company regularly exchanged guest performances with Moscow and Leningrad.

The influx of well-trained young professionals was remarkable in the 1970s. The debut of dancers Maira Kadyrova, Zarema Kasteeva, Maira Karakulova, and Murat Adyrkhaev, and of the choreographers M. Tleubaev and Zhanat Baidaralin appreciably enhanced the standards of Kazakh ballet. Tleubaev choreographed *Aksak Kulan* (Dame Wild Hare) to music by Almaz Serkebaev and *My Brother, Mougly,* a rock opera and ballet; Baidaralin set *Alia* to music by Mansur Sagatov; and Raibayev contributed Stravinsky's *Jeu de Cartes* and *Man and Woman* to music by Arthur Honegger. In the 1980s the ninety-member company was officially called the Abai Academic Opera and Ballet Theater of Kazakhstan, with Raibayev its artistic director. In 1984 the company presented Ksenia Ter-Stepanova's staging of the Kirov Ballet's *La Sylphide.* (A full list of the company's productions to 1981 appears in the *Soviet Encyclopedia of Ballet* [in Russian].) Among the principal dancers of the era were Raushan Baiseitova, Larisa Lee, Larisa Akylbekova, Ramazam Bapov, Bourdzhan Eshmukhambetov, Eduard Malbekov, Timur Nurkalev, Bulat Valev, Murat Adyrkhaev, and Kairat Mazhikov.

A ballet school with an eight-year program has been functioning in the capital, Alma-Ata, since 1934. The school trains ballet dancers and dancers for folk dance ensembles. Besides the ballet company of the Abai Theater there are other professional ballet troupes in Alma-Ata: the Classical Dance Ensemble of Kazakhstan, the ballet group of the Gulder variety dance company, the ballet group in the Song and Dance Company of Kazakhstan, the professional ballet troupe at the Uigur Drama Theater, and the ballet troupe at the Korean Drama Theater. There are also many amateur dance companies around the state, including folk ensembles with a ballet repertory, dance groups, and ballet dance circles. The theory of dance is studied at the Auezov Institute of Literature and the Arts under the Academy of Sciences of Kazakhstan, the House of Folk Art, and the Research and Methodological Center under the Ministry of Culture of Kazakhstan.

BIBLIOGRAPHY
Abirov, Daurent, and A. Ismailov. *Kazakhskie narodnye tantsy.* Alma-Ata, 1961.
Sarynova, Lydia. *Baletnoe iskusstvo Kazakhstana.* Alma-Ata, 1976.

LYDIA P. SARYNOVA
Translated from Russian

KEBIAR. The genre of dance and music known as *ke-biar* was initiated in the Bulelang district of North Bali shortly after the Dutch takeover of the island in 1908. The word itself refers to a sudden outburst, such as lightning or the bursting open of a flower; the style made great use of sudden shifts of tempo and dynamics, richly embellished melodic forms, and overwhelming energy. The *gamelan gong* instrumentation was transformed to allow greater dynamics and melodic ornamentation as well as an embellished shimmering effect. [*See* Gamelan.]

Some new dances, such as *kebiar légong*, had no plot but focused entirely on the dynamic relationship between dancer and gamelan. I Mario, a dancer from Tabanan, South Bali, is credited with bringing *kebiar* to its full flowering in the 1920s. [*See the entry on Mario.*]

Kebiar duduk employs a dancer who enters with a fan, exchanges it for the mallets of a *trompong* (a row of tuned gongs), and plays the instrument with great flourish. The dancer remains in a low, squatting position throughout the dance, on level with the *trompong*, but this does not hinder his fluidity of movement. Even his semi-squatting walks across the dance space, one foot crossed in front of the other, somehow allows a graceful, sweeping line of movement. Dance follows music with great precision but incorporates a great deal of expression, alternately suggesting coyness, shyness, sadness, and alarm.

More recent dances in the *kebiar* style include *Panji Semirang*, in which a female dancer portrays Princess Candra Kirana of the Malat legendary chronicles. Other female dances are *Mergapati* (King of the Lions), *Yudapati* (King of Battle), and *Wiranata* (Brave King). *Oleg Tumulil-*

KEBIAR. The *kebiar duduk* is a virtuosic solo for a male dancer who moves fluidly, low to the ground, as he manipulates a fan and plays the *trompong* (row of tuned gongs). Here, Gedé Sukraka performs the *kebiar duduk* with the gamelan ensemble from the village of Sebatu, Bali. (Photograph from the Dance Collection, New York Public Library for the Performing Arts.)

KEBIAR. A scene from a 1989 performance of the *kebiar*-style *Oleg Tumulilingan* (Bumblebees) by dancers and musicians from Miaton, Bali. Depicting the flirtation of two bees in a flower garden, this dance was created by I Ketut Mario for his company's 1952/53 tour of the United States and Europe. It remains a popular work, although innovations and variations have been introduced by later generations of dancers. (Photograph © 1989 by Jack Vartoogian; used by permission.)

ingan (Bumblebees) is a courtship dance between a female and a refined male, originally composed for a European tour in the 1950s. In *Panyembrama* (Greeting), five female dancers carry bowls containing flower petals and incense. Just as other dances are performed to honor deities in a temple *odalan* ceremony, *Panyembrama* honors the human guests in the audience. It has become the standard opening dance in revue performances for audiences of tourists.

Sendratari is a contemporary dance theater genre that has developed as a manifestation of the *kebiar* musical style. Relying heavily on gesture and pantomime, the term is a composite of *seni* (art), drama, and *tari* (dance). A *juru tandak* (singer–reciter) or *dalang* (shadow-puppet master) functions as solo vocalist and narrator, sitting amid the *gong kebiar* musicians with a microphone. *Sendratari* stems from the Javanese *Rāmāyaṇa* ballet, developed in 1962 under government sponsorship as an entertainment that could be understood by foreigners as well as Indonesians. In Bali the government high school of performing arts, KOKAR, adapted the Javanese idea to a Balinese style, using *gamelan gong kebiar*. Originally enacting the Balinese *Jayaprana* romance, they soon moved on to the *Rāmāyaṇa* epic. The drama was conceived with a proscenium stage in mind, but as its popularity spread throughout the island's villages, local groups made use of whatever stage arrangements they had available. The three-sided *kalangan* space of traditional dance theater has been rejected whenever possible in favor of an end stage or proscenium. The skill of combining dance and vocalization is not required of *Sendratari* performers; instead, special attention is given to new choreography, often on a grand scale incorporating elaborate props such as chariots. Many styles of music are brought together in new compositions and arrangements. The strong *kebiar* accent on music–dance integration, plus a simplified, easy-to-follow story line, have made *Sendratari* a very popular Balinese genre. Recent projects at the State Dance College of Bali (S.T.S.I.) have adapted the *Mahābhārata* epic to this format.

Since the 1920s, when *kebiar* music and dance swept the island, village *gamelan* clubs have been sending their old instruments to the gong-smiths to be melted down and reforged in *gong kebiar* style. *Kebiar* has become the dominant genre of Balinese music, replacing the tradi-

tional *gaguntangan* ensemble for *arja* theater as well as
pelegongan, which accompanied *légong* dance. In addition, the great popularity of *kebiar* dance styles and
Sendratari have ensured *gamelan gong kebiar* a dominant
place in the ears of the Balinese people.

[*See also* Indonesia, *articles on Balinese dance traditions.*]

BIBLIOGRAPHY
Bandem, I Madé, and Fredrik Eugene DeBoer. *Balinese Dance in Tran-
sition: Kaja and Kelod.* 2d ed. New York, 1995.
Coast, John. *Dancing Out of Bali.* London, 1954.
Covarrubias, Miguel. *Island of Bali.* New York, 1937.
de Zoete, Beryl, and Walter Spies. *Dance and Drama in Bali* (1938).
New ed. New York, 1973.
Dibia, I Wayan. "Arja: A Sung Dance-Drama of Bali; A Study of
Change and Transformation." Ph.D. diss., University of California,
Los Angeles, 1992.
Herbst, Edward. *Voices in Bali: Energy and Perceptions in Vocal Music
and Dance Theater.* Hanover and London, 1997.
Hitchcock, Michael, and Lucy Norris. *Bali, the Imaginary Museum:
The Photographs of Walter Spies and Beryl de Zoete.* New York, 1995.
Hood, Mantle. "The Enduring Tradition: Music and Theater in Java
and Bali." In *Indonesia,* edited by Ruth McVey, pp. 438–560. New
Haven 1983.
Lendra, I Wayan. "Bali and Grotowski: Some Parallels in the Training
Process." *Drama Review* 35 (1991): 113–128.
McPhee, Colin. *Music in Bali.* New Haven, 1966.
McPhee, Colin. "Dance in Bali." In *Traditional Balinese Culture,* edited
by Jane Belo, pp. 290–321. New York, 1970.
Ornstein, Ruby. "Gamelan Gong Kebjar: The Development of a Bali-
nese Musical Tradition." Ph.D. diss., University of California, Los
Angeles, 1971.
Seebass, Tilman. "A Note on Kebyar in Modern Bali." *Orbis Musicae* 9
(Essays in honor of Edith Gerson Kiwi), 1985: 103–121.
Tenzer, Michael. *Balinese Music.* Singapore, 1992.

EDWARD HERBST

KEHLET, NIELS (born 6 September 1938 in Copenhagen), Danish dancer and teacher. The repertory of the
Royal Danish Ballet traditionally has offered great scope
for the *demi-caractère* dancer. Kehlet saw this opportunity
and used it. In 1948 he entered the ballet school of the
Royal Theater in Copenhagen, where his most important
teachers were Vera Volkova, Stanley Williams, and Hans
Brenaa. Kehlet joined the Royal Danish Ballet in 1957 and
became a principal dancer in 1961. From his debut it was
obvious that in Kehlet the ballet had found a fantastic
jumper with a light and subtle technique. He also had a
boyish and audacious charm that endeared him to audiences in such ballets as *Graduation Ball* and *La Fille Mal
Gardée.* His first success was in 1965 as Franz in *Coppélia,*
which became his most celebrated role as a gamin.

Kehlet's interpretations have expanded *demi-caractère*
roles that are usually rather limited; these range from the
Joker in John Cranko's *Jeu de Cartes* to the sensual Faun
in Jerome Robbins's *Afternoon of a Faun.* In *The Prodigal*

KEHLET. The title role in Fokine's *Le Spectre de la Rose* provided Kehlet with ample opportunity to display his elevation, *ballon*, and speed. Here, the Spirit of the Rose is seen making his spectacular entrance, bounding through the open window while the weary Girl (Solveig Østergaard), home from the ball, dozes in her chair. (Photograph by Rigmor Mydtskov; used by permission.)

Son, Petrouchka, and Glen Tetley's *Pierrot Lunaire,* Kehlet transformed the gamin into a character of tragic dimensions. As Mercutio in John Neumeier's *Romeo and Juliet* in 1974, Kehlet demonstrated his growth—becoming a great actor while retaining his light technique. In roles such as the Dancing Master in Flemming Flindt's *The Lesson* and as Thisbe, the Craftsman in drag, in Neumeier's *A Midsummer Night's Dream,* Kehlet covered the range from the demonic to the grotesque.

Kehlet was particularly well suited to the Bournonville repertory. He mastered the Bournonville style better than most, shifting easily from the joyful Gennaro in *Napoli* to the melancholy James in *La Sylphide.* Over nearly three decades of dancing Kehlet depicted a long series of fantastic, funny, and touching figures in the Bournonville ballets.

Early on in Kehlet's career, French choreographers such as Roland Petit and Jean Coralli saw his potential and created works for him to dance both at home and abroad. As a result, Kehlet traveled widely as a guest artist, but unlike his peers Erik Bruhn and Peter Schaufuss, he never left the Royal Danish Ballet. After having danced the young heroes, Kehlet continued on as a character dancer and also taught. He retired as a dancer in 1994.

BIBLIOGRAPHY

Aschengreen, Erik. "Niels Kehlet." *Saisons de la Danse,* no. 22 (March 1970): 10–13.

Aschengreen, Erik. "Kehlet, Niels." In *Dansk biografisk leksikon.* 3d ed. Copenhagen, 1979–.

Hunt, Marilyn. "A Conversation with Niels Kehlet." *Ballet Review* 16 (Summer 1988): 76–96.

ERIK ASCHENGREEN